MANAGERIAL ECONOMICS: APPLICATIONS, STRATEGY, AND TACTICS

JAMES R. McGUIGAN
JRM Investments

R. CHARLES MOYER
Babcock Graduate School of Management
Wake Forest University

FREDERICK H. deB. HARRIS
Babcock Graduate School of Management
Wake Forest University

 South-Western College Publishing
an International Thomson Publishing company I T P®

Cincinnati • Albany • Boston • Detroit • Johannesburg • London • Madrid • Melbourne • Mexico City
New York • Pacific Grove • San Francisco • Scottsdale • Singapore • Tokyo • Toronto

Publishing Team Director: Jack W. Calhoun
Acquisitions Editor: Keri Witman
Developmental Editor: Susanna C. Smart
Production Editor: Brenda Owens
Media Technology Editor: Mary Hufford
Media Production Editor: Kurt Gerdenich
Production House: Carlisle Publishers Services
Photo Research: Cary Benbow
Marketing Manager: Lisa L. Lysne
Manufacturing Coordinator: Georgina Calderon
Internal Design: Maureen McCutcheon Design
Cover Design: Matulionis Photography & Design
Cover Images: © 1998 Photo Disc

Library of Congress Cataloging-in-Publication Data

McGuigan, James R.
    Managerial economics : applications, strategy, and tactics / James
  R. McGuigan, R. Charles Moyer, Frederick H. deB. Harris. — 8th ed.
      p.   cm.
    Includes index.
    ISBN 0-538-88106-2
    1. Managerial economics. 2. Managerial economics–Problems,
exercises, etc. I. Moyer, R. Charles, 1945– . II. Harris,
Frederick H. deB.   III. Title.
HD30.22.M32 1999   98-21497
338.5'024'658—DC21   CIP

    2 3 4 5 6 7 8 9 Cl 6 5 4 3 2 1 0 9 8

Printed in the United States of America

I(T)P®

International Thomson Publishing
South-Western College Publishing is an ITP Company
The ITP trademark is used under license

RISF

a part of Bishop B
Learning Reso

To my family
J.R.M.

■

To Sally, Laura, and Craig
R.C.M.

■

To Nancy, Taylor, and Sarah
F.H.B.H.

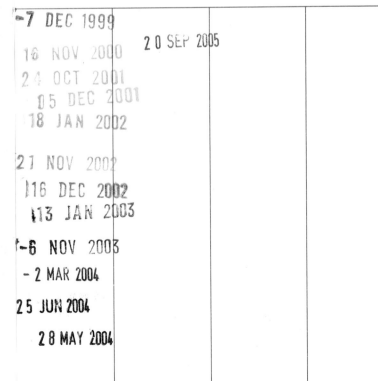

CONTENTS

Managerial economics is concerned with resource-allocation, strategic decisions, and tactical decisions that are made by analysts, managers, and consultants in the private, public, and not-for-profit sectors of the economy. Managerial economic techniques seek to achieve the objectives of the organization in the most efficient manner, while considering both explicit and implicit constraints on achieving the objective(s). The book is organized around the twin themes of product-line rivalry and shareholder wealth maximization for private sector enterprises. In addition, the theme of managerial efficiency provides a common basis for making resource-allocation decisions in all enterprises.

The major emphasis is to provide the analytical tools and managerial insights essential to the analysis and solution of those problems that have significant economic consequences, both for the firm and society at large. Effective decision making requires an understanding of the constraints (limitations) imposed on the decision maker by the business environment. To accomplish this, major issues associated with government regulation of the firm, as well as implicit constraints on the actions of private and public sector enterprises, are examined throughout the text and in two dedicated chapters. These issues include a consideration of the externalities associated with economic decisions.

PEDAGOGICAL APPROACH: THEORY-IN-CONTEXT

Managerial Economics is an applied branch of microeconomics. Because of this emphasis on applications, economic theory in this text is always presented within a deep fact-situation context. Thus the theory-in-context approach brings theory to bear on relevant situations whose facts fit the theoretical assumptions not merely on two dimensions, but on five, or eight, or twelve. Teaching potential managers with this approach is far preferable to teaching either applications alone or theory alone. Theory-in-context not only stimulates student interest at the inception of the learning process, but also promotes mastery of challenging analytical tools and facilitates the acquisition of complex managerial insights. Perhaps most importantly, theory-in-context empowers students to spot analogous real-world situations and apply appropriate tools and insights outside of the classroom and beyond the final exam.

To this end, we motivate the topics in each chapter with a "managerial challenge" taken from the business press or our own management consulting experience. The individual topics within chapters are then illustrated with 258 real-world applications, in-depth examples, or case exercises. We have deliberately doubled the number of such applications, examples, and exercises relative to other books while retaining a focus on rigorous analytical tools. We believe this theory-in-context approach elicits the students' commitment to the lifelong learning required for best-practices management throughout their careers. An appreciation for best practices, the application of careful analysis, and a healthy dose of managerial insight provide the formula for management who can make a difference—i.e., for increases in capitalized value.

Course Content

A survey of managerial economics and business economics courses in a wide range of universities has led to a broad consensus on topic coverage in some areas, but a wide diversity of coverage in other areas. In organizing the book, we have recognized the differences existing in various curricula. The broad topic coverage provided in the text gives instructors a great deal of flexibility in designating a course suited to the needs of their students and the demands of their curricula.

Part I of the book provides an overview of managerial economics and introduces key economic concepts and tools. In these introductory chapters, the goal of the enterprise (shareholder wealth maximization) is established, the decision-making process and philosophy of optimization are introduced, the role of profit is discussed, and the relationship between managerial economics and other areas of business and economic analysis is developed. In addition, this section introduces the fundamental economic concepts of marginal analysis, net present value, risk, risk versus return analysis, and classical optimization.

Part II examines the areas of demand analysis and forecasting techniques in domestic and export markets. Part III deals with production and cost analysis, and Part IV focuses on price determination and capacity choice in theory and practice. The strategic framework of Michael Porter and the new tactical insights from business games are highlighted. The extent of, rationale for, and consequences of government regulation also are covered in Part IV. Part V includes a coverage of capital budgeting, cost-benefit analysis, and risk analysis and management.

Although the primary focus of the book is on private sector management, the text is written with a recognition that many students of economics and business management pursue careers in the public and not-for-profit sectors of the economy. Consequently, we have included a discussion of the philosophy of public involvement in the economy, the objective of public and not-for-profit organizations, and coverage of specific analytical tools that are of use in these sectors.

This eighth edition represents a major revision of the text. Five new chapters and Appendices have been added. Chapter 7 addresses the international finance and economics concepts required to manage export sales, including the foreign exchange market, pricing export products, free trade areas, and trade imbalances. Chapter 13 provides a contemporary, in-depth look at competitive decision making under information asymmetry. Specific topics include asymmetric information exchange, the "lemons market," solutions to adverse selection problems, principal-agent problems, and incentive signaling. Chapter 16 provides extensive coverage of game theory in the context of oligopolistic rivalry. The chapter covers business strategy games, sequential games, simultaneous games, and applications to the problems of capital equipment leasing, excess capacity, scale of entry, pricing tactics, entry deterrence, and industry standards. A new Appendix 16A has been added on bidding tactics in auctions, optimal mechanism design, franchise arrangements, and vertical requirements contracting. Appendix 17A develops the techniques and practical applications of one of the hottest areas in management consulting—yield management. In addition to these new features, we have retained, expanded, and updated the most popular features from the seventh edition, including many new Managerial Challenge sections and an expanded use of 258 examples and applications throughout the text.

Student Preparation

The text is designed for use by upper-level undergraduates and first-level graduate students in departments of economics, schools of business, schools of management, and schools of public administration. Students are presumed to have a background in the basic principles of economics. Prior course work in statistics and quantitative methods is desirable, but not essential because all of the concepts employed in the text are fully developed within the text itself. The book makes occasional use of elementary concepts of differential calculus. A review of these basic concepts is contained in Chapter 3. However, in all cases where calculus is employed, one or more alternative approaches, such as graphical, algebraic, or tabular analysis, are also presented.

Pedagogical Features of the Eighth Edition

The eighth edition of *Managerial Economics* makes extensive use of pedagogical learning aids to enhance student learning. The key features of the book are:

1. **Part Openers.** Each major section of the book opens with a brief discussion of the material contained in the following chapters. The relationship of the material in the section to the goal of shareholder wealth maximization and efficient resource allocation is illustrated with a schematic diagram appearing on the first page of each part opener.

2. **Managerial Challenges.** Each chapter opens with a Managerial Challenge that illustrates a real-life economic analysis problem faced by managers that is related to the material to be covered in the chapter. Many of these challenges have been updated with more contemporary illustrations.

3. **Chapter Glossaries.** In the margins of the text, new terms are defined as they are introduced. The placement of the glossary terms next to the location where the term is first used reinforces the importance of these new concepts and aids in later studying. An index to the glossary is provided at the end of the text.

4. **Chapter Preview.** Each chapter begins with a Chapter Preview that briefly summarizes the major issues that are covered in the chapter.

5. **International Perspectives.** Throughout the book, special International Perspectives sections are provided that illustrate the application of managerial economics concepts to problems faced by managers in an increasingly global economy.

6. **Extensive Use of Examples.** More than 250 examples, derived from both actual practice and hypothetical data, are provided and highlighted throughout the text. These examples help the tools and concepts to come alive and thereby enhance student learning. They are listed on the inside front and back covers to highlight the prominence of this feature of the book.

7. **Point-by-Point Summaries.** Each chapter ends with a detailed, point-by-point summary of important concepts from the chapter.

8. **Diversity of Presentation Approaches.** Important analytical concepts are presented in several different ways, including tabular analysis, graphical analysis, and algebraic analysis. When elementary differential calculus is used, at least one alternative mode of analysis also is presented for the student.

9. **Exercises.** Each chapter contains a large problem analysis set. Many new problems have been added to this edition. Check answers to selected problems are provided at the end of the text.

10. **Short Cases.** Many chapters include short case problems that extend the concepts and tools developed in the text.

11. **Internet Margin Notes.** Internet addresses in the margins tie applications and examples to the sites of companies being discussed or to other relevant sites. Students gain not only the additional information and data found at the sites but also the experience of using the Web to find financial and economic information.

12. **Internet Exercises.** Exercises at the ends of chapters provide further practice on the Internet by having students apply information and/or data from the Web sites to a problem or question posed in the exercise.

Significant Changes in the Eighth Edition

The eighth edition has been heavily revised and updated to streamline the presentation, to provide additional contemporary applications, and to enhance student learning. Many new topics have been added to reflect recent developments in the field—especially in the fields of international economics, management strategy, the tactics of applied game theory, and decision making under asymmetric information. The most important changes are enumerated below.

- **Chapter 1 (Introduction and Goals of the Firm):** There is an expanded coverage of incomplete markets, recontracting, and the principal-agent problem in market economies. The section dealing with the implications of the shareholder wealth maximization goal has been expanded, and many new examples have been added.

- **Chapter 2 (Fundamental Economic Concepts):** A new Managerial Challenge has been added.

- **Chapter 4 (Demand Analysis):** The discussion of utility maximization and demand has been expanded to include revealed preference techniques in pricing new products and measuring the effect on the cost of living of new products. Several new examples have been added, including some with international implications.

- **Chapter 5 (Estimation of Demand):** New coverage appears on omitted variable bias and the simultaneity between advertising and sales. New examples, based on empirical research, and a case exercise on soft-drink demand have been added.

- **Chapter 6 (Business and Economic Forecasting):** New material on leading indicators, business-cycle duration, and expected inflation has been added.

- **Chapter 7 (Exchange Rates and International Trade-Managing Exports):** This is a totally new chapter. See the table of contents for a listing of topics.

- **Chapter 8 (Production Economics):** There is an expanded discussion of process choice, technical efficiency, and allocative efficiency. Many new examples have been added.

- **Chapter 9 (Cost Analysis):** New examples have been added, and discussion of optimal capacity utilization has been expanded.

- **Chapter 10 (Applications of Cost Theory):** A new section on the optimal scale of operations has been added.

- **Chapter 12 (Price, Output, and Strategy):** Two new sections on Porter's five forces strategic framework and on optimal advertising intensity along with many new examples have been added.

- **Chapter 13 (Competitive Markets under Asymmetric Information):** This chapter new to the seventh edition has been revised and expanded with many new examples.

- **Chapter 14 (Price and Output Determination: Monopoly):** New examples and a new section on mark-ups and components of the gross margin have been added.

- **Chapter 15 (Price and Output Determination: Strategy and Tactics):** Discussion of cooperative and noncooperative games in the context of oligopolistic price and output determination has been greatly expanded. A new section on avoiding price wars and several new examples have been added.

- **Chapter 16 (Game-Theoretic Rivalry: Best-Practice Tactics):** This chapter, new to the seventh edition, has been substantially expanded with manufacturer-distributor games, double-money-back pricing games, licensing and leasing and excess capacity commitment games, predation games, and a new section on industry standards as a mechanism for escaping the prisoner's dilemma. Many new examples as well as an international case exercise on Boeing and Airbus have been added.

- **Appendix 16A (Optimal Mechanism Design):** A totally new Appendix has been added on mechanism design in queue service, vertical integration and vertical requirements contracting and optimal auction design.
- **Chapter 17 (Pricing Techniques and Analysis):** This chapter incorporates three new sections on the conceptual framework for proactive value-based pricing, on two-part pricing, and on pricing across the product life cycle. New examples have been added. The Appendix on yield management has been expanded to discuss the systems management approach to pricing and sources of sustainable price premiums as well as several new examples.
- **Chapter 18 (Government Regulation and Antitrust):** This chapter has been updated to reflect new developments in predatory pricing and refusals to deal. The Appendix on externalities now includes a discussion of Coase's railroad-farmer reciprocal externality.

Ancillary Materials

A complete set of ancillary materials is available to adopters to supplement the text, including the following:

- An *Instructor's Manual* and *Test Bank*, prepared by the authors, contain suggested answers to the end-of-chapter exercises and cases. The authors have taken great care to provide an error-free manual for instructors to use. The manual will be available both in a hard copy form and on disk (MS-Word) to make it easy for instructors to provide portions of these solutions to students, if desired. The *Test Bank*, containing a large collection of true-false, multiple choice, and numerical problems, is available to adopters for test use. The computerized *WestTest* software and diskette of the *Test Bank* are available to simplify the preparation of quizzes and exams.
- A revised and updated *Study Guide*, prepared by Professor Richard D. Marcus at the University of Wisconsin-Milwaukee, is available for purchase by students. The *Study Guide* provides valuable assistance to students when reviewing and applying the material presented in the text.
- Transparency masters have been prepared for the key tables and figures from the book.
- A PowerPoint Presentation package, prepared by Richard D. Marcus at the University of Wisconsin-Milwaukee, provides lecture aids covering many of the most important topics from the text. It can be customized by instructors to meet their specific course needs.
- A text Internet site can be found at http://mcguigan.swcollege.com and contains some of the supplements. The site also provides teaching resources, learning resources, Internet application links and updates, and an interactive Talk-to-the-Author link.
- Two packages of computer software are provided free to adopters of the book. The ForeProfit software, prepared by Professor Joe Kreitzer at the University of St. Thomas, is a user-friendly, free-standing package that provides on-screen help and user diagnostics. The software can be used to solve regression analysis, forecasting, linear programming, capital expenditure, and cost-benefit analysis problems. The ForeProfit software is also available on the text Internet site. In addition, for those

users who prefer a Lotus-based software package, a Lotus-based software supplement is available that has been prepared by Professor Robert Ritchey at Texas Tech University. This software performs regression analysis, forecasting, linear programming, and capital budgeting analysis.

Acknowledgments

A number of reviewers, users, and colleagues have been particularly helpful in providing us with many worthwhile comments and suggestions at various stages in the development of this and earlier editions of the book. Included among these individuals are:

William Beranek, J. Walter Elliott, William J. Kretlow, William Gunther, J. William Hanlon, Robert Knapp, Robert S. Main, Edward Sussna, Bruce T. Allen, Allen Moran, Edward Oppermann, Dwight Porter, Robert L. Conn, Allen Parkman, Daniel Slate, Richard L. Pfister, J.P. Magaddino, Richard A. Stanford, Donald Bumpass, Barry P. Keating, John Wittman, Sisay Asefa, James R. Ashley, David Bunting, Amy H. Dalton, Richard D. Evans, Gordon V. Karels, Richard S. Bower, Massoud M. Saghafi, John C. Callahan, Frank Falero, Ramon Rabinovitch, D. Steinnes, Jay Damon Hobson, Clifford Fry, John Crockett, Marvin Frankel, James T. Peach, Paul Kozlowski, Dennis Fixler, Steven Crane, Scott L. Smith, Edward Miller, Fred Kolb, Bill Carson, Jack W. Thornton, Changhee Chae, Robert B. Dallin, Christopher J. Zappe, Anthony V. Popp, Phillip M. Sisneros, Richard D. Marcus, George Brower, Carlos Sevilla, Dean Baim, Charles Callahan, Phillip Robins, Bruce Jaffee, Alwyn du Plessis, Darly Winn, Gary Shoesmith, Richard J. Ward, William H. Hoyt, Irvin Grossack, William Simeone, Satyajit Ghosh, David Levy, Audie Brewton, Simon Hakim, Patricia Sanderson, David P. Ely, Albert A. O'Kunade, Doug Sharp, Arne Dag Sti, Walker Davidson, David Buschena, George M. Radakovic, Harpal S. Grewal, Stephen J. Silver, Michael J. O'Hara, Luke M. Froeb, Dean Waters, Jake Vogelsang, and Tim Mages.

Individuals who have been especially helpful in the preparation of the eighth edition include Lynda Y. de la Viña, Audie R. Brewton, Paul M. Hayashi, Richard D. Marcus, and Lawrence B. Pulley.

We are also indebted to Richard Marcus, Bob Hebert, Sarah Harris, and Wake Forest University for the support they provided and owe thanks to our faculty colleagues for the encouragement and assistance provided on a continuing basis during the preparation of the manuscript. We wish to express our appreciation to the members of the South-Western/ITP staff—particularly, Lisa Lysne, Brenda Owens, and Keri Witman— for their help in the preparation and promotion of this book. We also wish to express our appreciation for the sound advice and extensive assistance of Chad Thomas and the rest of the staff at Carlisle Publishers Services. Most of all we would like to thank our editor, Susanna Smart, who is a constant source of excellent advice and encouragement. Susan's high standards of performance and her total knowledge of the publishing field have helped immensely with this project.

We are grateful to the Literary Executor of the late Sir Ronald A. Fisher, F.R.S.; to Dr. Frank Yates, F.R.S.; and to Longman Group, Ltd., London, for permission to reprint Table III from their book *Statistical Tables for Biological, Agriculture, and Medical Research* (6th ed., 1974).

James R. McGuigan
R. Charles Moyer
Frederick H. deB. Harris

INTRODUCTION

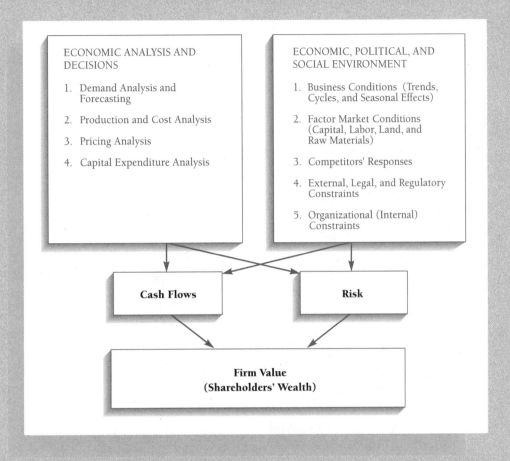

ECONOMIC ANALYSIS AND
DECISIONS

1. Demand Analysis and
   Forecasting

2. Production and Cost Analysis

3. Pricing Analysis

4. Capital Expenditure Analysis

ECONOMIC, POLITICAL, AND
SOCIAL ENVIRONMENT

1. Business Conditions (Trends,
   Cycles, and Seasonal Effects)

2. Factor Market Conditions
   (Capital, Labor, Land, and
   Raw Materials)

3. Competitors' Responses

4. External, Legal, and Regulatory
   Constraints

5. Organizational (Internal)
   Constraints

Cash Flows

Risk

Firm Value
(Shareholders' Wealth)

Part I (Introduction) presents an overview of managerial economics analysis and introduces some key economic concepts and tools. In the first chapter, the goals of the enterprise (both the for-profit firm and the not-for-profit organization) are developed; the decision-making process and the philosophy of optimization are introduced; the role of profit is discussed; and the relationship between managerial economics techniques and accounting, finance, marketing, operations management, and labor relations are highlighted. Chapter 2 reviews fundamental economic concepts, including marginal analysis, net present value, risk versus return analysis, and the measurement of risk. Chapter 3 provides a self-contained introduction to optimization and constrained optimization techniques, including applications of basic calculus. Linear programming applications appear later (in Chapter 10), following the discussion of production and cost. The tools and concepts developed in Part I are central to the analyses used throughout the balance of the text.

1

Introduction and Goals of the Firm

CHAPTER PREVIEW

Managerial economics is the application of microeconomic theory and methodology to decision-making problems faced by private, public, and not-for-profit institutions. Managerial economics assists decision makers (managers) in efficiently allocating scarce resources, planning corporate strategy, and executing effective tactics. Economic profit is defined and the role of profits in allocating resources in a free enterprise system is examined. The primary normative goal of the firm, namely, shareholder wealth maximization, is developed along with a discussion of how managerial decisions influence shareholder wealth. Next, the problems associated with the separation of ownership and control and agency relationships in large corporations are explored. Finally, appropriate normative goals to guide resource-allocation decisions in public sector and not-for-profit enterprises are discussed.

WHAT IS MANAGERIAL ECONOMICS?

Managerial economics deals with the application of microeconomic theory and methodology to decision-making problems faced by private, public, and not-for-profit institutions. The field of managerial economics has experienced rapid growth over the past three decades. This growth reflects a realization that analysts, directors, and senior managers can use economic theory to make decisions consistent with the goals of the organization. Managerial economics extracts from microeconomic theory those concepts and techniques that enable the decision maker to allocate efficiently the resources of the organization and to respond effectively to tactical issues.

The tools of managerial economics can be applied by managers in profit-seeking firms and in the public and not-for-profit sectors of the economy, because managers in all types of enterprises face a common set of problems. Despite some unique complexities, managerial problems generally follow this form:

> To identify the alternative means of achieving given objective(s), and then to select the alternative that accomplishes the objective(s) in the most resource efficient manner, taking into account the likely actions and reactions of interdependent rival decision makers.

EXAMPLE

www . . . .
You can learn more about Toyota's operations by accessing their website at http://www.toyota.com/times
For example, on July 8, 1997, Toyota completed the construction of a new $700 million manufacturing facility in Princeton, Indiana.

DECISION PROBLEM: TOYOTA MOTORS

Consider Toyota Motors operations in the United States. Toyota faces increasing demand for its U.S.-manufactured vehicles. It has identified two possible strategies (S1 and S2) to meet the growing demand for its products. Strategy S1 represents an internal expansion of capacity. Strategy S2 represents the purchase of a surplus plant now owned by General Motors. The objective of Toyota's managers is to maximize the value today (present value) of expected future returns (profit) from the capacity expansion. This problem can be summarized as follows:

$$\text{Objective function: Maximize (present value) profit (S1, S2)}$$

In this example, the following decision rule can be created:

$$\text{Decision rule: Choose strategy S1 if Profit (S1)} \geq \text{Profit (S2)}$$
$$\text{Choose strategy S2 if Profit (S1)} < \text{Profit (S2)}$$

Although this is a simple problem, it illustrates the essential elements of resource-allocation problems. Economic theory can assist a manager in deciding on the appropriate objective function and in clarifying the decision rules.

MANAGERIAL ECONOMICS AND ECONOMIC THEORY

Economics traditionally is divided into *microeconomics* and *macroeconomics*. Microeconomics deals with the theory of individual choice; that is, decisions made by a particular consuming unit, such as an individual, or a producing unit, such as a business firm. Macroeconomics focuses on the overall economy and general economic equilibrium conditions. Managerial economists draw on both of these branches of economics during the decision-making process. Although a firm's managers can do little to affect the aggregate economy, their decisions should be consistent with the current economic outlook.

The types of decisions made by managers usually involve questions of resource allocation within the organization in both the short and the long run. In the short run, a

SALOMON BROTHERS' EXECUTIVE OFFICER PERFORMANCE BONUS PLAN[1]

Separation of ownership (shareholders) and control (management) in large corporations permits managers to pursue goals, such as maximization of their own personal welfare, that are not always in the long-term interests of shareholders. As the result of pressure from large institutional shareholders and recent tax law changes,[2] a growing number of corporations are seeking to forge a closer alliance between the interests of shareholders and managers by structuring compensation plans that have a larger proportion of the manager's compensation in the form of performance-based payments.

One such unusual plan, devised by Salomon Brothers, a large investment banking firm, pays its chairman, Deryck C. Maughan, an annual base salary of $1 million plus an annual performance bonus of up to $24 million. This bonus is based on Salomon's overall rate of return on equity and its rate of return *relative to* the firm's five major competitors.[3] The following table shows the possible performance bonuses that the chairman can earn. For example, if Salomon's annual return on equity is 5 percent, and is equal to that of the average rate of return of the five

rival firms (i.e., 5 percent, 0), then the chairman would earn no performance bonus. On the other hand, the payment of the maximum $24 million bonus would require the firm to have a very extraordinary year—Salomon's return on equity would have to be 30 percent (or more) and this rate of return would have to be 10 (or more) percentage points above the average of its five major competitors.

The objectives of the firm and how to motivate managers to pursue these objectives are some of the topics discussed in this chapter.

WWW . . . .

You can access financial information as well as the annual report for Salomon Brothers on the Internet at http://www.salomon.com/investor.htm

---

[1] Michael Siconofli, "Salomon's Chief Stands to Hit the Jackpot," *Wall Street Journal*, 5 May 1994, p. C1.

[2] Changes in the tax laws (1993) bar publicly held corporations from deducting (in computing taxable income) compensation of more than $1 million for each of its top executives, unless it is based on performance goals approved by shareholders.

[3] These competitors are Merrill Lynch, Morgan Stanley, Bear Sterns, J. P. Morgan, and Bankers Trust.

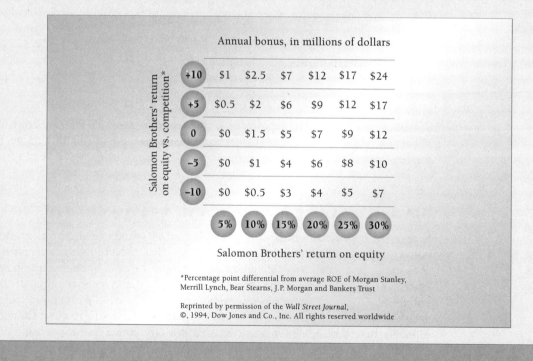

Annual bonus, in millions of dollars

Salomon Brothers' return on equity vs. competition*	5%	10%	15%	20%	25%	30%
+10	$1	$2.5	$7	$12	$17	$24
+5	$0.5	$2	$6	$9	$12	$17
0	$0	$1.5	$5	$7	$9	$12
−5	$0	$1	$4	$6	$8	$10
−10	$0	$0.5	$3	$4	$5	$7

Salomon Brothers' return on equity

*Percentage point differential from average ROE of Morgan Stanley, Merrill Lynch, Bear Stearns, J.P. Morgan and Bankers Trust

manager may be interested in estimating demand and cost relationships to make decisions about the price to charge for a product and the quantity of output to produce. The areas of microeconomics dealing with demand theory and with the theory of cost and production are obviously useful in making decisions on such matters. Macroeconomic theory also enters into decision making when a manager attempts to forecast future demand based on forces influencing the overall economy.

In the long run, decisions must be made about expanding or contracting production and distribution facilities, developing and marketing new products, and possibly acquiring other firms. Basically, these decisions are concerned with economies (or diseconomies) of scale and typically require the organization to make capital expenditures; that is, expenditures made in the current period that are expected to yield returns in future periods. Economists have developed a theory of capital that can be used in deciding whether to undertake specific capital expenditures.

THE DECISION-MAKING MODEL

The ability to make good decisions is the key to successful managerial performance. Managers of profit-seeking firms are faced with a wide range of important decisions in the areas of pricing, product choice, cost control, advertising, capital investments, and dividend policy, to name but a few. Managers in the not-for-profit and the public sectors are faced with a similarly wide range of decisions. For example, the dean of your school must decide how to allocate funds among such competing needs as travel, phone services, and secretarial support. Longer-range decisions must be made about new facilities, new programs, the purchase or lease of a new computer, and the decision to establish an executive training center. Public sector managers face such decisions as the need for a "Stealth" bomber, the need to support public transit systems, the enforcement of antitrust laws, the economic viability of passive restraint devices in automobiles, and alternatives to reduce energy consumption.

Decision making in each of these areas shares several common elements. First, the decision maker must establish or identify the objectives of the organization. The failure to identify organizational objectives correctly can result in the complete rejection of an otherwise well-conceived and well-implemented plan. Later sections of this chapter deal with the issue of organizational objectives.

Next, the decision maker must identify the problem requiring a solution. For example, the manager of a brewing plant in Milwaukee may note that the plant's profit margin on sales has been decreasing. This could be caused by pricing errors, labor force problems, or the use of outdated production equipment. Once the source or sources of the problem are identified, the manager can move to an examination of potential solutions. If the problem is the use of technologically inefficient equipment, two possible solutions are (1) updating and replacing the plant's equipment or (2) building a completely new plant. The choice between these alternatives depends on the relative costs and benefits, as well as other organizational and societal constraints that may make one alternative preferable to another. For example, the decision to build a new brewery in a suburban area may not be politically desirable if it means a major inner-city facility must be closed.

The final step in the process, after all alternatives have been identified and evaluated and the best alternative has been chosen, is the implementation of the decision. This phase often requires constant monitoring to ensure that results are as expected. If they are not, corrective action needs to be taken when possible. This five-step decision-making process is illustrated in Figure 1.1.

FIGURE   1.1

The Decision-Making
Process

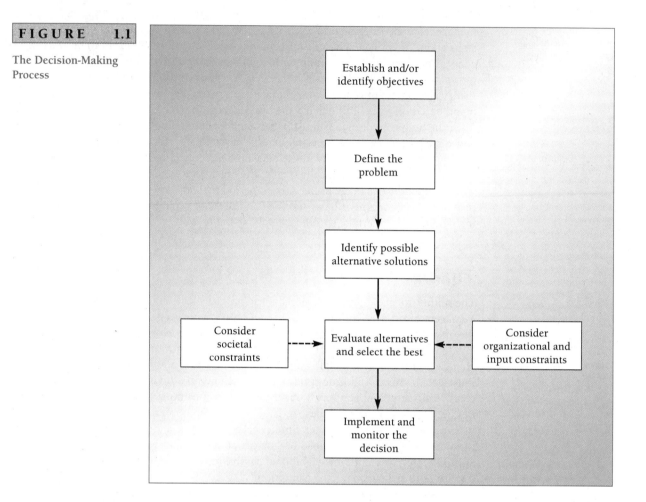

THE ROLE OF PROFITS

Economic Profit
The difference between
total revenue and total
economic cost. Economic
cost includes a "normal"
rate of return on the capital
contributions of the firm's
owners.

Economic profit is the difference between total revenue and total economic cost. *Total
revenue* is measured as the sales receipts of a firm, that is, price times quantity sold. The
economic cost of any activity may be thought of as the highest valued alternative opportunity that is foregone. To attract economic resources to some activity, the firm must pay
a price for these factors (labor, capital, and natural resources) that is sufficient to convince the owners of these resources to sacrifice other alternatives and commit the resources to this use. Thus, economic costs may be thought of as *opportunity costs,* or the
costs of attracting a resource from its next best alternative use. In a general sense, economic profit may be defined as *the difference between total revenue and total economic cost.*

Throughout this text the term *profit* refers to economic profits. Accordingly, the term
cost includes all economic costs, both explicit and implicit,[4] and includes in it a normal
return (profit) for the owners who have contributed their financial resources. When we
refer to profit maximization in this book, we mean an objective of maximizing the economic profit of the firm.

---

[4]The concepts of economic costs and profits are discussed in more detail in Chapter 9.

Why Are Profits Necessary?

In a free enterprise system, economic profits play an important role in guiding the decisions made by the thousands of competing, independent economic units. The existence of profits (resulting from the excess of revenues over costs) determines the type and quantity of goods and services that are produced and sold. It also determines the demand for various factors of production—labor, capital, and natural resources. Because of the important role played by profits in our system, we review several theories of profit.

Risk-Bearing Theory of Profit   Some economists have argued that economic profits above a normal rate of return are necessary to compensate the owners of the firm for the risk they assume when making their investments. Because a firm's shareholders are not entitled to a fixed rate of return on their investment—that is, they are residual claimants to the firm's resources—they need to be compensated for this risk in the form of a higher rate of return.

<table>
<tr><td>

EXAMPLE

www. . . . .
The website for Circus Circus Enterprises is http://www.circuscircus.com

</td><td>

RISK AND PROFITABILITY: CIRCUS CIRCUS

The relationship between risk and profit levels can be seen in the case of Circus Circus, the Las Vegas hotel and casino operator. During 1994 Circus Circus earned a return on net worth of about 20.5 percent, compared with a mean return on net worth of 12.5 percent for all firms in the hotel/gaming industry and of 15.0 percent for all industrial, retail, and transportation firms followed by *Value Line*. The hotel and gaming industries are subject to substantial swings in profitability over time. Firms operating in these industries also are subject to severe competitive pressures. In addition, Circus Circus is financed with a high proportion of debt (50 percent of total capital), compared with an average of 39 percent for the other firms followed by *Value Line*. Other firms in this industry did not perform as well as Circus Circus during 1994. Mirage Resorts earned 11.5 percent on net worth, Hilton earned 10.5 percent, and Bally earned 2.5 percent. Firms that operate in a high-risk industry such as this one require the incentive of high potential profits to attract capital. The high returns of Circus Circus come with high risk (variability), however.

</td></tr>
</table>

The risk-bearing theory of profits is explained in the context of normal profits, where *normal* is defined in terms of the relative risk of alternative investments. Normal profits for a high-risk firm, such as a casino operator, should be higher than normal profits for firms of lesser risk, such as water utilities. Indeed, the industry average return on net worth for the hotel/gaming industry was 12.5 percent in 1994, compared with 10.0 percent for the water utility industry.

Dynamic Equilibrium (Friction) Theory of Profit   According to the dynamic equilibrium or friction theory of profit, there exists a long-run equilibrium normal rate of profit (adjusted for risk) that all firms should tend to earn. At any point in time, however, an individual firm or the firms in a specific industry might earn a rate of return above or below this long-run normal return level. This can occur because of temporary dislocations (shocks) in various sectors of the economy. For example, U.S. firms that produced oil and natural gas experienced a dramatic increase in profits in response to supply shortages following the invasion of Kuwait by Iraq in 1990. Rates of return rose substantially. However, those high returns declined shortly after the war ended when market conditions led to excess supplies.

Similarly, if a new, inexpensive, and readily available energy source were to be discovered, oil prices would decline substantially. Over time, some producers would leave this increasingly unprofitable market until a normal rate of profit is restored for the remaining firms. The inability of our economic system to adjust instantaneously to changes in market conditions may result in short-term profits above or below normal levels.

Monopoly Theory of Profit   In some industries one firm is effectively able to dominate the market and potentially earn above-normal rates of return for a long period of time. This ability to dominate the market may arise from economies of scale (a situation in which one large firm can produce additional units of output at a lower cost than can smaller firms), control of essential natural resources, control of critical patents, or governmental restrictions that prohibit competition. The conditions under which a monopolist can earn above-normal profits are discussed in greater depth in Chapter 14.

Innovation Theory of Profit   The innovation theory of profit suggests that above-normal profits are the reward for successful innovations. Firms that develop unique, high-quality products (such as Microsoft in the computer software industry) or firms that are successful in identifying unique market opportunities (such as Federal Express) are rewarded with the potential for above-normal profits. Indeed, the U.S. patent system is designed to ensure that these above-normal return opportunities furnish strong incentives for continued innovation.

Managerial Efficiency Theory of Profit   Closely related to the innovation theory is the managerial efficiency theory of profit. This theory maintains that above-normal profits can arise because of the exceptional managerial skills of well-managed firms. The ability to earn above-normal profits by exercising high-quality managerial skills is a continuing incentive for greater efficiency in our economic system.

No single theory of profit can explain the observed profit rates in each industry, nor are these theories necessarily mutually exclusive. Profit performance is invariably the result of many factors, including differential risk, innovation, managerial skills, the existence of monopoly power, and chance occurrences. The important thing to remember is that profit and profit opportunities play a major role in determining the efficient allocation of resources in our economy. Without the market signals that profits give, it would be necessary to develop alternative schemes on which to base resource-allocation decisions. These alternatives are often highly bureaucratic and frequently lack the responsiveness to changing market conditions that a free enterprise system provides.

OBJECTIVE OF THE FIRM

One common economic model of the firm assumes that the objective of the owners of the firm is to maximize profits. This profit-maximization model of firm behavior has been extremely rich in its decision-making implications. The marginal (and incremental) decision rules that have been derived from this theory provide very useful guidelines for making a wide range of resource-allocation decisions. For example, if incremental cost is defined as the change in total cost resulting from a decision, and if incremental revenue is defined as the change in total revenue resulting from a decision, then any business decision is profitable if one of these results occurs:

1. It increases revenue more than costs.
2. It decreases some costs more than it increases others (assuming revenues remain constant).

3. It increases some revenues more than it decreases others (assuming costs remain constant).
4. It reduces costs more than revenue.

The simple profit-maximization model of the firm has provided decision makers with useful insights regarding efficient resource management and allocation. However, the profit-maximization model is limited because it does not incorporate the time dimension in the decision process and it does not consider risk. The shareholder wealth-maximization model of the firm overcomes these limitations.

The Shareholder Wealth-Maximization Model of the Firm

Effective economic decision making requires an understanding of the goal(s) of the firm. What objective(s) should guide business decision making? That is, what *should* management try to achieve for the owners of the firm? The most widely accepted objective of the firm is to maximize the value of the firm for its owners; that is, to *maximize* **shareholder wealth.** Shareholder wealth is measured by the market price of a firm's common stock.

The shareholder wealth-maximization goal states that a firm's management should maximize the *present value* of the *expected future returns* to the owners (shareholders). As we shall see in Chapter 19, these returns are in the form of cash flows. For simplicity, at this point let us consider cash flows to be the same as profits. Hence, the value of a firm's stock is equal to the present value of all expected future profits, discounted at the shareholders' required rate of return, or

Shareholder Wealth
A measure of the value of a firm. Shareholder wealth is equal to the value of a firm's common stock, which, in turn, is equal to the present value of all future cash returns expected to be generated by the firm for the benefit of its owners.

$$V_0 = \frac{\pi_1}{(1+k_e)^1} + \frac{\pi_2}{(1+k_e)^2} + \frac{\pi_3}{(1+k_e)^3} + \ldots + \frac{\pi_\infty}{(1+k_e)^\infty}$$

$$V_0 = \sum_{t=1}^{\infty} \frac{\pi_t}{(1+k_e)^t} \qquad [1.1]$$

where V_0 is the current (present) value of a share of stock, π_t represents the profits expected in each of the future periods (1 through ∞), and k_e equals the investors' required rate of return. Equation 1.1 assumes that the reader is familiar with the concept of discounting and present values. (A review of this concept is found in Appendix A at the end of the book.) For the purposes of analysis here, it is only necessary to recognize that \$1 received one year from today is generally worth less than \$1 received today because \$1 today can be invested at some rate of interest, for example, 15 percent, to yield \$1.15 at the end of one year. Thus, an investor who requires (or has an opportunity to earn) a 15 percent annual rate of return on an investment would place a current value of \$1 on \$1.15 expected to be received in one year.

Equation 1.1 explicitly considers the *timing* of future profits. By discounting all future profits at the required rate of return, k_e, Equation 1.1 recognizes that a dollar received in the future is worth less than a dollar received immediately.

Equation 1.1 also provides a conceptual basis for evaluating differential levels of *risk*. For example, if a series of future profits is highly uncertain (i.e., likely to diverge substantially from their expected values), the discount rate, k_e, can be increased to account for this risk. Thus, the greater the risk associated with receiving a future benefit (profit), the lower the value placed by investors on that benefit. The shareholder wealth-maximization model of the firm is therefore capable of dealing with the two primary shortcomings of the static profit-maximization model.

www . . . .
You can access interim
shareholder reports and
book value information for
Berkshire Hathaway on the
Internet at
http://www.
berkshirehathaway.com
For example, as of June 30,
1997, their net book value
per share of Class A
common stock was
$22,732.

SHAREHOLDER WEALTH MAXIMIZATION: BERKSHIRE HATHAWAY CORPORATION

Warren E. Buffett, chairman and CEO of Berkshire Hathaway, Inc., has described the long-term economic goal of Berkshire Hathaway as follows: "to maximize the average annual rate of gain in intrinsic business value on a per-share basis."[5] Berkshire's book value per share has increased from $19.46 in 1964, when he acquired the firm, to $19,011 at the end of 1996, a compound annual rate of growth of about 23 percent. The growth rate in the market value of Berkshire's shares has been even greater, with the market value per share reaching $36,500 at the end of 1996. Berkshire's directors are all major stockholders. At least four of the directors have over 50 percent of their family's net worth invested in Berkshire. Insiders own over 47 percent of the firm's stock. Buffet's firm has placed a high premium on the goal of maximizing shareholder wealth, that is, maximizing the value of the owners' portion of the firm.

Additional insight regarding the achievement of the shareholder wealth-maximization goal can be gained by decomposing the profit concept, π, into its important elements. Profit in period t, π_t, is equal to total revenue (TR_t) minus total costs (TC_t), or

$$\pi_t = TR_t - TC_t \qquad [1.2]$$

Similarly, total revenue in period t equals price per unit (P_t) times quantity sold (Q_t), or

$$TR_t = P_t \cdot Q_t \qquad [1.3]$$

Total cost in period t equals variable cost per unit (V_t) times the number of units of output (Q_t) plus fixed costs in period t, or

$$TC_t = V_t \cdot Q_t + F_t \qquad [1.4]$$

By combining Equations 1.2, 1.3, and 1.4 with Equation 1.1, we get

$$V_0 \cdot (\text{Shares Outstanding}) = \sum_{t=1}^{\infty} \frac{P_t \cdot Q_t - V_t \cdot Q_t - F_t}{(1 + k_e)^t} \qquad [1.5]$$

The term $P_t \cdot Q_t$ represents the total revenue generated by the firm. From a decision-making perspective, this value is dependent on the firm's demand function (discussed in Chapters 4–6) and the firm's pricing decisions (see Chapters 12–17).

The firm's costs, both fixed (F_t) and variable (V_t) are discussed in Chapters 8–11. In addition, the choice of investments made by the firm—the capital budgeting decisions—determines what proportion of total cost will be fixed and what proportion will be variable. A firm that chooses a capital-intensive production technology will tend to have a higher proportion of its total costs of operation represented as fixed costs than will a firm that chooses a more labor-intensive technology. Capital budgeting decisions are considered in Chapter 19.

The discount rate, k_e, that investors use to value the stream of income generated by a firm is determined by the perceived risk of the firm and by conditions in the financial markets, including the level of expected inflation. Risk and its relationship to required rates of return are discussed in Chapters 2 and 20.

[5]*Annual Report*, Berkshire Hathaway, Inc., 1996.

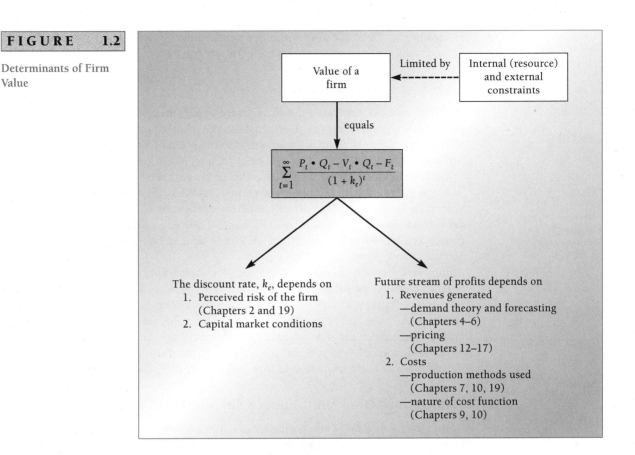

FIGURE 1.2

Determinants of Firm Value

Value of a firm — Limited by → Internal (resource) and external constraints

↓ equals

$$\sum_{t=1}^{\infty} \frac{P_t \cdot Q_t - V_t \cdot Q_t - F_t}{(1 + k_e)^t}$$

The discount rate, k_e, depends on
1. Perceived risk of the firm (Chapters 2 and 19)
2. Capital market conditions

Future stream of profits depends on
1. Revenues generated
   —demand theory and forecasting (Chapters 4–6)
   —pricing (Chapters 12–17)
2. Costs
   —production methods used (Chapters 7, 10, 19)
   —nature of cost function (Chapters 9, 10)

In making its pricing, output, production, and cost decisions, management is faced with several legal, behavioral, value-based, and environmental constraints on its actions. These constraints are briefly considered in the next section and discussed in greater detail in Chapter 18.

The integrative nature of the wealth-maximization model is illustrated in Figure 1.2.

EXAMPLE

www..............
Firms such as IBM can also develop the expertise to produce complementary products through the acquisition process. You can learn about IBM's most recent acquisitions at their website at
http://www.ibm.com/
Investor/acquisitions.
html

RESOURCE-ALLOCATION DECISIONS AND SHAREHOLDER WEALTH MAXIMIZATION: IBM CORPORATION

Consider the case of IBM. Its research and development personnel must develop products that will appeal to its customers and/or increase current operating efficiency. Engineers design production facilities to produce products in the most cost-efficient manner. Marketing researchers try to identify customer needs and provide important information about competitors that influences pricing, product quality, and product feature decisions. Financial managers must acquire the funds needed to produce IBM's products and fund its capital outlays. Personnel managers work to attract and retain a cost-effective workforce. These decisions are made against a backdrop of internal resource constraints, government regulation, and legal constraints. By working together toward the common goal, shareholder wealth can be maximized.

In summary, the value of an enterprise is determined by the amount, timing, and risk of the profits expected to be generated by the enterprise.

Profits versus Cash Flows

In the previous discussion of the shareholder wealth-maximization objective, we have talked about maximizing the present value of expected future *profits*. The economic profit concept we are using is *not* the same as the accounting definition of earnings, or net income. Accounting profits are subject to ambiguous interpretation because of the broad latitude provided by generally accepted accounting principles in its definition. Also, the accounting profit concept does not consider some important economic costs, such as the opportunity cost of the capital invested by owners. In addition, accounting profit concepts may not be reflective of the actual *cash flows* collected and paid by a company over time, especially when one considers differential methods of computing depreciation and of inventory valuation.

In practice, managers who seek to maximize shareholder wealth focus on maximizing the present value of the cash flows available to the equity (owners) of the firm. The cash flow definition of benefits available to a firm's owners is unambiguous and consistent with the objective of maximizing the present value of expected future economic profits. Throughout the text, when the term *profit* is used, it means economic, not accounting-defined profits. When used in this way, the profit concept is consistent with the cash flow concept and will lead to wealth-maximizing decisions by managers.

Managerial Actions to Influence Shareholder Wealth

How can managers influence the magnitude, timing, and risk of the profits expected to be generated by the firm to maximize shareholder wealth? Many factors ultimately influence the magnitude, timing, and risk of a firm's profits and thus the price of the firm's stock. (A firm's stock price is the tangible measure of shareholder wealth.) Some of these factors are related to the external economic environment and are largely outside the direct control of managers. Other factors can be directly manipulated by the managers. Figure 1.3 illustrates the factors affecting stock prices. The top panel enumerates some of the factors in the economic environment that have an impact on the strategic decisions managers can make. The economic environment factors are largely outside the direct control of managers (e.g., antitrust policy or the yen/dollar exchange rate), but managers must be aware of how these factors affect the policy decisions under the control of management. Many of these economic environment factors act as constraints, or limitations, on the value-maximizing decisions available to managers.

In this context, it is useful to consider a competitive strategy framework developed initially by Michael E. Porter and developed further by Alfred Rappaport.[6,7] Porter and Rappaport recommend that managers formulate an overall competitive strategy analyzing five competitive forces that can influence an industry's structure and can therefore ultimately affect the market prices of stocks of individual companies in a particular industry. The five competitive forces are

1. The threat of new entrants.
2. The threat of substitute products.
3. The bargaining power of buyers.

---

[6] Michael E. Porter, *Competitive Advantage* (New York: Free Press, 1985), chapter 1.

[7] Alfred Rappaport, *Creating Shareholder Value* (New York: Free Press, 1986), chapter 4.

4. The bargaining power of suppliers.
5. The rivalry among current competitors.

By making policy decisions using such a competitive framework, managers can be in a position to create value for shareholders.

The policy decision areas are enumerated in the next panel of Figure 1.3. Managers make choices regarding the products to be produced, the technology used to produce them, the marketing effort and distribution channels, and the selection of employees and their compensation. In addition, managers establish investment policies, the ownership structure of the firm, the capital structure (use of debt) of the firm, working capital management policies, and dividend policies. Managers also initiate restructuring

FIGURE   1.3

Factors Affecting Stock
Prices

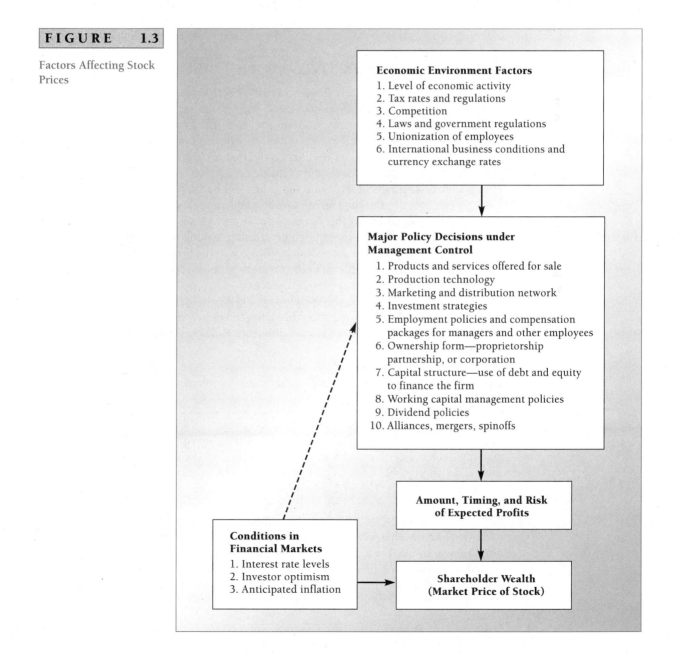

events, such as mergers, spinoffs, and alliances in an attempt to increase capitalized value. The decisions made in these key policy decision areas determine the amount, timing, and risk of the firm's expected cash flows. Participants in the financial markets evaluate the profits expected by the firm in relation to alternative streams of profits expected from other firms and ultimately establish the price of the firm's stock. The value of a firm's stock is influenced at any point in time by general conditions in the financial markets, including the level of interest rates, anticipated inflation rates, and the level of investor optimism regarding the future. Financial market conditions also affect the major policy decisions made by management.

The resource-allocation decisions of managers must be made according to resource, legal, environmental, and behavioral constraints. The focus of this book is on making decisions subject to constraints that can improve the amount, the timing, or the risk profile of a firm's profit stream, thus leading to increases in shareholder wealth.

ALTERNATIVE OBJECTIVES OF THE FIRM

The marginal (or incremental) decision criteria, derived from the static profit-maximization objectives and the dynamic shareholder wealth-maximization objectives, are useful in cases where alternative decisions are easily enumerated and outcomes (costs and revenues) associated with these alternatives can be estimated. These cases include such problems as scheduling for optimal production, determining an optimal inventory policy given some pattern of sales and available production facilities, and choosing from among alternative means of achieving some desirable end result (for example, buying or leasing a machine or refunding an outstanding bond issue). In practice, the techniques of optimization suggested by the marginal decision rules and the wealth-maximization objective are frequently employed to guide decision making in the corporation.

By observing the way decisions are actually made in the firm and comparing these decisions with the efficiency criteria in the previous sections, economists have frequently found a divergence between theory and practice. What are the reasons for this divergence? As the small business enterprise grew and expanded into the modern corporation of today, the roles of ownership and management became increasingly separated,[8] permitting managers to pursue their self-interests. A discussion of divergent objectives follows.

Divergent Objectives

Separation of ownership and control has permitted managers to pursue goals more consistent with their own self-interests, subject, of course, to the constraint that they satisfy shareholders sufficiently to maintain control of the corporation. Instead of seeking to maximize some objective (such as shareholder wealth), management is said to "satisfice" or seek acceptable levels of performance, while maximizing their own welfare. For example, in the early 1980s, Exxon managers diversified the general administrative function of the company into product lines, such as computer software development, where Exxon had little or no competitive advantage. Although wild fluctuations in the executive bonuses that were tied to quarterly earnings did smooth out, the diversification decision resulted in a decline in the value of Exxon stock.

Maximization of their own personal welfare (or utility) may also lead managers to be concerned with long-run survival (job security). The concern for long-run survival may

---

[8] Adolf Berle and Gardiner C. Means, *The Modern Corporation and Private Property* (New York: Macmillan, 1932).

lead management to minimize (or limit) the amount of risk incurred by the firm, because unfavorable outcomes can lead to their dismissal or possible bankruptcy for the firm. Likewise, the desire for job security is cited as one reason management often opposes takeover offers (mergers) by other companies. Giving senior management "golden parachute" contracts to compensate them if they lose their positions as the result of a merger is one approach designed to ensure that they will act in the interests of shareholders in merger decisions, rather than in their own interests.

EXAMPLE

WWW . . . .
PepsiCo pays its CEO and executive officers bonus awards based on factors such as financial earnings and market share. This information is usually contained in proxy statements, which you can find on the Internet at http://www.pepsico.com/web_pages/resource/financial_info.html

EXECUTIVE COMPENSATION AND SHAREHOLDER WEALTH MAXIMIZATION

How should corporations structure the compensation (i.e., salary and incentives) of officers and directors to motivate these managers to make decisions that maximize shareholder wealth? One approach, such as the Salomon Brothers example cited earlier in the Managerial Challenge, is to offer managers cash bonuses based on the overall performance of the firm or division in the firm. Another approach is to offer executives options to buy stock in the company at some predetermined price. If the firm prospers, then both the owners and managers will reap the rewards of higher stock prices. However, this approach does not always lead to a long-term wealth-maximization perspective on the part of managers. Instead of retaining their ownership interest in the company, executives sometimes exercise the options and sell the stock relatively quickly.

Several corporations have tried an alternative approach to getting officers and directors to think of themselves as owners, rather than as hired help, by requiring (or voluntarily encouraging) them to own stock in the company. Kodak, for example, requires 40 of its top executives to invest one to four times their base salary in Kodak stock.[9] General Motors instituted a similar plan by requiring its top 65 executives to hold General Motors common stock equivalent in market value to the manager's annual salary.[10] Other companies that have instituted either mandatory or voluntary stock ownership guidelines include Xerox, CSX, Union Carbide, and Hershey Foods. A survey found that nearly 10 percent of U.S. firms with sales exceeding $5 billion require senior executives to hold common stock in the company.[11] This requirement appears to be a growing trend—over 50 percent of the CEOs of 561 major corporations believe executives should be required to own significant amounts of stock in the companies where they are employed.[12]

Another approach to encourage officers and directors to act in the interests of shareholders, which has not yet gained widespread use, is to compensate them in shares of the common stock of the company. For example, Panhandle Eastern's president is paid entirely in common stock of the company—25,000 shares per quarter (plus medical benefits)—and receives no retirement or severance benefits.[13] Similarly, Scott Paper and Travelers pay their outside directors solely in common stock.[14]

---

[9] Grace M. Kang, "Now, a Big Job at Kodak Means You'll Buy a Big Stake," *Business Week,* 1 February 1993, p. 26.

[10] Robert L. Simison, "GM in Bid to Retain Talent, Awards Hefty Raises to 3,400 Top Executives," *Wall Street Journal,* 3 March 1994, p. A2.

[11] Joann S. Lublin, "Buy or Bye," *Wall Street Journal,* 21 April 1993, p. R9.

[12] Ibid., p. R9.

[13] "Panhandle Eastern Prospers by Hauling Others' Fuel," *Wall Street Journal,* 2 February 1993, p. B4.

[14] Martha Irvine, "Scott Paper Chief Tells Nine Directors: Think Like a Holder," *Wall Street Journal,* 31 August 1994, p. C15.

The trend toward long-term, performance-based compensation plans is not limited just to a firm's top layer of managers. For example, in 1989 PepsiCo announced a stock option plan for all of its 100,000 employees who work 30 hours or more per week—from truck drivers to plant managers. Although the PepsiCo plan is the exception, there has been a growing tendency for stock option plans to be widened in their coverage. The average large firm now has 300 to 400 of its top employees covered by stock option plans, up from about 100 employees just 10 years ago.[15] In addition, the size of the long-term compensation received by managers has grown dramatically. For example, Michael Eisner received over $20.2 million in long-term compensation (in addition to his $750,000 salary) as a reward for increasing Walt Disney's market value over 10-fold to $22.7 billion during his 10 years as chairman.[16]

The growth of performance-based compensation plans is an attempt to realign the interests of managers with those of stockholders, and thereby avoid costly inefficiencies that can arise due to a divergence of interests.

Agency Problems

The existence of divergent objectives between owners and managers is one example of a class of problems arising from agency relationships. *Agency relationships* occur when one or more individuals (the principals) employ another individual (the agent) to perform a service on behalf of the principals.[17] In an agency relationship, decision-making authority often is delegated to the agent from the principals. In the context of managerial economics, the most important agency relationship is the relationship between stockholders (owners) and managers.

Stockholders and Managers   Inefficiencies that arise because of agency relationships have been called *agency problems*. These problems occur because each party to a transaction is assumed to act in a manner consistent with maximizing his or her own utility (welfare). The concern by some managers for long-run survival (job security), rather than shareholder wealth maximization, is an example of an agency problem. Another example is the consumption of on-the-job perquisites (such as the use of company airplanes, limousines, and luxurious offices) by managers who have no (or only a partial) ownership interest in the firm. Shirking by managers is also an agency-related problem.

The common factors that give rise to all principal-agent problems are the unobservability of some manager-agent action and the presence of random disturbances in team production. The job performance of parking gate attendants and piecework garment workers is easily monitored, but the work effort of salespeople and manufacturer's trade representatives may not be observable at less-than-prohibitive cost. Observing the managerial input is even more problematic because managers contribute an input one might call "creative ingenuity." Creative ingenuity in making the company's decisions is inherently unobservable; owners know it when they see it, but do not recognize when it is missing. As a result, the managerial input is inseparable from good and bad luck in explaining fluctuations in company performance. Owners therefore find it difficult to know when to reward managers and when to blame them for poor performance.

---

[15] Jolie Solomon, "Pepsi Offers Stock Options to All, Not Just Honchos," *Wall Street Journal,* 28 June 1989.

[16] "That Eye-Popping Executive Pay," *Business Week,* 25 April 1994, pp. 52–58.

[17] See Amir Barnea, R. Haugen, and L. Senbet, *Agency Problems and Financial Contracting* (Englewood Cliffs, N.J.: Prentice-Hall, 1985), for an overview of the agency problem issue. See also Michael Jensen and William Meckling, "Theory of the Firm: Managerial Behavior, Agency Costs, and Ownership Structure," *Journal of Financial Economics,* October 1976, pp. 305–360, and Eugene Fama, "Agency Problems and the Theory of the Firm," *Journal of Political Economy,* April 1980, pp. 288–307.

Agency Costs

Costs associated with resolving conflicts of interest among shareholders, managers, and lenders. Agency costs include the cost of monitoring and bonding performance, the cost of constructing contracts designed to minimize agency conflicts, and the loss in efficiency resulting from unresolved agent-principal conflicts.

To mitigate these agency problems the firm incurs several **agency costs.** Examples of these agency costs include

1. Expenditures to structure the organization in such a way as to minimize the incentives for management to take actions contrary to shareholder interests, such as providing a portion of management's compensation in the form of stock of the corporation.
2. Expenditures to monitor management's actions, such as paying for audits of managerial performance and internal audits of the firm's expenditures.
3. Bonding expenditures to protect the owners from managerial dishonesty.
4. The opportunity cost of lost profits arising from complex organizational structures that prevent management from making timely responses to opportunities.

Managerial motivations to act in the interests of stockholders include the structure of their compensation package, the threat of dismissal, and the threat of takeover by a new group of owners. Economic theory has shown that agency problems and their associated costs can be reduced greatly if the financial markets operate efficiently. Some agency problems can be reduced by the use of complex managerial incentive contracts, which are discussed in Chapter 13. Remaining agency problems give rise to costs that show up as a reduction in the value of the firm's shares in the marketplace.

EXAMPLE

www..............
You can learn about RJR Nabisco's financial performance since the KKR takeover at their Internet site:
http://www.rjrnabisco.com/

AGENCY COSTS AND CORPORATE TAKEOVERS: RJR NABISCO

When managers do not have a significant ownership stake in the firm they manage, there is the potential that shareholder resources will be diverted from their most productive uses to provide perquisites for managers that are inconsistent with the most efficient allocation of resources. When this happens, pressure may build for a change in management. For example, in 1988 RJR Nabisco was a firm that had become bloated with resources that were frequently being allocated in an unwise manner. The executive beach homes in Florida; the gargantuan airplane hangar in Atlanta for the firm's extensive fleet of corporate aircraft; the expensive, but failed, "smokeless" cigarette, Premier; and the trail of failed former acquisitions had left RJR Nabisco with substantially less value in the marketplace than was possible with better management. Recognizing this, Kohlberg Kravis Roberts & Co. (KKR) initiated an unfriendly takeover bid and paid a record $25 billion to acquire RJR Nabisco in early 1989. This represented a price of about $109 per share, compared with a pre-takeover price in the range of $50 to $55. The deal was heavily leveraged with debt. The new owners moved quickly to sell many of RJR's poorly performing assets, slash operating expenses, reduce the company's workforce, and cancel the Premier project.

The RJR takeover illustrates what can happen when managers stray from the goal of wealth maximization and pursue, instead, self-interests. The takeover market, as well as competition from better managed firms, domestically and increasingly from abroad, eventually force most firms to take drastic corrective actions or to face extinction.

EXAMPLE

AGENCY COSTS AND CORPORATE RESTRUCTURING: O.M. SCOTT & SONS

The existence of high agency costs associated with the separation of ownership from management has prompted many firms to financially restructure themselves to achieve higher operating efficiencies. For example, in December 1986, the lawn products firm

O.M. Scott & Sons, prior to that time a subsidiary of ITT, was purchased by the Scott managers in a highly financially leveraged buyout (often referred to as an LBO). Faced with the heavy interest and principal burdens of the debt-financed transaction and having the potential to profit from more efficient operation of the firm, the new owner-managers quickly put in place strategies designed to improve Scott's performance. By monitoring inventory levels more closely and negotiating more aggressively with suppliers, the firm was able to reduce its average monthly working capital investment from an initial level of $75 million to $35 million. At the same time, sales increased from $160 million to a new level of $200 million.[18] One of the motivations for LBO transactions is to reduce the agency costs associated with a separation of ownership from management.

IMPLICATIONS OF SHAREHOLDER WEALTH MAXIMIZATION

Critics of aligning management interests with equity owner interests often allege that shareholder wealth maximization focuses on short-term payoffs to the exclusion of long-term investment. The evidence suggests just the opposite. Near-term cash flows can explain only a small fraction of the capitalized market value reflected in a firm's share price. For example, only 18 percent of 1988 share values can be explained by the first five years of expected dividends and only 35 percent by the entire first ten years.[19] Shareholder wealth maximization is long term not short term in focus. Moreover, it is forward looking, not merely extrapolative. For example, despite consistent upward trends in cash flows and stock price appreciation over the previous ten years, declining share prices of tobacco companies in 1990–1992 anticipated the ongoing switch to generic cigarettes and the additional smoking location restrictions announced in 1992–1994. This also illustrates another implication of shareholder wealth maximization. Value-maximizing managers must manage change, sometimes radical change in competition (e.g., in airlines), technology (e.g., in PCs), and regulation (e.g., in cigarettes), and they must do so three and four steps ahead of current events. Even in periods of relative stability in the business environment, they must focus continuously on change-management questions, like whether to ramp up or phase out capacity in particular product lines.

Shareholder wealth maximization is also a dynamic objective reflecting the currently available public information regarding a company's expected future cash flows and foreseeable risks. As such, it reflects the strategic investment opportunities a management team develops, not only the firm's preexisting positive net present value investments. Amgen, a biotechnology company, had shareholder value of $42 million in 1983 despite no sales, no cash flow, no capital assets, no patents, and poorly protected trade secrets. In 1996, Amgen had sales of over $2.23 billion and cash flow of $781 million annually. In general, only about 85 percent of shareholder value can be explained by even 30 years of cash flows. The remainder reflects the capitalized value of strategic options to expand some profitable lines of business, to cancel and abandon others, and to retain but delay investment until more information becomes available on still other projects.

---

[18] A more complete discussion of the Scott experience can be found in Brett Duval Fromson, "Life After Debt: How LBOs Do It," *Fortune*, 13 March 1989, pp. 91–92.

[19] J.R. Woolridge, "Competitive Decline: Is a Myopic Stock Market to Blame?" *Journal of Applied Corporate Finance*, Spring 1988, pp. 26–36.

Value-maximizing behavior as the objective of management is also distinguishable from satisfiying behavior.[20] Rather than seeking to achieve an incremental moving standard such as 97 percent, 99 percent, 99.9 percent error-free takeoffs and landings from O'Hare airport or 9 percent, 11 percent, 12.1 percent return on equity, the value-maximizing manager commits himself or herself to continuous marginal improvements in accordance with an unambiguous rule of rational life. In particular, any time the marginal benefits of an action exceed their marginal cost, just do it! We discuss this optimization approach to decision-making further in Chapter 3.

In general, then, shareholder wealth maximization implies that management should seek to develop a forward-looking, dynamic, and long-term outlook; anticipate and manage change; acquire strategic investment opportunities; and maximize the present value of expected cash flows to owners, as allowed by legal and regulatory constraints. This maximization of shareholder value is the only objective on which managers need to focus if three conditions hold: complete markets, no significant asymmetric information, and known recontracting costs.

Complete Markets   For all the effects of management decisions to influence a company's cash flows, there must be liquid markets for the firm's inputs, products, and byproducts. For example, if a market in transferable pollution allowances (pollution permits) establishes a price for sulfur dioxide (acid rain) emissions, then managers of power plants can make value-maximizing decisions about whether to install smokestack scrubbers or purchase additional pollution permits. Economically profitable pollution abatement will occur, and over time the number of pollution permits issued and pollution released into the environment can be reduced. Similarly, more complete futures and options markets for crude oil and coffee bean inputs allow Texaco and Starbuck's Coffeehouses to plan with more accurate cash flow projections. For a small 3–5 percent expense known in advance, value-maximizing managers can employ these "derivative markets" to hedge against unexpected cost increases and reduce the respective cost-covering prices of gasoline and cappuccino.

EXAMPLE

TRADABLE POLLUTION PERMITS AT DUKE POWER[21]

Sulfur dioxide (SO_2) byproducts of burning high-sulfur coal in power plants and other heavy industry has raised the acidity of eastern forests from Maine to Georgia to levels almost 100 times higher than in the Grand Tetons and the Cascades of the far Northwest. Dead trees, peeling paint, and stone decomposition on buildings and monuments have been the result. To elicit substantial pollution abatement at the least cost, the Clean Air Act of 1990 created a market in the rights to emit SO_2. The result was tradable pollution permits or allowances (TPAs) issued by the Environmental Protection Agency to 467 known SO_2 polluters for approximately 70 percent of preexisting emissions. The

---

[20] Herbert Simon stated the case for satisficing behavior in "Theories of Decision-Making in Economic and Behavioral Science" reprinted in E. Mansfield, *Microeconomics: Selected Readings,* 5th ed. (New York: Norton, 1985).

[21] Based on "Cornering the Market," *Wall Street Journal,* and Jean-Jacques Laffont and Jean Tirole, "Pollution Permits and Compliance Strategies" and "Pollution Permits and Environmental Innovation," *Journal of Public Economics,* October 1996, p. 127ff.

www................
The EPA keeps track of
allowance transactions and
holdings by way of the
Allowance Tracking System.
You can learn more about
the mechanics of how
allowance trading occurs,
as well as find out about
current allowance prices
and trade volumes, at the
following EPA Internet site:
http://www.epa.gov/
docs/acidrain/trading.
html

utilities then began to trade the allowances. Low-abatement-cost plants sold allowances, and high-abatement-cost plants bought allowances. As a result of the growing completeness of this market, electric utilities like Duke Power now know what expense line to incorporate in their cash flow projections for the SO_2 byproducts of operating with high-sulfur coal. Recently, the TPAs have sold for $131/ton, and a single utility plant operation may require 15,000 tons of permits or more. The continuous tradeoff between installing pollution abatement equipment (e.g., smokestack scrubbers), utilizing higher cost alternative fuels (e.g., low-sulfur coal and natural gas), or paying the current market price of these EPA-issued pollution permits can now be analyzed.

Of course, what would be really useful for value-maximizing managers to know is the forecasted future cost of the permits relative to the life cycle cost of pollution abatement equipment. Futures and forward markets in pollution allowances have emerged to assist polluters in making these determinations. It is now possible to hedge the cost of pollution permits by buying today a futures contract for the delivery of a TPA in, for instance, 1, 2, or 3 years. This locks in the expense of the SO_2 byproduct over that time frame. Should the TPA permits become more expensive, the futures contract holder will receive a rise in contract value which simply offsets the increase in cost of the permit. Should the TPA permits become cheaper, the futures contract holder will suffer a decline in contract value which again simply offsets the reduced cost of the permits. For about 3–5 percent of the value at risk, the power utility can "lock in" its future byproduct expense.

One drawback of these allowance spot markets and futures markets is that the incentives for pollution abatement innovation are reduced. The discoverers of new pollution abatement technology must license their innovation for less money because of the existence of the allowances. In essence, the EPA-issued allowances have created a competing "technology" which reduces the returns to pollution abatement innovation. As a result, an option contract to pollute would be preferable to the current spot market in allowances. For an up-front payment of an option premium, an EPA-issued pollution option would allow companies to elect to pollute over a given exercise period for a given "striking price." The EPA could set the striking price and the allowable exercise period. This public policy mechanism would better preserve the private incentive for value-maximizing managers to develop and adopt innovative pollution abatement technology.

No Asymmetric Information   Monitoring and coordination problems within the corporation and contracting problems between sellers and buyers often arise because of asymmetric information. Line managers and employees can misunderstand what senior executives intend. A Food Lion memo challenging employees to find a thousand different ways to save 1 percent of their own costs elicited undesirable shortcuts in food preparation and storage. Also, asymmetric information can cause customers to rationally discount products such as used cars or computer components for which quality information is often unverifiable at the point of purchase. Reputation with customers, workers, and the surrounding tax jurisdiction is one way companies deal with the problem of asymmetric information, and managers must attend to these effects of reputation on shareholder value. We address the managerial implications of asymmetric information in Chapter 13.

Known Recontracting Costs   Finally, to focus exclusively on the discounted present value of future cash flows necessitates that managers obtain not only sales revenue and expense estimates but also future recontracting costs for pivotal inputs. Owners of professional baseball teams have recently emphasized the importance of known recontracting costs (with star players) to the value of their franchises. In another instance, Westinghouse entered into long-term contracts to resupply fuel rods to nuclear power plants without such knowledge. Thereafter, the market price of uranium quadrupled. Although Westinghouse was allowed to breach its contracts, and the nation's power suppliers were the immediate losers, Westinghouse's reputation suffered and capitalized value declined. By hedging this commodity price risk in the metals futures market, both Westinghouse and its customers would have increased shareholder value. Complete derivative markets go a long way toward solving the problems introduced by recontracting costs. Nevertheless, a pivotal input can often "hold up" the firm's owners when the time comes for contract renewals, and value-maximizing managers must anticipate and mitigate these recontracting problems.

EXAMPLE

LOW EARTH ORBIT SPACE JUNK: WESTINGHOUSE[22]

To the extent markets are incomplete, information is asymmetric, or recontracting costs are unknown, managers must attend to these matters rather than simply focus on expected future cash flows. For example, satellite orbital paths are becoming congested with space junk. The U.S. Air Force's Space Command tracks 8,500 objects 10 centimeters or larger in low earth orbit (6–125 miles up) and 1 meter or larger in geosynchronous orbit (20,000 miles up). A collision with a 0.5 centimeter object will depressurize the space shuttle resulting in "mission loss." In July 1996, Cerise, a French satellite, tumbled out of orbit after colliding with pieces of an exploded Arienne 4 French rocket. The vastness of interstellar space is just that—vast—but geosynchronous and low earth orbits are becoming congested.

The problem is that satellite orbital paths are common property resources like deep sea fisheries. No company or nation has an incentive to economize on their use in order to achieve maximum sustainable yield because no one can appropriate the benefits of doing so. No property rights are specified, assigned, or enforced. As a result, each producer has an incentive to overutilize the resource. When congestion occurs, the costs are widespread, but the catastrophic accident befalls only isolated parties. Who owes what to whom when a future Cerise plows into a Westinghouse satellite has not been determined. This difficulty prevents all but the most vague analysis of projected cash flows.

About 70 to 100 new commercial and military satellites are launched per year worldwide at a cost of about $8,000 to $25,000 per pound. Lockheed Martin is testing an X-33 rocket that will reduce this cost to $1,000 per pound. As companies like Aeroastro and Kelly Space develop still cheaper launch systems that can achieve escape velocity, the congestion will surely worsen. Westinghouse and Motorola are contracting with Teledesio to launch a swarm of 924 new communication satellites into low earth orbit. Before they do so, managers will need to press for the privatization of the common property resources associated with satellite orbital paths. Markets can then emerge to price the paths which will enable meaningful analysis of the projected cash flow from operating a satellite.

The same type of problem arose recently in the case of the electromagnetic spectrum. Radio, television, and broadband cellular phone frequencies were once common property available to anyone who wished to transmit signals. As demand by broadcasters and cellular phone users in a geographic area grew, the Federal Communications Commission assigned unique blocks of frequencies closer and closer to one another and kept a watchful eye on all the signal interference. However, the FCC was powerless to stop the

---

[22] Based on "To Boldly Dump," *The Economist,* 29 March, 1997, p. 87, and "They're Going Crazy in Space," *Business Week,* 28 July, 1997, p. 89.

growing congestion and resulting signal degradation. Only when Congress empowered the FCC to auction off the electromagnetic spectrum did the projected cost of clear signal quality become identifiable. The auctions then created an incentive for the development of innovative communications technologies to reduce cost. For example, the 1995 auction of broadband frequencies for personal communication systems coincided with the announcement of signal compression technology to mitigate the signal congestion problem.

Residual Claimants

There is a growing consensus that the primary duty of management and the board of directors of a company is to the shareholders and not to other stakeholders. Shareholders have a residual claim on the firm's net cash flows after all expected contractual returns have been paid. All the other stakeholders (employees, customers, bondholders, banks, suppliers, the surrounding tax jurisdictions, the community in which plants are located, etc.) have *contractual* expected returns. If expectations created by those contracts are not met, any of these stakeholders has access to the full force of the contract law in securing whatever they are due. Shareholders have contractual rights, too, but those rights simply entitle them to whatever is left over, i.e., to the residual. As a consequence, when shareholder owners hire a CEO and a board, they create a fiduciary duty to husband the company's resources in such a way as to maximize the net present value of the residual claims. This is what constitutes the objective of shareholder wealth maximization.

Be very clear, however, that the value of any company's stock is quite dependent on reputation effects. Underfunding a pension plan or polluting the environment results in massive losses of capitalized value because the financial markets anticipate (correctly) that such a company will have reduced future cash flows. Recontracting costs and labor costs to attract new employees will rise; tax jurisdictions will reduce the tax preferences offered in new plant locations; customers may boycott; and the public relations, lobbying, and legal costs of such a company will surely rise. All this implies that value-maximizing managers must be very carefully attuned to stakeholder interests precisely because it is in their shareholders' best interests to do so.

GOALS IN THE PUBLIC SECTOR AND THE NOT-FOR-PROFIT ENTERPRISE

The value-maximization objective developed for private sector firms is not an appropriate objective in the public sector or in not-for-profit (NFP) organizations.[23] These organizations pursue a different set of objectives because of the nature of the good or service they supply and the manner in which they are funded.

There are three characteristics of NFP organizations that distinguish them from for-profit enterprises and influence decision making in the enterprise. First, no one possesses a right to receive profit or surpluses in an NFP enterprise. The absence of a profit motive can have a serious impact on the incentive to be efficient. Second, NFP enterprises are exempt from taxes on corporate income. Finally, many NFP enterprises benefit from the fact that donations to them are tax deductible. These tax benefits give NFP enterprises an advantage when competing with for-profit enterprises.

---

[23] This section draws heavily on Burton A. Weisbrod, *The Nonprofit Economy* (Cambridge, Mass.: Harvard University Press, 1988).

Not-for-profit organizations include performing arts groups, museums, libraries, hospitals, churches, volunteer organizations, cooperatives, credit unions, labor unions, professional societies, foundations, and fraternal organizations. Some of these organizations offer services to a group of clients, such as the patients of a hospital. Others provide services primarily to members, such as the members of a country club or credit union. Finally, some NFP organizations produce public benefits, as does a local symphony or theater company.

The most important feature that distinguishes NFP organizations from private sector and public (government) sector organizations is their sources of financial support. NFP organizations receive a large percentage of their externally generated funds from voluntary contributions. The greater the proportion of external funds from contributions as a percentage of total revenue, the closer the organization is to being a pure NFP organization. In contrast, the lower the percentage of contributions to total revenue, the closer the organization is to being a business firm or government agency. For example, by this criterion a credit union would be expected to have organizational objectives that are very similar to those of banks, whereas the American Economic Association, a professional association of economists, is more nearly like an NFP organization.

Public sector (government) agencies tend to provide services with a significant *public-good* character. In contrast to private goods like bite-sized candy bars, **public goods** may be consumed by more than one person at the same time and entail high transaction costs of excluding those who do not pay. Examples of public goods include national defense and flood control. If an antiballistic missile system or a flood control levy is constructed, those behind the shield cannot be excluded from its protection even if they refuse to contribute to the cost. Even if one could charge market prices, the indivisibility in consumption of a public good makes the incremental cost (and therefore the efficient price) of another participant quite low. Some goods, such as recreational facilities and the performing arts, have both private- and public-good characteristics. For example, concerts and parks may be shared (within limits) and are partially nonexcludable since quality performing arts and recreational facilities convey prestige and quality-of-life benefits to the entire community.[24] The more costly the exclusion, the more likely the good or service will be provided by the public sector rather than the private sector. Portrait artists and personal fitness trainers offer pay-as-you-go private fee arrangements. On the other hand, chamber music fans and tennis court users often organize in consumption-sharing and cost-sharing clubs, and open-air symphony concerts and large parks usually necessitate some public financing.

Public Goods

Goods that may be consumed by more than one person at the same time with little or no extra cost, and for which it is expensive or impossible to exclude those who do not pay.

Not-for-Profit Objectives

Several organizational objectives have been suggested for the NFP enterprise. These include the following:

1. Maximization of the quantity and quality of output subject to a break-even budget constraint
2. Utility maximization of the administrators
3. Maximization of cash flows
4. Maximization of the utility (satisfaction) of contributors

---

[24] William J. Baumol and W. G. Bowen, *Performing Arts: The Economic Dilemma* (Brookfield, VT: Ashgate Publishing Co., 1993).

For NFP organizations that rely heavily on external contributions, the overriding objective is to satisfy current and prospective contributors. This does not mean that the other objectives are mutually exclusive. It is common to find an NFP organization that seeks to satisfy its contributors by (1) efficiently managing its resources, (2) increasing its capacity to supply high-quality goods or services, and (3) providing a rewarding work environment for its administrators. As reliance on outside contributors lessens, the other objectives gain importance to the organization.

The Efficiency Objective

Although both the public sector agency and the NFP organization may pursue many objectives, a major focus of economists is on the efficiency dimension of organizational objectives. Whatever set of objectives the organization decides to pursue, these objectives should be pursued in the most resource-efficient fashion.

Cost-Benefit Analysis
A resource-allocation model that can be used by public sector and not-for-profit organizations to evaluate programs or investments on the basis of the magnitude of the discounted costs and benefits.

The model that has been developed to provide a framework for the allocation of public and NFP resources among competing uses primarily has been the **cost-benefit analysis** model. This model is the analogue to the capital budgeting model in the private sector. Benefits and costs associated with investments are estimated and discounted by an appropriate discount rate, and projects are evaluated on the basis of the magnitude of the discounted benefits in relation to the costs. Because government and NFP organization spending is normally constrained by a budget ceiling, the criterion actually used in evaluating expenditures for any public purpose may be one of the following:

1. Maximize benefits for given costs
2. Minimize costs while achieving a fixed level of benefits
3. Maximize net benefits (benefits minus costs)

Cost-benefit analysis, as a guide to a more efficient allocation of resources by a public agency or an NFP institution, is only one input necessary to the final decision. It *does* furnish decision makers with the results of a careful analysis of the costs and returns associated with alternative actions. It *does not,* however, incorporate many of the more subjective considerations or less easily quantifiable objectives into the analysis. For example, a cost-benefit analysis typically does not consider the effect of a proposed project on income distribution. Concern for these matters must be introduced at a later stage in the analysis, generally through the political process.

NFP institutions normally are faced with decision problems not markedly different from those of a public agency; they exist to supply some good (or service) in the most efficient manner. An NFP hospital, for example, may seek to provide a certain quantity and quality of medical service to the citizens of a community, given a resource or budget constraint. Decisions about what programs to emphasize (where to allocate funds) should be based on an analysis of benefits that may be generated from competing programs. The identification of specific functional goals or objectives for both governmental and NFP institutions remains a critical problem. In some cases efficiency analyses may help to identify specific goals, whereas in other cases these goals and objectives will be established (often via a political process) before any analysis about how they might best be achieved. Once established, the *normative objective,* which is assumed in this text, is that decision makers seek to achieve the goal in the most efficient manner; that is, with the least possible expenditure of real resources. The tools and techniques presented in the following chapters are developed with this purpose in mind. Chapter 19 discusses the capital budgeting problems associated with resource allocation and the efficient achievement of objectives in public agencies and NFP institutions.

MANAGING IN A GLOBAL COMPETITIVE ECONOMY

U.S. manufacturers face serious economic challenges from firms located in Japan, Korea, other countries in the Far East, the European Community, Canada, and others. As other economies have developed and trade barriers have been lowered, American firms have found themselves facing increasingly intense competition from abroad. The U.S. foreign trade deficit (i.e., the dollar value of exports minus imports) has grown from an annual level of approximately $30 billion during the late 1970s and early 1980s to well over $100 billion in the late 1990s.

Many industries have seen substantial portions of industry output move overseas, either to foreign firms or subsidiaries of U.S. firms. For example, in 1980 nearly 94 percent of the computers bought in the United States were made there. By 1990, that figure had declined to less than 66 percent. The figure is even lower if one counts the foreign component contents of U.S.-assembled computers. Dramatic domestic market share declines have been experienced in the machine tool, semiconductor, telephone equipment, and apparel industries. Indeed, very few industries have witnessed increases in the domestically produced portion of their U.S. market share. With more import transactions by Americans purchasing yen, DM, and Canadian dollar-denominated products than export transactions to foreigners purchasing U.S. dollar-denominated products, the value of the U.S. dollar declined relative to the currencies of most developed countries from 1986 through 1996. A weaker dollar automatically makes U.S. exports cheaper abroad and imports more expensive, so some stabilization of these trade flow imbalances has begun.

Another challenge for U.S. manufactures, however, is the increased competition from foreign firms that have set up plants in the United States. As the dollar declined in value, foreign investors found it cheaper to purchase not only Cadillacs and IBM PCs but also dollar-denominated *assets.* The buying spree included not only T-bills, bonds, and stocks but also real estate and factories. This trend has reduced the U.S.-owned share of U.S. production capacity in the cement industry, for example, from 90 percent in 1979 to 30 percent in 1989. Domestic automobile manufacturers also face substantial competition from domestic plants owned by foreign firms from Japan and Europe. Sustained international trade deficits necessarily result in either asset sales or borrowing. As a result, since 1985 the U.S. has been a net debtor nation. On the one hand, this situation is attractive; more foreign goods today in exchange for U.S. promissory notes to repay tomorrow. On the other hand, a shrinking manufacturing sector entails the limited employment prospects of the service economy.

The study of managerial economics is important for future managers who face the growing challenge of global competition. Many times U.S. managers can learn from the successful experiences of their foreign competitors. For example, the "just-in-time" inventory management techniques and quality management practices that have exploded in popularity over the past decade have been adapted from successful Japanese firms. Managers who face the challenge of global competition must pay even closer attention to the principles of efficient resource allocation that are at the core of managerial economics. Our global competitors understand these principles and, in many cases, have applied them effectively to enhance their competitive position. Chapter 7 addresses import-export trade in Japanese and European companies. Throughout the text we will highlight specific issues and opportunities that face managers in a global, competitive economy.

SUMMARY

- *Managerial economics* is the application of economic theory and analytical tools to decision-making problems faced by private, not-for-profit, and public institutions. Increasingly, these decision-making problems have an international dimension.

- Managerial economics draws on microeconomic theory and macroeconomic models to assist managers in making optimal resource-allocation decisions.

- *Economic profit* is defined as the difference between total revenues and *total economic costs*. Economic costs include a normal rate of return on the capital contributed by the firm's owners. Economic profits exist to compensate investors for the risk they assume, because of temporary disequilibrium conditions that may occur in a market, because of the existence of monopoly power, and as a reward to firms that are especially successful in innovation or are managed in a highly efficient manner.

- As an overall objective of the firm, the *shareholder wealth-maximization* model is very appealing. It is flexible enough to account for differential levels of risk and timing differences in the receipt of benefits and the incurring of future costs. Because shareholder wealth is defined in terms of the value of the stock, this goal provides a precise measure of performance, which is free from the problems associated with using various accounting measures.

- Managers may not always behave in a manner consistent with the wealth-maximization objective. The costs associated with these deviations from the objective are often called *agency costs*.

- *Not-for-profit* enterprises exist to supply a good or service desired by their primary contributors. Public sector organizations often provide services having significant public-good characteristics; that is, they may be consumed by more than one person at a time with little additional cost, and the transaction cost of excluding those who do not pay exceeds the benefits that are derived by charging the efficient price.

- Regardless of their specific objectives, both public and private institutions should seek to furnish their goods or services in the most resource-efficient manner. The marginal decision rules from the profit-maximization model are often very valuable in this context.

EXERCISES

1. In the period following the invasion of Kuwait by Iraq, oil prices increased significantly, as did the profits earned by many oil companies. Some politicians argued that these profits are undeserved and called for price rollbacks and/or increased taxes. Discuss the pros and cons of these proposals in the context of the various theories of profit.

2. In 1994, firms in the drug industry earned an average return on net worth of 26.5 percent, compared with an average return by over 1,400 firms followed by *Value Line* of 15.0 percent. Which theory or theories of profit do you think best explain the performance of the drug industry?

3. Try to define, in as operational a manner as possible, the objectives that your college or university seeks to pursue.

    a. How may success in achieving these objectives be measured?

    b. To what extent do the objectives of various subunits of your college or university complement (or contradict) each other?

    c. Who are the major constituencies served by your university? What role do they play in the formation of these objectives?

    d. You may want to talk with some of your school's administrators and compare their views on the college's goals and objectives with your own.

4. Why do organizations frequently diverge from "optimal" performance in a normative sense and pursue some objective other than (or in addition to) the efficiency objective? Would you expect a greater divergence from the efficiency objective in

   a. Small individual proprietorships?
   b. Large corporations?
   c. Public corporations?
   d. Other government agencies? Why?

5. In the context of the shareholder wealth-maximization model of the firm, what is the expected impact of each of the following events on the value of the firm?

   a. New foreign competitors enter the market.
   b. Strict pollution control requirements are implemented by the government.
   c. A previously nonunion workforce votes to unionize.
   d. The rate of inflation increases substantially.
   e. A major technological breakthrough is achieved by the firm, reducing its costs of production.

6. After the invasion of Kuwait by Iraq, the price of jet fuel used by airlines increased dramatically. As the CEO of US Airways, you have been presented with the following options to deal with this problem:

   a. Raise airfares to offset cost increases.
   b. Reduce the number of flights per day in some markets.
   c. Make long-term contracts to buy jet fuel at a fixed price for the next two years and set airfares to a level that will cover these costs.

   Evaluate these options in the context of the decision-making model presented in the text.

7. How would each of the following actions be expected to affect shareholder wealth?

   a. RJR Nabisco sells its Del Monte division for over $1 billion.
   b. Ford Motor Company pays $2.5 billion for Jaguar.
   c. General Motors offers large rebates to stimulate sales of its automobiles.
   d. Rising interest rates cause the required returns of shareholders to increase.
   e. Import restrictions are placed on the Japanese competitors of Chrysler.
   f. There is a sudden drop in the expected future rate of inflation.
   g. A new, labor-saving machine is purchased by Wonder Bread and results in the layoff of 300 employees.

www exercise

Incentive Compensation

8. Access the Towers Perrin Internet site http://www.towers.com. Click the "Publications" button, then scroll down and click the "Perspectives on Management Pay" button. Several full-text issues should be accessible. In a past issue (September 1996) Towers Perrin reported, for example, that only about 27 percent of typical CEO compensation in large U.S. corporations was in the form of salary, while annual and long-term incentive pay made up 66 percent, with the remainder of compensation being in the form of benefits

   Use the information that you find at this site to write a two-paragraph executive summary of current practices in CEO incentive compensation, and relate your findings to the agency problem mentioned in the text.

CASE EXERCISES   **REFORMING THE FORMER SOVIET ECONOMY**

The failure of the state-controlled, centrally planned economies of the Eastern European countries and of the former Soviet Union to produce adequate quantities of high-quality products that are desired by consumers has led to major economic and political reform in these countries. East Germany ceased to exist as an independent nation-state in a little over one year and was merged into a united Germany in late 1990. Economic and political pressures have led to major changes in the organization of the economies (and governments) of Hungary, Poland, Rumania, and the Soviet Union itself.

The failure of state-controlled economies that did not permit the private ownership of property or capital and did not permit competition among profit-seeking enterprises can be viewed as a reflection of a major agency problem. Plant managers had little to gain from more efficient operations. There was neither the pressure from competitors nor from potential takeovers by a more efficient group of owner-managers, as is true in Western economies. Furthermore, as state-chartered monopolies, there was no risk of failure of the enterprise.

The Soviet Union finally collapsed under the pressure of a failed economic system and political reforms that permitted open criticism of the government. President Yeltsin of Russia quickly moved to reform the economic system. Price controls were lifted on most goods and services, state subsidies were eliminated, and steps were taken that should lead to the international convertibility of the currency, the ruble. These steps were designed to increase the accountability of managers to the new owners, add an important element of competition to the former Soviet economy, and increase the efficiency of economic enterprises in the former Soviet Union. This ambitious plan to privatize the former Soviet economy raises a host of interesting challenges for managers.

QUESTIONS

1. When state-owned enterprises are sold, how should their value be established? Should the value be based on the cost of the assets in place, the past earning power of the enterprise, or the future earning potential in a competitive economy?

2. How can the future earning capacity of privatized enterprises be estimated?

3. What long-term effect do you think the lifting of price controls will have on inflation in the former Soviet Union?

4. What effect do you think the privatization of currently state-run enterprises will have on the employment levels in these enterprises in the near term? In the longer term?

2

Fundamental Economic Concepts

CHAPTER PREVIEW

Managerial economic analysis is based largely on a few fundamental economic concepts. Four of the most important concepts are marginal analysis, net present value, the meaning and measurement of risk, and the trade-offs that must be made between risk and return. Marginal analysis tools are central when a decision maker is seeking to optimize some objective, such as profits or shareholder wealth. The net present value concept provides the linkage between the long-term decisions made by a firm and the shareholder wealth-maximization objective. Because most economic decisions involve an element of risk, the meaning and measurement of risk is an important concept for managers. Risk-return analysis is important to an understanding of the many trade-offs that managers must make as they plan new products, increases in capacity, pricing changes, and so on. These fundamental concepts are cornerstones to further analysis in the managerial economics arena. By understanding and applying these fundamental concepts, a manager will be able to make decisions that contribute to the ultimate goal of efficient resource allocation and shareholder wealth maximization.

MANAGERIAL CHALLENGE

REVENUE MANAGEMENT AT DELTA AIRLINES[1]

The airline industry has escaped another series of price wars and returned to profitability. In 1996, American Airlines reported profit of $450 million up from $228 million a year earlier. Delta reported $920 million in 1997 up from $294 million in 1995 and $156 million in 1996. Even US Airways has returned to profitability after a long stretch of losses. One of the key developments contributing to these trends has been the success of revenue management techniques. Revenue or "yield" management (RM) is an integrated demand-management, order-booking, and capacity-planning process that focuses on marginal analysis. It was first introduced at Delta Airlines in 1979 in response to a low-cost discounter and was quickly advanced by other travel industry companies. The first computer-aided reservation and decision-analysis system was SABRE, installed by IBM at American Airlines. More recent revenue management applications have spread into hotels, rental cars, cruise ships, broadcasting, sports facilities, entertainment, hospitals, consulting and other professional services.

To win orders in a service industry *without slashing prices* requires that companies create perceived value for segmented classes of differentiated customers. Business travelers on airlines, for example, want and will pay for last-minute responsiveness to their change orders. Other business travelers demand exceptional delivery reliability and on-time performance. In contrast, most vacation excursion travelers want commodity-like service at rock-bottom prices. Although only 15–20 percent of most airlines' seats are in the business segment, 65–75 percent of the profit contribution on a typical flight comes from this group. The problem is that airline capacity must be planned and allocated well in advance of customer arrivals, often before demand is fully known, yet unsold inventory perishes at the moment of departure. This same management challenge faces hospitals, consulting firms, TV stations, and printing businesses, all of whom must acquire and schedule capacity before the demands for Thursday's elective surgeries, next week's crisis

management, the 11 A.M. network ad segment, or the afternoon press run are fully known.

One approach to minimizing unsold inventory and yet capturing all last-minute high-profit business is to auction off capacity to the highest bidder. The auction for free-wheeling electricity works just that way: power companies bid at quarter 'til the hour for excess supplies that other utilities agree to deliver on the hour. However, in airlines (like many other service businesses) prices cannot be adjusted quickly as the moment of departure approaches. Instead, revenue managers employ large historical databases to predict segmented customer demand in light of current arrivals on the reservation system and then compare the expected marginal profit from holding another seat in business class in anticipation of "last-minute" demand to the expected marginal contribution from accepting another reservation request in a discount class.

On a 9 A.M. Atlanta to Chicago flight next Monday, 63 of the 170 seats have been protected for first class, business class, and full coach fares but only 50 have been sold; the remaining 103 seats have been authorized for sale at a discount. A new reservation request arrives in the discount class which is presently full.[2] Should the airline reallocate capacity and take on the new discount passenger? The answer is "maybe"; it depends on the relative profit margins from each class and the predicted probability today three days before departure of excess demand (beyond 63 seats) next week in the business classes. If the $721 full coach fare has a $500 profit margin and the $155 discount fare has a $100

[1] Based on Robert Cross, *Revenue Management* (New York: Broadway Books, 1995), and Frederick Harris and Peter Peacock, "Hold My Place Please: Yield Management Improves Capacity Allocation Guesswork," *Marketing Management*, Fall, 1995, pp. 34–46.

[2] Appendix 17A explains how these demand assessments take into account the likely incidence of cancellations and no-shows and then authorize an optimal level of overbooking.

profit margin, the seat in question should not be re-allocated from business to discount customers if the probability of "stocking out" in business is greater than 0.20. For example, if the probability is 0.25, the expected marginal profit from holding an empty seat for another potential business customer is $125, whereas the marginal profit from selling that seat to the discount customer is only $100. Even an advance-payment no-refund seat request from the discount class should be refused. Every company has some viable orders that should be refused; excess capacity is not "idle capacity" but rather a predictable revenue opportunity waiting to happen.

In this chapter, we discuss the methods of "marginal analysis" that can be used to solve an airline's seat allocation decision problem. Chapter 17 discusses the price discrimination analysis that underlies revenue management, and Appendix 17A applies the techniques of revenue management.

www . . . .
The firm Aeronomics Incorporated specializes in revenue management and sponsors the annual International Revenue Management Conference. Information on this conference is found at
http://www.aeronomics.com/news

MARGINAL ANALYSIS

Marginal Analysis
A basis for making various economic decisions that analyzes the additional (marginal) benefits derived from a particular decision and compares them with the additional (marginal) costs incurred.

Marginal analysis is one of the most useful concepts of economic decision making. Resource-allocation decisions typically are expressed in terms of the marginal conditions that must be satisfied to attain an optimal solution. The familiar profit-maximization rule for the firm of setting output at the point where "marginal cost equals marginal revenue" is one such example. Long-term investment decisions (capital expenditures) also are made using marginal analysis decision rules. If the expected return from an investment project (that is, the *marginal return* to the firm) exceeds the cost of funds that must be acquired to finance the project (the *marginal cost* of capital), then the project should be undertaken. Following this important marginal decision rule leads to the maximization of shareholder wealth.

In the marginal analysis framework, resource-allocation decisions are made by comparing the marginal (or incremental) benefits of a change in the level of an activity with the marginal (or incremental) costs of the change. *Marginal benefit* is defined as the change in total benefits that are derived from undertaking some economic activity, such as additional shipbuilding at Tenneco Shipyards. For example, the marginal revenue (a benefit) derived from producing and selling one more supertanker is equal to the difference between total revenue, assuming the additional unit is not sold, and total revenue including the additional sale. Similarly, *marginal cost* is defined as the change in total costs that occurs from undertaking some economic activity, such as the production of an additional unit of output. Recall from the previous chapter that total (economic) costs include opportunity costs, and therefore may not necessarily always be equal to the cash outlays alone.[3] Perhaps the Tenneco design team has an opportunity for higher net profit as subcontractors on Boeing projects. If so, Tenneco's routine, ship-design work should be contracted out to lower-cost firms.

A change in the level of an economic activity is desirable if the marginal benefits exceed the marginal costs. This is equivalent to saying that the increase in total revenues,

[3] The concept of economic cost is examined in more detail in Chapter 9.

for example, exceeds the increase in total costs. Therefore, in decisions involving the expansion of an economic activity, the optimal level occurs at the point where the marginal benefits are equal to the marginal costs. If we define *net marginal return* as the *difference* between marginal benefits and marginal costs, then an equivalent optimality condition is that the level of the activity should be increased to the point where the net marginal return is zero.

EXAMPLE

www..............
Financial information on the Sara Lee Corporation can be found at
http://www.saralee.com/
financial/stock/index.htm

MARGINAL ANALYSIS AND CAPITAL BUDGETING DECISIONS: SARA LEE CORPORATION

The capital budgeting decision problem facing a typical firm, such as Sara Lee Corporation, can be used to illustrate the application of marginal analysis decision rules. Sara Lee has the following schedule of potential investment projects (all assumed to be of equal risk) available to it:

Project	Investment Required ($ Million)	Expected Rate of Return	Cumulative Investment ($ Million)
A	$25.0	27.0%	$ 25.0
B	15.0	24.0	40.0
C	40.0	21.0	80.0
D	35.0	18.0	115.0
E	12.0	15.0	127.0
F	20.0	14.0	147.0
G	18.0	13.0	165.0
H	13.0	11.0	178.0
I	7.0	8.0	185.0

Sara Lee has estimated the cost of acquiring the funds needed to finance these investment projects as follows:

Block of Funds ($ Million)	Cost of Capital	Cumulative Funds Raised ($ Million)
First $50.0	10.0%	$50.0
Next 25.0	10.5	75.0
Next 40.0	11.0	115.0
Next 50.0	12.2	165.0
Next 20.0	14.5	185.0

The expected rate of return on the projects listed above can be thought of as the marginal (or incremental) return available to Sara Lee as it undertakes each additional investment project. Similarly, the cost-of-capital schedule may be thought of as the marginal cost of acquiring the needed funds. Following the marginal analysis rules means that Sara Lee should invest in additional projects as long as the expected rate of return on the project exceeds the marginal cost of capital funds needed to finance the project.

Project A, which offers an expected return of 27 percent and requires an outlay of $25 million, is acceptable because the marginal return exceeds the marginal cost of capital (10.0 percent for the first $50 million of funds raised by Sara Lee). In fact, an examination of the tables indicates that projects A through G all meet the marginal analysis test because the marginal return from each of these projects exceeds the marginal cost of capital funds needed to finance these projects. In contrast, projects H and I should not be undertaken because they offer returns of 11 and 8 percent, respectively, compared with a marginal cost of capital of 14.5 percent for the $20 million in funds needed to finance these projects.

In summary, marginal analysis instructs decision makers to determine the additional (marginal) costs and additional (marginal) benefits associated with a proposed action. *Only if the marginal benefits exceed the marginal costs* (that is, if net marginal benefits are positive) should the action be taken.[4]

Total, Marginal, and Average Relationships

Economic relationships can be presented using tabular, graphic, and algebraic frameworks. Let us first use a tabular presentation. Suppose that the total profit π_T of a firm is a function of the number of units of output produced Q, as shown in columns 1 and 2 of Table 2.1. Marginal profit, which represents the change in total profit resulting from a one-unit increase in output, is shown in column 3 of the table. (A Δ is used to represent a "change" in some variable.) The marginal profit $\Delta\pi(Q)$ of any level of output Q is calculated by taking the difference between the total profit at this level $\pi_T(Q)$ and at one unit below this level $\pi_T(Q-1)$.[5] In comparing the marginal and total profit functions, we note that for increasing output levels, the marginal profit values remain positive as long as the total profit function is increasing. Only when the total profit function begins decreasing—that is, at $Q = 10$ units—does the marginal profit become negative. The average profit function values $\pi_A(Q)$, shown in column 4 of Table 2.1, are obtained by dividing the total profit figure $\pi_T(Q)$ by the output level Q. In comparing the marginal and the average profit function values, we see that the average profit function $\pi_A(Q)$ is increasing as long as the marginal profit is greater than the average profit; that is, up to $Q = 7$ units. Beyond an output level of $Q = 7$ units, the marginal profit is less than the average profit and the average profit function values are decreasing.

By examining the total profit function $\pi_T(Q)$ in Table 2.1, we see that profit is maximized at an output level of $Q = 9$ units. Given that the objective is to maximize total profit, then the optimal output decision would be to produce and sell 9 units. If the marginal analysis decision rule discussed earlier in this section is used, the same (optimal) decision is obtained. Applying the rule to this problem, the firm would expand production as long as the *net* marginal return—that is, marginal revenue minus marginal cost (marginal profit)—is positive. From column 3 of Table 2.1, we can see that the marginal profit is positive for output levels up to $Q = 9$. Therefore, the marginal profit decision

---

[4] Strictly speaking, an action may also be undertaken if marginal benefits *equal* marginal costs. In this case, the manager will be indifferent to taking the action.

[5] The marginal profit of the 0th unit—that is, $Q = 0$—is defined as zero.

TABLE   2.1

Total, Marginal, and Average Profit Relationships

(1) Number of Units of Output Per Unit of Time Q	(2) Total Profit $\pi_T(Q)$ ($)	(3) Marginal Profit $\Delta\pi(Q) = \pi_T(Q) - \pi_T(Q-1)$ ($/Unit)	(4) Average Profit $\pi_A(Q) = \pi_T(Q)/Q$ ($/Unit)
0	−200	0	—
1	−150	50	−150.00
2	−25	125	−12.50
3	200	225	66.67
4	475	275	118.75
5	775	300	155.00
6	1,075	300	179.17
7	1,325	250	189.29
8	1,475	150	184.38
9	1,500	25	166.67
10	1,350	−150	135.00

rule would indicate that 9 units should be produced—the same decision that was obtained from the total profit function.

The relationships among the total, marginal, and average profit functions and the optimal output decision also can be represented graphically. A set of *continuous* profit functions, analogous to those presented previously in Table 2.1 for *discrete* integer values of output (*Q*), is shown in Figure 2.1. At the break-even output level Q_1, both total profits and average profits are zero. The marginal profit function, which equals the *slope* of the total profit function, takes on its maximum value at an output of Q_2 units. This point corresponds to the *inflection point.* Below the inflection point, total profits are increasing at an increasing rate, and hence marginal profits are increasing. Above the inflection point, up to an output level Q_4, total profits are increasing at a decreasing rate and consequently marginal profits are decreasing. The average profit function, which represents the slope of a straight line drawn from the origin 0 to each point on the total profit function, takes on its maximum value at an output of Q_3 units. The average profit necessarily equals the marginal profit at this point. This follows because the slope of the 0*A* line, which defines the average profit, is also equal to the slope of the total profit function at point *A,* which defines the marginal profit. Finally, total profit is maximized at an output of Q_4 units where marginal profit equals 0. Beyond Q_4 the total profit function is decreasing, and consequently the marginal profit function takes on negative values.

THE NET PRESENT VALUE CONCEPT

To achieve the objective of shareholder wealth maximization, a set of appropriate decision rules must be specified. We just saw that the decision rule of setting *marginal revenue (benefit) equal to marginal cost* (MR = MC) provides a framework for making many important resource-allocation decisions. The MR = MC rule is best suited for situations when the costs and benefits occur at approximately the same time. Many economic decisions require that costs be incurred immediately but result in a stream of benefits over

FIGURE   **2.1**

Total, Average,
and Marginal
Profit Functions

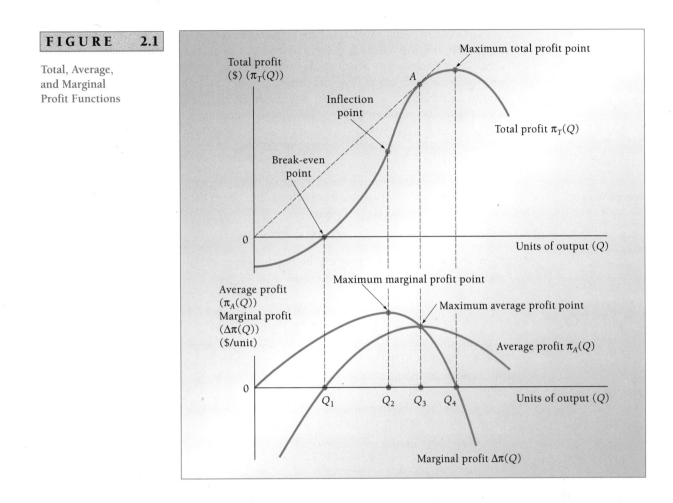

several future time periods. In these cases, the *net present value (NPV) rule* provides appropriate guidance for decision makers.

Determining the Net Present Value of an Investment

To understand the NPV rule, consider the following situation. You have just inherited $1 million. Your financial advisor has suggested that you use these funds to purchase a piece of land near a proposed new highway interchange. Your advisor, who is also a state road commissioner, is certain that the interchange will be built and that in one year the value of this land will increase to $1.2 million. Hence, you believe initially that this is a riskless investment. At the end of one year you plan to sell the land. You are being asked to invest $1 million today in the anticipation of receiving $1.2 million a year from today, or a profit of $200,000. You wonder whether this profit represents a sufficient return on your investment.

You feel it is important to recognize that there is a one-year difference between the time you make your outlay of $1 million and the time you receive $1.2 million from the sale of the land. A return of $1.2 million received one year from today must be worth less than $1.2 million today because you could invest your $1 million today to earn interest over the coming year. *A dollar received in the future is worth less than a dollar in hand today because a dollar today can be invested to earn a return immediately.* Therefore, to compare a dollar received in the future with a dollar in hand today, it is necessary to multiply the future dollar by a *discount factor* that reflects the alternative investment opportunities that are available.

Instead of investing your $1 million in the land venture, you are aware that you could also invest in a one-year U.S. government bond that currently offers a return of 9 percent. The 9 percent return represents the return (the opportunity cost) forgone by investing in the land project. The 9 percent rate also can be thought of as the compensation to an investor who agrees to postpone receiving a cash return for one year. The appropriate discount factor, also called a *present value interest factor (PVIF)*, is equal to

$$PVIF = \frac{1}{1 + i}$$

Present Value
The value today of a future amount of money or a series of future payments evaluated at the appropriate discount rate.

where i is the compensation for postponing receipt of a cash return for one year. The **present value** (PV_0) of an amount received one year in the future (FV_1) is equal to that amount times the discount factor, or

$$PV_0 = FV_1 \times (PVIF) \qquad [2.1]$$

In the case of the land project, the present value of the promised $1.2 million expected to be received in one year is equal to

$$PV_0 = \$1.2 \text{ million} \left(\frac{1}{1 + 0.09} \right) = \$1,100,917$$

If you invested $1,100,917 today to earn 9 percent for the coming year, you would have $1.2 million at the end of the year. You are clearly better off with the proposed land investment (assuming that it really is riskless like the U.S. government bond investment). How much better off are you?

The answer to this question is at the heart of NPV calculations. The land investment project is worth $1,100,917 today to an investor who demands a 9 percent return on this type of investment. You, however, have been able to acquire this investment for only $1,000,000. Thus your present wealth has increased by undertaking this investment by $100,917 ($1,100,917 present value of the projected investment opportunity payoffs minus the required initial investment of $1,000,000). The net present value (NPV) of this investment is $100,917. In general, the NPV of an investment is equal to

$$NPV = \text{Present value of future returns} - \text{Initial outlay} \qquad [2.2]$$

This example was simplified by assuming that the returns from the investment were received exactly one year from the date of the initial outlay. The NPV rule can be generalized to cover returns received over any number of future time periods. In Appendix A the present value concept is developed in more detail so that it can be applied in more complex investment settings.

Net Present Value and Shareholder Wealth Maximization

The net present value of an investment made by a firm represents the contribution of that investment to the value of the firm and accordingly, to the wealth of shareholders. The net present value concept is used to evaluate the *cash flows* generated from the firm's activities. Hence, the NPV concept plays a central role in the achievement of shareholder wealth maximization.

Market Efficiency   A central theme of much of the financial economics research since the 1960s has been the *efficiency* of the capital markets. The more efficient capital markets are, the more likely it is that resources will find their highest value (risk-adjusted) uses.

In an efficient capital market, stock prices provide an unbiased estimate of the true value of an enterprise. Stock prices reflect a *present value* estimate of the firm's *expected cash flows,* evaluated at an appropriate *required rate of return.* The required rate of return is determined by conditions in the financial markets, including the supply of funds from savers, the investment demand for funds, and expectations regarding future inflation rates. The required rate of return on a security also depends on the seniority of the security, the maturity of that security, the business and financial risk of the firm issuing the security, the risk of default, and the marketability of the security. The *efficiency of the capital markets* is the important "glue" that bonds the present value of a firm's net cash flows—discounted at the appropriate risk-adjusted required rate of return—to shareholder wealth as measured by the market value of a company's common stock.

Sources of Positive Net Present Value Projects

What causes some projects to have a positive net present value and others to have a negative net present value? When product and factor markets are other than perfectly competitive, it is possible for a firm to earn above-normal profits (economic rents) that result in positive net present value projects. The reasons why these above-normal profits may be available arise from conditions that define each type of product and factor market and distinguish it from a perfectly competitive market. These reasons include the following barriers to entry and other factors.

1. Buyer preferences for established brand names.
2. Ownership or control of favored distribution systems (such as exclusive auto dealerships or airline hubs).
3. Patent control of superior product designs or production techniques.
4. Exclusive ownership of superior natural resource deposits.
5. Inability of new firms to acquire necessary factors of production (management, labor, equipment).
6. Superior access to financial resources at lower costs (economies of scale in attracting capital).
7. Economies of large-scale production and distribution arising from
   a. Capital-intensive production processes.
   b. High initial start-up costs.

These factors can permit a firm to identify positive net present value projects for internal investment. If the barriers to entry are sufficiently high (such as a patent on key technology) so as to prevent any new competition or if the start-up period for competitive ventures is sufficiently long, then it is possible that a project may have a positive net present value. However, in assessing the viability of such a project, the manager or analyst must consider the likely period of time when above-normal returns can be earned before new competitors emerge and force cash flows back to a more normal level. It is generally unrealistic to expect to be able to earn above-normal returns over the entire life of an investment project.

Risk and the NPV Rule

The land investment example above assumed that the investment was riskless. Therefore, the rate of return used to compute the discount factor and the net present value was the riskless rate of return available on a U.S. government bond having a one-year maturity. What if you do not believe your investment advisor who says that the construction of the new interchange is a certainty or you are not confident about your advisor's estimate of the value of the land in one year? To compensate for the perceived risk of this investment, you decide that you require a 19 percent rate of return on your investment. Using a 19 percent required rate of return in calculating the discount factor, the present value of the expected \$1.2 million sales price of the land is \$1,008,403 [\$1.2 million times (1/1.19)]. Thus, the NPV of this investment declines to \$8,403. The increase in the perceived risk of the investment results in a dramatic decline in its NPV.

A primary problem facing managers is the difficulty of evaluating the risk associated with investments and then translating that risk into a discount rate that reflects an adequate level of risk compensation. In the next section of this chapter we discuss the risk concept and the factors that affect investment risk and influence the required rate of return on an investment.

MEANING AND MEASUREMENT OF RISK

We begin the discussion of risk analysis by defining several key terms and concepts. Although the examples presented here deal primarily with investment decisions, the ideas are applicable to all other types of economic decisions, such as those of pricing and production.

The Meaning of Risk

Risk
A decision-making situation in which there is variability in the possible outcomes, and the probabilities of these outcomes can be specified by the decision maker.

Risk is defined as the "possibility of loss or injury; hazard; peril; danger."[6] Hence, risk implies a chance for some unfavorable event to occur. From the perspective of security analysis or the analysis of an investment project, risk is the *possibility that actual cash flows (returns) will be less than forecasted cash flows (returns)*. More generally, **risk** refers to the chance that you will encounter an outcome that differs from the expected outcome. When a range of potential outcomes is associated with a decision and the decision maker is able to assign probabilities to each of these possible outcomes, risk is said to exist.

An investment decision is said to be *risk free* if the outcome (dollar returns) from the initial investment is known with certainty. A good example of a risk-free investment is U.S. Treasury securities. There is virtually no chance that the Treasury will fail to redeem these securities at maturity or that the Treasury will default on any interest payments owed.[7]

In contrast, US Airways bonds constitute a *risky* investment opportunity because it is possible that US Airways will default on one or more interest payments and will lack sufficient funds at maturity to redeem the bonds at face value. In other words, the possible returns from this investment are *variable,* and each potential outcome can be assigned a *probability.*

In summary, *risk* refers to the potential variability of outcomes from a decision alternative. The more variable these outcomes are, the greater the risk associated with the decision alternative.

---

[6] *Webster's Third New International Dictionary,* s.v. "risk" (Chicago: Encyclopedia Brittanica, Inc., 1981).

[7] Note this discussion of risk deals with *dollar returns* and ignores such other considerations as potential losses in purchasing power. In addition, it assumes that securities are held until maturity, which is not always the case. Sometimes a security must be sold before maturity for less than face value because of changes in the level of interest rates.

Probability Distributions

Probability
The percentage chance that
a particular outcome will
occur.

The **probability** that a particular outcome will occur is defined as the *percentage chance* of its occurrence. Probabilities may be either objectively or subjectively determined. An objective determination is based on past outcomes of similar events, whereas a subjective determination is merely an opinion made by an individual about the likelihood that a given event will occur. In the case of decisions that are frequently repeated, such as the drilling of developmental oil wells in an established oil field, reasonably good objective estimates can be made about the success of a new well. In contrast, for totally new decisions or one-of-a-kind investments, subjective estimates about the likelihood of various outcomes are necessary. The fact that many probability estimates in business are at least partially subjective does not diminish their usefulness.

EXAMPLE

PROBABILITY DISTRIBUTIONS AND RISK: US AIRWAYS BONDS

www
The annual report for the
US Airways Corporation
can be found at
http://www.usair.com/
company/financial/
indexj.htm

Consider an investor who is contemplating the purchase of US Airways bonds. That investor might assign the probabilities associated with the three possible outcomes from this investment as shown in Table 2.2. These probabilities are interpreted to mean that a 30 percent chance exists that the bonds will not be in default over their life and will be redeemed at maturity, a 65 percent chance of interest default during the life of the bonds, and a 5 percent chance that the bonds will not be redeemed at maturity. In this example, no other outcomes are deemed possible.

Using either objective or subjective methods, the decision maker can develop a probability distribution for the possible outcomes. Table 2.3 shows the probability distribution of net cash flows for two sample investments. The lowest estimated annual net cash flow (NCF) for each investment—$200 for Investment I and $100 for Investment II—represents pessimistic forecasts about the investments' performance; the middle values—$300 and $300—could be considered normal performance levels; and the highest values—$400 and $500—are optimistic estimates.

TABLE   2.2

Possible Outcomes from Investing in US Airways Bonds

Outcome	Probability
No default, bonds redeemed at maturity	0.30
Default on interest for one or more periods	0.65
No interest default, but bonds not redeemed at maturity	0.05
	1.00

TABLE   2.3

Probability Distributions of the Annual Net Cash Flows (NCF) from Two Investments

Investment I		Investment II	
Possible NCF	Probability	Possible NCF	Probability
$200	0.2	$100	0.2
300	0.6	300	0.6
400	0.2	500	0.2
	1.0		1.0

Expected Values

Expected Value
The weighted average of the possible outcomes where the weights are the probabilities of the respective outcomes.

From this information, the expected value of each decision alternative can be calculated. The **expected value** is defined as the weighted average of the possible outcomes. It is the value that is expected to occur on average if the decision (such as an investment) were repeated a large number of times.

Algebraically, the expected value may be defined as

$$\hat{r} = \sum_{j=1}^{n} r_j p_j \tag{2.3}$$

where $\hat{r}$ is the expected value; r_j is the outcome for the jth case, where there are n possible outcomes; and p_j is the probability that the jth outcome will occur. The expected cash flows for Investments I and II are calculated in Table 2.4 using Equation 2.3. In this example both investments have expected values of annual net cash flows equaling $300.

Standard Deviation: An Absolute Measure of Risk

Standard Deviation
A statistical measure of the dispersion or variability of possible outcomes.

The **standard deviation** is a statistical measure of the dispersion of a variable about its mean. It is defined as the square root of the weighted average squared deviations of individual outcomes from the mean:

$$\sigma = \sqrt{\sum_{j=1}^{n} (r_j - r)^2 p_j} \tag{2.4}$$

where σ is the standard deviation.

The standard deviation can be used to measure the variability of a decision alternative. As such, it gives an indication of the risk involved in the alternative. The larger the standard deviation, the more variable the possible outcomes and the riskier the decision alternative. A standard deviation of zero indicates no variability and thus no risk.

Table 2.5 shows the calculation of the standard deviations for Investments I and II. These calculations show that Investment II appears to be *riskier* than Investment I because the expected cash flows from Investment II are *more variable*.

This example dealt with a *discrete* probability distribution of outcomes (net cash flows) for each investment; that is, a *limited* number of possible outcomes were identified and probabilities were assigned to them. In reality, however, many different outcomes are possible for each investment decision, ranging from losses each year to annual net cash flows in excess of the optimistic estimates of $400 and $500. To indicate the probability of *all* possible outcomes, it is necessary to construct a *continuous* probability distribution. Conceptually, this involves assigning probabilities to each possible outcome such that the sum of the probabilities over possible outcomes total 1.0 (see Figure 2.2). This figure shows that Investment I has a tighter probability distribution and

TABLE 2.4	Investment I			Investment II		
Computation of the Expected Returns from Two Investments	r_j	p_j	$r_j \times p_j$	r_j	p_j	$r_j \times p_j$
	$200	0.2	$ 40	$100	0.2	$ 20
	300	0.6	180	300	0.6	180
	400	0.2	80	500	0.2	100
		Expected value: $\hat{r}_\mathrm{I} = \$300$				$\hat{r}_\mathrm{II} = \$300$

smaller standard deviation, indicating a lower variability of returns, and Investment II has a flatter distribution and larger standard deviation, indicating higher variability and, by extension, more risk.

Normal Probability Distribution

The outcomes from many decisions can be estimated by assuming that they follow the *normal* probability distribution. This assumption is often correct or nearly correct, and it greatly simplifies the analysis. The normal probability distribution is characterized by a symmetrical, bell-like curve. If the expected continuous probability distribution for

	j	r_j	$\hat{r}$	$r_j - \hat{r}$	$(r_j - \hat{r})^2$	p_j	$(r_j - \hat{r})^2 p_j$
Investment I	1	$200	$300	$-100	$10,000	0.2	$2,000
	2	300	300	0	0	0.6	0
	3	400	300	100	10,000	0.2	2,000

TABLE 2.5

Computation of the Standard Deviations for Two Investments

$$\sum_{j=1}^{3} (r_j - \hat{r})^2 p_j = \$4,000$$

$$\sigma = \sqrt{\sum_{j=1}^{n} (r_j - \hat{r})^2 p_j} = \sqrt{4,000} = \underline{\underline{\$63.25}}$$

	j	r_j	$\hat{r}$	$r_j - \hat{r}$	$(r_j - \hat{r})^2$	p_j	$(r_j - \hat{r})^2 p_j$
Investment II	1	$100	$300	$-200	$40,000	0.2	$8,000
	2	300	300	0	0	0.6	0
	3	500	300	200	40,000	0.2	8,000

$$\sum_{j=1}^{3} (r_j - \hat{r})^2 p_j = \$16,000$$

$$\sigma = \sqrt{\sum_{j=1}^{n} (r_j - \hat{r})^2 p_j} = \sqrt{16,000} = \underline{\underline{\$126.49}}$$

FIGURE 2.2

Continuous Probability Distributions for Two Investments

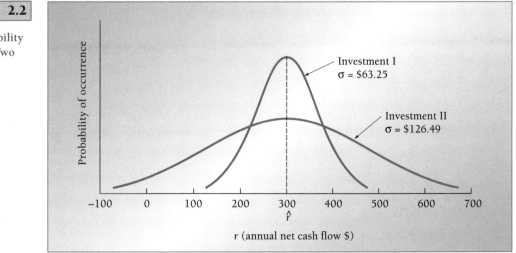

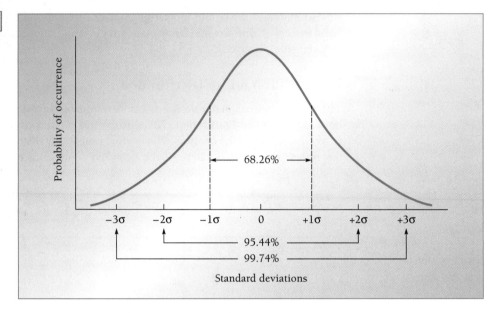

the possible outcomes is approximately normal, a table of the *standard normal probability function* (Table 1 in Appendix B at the end of this book) can be used to compute the probability of occurrence of any particular outcome. From this table, for example, it is apparent that the actual outcome should be between plus and minus 1 standard deviation from the expected value 68.26 percent of the time,[8] between plus and minus 2 standard deviations 95.44 percent of the time, and between plus and minus 3 standard deviations 99.74 percent of the time (see Figure 2.3).

The number of standard deviations z that a particular value of r is from the mean $\hat{r}$ can be computed as

$$z = \frac{r - \hat{r}}{\sigma} \qquad [2.5]$$

Table 1 and Equation 2.5 can be used to compute the probability of an annual net cash flow for Investment I being less than some value r—for example, $205. First, the number of standard deviations that $205 is from the mean must be calculated. Substituting the mean and the standard deviation from Tables 2.4 and 2.5 into Equation 2.5 yields

$$z = \frac{\$205 - \$300}{\$63.25}$$

$$= -1.50$$

In other words, the annual cash flow value of $205 is 1.5 standard deviations *below* the mean. Reading from the 1.5 row in Table 1 gives a value of 0.0668 or 6.68 percent. Thus a 6.68 percent probability exists that Investment I will have annual net cash flows less than $205. Conversely, there is a 93.32 percent probability $(1 - 0.0668)$ that the investment will have a cash flow greater than $205.

---

[8]For example, Table 1 indicates a probability of 0.1587 of a value occurring that is greater than $+1\sigma$ from the mean *and* a probability of 0.1587 of a value occurring that is less than -1σ from the mean. Hence the probability of a value *between* $+1\sigma$ and -1σ is 68.26 percent—that is, $1.00 - (2 \times 0.1587)$.

A Practical Approach for Estimating Standard Deviations

Most business decisions have outcomes best represented by a continuous probability distribution of possible outcomes, not the discrete distribution of outcomes, such as those shown in Tables 2.2 and 2.3. Under these circumstances, a simple technique can be used to derive the standard deviation of possible outcomes. Assuming that the distribution of possible outcomes is approximately normally distributed, information can be developed in a form useful for making the necessary computations.

For example, the individual responsible for making estimates of the expected return and risk from a decision, such as an investment project or the pricing of a new product, could be asked to supply the following information:

1. Estimate the most optimistic outcome. The most optimistic outcome is defined to be an outcome that would not be exceeded more than 5 percent (or any other prespecified percentage) of the time.
2. Estimate the most pessimistic outcome. The most pessimistic outcome is defined to be an outcome that you would not expect to do worse than more than 5 percent of the time.
3. With a normal distribution, the expected value will be midway between the most optimistic and the most pessimistic estimate.
4. Calculate the value of one standard deviation from Table 1, Appendix B.

EXAMPLE

ESTIMATION OF THE STANDARD DEVIATION: PROCTER & GAMBLE

When pricing a new product, the product manager of Procter & Gamble estimates that the most optimistic (not expected to be exceeded more than 5 percent of the time) price the firm can charge is $5.00 per unit. The most pessimistic (not expected to be less than this amount more than 5 percent of the time) estimate of the price that can be charged is $3.50. Assuming normality, the expected price is $4.25. From Table 1 in Appendix B, the z-value that leaves 5 percent in either tail of the normal distribution is approximately 1.645 standard deviations (σ) to the right or left of the expected value. This z-value corresponds to the distance between the expected value and either the most optimistic or the most pessimistic estimate of price. Hence, the probability of a price of at least $5.00 is equal to the probability of a z-value *greater* than $+1.645$. To calculate the standard deviation (σ) of this distribution, use the most optimistic outcome ($5.00), the expected outcome ($4.25), and the z-value:

$$z = 1.645 = \frac{(\$5.00 - \$4.25)}{\sigma}$$

$$\sigma = \frac{\$0.75}{1.645}$$

$$= \$0.46$$

In this case the expected value is $4.25 with a standard deviation of $0.46.

Coefficient of Variation: A Relative Measure of Risk

The standard deviation is an appropriate measure of risk when the decision alternatives being compared are approximately equal in size (that is, have similar expected values of the outcomes) and the outcomes are estimated to have symmetrical probability distributions.

Because the standard deviation is an *absolute* measure of variability, however, it is generally not suitable for comparing alternatives of differing size. In these cases the **coefficient of variation** provides a better measure of risk.

Coefficient of Variation
The ratio of the standard deviation to the expected value. A relative measure of risk.

The coefficient of variation (v) considers relative variation and thus is well suited for use when a comparison is being made between two unequally sized decision alternatives. It is defined as the ratio of the standard deviation σ to the expected value $\hat{r}$, or

$$v = \frac{\sigma}{\hat{r}} \qquad [2.6]$$

In general, when comparing two equally sized decision alternatives, the standard deviation is an appropriate measure of risk. When comparing two unequally sized alternatives, the coefficient of variation is the more appropriate measure of risk.

EXAMPLE

RELATIVE RISK MEASUREMENT: ARROW TOOL COMPANY

Arrow Tool Company is considering two investments, T and S. Investment T has expected annual net cash flows of $100,000 and a standard deviation of $20,000, whereas Investment S has expected annual net cash flows of $4,000 and a $2,000 standard deviation. Intuition tells us that Investment T is less risky because its *relative* variation is smaller. As the coefficient of variation increases, so does the relative risk of the decision alternative. The coefficients of variation for Investments T and S are computed as

Investment T:

$$v = \frac{\sigma}{\hat{r}}$$

$$= \frac{\$20,000}{\$100,000}$$

$$= 0.20$$

Investment S:

$$v = \frac{\sigma}{\hat{r}}$$

$$= \frac{\$2,000}{\$4,000}$$

$$= 0.5$$

Cash flows of Investment S have a *larger* coefficient of variation (0.50) than do cash flows of Investment T (0.20); therefore, even though the standard deviation is smaller, Investment S is the *more* risky of the two alternatives.

THE RELATIONSHIP BETWEEN RISK AND RETURN

Understanding the trade-off between risk and required (and expected) rates of return is integral to effective decision making. For example, investors who purchase shares of common stock hope to receive returns that will exceed those that might be earned from alternative investments, such as a savings account, U.S. government bonds, or high-quality corporate bonds. Investors recognize that the expected return from common stock over the long run tends to be higher than the expected return from less risky investments. To receive higher returns, however, investors must be prepared to accept a higher level of risk.

Risk and Required Return

The relationship between risk and required return on an investment in either a physical asset or financial asset (security) can be defined as

$$\text{Required return} = \text{Risk-free return} + \text{Risk premium} \qquad [2.7]$$

The risk-free rate of return refers to the return available on an investment with no risk of default. For debt securities, no default risk means that promised interest and principal payments are guaranteed to be made. The best example of risk-free securities are short-term U.S. government securities, such as Treasury bills. There is no risk of default on these securities because the U.S. government always can print more money. Of course, if the government recklessly prints money to pay its obligations, the purchasing power of the money will decline. Nevertheless, the buyer of a U.S. government bond always is assured of receiving the promised *dollar* payments.

A *risk premium* is a potential "reward" that an investor can expect to receive from making a risky investment. Investors generally are considered to be *risk averse;* that is, they expect, on average, to be compensated for the risk they assume when making an investment. Over the long term, expected returns and required returns from securities will tend to be equal.

EXAMPLE

www.................
You can learn more about how Moody's Investors Service rates corporate bonds at http://www.moodys.com/index.shtml

RISK-RETURN TRADE-OFFS IN STOCKS AND BONDS

Investors require higher rates of return on securities subject to default risk. Bond rating agencies, such as Moody's, Standard and Poor's, Duff and Phelps, and Fitch, provide evaluations of the default risk of many corporate bonds in the form of bond ratings. Moody's, for example, rates bonds on a 9-point scale from Aaa, Aa through C, where Aaa-rated bonds have the lowest expected default risk. As can be seen in Table 2.6, the yields on bonds increase as the risk of default increases, reflecting the positive relationship between risk and required returns. Over time, the spread between the required returns on bonds having various levels of default risk varies, reflecting the economic prospects and the resulting probability of default.

The risk versus return trade-off also can be illustrated by examining the returns *achieved* by investors in various securities over long periods of time. Table 2.7 shows the realized returns (and the standard deviation of those returns) from small company common stock (highest risk), the common stocks in the S & P 500 index (next highest risk),

TABLE   2.6

Relationship between Default Risk and Required Returns

Security	Yield
U.S. Treasury bonds (30 year)	6.71%
Aaa-rated corporate bonds	7.37
Aa-rated corporate bonds	7.55
A-rated corporate bonds	7.69
Baa-rated corporate bonds	8.05

Source: Board of Governors of the Federal Reserve System, *Federal Reserve Bulletin* (Washington, D.C., July 1997), p. A23.

Relationship between
Realized Returns and
Risk of Various
Investments
(1926–1996)

Series	Arithmetic mean	Standard deviation	Distribution
Large company stocks	12.7%	20.3%	
Small company stocks	17.7%	34.1%	*
Long-term corporate bonds	6.0%	8.7%	
Long-term government bonds	5.4%	9.2%	
Intermediate-term government bonds	5.4%	5.8%	
U.S. Treasury bills	3.8%	3.3%	
			−90% 0% +90%

* The 1933 small company stock total return was 142.9%

Source: *Stocks, Bonds, Bills and Inflation: 1997 Yearbook* (Chicago Ibbotson Associates, Inc., 1997)
Table 2-1 p.33. Annually updates work by Roger G. Ibbotson and Rex A. Sinquefield.
Data reproduced with permission of Ibbotson Associates. All rights reserved

long-term U.S. government bonds (third highest risk), long-term corporate bonds (fourth highest risk), intermediate-term government bonds (fifth highest risk), and U.S. Treasury bills (lowest risk). The realized returns and the standard deviation (risk) of these returns over the period 1926–1996 are consistent with our expectation that there is a positive relationship between risk and return.

SUMMARY

▢ The *marginal analysis* concept requires that a decision maker determine the additional (marginal) costs and additional (marginal) benefits associated with a proposed action. If the marginal benefits exceed the marginal costs (that is, if the net marginal benefits are positive), the action should be taken.

▢ The *net present value* of an investment is equal to the present value of expected future returns (cash flows) minus the initial outlay.

▢ The net present value of an investment equals the contribution of that investment to the value of the firm and, accordingly, to the wealth of shareholders. The net present value of an investment depends on the return required by investors (the firm), which, in turn, is a function of the perceived risk of the investment.

▢ *Risk* refers to the potential variability of outcomes from a decision alternative. It can be measured either by the *standard deviation* (an absolute measure of risk) or *coefficient of variation* (a relative measure of risk).

▢ A positive relationship exists between risk and required rates of return on securities and physical asset investments. Investments involving greater risks must offer higher expected returns.

EXERCISES

1. Discuss how an airline might use the marginal analysis concept to decide on adding a new flight to its schedule. Identify the costs that should and should not be considered in this analysis.

2. To save money, the state legislature has mandated a 5 percent decrease in the enrollment at Major State University. At the same time the legislature reduced appropriations to the school by 5 percent. Evaluate this decision using the marginal analysis concepts developed in this chapter.

3. The Ajax Corporation has the following set of projects available to it:

Project*	Investment Required ($ Million)	Expected Rate of Return
A	500	23.0%
B	75	18.0
C	50	21.0
D	125	16.0
E	300	14.0
F	150	13.0
G	250	19.0

*Note: All projects have equal risk.

Ajax can raise funds with the following marginal costs:

First $250 million	14.0%
Next 250 million	15.5
Next 100 million	16.0
Next 250 million	16.5
Next 200 million	18.0
Next 200 million	21.0

Use the marginal cost and marginal revenue concepts developed in this chapter to derive an optimal capital budget for Ajax.

4. The Compatible Computer Company, a computer software developer, has estimated the probability of next year's revenues as follows:

Revenues ($000)	Probability
700	.10
800	.20
900	.40
1,000	.20
1,100	.10

a. Compute expected annual revenues.
b. Compute the standard deviation of annual revenues.
c. Compute the coefficient of variation of annual revenues.

48   PART I   Introduction

5. The demand for MICHTEC's products is related to the state of the economy. If the economy is expanding next year (an above-normal growth in GNP), the company expects sales to be $90 million. If there is a recession next year (a decline in GNP), sales are expected to be $75 million. If next year is normal (a moderate growth in GNP), sales are expected to be $85 million. MICHTEC's economists have estimated the chances that the economy will be either expanding, normal, or in a recession next year at 0.2, 0.5, and 0.3, respectively.

   a. Compute expected annual sales.
   b. Compute the standard deviation of annual sales.
   c. Compute the coefficient of variation of annual sales.

6. Two investments have the following expected returns (net present values) and standard deviation of returns:

Project	Expected Returns	Standard Deviation
A	$ 50,000	$ 40,000
B	250,000	125,000

   a. Based on the standard deviation, which project is riskier?
   b. Based on the coefficient of variation, which project is riskier?
   c. Which measure of risk do you think is appropriate to use in this case? Why?

7. An investment project has expected annual net cash flows of $100,000 with a standard deviation of $40,000. The distribution of annual net cash flows is approximately normal.

   a. Determine the probability that the annual net cash flows will be negative.
   b. Determine the probability that the annual net cash flows will be less than $20,000.

8. The manager of the aerospace division of General Aeronautics has estimated the price it can charge for providing satellite launch services to commercial firms. Her most optimistic estimate (a price not expected to be exceeded more than 10 percent of the time) is $2 million. Her most pessimistic estimate (a lower price than this one is not expected more than 10 percent of the time) is $1 million. The price distribution is believed to be approximately normal.

   a. What is the expected price?
   b. What is the standard deviation of the launch price?
   c. What is the probability of receiving a price less than $1.2 million?

9. Why do you think there should be a positive relationship between *risk* and *realized return* as well as between *risk* and *expected return?*

10. Given the following possible returns (dividends plus capital gains) over the coming year from a $10,000 investment in General Electric common stock:

State of Economy	Probability	Return
Recession	0.25	$-1,500
Normal year	0.50	2,000
Boom	0.25	3,500

a. Determine the expected return.
b. Determine the standard deviation of return.
c. Determine the coefficient of variation.

11. Given that the rate of return on Ford Motor Company common stock over the coming year is normally distributed with an expected value of 15 percent and a standard deviation of 10 percent, determine the probability of earning a

a. Negative rate of return.
b. Rate of return of at least 20 percent.
c. Rate of return of at least 15 percent.
d. Rate of return in excess of the Treasury bill rate (which is currently 5 percent).
e. Positive rate of return.

12. Amgen, Inc. uses state-of-the-art biotechnology to develop human pharmaceutical and diagnostic products. During 1983 and 1984 Amgen had losses of $4.9 million and $7.8 million, respectively. The firm barely broke even between 1985 and 1987 and had sizable losses ($8.2 million) in 1988. On the strength of royalty income from the sale of its Epogen product, a stimulator of red blood cell production, profits increased steadily from $19 million in 1989 to $355 million in 1993 to $670 million in 1996. Profits are expected to exceed $900 million per year by 1998–1999, according to forecasts prepared by the *Value Line Investment Survey.* *Value Line* rates the safety (a risk measure) of Amgen to be "average."

a. Discuss the past, present, and projected performance of Amgen in the context of risk-return trade-offs.
b. Amgen's 1993 return on equity (net income ÷ shareholders' equity) was about 30 percent. In 1993, its projected return on equity was 28.5 percent for 1995 and 22.5 percent during 1997–1999. The 1989 return on equity was 10.2 percent, and the 1985 to 1987 return on equity was about 0.9 percent. Do you believe Amgen is now earning "excessive profits" from its Epogen product? Why or why not?

www exercise

Risk-Return Analysis of Equities

13. Access the riskview.com website at http://www.riskview.com. Before you download their free riskview.com software, carefully read the configuration instructions. This software gives you access to historical return and volitility data and allows you to estimate risk and evaluate investment return for approximately 3,000 companies whose equity shares are traded on various exchanges.

Select a portfolio of various stocks based on their risk-return characteristics. Write a brief executive summary in which you justify the inclusion of each stock; you may do so by comparing their risk-return characteristics to those of similar stocks in their industry or sector of the economy.

CASE EXERCISES   THE TORO COMPANY AND THE PROBABILITY OF SNOW[9]

The Toro Company makes snow blowers that remove snow from walks and driveways. According to Richard Pollick, marketing director at Toro, "We found that the big barrier to buying one of our machines was the fear that there wouldn't be enough snow to justify the cost."

The company designed a promotional campaign to overcome this problem. It agreed to refund the entire price of its machines purchased before December 10 if the snowfall during the ensuing winter was less than 20 percent of the 40-year average for the purchase location. In effect, then, the customer would get the snowblower free! If the

---

[9] Based on Bill Richards, "Executives at Toro Are Dreaming of a White Winter—Very White," *Wall Street Journal,* 12 December 1983.

snowfall was less than 50 percent of the 40-year average, then Toro would refund part of the purchase price. According to the marketing director, this promotion led to significantly increased early season sales.

After the program ended, company management began to monitor closely reports from 172 weather stations located in the northern part of the country. Toro also hedged its bets by purchasing weather insurance from Good Weather International, a New York company. In the event of low snowfall amounts, Good Weather would reimburse Toro for its losses.

The probability that Good Weather would have to reimburse Toro under this agreement is very small. According to a meteorologist at the National Climatic Center, Minneapolis has *never* had a winter in its recorded history with a snowfall less than 20 percent of the average. Also, the city has had less than 50 percent of its average snowfall only four times in the past 40 years.

QUESTIONS

1.   What factors might have led Toro management to consider purchasing this type of insurance?
2.   What factors would the managers at Good Weather have to consider in determining a price (i.e., insurance premium) to charge Toro for this protection?

3

Optimization Techniques

CHAPTER PREVIEW

Normative economic decision analysis involves determining the action that best achieves a desired goal or objective. This means finding the action that optimizes (that is, maximizes or minimizes) the value of an objective function. For example, in a price-output decision-making problem, we may be interested in determining the output level that maximizes profits. In a production problem, the goal may be to find the combination of inputs (resources) that minimizes the cost of producing a desired level of output. In a capital budgeting problem, the objective may be to select those projects that maximize the net present value of the investments chosen. There are many techniques for solving optimization problems such as these. This chapter (and appendix) focuses on the use of differential calculus to solve certain types of optimization problems. In Chapter 11, linear-programming techniques, used in solving constrained optimization problems, are examined. Optimization techniques are a powerful set of tools that are important in efficiently managing an enterprise's resources and thereby maximizing shareholder wealth.

TYPES OF OPTIMIZATION TECHNIQUES

In Chapter 1 we defined the general form of a problem that managerial economics attempts to analyze. The basic form of the problem is to identify the alternative means of achieving a given objective and then to select the alternative that accomplishes the objective in the most efficient manner, subject to constraints on the means. In programming terminology, the problem is optimizing the value of some objective function, subject to any resource and/or other constraints such as legal, input, environmental, and behavioral restrictions.

Mathematically, we can represent the problem as

$$\text{Optimize } y = f(x_1, x_2, \ldots, x_n) \tag{3.1}$$

$$\text{subject to } g_j(x_1, x_2, \ldots, x_n) \begin{Bmatrix} \leq \\ = \\ \geq \end{Bmatrix} b_j \quad j = 1, 2, \ldots, m \tag{3.2}$$

where Equation 3.1 is the objective function and Equation 3.2 constitutes the set of constraints imposed on the solution. The x_i variables, $x_1, x_2, \ldots, x_n$, represent the set of decision variables, and $y = f(x_1, x_2, \ldots, x_n)$ is the objective function expressed in terms of these decision variables. Depending on the nature of the problem, the term *optimize* means either *maximize* or *minimize* the value of the objective function. As indicated in Equation 3.2, each constraint can take the form of an equality ($=$) or an inequality ($\leq$ or $\geq$) relationship.

Complicating Factors in Optimization

Several factors can make optimization problems fairly complex and difficult to solve. One such complicating factor is the *existence of multiple decision variables* in a problem. Relatively simple procedures exist for determining the profit-maximizing output level for the single-product firm. However, the typical medium- or large-size firm often produces a large number of different products, and as a result, the profit-maximization problem for such a firm requires a series of output decisions—one for each product. Another factor that may add to the difficulty of solving a problem is the *complex nature of the relationships between the decision variables and the associated outcome.* For example, in public policy decisions on government spending for such items as education, it is extremely difficult to determine the relationship between a given expenditure and the benefits of increased income, employment, and productivity it provides. No simple relationship exists among the variables. Many of the optimization techniques discussed here are only applicable to situations in which a relatively simple function or relationship can be postulated between the decision variables and the outcome variable. A third complicating factor is the possible *existence of one or more complex constraints on the decision variables.* For example, virtually every organization has constraints imposed on its decision variables by the limited resources—such as capital, personnel, and facilities—over which it has control. These constraints must be incorporated into the decision problem. Otherwise, the optimization techniques that are applied to the problem may yield a solution that is unacceptable from a practical standpoint. Another complicating factor is the presence of *uncertainty* or *risk.* In this chapter, we limit the analysis to decision making under *certainty,* that is, problems in which each action is known to lead to a specific outcome. Chapters 2 and 20 examine methods for analyzing decisions involving risk and uncertainty. These factors illustrate the difficulties that may be encountered and may render a problem unsolvable by formal optimization procedures.

MANAGERIAL CHALLENGE

A SKELETON IN THE STEALTH BOMBER'S CLOSET[1]

In 1990 the U.S. Air Force publicly unveiled its newest long-range strategic bomber—the B-2 or "Stealth" bomber. This plane is characterized by a unique flying wing design engineered to evade detection by enemy radar. The plane has been controversial because of its high cost. However, a lesser known controversy relates to its fundamental design.

The plane's flying wing design originated from a secret study of promising military technologies that was undertaken at the end of World War II. The group of prominent scientists who undertook the study concluded that a plane can achieve maximum range if it has a design in which virtually all the volume of the plane is contained in the wing. A complex mathematical appendix was attached to the study that purported to show that range could be *maximized* with the flying wing design.

However, a closer examination of the technical appendix by Joseph Foa, now an emeritus professor of engineering at George Washington University, discovered that a fundamental error had been made in the initial report. It turned out that the original researchers had taken the first derivative of a complex equation for the range of a plane and found that it had two solutions. The original researchers mistakenly concluded that the all-wing design was the one that maximized range, when, in fact, it *minimized* range.

In this chapter we introduce some of the same optimization techniques applied to an analysis of the Stealth bomber project. We develop tools designed to maximize profits or minimize costs. Fortunately, the mathematical functions we deal with in this chapter and throughout the book are much simpler than those that confronted the original "flying wing" engineers. We introduce techniques that can be used to check whether a function, such as profits or costs, is being minimized or maximized at a particular level of output.

---

[1] This Managerial Challenge is based primarily on W. Biddle, "Skeleton Alleged in the Stealth Bomber's Closet," *Science,* 12 May 1989, pp. 650–651.

Constrained versus Unconstrained Optimization

The mathematical techniques used to solve an optimization problem represented by Equations 3.1 and 3.2 depend on the form of the criterion and constraint functions. The simplest situation to be considered is the *unconstrained* optimization problem. In such a problem no constraints are imposed on the decision variables, and *differential calculus* can be used to analyze them. Another relatively simple form of the general optimization problem is the case in which all the constraints of the problem can be expressed as *equality* (=) relationships. The technique of *Lagrangian multipliers* can be used to find the optimal solution to many of these problems.

Often, however, the constraints in an economic decision-making problem take the form of *inequality* relationships (≤ or ≥) rather than equalities. For example, limitations on the resources—such as personnel and capital—of an organization place an *upper bound* or budget ceiling on the quantity of these resources that can be employed in maximizing (or minimizing) the objective function. With this type of constraint, all of a given resource need not be used in an optimal solution to the problem. An example of a *lower bound* would be a loan agreement that requires a firm to maintain a *current ratio* (that is, ratio of current assets to current liabilities) of at least 2.00. Any combination of current assets and current liabilities having a ratio greater than or equal to 2.00 would meet the provisions of the loan agreement. Such optimization procedures as the Lagrangian multiplier method are not suited to solving problems of this type efficiently; however, modern mathematical programming techniques have been developed that can efficiently solve several classes of problems with these inequality restrictions.

Linear-programming problems constitute the most important class for which efficient solution techniques have been developed. In a linear-programming problem, both the objective and the constraint relationships are expressed as linear functions of decision variables.[2] Other classes of problems include *integer-programming* problems, in which some (or all) of the decision variables are required to take on integer values, and *quadratic-programming* problems, in which the objective relationship is a quadratic function of the decision variables.[3] Generalized computing algorithms exist for solving optimization problems that meet these requirements.

The remainder of this chapter deals with the classical optimization procedures of differential calculus. Lagrangian multiplier techniques are covered in Appendix 3A. Linear programming is encountered in Chapter 11.

EXAMPLE

www . . . .
Decision science modeling at American Airlines is described at http://www.sabre.com/its/

CONSTRAINED OPTIMIZATION: OPTIMIZING FLIGHT CREW SCHEDULES AT AMERICAN AIRLINES[4]

One problem that faces major airlines, such as American Airlines, is the development of a schedule for airline crews (pilots and flight attendants) that results in a high level of crew utilization. This scheduling problem is rather complex because of Federal Aviation Administration (FAA) rules designed to ensure that a crew can perform its duties without risk from fatigue. Union agreements require that flight crews receive pay for a contractually set number of hours of each day or trip. The goal for airline planners is to construct a crew schedule that meets or exceeds crew pay guarantees and does not violate FAA rules. With the salary of airline captains at $140,000 per year or more, it is important that an airline make the maximum possible usage of its crew personnel. Crew costs are the second largest direct operating cost of an airline.

The nature of the constrained optimization problem facing an airline planner is to *minimize the cost of flying the published schedule,* subject to the following constraints:

1. Each flight is assigned only one crew.
2. Each pairing of a crew and a flight must begin and end at a home "crew base," such as Chicago or Dallas for American.
3. Each pairing must be consistent with union work rules and FAA rules.
4. The number of jobs at each crew base must be within targeted minimum and maximum limits as specified in American's personnel plan.

American was able to develop a sophisticated constrained optimization model that saved $18 million per year compared with previous crew allocation models used.

---

[2] A linear relationship of the variables $x_1, x_2, \ldots, x_n$ is a function of the form:

$$a_1 x_1 + a_2 x_2 + \ldots + a_n x_n$$

where all the x variables have exponents of 1.

[3] A quadratic function contains either squared terms (x_i^2) or cross-product terms ($x_i x_j$).

[4] Ira Gershkoff, "Optimizing Flight Crew Schedules," *Interfaces,* July–August 1989, pp. 29–43.

DIFFERENTIAL CALCULUS

In Chapter 2, marginal analysis was introduced as one of the fundamental concepts of economic decision making. In the marginal analysis framework, resource-allocation decisions are made by comparing the marginal benefits of a change in the level of an activity with the marginal costs of the change. A change should be made as long as the marginal benefits exceed the marginal costs. By following this basic rule, resources can be allocated efficiently and profits or shareholder wealth can be maximized.

In the profit-maximization example developed in Chapter 2, the application of the marginal analysis principles required that the relationship between the objective (profit) and the decision variable (output level) be expressed in either tabular or graphic form. This framework, however, can become cumbersome when dealing with several decision variables or with complex relationships between the decision variables and the objective. When the relationship between the decision variables and criterion can be expressed in *algebraic* form, the more powerful concepts of differential calculus can be used to find optimal solutions to these problems.

Relationship between Marginal Analysis and Differential Calculus

Initially, let us assume that the objective we are seeking to optimize, Y, can be expressed algebraically as a function of *one* decision variable, X,

$$Y = f(X) \qquad [3.3]$$

Recall that marginal profit is defined as the change in profit resulting from a one-unit change in output. In general, the marginal value of any variable Y, which is a function of another variable X, is defined as the change in the value of Y resulting from a one-unit change in X. The marginal value of Y, M_y, can be calculated from the change in Y, ΔY, that occurs as the result of a given change in X, ΔX:

$$M_y = \frac{\Delta Y}{\Delta X} \qquad [3.4]$$

Derivative
Measures the marginal effect of a change in one variable on the value of a function. Graphically, it represents the slope of the function at a given point.

When calculated with this expression, different estimates for the marginal value of Y may be obtained, depending on the size of the change in X that we use in the computation. The true marginal value of a function (e.g., an economic relationship) is obtained from Equation 3.4 when ΔX is made as small as possible. If ΔX can be thought of as a *continuous* (rather than a discrete) variable that can take on fractional values,[5] then in calculating M_y by Equation 3.4, we can let ΔX approach zero. In concept, this is the approach taken in differential calculus. The **derivative**, or more precisely, *first derivative*,[6] dY/dX, of a function is defined as the *limit* of the ratio $\Delta Y/\Delta X$ as ΔX approaches zero; that is,

$$\frac{dY}{dX} = \lim_{\Delta X \to 0} \frac{\Delta Y}{\Delta X} \qquad [3.5]$$

Graphically, the first derivative of a function represents the *slope* of the curve at a given point on the curve. The definition of a derivative as the limit of the change in Y (that is, ΔY) as ΔX approaches zero is illustrated in Figure 3.1(a). Suppose we are interested in

---

[5] For example, if X is a continuous variable measured in feet, pounds, and so on, then ΔX can in theory take on fractional values such as 0.5, 0.10, 0.05, 0.001, 0.0001 feet or pounds. When X is a continuous variable, ΔX can be made as small as desired.

[6] It is also possible to compute second, third, fourth, and so on, derivatives. Second derivatives are discussed later in this chapter.

FIGURE   3.1

First Derivative of a
Function

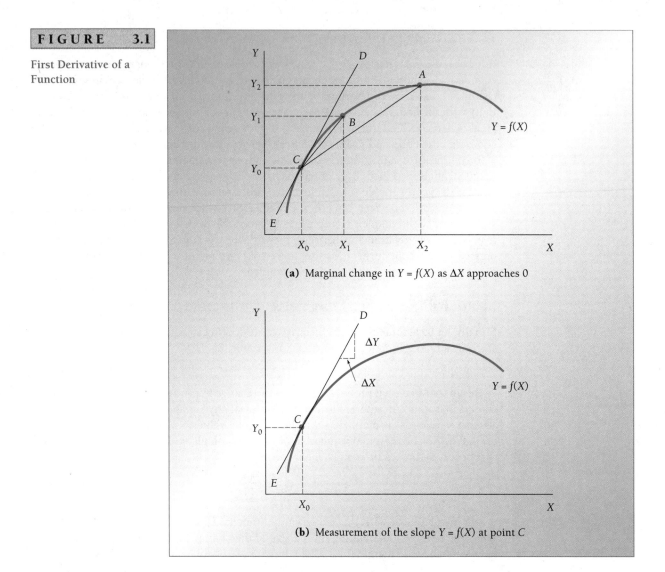

(a) Marginal change in $Y = f(X)$ as ΔX approaches 0

(b) Measurement of the slope $Y = f(X)$ at point C

the derivative of the $Y = f(X)$ function at the point X_0. The derivative dY/dX measures the slope of the tangent line ECD. An estimate of this slope, albeit a poor estimate, can be obtained by calculating the marginal value of Y over the interval X_0 to X_2. Using Equation 3.4, a value of

$$M'_y = \frac{\Delta Y}{\Delta X} = \frac{Y_2 - Y_0}{X_2 - X_0}$$

is obtained for the slope of the CA line. Now let us calculate the marginal value of Y using a smaller interval, for example, X_0 to X_1. The slope of the line C to B, which is equal to

$$M''_y = \frac{\Delta Y}{\Delta X} = \frac{Y_1 - Y_0}{X_1 - X_0}$$

gives a much better estimate of the true marginal value as represented by the slope of the ECD tangent line. Thus we see that the smaller the ΔX value, the better the estimate of the slope of the curve. Letting ΔX approach zero allows us to find the slope of the $Y = f(X)$

curve at point *C*. As shown in Figure 3.1(b), the slope of the *ECD* tangent line (and the *Y* = *f*(*X*) function at point *C*) is measured by the change in *Y*, or rise, ΔY, divided by the change in *X*, or run, ΔX.

Process of Differentiation

The process of differentiation—that is, finding the derivative of a function—involves determining the limiting value of the ratio $\Delta Y/\Delta X$ as ΔX approaches zero. Before offering some general rules for finding the derivative of a function, we illustrate with an example the algebraic process used to obtain the derivative without the aid of these general rules. The specific rules that simplify this process are presented in the following section.

<table>
<tr><td>

EXAMPLE

www..............

You can connect to Illinois Power Company, a subsidiary of Illinova, at http://www.illinova.com/ Clicking on the "inside Illinova" button will give you access to financial information.

</td><td>

PROCESS OF DIFFERENTIATION: PROFIT MAXIMIZATION AT ILLINOIS POWER

Suppose the profit, π, of Illinois Power can be represented as a function of the output level *Q* using the expression

$$\pi = -40 + 140Q - 10Q^2 \qquad [3.6]$$

We wish to determine $d\pi/dQ$ by first finding the marginal-profit expression $\Delta\pi/\Delta Q$ and then taking the limit of this expression as ΔQ approaches zero. Let us begin by expressing the new level of profit ($\pi + \Delta\pi$) that will result from an increase in output to ($Q + \Delta Q$). From Equation 3.6, we know that

$$(\pi + \Delta\pi) = -40 + 140(Q + \Delta Q) - 10(Q + \Delta Q)^2 \qquad [3.7]$$

Expanding this expression and then doing some algebraic simplifying, we obtain

$$(\pi + \Delta\pi) = -40 + 140Q + 140\Delta Q - 10[Q^2 + 2Q\Delta Q + (\Delta Q)^2]$$

$$= -40 + 140Q - 10Q^2 + 140\Delta Q - 20Q\Delta Q - 10(\Delta Q)^2 \qquad [3.8]$$

Subtracting Equation 3.6 from Equation 3.8 yields

$$\Delta\pi = 140\Delta Q - 20Q\Delta Q - 10(\Delta Q)^2 \qquad [3.9]$$

Forming the marginal-profit ratio $\Delta\pi/\Delta Q$, and doing some canceling, we get

$$\frac{\Delta\pi}{\Delta Q} = \frac{140\Delta Q - 20Q\Delta Q - 10(\Delta Q)^2}{\Delta Q}$$

$$= 140 - 20Q - 10\Delta Q \qquad [3.10]$$

Taking the limit of Equation 3.10 as ΔQ approaches zero yields the expression for the derivative of Illinois Power's profit function (Equation 3.6)

$$\frac{d\pi}{dQ} = \underset{\Delta Q \to 0}{\text{limit}} [140 - 20Q - 10\Delta Q]$$

$$= 140 - 20Q \qquad [3.11]$$

If we are interested in the derivative of the profit function at a particular value of *Q*, Equation 3.11 can be evaluated for this value. For example, suppose we want to know the marginal profit, or slope of the profit function, at *Q* = 3 units. Substituting *Q* = 3 in Equation 3.11 yields

$$\underset{\text{profit}}{\text{Marginal}} = \frac{d\pi}{dQ} = 140 - 20(3) = \$80 \text{ per unit}$$

</td></tr>
</table>

Rules of Differentiation

Fortunately, we do not need to go through this lengthy process every time we want the derivative of a function. A series of general rules, derived in a manner similar to the process just described, exists for differentiating various types of functions.[7]

Constant Functions   A constant function can be expressed as

$$Y = a \qquad\qquad [3.12]$$

where a is a constant (that is, Y is independent of X). The derivative of a constant function is equal to zero:

$$\frac{dY}{dX} = 0 \qquad\qquad [3.13]$$

For example, consider the constant function

$$Y = 4$$

which is graphed in Figure 3.2(a). Recall that the first derivative of a function (dY/dX) measures the slope of the function. Because this constant function is a horizontal straight line with zero slope, its derivative (dY/dX) is therefore equal to zero.

Power Functions   A power function takes the form of

$$Y = aX^b \qquad\qquad [3.14]$$

where a and b are constants. The derivative of a power function is equal to b times a, times X raised to the $(b - 1)$ power:

$$\frac{dY}{dX} = b \cdot a \cdot X^{b-1} \qquad\qquad [3.15]$$

A couple of examples are used to illustrate the application of this rule. First, consider the function

$$Y = 2X$$

which is graphed in Figure 3.2(b). Note that the slope of this function is equal to 2 and is constant over the entire range of X values. Applying the power function rule to this example, where $a = 2$ and $b = 1$, yields

$$\frac{dY}{dX} = 1 \cdot 2 \cdot X^{1-1} = 2X^0$$

$$= 2$$

Note that any variable to the zero power, e.g., X^0, is equal to 1.

Next, consider the function

$$Y = X^2$$

which is graphed in Figure 3.2(c). Note that the slope of this function varies depending on the value of X. Application of the power function rule to this example yields ($a = 1$, $b = 2$):

---

[7]A more expanded treatment of these rules can be found in any introductory calculus book such as André L. Yandl, *Applied Calculus* (Belmont, Calif.: Wadsworth, 1991).

FIGURE   3.2   Constant, Linear, and Quadratic Functions

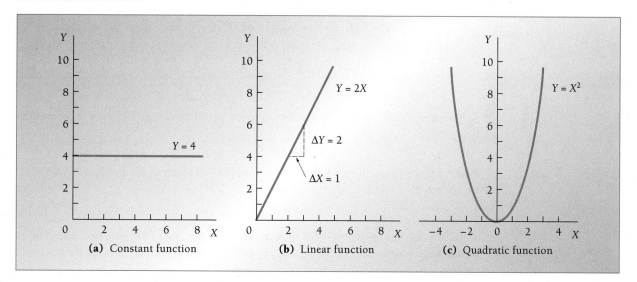

(a) Constant function   **(b)** Linear function   **(c)** Quadratic function

$$\frac{dY}{dX} = 2 \cdot 1 \cdot X^{2-1}$$

$$= 2X$$

As we can see, this derivative (or slope) function is negative when $X < 0$, zero when $X = 0$, and positive when $X > 0$.

Sums of Functions   Suppose a function $Y = f(X)$ represents the sum of two (or more) separate functions, $f_1(X)$, $f_2(X)$, that is,

$$Y = f_1(X) + f_2(X) \qquad\qquad [3.16]$$

The derivative of Y with respect to X is found by differentiating each of the separate functions and then adding the results:

$$\frac{dY}{dX} = \frac{df_1(X)}{dX} + \frac{df_2(X)}{dX} \qquad\qquad [3.17]$$

This result can be extended to finding the derivative of the sum of any number of functions.

EXAMPLE

RULES OF DIFFERENTIATION: PROFIT MAXIMIZATION AT ILLINOIS POWER (CONTINUED)

As an example of the application of these rules, consider again the profit function for Illinois Power, given by Equation 3.6, that was discussed earlier:

$$\pi = -40 + 140Q - 10Q^2$$

In this example Q represents the X variable and π represents the Y variable; that is, $\pi = f(Q)$. The function $f(Q)$ is the sum of *three* separate functions—a constant function, $f_1(Q) = -40$, and two power functions, $f_2(Q) = 140Q$ and $f_3(Q) = -10Q^2$. Therefore, applying the differentiation rules yields

$$\frac{d\pi}{dQ} = \frac{df_1(Q)}{dQ} + \frac{df_2(Q)}{dQ} + \frac{df_3(Q)}{dQ}$$

$$= 0 + 1 \cdot 140 \cdot Q^{1-1} + 2 \cdot (-10) \cdot Q^{2-1}$$

$$= 140 - 20Q$$

This is the same result that was obtained earlier in Equation 3.11 by the differentiation process.

Product of Two Functions   Suppose the variable Y is equal to the product of two separate functions $f_1(X)$ and $f_2(X)$:

$$Y = f_1(X) \cdot f_2(X) \tag{3.18}$$

In this case the derivative of Y with respect to X is equal to the sum of the first function times the derivative of the second, plus the second function times the derivative of the first.

$$\frac{dY}{dX} = f_1(X) \cdot \frac{df_2(X)}{dX} + f_2(X) \cdot \frac{df_1(X)}{dX} \tag{3.19}$$

For example, suppose we are interested in the derivative of the expression

$$Y = X^2(2X - 3)$$

Let $f_1(X) = X^2$ and $f_2(X) = (2X - 3)$. By the above rule (and the earlier rules for differentiating constant and power functions), we obtain

$$\frac{dY}{dX} = X^2 \cdot \frac{d}{dX}[(2X - 3)] + (2X - 3) \cdot \frac{d}{dX}[X^2]$$

$$= X^2 \cdot (2 - 0) + (2X - 3) \cdot (2X)$$

$$= 2X^2 + 4X^2 - 6X$$

$$= 6X^2 - 6X$$

$$= 6X(X - 1)$$

Quotient of Two Functions   Suppose the variable Y is equal to the quotient of two separate functions $f_1(X)$ and $f_2(X)$:

$$Y = \frac{f_1(X)}{f_2(X)} \tag{3.20}$$

For such a relationship the derivative of Y with respect to X is obtained as follows:

$$\frac{dY}{dX} = \frac{f_2(X) \cdot \dfrac{df_1(X)}{dX} - f_1(X) \cdot \dfrac{df_2(X)}{dX}}{[f_2(X)]^2} \tag{3.21}$$

As an example, consider the problem of finding the derivative of the expression

$$Y = \frac{10X^2}{5X - 1}$$

Letting $f_1(X) = 10X^2$ and $f_2(X) = 5X - 1$, we have

$$\frac{dY}{dX} = \frac{(5X - 1) \cdot 20X - 10X^2 \cdot 5}{(5X - 1)^2}$$

$$= \frac{100X^2 - 20X - 50X^2}{(5X - 1)^2}$$

$$= \frac{50X^2 - 20X}{(5X - 1)^2}$$

$$= \frac{10X(5X - 2)}{(5X - 1)^2}$$

Functions of a Function (Chain Rule)   Suppose Y is a function of the variable Z, $Y = f_1(Z)$; and Z is in turn a function of the variable X, $Z = f_2(X)$. The derivative of Y with respect to X can be determined by first finding dY/dZ and dZ/dX and then multiplying the two expressions together:

$$\frac{dY}{dX} = \frac{dY}{dZ} \cdot \frac{dZ}{dX}$$

$$= \frac{df_1(Z)}{dZ} \cdot \frac{df_2(X)}{dX} \qquad [3.22]$$

To illustrate the application of this rule, suppose we are interested in finding the derivative (with respect to X) of the function

$$Y = 10Z - 2Z^2 - 3$$

where Z is related to X in the following way:[8]

$$Z = 2X^2 - 1$$

First, we find (by the earlier differentiation rules)

$$\frac{dY}{dZ} = 10 - 4Z$$

$$\frac{dZ}{dX} = 4X$$

and then

$$\frac{dY}{dX} = (10 - 4Z) \cdot 4X$$

Substituting the expression for Z in terms of X into this equation yields

$$\frac{dY}{dX} = [10 - 4(2X^2 - 1)] \cdot 4X$$

$$= (10 - 8X^2 + 4) \cdot 4X$$

$$= 40X - 32X^3 + 16X$$

$$= 56X - 32X^3$$

$$= 8X(7 - 4X^2)$$

These rules for differentiating functions are summarized in Table 3.1.

---

[8]Alternatively, one can substitute $Z = 2X^2 - 1$ into $Y = 10Z - 2Z^2 - 3$ and differentiate Y with respect to X. The reader is asked to demonstrate in Exercise 24 that this approach yields the same answer as the chain rule.

Function	Derivative
1. Constant Function $Y = a$	$\dfrac{dY}{dX} = 0$
2. Power Function $Y = aX^b$	$\dfrac{dY}{dX} = b \cdot a \cdot X^{b-1}$
3. Sums of Functions $Y = f_1(X) + f_2(X)$	$\dfrac{dY}{dX} = \dfrac{df_1(X)}{dX} + \dfrac{df_2(X)}{dX}$
4. Product of Two Functions $Y = f_1(X) \cdot f_2(X)$	$\dfrac{dY}{dX} = f_1(X) \cdot \dfrac{df_2(X)}{dX} + f_2(X) \cdot \dfrac{df_1(X)}{dX}$
5. Quotient of Two Functions $Y = \dfrac{f_1(X)}{f_2(X)}$	$\dfrac{dY}{dX} = \dfrac{f_2(X) \cdot \dfrac{df_1(X)}{dX} - f_1(X) \cdot \dfrac{df_2(X)}{dX}}{[f_2(X)]^2}$
6. Functions of a Function $Y = f_1(Z)$, where $Z = f_2(X)$	$\dfrac{dY}{dX} = \dfrac{dY}{dZ} \cdot \dfrac{dZ}{dX}$

APPLICATIONS OF DIFFERENTIAL CALCULUS TO OPTIMIZATION PROBLEMS

The reason for studying the process of differentiation and the rules for differentiating functions is that these methods can be used to find optimal solutions to many kinds of maximization and minimization problems in managerial economics.

Maximization Problem

Recall from the discussion of marginal analysis, a necessary (but not sufficient) condition for finding the maximum point on a curve (for example, maximum profits) is that the marginal value or slope of the curve at this point must be equal to zero. We can now express this condition within the framework of differential calculus. Because the derivative of a function measures the slope or marginal value at any given point, an equivalent necessary condition for finding the maximum value of a function $Y = f(X)$ is that the derivative dY/dX at this point must be equal to zero. This is known as the **first-order condition** for locating one or more maximum or minimum points of an algebraic function.

First-Order Condition
A test to locate one or more maximum or minimum points of an algebraic function.

EXAMPLE

FIRST-ORDER CONDITION: PROFIT MAXIMIZATION AT ILLINOIS POWER (CONTINUED)

Using the profit function (Equation 3.6)

$$\pi = -40 + 140Q - 10Q^2$$

discussed earlier, we can illustrate how to find the profit-maximizing output level Q by means of this condition. Setting the first derivative of this function (which was computed previously) to zero, we obtain

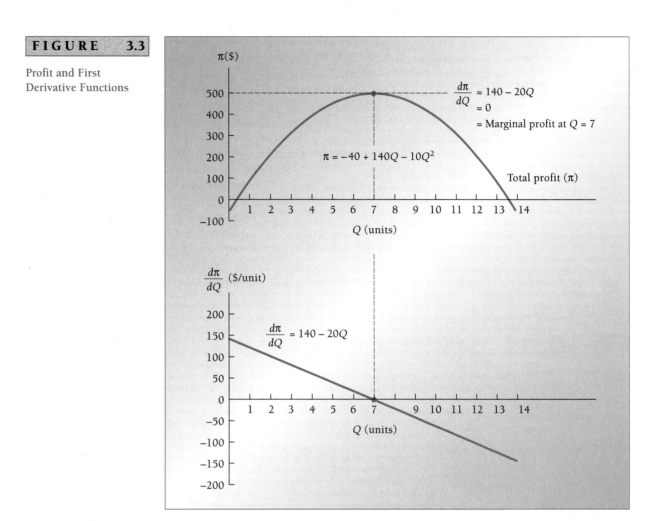

FIGURE   3.3

Profit and First
Derivative Functions

$$\frac{d\pi}{dQ} = 140 - 20Q$$

$$0 = 140 - 20Q$$

Solving this equation for Q yields $Q^* = 7$ units as the profit-maximizing output level. The profit and first derivative functions and optimal solution are shown in Figure 3.3. As we can see, profits are maximized at the point where the function is neither increasing nor decreasing; in other words, where the slope (or first derivative) is equal to zero.

Second Derivatives and the Second-Order Condition

Setting the derivative of a function equal to zero and solving the resulting equation for the value of the decision variable does not guarantee that the point will be obtained at which the function takes on its maximum value. (Recall the Stealth bomber example at the start of the chapter.) The slope of a U-shaped function will also be equal to zero at its low point and the function will take on its *minimum* value at the given point. In other words, setting the derivative to zero is only a *necessary* condition for finding the maximum value of a function; it is not a *sufficient* condition. Another condition,

Second-Order Condition

A test to determine whether a point that has been determined from the first-order condition is either a maximum point or a minimum point of the algebraic function.

known as the **second-order condition,** is required to determine whether a point that has been determined from the first-order condition is either a maximum point or minimum point of the algebraic function.

This situation is illustrated in Figure 3.4. At both points A and B the slope of the function (first derivative, dY/dX) is zero; however, only at point B does the function take on its maximum value. We note in Figure 3.4 that the marginal value (slope) is continually *decreasing* in the neighborhood of the maximum value (point B) of the $Y = f(X)$ function. First the slope is positive up to the point where $dY/dX = 0$, and thereafter the slope becomes negative. Thus we must determine whether the slope's marginal value (slope of the slope) is declining. A test to see whether the marginal value is decreasing is to take the derivative of the marginal value and check to see if it is negative at the given point on the function. In effect, we need to find the derivative of the derivative—that is, the *second derivative* of the function—and then test to see if it is less than zero. Formally, the second derivative of the function $Y = f(X)$ is written as d^2Y/dX^2 and is found by applying the previously described differentiation rules to the first derivative. A *maximum point is obtained if the second derivative is negative; that is, $d^2Y/dX^2 < 0$.*

FIGURE   3.4

Maximum and Minimum
Values of a Function

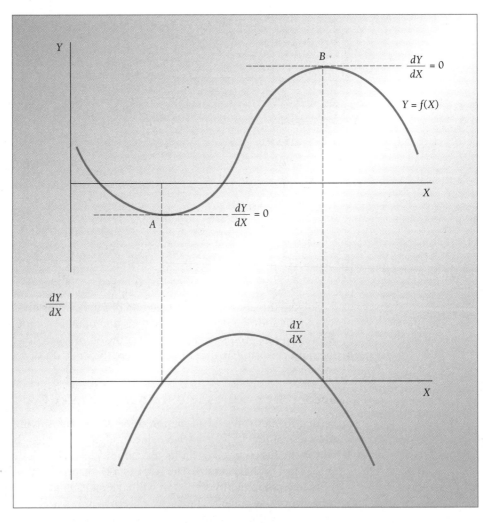

EXAMPLE

SECOND-ORDER CONDITION: PROFIT MAXIMIZATION AT ILLINOIS POWER (CONTINUED)

Returning to the profit-maximization example, the second derivative is obtained from the first derivative as follows:

$$\frac{d\pi}{dQ} = 140 - 20Q$$

$$\frac{d^2\pi}{dQ^2} = 0 + 1 \cdot (-20) \cdot Q^{1-1}$$

$$= -20$$

Because $d^2\pi/dQ^2 < 0$, we know that a maximum-profit point has been obtained.

An opposite condition holds for obtaining the point at which the function takes on a minimum value. Note again in Figure 3.4 that the marginal value (slope) is continually *increasing* in the neighborhood of the minimum value (point A) of the $Y = f(X)$ function. First the slope is negative up to the point where $dY/dX = 0$, and thereafter the slope becomes positive. Therefore, we test to see if $d^2Y/dX^2 > 0$ at the given point. *A minimum point is obtained if the second derivative is positive; that is, $d^2Y/dX^2 > 0$.*

Minimization Problem

In some decision-making situations, cost minimization may be the objective. As in profit-maximization problems, differential calculus can be used to locate the optimal points.

EXAMPLE

www . . . .
Brooklyn Union is a natural gas distribution company. You can access financial information on Brooklyn Union at their Internet site: http://www.bug.com/finance/financ.htm

COST MINIMIZATION: BROOKLYN UNION GAS CORPORATION

Suppose we are interested in determining the output level that minimizes average total costs for Brooklyn Union Gas Corporation, where the average total cost function might be approximated by the following relationship (Q represents output):

$$C = 15 - .040Q + .000080Q^2 \qquad [3.23]$$

Differentiating C with respect to Q gives

$$\frac{dC}{dQ} = - .040 + .000160Q$$

Setting this derivative equal to zero and solving for Q yields

$$0 = -.040 + .000160Q$$

$$Q^* = 250$$

Taking the second derivative, we obtain

$$\frac{d^2C}{dQ^2} = + .000160$$

Because the second derivative is positive, the output level of $Q = 250$ is indeed the value that minimizes average total costs.

Summarizing, we see that *two* conditions are required for locating a maximum or minimum value of a function using differential calculus. The *first-order* condition determines the point(s) at which the first derivative dY/dX is equal to zero. Having obtained one or more points, a *second-order* condition is used to determine whether the function takes on a maximum or minimum value at the given point(s). The second derivative d^2Y/dX^2 indicates whether a given point is a maximum ($d^2Y/dX^2 < 0$) or a minimum ($d^2Y/dX^2 > 0$) value of the function.

PARTIAL DIFFERENTIATION AND MULTIVARIATE OPTIMIZATION

Thus far in the chapter, the analysis has been limited to a criterion variable Y that can be expressed as a function of *one* decision variable X. However, many commonly used economic relationships contain two or more decision variables. For example, a *production function* relates the output of a plant, firm, industry, or country to the inputs employed—such as capital, labor, and raw materials. Another example is a *demand function,* which relates sales of a product or service to such variables as price, advertising, promotion expenses, price of substitutes, and income.

Partial Derivatives

Consider a criterion variable Y that is a function of two decision variables X_1 and X_2:[9]

$$Y = f(X_1, X_2)$$

Let us now examine the change in Y that results from a given change in either X_1 or X_2. To isolate the marginal effect on Y from a given change in X_1—that is, $\Delta Y/\Delta X_1$—we must hold X_2 constant. Similarly, if we wish to isolate the marginal effect on Y from a given change in X_2—that is, $\Delta Y/\Delta X_2$—the variable X_1 must be held constant. A measure of the marginal effect of a change in any one variable on the change in Y, holding all other variables in the relationship constant, is obtained from the **partial derivative** of the function. The partial derivative of Y with respect to X_1 is written as $\partial Y/\partial X_1$ and is found by applying the previously described differentiation rules to the $Y = f(X_1, X_2)$ function, where the variable X_2 is treated as a constant. Similarly, the partial derivative of Y with respect to X_2 is written as $\partial Y/\partial X_2$ and is found by applying the differentiation rules to the function, where the variable X_1 is treated as a constant.

Partial Derivative

Measures the marginal effect of a change in one variable on the value of a multivariate function, while holding constant all other variables.

EXAMPLE

PARTIAL DERIVATIVES: INDIANA PETROLEUM COMPANY

To illustrate the procedure for obtaining partial derivatives, let us consider the following relationship in which the profit variable, π, is a function of the output level of *two* products (heating oil and gasoline) Q_1 and Q_2:

$$\pi = -60 + 140Q_1 + 100Q_2 - 10Q_1^2 - 8Q_2^2 - 6Q_1Q_2 \qquad [3.24]$$

Treating Q_2 as a constant, the partial derivative of π with respect to Q_1 is obtained:

$$\frac{\partial \pi}{\partial Q_1} = 0 + 140 + 0 + 2 \cdot (-10) \cdot Q_1 - 0 - 6Q_2$$

$$= 140 - 20Q_1 - 6Q_2 \qquad [3.25]$$

---

[9] The following analysis is not limited to two decision variables. Relationships containing any number of variables can be analyzed within this framework.

Similarly, with Q_1 treated as a constant, the partial derivative of π with respect to Q_2 is equal to

$$\frac{\partial \pi}{\partial Q_2} = 0 + 0 + 100 - 0 + 2 \cdot (-8) \cdot Q_2 - 6Q_1$$

$$= 100 - 16Q_2 - 6Q_1 \qquad [3.26]$$

EXAMPLE

PARTIAL DERIVATIVES: DEMAND FUNCTION FOR SHIELD TOOTHPASTE

As another example, consider the following (multiplicative) demand function, where Q = quantity sold, P = selling price, and A = advertising expenditures:

$$Q = 3.0P^{-.50}A^{.25} \qquad [3.27]$$

The partial derivative of Q with respect to P is

$$\frac{\partial Q}{\partial P} = 3.0A^{.25}(-.50P^{-.50-1})$$

$$= -1.5P^{-1.50}A^{.25}$$

Similarly, the partial derivative of Q with respect to A is

$$\frac{\partial Q}{\partial A} = 3.0P^{-.50}(.25A^{.25-1})$$

$$= .75P^{-.50}A^{-.75}$$

Maximization Problem

The partial derivatives can be used to obtain the optimal solution to a maximization or minimization problem containing two or more X variables. Analogous to the first-order conditions discussed earlier for the one-variable case, we set *each* of the partial derivatives equal to zero and solve the resulting set of simultaneous equations for the optimal X values.

EXAMPLE

PROFIT MAXIMIZATION: INDIANA PETROLEUM COMPANY (CONTINUED)

Suppose we are interested in determining the values of Q_1 and Q_2 that maximize the company's profits given in Equation 3.24. In this case, each of the two partial derivative functions (Equations 3.25 and 3.26) would be set equal to zero:

$$0 = 140 - 20Q_1 - 6Q_2 \qquad [3.28]$$

$$0 = 100 - 16Q_2 - 6Q_1 \qquad [3.29]$$

This system of equations can be solved for the profit-maximizing values of Q_1 and Q_2.[10] The optimal values are $Q_1^* = 5.77$ units and $Q_2^* = 4.08$ units.[11] The optimal total profit is equal to

$$\pi^* = -60 + 140(5.77) + 100(4.08) - 10(5.77)^2 - 8(4.08)^2 - 6(5.77)(4.08)$$

$$= 548.45$$

---

[10] The second-order conditions for obtaining a maximum or minimum in the multiple-variable case are somewhat complex. A discussion of these conditions can be found in most basic calculus texts.

[11] Exercise 25 at the end of the chapter requires the determination of these optimal values.

INTERNATIONAL
PERSPECTIVES

www...............
You can read more about
trade tariffs and quotas at
the Internet site maintained
by the National Center for
Policy Analysis:
http://www.public-policy.
org/~ncpa/studies/s171/
s171.html

DEALING WITH IMPORT RESTRAINTS: TOYOTA

During the 1992 U.S. presidential campaign, there was extensive rhetoric about the "problem" of the U.S. balance of trade deficit with Japan, particularly about the level of Japanese auto imports into the United States. Some of the proposals that have been advanced to reduce the magnitude of this "problem," and thereby assist the U.S. auto industry, include the imposition of rigid car import quotas. Japanese manufacturers would be forced to restrict the number of cars that are exported to the United States.

Had rigid import quotas been imposed, Japanese manufacturers would have had to take this constraint into consideration when making production, distribution, and new car introduction plans. Japanese manufacturers could no longer just seek to maximize profits. Profits could only be maximized subject to an aggregate constrained level of exports that could be sent to the U.S. market.

Shortly after, Japanese manufacturers responded to import constraints by raising prices, thereby making Japanese cars less price competitive with U.S.-built autos. Increases in prices by Japanese firms would give U.S. manufacturers additional room for raising their own prices. Indeed, in early 1992 in the face of threatened import quotas, Toyota announced significant price increases on the cars it sold in the United States. Over the longer term, Japanese firms have shifted their product mix to more profitable, larger (luxury) cars, abandoning some of their market share in smaller, less profitable vehicles to U.S. manufacturers.

As can be seen in this example, the imposition of additional constraints on the operating activities of a firm can have a substantial impact on its short- and long-term pricing and output strategies.

SUMMARY

- ▫ Within the area of decision making under certainty are two broad classes of problems—*unconstrained* optimization problems and *constrained* optimization problems.
- ▫ *Marginal analysis* is useful in making decisions about the expansion or contraction of an economic activity.
- ▫ *Differential calculus,* which bears a close relationship to marginal analysis, can be applied whenever an algebraic relationship can be specified between the decision variables and the objective or criterion variable.
- ▫ The *first derivative* measures the slope or rate of change of a function at a given point and is equal to the limiting value of the marginal function as the marginal value is calculated over smaller and smaller intervals, that is, as the interval approaches zero.
- ▫ Various rules are available (see Table 3.1) for finding the derivative of specific types of functions.
- ▫ A necessary, but not sufficient, condition for finding the maximum or minimum points of a function is that the first derivative be equal to zero. This is known as the *first-order condition.*
- ▫ A *second-order condition* is required to determine whether a given point is a maximum or minimum. The *second derivative* indicates that a given point is a maximum if the second derivative is less than zero or a minimum if the second derivative is greater than zero.
- ▫ The *partial derivative* of a multivariate function measures the marginal effect of a change in one variable on the value of the function, holding constant all other variables.

■ In constrained optimization problems, *Lagrangian multiplier techniques* can be used to find the optimal value of a function that is subject to *equality* constraints. Through the introduction of additional (artificial) variables into the problem, the Lagrangian multiplier method converts the constrained problem into an unconstrained problem, which can then be solved using ordinary differential calculus procedures. Lagrangian multiplier techniques are discussed and illustrated in Appendix 3A.

EXERCISES

1. Explain how the first and second derivatives of a function are used to find the maximum or minimum points of a function $Y = f(X)$. Illustrate your discussion with graphs.

2. Why is the first-order condition for finding a maximum (or minimum) of a function referred to as a necessary, but not sufficient, condition?

3. Defining Q to be the level of output produced and sold, suppose that the firm's total revenue (*TR*) and total cost (*TC*) functions can be represented in tabular form as shown below.

Output Q	Total Revenue TR	Total Cost TC	Output Q	Total Revenue TR	Total Cost TC
0	0	20	11	264	196
1	34	26	12	276	224
2	66	34	13	286	254
3	96	44	14	294	286
4	124	56	15	300	320
5	150	70	16	304	356
6	174	86	17	306	394
7	196	104	18	306	434
8	216	124	19	304	476
9	234	146	20	300	520
10	250	170			

a. Compute the marginal revenue and average revenue functions.
b. Compute the marginal cost and average cost functions.
c. On a single graph, plot the total revenue, total cost, marginal revenue, and marginal cost functions.
d. Determine the output level in the *graph* that maximizes profits (that is, profit = total revenue − total cost) by finding the point where marginal revenue equals marginal cost.
e. Check your result in part (d) by finding the output level in the *tables* developed in parts (a) and (b) that likewise satisfies the condition that marginal revenue equals marginal cost.

4. Consider again the total revenue and total cost functions shown in tabular form in the previous problem.
    a. Compute the total, marginal, and average profit functions.
    b. On a single graph, plot the total profit and marginal profit functions.
    c. Determine the output level in the graph and table where the total profit function takes on its maximum value.
    d. How does the result in part (c) in this exercise compare with the result in part (d) of the previous exercise?
    e. Determine total profits at the profit-maximizing output level.

5. Differentiate the following functions:
    a. $TC = 50 + 100Q - 6Q^2 + .5Q^3$
    b. $ATC = 50/Q + 100 - 6Q + .5Q^2$
    c. $MC = 100 - 12Q + 1.5Q^2$
    d. $Q = 50 - .75P$
    e. $Q = .40X^{1.50}$

6. Differentiate the following functions:
    a. $Y = 2X^3/(4X^2 - 1)$
    b. $Y = 2X^3(4X^2 - 1)$
    c. $Y = 8Z^2 - 4Z + 1$, where $Z = 2X^2 - 1$ (differentiate Y with respect to X)

7. Defining Q to be the level of output produced and sold, assume that the firm's cost function is given by the relationship

    $$TC = 20 + 5Q + Q^2$$

    Furthermore, assume that the demand for the output of the firm is a function of price P given by the relationship

    $$Q = 25 - P$$

    a. Defining total profit as the difference between total revenue and total cost, express in terms of Q the total profit function for the firm. (*Note:* Total revenue equals price per unit times the number of units sold.)
    b. Determine the output level where total profits are maximized.
    c. Calculate total profits and selling price at the profit-maximizing output level.
    d. If fixed costs increase from $20 to $25 in the total cost relationship, determine the effects of such an increase on the profit-maximizing output level and total profits.

8. Using the cost and demand functions in Exercise 7:
    a. Determine the marginal revenue and marginal cost functions.
    b. Show that, at the profit-maximizing output level determined in part (b) of the previous exercise, marginal revenue equals marginal cost. This illustrates the economic principle that profits are maximized at the output level where marginal revenue equals marginal cost.

9. Using the cost and demand functions in Exercise 7, suppose the government imposes a 20 percent *tax on the net profits* (that is, a tax on the difference between revenues and costs) of the firm.
    a. Determine the new profit function for the firm.
    b. Determine the output level at which total profits are maximized.
    c. Calculate total profits (after taxes) and the selling price at the profit-maximizing output level.
    d. Compare the results in parts (b) and (c) with the results in Exercise 7 above.

10. Suppose the government imposes a 20 percent *sales tax* (that is, a tax on revenue) on the output of the firm. Answer questions (a), (b), (c), and (d) of the previous exercise according to this new condition.

11. The Bowden Corporation's average variable cost function is given by the following relationship (where Q is the number of units produced and sold):

$$AVC = 25,000 - 180Q + .50Q^2$$

   a. Determine the output level (Q) that minimizes average variable cost.
   b. How does one know that the value of Q determined in part (a) *minimizes* rather than *maximizes AVC?*

12. Determine the partial derivatives with respect to all of the variables in the following functions:

   a. $TC = 50 + 5Q_1 + 10\,Q_2 + .5Q_1Q_2$
   b. $Q = 1.5L^{.60}\,K^{.50}$
   c. $Q_A = 2.5P_A^{-1.30}Y^{.20}P_B^{.40}$

13. Bounds Inc. has determined through regression analysis that its sales (S) are a function of the amount of advertising (measured in units) in two different media. This is given by the following relationship (X = newspapers, Y = magazines):

$$S(X,Y) = 200X + 100Y - 10X^2 - 20Y^2 + 20XY$$

   a. Find the level of newspaper and magazine advertising that maximizes the firm's sales.
   b. Calculate the firm's sales at the optimal values of newspaper and magazine advertising determined in part (a).

14. The Santa Fe Cookie Factory is considering an expansion of its retail piñon cookie business to other cities. The firm's owners lack the funds needed to undertake the expansion on their own. They are considering a franchise arrangement for the new outlets. The company incurs variable costs of $6 for each pound of cookies sold. The fixed costs of operating a typical retail outlet are estimated to be $300,000 per year. The demand function facing each retail outlet is estimated to be

$$P = \$50 - .001Q$$

   where P is the price per pound of cookies and Q is the number of pounds of cookies sold. (*Note:* Total revenue equals price (P) times quantity (Q) sold.)

   a. What price, output, total revenue, total cost, and total profit level will each profit-maximizing franchise experience?
   b. Assuming that the parent company charges each franchisee a fee equal to 5 percent of total revenues, recompute the values in part (a) above.
   c. The Santa Fe Cookie Factory is considering a combined fixed/variable franchise fee structure. Under this arrangement each franchisee would pay the parent company $25,000 plus 1 percent of total revenues. Recompute the values in part (a) above.
   d. What franchise fee arrangement do you recommend that the Santa Fe Cookie Factory adopt? What are the advantages and disadvantages of each plan?

15. Several fast-food chains, including McDonald's, announced that they have shifted from the use of beef tallow, which is high in saturated fat, to unsaturated vegetable fat. This change was made in response to increasing consumer awareness of the relationship between food and health.

a. Why do you believe McDonald's used beef tallow prior to the change?
b. What impact would you expect the change to have on McDonald's profits (i) in the near term, (ii) in the long term?
c. Structure this situation as a constrained-optimization problem. What is the objective function? What are the constraints?

16. Differentiate the following functions:
    a. $TR = 50Q - 4Q^2$
    b. $VC = 75Q - 5Q^2 + .25Q^3$
    c. $MC = 75 - 10Q + .75Q^2$
    d. $Q = 50 - 4P$
    e. $Q = 2.0 L^{.75}$

17. Determine the marginal cost function by differentiating the following total cost function with respect to Q (output):
$$TC = a + bQ + cQ^2 + dQ^3$$
where a, b, c, and d, are constants.

18. Differentiate the following functions:
    a. $Y = \frac{1}{3}X^3/(\frac{1}{2}X^2 - 1)$
    b. $Y = \frac{1}{3}X^3(\frac{1}{2}X^2 - 1)$
    c. $Y = 2Z^2 + 2Z + 3$, where $Z = X^2 - 2$ (differentiate Y with respect to X)

19. Determine the partial derivatives with respect to all the variables in the following functions:
    a. $Y = \alpha + \beta_1 X_1 + \beta_2 X_2 + \beta_3 X_3$, where α, β_1, β_2, and β_3 are constants
    b. $Q = \alpha L^{\beta_1} K^{\beta_2}$, where α, β_1, and β_2 are constants
    c. $Q_A = aP_A^b Y^c P_B^d$, where a, b, c, and d are constants

20. Given the following total revenue function (where Q = output):
$$TR = 100 Q - 2Q^2$$
    a. Determine the level of output that maximizes revenues.
    b. Show that the value of Q determined in part (a) maximizes, rather then minimizes, revenues.

21. Given the following total profit function (where Q = output):
$$\pi = -250,000 + 20,000 Q - 2Q^2$$
    a. Determine the level of output that maximizes profits.
    b. Show that the value of Q determined in part (a) maximizes, rather then minimizes, profits.

22. Given the following average total cost function (where Q = output):
$$ATC = 5,000 - 100Q + 1.0Q^2$$
    a. Determine the level of output that minimizes average total costs.
    b. Show that the value of Q determined in part (a) minimizes, rather then maximizes, average total costs.

23. Determine the value(s) of X that maximize or minimize the following functions and indicate whether each value represents either a maximum or minimum point of the function. (Hint: The roots of the quadratic equation: $aX^2 + bX + c = 0$ are $X = \dfrac{-b \pm \sqrt{b^2 - 4ac}}{2a}$.)

    a. $Y = \frac{1}{3}X^3 - 60X^2 + 2{,}000X + 50{,}000$

    b. $Y = -\frac{1}{3}X^3 + 60X^2 - 2{,}000X + 50{,}000$

24. Show that substituting

$$Z = 2X^2 - 1$$

into

$$Y = 10Z - 2Z^2 - 3$$

and differentiating Y with respect to X yields the same result as application of the chain rule $[dY/dX = 8X(7 - 4X^2)]$.

25. Show that the optimal solution to the set of simultaneous equations in the Indiana Petroleum example, Equations 3.28 and 3.29, are $Q_1^* = 5.77$ and $Q_2^* = 4.08$.

www exercise

Import Quotas as an
Optimization Constraint

26. As suggested in the text, import restrictions such as tariffs and quotas serve as constraints on the profit-maximization objective of importers. While international free trade agreements such as the North American Free Trade Agreement have generally reduced or eliminated tariffs and quotas, some still remain. One of the import quotas still in force in the United States applies to textiles. You can access information on textile quotas from several sites on the Internet, including the World Trade Organization's website at http://www.wto.org/goods/textiles.htm and the Cato Institute website at http://www. cato.org/pubs/pas/pa-140es.html and write a two-paragraph executive summary of how this import quota modifies the profit-maximizing choices of both domestic and foreign textile manufacturers.

Constrained Optimization and Lagrangian Multiplier Techniques

SIMPLE CONSTRAINED OPTIMIZATION

Chapter 3 discussed some of the techniques for solving unconstrained optimization problems. In this appendix the Lagrangian multiplier technique is developed to deal with some classes of constrained optimization problems. In Chapter 11 linear programming, a more general technique for dealing with constrained optimization, is developed.

Most organizations have constraints on their decision variables. The most obvious constraints, and the easiest to quantify and incorporate into the analysis, are the limitations imposed by the quantities of resources (such as capital, personnel, facilities, and raw materials) available to the organization. Other more subjective constraints include legal, environmental, and behavioral limitations on the decisions of the organization.

When the constraints take the form of equality relationships, classical optimization procedures can be used to solve the problem. One method, which can be employed when the objective function is subject to only *one* constraint equation of a relatively simple form, is to solve the constraint equation for one of the decision variables and then substitute this expression into the objective function. This procedure converts the original problem into an unconstrained optimization problem, which can be solved using the calculus procedures developed in Chapter 3.

EXAMPLE

CONSTRAINED PROFIT MAXIMIZATION: INDIANA PETROLEUM COMPANY

Consider again the two-product profit-maximization problem (Equation 3.24) from Chapter 3. Suppose that the raw material (crude oil) needed to make the products is in short supply and that the firm has a contract with a supplier calling for the delivery of 200 units of the given raw material during the forthcoming period. No other sources of the raw material are available. Also, assume that *all the raw material must be used during the period* and that none can be carried over to the next period in inventory. Furthermore, suppose that Product 1 requires 20 units of the raw material to produce one unit of output and Product 2 requires 40 units of raw material to produce one unit of output. The constrained optimization problem can be written as follows:

$$\text{Maximize } \pi = -60 + 140Q_1 + 100Q_2 - 10Q_1^2 - 8Q_2^2 - 6Q_1Q_2 \qquad [3A.1]$$

$$\text{subject to } 20Q_1 + 40Q_2 = 200 \qquad [3A.2]$$

The raw material constraint line and the profit function (curve) that is tangent to the constraint line are shown together in Figure 3A.1. Note that the solution to the unconstrained problem obtained earlier—$Q_1 = 5.77$ and $Q_2 = 4.08$—is not a feasible solution to the constrained problem because it requires $20(5.77) + 40(4.08) = 278.6$ units of raw material when in fact only 200 units are available. Following the procedure just described, we solve the constraint for Q_1:

FIGURE   3A.1   Constrained Profit Maximization: Indiana Petroleum Company

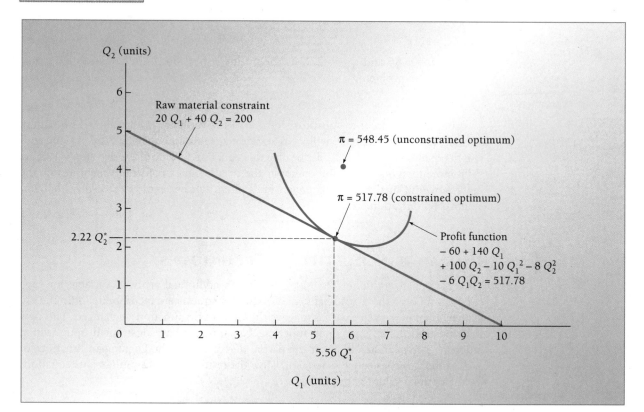

$$Q_1 = \frac{200}{20} - \frac{40Q_2}{20}$$

$$= 10 - 2Q_2$$

Substituting this expression for Q_1 in the objective function, we obtain

$$\pi = -60 + 140(10 - 2Q_2) + 100Q_2 - 10(10 - 2Q_2)^2$$

$$-8Q_2^2 - 6(10 - 2Q_2)Q_2$$

$$= -60 + 1400 - 280Q_2 + 100Q_2 - 1000 + 400Q_2$$

$$-40Q_2^2 - 8Q_2^2 - 60Q_2 + 12Q_2^2$$

$$= 340 + 160Q_2 - 36Q_2^2$$

Taking the derivative of this expression with respect to Q_2 yields

$$\frac{d\pi}{dQ_2} = 160 - 72Q_2$$

Setting $d\pi/dQ_2$ equal to zero and solving for Q_2, we obtain

$$0 = 160 - 72Q_2$$

$$Q_2^* = \frac{160}{72}$$

$$= 2.22 \text{ units}$$

In turn solving for Q_1, we obtain

$$Q_1^* = 10 - 2(2.22)$$

$$= 5.56 \text{ units}$$

Thus $Q_1^* = 5.56$ and $Q_2^* = 2.22$ is the optimal solution to the constrained profit-maximization problem.

Using the constraint to substitute for one of the variables in the objective function, as in the preceding example, will yield an optimal solution only when there is one constraint equation and it is possible to solve this equation for one of the decision variables. With more than one constraint equation and/or a complex constraint relationship, the more powerful method of Lagrangian multipliers can be employed to solve the constrained optimization problem.

LAGRANGIAN MULTIPLIER TECHNIQUES

The Lagrangian multiplier technique creates an additional artificial variable for each constraint. Using these artificial variables, the constraints are incorporated into the objective function in such a way as to leave the value of the function unchanged. This new function, called the Lagrangian function, constitutes an unconstrained optimization problem. The next step is to set the partial derivatives of the Lagrangian function for each of the variables equal to zero and solve the resulting set of simultaneous equations for the optimal values of the variables.

EXAMPLE

LAGRANGIAN MULTIPLIERS: INDIANA PETROLEUM COMPANY (CONTINUED)

The Lagrangian multiplier method can be illustrated using the example discussed in the previous section. First, the constraint equation, which is a function ∂ of the two variables Q_1 and Q_2, is rearranged to form an expression equal to zero:

$$\partial(Q_1, Q_2) = 20Q_1 + 40Q_2 - 200 = 0$$

Next we define an artificial variable λ (lambda) and form the Lagrangian function.[12]

$$L_\pi = \pi(Q_1, Q_2) - \lambda\delta(Q_1, Q_2)$$

$$= -60 + 140Q_1 + 100Q_2 - 10Q_1^2 - 8Q_2^2 - 6Q_1Q_2$$

$$-\lambda(20Q_1 + 40Q_2 - 200)$$

As long as $\partial(Q_1, Q_2)$ is *maintained equal to zero*, the Lagrangian function L_π will not differ in value from the profit function π. Maximizing L_π will also maximize π. L_π is seen to be a function of Q_1, Q_2, and λ. Therefore, to maximize L_π (and also π), we need to partially differentiate L_π with respect to each of the variables, set the partial deriva-

---

[12] To assist in the interpretation of the results, it is often useful to adopt the arbitrary convention that in the case of a *maximization* problem the lambda term should be *subtracted* in the Lagrangian function. In the case of a *minimization* problem, the lambda term should be *added* in the Lagrangian function.

tives equal to zero, and solve the resulting set of equations for the optimal values of Q_1, Q_2, and λ. The partial derivatives are equal to

$$\frac{\partial L_\pi}{\partial Q_1} = 140 - 20Q_1 - 6Q_2 - 20\lambda$$

$$\frac{\partial L_\pi}{\partial Q_2} = 100 - 16Q_2 - 6Q_1 - 40\lambda$$

$$\frac{\partial L_\pi}{\partial \lambda} = -20Q_1 - 40Q_2 + 200$$

Setting the partial derivatives equal to zero yields the equations

$$20Q_1 + 6Q_2 + 20\lambda = 140$$

$$6Q_1 + 16Q_2 + 40\lambda = 100$$

$$20Q_1 + 40Q_2 = 200$$

After solving this set of simultaneous equations, we obtain $Q_1^* = 5.56$, $Q_2^* = 2.22$, and $\lambda^* = +.774$. (*Note:* These are the same values of Q_1 and Q_2 that were obtained earlier in this section by the substitution method.)

If a problem has two or more constraints, then a separate λ variable is defined for each constraint and incorporated into the Lagrangian function. In general, λ measures the marginal change in the value of the objective function resulting from a one-unit change in the value on the righthand side of the equality sign in the constraint relationship. In the example above, λ^* equals $\$.774$ and indicates that profits could be increased by this amount if one more unit of raw material was available; that is, an increase from 200 units to 201 units. The λ values are analogous to the dual variables of linear programming, which are discussed in Chapter 11.

EXERCISES

1. What purpose do the artificial variables (λs) serve in the solution of a constrained optimization problem by Lagrangian multiplier techniques?

2. What do the artificial variables (λs) measure in the solution of a constrained optimization problem using Lagrangian multiplier techniques?

3. Bounds, Inc. has determined through regression analysis that its sales (S) are a function of the amount of advertising (measured in units) in two different media. This is given by the following relationship ($X =$ newspapers, $Y =$ magazines):

$$S(X,Y) = 200X + 100Y - 10X^2 - 20Y^2 + 20XY$$

Assume the advertising budget is restricted to 20 units.

a. Determine (using Lagrangian multiplier techniques) the level of newspaper and magazine advertising that maximizes sales subject to this budget constraint.

b. Calculate the firm's sales at this constrained optimum level.

c. Give an economic interpretation for the value of the Lagrangian multiplier (λ) obtained in part (a).

d. Compare the answer obtained in parts (a) and (b) above with the optimal solution to the *unconstrained* problem in Exercise 13 of Chapter 3.

DEMAND AND FORECASTING

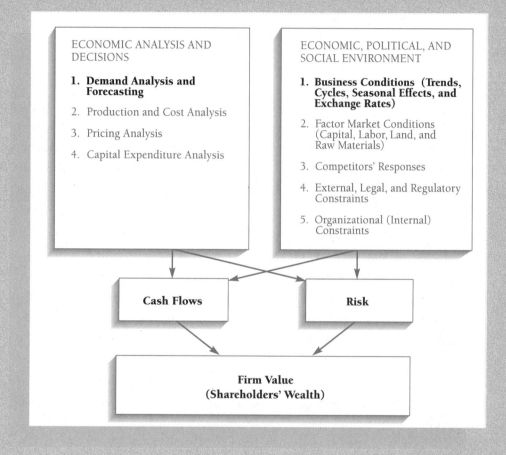

ECONOMIC ANALYSIS AND
DECISIONS

1. **Demand Analysis and
   Forecasting**

2. Production and Cost Analysis

3. Pricing Analysis

4. Capital Expenditure Analysis

ECONOMIC, POLITICAL, AND
SOCIAL ENVIRONMENT

1. **Business Conditions (Trends,
   Cycles, Seasonal Effects, and
   Exchange Rates)**

2. Factor Market Conditions
   (Capital, Labor, Land, and
   Raw Materials)

3. Competitors' Responses

4. External, Legal, and Regulatory
   Constraints

5. Organizational (Internal)
   Constraints

Cash Flows

Risk

**Firm Value
(Shareholders' Wealth)**

Part II (Demand and Forecasting) considers the elements determining the demand for a firm's output. Chapter 4 develops the theory of demand and introduces the elasticity properties of the demand function. Chapter 5 examines the procedures that may be used in making empirical estimates of the demand relationships developed in Chapter 4. Business and economic forecasting is the topic in Chapter 6. We consider forecasting at both the level of the firm and the overall economy. Chapter 7 examines the determinants of exchange rates, trade policy, and other factors crucial for effectively managing import-export trade. Understanding the determinants of demand is central to estimating the level and risk of the cash flows facing a firm. Forecasts of future economic activity and assessments of the impact of differing levels of economic activity on the demand of a firm are important inputs in the pricing, production, and resource-allocation decisions that wealth-maximizing managers must make.

4

Demand Analysis

CHAPTER PREVIEW

Demand analysis serves two major managerial objectives. First, it provides the insights necessary for the effective manipulation of demand. Second, it aids in forecasting sales and revenues. This chapter develops the theory of demand and introduces the elasticity properties of the demand function. The chapter begins by examining only the relationship between price and quantity, thereby assuming that the other factors that influence demand, such as income levels and advertising, remain unchanged or are held constant. Later the effects of these other factors are added to the analysis. One of the most important concepts from the theory of demand, the concept of elasticity, is developed in this chapter. In the general context of demand analysis, elasticity is a measure of the responsiveness of quantity demanded to a change in one of the factors influencing demand, such as price, advertising, income levels, or the price of substitute and complementary goods. The appendix to the chapter employs consumer indifference curves to develop the relationship between cost-of-living price indices and new product introductions. A thorough understanding of demand theory and its applications is central to effective, wealth-maximizing decision making by a firm's managers because demand relationships determine the revenue portion of a firm's cash flow stream.

DEMAND RELATIONSHIPS: THE DEMAND SCHEDULE AND THE DEMAND CURVE

Demand relationships can be represented in the form of a schedule (table), graph, or algebraic function. Each of these forms of presentation provides insights into demand relationships. This section focuses on schedules and graphs; the next section discusses algebraic functions.

The Demand Schedule Defined

The demand schedule is the simplest form of the demand relationship. It is merely a list of prices and corresponding quantities of a commodity that would be demanded by some individual or group of individuals at those prices.[1] Table 4.1 shows the demand schedule for pizzas at a local Pizza Hut restaurant. This demand schedule indicates that *if* the price of pizzas were $9.00, 60 pizzas would be purchased by consumers. Note that the lower the price, the greater the quantity of pizzas that would be demanded. This inverse or negative relationship between price and quantity demanded is generally referred to as the "law of demand." At lower prices people are able and willing to purchase more of a commodity than at a higher price.

Utility Maximization and Demand

The concept of demand is based on the theory of consumer choice. This theory assumes that consumers are rational. As rational individuals they seek to maximize the satisfaction gained from their consumption or expenditure decisions. This satisfaction may be defined as *utility*. Their consumption decisions (and hence amount of satisfaction) are limited by the amount of funds available to purchase various goods. Within a programming framework, each consumer faces a constrained optimization problem, where the objective is to choose the combinations of goods that maximize his or her utility, subject to a constraint on the amount of funds available (i.e., budget) to purchase these goods. Think of a food and entertainment budget allowance from your employer while you are traveling on an extended business trip or, alternatively, a set of friends who share these expenses while rooming together.

Marginal utility is defined as the change in utility per unit change in the consumption of a given good, holding constant the quantity of other goods. To maximize their utility, consumers should allocate their available funds in such a manner that they receive the same marginal, or additional, satisfaction for the last dollar spent on each good

Marginal Utility
The change in satisfaction per unit change in consumption of a good, holding constant the quantity of other goods.

---

[1]The terms *commodity, good,* and *product* are used interchangeably throughout the text to describe both physical goods and services.

TABLE 4.1	Price of Pizza ($/Unit)	Quantity of Pizzas Sold (Units Per Time Period)
Simplified Demand Schedule: Pizza Hut Restaurant	10	50
	9	60
	8	70
	7	80
	6	90

MANAGERIAL CHALLENGE

HEALTH-CARE REFORM AND CIGARETTE TAXES[2]

During 1993, the Clinton administration proposed a substantial increase in the tax on a pack of cigarettes as one way to help fund the proposed reforms to the nation's health-care system. Initial proposals were for an increase in the per pack tax ranging from $0.50 to $2. In addition to serving as a source of income to fund health-care reform, the tax increase was being justified as "a way to force smokers to pay for the costs they impose on society and would induce many people to quit smoking or avoid the habit."[3]

In 1997, the same proposal resurfaced as a mechanism to fund the "Tobacco settlement," an agreement under which Philip Morris, Reynolds Tobacco, Liggett, and other cigarette manufacturers would pay $368 billion over 25 years to achieve immunity from civil liability in personal injury and class action damage cases. The States Attorney Generals had sued the manufacturers to recover the additional Medicare and Medicaid costs of smoking-related illnesses. Under the settlement, wholesale prices averaging $1.43 per pack would rise by 62 cents to $2.05. Some critics of the proposal insist that the tobacco tax must be higher (perhaps as much as $1.50 higher) to deter young smokers from acquiring the habit. The stated objective for reducing teenage smoking is 30 percent in 5 years and 50 percent in 7 years.

One important element of the debate regarding the "optimal" cigarette tax increase revolves around the impact of a price increase on the quantity demanded. The effect on quantity demanded depends on how sensitive demand is to changes in price. A measure of this sensitivity is the price elasticity of demand. In general, the price elasticity of demand represents the percentage change in quantity demanded that occurs as a result of a 1 percent change in price. Economists have estimated the price elasticity of demand to be around -0.4, indicating that for a 10 percent increase in price, quantity demanded can be expected to decline by 4 percent. For teenagers, however, the price elasticity is thought to be fifty percent higher—around -0.6—indicating

that for a 10 percent increase in price, quantity demanded can be expected to decline by 6 percent.

The Canadian experience indicates the effect that substantial price increases can have on quantity demanded. In the 1980s, Canada began a series of dramatic increases in cigarette taxes that ultimately have pushed the price of a pack of cigarettes to over $4 today. Between 1982 and 1992, per capita consumption of cigarettes declined by 38 percent. These large price increases have had even more dramatic effects on teenage smoking, where per capita consumption declined by 61 percent over the same period.

In the debate over the amount of cigarette tax increase that might be included as part of a health-care reform proposal, policy makers faced a difficult set of trade-offs. On the one hand, if the primary objective is to generate income to fund health-care reform, the tax should be set such that it will maximize tax income to the U.S. Treasury. On the other hand, if the primary objective is to discourage smoking, a much higher tax could be justified. In either case, however, knowledge of the relationship between cigarette prices and quantity demanded is an essential input in this important policy decision.

www . . . .
The National Center for Policy Analysis Internet site provides additional information on cigarette tax policy at the following address:
http://www.public-policy.org/~ncpa/ba/ba231.html
The Internet site for the Federation of Tax Administrators lists current state excise tax rates for cigarettes at the following address:
http://www.taxadmin.org/fta/rate/cigarett.html

---

[2]Based in part on "Add $2 to the Cost of a Pack of Cigarettes . . . ," and ". . . And Even Teen Smokers May Kick the Habit," *Business Week,* 15 March 1993, p. 18, and "Critics Question Tobacco Pact's Effect on Teen Smoking," *Wall Street Journal,* 19 August 1997, p. A20.

[3]Quote from Matthew Myers, counsel to the Coalition on Smoking or Health, in "Add $2 to the Cost of a Pack of Cigarettes . . . ," *Business Week,* 15 March 1993, p. 18.

purchased. In other words, to maximize utility, the ratio of marginal utility (*MU*) to price (*P*) for all goods must be equal. In the case of two goods, food (*F*) and entertainment (*E*), this optimality condition is

$$\frac{MU_F}{P_F} = \frac{MU_E}{P_E}$$

[4.1]

If this condition does not hold (perhaps because of a price change for one of the goods), a consumer will reallocate his or her expenditures in such a manner that would result in an increase in satisfaction (utility). For example, if the price of food were to increase, the consumer would receive more satisfaction per dollar spent on entertainment than on food. As a result, the consumer will increase purchases of entertainment and reduce purchases of food. Each additional unit of entertainment that is purchased will provide less satisfaction (marginal utility) than the prior unit. Similarly, the reduction in purchases of food will increase the marginal utility of the last unit of food that is purchased. (If you have seven late-night snacks per week, you do not mind greatly forgoing one of them. However, if you have only one snack, you will be much less willing to give that one away.) Increased purchases of entertainment and reduced purchases of food will continue until the equilibrium condition in Equation 4.1 is restored. These concepts are developed in more detail in the appendix to this chapter.

Economists have identified two basic reasons for the increase in quantity demanded as the result of a price reduction. These factors are known as the *income* and *substitution effects*.

Income Effect   When the price of a good—for example, steak—declines, the effect of this decline is that the real income or purchasing power of the consumer has increased. This is known as the *income effect*. For example, if an individual normally purchases two pounds of steak per week at $5 per pound, a price decline to $4 per pound would enable the consumer to purchase the same amount of steak for $2 less per week. This savings of $2 represents an increase in real income of $2, which may be used to purchase greater quantities of steak (as well as other goods) each week. Sometimes the income effect of a price reduction is miniscule because so little of the household's budget is expended on the good (consider salt), but at other times the change in purchasing power is enormous. Consider a young family who spends 40 percent of their disposable income on apartment housing.

Substitution Effect   When the price of a good—such as steak—declines, it becomes less expensive in relation to other goods—for example, chicken. As a result of the price decline, the rational consumer can increase his or her satisfaction (or utility) by purchasing more of the good whose price has declined and less of the other goods. This is known as the *substitution effect*.

For example, suppose that the prices of steak and chicken are $5 and $2 per pound, respectively. Furthermore, assume that an individual purchases two pounds of steak and two pounds of chicken per week for a total expenditure of $14. Suppose that the price of steak declines to $4 per pound. As a result of this price decrease, an individual who has a preference for steak may decide to increase his or her consumption of steak to three pounds per week and decrease his or her consumption of chicken to one pound per week—which requires the same total expenditure of $14 per week. Thus we see that a decrease in the price of steak (relative to chicken) has led to an increase in the demand for steak.

In summary, because of the combined impact of the income and substitution effects, a decline in the price will always have an impact on the quantity demanded. For normal (income superior) goods for which more is preferred to less as income rises (e.g., single family housing), both the substitution and income effects dictate an increase in quantity demanded at lower prices. For income inferior goods like efficiency apartments, mackerel, and subcompact cars,[4] the income and substitution effects have opposite and partially offsetting impacts on the quantity demanded. The net effect of both actions, even in the case of inferior goods, is that more will likely be demanded at lower prices.[5]

The Demand Curve Defined

The demand relationship may be represented graphically in the form of a demand curve. Using the data from the Pizza Hut example (Table 4.1), we may plot and hence define the demand curve for pizza. In graphing demand relationships, it is common practice to plot the quantity demanded on the horizontal axis and the price level on the vertical axis. Figure 4.1 shows a demand curve. The curve indicates that at a price of $8, for example, 70 pizzas would be demanded. Along this straight demand curve, the rate of change of quantity demanded per unit price (i.e., the slope of *DD*) is *AB* ÷ *AC* or −4 ÷ 40 = −1/10. A nonlinear demand curve has its slope calculated along a tangent line like *TT′* in Figure 4.2.

Individual and Market Demand Curves

The expenditure decisions made by each individual determine his or her demand for a given good. The market demand curve for a good is equal to the sum of the indi-

---

[4]"Inferior goods" are those that are consumed less as income rises, and vice versa.

[5]As Baumol has noted, "In practice, the income effect for most consumers' goods is likely to be small because a buyer's outlay on any one commodity constitutes a relatively small proportion of this budget, so that a fall in the price of that item alone will not increase his real income significantly." This suggests that more will be demanded at lower prices, even for inferior goods. See William J. Baumol, *Economic Theory and Operations Analysis,* 4th ed. (Englewood Cliffs, N.J.: Prentice-Hall, 1977), p. 210.

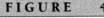

FIGURE   4.1

Straight-Line Demand
Curve: Pizza Hut
Restaurant

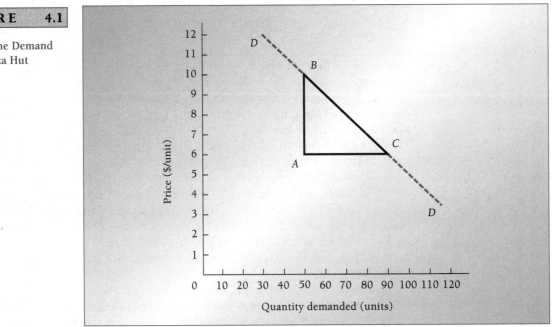

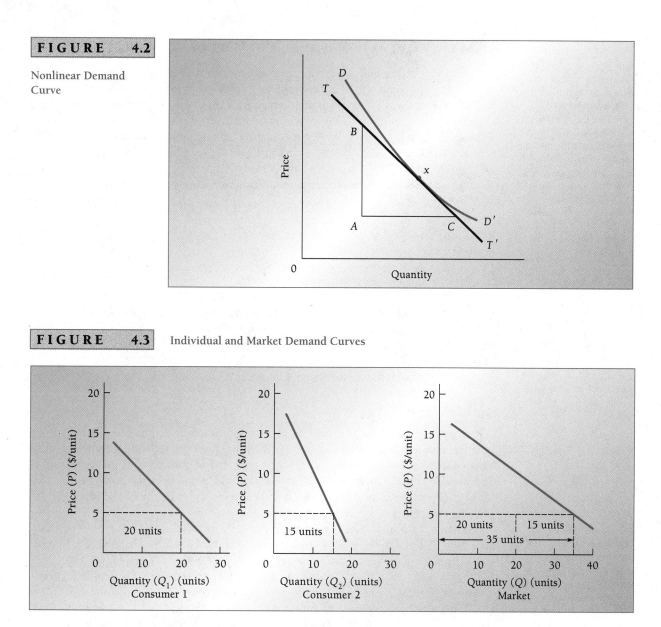

FIGURE   4.2

Nonlinear Demand
Curve

FIGURE   4.3   Individual and Market Demand Curves

vidual demands. As shown in Figure 4.3, for two individuals, the market demand curve is obtained through the horizontal summation of the quantities demanded at each price.[6] For example, at a price of $5 per unit, consumers 1 and 2 would purchase 20 and 15 units, respectively, yielding a market demand of 35 units. Other points on the market demand curve are obtained in a similar manner. Market demand is generally of more interest than individual demand relationships to the firm's managers because the market demand curve serves as a basis for making many pricing and output decisions.

---

[6]For goods that can be shared, like pools, concerts, and flood control projects, market demand is the vertical summation of the willingness to pay of the individual demanders.

DEMAND RELATIONSHIPS: THE DEMAND FUNCTION

Demand Function

Describes the relationship that exists during some period of time between the number of units of a good or service that consumers are willing to buy and a given set of conditions that influence the willingness to purchase, such as price, income level, and advertising.

Complementary Goods

Two goods are complementary if the quantity demanded of one *decreases* (increases) when the price of the other is *increased* (decreased), assuming all other factors affecting demand remain unchanged.

Substitute Goods

Two goods are substitutes if the quantity demanded of one *increases* (decreases) when the price of the other is *increased* (decreased), assuming all other factors affecting demand remain unchanged.

The demand schedule and the demand curve specify the relationship between prices and the quantity of a commodity that will be demanded at those prices at some point in time, *holding constant the influence of all other factors.* A number of these other factors may effect a change in the shape as well as the position of the demand curve as time passes. Decision variables that management will often consider include the design and packaging of products, the amount and distribution of the firm's advertising budget, the size of the sales force, promotional expenditures, the time period of adjustment for any price changes, and taxes or subsidies. Algebraically, the **demand function** can be represented as

$$Q_D = f(P, P^S, P^C, Y, A, A^C, N, C^P, P^E, T^A, T/S \ldots) \qquad [4.2]$$

where Q_D = quantity demanded of the product
  P = price of the product
  P^S = price of **substitute product(s)**
  P^C = price of **complementary product(s)**
  Y = income of consumers
  A = advertising expenditures (and other marketing expenditures)
  A^C = competitors' advertising expenditures on the product
  N = population (and other demographic factors)
  C^P = consumer tastes and preferences for the product
  P^E = expected (future) changes in price
  T^A = adjustment time period
  T/S = taxes or subsidies

This representation of the demand function indicates that quantity demanded is a function of a number of different factors (i.e., independent variables). Table 4.2 summarizes some of the factors that affect the shape and/or position of the demand curve. The variables listed above represent only some of the possible explanatory variables affecting demand. For any given product, other variables may be equally important in explaining demand.

The demand schedule or demand curve merely deals with the price-quantity relationship. *Changes in the price (i.e., P) of the commodity will result only in movement along the demand curve, whereas changes in any of the other independent variables (i.e., P^S, P^C, Y, A, A^C, N, C^P, P^E, . . .) in the demand function result in a shift of that curve.*

This is illustrated graphically in Figure 4.4. The initial demand relationship is line DD'. If the original price were P_1, quantity Q_1 would be demanded. If the price declined to P_2, the quantity demanded would increase to Q_2. If, however, changes occurred in the other independent variables, we would expect to have a shift in the entire curve. If, for example, a tax reduction were approved and consumer disposable income increased, the new demand curve might become $D_1 D_1'$. At any price, P_1, along $D_1 D_1'$, a greater quantity, Q_3, will be demanded than at the same price on the original curve DD'. Similarly, if the prices of substitute products were to decline, the demand curve would shift downward and to the left. At any price, P_1, along the new curve $D_2 D_2'$, a smaller quantity, Q_4, would be demanded than at the same price on either DD' or $D_1 D_1'$.

In summary, movement *along* a demand curve is often referred to as *a change in the quantity demanded,* while holding constant the effects of factors other than price that affect demand. Movement *of* the entire demand curve is often referred to as *a change in demand.* Demand curve movement is caused by factors other than price that influence the desire of consumers to buy a particular product.

TABLE 4.2	Factor	Expected Effect
Partial List of Factors Affecting Demand	Increase (decrease) in price of substitute goods[a] (P^S)	Increase (decrease) in demand (Q_D)
	Increase (decrease) in price of complementary goods[b] (P^C)	Decrease (increase) in Q_D
	Increase (decrease) in consumer income levels[c] (Y)	Increase (decrease) in Q_D
	Increase (decrease) in the amount of advertising and marketing expenditures (A)	Increase (decrease) in Q_D
	Increase (decrease) in level of advertising and marketing by competitors (A^C)	Decrease (increase) in Q_D
	Increase (decrease) in population (N)	Increase (decrease) in Q_D
	Increase (decrease) in consumer preferences for the good or service (C^P)	Increase (decrease) in Q_D
	Expected future price increases (decreases) for the good (P^E)	Increase (decrease) in Q_D
	Time period of adjustment increases (decreases) (T^A)	Increase (decrease) in Q_D
	Taxes (subsidies) on the good increase (decrease) (T/S)	Decrease (increase) in Q_D

[a]Two goods are substitutes if an increase (decrease) in the price of Good 1 results in an increase (decrease) in the quantity demanded of Good 2, holding other factors constant, such as the price of Good 2, other prices, income, and so on, or vice versa. For example, margarine may be viewed as a rather good substitute for butter. As the price of butter increases, more people will decrease their consumption of butter and increase their consumption of margarine.

[b]Goods that are used in conjunction with each other, either in production or consumption, are called *complementary goods*. For example, video tapes are used in conjunction with VCRs. An increase in the price of VCRs would have the effect of decreasing the demand for magnetic tapes, ceteris paribus. In other words, two goods are complementary if a decrease in the price of Good 1 results in an increase in the quantity demanded of Good 2, ceteris paribus. Similarly, two goods are complements if an increase in the price of Good 1 results in a decrease in the quantity demanded of Good 2.

[c]The case of inferior goods—that is, those goods that are purchased in smaller total quantities as income levels rise—will be discussed below in a consideration of the concept of income elasticity.

FIGURE 4.4	
Shifts in Demand	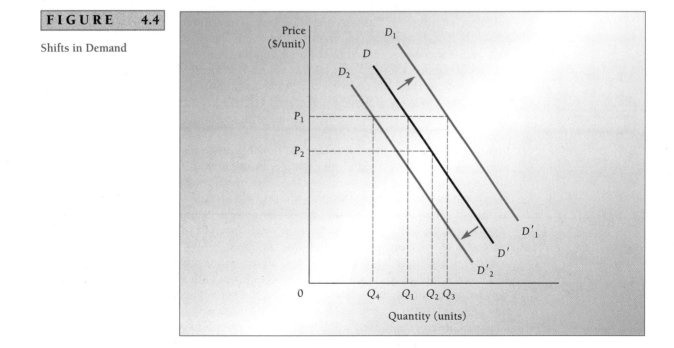

The demand function given in Equation 4.2 expresses the general relationship between quantity demanded and the various explanatory variables. A specific demand function can be developed for any good (or service).

The following equation expresses the market demand for Christmas trees in Youngstown as a function of the price of trees and per capita disposable personal income:

$$Q_D = 15,000 - 2500P + 2.50Y \qquad [4.3]$$

where Q_D = number of trees (quantity) sold
     P = price of trees (measured in dollars)
     Y = per capita disposable personal income (measured in dollars)

Note that this demand function contains only two explanatory variables—namely, price (P) and income (Y). Any number of explanatory variables can be used in the demand function. Note also that the equation is a linear relationship. As is shown in the following chapter, it is possible to develop nonlinear demand functions, such as logarithmic models. Such models introduce a limit to the quantity demanded (e.g., Christmas trees that households wish to buy even at very low prices).

Other Factors Affecting Demand

Up to this point it has been implicitly assumed that we are considering the demand for consumer goods of a nondurable nature. These are goods purchased largely to meet current needs, and they generally provide service on a short-term basis. Food items, Christmas trees, and virtually all services fall in this category, but housing and VCRs are clearly different. Although much of the foregoing discussion is relevant to the demand for durable as well as producers' goods, some unique characteristics about the demand for these items can be noted.

Durable Good

A good that yields benefits to the owner over a number of future time periods.

Durable Goods **Durable goods** may be broadly defined as those that *yield services to their owners over a number of future time periods.* Because of the relatively long-term nature of the services provided by durables, the demand for these items is generally more volatile. One reason for this is that by their very nature, durable goods *may be stored for periods of time.* If distributors, producers, and consumers (both final or intermediate) have accumulated large inventories of some durable good, an increase in the demand for that good may not show up in production for a considerable period of time, until inventories are worked off. Conversely, when inventories of the durable good are low, a small increase in demand may be magnified as distributors and producers stockpile inventories to accommodate even larger demand increases anticipated in the future. Another reason for this volatility is that the *replacement of a durable item may be delayed* from period to period by performing additional maintenance on existing items or by merely tolerating an old model. For example, an automobile may be repaired (or its out-of-date styling merely endured); an electric range may be fixed (at considerably less cost than buying a new range); or the discomforts of old furniture may be tolerated for "one more year." Thus an analysis of the demand for durable items must take account of both consumer desires and needs to expand the total stock of the durable good and the replacement of old, worn-out, or out-of-style products.

Obsolescence in style, convenience, and prestige value probably plays a larger role in affecting the replacement of durables than does physical deterioration. Also, *consumer expectations* regarding future levels of income, the availability of complements, and future product price play a major role in explaining the demand for durable goods. For example, a consumer may ask the following sorts of questions when embarking on a personal computer purchase:

- Will new products soon make my computer obsolete?
- Will my income be sufficient and steady enough to make the payments on the computer?
- Are prices likely to rise or fall over the next year?
- Will adequate software be available over the economic working life of my PC?

These factors also come into play in evaluating replacement demand. For these reasons an analysis of the demand for durable goods is more complex than a similar analysis for nondurables. As a result, the fluctuations in demand will be greater as consumers postpone or expand purchases based on their pessimism or optimism about future economic developments.

EXAMPLE

www . . . .
You can access financial and product line information on General Motors at the following Internet address:
http://www.gm.com/index.cgi

COMPLEMENT STRATEGY AT GENERAL MOTORS AND INTEL

Identifying, developing, and managing relationships with complement products in order to increase demand for one's own product has become a key element of corporate strategy. The other five forces of competition are much more difficult to influence.[7] To eliminate the competition from substitute products requires a never-ending upstaging of new imitators and can seldom provide sustainable competitive advantage. To cooperate effectively with rivals often constitutes a violation of the antitrust laws of the U.S. or the tougher antitrust laws of the European Union. To erect permanent barriers to entry requires the best product differentiation ad campaigns and relationship marketing. And, after improving coordination with vertical integration and total quality management, the remaining power of buyers and suppliers is often beyond a firm's control. Consequently, many companies today seek to develop complementary products as a driver of demand for their own product.

GM invests heavily in and thereby expands the capacity of high-end auto loans (GMAC) and specialty auto insurance (Integon). GM does so not because these are particularly profitable assets on their own, but rather because reduced time and inconvenience in arranging such loans and insurance are strong complements to the sale of very profitable Suburbans, Cadillacs, and other luxury cars and trucks. Similarly, Intel engineers responsible for designing computer chips now regularly outpace the demands of current PC applications for speed and computation capacity. So, Intel has entered into a joint venture with ProShare to accelerate the development of inexpensive interactive video, desktop video conferencing, and video telephone. The new complementary technologies will require much larger and faster computer chips.

Other examples that illustrate a company's astute use of complements to increase demand for their primary products are Michelin tires and travel guides, Borders books and in-store coffee bars, and inexpensive reading glasses displayed alongside Hallmark greeting cards.

Producers' Good
A good that is not produced for direct consumption but rather is the raw material or capital equipment that is used to produce a consumer good (or some other producers' good).

Derived Demand In addition to the factors just discussed, the demand functions for some goods include the demand for another good as one of the independent variables. For example, the demand for automobile loans is not determined directly. Rather, it is *derived* from the demand for automobiles. This is also the case for producers' goods.

Producers' goods differ from consumer goods in that they are not produced for direct consumption but rather are the raw materials, capital equipment, and parts that are

---

[7]Michael Porter's five forces of competition are described in Chapter 1 (see Figure 1.3). Adam Brandenberg and Barry Nalebuff explain this role of complementary products in *Co-Opetition* (New York: Bantam Books, 1996).

combined to produce a consumer good (or some other producers' good). As such, the demand for producers' goods may be thought of as a *derived demand* because it is derived from some ultimate consumer desire. For example, the demand for aluminum, a raw material, is dependent on consumer desires and tastes for those products that are wholly or partially made of aluminum such as window awnings, rain gutters, and plane travel. These consumer preferences may be completely independent of the fact that aluminum is used in the production of the good.

Therefore, in an analysis of derived demand for producers' goods, an account must be taken of two new sets of factors. First, we must consider the criteria or specifications used by the purchasing agent of the producing company that guide the agent in selecting one material, machine, process, or product over competitive alternatives. Second, and perhaps more important, we must take account of the significant factors affecting the demand for the ultimate consumer goods for which the producers' goods are inputs. Once this has been done, a demand analysis of producers' goods is conceptually the same as an analysis for a consumer good.

Exchange Rate Considerations   In addition to the above determinants of demand, the demand for goods traded in foreign markets is also influenced by external factors such as exchange rate fluctuations. When Microsoft sells computer software overseas, it prefers to be paid in dollars. This is because a company like Microsoft incurs few offshore expenses beyond advertising and therefore cannot simply match payables and receivables in a foreign currency. To accept Italian lira, French francs, or Australian dollars in payment for software purchase orders would introduce an exchange rate risk exposure for which Microsoft would want to be compensated in the form of higher prices on its software. Consequently, the foreign exports of Microsoft are typically transacted in dollars and are therefore tied inextricably to the price of the dollar against other currencies. As the value of the dollar rises, offshore buyers must pay a larger amount of their own currency to obtain the dollars required to pay for Microsoft's software, and this decreases the demand. Similarly, a lower value of the dollar reduces the lira or franc price of the product, raising the demand for Microsoft software.

EXAMPLE

www . . . .
The U.S. International Trade Administration provides news and other information on international trade issues affecting U.S. companies at the following Internet address: http://www.ita.doc.gov/media/

EXCHANGE RATE IMPACTS ON DEMAND: CUMMINS ENGINE COMPANY

Cummins Engine Company of Columbus, Indiana, is the largest independent manufacturer of new and replacement diesel engines for heavy trucks, construction, mining, and agricultural machinery. GMC, Ford, and Daimler-Benz are their major competitors, and 38 percent of sales occur offshore. The Cummins and Daimler-Benz large diesel truck engines sell for approximately $40,000 and DM100,000, respectively. Twice in the last two decades Cummins has suffered substantial declines in cash flow: during the period 1982–1985 and during the recession of 1990–1991.

In the earlier period, the price of the dollar against the mark (i.e., the dollar exchange rate quoted in deutschmarks) rose from DM2.43 to a high of DM2.94. This meant that a $40,000 Cummins diesel engine that had sold for DM97,200 in Munich in 1982 became DM117,600, whereas the DM100,000 Mercedes diesel that had been $41,152 declined to $34,014 in Detroit. Cummins faced two unattractive options, either of which would reduce cash flow. It could either cut its profit margins and maintain unit sales or maintain margins but have both offshore and domestic unit sales collapse because of the rapid appreciation of the dollar. The company chose to cut margins and maintain sales. By 1987 the dollar's value had declined and Cummins' performance improved. In the interim, demand for Cummins' engines was adversely affected by the temporary appreciation of the dollar.

PRICE ELASTICITY OF DEMAND

Price Elasticity
The ratio of the percentage change in quantity demanded to the percentage change in price, assuming that all other factors influencing demand remain unchanged. Also called *own* price elasticity.

From a decision-making perspective, the firm needs to know the effect of changes in any of the independent variables in the demand function on the quantity demanded. Some of these variables are under the control of management, such as price, advertising, product quality, and customer service. For these variables, management must know the effects of changes on quantity to assess the desirability of instituting the change. Other variables, including income, prices of competitors' products, and expectations of consumers regarding future prices, are outside the direct control of the firm. Nevertheless, effective forecasting of demand requires that the firm be able to measure the impact of changes in these variables on the quantity demanded.

Price Elasticity Defined

Ceteris Paribus
Latin for "all other things held constant."

The most commonly used measure of the responsiveness of quantity demanded to changes in any of the variables that influence the demand function is *elasticity*. In general, *elasticity* may be thought of as a ratio of the percentage change in one quantity (or variable) to the percentage change in another, **ceteris paribus** (all other things remaining unchanged). In other words, how responsive is some dependent variable to changes in a particular variable? With this in mind, we define the **price elasticity of demand** (E_D) as the ratio of the percentage change in quantity demanded to a percentage change in price:

$$E_D = \frac{\%\Delta Q}{\%\Delta P}, \text{ ceteris paribus} \qquad [4.4]$$

where ΔQ = change in quantity demanded
   ΔP = change in price

Because of the normal inverse relationship between price and quantity demanded, the sign of the price elasticity coefficient will be negative. Occasionally, price elasticities are referred to as absolute values. In the passages that follow, the use of absolute values will be indicated where appropriate.

Arc Price Elasticity

The *arc* price elasticity of demand is a technique for calculating price elasticity between two prices.[8] It indicates the effect of a change in price, from P_1 to P_2, on the quantity demanded. The following formula is used to compute this elasticity measure:

$$E_D = \frac{\dfrac{Q_2 - Q_1}{\left(\dfrac{Q_2 + Q_1}{2}\right)}}{\dfrac{P_2 - P_1}{\left(\dfrac{P_2 + P_1}{2}\right)}} = \frac{Q_2 - Q_1}{P_2 - P_1} \cdot \frac{P_2 + P_1}{Q_2 + Q_1} \qquad [4.5]$$

---

[8]As we will see in the following section dealing with "point price elasticities," the price elasticity of a straight-line demand curve is different at each point on the demand curve. Hence an "arc price elasticity" computed between two prices may be thought of as an "average" of the various point elasticities between the two prices.

where Q_1 = quantity sold before a price change
$\quad\quad Q_2$ = quantity sold after a price change
$\quad\quad P_1$ = original price
$\quad\quad P_2$ = price after a price change

The fraction $(Q_2 + Q_1)/2$ represents average quantity demanded in the range over which the price elasticity is being calculated. $(P_2 + P_1)/2$ also represents the average price over this range.

Rearranging Equation 4.5 shows that the elasticity measurement depends on the inverse of the *slope* of the ordinary demand curve (i.e., the sensitivity of demand to price *changes*)

$$\frac{Q_2 - Q_1}{P_2 - P_1}$$

as well as the *position* on the curve or schedule (i.e., the price point positioning) where elasticity is calculated

$$\frac{P_2 + P_1}{Q_2 + Q_1}$$

Because the slope (or its inverse) remains constant over the entire schedule (*assuming linearity*), but the value of $(P_2 + P_1)/(Q_2 + Q_1)$ changes, depending on where on the demand curve elasticity is being calculated, *the value of the elasticity measure generally changes throughout the length of the demand curve*. Price elasticity at higher prices and small volume is therefore larger (in absolute value) than price elasticity for the same product and same demanders at lower price points and large volume.

To illustrate, consider the demand schedule shown in Table 4.3 for men's Levi's jeans in a local Sears store. Calculate the price elasticity between an original price of $19 (14 units are demanded) and a new price of $18. Substituting the relevant data from Table 4.3 into Equation 4.5 yields

$$E_D = \frac{\dfrac{16 - 14}{(16 + 14)/2}}{\dfrac{\$18 - \$19}{(\$18 + \$19)/2}}$$

$$= -2.46$$

TABLE 4.3	Price, P ($/Unit)	Quantity Sold, Q_D (Units Per Period)
Demand Schedule: Levi's Jeans	20	12
	19	14
	18	16
	17	18
	16	20
	12	28
	11	30

A price elasticity of demand coefficient of -2.46 means that a 1 percent increase (decrease) in price can be expected to result in a 2.46 percent decrease (increase) in quantity demanded, ceteris paribus.

Now assume the original price was \$12, and a new price of \$11 is set. Determine the price elasticity of demand. Employing Equation 4.5 and the relevant data from Table 4.3 yields

$$E_D = \frac{\dfrac{30 - 28}{(30 + 28)/2}}{\dfrac{\$11 - \$12}{(\$11 + \$12)/2}} = -0.79$$

A price elasticity of demand of -0.79 means that a 1 percent increase (decrease) in price can be expected to result in a 0.79 percent decrease (increase) in quantity demanded, ceteris paribus.

We can also use Equation 4.5 to compute a price that would have to be charged to achieve a particular level of sales. Consider the NBA Corporation, which had monthly basketball shoe sales of 10,000 pairs (at \$100 per pair) before a price cut by its major competitor. After this competitor's price reduction, NBA's sales declined to 8,000 pairs a month. From the past experience NBA has estimated the price elasticity of demand to be about -2.0 in this price-quantity range. If the NBA wishes to restore its sales to 10,000 pairs a month, determine the price that must be charged.

Letting $Q_2 = 10{,}000$, $Q_1 = 8{,}000$, $P_1 = \$100$, and $E_D = -2.0$, the required price, P_2, may be computed using Equation 4.5:

$$-2.0 = \frac{\dfrac{10{,}000 - 8{,}000}{(10{,}000 + 8{,}000)/2}}{\dfrac{P_2 - \$100}{(P_2 + \$100)/2}}$$

$$P_2 = \$89.50$$

A price cut to \$89.50 would be required to restore sales to 10,000 pairs a month.

EXAMPLE

PRICE ELASTICITY OF DEMAND: THE *MACON TELEGRAPH*[9]

The *Macon Telegraph* newspaper is the principal sponsor of the Macon Labor Day Road Race, a 5K and 10K running event held annually in Macon, Georgia. The entry fee for the race in 1990 was \$12 per runner. The fee was raised to \$20 per runner for the 1991 race, in hopes of increasing revenues from the race. Prior to the race, there were complaints that the fee was too high for that kind of race and that it precluded many families from being able to afford entry fees.

The newspaper learned a lesson in price elasticity for running events from this experience. In 1990 the race attracted 1,600 runners, and thus generated income of \$19,200. In 1991, under similar weather conditions, the race attracted only 900 runners, and thus generated income of only \$18,000. Because a $(\$20 - \$12)/\$16 = 50$ percent increase in price resulted in a massive $(-700/1250) = 56$ percent decrease in quantity demanded,

---

[9]Based on Margaret Chivers, "They Voted with Their Feet," *Running Journal,* October 1991, pp. 1–2.

the total revenue *declined,* and the price elasticity of demand over this range is "elastic" (greater than 1.0 in absolute value). Specifically, the price elasticity can be estimated as

$$E_D = [(Q_2 - Q_1)/(Q_2 + Q_1)]/[(P_2 - P_1)/(P_2 + P_1)]$$

$$= [(900 - 1,600)/(900 + 1,600)]/[(\$20 - \$12)/(\$20 + \$12)]$$

$$= -1.12$$

That is, the $\%\Delta Q_D = -56$ percent is 1.12 times as large as the $\%\Delta P = 50$ percent.

In this case, the strategy of raising the price backfired because the newspaper misunderstood or incorrectly estimated the price elasticity of demand.

Point Price Elasticity

The preceding formulas measure the *arc elasticity* of demand; that is, elasticity is computed over a discrete range of the demand curve or schedule. Because elasticity is normally different at each point on the curve, arc elasticity is a measure of the average elasticity over that range.

By employing some elementary calculus, the elasticity of demand at any *point* along the curve may be calculated with the following expression:

$$E_D = \frac{\partial Q_D}{\partial P} \cdot \frac{P}{Q_D} \qquad [4.6]$$

where $\dfrac{\partial Q_D}{\partial P}$ = the partial derivative of quantity with respect to price (that verse of the slope of the demand curve)

Q_D = the quantity demanded at price P

P = the price at some specific point on the demand curve

The partial derivative of quantity with respect to price, $\partial Q_D/\partial P$, is merely an indication of the rate of change in quantity demanded as price changes. It is analogous to the

$$\frac{Q_2 - Q_1}{P_2 - P_1}$$

terms in the arc elasticity measure.

The algebraic demand function for Christmas trees (Equation 4.3) introduced in the previous section can be used to illustrate the calculation of the point price elasticity. Suppose one is interested in determining the point price elasticity when the price (P) is equal to $8 and per capita disposable personal income (Y) is equal to $6,000. Taking the partial derivative of Equation 4.3 with respect to P yields

$$\frac{\partial Q_D}{\partial P} = -2500$$

Substituting the relevant values of P and Y into Equation 4.3 gives

$$Q_D = 15,000 - 2500(8) + 2.50(6,000) = 10,000$$

From Equation 4.6 one obtains

$$E_D = -2500 \left(\frac{\$8}{10,000} \right) = -2.0$$

PRICE ELASTICITY OF DEMAND:
THE CASE OF HORSE RACE PARI-MUTUEL BETTING[10]

Faced with tight budgets and the need to raise additional revenues, many states have turned to various forms of state-operated legalized gambling. One of the earliest forms of betting, and still among the most prevalent, is the pari-mutuel wagering system of horse racing. The revenue from horse race betting comes from a tax (called the "takeout rate") on the total of money wagered (called the "handle"). This revenue is distributed between the state and the racing industry according to state law. The handle is thought to vary inversely with the takeout rate because "(1) smaller takeout rates . . . generate larger mutuel payouts giving the betting public more returns to rewager, and (2) smaller takeout rates and associated greater payouts tend to attract patrons, particularly from other forms of legal and illegal gambling." Hence, from a policy perspective, it is very important to know how responsive the *handle* is to changes in the takeout rate (which can be considered as equivalent to the price of gambling). If the demand for horse race wagering is price inelastic, then states could increase their revenues by increasing the takeout rate. In contrast, if demand is price elastic, then increases in the takeout rate are likely to lead to declines in state revenues.

Early studies of the price elasticity of betting indicated an elastic relationship, suggesting that price increases would lead to revenue declines. In contrast, Pescatrice estimated the price elasticity of demand for horse race betting using an improved model and employing data from one racetrack in New Orleans and two tracks in New York City. The results of these estimates of the demand function for the handle at these tracks indicated a price elasticity for betting of about -0.98. This result helps to explain why the New York racetracks lost revenue when they cut the takeout rate from 17 percent to 14 percent. With an inelastic demand, a reduction in "price" results in a decline in total revenue. Conversely, under conditions of inelastic demand, an *increase* in price results in increased total revenue. A careful analysis of the experience at 22 racetracks indicated that in 21 instances, increases in the takeout rate resulted in increases in total revenues to both the state and the racing industry.

Interpreting the Price Elasticity: Relationship between the Price Elasticity and Revenues

Once the price elasticity of demand has been calculated, it is necessary to interpret the meaning of the number obtained. The elasticity coefficient may take on *absolute values* over the range from 0 to ∞ (infinity). Values in the indicated ranges are described in Table 4.4.

---

[10]Based on Donn R. Pescatrice, "The Inelastic Demand for Wagering," *Applied Economics* 12 (1980), pp. 1–10.

TABLE   4.4

Price Elasticity of
Demand in Absolute
Values

Range	Description
$E_D = 0$	Perfectly inelastic
$0 < |E_D| < 1$	Inelastic
$|E_D| = 1$	Unit elastic
$1 < |E_D| < \infty$	Elastic
$|E_D| = \infty$	Perfectly elastic

Perfectly Elastic and Inelastic Demand Curves

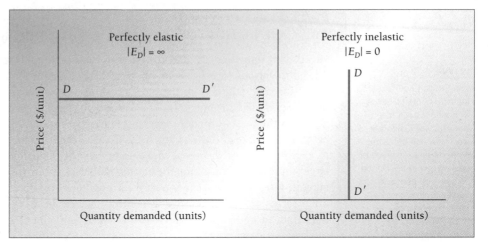

When demand is *unit* elastic, a percentage change in price P is matched by an *equal* percentage change in quantity demanded Q_D. When demand is *elastic,* a percentage change in P is exceeded by the percentage change in Q_D. For *inelastic* demand, a percentage change in P results in a smaller percentage change in Q_D. The theoretical extremes of perfect elasticity and perfect inelasticity are illustrated in Figure 4.5. (AAA grade January wheat sells on the Kansas City spot market with perfectly elastic demand facing any particular grain dealer. Drug addicts have almost perfectly inelastic demand. However, these extremes are rarely encountered. Rather they illustrate the limits of price elasticity.)

The price elasticity of demand indicates the effect a change in price will have on the total revenue that is generated. Because total revenue TR is equal to price (average revenue), P, times the number of units sold, Q_D, we may determine, from our knowledge of demand elasticity, the effect on total revenue when price changes.

When demand elasticity is less than 1 in absolute value (i.e., inelastic), an increase (decrease) in price will result in an increase (decrease) in total consumer expenditures ($P \cdot Q_D$). This occurs because an inelastic demand indicates that a given percentage increase in price results in a smaller percentage decrease in quantity sold, the net effect being an increase in the total expenditures, $P \cdot Q_D$. Table 4.5 illustrates this point. When demand is *inelastic*—that is, $|E_D| < 1$—an increase in price from \$2 to \$3, for example, results in an increase in total revenue from \$18 to \$24.[11]

In contrast, when demand is *elastic*—that is, $|E_D| > 1$—a given percentage increase (decrease) in price is more than offset by a larger percentage decrease (increase) in quantity sold. An increase in price from \$9 to \$10 results in a reduction in total consumer expenditure from \$18 to \$10 (see Table 4.5).

When demand is *unit elastic,* a given percentage change in price is exactly offset by the same percentage change in quantity demanded, the net result being a constant total consumer expenditure. If the price is increased from \$5 to \$6, total revenue would remain constant at \$30, because the decrease in quantity demanded at the new price just offsets the price increase (see Table 4.5). When the price elasticity of demand $|E_D|$ is equal to 1 (or is

---

[11]The symbol $|E_D| < 1$ indicates that we are talking about the absolute value of the elasticity coefficient, rather than its actual negative value. This symbol (| |) is used whenever we refer to absolute values.

TABLE 4.5 Relationship between Elasticity and Marginal Revenue				

Price, P ($/Unit)	Quantity, Q_D (Units)	Elasticity E_D	Total Revenue $P \cdot Q_D$ ($)	Marginal Revenue ($/Unit)
10	1		10	
9	2	−6.33	18	8
8	3	−3.40	24	6
7	4	−2.14	28	4
6	5	−1.44	30	2
5	6	−1.00	30	0
4	7	−0.69	28	−2
3	8	−0.46	24	−4
2	9	−0.29	18	−6
1	10	−0.15	10	−8

Marginal Revenue

The change in total revenue that results from a one-unit change in quantity demanded.

unit elastic), the total revenue function is maximized. In the example, total revenue equals $30 when price P equals either $5 or $6 and quantity demanded Q_D equals either 6 or 5.

The relationship among price, quantity, elasticity measures, **marginal revenue,** and total revenue is illustrated graphically in Figure 4.6. When total revenue is maximized, marginal revenue equals zero and demand is unit elastic. At any price higher than P_1 (unit elasticity), the demand function is elastic. At lower prices the demand function is inelastic. Hence, successive equal percentage increases in price may be expected to generate greater and greater percentage decreases in quantity demanded because the demand function is becoming increasingly elastic (see Figure 4.6). Alternatively, successive equal percentage reductions in price may be expected to generate ever lower percentage increases in quantity demanded because the demand function is more inelastic at lower prices.

The relationship between a product's price elasticity of demand and the marginal revenue at that price point is one of the most important in managerial economics. This relationship can be derived by analyzing the change in revenue resulting from a price change. To start, marginal revenue is defined as the change in total revenue resulting from lowering price to make an additional unit sale. Lowering price from P_1 to P_2 in Figure 4.6 to increase quantity demanded from Q_1 to Q_2 results in a change in the initial revenue P_1AQ_10 to P_2BQ_20. The difference in these two areas is illustrated in Figure 4.6 as the two shaded rectangles. The horizontal shaded rectangle is the loss of revenue caused by the price reduction $(P_1 - P_2)$ over the previous units sold Q_1. The vertical shaded rectangle is the gain in revenue from selling $(Q_2 - Q_1)$ additional units at the new price P_2. That is, the change in total revenue from lowering price to sell another unit can always be written as follows:

$$MR = \frac{\Delta TR}{\Delta Q} = \frac{P_2(Q_2 - Q_1) + (P_1 - P_2)Q_1}{(Q_2 - Q_1)}$$

where $P_2(Q_2 - Q_1)$ is the vertical shaded rectangle and $(P_1 - P_2)Q_1$ is the horizontal shaded rectangle. Rearranging, we have

$$MR = P_2 + \frac{(P_1 - P_2)Q_1}{(Q_2 - Q_1)}$$

$$= P_2\left(1 + \frac{(P_1 - P_2)Q_1}{(Q_2 - Q_1)P_2}\right)$$

Price Elasticity over
Demand Function

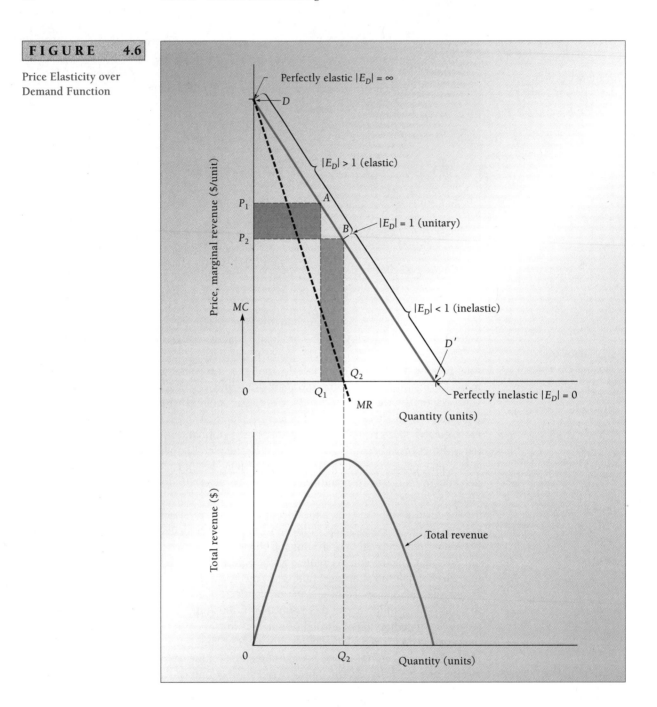

$$MR = P_2 \left(1 + \frac{\Delta P Q_1}{\Delta Q P_2} \right)$$

The ratio term is the inverse of the price elasticity at the price point P_2 using the quantity Q_1. For small price and quantity changes this number closely approximates the arc price elasticity in Equation 4.5. Therefore, the relationship between marginal revenue and price elasticity can be expressed algebraically as follows:[12]

$$MR = P\left(1 + \frac{1}{E_D}\right) \qquad\qquad [4.7]$$

Using this equation, one can demonstrate that when demand is unit elastic, marginal revenue is equal to zero. Substituting $E_D = -1$ into Equation 4.7 yields

$$MR = P\left(1 + \frac{1}{-1}\right)$$

$$= P(0)$$

$$= 0$$

EXAMPLE

AUTHORS PRESS WEST PUBLISHING TO INCREASE SALES REVENUE

Entertainment and publishing companies pay composers, playwrights, and authors a fixed percentage of realized sales revenue as a royalty. The two groups often therefore differ as to the preferred price and unit sales. Referring to Figure 4.6, total revenue can be increased by lowering the price anytime the quantity sold is less than Q_1. That is, at any price above P_1 (where marginal revenue remains positive) the total revenue will continue to climb only if prices are lowered and additional units sold. Composers and authors often therefore press their publishers to lower prices until revenue is maximized— i.e., to the point where demand is unit elastic. The publisher, on the other hand, will

---

[12]This equation also can be derived from the definitions of marginal revenue and price elasticity using calculus. Marginal revenue is equal to the first derivative of total revenue:

$$MR = \frac{d(TR)}{dQ_D} = \frac{d(P \cdot Q_D)}{dQ_D}$$

Using the rule for taking the derivative of a product yields

$$MR = P \cdot \frac{dQ_D}{dQ_D} + Q_D\frac{dP}{dQ_D}$$

$$= P + Q_D\frac{dP}{dQ_D}$$

This equation may be rewritten as

$$MR = P\left(1 + \frac{Q_D}{P} \cdot \frac{dP}{dQ_D}\right)$$

Recalling that the point price elasticity of demand is

$$E_D = \frac{dQ_D}{dP} \cdot \frac{P}{Q_D}$$

it can be seen that the term $\frac{Q_D}{P} \cdot \frac{dP}{dQ_D}$ is the reciprocal of the point price elasticity measure.

Hence, substituting $\frac{1}{E_D}$ for $\frac{Q_D}{P} \cdot \frac{dP}{dQ_D}$, results in Equation 4.7:

$$MR = P\left(1 + \frac{1}{E_D}\right)$$

wish to charge higher prices and sell less quantity because operating profits arise from marginal revenue in excess of marginal cost. Unless marginal cost is zero, the publisher always wants a positive marginal revenue and therefore a price greater than P_1 (for example, P_2). A commission-based sales force and the senior management have this same conflict; sales people often develop ingenious hidden discounts to try to circumvent a company's list pricing policies. Lowering price to set $|E_D| = 1$ will always maximize sales revenue (and therefore, maximize total commissions).

The fact that total revenue is maximized (and marginal revenue is equal to zero) when $|E_D| = 1$ can be shown with the following example.

EXAMPLE

TOTAL REVENUE, MARGINAL REVENUE, AND ELASTICITY: CUSTOM-TEES, INC.

Custom-Tees, Inc., operates a kiosk in Hanes Mall where it sells custom-printed T-shirts. The demand function for the shirts is

$$Q_D = 150 - 10P \qquad [4.8]$$

where P is the price in dollars per unit and Q_D is the quantity demanded in units per period.
The demand curve can be rewritten in terms of P as a function of Q_D.

$$P = 15 - \frac{Q_D}{10} \qquad [4.9]$$

Total revenue (TR) is equal to price times quantity sold.

$$TR = P \cdot Q_D$$

$$= \left(15 - \frac{Q_D}{10}\right) Q_D$$

$$= 15\,Q_D - \frac{Q_D^2}{10}$$

Marginal revenue (MR) is equal to the first derivative of total revenue with respect to Q_D:

$$MR = \frac{d(TR)}{dQ_D}$$

$$= 15 - \frac{Q_D}{5}$$

To find the value of Q_D where total revenue is maximized, set marginal revenue equal to zero:[13]

$$MR = 0$$

$$15 - \frac{Q_D}{5} = 0$$

$$Q_D^* = 75 \text{ units}$$

---

[13]To be certain one has found values for P and Q_D, where total revenue is maximized rather than minimized, check the second derivative of TR to see that it is negative. In this case $d^2\,TR/dQ_D^2 = -1/5$, so the total revenue function is maximized.

Substituting this value into Equation 4.9 yields

$$P^* = 15 - \frac{75}{10} = \$7.50 \text{ per unit}$$

Thus, total revenue is maximized at $Q_D^* = 75$ and $P^* = \$7.50$ *Checking:*

$$E_D = \frac{\partial Q_D}{\partial P} \cdot \frac{P}{Q_D} = (-10)\frac{(7.5)}{75} = -1$$

$$|E_D| = 1$$

In addition to showing that $|E_D| = 1$ when the total revenue function is at its maximum, this example also demonstrates that marginal revenue *MR* is equal to zero when total revenue is maximized. This finding is not surprising when reminded that the definition of marginal revenue is the increase in total revenue resulting from the sale of one additional unit. Beyond the output level where total revenue is maximized, marginal revenue becomes negative and total revenue declines; that is, $|E_D| < 1$.[14]

Importance of Elasticity-Revenue Relationships

Decision makers must be aware of the relationship among price, elasticity, and total revenue. For example, an urban transit system faced with large, continuous operating deficits may be tempted to raise its fares to increase revenues. This strategy will only be successful if the current fare structure is such that demand is inelastic. In the unhappy case that total revenues are already being maximized by present fares—that is, the elasticity of demand is unitary—any further increases in fares will be self-defeating, leading to a reduction in total revenues and increased losses if service levels are maintained. This problem was also illustrated in the *Macon Telegraph* example above.

In addition, elasticity is often the key to marketing plans. A product-line manager will attempt to maximize revenue by allocating a marketing expense budget among price promotions, advertising, retail displays, trade allowances, direct mail, and in-store couponing. Knowing whether and at what magnitude demand is responsive to each of these marketing initiatives (e.g., to price reductions at each price point) depends on careful estimates of the elasticities.

VW Invasion of North America

www ....
You can reach Volkswagen
on the Internet at:
http://www.vw.com/

When Volkswagon entered the U.S. market with their basic no-frills automobile, the Beetle, VW was experiencing little success in Europe. Excess inventory had stockpiled at ports and road terminals awaiting export to a new market. Consequently, VW focused for a time on any demand stimulus that would increase revenue. In the U.S. market, VW had no dealer network and initially provided sales and service only at the docks in New Jersey, Charleston, SC, and Houston, TX. General Motors and Ford were developing compact cars as well, so VW decided to enter the market at a ridiculously low promotional price of $800. Two years later a 25 percent price increase was introduced. Although VW lost some potential customers at $1000 who were willing to pay between $800 and $999, the extra $200 per car on all the cars they continued to sell (see Figure 4.7) easily offset

---

[14]Additional applications of the relationship among price, marginal revenue, and elasticity (Equation 4.7) are examined in the discussions of pricing by monopolists (Chapter 14) and the practice of price discrimination (Chapter 17).

FIGURE   4.7   Raising Price with Demand in the Elastic Range

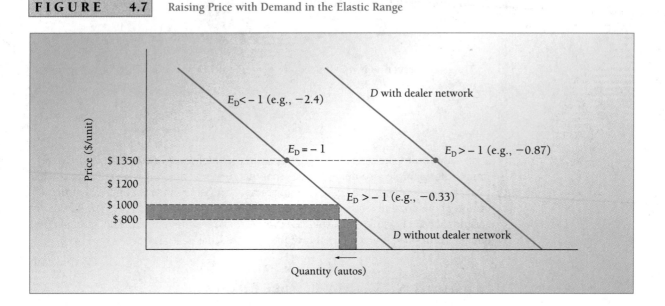

the revenue loss at old $800 prices from a few lost sales. (Compare the two shaded areas in Figure 4.7.) The price elasticity of demand was in the elastic range of demand. By 1960, VW had raised the price another 20 percent to $1,200, and again revenue rose. Finally, in 1964 at $1,350, the extra receipts from the $150 price increase across all remaining sales were just sufficient to offset the loss in revenue from the lost sales. At $1,350, price elasticity had reached the unit elastic price point. Volkswagon then proceeded to build a U.S. dealer network and develop a new product, the more powerful and better appointed Super Beetle. These changes increased the potential size of the market in the United States and shifted the demand for Volkswagon products to the right. At $1,350 with a dealer network and a larger quantity base, the measured price elasticity then declined (again into the inelastic range), and Volkswagon was again in a position to raise price.

One managerial insight that this example illustrates is that firms should always seek to raise prices for any products in the inelastic range of their demand. To lower prices in such a range would both *increase* costs (of producing and distributing additional output) and *decrease* revenue. Better to approach unit elasticity by raising prices, and thereby increase revenue and save the production and distribution costs. In fact, profit-maximizing firms will carry these price increases right on into the elastic range beyond the point of maximum revenue and unit elasticity (above and beyond point B at P_2 and Q_2 in Figure 4.6). Starting from zero output, a profit-maximizing firm will lower price to increase revenue as long as the incremental change in total revenue (the MR in Figure 4.6) exceeds the change in marginal cost (labeled height MC). That is, the profit-maximizing output will always occur in the elastic region of the firm's demand—for example, at a price above the unit elastic price point.

Unit elasticity is also of special significance for commission-based employees or anyone whose paycheck rises as sales revenue increases. For example, entertainers and publishing companies pay a royalty as a fixed percentage of realized sales revenue to composers, playwrights, and authors. The two groups often differ as to the preferred price.

Referring again to Figure 4.6, total revenue can be increased by lowering the price any-time the quantity sold is less than Q_2. That is, at any price above P_2, where marginal revenue remains positive, the total revenue will continue to climb by lowering price and selling another record or book. Composers and authors often therefore press their publishers to lower prices until revenue is maximized—for example, to the point where demand is unit elastic. The publisher, on the other hand, will wish to charge higher prices and sell less quantity because operating profits arise from marginal revenue in excess of marginal cost. Unless marginal cost is zero, the publisher will always want a positive marginal revenue and therefore a price greater than P_2 (for example, P_1). A commission-based sales force and senior management have this same conflict; sales people often develop ingenious hidden discounts to try to circumvent a company's list pricing policies. The managers, on the other hand, want higher prices with somewhat reduced revenue, much reduced costs, and therefore higher profits. One solution to this incentives conflict is to involve sales personnel (and authors) in the company's profit-sharing plan.

EXAMPLE

www . . . .
Rothstein-Tauber, Inc. is one of a number of consulting firms that estimates price elasticities. You can access their Internet site at:
http://www.rtimarketresearch.com/rt03008.htm

PRICE ELASTICITIES: EMPIRICAL ESTIMATES

Economists have made estimates of the price elasticity of demand for a wide variety of goods and services. A number of empirically determined price elasticities are shown in Table 4.6. This table indicates that the market demand for furniture, a durable good, is extremely price elastic (-3.04), whereas the market demand for regular coffee (-0.16) is extremely price inelastic.

A study by Huang, Siegfried, and Zardoshty on the demand for coffee confirms the relationship between price levels and the price elasticity of demand shown in Figure 4.6.[15] After studying coffee demand for the period 1963–1977, they found that the price elasticity of demand for that period ranged from -0.10 for price levels prevailing throughout most of the period to -0.89 for the peak price level, which occurred in the second quarter of 1977. Thus coffee users are nearly nine times more sensitive to price changes at high prices than at lower price levels.

Factors Affecting the Price Elasticity of Demand

As shown in Table 4.6, price elasticities vary greatly among different products and services. Some of the factors that account for the differing responsiveness of consumers to price changes are examined below.

Availability and Closeness of Substitutes   The most important determinant of the price elasticity of demand is the availability and closeness of substitutes. The greater the number of substitute goods, the more price elastic is the demand for a product because a customer can easily shift to a substitute good if the price of a product in question increases. The availability and closeness of substitutes relates not only to different products, such as butter and margarine or beef and pork, but also to the availability of the same product from different producers. For example, the demand for Chevrolets is likely to be very price elastic because of the ready availability of close substitutes such as Fords, Plymouths, and Hondas. Intravenous feeding solution has few (if any) substitutes for hospital patients in

[15]Cliff J. Huang, J.J. Siegfried, and F. Zardoshty, "The Demand for Coffee in the United States, 1963–1977," *Quarterly Review of Economics and Business* (Summer 1980), pp. 36–50. Another more recent estimate of the demand elasticity for coffee can be found in Albert A. Okunade, "Functional Forms and Habits Effects in the U.S. Demand for Coffee," *Applied Economics* (November 1992).

TABLE 4.6		

Empirical Price Elasticities

Commodity (Good/Service)	Price Elasticity
Alcoholic beverages (consumed at home)	
Beer	−.84[a]
Wine	−.55[a]
Liquor	−.50[a]
Beef	−.65[b]
Chicken	−.65[b]
Coffee	
Regular	−.16[c]
Instant	−.36[c]
Credit charges on bank cards	
Small banks	−2.44[d]
Large banks	−0.69[d]
Dental visits	
Adult males	−.65[e]
Adult females	−.78[e]
Children	−1.40[e]
Furniture	−3.04[f]
Glassware/China	−1.20[g]
Household appliances	−.64[g]
International air transportation	
United States/Europe	−1.25[h]
Canada/Europe	−.82[h]
Milk	−.49[b]
Outdoor recreation	−.12 to −.56[i]
Potatoes	−.27[b]
School lunches	−.47[j]
Shoes	−.73[g]
Soybean meal	−1.65[k]
Telephones	−0.10[l]
Tires	−0.60[g]
Tobacco products	−.46[g]
Tomatoes	−2.22[b]
Wool	−1.32[m]

[a]Dale Heien and Greg Pompelli, "The Demand for Alcoholic Beverages: Economic and Demographic Effects," *Southern Economic Journal* (January 1989), pp. 759–769.

[b]Daniel B. Suits, "Agriculture," in *Structure of American Industry*, 7th ed., ed. W. Adams (New York: Macmillan, 1986).

[c]Cliff J. Huang, John J. Siegfried, and Farangis Zardoshty, "The Demand for Coffee in the United States, 1963–1977," *Quarterly Review of Economics and Business* 20, no. 2 (Summer 1980), pp. 36–50.

[d]J. Starvins, "Can Demand Elasticity Explain Sticky Credit Card Rates?" *New England Economic Review* (July/August 1996), pp. 43–54.

[e]Willard G. Manning, Jr. and Charles E. Phelps, "The Demand for Dental Care," *The Bell Journal of Economics* 10, no. 2 (Autumn 1979), pp. 503–525.

[f]Richard D. Stone and D.A. Rowe, "The Durability of Consumers' Durable Goods," *Econometrica* 28 (1960), pp. 407–416.

[g]H.S. Houthakker and Lester D. Taylor, *Consumer Demand in the United States*, 2d ed. (Cambridge, Mass.: Harvard University Press, 1970).

[h]J.M. Cigliano, "Price and Income Elasticities for Airline Travel: The North Atlantic Market," *Business Economics* (September 1980), pp. 17–21.

[i]Russel L. Gum and W.E. Martin, "Problems and Solutions in Estimating the Demand for and Value of Rural Outdoor Recreation," *American Journal of Agricultural Economics* (November 1975), pp. 558–566.

[j]George A. Braley and P.E. Nelson, Jr., "Effect of a Controlled Price Increase on School Lunch Participation: Pittsburgh, 1973," *American Journal of Agricultural Economics* (February 1975), pp. 90–96.

[k]H. Knipscheer, L. Hill, and B. Dixon, "Demand Elasticities for Soybean Meal in the European Community," *American Journal of Agricultural Economics* (May 1982), pp. 249–253.

[l]D. Cracknell and M. Knott, "The Measurement of Price Elasticities—The BT Experience," *International Journal of Forecasting* 11(1995), pp. 321–329.

[m]C.E. Ferguson and M. Polasek, "The Elasticity of Import Demand for Raw Apparel Wool in the United States," *Econometrica* 30 (1962), pp. 670–699.

shock or otherwise unable to digest food, but the price elasticity of demand for Johnson & Johnson's product is high because numerous companies offer an identical product.

Durable Goods   The demand for durable goods tends to be more price elastic than the demand for nondurables. This is true because of the ready availability of a relatively inexpensive substitute in many cases—for instance, the repair of a used television, car, or refrigerator, rather than buying a new one. Consumers of durable goods are often in a position to wait for a more favorable price, a sale, or a special deal when buying these items. This accounts for some of the volatility in the demand for durable goods.

Percentage of Budget   The demand for relatively high-priced goods tends to be more price elastic than the demand for inexpensive items. This is true because expensive items account for a greater proportion of a person's income and potential expenditures than do low-priced items. Consequently, we would expect the demand for automobiles to be more price elastic than the demand for children's toys. The greater the percentage of the budget spent on a good, the larger the income effect of a price change; and the larger the income effect, the greater the price elasticity for normal goods. German households often spend as much as 20–30 percent of their disposable income on cars; French households do the same with food, but spend half as much as Germans on automobile transportation. Therefore, ceteris paribus, we would expect the price elasticity of demand for standard sedan autos to be higher in Germany than in France.

Time Frame of Analysis   Over time, the demand for many products tends to become more elastic because of the increase in the number of effective substitutes that become available. For example, in the short run, the demand for gasoline may be relatively price inelastic because the only available alternatives are not taking a trip or using some form of public transportation. Over time, as consumers replace their cars, they find another excellent substitute for gasoline—namely, more fuel-efficient vehicles. Also, other product alternatives may come available, such as electric cars or cars powered by natural gas.

Another reason the time frame of analysis affects the elasticity involves transaction costs. Almost all purchases necessitate a certain transportation and time expense on the part of both buyer and seller. In addition, to respond to a price decrease, potential customers must first learn about the discount and then incur, in their own schedules, the adjustment costs required to complete a purchase during the sale period. Because both search and adjustment costs for consumers are higher if sale prices last only a few minutes, the demand response to price changes is enhanced the longer the time period of adjustment. Predictable end-of-model-year promotions in the auto industry lasting throughout the month of August stimulate much more elastic demand than unannounced "Midnight Madness" sales that last only a few hours.

<table>
<tr><td>EXAMPLE</td></tr>
</table>

www . . . .
The Internet site maintained by the U.S. Census Bureau contains information on housing, home ownership, and affordability. The site address is: http://www.census.gov/ hhes/www/housing.html

DETERMINANTS OF PRICE ELASTICITY OF DEMAND FOR HOUSING IN SAN FRANCISCO, KANSAS CITY, AND HOUSTON

Residents of San Francisco spend 39.7 percent of their after-tax income on housing while residents of Kansas City and Houston spend only 18.4 percent and 18.7 percent, respectively.[16] This difference in the allocation of a typical household's budget implies that the increase in a San Franciscan's purchasing power for all goods and services, if housing costs in general fall by 10 percent, will be more than twice as large

---

[16]Based on "The Home Front," *Wall Street Journal,* 11 July 1997, p. B6.

as the increase in purchasing power enjoyed by a Kansas Citian or Houstonian for the same 10 percent decline in housing costs. The demand for all "normal" or income superior goods (i.e., goods whose demand increases with the real income available to the household) should rise more in San Francisco than in Kansas City or Houston. Because housing is an income superior good, one might expect the percentage increase in demand for housing in San Francisco to be larger than in Kansas City or Houston. That is, taken by itself, a larger (real) income effect implies a more price elastic demand for housing in San Francisco.

Remember, however, that not only the percentage of the budget spent on an item but also its durability, the time period of adjustment, and the availability and closeness of substitutes affect the price elasticity of demand across products and markets. The space constraints of the narrow peninsula between San Francisco Bay and the Pacific reduce significantly the availability of substitute housing in San Francisco. In Kansas City and Houston, by contrast, subdivisions and apartment complexes with identically desirable housing features stretch as far as the eye can see. Any Kansas City or Houston household with increased purchasing power for any reason can easily find marginally larger substitute housing available in many alternative locations. And if rents rise, the Kansas City and Houston households can easily move back to smaller accommodations. In contrast, the San Franciscan faces many fewer choices. If rents fall, the San Francisco families may well stay put; and if rents rise, they may have little or no choice but to pay the higher rates.

Consequently, a 10 percent decline (projected to last 18 months) in housing prices for two bedroom apartments is likely to result in a greater percentage increase in apartment housing demand in Kansas City and Houston than in San Francisco.

Overall, because of the reduced availability of substitutes, the price elasticity of demand for apartment housing may well be less price elastic in San Francisco, despite the substantially larger percentage of the household budget spent on housing in that location.

INTERNATIONAL PERSPECTIVES

FREE TRADE AND THE PRICE ELASTICITY OF DEMAND: NESTLE

The period from the late 1980s to the early 1990s was characterized by an explosion of free-trade agreements among important trading partners. The Europe 1992 plan virtually eliminated trade barriers among the major Common Market countries. Most goods now flow freely and without tariffs from one country to another. Increasing standardization of products in these markets will further reduce trading barriers. On the North American continent, the North American Free Trade Agreement (NAFTA) has been ratified by the United States, Canada, and Mexico. In 1994, the General Agreement on Tariffs and Trade (GATT) was implemented, leading to a worldwide reduction in tariffs and other trade barriers.

What are the implications of these reduced trading barriers to estimates of price elasticity of demand for the products produced by manufacturers in the individual countries? Free trade results in an effective increase in the number of substitute goods that are available to consumers and businesses in any country. Consequently, as barriers to free trade come down, the demand will become more price elastic for goods that historically have not been able to flow easily (without significant tariffs or quotas) between countries. Nestle's yogurt and custard products now travel from manufacturing sites in the British Midlands to Milan in 17 hours; the customs processing and transportation bottlenecks once required 38 hours. Accordingly, some industries will experience pressure on their prices and market share. Greater efficiency in production and distribution and increasing attention to quality will be required if formerly protected, inefficient producers are to survive in a globally competitive world. The winners in this process should be consumers, who will have a wider variety of products to choose from at competitive prices. The losers will be those firms that cannot compete in a global market on the basis of cost, quality, and service.

INCOME ELASTICITY OF DEMAND

Among the variables that affect demand, income is often one of the most important. Analogous to the price elasticity of demand, one can also compute an income elasticity of demand.

Income Elasticity Defined

Income Elasticity
The ratio of the percentage change in quantity demanded to the percentage change in income, assuming that all other factors influencing demand remain unchanged.

Income elasticity of demand measures the responsiveness of a change in quantity demanded of some commodity to a change in income. It can be expressed as

$$E_y = \frac{\%\Delta Q_D}{\%\Delta Y}, \ ceteris \ paribus \qquad [4.10]$$

where ΔQ_D = change in quantity demanded
ΔY = change in income

Various measures of income can be used in the analysis. One commonly used measure is consumer disposable income, calculated on an aggregate, household, or per capita basis.

Arc Income Elasticity

The *arc* income elasticity is a technique for calculating income elasticity between two income levels. It is computed as

$$E_y = \frac{\dfrac{Q_2 - Q_1}{(Q_2 + Q_1)/2}}{\dfrac{Y_2 - Y_1}{(Y_2 + Y_1)/2}} \qquad [4.11]$$

where Q_2 = quantity sold after an income change
Q_1 = quantity sold before an income change
Y_2 = new level of income
Y_1 = original level of income

For example, assume that an increase in disposable personal income in Rhode Island from $1.00 billion to $1.10 billion is associated with an increase in boat sales in the state from 5,000 to 6,000 units. Determine the income elasticity over this range. Substituting the relevant data into Equation 4.11 yields

$$E_y = \frac{\dfrac{6,000 - 5,000}{(6,000 + 5,000)/2}}{\dfrac{\$1.10 - \$1.00}{(\$1.10 + \$1.00)/2}}$$

$$= 1.91$$

Thus, a 1 percent increase in income would be expected to result in a 1.91 percent increase in quantity demanded, ceteris paribus. Recall that this calculation assumes that all other factors influencing quantity demanded have remained unchanged. If this assumption (ceteris paribus) is not met, the calculated elasticity measure may be quite misleading. This warning applies to all elasticity calculations.

Point Income Elasticity

The arc income elasticity measures the responsiveness of quantity demanded to changes in income levels over a range. In contrast, the *point* income elasticity provides a measure of this responsiveness at a specific point on the demand function. The point income elasticity is defined as

$$E_y = \frac{\partial Q_D}{\partial Y} \cdot \frac{Y}{Q_D}$$

[4.12]

where Y = income

Q_D = quantity demanded of some commodity

$\dfrac{\partial Q_D}{\partial Y}$ = the partial derivative of quantity with respect to income

The algebraic demand function for Christmas trees (Equation 4.3) introduced earlier in the chapter can be used to illustrate the calculation of the point income elasticity. Suppose one is interested in determining the point income elasticity when the price is equal to $8 and per capita personal disposable income is equal to $6,000. Taking the partial derivative of Equation 4.3 with respect to Y yields

$$\frac{\partial Q_D}{\partial Y} = 2.50$$

Recall from the point price elasticity calculation described earlier in the chapter that substituting $P = \$8$ and $Y = \$6,000$ into Equation 4.3 gave Q_D equal to 10,000 units. Therefore, from Equation 4.12, one obtains

$$E_y = 2.50 \left(\frac{\$6,000}{10,000} \right) = 1.50$$

Thus, from an income level of $6,000, one could expect demand for Christmas trees to increase by 1.5 percent for each 1 percent increase in per capita disposable income, ceteris paribus.

Interpreting the Income Elasticity

For most products, income elasticity is expected to be positive; that is, $E_y > 0$. Such goods are referred to as *normal* or *income superior* goods. Those goods having a calculated income elasticity that is negative are called *inferior* goods. Inferior goods are those that are purchased in smaller absolute quantities as the income of the consumer increases. Such food items as pork and beans or subcompact autos are frequently cited as examples of inferior goods. They may compose a large part of a low-income diet or transportation budget but may virtually disappear as income levels increase.

Income elasticity is typically defined as being *low* when it is between 0 and 1 and *high* if it is greater than 1. Goods that are normally considered luxury items generally have a high income elasticity, whereas goods that are necessities (or perceived as necessities) have low income elasticities.

Knowledge of the magnitude of the income elasticity of demand for a particular product is especially useful in relating forecasts of economic activity, such as an expected increase in disposable personal income, to the effects it will have on a particular product or industry. In industries that produce goods having high income elasticities (such as most durable goods producers), a major increase or decrease in economic activity will have a significant impact on the performance of firms in that industry during the period of projection. Knowledge of income elasticities is also useful in developing marketing strategies for products. For example, products having a high income elasticity can be promoted as being luxurious and stylish, whereas goods having a low income elasticity can be promoted as being economical.

EXAMPLE

INCOME ELASTICITIES: EMPIRICAL ESTIMATES

Estimates of the income elasticity of demand have been made for a wide variety of goods and services. A number of these empirically determined income elasticities are shown in Table 4.7. Note that the income elasticities for goods that are often perceived as necessities (e.g., many food items, housing) are less than 1.0, whereas the income elasticities for items that are usually viewed as luxuries (e.g., European travel) are greater than 1.0.

Demand is a function of more than just consumer income levels. For example, an expected increase in industry sales brought about by anticipated increases in consumer income might be more than offset by a decline in the price of a close substitute product or by an increase in the price of a required complement. As will become more apparent in Chapters 5 and 6, a meaningful analysis and forecast of demand requires a consideration of all major variables influencing the demand for a particular commodity.

TABLE   4.7

Empirical Income
Elasticities

Commodity (Good/Service)	Income Elasticity
Apples	1.32[a]
Beef	1.05[a]
Chicken	.28[a]
Dental visits	
Adult males	.61[b]
Adult females	.55[b]
Children	.87[b]
Housing (low-income renters)	.22[c]
International air transportation	
United States/Europe	1.91[d]
Canada/Europe	1.77[d]
Milk	.50[a]
Oranges	.83[a]
Potatoes	.15[a]
Tomatoes	.24[a]

[a]Daniel B. Suits, "Agriculture," In *Structure of American Industry,* 7th ed., ed. W. Adams (New York: Macmillan, 1986).

[b]Willand G. Manning, Jr. and Charles E. Phelps, "The Demand for Dental Care," *The Bell Journal of Economics* 10, no. 2 (Autumn 1979), pp. 503–525.

[c]Elizabeth A. Roistacher, "Short-Run Housing Responses to Changes in Income," *American Economic Review* (February 1977), pp. 381–386.

[d]J. M. Cigliano, Price and Income Elasticities for Airline Travel: The North Atlantic Market," *Business Economics* (September 1980), pp. 17–21.

CROSS ELASTICITY OF DEMAND

Another variable that often affects the demand for a product is the price of a related (substitute or complementary) product.

Cross Elasticity Defined

Cross Elasticity
The ratio of the percentage change in the quantity demanded of Good A to the percentage change in the price of Good B, assuming that all other factors influencing demand remain unchanged. Also called *cross-price elasticity.*

The **cross elasticity of demand,** E_x, (also called *cross-price elasticity*) is a measure of the responsiveness of changes in the quantity demanded (Q_{DA}) of Product A to price changes for Product B (P_B).

$$E_x = \frac{\%\Delta Q_{DA}}{\%\Delta P_B}, \text{ ceteris paribus} \qquad [4.13]$$

where ΔQ_{DA} = change in quantity demanded of Product A
ΔP_B = change in price of Product B

Arc Cross Elasticity

The *arc* cross elasticity is a technique for computing cross elasticity between two price levels. It is calculated as

$$E_x = \frac{\dfrac{Q_{A2} - Q_{A1}}{(Q_{A2} + Q_{A1})/2}}{\dfrac{P_{B2} - P_{B1}}{(P_{B2} + P_{B1})/2}} \qquad [4.14]$$

where Q_{A2} = quantity demanded of A after a price change in B
Q_{A1} = original quantity demanded of A
P_{B2} = new price for Product B
P_{B1} = original price for Product B

For example, suppose the price of butter P_B increases from \$1 to \$1.50 per pound. As a result, the quantity demanded of margarine Q_A increases from 500 pounds to 600 pounds a month at a local grocery store. Compute the arc cross elasticity of demand. Substituting the relevant data into Equation 4.14 yields

$$E_x = \frac{\dfrac{600 - 500}{(600 + 500)/2}}{\dfrac{\$1.50 - \$1.00}{(\$1.50 + \$1.00)/2}}$$

$$= 0.45$$

This indicates that a 1 percent increase in the price of butter will lead to a 0.45 percent increase in the quantity demanded of margarine, which is, of course, a butter substitute, ceteris paribus.

Point Cross Elasticity

In similar fashion, the *point* cross elasticity between Products A and B may be computed as

$$E_x = \frac{\partial Q_A}{\partial P_B} \cdot \frac{P_B}{Q_A} \qquad [4.15]$$

where P_B = price of Product B

Q_A = quantity demanded of Product A when the price of Product B equals P_B

$\dfrac{\partial Q_A}{\partial P_B}$ = the partial derivative of Q_A with respect to P_B

Interpreting the Cross Elasticity

If the cross elasticity measured between Items A and B is *positive* (as might be expected in our butter/margarine example or between such products as plastic wrap and aluminum foil), the two products are referred to as *substitutes* for each other. The higher the cross elasticity, the closer the substitute relationship. A *negative* cross elasticity, on the other hand, indicates that two products are *complementary*. For example, a significant decrease in the price of CDs would probably result in an increase in the demand for CD players.

The following example illustrates how cross elasticities have been used by the courts in the interpretation of U.S. antitrust laws.

EXAMPLE

ANTITRUST AND CROSS ELASTICITIES: DUPONT CORPORATION

The number of close substitutes that a product has may be an important determinant of market structure. The fewer and poorer the number of close substitutes that exist for a product, the greater the amount of monopoly power that is possessed by the producing or selling firm. An important issue in antitrust cases involves the appropriate definition of the relevant product market to be used in computing statistics of market control (e.g., market share). A case involving DuPont's production of cellophane was concerned with this issue. Does the relevant product market include just the product cellophane or is it the much broader flexible packaging materials market? The Supreme Court found the cross elasticity of demand between cellophane and other flexible packaging materials to be sufficiently high so as to exonerate DuPont from a charge of monopolizing the market.[17] Had the relevant product been considered to be cellophane alone, DuPont would have clearly lost, because it produced 75 percent of the market output and its only licensee, Sylvania, produced the rest. But when other flexible packaging materials were included in the product market definition, DuPont's share dropped to an acceptable 18 percent level. The importance of the definition of the relevant product market and the determination of the cross elasticity of demand among close substitute products is emphasized in this and many other cases.[18]

EXAMPLE

www...............
Read more about the FTC case against Office Depot and Staples by searching the FTC Internet site under the keyword "Staples" at the following address: http://www.ftc.gov/search/search.htm

WHY PAY MORE FOR FAX PAPER AND STAPLES AT STAPLES?[19]

Just what constitutes an available substitute has as much to do with the cross-price elasticity of demand as it does with the cross-price elasticity of rival firm supply. In a hotly contested recent merger proposal, the Federal Trade Commission (FTC) has argued that office superstores like Office Max, Office Depot, and Staples are a separate relevant market. Office Depot had 46 percent of the $13.22 billion in 1996 superstore sales of office supplies; Staples had 30 percent, and Office Max had the remaining 24 percent. Office

[17] U.S. v. DuPont, 118 F. Supp. 41 (1953).

[18] See, for example, U.S. v. Alcoa, 148 F. 2d., 416, 424; Times Picayune Publishing Co. v. U.S., 345 U.S. 594; Continental Can Co. v. U.S., 378 U.S., 441, 489. See William G. Shepherd, *Public Policies Toward Business,* 8th ed. (Homewood, Ill.: Richard D. Irwin, 1990) and Irwin M. Stelzer and Howard Kitt, *Selected Antitrust Cases: Landmark Decisions,* 7th ed. (Homewood, Ill.: Richard D. Irwin, 1985) for a further discussion of some of the economic issues involved in antitrust laws.

[19] Based on "FTC Votes to Bar Staples' Bid for Rival," *Wall Street Journal,* 11 March 1997, p. A3.

Depot and Staples proposed to merge thereby creating a combined firm with 76 percent of the market. Such mergers have been disallowed many times under the Sherman Antitrust Act's prohibition of monopolization.

The two companies insisted, however, that their competitors included not only Office Max but all office supply distribution channels including small paper goods specialty stores, department stores, discount stores like K-Mart, warehouse clubs like Sam's Club, office supply catalogs, and some computer retailers. This larger office supply industry is very fragmented, easy to enter (or exit), and huge; 1996 sales topped $185 billion. By this latter standard, the proposed merger involved admittedly the largest players in the industry, but companies with only 3–5 percent market shares. Under this alternative interpretation of the relevant market, Office Depot and Staples should be allowed to proceed with their merger.

Have superstores like Home Depot and Lowes in do-it-yourself building supplies, PetSmart in pet supplies, and Office Depot, Office Max, and Staples created a new customer shopping experience and demand pattern where they are clustered? Office supply products are search goods for which the customer can detect quality prior to purchase and locate just the quality-price combination he or she desires. Brand name reputations should therefore have little effect on repeat purchase shopping patterns at Office Depot and Staples. Is this case devoid of a rationale for antitrust action? Have successful entrepreneurs simply created a new segment within the traditional relevant market for office products? The FTC undertook two sets of experiments to advise the commissioners who voted to deny the proposed merger. Prices for everything from paper clips to fax paper were sampled in 40 cities and towns where Office Depot and Staples competed and in other similar locations where only one of the superstores was present. The prices were significantly higher in the single store markets. Apparently, despite an enormous rival supply of traditional office product retailers, customers are willing to pay more for staples at Staples.

As Wal-Mart has demonstrated in other search good categories, shoppers will flock to a superstore despite numerous closer small retailers. So, despite the enormous preexisting supply of traditional rivals and the exceptional ease of entry (and exit) at small scale, competition for superstore retailers comes only from other superstore retailers. As a result, the Sherman Act warrants denying the proposed merger in office supply superstores. Any superstore company can become a "category killer" on its own sales growth, like Toy-R-Us, but the FTC has decided to bar superstore mergers as a route to near monopoly status. Staples is entitled and determined to appeal this regulatory decision in the courts.

An Empirical Illustration of Price, Income, and Cross Elasticities

Economists have done much empirical work to estimate the various elasticity measures for a wide range of goods and services. With the increased emphasis on the price and availability of energy resources in the United States, an obvious need exists for accurate elasticity measures of the demand for such goods as electric power.

A study by Chapman, Tyrrell, and Mount examined the elasticity of energy use by residential, commercial, and industrial users during the period 1946–1972.[20] They

---

[20] D. Chapman, T. Tyrrell, and T. Mount, "Electricity Demand Growth and the Energy Crisis," *Science,* 17 November 1972, p. 705.

	Price Elasticity	Income Elasticity	Cross Elasticity (Gas)
Residential market	−1.3	0.3	0.15
Commercial market	−1.5	0.9	0.15
Industrial market	−1.7	1.1	0.15

TABLE 4.8

Electricity-Use Elasticities

hypothesized that the demand for electricity was determined by the price of electricity, income levels, and the price of a substitute good—natural gas.

Table 4.8 summarizes the electricity-use elasticities with respect to price, income, and natural gas prices. As shown in the table, price elasticity of demand for electricity is relatively elastic in all markets, with the highest price elasticity being in the industrial market. The significant decline in the growth rate of demand for electricity since the energy crisis-induced price increases is consistent with these results. For example, many assembly plants, foundries, and other heavy industrial users switched to self-generated power with natural gas-fired turbines. The income elasticity figures indicate that electricity use tends to increase with increases in income. The positive cross-elasticity values show that electricity and natural gas are, indeed, substitute goods.

OTHER DEMAND ELASTICITY MEASURES

Price, income, and cross-elasticity measures are the most common applications of the elasticity concept to demand analysis. However, elasticity is a general concept relating the responsiveness (or relative change) of one variable to changes in another variable. With this in mind, this section briefly defines some less common elasticities.[21]

Advertising Elasticity

Advertising elasticity measures the responsiveness of sales to changes in advertising expenditures. It is measured by the ratio of the percentage change in sales to a percentage change in advertising expenditures. The higher the advertising elasticity coefficient, the more responsive sales are to changes in the advertising budget. An awareness of this elasticity measure may assist advertising or marketing managers in their determination of appropriate levels of advertising outlays relative to price promotions or display and packaging expenditures.

Elasticity of Price Expectations

In an inflationary environment, the elasticity of price expectations may provide helpful insights. It is defined as the percentage change in *future* prices expected as a result of current percentage price changes. A coefficient that exceeds unity indicates that buyers expect future prices to rise (or fall) by a greater percentage amount than current prices.

---

[21]In addition to demand elasticities, one can also define a price elasticity of *supply*. The price elasticity of supply measures the responsiveness of quantity supplied by producers to changes in prices. An inelastic supply function is one whose price elasticity coefficient is less than unity. It indicates that a 1 percent change in price will lead to a less than 1 percent change in quantity supplied. An elastic supply function has an elasticity coefficient greater than unity, indicating that a 1 percent change in price will result in a greater than 1 percent change in quantity supplied. Because producers are normally willing to supply more at higher prices, the sign of the price elasticity coefficient of supply will normally be positive.

A positive coefficient that is less than unity indicates that buyers expect future prices to increase (or decrease) but by a lesser percentage amount than current price changes. A zero coefficient indicates that consumers feel that current price changes have no influence on future changes. Finally, a negative coefficient indicates that consumers believe an increase (decrease) in current prices will lead to a decrease (increase) in future prices.

A positive coefficient of price expectations (especially one greater than unity) suggests that current price increases may shift the demand function to the right. This may result in the same or greater sales at the higher prices, as consumers try to beat future price increases by stockpiling the commodity. The stockpiling that occurs when crops freeze (e.g., coffee beans in South America) or otherwise appear in short supply (e.g., during the sugar shortages of 1975) can be explained, at least in part, by the effects of a high elasticity of price expectations. Eventually a competitor's reactions or the large inventory of the product in the consumers' hands will tend to lower the price expectations elasticity, perhaps turning it negative, and result in a shift to the left in the demand function.

COMBINED EFFECT OF DEMAND ELASTICITIES

When two or more of the factors that affect demand change simultaneously, one is often interested in determining their combined impact on quantity demanded. For example, suppose that a firm plans to increase the price of its product next period and anticipates that consumers' incomes will also increase next period. Other factors affecting demand such as advertising expenditures and competitors' prices are expected to remain the same in the next period. From the formula for the price elasticity (Equation 4.4), the effect on quantity demanded of a price increase would be equal to

$$\%\Delta Q_D = E_D(\%\Delta P)$$

Similarly, from the formula for the income elasticity (Equation 4.11), the effect on quantity demanded of an increase in consumers' incomes would be equal to

$$\%\Delta Q_D = E_y(\%\Delta Y)$$

Each of these percentage changes (divided by 100 to put them in a decimal form) would be multiplied by current period demand (Q_1) to get the respective changes in quantity demanded caused by the price and income increases. Assuming that the price and income effects are *independent* and *additive*, the quantity demanded next period (Q_2) would be equal to current period demand (Q_1) plus the changes caused by the price and income increases:

$$Q_2 = Q_1 + Q_1 [E_D(\%\Delta P)] + Q_1[E_y(\%\Delta Y)]$$

or

$$Q_2 = Q_1 [1 + E_D(\%\Delta P) + E_y(\%\Delta Y)] \qquad [4.16]$$

The combined use of income and price elasticities, illustrated here for forecasting demand, can be generalized to include any of the elasticity concepts that were developed in the preceding sections of this chapter.

EXAMPLE

PRICE AND INCOME EFFECTS: THE SEIKO COMPANY

Seiko is planning to increase the price of its watches by 10 percent in the coming year. Economic forecasters expect real disposable personal income to increase by 6 percent during the same period. From past experience, the price elasticity of demand has been estimated to be approximately -1.3 and the income elasticity has been estimated at 2.0.

These elasticities are assumed to remain constant over the range of price and income changes anticipated. Seiko currently sells 2 million watches per year. Determine the forecasted demand for next year (assuming that the percentage price and income effects are independent and additive). Substituting the relevant data into Equation 4.16 yields

$$Q_2 = 2,000,000 [1 + (-1.3)(.10) + (2.0)(.06)]$$

$$= 1,980,000 \text{ units}$$

The forecasted demand for next year is 1.98 million watches assuming that other factors that influence demand, such as advertising and competitors' prices, remain unchanged. In this case, the positive impact of the projected increase in household income is more than offset by the decline in quantity demanded associated with a price increase.

SUMMARY

- Demand relationships can be represented in the form of a schedule (table), graph, or algebraic function. Each of these methods of presentation provides insights into the demand concept.

- The demand curve is typically downward sloping, indicating that consumers are willing to purchase more units of a good or service at lower prices. The downward-sloping demand curve can be explained by the law of diminishing marginal utility.

- Changes in price result in *movement* along the demand curve, whereas changes in any of the other variables in the demand function result in *shifts* of the entire demand curve. Thus changes in quantity demanded along a particular demand curve result from price changes. In contrast, when one speaks of changes in demand, one is referring to shifts in the entire demand curve.

- Some of the factors that cause a shift in the entire demand curve are changes in the income level of consumers, the price of substitute and complementary goods, the level of advertising, competitors' advertising expenditures, population, consumer preferences, time period of adjustment, taxes or subsidies, and price expectations.

- Elasticity refers to the responsiveness of one economic variable to changes in another, related variable. Thus *price elasticity* of demand refers to the percentage change in quantity demanded associated with a percentage change in price, holding constant the effects of other factors thought to influence demand. Demand is said to be relatively price *elastic* if a given percentage change in price results in a greater percentage change in quantity demanded. Demand is said to be relatively price *inelastic* if a given percentage change in price results in a lesser percentage change in quantity demanded.

- When demand is unit elastic, marginal revenue equals zero and total revenue is maximized. When demand is elastic, an increase (decrease) in price will result in a decrease (increase) in total revenue. When demand is inelastic, an increase (decrease) in price will result in an increase (decrease) in total revenue.

- *Income elasticity* of demand refers to the percentage change in quantity demanded associated with a percentage change in income, holding constant the effects of other factors thought to influence demand.

- *Cross elasticity* of demand refers to the percentage change in quantity demanded of Good *A* associated with a percentage change in the price of Good *B*.

- An understanding of the magnitude of various elasticity measures for a product can be extremely helpful when forecasting demand and formulating marketing or operations plans.

EXERCISES

1. Jenkins Photo Company manufactures an automatic camera that currently sells for $90. Sales volume is about 2,000 cameras per month. A close competitor, the B.J. Photo Company, has cut the price of a similar camera it makes from $100 to $80. Jenkins' economist has estimated the cross elasticity of demand between the two firms' products at about 0.4, given current income and price levels.

   What impact, if any, will the action by B.J. have on total revenue generated by Jenkins, if Jenkins leaves its current price unchanged?

2. The Potomac Range Corporation manufactures a line of microwave ovens costing $500 each. Its sales have averaged about 6,000 units per month during the past year. In August, Potomac's closest competitor, Spring City Stove Works, cut its price for a closely competitive model from $600 to $450. Potomac noticed that its sales volume declined to 4,500 units per month after Spring City announced its price cut.

   a. What is the arc cross elasticity of demand between Potomac's oven and the competitive Spring City model?

   b. Would you say that these two firms are very close competitors? What other factors could have influenced the observed relationship?

   c. If Potomac knows that the arc price elasticity of demand for its ovens is -3.0, what price would Potomac have to charge to sell the same number of units it did before the Spring City price cut?

3. The price elasticity of demand for personal computers is estimated to be -2.2. If the price of personal computers declines by 20 percent, what will be the expected percentage increase in the quantity of computers sold?

4. The Olde Yogurt Factory has reduced the price of its popular Mmmm Sundae from $2.25 to $1.75. As a result, the firm's daily sales of these sundaes have increased from 1,500/day to 1,800/day. Compute the arc price elasticity of demand over this price and consumption quantity range.

5. The subway fare in your town has just been increased from a current level of 50 cents to $1.00 per ride. As a result, the transit authority notes a decline in ridership of 30 percent.

   a. Compute the price elasticity of demand for subway rides.

   b. If the transit authority reduces the fare back to 50 cents, what impact would you expect on the ridership? Why?

6. The demand for mobile homes in Azerpajama, a small, oil-rich sheikdom, has been estimated to be $Q_D = 250,000 - 35P$. If this relationship remains approximately valid in the future:

   a. How many mobile homes would be demanded at a price of $2,000? $4,000? $6,000?

   b. What is the *arc* price elasticity of demand between $2,000 and $4,000? Between $4,000 and $6,000?

   c. What is the *point* price elasticity of demand at $2,000, $4,000, and $6,000?

   d. If 25,000 mobile homes were sold last year, what would you expect the average price to have been?

   e. In a move to increase his popularity (and in the face of rapidly accumulating oil royalties) Sheik Archie has decided to subsidize the price of mobile homes and offer them to all who want them at a price of only $1,000. As the sheik's chief adviser, how many homes would you expect to be bought at this bargain-basement price? At this price, how confident are you of the estimated demand equation?

   f. Without subsidy, what is the highest theoretical price that anyone would pay for a mobile home in the sheikdom?

7. A number of empirical studies of automobile demand have been made yielding the following estimates of income and price elasticities:

Study	Income Elasticity	Price Elasticity
Chow	+3.0	−1.2
Alkinson	+2.5	−1.4
Roos and Von Szeliski	+2.5	−1.5
Suits (as reworked)	+3.9	−1.2

Assume also that income and price effects on automobile sales are *independent* and *additive*. Assume also that the auto companies intend to increase the average price of an automobile by about 6 percent in the next year and that next year's disposable personal income is expected to be 4 percent higher than this year's. If this year's automobile sales were 11 million units, how many would you expect to be sold under each pair of price and income demand elasticity estimates?

8. A typical consumer behaved in the following manner with respect to purchases of butter over the past eight years:

Year	Price of Butter ($/Pound)	Quantity of Butter Purchased (Pounds)	Real Income (Dollars)	Price of Margarine ($/Pound)
1	$ .95	200	$11,000	$.65
2	1.10	180	11,000	.65
3	1.10	190	11,500	.65
4	1.10	200	11,500	.90
5	1.15	170	11,500	.90
6	.99	190	11,500	.90
7	.99	175	10,500	.90
8	.99	150	10,500	.65

Compute all meaningful price, income, and cross-elasticity coefficients. (Remember that the effects of other factors need to be held constant when computing any one of these coefficients.)

9. If the marginal revenue from a product is $15 and the price elasticity of demand is −1.2, what is the price of the product?

10. If the price elasticity of demand for cable TV connections is high (for example, greater than 1.5) and the price elasticity of demand for movies shown in theaters is less than 1, what strategy would you expect cable TV firms to follow in arranging for initial hookups?

11. The demand function for bicycles in Holland has been estimated to be

$$Q = 2,000 + 15Y - 5.5P$$

where Y is income in *thousands* of guilders, Q is the quantity demanded in units, and P is the price per unit. When $P = 150$ guilders and $Y = 15(000)$ guilders, determine the following:

a. Price elasticity of demand
b. Income elasticity of demand

12. Two goods have a cross-price elasticity of $+1.2$.

a. Would you describe these goods as substitutes or complements?
b. If the price of one of the goods increases by 5 percent, what will happen to the demand for the other product, holding constant the effects of all other factors?

13. In an attempt to increase revenues and profits, a firm is considering a 4 percent increase in price and an 11 percent increase in advertising. If the price elasticity of demand is -1.5 and the advertising elasticity of demand is $+0.6$, would you expect an increase or decrease in total revenues?

14. During 19X5 the demand for a firm's product has been estimated to be

$$Q = 1000 - 200P$$

During 19X6 the demand for that same firm's product has been estimated to be

$$Q = 1150 - 225P$$

If the price was $2 during 19X5 and $3 during 19X6, has the price elasticity of demand for this product been increasing or decreasing?

15. Between 19X1 and 19X2, the quantity of automobiles produced and sold declined by 20 percent. During this period the real price of cars increased by 5 percent, real income levels declined by 2 percent, and the real cost of gasoline increased by 20 percent. Knowing that the income elasticity of demand is $+1.5$ and the cross-price elasticity of gasoline and cars is -0.3,

a. Compute the impact of the decline in real income levels on the demand for cars.
b. Compute the impact of the gasoline price increase on the demand for cars.
c. Compute the price elasticity of the demand for cars during this period.

16. Compute the price elasticity of demand and the income elasticity of demand at the prices and income specified in the following demand function:

$$Q = 25 - 4P + 6I$$

a. When $I = 10$ and $P = 4$
b. When $I = 4$ and $P = 6$

17. The demand function for school lunches in Pittsburgh has been estimated to be

$$Q = 16,415.21 - 262.743P$$

where Q = lunches served
      P = price in cents

a. Compute the point elasticity of demand for school lunches at a price of
    (i) 40 cents per lunch
    (ii) 50 cents per lunch
b. What is the arc price elasticity of demand between a price of 40 cents and 50 cents?

18. Over the past six months Heads-Up Hair Care, Inc., has normally had sales of 500 bottles of A-6 Hair Conditioner per week. On the weeks when Heads-Up ran sales on its B-8 Hair Conditioner, cutting the price of B-8 from $10 to $8, sales of A-6 declined to 300 bottles.

a. What is the arc cross elasticity of demand between A-6 and B-8?

    b. If the price of B-8 were increased to $12, what effect would you expect this to have on the quantity demanded of A-6?

    c. What does the evidence indicate about the relationship between B-8 and A-6?

19. Ms. Jones consumes three products, A, B, and C. She has decided that her last purchase of A gave her 8 units of satisfaction, her last purchase of B gave her 10 units of satisfaction, and her last purchase of C gave her 5 units of satisfaction. The prices of A, B, and C are $4, $5, and $3 per unit, respectively.

    As a rational consumer, what should Ms. Jones purchase?

20. The income elasticity of demand for residential use of electricity has been estimated as 0.3. If the price of electricity is expected to remain constant and the price of substitute goods is expected to remain constant, what would you expect to happen to the demand for electricity by residential customers if disposable personal income were expected to decline by 10 percent over the next year?

21. A study of the long-term income elasticity of demand for housing by renters is in the range of 0.8 to 1.0, whereas the income elasticity for owner-occupants is between 0.7 and 1.15.

    a. If income levels are expected to increase at a compound annual rate of 4 percent per year for the next five years, forecast the impact of this increase in income levels on the quantity of housing demanded in the two markets (rental and owner-occupants) in five years (assume that the price of housing does not change over this period).

    b. What would be the impact of price increases during this period on the levels of demand forecasted in part (a)?

22. Given the following demand function:

Price P ($)	Quantity Q_D (Units)	ARC Elasticity E_D	Total Revenue ($)	Marginal Revenue ($/Unit)
$12	30		—	
11	40	—	—	—
10	50	—	—	—
9	60	—	—	—
8	70	—	—	—
7	80	—	—	—
6	90	—	—	—
5	100	—	—	—
4	110	—	—	—

    a. Compute the associated arc elasticity, total revenue, and marginal revenue values.

    b. On separate graphs, plot the demand function, total revenue function, and marginal revenue function.

23. The Stopdecay Company sells an electric toothbrush for $25. Its sales have averaged 8,000 units per month over the last year. Recently, its closest competitor, Decayfighter, reduced the price of its electric toothbrush from $35 to $30. As a result, Stopdecay's sales declined by 1,500 units per month.

    a. What is the arc cross elasticity of demand between Stopdecay's toothbrush and Decayfighter's toothbrush? What does this indicate about the relationship between the two products?

b. If Stopdecay knows that the arc price elasticity of demand for its toothbrush is -1.5, what price would Stopdecay have to charge to sell the same number of units as it did before the Decayfighter price cut? Assume that Decayfighter holds the price of its toothbrush constant at $30.

c. What is Stopdecay's average monthly total revenue from the sale of electric toothbrushes before and after the price change determined in part (b)?

d. Is the result in part (c) necessarily desirable? What other factors would have to be taken into consideration?

24. The demand for renting motorboats in a resort town has been estimated to be $Q_D = 5000 - 50P$ where Q_D is the quantity of boats demanded (boat-hours) and P is the average price per hour to rent a motorboat. If this relationship holds true in the future:

a. How many motorboats will be demanded at a rental price of $10, $20, and $30 per hour?

b. What is the *arc* price elasticity of demand between $10 and $20? Between $20 and $30?

c. What is the *point* price elasticity of demand at $10, $20, and $30?

d. If the number of boat rental hours was 4,250 last year, what would you expect the average rental rate per hour to have been?

25. The following table gives hypothetical data for the weekly purchase of sirloin steak by a college fraternity house. Compute all meaningful arc elasticity coefficients (price, cross, and income). Remember that the effects of the other factors must be held constant when computing any of these elasticities.

Week	Price per Pound of Steak	Quantity of Steak Purchased (Pounds)	Income (Member Dues)	Price Per Pound of Hamburger
1	$2.50	100	$500	$.90
2	2.60	95	500	.90
3	2.60	100	550	.90
4	2.60	105	550	.95
5	2.50	115	550	.95
6	2.50	105	550	.90
7	2.50	100	500	.90
8	2.65	90	500	.90
9	2.65	110	500	1.00
10	2.65	90	400	1.00

26. "Because of the American love affair with driving the automobile, increases in the price of gasoline will not affect consumption." What type of demand curve is implied by this statement? Do you believe this is true? Why?

27. Some proposals for tax reform would eliminate the interest deduction for second homes. Explain the impact this would have on the disposable income of owners of second homes and on the price of second homes in the marketplace.

28. If the price of VCRs declines by 20 percent and the total revenue from the sale of VCRs rises, what can you say about the price elasticity of demand for VCRs? Will this price reduction necessarily lead to an increase in profits for VCR manufacturers?

Average Daily Transit Riders (19X1)	Round-Trip Fare	Average Downtown Parking Rate
5,000	$1.00	$5.50

29. The Genessee Transportation Company operates an urban bus system in the city of Genessee, Pennsylvania. Economic analysis performed by the firm indicates that two major factors influence the demand for its services: fare levels and downtown parking rates. Table 1 presents information available from 19X1 operations. Forecasts of future fares and daily parking rates are presented in Table 2.

Genessee's economists supplied the following information so that the firm can estimate ridership in 19X2 and 19X3. Based on past experience, the coefficient of cross elasticity between bus ridership and downtown parking rates is estimated at 0.2, given a fare of $1.00 per round trip. This is not expected to change for a fare increase to $1.25. The price elasticity of demand is currently estimated at −1.1, given daily parking rates of $5.50. It is estimated, however, that the price elasticity will change to −1.2 when parking rates increase to $6.50. Using these data, estimate the average daily ridership for 19X2 and 19X3.

Year	Round-Trip Fare	Average Parking Rates
19X2	$1.00	$6.50
19X3	$1.25	$6.50

30. Many states offer drivers an opportunity to express their individuality with their automobile license plates. For the privilege of having your license plate imprinted with your own custom message—such as SINGLE, PISCES, AG OF 81, PLIBIT, MY BENZ, B-PHIT—drivers normally pay a small premium to the state.
In 1965 when vanity license plates were introduced in Texas, they could be acquired for a mere $10 over the cost of a normal license plate. By 1985 the price had jumped to $25. At this price 154,000 Texans invested in "their own automotive identity." As Texas entered the oil price recession of the mid-eighties, however, legislative leaders frantically scrambled for new sources of revenue. In 1986 the Texas legislature tripled the price to $75. Sales tumbled to only 56,000 custom plates. Faced with this sudden decline in demand, the legislature cut the price to $40 for 1987. The Texas legislators learned a quick lesson in the concept of price elasticity.
a. What assumptions do you believe led the legislature to increase the price in 1986?
b. Compute the arc price elasticity of demand between $25 and $75, assuming no other factors affecting the demand for license plates changed between 1985 and 1986. Given this calculation, why do you feel the legislature cut the price to $40 for 1987?
c. What other factors should be considered in future pricing decisions by the legislature?
31. The Reliable Aircraft Company manufactures small, pleasure-use aircraft. Based on past experience, sales volume appears to be affected by changes in the price of the planes and by the state of the economy as measured by consumers' disposable

personal income. The following data pertaining to Reliable's aircraft sales, selling prices, and consumers' personal income were collected:

Year	Aircraft Sales	Average Price	Disposable Personal Income (in Constant 19X0 Dollars—Billions)
19X3	525	$7200	$610
19X4	450	8000	610
19X5	400	8000	590

    a. Estimate the arc price elasticity of demand using the 19X3 and 19X4 data.

    b. Estimate the arc income elasticity of demand using the 19X4 and 19X5 data.

    c. Assume that these estimates are expected to remain stable during 19X6. Forecast 19X6 sales for Reliable assuming that its aircraft prices remain constant at 19X5 levels and that disposable personal income will increase by $40 billion. Also assume that arc income elasticity computed in (b) above is the best available estimate of income elasticity.

    d. Forecast 19X6 sales for Reliable given that its aircraft prices increase by $500 from 19X5 levels and that disposable personal income will increase by $40 billion. Assume that the price and income effects are *independent* and *additive* and that the arc income and price elasticities computed in parts (a) and (b) are the best available estimates of these elasticities to be used in making the forecast.

32. In 19X2 the fare on Chicago's transit system was 60 cents per ride. This resulted in 711.6 million trips being taken on the system. In 19X3 the fare was increased to 80 cents and ridership declined to 692.4 million trips.

    a. Compute the arc price elasticity of demand for transit ridership in Chicago assuming that all other factors influencing demand remained constant during this period.

    b. Based on your answer to part (a), do you believe the fare increase was a rational action for the Chicago Transit Authority?

    c. What other factors do you feel may have had an impact on ridership during this period? Do you believe the decline in ridership experienced in 19X3 tends to overstate or understate the actual impact of the fare increase?

    d. In 19X4 the fare increased to 90 cents and ridership declined to 640 million trips. Compute the arc price elasticity between 19X3 and 19X4. How can you account for the differences between the 19X2–19X3 elasticity coefficient and the 19X3–19X4 elasticity coefficient?

33. A Department of Energy report showed that during the period between March 19X0 and March 19X1, energy consumption per U.S. household dropped 9 percent. During the same period, energy prices rose by 24 percent.

    a. Assuming all other factors influencing demand remained constant during this period, what was the price elasticity of demand for household energy consumption?

    b. What other factors may have influenced the results for this period?

    c. If household energy consumption had been increasing at a rate of 2 percent per year before this price increase, what impact would this have on the computed price elasticity?

www exercise

Further Research on the
Proposed Office
Depot–Staples Merger

34. In late June 1997 a federal district court in Washington, D.C., granted the Federal Trade Commission's (FTC's) request for a preliminary injunction blocking the Staples–Office Depot merger. The antitrust case involving Staples was significant in part for the role of econometric analysis of the pricing behavior of Staples. Access the Federal Trade Commission Internet site at: http://www.ftc.gov/ search/search.htm. Search under the "Staples" keyword and read the summary of econometric analysis. By how much did the FTC's empirical analysis determine that average office supply prices would rise as a consequence of the merger between Office Depot and Staples? A key issue of contention in the case was that Staples charged higher prices in those geographical markets that lacked an Office Depot outlet. What were the alternative methods used by the FTC and the merging firms to determine whether or not an Office Depot and a Staples outlet were in the same geographical market? How did these differences in measurement of geographical market affect the pricing behavior estimated by the FTC and by the merging firms?

Indifference Curve Analysis of Demand

MANAGERIAL CHALLENGE

NEW PRODUCT PRICING AT MOTOROLA[22]

What's a cell phone worth? When cell phones first began replacing two-way mobile radios in 1983, one of the hardest questions for Motorola to answer was what price elasticity of demand would characterize the new product. Clearly, no close substitutes existed. Returning to one's car to check in with the office or regularly calling the office from a pay phone imposed substantial inconvenience relative to a small light cell phone carried in one's coat pocket. Consumers would presumably pay substantially higher prices for the convenience of the new technology. But how much higher and what sensitivity would the new demand exhibit to price promotions? These are difficult questions requiring careful analysis when an extensive history of product sales and price data are present. They are virtually impossible to answer with new products, not yet introduced.

One approach to estimating the value of a new product is to conduct marketing research experiments that benchmark the product against other similar technologies. Thus, when digital technology made pagers a practical extension of cell phones in 1992, it was possible to ask cell phone users what extra amount per month they would pay to have access to a pager. Similarly, buyers of Cheerios, a ready-to-eat cereal, can be surveyed about their willingness to pay extra for Apple Cinnamon Cheerios, and music cassette buyers can be asked the same question about music CDs. Often, however, the technological leaps associated with new product introductions make these comparisons infeasible. In 1972, few engineers could assess their willingness to pay for pocket calculators relative to slide rules. In 1981, few secretaries could assess their improved efficiency with electronic word processors rather than manual typewriters. Some other method was required to identify the extra quality and value contributed by the new products.

In this appendix, we will see how the techniques of indifference curve analysis can identify the value of a new product. These methods have application in measuring the effect of higher quality products on the cost of living and in pricing decisions affecting new product introductions.

WWW . . . .
Motorola's Internet site can be accessed at:
http://www.mot.com/

---

[22]Based on "It Overstates Inflation," *Business Week,* 9 June 1997, pp. 68–69, and "Now Prices Can be 'Virtual' Too," *The Economist,* 14 June 1997, p. 88.

Indifference Curves

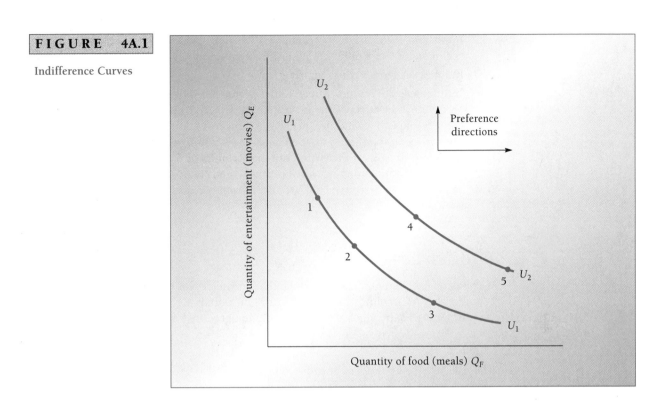

INDIFFERENCE CURVES

The derivation of a consumer's demand function is based on indifference curves and budget lines. *Indifference curves* reveal the consumer's consumption preferences, or utility, for various combinations of goods. *Budget lines,* which are based on the prices of various goods and on the consumer's income, limit the choices available for consumption.

Consider the situation of a consumer who wishes to allocate an available subbudget of income between two commodities, restaurant food (*F*)and entertainment (*E*). The utility, *U,* or satisfaction the consumer receives from the two goods, can be expressed as

$$U = f(Q_F, Q_E) \qquad\qquad [4A.1]$$

where Q_F and Q_E are the respective quantities of food and entertainment consumed. The utility received from consuming various combinations of goods *F* and *E* can be ranked in an ordinal fashion. That is, it is possible to indicate that a consumer prefers 8 restaurant meals and 3 movies per month to an alternative combination, such as 10 meals and 1 movie. This notion of ordinal utility can be depicted by *indifference curves*. An indifference curve is a plotting of points representing various combinations of two goods, for example *F* and *E*, such that the consumer is *indifferent* among any combinations along a specific indifference curve.

Figure 4A.1 shows two indifference curves, U_1 and U_2. The consumer is indifferent among combinations 1, 2, and 3 on curve U_1, but prefers any combination of *E* and *F*, such as points 4 and 5 on curve U_2 to any combination available on curve U_1. The most important properties of indifference curves are:

1. Any combination of commodities lying on an indifference curve (U_2, for example) that is above and to the right of another indifference curve (such as U_1) is the preferred combination.

2. Indifference curves have a negative (downward) slope to the right, indicating that more of E can only be obtained by consuming less of F.

3. Indifference curves never intersect.

4. Indifference curves are convex to the origin. The absolute value of the slope of an indifference curve is the marginal rate of substitution of F for E. The convex shape of an indifference curve indicates that the slope diminishes as one moves to the right; i.e., the consumer is willing to give up fewer and fewer units of F to gain an increasing number of units of E. This is consistent with the law of diminishing marginal utility, which states that the additional satisfaction, or marginal utility, derived from successive units of a good is thought to decline.

BUDGET LINES

In choosing the amount of goods F and E that maximizes his or her utility, the consumer is limited by the amount of income available to purchase these goods. The consumer faces an (F + E) subbudget of the household budget constraint, of the form

$$M = P_F Q_F + P_E Q_E \qquad [4A.2]$$

where M represents the amount of income available to the consumer to be spent on goods F and E. P_F and P_E represent the price of a unit of F and E, respectively. The amount spent on F—$P_F Q_F$—plus the amount spent on E—$P_E Q_E$—equals the total amount of income available, M. This budget line is shown in Figure 4A.2. It intersects the y-axis (vertical) at M/P_E—the number of movies consumed if the entire subbudget is spent on movies. The budget line intersects the x-axis (horizontal) at M/P_F—the number of meals consumed if all the subbudget is spent on F. Any combination of meals and movies lying on or below the budget line is available to the consumer. Any household that prefers more meals and movies to less will select for consumption some combination of F and E which lies on the subbudget constraint—i.e., a consumption bundle which exhausts the subbudget.

Knowing that all interior combinations of food and entertainment (below the budget constraint) are less preferred than the chosen combination (F_1, E_1) allows a practical mechanism for locating a regular buyer's indifference curve. In a so-called revealed preference experiment, a household agrees to keep a diary of their food and entertainment consumption over an extended time period. Various coupon and subsidy schemes change the effective price of items the household buys regularly. If a consumption experimenter lowers the price of food and raises the price of entertainment such that the household now can select between (F_1, E_1) or any other combination allowed by the new flatter budget line in Figure 4A.2, and if the household responds that they still prefer (F_1, E_1), the new shaded area of consumption choices has been identified as less preferred. Conducting the same experiment in reverse (i.e., with increased food prices and lower entertainment prices along the steepest budget constraint in Figure 4A.2), another shaded set of consumption bundles less preferred than (F_1, E_1) can be identified. Continuing in this fashion until the household switches to a new subsidized food combination like (F_2, E_2) or a new subsidized entertainment combination like (F_3, E_3) reveals the shape and location of the household's indifference curve. These techniques are important in pricing new products and in measuring the cost of living before and after new product introductions.

FIGURE   4A.2

Budget Line

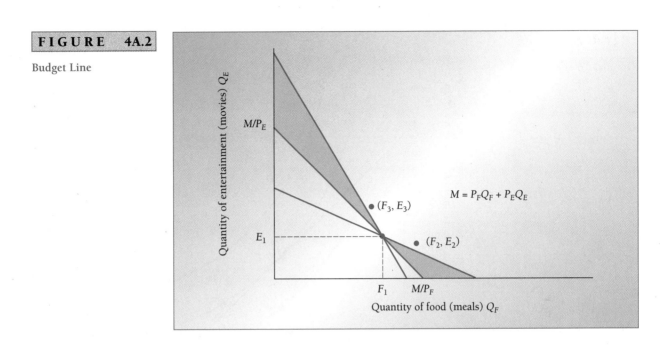

$M = P_F Q_F + P_E Q_E$

(F_3, E_3)

(F_2, E_2)

GRAPHICAL DETERMINATION OF THE OPTIMAL COMBINATION

Given the indifference curves and budget constraint, the consumer's problem is to choose the combination of F and E that *maximizes* the utility derived without overspending the budget. Because a consumer's satisfaction increases with combinations moving upward and/or to the right, utility is maximized at the point of *tangency* between the budget constraint and the highest consumer indifference curve, as illustrated in Figure 4A.3. Given three possible indifference curves and a budget constraint, the optimal combination of goods F and E for this consumer is given at point D. At this point the consumer can achieve a U_2 level of satisfaction by consuming Q_F^* units of F and Q_E^* units of E. These levels provide the highest utility without violating the budget constraint.

At the point of tangency of the indifference curve (U_2) and the budget line in Figure 4A.3, the slope[23] of the indifference curve is equal to the slope of the budget line. The slope $(\Delta Q_E / \Delta Q_F)$ of the budget line is equal to the ratio of the price of commodity $F(P_F)$ to the price of commodity $E(P_E)$; that is

$$\frac{\Delta Q_E}{\Delta Q_F} = \frac{(M/P_E - 0)}{(M/P_F - 0)} = \frac{P_F}{P_E} \qquad [4A.3]$$

The slope of the indifference curve $(\Delta Q_E / \Delta Q_F)$ at any point measures the consumer's *marginal rate of substitution (MRS)* of commodity E for commodity F (holding utility constant). This slope is equal to the ratio of the marginal utility of F ($MU_F = \partial U/\partial Q_E$) to the marginal utility of E ($MU_E = \partial U/\partial Q_E$), that is

$$\frac{\Delta Q_E}{\Delta Q_F} = MRS = \frac{MU_F}{MU_E} \qquad [4A.4]$$

---

[23]Note that the slopes of the indifference curves and budget line are both negative. In the remainder of this appendix, slope will be taken to mean *absolute value.*

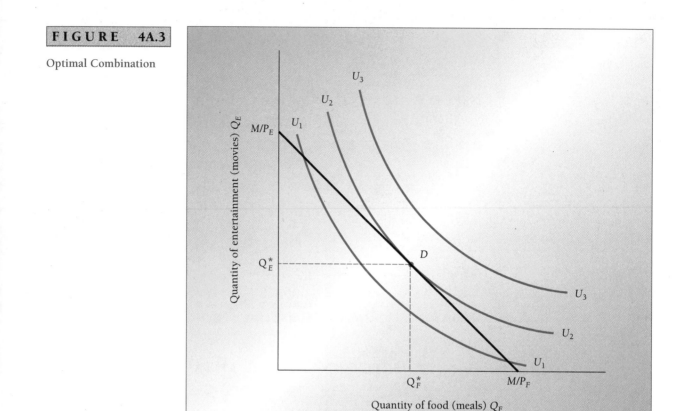

At the optimum (tangency) point, setting Equation 4A.3 equal to Equation 4A.4 yields

$$\frac{MU_F}{MU_E} = \frac{P_F}{P_E} \qquad [4A.5]$$

or

$$\frac{MU_F}{P_F} = \frac{MU_E}{P_E} \qquad [4A.6]$$

which is equivalent to (for the two-commodity case) the optimality condition (Equation 4.1) presented earlier in Chapter 4.

GRAPHICAL DERIVATION OF THE DEMAND FUNCTION

A consumer's demand function for a good can be derived graphically based on his or her indifference curves and budget line.

Consider a consumer whose indifference curves and budget line are shown in Figure 4A.4. Assume the consumer has $350 to spend on products F and E. The initial price of E is $5 per movie and the initial price of F is $10 per restaurant meal. Under these conditions, the consumer could acquire 70 movies or 35 meals or any combination thereof (illustrated by the lower budget line). Three indifference curves are plotted, U_1, U_2, and U_3. Given the income constraint of $350 and the initial prices of F ($10) and E ($5), the consumer would choose combination X on curve U_1. At this point the consumer would acquire 16 units of F. Hence at a price of $10 per unit, the

FIGURE 4A.4

Derivation of a Demand Function

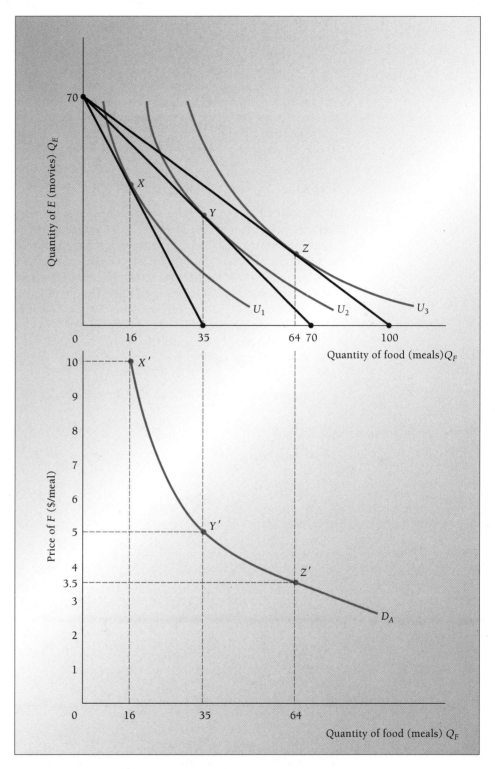

consumer would demand 16 meals. This point is now plotted on the lower panel of Figure 4A.4 as point X'.

If the price of F declines to \$5, a new budget line is defined which intersects the Q_F axis at 70 units. The new optimum occurs at point Y with 35 units of F being demanded at a price of \$5. This point is plotted on the lower panel at Y'.

Finally, at a price of \$3.50 for a unit of F, a new optimum point occurs at Z with 64 units of F being demanded. By plotting in the lower panel of Figure 4A.4 the three prices and associated quantities demanded, the familiar demand curve, D_A, for food is derived. This is illustrated by the curve that connects points X', Y', and Z'.

INCOME AND SUBSTITUTION EFFECTS

Indifference curve analysis can also be used to illustrate the income and substitution effects of a price decline. Consider the case of a consumer who consumes food and entertainment with an initial budget constraint given in Figure 4A.5 as XV. The consumer will buy Q_1 units of F and Q_4 units of E, as indicated at Point 1.

If the price of food declines such that the new budget line becomes XV', Point 2 represents the new optimum for the consumer. This point falls on the higher of the two indifference curves, U_2, plotted on the figure. Given the new lower price for food, the consumer demands Q_2 units of F.

Next, we construct a new, artificial budget line, ZW, which is parallel to XV' and tangent to the original indifference curve U_1. From the original optimal combination of

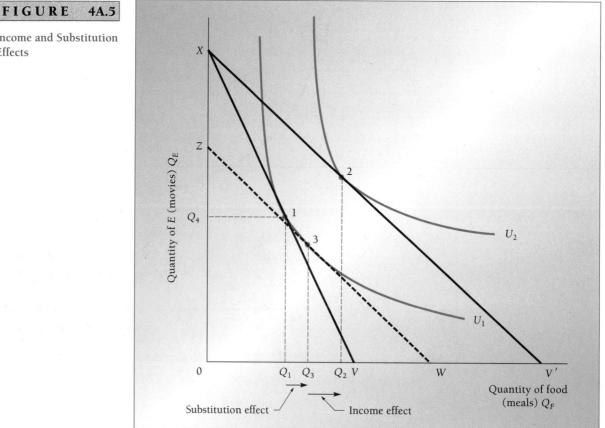

FIGURE   4A.5

Income and Substitution Effects

food and entertainment, Point 1, to the artificial optimum, Point 3, "real" income of the consumer has remained the same in the sense that the consumer experiences the same utility at Point 1 and Point 3. The change in quantity demanded for F from Q_1 to Q_3 may be thought of as representing the "pure" substitution effect of food for entertainment resulting from the price reduction for food. In contrast, the increased consumption of food measured from Points Q_3 to Q_2 may be thought of as the "pure" income effect. This is so because the only difference between ZW and XV' is the level of income that each reflects. In summary, a decline in price for food results in the consumer demanding $Q_3 - Q_1$ more units of food because of the substitution effect, and $Q_2 - Q_3$ more units of food because of the income effect.

ALGEBRAIC DETERMINATION OF THE OPTIMAL COMBINATION

The determination of the optimal combination of goods F and E that maximizes a consumer's utility subject to a budget constraint can also be obtained algebraically using Lagrangian multiplier techniques. The objective is to maximize utility, represented by Equation 4A.1,

$$U = f(Q_F, Q_E)$$

subject to the budget constraint, represented by Equation 4A.2,

$$M = P_F Q_F + P_E Q_E$$

We begin by forming the Lagrangian function

$$U_\lambda = f(Q_F, Q_E) - \lambda (P_F Q_F + P_E Q_E - M) \qquad [4A.7]$$

Differentiating Equation 4A.7 with respect to Q_F, Q_E, and λ and setting the derivatives equal to 0 yields

$$\frac{\partial U_\lambda}{\partial Q_F} = \frac{\partial f}{\partial Q_F} - \lambda P_F = 0 \qquad [4A.8]$$

$$\frac{\partial U_\lambda}{\partial Q_E} = \frac{\partial f}{\partial Q_E} - \lambda P_E = 0 \qquad [4A.9]$$

$$\frac{\partial U_\lambda}{\partial \lambda} = -P_F Q_F - P_E Q_E + M = 0 \qquad [4A.10]$$

Recognizing that $\partial f / \partial Q_F = MU_F$ and $\partial f / \partial Q_E = MU_E$, we substitute these quantities into Equations 4A.8 and 4A.9 to give

$$MU_F = \lambda P_F$$

$$\lambda = \frac{MU_F}{P_F} \qquad [4A.11]$$

and

$$MU_E = \lambda P_E$$

$$\lambda = \frac{MU_E}{P_E} \qquad [4A.12]$$

Setting Equation 4A.11 equal to Equation 4A.12 yields the optimality condition (Equation 4A.6 and Equation 4.1 from the chapter).

$$\frac{MU_F}{P_F} = \frac{MU_E}{P_E}$$

MEASURING THE VALUE OF CELLULAR PHONES[24]

When Motorola introduced the cellular phone, the quality of telecommunications services clearly rose. The difficult question was what value to place on this enhanced convenience for "staying in touch." Public as well as private managers are interested in such a question because quality enhancements offered by new products like open heart surgery, central air conditioning, and cellular phones lower the cost of living. Official cost-of-living indices for medical services, housing, and telecommunications determine everything from wage indexation agreements in union bargaining to hospital cost reimbursements and therefore become embedded in the underlying rate of inflation. In 1997, estimating correctly the value of the quality improvements from a new product became a serious issue in boardrooms, central banks, on Wall Street, and in congressional debates about social security cost-of-living adjustments.

To calculate the value of a new product consumed at P_{NP} in the quantity Q_{NP}, consider the following procedure with a representative household or business who chooses between two-way radio mobile phones and cellular phones. Raise the price of the new cellular phone service until the last most valuable use is discouraged and quantity demanded falls to zero. Figure 4A.6 illustrates this idea as a steepening of the initial budget constraint whose x-intercept is M/P_{NP} until the preferred quantity declines from Q_{NP} to zero at Point 2′. Identify the price that is high enough to accomplish the collapse of all new product sales as P_{MAX}, the "virtual price" beyond which no one would purchase the new cellular phone product. Then, maintaining relative prices at this P_{MAX} level (namely, P_{MAX}/P_{RADIO}), calculate the purchasing power required to leave the household as well off as they were with Q_{NP} at Point 1′. After subtracting the money income of the household (M), the additional dollars required to restore utility to the level U_1 associated with current sales of the new product is the value of the enhanced quality attributable to the new product. In Figure 4A.6, hold utility constant at U_1 while raising cellular phone prices to P_{MAX}; the tangency at Point 3′ identifies $M + V_{NP}$ as the amount of purchasing power required. Therefore, V_{NP} is the additional value attributable to the new cellular phone product.

With revealed preference techniques for identifying the household's indifference curve data and linear programming to identify the budget constraints in question, estimates of V_{NP} are obtainable for both Motorola's pricing analysts and the cost-of-living analysts in the Bureau of Labor Statistics.

EXERCISE

1. Suppose an individual's utility (that is, satisfaction) received from two goods can be represented by the following relationship:

$$U = f(Q_A, Q_B) = 2Q_A + 2Q_B - .5Q_A^2 + Q_A Q_B - .6Q_B^2$$

where Q_A and Q_B are the amounts consumed of the respective goods. Furthermore, assume that the cost per unit of good A is $4 and the cost per unit of good

---

[24] Based on "It Overstates Inflation," *Business Week,* 9 June 1997, pp. 68–69, "Costing a Packet," *The Economist,* May 6, 1996, p. 75, and J. Hausman, "Cellular Telephones: New Products and the CPI," NBER Working Paper, No. 5982, March 1997.

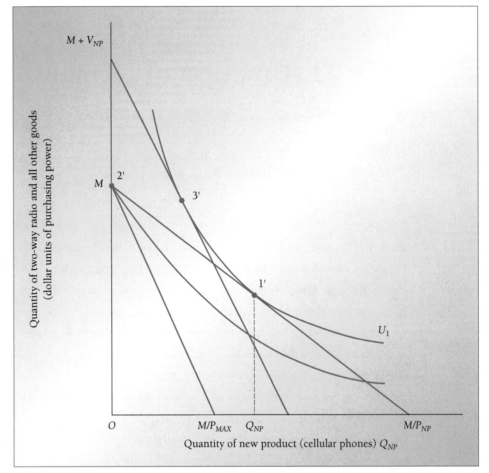

B is $6. The individual has $48 available to spend on the two goods and desires to maximize the utility received from consumption of the two goods subject to his budget constraint.

a. Formulate the problem in a programming format.

b. Convert this constrained optimization problem into an unconstrained problem by forming the Lagrangian function.

c. Solve this unconstrained problem using the techniques of differential calculus.

d. Defining $MU_A = \partial f/\partial Q_A$ and $MU_B = \partial f/\partial Q_B$ to be the marginal utility functions, show that the ratio of the marginal utilities

$$\frac{MU_A}{MU_B}$$

evaluated at optimal values of Q_A and Q_B obtained in part (c), is equal to the ratio of the prices of the two goods. This illustrates the economic principle that in equilibrium the ratio of the prices of two goods must be equal to the ratio of the marginal utilities (i.e., Equation 4A.5).

e. Give an economic interpretation of the value of the Lagrangian multiplier (λ) obtained in part (c).

Estimation of Demand

CHAPTER PREVIEW

The preceding chapter developed the theory of demand, including the concepts of price elasticity, income elasticity, and cross elasticity of demand. A manager who is contemplating an increase in the price of one of the firm's products needs to know the impact of this increase on quantity demanded, total revenue, and profits. Is the demand elastic, inelastic, or unit elastic with respect to price over the range of the contemplated price increase? What will happen to demand if consumer incomes increase or decrease as a result of an economic expansion or contraction? Managers face these types of problems every day. A concern for empirical demand relationships is not limited to profit-seeking enterprises. Governments and not-for-profit institutions are faced with similar relationships. What will be the impact of an increase in cigarette taxes? Will teenager demand increase, decrease, or remain constant? What effect will a tuition increase have on local state university revenues? These and a multitude of similar questions illustrate the importance of developing empirical estimates of demand relationships. This chapter discusses some of the techniques and problems associated with making such estimates. The more knowledge a manager has regarding the demand for the firm's product, the more likely that manager will be to take actions that can maximize the profits and cash flows accruing to the firm and therefore contribute to the goal of maximizing shareholder wealth.

MANAGERIAL CHALLENGE

DEMAND FOR PUBLIC TRANSPORTATION[1]

Port Authority Transit (PAT) provides public transportation services to the residents of Allegheny County (Pittsburgh and suburbs). It operates a fleet of 925 buses and 71 light rail vehicles and trolleys in providing nearly 90 million rides per year. In June 1990 PAT adopted a $173.7 million budget for the 1990–91 fiscal year. By state law PAT is required to operate on a balanced budget. PAT's cash base fare is $1.10. Fares cover only part of its costs—with the balance of its revenues coming from federal, state, and county subsidies.

As a result of the Persian Gulf crisis beginning in August 1990, the cost of diesel fuel (used to operate buses) increased from $0.61 per gallon to $1.09 per gallon—which produced a projected $3.2 million budget deficit. (Each 1-cent increase in the price of diesel fuel costs PAT more than $100,000 per year, because its vehicles use more than 10 million gallons annually.)

Faced with this projected deficit and the need to balance its budget, PAT could attempt to either reduce costs or increase revenues. Cutting costs is difficult because most administrative expenses (e.g., salaries) are relatively fixed in the short run. Likewise, hourly wage rates paid to drivers and mechanics are set by union contracts and cannot be lowered unilaterally. Service cutbacks are possible; however, this may also reduce revenues and thus be counterproductive. Instead of attempting to reduce costs, the executive director of PAT proposed a 15-cent increase in fares to offset the increased cost of diesel fuel.

In analyzing the effects of this fare increase, a number of issues have to be addressed. For example:

- How will the fare (price) increase affect demand and overall revenues?
- What other factors, besides fares, affect demand?

Examination of the data in the graph on the following page gives some possible answers to these questions. Note that ridership declined every year (i.e., 1969, 1971, 1976, 1980, 1982, and 1990) that PAT raised fares. Note also that ridership increased during the mid to late 1970s when there were gasoline shortages and (relatively) higher gasoline prices. Finally, note that ridership declined in the early 1980s—a period during which there was higher unemployment, population declines, and (relatively) lower gasoline prices.

www. . . . .
The U.S. Department of Transportation maintains the National Transportation Library on the Internet, which contains travel demand forecasting studies. The site address is:
http://www.bts.gov/NTL/

---

[1] Based on an article in *The Pittsburgh Press* by Joe Grata, 26 October 1990, p. A1. Reprinted by permission of *The Pittsburgh Press*.

DEMAND ESTIMATION USING MARKETING RESEARCH TECHNIQUES

Before examining some of the statistical techniques that are useful in estimating demand relationships, this section looks at three different marketing research methods that can be used in analyzing demand. These techniques are consumer surveys, consumer clinics, and market experiments.

MANAGERIAL CHALLENGE

DEMAND FOR PUBLIC TRANSPORTATION—CONT'D

Econometric models can be developed that incorporate price and other relevant variables in explaining demand for various goods and services. Such models can be used to make forecasts of demand (and revenues) based on expected changes in any of the relevant variables. This chapter focuses on the techniques that are used in developing such models.

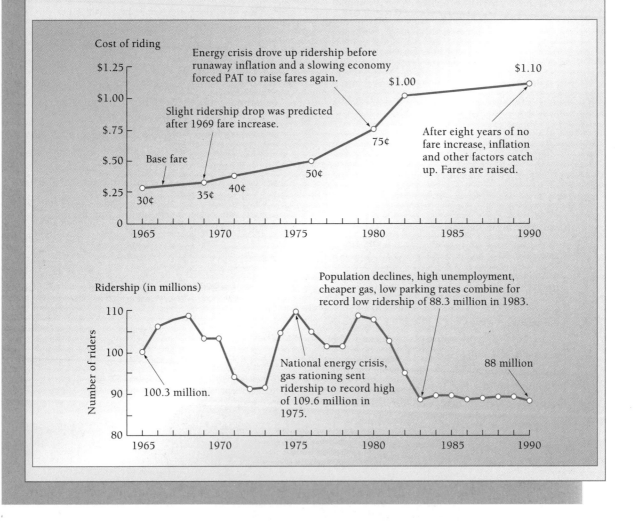

Consumer Surveys

Consumer surveys involve questioning a sample of consumers to determine such factors as their willingness to buy, their sensitivity to price changes or relative price levels, and their awareness of advertising campaigns. Consumer surveys can provide a great deal of useful information to a firm. However, many consumers are not able or not willing to give accurate answers to these types of questions. For example, can you specify what your response would be to a 25-cent rise in the price of hamburgers at your favorite fast-food restaurant? How many fewer hamburgers would you buy per month? Do you know how many you buy now? The approach of direct consumer interviewing has many potential pitfalls. As unrealistic as it may be to expect even the most earnest of consumers to be able to specify his or her response to hypothetical price changes, questions about reactions to changes in the quantity or emphasis of advertising and to changes in income levels produce responses that may be even more suspect.

This is not to say that nothing can be learned from consumer interviews. Consumer expectations about future business and credit conditions may provide significant insights into their propensity to purchase many items, especially durable goods. Using a little imagination and asking less direct questions may also offer insights. If questioning reveals that consumers are unaware of price differences among several competing goods, it might be concluded that at least within the current range of prices, consumers are not terribly price conscious; that is, demand may be price inelastic. Also, the effectiveness of advertising campaigns may be tested by sampling the awareness of a group of consumers to the campaign.

Consumer Clinics

Another means of recording consumer responses to changes in factors affecting demand is through the use of *consumer clinics*. In these situations, for example, experimental groups of consumers are given a small amount of money with which to buy certain items. The experimenter can observe the impact on actual purchases as price, prices of competing goods, and other variables are manipulated.[2]

Although consumer clinics of this sort are considerably more realistic than the hypothetical situations facing consumers in the direct interview method, they still have shortcomings. First, the costs of setting up and running such a clinic are substantial, and consequently the number of consumers actually participating is likely to be quite small. Second, the participants are generally aware that their actions are being observed, and hence they may seek to act in a manner somewhat different from normal—the "Hawthorne effect." An individual taking part in a consumer clinic may suspect that the experimenter is interested in sensitivity to prices and may be significantly more price conscious than otherwise would be the case.

In spite of these problems, interview and consumer clinic approaches often furnish useful information to aid in the decision-making process. It should be evident after the discussion of direct market experimentation and regression techniques that sometimes interviews and consumer clinics offer the only usable information.

Market Experiments

Another approach that is sometimes used to garner information about the demand function is the *market experiment,* which examines the way consumers behave in real market situations. A firm may vary one or more of the determinants of the amount sold, such as price and advertising, and observe the impact on quantity demanded. This approach may be especially useful in developing a feel for the price elasticity or cross elasticity of demand for a product.

---

[2] The use of laboratory experimentation to estimate demand elasticities is illustrated in J. F. Engle, *Consumer Behavior,* (Hinsdale, Ill: Dryden Press, 1993).

ESTIMATION OF CROSS ELASTICITY: SIMMONS MATTRESS COMPANY

The Simmons Mattress Company conducted an experiment involving the relative prices of its mattresses.[3] Two identical types of mattresses, some with the Simmons label and others with an unknown brand name, were offered for sale at the same prices and varying price spreads to determine cross elasticity. It was found that with identical prices, Simmons outsold the unknown brand 15 to 1; with a $5 premium over the unknown label, Simmons's margin was reduced to 8 to 1; and with a 25 percent premium over the unknown label, sales were about the same.

Market experimentation has several serious shortcomings. If done on a scale large enough to generate a high degree of confidence in the results, it may be quite risky. Customers lost by a change in advertising strategy or an increase in price may never be regained. Market experimentation is also extremely expensive on such a large scale. And its cost is even higher when a controlled experiment is attempted. As a result, few of these well-controlled, expensive experiments are conducted, so results can be unreliable. Observed changes that occur in an uncontrolled experiment may be due to all sorts of disturbance factors, such as unusually bad weather, competitive advertising or competitive price reductions, and even local strikes or large layoffs that change consumer incomes significantly. Because of the high cost and risk of a market experiment, the duration of the test is likely to be short and the number of possible variations in parameters, such as price or advertising outlays, are likely to be few. Hence long-run decisions must be made on the basis of a few short-run observations.

In spite of these limitations, direct market experimentation may be useful in a number of situations. For example, statistical demand studies may be impossible when the marketing of a new product is being considered and no price-output data are available. Also, market experiments may provide important data for verifying the results of a statistical study. The information that a statistical demand analysis can provide, however, is generally more comprehensive and often significantly lower in cost than the alternatives outlined above. Hence, this method is often superior to consumer surveys, clinics, or market experimentation. The following sections discuss the application of regression analysis to the estimation of demand functions.

STATISTICAL ESTIMATION OF THE DEMAND FUNCTION

Econometrics
A collection of statistical
techniques available for
testing economic theories
by empirically measuring
relationships among
economic variables.

Econometrics is a collection of statistical techniques available for testing economic theories by empirically measuring relationships among economic variables. The measurement of economic relationships is a necessary step in using economic theories and models to obtain estimates of the numerical values of variables that are of interest to the decision maker. For example, when forecasting demand the manager must have an estimate of the responsiveness of quantity demanded to changes in other variables such as price, income levels, and advertising expenditures. Similarly, when considering the construction of a larger plant, an efficient manager must have an estimate of the impact of this new plant on the firm's cost of operations. Will the plant reduce or increase the average cost of production? The principal econometric techniques used in measuring demand (as well as other economic) relationships are *regression* and *correlation analysis*. The remainder of this chapter illustrates the application of regression and correlation models to demand estimation. The simple (two-variable) linear regression model and the more complex cases of multiple linear regression models and nonlinear models (in

---

[3] Joel Dean, *Managerial Economics* (Englewood Cliffs, N.J.: Prentice-Hall, 1960).

Appendix 5A) are developed. These models also play a key role in the discussions of economic forecasting and the estimation of production and cost functions in later chapters.

The estimation of a demand function using econometric techniques involves the following steps:

1. Identification of the variables
2. Collection of the data
3. Specification of the demand model
4. Estimation of the parameters of the model
5. Development of forecasts (estimates) based on the model

The remainder of this section discusses the first three of these steps. Subsequent sections of the chapter are concerned with the final two steps.

Identification of the Variables

As discussed in the previous chapter, the demand function (Equation 4.2) may be viewed as the relationship between quantity demanded (the dependent variable) and several independent variables. The first task in developing a statistical demand model is to identify the independent variables that are likely to influence quantity demanded. These might include such factors as price of the good in question, price of competing or substitute goods, population, per capita income, and advertising and promotional expenditures. The researcher should seek to learn as much as possible about factors that may influence the demand for a product before specifying which independent variables are to be used in the initial demand equation. If an important variable is omitted in the specification process, the regression statistics that are ultimately computed may be badly distorted.[4] When the model is being formulated, the researcher must attempt to include *all* the *important* variables. However, because data are not always readily available or are expensive to generate, one must frequently be content with a model containing relatively few variables. Rarely will an empirical demand equation be encountered that contains more than six or seven independent variables.

The variable that we are trying to predict is known as the *dependent* variable (designated Y). The variables that are used in predicting the value of the dependent variable are defined as *independent* variables (such as X_1, X_2, and X_3).

Collection of the Data

Once the variables have been identified, the next step is to collect data on the variables. Data can be obtained from a number of different sources. When estimating company demand, price and sales data can be gathered from past records of the firm. When estimating industry demand for a commodity, data may be gathered from information collected and published by various federal, state, and local government agencies, industry trade associations, and commercial banks. In addition to aggregate data for the entire economy, these institutions frequently provide information (e.g., employment, income, prices, and population) for individual metropolitan areas, states, and regions of the country. Sometimes, the data will not be available in the form originally desired. This may require that some variables in the model be respecified or transformations be made to put the data in the required form.

---

[4] See the "Problems in Applying the Linear Regression Model" section of this chapter for a discussion of specification error and how it can affect regression results.

VARIABLE IDENTIFICATION AND DATA COLLECTION: SHERWIN-WILLIAMS COMPANY

Sherwin-Williams Company is attempting to develop a demand model for its line of exterior house paints. The company's chief economist feels that the most important variables affecting paint sales (Y) (measured in gallons) are

1. Promotional expenditures (A) (measured in dollars). These include expenditures on advertising (radio, TV, and newspapers), in-store displays and literature, and customer rebate programs.
2. Selling price (P) (measured in dollars per gallon).
3. Disposable income per household (M) (measured in dollars).

The chief economist decides to collect data on the variables in a sample of 10 company sales regions that are roughly equal in population.[5] Data on paint sales, promotional expenditures, and selling prices were obtained from the company's marketing department. Data on disposable income (per capita) was obtained from the Bureau of Labor Statistics. The data are shown in Table 5.1.

Specification of the Model

The next step is to specify the form of the equation, or model, that indicates the relationship between the independent variables and the dependent variable(s). The specific form of the demand function, which the econometrician estimates, normally is chosen to depict the true relationships as closely as possible. Many alternatives and variations may be tried. Because there is often no a priori reason for expecting one form to model the true relationship better than another, many variations are usually estimated to obtain the best fit between the data for the dependent and independent variables. A clue to which functional form should initially be tried may be gained by

---

[5] A sample size of 10 observations was chosen to keep the arithmetic simple. Much larger samples are used (when the data are available) in actual applications. The desired accuracy and the cost of sampling must be weighed in determining the optimal sample size to use in a given problem.

TABLE 5.1				
Sherwin-Williams Company Data				

Sales Region	Sales (Y) (×1,000 gallons)	Promotional Expenditures (A) (×$1,000)	Selling Price (P) ($/gallon)	Disposable Income (M) (×$1,000)
1	160	150	15.00	19.0
2	220	160	13.50	17.5
3	140	50	16.50	14.0
4	190	190	14.50	21.0
5	130	90	17.00	15.5
6	160	60	16.00	14.5
7	200	140	13.00	21.5
8	150	110	18.00	18.0
9	210	200	12.00	18.5
10	190	100	15.50	20.0

graphing such relationships as the dependent variable over time (when working with time-series data) and each independent variable against the dependent variable. The results of this preliminary analysis often will tell, for example, whether a linear equation is most appropriate or whether logarithmic, exponential, or other transformations are more appropriate.[6]

Linear Model   The most common form of estimation equation in demand studies is a linear relationship.

In the Sherwin-Williams example, a linear demand model would be specified as follows:

$$Y = \alpha + \beta_1 A + \beta_2 P + \beta_3 M + \epsilon \qquad [5.1]$$

where α, β_1, β_2, and β_3 are the parameters of the model and ϵ is the error term. The values of the parameters are estimated using the regression techniques described later in the chapter. An error term is included in the model to reflect the fact that the relationship is not an exact one, i.e., the observed demand value may not always be equal to the theoretical value.[7] Based on economic theory, one would hypothesize that price (P) would have a negative impact on gallons of paint sold (Y) (i.e., as the price rises, quantity demanded declines, holding constant all other variables) and that promotional expenditures (A) and income (M) would have a positive impact on paint sales.

The parameter estimates may be interpreted in the following manner. The constant or intercept term, α, has little economic significance in Equation 5.1 because it represents the quantity of paint demanded when all the independent variables (i.e., promotional expenditures, price, and income) are equal to zero. However, if we rearrange Equation 5.1 to solve for price (P), the intercept of the resulting *inverse demand function* identifies the maximum price that can be charged.

The value of each β coefficient provides an estimate of the change in quantity demanded associated with a *one-unit* change in the given independent variable, holding constant all other independent variables. The β coefficients are equivalent to the partial derivatives of the demand function:

$$\beta_1 = \frac{\partial Y}{\partial A}, \beta_2 = \frac{\partial Y}{\partial P}, \beta_3 = \frac{\partial Y}{\partial M} \qquad [5.2]$$

Thus, each independent variable has a *constant marginal impact* on quantity demanded, regardless of the level of the other independent variables (i.e., regardless of the point on the demand curve where it is measured). Note also that the elasticity of demand with respect to each independent variable is *not* constant, but instead varies with the point on the demand curve where it is measured. This can be shown as follows for the price elasticity. Recalling from Chapter 4 that the point price elasticity of demand was defined as

$$E_D = \frac{\partial Y}{\partial P} \cdot \frac{P}{Y} \qquad [5.3]$$

and substituting Equation 5.2 into Equation 5.3 yields

$$E_D = \beta_2 \cdot \frac{P}{Y} \qquad [5.4]$$

---

[6] See Appendix 5A for a discussion of these transformations. See also any standard econometrics text, such as R. S. Pindyck and D. L. Rubinfeld, *Econometric Models and Economic Forecasts,* 3d ed. (New York: McGraw-Hill, 1991), for additional information concerning some of the alternative functional forms that may be tried.

[7] The error term is examined in more detail in the discussion of regression analysis later in the chapter.

Equation 5.4 shows that price elasticity is a function of the values of price (P) and quantity demanded (Y).

Linear demand equations have been used extensively in empirical work because of their ease of estimation and the realism with which they approximate many true demand relationships.

Multiplicative Exponential Model   Another commonly used demand relationship is the multiplicative exponential model. In the Sherwin-Williams example, such a model would be specified as follows:

$$Y = \alpha A^{\beta_1} P^{\beta_2} M^{\beta_3} \tag{5.5}$$

This model is popular because of both its ease of estimation and its intuitive appeal. For instance, Equation 5.5 may be transformed to a simple linear relationship in logarithms (and adding an error term) as follows:

$$\log Y = \log \alpha + \beta_1 \log A + \beta_2 \log P + \beta_3 \log M + \epsilon \tag{5.6}$$

and the parameters $\log \alpha$, β_1, β_2, and β_3 can be estimated by the standard least-squares technique. Most computer regression packages allow the transformation from Equation 5.5 to Equation 5.6 by merely changing one or two commands, thus making it unnecessary for the researcher to convert all data to logarithmic values by hand.

The intuitive appeal of this multiplicative exponential functional form is based on the fact that the marginal impact of any one independent variable is interdependent with the value of all other independent variables in the equation. In the Sherwin-Williams example, the marginal impact of a change in price on quantity demanded is dependent not only on the price change but also on the level of promotional expenditures and income.

Demand functions in the multiplicative exponential form possess the useful feature that the *elasticities are constant* over the range of data used in estimating the parameters and are equal to the estimated values of the respective parameters.[8]

In the Sherwin-Williams example, the price elasticity of demand is defined as

$$E_D = \frac{\partial Y}{\partial P} \cdot \frac{P}{Y} \tag{5.7}$$

Differentiating Equation 5.5 with respect to price results in

$$\frac{\partial Y}{\partial P} = \beta_2 \alpha A^{\beta_1} P^{\beta_2-1} M^{\beta_3} \tag{5.8}$$

Hence

$$E_D = \beta_2 \alpha A^{\beta_1} P^{\beta_2-1} M^{\beta_3} \left(\frac{P}{M}\right) \tag{5.9}$$

Substituting Equation 5.5 for Y and canceling and combining terms where possible yields

$$E_D = \beta_2$$

The property of constant elasticity is useful, because it means that a given percentage change in one of the independent variables, such as price or income, will result in the

---

[8] Note that a constant percentage increase in an exponential function plots as a straight line on a logarithmic graph. This is illustrated in the context of cost analysis in Appendix 10A, Figures 10A.1 and 10A.2.

same proportionate percentage change in quantity demanded at all points on the demand curve. This is a peculiar property of the multiplicative exponential demand function in comparison with the more typical linear demand function. As was shown earlier, the elasticity of a linear function changes over the entire range of the demand curve. However, pricing analysts at Sherwin-Williams may be able to tell us that the percentage change in quantity demanded for either a 10 percent price increase or a 10 percent price cut is a constant 15 percent. If so, a multiplicative exponential demand model is appropriate.

The cautions against extrapolating the results from the estimated equation too far beyond the values of the data used in obtaining the original parameter estimates are just as applicable for the multiplicative or any other specified form of the demand equation as for the linear equation. For example, prior to 1980, the growth in peak electric demand was exponential. Utility companies planned additions to capacity to meet this demand growth. However, this exponential growth relationship ceased to hold after 1980, resulting in massive overbuilding of electric generating capacity and increasing the pressure to restructure the industry to bring the forces of competition to bear on the situation.

Having completed the discussion of the first three steps in estimating a demand function, we now focus on the statistical techniques used to estimate the parameters of the demand model and make forecasts of demand.

SIMPLE LINEAR REGRESSION MODEL

The analysis in this section is limited to the case of one independent and one dependent variable (two-variable case), where the form of the relationship between the two variables is *linear*.[9]

$$Y = \alpha + \beta X + \epsilon \qquad [5.10]$$

The simple linear regression model that is used in this problem involves several basic underlying assumptions.

Assumptions Underlying the Simple Linear Regression Model[10]

A standard convention in regression analysis, which will be followed here, is to use X to represent the independent variable and Y to represent the dependent variable.[11]

Assumption 1   The value of the dependent variable Y is postulated to be a random variable, which is dependent on fixed (i.e., nonrandom) values of the independent variable X.[12]

Assumption 2   A theoretical straight-line relationship (see Figure 5.1) exists between X and the expected value of Y for each of the possible values of X. This theoretical regression line

$$E(Y \mid X) = \alpha + \beta X \qquad [5.11]$$

---

[9] Nonlinear relationships are considered in the appendix for this chapter.

[10] See L. Lardaro *Applied Econometrics* (New York: Harper Collins College Publishers, 1993), chap. 4, for an expanded discussion of the assumptions underlying simple linear regression.

[11] Capitalized letters X and Y represent the *name* of the random variables. Lower case x and y represent *specific values* of the random variables.

[12] Stochastic (i.e., random) values of the independent variable are addressed later in the chapter under simultaneous equations regression.

FIGURE   5.1

Theoretical Regression
Line

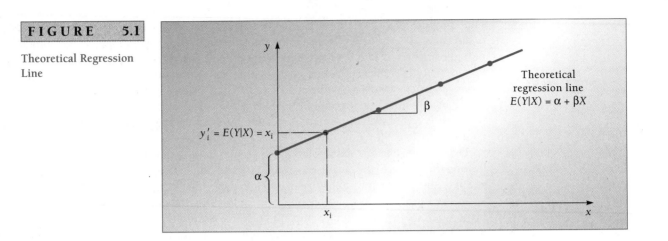

has a slope of β and an intercept of α. The regression coefficients α and β constitute population parameters whose values are unknown and we desire to estimate them.

Assumption 3   Associated with each value of X is a probability distribution, $f(y|x)$, of the possible values of the random variable Y. When X is set equal to some value x_i, the value of Y that is observed will be drawn from the $f(y|x_i)$ probability distribution and will not necessarily lie on the theoretical regression line (see Figure 5.2). When a sample of n pairs of observations is collected, a series of (x_i, y_i) values is obtained that is scattered around the theoretical regression line (see Figure 5.3). If ϵ_i is the *deviation* of the *observed* y_i value from the true theoretical value y_i', then

$$y_i = y_i' + \epsilon_i \qquad\qquad [5.12]$$

$$y_i = \alpha + \beta x_i + \epsilon_i$$

or, in general, the *theoretical regression equation* becomes

$$Y = \alpha + \beta X + \epsilon \qquad\qquad [5.13]$$

where ϵ is called the *stochastic disturbance* (or *error*) *term*.

Assumption 4   The disturbance term (ϵ_i) is assumed to be an independent random variable [that is, $E(\epsilon_i \epsilon_j) = 0$ for $i \neq j$] with an expected value equal to zero [that is, $E(\epsilon_i) = 0$] and with a constant variance equal to σ_ϵ^2 [that is, $E(\epsilon_i^2) = \sigma_\epsilon^2$ for all i]. Furthermore, to perform the statistical tests of significance (i.e., t-tests and F-tests) later in the chapter, we also must assume that the disturbance term (ϵ_i) follows the normal probability distribution.

Together, assumptions 1 and 4 imply that the disturbance term is expected to be uncorrelated with the independent variables in the regression model.

Estimating the Population Regression Coefficients

Once the regression model is specified, the unknown values of the population regression coefficients α and β are estimated by using the n pairs of sample observations $(x_1, y_1), (x_2, y_2), \ldots, (x_n, y_n)$. This process involves finding a *sample regression line* that best fits the sample of observations the analyst has gathered.

Conditional Probability
Distribution of
Dependent Variable

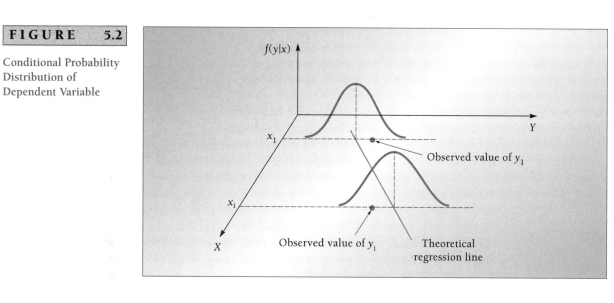

Deviation of the
Observations about the
Theoretical Regression
Line

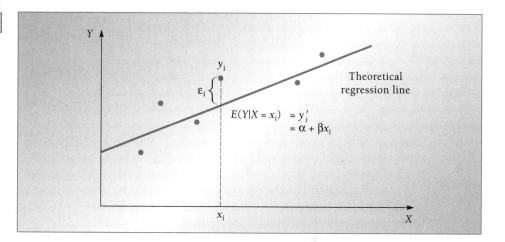

The sample estimates of α and β can be designated by a and b, respectively. The estimated or predicted value of Y, y_i' for a given value of X (see Figure 5.4) is

$$y_i' = a + bx_i \qquad [5.14]$$

Letting e_i be the *deviation* of the *observed* y_i value from the *estimated value* y_i', then

$$y_i = y_i' + e_i$$
$$= a + bx_i + e_i \qquad [5.15]$$

or, in general, the *sample regression equation* becomes

$$Y = a + bX + e \qquad [5.16]$$

Although there are several methods for determining the values of a and b (that is, finding the regression equation that provides the best fit to the series of observations), the best known and most widely used is the method of *least squares*. The objective of least-squares analysis is to find values of a and b that *minimize* the sum of the squares of

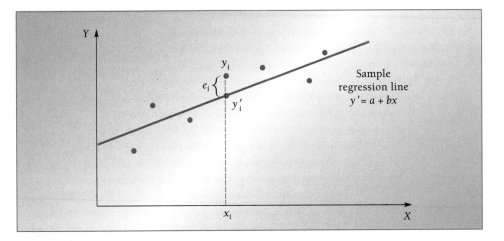

the e_i deviations. (By squaring the errors, positive and negative errors cumulate and do not cancel each other out.) From Equation 5.15, the value of e_i is given by

$$e_i = y_i - a - bx_i \tag{5.17}$$

Squaring this term and summing over all n pairs of sample observations, one obtains

$$\sum_{i=1}^{n} e_i^2 = \sum_{i=1}^{n} (y_i - a - bx_i)^2 \tag{5.18}$$

Using calculus, the values of a and b that minimize this sum of squared deviations expression are given by

$$b = \frac{n\Sigma x_i y_i - \Sigma x_i \Sigma y_i}{n\Sigma x_i^2 - (\Sigma x_i)^2} \tag{5.19}$$

$$a = \bar{y} - b\bar{x} \tag{5.20}$$

where $\bar{x}$ and $\bar{y}$ are the arithmetic means of X and Y, respectively (that is, $\bar{x} = \Sigma x /n$ and $\bar{y} = \Sigma y/n$) and where the summations range over all the observations ($i = 1, 2, \ldots, n$).

ESTIMATING REGRESSION PARAMETERS: SHERWIN-WILLIAMS COMPANY (CONTINUED)

Returning to the Sherwin-Williams Company example, suppose that only promotional expenditures are used to predict paint sales. Using the notation of the simple linear regression model, Y will be used to represent paint sales and X to represent promotional expenditures. The regression model can be represented by Equation 5.13 discussed earlier. If promotional expenditures are used to predict paint sales in a given metropolitan area, then estimates of α and β must be calculated from the sample data presented earlier in Table 5.1. These data are reproduced here in columns 1–3 of Table 5.2 and shown graphically in Figure 5.5.

The estimated slope of the regression line is calculated as follows using Equation 5.19:

$$b = \frac{10(229,100) - (1,250)(1,750)}{10(180,100) - (1,250)^2}$$

$$= .433962$$

TABLE 5.2	Sales Region (1) i	Promotional Expenditures (× $1,000) (2) x_i	Sales (× 1,000 gal) (3) y_i	(4) x_iy_i	(5) x_i^2	(6) y_i^2
Worksheet for Estimation of the Simple Regression Equation: Sherwin-Williams Company	1	150	160	24,000	22,500	25,600
	2	160	220	35,200	25,600	48,400
	3	50	140	7,000	2,500	19,600
	4	190	190	36,100	36,100	36,100
	5	90	130	11,700	8,100	16,900
	6	60	160	9,600	3,600	25,600
	7	140	200	28,000	19,600	40,000
	8	110	150	16,500	12,100	22,500
	9	200	210	42,000	40,000	44,100
	10	100	190	19,000	10,000	36,100
	Total	1,250	1,750	229,100	180,100	314,900
		Σx_i	Σy_i	Σx_iy_i	Σx_i^2	Σy_i^2

$$\bar{x} = \Sigma x_i/n = 1,250/10 = 125$$
$$\bar{y} = \Sigma y_i/n = 1,750/10 = 175$$

Similarly, using Equation 5.20 the intercept is estimated as

$$a = 175 - .433962(125)$$

$$= 120.75475$$

Therefore, the equation for estimating paint sales (in thousands of gallons) based on promotional expenditures (in thousands of dollars) is

$$Y = 120.755 + .434X \qquad [5.21]$$

and is graphed in Figure 5.5. The coefficient of X (.434) indicates that for a one-unit increase in X ($1,000 in additional promotional expenditures), expected sales (Y) will increase by .434 (×1,000) = 434 gallons in a given sales region.

Using the Regression Equation to Make Predictions

A regression equation can be used to make predictions concerning the value of Y, given any particular value of X. This is done by substituting the particular value of X, namely, x_p, into the sample regression equation (Equation 5.14):

$$y' = a + bx_p$$

where, recall, y' the hypothesized expected value for the dependent variable from the probability distribution $f(Y/X)$.[13]

Suppose one is interested in estimating Sherwin-Williams' paint sales for a metropolitan area with promotional expenditures equal to $185,000 (i.e., $x_p = 185$).

---

[13] The expected value of the error term (e) is zero, as indicated earlier in assumption 4.

FIGURE   5.5

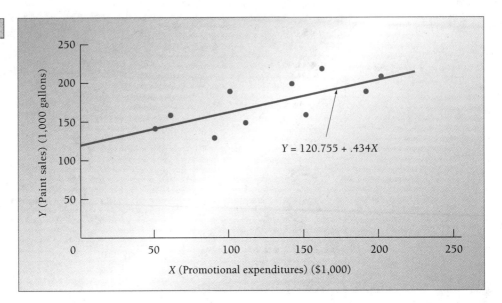

FIGURE   5.5

Estimated Regression
Line: Sherwin-Williams
Company

$$Y = 120.755 + .434X$$

Substituting $x_p = 185$ into the estimated regression equation (Equation 5.21) yields

$$y' = 120.755 + .434 (185)$$

$$= 201.045$$

or 201,045 gallons.

Caution must be exercised in using regression models for prediction, particularly when the value of the independent variable lies *outside* the range of observations from which the model was estimated. In many cases the linear relationship is not valid for extremely large or small values of the independent variable. For example, suppose we want to estimate paint sales for a sales region with promotional expenditures equal to $300,000 (i.e., $x_p = 300$). Because this value of X falls well outside of the series of observations for which the regression line was calculated, we cannot be certain that the prediction of paint sales based on the linear regression model would be reasonable. Such factors as diminishing returns and the existence of saturation levels can cause relationships between economic variables to be nonlinear.

A measure of the accuracy of estimation with the regression equation can be obtained by calculating the standard deviation of the errors of prediction. The error term e_i was defined earlier in Equation 5.17 to be the difference between the observed and predicted value of the dependent variable. The standard deviation of the e_i term is calculated as

$$s_e = \sqrt{\frac{\Sigma e_i^2}{n - 2}} = \sqrt{\frac{\Sigma(y_i - a - bx_i)^2}{n - 2}}$$

or, when this expression is simplified, by

$$s_e = \sqrt{\frac{\Sigma y_i^2 - a\Sigma y_i - b\Sigma x_i y_i}{n - 2}} \qquad [5.22]$$

Standard Error of the Estimate
The standard deviation of the error term in a linear regression model.

If the observations are tightly clustered about the regression line, the value of s_e (also known as the **standard error of the estimate**) will be small and prediction errors will tend to be small. Conversely, if the deviations e_i between the observed and predicted values of Y are fairly large, both s_e and the prediction errors will be large.

In the Sherwin-Williams Company example, substituting the relevant data from Table 5.2 into Equation 5.22 yields

$$s_e = \sqrt{\frac{314{,}900 - 120.75475(1{,}750) - .433962(229{,}100)}{10 - 2}}$$

$$= 22.799$$

or a standard error of 22,799 gallons.

The standard error of the estimate (s_e) can be used to construct prediction *intervals* for Y.[14] An *approximate* 95 percent prediction interval is equal to[15]

$$y' \pm 2s_e \qquad\qquad [5.23]$$

Returning to the Sherwin-Williams Company example, suppose we want to construct an approximate 95 percent prediction interval for paint sales in a sales region with promotional expenditures equal to $185,000 (i.e., $x_p = 185$). Substituting $y' = 201.045$ and $s_e = 22.799$ into Equation 5.23 yields

$$201.045 \pm 2(22.799)$$

or a prediction interval from 155.447 to 246.643 (that is, from 155,447 gallons to 246,643 gallons).

Inferences about the Population Regression Coefficients

For repeated samples of size n, the sample estimates of α and β—that is, a and b—will tend to vary from sample to sample. In addition to prediction, often one of the purposes of regression analysis is testing whether the slope parameter β is equal to some particular value β_0. One standard hypothesis is to test whether β is equal to zero.[16] In such a test the concern is with determining whether X has a significant effect on Y. If β is either zero or close to zero, then the independent variable X will be of no practical benefit in predicting or explaining the value of the dependent variable Y. When $\beta = 0$, a one-unit change in X causes Y to change by zero units, and hence X has no effect on Y.

To test hypotheses about the value of β, the sampling distribution of the statistic b must be known.[17] It can be shown that b has a t-distribution with $n - 2$ degrees of

---

[14] An *exact* $(1 - k)$ percent prediction interval is a function of both the sample size (n) and how close x_p is to $\bar{x}$ and is given by the following expression:

$$y' \pm t_{k/2,n-2} s_e \sqrt{1 + \frac{1}{n} + \frac{(x_p - \bar{x})^2}{\Sigma(x_i - \bar{x})^2}}$$

where $t_{k/2,n-2}$ is the value from the t-distribution (with $n - 2$ degrees of freedom) in Table 2 of the Statistical Tables (Appendix B) in the back of the book.

[15] For large n ($n > 30$), the t-distribution approximates a normal distribution and the t-value for a 95 percent prediction interval approaches 1.96 or approximately 2. For most applications, the approximation methods give satisfactory results.

[16] The intercept parameter, α, is of less interest in most economic studies and will be excluded from further analysis.

[17] In addition to testing hypotheses about β, one can also calculate confidence intervals for β. See L. Lardaro, *Applied Econometrics* (New York: HarperCollins, 1993), pp. 225–226 for a discussion of the procedures for calculating confidence intervals.

freedom.[18,19] The mean of this distribution is equal to the true underlying regression coefficient β, and an estimate of the standard deviation can be calculated as

$$s_b = \sqrt{\frac{s_e^2}{\Sigma x_i^2 - (\Sigma x_i)^2/n}}$$ [5.24]

where s_e is the standard deviation of the error terms from Equation 5.22.

Suppose that we want to test the null hypothesis:

$$H_0: \beta = \beta_0$$

against the alternative hypothesis:

$$H_a: \beta \neq \beta_0$$

at the k percent level of significance.[20] We calculate the statistic

$$t = \frac{b - \beta_0}{s_b}$$ [5.25]

and the decision is to reject the null hypothesis, if t is either less than $-t_{k/2,n-2}$ or greater than $+ t_{k/2,n-2}$ where the $t_{k/2,n-2}$ value is obtained from the t-distribution (with $n - 2$ degrees of freedom) in Table 2 (Appendix B).[21] Business applications of hypothesis testing are well advised to keep k small (i.e., no larger than 1 percent or 5 percent). One cannot justify building a marketing plan around advertising and retail displays incurring millions of dollars of promotional expense unless the demand estimation yields a very high degree of confidence that promotional expenditures actually "drive" sales (i.e., $\beta \neq 0$).

In the Sherwin-Williams Company example, suppose that we want to test (at the $k = .05$ level of significance) whether promotional expenditures is a useful variable

---

[18] A t-test is usually used to test for the significance of individual regression parameters when the sample size is relatively small (30 or less). For larger samples, tests of statistical significance may be made using the standard normal probability distribution, which the t-distribution approaches in the limit.

[19] *Degrees of freedom* are the number of observations beyond the minimum necessary to calculate a given regression coefficient or statistic. In a regression model, the number of degrees of freedom is equal to the number of observations less the number of parameters (α and βs) being estimated. For example, in a simple (two-variable) regression model, a minimum of two observations is needed to calculate the slope (β) and intercept (α) parameters—hence the number of degrees of freedom is equal to the number of observations minus two.

[20] The *level of significance* (k) used in testing hypotheses indicates the probability of making an incorrect decision with the decision rule—that is, rejecting the null hypothesis when it is true. For example, with H_0: $\beta = 0$, setting k equal .05 (i.e., 5 percent) indicates that there is one chance in 20 that we will conclude that an effect (positive or negative) exists when no effect is present—i.e., a 5 percent chance of "false positive" outcomes. Medical researchers trying to identify statistically significant therapies that could save lives and research and development (R&D) researchers trying to identify potential blockbuster drugs worry more about reducing the risk of "false negatives"—i.e., of concluding they have nothing when their research could save a life or a company. Medical and R&D researchers therefore often perform hypothesis tests with $k = 0.35$ (i.e., with 65 percent confidence that the null hypothesis $\beta = 0$ should be rejected).

[21] *One-tail* tests can also be performed. To test H_0: $\beta \leq \beta_0$ against H_a: $\beta > \beta_0$, one calculates t using Equation 5.25 and rejects H_0 at the k level of significance of $t > t_{k,n-2}$, where $t_{k,n-2}$ is obtained from the t-distribution (Table 2 of Appendix B) with $n - 2$ degrees of freedom. Similarly, to test H_0: $\beta \geq \beta_0$ against H_a: $\beta < \beta_0$, one calculates t using Equation 5.25 and rejects H_0 at the k level of significance if $t < - t_{k,n-2}$.

in predicting paint sales. In effect, we wish to perform a statistical test to determine whether the sample value—that is, $b = .433962$—is significantly different from zero. The null and alternative hypotheses are

$$H_0: \beta = 0 \text{ (No relationship between } X \text{ and } Y)$$

$$H_a: \beta \neq 0 \text{ (Linear relationship between } X \text{ and } Y)$$

Because there were 10 observations in the sample used to compute the regression equation, the sample statistic b will have a t-distribution with $8(=n-2)$ degrees of freedom. From the t-distribution (Table 2 of Appendix B), we obtain a value of 2.306 for $t_{.025,8}$. Therefore, the decision rule is to reject H_0—in other words, to conclude that $\beta \neq 0$ and that a statistically significant relationship exists between promotional expenditures and paint sales—if the calculated value of t is either less than -2.306 or greater than $+2.306$.

Using Equation 5.24, s_b is calculated as

$$s_b = \sqrt{\frac{(22.799)^2}{180,100 - (1,250)^2/10}}$$

$$= .14763$$

The calculated value of t, from Equation 5.25 becomes

$$t = \frac{.433962 - 0}{.14763}$$

$$= 2.939$$

Because this value is greater than $+2.306$, we reject H_0. Therefore, based on the sample evidence, we conclude at the 5 percent level of significance that a linear, positive relationship exists between promotional expenditures and paint sales.

Correlation Coefficient

In linear correlation analysis we can determine the strength or degree to which two variables tend to vary together. In other words, we analyze the extent to which high (or low) values of one variable tend to be associated with high (or low) values of the other variable. In linear correlation analysis it is unnecessary to label the variables under consideration as being either dependent or independent. The measure of the degree of association between two variables is called the linear *correlation coefficient*. Given n pairs of observations from the population, $(x_1, y_1), (x_2, y_2), \ldots, (x_n, y_n)$, the sample correlation coefficient is defined as

$$r = \frac{\Sigma(x_i - \bar{x})(y_i - \bar{y})}{\sqrt{\Sigma(x_i - \bar{x})^2 \Sigma(y_i - \bar{y})^2}}$$

and, when this expression is simplified, calculated as

$$r = \frac{n\Sigma x_i y_i - \Sigma x_i \Sigma y_i}{\sqrt{[n\Sigma x_i^2 - (\Sigma x_i)^2][n\Sigma y_i^2 - (\Sigma y_i)^2]}} \qquad [5.26]$$

The value of the correlation coefficient (r) ranges from $+1$ for two variables with perfect positive correlation to -1 for two variables with perfect negative correlation. Figures 5.6 (a) and (b) illustrate two variables that exhibit perfect positive and negative correlation, respectively. Very few, if any, relationships between economic variables exhibit perfect correlation. Figure 5.6(c) illustrates zero correlation—no discernible relationship exists between

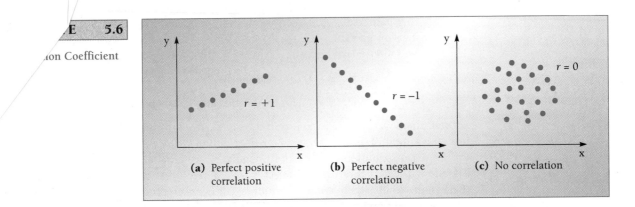

(a) Perfect positive correlation

(b) Perfect negative correlation

(c) No correlation

the observed values of the two variables. A positive correlation coefficient indicates that high values of one variable tend to be associated with high values of the other variable, whereas a negative correlation coefficient indicates just the opposite—high values of one variable tend to be associated with low values of the other variable.

The Sherwin-Williams Company example discussed earlier can be used to illustrate the calculation of the sample correlation coefficient. Substituting the relevant quantities from Table 5.2 into Equation 5.26, we obtain a value of

$$r = \frac{10(229,100) - (1,250)(1,750)}{\sqrt{[10(180,100) - (1,250)^2][10(314,900) - (1,750)^2]}}$$

$$= .72059 \text{ or } .721$$

for the correlation between the sample observations of promotional expenditures and paint sales.[22]

Correlation analysis is useful in exploratory studies of the relationships among economic variables. The information obtained in the correlation analysis can then be used as a guide in building descriptive models of economic phenomena that can serve as a basis for prediction and decision making.

The Analysis of Variance

The section on "Estimating the Population Regression Coefficients" illustrated a method for testing the statistical significance of individual regression coefficients. Now we will examine some techniques for evaluating the overall "fit" of the regression line to the sample of observations.

We begin by examining a typical observation (y_i) in Figure 5.7. Suppose we want to predict the value of Y for a value of X equal to x_i. While ignoring the regression line for the moment, what error is incurred if we use the average value of Y (that is, $\bar{y}$) as the best estimate of Y? The graph shows that the error involved, labeled the "total error," is the difference between the observed value (y_i) and $\bar{y}$. Suppose we now use the sample regression line to estimate Y. The best estimate of Y, given $X = x_i$, is y_i'. As a result of using the regression line to estimate Y, the estimation error has been reduced to the difference between the observed value (y_i) and y_i'. In the graph, the total error $(y_i - \bar{y})$ has

---

[22] Statistical techniques exist for testing whether the degree of correlation within the population is significantly different from zero. See D. R. Anderson, D. J. Sweeney, and T. A. Williams, *Statistics for Business and Economics,* 5th ed. (St. Paul, Minn.: West, 1993), for a discussion of these techniques.

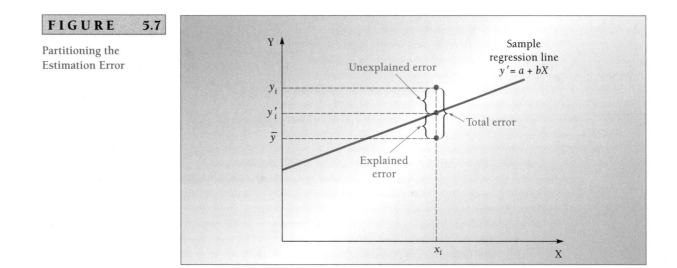

FIGURE   5.7

Partitioning the
Estimation Error

been partitioned into two parts—the unexplained portion of the total error $(y_i - y_i')$ and that portion of the total error explained by the regression line $(y_i' - \bar{y})$; that is,

Total error = Unexplained error + Explained error

$$(y_i - \bar{y}) = (y_i - y_i') + (y_i' - \bar{y})$$

If we decompose the total error of each observation in the sample using this procedure and then sum the squares of both sides of the equation, we obtain (after some algebraic simplification):[23]

Total SS = Unexplained SS + Explained SS

$$\Sigma(y_i - \bar{y})^2 = \Sigma(y_i - y_i')^2 + \Sigma(y_i' - \bar{y})^2 \qquad [5.27]$$

This equation indicates that the sum of the squared errors, over all the observations in the sample, can be partitioned into two independent parts—the Unexplained SS and the Explained SS.

By using this sum-of-squares analysis, we can now illustrate two techniques for evaluating the overall explanatory power of the regression equation. One measure of the fit of the regression line to the sample observations is the sample **coefficient of determination.** The coefficient of determination (r^2) is equal to the ratio of the Explained SS to the Total SS:

**Coefficient of
Determination**
A measure of the
proportion of total variation
in the dependent variable
that is explained by the
independent variable(s).

$$r^2 = \frac{(y_i' - \bar{y})^2}{(y_i - \bar{y})^2} \qquad [5.28]$$

It measures the proportion of the variation in the dependent variable that is explained by the regression line (the independent variable). The coefficient of determination ranges in value from 0—when none of the variation in Y is explained by the regression—to 1—when all the variation in Y is explained by regression.

Table 5.3 shows the calculation of the Explained, Unexplained, and Total SS for the Sherwin-Williams Company example that was introduced earlier.[24] The Explained SS is

---

[23] A standard convention in statistics is to let "SS" represent the "Sum of Squares" or, more accurately the "Sum of Squared Errors."

[24] Only two of the three SS need to be calculated in the manner shown in Table 5.3, because the third SS can be obtained from Equation 5.27 once the other two SS are calculated.

			$y' =$ 120.75475 + .433962 x_i	Explained SS $(y_i' - \bar{y})^2$	Unexplained SS $(y_i - y_i^1)^2$	Total SS $(y_i - \bar{y})^2$
i	x_i	y_i				
1	150	160	185.849	117.702	668.171	225.000
2	160	220	190.189	230.696	888.696	2,025.000
3	50	140	142.453	1,059.317	6.017	1,225.000
4	190	190	203.208	795.665	174.451	225.000
5	90	130	159.811	230.696	888.696	2,025.000
6	60	160	146.792	795.665	174.451	225.000
7	140	200	181.509	42.373	341.917	625.000
8	110	150	168.491	42.373	341.917	625.000
9	200	210	207.547	1,059.317	6.017	1,225.000
10	100	190	164.151	117.702	668.171	225.000
				4,491.506	4,158.504	8,650.000*
				$\Sigma(y_i' - \bar{y})^2$	$\Sigma(y_i - y_i')^2$	$\Sigma(y_i - \bar{y})^2$

TABLE 5.3

Calculation of the Explained, Unexplained, and Total SS for the Sherwin-Williams Company

*"Total SS" differs slightly from the sum of "Explained SS" and "Unexplained SS" because of rounding.

4,491.506 and the Total SS is 8,650.000, and therefore, by Equation 5.28 the coefficient of determination is

$$r^2 = \frac{4,491.506}{8,650.000}$$

$$= .519$$

The regression equation, with promotional expenditures as the independent variable, explains about 52 percent of the variation in paint sales in the sample. Note also that, in the two-variable linear regression model, the coefficient of determination is equal to the square of the correlation coefficient, i.e., $r^2 = .519 = (r)^2 = (.72059)^2$.

A second technique for evaluating the explanatory power of the regression equation is an F-test of the sources of variation within the sample data.[25] Using the sum-of-squares framework discussed above, an analysis of variance table is constructed as shown in Table 5.4. The F-ratio

$$F = \frac{SSR}{SSE/d.f.} \tag{5.29}$$

then can be used to test whether the estimated regression equation explains a significant proportion of the variation in the dependent variable. The decision is to reject the null hypothesis of no relationship between X and Y (that is, no explanatory power) at the k level of significance if the calculated F-ratio is greater than the $F_{k,1,n-2}$ value obtained from the F-distribution in Table 3 of the Statistical Tables (Appendix B).

---

[25] For the simple (two-variable) regression model, the F-test can be shown to be equivalent to the t-test discussed in the section, "Inferences about the Population Regression Coefficients," for testing whether $\beta = 0$. See J. Johnston, *Econometric Methods* (New York: McGraw-Hill, 1984), sec. 2.6. For the multiple linear regression model (discussed in the section, "Multiple Linear Regression Model"), the F-test is used to test the hypothesis that *all* the regression coefficients are zero.

TABLE   5.4

Analysis of Variance
Table for Regression
Model

Source of Variation	Sum of Squares	Degrees of Freedom
Regression $\left(\begin{array}{c}\text{explained}\\ \text{variation}\end{array}\right)$	$\text{SSR} = \Sigma(y_i' - \bar{y})^2$	1
Error $\left(\begin{array}{c}\text{unexplained}\\ \text{variation}\end{array}\right)$	$\text{SSE} = \Sigma(y_i - y_i')^2$ $= 4{,}158.5$	$n - 2$
Total	$\text{SST} = \Sigma(y_i - \bar{y})^2$ $= 8{,}650$	$n - 1$

An analysis of variance table for the Sherwin-Williams Company example appears in Table 5.4. Forming the F-ratio, we obtain

$$F = \frac{4{,}491.506}{4{,}158.5/8}$$

$$= 8.641$$

The value of $F_{.05,1,8}$ from the F-distribution (Table 3 of Appendix B) is 5.32. Therefore, we reject, at the .05 level of significance, the null hypothesis that there is no relationship between promotion expenditures and paint sales. In other words, we conclude that the regression model *does* explain a significant proportion of the variation in paint sales in the sample.

Association and Causation

Based on the finding of a statistically significant regression relationship, one may be tempted to conclude that a causal economic relationship exists—the independent variable being the cause and the dependent variable being the effect. However, *the presence of association (correlation) does not necessarily imply causation.* Statistical tests can only establish whether association exists between the variables. The existence of a cause-and-effect economic relationship can only be inferred from economic reasoning.

An association relationship may not imply a causal relationship for many reasons. First, even a 95 percent statistically significant association between two variables may result from 5 percent pure chance. Second, the association between two variables may be the result of the influence of a third common factor. For example, although per capita expenditures for food and clothing exhibit a close relationship over time, one cannot conclude that increases in food expenditures cause increases in clothing expenditures. The high degree of association between these variables can be attributed to a third variable—namely, per capita income. As per capita income increases over time, people tend to spend more on both food and clothing. Finally, both variables may be the cause and the effect at the same time. In other words, a simultaneous or interdependent relationship may exist between the variables. For example, one could hypothesize that a person's income is a function of his or her level of education—the more years of schooling the person has, the higher will be the income. However, one could argue that the opposite relationship is also true—namely, that education level is a function of income.

A higher income increases the likelihood that a person will be able to afford additional college or professional education.

MULTIPLE LINEAR REGRESSION MODEL

A functional relationship containing two or more independent variables is known as a *multiple linear regression model*. In the (completely) general multiple linear regression model, the dependent variable Y is hypothesized to be a function of m independent variables $X_1, X_2, \ldots, X_m$, and to be of the form

$$Y = \alpha + \beta_1 X_1 + \beta_2 X_2 + \cdots + \beta_m X_m + \epsilon \qquad [5.30]$$

In the Sherwin-Williams Company example, paint sales (Y) were hypothesized to be a function of three variables—promotional expenditures (A), price (P), and household disposable income (M) (see Equation 5.1):

$$Y = \alpha + \beta_1 A + \beta_2 P + \beta_3 M + \epsilon$$

Assumptions Underlying the Multiple Linear Regression Model   In addition to satisfying a set of four assumptions (or postulates) similar to those for the simple linear regression model (discussed earlier in the chapter), the application of the least-squares estimation procedure to the multiple linear regression model requires two further assumptions.

Assumption 5   The number of observations (n) must exceed the number of parameters to be estimated ($m + 1$).

Assumption 6   No exact linear relationships can exist between any of the independent variables. A definitional relationship or identity, like cash in the register is equal to initial cash plus receipts, cannot be estimated unless there is some source of randomness in the data. For example, the clerk on duty may commit occasional errors in making change.

Use of Computer Programs

Using matrix algebra, procedures similar to those explained for the simple linear regression model can be employed for calculating the estimated regression coefficients (a, b's) of Equation 5.30 and testing the statistical significance of the individual independent variables and overall explanatory power of the regression equation.[26] In most practical applications of multiple regression analysis, generalized computer programs are used in performing these procedures on a given set of data.

Although many different programs are available for doing multiple regression analysis, the output of these programs is fairly standardized. The output normally includes the estimated regression coefficients, t-statistics of the individual coefficients, R^2, analysis of variance, and F-test of overall significance. The particular program that is illustrated here is MYSTAT.[27]

Putting the data in Table 5.1 for the Sherwin-Williams Company along with the appropriate control statements into the MYSTAT program yields the output shown in Figure 5.8.

---

[26] See Lardaro, *Applied Econometrics,* (New York: HarperCollins, 1993), chap. 6, for a discussion of the multiple linear regression model.

[27] See MYSTAT (Evanston, Ill.: Systat, Inc., 1989). MYSTAT is a product of Systat, Inc., Evanston, Ill.

FIGURE   5.8   Computer Output: Sherwin-Williams Company

```
Dep var:   SALES (Y)   N:    10   Multiple R:    .889   Squared multiple R:    .790

Adjusted squared multiple R:       .684        Standard error of estimate:       17.417

   Variable     Coefficient   Std error    Std coef Tolerance      T         P(2 tail)


CONSTANT           310.245       95.075       0.000   .             3.263       0.017
 PROMEXP (X₁)        0.008        0.204       0.013  0.3054426      0.038       0.971
 SELLPR  (X₂)      -12.202        4.582      -0.741  0.4529372     -2.663       0.037
 DISPINC (X₃)        2.677        3.160       0.225  0.4961686      0.847       0.429




                          Analysis of Variance


   Source     Sum-of-squares    DF    Mean-square     F-ratio        P

Regression       6829.866        3     2276.622        7.505       0.019
  Residual       1820.134        6      303.356
```

Estimating the Population Regression Coefficients

From the computer output (coefficient column) the following regression equation is obtained:

$$Y = 310.245 + 0.008A - 12.202P + 2.677M \qquad [5.31]$$

The coefficient of the P variable (-12.202) indicates that, *all other things being equal*, a $1.00 price increase will reduce expected sales by $-12.202 \times 1,000$ or 12,202 gallons in a given sales region.

Using the Regression Model to Make Forecasts

As in the simple linear regression model, the multiple linear regression model can be used to make point or interval forecasts. Point forecasts can be made by substituting the particular values of the independent variables into the estimated regression equation.

In the Sherwin-Williams example, suppose we are interested in estimating sales in a sales region where promotional expenditures are $185,000 (i.e., $A = 185$), selling price is $15.00 ($P$), and disposable income per household is $19,500 (i.e., $M = 19.5$). Substituting these values into Equation 5.31 yields

$$y' = 310.245 + .008(185) - 12.202(15.00) + 2.677(19.5) = 180.897$$

or 180,897 gallons. Whether to include one, two, or all three independent variables in predicting y' depends on the mean prediction error (e.g., here $185,000 - 180,897 = 4,103$) in this and subsequent out-of-sample forecasts.

The standard error of the estimate (s_e) from the output in Figure 5.8 can be used to construct prediction intervals for Y. An *approximate* 95 percent prediction interval is equal to

$$y' \pm 2s_e$$

For a sales region with the characteristics cited in the previous paragraph (i.e., $A = 185$, $P = \$15.00$, and $M = 19.5$), an *approximate* 95 percent prediction interval for paint sales is equal to

$$180.897 \pm 2(17.417)$$

or from 146,063 to 215,731 gallons.

Inferences about the Population Regression Coefficients

Most regression programs test whether *each* of the independent variables (Xs) is statistically significant in explaining the dependent variable (Y). This tests the null hypothesis:

$$H_0: \beta_i = 0$$

against the alternative hypothesis:

$$H_a: \beta_i \neq 0$$

The decision rule is to reject the null hypothesis at the k level of significance if the t-value (labeled T) from the computer output ($t = b/s_b$) is either less than $-t_{k/2,n-m-1}$ or greater than $+t_{k/2,n-m-1}$ where the $t_{k/2,n-m-1}$ value is obtained from the t-distribution (with $n-m-1$ degrees of freedom) in Table 2 in the Tables (Appendix B).[28]
To test the null hypothesis of no relationship between paint sales (Y) and each of the independent variables at the .05 significance level, we would reject the null hypothesis if the respective t-value for each variable is less than $-t_{.025,6} = -2.447$ or greater than $t_{.025,6} = +2.447$. As shown in Figure 5.8, only the calculated t-value for the P variable is less than -2.447. Hence, we can conclude that only selling price (P) is statistically significant (at the .05 level) in explaining paint sales. This inference might determine that marketing plans for this type of paint should focus on price and not on the effects of promotional expenditures or the disposable income of the target households.

The Analysis of Variance

Techniques similar to those described for the simple linear regression model are used to evaluate the *overall* explanatory power of the multiple linear regression model.
The multiple coefficient of determination (r^2) is a measure of the overall "fit" of the model. The squared multiple R value of .790 in Figure 5.8 indicates that the three-variable regression equation explains 79 percent of the total variation in the dependent variable (paint sales).
The F-value (labeled F-ratio in the computer output of Figure 5.8) is used to test the hypothesis that the independent variables ($X_1, X_2, \ldots, X_m$) explain a significant proportion of the variation in the dependent variable (Y). One is using the F-value to test the null hypothesis:

$$H_0: \text{All } \beta_i = 0$$

against the alternative hypothesis:

$$H_a: \text{At least one } \beta_i \neq 0$$

---

[28] Rather than having to look up the $t_{k/2,n-m-1}$ in the table, MYSTAT calculates the significance level at which one can reject the null hypothesis ($\beta_i = 0$). For example, if we are testing the null hypothesis at the $k = .05$ significance level, we would reject the null hypothesis (no relationship between Y and X_i) if the P (2 tail) value from the computer output is less than .05.

In other words, we are testing whether at least one of the explanatory variables contributes information for the prediction of Y. The decision is to reject the null hypothesis at the k level of significance if the F-value from the computer output is *greater* than the $F_{k,m,n-m-1}$ value from the F-distribution (with m and $n-m-1$ degrees of freedom). Table 3 (Appendix B) provides F-values.

In the Sherwin-Williams example, suppose we want to test whether the three independent variables explain a significant (at the .05 level) proportion of the variation in income. The decision rule is to reject the null hypothesis (no relationship) if the calculated F-value is greater than $F_{05,3,6} = 4.76$. Because the F-value of 7.505 (from Figure 5.8) exceeds 4.76, we reject the null hypothesis and conclude that the independent variables *are* useful in explaining paint sales.[29]

PROBLEMS IN APPLYING THE LINEAR REGRESSION MODEL

When the simple linear and multiple linear regression models were discussed earlier in this chapter, several assumptions were made about the nature of the relationships among the variables. Questions naturally arise on the applicability or validity of these assumptions in the actual analysis of economic relationships and data. How can we determine if the assumptions are being violated in a given situation? How does the violation of the assumptions affect the parameter estimates and prediction accuracy of the model? What methods (if any) exist for overcoming the difficulties caused by the inapplicability of the assumptions in a given situation?

Econometrics provides answers to some, but not all, of these questions. A thorough treatment of them is beyond the scope of this introductory chapter.[30] The (more limited) objective in this section is to make the reader aware of some of the potential problems that can arise in actual applications of the regression models and to suggest possible techniques for overcoming some of these problems. Some of the problems that may invalidate the regression results include the following:

1. Autocorrelation
2. Heteroscedasticity
3. Specification and measurement errors
4. Multicollinearity
5. Simultaneous equation relationships and the identification problem
6. Nonlinearities

The first five of these problems are discussed in this section, and the problem of nonlinear relationships is treated in the appendix to the chapter.

Autocorrelation

In many economic modeling and prediction problems, empirical data are in the form of a *time series*—a series of observations taken on the variables at different points in time. For example, we may be interested in predicting total (domestic U.S.) television sales by

---

[29] Rather than having to look up the $F_{k,m,n-m-1}$ value in the table, MYSTAT calculates the significance level at which we can reject the null hypothesis (All $\beta_i = 0$). This is shown in the P column of the Analysis of Variance table.

[30] See Lardaro, *Applied Econometrics,* for a more detailed explanation of these methodological issues.

using disposable income as the independent variable. The data used to calculate estimates of the regression parameters (that is, *a* and *b*) might consist of a series of yearly (or quarterly) measurements of the number of television sets sold and disposable income for a period of 10 to 15 years. In working with time-series data, a problem known as **autocorrelation** can arise.

Autocorrelation
An econometric problem characterized by the existence of a significant pattern in the successive values of the error terms in a linear regression model.

Recall that one of the assumptions underlying the regression model (specifically, assumption 4) is that the disturbance term e_t must be an independent random variable. In other words, we assume that each successive error e_t, is independent of earlier and later errors so that the regression equation produces no predictable pattern in the successive values of the disturbance term. The existence of a significant pattern in the successive values of the error term constitutes *autocorrelation*. Successive values of the disturbance term can exhibit either positive or negative autocorrelation. Positive autocorrelation, as shown in Figure 5.9 (a), is inferred whenever successive positive (or negative) disturbances tend to be followed by disturbances of the *same* sign. Negative autocorrelation, as shown in Figure 5.9 (b), is inferred whenever successive positive (or negative) disturbances tend to be followed by disturbances of the *opposite* sign.

Negative autocorrelation reflects an undershooting and overshooting process like purchases of storable consumer goods. If a household buys two much breakfast cereal one week, that household will probably buy less than average the next week, and again more than average the following week. Financial market returns can also exhibit such patterns. Returns temporarily above capital market equilibrium values will set in motion arbitrage activity that corrects (perhaps overcorrects) the return back toward the trend.

Positive autocorrelation can result from several factors. One is the existence of cyclical and seasonal variation in economic variables. The overall growth of the economy coupled with business cycles causes most economic time series to have an overall upward trend with periodic upturns and downturns around this trend. Likewise, seasonal patterns can cause weekly, monthly, or quarterly data to rise and fall in a predictable manner each year. Another cause of positive autocorrelation is self-reinforcing trends in consumer purchase patterns, for example, in fashion retailing. If Hermes scarves are in fashion, each successive week of sales data will be farther above trend than the previous week until the fad slows and the Hermes look goes out of fashion. Either positive or negative autocorrelation may also result if significant explanatory variables are omitted from the regression equation or if nonlinear relationships exist.

FIGURE   5.9   Types of Autocorrelation (Numbers 1, 2, 3, . . . , 10 refer to successive time periods.)

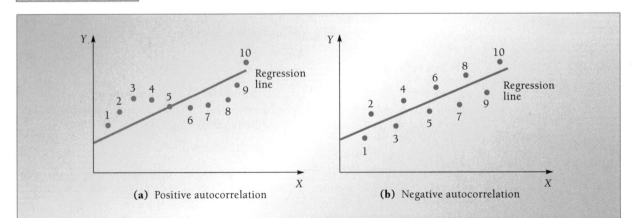

(a) Positive autocorrelation   (b) Negative autocorrelation

As a safeguard when working with time-series data, the disturbances (e_t values) should be examined for randomness. Statistical tests are also available to check for autocorrelation. One commonly used technique is the Durbin-Watson statistic. It is calculated as follows:[31]

$$d = \frac{\sum_{t=2}^{n}(e_t - e_{t-1})^2}{\sum_{t=1}^{n}e_t^2} \qquad [5.32]$$

where e_t is the estimated error term in period t and e_{t-1} is the error term in period $t - 1$. The Durbin-Watson statistic tests for first-order autocorrelation, that is, whether the error in period t is dependent on the error in the preceding period $t - 1$. The value of d ranges from 0 to 4. If there is *no* first-order autocorrelation, the expected value of d is 2. Values of d less than 2 indicate the possible presence of *positive* autocorrelation, whereas values of d greater than 2 indicate the possible presence of *negative* autocorrelation.

Formal hypothesis tests for first-order autocorrelation can be performed using the d statistic and the Durbin-Watson table (Table 6 in the Tables of Appendix B). The critical value of d from the table (at the .025 significance level for a one-tail test, that is, a test for positive autocorrelation or a test for negative autocorrelation, or at the .05 significance level for a two-tail test) is a function of both the number of observations (n) and the number of independent variables (m). The decision rules are summarized in Figure 5.10.

For example, suppose we wish to test for the presence of positive autocorrelation (at the .025 level of significance) in a regression equation with four independent variables (not counting the constant term) estimated from 25 observations. For $m = 4$ and $n = 25$, the values of d_L and d_U are 0.94 and 1.65, respectively (see Table 6, Appendix B). If the calculated d value is less than $d_L = 0.94$, one would *reject* H_0 and conclude that there is statistically significant evidence of the presence of positive autocorrelation. If the calculated d value is between 0.94 and 1.65, no conclusion could be drawn concerning the possible presence of positive autocorrelation. Finally, if the calculated d value is greater than 1.65, one would *not reject* H_0 and conclude that there is *no* statistically significant evidence of the presence of positive autocorrelation.

The presence of autocorrelation leads to several undesirable consequences in the regression results. First, although the estimates of α and β will be unbiased, the least-squares procedure will misestimate the sampling variances of these estimates. [An estimator is unbiased if its expected value is identical to the population parameter being estimated. The computed a and b values are unbiased estimators of α and β, respectively, because $E(a) = \alpha$ and $E(b) = \beta$.] In particular, the standard error (s_e in Equation 5.22) will either be inflated or deflated depending on whether we have positive or negative autocorrelation. As a result, the use of the t-statistic to test hypotheses about these parameters may yield incorrect conclusions about the importance of the individual predictor (that is, independent) variables. Second, overall measures of the fit and explanatory power of the regression model, such as the coefficient of determination (r^2) and F-test, will no longer provide reliable information about the significance of the economic relationships obtained. Finally, the use of the regression equation for prediction purposes will yield predictions with unnecessarily large sampling variances.

---

[31] Most computer regression programs will compute the Durbin-Watson statistic when specified by the user in the control statements.

| Type of Autocorrelation | One-tail Tests | | Two-tail Test* |
	Positive Autocorrelation	Negative Autocorrelation	Positive and Negative
Hypothesis			
Null	H_0: No Positive autocorrelation	H_0: No negative autocorrelation	H_0: No positive or negative autocorrelation
Alternative	H_a: Positive autocorrelation	H_a: Negative autocorrelation	H_a: Positive or negative autocorrelation
Decision Rule			
Reject H_0	$d < d_L$	$d > (4 - d_L)$	$d < d_L$ or $d > (4 - d_L)$
Do not reject H_0	$d > d_U$	$d < (4 - d_U)$	$d_U < d < (4 - d_U)$
Test is inconclusive (No conclusion can be made concerning the possible presence of autocorrelation)	$d_L \leq d \leq d_U$	$(4 - d_U) \leq d \leq (4 - d_L)$	$d_L \leq d \leq d_U$ or $(4 - d_U) \leq d \leq (4 - d_L)$

*Note that for a two-tail test, the significance level is double that shown in Table 6 of the Tables in Appendix B.

Several procedures are available for dealing with autocorrelation.[32] If one can determine the functional form of the dependence relationship in the successive values of the residuals, then the original variables can be transformed by a lag structure to remove this pattern. Another technique that may help to reduce autocorrelation is to include a new linear trend or time variable in the regression equation.[33] A third procedure is to calculate the first differences in the time series of each of the variables (that is, $Y_{t+1} - Y_t$, $X_{1,t+1} - X_{1,t}$, $X_{2,t+1} - X_{2,t}$, and so on) and then calculate the regression equation using these transformed variables. A fourth method is to include additional variables of the form X_1^2 or $X_1 X_2$ in the regression equation. Usually one of these procedures will yield satisfactory results consistent with the independent errors assumption.

Heteroscedasticity

Heteroscedasticity

An econometric problem characterized by the lack of a uniform variance of the error terms about the regression line.

In developing the ordinary least-squares regression model, another of the assumptions (assumption 4) is that the error terms have a constant variance. In other words, we assume that the observations have uniform variability about the theoretical regression line. This property is referred to as *homoscedasticity*. Departure from this assumption is known as **heteroscedasticity**, which is indicated whenever there is a systematic relationship between the absolute magnitude of the error term and the magnitude of one (or more) of the independent variables. Graphic or tabular comparisons between the absolute values of disturbance terms and the values of each of the independent variables will help to detect the existence of significant heteroscedasticity.

---

[32] See R. Pindyck and D. Rubinfeld, *Econometric Models and Economic Forecasting* (Boston, MA: Irwin-McGraw Hill, 1998) for a much more detailed discussion of procedures for dealing with autocorrelation.

[33] A linear trend variable is one in which each observation in the time series is given a successively larger integer value, such as 1, 2, 3, . . . , n, when n is the number of observations.

The presence of heteroscedasticity causes the estimate of the variance of the error terms (s_e) to be dependent on the particular set of values of the independent variables that was chosen. Another set of observations may yield a much different estimate of this variance. As a result, tests of the statistical significance of the individual regression coefficients (the t-test) and overall explanatory power of the regression equation (the F-test, r^2) may prove to be misleading.

One form of heteroscedasticity occurs when the variance of the error term increases with the size of the independent variable, such as in the case illustrated in Figure 5.11. For example, consider a regression model in which savings by households is postulated to be a function of household income. In this case it is likely that more variability will be found in the savings of high-income households compared with low-income households simply because high-income households have more money available for potential savings. Another example arising frequently with cross-sectional sales data is that the error variance with large-size retail stores, divisions, or firms exceeds the error variance for smaller entities. In many cases this form of heteroscedasticity can be reduced or eliminated by dividing all the variables in the regression equation by the independent variable that is thought to be causing the heteroscedasticity and then applying the least-squares analysis to the resulting set of transformed variables. This transformation, however, *does* alter the form of the hypothesized relationship among the variables and thus may be inappropriate in some situations. Another method for dealing with heteroscedasticity is to take logarithms of the data. Again, this transformation alters the form of the hypothesized relationship among the variables. More advanced, generalized least-squares techniques can account for the nonuniform error variance and preserve the original, hypothesized relationship.

Specification and Measurement Errors

Specification Error

An econometric problem characterized by the omission of one or more significant explanatory variables from the regression equation.

Specification errors can result whenever one or more significant explanatory variables are not included in the regression equation. If the omitted variable is moderately or highly correlated with one of the explanatory variables included in the regression equation, then the effect of the missing variable will be represented in the coefficient (b value) of the included variable. This may lead to overestimating or underestimating the economic effect of the explanatory variable included in the regression equation, that is, a

FIGURE   5.11

Illustration of Heteroscedasticity

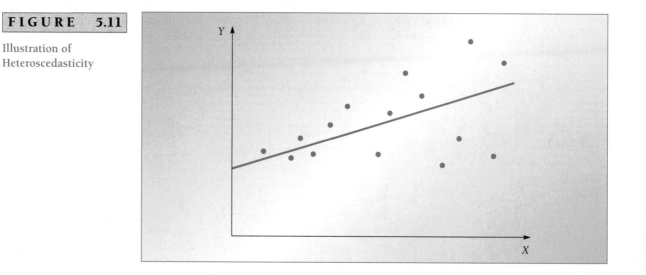

bias in the least-squares estimates of the theoretical regression coefficients (α, βs). Even if the missing variable is independent of (that is, uncorrelated with) all the other explanatory variables included in the regression equation, then the effect of the omitted variable will be to increase the magnitude of the residual errors and the resulting estimated standard deviation of the residuals (s_e). The omission of a significant explanatory variable from a time series regression equation (e.g., a time trend) may also produce autocorrelation problems.[34]

The formulation of a correctly specified model must therefore occupy a prominent role in the estimation of any economic relation. Sometimes relevant variables must be omitted because the estimation is supporting decisions that must be taken prior to complete data availability. When this occurs, a close proxy variable is often available and should be substituted for the omitted variable. The closer the proxy, the better the estimation. When no proxy is available, the direction of bias in the estimated parameters should be diagnosed. The misestimated parameter for X_1(b_1) may be written as the sum of the true parameter (β_1) plus the effect of the omitted variable j,

$$b_1 = \beta_1 + \beta_j r_{1,j} \qquad [5.33]$$

If one knows that the likely sign of the correlation coefficient between the omitted variable and the included explanatory variable ($r_{1,j}$) is positive, and if the hypothesized effect of the omitted variable on the dependent variable (β_j) is positive, the estimated parameter will be positively biased. For example, omitting household income from a demand estimation of luxury car rentals is likely to positively bias the parameter on the price variable since higher income and the price paid for a luxury car for a week are probably positively correlated and since household income itself is hypothesized to be a positive determinant of luxury car rentals. On the other hand, if the likely correlation between the omitted and the explanatory variable is negative or the hypothesized effect of the omitted variable on the dependent variable is negative, the estimated parameter will be negatively biased. In the Sherwin-Williams paint demand data, the correlation coefficient between disposable income and price is -0.514 (see Table 5.5). Omitting DISPINC from that demand estimation in Figure 5.8 would lead to a negative bias in the estimated effect of price on sales. Although these diagnoses of the omitted variable bias can never replace a fully and correctly specified model, they do allow much more informed decision making based on incomplete data.

The estimation of the parameters of the regression equation requires that a series of measurements be made on both the dependent and independent variables that are to be included in the relationship. Despite the many precautions taken, errors in the measurement of economic variables can arise. For example, the values of many economic

---

[34] Inclusion of irrelevant explanatory variables has a similar effect on the standard error of the residuals (s_e).

TABLE 5.5		SALES Y	PROMEXP X_1	SELLPR X_2	DISPINC X_3
Correlation Coefficients: Sherwin-Williams Company	SALES Y	1.000			
	PROMEXP X_1	0.721	1.000		
	SELLPR X_2	-0.866	-0.739	1.000	
	DISPINC X_3	0.615	0.710	-0.514	1.000

variables (such as unemployment, GNP, and prices) are obtained from samples, and sampling error is inherent in the data. Also, data based on a complete census of the population can contain errors caused by missing observations, interviewer biases, recording errors, and so forth. Finally, proxy variables always introduce some measurement error. Measurement errors in the dependent variable do not affect the validity of the assumptions underlying the regression model or the parameter estimates obtained by the least-squares procedure because these errors become part of the overall residual or unexplained error. However, measurement error in the explanatory variables introduces a stochastic component in the Xs and may cause the values of the error term e_i to be correlated with the observed values of these explanatory variables. Consequently, the assumption that the disturbance terms are independent random variables (assumption 4) is violated, and the resulting least-squares estimates of the regression coefficients (α, β's) are biased.

Simultaneous equation estimation techniques discussed in the next section are one method of dealing with stochastic explanatory variables. Measurement error can also be modeled, if the form of the error in the X variables can be specified.[35]

Multicollinearity

Multicollinearity
An econometric problem characterized by a high degree of intercorrelation among some or all of the explanatory variables in a regression equation.

Whenever a high degree of intercorrelation exists among some or all of the explanatory variables in the regression equation, it becomes difficult to determine the separate influences of each of the explanatory variables on the dependent variable because the standard deviations (s_b's) of their respective regression coefficients become large. Whenever two or more explanatory variables are highly correlated (or collinear), the t-test is no longer a reliable indicator of the statistical significance of the individual explanatory variables. Under such a condition, the least-squares procedure tends to yield highly unstable estimates of the regression coefficients from one sample to the next. The presence of **multicollinearity,** however, does not necessarily invalidate the use of the regression equation for prediction purposes. Provided that the intercorrelation pattern among the explanatory variables persists into the future, the equation can produce reliable forecasts of the value of the dependent variable.

A number of techniques exist for dealing with multicollinearity. One technique is to alter the model by removing all but one of the set of highly intercorrelated variables. For example, consider the variables that were used to explain paint sales in the Sherwin-Williams example discussed earlier. The correlation coefficients between each of the variables are shown in Table 5.5. The correlation coefficients between each of the possible pairs of explanatory (independent) variables are shown in the enclosed area of the table. Note the high degree of intercorrelation (in absolute value terms) between promotional expenditures and selling price and between promotional expenditures and disposable income, indicating that the standard deviations of the estimates of these three regression coefficients may be inflated. Therefore, the analyst may want to consider dropping one of these variables from the regression.[36]

When working with time-series data, another technique is to use cross-sectional data to obtain independent estimates of some of the regression parameters. Finally, the elimination of trends, through deflation procedures such as using a trend variable or first differences, will often reduce the multicollinearity problem.

---

[35] See Lardaro, *Applied Econometrics,* for some suggested procedures for overcoming the problems presented by measurement error.

[36] The analyst must carefully observe the effect of this procedure on the other parameters, however, because removing a partially collinear but relevant explanatory variable introduces omitted variable bias into the estimation.

Simultaneous Equation Relationships and the Identification Problem

Many economic relationships are characterized by simultaneous interactions. For example, recognition of simultaneous relationships is at the heart of marketing plans. The optimal advertising expenditure for a product line like Hanes Her Way hosiery depends on sales (i.e., on the quantity Hanes expects to sell). However, sales obviously also depend on advertising; a particularly effective ad campaign that just happens to match a random swing in customer fashion will drive sales substantially upward. And this sales boost will increase spending on advertising. Sales (i.e., demand) and advertising are simultaneously determined.

The emphasis of this chapter has been on building single-equation models of demand in which we attempt to explain or predict the value of one dependent variable (quantity demanded) using one or more independent variables. However, as Johnston emphasizes:

> It would appear that the most serious defect of the single-equation model is that attention is focused on a *single* equation, when the essence of economic theory is the interdependence of economic phenomena and the determination of the values of economic variables by the simultaneous interaction of relationships.[37]

The problems that are encountered in attempting to estimate the parameters in simultaneous equation relationships are beyond the scope of this introductory econometrics chapter.[38] However, one aspect—the **identification problem**—is examined below.

Identification Problem
A difficulty encountered in empirically estimating a demand function by regression analysis. This problem arises from the simultaneous relationship between two functions, such as supply and demand.

In developing demand functions from empirical data, one is faced with problems arising because of the simultaneous relationship between the demand function and the supply function. It is the interaction of the demand and supply functions that determines the price at which a product is sold. Suppose demand can be written as a function of price (P), income (M), and a random error ϵ_1,

$$Q_d = \beta_1 + \beta_2 P + \beta_3 M + \epsilon_1 \qquad [5.34]$$

and supply can be written as a function of price, input costs (I), and a random error ϵ_2,

$$Q_s = \alpha_1 + \alpha_2 P + \alpha_3 I + \epsilon_2 \qquad [5.35]$$

or rearranging,

$$P = \frac{-\alpha_1}{\alpha_2} + \frac{1}{\alpha_2}(Q_s - \epsilon_2) - \frac{\alpha_3}{\alpha_2} I \qquad [5.36]$$

Since quantity demanded will equal quantity supplied in market-clearing equilibrium (i.e., $Q_d = Q_s$), we can substitute Equation 5.34 for Q_s in 5.36 to obtain

$$P = \frac{-\alpha_1}{\alpha_2} + \frac{1}{\alpha_2}(\beta_1 + \beta_2 P + \beta_3 M + \epsilon_1 - \epsilon_2) - \frac{\alpha_3}{\alpha_2} I \qquad [5.37]$$

$$P = \frac{1}{\alpha_2 - \beta_2}(-\alpha_1 + \beta_1 + \beta_3 M + \epsilon_1 - \epsilon_2 - \alpha_3 I). \qquad [5.38]$$

---

[37] J. Johnston, *Econometric Methods,* 1st ed. (New York: McGraw-Hill, 1963), p. 146.

[38] See R. Pindyck and D. Rubinfeld, *Econometric Models and Forecasting,* 3rd ed., Chapter 12 (Boston, MA: Irwin-McGrawHill, 1998) for a more complete discussion of simultaneous equations estimation.

The price variable in 5.38 is quite obviously a stochastic explanatory variable; observed values of P will be correlated with the disturbance term in the demand function ϵ_1. An ordinary least-squares regression of Equation 5.34 therefore violates assumption 4 that disturbance terms must be independent of the Xs. As a result, the price coefficient in Equation 5.34 (β_2) will be biased.

To see the problem this poses when estimating the shape of an empirical demand function, note that one may observe only one actual price-output combination at any point in time. If one sought to estimate the demand curve for computer memory chips, one might observe historical data on quantity bought (sold) and the price at a specific time. A next step would be to plot these data on a graph, as shown in Figure 5.12. Is the line DD', drawn by connecting the four observed price-output combinations, equivalent to the demand curve for memory chips? Usually not. Although it does have the traditional negative slope of a demand curve, one cannot conclude that it represents the true demand-price relationship.

To see why this is so, recall that the price-output combinations actually observed result from an interaction of the supply and demand curves at a point in time. This is illustrated in Figure 5.13. If D_1, D_2, D_3, and D_4 represent the true demand curves at four different points in time and S_1, S_2, S_3, and S_4 the corresponding supply curves, one would have been seriously misled to conclude that the true demand relationship was depicted by DD' and was generally inelastic, when in fact demand was quite elastic and shifting (as was the supply curve). During the four successive time periods in which price-output combinations were observed, both the demand and supply curves had shifted. Recall from Chapter 4 that the simple demand function, relating price to quantity demanded, assumed that all other variables affecting the position of the functions were held *constant*. Hence to obtain a true estimate of the actual demand function, one

FIGURE   5.12

Quantity of Computer
Memory Chips
Purchased (Sold)

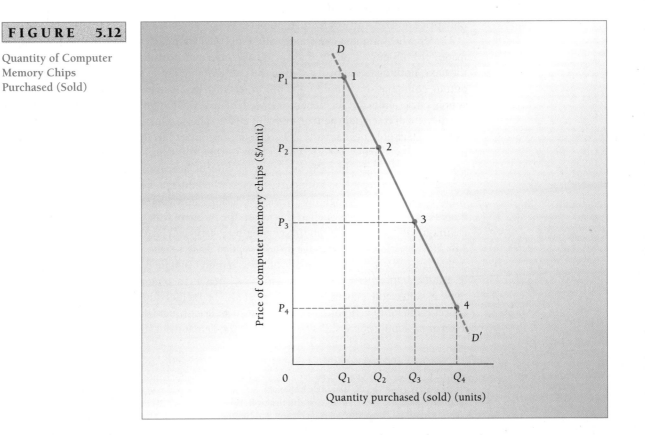

FIGURE   5.13

Quantity of Computer
Memory Chips
Purchased (Sold) with
Shifting Supply and
Demand

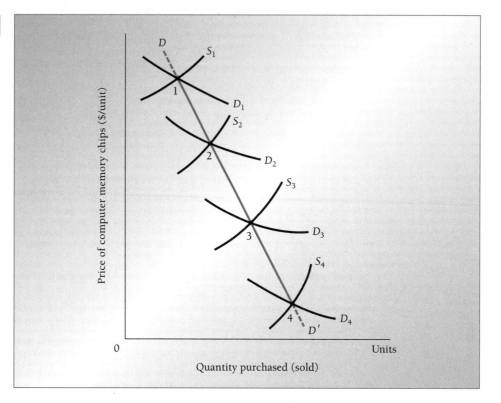

must hold constant the effects of all other variables in the demand functions, allowing only price and quantity demanded to vary.

Under what circumstances may valid empirical estimates of the demand function be made? If both curves retain their original shape and position from one time period to the next, nothing could be learned of the true demand curve because all observed price-output combinations would coincide or at least be closely clustered. If, however, the supply curve shifts but the demand curve remains constant, observed price-output combinations will trace out the true demand curve. This is illustrated in Figure 5.14. If, for example, technological advances were being introduced in the production of computer memory chips during periods 1, 2, 3, and 4, then the supply curve would shift downward and to the right, from S_1 to S_4, tracing out the actual demand curve.

A final possibility is that both curves have shifted during the time period under consideration, but one has enough information to *identify* how each curve has shifted. When simultaneous relationships such as this occur, the ordinary least-squares (OLS) curve-fitting techniques discussed earlier in this chapter may very well *break down and yield results that bear little or no relationship to the actual equation being sought.* Separating the effects of simultaneous relationships in demand analysis requires that more than just price-output data be available. In other words, other variables, such as income and advertising which may cause a shift in the demand function, must also be included in the model. Alternative statistical estimation techniques, such as two-stage least-squares (2SLS), must often be used to separate supply curve shifts from shifts in the demand curve.[39]

------

[39] A discussion of these alternative estimation procedures is beyond the scope of this book. The reader is referred to William J. Baumol, *Economic Theory and Operations Analysis,* 4th ed. (Englewood Cliffs, N.J.: Prentice-Hall, 1977), chap. 10 and its Appendix, for a further discussion of the identification problem and alternative estimation techniques. See also Ernest R. Berndt, *The Practice of Econometrics: Classic and Contemporary* (Reading, MA: Addison-Wesley Publishing Company, 1991), especially chapter 8.

Quantity of Computer
Memory Chips
Purchased (Sold) with
Stable Demand and
Shifting Supply

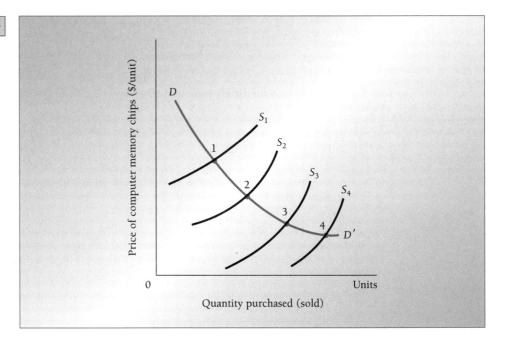

EXAMPLE

www . . . .
Techniques have also been
developed to estimate the
demand for outdoor
recreational activities. The
United States Geological
Survey's Midcontinent
Ecological Science Center
has estimated the
recreational demand for
fishing, hunting and wildlife,
accessible at the following
Internet site:
http://www.mesc.usgs.
gov/wildlife-nonmarket-
benefits.html

THE DEMAND FOR LEISURE ACTIVITIES: THE CASE OF CHESS

Although there has been much research dealing with the demand for specific goods and
services, there have been relatively few studies of the demand for individual leisure activities. The primary reason for the dearth of this type of research is the difficulty in securing the necessary data needed for the analysis.

Chressanthis[40] has estimated the per capita demand for chess membership in the
United States Chess Federation (USCF). Members of the USCF pay an annual membership fee that gives them the right to enter sanctioned tournaments, to receive a rating
(measure of one's chess playing ability), to purchase chess equipment at discounted prices,
and to receive the federation's monthly magazine. Although this study does not look at the
demand for all chess playing activity in the United States, it does consider an extremely
important segment of that activity. The empirical model used is designed to explain annual
variations in per capita USCF membership over the period from 1946 to 1990.

Membership is hypothesized to be a function of the following variables (the direction
of the relationship is shown in parentheses):

- *Price* = the one year regular membership price adjusted for inflation (−)
- *Youth* = a dummy variable to account for the enactment of special prices for
  individuals 19 and under, since 1967 (+)
- *Scholastic* = a dummy variable to account for the existence of a special student
  membership, since 1976 (+)
- *Income* = per capita disposable personal income adjusted for inflation (+)
- *Fischer* = a dummy variable to account for periods before, during, and after the
  Bobby Fischer reign as World Chess Champion (+)

---

[40] George A. Chressanthis, "The Demand for Chess in the United States, 1946–1990," *The American Economist,* (Spring 1994), pp. 17–26.

■ *TV stations* = commercial TV stations per 100,000 U.S. population adjusted for the percent of total households owning at least one TV set (−)

■ *Work* = average weekly work hours divided by 168, as a percent (−)

■ *Tournaments* = Number of USCF-sponsored national tournaments (+)

■ *OBSSQ* = a nonlinear time trend in per capita USCF membership (−)

The primary results of the ordinary least-squares estimates of this model are shown in Table 5.6. The signs of the independent variables are as hypothesized in the model and are generally significant. The R^2 and F-tests indicate an excellent fit, and the Durbin-Watson statistic suggests no problems of autocorrelation.

Overall this study indicates that demand for membership in the USCF conforms to economic theory and can be explained very well by the model presented. Based, in part, on the results from this study, the USCF has begun a number of promotional programs designed to increase its membership, including special exhibitions for youth groups, an increased number of nonrated beginner tournaments, the promotion of "chess camps," and the introduction of chess into inner-city schools. Furthermore, the USCF has increased the pace of play in tournaments to increase spectator interest. Finally, the USCF has sponsored promotions featuring the current world chess champion.

TABLE 5.6

OLS Estimates of the Determinants of the Demand for Chess in the United States, 1946–1990 (Dependent variable = Membership)

Explanatory Variables	Coefficient
Constant	146.816[a] (3.007)
Price	−0.263[c] (−1.520)
Youth	0.843 (0.245)
Scholastic	−0.891 (−0.382)
Income	0.003[b] 2.076
Fischer	5.036[a] (5.117)
TV stations	−24.241[b] (−1.919)
Work	−6.692[a] (−3.137)
Tournaments	1.879[b] (1.877)
OBBSQ	−0.019[a] (−3.491)
Adjusted R^2	0.968
Durbin-Watson	2.296
F	132.421
N	45

Notes: *t*-statistics in parentheses. Hypotheses tests are one-tailed.
[a,b,c]Statistical significance at the 1%, 5%, and 10% levels, respectively.

SUMMARY

☐ Empirical estimates of the demand for a good or service are essential if the firm is to achieve its goal of shareholder wealth maximization. Without good estimates of the demand function facing a firm, it is impossible for that firm to make profit-maximizing price and output decisions.

☐ Consumer surveys involve questioning a sample of consumers to determine such factors as their willingness to buy, their sensitivity to price changes or levels, and their awareness of promotional campaigns.

☐ Consumer clinics make use of experimental groups of consumers. These consumers are given money to spend in a closely monitored environment and their purchasing behavior is then analyzed. Consumer clinics tend to be expensive to operate, and they may be influenced by significant experimental bias if the consumers are aware that their behavior is being monitored.

☐ Market experiments observe consumer behavior in real-market situations. By varying product characteristics, price, advertising, or other factors in some markets but not in others, the effects of these variables on demand can be determined. Market experiments are very expensive.

☐ Statistical techniques are often found to be of great value and relatively inexpensive as a means to make empirical demand function estimates. Regression analysis is often used to estimate statistically the demand function for a good or service.

☐ The linear model and the multiplicative exponential (double-logarithmic) model are the two most commonly used functional relationships in demand studies.

☐ In a *linear* demand model, the coefficient of each independent variable provides an estimate of the change in quantity demanded associated with a one-unit change in the given variable, holding constant all other variables. This marginal impact is constant at all points on the demand curve. The elasticity of a linear demand model with respect to each independent variable (e.g., price elasticity and income elasticity) is not constant, but instead varies over the entire range of the demand curve.

☐ In a multiplicative exponential demand model, the marginal impact of each independent variable on quantity demanded is not constant, but instead varies over the entire range of the demand curve. The elasticity of a multiplicative exponential demand model with respect to each independent variable is constant and is equal to the estimated value of the respective parameter.

☐ The objective of *regression analysis* is to develop a functional relationship between the dependent and independent (explanatory) variable(s). Once a functional relationship (that is, regression equation) is developed, the equation can be used to make forecasts or predictions concerning the value of the dependent variable for given values of the independent variable(s).

☐ The *least-squares* technique is used to estimate the regression coefficients. Least squares minimizes the sum of the squares of the differences between the observed and estimated values of the dependent variable over the sample of observations.

☐ The *t*-test is used to test the hypothesis that a *given* independent variable is useful in explaining variation in the dependent variable.

☐ The *F*-test is used to test the hypothesis that *all* the independent variables (X_1, X_2, . . . , X_m) in the regression equation explain a significant proportion of the variation in the dependent variable.

☐ The *coefficient of determination* (r^2) measures the proportion of the variation in the dependent variable that is explained by the regression equation (that is, independent variables).

☐ The presence of association does not necessarily imply causation. Statistical tests can only establish whether or not an association exists between variables. The existence of a cause-and-effect economic relationship should be inferred from economic reasoning.

▣ Various methodological problems can occur when applying the single-equation linear regression model. These include autocorrelation, heteroscedasticity, specification and measurement errors, multicollinearity, simultaneous equation relationships, and nonlinearities. Many of these problems can invalidate the regression results. In some cases, methods are available for detecting and overcoming these problems.

▣ Because of the simultaneous equation relationship that exists between the demand function and the supply function in determining the market clearing price and quantity, econometricians must exercise great care when estimating and interpreting empirical demand functions.

EXERCISES

1. Consider the Sherwin-Williams Company example discussed in the chapter (see Table 5.1). Suppose one is interested in developing a simple regression model with paint sales (Y) as the dependent variable and selling price (P) as the independent variable.

    a. Determine the estimated regression line.
    b. Give an economic interpretation of the estimated intercept (a) and slope (b) coefficients.
    c. Test the hypothesis (at the .05 level of significance) that there is no relationship (that is, $\beta = 0$) between the variables.
    d. Calculate the coefficient of determination.
    e. Perform an analysis of variance on the regression, including an F-test of the overall significance of the results (at the .05 level).
    f. Based on the regression model, determine the best estimate of paint sales in a sales region where the selling price is $14.50. Construct an *approximate* 95 percent prediction interval.
    g. Determine the price elasticity of demand at a selling price of $14.50.

2. In a study of the demand for life insurance, Executive Insurers, Inc., is examining the factors that affect the amount of life insurance held by executives. The following data on the amount of insurance and annual incomes of a random sample of 12 executives was collected.

Observation	Amount of Life Insurance ($\times$$1,000)	Annual Income ($\times$$1,000)
1	90	50
2	180	84
3	225	74
4	210	115
5	150	104
6	150	96
7	60	56
8	135	102
9	150	104
10	150	108
11	60	65
12	90	58

a. Given the nature of the problem, which would be the dependent variable and which would be the independent variable?
b. Plot the data.
c. Determine the estimated regression line. Give an economic interpretation of the slope (b) coefficient.
d. Test the hypothesis that there is no relationship (i.e., $\beta = 0$) between the variables.
e. Calculate the coefficient of determination.
f. Perform an analysis of variance on the regression, including an F-test of the overall significance of the results.
g. Determine the best estimate, based on the regression model, of the amount of life insurance held by an executive whose annual income is $80,000. Construct an *approximate* 95 percent prediction interval.

3. The Pilot Pen Company has decided to use 15 test markets to examine the sensitivity of demand for its new product to various prices. Advertising effort was identical in each market. Each market had approximately the same level of business activity and population.

Test Market	Price Charged	Quantity Sold (thousands of pens)
1	50¢	20.0
2	50¢	21.0
3	55¢	19.0
4	55¢	19.5
5	60¢	20.5
6	60¢	19.0
7	65¢	16.0
8	65¢	15.0
9	70¢	14.5
10	70¢	15.5
11	80¢	13.0
12	80¢	14.0
13	90¢	11.5
14	90¢	11.0
15	40¢	17.0

a. Using a linear regression model, estimate the demand function for Pilot's new pen.
b. Evaluate this model by computing the coefficient of determination and by performing a t-test of the significance of the price variable.
c. What is the price elasticity of demand at a price of 50 cents?

4. In a study of housing demand, the county assessor is interested in developing a regression model to estimate the market value (i.e., selling price) of residential property within his jurisdiction. The assessor feels that the most important variable affecting selling price (measured in thousands of dollars) is the size of house (measured in hundreds of square feet). He randomly selected 15 houses and measured both the selling price and size, as shown in the table below.

Observation i	Selling Price ($\times\$1,000$) Y	Size ($\times100$ ft^2) X_2
1	65.2	12.0
2	79.6	20.2
3	111.2	27.0
4	128.0	30.0
5	152.0	30.0
6	81.2	21.4
7	88.4	21.6
8	92.8	25.2
9	156.0	37.2
10	63.2	14.4
11	72.4	15.0
12	91.2	22.4
13	99.6	23.9
14	107.6	26.6
15	120.4	30.7

a. Plot the data.
b. Determine the estimated regression line. Give an economic interpretation of the estimated slope (b) coefficient.
c. Determine if size is a statistically significant variable in estimating selling price.
d. Calculate the coefficient of determination.
e. Perform an F-test of the overall significance of the results.
f. Construct an *approximate* 95 percent prediction interval for the selling price of a house having an area (size) of 15 (hundred) square feet.

5. The supply function for Gooseberry Patch Dolls has been estimated to be

$$Q_s = -35,000 + 4,000P + 2000T$$

where T is a trend variable with a value $T = 0$ during 19X0, $T = 1$ during 19X1, $T = 2$ during 19X2, and so on. P is the price per doll and Q_s is the quantity supplied.
Over the past ten years, actual price and quantity sold have been as follows:

Year	Price	Quantity Sold
19X0	$15.00	25,000
19X1	14.00	23,100
19X2	13.50	22,700
19X3	13.20	24,100
19X4	12.50	22,700
19X5	12.00	23,200
19X6	12.00	24,600
19X7	11.50	25,700
19X8	11.20	25,800
19X9	11.00	26,800

a. Plot the supply curves year by year by first letting $T = 0$ for 19X0, then setting $T = 1$ for 19X1, and so on.

b. On the same graph with the 10 supply curves, plot the actual price and quantity sold data.

c. Estimate the demand function using the preceding data and a simple regression routine. What is the slope of the regression line?

d. What assumptions must you make to be confident about the demand function estimated in part (c)?

6. a. Fill in the missing information (blanks) in the following multiple regression computer output.

b. Determine which of the variables (if any) are statistically significant (at the .05 level).

c. Determine whether the independent variables explain a significant (.05 level) proportion of the variation in the dependent variable.

DEPENDENT VARIABLE: SALES

VARIABLE	DF	PARAMETER ESTIMATE	STANDARD ERROR	T-RATIO
INTERCEPT	1	————	1.105	2.205
PRICE	1	−.3750	————	−1.570
INCOME	1	————	.140	2.780
ADVERTISING	1	−6.2500	1.950	————

SOURCE OF VARIATION	DF	SUM OF SQUARES	MEAN SQUARES
REGRESSION	————	1187.343	————
RESIDUAL	————	————	18.625
TOTAL	25	————	

R-SQUARE: ————

F-RATIO: ————

7. Cascade Pharmaceuticals Company developed the following regression model, using time-series data from the past 33 quarters, for one of its nonprescription cold remedies:

$$Y = -1.04 + .24X_1 - .27X_2$$

where Y = quarterly sales (in thousands of cases) of the cold remedy
X_1 = Cascade's quarterly advertising ($\times\$1,000$) for the cold remedy
X_2 = competitors' advertising for similar products ($\times\$10,000$)

Additional information concerning the regression model:

$$s_{b_1} = .032 \quad s_{b_2} = .070$$

$$R^2 = .64 \quad s_e = 1.63 \quad F\text{-statistic} = 31.402$$

Durbin-Watson (d) statistic = .4995

a. Which of the independent variables (if any) appear to be statistically significant (at the .05 level) in explaining sales of the cold remedy?

      b. What proportion of the total variation in sales is explained by the regression equation?

      c. Perform an F-test (at the .05 level) of the overall explanatory power of the model.

      d. What conclusions can be drawn from the data about the possible presence of autocorrelation?

      e. How do the results in part (d) affect your answers to parts (a), (b), and (c)?

      f. What additional statistical information (if any) would you find useful in the evaluation of this model?

8. The following equation was estimated as the demand function for gasoline (number of observations equals 100, and standard errors are in parentheses):

$$\ln Q = 3.95 - 0.582 \ln P + 0.401 \ln Y - 0.211 \ln P_c$$
$$\qquad\qquad\;\;(0.105)\qquad(0.195)\qquad\;(0.156)$$

    where Q = gallons of gas demanded, P = price per gallon of gasoline, Y = income level of consumers, and P_c = an index of the price for automobiles.

      a. Interpret the coefficients of the various variables in the preceding demand equation.

      b. How much confidence do you have in each of these coefficient estimates?

9. In an article entitled "A Coherence Approach to Estimates of Price Elasticities in the Vacation Travel Market," Taplin reports the following regression equation for vacation leisure travel expenditures in Australia.[41] The dependent variable in the equation (X_1) is dollars spent on vacation travel overseas. The independent variables are household disposable income in dollars per week (Y) and age of household head in years (Z).

$$\log X_1 = -0.6858 + 0.7407 \log Y + 0.6267 \log Z$$
$$\qquad\qquad\qquad\;\;(2.181)\qquad\quad(0.432)$$

$$r^2 = 0.519$$

    (*Note:* t-values in parentheses; 8 degrees of freedom.)

      a. What interpretation would you give to the coefficient of the Y variable; that is, 0.7407?

      b. What interpretation would you give to the coefficient of the Z variable; that is, 0.6267?

      c. What conclusions can you draw about the significance of the income variable and the age variable?

      d. What interpretation can you give to r^2 from this equation?

10. Moyer Winery is the maker of a high-quality champagne. A linear regression model used to estimate the demand function for Moyer's champagne yielded the following results:

$$Q_D = 10,425 - 2,910P_x + .028A + 11,100P_{op}$$
$$\qquad\qquad\quad(1,010)\qquad(0.004)\quad(3,542)$$

    where Q_D = quantity of Moyer champagne demanded

            P_x = price of Moyer champagne

            A = Moyer Winery advertising in dollars

            P_{op} = percentage of the U.S. population over 21 years of age

[41] John Taplin, "A Coherence Approach to Estimates of Price Elasticities in the Vacation Travel Market," *Journal of Transport Economic Policy* 14 (1980).

a. Determine the point price elasticity for prices of $5 and $10, when $A = $ $1,000,000 and $P_{op} = .5$.
b. Determine the point advertising elasticity at an advertising level of $2,000,000, if price remains at $5 and $P_{op} = .5$.
c. The standard error for each coefficient is given in parentheses. If you know that the demand function was estimated using 25 observations, can you reject at the 95 percent confidence level the hypothesis that there is no relationship between each of the independent variables and Q_D?

11. General Cereals is using a regression model to estimate the demand for Tweetie Sweeties, a whistle-shaped, sugar-coated breakfast cereal for children. The following (multiplicative exponential) demand function is being used:

$$Q_D = 6{,}280 P^{-2.15} A^{1.05} N^{3.70}$$

where Q_D = quantity demanded, in 10 oz. boxes
   P = price per box, in dollars
   A = advertising expenditures on daytime television, in dollars
   N = proportion of the population under 12 years old

a. Determine the point price elasticity of demand for Tweetie Sweeties.
b. Determine the advertising elasticity of demand.
c. What interpretation would you give to the exponent of N?

12. The demand for gasoline sold by the Black Gold Refining Company has been estimated as

$$Q_B = .22 P_B^{-.95} I^{1.4} A_B^{.3} P_C^{.2} P_{op}^{.6}$$

where Q_B = number of gallons of gas sold each month (millions)
   P_B = price per gallon charged by Black Gold
     I = level of per capita disposable personal income in Black Gold's market area
   A_B = dollar amount of advertising expenditures made by Black Gold
   P_C = price per gallon charged by competitors
   P_{op} = driving age population in Black Gold's market area

a. What interpretation can you give to the exponents of P_B, I, A_B, P_C, P_{op}?
b. Are these values consistent with your expectations?
c. If Black Gold ceased advertising, what would be the impact on demand according to this demand equation? What problem does this illustrate in an interpretation of demand functions?

13. The demand for haddock has been estimated as[42]

$$\log Q = a + b \log P + c \log I + d \log P_m$$

where Q = quantity of haddock sold in New England
   P = price per pound of haddock
     I = a measure of personal income in the New England region
   P_m = an index of the price of meat and poultry

---

[42] F. W. Bell, "The Pope and the Price of Fish," *American Economic Review* (December 1958).

If $b = -2.174$, $c = .461$, and $d = 1.909$,

   a.   Determine the price elasticity of demand.

   b.   Determine the income elasticity of demand.

   c.   Determine the cross elasticity of demand.

   d.   How would you characterize the demand for haddock?

   e.   Suppose disposable income is expected to increase by 5 percent next year. Assuming all other factors remain constant, forecast the percentage change in the quantity of haddock demanded next year.

14.   An estimate of the demand function for household furniture produced the following results:

$$F = .0036Y^{1.08}R^{0.16}P^{-0.48} \qquad r^2 = .996$$

where F = furniture expenditures per household

      Y = disposable personal income per household

      R = value of private residential construction per household

      P = ratio of the furniture price index to the consumer price index

   a.   Determine the point price and income elasticities for household furniture.

   b.   What interpretation would you give to the exponent for R? Why do you suppose R was included in the equation as a variable?

   c.   If you were a furniture manufacturer, would you have preferred to see the analysis performed in physical (constant dollar) sales units rather than actual dollar units? If you change F to constant dollar terms, what other variable should you also change?

15.   The following demand function has been estimated for product A:

$$Q_A = aP_A^b\, I^c\, P_B^d\, P_{op}^e\, A_B^f\, A_A^g$$

where Q_A = quantity of A demanded in units

      P_A = price of A

      P_B = price of B

       I = per capita income

      P_{op} = total population

      A_A = advertising expenditures for A

      A_B = advertising expenditures for B

   a.   Determine the cross elasticity between A and B. Determine the price elasticity of A. Determine the income elasticity of A.

   b.   How would you interpret the values for e, f, and g?

   c.   If $c = -.8$, what could you say about product A?

   d.   If $f = -.3$ and $d = .9$, what can you say about products A and B?

16.   You wish to design an experiment aimed at estimating the price elasticity of demand for your firm's new Convertible Monster (CONMON) toy. The toy currently sells for $14.95 and is sold exclusively at FloorMart discount stores throughout the country. Design an experiment that will enable you to estimate the price elasticity of demand for these toys at the lowest possible cost to your firm.

17.   Suppose an appliance manufacturer is doing a regression analysis, using quarterly *time-series* data, of the factors affecting its sales of appliances. A regression equation was estimated between appliance sales (in dollars) as the dependent variable

and disposable personal income and new housing starts as the independent variables. The statistical tests of the model showed large t-values for both independent variables, along with a high r^2 value. However, analysis of the residuals indicated that substantial autocorrelation was present.

   a. What are some of the possible causes of this autocorrelation?

   b. How does this autocorrelation affect the conclusions concerning the significance of the individual explanatory variables and the overall explanatory power of the regression model?

   c. Given that a person uses the model for forecasting future appliance sales, how does this autocorrelation affect the accuracy of these forecasts?

   d. What techniques might be used to remove this autocorrelation from the model?

18. Suppose the appliance manufacturer discussed in Exercise 17 also developed another model, again using time-series data, where appliance sales was the dependent variable and disposable personal income and retail sales of durable goods were the independent variables. Although the r^2 statistic is high, the manufacturer also suspects that serious multicollinearity exists between the two independent variables.

   a. In what ways does the presence of this multicollinearity affect the results of the regression analysis?

   b. Under what conditions might the presence of multicollinearity cause problems in the use of this regression equation in designing a marketing plan for appliance sales?

Note: The following problems require the use of a multiple regression computer program.

19. Consider again the Sherwin-Williams Company example discussed in the chapter (see Table 5.1). Suppose one is interested in developing a multiple regression model with paint sales (Y) as the dependent variable and promotional expenditures (A) and selling price (P) as the independent variables.

   a. Determine the estimated regression line.

   b. Give an economic interpretation of the estimated slope (b's) coefficients.

   c. Test the hypothesis (at the .05 level of significance) that there is no relationship between the dependent variable and each of the independent variables.

   d. Determine the coefficient of determination.

   e. Perform an analysis of variance on the regression, including an F-test of the overall significance of the results (at the .05 level).

   f. Based on the regression model, determine the best estimate of paint sales in a sales region where promotional expenditures are \$80(000) and the selling price is \$12.50.

   g. Determine the point (i) promotional and (ii) price elasticities at the values of promotional expenditures and selling price given in part (f).

20. Executive Insurers, Inc. (see Exercise 2) feels the use of more independent variables might improve the overall explanatory power of the regression model. In the following table, data are shown on two additional variables (age of the executive and number of children) for the random sample of 12 executives along with the original data from Exercise 2:

   a. Determine the estimated regression equation with the three explanatory variables shown in the table.

   b. Give an economic interpretation of each of the regression coefficients.

Observation	Amount of Life Insurance (×$1,000)	Annual Income (×$1,000)	Age (Years)	Number of Children
1	90	50	34	2
2	180	84	40	4
3	225	74	46	3
4	210	115	63	3
5	150	104	62	4
6	150	96	54	2
7	60	56	31	1
8	135	102	57	3
9	150	104	40	3
10	150	108	42	4
11	60	65	45	2
12	90	58	35	1

c. Which of the independent variables (if any) are statistically significant (at the .05 level) in explaining the amount of insurance held by executives?

d. What proportion of the total variation in the amount of insurance is explained by the regression model?

e. Perform an F-test (at the .05 significance level) of the overall explanatory power of the model.

f. Construct an *approximate* 95 percent prediction interval for the amount of insurance held by an executive whose annual income is $90,000, whose age is 50, and who has three children.

21. The county assessor (see Exercise 4) feels that the use of more independent variables in the regression equation might improve the overall explanatory power of the model.

In addition to size, the assessor feels that the total number of rooms, age, and whether or not the house has an attached garage might be important variables affecting selling price. This data for the 15 randomly selected dwellings is shown in the table at the top of the next page.

a. Using a computer regression program, determine the estimated regression equation with the four explanatory variables shown in the table at the top of the next page.

b. Give an economic interpretation of each of the estimated regression coefficients.

c. Which of the independent variables (if any) are statistically significant (at the .05 level) in explaining selling price?

d. What proportion of the total variation in selling price is explained by the regression model?

e. Perform an F-test (at the .05 significance level) of the overall explanatory power of the model.

f. Construct an *approximate* 95 percent prediction interval for the selling price of a 15-year-old house having 1,800 square feet, 7 rooms, and an attached garage.

22. The county assessor (see Exercise 21) is concerned about possible multicollinearity between the size (X_1) and total number of rooms (X_2) variables. Calculate the correlation coefficient between these two variables.

Observation i	Selling Price ($\times$\$1,000) Y	Size ($\times$100 ft^2) X_1	Total No. of Rooms X_2	Age X_3	Attached Garage (No = 0, Yes = 1) X_4
1	65.2	12.0	6	17	0
2	79.6	20.2	7	18	0
3	111.2	27.0	7	17	1
4	128.0	30.0	8	18	1
5	152.0	30.0	8	15	1
6	81.2	21.4	8	20	1
7	88.4	21.6	7	8	0
8	92.8	25.2	7	15	1
9	156.0	37.2	9	31	1
10	63.2	14.4	7	8	0
11	72.4	15.0	7	17	0
12	91.2	22.4	6	9	0
13	99.6	23.9	7	20	1
14	107.6	26.6	6	23	1
15	120.4	30.7	7	23	1

www exercise

Computer Industry
Forecasts

23. The techniques discussed in this chapter are used by a large number of commercial market research companies, many who provide free information on the Internet. For example, the company Computer Industry Forecasts provides market data on software, peripherals, computers, communications equipment, and the Internet. The analyses they provide include sales and shipment forecasts, planned purchases, and market shares.

Access the Computer Industry Forecasts Internet site at http://www.cif1.com/. If you click on the button for "free data" and then browse you will arrive at a site (http://www.sonic.net/~punch/guest/browse.htm) that gives you free access to some recent issues of their quarterly publication. Use these free back issues to perform an economic profile of a sector of the computer industry listed in each issue, such as personal computers. Your profile should include forecast U.S. and worldwide shipments, market share by channel (brand name), and retail sales (for example, subdivided into home, school, and commercial).

CASE EXERCISE   DEMAND ESTIMATION

Early in 1993, the Southeastern Transportation Authority (STA), a public agency responsible for serving the commuter rail transportation needs of a large Eastern city, was faced with rising operating deficits on its system. Also, because of a fiscal austerity program at both the federal and state levels, the hope of receiving additional subsidy support was slim.

The board of directors of STA asked the system manager to explore alternatives to alleviate the financial plight of the system. The first suggestion made by the manager was to institute a major cutback in service. This cutback would result in no service after 7 P.M., no service on weekends, and a reduced schedule of service during the midday period Monday through Friday. The board of STA indicated that this alternative was not likely to be politically acceptable and could only be considered as a last resort.

The board suggested that because it had been over five years since the last basic fare increase, a fare increase from the current level of $1 to a new level of $1.50 should be considered. Accordingly, the board ordered the manager to conduct a study of the likely impact of this proposed fare hike.

The system manager has collected data on important variables thought to have a significant impact on the demand for rides on STA. These data have been collected over the past 24 years and include the following variables:

1. Price per ride (in cents)—This variable is designated P in Table 1. Price is expected to have a negative impact on the demand for rides on the system.

2. Population in the metropolitan area serviced by STA—It is expected that this variable has a positive impact on the demand for rides on the system. This variable is designated T in Table 1.

3. Disposable per capita income—This variable was initially thought to have a positive impact on the demand for rides on STA. This variable is designated I in Table 1.

4. Parking rate per hour in the downtown area (in cents)—This variable is expected to have a positive impact on demand for rides on the STA. It is designated H in Table 1.

The transit manager has decided to perform a multiple regression on the data to determine the impact of the rate increase.

QUESTIONS

1. What is the dependent variable in this demand study?
2. What are the independent variables?
3. What are the expected signs of the variables thought to affect transit ridership on STA?
4. Using a multiple regression program available on a computer to which you have access, estimate the coefficients of the demand model for the data given in Table 1.
5. Provide an economic interpretation for each of the coefficients in the regression equation you have computed.
6. What is the value of the coefficient of determination? How would you interpret this result?
7. Calculate the price elasticity using 1992 data.
8. Calculate the income elasticity using 1992 data.
9. What is the Durbin-Watson statistic for this regression? What does this indicate about the presence of autocorrelation in the data?
10. Based on an analysis of the correlation matrix of the independent variables, what can you say about the presence of multicollinearity in the model?
11. If the fare is increased to $1.50, what is the expected impact on weekly revenues to the transit system if all other variables remain at their 1992 levels?

TABLE 1					
Year	Weekly Riders (Y) (×1,000)	Price (P) per Ride (Cents)	Population (T) (×1,000)	Income (I)	Parking Rate (H) (Cents)
1966	1,200	15	1,800	2,900	50
1967	1,190	15	1,790	3,100	50
1968	1,195	15	1,780	3,200	60
1969	1,110	25	1,778	3,250	60
1970	1,105	25	1,750	3,275	60
1971	1,115	25	1,740	3,290	70
1972	1,130	25	1,725	4,100	75
1973	1,095	30	1,725	4,300	75
1974	1,090	30	1,720	4,400	75
1975	1,087	30	1,705	4,600	80
1976	1,080	30	1,710	4,815	80
1977	1,020	40	1,700	5,285	80
1978	1,010	40	1,695	5,665	85
1979	1,010	40	1,695	5,800	100
1980	1,005	40	1,690	5,900	105
1981	995	40	1,630	5,915	105
1982	930	75	1,640	6,325	105
1983	915	75	1,635	6,500	110
1984	920	75	1,630	6,612	125
1985	940	75	1,620	6,883	130
1986	950	75	1,615	7,005	150
1987	910	100	1,605	7,234	155
1988	930	100	1,590	7,500	165
1989	933	100	1,595	7,600	175
1990	940	100	1,590	7,800	175
1991	948	100	1,600	8,000	190
1992	955	100	1,610	8,100	200

Data on Transit Ridership

CASE EXERCISE   SOFT DRINKS

Demand can be estimated with experimental data, time-series data, or cross-section data. Sara Lee Corporation generates experimental data in test stores where the effect of an NFL-licensed Carolina Panthers logo on Champion sweatshirt sales can be carefully monitored. Demand forecasts usually rely on time-series data. In contrast, cross-section data appears in Table 2. Soft drink consumption in cans per capita per year is related to six-pack price, income per capita, and mean temperature across the 48 contiguous states in the United States.

QUESTIONS

1. Estimate the demand for soft drinks using a multiple regression program available on your computer.

TABLE 2

Soft Drink Demand Data

	Cans/Capita/Yr	6-Pack Price	Income/Capita	Mean Temp
Alabama	200	2.19	11.7	66
Arizona	150	1.99	15.3	62
Arkansas	237	1.93	9.9	63
California	135	2.59	22.5	56
Colorado	121	2.29	17.1	52
Connecticut	118	2.49	24.3	50
Delaware	217	1.99	25.2	52
Florida	242	2.29	16.2	72
Georgia	295	1.89	12.6	64
Idaho	85	2.39	14.4	46
Illinois	114	2.35	21.6	52
Indiana	184	2.19	18	52
Iowa	104	2.21	14.4	50
Kansas	143	2.17	15.3	56
Kentucky	230	2.05	11.7	56
Louisiana	269	1.97	13.5	69
Maine	111	2.19	14.4	41
Maryland	217	2.11	18.9	54
Massachusetts	114	2.29	19.8	47
Michigan	108	2.25	18.9	47
Minnesota	108	2.31	16.2	41
Mississippi	248	1.98	9	65
Missouri	203	1.94	17.1	57
Montana	77	2.31	17.1	44
Nebraska	97	2.28	14.4	49
Nevada	166	2.19	21.6	48
New Hampshire	177	2.27	16.2	35
New Jersey	143	2.31	21.6	54
New Mexico	157	2.17	13.5	56
New York	111	2.43	22.5	48
North Carolina	330	1.89	11.7	59
North Dakota	63	2.33	12.6	39
Ohio	165	2.21	19.8	51
Oklahoma	184	2.19	14.4	82
Oregon	68	2.25	17.1	51
Pennsylvania	121	2.31	18	50
Rhode Island	138	2.23	18	50
South Carolina	237	1.93	10.8	65
South Dakota	95	2.34	11.7	45
Tennessee	236	2.19	11.7	60
Texas	222	2.08	15.3	69
Utah	100	2.37	14.4	50
Vermont	64	2.36	14.4	44
Virginia	270	2.04	14.4	58
Washington	77	2.19	18	49
West Virginia	144	2.11	13.5	55
Wisconsin	97	2.38	17.1	46
Wyoming	102	2.31	17.1	46

2. Interpret the coefficients and calculate the price elasticity of soft drink demand.

3. Omit price from the regression equation and observe the bias introduced into the parameter estimate for income.

4. Now omit both price and temperature from the regression equation. Should a marketing plan for soft drinks be designed that relocates most canned drink machines into low income neighborhoods? Why or why not?

5. If the data in Table 2 represented Coca Cola consumption and prices, what problems might arise from incorporating the price of Pepsi into the regression model?

Nonlinear Regression Models

INTRODUCTION

Although the relationships among many economic variables can be satisfactorily represented using a linear regression model, situations do occur in which a nonlinear model is clearly required to portray adequately the relationship over the relevant range of observations. For example, economic theory postulates the existence of nonlinear diminishing returns relationships among many production and consumption variables. Also, many economic time series tend to exhibit a constant percentage rate of growth and thus yield a nonlinear relationship when plotted against time. Finally, although no underlying theoretical reasons may suggest the presence of nonlinearities, a plot of the variables in a scatter diagram may yield some form of nonlinear relationship.

Various models are available to deal with these situations. Through an appropriate transformation of the variables in the model, the standard linear regression procedures can be used to estimate the values of the parameters of these models. The transformations that are discussed here include the semilogarithmic transformation, the double-log transformation, reciprocal transformation, and polynomial transformations. These transformations normally can be handled with an appropriate instruction to the regression analysis computer program.

SEMILOGARITHMIC TRANSFORMATION

Sometimes, the relationship between one or more of the independent variables and the dependent variable can be estimated best by taking the logarithm of one or more of the independent variables.[43] This transformation is often useful when problems of heteroscedasticity exist with respect to one of the independent variables. For example, cross-section regression models, which use firm size as one of the independent variables, often take the log of firm size because of the potential problems caused by including in the same equation firms of $10 million in assets with firms of $10 billion in assets.

A semilog transformation is of the form

$$Y = a + b \log S + cX + dZ \qquad [5A.1]$$

where Y is the dependent variable, X and Z are independent variables expressed in a normal form, and $log S$ is an independent variable expressed in a logarithmic form. Standard least-squares techniques can be used to estimate Equation 5A.1.

---

[43] It is possible to transform many, but not all, nonlinear forms into a linear expression.

DOUBLE-LOG TRANSFORMATION

In the chapter, we saw that a multiplicative exponential model (see Equation 5.5) is often used in demand studies. Likewise, as will be seen later in Chapter 8, such models are useful for relating the quantities of various inputs used in a production process to the quantity of output obtained. A three-variable exponential regression function can be represented as

$$Z = AV^{\beta_1}W^{\beta_2} \qquad\qquad [5A.2]$$

where V and W are the explanatory variables; A, β_1, and β_2 are the parameters to be estimated. Multiplicative exponential functions such as these can be transformed to linear relationships. In Equation 5A.2, taking logarithms of both sides of the equation yields

$$\log Z = \log A + \beta_1 \log V + \beta_2 \log W$$

By defining the following transformations: $Y = \log Z$, $\alpha = \log A$, $X_1 = \log V$, $X_2 = \log W$, and adding an error term ϵ, the following multiple linear regression model is obtained:

$$Y = \alpha + \beta_1 X_1 + \beta_2 X_2 + \epsilon$$

Again, least-squares procedures can be used to estimate these regression coefficients.

RECIPROCAL TRANSFORMATION

Another transformation, which is useful in relationships that exhibit an asymptotic behavior, is the reciprocal transformation. The two possible cases are shown in Figure 5A.1. In Figure 5A.1 (a) the relationship is of the form

$$Y = \alpha + \frac{\beta}{Z} \qquad\qquad [5A.3]$$

and in Figure 5A.1 (b) it is of the form

$$Y = \alpha - \frac{\beta}{Z} \qquad\qquad [5A.4]$$

FIGURE   5A.1

Reciprocal
Transformations

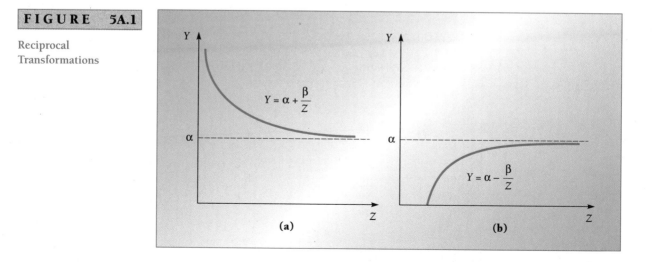

Defining the transformation $X = 1/Z$, Equations 5A.3 and 5A.4 yield the following respective simple linear regression models:

$$Y = \alpha + \beta X + \epsilon$$

and

$$Y = \alpha - \beta X + \epsilon$$

whose parameters can be estimated by the usual least-squares procedures.

POLYNOMIAL TRANSFORMATION

As will be seen in Chapter 10, the cost-output function for a firm is often postulated to follow a quadratic or cubic pattern. This type of relationship can be represented by means of a *polynomial function*. For example, a third-degree (that is, cubic) polynomial function can be represented as

$$Y = \alpha + \beta_1 Z + \beta_2 Z^2 + \beta_3 Z^3 \qquad [5A.5]$$

Letting $X_1 = Z$, $X_2 = Z^2$, $X_3 = Z^3$, Equation 5A.5 can be transformed into the following multiple linear regression model:

$$Y = \alpha + \beta_1 X_1 + \beta_2 X_2 + \beta_3 X_3$$

Standard least-squares procedures can be used in estimating the parameters of this model.

The transformations discussed illustrate the possibilities that are available to the model builder. These various transformations may, of course, be combined and used in the same equation. Further discussions of these and other more complex transformations are found in most econometrics books.

EXERCISES

1. A product manager has been reviewing selling expenses (that is, advertising, sales commissions, and so on) associated with marketing a line of household cleaning products. The manager suspects that there may be some sort of diminishing marginal returns relationship between selling expenses and the resulting sales generated by these expenditures. After examining the selling expense and sales data for various regions (all regions are similar in sales potential) shown in the following table and graph, however, the manager is uncertain about the nature of the relationship.

Region	Selling Expense ($000)	Sales (100,000 units)	Log (selling expense)	Log (sales)
A	5	1	3.6990	5.0000
B	30	4.25	4.4771	5.6284
C	25	4	4.3979	5.6021
D	10	2	4.0000	5.3010
E	55	5.5	4.7404	5.7404
F	40	5	4.6021	5.6990
G	10	1.75	4.0000	5.2430
H	45	5	4.6532	5.6990
I	20	3	4.3010	5.4771
J	60	5.75	4.7782	5.7597

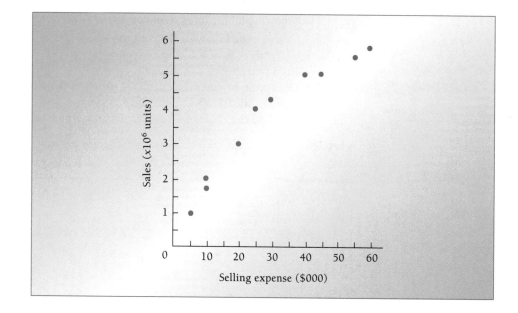

a.   Using the linear regression model

$$Y = \alpha + \beta X$$

where Y is sales and X is selling expenses, estimate α, β, and the r^2 statistic by the least-squares technique.

b.   Using the exponential function model

$$Y = \alpha X^{\beta}$$

apply the double-logarithmic transformation to obtain a linear relationship that can be estimated by the least-squares technique.

c.   Applying the least-squares technique, estimate α, β, and the r^2 statistic for the transformed (linear) model in part (b). (Note that the logarithms of the X and Y variables needed in the calculations are given in the table.)

d.   Based on the r^2 statistics calculated in parts (a) and (c), which model appears to give a better fit of the data?

e.   What implications does the result in part (d) have for the possible existence of a diminishing marginal returns relationship between sales and selling expenses as suggested by the manager?

f.   What other transformations of the variables might we try to give a better fit to the data?

Note: The following problems require the use of a multiple regression computer program, such as JMP, Minitab, SAS, SPSS, or MYSTAT.

2.   a.   Using the data in Table 5.1 for the Sherwin-Williams Company, estimate a multiplicative exponential demand model (see Equation 5.5) for paint sales.

b.   Compare the results in part (a) (i.e., parameter estimates, standard errors, statistical significance) with the linear model developed in the chapter.

3.   The following table presents data on sales (S), advertising (A), and price (P):

   a.   Estimate the following demand models:
        (i) $S = \alpha + \beta_1 A + \beta_2 P$
        (ii) $S = \alpha A^{\beta_1} P^{\beta_2}$

   b.   Determine whether the estimated values of β_1 and β_2 are statistically significant (at the .05 level).

   c.   Based on the value of R^2 and the F-ratio, which model gives the best fit?

Observation	Sales (S)	Advertising (A)	Price (P)
1	495	900	150
2	555	1,200	180
3	465	750	135
4	675	1,350	135
5	360	600	120
6	405	600	120
7	735	1,500	150
8	435	750	150
9	570	1,050	165
10	600	1,200	150

Business and Economic Forecasting

"With over 50 foreign cars already on sale here, the Japanese auto industry isn't likely to carve out a big slice of the U.S. market for itself."
    —Business Week, *1958*

    "TV won't be able to hold on to any market it captures after the first six months. People will soon get tired of staring at a plywood box every night."
    —20th Century Fox's Daryl F. Zanuck, *1946*

One of the central concerns of managers in all enterprises is forecasting the future demand for their products, forecasting the cost of producing their products, and forecasting the price at which their products will be sold. As the quotes above indicate, forecasting is often difficult. The forecasts at the firm level depend on the performance of the overall economy, including the growth rate in gross national product, the level of interest rates, the rate of unemployment, the value of the dollar in foreign exchange markets, and the rate of inflation. These macroeconomic forecasts are provided by economists employed by the government, large firms, and economic forecasting organizations. The forecasting models used to forecast the future macroeconomic environment are very complex and require considerable judgment in their use. Other forecasting techniques are more suitable for use at the firm level. In this chapter we discuss several classes of forecasting techniques and consider the strengths and weaknesses of each, including time-series analysis, smoothing techniques, barometric techniques, survey and opinion-polling techniques, and econometric methods. Appendix 6A provides an introduction to vector autoregression (VAR) forecasting techniques. Because the value of a firm depends on expected levels of future cash flows, forecasting the components of these future cash flows is very important if managers wish to make shareholder wealth-maximizing decisions.

MANAGERIAL CHALLENGE

FORD MOTOR COMPANY: THE DEMAND FOR SPORT UTILITY VEHICLES

The demand for motor vehicles underwent several important changes during the 1980s and the first half of the 1990s. The proportion of total vehicles sold in the United States that were traditional passenger cars declined substantially as light-duty pickup trucks, minivans, and sport utility (4-wheel drive) vehicles increased in popularity. Indeed, this change in consumer vehicle preferences may be responsible for the survival of Chrysler Corporation, which popularized the minivan during the 1980s and has a significant presence in the sport utility sector of the market, with its popular Jeep products. The profit margin on trucks, minivans, and sport utility vehicles tends to be much larger than on traditional passenger cars.

In 1994, Ford Motor Company announced a substantial increase in its capacity to produce its popular sport utility vehicle, the Explorer. Ford had been running its factories consistently on overtime to meet the surging demand. Ford hoped that its output capacity expansion would be a very profitable investment. This new capacity became available just as the newly designed Ford Explorer model was introduced. Ford announced substantial price increases for the 1995 Explorer relative to its 1994 model predecessor.

Industry analysts have questioned the wisdom of these price increases in the face of the dramatic increase in capacity. Furthermore, other auto companies have increased their offerings in this important market segment. General Motors introduced a redesigned Chevrolet sport utility vehicle in 1995. Chrysler also expanded its production capacity for its Jeep vehicles. Honda was planning a competitive entry in this market.

Time will tell whether Ford's investment in expanded capacity and its substantial price increases will prove to have been wise business decisions. Internally, Ford analysts have prepared forecasts of demand that suggest the wisdom of these moves. However, when introducing new products, one must be concerned about the responses of competitors. This makes many aspects of business forecasting quite difficult. Oftentimes, past patterns of demand may not hold in the future, as competitors' actions change the structure of the demand relationship.

In this chapter, we discuss several commonly used quantitative forecasting methods, including time-series analysis and econometric techniques. Other methods, such as survey and opinion-polling techniques and market experiments, can provide additional information that will be useful in reducing the error in making forecasts.

www . . . .
J. D. Power and Associates is an international market research firm that specializes in the automobile industry. You can read their most recent forecasts on the Internet at: http://www.jdpower.com/forecast.html

SIGNIFICANCE OF FORECASTING

In 1943, IBM chairman Thomas Watson said, "I think there's a world demand for about five computers." This quote illustrates the difficulty managers encounter in accurately forecasting future business prospects. Because management in both public and private enterprise typically operates under conditions of uncertainty, one of the most important functions of the managerial economist is that of forecasting. A forecast is merely a prediction concerning the future and is required in virtually all areas of the enterprise. Sales estimates are necessary to plan the proper future levels of production. The financial manager requires estimates of the future cash flows of the firm. This in turn requires a forecast of probable future levels of sales, production, receipts, and disbursements, as well as capital expenditures. In planning for capital investments, predictions about future economic activity are required so that returns accruing from the capital investment may be estimated. Forecasts of money and credit conditions must also be made so that the cash needs of the firm may be met at the lowest possible cost.

Public administrators and managers of not-for-profit institutions must also make forecasts. City government officials, for example, forecast the level of services that will be required of their various departments during a budget period. How many police officers will be needed to handle the public-safety problems of the community? How many streets will require repair next year, and how much will this cost? What will next year's school enrollment be at each grade level? Government officials continually make estimates of the revenues that a specific tax or package of taxes will generate. This requires an evaluation of the level of economic activity that will prevail during the budget period. The hospital administrator faces such problems as forecasting the health care needs of the community and the amount and cost of charity patient care the hospital will provide. To do this effectively, an estimate has to be made, not only of the growth in absolute size of population, but also of the changes in the number of people in various age groups and of the varying medical needs that these different age groups will have. Universities forecast student enrollments, costs of operations, and in many cases the level of funds that will be provided by tuition and government appropriations.

Obviously, good forecasting is essential to reduce the uncertainty of the environment in which most managerial decisions are made. The level of sophistication required in forecasting techniques varies directly with the significance of the problem being examined. Many decisions require that only very simple assumptions be made about the future. In cases where the decision is relatively insignificant (the potential gains or losses are small) and the decision has a short-run impact, an appropriate forecast may simply be based on the assumption that the future will be similar to the present. When the costs of an erroneous forecast increase and when the time period of the forecast increases, the use of more formal and sophisticated methodology becomes justifiable.

EXAMPLE

www . . . .
Domino's Pizza has extended its "pizza meter" to politics, sporting events, and television programming. Access the Domino's Pizza Internet site at:
http://www.dominos.com /info/search.html
and search under the keyword "pizza meter."

UNCONVENTIONAL FORECASTING: DOMINO'S PIZZA AND THE PENTAGON

Sometimes very unconventional forecasting techniques can be used to forecast significant events, such as takeover activity being conducted through Wall Street investment banking firms or major events planned in Washington. An interesting example of this type of unconventional forecasting was uncovered in Washington during the war with Iraq.

At the Pentagon, Domino's usually delivers an average of three pizzas a night. On Tuesday, January 8, 1991, the number of pizzas ordered began to rise slowly, reaching 20 by Sunday the 13th. That topped the Pentagon's previous record of 19 ordered the night before Ferdinand Marcos slipped out of the Philippines. On Monday, two days before the war began with Iraq, 50 pizzas were ordered. Tuesday the number grew to 101, and Wednesday, the night the war began, the number hit 125. Similar patterns of pizza ordering occurred at the CIA and the White House prior to the event. This pattern in pizza ordering in Washington has received such close attention from the press that it has been named the "Domino Principle." When world crises are developing, the manager of the Washington Domino's gets many calls from individuals who do not want to order a pizza. They just want to know how many pizzas have been ordered by the White House or the Pentagon. One wonders whether pizza deliveries to the Pentagon will become classified information.

SELECTION OF A FORECASTING TECHNIQUE

The forecasting technique used in any particular situation depends on a number of factors.

Hierarchy of Forecasts

One dimension that helps determine the appropriate technique is the level of aggregation of the items being forecast. The highest level of economic aggregation that is normally forecast is that of the national economy, although world economic forecasts have become increasingly common. The usual measure of overall economic activity is gross national product (GNP); however, a firm may be more interested in forecasting some subset of GNP. For example, a machine tool firm may be more concerned about expected plant and equipment expenditures than about the GNP as a whole. Retail establishments are more concerned about future levels and changes in disposable personal income than about the overall GNP estimate.

The next level in the hierarchy of economic forecasts is the industry sales forecast. This is usually dependent on the expected performance of the overall economy or on some major sector. Last are individual firm sales forecasts, which are in turn dependent on industry sales forecasts. For example, a simple, single firm forecast might take the industry sales estimate and relate this to the expected market share of the individual firm. Future market share might be estimated on the basis of historical market shares as well as on changes that are anticipated because of new marketing strategies, new products and model changes, and relative prices.

Within the firm, a hierarchy of forecasts also exists. The firm may estimate future total dollar sales, dollar and unit sales by product line, or regional sales in total dollars and units of specified product lines. These forecasts are used in planning orders for raw materials, employee-hiring needs, shipment schedules, and production runs. In addition, marketing managers use sales forecasts to determine optimal sales force allocations, to set sales goals, and to plan promotions. The sales forecast constitutes a crucial part of the financial manager's forecast of the cash needs of the firm. Long-term forecasts for the economy, the industry, and the firm are used in planning long-term capital expenditures for plant and equipment and for charting the general direction of the firm.

Criteria Used in the Selection of a Forecasting Technique

Some forecasting techniques are quite simple and rather inexpensive to develop and use, whereas others are extremely complex, require significant amounts of time to develop, and may be quite expensive. Some are best suited for short-term projections, whereas others are better for preparing intermediate- or long-term forecasts. The technique used in any specific instance depends on a number of factors, including the following:

1. The cost associated with developing the forecasting model compared with potential gains resulting from its use
2. The complexity of the relationships that are being forecast
3. The time period of the forecast (long-term or short-term)
4. The accuracy required of the model
5. The lead time necessary for making decisions dependent on the variables estimated in the forecast model

Testing the Accuracy of Forecasting Models

In determining the accuracy, or reliability, of a forecasting technique, one is concerned with the magnitude of the errors or differences between the observed (actual) (Y) and the forecasted values ($\hat{Y}$) of the variable(s) being examined. Various measures are available for evaluating the accuracy of a forecasting model. Recall, for example, in the discussion of regression analysis in the previous chapter, that the coefficient of determination, or R^2, was used as a measure of the "goodness of fit" in evaluating the explanatory power of a regression equation. In this chapter, the average forecast error, or root mean square error,

$$\text{RMSE} = \sqrt{\frac{1}{n}\Sigma(Y_t - \hat{Y}_t)^2} \qquad [6.1]$$

is used to evaluate the accuracy of a forecasting model (where n is the number of observations). The smaller the value of the RMSE, the greater the accuracy of the forecasting model. One can use the RMSE to compare the accuracy of alternative forecasting models.[1]

Alternative Forecasting Techniques

The managerial economist may choose from a wide range of forecasting techniques. These can be classified in the following general categories:[2]

- Time-series analysis
- Smoothing techniques
- Barometric techniques
- Survey and opinion-polling techniques
- Econometric models
- Input-output analysis
- Vector autoregression (VAR)

The remaining sections of this chapter (and the appendices) examine these forecasting techniques.

---

[1] Another commonly used measure of forecasting accuracy is the mean absolute deviation (MAD). It is defined as follows:

$$\text{MAD} = \frac{1}{n}\Sigma|(Y_t - \hat{Y}_t)|$$

where the variables have the same definitions as in Equation 6.1, and | | indicates the absolute value.

[2] The forecasting techniques examined in this chapter are based on the assumption that historical data are available and that these data will be of use in predicting future values of the variable in question. In some important instances, however, no such historical data are available or data are insufficient to permit the use of traditional forecasting techniques. One such instance is forecasting when a new process or product (e.g., solar energy for power generation) will be widely accepted. Another instance where traditional forecasting may be of little use is when predicting new discoveries and developments in such fields as medical research and space exploration. Various qualitative, or technological, forecasting techniques are available for dealing with these problems. Discussion of these techniques is beyond the scope of this chapter. See Steven C. Wheelwright and Spyros Makridakis, *Forecasting Methods for Management,* 5th ed. (New York: John Wiley, 1989), chap. 17. An excellent source of research on technological forecasting is the journal *Technological Forecasting and Social Change* published by Elsevier Science Publishing Company.

TIME-SERIES ANALYSIS

Time-Series Data

A series of observations taken on an economic variable at various past points in time.

Data collected for use in forecasting the value of a particular variable may be classified into two major categories—time-series and cross-sectional data. **Time-series data** are defined as a sequential array of the values of an economic variable at different points in time. **Cross-sectional data** are an array of the values of an economic variable observed at the same time. Data collected in a census are cross-sectional because they consist of a series of observations taken at approximately the same time on various aspects of the population. No matter what type of forecasting model is being used, one must decide whether time-series or cross-sectional data are most appropriate (and available).

Cross-Sectional Data

A series of observations taken on different observation units (for example, households, states, or countries) at the same point in time.

Time-series forecasting models are based *solely* on historical observations of the values of the variable being forecast. These models do not attempt to explain underlying causal relationships that produce the observed outcome. For example, if a university were interested in predicting student enrollments for the coming term, only past student enrollment figures would be used in developing the forecast.

Components of a Time Series

In the analysis of time-series data (see Figure 6.1a, b), time (in years, months, and so on) is represented on the horizontal axis and the values of the variable are on the vertical axis. The variations that are evident in the time series in Figure 6.1 (and in virtually all economic time series) can be decomposed into four components:

Secular Trends

Long-run changes (growth or decline) in an economic time-series variable.

1. **Secular trends**—These are long-run changes in an economic data series over time [*solid line* in Panel (a) of Figure 6.1]. For example, in empirical demand analyses, such factors as increasing population size or changes in the age distribution or evolving consumer tastes may result in gradual increases or decreases of a demand series over time.

Cyclical Variations

Major expansions and contractions in an economic series that usually are longer than a year in duration.

2. **Cyclical variations**—These are major expansions and contractions in an economic series that are usually greater than a year in duration [*broken line* in Panel (a) of Figure 6.1]. For example, the housing industry appears to experience regular, relatively long-term expansions and contractions in demand. In most industries, however, cyclical variations are not consistent or predictable over time. In addition, to make valid statistical adjustments for cyclical fluctuations in an economic series over time, one must assume that secular trend and cyclical fluctuations result from two different sets of causal factors. This is often difficult to establish. For these reasons, methods of adjusting time-series forecast models for cyclical variations will not be discussed here. When cyclical variations are present in a data series, regression estimates using those data will be distorted due to the presence of positive autocorrelation. Care must then be taken to specify a lag structure appropriate to remove the autocorrelation.[3]

Seasonal Effects

Variations in a time series during a year that tend to appear regularly from year to year.

3. **Seasonal effects**—These cause variations during a year that tend to be more or less consistent from year to year. The data in Panel (b) of Figure 6.1 (*broken line*) show significant seasonal variation. For example, two-thirds of Hickory Farms' (a retailer of holiday food gifts) annual sales occur in the November-December period.

4. **Random fluctuations**—Finally, an economic series may be influenced by random factors that are by and large not predictable [*solid line* in Panel (b) of Figure 6.1], such as wars, natural disasters, and extraordinary government actions (for example, a wage-price freeze).

---

[3] Tests for diagnosing the presence of autocorrelation are discussed in Chapter 5.

FIGURE   6.1

Secular, Cyclical, Seasonal, and Random Fluctuations in Time-Series Data

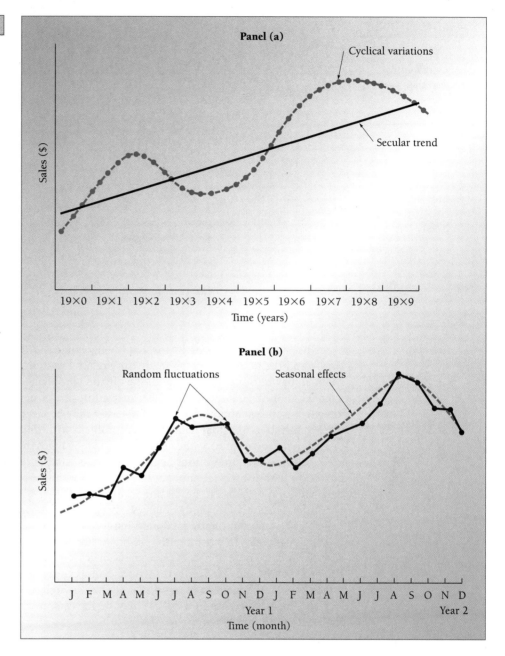

Some Elementary Models

The simplest model states that the forecast value of the variable for the next period will be the same as the value of that variable for the present period:

$$\hat{Y}_{t+1} = Y_t \tag{6.2}$$

For example, consider the sales data shown in Table 6.1 for the Buckeye Brewing Company. To forecast monthly sales, the model uses *actual* beer sales for March 19X3 of 2,738 (000) barrels as the forecast value for April.

A model such as this is quite easy to use and simple to understand. It is particularly useful for forecasting over a short time period when historical evidence indicates no

TABLE 6.1				

Buckeye Brewing
Company's Monthly
Beer Sales (thousands of
barrels)

		Year		
Month	**19X1**	**19X2**	**19X3**	
January	2,370	2,446	2,585	
February	2,100	2,520	2,693	
March	2,412	2,598	2,738	
April	2,376	2,533		
May	3,074	3,250		
June	3,695	3,446		
July	3,550	3,986		
August	4,172	4,222		
September	3,880	3,798		
October	2,931	2,941		
November	2,377	2,488		
December	2,983	2,878		

dramatic short-run changes in the data being forecast. Thus where changes occur slowly and the forecast is being made for a relatively short period in the future, such a model may be quite useful. One of the obvious problems that might exist with such a model is the availability of data. Because a forecast of next month's sales requires a knowledge of this month's sales, the forecaster may be faced with the task of speeding up the collection of actual data. Another problem with this model is that it makes no provision for incorporating the effects of known changes in the environment that may affect sales. Special promotions by the firm (or its competitors) could cause such great distortion in the observed values of the variable for one or more time periods that past data will be of little use in predicting future values.

Further examination of the Buckeye beer sales data in Table 6.1 indicates that monthly sales are not totally random. First we note that there is a slight upward trend in sales—beer sales in most months are higher than in the same month of the previous year. Second, we note that sales are somewhat seasonal—beer sales are high during the summer months and low during the winter. Failure to recognize and incorporate this information into the model will result in consistently high forecast errors.

If a recognizable pattern exists, it may be incorporated by adjusting Equation 6.2 slightly to yield this equation:

$$\hat{Y}_{t+1} = Y_t + (Y_t - Y_{t-1}) \qquad [6.3]$$

For example, Buckeye's sales forecast for April 19X3 using this model would be

$$Y_{t+1} = 2,738 + (2,738 - 2,693)$$

$$= 2,783 \ (000) \ \text{barrels}$$

The use of this model, however, is still somewhat inappropriate for the data in Table 6.1. Although the forecast value for April is probably within reason, the forecast for May would probably seriously understate actual sales in May due to strong seasonality. A better forecast might be that May 19X3 beer sales will assume the same value as (or some percentage above) May 19X2 sales or that May 19X3 sales will be some specified percentage above average sales of the first four months of the year.

FIGURE   6.2

Time-Series Growth
Patterns

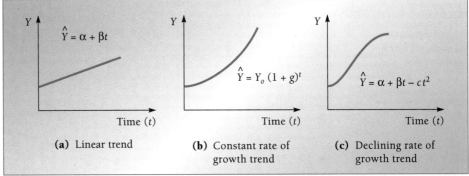

(a) Linear trend

(b) Constant rate of
growth trend

(c) Declining rate of
growth trend

Forecasting models that incorporate trends and seasonal effects such as these are discussed below.

Secular Trends

Long-run changes in an economic time series can follow a number of different types of trends. Three possible cases are shown in Figure 6.2. A *linear* trend is shown in Panel (a). Panels (b) and (c) depict *nonlinear* trends. In Panel (b), the economic time series follows a *constant rate of growth* pattern. The earnings of many corporations follow this type of trend. Panel (c) shows an economic time series that exhibits a declining rate of growth. Sales of a new product may follow this pattern. As market saturation occurs, the rate of growth will decline over time. Linear and constant rate of growth trends are examined in more detail below.

Linear Trends   A linear trend factor in a time series may be estimated in a number of ways. The easiest is to visually fit a straight line through the observed points in a graph relating the variable to points in time, but this method lacks sophistication and consistency because two different forecasters will rarely fit identical trend lines to the same set of data. The use of *least-squares* regression analysis, however, will provide an equation of a straight line of "best fit." (See Chapter 5 for a further discussion of the least-squares technique.) The equation of a linear trend line is given in the general form

$$\hat{Y}_t = \alpha + \beta t \qquad\qquad [6.4]$$

where $\hat{Y}_t$ is the forecast or predicted value for period t, α is the y intercept or constant term, t is a unit of time, and β is an estimate of this trend factor. Typically, some year, quarter, or month is identified as the starting time period (i.e., $t = 0$).

Linear trend forecasting is easy and inexpensive to do, but is generally too simple and inflexible to be used in many forecasting circumstances. However, when the need for precise forecasts is not great, this method may be adequate.

EXAMPLE

LINEAR TREND FORECASTING: PRIZER CREAMERY

Suppose one is interested in forecasting monthly ice cream sales of the Prizer Creamery for 19X5. A least-squares trend line could be estimated from the ice cream sales data for the past four years (48 monthly observations), as shown in Figure 6.3. Assume that the equation of this line is calculated to be

$$\hat{Y}_t = 30{,}464 + 121.3\, t \qquad\qquad [6.5]$$

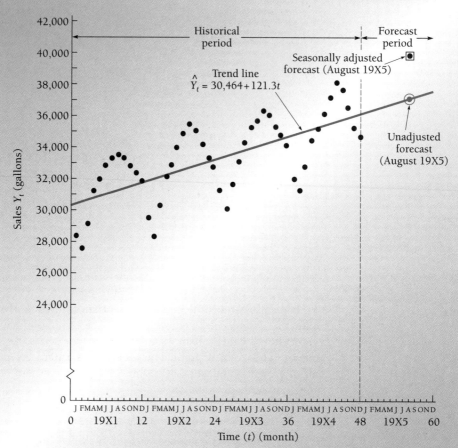

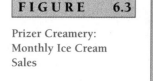

where $\hat{Y}_t =$ predicted monthly ice cream sales in gallons in month t

$30{,}464 =$ number of gallons sold when $t = 0$

$t =$ time period (months) (where December 19X0 = 0, January 19X1 = 1, February 19X1 = 2, March 19X1 = 3, . . .)

The coefficient (121.3) of t indicates that sales may be expected to increase by 121.3 gallons on the average each month. Based on this trend line and ignoring any seasonal effects, forecasted ice cream sales for August 19X5 ($t = 56$) would be

$$Y_{56} = 30{,}464 + 121.3 (56)$$

$$= 37{,}257 \text{ gallons}$$

This *seasonally unadjusted* forecast is given by the point (⊙) on the trend line in Figure 6.3. As can be seen in the graph, ice cream sales are subject to seasonal variations. Later in this section we will show how this seasonal effect can be incorporated into the forecast.

Constant Rate of Growth Trends   The formula for the constant rate of growth forecasting model is

$$\hat{Y}_t = Y_0(1 + g)^t \qquad [6.6]$$

where $\hat{Y}_t$ is the forecasted value for period t, Y_0 is the initial ($t = 0$) value of the time series, g is the constant growth rate per period, and t is a unit of time. The predicted value of the time series in period t $(\hat{Y}_t)$ is equal to the initial value of the series (Y_0) compounded at the growth rate (g) for t periods. Because Equation 6.6 is a nonlinear relationship, the parameters cannot be estimated directly with the ordinary least-squares method. However, taking logarithms of both sides of the equation gives

$$\log \hat{Y}_t = \log Y_0 + \log (1 + g) \cdot t$$

or

$$\hat{Y}_t' = \alpha + \beta t \qquad [6.7]$$

where $\hat{Y}_t' = \log \hat{Y}_t$, $\alpha = \log Y_0$, and $\beta = \log(1 + g)$. Equation 6.7 is a linear relationship whose parameters can be estimated using standard linear regression techniques.

For example, suppose that annual earnings data for the Fitzgerald Company for the past 10 years have been collected and that Equation 6.7 was fitted to the data using least-squares techniques. The annual rate of growth of company earnings was estimated to be 6 percent. If the company's earnings this year $(t = 0)$ are \$600,000, then next year's $(t = 1)$ forecasted earnings would be

$$\hat{Y}_1 = 600,000 (1 + .06)^1$$
$$= \$636,000$$

Similarly, forecasted earnings for the year after next $(t = 2)$ would be[4]

$$\hat{Y}_2 = 600,000 (1 + .06)^2$$
$$= \$674,160$$

Seasonal Variations

When *seasonal* variations are introduced into a forecasting model, its short-run predictive power may be improved significantly. Seasonal variations may be estimated in a number of ways.[5]

Ratio to Trend Method   One approach is the *ratio to trend method*. This method assumes that the trend value is *multiplied by* the seasonal effect.

EXAMPLE

SEASONALLY ADJUSTED FORECASTS: PRIZER CREAMERY (continued)

Recall in the Prizer Creamery example discussed earlier that a linear trend analysis (Equation 6.5) yielded a sales forecast for August 19X5 of 37,257 gallons. This estimate can be adjusted for seasonal effects in the following manner. Assume that over the past four years (19X1–19X4) the trend model predicted the August sales patterns shown in Table 6.2 and that actual sales are as indicated. These data indicate that, on the average, August sales have been 7.0 percent higher than the trend value. Hence, the August 19X5

[4] For large values of t, such calculations can become quite cumbersome. In these cases, present value (and/or compound value) tables or financial calculators can be used in performing the calculations.

[5] In addition to the methods discussed here, another time-series forecasting model that is often very effective in generating forecasts when there is a significant seasonal component is the exponentially weighted moving-average (EWMA) forecasting model. At each point in time, the EWMA model estimates a smoothed average from past data, an average trend gain, and the seasonal factor. These three components are then combined to compute a forecast. See Paul Newbold and Theodore Bos, *Introductory Business Forecasting,* 2nd ed. (Cincinnati, OH: South-Western Publishing, 1994), especially chap. 6.

TABLE 6.2			

Prizer Creamery's August Ice Cream Sales

Year (August)	Forecast	Actual	Actual/Forecast
19X1	31,434	33,600	1.0689
19X2	32,890	35,600	1.0824
19X3	34,346	36,400	1.0598
19X4	35,801	38,200	1.0670
19X5	37,257	—	—
		Sum =	4.2781

Adjustment factor = 4.2781/4 = 1.0695 (i.e., + 7.0%)

sales forecast should be seasonally adjusted *upward* by 7.0 percent to 39,865. The seasonally adjusted forecast is shown by the point (⊡) above the trend line in Figure 6.3. If however, the model predicted February 19X5 ($t = 50$) sales to be 36,529, but similar data indicated February sales to be 10.8 percent below trend on the average, the forecast would be adjusted *downward* to 36,529 $(1 - .108) = 32,584$ gallons.

Dummy Variables   Another approach for incorporating seasonal effects into the linear trend analysis model is the use of *dummy variables*. A dummy variable is a variable that normally takes on one of two values—either 0 or 1. Dummy variables, in general, are used to capture the impact of certain qualitative factors in an econometric relationship, such as sex—male-0 and female-1. This method, assumes that the seasonal effects are *added* to the trend value. If a time series consists of quarterly data, then the following model could be used to adjust for seasonal effects:

$$\hat{Y}_t = \alpha + \beta_1 t + \beta_2 D_{1t} + \beta_3 D_{2t} + \beta_4 D_{3t} \qquad [6.8]$$

where $D_{1t} = 1$ for first-quarter observations and 0 otherwise, $D_{2t} = 1$ for second-quarter observations and 0 otherwise, $D_{3t} = 1$ for third-quarter observations and 0 otherwise, and α and β are parameters to be estimated using least-squares techniques. In this model the values of the dummy variables (D_{1t}, D_{2t}, D_{3t}) for observations in the fourth quarter of each year (base period) would be equal to zero. In the estimated model the value $\beta_2 D_{1t}$ represents the impact of a first-quarter observation (D_1) on values of the forecast, Y_t, relative to the forecast from the omitted class (4th quarter), when D_{2t} and D_{3t} take values of 0.

EXAMPLE

DUMMY VARIABLES AND SEASONAL ADJUSTMENTS: VALUE-MART COMPANY

The Value-Mart Company (a small chain of discount department stores) is interested in forecasting quarterly sales for next year (19X9) based on Equation 6.8. Using quarterly sales data for the past eight years (19X1–19X8), the following model was estimated:

$$\hat{Y}_t = 22.50 + 0.250t - 4.50 D_{1t} - 3.20 D_{2t} - 2.10 D_{3t} \qquad [6.9]$$

where $\hat{Y}_t$ = predicted sales ($ million) in quarter t
  22.50 = quarterly sales ($ million) when $t = 0$
      t = time period (quarter) (where the fourth quarter of 19X0 = 0, first quarter of 19X1 = 1, second quarter of 19X1 = 2, . . .)

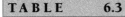

TABLE 6.3					
Value-Mart's Quarterly Sales Forecast (19X9)					

	Time Period	Dummy Variable			Sales Forecast ($ Million) $\hat{Y}_t = 22.50 + .250\,t - 4.50\,D_{1t} - 3.20\,D_{2t} - 2.10\,D_{3t}$
Quarter	t	D_{1t}	D_{2t}	D_{3t}	
1	33	1	0	0	26.25
2	34	0	1	0	27.80
3	35	0	0	1	29.15
4	36	0	0	0	31.50

The coefficient of t (0.250) indicates that sales may be expected to increase by $0.250 million on the average each quarter. The coefficients of the three dummy variables (−4.50, −3.20, and −2.10) indicate the change (i.e., reduction because the coefficients are negative) in sales in quarters 1, 2, and 3, respectively, because of seasonal effects. Based on Equation 6.9, Value-Mart's quarterly sales forecasts for 19X9 are shown in Table 6.3.

Trend projections such as this are most useful for intermediate- and long-term forecasting whereas a simplified trend model is generally inappropriate for estimating short-term variations and predicting the turning points in an economic series. Simple trend projections assume that historical relationships will continue into the future and do not try to discover the underlying causes that produced those historical relationships. If the causal factors change, a poor forecast may result.[6] The introduction of seasonality factors into a forecasting model, however, should significantly improve the model's ability to predict short-run turning points in the data series, provided the historical causal factors have not changed significantly.

The models of time-series forecasting discussed in this section may have substantial value in many areas of business. However, the business forecaster must not rely too heavily on time-series models alone. These models do not seek to relate changes in a data series to the causes underlying observed values in the series, so they are highly susceptible to making poor predictions when the underlying causal factors change. For example, narrow definitions of the nation's money supply have gradually broadened to include bank-card lines of credit in determining inflation forecasts. However, mutual fund balances on which one can now write withdrawal checks may have become a more important measure of household purchasing power in modeling inflationary pressures in the economy.

SMOOTHING TECHNIQUES

Smoothing techniques are another form of time-series forecasting models which assume that an underlying pattern can be found in the historical values of a variable that is being forecast. It is assumed that these historical observations represent not only the

---

[6] A more flexible (and more complex) technique for short-term time-series forecasting is the Box-Jenkins technique. See P. Newbold and T. Bos, *Introductory Business and Economic Forecasting*, 2nd ed. (Cincinnati, OH: South-Western, 1994), chapter 17.

underlying pattern but also random variations. By taking some form of an average of past observations, smoothing techniques attempt to eliminate the distortions arising from random variation in the series and to base the forecast on a smoothed average of several past observations.

In general, smoothing techniques work best when a data series tends to change slowly from one period to the next and when no frequent changes occur in the direction of the underlying pattern. Smoothing techniques, like many other time-series forecasting models, are cheap to develop, relatively inexpensive with respect to data storage needs, and inexpensive to operate; that is, they use up very little computer time.

Moving Averages

Moving averages are one of the simplest of the smoothing techniques. If a data series possesses a large random factor, a trend analysis forecast like those discussed in the previous section will tend to generate forecasts having large errors from period to period. In an effort to minimize the effects of this randomness, a series of recent observations can be averaged to arrive at a forecast. This is the moving average method. A number of observed values are chosen, their average is computed, and this average serves as a forecast for the next period. In general, a moving average may be defined as

$$\hat{Y}_{t+1} = \frac{Y_t + Y_{t-1} + \ldots + Y_{t-N+1}}{N} \qquad [6.10]$$

where $\hat{Y}_{t+1}$ = forecast value of Y for one period in the future
Y_t, Y_{t-1}, Y_{t-N+1} = observed values of Y in periods $t, t-1, \ldots,$
$t - N + 1$, respectively
N = number of observations in the moving average

The greater the number of observations N used in the moving average, the greater the smoothing effect because each new observation receives less weight ($1/N$) as N increases. Hence, generally, the greater the randomness in the data series and the slower the change in the underlying pattern, the more preferable it is to use a relatively large number of past observations in developing the forecast.

EXAMPLE

MOVING AVERAGE FORECASTS: WALKER CORPORATION

The Walker Corporation is examining the use of various smoothing techniques to forecast monthly sales. The company collected sales data for the last 12 months (19X0) as shown in Table 6.4 and Figure 6.4. One technique under consideration is a three-month moving average. Equation 6.10 can be used to generate the forecasts. The forecast for period 4 is computed by averaging the observed values for periods 1, 2, and 3.

$$\hat{Y}_4 = \frac{Y_3 + Y_2 + Y_1}{N} \qquad [6.11]$$

$$= \frac{1,925 + 1,400 + 1,950}{3}$$

$$= 1,758$$

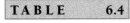

TABLE 6.4

Walker Corporation's
Three-Month Moving
Average Sales Forecast

		Sales ($1,000)		Error	
t	Month	Actual Y_t	Forecast $\hat{Y}_t$	$\overline{(Y_t - \hat{Y}_t)}$	$(Y_t - \hat{Y}_t)^2$
1	January 19X0	1,950	—	—	—
2	February	1,400	—	—	—
3	March	1,925	—	—	—
4	April	1,960	1,758	202	40,804
5	May	2,800	1,762	1,038	1,077,444
6	June	1,800	2,228	−428	183,184
7	July	1,600	2,187	−587	344,569
8	August	1,450	2,067	−617	380,689
9	September	2,000	1,617	383	146,689
10	October	2,250	1,683	567	321,489
11	November	1,950	1,900	50	2,500
12	December	2,650	2,067	583	339,889
13	January 19X1	*	2,283	—	—

Sum = 2,837,257

$$\text{RMSE} = \sqrt{2,837,257/9} = \$561(000)$$

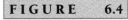

FIGURE 6.4

Walker Corporation's
Three-Month Moving
Average Sales Forecast

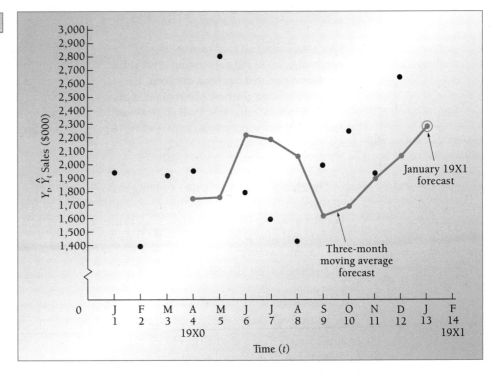

Similarly, the forecast for period 5 is computed as

$$\hat{Y}_5 = \frac{Y_4 + Y_3 + Y_2}{N} \qquad [6.12]$$

$$= \frac{1,960 + 1,925 + 1,400}{3}$$

$$= 1,762$$

Note that if one subtracts $\hat{Y}_4$ from $\hat{Y}_5$, the result is the change in the forecast from $\hat{Y}_4$, or

$$\Delta\hat{Y}_4 = \hat{Y}_5 - \hat{Y}_4 \qquad [6.13]$$

$$= \frac{Y_4 + Y_3 + Y_2}{N} - \frac{Y_3 + Y_2 + Y_1}{N}$$

$$= \frac{Y_4}{N} - \frac{Y_1}{N}$$

Adding this change to $\hat{Y}_4$, the following alternative expression for $\hat{Y}_5$ can be derived:

$$\hat{Y}_5 = \hat{Y}_4 + \frac{Y_4}{N} - \frac{Y_1}{N} \qquad [6.14]$$

or, in general,

$$\hat{Y}_{t+1} = \hat{Y}_t + \frac{Y_t}{N} - \frac{Y_{t-N}}{N} \qquad [6.15]$$

which indicates that each moving average forecast is equal to the past forecast, $\hat{Y}_t$, plus the weighted effect of the most recent observation, Y_t/N, minus the weighted effect of the oldest observation that has been dropped, Y_{t-N}/N. As N becomes larger, the smoothing effect increases because the new observation, Y_t, has a small impact on the moving average.

As shown in Table 6.4, Walker's forecast for January 19X1 ($t = 13$) is $2,283 (000). Note also that the root mean square error (RMSE) of the three-month (N) moving average period is $561(000).

The choice of an appropriate moving average period, that is, the choice of N, should be based on a comparison of the results of the model in forecasting past observations. For example, the forecaster might try a three-period average, a five-period average, and a seven-period average, and compare the accuracy (i.e., RMSE) of the alternatives. The best moving average is chosen on the basis of the value of N that minimizes the root mean square error (Equation 6.1).

First-Order Exponential Smoothing

One criticism of moving averages as smoothing techniques is that they normally give equal weight (a weight of $1/N$) to all observations used in preparing the forecast, even though intuition often indicates that the most recent observation probably contains more immediately useful information than more distant observations. Exponential smoothing is designed to overcome this objection.[7]

---

[7] More complex double exponential smoothing models generally give more satisfactory results than first-order exponential smoothing models when the data possess a linear trend over time. See Newbold and Bos, *Introductory Business Forecasting*.

Consider the following alternative forecasting model:

$$\hat{Y}_{t+1} = wY_t + (1 - w)\hat{Y}_t \qquad [6.16]$$

This model weights the most recent observation by w (some value between 0 and 1 inclusive), and the past forecast by $(1 - w)$. A large w indicates that a heavy weight is being placed on the most recent observation.[8]

Using Equation 6.16, a forecast for $\hat{Y}_t$ may also be written as

$$\hat{Y}_t = wY_{t-1} + (1 - w)(\hat{Y}_{t-1}) \qquad [6.17]$$

By substituting Equation 6.17 into 6.16, we get

$$\hat{Y}_{t+1} = wY_t + w(1 - w)Y_{t-1} + (1 - w)^2\hat{Y}_{t-1} \qquad [6.18]$$

By continuing this process of substitution for past forecasts, we obtain the general equation

$$\hat{Y}_{t+1} = wY_t + w(1 - w)Y_{t-1} + w(1 - w)^2Y_{t-2}$$

$$+ w(1 - w)^3Y_{t-3} + \ldots \qquad [6.19]$$

Equation 6.19 shows that the general formula (Equation 6.16) for an exponentially weighted moving average is a weighted average of all past observations, with the weights defined by the geometric progression:

$$w, (1 - w)w, (1 - w)^2w, (1 - w)^3w, (1 - w)^4w, (1 - w)^5w, \ldots \qquad [6.20]$$

For example, a w of 2/3 would produce the following series of weights:

$$w = .667$$

$$(1 - w)w = .222$$

$$(1 - w)^2w = .074$$

$$(1 - w)^3w = .024$$

$$(1 - w)^4w = .0082$$

$$(1 - w)^5w = .0027$$

With a high initial value of w, heavy weight is placed on the most recent observation, and rapidly declining weights are placed on older values.

Another way of writing Equation 6.16 is

$$\hat{Y}_{t+1} = \hat{Y}_t + w(Y_t - \hat{Y}_t) \qquad [6.21]$$

This indicates that the new forecast is equal to the old forecast plus w times the error in the most recent forecast. A w that is close to 1 indicates a desire to quickly adjust for any error in the preceding forecast. Similarly, a w closer to 0, suggests little desire to adjust the current forecast for last period's error.

It should be apparent from Equations 6.16 and 6.21 that exponential forecasting techniques can be very easy to use. All that is required is last period's forecast, last period's observation, plus a value for the weighting factor, w. The optimal weighting factor is normally determined by making successive forecasts using past data with various values of w and choosing the w that minimizes the root mean square error (RMSE) given in Equation 6.1.

---

[8] The greater the amount of serial correlation (correlation of values from period to period), the larger will be the optimal value of w.

| EXAMPLE |

EXPONENTIAL SMOOTHING: WALKER CORPORATION (continued)

Consider again the Walker Corporation example discussed earlier. Suppose that the company is interested in generating sales forecasts using the first-order exponential smoothing technique. The results are shown in Table 6.5. To illustrate the approach, an exponential weight w of .5 will be used. To get the process started, one needs to make an initial forecast of the variable. This forecast might be a weighted average or some simple forecast, such as Equation 6.2:

$$\hat{Y}_{t+1} = Y_t$$

The latter approach will be used. Hence the forecast for month 2 made in month 1 would be $1,950 (000) ($\hat{Y}_{t+1}$ = 1,950). The month 3 forecast value is (using Equation 6.21)

$$\hat{Y}_3 = 1,950 + .5(1,400 - 1,950)$$

$$= 1,950 - 275 = \$1,675 \ (000)$$

Similarly, the month 4 forecast equals

$$\hat{Y}_4 = 1,675 + .5(1,925 - 1,675)$$

$$= \$1,800 \ (000)$$

The remaining forecasts are calculated in a similar manner. This process is normally repeated for several different values of w until a w is found that minimizes the root mean square error (RMSE). The optimal w is then used to generate future forecasts.

As can be seen in Table 6.5, Walker's sales forecast for January 19X1 using the first-order exponential smoothing technique is $2,322 (000). Also, the root mean square error of this forecasting method (with w = .50) is $491 (000).

| TABLE   6.5 |

Walker Corporation:
First-Order Exponential
Smoothing Sales
Forecast

		Sales ($000)		Error	
t	Month	Actual Y_t	Forecast $\hat{Y}_t$	$(Y_t - \hat{Y}_t)$	$(Y_t - \hat{Y}_t)^2$
1	January 19X0	1,950	—	—	—
2	February	1,400	1,950	−550	302,500
3	March	1,925	1,675	250	62,500
4	April	1,960	1,800	160	25,600
5	May	2,800	1,880	920	846,400
6	June	1,800	2,340	−540	291,600
7	July	1,600	2,070	−470	220,900
8	August	1,450	1,835	−385	148,225
9	September	2,000	1,642	358	128,164
10	October	2,250	1,821	429	184,041
11	November	1,950	2,036	−86	7,396
12	December	2,650	1,993	657	431,649
13	January 19X1	*	2,322	—	—
					Sum = 2,648,975

$$\text{RMSE} = \sqrt{2,648,975/11} = \$491 \ (000)$$

Exponential smoothing gives the forecaster a great deal of flexibility in choosing the appropriate weights for past values. Furthermore, this approach only requires that two pieces of data be stored for each series forecast—the observed value for the last period and the last period forecast.

BAROMETRIC TECHNIQUES

www . . . .

National Bureau of
Economic Research on the
Internet is located at:
http://www.nberg.org

The time-series forecasting models discussed above assume that future patterns in an economic time series may be predicted by projecting past data from that same series. Recall that in our discussion of time-series analysis, cyclical variations were largely ignored because very few economic time series exhibit consistent enough cyclical variations to make simple projection forecasting of these variations a reliable tool. Table 6.6 conveys why the prediction of a business cycle's turning point proves to be so difficult. Although the duration of postwar U.S. business cycles averages 61 months (from peak to peak), two cycles have lasted over 100 months while others have been as short as 32 and even 18 months. Economists, however, have long recognized that if it were possible to isolate sets of time series that exhibited a close correlation of their movements over time, and if one or more of these time series normally *led* (in a consistent manner) the time series in which the forecaster has interest, then this leading series could be used as a predictor or barometer for short-term changes in the series of interest.

Although the concept of leading or barometric forecasting is not new,[9] current barometric forecasting is based largely on the work done at the National Bureau of Economic Research. The barometric forecasting model developed there is used primarily to identify potential future changes in *general business conditions*, rather than conditions for a specific industry or firm.

---

[9] Andrew Carnegie used to count the number of smoke-belching chimneys in Pittsburgh to forecast the level of business activity and consequently the demand for steel.

TABLE 6.6			Contraction*	Expansion†	Business Cycle‡	
Oct 1945	Nov 1948		8	37	88	45
Oct 1949	July 1953		11	45	48	56
May 1954	Aug 1957		10	39	55	49
Apr 1958	Apr 1960		8	24	47	32
Feb 1961	Dec 1969		10	106	34	116
Nov 1970	Nov 1973		11	36	117	47
Mar 1975	Jan 1980		16	58	52	74
July 1980	July 1981		6	12	64	18
Nov 1982	July 1990		16	92	28	108
Mar 1991			8	—	100	—
Average post-war cycle			11	50	61	61

Duration of U.S. Business Cycles (in months)

*Months from previous peak to trough.
†Months from trough to next peak.
‡Months from previous trough to next trough and months from previous peak to next peak.
Source: *Survey of Current Business*, October 1994, Table C-51.

Leading, Lagging, and Coincident Indicators

Economic indicators may be classified as leading, coincident, or lagging indicators (see Figure 6.5). The *Business Conditions Digest,* a monthly publication of the Department of Commerce, provides an extensive list of leading, lagging, and coincident indicators. The long list of indicators includes more than 300 time series that are useful to business analysts and forecasters.

A short list of indicators is also developed that includes 11 series that tend to lead the peaks and troughs of business cycles, 4 series of roughly coincident indicators of economic activity, and 7 series that tend to lag peaks and troughs of economic activity. Table 6.7 lists the economic series included in the short list. This table lists the series name, the mean lead or lag of the series in relation to peaks and troughs of economic activity. Periodically, the Department of Commerce assigns a score to each indicator on the basis of its performance in the following areas:

1. Overall economic significance
2. Statistical adequacy
3. Conformity with the direction and magnitude of changes in the level of economic activity
4. Smoothness
5. Currency in the availability of data
6. Consistency with respect to turning points in economic activity

A perfect score for an indicator according to these criteria would be 100.

The rationale for the use of many of the series listed in this table is obvious. Many of these series represent commitments to future levels of economic activity. Building permits precede housing starts, and orders for durable goods precede their actual production. For

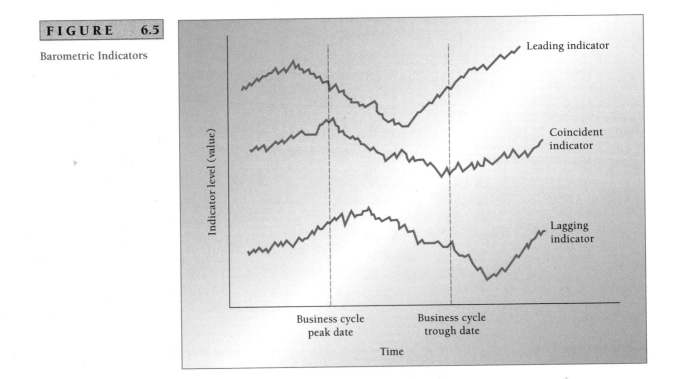

FIGURE   6.5

Barometric Indicators

TABLE	6.7	Cyclical Leads (−) and Lags (+) for Leading, Coincident, and Lagging Indicators (Length in months)

Series No.	Series Title	At reference peaks									
		July 1990	July 1981	Jan. 1980	Nov. 1973	Dec. 1969	Apr. 1960	Aug. 1957	July 1953	Nov. 1948	Mean
LEADING INDICATORS											
1	Average weekly hours, manufacturing	−15	−7	−10	−7	−14	−11	−21	−3	−11	−11.0
5	Average weekly initial claims for unemployment insurance (inverted)[1]	−22	0	−16	−9	−11	−12	−23	−10	−13	−12.9
8	Manufacturers' new orders in 1987 dollars, consumer goods and materials	−2	−2	−13	−8	−13	−13	−25	−3	−5	−9.3
32	Vendor performance, slower deliveries diffusion index	+1	−3	−9	0	−4	−14	−28	−12	−7	−8.4
20	Contracts and orders for plant and equipment in 1987 dollars	−7	−3	−10	−1	−11	−13	−9	−5	−7	−7.3
29	Building permits, new private housing units	−21	−10	−19	−11	−10	−17	−30	−8	−13	−15.4
92	Change in manufacturers' unfilled orders in 1987 dollars, durable goods (smoothed)[2]	−3	−6	−13	−6	−7	−12	−19	−26	−3	−10.6
99	Change in sensitive materials prices (smoothed)[2]	+2	−7	−7	+3	−10	−17	−17	−9	n.a.	−7.8
19	Index of stock prices, 500 common stocks	−1	−8	NST	−10	−12	−9	−13	−6	−30	−11.1
106	Money supply M2 in 1987 dollars	−7	NST	−24	−10	−11	NST	−16	NST	−17	−14.2
83	Index of consumer expectations	−18	−2	−38	−15	−10	−2	−9	−5	n.a.	−12.4
910	Composite index of 11 leading indicators	−18	−8	−15	−9	−11	−11	−20	−5	−7	−11.6
940	Ratio, coincident index to lagging index	−4	−4	−15	−11	−9	−12	−27	−9	−10	−11.2
COINCIDENT INDICATORS											
41	Employees on nonagricultural payrolls	−1	0	+2	+11	+3	0	−5	−1	−2	+0.8
51	Personal income less transfer payments in 1987 dollars	−3	+1	0	0	NST	+1	0	−1	−1	−.4
47	Index of industrial production	+2	0	+2	0	−2	−3	−5	0	−4	−1.1
57	Manufacturing and trade sales in 1987 dollars	−4	−6	−10	0	−2	−3	−6	−3	+1	−3.7
920	Composite index of 4 coincident indicators	−1	+1	0	0	−2	−3	−5	0	−1	−1.2
LAGGING INDICATORS											
91	Average duration of unemployment (inverted)[1]	−13	+5	−6	−2	−2	+2	+1	+2	0	−1.4
77	Ratio, manufacturing and trade inventories to sales in 1987 dollars	+6	+15	+5	+16	+11	+9	+8	+5	+8	+9.2
62	Change in index of labor cost per unit of output, manufacturing (smoothed)[2]	+8	+6	+5	+16	+1	+10	+6	+6	0	+6.4
109	Average prime rate charged by banks	−14	+1	+3	+10	+2	+3	+4	+7	NST	+2.0
101	Commercial and industrial loans outstanding in 1987 dollars	0	+14	+2	+10	+8	NST	+1	−1	+3	+4.6
95	Ratio, consumer installment credit to personal income	−10	NST	−7	+5	NST	+8	+5	+5	NST	+1.0
120	Change in Consumer Price Index for services (smoothed)[2]	+2	+2	+5	+11	+4	−6	−5	n.a.	n.a.	+1.9
930	Composite index of 7 lagging indicators	−8	+3	+3	+13	+3	+3	+4	+5	NST	+3.1

n.a. Not available. Data needed to determine a specific turning point are not available.

[1] This series is inverted; i.e., low values are peaks and high values are troughs.

[2] This series is smoothed by an autoregressive-moving-average filter developed by Statistics Canada.

NOTE:—Reference peaks and troughs are the cyclical turning points in overall business activity; specific peaks and troughs are the cyclical turning points in individual series. This table lists, for the composite indexes and their components, the leads (−) and lags (+) of the specific peaks and troughs in relation to the corresponding reference peaks and troughs. See *Measuring Business Cycles* by Arthur F. Burns and Wesley C. Mitchell (National Bureau of Economic Research, Inc., 1946) for information on the selection of cyclical peaks and troughs.

TABLE   6.7 Cyclical Leads (−) and Lags (+) for Leading, Coincident, and Lagging Indicators (Length in months)—cont'd

Series No.	Series Title	At reference troughs									
		Mar. 1991	Nov. 1982	July 1980	Mar. 1975	Nov. 1970	Feb. 1961	Apr. 1958	May 1954	Oct. 1949	Mean
	LEADING INDICATORS										
1	Average weekly hours, manufacturing	+1	−1	0	0	−2	−2	0	−1	−6	−1.2
5	Average weekly initial claims for unemployment insurance (inverted)	0	−2	−2	0	−1	0	0	+4	0	−.1
8	Manufacturers' new orders in 1987 dollars, consumer goods and materials	0	−1	−2	0	0	0	−2	−7	−4	−1.8
32	Vendor performance, slower deliveries diffusion index	0	−8	−2	−1	+1	−11	−4	−6	−7	−4.2
20	Contracts and orders for plant and equipment in 1987 dollars	+3	+4	−2	+9	−1	+1	−1	−2	−6	+.6
29	Building permits, new private housing units	−2	−13	−3	0	−10	−2	−2	−8	−9	−5.4
92	Change in manufacturers' unfilled orders in1987 dollars, durable goods (smoothed)[2]	+20	−2	−1	+1	−3	−9	−2	−5	−4	−.6
99	Change in sensitive materials prices (smoothed)[2]	0	−5	0	−2	−2	−1	−4	−4	−4	−2.4
19	Index of stock prices, 500 common stocks	−5	−4	NST	−3	−5	−4	−4	−8	−4	−4.6
106	Money supply M2 in 1987 dollars	−2	NST	−2	−2	−7	NST	−3	NST	−15	−5.2
83	Index of consumer expectations	−5	−8	−4	−1	−6	−3	+1	−6	n.a.	−4.0
910	Composite index of 11 leading indicators	−2	−10	−2	−1	−1	−2	−2	−4	−4	−3.1
940	Ratio, coincident index to lagging index	−2	−10	−2	0	−8	−1	0	−5	0	−2.9
	COINCIDENT INDICATORS										
41	Employees on nonagricultural payrolls	+11	0	0	+1	0	0	+1	+3	0	+1.8
51	Personal income less transfer payments in 1987 dollars	+8	0	0	−1	NST	−2	0	−1	−3	+.1
47	Index of industrial production	0	+1	0	0	0	0	0	−1	0	0
57	Manufacturing and trade sales in 1987 dollars	−2	+1	−1	0	0	−1	0	−5	−3	−1.2
920	Composite index of 4 coincident indicators	0	+1	0	0	0	0	0	+2	0	+.3
	LAGGING INDICATORS										
91	Average duration of unemployment (inverted)[1]	+19	+8	+6	+10	+19	+5	+6	+12	+8	+10.3
77	Ratio, manufacturing and trade inventories to sales in 1987 dollars	+36	+14	+6	+44	+27	+14	+13	+12	+9	+17.4
62	Change in index of labor cost per unit of output, manufacturing (smoothed)[2]	+6	+10	+7	+8	+12	+7	+6	+11	+1	+9.7
109	Average prime rate charged by banks	+35	+8	+1	+25	+16	+57	+4	+14	NST	+17.9
101	Commercial and industrial loans outstanding in 1987 dollars	+24	+11	+8	+18	+15	NST	+4	+3	−1	+10.2
95	Ratio, consumer installment credit to personal income	+21	0	NST	+11	NST	+9	+7	+6	NST	+9.0
120	Change in Consumer Price Index for services (smoothed)[2]	+18	+2	+3	+5	+27	+5	+8	n.a.	n.a.	+9.7
930	Composite index of 7 lagging indicators	+36	+7	+3	+21	+15	+6	+4	+9	NST	+9.3

NST No specific turn. No specific turning point is discernible in the data.

Source: *Survey of Current Business,* U.S. Department of Commerce, October 1994, no. C52.

some of the other indicators, the nature of the causal relationships involved is not quite so clear. The value of any particular time series as a predictor of future changes in another series depends on a number of factors. First, the user must be concerned with the success of the series in predicting the turning points in economic activity. Even the best series exhibit only 80 to 90 percent accuracy. In addition, a series is more valuable not only if it consistently leads (lags) business cycles but also if it lacks a large variability in the *length* of the lead (lag). Data for the series must also be available on a current basis. Finally, a series that is free of large random or seasonal fluctuations should be rated high because it will not give as many false signals.

The main value of leading and lagging indicators is in predicting the *direction* of future change in economic activity. These indicators reveal little or nothing about the *magnitude* of the changes.

<table>
<tr><td>

EXAMPLE

www . . . .
The Index of Leading
Economic Indicators can be
accessed at the following
Internet site:
http://www.
conference-board.org/
Descriptions of recent
revisions in this index can
be found at:
http://www.tcb-indicators.
org/rev96/rev96.htm

</td></tr>
</table>

LEADING INDICATORS CHANGE[10]

The Index of Leading Economic Indicators is constantly under scrutiny by both private and public forecasting agencies. When any series appears outdated or begins to generate misleading signals, a replacement can often emerge from a consensus of best practices in business forecasting. Recently, three of the series in Table 6.7 have been ranked "Poor" at predicting recessions and recoveries in the last decade by the Conference Board, a prominent trade association of major corporations that collects, analyzes, and distributes business cycle data. Two of the three (i.e., manufacturers' unfilled orders for durables and the change in sensitive materials prices) may be removed from the Index and replaced by the interest rate spread between 10-year Treasury bond yields and three-month Treasury bill yields. The interest rate spread is an attempt to capture the effects of monetary policy on the business cycle. A long-bond yield 1.21 percent higher than the T-bill yield implies less than a 0.05 probability of recession four quarters ahead. If the Federal Reserve tightens credit such that short-term interest rates rise as much as 0.82 percent above long-term rates, the probability of recession increases to 50 percent. At an interest rate spread of 2.40 percent, the probability of recession four quarters ahead rises to 90 percent. This new indicator of credit conditions should effectively supplement the generally poor third predictor, the M2 measure of the nation's money supply. If inventory policies or oil price hikes return to a position of prominence in business planning, then the manufacturers' unfilled orders and sensitive materials price series can easily be restored to the Index.

Diffusion and Composite Indexes

To overcome some of the weaknesses associated with forecasting based on leading series, economists have developed the *diffusion index*. The primary advantage of this index is that it reduces the chances of making a false prediction based on a short-term fluctuation in one series alone. When all indicators in the index are rising, the diffusion index equals 100; when all are falling it equals 0; and when one-fourth are rising it equals 25. During business cycle expansions, the National Bureau of Economic Research has found that this index is normally above 50 percent and during contractions it is normally below 50 percent. Diffusion indexes may be constructed using any combination of indicator series that the forecaster feels is appropriate.

---

[10] Based on "Makeup of Leading Indicators May Shift," *Wall Street Journal,* 11 August 1996, p. A2

Composite indexes, which are weighted averages of several indicators, are also de-signed to overcome the problem of making false predictions based on short-term fluc-tuations in a single series. The performance of the composite indexes for the 11 leading, 4 coincident, and 7 lagging indicators is summarized in Table 6.7.

In summary, barometric forecasting provides a better basis for predicting short-run turning points in an economic series than the methods discussed earlier. Nevertheless, barometric forecasting still suffers from the major weakness that it is generally incapable of predicting the magnitude of forecast changes.

SURVEY AND OPINION-POLLING TECHNIQUES

Survey and opinion-polling techniques are other forecasting tools that may be helpful in making short-period forecasts. These techniques may be used for forecasting the over-all level of economic activity (or some special portion of it), or they may be used within the firm for forecasting future sales. The rationale for the use of survey and opinion-polling techniques is that certain attitudes having an impact on economic decisions may be identified in advance of the actual implementation of the decision. If individuals who are responsible for making these decisions are polled, they may provide insights into their intended actions. Business firms normally plan additions to plant and equipment well in advance of the actual expenditures; consumers plan expenditures for many durable goods (as well as most other large expenditures such as vacations and educa-tion) in advance of the actual purchase; and governments at all levels prepare budgets indicating priorities and amounts of intended expenditures.

Survey techniques furnish a substantial amount of qualitative information that may be useful in economic forecasting. These techniques are usually used to supplement the other quantitative forecasting methods discussed in this chapter. The greatest value of survey and opinion-polling techniques is that they may help to uncover changes in past relationships that the quantitative techniques assume will remain stable. If consumer tastes are changing or if business executives begin to lose confidence in the economy, survey techniques may be able to uncover these trends before their impact is felt. In addition, survey techniques may provide the only source of data for predicting the demand for new products.

Forecasting Economic Activity

As mentioned, survey and opinion-polling techniques are used as an aid in forecasting economic activity in various sectors of the economy. Some of the best-known surveys available from private and governmental sources include the following:

www . . . .
You may contact the Survey of Current Business on the Internet at:
http://www.bea.doc.gov/bea/scbinf.html

1. *Plant and equipment expenditure plans*—Surveys of business intentions regarding plant and equipment expenditures are conducted by McGraw-Hill, the National Industrial Conference Board, the U.S. Department of Commerce, *Fortune* magazine, the Securities and Exchange Commission, and a number of individual trade associations. The McGraw-Hill survey, for example, is conducted twice yearly and covers all large corporations and many medium-sized firms. The survey reports plans for expenditures on fixed assets, as well as for expenditures on research and development. More than 50 percent of all new investment is accounted for by the McGraw-Hill survey.

   The Department of Commerce–Bureau of Economic Analysis plant and equipment expenditures survey is conducted quarterly and published regularly in the *Survey of Current Business.* The sample is larger and more comprehensive than that used by McGraw-Hill.

The National Industrial Conference Board surveys capital appropriations commitments made by the board of directors of 1,000 manufacturing firms. The survey picks up capital expenditure plans that are to be made sometime in the future and for which funds have been appropriated. It is especially useful to firms that sell heavily to manufacturers and may aid in picking turning points in plant and equipment expenditures. This survey is published in the *Survey of Current Business.*

www . . . .
National Association of Purchasing Managers is located on the Internet at: http://www.napm.org/indexedfiles/rob/main.html

2. *Plans for inventory changes and sales expectations*—Business executives' expectations about future sales and their intentions about changes in inventory levels are reported in surveys conducted by the U.S. Department of Commerce, McGraw-Hill, Dun and Bradstreet, and the National Association of Purchasing Agents. The National Association of Purchasing Agents survey, for example, is conducted monthly, using a large sample of purchasing executives from a broad range of geographical locations and industrial activities in manufacturing firms.

www . . . .
Also, the University of Michigan's Survey Research Center can be found on the Internet: http://www.isr.umich.edu/src/

3. *Consumer expenditure plans*—Consumer intentions to purchase specific products—including household appliances, automobiles, and homes—are reported by the Survey Research Center at the University of Michigan and by the Census Bureau. The Census Bureau survey, for example, is aimed at uncovering varying aspects of consumer expenditure plans, including income, holdings of liquid and nonliquid assets, the likelihood of making future durable goods purchases, and consumer indebtedness.

Sales Forecasting

Opinion polling and survey techniques are also used on a micro level within the firm for forecasting sales. Some of the variations of opinion polling that are used include the following:

1. *Jury of executive opinion model*—The subjective views of top management are averaged to generate one forecast about future sales. Usually, this method is used in conjunction with some quantitative method, such as trend extrapolation. The management jury then modifies the resulting forecast based on their own expectations and insights regarding the sales environment.

2. *Sales force polling*—Some firms survey their own salespeople in the field about their expectations for future sales by specific geographical area and product line. The idea is that the employees who are closest to the ultimate customers may have significant insights to the state of the future market. Forecasts based on sales force polling may then be used to modify other quantitative or qualitative forecasts that have been generated internally in the firm.

3. *Surveys of consumer intentions*—Some firms conduct their own surveys of specific consumer purchases. Such surveys are common in durable goods industries but too expensive or infeasible for less expensive items. Consider an auto dealer who pursues a "customer for life" relationship with his or her target market. Such a dealer or a furniture company may conduct a mail survey of a sample of consumers to estimate consumers' intentions of purchasing replacement autos or furniture. Among other things, the firms may analyze the intentions to buy in relation to consumers' income.

The results of such a survey then are used to project national or regional furniture sales and to predict the impact that changes in income will have on furniture sales.

ECONOMETRIC MODELS

Another forecasting tool that is available to the managerial economist is econometric methodology. Econometrics is a combination of theory, statistical analysis, and mathematical model building to explain economic relationships. Econometric models may vary in their level of sophistication from the simple to the extremely complex. Econometric techniques for demand estimation were discussed in detail in Chapter 5. The discussion in this section deals with the application of these techniques to economic forecasting.

Advantages of Econometric Forecasting Techniques

Forecasting models based on econometric methodology possess a number of significant advantages over time-series analysis (e.g., trend projection) models, barometric models, and survey or opinion poll-based models. The most significant advantage of econometric models is that they seek to actually *explain* the economic phenomenon being forecast. Because management frequently is able to manipulate some of the independent variables embodied in the model (such as price or advertising expenditures in a demand model), econometric models enable management to assess quantitatively the impact of changes in its policies.

Another advantage of econometric models is that they predict not only the direction of change in an economic series but also the magnitude of that change. This represents a substantial improvement over the trend projection models, which failed to identify turning points, and the barometric models, which did not forecast the magnitudes of expected changes.

A third advantage of econometric models is their adaptability. On the basis of a comparison between forecast values and actual values, the model can be modified (that is, existing parameters may be reestimated and new variables or relationships developed) to improve future forecasts.

Single-Equation Models

The simplest form of econometric model is the single-equation model. This is the type that is frequently used in empirical demand analysis. For example, in the previous chapter, a single-equation model was developed for explaining the demand for Sherwin-Williams house paint. Once the parameters of the demand equation were estimated, we showed how the model could be used to make forecasts of demand for house paint in a given region.

Applications of Single-Equation Forecasting Models

Single-equation econometric models have been widely used by firms to aid in forecasting the demand for their products. An example of single-equation forecasting models is presented below to illustrate the form and substance of many such models.

EXAMPLE

SINGLE-EQUATION FORECASTS: THE DEMAND FOR GAME-DAY ATTENDANCE IN THE NFL

Welki and Zlatoper report a model that explains the major determinants of the demand for game-day attendance at National Football League games.[11] The model is based on data from the 1991 season. A forecasting model such as this might be used by a team to

---

[11] Andrew M. Welki and Thomas J. Zlatoper, "U.S. Professional Football: The Demand for Game-Day Attendance in 1991," *Managerial and Decision Economics* (September-October 1994), pp. 489–495.

plan the most opportune times for special promotions and to predict demand for items sold at the stadium concession outlets. The following variables were used in the estimated model:

ATTENDANCE	game attendance
PRICE	average ticket price (1991 dollars)
INCOME	real per capita income (1987 dollars)
COMPCOST	price of parking at one game (1991 dollars)
HMTMRECORD	season's winning proportion of the home team prior to game day
VSTMRECORD	season's winning proportion of the visiting team prior to game day
GAME	number of the regular season game played by the home team
TEMP	high temperature on game day
RAIN	dummy variable 1 = rain, 0 = no rain
DOME	dummy variable 1 = indoors, 0 = outdoors
DIVRIVAL	dummy variable 1 = teams are in same division, 0 = teams are not in same division
CONRIVAL	dummy variable 1 = conference game, 0 = nonconference game
NONSUNDAY	dummy variable 1 = game day is not Sunday, 0 = game day is Sunday
SUNNIGHT	dummy variable 1 = game moved to Sunday night for coverage on ESPN, 0 otherwise
BLACKOUT	dummy variable = 1 if game is blacked out for local TV, 0 otherwise

The estimated values of the coefficients for each of these variables are as follows:

Independent Variable	Expected Sign	Estimated Coefficient	T-Statistic
INTERCEPT		98053.00	11.49
PRICE	−	−642.02	−3.08
INCOME	?	−1.14	−3.12
COMPCOST	−	574.94	1.34
HMTMRECORD	+	16535.00	6.38
VSTMRECORD	?	2588.70	1.05
GAME	?	−718.65	−3.64
TEMP	?	−66.17	−1.27
RAIN	−	−2184.40	−1.23
DOME	?	−3171.70	−1.66
DIVRIVAL	+	−1198.00	−0.70
CONRIVAL	?	−1160.00	−0.58
NONSUNDAY	+	4114.80	1.74
SUNNIGHT	+	804.60	0.28
BLACKOUT		−5261.00	−3.15

These results indicate that weather conditions have little impact on the attendance at games. Fans appear to favor games played outdoors rather than in domed stadiums. Conference and divisional rivalries do not appear to impact demand greatly. Higher prices negatively impact attendance, but demand appears to be inelastic at current price levels. The quality of the team, as measured by its winning percentage, has a significant positive impact on attendance. A model similar to this could be used as the basis for forecasting demand for any type of athletic event.

Multiple-Equation Models

Although in many cases single-equation models may accurately specify the relationship that is being examined, frequently the interrelationships may be so complex that a system of several equations becomes necessary. Before examining a simple five-equation model of the national economy, it may be helpful to define some of the more important terms encountered in a discussion of econometric models.

Endogenous Variables
The variables that the econometric model seeks to explain or predict through the solution of a system of equations.

Exogenous Variables
The variables that are explained or determined by factors external to the econometric model.

Endogenous and Exogenous Variables **Endogenous variables** are those that the model seeks to explain, or predict, via the solution of the system of equations. **Exogenous variables** are explained outside the model. Exogenous variables are determined by factors external to the model and may include such things as the level of government expenditures or the level of exports. They may also include variables that are specified by earlier data. If corporate investment were expressed as a function of corporate profits lagged by one period, the corporate profit variable would be considered an exogenous variable. Remember that every econometric model may have a different set of endogenous and exogenous variables and that a variable considered exogenous in one model may be endogenous in another.

Structural and Definitional Equations An econometric model consists of two types of equations: *structural* (or *behavioral*) equations and *definitional* equations. A structural equation explains the relationship between a particular endogenous variable and other variables in the system. In addition, a number of definitional equations will be included in the model that specify relationships that are true by definition. The statement that gross national product (*GNP*) equals consumption expenditures *C* plus gross capital investment *I* plus government expenditures *G* is an example of a definitional equation.

EXAMPLE

MULTIPLE-EQUATION MODELS: THE U.S. ECONOMY

An econometric model based on a system of equations can best be illustrated by examining a simple model of the national economy:

$$C = \alpha_1 + \beta_1 Y + \epsilon_1 \tag{6.22}$$

$$I = \alpha_2 + \beta_2 P_{t-1} + \epsilon_2 \tag{6.23}$$

$$T = \beta_3 GNP + \epsilon_3 \tag{6.24}$$

$$GNP = C + I + G \tag{6.25}$$

$$Y = GNP - T \tag{6.26}$$

where *C* = consumption expenditures
  I = investment
  P_{t-1} = profits, lagged one period

GNP = gross national product
T = taxes
Y = national income
G = government expenditures

Equations 6.22, 6.23, and 6.24 are behavioral or structural equations, whereas Equations 6.25 and 6.26 are identities or definitional equations. Once the system of equations has been specified, the next task is to estimate the value of the parameters (α_1, α_2, β_1, β_2, β_3) based on historical data. The ϵ's are included in Equations 6.22, 6.23, and 6.24 to reflect the fact that the theoretical relationships are not exact. To make unbiased estimates of the model's parameters, one must assume that the ϵ's (disturbance terms) are randomly distributed with an expected value of zero. The econometric techniques used to solve for the values of the parameters in a system of equations are beyond the scope of this book.[12] Once parameters have been estimated, forecasts may be generated by substituting known or estimated values for the exogenous variables into the system and solving for the endogenous variables.

Complex Models of the U.S. Economy   A number of complex multiple-equation econometric models of the U.S. economy have been developed and are used to forecast business activity. Information on three of these models is summarized in Table 6.8. As can be seen, some of the large econometric models still rely heavily on the judgment of their staffs of economists and on a subjective interpretation of current economic data. In choosing an econometric model, a manager should determine that the model provides *timely* forecasts of variables of particular importance to the firm. The manager should

---

[12] See, for example, Ernest R. Berndt, *The Practice of Econometrics* (Reading, Mass.: Addison-Wesley Publishing Co., 1991), chapter 8.

TABLE   6.8

Characteristics of Three Econometric Models of the U.S. Economy

	Model		
Characteristic	**Wharton Econometric Forecasting Associates**	**Chase Econometric Associates**	**Townsend-Greenspan**
Approximate number of variables forecasted	10,000	700	800
Forecast horizon (quarters)	2	10–12	6–10
Frequency of model updates (times per year)	12	12	4
Date model forecast first regularly issued	1963	1970	1965
Forecasting techniques			
(a) Econometric model	60%	70%	45%
(b) Judgment	30%	20%	45%
(c) Time-series methods	—	5%	—
(d) Current data analysis	10%	5%	10%

SOURCE: Stephen K. McNees, "The Recent Record of Thirteen Forecasters," *New England Economic Review* (September-October 1981), pp. 5–21.

also check the past forecasting accuracy of the model compared with alternative, available models.

Appendix 6A introduces a relatively new class of econometric forecasting models known as *vector autoregression* (VAR) models. These models combine elements of time-series analysis with elements of structural (multiequation) models and, under certain circumstances, have produced excellent forecasts of future economic activity.

EXAMPLE

CONSENSUS FORECASTS: THE LIVINGSTON SURVEYS[13]

From 1946 until his death in 1989, Joseph A. Livingston conducted a semiannual survey of leading U.S. economists regarding their forecasts of unemployment, inflation, stock prices, and economic growth. The 50 to 60 economists who were regularly surveyed represented a cross section from large corporations and banks, labor unions, government, investment banking firms, and universities. In addition to providing a broad consensus forecast of the economy, the Livingston surveys have been used by researchers as direct measures of economic expectations when testing various economic theories. The Livingston surveys also have been used to test theories regarding the way expectations are formed. The Federal Reserve Bank of Philadelphia took over the survey after Livingston's death.

The Livingston survey provides an indication of expectations regarding the future course of the economy. As a broad-based consensus forecast, it tends to be more stable over time than any individual forecast. Indeed, there is evidence that consensus forecasts such as this tend to be more accurate than any individual forecast, because individual forecast errors tend to cancel out each period. Figure 6.6 indicates the record of the Livingston forecasts in predicting major expansions and recessions. As can be seen in that figure, these economists have tended to predict relatively moderate recessions and expansions, with the exception of the 1949 period and the 1980–82 period. In contrast, there is evidence that economists have tended to underestimate both increases and decreases in the inflation rate. However, forecasts of inflation are improving. Figure 6.7 shows that actual and expected inflation have mirrored one another in the 1990s.[14]

[13] Based on Herb Taylor, "The Livingston Surveys: A History of Hopes and Fears," *Business Review*, Federal Reserve Bank of Philadelphia (January-February 1992), pp. 15–27.

[14] Based on Dean Croushore, "Inflation Forecasts: How Good Are They?" *Business Review*, Federal Reserve Bank of Philadelphia (May/June 1996), pp. 15–25.

FIGURE 6.6	Livingston Forecasts

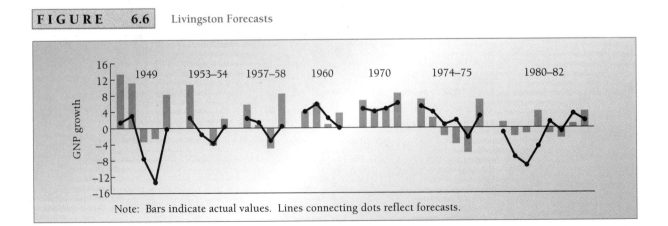

Note: Bars indicate actual values. Lines connecting dots reflect forecasts.

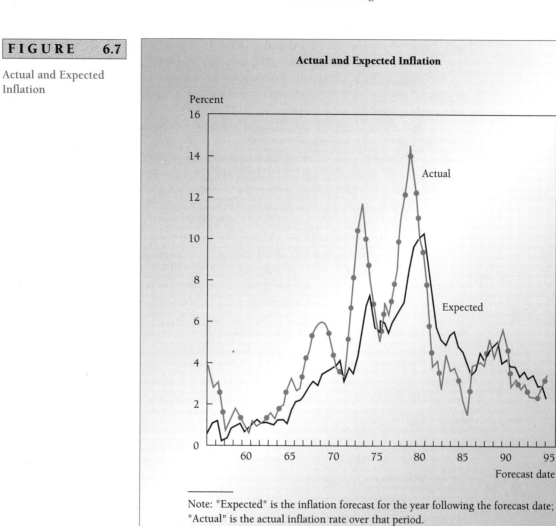

FIGURE   6.7

Actual and Expected
Inflation

Note: "Expected" is the inflation forecast for the year following the forecast date;
"Actual" is the actual inflation rate over that period.

Source: Federal Reserve Bank of Philadelphia.

Consensus forecasts of macroeconomic activity, such as the Livingston forecasts, can provide an extremely useful and low-cost source of key macroeconomic variables that can be used by both large and small firms in their own forecasting and business planning efforts.

**INTERNATIONAL
PERSPECTIVES**

LONG-TERM SALES FORECASTING BY GENERAL MOTORS IN OVERSEAS MARKETS[15]

General Motors has an extensive forecasting system for both its North American and its overseas operations that is implemented by the Corporate Product Planning and Economics Staff. The process generates short- and long-term forecasts of the U.S. vehicle market and long-term forecasts for overseas markets. A discussion of the overseas forecasting process follows.

General Motors produces forecasts for motor vehicle sales in nearly 60 countries. These countries vary in the number of cars per 1,000 people (car density), from less than 10 to over 500. The primary factor used to explain the growth in car density is the level

www . . . .
The International Institute of
Forecasters maintains an
Internet site at:
http://weatherhead.
cwru.edu/forecasting/

[15] This section was adapted from Richard DeRoeck, "Sales Forecasting at General Motors," *International Institute of Forecasters Newsletter* (December 1990), pp. 2–4.

and changes in income in each country. In the first step of the forecasting process, the macroeconomic relationship between key economic variables, including income levels and motor vehicle sales, is estimated. Specifically, estimates are made of the income elasticity of demand in each country. The second step attempts to monitor changes over time in the relationships established in step one.

The third step consists of consultations between the Product Planning and Economics Staff and the Marketing Staffs of each GM overseas operation. The objective of this phase is to identify any special factors in each country that might require a significant modification in the forecasts generated from the econometric models. For example, in the early and mid-1980s, it was felt that certain fiscal and infrastructure policies that had been adopted by government would hold down demand by up to 50 percent, relative to the forecasts from the econometric model. When these policy barriers were removed, car sales increased greatly, returning to levels predicted by the econometric model.

The final step provides models of alternative future scenarios that reflect the impact of major changes in the economic environment for which full information is unavailable. For example, GM has developed an alternative model scenario that reflects the impact of the creation of a single West European market and the dissolution of the former Soviet-bloc countries. Events then are monitored to determine which alternative scenario appears to provide the best basis for making future forecasts.

The types of sales forecasting models that are available to managers of global corporations are really no different than those available to domestic firms. However, these models must be customized to reflect the specific economic conditions in each country. Important relationships, such as the income and price elasticity of demand, are likely to vary substantially between countries. And deriving cash flow forecasts from foreign sales necessitates modeling (and managing) the exchange rate risk exposure. Furthermore, one often finds that the data desired to develop and implement an econometric forecasting model are not readily available, especially in lesser developed economies. These data problems increase the difficulty of developing accurate forecasting models for use by a multinational firm.

FORECASTING WITH INPUT-OUTPUT ANALYSIS

Another forecasting approach that capitalizes on the interdependence between various intermediate product and final product industries is *input-output analysis*. Input-output analysis enables the forecaster to trace the effects of an increase in demand for one product to other industries. An increase in the demand for automobiles will first lead to an increase in the output of the auto industry. This in turn will lead to an increase in the demand for steel, glass, plastics, tires, and upholstery fabric. In addition, secondary impacts will occur as the increase in the demand for upholstery fabric, for example, requires an increase in the production of fibers used to make the fabric. The demand for machinery may also increase as a result of the fabric demand, and so the pattern continues. Input-output analysis permits the forecaster to trace through all the interindustry effects that occur as a result of the initial increase in the demand for automobiles.

Input-Output Tables

Input-output forecasting requires the use of a complicated set of tables specifying the interdependence among the various industries in the economy.[16] The construction of

---

[16] The most recent input-output tables may be found for 85 industries in "Benchmark Input-Output Accounts for the U.S. Economy, 1987: Requirements Tables", *Survey of Current Business* (May 1994), pp. 62–86. These tables are slightly modified from time to time to reflect changes in the computation of the National Income and Product Accounts and other minor changes.

these tables is a massive undertaking. Fortunately for most managerial economists, it is done periodically and made available by the Bureau of Economic Analysis (BEA) of the Department of Commerce.

SUMMARY

- A forecast is a prediction concerning the future.
- The choice of a forecasting technique depends on the cost of developing the forecasting model relative to the potential benefits to be derived, the complexity of the relationship being forecast, the time period for the forecast, the accuracy required of the model, and the lead time required to obtain inputs for the forecasting model.
- Data used in forecasting may be in the form of a time series—that is, a series of observations of a variable over a number of past time periods—or they may be cross-sectional—that is, observations are taken at a single point in time for a sample of individuals, firms, geographic regions, communities, or some other set of observable units.
- Time-series forecasting models are based on an extrapolation of past values into the future. Time-series forecasting models may be adjusted for seasonal, secular, and cyclical trends in the data.
- When a data series possesses a great deal of randomness, *smoothing techniques,* such as moving averages and exponential smoothing, may improve the forecast accuracy.
- Neither trend analysis models nor smoothing techniques are capable of identifying major future changes in the direction of an economic data series.
- *Barometric techniques,* which employ leading, lagging, and coincident indicators, are designed to forecast changes in the direction of a data series but are poorly suited for forecasting the magnitude of the change.
- *Survey and opinion-polling techniques* are often useful in forecasting such variables as business capital spending and major consumer expenditure plans and for generating product-specific or regional sales forecasts for a firm.
- *Econometric methods* seek to explain the reasons for a change in an economic data series and to use this quantitative, explanatory model to make future forecasts. Econometric models are one of the most useful business forecasting tools, but they tend to be expensive to develop and maintain.
- The ultimate measure of the effectiveness of a forecast is not its level of mathematical or theoretical sophistication, but rather its ability to generate cost-effective estimates of the future that are sufficiently accurate to meet the needs of the decision maker.

EXERCISES

1. An economist for Pittsburgh Brewing Company has hypothesized a forecasting model in which the sales in any particular month are directly proportional to the square of the wages of Pittsburgh steelworkers in the previous month, plus a random error.

   a. If S = sales, W = steelworkers' wages, t = time, and e = the random error term, formulate an equation for this month's sales and another equation to forecast next month's sales.

   b. If the random errors average out to zero, and if sales this month are $900,000 and wages last month were $2,000, what should next month's sales be if this month's wages decline to $1,800?

2. The forecasting staff for the Prizer Corporation has developed a model to predict sales of its air-cushioned-ride snowmobiles. The model specifies that sales S vary jointly with disposable personal income Y and the population between ages 15 and 40, Z, and *inversely* with the price of the snowmobiles P. Based on past data, the best estimate of this relationship is

$$S = k \, \frac{YZ}{P}$$

where k has been estimated (with past data) to equal 100.

a. If $Y = \$11,000$, $Z = \$1,200$, and $P = \$20,000$, what value would you predict for S?

b. What happens if P is reduced to $\$17,500$?

c. How would you go about developing a value for k?

d. What are the potential weaknesses of this model?

3. Forecast errors can usually be reduced by increasing the amount of time and money spent on preparing the forecast. Under what circumstances might such an increase in expenditures not be undertaken by profit-maximizing managers?

4. Stowe Automotive is considering an offer from Indula to build a plant making automotive parts for use in that country. In preparation for a final decision, Stowe's economists have been hard at work constructing a basic econometric model for Indula to aid the company in predicting future levels of economic activity. Because of the cyclical nature of the automotive parts industry, forecasts of future economic activity are quite important in Stowe's decision process.

Corporate profits (P_{t-1}) for all firms in Indula were about $100 billion. *GNP* for the nation is composed of consumption C, investment I, and government spending G. It is anticipated that Indula's federal, state, and local governments will spend in the range of $200 billion next year. On the basis of an analysis of recent economic activity in Indula, consumption expenditures are assumed to be $100 billion plus 80 percent of national income. National income is equal to *GNP* minus taxes T. Taxes are estimated to be at a rate of about 30 percent of *GNP*. Finally, corporate investments have historically equaled $30 billion plus 90 percent of last year's corporate profits (P_{t-1}).

a. Construct a five-equation econometric model of the state of Indula. There will be a consumption equation, an investment equation, a tax receipt equation, an equation representing the *GNP* identity, and a national income equation.

b. Assuming that all random disturbances average to zero, solve the system of equations to arrive at next year's forecast values for C, I, T, *GNP*, Y. (*Hint:* It is easiest to start by solving the investment equation and then working through the appropriate substitutions in the other equations.)

5. a. Fred's Hardware and Hobby House expects its sales to increase at a constant rate of 8 percent per year over the next three years. Current sales are $100,000. Forecast sales for each of the next three years.

b. If sales in 19X0 were $60,000 and they grew to $100,000 by 19X4 (a four-year period), what was the actual annual compound growth rate?

6. Metropolitan Hospital has estimated its average monthly bed needs as

$$N = 1,000 + 9X$$

where X = time period (months); January 19X6 = 0

N = monthly bed needs

Assume that no new hospital additions are expected in the area in the foreseeable future. The following monthly seasonal adjustment factors have been estimated, using data from the past five years:

Month	Adjustment Factor
January	+5%
April	−15%
July	+4%
November	−5%
December	−25%

    a. Forecast Metropolitan's bed demand for: January, April, July, November, and December of 19X8.

    b. If the following actual and forecast values for June bed demands have been recorded, what seasonal adjustment factor would you recommend be used in making future June forecasts?

Year	Forecast	Actual
19X6	1,045	1,096
19X5	937	993
19X4	829	897
19X3	721	751
19X2	613	628
19X1	505	560

7. A firm has experienced the demand shown in the table below over the past ten years.

Year	Demand	5-Year Moving Average	3-Year Moving Average	Exponential Smoothing ($w = .9$)	Exponential Smoothing ($w = .3$)
19X0	800	xxxxx	xxxxx	xxxxx	xxxxx
19X1	925	xxxxx	xxxxx	—	—
19X2	900	xxxxx	xxxxx	—	—
19X3	1025	xxxxx	—	—	—
19X4	1150	xxxxx	—	—	—
19X5	1160	—	—	—	—
19X6	1200	—	—	—	—
19X7	1150	—	—	—	—
19X8	1270	—	—	—	—
19X9	1290	—	—	—	—
19Y0	*	—	—	—	—

*Unknown future value to be forecast.

a.   Fill in the table above by preparing forecasts based on a five-year moving average, a three-year moving average, and exponential smoothing (with a $w = .9$ and a $w = .3$). *Note:* The exponential smoothing forecasts may be begun by assuming $\hat{Y}_{t+1} = Y_t$.

b.   Using the forecasts from 19X5 through 19X9, compare the accuracy of each of the forecasting methods based on the RMSE criterion.

c.   Which forecast would you use for 19Y0? Why?

8.   The economic analysis division of Mapco Enterprises has estimated the demand function for its line of weed trimmers as

$$Q_D = 18{,}000 + 0.4N - 350P_M + 90P_S$$

where N = number of new homes completed in the primary market area

   P_M = price of the Mapco trimmer

   P_S = price of its competitor's Surefire trimmer

   In 19X1, 15,000 new homes are expected to be completed in the primary market area. Mapco plans to charge $50 for its trimmer. The Surefire trimmer is expected to sell for $55.

a.   What sales are forecast for 19X1 under these conditions?

b.   If its competitor cuts the price of the Surefire trimmer to $50, what effect will this have on Mapco's sales?

c.   What effect would a 30 percent reduction in the number of new homes completed have on Mapco's sales (ignore the impact of the price cut of the Surefire trimmer)?

9.   The sales of Cycle City, a large motorcycle and moped distributor, have been growing significantly over the past ten years. This past history of sales growth is indicated in the table below:

Year	Sales
19X0	$100,000
19X1	130,000
19X2	166,400
19X3	209,664
19X4	259,983
19X5	317,180
19X6	380,615
19X7	449,126
19X8	520,986
19X9	593,924
19Y0	665,195

a.   What has been the compound annual rate of growth in sales for Cycle City over this ten-year period?

b.   Based on your answer in part (a), what sales do you forecast for the next year (19Y1)?

c.   Graph the growth in sales over the past ten years. What has been happening to the rate of growth over this period?

d.   Based on your answer to part (c), what sales do you forecast for 19Y1?

10. The Questor Corporation has experienced the following sales pattern over the past ten years:

Year	Sales ($000)
19X0	121
19X1	130
19X2	145
19X3	160
19X4	155
19X5	179
19X6	215
19X7	208
19X8	235
19X9	262
19Y0	*

*Unknown future value to be forecast.

a. Compute the equation of a trend line (similar to Equation 6.4) for these sales data to forecast sales for the next year. (Let 19X0 = 0, 19X1 = 1, etc. for the time variable.) What does this equation forecast for sales in the year 19Y0?

b. Use a first-order exponential smoothing model with a w of 0.9 to forecast sales for the year 19Y0.

11. The following table provides corporate average bond yields for each month of 19X4:

Month	Yield
January	12.92%
February	12.88
March	13.33
April	13.59
May	14.13
June	14.40
July	14.32
August	13.78
September	13.56
October	13.33
November	12.88
December	12.74

a. Use the models in Equations 6.2, 6.3, 6.4, plus a three-month moving average to forecast the interest rate for January 19X5.

b. Compare the results of each of these forecasts with the actual January 19X5 figure of 12.64 percent.

12. Bell Greenhouses has estimated its monthly demand for potting soil to be the following:

$$N = 400 + 4X$$

where N = monthly demand for bags of potting soil

   X = time periods in months (March 19X4 = 0)

Assume this trend factor is expected to remain stable in the foreseeable future. The following table contains the monthly seasonal adjustment factors, which have been estimated using actual sales data from the past five years:

Month	Adjustment Factor
March	+2%
June	+15%
August	+10%
December	-12%

a. Forecast Bell Greenhouses' demand for potting soil in March, June, August, and December 19X6.

b. If the following table shows the forecasted and actual potting soil sales by Bell Greenhouses for April in each of the past five years, determine the seasonal adjustment factor to be used in making an April 19X6 forecast.

Year	Forecast	Actual
19X5	500	515
19X4	452	438
19X3	404	420
19X2	356	380
19X1	308	320

13. Savings-Mart (a chain of discount department stores) sells patio and lawn furniture. Sales are seasonal, with higher sales during the spring and summer quarters and lower sales during the fall and winter quarters. The company developed the following quarterly sales forecasting model:

$$\hat{Y}_t = 8.25 + .125t - 2.75D_{1t} + 2.25D_{2t} + 3.50D_{3t}$$

where $\hat{Y}_t$ = predicted sales ($ million) in quarter t

   8.25 = quarterly sales ($ million) when $t = 0$

   t = time period (quarter) where the fourth quarter of 19X0 = 0, first quarter of 19X1 = 1, second quarter of 19X1 = 2, . . .

   $D_{1t} = \begin{cases} 1 \text{ for first-quarter observations} \\ 0 \text{ otherwise} \end{cases}$

   $D_{2t} = \begin{cases} 1 \text{ for second-quarter observations} \\ 0 \text{ otherwise} \end{cases}$

   $D_{3t} = \begin{cases} 1 \text{ for third-quarter observations} \\ 0 \text{ otherwise} \end{cases}$

Forecast Savings-Mart's sales of patio and lawn furniture for each quarter of 19X6.

14. The demand for tea has been estimated as

$$Q = 7,000 - 550P + 210I + 425P_c$$

where Q = thousands of pounds of tea sold

   P = price per pound of tea

   I = per capita disposable personal income in thousands of dollars

   P_c = price per pound of coffee

   a. If next year's tea price is forecast to be $3, per capita disposable personal income is estimated to be $15,000 (that is, 15), and the price per pound of coffee is estimated to be $4, compute the expected quantity demanded for the coming year.

   b. Economic forecasters think there is a high probability of a major recession next year that would reduce per capita income to $13,000 (13). In addition, a frost in Brazil is likely to increase the price of coffee to $7 per pound. What impact would these changes in the economic outlook have on the demand for tea?

15. A university is typically required to prepare operating budgets well in advance of actually receiving its revenues and incurring the expenditures. An important source of revenue is student tuition, which is obviously a function of the number of students enrolled. A university was having problems in preparing accurate budgets because past forecasts of enrollment, made each February before the start of the academic year in September, were subject to considerable error. One aspect of the problem was determining the relationship between the numbers of applications received by February 1 and the number of new students entering the university in the following September. The data tabulated below were collected on September registrations and February 1 applications.

Year	Number of Applications Received by February 1 (Hundreds)	Number of New Students Enrolled in September (Hundreds)
19X0	28	24
19X1	26	20
19X2	28	18
19X3	28	22
19X4	36	32
19X5	36	33
19X6	42	34
19X7	46	34
19X8	46	35
19X9	50	38

   a. Given the nature of the forecasting problem, which variable would be the dependent variable and which would be the independent variable?

   b. Plot the data.

   c. Determine the estimated regression line. Give an economic interpretation of the slope (β) coefficient.

   d. Test the hypothesis that there is no relationship (that is, $\beta = 0$) between the variables.

e.   Calculate the coefficient of determination.

f.   Perform an analysis of variance on the regression, including an *F*-test of the overall significance of the results.

g.   Suppose 4,200 applications are received by February 1. What is the best estimate, based on the regression model, of the number of new students that will be enrolled in the following September? Construct an approximate 95 percent prediction interval.

h.   Suppose that as the result of changes in the deadlines for scholarship and loan selection requests, applications received by February 1 increase to 6,000. What would be the estimate of enrollment for the following September?

i.   Would the estimate of enrollment in part (h) be reliable? Why or why not?

www exercise

Economic Forecasting

16. Use the monthly series on the Consumer Price Index (all items) from the previous 2 years to produce a forecast of the CPI for each of the next 3 years. Is the precision of your forecast greater or less at 36 months ahead than at 12 months ahead? Why? Compare your answer to that of the Dismal Scientist, a company that provides economic data, analysis, and forecasts on the Internet at: http://www.dismal.com/. Once you have accessed their site, click the "forecasts" button, and then request annual forecasts for prices.

CASE EXERCISE   SOUTH POLE ICE CREAM COMPANY

Monthly sales (× $100,000) of the South Pole Ice Cream Company are shown in the table below.

Month	19X0	19X1	19X2
January	2.30	2.65	3.30
February	2.60	2.80	3.60
March	2.70	3.00	3.60
April	2.85	3.20	4.20
May	3.25	3.85	4.20
June	3.30	3.90	5.00
July	3.25	3.80	*
August	3.35	3.90	*
September	3.20	3.60	*
October	3.10	3.55	*
November	2.75	3.30	*
December	2.65	3.20	*

QUESTIONS

1.   Plot the data on a graph with time on the horizontal axis and sales (× $100,000) on the vertical axis.

2.   Fit a linear trend equation to the data using the least-squares method. (*Note:* This can be done using either a calculator or computer.)

3.   Based on your answer to question 2, forecast (seasonally unadjusted) sales for each of the last six months of 19X2.

4.   Calculate seasonally adjusted monthly sales by the ratio to trend method for the last six months of 19X2.

Forecasting with Vector Autoregressions[17]

INTRODUCTION

Vector autoregression (VAR) was introduced in the late 1970s as an alternative to large structural forecasting models, such as those used at Data Resources, Inc. (DRI) and Wharton Econometric Forecasting Associates (WEFA). As explained in Chapter 6, structural models rely on complex economic theory to econometrically model explicit relationships among large numbers of macroeconomic variables. In many cases, structural models consist of several hundred equations and more than a thousand variables. Unfortunately, despite the substantial effort and cost invested in building and maintaining structural models, the forecasting accuracy of the models has not been particularly good.

In contrast to structural models, VAR models rely on recurrent past patterns in economic data to forecast only a few key macroeconomic variables, such as gross national product (GNP), inflation, and interest rates. "Unrestricted" VAR models are particularly attractive in that economic theory is required only in selecting the variables to include and their lag lengths. In addition, unrestricted VAR models require only ordinary least squares (OLS) for estimation. The primary problem with unrestricted VARs is that the number of right-hand-side (*rhs*) variables is often quite large. Due to frequent problems of multicollinearity and loss of degrees of freedom (so-called overparameterization), VAR models also have not performed particularly well in comparative forecasting studies. (For a discussion of multicollinearity, see Chapter 5.)

The problem of overparameterization has been addressed in various ways. Perhaps the most popular approach is known as Bayesian VAR (BVAR), which was introduced in 1979 along with VAR. BVAR uses "mixed estimation" to place restrictions on the coefficient estimates of the model so that the estimates are more efficient (smaller variance). BVAR models have been shown in several studies to forecast as well as (if not better than) the structural models of the best-known forecasting services.

Statistical tests have also been applied to VAR models to eliminate variables and lags of variables in an effort to reduce the degree of overparameterization and, thereby, improve forecasting accuracy. More recent experimental work, however, has shown that relatively simple general restrictions related to lag length also can be placed on VAR models to obtain more efficient estimates and improve forecasting accuracy. As a result, VAR models still can be used effectively in many forecasting applications. VAR and BVAR models are discussed next, followed by a comparative forecasting experiment.

---

[17] This appendix has been prepared by Professor Gary L. Shoesmith, Babcock Graduate School of Management, Wake Forest University.

UNRESTRICTED VAR

An unrestricted VAR model consisting of n time series Y_{it} with p lags of each variable can be represented by

$$Y_{it} = a_{i0} + \left[\sum_{j=1}^{n} a_{ij1}Y_{jt-1} + a_{ij2}Y_{jt-2} + \ldots + a_{ijp}Y_{jt-p} \right] \qquad [6A.1]$$

$$+ u_{it}, i = 1, 2, \ldots, n$$

Thus, estimating a basic VAR model involves regressing each variable on a constant term and p time lags of itself and all other variables. From the above, the number of coefficient estimates for each equation is $(n \times p) + 1$. The k period forecast is then generated recursively using actual lagged values to forecast period $t + 1$ and actual plus forecasted lagged values for periods $t + 2$ through $t +$ k. VAR models are used in most cases to forecast one to two years ahead.

As an example of Equation 6A.1, a VAR model consisting of two variables, X_t and Y_t, with four lags of each variable can be represented by

$$X_t = a_0 + a_{11}X_{t-1} + a_{12}X_{t-2} + a_{13}X_{t-3} + a_{14}X_{t-4}$$
$$+ a_{21}Y_{t-1} + a_{22}Y_{t-2} + a_{23}Y_{t-3} + a_{24}Y_{t-4} + u_{1t} \qquad [6A.2a]$$

$$Y_t = b_0 + b_{11}X_{t-1} + b_{12}X_{t-2} + b_{13}X_{t-3} + b_{14}X_{t-4} + b_{21}Y_{t-1}$$
$$+ b_{22}Y_{t-2} + b_{23}Y_{t-3} + b_{24}Y_{t-4} + u_{2t} \qquad [6A.2b]$$

where u_{1t} and u_{2t} are independent, normally distributed error terms with a mean of 0 and a standard deviation of σ_1 and σ_2, respectively. Given that the lag lengths are equal for both X_t and Y_t equations, OLS can be used to estimate the nine coefficients of each equation.

In contrast to the system in Equation 6A.2, national and regional VAR models typically include five to ten variables and at least one year of lags using monthly or quarterly data. A quarterly model consisting of seven variables and six lags would have $(7 \times 6) + 1 = 43$ *rhs* variables for each equation. A monthly model having 7 variables and 18 lags would have 127 *rhs* variables.

From the above, VAR models have the obvious advantage of less data requirements and cost compared with more complex structural models. The disadvantages of VAR models include (1) the number of variables is restricted, resulting in less detailed forecasts, (2) VAR forecasts cannot be managed in the same way expert judgment can be applied to structural model forecasts, and (3) VAR models are not well designed for conventional policy analysis.

The most significant problem with the model in Equation 6A.1, however, is that, with five to ten variables and even one year of time lags, the available data are quickly depleted in terms of degrees of freedom. This is particularly troublesome in regional models in that many regional variables are not available with long histories. Even if long histories are available, it is often inadvisable to use the entire series if significant changes have occurred in the composition of the real economy or in the collection of the data. Together with the high degree of multicollinearity that results from using several time lags of each variable, the resulting overparameterization often leads to inefficient coefficient estimates and large out-of-sample forecast errors.

Various statistical tests have been used to eliminate unnecessary lags and variables in VAR models to reduce the degree of overparameterization and improve their forecasting accuracy.[18] This approach usually involves testing numerous hypotheses using F-tests and t-tests. (F-tests and t-tests are discussed in Chapter 5.) Compared to the basic VAR in Equation 6A.1, however, determining these restrictions can be time consuming and requires considerably more statistical skills than OLS. The restrictions are also model specific in that adding or subtracting a variable or lag in the original system of equations requires performing all the tests again.

Fortunately, recent experimentation with generalized restrictions on the number of lags suggests a more practical means of improving the forecasting accuracy of VAR models.[19] As a simple guideline, the greater the number of variables, the fewer the number of lags that should be used. For example, with only two or three variables, a lag length of four to six periods would probably be appropriate. However, in the more common case of five to ten variables, a lag length as short as one or two periods will generally lead to improved forecasting accuracy over longer lag-length versions of the same model. An example of this is provided in the last section.

Bayesian VAR

The BVAR method pioneered by Litterman approaches the problem of overparameterization in a systematic fashion using a technique known as *mixed estimation*.[20] Instead of eliminating variables, the BVAR approach imposes normal "prior" distributions on the coefficient estimates of the basic VAR model in Equation 6A.1 such that the coefficients of variables and lags of variables thought to be less important have normal distributions with means of zero and small standard deviations.

The use of mixed estimation in BVAR forecasting has specific implications with respect to degrees of freedom in that the technique involves supplementing actual observed data with stochastic "prior" information regarding the distributions of the coefficient estimates. Restrictions are typically imposed on each of the parameter estimates except the constant term. For each restriction, an artificial "observation" is added reflecting the "prior" mean. The "prior" standard deviation is then imposed during estimation. This approach addresses overparameterization in two ways. First, because the coefficient estimates are restricted according to the "prior" mean and standard deviation, the variability of the estimates is reduced. Second, with each additional observation, the "adjusted" degrees of freedom are increased by one and, consequently, always equal $T-1$, where T is the number of actual observations.

The most common "prior" for the means of the coefficient estimates is to let the coefficient on each first own lag be 1.0, with all other means equal to zero. The "prior" standard deviations are then specified for each equation such that the distributions are generally looser (greater standard deviations) for the own lags and tighter (smaller standard deviations) for more distant lags of both own and cross variables. These restrictions

---

[18] See, for example, J. G. Hoehn, W. C. Gruben, and T. B. Fomby, "Time Series Forecasting Models of the Texas Economy: A Comparison," *Federal Reserve Bank of Dallas Economic Review* (May 1984), pp. 11–24.

[19] For a comparison of alternative approaches to determining lag lengths, see R.W. Hafer and R.G. Sheehan, "The Sensitivity of VAR Forecasts to Alternative Lag Structures," *International Journal of Forecasting* 5 (1989), pp. 399–408.

[20] For a detailed description of Litterman's original national BVAR model and its forecasting performance compared to several leading forecasting services, see R.B. Litterman, "Forecasting with Bayesian Vector Autoregressions—Five Years of Experience," *Journal of Business & Economic Statistics* 4(1) (1986), pp. 25–38.

can be specified generally across all equations without much difficulty using software packages such as RATS.[21]

EXAMPLE

COMPARATIVE FORECASTING ACCURACY: SIX VAR MODELS

This section provides a forecasting example using VAR and BVAR models. Each model consists of six variables: real gross national product (*RGNP*), the implicit price deflator for GNP (*PGNP*), the unemployment rate (*RU*), gross private domestic investment (*GPDI*), the three-month Treasury bill rate (*TBILL*), and the money supply (*M1*). *RGNP*, *PGNP*, *GPDI*, and *M1* are used in natural log form.

The BVAR model includes six lags of each variable and applies the same Bayesian prior used by Litterman. The forecasting performance of the BVAR model is compared to two VAR models. The first VAR model includes six lags of each variable, requiring the estimation of 37 *rhs* variables for each equation. The second VAR model includes two lags of each variable, requiring the estimation of only 13 *rhs* variables for each equation. Both VAR models are estimated with OLS. The time-series forecasting package RATS is used to make all the forecasting computations.

Table 6A.1 compares the forecasting performance of the three models over 20 successive, eight-quarter-ahead experimental forecasts. The first forecasts are for 1984:1Q through 1985:4Q, having estimated each model with data through 1983:4Q. The second forecasts are for 1984:2Q through 1986:1Q, having estimated each model with data through 1984:1Q, and so on.

The forecasting accuracy of each model is based on the mean absolute error (MAE) in forecasting each variable over steps 1 through 8. The MAE measure of the *s*-quarter-ahead forecast for each variable is given by

$$MAE_s = \frac{1}{T}\sum_{t=1}^{T} |A_t - {}_sF_t| \qquad [6A.3]$$

where A_t is the actual value at time t, ${}_sF_t$ is the forecast made s quarters earlier, and T is the number of forecasts made ($T = 20$). This simply means that, for each variable and forecast step 1 through 8, the absolute error of the forecast is computed and stored. RATS then reestimates the model with one additional observation, forecasts and computes the absolute error for each variable at each step, stores each amount again, and so on. Once the 20 eight-quarter-ahead forecasts are completed, the program then averages the 20 absolute errors at each step for each variable.

Table 6A.1 shows that the BVAR model is consistently more accurate than either of the VAR models. The BVAR model MAEs are lower in 39 of 48 cases compared with either of the VAR models. The two-lag VAR model, however, clearly outperforms the six-lag VAR model. The two-lag VAR model is more accurate in 40 of 48 cases compared with the six-lag model, and substantially more accurate in most cases.

The results in Table 6A.1 are typical of comparisons of BVAR and VAR accuracy. Although BVAR models have been shown to be consistently superior, VAR models can still be used effectively provided appropriate steps are taken to reduce the degree of overparameterization. In the experiment above, the two-lag VAR model offers an attractive alternative to forecasters without the convenience of BVAR software. In fact, most spreadsheet software is adequate for VAR modeling and forecasting.

---

[21] See T.A. Doan, *User's Manual, RATS, Version 3.10* (Evanston Ill.: VAR Econometrics, 1990).

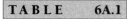

TABLE   6A.1

BVAR and VAR Mean
Absolute Forecast Errors
(Observations = 20)

Forecast Step	1	2	3	4	5	6	7	8	1–8
BVAR									
RGNP	0.48	0.77	1.02	1.24	1.67	1.90	2.06	2.16	1.41
PGNP	0.33	0.70	1.04	1.47	1.99	2.52	3.06	3.68	1.85
RU	0.11	0.18	0.21	0.25	0.28	0.31	0.41	0.56	0.29
GPDI	3.51	5.13	6.56	8.51	9.30	10.09	10.91	11.26	8.16
TBILL	0.62	1.32	1.99	2.61	3.15	3.62	4.03	4.41	2.72
M1	0.93	2.01	3.36	4.80	6.11	7.55	8.91	10.30	5.50
VAR (Lags = 6)									
RGNP	1.04	1.94	2.44	2.99	3.66	4.17	4.58	5.13	3.24
PGNP	0.36	0.85	1.52	2.31	3.17	4.05	4.91	5.81	2.87
RU	0.25	0.50	0.78	1.09	1.38	1.57	1.72	1.89	1.15
GPDI	4.19	8.18	9.96	11.39	12.18	12.14	10.74	10.24	9.88
TBILL	0.88	2.05	3.05	3.93	4.77	5.56	6.18	6.57	4.12
M1	0.71	1.66	3.07	4.53	5.83	7.41	8.89	10.48	5.32
VAR (Lags = 2)									
RGNP	0.60	0.95	1.10	1.38	1.86	2.20	2.49	2.76	1.67
PGNP	0.33	0.76	1.28	1.88	2.58	3.33	4.17	5.05	2.42
RU	0.16	0.28	0.31	0.32	0.37	0.44	0.60	0.79	0.41
GPDI	2.94	5.10	6.13	6.67	6.85	7.01	6.85	7.15	6.09
TBILL	0.83	1.64	2.32	3.00	3.65	4.23	4.72	5.16	3.19
M1	0.80	2.02	3.46	5.01	6.45	8.05	9.52	11.15	5.81

EXERCISE

1.   Estimate a three-equation VAR model with four lags using the data in Table 6A.2. Generate forecasts for eight quarters, that is, 1989:1 through 1990:4.

TABLE   6A.2

Historical Data: Real GNP (Billions of Constant 1982 Dollars); Implicit Price Deflator for GNP (1982 = 100); 3-Month T-Bill Rate (%)

Entry	RGNP 8	PGNP 9	TBILL 10
79: 1	3181.70	76.100	9.35767
79: 2	3178.70	77.800	9.37233
79: 3	3207.40	79.400	9.63133
79: 4	3201.30	81.000	11.80370
80: 1	3233.40	82.700	13.45870
80: 2	3157.00	84.600	10.04930
80: 3	3159.10	86.500	9.23533
80: 4	3199.20	89.000	13.70970
81: 1	3261.10	91.300	14.36900
81: 2	3250.20	92.800	14.82900
81: 3	3264.60	94.900	15.08730
81: 4	3219.00	96.700	12.02270
82: 1	3170.40	98.200	12.89500
82: 2	3179.90	99.400	12.35900
82: 3	3154.50	100.800	9.70533
82: 4	3159.30	101.700	7.93500
83: 1	3186.60	102.500	8.08133
83: 2	3258.30	103.300	8.41900
83: 3	3306.40	104.200	9.18667
83: 4	3365.10	105.400	8.79333
84: 1	3451.70	106.500	9.13333
84: 2	3498.00	107.300	9.84333
84: 3	3520.60	108.200	10.34330
84: 4	3535.20	109.000	8.97333
85: 1	3577.50	109.700	8.18333
85: 2	3599.20	110.600	7.52333
85: 3	3635.80	111.300	7.10333
85: 4	3662.40	112.200	7.14667
86: 1	3721.10	112.400	6.88667
86: 2	3704.60	113.200	6.13000
86: 3	3712.40	114.600	5.53333
86: 4	3733.60	115.100	5.34000
87: 1	3781.20	116.100	5.53333
87: 2	3820.30	117.000	5.73333
87: 3	3858.90	118.000	6.03333
87: 4	3920.70	118.500	6.00333
88: 1	3970.20	119.300	5.76000
88: 2	4005.80	120.600	6.23000
88: 3	4032.10	122.000	6.99333
88: 4	4059.30	123.400	7.70333

7

Exchange Rates and International Trade: Managing Exports

CHAPTER PREVIEW

Today, business plans involve purchasing, production, and marketing operations on several continents. Most companies, whether American, Dutch, German, Japanese, Brazilian, or Korean, engage in foreign direct investment and manufacture abroad. Some companies outsource manufacturing to low-wage partners, affiliates, or operating divisions in places like Mexico, Portugal, Indonesia, and the Caribbean. Others buy parts and supplies or assembled components from foreign firms. And almost all manufacturers produce an export product to sell abroad. Indeed, export markets are increasingly the primary source of sales growth for many manufacturers. Careful analysis and accurate forecasting of these international purchases and international sales provide pivotal information for capacity planning, production scheduling, and pricing, promotion, and distribution plans in many companies.

In this chapter, we investigate the relationship between exchange rates and international trade. Import and export sales vary with long-term trends in exchange rates. First, we analyze the determinants of long-term trends in exchange rates by examining the market for U.S. dollars as foreign exchange. Purchasing power parity conditions provide a way to assess these trends. We then explore the reasons for and patterns of free trade in the world's economy with special attention to regional trading blocs, like the European Union and NAFTA. The chapter closes with an explanation of the U.S. balance of payments and perspectives on the U.S. trade deficit.

MANAGERIAL CHALLENGE

EXPORT MARKET PRICING AT TOYOTA[1]

On January 5, 1994, the U.S. dollar exchanged for ¥113. A 1994 Toyota Celica ST Coupe made in Japan and shipped to Eastern U.S. dealers sold for $16,968—i.e., each sale realized revenue approximately equal to ¥2 million (i.e., ¥1,917,384). Just 16 months later on April 19, 1995, the dollar was worth only ¥80. This 34 percent decline in the value of the dollar and corresponding 34 percent appreciation of the yen made Japanese exports to the United States potentially much more expensive. To recover costs and maintain their 1994 profit margin, Toyota was presented with the prospect of pricing that same Toyota Celica ST Coupe at $23,967 (i.e., ¥1,917,384/¥80). Since domestic U.S. producers of comparable small sporty cars had raised prices only 5–10% over the intervening period, Toyota faced a tough decision. Increase the car's price well ahead of the competition and try to limit the erosion of market share by emphasizing manufacturing quality and service or, alternatively, reduce margins and protect current market share.

As we shall see in this chapter, different companies react in different ways to the pricing challenges presented by severe currency fluctuations. GM and Ford tend to maintain margins. In contrast, Toyota chose to increase the 1995 Celica ST Coupe price by only 2 percent to $17,285, despite the consequential 32 percent decline in realized yen per sale. Because of these pricing and related decisions, between 1994 and 1997, the Big Three's share of the U.S. passenger car market fell from 64.6 percent to 61.1 percent, while Toyota's share of the U.S. passenger car market jumped from 8.5 percent to 10.5 percent.

www . . . .
The U.S. International Trade Administration provides news and other information on international trade issues affecting U.S. companies at the following Internet address:.
http://www.ita.doc.gov/media

---

[1]Based on G. Gardner, "The Fading Big Three Car Market," *Ward's Automotive World*, September 1997, pp. 41–46, and Jack Gillis, *The Car Book*, 1997.

IMPORT-EXPORT SALES AND EXCHANGE RATES

The reduction of trade barriers and the opening of markets to foreign imports has increased the competitive pressure on manufacturers who once dominated their domestic industries. Tennis shoes and dress footwear once produced in large factories in the United States now come from Korea, Britain, and Italy. Automobiles once dominated by Ford, General Motors, and Chrysler now come in large numbers from Japan. Boeing now dominates airplane sales all over the world, including Japan, where the United States enjoyed a $5.5 billion 1997 trade surplus in aviation products. And Microsoft just became the second largest U.S. exporter, with foreign sales greater than GM, Ford, and Chrysler *combined*. In retailing, McDonald's operates in over 100 foreign countries, and Coca-Cola's international sales now exceed those in the United States. Exports have become the key to growth for many leading manufacturing firms, service companies, and franchise retailers.

Export and import sales are very sensitive to changes in exchange rates. A BMW automobile that retails in Munich for 95,000 deutsche marks can be transported to New York for about $300. In 1997 if the deutsche mark (abbreviated DM) exchanges for 0.5319 U.S.

dollars, the Munich manufacturer must charge DM95,0000 × 0.5319 $/DM = $50,531 to replace the deutsche mark revenue from a foregone domestic sale in Germany. Including the transportation cost, a BMW in New York would therefore retail for $53,831. Now suppose the exchange rate changes, and the value of the dollar trends downward for an extended period. If only 1.50 DM exchange for a U.S. dollar (i.e., 0.66 $/DM), a New York BMW dealer will need to raise the import price to (0.66 $/DM) × DM95,000 = $62,700 to match the revenue available from a domestic sale in Germany. If competition for luxury cars is stiff, this price increase may substantially diminish sales, and a rollback of the price increase would then reduce margins.

No feature of the car has changed. No service offering has changed. No warranty has changed. The exports by BMW to the United States became $9,169 more expensive simply because the currency of the foreign buyers in the United States became weaker. Price increases of this magnitude in export markets due to changes in long-term trend exchange rates are common. Analyzing and forecasting such changes provide key information for the marketing and operations plans of companies like BMW, Boeing, and Microsoft.

COLLAPSE OF EXPORT SALES AT CUMMINS ENGINE[2]

Cummins Engine Co. of Columbus, Indiana, is the world's leading producer of replacement diesel engines for trucks. Like all capital equipment manufacturers, Cummins' sales are highly cyclical, declining steeply in economic downturns. If households buy fewer appliances, clothing, and furniture, less shipping by truck is required to deliver supplies, refill inventories in warehouses, and restock store shelves. Less shipping means less truck mileage, and less truck mileage means a slower replacement demand for diesel engines. For example, in the short steep recession of 1982, Cummins's dollar sales fell off 20 percent and cash flow declined 55 percent. As the U.S. economy improved 1983–84, Cummins' sales recovered to record levels. By 1985, the U.S. economy was booming with real GNP growth at 5.8 percent. Yet that year, Cummins' sales declined 8 percent, operating margins declined 44 percent, and cash flow declined 51 percent.

Cummins Engine sells 38 percent of its replacement diesel engines in the export market and its biggest competitor is the Mercedes-Benz diesel. What deutsche mark or pound price a Cummins engine can sell for in Munich or London (and still recover its cost plus a small profit) is as important to Cummins' cash flow as steel costs or their wage bargain with the United Machinists union. A $40,000 Cummins diesel sold for approximately DM72,000 in 1978, 1988, and again in 1998. In each of these years, the exchange rate between the deutsche mark and the U.S. dollar stood at approximately 1.8—i.e., 1.8 deutsche marks per dollar. In one intervening time period, however, the dollar appreciated substantially against the mark. Between 1980–1985, the value of the dollar soared almost 47 percent from DM1.82 to DM2.94. (See the Price of the Dollar graph in Figure 7.1.) Similar exchange rate movements occurred against the British pound where the U.S. currency appreciated 54 percent (from £0.44 per $ to £0.77 per $).[3]

The effect of the massive dollar appreciation on Cummins' export sales was catastrophic. For a German to buy a $40,000 Cummins diesel engine in 1985 required not

---

[2] Based on *Value Line Investment Survey, Part III: Ratings and Reports,* various issues.

[3] Exchange rate percentage changes are calculated as the difference from one period to the next divided by the average exchange rate over the period. For example £0.44 per U.S. dollar to £0.77 equals a 0.33/60.5 = 54% change. Similarly, DM 1.82 to DM 2.94 equals a 1.12/2.38 or 47% change. The reason for this midpoint procedure is that when the DM/$ exchange rate returns by 1988 to very nearly its original level (i.e., see DM 1.88 for 1988 in Figure 7.1), the midpoint calculation yields −44 percent, nearly equal and opposite to the +47 percent rise.

FIGURE   7.1   Price of U.S. Dollar

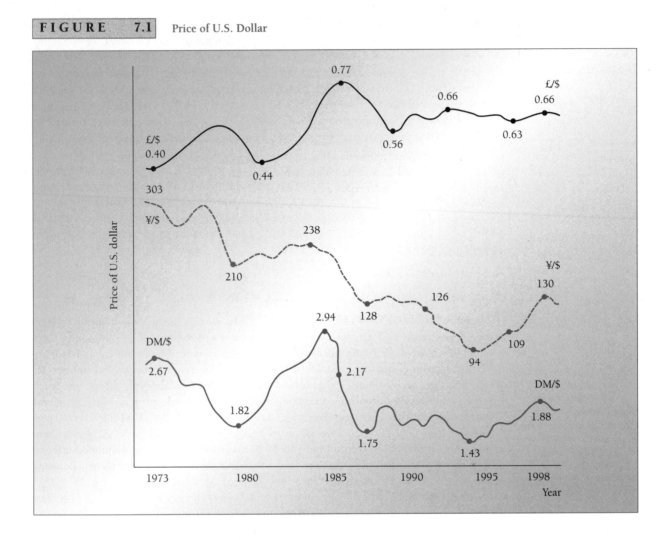

1.82 × \$40,000 = DM72,600 but rather 2.94 × \$40,000 = DM117,600! This enormous price increase of the Cummins export product (attributable solely to the change in exchange rates) made substitute products, like a domestic DM100,000 Mercedes-Benz diesel, much more attractive to German trucking companies than before. Moreover, Mercedes-Benz perceived a real opportunity to sell their own diesel in Cummins's home territory in the United States. An import diesel made by Mercedes-Benz (which had sold in Columbus, Cleveland, and Chicago for DM100,000/1.82 = \$54,945 in 1980) could now sell for just DM100,000/2.94 = \$34,014. Consequently, not only did Cummins' export sales collapse, but so did Cummins's domestic sales (and margins). The steep appreciation of the dollar in this 1980–85 period put U.S. manufacturers of traded goods, like diesel engines, at a very big disadvantage.

THE MARKET FOR U.S. DOLLARS AS FOREIGN EXCHANGE

Since American manufacturers, like Cummins Engine, incur most of their expenses at domestic manufacturing sites in the United States, American manufacturers ask that export purchase orders be made payable in U.S. dollars. This receivables policy requires that Munich dealers wishing to buy Cummins diesels transact simultaneously in the foreign exchange and diesel markets. To buy a Cummins diesel, Munich companies (or their financial intermediaries) will supply deutsche marks and demand dollars to secure the currency required for the dollar-denominated purchase order and payment draft awaited by the Cummins shipping department. This additional demand for the dollar and the concurrent additional supply of marks drive the price of the dollar higher than it otherwise would have settled on the currency markets on that particular day. Thus, the equilibrium exchange rate in deutsche marks per dollar (i.e., the price of the dollar as foreign exchange exhibited in Figure 7.1) rises.

In general, any unanticipated increase in export sales results in an appreciation of the domestic currency. Any unanticipated decrease in export sales, like that experienced by Cummins Engine in 1984–85, results in a depreciation of the domestic currency. After 1985, Figure 7.1 shows that the dollar did reverse course and depreciate from DM 2.94 per dollar to DM 2.17 per dollar by 1986. This downward price trend of the dollar assisted Cummins in stabilizing its sales and cash flows both at home and abroad. With the dollar worth fewer marks, American imports priced in dollars by Mercedes-Benz dealers in the United States became more expensive while American exports priced in marks by Cummins dealers in Germany became cheaper. This automatic self-correcting adjustment of flexible exchange rates in response to trade flow imbalances is one of the primary arguments for adopting a freely fluctuating exchange rate policy.

Import Flows and the Transaction Demand for Currency

To examine these effects more closely, let's turn the argument around and trace the currency flows when Americans increase their demand for imported goods. Suppose an unexpectedly large number of baby boomers wish to recapture their youth by purchasing sporty Miata or Mercedes convertibles. The Mercedes dealers would have some inventory stock on hand. Moreover, in anticipation of some custom orders, the dealers' banks would have a carefully selected amount of foreign currency on hand to support the necessary purchase order transactions with Mercedes headquarters in Stuttgart. Our interest lies in tracing the consequences of an unanticipated upswing in American demand for these imported convertibles. What exactly happens in the currency markets?

First, just as Cummins Engine prefers to be paid in U.S. dollars, so too Mercedes-Benz Stuttgart wishes to be paid in deutsche marks. Therefore, Mercedes purchase orders must be accompanied by DM cash payments. The local Mercedes-Benz dealer in Atlanta therefore requests a wire transfer from her banker at NationsBank. NationsBank debits the dollar account of the dealer, then authorizes payment from the deutsche mark cash balances of NationsBank and presents a wire transfer for an equivalent sum (minus fees) to the Stuttgart branch of Deutsche Bank for deposit in the Mercedes account. Both import buyer and foreign seller have done business in their home currencies and exchanged a handsome new car. And the merchandise trade account of the U.S. balance of payments would show one additional import transaction valued at the Mercedes convertible's purchase price.

If NationsBank anticipated fewer such import transactions and deutsche mark requests than actually occurred, the bank's foreign currency portfolio would now be out of balance. Deutsche mark balances must be restored to support future export transactions. NationsBank therefore goes (electronically) into the foreign currency markets and demands marks. Although the American bank might pay with any currency in excess supply in its foreign currency portfolio, it would normally pay in U.S. dollars. In particular, if no other unanticipated import or export flows (nor any unanticipated capital flows) have occurred, NationsBank would pay in U.S. dollars. Therefore, unanticipated demand by Americans for German imports both raises the demand for deutsche marks and increases the supply of U.S. dollars.

Equilibrium Price of the U.S. Dollar

In the market for U.S. dollars as foreign exchange (see Figure 7.2), the supply curve shifts to the right. This shift of market supply represents NationsBank and many other correspondent banks supporting import transactions by selling dollars to acquire other foreign currencies. The equilibrium price on the y-axis of Figure 7.2 is the price of the dollar expressed in amounts of any foreign currency, for example, the deutsche marks per U.S. dollar, yen per U.S. dollar, or British pounds per U.S. dollar. As the supply of U.S. dollars increases S_0 to S_1, the equilibrium price of the dollar declines.

For example, as imports of Mercedes-Benz replacement diesel truck engines and other German imports increased in 1985–86, the supply of U.S. dollars in the foreign currency market had to increase. Again, American consumers and companies needed to acquire marks to purchase German imports. U.S. financial intermediaries supplied dollars to acquire the foreign currency their local customers requested. Thus, the spectacular dollar appreciation of the previous four years slowed and the dollar actually began to depreciate (see Figure 7.1). The dollar's price decline is expressed as a falling exchange rate in Figure 7.2, for example, DM2.94 per U.S. dollar in 1985 to DM2.17 per U.S. dollar in 1986.

FIGURE   7.2

Market for U.S. Dollars as Foreign Exchange (Depreciation of the Dollar, 1985–86)

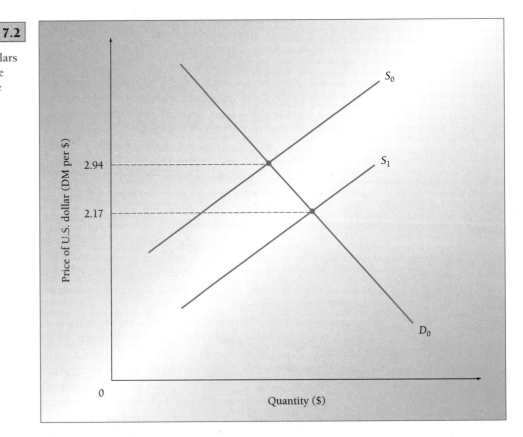

Foreign Exchange Risk Management

Internal Hedges

Internal Hedge
A balance sheet offset to foreign currency cash flows.

These foreign currency flows to support import-export transactions would have been unnecessary if Mercedes-Benz had set up an **internal hedge** in the form of offsetting payables in U.S. dollars. The North American subsidiary of Mercedes would simply accept purchase orders with payment in U.S. dollars and then use those same dollars to pay Mercedes expenses owed in the United States. Or Mercedes might have used the U.S. dollar receivables to buy American parts and supplies or fixed assets. For example, in 1997, Mercedes-Benz built a Birmingham, Alabama, plant to assemble their new sport utility vehicle. Such offsetting positions in payables and receivables is a way of balancing Mercedes assets and liabilities in U.S. dollars so as to avoid the foreign exchange risk of being a company with U.S. dollar receivables abroad and deutsche mark payables at home. With an internal hedge provided by a German ball-bearing plant, Cummins Engine could accomplish the same thing.

INTERNATIONAL PERSPECTIVES

Honda Buys U.S. Assembly Capacity[4]

When a manufacturer's home currency is strong, foreign direct investment in overseas plant and equipment is especially attractive. As the yen rocketed from ¥238 per U.S. dollar in 1985 to ¥94 per U.S. dollar in 1995 (see Figure 7.1), Honda and Toyota employed the strengthening yen to acquire U.S. manufacturing capacity. A $1 billion U.S. assembly plant cost ¥94 billion in 1995, down from ¥238 billion ten years earlier. At the same time, the U.S. demand for the Toyota Camry and Honda Accord outpaced the capacities of the Japanese manufacturers, and their market share of the North American market rose from 20 percent to 30 percent. In the late 1980s and early 1990s, the U.S. Congress responded with "voluntary import restraints" on Japanese cars and imposed a 25 percent tariff on Japanese light trucks.

To ease the trade policy pressure, to exempt their cars and trucks from U.S. tariffs, and to improve the delivery time and reliability for their most popular models, Toyota and Honda each built four assembly plants in North America. Nissan also built one plant in the United States and one plant in Mexico, and Mazda and Mitsubishi each built one plant in the United States. The combined capacity of these 12 Japanese-owned factories is 3.2 million vehicles a year, 18 percent of the total 17.2 million North American auto manufacturing capacity. By 1996, Honda assembled in North America 80 percent (and Toyota assembled 60 percent) of their vehicles sold in North America. Both Honda and Toyota plan to expand their light truck and minivan assembly capacity still further in the United States and Canada.

By acquiring plant and equipment in North America while the yen was appreciating against the dollar, Honda and Toyota clearly acquired fixed assets at very favorable home currency cost. And massive purchases of struts and shock absorbers from Tenneco of Greenwich, Connecticut, had a similar objective. At the same time, however, these transactions established a substantial internal hedge that complemented other cost-cutting measures initiated by Toyota and Honda. Thus, despite the plummeting yen value of the dollar receivables on each Camry sold, the purchase of less expensive U.S.

[4] Based on "Japanese Carmakers Plan Major Expansion of American Capacity," *Wall Street Journal*, 24 September 1997, p. A1, and "Detroit Is Getting Sideswiped by the Yen," *Business Week*, 11 November 1996, p. 54.

parts and assembly plants provided a cost savings. As the value of the dollar declined and the yen rose, these low-cost dollar payables for U.S. parts and U.S. assembly plants made it possible to hold price increases on Corollas, Camrys, and Accords to a minimum. As a result, the Camry has become the highest volume model of any car selling in the United States.

Other Risk Management Alternatives

In addition to internal hedges, any company can reduce the cash flow effects of exchange rate fluctuations by establishing a short position in the foreign currency futures or options market to hedge the domestic cash flow from their export sales receipts. For example, suppose Cummins Engine had sales contracts with their German dealers for future delivery in 1985 of DM10 million of diesel engines. Cummins has risk exposure to a decline in the value of the export sales receipts. So, to lay off this exchange rate risk, in 1984 Cummins might have sold deutsche mark futures in the foreign exchange futures markets to establish a hedge. Cummins transaction is described as a covered hedge because Cummins has a contract for deutsche mark receivables (from their German dealers) equal to the amount of their short futures position.

Selling futures contracts in 1984 that agree to deliver DM10 million at some pre-specified forward price (say, $0.41/DM) and future settlement date in 1985 would make money for Cummins Engine if the dollar appreciated and the mark declined in value. For example, at DM2.94 per dollar in 1985 (i.e., $0.34/DM), Cummins is entitled to receive $0.41 per deutsche mark, deliverable by purchasing the currency in the spot market for $0.34. Therefore, Cummins cancels its position and can collect from the futures market settlements process $0.07/DM $\times$ 10 million = $700,000 on their futures market contract. This cash flow would be just sufficient to cover their $0.41 to $0.34 per deutsche mark loss in value on the 10 million marks received in 1985 from their German dealers. As intended, these two cash flows from a covered hedge just offset.

Besides setting up internal hedges or short futures positions, Mercedes and Cummins Engine could also have entered into a currency-swap contract to exchange their anticipated future streams of dollar and deutsche mark cash flows from export sales.[5] However, all these alternatives to demanding payment in their domestic (home) currency impose some cost on Mercedes-Benz and Cummins Engine. Therefore, Mercedes generally will offer its best fixed price on an export transaction to an American or other foreign buyer on a purchase order payable only in deutsche marks. And for the same reason, the best fixed price from Cummins Engine generally will be available on a purchase order payable only in U.S. dollars.

DETERMINANTS OF LONG-RUN TRENDS IN EXCHANGE RATES

The Role of Real Growth Rates

As we have seen, a primary determinant of the year-to-year exchange rate fluctuations in Figure 7.1 is the net direction of trade flows. Unanticipated increases in imports lower a local currency's value, whereas unanticipated increases in exports raise a local

---

[5] At each future settlement date in a swap contract, the difference between the spot market exchange rate and the forward rates prespecified at the start of the swap contract actually determine who pays whom. For complete explanations of the use of futures, options, and swap contracts in managing foreign exchange risk, see C. Eun and B. Resnick, *International Finance* (Burr Ridge, Ill.: Irwin, 1997).

currency's value. The stimulus underlying trade flow imbalances may be either business cycles, productivity increases, or the introduction of protectionist trade barriers. When cyclical expansions in one economy are met with cyclical downturns in a second economy, net trade imbalances often result. In a business-cycle or productivity-based expansion, consumption (including import consumption) increases; in a contraction, import consumption decreases.

During the period from 1994 to 1997, for example, U.S. gross domestic product (GDP) grew at 4.1 percent, 2.9 percent, 2.4 percent, and 2.3 percent, respectively. The United States had a healthy but slowing economy. Japanese real GDP, on the other hand, exhibited only 0.5 percent growth in 1994 and 1995 but 3.7 percent growth in 1996. Canada and Mexico, the United States's largest and third largest trading partners, respectively, experienced rising growth too—Canada from 1.2 percent in 1996 to 3.7 percent in 1997 and Mexico from 6.4 percent to 8.8 percent. British and German growth rates also rose over this period. These growth-rate trends among the five largest U.S. trading partners led to increased exports from the United States of goods like computer software, PCs, grains, aircraft, professional services, and diesel engines while causing decreased imports into the United States of goods like autos and consumer electronics.

As exports from the United States rose, foreign buyers had to acquire dollars to complete transactions with U.S. companies like Microsoft, IBM, ADM, Boeing, McKinsey, and Cummins Engine. In the market for dollars as foreign exchange, this increases the demand for dollars; D_0 in Figure 7.3 shifts out to D_1. At the same time, decreased purchases of foreign imports by Americans decreases the supply of dollars. That is, in the market for dollars as foreign exchange, S_0 shifts left to S_1. Both factors cause an appreciation of the U.S. dollar, such as occurred in 1996–97. In sum, the increase in exports and decrease in imports led to a rise in the price of the dollar against the yen from an average ¥94 per dollar in 1995 to ¥109 per dollar in 1996, and ¥121 per dollar in 1997. The ¥/$ exchange rates in Figure 7.1 mirror these market demand and supply shifts shown in Figure 7.3.

The Role of Real Interest Rates

The second factor determining long-run trends in exchange rates is comparable interest rates adjusted for inflation. The higher the real rate of interest in an economy, the greater the demand for the financial assets offered by that economy. If a Japanese, German, or Swiss investor or financial institution can earn higher returns (for equivalent risk) from U.S. bonds than from German or Japanese bonds, foreign owners of capital will move quickly toward U.S. financial markets as foreign portfolios are rebalanced to incorporate more U.S. assets. Since the New York Federal Reserve Bank auctioning off new T-bills, Solomon Brothers underwriting a new issue of DuPont bonds, Merrill-Lynch selling T-bills, T-bonds, and DuPont bonds in the secondary (resale) market, and the New York Stock Exchange settlements department all require payment in U.S. dollars, the foreign investor who desires U.S. financial assets must first acquire U.S. dollars to complete her transactions. So, a higher real interest rate in the United States (relative to German, Japanese, and British rates) implies international capital inflow into the United States and an increased demand for and appreciation of U.S. dollars.

In September 1997, 90-day T-bill rates in the United States stood at 5.6 percent up from 5.2 percent a year earlier. With consumer inflation in the United States running at 2.2 percent in the third quarter of 1997, down from 2.5 percent a year earlier, the real rate of return in the United States was rising—i.e., $5.2 - 2.5 = 2.7\%$ in the third quarter of 1996 versus $5.6 - 2.2 = 3.4\%$ in the third quarter of 1997. In contrast, real rates of interest in Germany on government-issued 90-day bills were lower relative to U.S.

Market for U.S. Dollars
as Foreign Exchange
(Appreciation of the
Dollar, 1995–97)

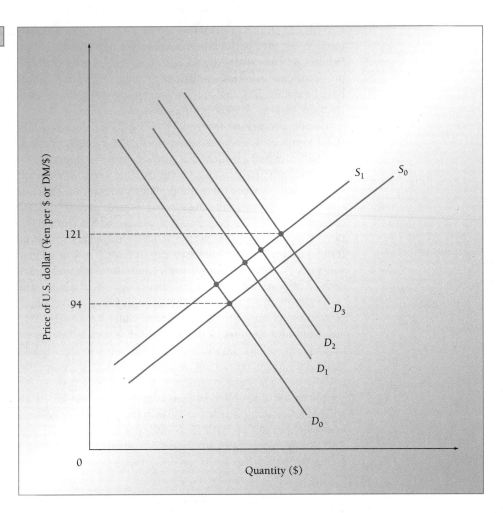

rates and unchanged from 1996 to 1997 (i.e., $3.1 - 1.7 = 1.4\%$ in 1996 and $3.3 - 1.9 = 1.4\%$ in 1997). Japanese 90-day real rates were also lower relative to U.S. rates and unchanged from 1996 to 1997 (i.e., 0.5% in both 1996 and 1997).

These real interest rate differentials favoring investment in the United States increase the foreign demand for U.S. financial assets, and increased foreign demand for U.S. financial assets raises the demand for U.S. dollars. Again referring to Figure 7.3, the demand for the dollar as foreign exchange increases from D_1 to D_2, and the dollar appreciates.

The Role of Expected Inflation

Inflationary expectations provide an important third determinant of long-term trends in exchange rates. Suppose you were entering into a long-term contract to replace the diesel engines installed in a fleet of trucks over the next three to five years. Would you be inclined to approach and enter into negotiation with Cummins Engine where recent material costs have been low, cost-saving productivity increases have been substantial, and union bargaining pressure may be declining? Or would you approach a substitute supplier like Mercedes-Benz where all those factors are reversed, suggesting the strong possibility of an upsurging inflationary trend underlying the costs of a German diesel engine?

Cost inflation is usually compared across economies by examining an index of producer prices or wholesale prices. From August 1996 to August 1997, the percentage change in producer prices in the United States was −0.2 percent (negative), whereas in Germany producer prices increased by 3.3 percent. Clearly, the lower price in a long-term fixed price contract for replacement diesels will be available from Cummins, the company in a country experiencing little in the way of cost-push inflation. In general, when producer price inflation is low in one country relative to another, export sales on traded goods like diesel engines increase. Eventually, if producer price inflation differentials between the United States and Germany persist, import-export companies will join the surging demand for American products and buy replacement diesels cheaply in the United States for resale at a profit in Germany.

These trade flows swell U.S. exports and German imports, thereby putting upward pressure on the DM/$ exchange rate. In Figure 7.3, demand for the dollar again shifts to the right (i.e., D_2 to D_3), and the dollar appreciates still further. Indeed, the relative purchasing power parity (PPP) hypothesis says that goods arbitrage of this sort will continue until the DM/$ exchange rate adjusts upward sufficiently to reflect entirely the inflation differential. That is, between the United States and Germany, a 3.5 percent differential in the producer price index favoring the United States should, according to PPP, raise the value of the dollar 3.5 percent against the mark. We discuss purchasing power parity below.

Trade-Weighted Exchange Rate

Figure 7.4 shows the value of the U.S. dollar against the currencies of the United States' largest trading partners from 1973–1998. This trade-weighted exchange rate calculates the weighted average value of the dollar against 19 currencies where the weights are determined by the volume of import plus export trade between the two countries. From 1996–98, the trade-weighted U.S. dollar appreciated substantially. All three factors de-

FIGURE   7.4   Trade-Weighted Exchange Rate, U.S. Dollar (1973–98)

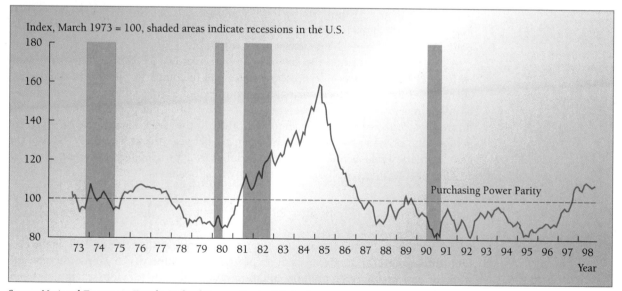

Source: National Economic Trends, *Federal Reserve Bank of St. Louis.*

termining long-run trends in exchange rates were involved. Real growth rates in the United States declined over this period relative to several of the United States's largest trading partners. Real interest rates on U.S. T-bills were high and rising relative to those same economies. And finally, cost inflation in the U.S. producer price index was at a post–World War II low relative to the United States's largest trading partners, so U.S. export trade rose dramatically.

Like their Japanese and European competitors in the 1980s, export trade has become the engine of growth for many U.S. companies in the 1990s. From the 1950s to the 1990s, the share of exports in U.S. GNP grew from 4 percent to 10 percent. By 1993, merchandise exports represented a 19 percent share of total U.S. manufacturing output. In 1996, U.S. exports increased 16 percent followed in 1997 by 27 percent additional growth. The continuing growth of the U.S. export sector suggests that the value of the dollar has not yet reached a level that will dampen export sales. At the highest 1997 value of DM1.88 and ¥134, the dollar is still well below its spectacular 1985 peak of DM2.94 and ¥238. This historical perspective, reflected in Figure 7.4, can be quite useful for assessing the relative strength of a currency.

PURCHASING POWER PARITY

When there are no significant costs or other barriers associated with moving goods or services between markets, then the price of each product should be the same in each market. This is known as the *law of one price*. When the different markets represent different countries, the law of one price says that prices will be the same in each country after making the appropriate conversion from one currency to another. Alternatively one can say that exchange rates between two currencies will equal the ratio of the price indexes between the countries. In international finance and trade, this relationship is known as the absolute version of **purchasing power parity.**

Purchasing Power Parity
A relationship between differential inflation rates and long-term trends in exchange rates.

Absolute purchasing power parity implies that a doubling of UK prices for a Dickens' novel (and other traded goods) will result in a depreciation of the British currency by 50 percent. For example, if after a sustained period of British inflation, one needs £20 to buy a Dickens' novel that before the inflation cost £10, and if German publishers will continue to print and sell that same novel (in English) for DM10, the novel will be exported to Britain. Such imports by the British will persist until the exchange rate reflecting the price of the British pound declines from DM10/£10 = 1.0 deutsche mark per pound to DM10/ £20 = 0.5 deutsche mark per pound.

A less restrictive form of the law of one price is known as *relative purchasing power parity* (PPP). The relative PPP principle states that in comparison to a period when exchange rates between two countries are in equilibrium, changes in the differential rates of inflation between two countries will be offset by equal, but opposite, changes in the future spot exchange rate. For example, if prices in the United States rise by 4 percent per year and prices in Germany rise by 6 percent per year, then relative PPP holds if the German mark weakens relative to the U.S. dollar by approximately 2 percent.

The exact relative purchasing power parity relationship is

$$\text{Relative PPP:} \qquad \left(\frac{S_1}{S_0}\right) = \left(\frac{1 + \pi_h}{1 + \pi_f}\right) \qquad\qquad [7.1]$$

where S_1 is the expected future (direct quote) spot rate at time period 1, S_0 is the current (direct quote) spot rate, π_h is the expected home country (U.S.) inflation rate, and π_f is the expected foreign country inflation rate. Using the previous example, if U.S. prices are expected to rise by 4 percent over the coming year, prices in Germany are expected to rise by 6 percent during the same time, and the current spot exchange rate (S_0), is \$0.60/DM, then the expected spot rate in one year (S_1), will be

$$S_1/\$0.60 = (1 + 0.04)/(1 + 0.06)$$

$$S_1 = \$0.5887$$

The higher German inflation rate can be expected to result in a decline in the future spot value of the DM relative to the dollar by 1.89 percent.[6]

The dashed lines in Figure 7.5 indicate purchasing power parity between the deutsche mark and the U.S. dollar accounting for cumulative inflation in the United States and Germany from 1973–1996. Over this period, the consumer price index in Germany rose from 67.1 to 132.6 (a 98 percent increase), and the consumer price index in the U.S. rose from 49.3 to 156.9 (a 219 percent increase). Starting from a March 1973 exchange rate of DM 2.81/\$, the predicted equilibrium exchange rate in 1997 implied by the hypothesis of purchasing power parity would be (DM2.81/\$1.00) × (1.98/3.19) = 1.76, close to the actual average exchange rate for 1997 of DM1.75/\$. Therefore, referring again to Figure 7.5, the dollar was substantially above its purchasing power parity level in 1984–86 but not in 1996–98.

Qualifications of PPP

Purchasing power parity calculations can be very sensitive to the starting point for the analysis. In 1972, the DM/\$ exchange rate averaged DM3.19/\$ whereas in 1973 the average value of the dollar fell to DM2.67/\$. The 1972 starting point implies a 1997 exchange rate predicted by PPP of DM1.91/\$, while the 1973 starting point implies a predicted 1997 exchange rate of only DM1.66/\$. Clearly, the difference is nontrivial, and many such applications of the PPP hypothesis will hinge on which year the analyst chooses to start. Figure 7.5 indicates this qualification by displaying a band of exchange rates within which PPP holds.

---

[6]Several other parity conditions in international finance are discussed in R. C. Moyer, W. Kretlow, and J. McGuigan, *Contemporary Financial Management*, 7th ed. (Cincinnati, OH.: Southwestern, 1997), chapter 21.

FIGURE   7.5   Purchasing Power Parity (DM/\$, 1973–98)

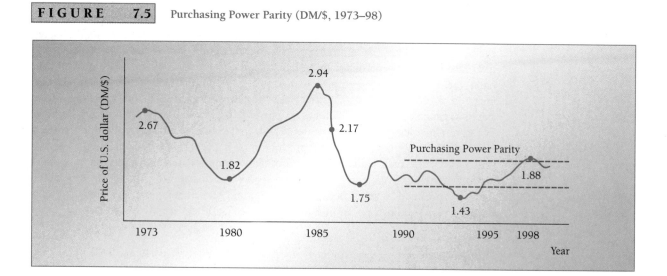

Purchasing power parity has several other qualifications as well. For the full PPP adjustments to take place in exchange rates as domestic prices inflate, the traded goods must be nearly identical in quality and use in the two economies. Cross-cultural differences (e.g., the Islamic aversion to Western clothing for women) can short-circuit these adjustments. In addition, both economies must have similar trade policies. If the French have much higher agricultural subsidies and trade barriers than their European neighbors, that policy may prevent the trade flows and subsequent exchange rate adjustments hypothesized by PPP. Similar qualifications apply to differences in value-added and other sales taxes across economies. Finally, the mark-ups and profit margins arising from the degree of competition in an economy must be comparable for purchasing power parity to hold. Despite these caveats, purchasing power parity has proved to be a useful benchmark for assessing trends in currency values.

EXAMPLE	### BIG MAC INDEX OF PURCHASING POWER PARITY[7]

Big Mac hamburgers bought anywhere in the world are as close to identical as MacDonald's can make them. In 1974, the Big Mac sold for approximately $1.00 in the United States and DM2.50 in Germany. In that same year, 2.50 German marks exchanged for one U.S. dollar in the foreign currency markets. The cost of a Big Mac in downtown Munich in 1996 was $4.90, slightly higher than implied by the 93 percent cumulative German inflation between 1974–96 (i.e., $1.93 \times DM2.50 = DM4.82$). In 1996 in Atlanta, the Big Mac sold for $2.36, considerably lower than implied by the 219 percent cumulative U.S. inflation (i.e., $3.19 \times \$1.00 = \$3.19$). Consequently, the Big Mac index of purchasing power parity (i.e., $DM4.90/\$2.36 = 2.08$) at the end of 1996 implied that the U.S. dollar should exchange for DM208/$—for example, that the dollar was substantially undervalued. Dollar appreciation against the mark in 1997 from DM1.53/$ to DM1.88/$ suggests that "burger economics" may have some merit.

The Big Mac relationships are not a perfect application of the relative PPP hypothesis for several reasons: (1) because the German VAT tax exceeds the U.S. sales tax, (2) because downtown land rents in Munich exceed those in Atlanta, and (3) because the degree of fast food industry competition facing a Munich MacDonald's is lower than that facing an Atlanta MacDonald's. Also, of course, a prepared Big Mac cannot be purchased in Munich for effective resale in Atlanta; goods arbitrage with perishable commodities is infeasible. Nevertheless, again, such PPP measures can help evaluate trends in currency value, like the appreciation of the dollar in 1996–98.

No one would ever execute a currency arbitrage trade based on the predictions of the purchasing power parity hypothesis. Currency arbitrage is triggered by unanticipated events that generate very temporary profit opportunities lasting only several hours or days. The trade flows predicted by PPP in response to inflation differentials, on the other hand, are a much longer-term process requiring several quarters or even years. Companies with a substantial proportion of their sales abroad must identify these longer-term trends in exchange rates, and purchasing power parity proves useful for just that purpose. For example, a realization that the dollar was well above purchasing power parity levels in 1984–85 should have influenced production and pricing policies in that era. Being attuned to the international business environment supports increased production volume, proactive pricing, targeted marketing, and segmented distribution channels, all of which may offer profit advantages. Some companies make these considerations a focus of their business plans and prosper in international markets; others are less successful.

---

[7] Based on "McCurrencies: Where's the Beef?" *The Economist,* 27 April 1996, p. 110, and "Big MacCurrencies," *The Economist,* 9 April 1994, p. 88.

EXAMPLE

GM, NISSAN, AND THE VALUE OF THE DOLLAR 1980–1988[8]

In 1980 with exchange rates at ¥226/$ and DM1.82/$, the Buick Century sold for approximately $10,000. Nissan priced their competing four-door standard sedan, the Maxima, at ¥2,250,000 or $9,956. As the dollar appreciated spectacularly in 1980–84 against the German mark (i.e., 1.82 to 2.94) and appreciated somewhat against the yen (i.e., 226 to 238), GM took four price increases averaging 10.2 percent per year across all their models, which added 48 percent ($1.102 = 1.48^4$) to the domestic (dollar) price of cars like the Century. Nissan took four price increases averaging 13.8 percent which added 68 percent to the dollar price of a Maxima. The dollar had risen 5 percent, so Nissan's effective price increase in their home currency was (68% − 5%)—i.e., 63 percent in yen. For GM, the export price to Japan was (48% + 5% =) 53 percent higher.

Consider, however, the net price increases in deutsche marks. Because the dollar had risen 47 percent against the mark in 1980–84, the net price increase for overseas sales in Germany in 1985 was a whopping (48% + 47% =) 95 percent higher in deutsche marks. The Opel Division of General Motors found it difficult to explain to potential German customers why asking prices should double in so short a period. Accordingly, Opel received permission to roll back many of these price increases.

In the subsequent period, 1985–88, the dollar depreciated almost as spectacularly as it had risen in 1980–84 (i.e., −44% against the mark and −60% against the yen). It is instructive to examine how Nissan and GM reacted when their roles in managing the exchange rate trends reversed. Now, Nissan had to deal with a strengthening currency and the deterioration of export sales that might follow. Nissan's response was to slash their profit margins by taking only 5.7 percent per-year dollar price increases (i.e., $1.057^4 = 1.25 = 25$ percent price increase) at a time when their currency was steeply appreciating by 60 percent. Over this four-year period, therefore, the net receipts in yen from selling a Maxima in the U.S. export market declined by 25 percent − 60 percent = −35 percent. That is, the 25 percent additional dollars charged were worth so much less yen that the net receipts in the home currency actually fell by 35 percent. General Motors, in this 1985–88 time period, took 7.2 percent price increases, raising dollar receipts 32 percent ($1.072^4 = 1.32$).

Altogether, between 1980 and 1988, the cumulative dollar price increase on the competing cars were similar. A $10,000 GM car rose in price to $19,479, and a competing $9,956 Nissan car rose in price to $20,837. However, the exchange rate trend from ¥226/$ in 1980 to ¥128/$ in 1988 reveals that the Japanese accepted a much smaller price increase in their home currency. Multiplying $20,837 by ¥128 to the dollar identifies the Nissan gross receipts on an export Maxima in 1988 as ¥2,667,136. This figure represents only a cumulative 20 percent yen price increase over the eight years, while GM's cumulative dollar price increase was 95 percent. Not surprisingly, the Japanese share of the U.S. new car market grew rapidly over this period, from 19.8 percent to 23.7 percent. General Motors's market share plummeted from 45.9 percent in 1980 to 36.1 percent in 1988.

Why did GM and Nissan have such different pricing and mark-up policies? One might suspect that costs were higher in the United States during 1980–88. In fact, the unit labor costs in auto manufacturing were lower in the United States than in Japan over this period. Perhaps Nissan sought greater sales volume to realize scale economies or take advantage of learning curve-related reductions in unit cost as cumulative volume increased. Total quality initiatives in Japanese manufacturing in this period did realize

---

[8] Based on "General Motors and the Dollar," Harvard Business School, Publishing Division, Harvard University, 1989.

much-heralded cost savings on the assembly plant floor as more vehicles passed quality inspections without requiring rework. And cost savings from manufacturing quality initiatives are related to volume. Finally, Toyota, Honda, and Nissan certainly are export-driven companies. Between 1985 and 1988, Nissan generated 50 percent of its sales abroad (fully 45 percent in the United States itself).

General Motors, in contrast, had 72 percent domestic sales, 12 percent export sales, and 16 percent sales from overseas production divisions. Consequently, GM does not focus marketing and operations planning on export sales. Every company should, however, always analyze their import market competition. Fundamentally, GM simply maintained higher net profit margins (i.e., 3.2 percent return on sales) over 1980–88, while Nissan cut net margins (i.e., from 2.4 percent to 1.2 percent) to achieve market penetration and realize greater production volume.

INTERNATIONAL TRADE: A MANAGERIAL PERSPECTIVE

Shares of World Trade and Regional Trading Blocs

The United States is both the largest exporter and the largest importer in the world's economy. Thus, the United States has the largest share of bilateral world trade (13.5 percent), and this proportion has remained remarkably stable for three decades. The remaining top 10 countries with the largest shares of world trade in 1996 were Germany (9 percent), Japan (7.1 percent), France (5.3 percent), Britain (5.1 percent), Italy (4.3 percent), Hong Kong (3.6 percent), Canada (3.5 percent), the Netherlands (3.2 percent), and Belgium (2.9 percent). Although these largest trading nations are predominantly Western-developed economies, the next 10 largest trading nations are mostly Asian rapidly developing economies: China (2.7 percent), South Korea (2.6 percent), Singapore (2.4 percent), Spain (2.1 percent), Taiwan (2.0 percent), Mexico (1.7 percent), Malaysia (1.5 percent), Sweden (1.4 percent), Thailand (1.2 percent), and Australia (1.1 percent). Altogether, the World Trade Organization includes 161 nations who have agreed to share trade statistics and coordinate the liberalization of trade policy (i.e., the opening of markets). In the last decade of the 20th century, not only capitalism but also free trade is spreading across the world economy.

Most nations continue to protect with tariffs and other trade barriers some infant or politically sensitive industries. France, for example, remains a largely agricultural polity and therefore lowers its agricultural trade barriers only after great hand-wringing and extended periods of tough negotiations with its European neighbors. Until recently, the United States imposed import restraints on Japanese automobiles and maintained 30 percent tariffs on textiles, apparel, and carbon steel imports. Fortunately, regional trading blocs like the European Union (EU) and the North American Free Trade Area (NAFTA) have been highly successful in the 1990s at removing trade barriers, negotiating multilateral reactions in tariffs, and promoting free trade as a mechanism of peaceful competition between nations.

Across the world economy, six such regional trading blocs have emerged (see Figure 7.6). In the Americas, Argentina, Brazil, Paraguay, and Uruguay have formed a trading block (MERCOSUR) to mirror the NAFTA free trade agreements of Canada, the United States, and Mexico. In addition, the Free Trade Area of the Americas (FTAA) includes 34 North and South American nations. Seven Southeast Asian (ASEAN) and 16 trans-Pacific economies including Japan and Mexico (APEC) have also formed trading blocs. Because of greater commonality of interest and pre-existing defense and regional cooperation treaties, these regional trading blocs have been the focus for most trade policy initiatives in recent years.

www...............
Access the MERCOSUR
Internet site at:
http://www.americasnet.
com/mauritz/mercosur/
english/

FIGURE   7.6   Regional Trading Blocs (Percentage of World Trade)

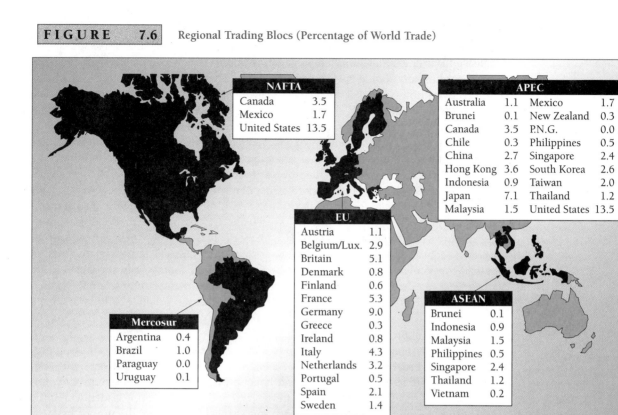

NAFTA	
Canada	3.5
Mexico	1.7
United States	13.5

APEC			
Australia	1.1	Mexico	1.7
Brunei	0.1	New Zealand	0.3
Canada	3.5	P.N.G.	0.0
Chile	0.3	Philippines	0.5
China	2.7	Singapore	2.4
Hong Kong	3.6	South Korea	2.6
Indonesia	0.9	Taiwan	2.0
Japan	7.1	Thailand	1.2
Malaysia	1.5	United States	13.5

EU	
Austria	1.1
Belgium/Lux.	2.9
Britain	5.1
Denmark	0.8
Finland	0.6
France	5.3
Germany	9.0
Greece	0.3
Ireland	0.8
Italy	4.3
Netherlands	3.2
Portugal	0.5
Spain	2.1
Sweden	1.4

Mercosur	
Argentina	0.4
Brazil	1.0
Paraguay	0.0
Uruguay	0.1

ASEAN	
Brunei	0.1
Indonesia	0.9
Malaysia	1.5
Philippines	0.5
Singapore	2.4
Thailand	1.2
Vietnam	0.2

Source: The Economist, *27 September 1997.*

Comparative Advantage and Free Trade

Within a regional trading bloc like EU, NAFTA, or APEC, each member can improve its economic growth by specializing in accordance with comparative advantage and then engaging in free trade. Intuitively, low-wage countries like Spain, Mexico, and Thailand enjoy a cost advantage in the manufacture of labor-intensive goods like garment sewing and the provision of labor-intensive services like coupon or insurance claims processing. Suppose one of these economies also enjoys a cost advantage in more capital-intensive manufacturing like auto assembly. One of the powerful insights of international microeconomics is that in such circumstances, the low-cost economy should not produce both goods, but rather it should specialize in that production for which it has the lower relative cost while buying the other product from its higher-cost trading partner. Let's see how this law of comparative advantage in bilateral trade reaches such an apparently odd conclusion.

Consider the bilateral trade between the United States and Japan in automobile carburetors and computer memory chips. Suppose the cost of production of carburetors in Japan is ¥10,000 compared to $120 in the United States. At an exchange rate of 100 yen to the dollar, the Japanese dollar price of $100 is lower than the U.S. price of $120. Suppose, in addition, that memory chips cost ¥8,000 in Japan compared to $300 in the U.S. Again, the dollar price of the Japanese product (i.e., $80) is lower than the price of the U.S. product. Japan is said to enjoy an absolute cost advantage in the manufacture of both products. However, Japan is 83 percent (i.e., $100/$120) as expensive in producing carburetors as the United States while being only 27 percent (i.e., $80/$300) as expensive in producing memory chips. Japan is said to have a comparative advantage in memory chips and should specialize in the manufacture of that product.

The gains from specialization in accordance with comparative advantage and trade are best demonstrated using the real terms of trade. **Real terms of trade** identify what amounts of labor effort, material, and other resources are required to produce a product in one economy relative to another. In Japan, the manufacture of memory chips requires the sacrifice of resources capable of manufacturing 0.8 carburetors (see Table 7.1), whereas in the United States the manufacture of a memory chip requires the sacrifice of 2.5 carburetors. That is, Japan's relative cost of memory chips (in terms of carburetor production that must be foregone) is less than a third as great as the relative cost of memory chips in the United States. On the other hand, U.S. carburetor production requires the resources associated with only 0.4 U.S. memory chips while Japanese carburetor production requires the sacrifice of 1.25 Japanese memory chips. The U.S. relative cost of carburetors is much lower than that of the Japanese. Said another way, the Japanese are particularly productive in using resources to manufacture memory chips, and the United States is particularly productive in using similar resources to produce carburetors. Each country has a comparative advantage: The Japanese in producing memory chips and the United States in producing carburetors.

Assess what happens to the total goods produced if each economy specializes in production in accordance with comparative advantage and then trades to diversify its consumption. Assume the United States and Japan produced one unit of each product initially, and that the quality of both carburetors and both memory chips is identical. If the Japanese cease production of carburetors and specialize in the production of memory chips, they increase memory chip production to 2.25 chips (see Table 7.1). Similarly, if the United States ceases production of memory chips and specializes in the production of carburetors, it increases carburetor production to 3.5 carburetors. In these circumstances, the United States could offer Japan 1.5 carburetors for a memory chip, and both parties would end up unambiguously better off. The United States would enjoy a residual domestic production after trade of 2.0 carburetors plus the import memory chip.

Real Terms of Trade
A comparison of relative costs of production across economies.

TABLE 7.1		**Absolute Cost, U.S.**	**Absolute Cost, Japan**
Real Terms of Trade and Comparative Advantage	Automobile carburetors	$120	¥10,000
	Computer memory chips	$300	¥8,000
		Relative Cost, U.S.	**Relative Cost, Japan**
	Automobile carburetors	$120/$300 = 0.4 Chips	¥10K/¥8K = 1.25 Chips
	Computer memory chips	$300/$120 = 2.5 Carbs	¥8K/¥10K = 0.8 Carbs
		Gains from Trade, U.S.	**Gains from Trade, Japan**
	Initial Goods	1.0 Carb + 1.0 Chip	1.0 Carb + 1.0 Chip
	After specialization:		
	Carburetors produced	(1.0 + 2.5) Carbs	0
	Memory chips produced	0	(1.0 + 1.25) Chips
	Trade	+ 1.0 Chip	+1.5 Carb
		−1.5 Carb	−1.0 Chip
	Net goods	2.0 Carbs + 1.0 Chip	1.5 Carbs + 1.25 Chips

And the Japanese would enjoy a residual domestic production after trade of 1.25 memory chips plus the import 1.5 carburetors. As demonstrated in Table 7.1, each economy would have replaced all the products they initially produced, plus each would enjoy additional amounts of both goods—i.e., unambiguous gains from trade.

Free Trade Areas: The European Union and NAFTA

www . . . .
The European Union on the Internet: http://europa.eu.int/en/eu.html

Free Trade Area
A group of nations who have agreed to reduce tariffs and other trade barriers.

Free trade and specialization in accordance with comparative advantage leaves economies vulnerable to trade interruptions and punitive tariffs. Nevertheless, the European Union provides an example of what can be accomplished. Starting with the Treaty of Rome in 1957, 12 original European Community members established the groundwork for a **free trade area** which they subsequently consolidated in the Single Europe Act of 1986. Between 1986 and 1992, 12 very dissimilar European economies realized 5 percent additional cumulative growth of GDP attributable to the increased intra-European trade.

Increased specialization in accordance with comparative advantage has the Spaniards and Portuguese assembling high value-added German components for BMWs and Blaupunkt radios. Reduced trade barriers at borders have cut transportation time. The Channel ferry now unloads in 15 minutes rather than the previous 1 1/2 hours, and yogurt from Nestle's subsidiary in Birmingham, England, now speeds across Europe to heavy buyers in Milan in 11 hours rather than the previous 38. Reduced intra-European tariffs on foodstuffs, beer, wine, and autos have markedly reduced the cost of living. Wide differences in value-added taxes have been reconciled at uniform lower tax rates in most cases. Just the mere act of exchanging money, which now employs 1 in every 200 full-time employees in Europe, may soon become much more efficient under the plans for a single European currency.

All of this free trade euphoria occurred in a region where the output per capita differs by 100 percent between wealthy Milan, Munich, and the Rhineland versus poor Greece, Southern Italy, Spain, Portugal, and Ireland. Manufacturing-unit-labor cost runs close to $30 an hour in Germany and only $14 to $16 an hour in Spain, Ireland, and Britain. Marketing plans are just as divergent. The peak penetration of TV into Spanish households (20 percent viewership) occurs at 2 to 4 in the afternoon. Only 5 percent of Spanish households are tuned in from 6 to 8 in the evening when the 22 percent peak British viewership is "watching the tele." The Spanish consider packaged pet food a luxury and purchase yogurt through the pharmacy. Milanese brag about overpaying for a Sony television while Munich shoppers search for days to find 5 percent discounts on Sony products. In short, few pan-European marketing plans succeed. Yet, intra-European trade dominates the landscape. Italy, Spain, and France do 60 percent of their total trade with other European countries. Portugal and Holland do close to 80 percent. Even Britain and Germany now trade more with their regional trading bloc partners than with the rest of the world combined.

Largest U.S. Trading Partners

www . . . .
You can access current information on U.S. trading partners and other trade issues on the Internet at the following site maintained by the Federal Reserve Bank of St. Louis: http://www.stls.frb.org/publ/net/

Canada, not Japan, is by far the largest trading partner of the United States with almost twice the share (22 percent) of American goods exported there than anywhere else in the world's economy (see Figure 7.7). U.S. exports to Canada include everything from merchandise, like Microsoft's software and Chrysler's automobile components for assembly at an automated minivan plant in Ontario, to professional services like strategic management consulting by McKinsey & Co. Canada is also the largest source of U.S. imports (19.4 percent), with natural resources and finished goods manufacturing leading the list. Japanese goods like Toyota and Honda autos, Sony consumer electronics,

FIGURE   7.7   Largest U.S. Trading Partners

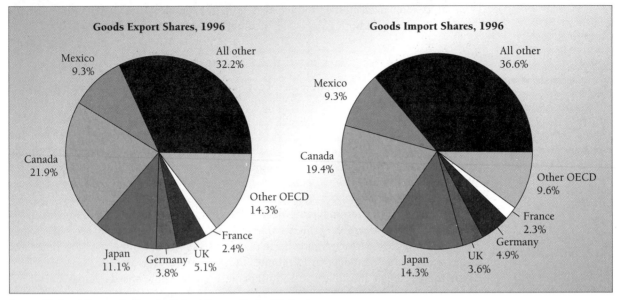

Source: National Economic Trends, *Federal Reserve Bank of St. Louis.*

Canon copiers, and Fuji film constitute 14.3 percent of total U.S. imports, and the Japanese absorb 11 percent of U.S. exports, primarily aircraft, chemicals, computers, timber, corn, and coal.

Mexico has a 9.3 percent share of U.S. goods exports and provides 9.3 percent of U.S. imports. Mexico exports large quantities of steel and oil to the United States. From 1993–1997, following the passage of NAFTA, Mexican tariffs declined from 40 percent to 16 percent, and U.S. imports increased from 67 percent to 72 percent of total imports. NAFTA reduced the trade barriers for American companies like General Motors and Wal-Mart, who now operate extensive retail operations through subsidiaries in Mexico. U.S.-owned manufacturing and processing plants have long employed the less-expensive skilled and semiskilled labor force in Mexico. This trade activity mirrors the labor-intensive assembly that German manufacturing companies perform in Spain and Portugal.

Germany is the fourth largest trading partner of the United States. Germany exports principally motor vehicles and parts (e.g., Mercedes-Benz diesel engines), specialized machinery, and chemicals to the United States and imports aircraft, computers, motor vehicles and parts (e.g., Cummins' engines), and scientific equipment from the United States.

A Comparison of the EU and NAFTA

Between the EU and NAFTA regional trading blocs, Europe has the larger share of world output (32 percent in 1995) and the larger share of world trade (37 percent in 1995). Recall, however, that much of the EU trade is with other members inside the regional trading bloc. Another important perspective can be obtained by considering competitiveness in the world economy. EU unit-labor costs and intermediate costs declined between 1987 and 1994 in motor vehicles and electrical equipment; these are Germany's two largest export categories to Britain and the United States. However, Japanese and U.S. costs in these industries declined even further. In other cases, like aerospace equipment, basic chemicals, and office machinery, EU competitiveness suffered still more. Between 1990 and 1996, the U.S. share of world exports rose from 11.7 percent to 13.1 percent and Japan's share rose from 8.5 percent to 9.4 percent. In that same period, the German, French, Italian, and British shares all declined; e.g., the German share of world trade declined from 12.6 percent to 10 percent.

Labor laws and social programs in Europe impose a heavy burden on manufacturing competitiveness. Six weeks' paid vacation in Germany is now standard, and the Germans spend 8.4 percent of GDP on pension payments. Compare two weeks' paid vacation in the United States and the 5 percent of GDP Americans spend on pension payments. Opting out of the EU's social programme has allowed the British economy to stay almost head-to-head with U.S. total labor costs. As a consequence, although wages for time worked in the U.S., British, and German manufacturing sectors are very similar (approximately $15 to $15.50 an hour in 1994), labor costs for holiday and leave pay add $5.70 an hour in Germany and only $1.03 an hour in the United States. When Social Security and other wage taxes are included, the total labor cost in Germany rises to $27.23 an hour versus $17.05 an hour in the United States and Britain.

In addition, workers on the senior management councils of German corporations often vote to stop or substantially delay plant closings. Plant closing legislation in the United States, on the other hand, has sensibly left the ultimate decision-making and contracting authority with boards of directors (and the courts). Also, French labor law makes it nearly impossible to lay off and furlough workers. Consequently, few entrepreneurial businesses in France proceed beyond very small sole proprietorships. One interesting development has been the emergence of foreign subsidiaries in France operating under less restrictive EU labor regulations. Consequently, despite the marketing power of a "made in Germany" label on an automobile, Mercedes-Benz recently announced plans to build its Swatch minicar in France.[9]

What all this demonstrates is that the institutional arrangements in the country surrounding a company are as important to its ultimate competitive success as the business plan, the quality of management decisions, and the commitment of dedicated employees. The enhanced competitive pressure arising from free trade and the opening of markets has only served to highlight the disadvantages of costly institutional arrangements.

TRADE DEFICITS AND THE BALANCE OF PAYMENTS

International trade is just one component of a country's balance of payments with the rest of the world. Capital flows and transfer payments are other important components. The U.S. balance of payments is divided into a current account and a capital account (see Table 7.2). The current account reflects goods and service trade flows, factor income receipts and payments on U.S. assets abroad and foreign assets in the United States, plus unilateral governmental and private transfers (e.g., foreign aid and legal judgments). The capital account reflects the sale or purchase of the nation's assets and liabilities, like office buildings, real estate, government securities, stocks and corporate bonds, private plant and equipment, and official reserves of foreign currencies, International Monetary Fund balances, and gold.

---

[9] Two useful surveys on these issues are "Business in Europe Survey," *The Economist,* 23 November 1996, and "Survey of the World Economy," *The Economist,* 20 September 1997.

TABLE 7.2		
1996 U.S. Balance of Payments (Billions of Dollars)		

Current Account, Net Inflow	−148
Exports & Factor Income, Total Inflow	1,056
Goods	612
Services	237
Receipts of Factor Income	207
Imports & Factor Income, Total Outflow	−1,164
Goods	−803
Services	−157
Payments of Factor Income	−204
Unilateral Transfers, Net,	−40
Foreign Aid, Pensions to U.S. Citizens Abroad, Private Remittances	
Capital Account, Net Inflow	148
Sale of U.S. Assets to Foreigners, Total Inflow	547
Foreign Direct Investment in U.S.	77
Foreign Official Assets in U.S., Net	122
Treasury Securities & U.S. Currency	173
Other Securities	134
U.S. Bank Liabilities, Other Claims	41
Purchase of Foreign Assets, Total Outflow	−399
U.S. Direct Investment Abroad	−88
U.S. Government Assets/Errors & Omissions, Net	−48
Foreign Securities	−108
Foreign Bank Liabilities, Other Claims	−162
U.S. Official Reserves, Net	7

The Current Account

On the inflow side of the current account, U.S. export goods and U.S. export services in 1996 generated $612 billion and $237 billion, respectively, in dollar inflows to the United States. Table 7.2 shows that the United States also earned $207 billion in factor income receipts on U.S. assets abroad. These receipts were approximately evenly divided in 1996 between (a) the net revenues from direct investment abroad of U.S. corporations like the Chrysler minivan plant in Canada and (b) the interest plus capital gains of private U.S. owners of foreign stocks, bonds, and real estate. On the outflow side of the **current account,** the U.S. imported $803 billion of goods and $157 billion of services in 1996 and made factor income payments to foreign owners of investments in the United States equaling $204 billion. Thus, the payment of factor income approximately balanced in 1996 ($207 billion inflow and $204 billion outflow) as depicted in Figure 7.8. However, the U.S. ran a balance of trade deficit in goods and services in 1996 of $111 billion (i.e., 612 + 237 − 803 − 157 = −111).

To balance the international transactions of the United States for the year 1996 required either asset sales to foreigners or increased borrowing from foreigners as described in the capital account. Indeed, the total deficit in the current account to be financed by net inflow to the capital account was somewhat larger—i.e., a $111 billion trade deficit plus a $40 billion transfer payments deficit plus a $3 billion factor income surplus totaling −$148 billion.

Current Account

A balance of payments tabulation of import-export goods, services, factor income, and net transfers.

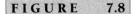

FIGURE   7.8   Quarterly Trade Balance

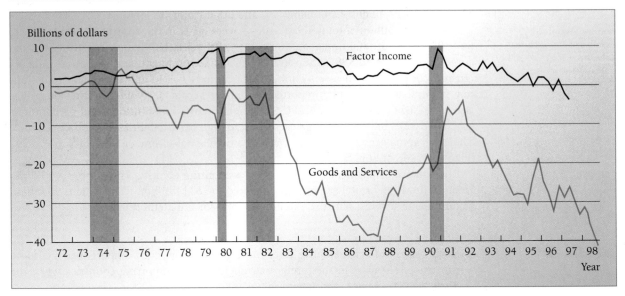

Source: National Economic Trends, *Federal Reserve Bank of St. Louis, November 1997.*

Perspectives on the Export Sector in the United States

The $848 billion export sector in the United States compares to a $7,253 billion gross *domestic* product (GDP) in 1996. That is, U.S. exports are approximately 10 percent of U.S. gross national product (GNP). For some quarterly growth statistics and for some companies like Cummins Engine, these annual averages can be very misleading. Fully 34 percent of Cummins's sales are export sales, and 43 percent of the *growth* in U.S. GNP in the third quarter of 1997 occurred in the export sector. By way of perspective, in net export countries like Japan, Belgium, or Singapore, the export sector constitutes 50 percent or more of the nation's GNP.

Figure 7.8 shows that in every year since 1975, the dollar value of foreign imports sold in the United States exceeded the value of U.S. exports sold abroad and converted to dollar values at the prevailing exchange rates. After the 1991–92 recession, U.S. import demand slowed, and U.S. trade flows almost balanced. More recently, the U.S. trade deficit has increased to record levels. The competitiveness of U.S. manufacturers in world markets continues to improve, and the U.S. export sector therefore continues to grow, but the volume of U.S. imports grows even faster. The U.S. trade deficits in 1995–97 were approximately equal to the size of the federal budget deficit for those years—between $50 and $150 billion. Since the Reagan era of the early 1980s, high real interest rates in the U.S. (relative to other economies) and a stable dollar have attracted the requisite flow of foreign capital to finance these "twin deficits."

The Capital Account

The capital account of the U.S. balance of payments in Table 7.2 tabulates these capital inflows and outflows. In 1996, foreigners bought $77 billion of real estate, plants, and equipment located in the United States (i.e., foreign direct investment in the United States). Also in 1996, the U.S. Treasury, public agencies, and the Federal Reserve sold $122 billion of U.S. government securities to foreign governments and another $173 billion of U.S. government securities and U.S. currency to foreign citizens and foreign corporations. Private U.S. corporations, banks, and other financial institutions sold $176 billion of stocks, bonds, bank liabilities, and other claims to foreigners.

These $547 billion of total dollar inflows were offset in the **capital account** in 1996 by $399 billion of total dollar outflows. First, U.S. citizens, financial institutions, and corporations invested $88 billion in foreign plant, equipment, and real estate. Net acquisition of government assets abroad (e.g., military bases) and errors and omissions (e.g., contraband trade and unreported capital flows from tax avoidance and smuggling) also increased by $46 billion. And U.S. citizens, financial institutions, and corporations purchased $270 billion of foreign securities, foreign bank liabilities, and other claims.[10] The U.S. capital account therefore showed a net capital inflow of $547 billion − $399 billion = $148 billion.

The balance of payment accounts is an accounting identity. Thus, the $148 billion credit in the 1996 capital account just covered the $111 billion trade deficit, $3 billion factor income surplus, plus the $40 billion debit for unilateral transfers.

Capital Account
A balance of payments tabulation of asset/liability sales and purchases.

SUMMARY

- Export sales are very sensitive to changes in exchange rates. Exports become more expensive (cheaper) in the foreign currencies of the importing countries when the domestic (i.e., home) currency of the manufacturer strengthens (weakens).

- Major currencies are traded in the foreign exchange markets; there are markets for U.S. dollars as foreign exchange, British pounds as foreign exchange, German deutsche marks as foreign exchange, etc. Demand and supply in these markets reflects the speculative and transactions demands of investors, import-export dealers, corporations, financial institutions, the International Monetary Fund, central bankers, and governments throughout the global economy.

- Export-oriented companies often demand payment and offer their best fixed price quotes in their domestic currency. Alternatively, such companies can manage the risk of exchange rate fluctuations themselves by setting up internal balance sheet hedges, futures market hedges, options market hedges, or currency swap contracts.

- Foreign buyers (or their financial intermediaries) usually must acquire deutsche marks to execute a purchase from Mercedes-Benz, U.S. dollars to execute a purchase from General Motors, or yen to execute a purchase from Toyota. Each buyer in these international sales transactions usually supplies their own domestic currency. Additional imports by Americans of Japanese automobiles would normally therefore result in an increased demand for the yen and an increased supply of dollars in the foreign currency markets, i.e., a dollar depreciation.

- Three transaction demand factors determine long-run trends in exchange rates: expected cost inflation, real (inflation-adjusted) growth rates, and real (inflation-adjusted) interest rates. The lower the expected cost inflation, the lower the real growth rate, and the higher the real rate of interest in one economy relative to another, the higher the exports, the lower the import demand, and the higher the demand for financial instruments from that economy. All three determinants imply an increased demand or decreased supply of the domestic currency, i.e., a currency appreciation.

[10] A small offset to the outflows side of the capital account resulted from a +$7 billion net change in the official reserve position of the United States in 1996—i.e., a $7.7 billion sale of foreign currencies, $0.7 billion net purchase of IMF reserves and special drawing rights, and no change in gold.

■ Speculative demand and central bank or IMF interventions especially influence short-term changes in exchange rates.

■ International capital flows and the flow of tradable goods across nations respond to arbitrage opportunities. Arbitrage trading ceases when parity conditions are met. One such condition is relative purchasing power parity.

■ Relative purchasing power parity (PPP) hypothesizes that a doubling of prices in one economy will lead to trade flows that cut in half the value of the currency. Over long periods of time and on an approximate basis, exchange rates do appear related to differential rates of inflation across economies. PPP serves a useful benchmark role in assessing long-term trends in exchange rates.

■ The European Union (EU) and the North American Free Trade Area (NAFTA) are two of several large trading blocks which have organized to open markets to free trade. The EU is the largest producer of world output with very dissimilar economies who have reduced trade barriers and specialized in accordance with comparative advantage. Marketing across the EU must address clusters of very different consumers.

■ The United States is both the largest single-nation exporter and the largest importer in the world economy. The largest trading partner of the United States is Canada followed by Japan, Mexico, and Germany. The U.S. share of world trade (13 percent) has grown in recent years, while that of Germany and other EU nations has declined. Extensive social programs, supplemental labor costs, and institutions which discourage business formation in Europe seem responsible for these trends.

■ The trade flows of the United States are often in deficit (i.e., imports exceed exports); the last time there was a trade surplus in the United States was 1975 (and a near surplus just after the recession of 1991–92). The balance of trade deficit of the United States is offset by international capital flows into the United States. The balance of payments accounts reflect this accounting identity.

■ The United States 1996 trade deficit was generated by $200 billion more merchandise imported into the United States than exported. Services generated a $80 billion trade surplus. In recent years, these trade deficits have been approximately the same size as the federal budget deficit—i.e., $50 to $150 billion, or between 1 and 2 percent of a $7.5 trillion gross domestic product in the United States.

EXERCISES

1. If the U.S dollar depreciates 20 percent, how does this affect the export and domestic sales of a U.S. manufacturer? Explain.

2. If the U.S. dollar were to appreciate substantially, what steps could a domestic manufacturer like Cummins Engine Co. of Columbus, Indiana, have taken in advance to reduce the effect of the exchange rate fluctuation on company profitability?

3. After an unanticipated dollar appreciation has occurred, what would you recommend a company like Cummins Engine do with its strong domestic currency?

4. What is the difference between transaction demand, speculative demand, and autonomous transactions by central banks, the World Bank, and the IMF in the foreign exchange markets? Which of these factors determines the long-term quarterly trends in exchange rates?

5. Would increased cost inflation in the United States relative to its major trading partners likely increase or decrease the value of the U.S. dollar? Why?

6. If the domestic prices for traded goods rise 50 percent over ten years in Japan and 100 percent over that same ten years in the United States, what would happen to the yen/dollar exchange rate? Why?

7. If Boeing's dollar aircraft prices increase 20 percent and the yen/dollar exchange rate declines 15 percent, what effective price increase is facing Japan Air Lines for the purchase of a Boeing 747? Would Boeing's margin likely rise or fall if the yen then depreciated and competitor prices were unchanged? Why?

8. Unit labor costs in Germany approach $30 per hour whereas in Britain unit labor costs are only $17 per hour. Why does such a large difference persist between two members of the EU free trade area?

9. If U.S. citizens and corporations earn more investment income on their foreign investments than is paid to foreigners on their U.S. investments, and if foreigners purchase more U.S. securities, loans, and real assets than U.S citizens and corporations purchase abroad, will the U.S. be a net importer or net exporter? Explain.

www exercise
Simulated Currency Trading

10. The Chicago Mercantile Exchange (CME) has developed an Internet site with a simulation that helps people learn more about how to trade currency futures and options. Access this site at: http://www.cme.com/market/cfot/simulation/. Once you are there, first read the material provided by the CME on how to trade currency futures and options. When you are ready, click the button to start the simulation.

CASE EXERCISE

THE VALUE OF THE U.S. DOLLAR, 1998

Analyze the following data on inflation rates, interest rates, and growth rate forecasts to determine the likely long-term trend movement of the U.S. dollar during 1998 against the German deutsche mark. Will the DM/$ exchange rate increase or decrease? Why?

	1996, %	1997, %	1998, %
U.S. nominal interest rate (90-day bills)	5.23	5.43	
German nominal interest rate (90-day bills)	3.13	3.40	
Quarterly U.S. consumer inflation	2.2	1.5	
Quarterly German consumer inflation	2.1	3.3	
U.S. real growth rate of GDP	3.3	3.4	2.5
German real growth rate of GDP	1.7	2.4	2.9
U.S. producer price index	1.5	−0.2	
German producer price index	1.4	1.8	

PRODUCTION AND COST

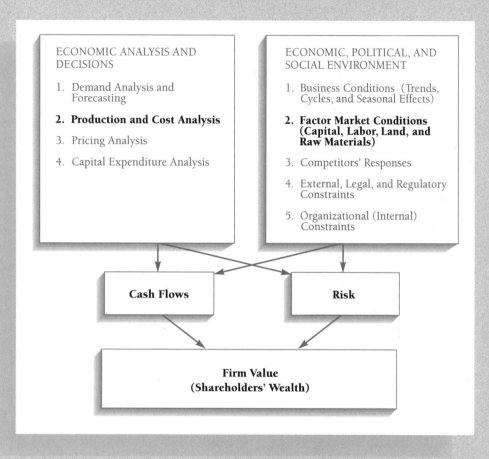

ECONOMIC ANALYSIS AND
DECISIONS

1. Demand Analysis and
   Forecasting

2. **Production and Cost Analysis**

3. Pricing Analysis

4. Capital Expenditure Analysis

ECONOMIC, POLITICAL, AND
SOCIAL ENVIRONMENT

1. Business Conditions (Trends,
   Cycles, and Seasonal Effects)

2. **Factor Market Conditions
   (Capital, Labor, Land, and
   Raw Materials)**

3. Competitors' Responses

4. External, Legal, and Regulatory
   Constraints

5. Organizational (Internal)
   Constraints

Cash Flows

Risk

**Firm Value
(Shareholders' Wealth)**

Part III deals with the production and cost analysis decisions facing managers of an economic enterprise. In Chapter 8 the theory of production decisions is developed. Production decisions include the determination of the type and amount of resources—such as land, labor, materials, capital equipment, and managerial skills—that are used in the production of a desired amount of output. The objective is to combine these inputs in the most efficient manner to produce the output of the enterprise. Appendix 8A examines constrained optimization techniques. Appendix 8B looks at production problems in a linear programming framework. In Chapter 9 the theory of cost analysis is developed. These cost figures are combined with revenue estimates to determine optimal (wealth-maximizing) levels and mixes of output. Chapter 10 discusses the applications of cost theory, including the measurement of short- and long-run cost relationships, the use of break-even analysis, and operating leverage concepts. The learning curve concept, as applied to manufacturing, is developed in Appendix 10A. Linear-programming approaches to constrained profit-maximization and cost-minimization problems are presented in Chapter 11.

Production Economics

CHAPTER PREVIEW

Managers are required to make decisions about the employment of the various types of resources within the firm. Traditionally, these have been classified into production, marketing, financing, and personnel decisions. Although these decisions are interrelated, it is
useful to discuss each of them separately. Production decisions include the determination
of the type and amount of resources or inputs—such as land, labor, raw and processed materials, factories, machinery, equipment, and managerial talent—to be used in the production of a desired quantity of output. The objective of the private sector manager is to
combine the resources of the firm in the most efficient manner to contribute to the goal of
maximizing shareholder wealth. In government agencies and other not-for-profit institutions, managers often are faced with binding budget constraints. In this context, their goal
is to maximize output (the provision of services) given the budget constraint. This can be
accomplished by finding the lowest cost combination of inputs to produce the organization's output. This chapter discusses the use of the economic theory of production in making wealth-maximizing production decisions.

PRODUCTION DEFINED

Production
The creation of any good or service that has value to either consumers or other producers.

In a very general sense, **production** is the creation of any good or service that has economic value to either consumers or other producers. This definition includes more than just the physical processing or manufacturing of material goods. It also includes production of transportation services, legal advice, education (teaching students), and invention (research and development). The list of goods and services produced by industry, not-for-profit organizations, and government is endless. The economic theory of *production* consists of a formal framework to assist the manager in deciding how to combine most efficiently the various inputs[1] needed to produce the desired output (product or service), given the existing technology. This technology consists of available production processes, equipment, labor and management skills, and information-processing capabilities. Production analysis is often applied by managers in assigning costs to the various feasible output levels and in communicating with plant engineers the operations plans of the company.

www . . . .
You can access a slide show on production economics at the following Internet site:
http://price.bus.okstate.edu/archive/Econ3113_963/Shows/Chapter6/index.htm

THE PRODUCTION FUNCTION

The theory of production is centered around the concept of a production function. A **production function** relates the maximum quantity of output that can be produced from given amounts of various inputs for a given technology. It can be expressed in the form of a mathematical model, schedule (table), or graph. A change in technology, such as the introduction of more automated equipment or the substitution of skilled for unskilled workers, results in a new production function. The production of most outputs (goods and services) requires the use of large numbers of inputs. The production of a house, for example, requires the use of many different labor skills (carpenters, plumbers, and electricians), raw materials (lumber, cement, bricks, and insulating materials), and types of equipment (bulldozers, saws, and cement mixers). Also, many production processes result in more than one output. For example, in the meat-processing industry, the slaughtering of a steer results in the joint output of various cuts of meat, hides, and fertilizer. To simplify the analysis and to illustrate the basic theory, the following discussion is limited to a two-input, one-output production function.[2]

Production Function
A mathematical model, schedule (table), or graph that relates the maximum feasible quantity of output that can be produced from given amounts of various inputs.

Letting X and Y represent the quantities of two inputs used in producing a quantity Q of output, a production function can be represented in the form of a mathematical model as

$$Q = f(X, Y) \qquad [8.1]$$

Input
A resource or factor of production, such as a raw material, labor skill, or piece of equipment, that is employed in a production process.

The function f incorporates the existing state of technology in producing Q from X and Y. The general function, f, can take many different forms. One commonly used function is

$$Q = \alpha L^{\beta_1} K^{\beta_2} \qquad [8.2]$$

where L is the amount of labor and K is the amount of capital used in the production process (α, β_1, and β_2 are constants). This particular multiplicative model is known as the **Cobb-Douglas production function** and is examined in more detail later in the chapter. Production functions also can be expressed in the form of a *schedule* (or table), as illustrated in the following ore-mining example.

Cobb-Douglas Production Function
A particular type of mathematical model, known as a power function, which is used to represent the relationship between the inputs employed in a production process and the output obtained from the process.

---

[1] The terms *input, factor,* and *resource* are used interchangeably throughout the chapter. They all have the same meaning in production theory.

[2] A text on microeconomic theory can be consulted for a treatment of the general case of m inputs and n outputs. See, for example, Robert S. Pindyck and Daniel L. Rubinfeld, *Microeconomics* (New York: Macmillan, 1997), chaps. 6 and 7.

MANAGERIAL CHALLENGE

ELECTRIC UTILITY DEREGULATION AND ECONOMIES OF SCALE

The electric utility industry in the United States long has been subject to intense regulation of its prices, service standards, and the choice of production technologies it employs. This regulation is provided by state-level regulatory commissions and the Federal Energy Regulatory Commission. When building a new power plant, a utility normally asks permission of the appropriate regulatory bodies. In making the decision, regulators consider the needs of utility customers and the projected costs of the new plant.

Many of the power plants constructed during the 1970s and 1980s were very large base-load generating plants using coal or nuclear energy as their power source. During that time there was a belief that these larger plants would provide the lowest cost sources of power due to economies of scale. However, in many cases the final cost of these plants has greatly exceeded initial estimates.

As the electric utility industry has entered an era of deregulation and market competition, these old assumptions of economies of scale have been called into question. Independent power producers, who produce electricity for sale to utility companies or directly to end users have built many smaller, less capital-intensive plants that often rely on natural gas as the power source. These producers have learned that substantial cost savings can be achieved by substituting the cheap variable input, natural gas, for the expensive capital equipment required in nuclear and coal-fired power plants.

Understanding the relationships between the inputs (resources) and outputs (products or services) of a production process is crucial in analyzing the trade-offs between capital costs and variable costs (such as labor and raw materials). The goal of the analysis discussed in this chapter is to permit management to make the proper production choices that will increase operating efficiency, lower costs, and contribute to shareholder wealth maximization.

www . . . .
http://www.sel.com/retail.html
You can learn more about recent developments in state-level electric utility deregulation and wheeling legislation at this Internet site maintained by Strategic Energy Ltd.

EXAMPLE

AN ILLUSTRATIVE PRODUCTION FUNCTION: DEEP CREEK MINING COMPANY

The Deep Creek Mining Company uses capital (mining equipment) and labor (workers) to mine uranium ore. Various sizes of ore-mining equipment, as measured by its horsepower rating, are available to the company. The amount of ore mined during a given period is a function only of the number of workers assigned to the crew operating a given piece of equipment. The data in Table 8.1 show the amount of ore produced (measured in tons) when various sizes of crews are used to operate the equipment efficiently. In this example, the two inputs are labor, X—that is, number of workers—and capital, Y—that is, size of equipment—and the output Q is the number of tons of ore produced with the given combination of inputs.

A two-input, one-output production function can also be represented *graphically* as a three-dimensional production surface, where the height of the bar associated with each input combination indicates the amount of output produced. The production surface for the ore-mining example is shown in Figure 8.1.

		Capital Input Y (Horsepower)							
		250	500	750	1,000	1,250	1,500	1,750	2,000
LABOR INPUT X	1	1	3	6	10	16	16	16	13
(NUMBER OF	2	2	6	16	24	29	29	44	44
WORKERS)	3	4	16	29	44	55	55	55	50
	4	6	29	44	55	58	60	60	55
	5	16	43	55	60	61	62	62	60
	6	29	55	60	62	63	63	63	62
	7	44	58	62	63	64	64	64	64
	8	50	60	62	63	64	65	65	65
	9	55	59	61	63	64	65	66	66
	10	52	56	59	62	64	65	66	67

TABLE   8.1

Total Output Table—
Deep Creek Mining
Company

FIGURE   8.1

Production Function—
Deep Creek Mining
Company

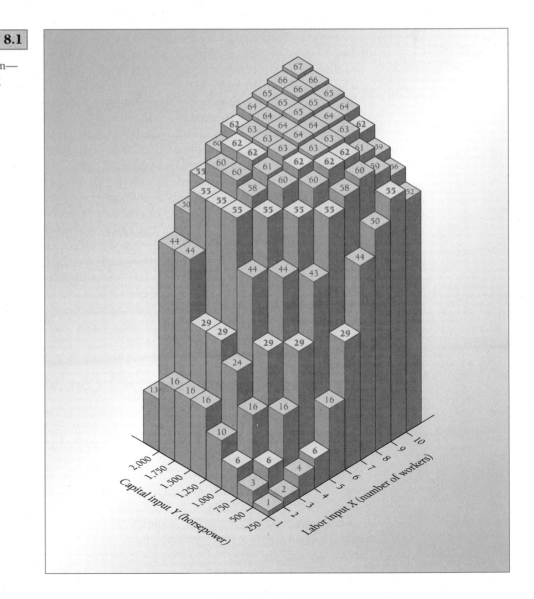

Fixed and Variable Inputs

In deciding how to combine the various inputs (X and Y) to produce the desired output, inputs are usually classified as being either fixed or variable. A *fixed* input is defined as one required in the production process but whose quantity employed in the process is constant over a given period of time regardless of the quantity of output produced. The costs of a fixed input must be incurred regardless of whether the production process is operated at a high or a low level. A *variable* input is defined as one whose quantity employed in the process changes, depending on the desired quantity of output to be produced.

Short Run

The period of time in which one (or more) of the resources employed in a production process is fixed or incapable of being varied.

The **short run** corresponds to the period of time in which one (or more) of the inputs is fixed. This means that to increase output, the firm must employ more of the variable input(s) with the given quantity of fixed input(s). Thus, for example, with an auto assembly plant of fixed size and capacity, the firm can increase output only by employing more labor, such as by paying workers overtime or by scheduling additional shifts.

As the time period under consideration (planning horizon) is lengthened, however, more of the fixed inputs become variable. Over a planning horizon of about six months or more, the firm could possibly acquire or build additional plant capacity and order more manufacturing equipment. Production facilities would no longer be a fixed factor. In lengthening the planning horizon, a point is eventually reached where all inputs are variable. The **long run** corresponds to this period of time in which *all* the inputs of the production function are variable.

Long Run

The period of time in which *all* the resources employed in a production process can be varied.

In the short run, because some of the inputs are fixed, only a subset of the total possible input combinations are available to the firm. By contrast, in the long run all possible input combinations are available to the firm. Consequently, in the long run the firm can choose between increasing production through the use of more labor (overtime or hiring more workers) or through plant expansion, depending on which combination of labor and plant size is most efficient at producing the desired output.

In developing some of the concepts of production theory, a production function with one fixed and one variable input is examined first. The objective of the analysis is to determine how to combine different quantities of the variable input with a given amount of the fixed input to produce various quantities of output. The total, average, and marginal products are defined and illustrated, and the law of diminishing returns and marginal revenue product are discussed. Then a slightly more complex situation is considered—a production function with two variable inputs. The objective in this situation is to determine how to combine the two variable inputs, based on the relative costs of producing a desired output by different input combinations. This situation is used to illustrate isoquants and returns to scale.

PRODUCTION FUNCTIONS WITH ONE VARIABLE INPUT

Suppose in the Deep Creek Mining Company example of the previous section that the amount of capital input Y—that is, the size of mining equipment—employed in the production process is a fixed factor. Specifically, suppose that the firm owns or leases a piece of mining equipment having a 750-horsepower rating. Depending on the amount of labor input X—that is, number of workers—used to operate the 750-horsepower equipment, varying quantities of output will be obtained, as shown in the "$Y = 750$" column of Table 8.1 and again in the "Q" column of Table 8.2. This *total product* function can be represented graphically, as shown in Figure 8.2 where output Q is measured along the vertical axis and the variable input, labor (X), is measured along the horizontal axis.

TABLE 8.2					

Total Product, Marginal Product, Average Product, and Elasticity—Deep Creek Mining Company (Capital input, horsepower, = 750)

Labor Input X (Number of Workers)	Total Product, TP_x (= Q) (Tons of Ore)	Marginal Product of Labor, MP_x ($\Delta Q \div \Delta X$)	Average Product of Labor, AP_x ($Q \div X$)	Elasticity, E_x ($MP_x \div AP_x$)
0	0	—	—	—
1	6	+ 6	6	1.0
2	16	+10	8	1.25
3	29	+13	9.67	1.34
4	44	+15	11	1.36
5	55	+11	11	1.0
6	60	+ 5	10	.50
7	62	+ 2	8.86	.23
8	62	0	7.75	0.0
9	61	− 1	6.78	−.15
10	59	− 2	5.90	−.34

FIGURE 8.2	

Total Product Curve—Deep Creek Mining Company

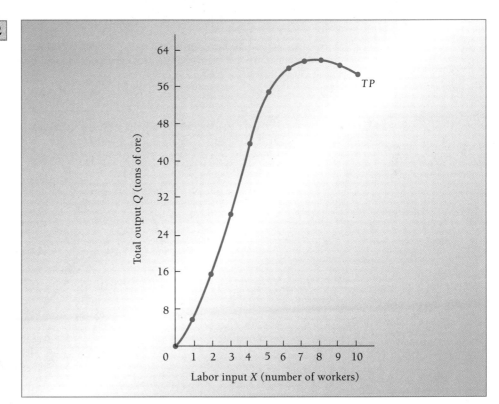

Marginal and Average Product Functions

Once the total product function is given (in tabular, graphic, or algebraic form), the marginal and average product functions can be derived. The marginal product is defined as the incremental change in total output that can be produced by the use of one more unit of the variable input in the production process. Letting ΔQ be the change in

Marginal Product
The incremental change in total output that can be obtained from the use of one more unit of an input in the production process (while holding constant all other inputs).

total output brought about by a change in the variable input ΔX, while Y remains fixed, then the **marginal product** is equal to[3]

$$MP_x = \frac{\Delta Q}{\Delta X}$$ [8.3]

The marginal product of labor in the ore-mining example is shown in the MP_x column of Table 8.2 and in Figure 8.3.

If input X is infinitely divisible, and hence a continuous variable, then the marginal product can be obtained by taking the partial derivative of Q (Equation 8.1) with respect to X:

$$MP_x = \frac{\partial Q}{\partial X}$$ [8.4]

The *average product* is defined as the ratio of total output to the amount of the variable input used in producing the output. For the variables that have been defined, the average product is equal to

$$AP_x = \frac{Q}{X}$$ [8.5]

The average product of labor for the Deep Creek ore-mining example is shown in the AP_x column of Table 8.2 and in Figure 8.3.

---

[3] Strictly speaking, the ratio $\Delta Q/\Delta X$ represents the *incremental* product rather than the *marginal* product. For clarity, we continue to use the term *marginal,* even though this and similar ratios throughout the text are calculated on an incremental basis.

FIGURE   8.3

Marginal and Average Product Curves—Deep Creek Mining Company

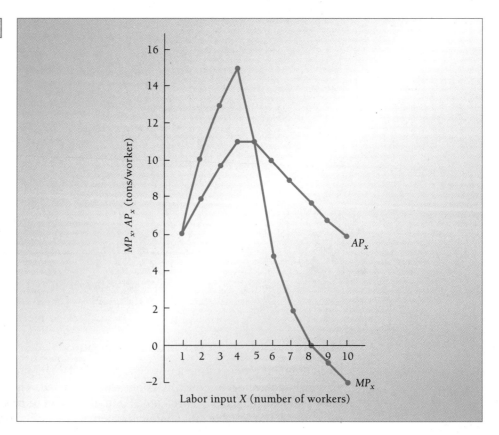

EXAMPLE

ALGEBRAIC DETERMINATION OF MARGINAL AND AVERAGE PRODUCT: ECLIPSE CORPORATION

Consider the following short-run algebraic production function for the Eclipse Company:

$$Q = 6X^2 - .2X^3 \qquad [8.6]$$

Taking the first derivative of Equation 8.6 with respect to X yields the following marginal product function:

$$MP_x = 12X - .6X^2 \qquad [8.7]$$

For Eclipse's algebraic production function given in Equation 8.6, the average product function is equal to

$$AP_x = \frac{6X^2 - .2X^3}{X}$$

$$= 6X - .2X^2 \qquad [8.8]$$

Production Elasticity

The discussion of the theory of demand in Chapter 4 introduced the concept of price elasticity. The price elasticity at any point on the demand curve or schedule was defined as the ratio of the percentage change in the quantity demanded brought about by a given percentage change in the price of the good, all other factors remaining the same. Similarly in production analysis, it is useful to define production elasticity. The elasticity of production is defined as the percentage change in output Q resulting from a given percentage change in the amount of the variable input X employed in the production process, with Y remaining constant. The production elasticity indicates the responsiveness of output to changes in the given input. Expressed in terms of the quantities previously defined, the elasticity of production is equal to

$$E_x = \frac{\%\Delta Q}{\%\Delta X} \qquad [8.9]$$

$$= \frac{\frac{\Delta Q}{Q}}{\frac{\Delta X}{X}}$$

Rearranging terms yields

$$E_x = \frac{\frac{\Delta Q}{\Delta X}}{\frac{Q}{X}} \text{ or } \frac{\Delta Q}{\Delta X} \times \frac{X}{Q}$$

or, because $MP_x = \Delta Q/\Delta X$ and $AP_x = Q/X$:

$$E_x = \frac{MP_x}{AP_x} \qquad [8.10]$$

which shows that the elasticity of production is equal to the ratio of the marginal product to the average product of input X.

The elasticity of production for the Deep Creek ore-mining example is shown in the E_x column of Table 8.2. A production elasticity greater than (less than) 1.0 indicates that output increases more than (less than) proportionately with a given percentage increase in the variable input. An elasticity of zero indicates that no change takes place in output as a result of a given percentage increase in the input, and a negative elasticity indicates that output *decreases* with a given percentage increase in the input. The elasticity-of-production concept is examined later in the discussion of the empirical determination of production functions.

Law of Diminishing Marginal Returns

The tabular production function just discussed illustrates the production law of diminishing marginal returns. Initially, the assignment of more workers to the crew operating the mining equipment (the fixed factor) allows greater labor specialization in the use of the equipment. As a result, the marginal output of each worker added to the crew at first increases, and total output increases at an increasing rate. Thus, as shown in Table 8.2, the addition of a second worker to the crew results in 10 additional tons of output; the addition of a third worker results in 13 additional tons of output; and the addition of a fourth worker yields 15 additional tons. However, in adding more workers to the crew, a point is eventually reached where the marginal increase in output for each worker added to the crew begins to decline. This occurs because only a limited number of ways exist to increase significantly the output of the equipment through greater labor specialization. Thus, the addition of a fifth worker to the crew yields a marginal increase in output of 11 additional tons, compared with the marginal increase of 15 additional tons for the fourth worker. Similarly, the additions of the sixth and seventh workers to the crew yield successively smaller increases of 5 and 2 tons, respectively. Note, however, the total output is still increasing. It still may be profitable to operate a crew of five, six, or seven workers.

In some cases, total output may level off or decline when even larger crew sizes are used to operate the equipment. Under these conditions the marginal product of each additional worker becomes zero or even negative. Note that the eighth, ninth, and tenth workers have marginal products of 0, -1, and -2 tons, respectively. A zero or negative marginal product for labor may result, for example, from the inability to supervise adequately the excessive number of workers operating the equipment. In addition, some work may be more difficult to accomplish when superfluous personnel are present. Such crowding effects can overwhelm the small additional output from the extra worker.

The law of diminishing marginal returns (sometimes also known as the diminishing marginal productivity law, or law of variable proportions) can be formally stated as follows:

> Given that the amount of all other productive factors remains unchanged, the use of increasing amounts of a variable factor in the production process beyond some point will eventually result in diminishing marginal increases in total output.

Note that the law does not state that each and every increase in the amount of the variable factor used in the production process will yield diminishing marginal returns. As the preceding example illustrates, it is possible that initial increases in the amount of the variable factor used in the production process may yield increasing marginal returns. However, by increasing the amount of the variable factor used, a point will always be reached where the marginal increases in total output will begin declining. The law of diminishing marginal returns is *not* a mathematical theorem but an empirical assertion that has been observed in almost every economic production process as the amount of the variable input increases. An interesting exception occurs with marketing expenses after the adoption of a new industry standard (e.g., digital HDTV).

INCREASING RETURNS AT SONY, MICROSOFT, AND INTEL[4]

Like service firms, many manufacturers today compete on customer inquiry systems, change order responsiveness, schedule conformance, product reliability, and technological updates, not just product delivery and warranty repairs. Qualifying for and actually winning a customer order often requires quality characteristics and support services beyond the physical unit of production. For example, Ford Motor wants all its manufacturing suppliers to meet the ISO9000 manufacturing quality standards for continuous improvement processes. Wal-Mart requires that their fashion clothing suppliers deliver shipments just-in time (JIT) for planned departure from Wal-Mart distribution centers. Disney chooses gift item manufacturers who can alter production schedules on short notice in order to provide much greater change order responsiveness than traditional make-to-order manufacturing. Consequently, product line costs usually now include marketing, distribution, and operations activities quite different from standard production and assembly.

At times, these additional supply activities can exhibit increasing returns and declining cost. For example, securing the adoption of an industry standard favorable to one's own product (e.g., digital high-definition television—HDTV) involves promotional and other marketing efforts which grow *more productive* the larger the product's market share. The greater the installed base of Sony digital TV receivers, the more programs are produced to transmit with this technology, and the more programs available, the easier and cheaper it is to secure the next household's adoption of the innovation. To take another example, the more adoptions Microsoft Windows secures, the more applications independent software developers introduce, and the more applications introduced the greater the chance for further adoptions. Normal sales penetration or saturation curves (like Figure 8.4) exhibit initially increasing marginal returns to promotional expenses followed by eventually diminishing marginal returns. However, with the adoption of new industry standards or a new technology, increasing returns can persist. For example, the higher the Intel Pentium processor's market share goes, the lower the promotional costs required to trigger another adoption. The limiting factor in the adoption of such innovations is the appearance of still newer technologies (e.g., networked computers need much less processing power than stand-alone PCs).

Relationship between Total, Marginal, and Average Product

To illustrate some additional properties of production functions with one variable input, assume now that the variable input, rather than being composed of finitely divisible units (workers), is infinitely divisible. In other words, the variable input is now considered to be a *continuous* variable rather than a discrete variable, as in the ore-mining example discussed previously. Figure 8.4 illustrates a production function (*TP*) with a continuously variable input exhibiting the law of diminishing marginal returns. Also shown are the corresponding average product (*AP*) and marginal product (*MP*) functions.

Several relationships among the *TP*, *AP*, and *MP* curves can be seen in the graph. In the first region labeled "increasing returns," the *TP* function (total output) is increasing

---

[4] Based on "The Theory That Made Microsoft: Increasing Returns," *Fortune,* 29 April 1996, pp. 65–68.

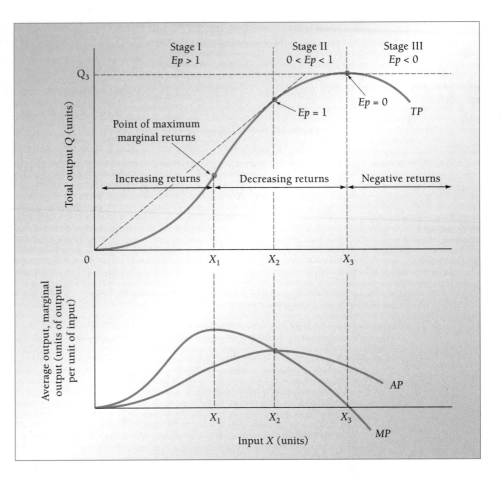

at an *increasing rate*. Because the *MP* curve measures the slope of the *TP* curve ($MP = \partial Q/\partial X$), the *MP* curve is increasing up to X_1. In the region labeled "decreasing returns," the *TP* function is increasing at a *decreasing rate,* and the *MP* curve is decreasing up to X_3. In the region labeled "negative returns," the *TP* function is *decreasing,* and the *MP* curve continues decreasing and becomes negative beyond X_3. An *inflection point* occurs at X_1. At this point the *TP* curve switches from being *convex* to the horizontal axis (U-shaped) to being *concave* to the horizontal axis (inverted U-shaped). X_3 is the point of maximum output for the given or fixed amount of other inputs, *Y,* employed in the production process. Next, if a line is drawn from the origin 0 to any point on the *TP* curve, it can be seen that the slope of this line, Q/X, is at a maximum when the line touches the *TP* curve at an input value of X_2. The slope of this line, Q/X, measures the average product *AP.* Hence we see that the *AP* curve reaches a maximum at this point. Note also that the marginal product *MP* equals the average product *AP* at X_2. This follows because the marginal product *MP* is equal to the slope of the *TP* curve ($MP = \partial Q/\partial X$), and at X_2 the average product *AP* is also equal to the slope of the *TP* curve.

Consider, for example, the following analogy. A baseball player's batting *average* for the season is 0.250. If that player has an excellent night at bat (his *marginal* performance) and goes 4 for 4 (1.000), then his season average will be pulled up. On the other hand if he goes hitless, this poor *marginal* performance will pull down his season average. If he goes 1 for 4, this marginal performance will have no impact on his season average (marginal performance equals average performance). Hence the *MP* curve will always intersect with the *AP* curve when it is at a maximum. As we will see in the next chapter, a firm's marginal cost curve always intersects the average cost curve at its minimum point, for the same reasons.

Three Stages of Production

In analyzing several useful special cases of the production function, economists have identified three different stages of production based on the relationships among the *TP*, *AP*, and *MP* functions. Stage I is defined as the *range of X over which the average product is increasing*. This occurs from the origin (0) up to X_2 and represents the region of net gains from specialization. Stage II corresponds to the *range of X from the point at which the average product is a maximum* (X_2) *to the point where the marginal product (MP) declines to zero* (X_3). The endpoint of Stage II thus corresponds to the point of maximum output on the *TP* curve. Stage III encompasses the *range of X over which the total product is declining* or, equivalently, *the marginal product is negative*. Stage III thus corresponds to all values of *X* greater than (i.e., to the right of) X_3 where crowding effects overwhelm any output attributable to additional workers.

The determination of the optimal quantity of input *X* to be used in producing a given amount of output *Q* is described in the next section; however, one can eliminate several values of *X* from consideration at this point. First, the rational producer would not operate the production process over the range of values of input *X* contained in Stage III. In Stage III an excessive amount of the variable input, relative to the fixed input *Y*, is being used to produce the desired output. In other words, because the marginal product of input *X* is negative beyond X_3, using more than X_3 units would cause a *reduction* in total output. Any desired output (up to the maximum obtainable with the given amount of the fixed input, that is, Q_3) could be produced by using less than X_3 units of the variable input. No manager would ever knowingly increase labor expenses to hire additional workers whose presence reduces output (e.g., Stage III). Even if the variable input were free, the rational producer would not wish to proceed into Stage III. By the same token, no manager whose productivity per worker is rising due to the gains from specialization (i.e., *AP* increasing in Stage I) should stop adding workers as long as the incremental cost for additional workers remains constant.

In general, then, how much of the variable input to employ over the remaining range of potentially optimal input choice (Stage II) depends on variable input costs. If labor costs are high, as in a United Auto Workers' assembly plant, production may proceed just a short distance into Stage II in hiring labor. Where labor costs are lower in a non-unionized plant, labor hiring may proceed well across Stage II to include relatively low-level incremental productivity workers, like apprentices. Of course, some inputs are subsidized (e.g., job training programs). Others may have input prices that are effectively negative such that revenues actually increase the more the input is used. For example, in order to ensure that dredge spoil once removed does not flow back into harbors and navigable waterways, the U.S. Army Corps of Engineers will actually pay concrete block manufacturers for every cubic yard used in the production process. Too much of the dredge spoil slurry in combination with concrete mix and sand results in more cracked blocks leaving the kilns. However, with a negative price on the input, the manufacturers employ dredge spoil into the range of Stage III production. Such exceptions prove the general rule that optimal production with a single variable input and positive input prices will reside in Stage II.

EXAMPLE

THREE STAGES OF PRODUCTION: DEEP CREEK MINING COMPANY (CONTINUED)

The three stages of production for the Deep Creek Mining Company example are shown in Table 8.3. In Stage I, from 0 to 5 workers, the average product of labor (AP_x) is increasing and the marginal product of labor (MP_x) is greater than or equal to the average product of labor.[5] In Stage II, from 5 to 8 workers, the marginal product of labor is greater than or equal to zero and the average product of labor is decreasing. Finally, in Stage III, beyond 8 workers, the marginal product of labor is negative.

www..............
For further reading on marginal revenue product see David Friedman's Internet textbook at: http://www.best.com/~ddfr/Academic/Price_Theory/PThy_Chapter_9.html

DETERMINING THE OPTIMAL USE OF THE VARIABLE INPUT

With one of the inputs (Y) fixed in the short run, the producer must determine the optimal quantity of the variable input (X) to employ in the production process. Such a determination requires the introduction into the analysis of product (output) prices and factor costs. Therefore, the analysis begins by defining marginal revenue product and marginal factor cost.

Marginal Revenue Product

Marginal Revenue Product
The amount that an additional unit of the variable production input adds to total revenue.

Marginal revenue product (MRP_x) is defined as *the amount that an additional unit of the variable input adds to total revenue,* or

$$MRP_x = \frac{\Delta TR}{\Delta X} \qquad [8.11]$$

where ΔTR is the change in total revenue associated with the given change (ΔX) in the variable input, and MRP_x is equal to the marginal product of X (MP_x) times the marginal revenue (MR_Q) resulting from the increase in output obtained:

$$MRP_x = MP_x \cdot MR_Q \qquad [8.12]$$

Consider again the Deep Creek Mining Company example (Table 8.2) of the previous section where Y (capital) is fixed at 750 horsepower. Suppose that the firm can sell all the ore it can produce at a price of $10 per ton (that is, in a *perfectly competitive market*). The marginal revenue product of labor (MRP_x) is computed using Equation 8.12

---

[5] The average product of labor is actually constant (i.e., not decreasing) between 4 and 5 workers.

TABLE	8.3

Three Stages of Production—Deep Creek Mining Company

Stage	Variable Input, X (Number of Workers)	Production Relationships
I	0–5	AP_x is increasing;* $MP_x \geq AP_x$; $E_p > 1$
Boundary	5	AP_x is a maximum; $MP_x = AP_x$; $E_p = 1$
II	5^+–8	AP_x is decreasing; $MP_x \geq 0$; $MP_x < AP_x$; $0 < E_p < 1$
Boundary	8	TP_x is a maximum; $MP_x = 0$; $E_p = 0$
III	8^+–10	$MP_x < 0$; $E_p < 0$

*Note that the AP_x function is actually *constant* between $X = 4$ and $X = 5$. This anomaly arises because labor (X) is a discrete variable, rather than a continuous variable as illustrated in Figure 8.4.

and is shown in Table 8.4.[6] Note that in a perfectly competitive market, marginal revenue is equal to the selling price.[7]

Marginal Factor Cost

Marginal Factor Cost
The amount that an additional unit of the variable production input adds to total cost.

Marginal factor cost (MFC$_x$) is defined as *the amount that an additional unit of the variable input adds to total cost,* or

$$MFC_x = \frac{\Delta TC}{\Delta X}$$ [8.13]

where ΔTC is the change in cost associated with the given change (ΔX) in the variable input.

In the ore-mining example, suppose that the firm can employ as much labor (X) as it needs by paying the workers $50 per period ($C_x$). In other words, the labor market is assumed to be *perfectly competitive.* Under these conditions, the marginal factor cost (MFC_x) is equal to C_x, or $50 per worker. It is constant regardless of the level of operation of the mine (see Table 8.4).

Optimal Input Level

Given the marginal revenue product and marginal factor cost, we can compute the optimal amount of the variable input to use in the production process. Recall from the discussion of marginal analysis in Chapter 2 that an economic activity (for example,

---

[6] Input levels in Stage III ($MP_x < 0$) have been eliminated from consideration.

[7] This relationship is discussed further in Chapter 12.

TABLE   8.4   Marginal Revenue Product and Marginal Factor Cost—Deep Creek Mining Company

Labor Input X (Number of Workers)	Total Product Q = (TP$_x$) (Tons of Ore)	Marginal Product of Labor MP$_x$ (Tons Per Worker)	Total Revenue TR = P · Q ($)	Marginal Revenue $MR_Q = \frac{\Delta TR}{\Delta Q}$ ($/Ton)	Marginal Revenue Product $MRP_x = MP_x \cdot MR_Q$ ($/Worker)	Marginal Factor Cost MFC$_x$ ($/Worker)
0	0	—	0	—	—	—
1	6	6	60	10	60	50
2	16	10	160	10	100	50
3	29	13	290	10	130	50
4	44	15	440	10	150	50
5	55	11	550	10	110	50
6*	60	5	600	10	50	50
7	62	2	620	10	20	50
8	62	0	620	10	0	50

production) should be expanded as long as the marginal benefits (revenues) exceed the marginal costs. The optimal level occurs at the point where the marginal benefits are equal to the marginal costs. For the short-run production decision, the optimal level of the variable input occurs where

$$MRP_x = MFC_x \qquad\qquad [8.14]$$

As can be seen in Table 8.4, the optimal input is $X^* = 6$ workers because $MRP_x = MFC_x = \$50$ at this point. At less than six workers, $MRP_x > MFC_x$ and the addition of more labor (workers) to the production process will increase revenues more than it will increase costs. Beyond six workers the opposite is true—costs increase more than revenues.

Having completed the discussion of production functions with one variable input, we now examine the slightly more complex situation of a production function with two variable inputs.

PRODUCTION FUNCTIONS WITH TWO VARIABLE INPUTS

Using the Deep Creek Mining Company example, suppose now that both capital—as measured by the horsepower rating of the equipment—and labor—as measured by the number of workers—are variable inputs to the ore-mining process. The firm can choose to operate the production process using any of the capital-labor combinations shown previously in Table 8.1. Note that the law of diminishing returns holds true in every row and column of the table. If one holds the number of workers X fixed and increases the size of the equipment Y, total output eventually increases at a decreasing rate, and for some (but not all) values of X, total output also declines. Similarly, if one holds the size of the equipment Y fixed and increases the number of workers X, total output eventually increases at a decreasing rate; and in some cases it also declines.

Production Isoquants

Production Isoquant

An algebraic function or a geometric curve representing all the various combinations of two inputs that can be used in producing a given level of output.

A production function with two variable inputs and one output can be represented graphically in either two or three dimensions. (A three-dimensional example was shown earlier in Figure 8.1.) A two-dimensional graph is more amenable to further analysis, so this method of illustration will be used. A production function is represented by a set of two-dimensional *production isoquants*. A **production isoquant** is either a geometric curve or an algebraic function representing all the various combinations of the two inputs that can be used in producing a given level of output. In the Deep Creek example, a production isoquant shows all the alternative ways in which labor input (number of workers) and capital input (size of equipment) can be combined to produce any desired level of output (tons of ore). Several of the production isoquants for the ore-mining example are shown in Figure 8.5. Each production isoquant is constructed by plotting all the various labor-capital combinations that can be used in producing a given level of output and then connecting these points by a series of straight lines. For example, an output of 6 tons can be produced using any of three different labor-capital combinations—by 1 unit of labor (1 worker) and 750 units of capital (750-horsepower mining equipment), by 2 units of labor and 500 units of capital, or by 4 units of labor and 250 units of capital. Similarly, as seen in the graph, an output of 62 tons can be produced using any one of six different labor-capital combinations. Each isoquant indicates how quantities of the two inputs may be *substituted* for one another in producing the desired level of output.

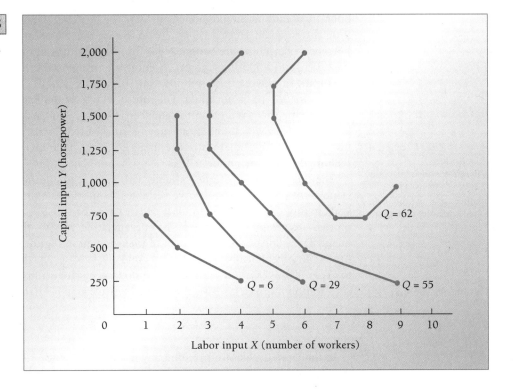

FIGURE   8.5

Production Isoquants—
Deep Creek Mining
Company

These input substitution choices are normally limited for two reasons. First, some input combinations in Figure 8.5 employ an excessive quantity of one input. Just as more than 8 workers result in negative marginal returns in choosing a single variable input for Deep Creek Mining (see Figures 8.2 and 8.3), so too here with 750-horsepower machinery, the eighth worker contributes no additional output along the isoquant $Q = 62$ in Figure 8.5. The presence of a ninth worker necessitates additional capital equipment investment simply to maintain output at 62 tons. That is, in the absence of additional capital equipment, the crowding effects introduced by the ninth worker would actually reduce output. Similarly, more than 1,750-horsepower machinery results in negative marginal returns with only 5 workers; another 250 horsepower (from 1,750 to 2,000 h.p. in Figure 8.5) requires an additional (sixth) worker just to maintain output at 62 tons. Because all such inefficient mixes of capital and labor increase the input requirements (and therefore costs) without increasing output, they should be excluded from consideration in making input substitution choices.

Input substitution choices are also limited by the technology of production, which often involves machinery that is not divisible. Although one can find smaller and larger mining equipment, not every horsepower machine listed on the Y axis of Figure 8.5 will be available. The industrial engineering of mining operations often requires that we select from three or four possible fixed proportions production processes involving a particular size mining drill and a particular size labor force to run it. We discuss the optimal choice of a fixed proportions production process in the next section.

Marginal Rate of Technical Substitution

In addition to indicating the quantity of output that can be produced with any of the various input combinations that lie on the isoquant curve, the isoquant also indicates the *rate* at which one input may be substituted for the other input in producing the given quantity of output. Suppose one considers the meaning of a shift from point *A* to point *B* on the isoquant labeled "*Q* = 29" in Figure 8.6. At point *A*, 3 workers and a 750-horsepower machine are being used to produce 29 tons of output, whereas at point *B*, 4 workers and a 500-horsepower machine are being used to produce the same amount of output. In moving from point *A* to point *B*, one has substituted one additional unit of labor for 250 units of capital. The rate at which capital has been replaced with labor in producing the given output is equal to 250/1 or 250 units of capital per unit of labor. The rate at which one input may be substituted for another input in the production process, while total output remains constant, is known as the **marginal rate of technical substitution,** or *MRTS*.

Marginal Rate of Technical Substitution

The *rate* at which one input may be substituted for another input in producing a given quantity of output.

The rate of change of one variable with respect to another variable is given by the slope of the curve relating the two variables. Thus, the rate of change of input *Y* with respect to input *X*—that is, the rate at which *Y* may be substituted for *X* in the production process—is given by the slope of the curve relating *Y* to *X*—that is, the slope of the isoquant. The slope of the *AB* segment of the isoquant in Figure 8.6 is equal to the ratio of *AC* to *CB*. Algebraically, $AC = Y_1 - Y_2$ and $CB = X_1 - X_2$; therefore the slope is equal to $(Y_1 - Y_2) \div (X_1 - X_2)$. Because the slope is negative and one wishes to express the substitution rate as a positive quantity, a negative sign is attached to the slope:

$$MRTS = -\frac{Y_1 - Y_2}{X_1 - X_2} = -\frac{\Delta Y}{\Delta X}$$ [8.15]

In the Deep Creek Mining Company example, $\Delta X = 3 - 4 = -1$, $\Delta Y = 750 - 500 = 250$. Substituting these values into Equation 8.15 yields

$$MRTS = -\frac{250}{-1} = 250$$

FIGURE   8.6

Production Isoquant Curve—Deep Creek Mining Company

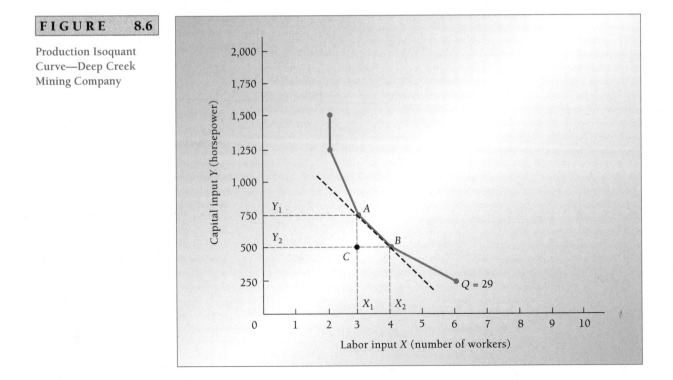

It can be shown that the *MRTS* is equal to the ratio of the marginal products of X and Y by using the definition of the marginal product (Equation 8.3). This definition yields $\Delta X = \Delta Q/MP_x$ and $\Delta Y = \Delta Q/MP_y$. Substituting these expressions into Equation 8.15 (and dropping the minus sign) yields

$$MRTS = \frac{\Delta Q/MP_y}{\Delta Q/MP_x}$$

$$MRTS = \frac{MP_x}{MP_y} \qquad [8.16]$$

For the Deep Creek Mining Company example, $MP_x = \Delta Q/\Delta X = (29 - 16)/(4 - 3)$ $= 13, MP_y = \Delta Q/\Delta Y = (29 - 16)/(750 - 500) = 13/250$. Substituting these values into Equation 8.16 yields

$$MRTS = \frac{13}{13/250} = 250$$

This is the same as the result obtained previously.

When the two inputs are continuous variables and the isoquants are continuous functions like $Q^{(2)}$ in Figure 8.7, the marginal rate of technical substitution (*MRTS*) at any point on the isoquant is equal to the negative of the slope of the isoquant at the point. For our general two-variable input production function (Equation 8.1)

$$Q = f(X, Y)$$

the slope of an isoquant at any point, such as point A in Figure 8.7, is equal to dY/dX, and therefore

$$MRTS = -\frac{dY}{dX} \qquad [8.17]$$

In a manner analogous to that described earlier for the case of discrete input variables (Equation 8.16), it can be shown that the marginal rate of technical substitution in the continuous input variables case is likewise equal to the ratio of the marginal products of the two inputs (and dropping the minus sign)

$$MRTS = \frac{MP_x}{MP_y} \qquad [8.18]$$

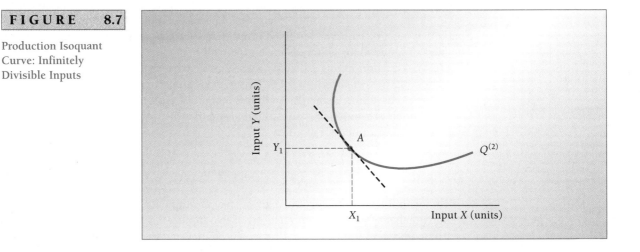

FIGURE   8.7

Production Isoquant
Curve: Infinitely
Divisible Inputs

Production Isoquants:
Perfect Substitute and
Complementary Inputs

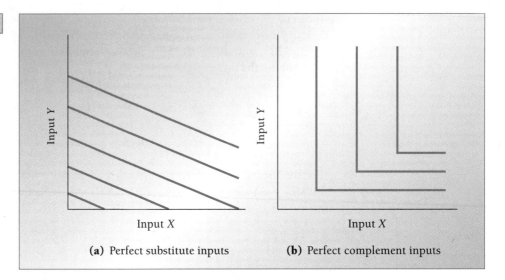

(a) Perfect substitute inputs   (b) Perfect complement inputs

where

$$MP_x = \frac{\partial Q}{\partial X} \text{ and } MP_y = \frac{\partial Q}{\partial Y}$$ [8.19]

As will be seen later in the chapter, the marginal rate of technical substitution is a very important concept in the derivation of the optimum combination of inputs to be used in producing a given quantity of output.

Perfect Substitute and Complementary Inputs

Production inputs vary in the degree to which they can be substituted for one another in a given process. The extreme cases are *perfect substitutes* and *perfect complements*. Isoquants for these two cases are shown in Figure 8.8. The isoquants for inputs that are *perfect substitutes* for one another consist of a series of parallel lines, as shown in Figure 8.8 (a). Examples of perfect substitutes are the use of alternative fuels (inputs) such as oil or coal in the production of electricity or the use of soybeans or oats in the production of nutrients in animal feeds. The isoquants for inputs that are *perfect complements* for one another consist of a series of right angles, as shown in Figure 8.8 (b). Such inputs are said to have zero substitutability. Examples of perfect complements include component parts that must be combined in fixed proportions, such as wheels and frames for automobiles or foundations and roofs for houses.

Most production inputs fall somewhere between the extreme cases of perfect complements and perfect substitutes. For most production functions, isoquants are convex to the origin as shown earlier in Figures 8.6 and 8.7. This shape implies that the production inputs are imperfectly substitutable and that the rate of substitution declines as one input is substituted for another.

www. . . . .
The following Internet site
applies the economic theory
of the optimal combination
of inputs to evaluate the
efficiency of Canadian milk
production:
http://www.afns.ualberta.
ca/wcdairy/wcd96/wcd96
333.htm

DETERMINING THE OPTIMAL COMBINATION OF INPUTS

As shown in the previous section, a given level of output can be produced using any of a large number of possible combinations of two inputs. Given that positive prices exist for these resources, differing total costs will be incurred in producing the desired output, depending on which combination of inputs is used. The firm is thus faced with determining the optimal combination of resources to employ in the production process.

Isocost Lines

The total cost of each possible input combination is a function of the market prices of these inputs. Assuming that the inputs are supplied in perfectly elastic input markets to the firm choosing its production input mix, the per unit price of each input will be constant, regardless of the amount of the input that is purchased. Letting C_x and C_y be the per unit prices of inputs X and Y, respectively, then the total cost (C) of any given input combination is

$$C = C_x X + C_y Y \qquad [8.20]$$

EXAMPLE

ISOCOST DETERMINATION: DEEP CREEK MINING COMPANY (CONTINUED)

In the Deep Creek Mining Company example discussed earlier, suppose that the price for workers is $50 per period ($C_x$) and that mining equipment can be leased at a price of $.20 per horsepower per period (C_y). The total cost per period of using X workers and equipment having Y horsepower to produce a given amount of output is

$$C = 50X + .20Y \qquad [8.21]$$

From this relationship, it can be seen that the mining of 55 tons of ore per period using 5 workers (X) and equipment having 750 horsepower (Y) would cost $50(5) + .20(750) = \$400$. However, this is not the only combination of workers and equipment costing $400. Any combination of inputs satisfying the equation

$$\$400 = 50X + .20Y$$

would cost $400. Solving this equation for Y yields

$$Y = \frac{\$400}{.20} - \frac{50}{.20}X$$

$$= \$2{,}000 - 250X$$

Thus the combinations $X = 1$ and $Y = 1{,}750$, $X = 2$ and $Y = 1{,}500$, $X = 3$ and $Y = 1{,}250$ (plus many other combinations) all cost $400.

The combinations of inputs costing $400 can be represented as the line in Figure 8.9 labeled "$C = \$400$." This line is called an *isocost* line, because it shows all the combinations of inputs having *equal* total costs. An isocost line exists for every possible total cost C. Solving Equation 8.21 for Y gives the equation of each isocost line

$$Y = \frac{C}{.20} - 250X \qquad [8.22]$$

A series of isocost lines is shown in Figure 8.9. Note that all the isocost lines are parallel, each one having a slope of -250. In general, the set of isocost lines consists of the set of equations given by the solution of Equation 8.20 for various values of C:

$$Y = \frac{C}{C_y} - \frac{C_x}{C_y}X \qquad [8.23]$$

FIGURE   8.9

Isocost Lines—Deep
Creek Mining Company

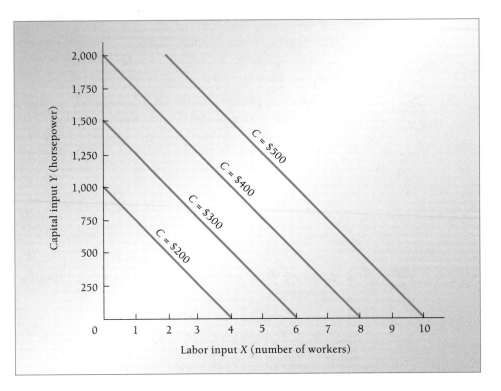

www

You can access a slide
show on the optimal
combination of inputs at the
following Internet site:
http://price.bus.okstate.
edu/archive/Econ3113
_963/Shows/Chapter7/
index.htm

Once the isoquants and isocosts are specified, it is possible to solve for the optimum combination of inputs. The production decision problem can be formulated in two different ways, depending on the manner in which the production objective or goal is stated. One can solve for the combination of inputs that either

1. minimizes total cost subject to a given constraint on output, or
2. maximizes output subject to a given total cost constraint.

Constrained cost minimization is the dual problem to the constrained output maximization problem.[8] To illustrate the general conditions for an optimum solution to each of these two types of production problems, one must assume, as was done earlier in this chapter, that the two inputs, X and Y, are infinitely divisible and can be represented as continuous variables. A graphic solution can be obtained by combining the isoquant and isocost curves on one set of axes. A set of isoquants for the general two-variable input production function and a set of isocosts are shown together in Figures 8.10 and 8.11.

Minimizing Cost Subject to an Output Constraint

Consider first the problem of minimizing the total cost of producing a given desired quantity of output. Suppose that the director of plant ops desires to release to production orders for at least $Q^{(2)}$ units of output. As shown in Figure 8.10, this constraint requires that the solution be in the feasible region containing the input combinations that lie either on the $Q^{(2)}$ isoquant or on isoquants that fall above and to the right having larger output values (the shaded area). The total cost of producing the required output

---

[8] The concept of the dual problem as it pertains to linear programming is discussed in Chapter 11.

Cost Minimization
Subject to an Output
Constraint

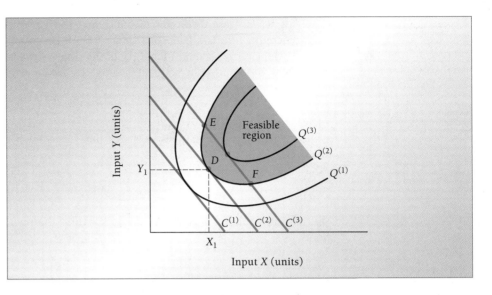

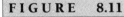

Output Maximization
Subject to a Cost
Constraint

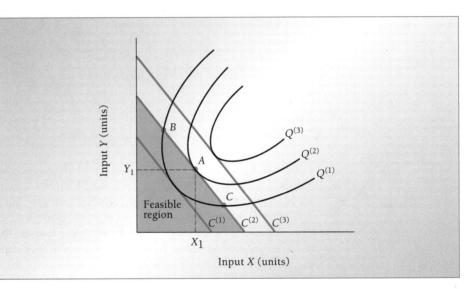

is minimized by finding the input combinations within this region that lie on the lowest cost isocost line. Combination D on the $C^{(2)}$ isocost line satisfies this condition. Combinations E and F, which also lie on the $Q^{(2)}$ isoquant, yield higher total costs, because they fall on the $C^{(3)}$ isocost line. No other point within the feasible region lies on an isocost line with a lower total cost than does point D. Thus, the use of X_1 units of input X and Y_1 units of input Y will yield a (constrained) minimum cost solution of $C^{(2)}$ dollars.

Two important characteristics of this solution permit us to state the necessary algebraic conditions needed to solve for the particular combination of inputs (X_1, Y_1).[9] First, note that the optimal solution occurs at the *boundary* of the feasible region of input combinations. Hence, one needs only to examine the $Q^{(2)}$ isoquant and the $C^{(2)}$ isocost line

---

[9] A set of *sufficient* conditions for an optimal solution must also include that the isoquants be convex to the origin.

in solving for an optimal solution. Second, note that the optimal solution occurs at the point where the isoquant is *tangent* to the isocost line. At the optimal input combination, the slope of the isoquant must equal the slope of the isocost line. As in the previous section, the slope of an isoquant is equal to dY/dX and

$$-\frac{dY}{dX} = MRTS = \frac{MP_x}{MP_y} \qquad [8.24]$$

Taking the derivative of the isocost equation (Equation 8.23), the slope of the isocost line is given by

$$\frac{dY}{dX} = -\frac{C_x}{C_y} \qquad [8.25]$$

Multiplying Equation 8.25 by (-1), and setting the result equal to Equation 8.24 yields

$$-\frac{dY}{dX} = -\left(-\frac{C_x}{C_y}\right)$$

$$= \frac{MP_x}{MP_y}$$

Thus the following condition, the "equimarginal criterion,"

$$\frac{MP_x}{MP_y} = \frac{C_x}{C_y}$$

or equivalently,

$$\frac{MP_x}{C_x} = \frac{MP_y}{C_y} \qquad [8.26]$$

must be satisfied in order that an input combination be an optimal solution to the problem of minimizing cost subject to an output constraint. Equation 8.26 indicates that the marginal product per dollar input cost of one factor must be equal to the marginal product per dollar input cost of the other factor. Note that the logic of this optimality condition is equivalent to that developed in Equation 4.1 for consumer demand choices that maximize utility subject to a household budget constraint. Further discussion of these optimization concepts is contained in Appendix 8A.

DETERMINING THE COST-MINIMIZING PRODUCTION PROCESS

The previous section analyzed the least-cost combination of divisible inputs in variable proportions production, where one input substituted continuously for another. However, Deep Creek Mining's production choices involve indivisible capital equipment, like a large mining drill that is controlled by a fixed number of workers. Similarly, an auto fender stamping machine in an assembly plant must be used in fixed proportion to a certain quantity of labor and sheet metal supplies. And 3 hours of setups, maintenance, and cleaning may be required to support a 5-hour printing press run. Three additional hours of work by a second shift of maintenance personnel would be required for a second press run, and a third shift of workers would be required for 24-hour printing operations. Although a higher output rate can be achieved by scaling up all the inputs, each of these production process is one of fixed not variable proportions.

Linear programming techniques are available to determine the least-cost process for fixed proportions production. The Deep Creek Mining Company example can be used to illustrate the graphic approach to finding such a solution.

COST MINIMIZATION: DEEP CREEK MINING COMPANY (CONTINUED)

Suppose one is interested in finding the combination of labor input (workers) and capital input (horsepower) that minimizes the cost of producing at least 29 tons of ore. Assume that the isocost lines are the ones defined by Equation 8.21 and graphed in Figure 8.9 earlier in this section. Figure 8.12 combines several isoquants and isocost lines for the ore-mining problem. The shaded area in the graph represents the set of feasible input combinations, that is, those labor and capital production processes that yield at least $Q = 29$ tons of output.

Production Processes and Process Rays

Production Process

A fixed proportions production relationship.

A **production process** can be defined as one in which the inputs are combined in fixed proportion to obtain the output. By this definition, a production process can be represented graphically as a ray through the origin having a slope equal to the ratio of the number of units of the respective resources required to produce one unit of output. Three production process rays for Deep Creek Mining are shown in Figure 8.12. Along process ray M_1, the inputs are combined in the ratio of two workers to a 1,250-horsepower (h.p.) drilling machine. Hence, ray M_1 has a slope of 625 h.p. per mine worker.

Operating multiple production processes like M_1, M_2, and M_3 can offer a firm flexibility in dealing with unusual orders, interruptions in the availability of resources, or

FIGURE   8.12

Isoquant Curves and Isocost Lines—Deep Creek Mining Company

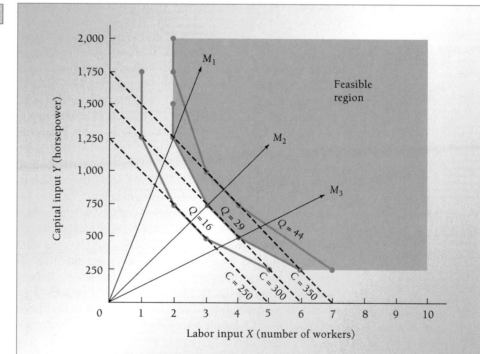

binding resource constraints. However, not all fixed proportions production processes are equally efficient. At times the firm will prefer to use one or two production processes exclusively if they offer the advantage of substantial cost savings. Mine 1 employs process M_1 to produce 29 tons with 2 workers and a 1,250-h.p. drilling machine at a total cost of 50 (2) + .20 (1250) = \$350 or \$350/29 = \$12.07 per ton. Mine 2 uses a more labor-intensive process (M_2) with 3 workers and a smaller 750-h.p. machine and incurs a lower total cost of \$300. Mine 2 is the benchmark operation for Deep Creek in that this M_2 process produces 29 tons at minimum cost—for example, \$300/29 = \$10.34 a ton.

Measuring the Efficiency of a Production Process

Allocative Efficiency
A measure of how closely production achieves the least-cost input mix or process, given the desired level of output.

Mine 1 with production process M_1 is said to be **allocatively inefficient** because it has chosen the wrong input mix; Mine 1 has allocated its input budget incorrectly. Its 1,250-h.p. machine is too large for the number of workers hired and the output desired. By producing 29 tons of output for \$350 relative to the lowest cost benchmark at \$300, process M_1 exhibits only \$300/\$350 = 85.7% allocative efficiency.

In addition to allocative inefficiency involving the incorrect input mix, a production operation can also exhibit technical inefficiency. For example, the industrial engineering indicated by the production isoquants in Figure 8.12 suggests that the process M_3 also should be capable of producing 29 tons. The "C = \$300" isocost line is tangent to the boundary of the feasible region (i.e., the "Q = 29" isoquant) at not only 3 workers and a 750-h.p. machine (M_2) but also at 4 workers and 500-h.p. machine (M_3). In principle, both production processes yield the desired 29 tons of ore at a minimum total cost of \$300 and will thereby satisfy the condition in Equation 8.26. But suppose Mine 3 has been unable to achieve more than 27 tons of output. Although it has adopted a least-cost process, Mine 3 would then be characterized as *technically inefficient*. In particular, Mine 3 exhibits only 27 tons/29 tons = 93 percent **technical efficiency** despite its least-cost process.

Technical Efficiency
A measure of how closely production achieves maximum potential output given the input mix or process.

However, 93 percent technical efficiency may be inadequate. Benchmark plants often do substantially better, with many processes meeting 98 percent and 99 percent of their production goals. In addition, as technically inefficient plants approach the current standard of excellence, continuous quality improvement initiatives may raise the standards. For example, just-in-time delivery systems have accentuated the need for very high reliability and technical efficiency to produce on time as promised with near zero defects. One A-frame supplier to General Motors assembly plants has reduced defective parts to five per million (i.e., 0.002 of 1 percent) and has agreed to pay a \$4,000 *per minute* "charge back" for any late deliveries resulting in assembly line delays. Such a company must constantly monitor and proactively solve production problems before they arise in order to ensure near 100% technical efficiency.

Overall Production Efficiency
A measure of technical and allocative efficiency.

Overall production efficiency is defined as the product of technical and allocative efficiency. If a plant has 93 percent technical efficiency and 85.7 percent allocative efficiency, then its overall production efficiency is 0.93 × 0.857 = 0.797, or 79.7 percent. Your job as an operations manager might be to decide which least-cost process Mine 1 in Figure 8.12 should now adopt. Because M_2 and M_3 are both allocatively efficient for 29 tons of output but process M_3 has experienced technical inefficiency problems resulting in an inability to realize its maximum potential output, process M_2 would be preferred.

TECHNICAL AND ALLOCATIVE EFFICIENCY IN COMMERCIAL BANKS[10]

Wave after wave of bank merger activity continues in almost every region of the United States. One reason is the potential for substantial improvements in operating efficiency. Combining loan officers, facilities, and deposits of various kinds, the representative commercial bank in the United States produces only 63 percent of the current-status loans (i.e., loans not in default) that benchmark banks produce. The problem (and opportunity for improvement) is twofold. First, some banks adopt inefficient processes which fail to allocate the appropriate proportion of scarce company resources to personnel, facilities, and to attracting deposits. Linear programming studies show that allocative efficiency in U.S. commercial banking averages only 81 percent; the least-cost process is 19 percent cheaper. In a service industry like banking, least-cost processes are the key to success, but one bank may not find another bank's deposit acquisition, borrower screening, or loan monitoring processes easy to imitate.

When several banks do manage to adopt identical least-cost processes, yet one produces more current-status loans than the others, the maximum feasible potential output in that type of institution can be identified. Technical efficiency then measures the observed bank output divided by the maximum potential output of benchmark banks with identical processes. The smaller a bank's comparative output, the lower the technical efficiency. The representative commercial bank in the United States is only 78 percent technically efficient. Bank takeovers, buyouts, and mergers often result in changes in the personnel, facilities, and processes of the acquired institution in a concerted effort to improve allocative and technical efficiency. After these restructurings, the ratio of noninterest operating expenses to total bank income often declines enough and capitalized value rises enough to allow recovery of a 20–30 percent merger premium paid by the new owners in excess of the bank's premerger value.

Maximizing Output Subject to a Cost Constraint

Consider next the problem of maximizing output subject to an upper limit or constraint on the total cost to be incurred in producing the output. Suppose that a total cost constraint of $C^{(2)}$ dollars is imposed on the production process. As shown in Figure 8.11, this constraint requires that the solution fall in the feasible region consisting of the input combinations that lie on or below the $C^{(2)}$ isocost line (the shaded area). Output is maximized by finding the input combinations within the feasible region that lie on the isoquant with the largest output value. Combination A on the $Q^{(2)}$ isoquant satisfies this condition. Combinations B and C, which also lie on the $C^{(2)}$ isocost line, yield lower outputs, because they fall on the $Q^{(1)}$ isoquant. No other point within the feasible region lies on an isoquant with a larger output value than does point A. Thus the use of X_1 units of input X and Y_1 units of input Y will yield a (constrained) maximum output of $Q^{(2)}$ units.

As in the previously discussed cost-minimization problem, the optimal input combination or optimal production process occurs at the boundary of the feasible region of input combinations and at a point of tangency between the isocost and isoquant curves. As before, the slope of the isocost line is equal to the slope of the isoquant at the optimal in-

[10] Based on D. Wheelock and P. Wilson, "Evaluating the Efficiency of Commercial Banks," *St. Louis Federal Reserve Review*, July/August 1995, pp. 39–52.

put combination point. From this characteristic of the solution, and using similar reasoning, it can be shown that the same condition

$$\frac{MP_x}{C_x} = \frac{MP_y}{C_y} \qquad [8.27]$$

that had to be satisfied in the cost-minimization problem must also hold true for an input combination to be an optimal solution to the problem of output maximization subject to a cost constraint. A linear programming explanation of the duality between cost minimization and output maximization subject to appropriate constraints is presented in Appendix 8B.

Effect of a Change in Input Prices

As shown above, the optimal combination of inputs in both the cost-minimization and output-maximization problems is a function of the relative prices of the inputs, that is, C_x and C_y. As the price of input X rises, one would expect the firm to use less of this input and more of the other input Y in the production process, all other things being equal. This shift is demonstrated in Figure 8.13. The firm is interested in minimizing the cost of producing a given quantity of output $Q^{(0)}$. Initially, the prices of inputs X and Y are C_x and C_y, respectively, resulting in the isocost line $C = C_x X + C_y Y$. Given these conditions, the firm would operate at tangency point A—using X_1 units of input X and Y_1 units of input Y. Now suppose that the price of input X is increased to C'_x. This has the effect of increasing the slope of the isocost lines, such as isocost line $C' = C'_x X + C_y Y$ shown in the graph. To produce the same $Q^{(0)}$ units of output at minimum cost, the firm would operate at tangency point B—using X_2 units of input X and Y_2 units of input Y. Oftentimes, these *input substitution effects* are reinforced by a negative *output effect*—that is, higher input costs are passed through to consumers who respond by cutting back their consumption. As less output than $Q^{(0)}$ is ordered, X falls below X_2.

From this analysis one can see that as the price of one input increases, the firm will substitute away from this input and use more of the relatively less expensive input. Since the Industrial Revolution, this phenomenon has been observed in the shift toward more capital-intensive production processes (that is, greater use of labor-saving equipment) because the price of labor has increased relative to the price of capital. Recently, Chrysler

FIGURE   8.13

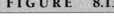

Effect of a Change in Input Prices

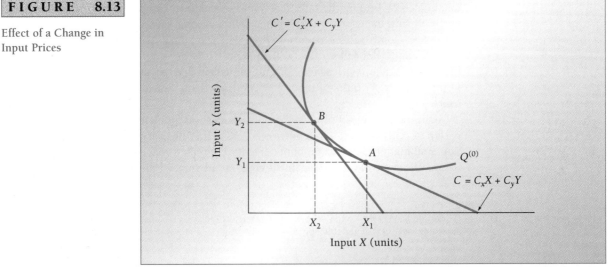

Corporation decided to assemble their most successful product line, the minivan, in an automated Canadian factory, in part because of rising union wages and restrictive workplace rules in their Detroit assembly plants.

This and the previous sections have been concerned with the effect on production output of arbitrary changes in either or both of the two inputs and in finding the optimal combination of inputs. The following section examines the effects on output of proportional changes in both inputs simultaneously, in other words, an investigation of the effects of a change in the overall scale of production.

RETURNS TO SCALE

This section begins with a definition of returns to scale, followed by discussions of measurement of returns to scale, homogeneous production functions and returns to scale, and the economic rationale for increasing and decreasing returns to scale.

Definition of Returns to Scale

Returns to Scale
The proportionate increase in output that results from a given proportionate increase in *all* the inputs employed in the production process.

In addition to providing a framework for determining the optimal combination of inputs to use in producing a desired level of output, production theory also offers a means for analysis of the effects on output of changes in the *scale* of production. An increase in the scale of production consists of a simultaneous proportionate increase in *all* the inputs used in the production process. The proportionate increase in output that results from the given proportionate increase in all the inputs is defined as the physical **returns to scale.** Suppose, in the Deep Creek Mining Company example introduced earlier, one is interested in determining the effect on the number of tons of ore produced (output) of a 1.50 factor increase in the scale of production from a given labor-capital combination of 4 workers and equipment having 500 horsepower. A 1.50 factor increase in the scale of production would constitute a labor-capital combination of $4 \times 1.5 = 6$ workers and equipment having $500 \times 1.5 = 750$ horsepower. From Table 8.1 note that the labor-capital combination of 4 workers and 500 horsepower yields 29 tons of output, whereas the combination of 6 workers and 750 horsepower yields 60 tons of output. Output has increased by the ratio of $60/29 = 2.07$. Thus, a 1.50 factor increase in input use has resulted in more than a 1.50 factor increase (that is, 2.07) in the quantity of output produced. Clearly, this relationship between the proportionate increases in inputs and outputs is not required to be the same for all increases in the scale of production. A 1.50 factor increase in the scale of production from 6 workers and 500 horsepower to 9 workers and 750 horsepower results in an increase in output from 55 to 61 tons—an increase by a factor of only 1.10.

Measurement of Returns to Scale

To present a general framework for analyzing physical returns to scale, assume, as in previous sections, that the two inputs of the production function can be represented as continuous variables. An increase in the scale of production can be represented graphically in a two-dimensional isoquant map, as is shown in Figure 8.14. Increasing the scale of production by a factor of λ from the combination of X_1 units of input X and Y_1 units of input Y (point A on the graph) constitutes a shift to the combination consisting of $X_2 = \lambda X_1$ units of input X and $Y_2 = \lambda Y_1$ units of input Y (point B on the graph). Any increase (or decrease) in the scale of production from a given point must lie along a line from the origin through the given point on the isoquant map. This follows because an increase in the scale of production requires that the inputs in the production process continue to be

FIGURE   8.14

Returns to Scale

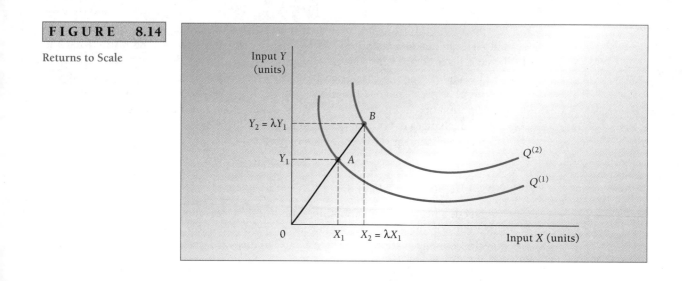

combined in the same proportion as that at the given point. At point A in the graph, the inputs are being combined in the proportion X_1/Y_1. At point B, the inputs are being combined in the same proportion because

$$\frac{X_2}{Y_2} = \frac{\lambda X_1}{\lambda Y_1} = \frac{X_1}{Y_1}$$

The increase in the quantity of output from $Q^{(1)}$ to $Q^{(2)}$ represents the returns to scale of an increase in the amounts of both inputs employed in the production process by a factor of λ. Three possible relationships exist between the increase in inputs and the increase in outputs. For an increase in all inputs by a factor of λ:

1. *Increasing* returns to scale case: Output increases by *more than* λ; that is, $Q^{(2)} > \lambda Q^{(1)}$.

2. *Decreasing* returns to scale case: Output increases by *less than* λ; that is, $Q^{(2)} < \lambda Q^{(1)}$.

3. *Constant* returns to scale case: Output increases by *exactly* λ; that is, $Q^{(2)} = \lambda Q^{(1)}$.

Depending on whether $Q^{(2)}$ is more than, less than, or equal to $\lambda Q^{(1)}$, the production function is said to exhibit increasing, decreasing, or constant physical returns to scale over the range of input combinations from A to B in Figure 8.14.

Figure 8.15 illustrates three different production functions that exhibit these types of returns to scale. In Panel (a), showing increasing returns to scale, doubling input X from 10 to 20 units and input Y from 100 to 200 units yields more than double the amount of output—an increase from 1,000 to 2,500 units. In Panel (b), showing decreasing returns to scale, a similar doubling of two inputs, X and Y, yields less than double the amount of output—an increase from 10,000 to 15,000 units. Finally in Panel (c), showing constant returns to scale, a similar doubling of inputs X and Y yields exactly double the amount of output—an increase from 100 to 200 units.

As one makes successive increases in the scale of production, the production function does not need to exhibit the same type (increasing, decreasing, or constant) of scale relationship. Suppose that starting from the labor-capital combination of 2 workers and 500 horsepower in the Deep Creek Mining Company example discussed earlier, we successively double ($\lambda = 2.0$) the scale of production. From Table 8.1 note that output first

FIGURE   8.15   Production Isoquants Exhibiting Increasing, Decreasing, and Constant Returns to Scale

increases from 6 tons to 55 tons, a 9.17 factor increase, and then increases from 55 tons to 65 tons, which is only a 1.18 factor increase. Over the given change in the scale of production, this production function first exhibits increasing and then decreasing returns to scale.

If the production function is given in algebraic form, returns to scale can be measured by increasing each of the inputs by a factor of λ and determining the effect on output.

For example, suppose one is interested in determining the returns to scale for the following production function of the Wellington Company:

$$Q = 10XY - 2X^2 - Y^2 \qquad [8.28]$$

First, increase each of the inputs by a factor of λ; that is $X' = \lambda X$ and $Y' = \lambda Y$. Next, substitute these values into the production function as follows:

$$Q' = 10(\lambda X)(\lambda Y) - 2(\lambda X)^2 - (\lambda Y)^2$$
$$= 10\lambda^2 XY - 2\lambda^2 X^2 - \lambda^2 Y^2$$
$$= \lambda^2(10XY - 2X^2 - Y^2)$$
$$= \lambda^2 Q$$

Because output increases by *more than* λ—by a factor of λ^2—Wellington's production function exhibits *increasing* returns to scale.

Homogeneous Production Functions and Returns to Scale

Many of the algebraic production functions used in analyzing production processes, such as the Cobb-Douglas power function (Equation 8.2), are said to be homogeneous. Homogeneous functions have certain mathematical properties that make them desirable in modeling production processes. If each input in the production function is multiplied by an arbitrary constant λ and if this constant can be factored out of the function, then the production function is defined as *homogeneous*.

One can also measure the degree of homogeneity of a production function. A production function $Q = f(X,Y)$ is said to be *homogeneous of degree n* if

$$f(\lambda X, \lambda Y) = \lambda^n f(X,Y) \text{ for } \lambda \neq 0 \qquad [8.29]$$

where λ is some constant. The following production function of the Fletcher Company

$$f(X,Y) = .6X + .2Y \qquad\qquad [8.30]$$

is homogeneous of degree 1.0 because

$$f(\lambda X, \lambda Y) = .6(\lambda X) + .2(\lambda Y)$$
$$= \lambda^1(.6X + .2Y)$$
$$= \lambda^1 f(X,Y)$$

If the degree of homogeneity (n) is equal to 1.0, then the production function is said to be *linearly homogeneous*.

The degree of homogeneity (n) indicates the type of returns to scale (i.e., increasing, decreasing, or constant) that characterize a production function. If $n = 1$, the production function exhibits constant returns to scale; if $n > 1$ the production function exhibits increasing returns to scale; and if $n < 1$ the production function exhibits decreasing returns to scale. Thus, Fletcher Company's linear production function given by Equation 8.30, with a degree of homogeneity (n) equal to 1.0, exhibits constant returns to scale. The nonlinear production function of the Wellington Company represented by Equation 8.28, which has a degree of homogeneity (n) equal to 2.0, exhibits increasing returns to scale.

Increasing and Decreasing Returns to Scale

In addition to satisfying the law of diminishing marginal returns discussed earlier, a firm's production function is often characterized by first increasing and then decreasing physical returns to scale. A number of industrial engineering arguments have been presented to justify this characteristic of the production function. The major argument given for initial increasing returns, as the scale of production is first increased, is the opportunity for *specialization in the use of capital and labor.* As the scale of production is increased, equipment that is more efficient in performing a limited set of tasks can be substituted for less efficient all-purpose equipment. Similarly, the efficiency of workers in performing a small number of related tasks is greater than that of less highly skilled but more versatile workers. Practical limits on the degree of specialization, however, may prevent increasing returns from being realized in producing ever-larger quantities of output.

A principal argument given for the existence of decreasing returns to scale is the increasingly complex *problems of coordination and control* faced by management as the scale of production is increased. Limitations on the ability of management to transmit and receive information (such as decisions and reports on performance) may diminish the effectiveness of management in exercising control and coordination of increasingly larger scales of production. As a result, proportionate increases in all of the inputs of the production process, including the input labeled "management," may eventually yield less than proportionate increases in total output.

Whether a production function for a particular production process exhibits any one or a combination of increasing, decreasing, and constant returns to scale is a question that usually can be answered best by statistical methods.

STATISTICAL ESTIMATION OF PRODUCTION FUNCTIONS

For most production processes, extensive data such as that contained in Table 8.1 for the Deep Creek Mining Company is seldom available for analysis. Instead, one must attempt to measure the relationships between inputs and outputs using data gathered from the day-to-day operations of the production process. Econometric techniques, which were developed earlier in the statistical estimation of demand functions (Chapter 5), are used in measuring production functions. The methodology consists of developing a mathematical model of the production process, collecting data on the production process, and then using regression analysis (or a related technique) to estimate the parameters of the model.

Production functions can be estimated for *individual* economic units—such as a plant or firm—or an *aggregation* of economic units—such as an industry, geographical region, sector of the economy, or entire economy.

Although the functional form and procedures for estimating the parameters of an aggregate production relationship generally are similar to those used in estimating the corresponding relationships for individual firms, it is more difficult to give a meaningful physical interpretation to the aggregate relationship. For the individual firm, the production function is an expression of the industrial engineering of the specific technological process employed in transforming inputs into outputs. In contrast, a production function for the entire economy (or major sector of it), in which aggregate variables are used to represent the thousands of different inputs and outputs, constitutes a descriptive model of the many different technological processes employed by all the productive entities within the economy. Because of the aggregative nature of the variables, the resulting model is not representative of the production process of either an "average" firm or any specific individual firm.[11]

An aggregate relationship that comes closer to representing the production process of an individual firm would be the industry production function. Within a given industry (for example, steel, aluminum, and shipbuilding) the production processes of most firms are somewhat similar. Also, the input and output variables in an industry production function, whether measured from cross-sectional or time-series data, would be relatively homogeneous; that is, the types and mix of products, labor skills, capital equipment, and raw materials would be similar among the firms in the industry.

Despite the similarities, one must exercise care in making inferences about the production function of an individual firm within the industry based on the aggregate production function for the entire industry. For example, some inputs, such as specialized labor skills, may constitute a *fixed* factor (input) of production from the standpoint of the industry and yet be a *variable* factor from the standpoint of the individual firm.[12] Also, even if all the firms in the industry are faced with increasing returns to scale, it does not necessarily follow that the industry as a whole will encounter similar returns to scale. Returns to scale for the industry may be limited by such factors as a lack of suitable production or marketing sites and limited supplies of raw materials.

The remainder of this section examines the Cobb-Douglas production function—one of the most commonly used models in empirical production studies—along with a couple of examples of statistically estimated production functions.

Cobb-Douglas Production Functions

www . . . .
You can work with interactive, animated Cobb-Douglas production functions at the following Internet site:
http://medusa.be.udel.edu/WWW_Sites/oo_Micro%20Models!/Index.html

In their first studies of production functions, Cobb and Douglas used a power function of the form

$$Q = \alpha L^{\beta} K^{1-\beta} \qquad [8.31]$$

---

[11] Although the aggregate production function may not be representative of any specific firm, it still can be useful as a descriptive or predictive *macroeconomic* model of the economy. The emphasis of the discussion (and the book), however, is on the usefulness of such models as *microeconomic* decision-making tools.

[12] The individual firm can increase the use of the given factor (for example, labor) by paying more than the going market rate for the factor. This will cause a shift in some of this factor to the firm and away from other firms.

where α and β are the parameters to be estimated and Q, L, and K are indices of output, labor input, and capital input, respectively. Because the exponents of the labor and capital variables sum to 1, such a model *assumes* there are no increasing or decreasing returns to scale.[13] In other words, if the quantities of both labor and capital inputs are increased by a factor of λ, then output will also increase exactly by a factor of λ. This can be shown as follows:

$$Q' = \alpha[\lambda L]^{\beta}[\lambda K]^{1-\beta}$$
$$= \alpha[\lambda^{\beta}L^{\beta}][\lambda^{1-\beta}K^{1-\beta}]$$
$$= (\lambda)^{\beta+(1-\beta)}(\alpha L^{\beta}K^{1-\beta})$$
$$= (\lambda)^{1}Q$$

In later studies by Cobb and Douglas and others, the assumption of constant returns to scale was relaxed by employing a function of the form

$$Q = \alpha L^{\beta_1}K^{\beta_2} \qquad [8.32]$$

where β_1 and β_2 are completely independent parameters that do *not* necessarily sum to 1.

The Cobb-Douglas power function has several important mathematical and economic properties that make the function an appealing one for representing the input-output production relationship.

Nonlinear Relationship   In the Cobb-Douglas power function, output is a (nonlinear) monotonically increasing function of each of the inputs.[14] As can be seen in Figure 8.16, with capital input held constant, output increases at a decreasing rate (marginal product falls) as labor input is increased. In other words, for any given amount of capital input (for instance, $K^{(0)}$, $K^{(1)}$, $K^{(2)}$), the slope of the output-labor input curve decreases as labor is added. A similar relationship exists between output and capital input if labor input is held constant. Also, the Cobb-Douglas production function can provide a good fit to the traditional S-shaped production function of economic theory over a wide range of values for the input variables (see Figure 8.17).

Linear Logarithmic Relationship   The nonlinear Cobb-Douglas production function (Equation 8.32) can be transformed into a linear relationship by taking logarithms of all the variables:

$$\log Q = \log \alpha + \beta_1 \log L + \beta_2 \log K \qquad [8.33]$$

or

$$Q' = \alpha' + \beta_1 L' + \beta_2 K'$$

where $Q' = \log Q$, $\alpha' = \log \alpha$, $L' = \log L$, and $K' = \log K$. With this transformation, the parameters of the model (α, β_1, β_2) can be estimated for input-output data using the standard least-squares regression techniques that were discussed in Chapter 5.

---

[13]In Equation 8.31 the sum of the exponents of the L and K variables is $\beta + (1 - \beta) = 1$.

[14]A "monotonically increasing function," $Y = f(X)$, means that Y *never decreases* (either increases or remains constant) as X increases.

FIGURE   8.16

Output as a Function of
Labor Input

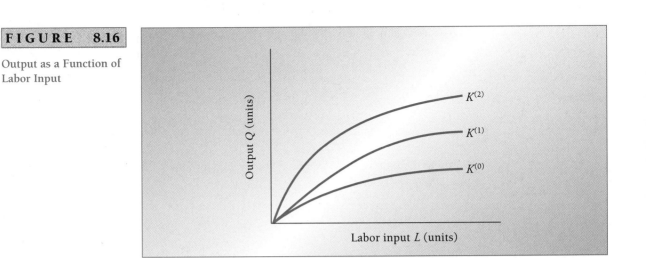

FIGURE   8.17

Cobb-Douglas
Production Function and
the Traditional S-shaped
Production Function

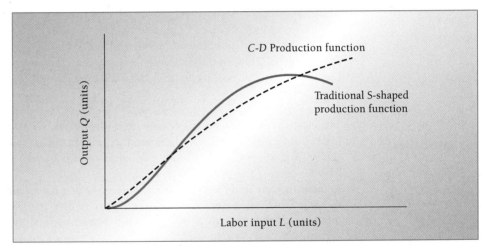

Constant Production Elasticities   The elasticity of production was defined earlier as the percentage change in output that occurs as the result of a given percentage change in one input with all other inputs held constant. The elasticity of production was shown to be equal to the ratio of the marginal product to the average product of the given input. Consider first the labor input.[15] The marginal productivity of labor is equal to[16]

$$MP_L = \frac{\partial Q}{\partial L}$$

$$= \alpha \beta_1 L^{\beta_1 - 1} K^{\beta_2}$$

Note that the marginal product of labor and capital can never be negative, indicating that a Cobb-Douglas function is always in Stage II.

---

[15] The reader who is unfamiliar with differential calculus can go directly to the final result in Equation 8.34.

[16] The concept of partial differentiation is discussed in Chapter 3.

The average productivity of labor is equal to

$$AP_L = \frac{Q}{L}$$

$$= \frac{\alpha L^{\beta_1} K^{\beta_2}}{L}$$

$$= \alpha L^{\beta_1 - 1} K^{\beta_2}$$

Forming the ratio of these marginal and average products, one obtains the elasticity of production for labor input:

$$E_L = \frac{MP_L}{AP_L}$$

$$= \frac{\alpha \beta_1 L^{\beta_1 - 1} K^{\beta_2}}{\alpha L^{\beta_1 - 1} K^{\beta_2}}$$

$$E_L = \beta_1 \qquad\qquad [8.34]$$

This result indicates that the elasticity of production for labor input is *constant* and is equal to the exponent of the labor variable in the production function. It shows that if the amount of labor input is increased by 1 percent, then output will increase by β_1 percent. A similar expression can be derived for capital input:[17]

$$E_K = \beta_2 \qquad\qquad [8.35]$$

The elasticity of production for capital input is likewise *constant* and is equal to the exponent of the capital variable in the production function. It indicates that output will increase by β_2 percent if the amount of capital input is increased by 1 percent.

Returns to Scale and Degree of Homogeneity   For a *homogeneous* production function, the degree of homogeneity indicates the type of returns to scale. The Cobb-Douglas production function (Equation 8.32) is a homogeneous function with a degree of homogeneity (n) equal to ($\beta_1 + \beta_2$). This can be shown as follows. Define $Q = f(L, K) = \alpha L^{\beta_1} K^{\beta_2}$. Multiplying L and K by a constant λ yields

$$f(\lambda L, \lambda K) = \alpha(\lambda L)^{\beta_1}(\lambda K)^{\beta_2}$$

$$= \alpha(\lambda^{\beta_1} L^{\beta_1})(\lambda^{\beta_2} K^{\beta_2})$$

$$= \lambda^{\beta_1 + \beta_2}(\alpha L^{\beta_1} K^{\beta_2})$$

$$= \lambda^{\beta_1 + \beta_2} f(L, K)$$

Because the exponent of λ is equal to ($\beta_1 + \beta_2$), the degree of homogeneity is equal to ($\beta_1 + \beta_2$). Depending on whether $n = \beta_1 + \beta_2$ is less than, equal to, or greater than 1, the Cobb-Douglas production function will exhibit decreasing, constant, or increasing returns, respectively. Thus once the parameters of the Cobb-Douglas model are estimated, the sum of the exponents of the labor (β_1) and capital (β_2) variables can be used to test for the presence of increasing, constant, or decreasing returns to scale.

---

[17]The reader is asked to demonstrate this relationship as one of the problems at the end of the chapter.

EXAMPLE

EMPIRICAL STUDIES OF THE COBB-DOUGLAS PRODUCTION FUNCTION

Since the original production function studies of Cobb and Douglas in the late 1920s,[18] literally dozens of similar studies have been undertaken.[19] Using time-series data, production functions have been developed for entire economies (for example, the United States, Norway, Finland, New Zealand), geographical regions (Massachusetts, and Victoria and New South Wales in Australia), and major sectors of the economy (manufacturing, mining, agriculture). Also, Cobb-Douglas functions have been estimated for various sectors of an economy using cross-sectional industry data (the United States, Australia, Canada) and for various industries using cross-sectional data on firms within an industry (railroads, coal, clothing, chemicals, electricity, milk, and rice).

This section examines three production function studies that illustrate the basic methodology used and the type of results obtained: first, a study employing aggregate time-series data on the economy; second, a study using cross-sectional data on individual industries; and third, a study that develops a production function for major league baseball.

Time-Series Analysis: U.S. Manufacturing Sector Example

In their original study Cobb and Douglas fitted a production function of the form in Equation 8.31 to indices of production Q, labor L, and capital K in the U.S. manufacturing sector for the period from 1899 to 1922. Q was an index of physical volume of manufacturing; L was an index of the average number of employed wage earners only (that is, salaried employees, officials, and working proprietors were excluded); and K was an index of the value of plants, buildings, tools, and machinery reduced to dollars of constant purchasing power. With the sum of the exponents restricted to one (constant returns to scale), the following function was obtained:

$$Q = 1.01 \, L^{.75} K^{.25} \qquad [8.36]$$

In later studies Cobb and Douglas made several modifications that altered their results somewhat. These modifications included revisions in the output and labor indices, removing the secular trend from each index by expressing each yearly index value as a percentage of its overall trend value, and dropping the assumption of constant returns to scale. With these modifications the estimated production function for the manufacturing sector was

$$Q = .84 \, L^{.63} K^{.30} \qquad [8.37]$$

These results are fairly typical of other time-series and cross-sectional production functions developed from data collected on the U.S. manufacturing sector in the early twentieth century. A 1 percent increase in labor input results in about a $\frac{2}{3}$-percent increase in output, and a 1 percent increase in capital input results in approximately a $\frac{1}{3}$-percent increase in output. Also, as in this function, the sum of the exponents (that is, elasticities) of the labor and capital variables is typically slightly less than 1. Although this would seem to indicate the presence of decreasing returns to scale in the broadly defined manufacturing sector, statistically speaking the sum of the exponents was not significantly different from 1.0.

---

[18] P.H. Douglas, "Are There Laws of Production?" *American Economic Review* 38, no. 1 (March 1948), pp. 1–41.

[19] See R.G. Chambers, *Applied Production Analysis* (New York: Cambridge University Press, 1988).

Cross-Sectional Analysis: U.S. Manufacturing Industries Example

In a study of more recent vintage, Moroney used cross-sectional data to estimate Cobb-Douglas production functions for 18 U.S. manufacturing industries.[20] Using aggregate data on plants located within each state, the following three-variable model was fitted:

$$Q = \alpha L_p^{\beta_1} L_n^{\beta_2} K^{\beta_3} \qquad\qquad [8.38]$$

where Q is the value added by the production plants, L_p is production worker work-hours, L_n is nonproduction work-years, and K is gross book values of depreciable and depletable assets.[21] The results for several of the industries are shown in Table 8.5. The sum of the exponents ($\beta_1 + \beta_2 + \beta_3$), that is, elasticities, ranged from a low of .947 for petroleum to a high of 1.109 for furniture. In 13 of the 18 industries studied, the statistical tests showed that the sum of the exponents was not significantly different from 1.0. This evidence supports the hypothesis that most manufacturing industries exhibit constant returns to scale.

---

[20] John R. Moroney, "Cobb-Douglas Production Functions and Returns to Scale in U.S. Manufacturing Industry," *Western Economic Journal* 6, no. 1 (December 1967), pp. 34–51.

[21] "Book values" of assets are the *historic* values of these assets as they appear on the balance sheet of the firm. Book values may differ significantly from current replacement values and hence may overstate or understate the actual amount of capital employed in the firm. Nonproduction workers are management and other staff personnel.

| TABLE 8.5 | Production Elasticities for Several Industries |

Industry	Capital Elasticity* β_1	Production Worker Elasticity β_2	Non-Production Worker Elasticity β_3	Sum of Elasticities $\beta_1 + \beta_2 + \beta_3$
Food and beverages	.555 (.121)	.439 (.128)	.076 (.037)	1.070* (.021)
Textiles	.121 (.173)	.549 (.216)	.335 (.086)	1.004 (.024)
Furniture	.205 (.153)	.802 (.186)	.103 (.079)	1.109* (.051)
Petroleum	.308 (.112)	.546 (.222)	.093 (.168)	.947 (.045)
Stone, clay, etc.	.632 (.105)	.032 (.224)	.366 (.201)	1.029 (.045)
Primary metals	.371 (.103)	.077 (.188)	.509 (.164)	.958 (.035)

*Numbers in parentheses below each elasticity coefficient is the standard error.
**Significantly greater than 1.0 at the .05 level (one-tail).

Source: John R. Moroney, "Cobb-Douglas Production Functions and Returns to Scale in U.S. Manufacturing Industry," *Western Economic Journal* 6, no. 1 (December 1967), Table 1, p. 46.

Empirical Estimation of a Production Function for Major League Baseball[22]

Team sports such as major league baseball are similar to other enterprises in that they attempt to provide a product (team victories) by employing various inputs (skills of team members). In acquiring team members through trades, the free agent market, and minor leagues/colleges, the owner is faced with various input trade-offs. For example, a baseball team owner may have to decide whether to trade a starting pitcher to obtain a power hitter or whether to sign a free agent relief pitcher (and release another player from the roster). These decisions are all made in the context of an intuitive baseball production function, possibly subject to various constraints (e.g., budgetary limits, league rules).

In an attempt to quantify the factors that contribute to the team's success, a Cobb-Douglas production function was developed using data from the 26 major league baseball teams in 1977. Output (Q) was measured by team victories. Inputs (X_1, X_2, X_3, etc.) from five different categories were included in the model:

▣ *Hitting.* This factor involves two different subskills—hitting frequency, as measured by the team *batting average,* and hitting with power, as measured by the team's *home runs.*

▣ *Running.* One measure of speed is a team's *stolen base total.*

▣ *Defense.* This factor also involves two subskills—catching those chances that the player is able to reach, as measured by *fielding percentage,* and catching difficult chances that many players would not be able to reach, as measured by *total chances accepted.* Because these two variables are correlated with one another (i.e., multicollinearity), separate regressions must be run with each variable.

▣ *Pitching.* The most obvious measure of the pitching factor is the team's earned run average (ERA). However, ERA depends not only on pitching skill, but also on the team's defensive skills. A better measure of pure pitching skills is the *strikeouts-to-walks* ratio for the pitching staff.

▣ *Coaching.* Teams often change managers when they are performing unsatisfactorily, so this is thought to be an important factor. However, the ability of a manager (coach) is difficult to measure. Two different measures are used in this study—the manager's *lifetime won-lost percentage* and *number of years spent managing in the major leagues.* Separate regressions are run with each variable.

Finally, a dummy variable ($NL = 0$, $AL = 1$) was used to control for any differences between leagues, such as the designated hitter rule.

The results of four regressions are shown in Table 8.6. Several conclusions can be drawn from these results:

1. Hitting average contributes almost six times as much as pitching to a team's success. This tends to contradict conventional wisdom, which says that pitching is the most important part of the game.

2. Home runs contribute about twice as much as stolen bases to a team's success.

3. Coaching skills are not significant in any of the regression equations.

---

[22] Charles E. Zech, "An Empirical Estimation of a Production Function: The Case of Major League Baseball," *The American Economist,* vol. XXV, no. 2 (Fall 1981), pp. 19–23.

TABLE   8.6

Empirical Estimates of
Baseball Production
Functions

Variable	Equation 1	Equation 2	Equation 3	Equation 4
Constant	.017	.018	.010	.008
League dummy	−.002	−.003	.004	.003
Batting average	2.017*	1.986*	1.969*	1.927*
Home runs	.229*	.299*	.208*	.215*
Stolen bases	.119*	.120*	.110*	.112*
Strikeouts/walks	.343*	.355*	.324*	.334*
Total fielding chances	1.235	1.200		
Fielding percentage			5.62	5.96
Manager W/L percentage		−.003		−.004
Manager years	−.004		−.002	
$\bar{R}^2$ (coef. of determination)	.789	.790	.773	.774

*Statistically significant at the .05 level.

4. Defensive skills are not significant in any of the regression equations.
5. Finally, the sums of the statistically significant variables in each of the four equations range from 2.588 to 2.709. Because these are all much greater than 1.0, the baseball production functions examined all exhibit *increasing returns to scale*.

SUMMARY

▢ A *production function* is a schedule, graph, or mathematical model relating the maximum quantity of output that can be produced from various quantities of inputs.

▢ For a production function with one variable input, the *marginal product* is defined as the incremental change in total output that can be produced by the use of one more unit of the variable input in the production process.

▢ For a production function with one variable input, the *average product* is defined as the ratio of total output to the amount of the variable input used in producing the output.

▢ The *law of diminishing marginal returns* states that, with all other productive factors held constant, the use of increasing amounts of the variable factor in the production process beyond some point will result in diminishing marginal increases in total output.

▢ In the short run, with one of the productive factors fixed, the optimal output level (and optimal level of the variable input) occurs where marginal revenue product equals marginal factor cost. *Marginal revenue product* is defined as the amount that an additional unit of the variable input adds to total revenue. *Marginal factor cost* is defined as the amount that an additional unit of the variable input adds to total cost.

▢ A *production isoquant* is either a geometric curve or algebraic function representing all the various combinations of inputs that can be used in producing a given level of output.

▢ The *marginal rate of technical substitution* is the rate at which one input may be substituted for another input in the production process, while total output remains constant. It is equal to the ratio of the marginal products of the two inputs.

■ In the long run, with both inputs being variable, minimizing cost subject to an output constraint (or maximizing output subject to a cost constraint) requires that the production process be operated at the point where the marginal product per dollar input cost of each factor is equal.

■ The degree of *technical efficiency* of a production process is the ratio of observed output to the maximum potentially feasible output for that process, given the same inputs.

■ The degree of *allocative efficiency* of a production process is the ratio of total cost for producing a given output level with the least cost process to the observed total cost of producing that output.

■ Physical *returns to scale* is defined as the proportionate increase in the output of a production process that results from a given proportionate increase in all the inputs.

■ The production function of economic theory, in addition to satisfying the law of diminishing marginal returns, is hypothesized to have a shape characterized by first increasing and then decreasing physical returns to scale.

■ The Cobb-Douglas production function, which is used extensively in empirical studies, is a power (multiplicative) function in which output is a (nonlinear) monotonically increasing function of each of the inputs.

■ The Cobb-Douglas production function has various properties that allow one to draw conclusions, based on parameter estimates, about economies of scale and the increase in output that will result from a given increase in any one (or more) of the inputs to the production process.

EXERCISES

1. In the Deep Creek Mining Company example described in the chapter (Table 8.1), suppose again that labor is the variable input and capital is the fixed input. Specifically, assume that the firm owns a piece of equipment having a 500-horsepower rating.

    a. Complete the following table:

Labor Input X (No. of Workers)	Total Product $TP_x\ (= Q)$	Marginal Product MP_x	Average Product AP_x	Elasticity of Production E_x
1				
2				
3				
4				
5				
6				
7				
8				
9				
10				

    b. Plot the (i) total product, (ii) marginal product, and (iii) average product functions.

    c. Determine the boundaries of the three stages of production.

2. From your knowledge of the relationships among the various production functions, complete the following table:

Variable Input X	Total Product $TP_x (= Q)$	Average Product AP_x	Marginal Product MP_x
0	0	—	—
1	___	___	8
2	28	___	___
3	___	18	___
4	___	___	26
5	___	20	___
6	108	___	___
7	___	___	−10

3. Suppose the short-run total product curve (TP_x) is a linear function of the variable input over some range of values. Determine the shape of the corresponding marginal product (MP_x) and average product (AP_x) functions.

4. The amount of fish caught per week on a trawler is a function of the crew size assigned to operate the boat. Based on past data, the following production schedule was developed:

Crew Size (Number of Men)	Amount of Fish Caught per Week (Hundreds of Pounds)
2	3
3	6
4	11
5	19
6	24
7	28
8	31
9	33
10	34
11	34
12	33

a. Over what ranges of workers are there (i) increasing, (ii) constant, (iii) decreasing, and (iv) negative returns?
b. How large a crew should be used if the trawler owner is interested in maximizing the total amount of fish caught?
c. How large a crew should be used if the trawler owner is interested in maximizing the average amount of fish caught per man?

5. Consider Exercise 4 again. Suppose the owner of the trawler can sell all the fish he can catch for $75 per 100 pounds and can hire as many crew members as he wants

by paying them $150 per week. Assuming that the owner of the trawler is interested in maximizing profits, determine the optimal crew size.

6. Consider the following short-run production function (where X = variable input, Q = output):

$$Q = 6X^2 - .4X^3$$

a. Determine the marginal product function (MP_x).
b. Determine the average product function (AP_x).
c. Find the value of X that maximizes Q.
d. Find the value of X at which the marginal product function takes on its maximum value.
e. Find the value of X at which the average product function takes on its maximum value.
f. Plot the (i) total, (ii) marginal, and (iii) average product functions for values of $X = 0, 1, 2, 3, \ldots, 12$.

7. Consider the following short-run production function (where X = variable input, Q = output):

$$Q = 10X - .5X^2$$

Suppose that output can be sold for $10 per unit. Also assume that the firm can obtain as much of the variable input (X) as it needs at $20 per unit.

a. Determine the marginal revenue product function.
b. Determine the marginal factor cost function.
c. Determine the optimal value of X, given that the objective is to maximize profits.

8. In the Deep Creek Mining Company example described in the chapter (Table 8.1), suppose one is interested in maximizing output subject to a cost constraint. Assume that the per-unit prices of labor and capital are $45 and $.24 respectively. Total costs (the sum of labor and capital costs) are constrained to $360 or less.

a. Using graphical isoquant-isocost analysis, determine the optimal combination of labor and capital to employ in the ore-mining process and the optimal output level.
b. Determine the optimal combination of labor and capital and optimal output level if the per-unit prices of labor and capital are $60 and $.18, respectively.

9. Suppose that as the result of recent labor negotiations, wage rates are *reduced* by 10 percent in a production process employing only capital and labor. Assuming that other conditions (for example, productivity) remain constant, determine what effect this decrease will have on the desired proportions of capital and labor used in producing the given level of output at minimum total cost. Illustrate your answer with an isoquant-isocost diagram.

10. The production schedule on the next page was developed for a production process (where the entries represent output measured in units):

a. Plot isoquants for 99, 109, 117, 129, 136, 141, 145, and 147 units of output.
b. Assume that labor costs are $10 per worker hour and machine costs are $15 per machine hour. Determine the maximum output that can be obtained given a cost constraint of $120.

Labor Input X	Capital Input Y (Machine Hours)							
(Worker Hours)	1	2	3	4	5	6	7	8
1	39	55	69	81	91	99	105	109
2	57	72	86	96	105	112	117	120
3	73	88	99	109	117	123	127	129
4	87	100	111	120	127	132	135	136
5	99	111	121	129	135	139	141	141
6	109	120	129	136	141	144	145	144
7	117	127	135	141	145	147	147	145
8	123	132	139	144	147	148	147	144
9	127	135	141	145	147	147	145	141
10	129	136	141	144	145	144	141	136

11. A firm uses two variable inputs, labor (L) and raw materials (M), in producing its output. At its current level of output:

$$C_L = \$10/\text{unit} \qquad MP_L = 25$$

$$C_M = \$2/\text{unit} \qquad MP_M = 4$$

   a. Determine whether the firm is operating efficiently, given that its objective is to minimize the cost of producing the given level of output.
   b. Determine what changes (if any) in the relative proportions of labor and raw materials need to be made to operate efficiently.

12. Suppose that a firm's production function is given by the following relationship:

$$Q = 2.5 \sqrt{LC} \qquad (\text{i.e., } Q = 2.5L^{.5}C^{.5})$$

   where Q = output
         L = labor input
         C = capital input

   a. Determine the percentage increase in output if labor input is increased by 10 percent (assuming that capital input is held constant).
   b. Determine the percentage increase in output if capital input is increased by 25 percent (assuming that labor input is held constant).
   c. Determine the percentage increase in output if *both* labor and capital are increased by 20 percent.

13. Based on the production function parameter estimates reported in Table 8.5:
   a. Which industry (or industries) appears to exhibit decreasing returns to scale (ignore the issue of statistical significance)?
   b. Which industry comes closest to exhibiting constant returns to scale?
   c. In which industry will a given percentage increase in capital result in the largest percentage increase in output?
   d. In what industry will a given percentage increase in production workers result in the largest percentage increase in output?

14. Given the following production function:

$$Q = 1.40L^{.70}K^{.35}$$

    a. Determine the elasticity of production with respect to
      (i) Labor (L)
      (ii) Capital (K)
    b. Give an economic interpretation of each value determined in part (a).

15. Consider the following Cobb-Douglas production function for the bus transportation system in a particular city:

$$Q = \alpha L^{\beta_1} F^{\beta_2} B^{\beta_3}$$

where L = labor input in worker hours
       F = fuel input in gallons
       B = capital input in number of buses
       Q = output measured in millions of bus miles

Suppose that the parameters (α, β_1, β_2, and β_3) of this model were estimated using annual data for the past 25 years. The following results were obtained:

$$\alpha = .0012 \qquad \beta_1 = .45 \qquad \beta_2 = .20 \qquad \beta_3 = .30$$

    a. Determine the (i) labor, (ii) fuel, and (iii) capital-input production elasticities.
    b. Suppose that labor input (worker hours) is increased by 2 percent next year (with the other inputs held constant). Determine the approximate percentage change in output.
    c. Suppose that capital input (number of buses) is decreased by 3 percent next year (that is, certain older buses are taken out of service). Assuming that the other inputs are held constant, determine the approximate percentage change in output.
    d. What type of returns to scale appears to characterize this bus transportation system (ignore the issue of statistical significance)?
    e. Discuss some of the methodological and measurement problems one might encounter in using time-series data to estimate the parameters of this model.

16. Determine whether each of the following production functions exhibits increasing, constant, or decreasing returns to scale:
    a. $Q = 1.5X^{.70}Y^{.30}$
    b. $Q = .4X + .5Y$
    c. $Q = 2.0XY$
    d. $Q = 1.0X^{.6}Y^{.5}$

17. Determine if the following production functions are homogeneous and, if so, the degree of homogeneity:
    a. $Q = 2X^{.7} + 3Y^{.7}$
    b. $Q = 2X^{.5}Y^{.5}$
    c. $Q = \dfrac{2X^3 + 3Y^3}{6X^2 - 2Y^2}$
    d. $Q = 3X^2Y^2 - .1X^3Y^3$
    e. $Q = 2X^{.8} + 3Y^{.7}$

18. Show that elasticity of production for capital input is constant and equal to β_2 for the Cobb-Douglas production function (Equation 8.31).

19. *Extension of the Cobb-Douglas Production Function*—The Cobb-Douglas power production function (Equation 8.31) can be shown to be a special case of a larger class of production functions having the following mathematical form:[23]

$$Q = \gamma[\partial K^{-\rho} + (1 - \partial)L^{-\rho}]^{-\nu/\rho}$$

—————
[23]See R.G. Chambers, *Applied Production Analysis* (Cambridge: Cambridge University Press, 1988).

where γ is an efficiency parameter which shows the output that results from given quantities of inputs; ∂ is a distribution parameter ($0 \leq \partial \leq 1$) that indicates the division of factor income between capital and labor; ρ is a substitution parameter that is a measure of substitutability of capital for labor (or vice versa) in the production process; and v is a scale parameter ($v > 0$) that indicates the type of returns to scale (increasing, constant, or decreasing). Show that when $v = 1$, this function exhibits constant returns to scale. (*Hint:* Increase capital K and labor L each by a factor of λ—$K^* = (\lambda)K$ and $L^* = (\lambda)L$—and show that output Q also increases by a factor of λ—$Q^* = (\lambda)(Q)$.)

20. Lobo Lighting Corporation currently employs 100 unskilled laborers, 80 factory technicians, 30 skilled machinists, and 40 skilled electricians. Lobo feels that the marginal product of the last unskilled laborer is 400 lights per week, the marginal product of the last factory technician is 450 lights per week, the marginal product of the last skilled machinist is 550 lights per week, and the marginal product of the last skilled electrician is 600 lights per week. Unskilled laborers earn $400 per week, factory technicians earn $500 per week, machinists earn $700 per week, and electricians earn $750 per week.

    Is Lobo using the lowest cost combination of workers to produce its targeted output? If not, what recommendations can you make to assist the company?

21. Consider the following short-run cubic production functions, holding constant the firm's capital inputs:

$$Q = -0.005\,L^3 + 0.30L^2$$

where: Q = units of output
             L = units of labor input

  a. What output is produced when $L = 0$?
  b. What is the average product of labor?
  c. What is the marginal product of labor?
  d. At what level of labor input is the marginal product of labor maximized?
  e. At what level of labor input is the marginal product of labor equal to the average product of labor? What happens to total product of labor at this point?

www exercise

Electric Utility Deregulation

22. Access the Internet site maintained by Strategic Energy Ltd: http://www.sel.com/retail. html. Research the status of electric utility deregulation in your state. Find out how deregulation has affected plant-level economies of scale in electricity generation.

CASE EXERCISE   PRODUCTION FUNCTION: WILSON COMPANY

(Note: The following exercise requires the use of a standard regression analysis program.)

Economists at the Wilson Company are interested in developing a production function for fertilizer plants. They have collected data on 15 different plants that produce fertilizer (see the following page).

QUESTIONS

1. Estimate the Cobb-Douglas production function $Q = \alpha L^{\beta_1} K^{\beta_2}$ where Q = output, L = labor input, K = capital input, and α, β_1, and β_2 are the parameters to be estimated. (*Note:* If the regression program on your computer does not have a loga-

rithmic transformation, manually transform the preceding data into the logarithms before entering the data into the computer.)

2.   Test whether the coefficients of capital and labor are statistically significant.

3.   Determine the percentage of the variation in output that is "explained" by the regression equation.

4.   Determine the labor and capital production elasticities and give an economic interpretation of each value.

5.   Determine whether this production function exhibits increasing, decreasing, or constant returns to scale (ignore the issue of statistical significance).

Plant	Output (000 Tons)	Capital ($000)	Labor (000 Worker Hours)
1	605.3	18,891	700.2
2	566.1	19,201	651.8
3	647.1	20,655	822.9
4	523.7	15,082	650.3
5	712.3	20,300	859.0
6	487.5	16,079	613.0
7	761.6	24,194	851.3
8	442.5	11,504	655.4
9	821.1	25,970	900.6
10	397.8	10,127	550.4
11	896.7	25,622	842.2
12	359.3	12,477	540.5
13	979.1	24,002	949.4
14	331.7	8,042	575.7
15	1064.9	23,972	925.8

Maximization of Production Output Subject to a Cost Constraint

Using graphical analysis, we illustrated in the chapter that the following condition (Equation 8.27)

$$\frac{MP_x}{C_x} = \frac{MP_y}{C_y}$$

must be satisfied in determining the combination of inputs $(X$ and $Y)$ that maximizes output (Q) subject to a cost constraint. This condition can also be derived algebraically using Lagrangian multiplier techniques.

Given the production function

$$Q = f(X,Y) \qquad [8A.1]$$

and the cost constraint

$$C = C_x X + C_y Y \qquad [8A.2]$$

we define an artificial variable λ (lambda) and form the Lagrangian function

$$L_Q = Q - \lambda(C_x X + C_y Y - C) \qquad [8A.3]$$

Differentiating L_Q with respect to X, Y, and λ and setting the (partial) derivatives equal to zero (condition for a maximum) yields

$$\frac{\partial L}{\partial X} = \frac{\partial f(X,Y)}{\partial X} - \lambda C_x = 0 \qquad [8A.4]$$

$$\frac{\partial L}{\partial Y} = \frac{\partial f(X,Y)}{\partial Y} - \lambda C_y - 0 \qquad [8A.5]$$

$$\frac{\partial L}{\partial \lambda} = C_x X + C_y Y - C = 0 \qquad [8A.6]$$

Recognizing that $\dfrac{\partial f(X,Y)}{\partial X} = MP_x$ and $\dfrac{\partial f(X,Y)}{\partial Y} = MP_y$, solve Equations 8A.4 and 8A.5 for λ

$$\lambda = \frac{MP_x}{C_x} \qquad [8A.7]$$

$$\lambda = \frac{MP_y}{C_y} \qquad [8A.8]$$

Setting Equations 8A.7 and 8A.8 equal to each other gives the optimality condition

$$\frac{MP_x}{C_x} = \frac{MP_y}{C_y} \qquad [8A.9]$$

EXERCISE

1. The output (Q) of a production process is a function of two inputs (X and Y) and is given by the following relationship:

$$Q = .50XY - .10X^2 - .05Y^2$$

The per-unit prices of inputs X and Y are \$20 and \$25, respectively. The firm is interested in maximizing output subject to a cost constraint of \$500.

a. Formulate the Lagrangian function:

$$L_Q = Q - \lambda(C_xX + C_yY - C)$$

b. Take the partial derivatives of L_Q with respect to X, Y, and λ and set them equal to zero.

c. Solve the set of simultaneous equations in part (b) for the optimal values of X, Y, and λ.

d. Based on your answers to part (c), how many units of X and Y should be used by the firm? What is the total output of this combination?

e. Give an economic interpretation of the λ value determined in part (c).

f. Check to see if the optimality condition (Equation 8A.9) is satisfied for the solution obtained above.

Production and Linear Programming

In Chapter 8, cost minimization subject to an output constraint in Figure 8.12 illustrated the graphical approach to a linear-programming problem. This Appendix relates the more formal mathematical approach of linear programming to a graphical solution of the output-maximization problem. The focus of the analysis is on *inputs* and the alternative production processes which can be used to obtain the product. The production problem involves determining the combination of production processes that maximizes output (or profits), subject to the restrictions on the required resources (inputs).[24] When the problem is stated in this form, the production isoquant framework can be used to illustrate the optimal choice of alternative production processes and the concept of input substitution. First, the output-maximization problem is formulated and solved. Later, the profit-maximization problem is examined.

ALGEBRAIC FORMULATION OF THE OUTPUT-MAXIMIZATION PROBLEM

Lumins Lamp Company employs capital (machine-hours) and labor (work-hours) in its operation. Three different production processes (P_1, P_2, and P_3) are available for manufacturing a certain type of lamp. Each process involves a different combination of labor and capital—process P_1 requires 1 machine-hour of capital and 4 work-hours of labor to produce each lamp; process P_2 requires 2 machine-hours and 2 work-hours to produce each lamp; and process P_3 requires 5 machine-hours and 1 work-hour to produce each lamp. Production resources are limited—5 machine-hours of capital and 8 work-hours of labor are available per day to manufacture these lamps.

Define Q_1, Q_2, and Q_3 to be the number of lamps produced per day by process, P_1, P_2, and P_3, respectively. Given that the objective is to maximize output subject to the input (capital and labor) constraints, the problem can be formulated in the linear-programming framework as follows:

Max	$Q_1 + Q_2 + Q_3$	(objective function)	[8B.1]
Subject to	$Q_1 + 2Q_2 + 5Q_3 \leq 5$	(capital constraint)	[8B.2]
	$4Q_1 + 2Q_2 + Q_3 \leq 8$	(labor constraint)	[8B.3]
	$Q_1, Q_2, Q_3, \geq 0$	(nonnegativity constraint)	[8B.4]

The objective function represents the total output from the three production processes. The first two constraints represent the respective limitations on the amounts of capital and labor that are available to operate the three production processes. The co-

---

[24]The linear-programming analysis described here can be expanded to cover the case of multiple products (outputs). See Chapter 11 for further applications of linear-programming techniques.

efficients of the Q_i variables in these constraints represent the number of units of the given resource required to manufacture one lamp by the ith production process. For example, the coefficient of Q_3 in the capital constraint indicates that 5 machine-hours of capital are required to produce one lamp using process P_3. The other coefficients have similar interpretations. The final constraint rules out negative production quantities.

GRAPHICAL REPRESENTATION AND SOLUTION OF THE OUTPUT-MAXIMIZATION PROBLEM

The linear-programming problem just described can be illustrated and solved graphically, using *process rays* to represent the production processes, *production isoquants* to represent the objective function, and a *feasible region* to represent the resource constraints.

Each production process is assumed to exhibit *constant returns to scale*. This means that output along each ray increases proportionately with increases in the inputs. For example, at point A on process ray P_1 in Figure 8B.1 1 machine-hour of capital and 4 work-hours of labor are used to produce one unit of output. Doubling the amount of capital and labor yields two units of output (point B), and tripling the amount of capital and labor yields three units of output (point C).

The production isoquants for the example problem can be constructed by drawing straight lines between the points of equal output on *adjacent* process rays. Four production isoquants representing output levels Q of 1, 2, 3, and 4 lamps, respectively, are

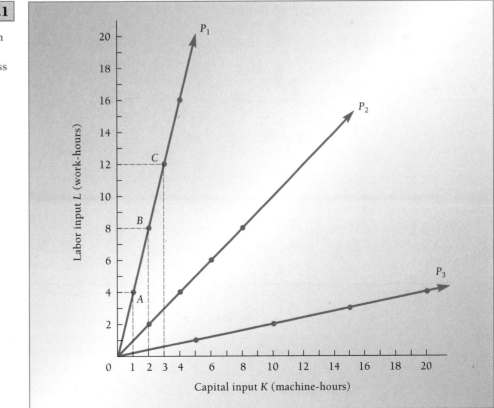

FIGURE 8B.1

Alternative Production Processes As Represented by Process Rays shown in Figure 8B.2.[25] Note that these linear-programming production isoquants have the same basic shape as the isoquants of production theory. Note also that the linear-programming production isoquants have parallel line segments between adjacent process rays. For example, line segment *AB* is parallel to *DE,* and line segment *BC* is parallel to *EF.* This occurs because the coefficients of the Q_i variables in the resource constraints are constants.

As indicated earlier, points *along* each process ray represent the output obtained if the two inputs (labor and capital) are combined in the ratio of the respective number of units of each resource required to produce a given unit of output. However, the points that lie on isoquants *between* adjacent process rays have a slightly different interpretation. These points represent a combination of output from each of the adjacent production processes. For example, point *H* on the "*Q* = 4" isoquant in Figure 8B.2 represents a production combination using both processes P_2 and P_3. The quantity of output that is produced by each process can be obtained by constructing a parallelogram such as the one shown in Figure 8B.2.[26] A line is drawn from point *H* parallel to process ray P_2, intersecting process ray P_3 at point *G.* Another line is drawn from point *H* parallel to process ray P_3, intersecting process ray P_2 at point *B.* From the parallelogram *0BHG,* we

---

[25] Production isoquants for *noninteger* output levels also can be constructed, although none are shown here.

[26] See William J. Baumol, *Economic Theory and Operations Analysis,* 4th ed. (Englewood Cliffs, N.J.: Prentice-Hall, 1977), footnote 5, p. 305, for a geometrical proof of this assertion.

FIGURE   8B.2

Production Isoquants

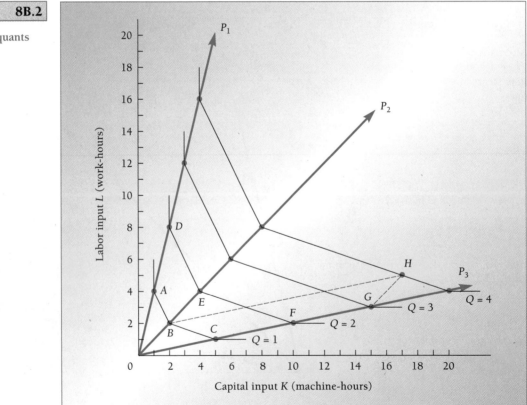

can determine both the quantity of output produced by each process and the respective amount of inputs used in each process. The firm should produce one unit of output using P_2, because point B is on the "$Q = 1$" isoquant, and three units of output using process P_3, because point G is one the "$Q = 3$" isoquant. This combination will yield the four units of output. At point B, 2 machine-hours of capital and 2 work-hours of labor are used in process P_2; and at point G, 15 machine-hours of capital and 3 work-hours of labor are used in process P_3. Total capital and labor resources used in producing the four units of output are 17 machine-hours and 5 work-hours, respectively. All other points that lie between process rays can be interpreted in a similar manner.

Feasible Region

The feasible region consists of all the capital and labor input combinations that simultaneously satisfy all constraints of the linear-programming problem. The shaded rectangle $0ABC$ shown in Figure 8B.3 represents the feasible region for the example problem. Because a maximum of 5 machine-hours of capital is available per day to produce lamps, only input combinations on or to the left of the BC line represent possible solutions to the linear-programming problem. Similarly, because a maximum of 8 work-hours of labor is available per day, possible solutions must lie on or below the AB line. Finally, the nonnegativity constraints preclude input combinations to the left of the $0A$ line and below the horizontal axis.

FIGURE   8B.3

Solution of Output-Maximization Problem

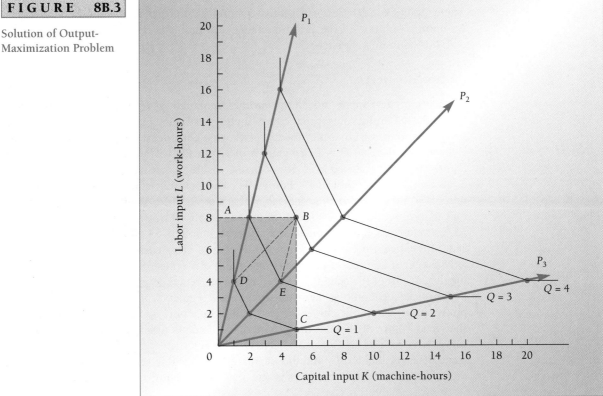

Optimal Solution

The combination of production processes that maximizes output subject to the resource constraints occurs at the point on the boundary of the feasible region that lies on the highest production isoquant. For the example problem shown in Figure 8B.3, the optimal solution occurs at point B. At point B, three units of output (lamps) are obtained by using 5 machine-hours of capital and 8 work-hours of labor. Constructing the parallelogram 0DBE shows that one unit of output should be produced using process P_1 and two units of output using process P_2. Production process P_1 should employ 1 machine-hour of capital and 4 work-hours of labor, and process P_2 should use 4 machine-hours of capital and 4 work-hours of labor.

PROFIT-MAXIMIZATION PROBLEM

The production problem also can be formulated as a profit-maximization problem. Assume that the firm has analyzed the costs of the three different production processes in the example problem described earlier in the appendix. It has been determined that each unit of output produced by process P_1 contributes $6 to profit and overhead; that is, revenue less variable cost is $6 per unit. Similarly, the profit contribution of output produced by processes P_2 and P_3 are $5 and $4 per unit, respectively.

Given that the firm desires to maximize profits rather than output, the only change in the linear-programming problem formulated earlier is the objective function. The objective function now becomes

$$\text{Max } \pi = 6Q_1 + 5Q_2 + 4Q_3 \qquad [8\text{B}.5]$$

where Q_1, Q_2, and Q_3 are the respective quantities produced by processes P_1, P_2, and P_3. An optimal solution of the profit-maximization problem can be obtained graphically with the aid of *isoprofit* curves.

Isoprofit Curves

An isoprofit curve represents all the various combinations of the two inputs that yield the same total profit. An isoprofit curve can be constructed by drawing straight lines between the points on adjacent process rays having equal total profits. To show how this is done, consider the "Q = 1" isoquant from Figure 8B.3. The isoquant is reproduced in Figure 8B.4 and is labeled ECA. Suppose one wishes to construct an isoprofit curve (π) corresponding to a profit of $4. Point A is clearly on this isoprofit curve, because one unit of output produced by process P_3 yields a profit of $4. Point C also represents one unit of output; however, each unit of output produced by process P_2 yields a profit of $5. Therefore, the point on process ray P_2 having profit of $4 must be $4 ÷ $5 = 80 percent of the distance from the origin (0) to point C. This corresponds to point B. Similarly, the point on process ray P_1 having a profit of $4 must be $4 ÷ $6 = 67 percent of the distance from the origin (0) to point E. This occurs at point D. By connecting the points on adjacent process rays with straight-line segments, one obtains the "$\pi = 4$" isoprofit curve. The profit curves corresponding to profits of $8, $12, and $16 are also shown in Figure 8B.4. Like the production isoquants described earlier, the isoprofit curves have parallel line segments between adjacent process rays. For example, line segment DB is parallel to FG, and line segment BA is parallel to GH. This occurs because the coefficients of the Q_i variables in the objective function are constants.

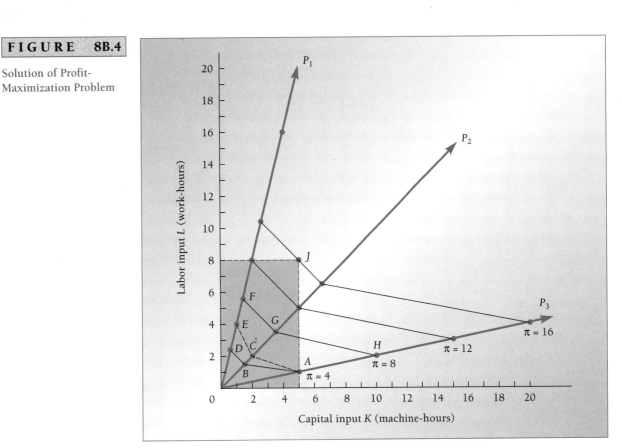

FIGURE   8B.4

Solution of Profit-
Maximization Problem

Optimal Solution

The combination of production processes that maximizes total profits subject to the resource constraints occurs at the point on the boundary of the feasible region that lies on
the highest isoprofit curve. For the example problem shown in Figure 8B.4, the optimal
solution is at point *J*, which lies on the "$\pi = 16$" isoprofit curve. Recalling that this solution corresponds to point *B* in Figure 8B.3, the firm should produce one lamp using
process P_1 and two lamps using process P_2 to maximize profits. Substituting these values for Q_1 and Q_2, respectively ($Q_3 = 0$), into the objective function shows that a profit
of ($\$6 \times 1$) + ($\$5 \times 2$) + ($\$4 \times 0$) = $16 is obtained.

EXERCISE

1. In the Lumins Lamp Company output-maximization problem described in the Ap-
    pendix, assume that production resources are limited to 14 machine-hours of cap-
    ital and 6 work-hours of labor.

    a. Formulate the problem algebraically in the linear-programming framework.
    b. Determine graphically the optimal amount of resources (capital and labor) to
        employ in each of the production processes and the total output obtained.

Cost Analysis

CHAPTER PREVIEW

Economic cost refers to the sacrifice that is made whenever an exchange or transformation of resources takes place. Economic costs are measured as opportunity costs. The opportunity cost of a resource is the cost of attracting that resource from its next best alternative use. Managers seeking to make the most efficient use of the organization's resources to maximize the value of the enterprise must be concerned with both short- and long-run cost-output relationships. Short-run cost-output relationships help managers to plan for the most profitable level of output, given the capital resources that are immediately available. Long-run cost-output relationships are important inputs into the decision to expand or contract the size of the enterprise. By making the most efficient use of resources in the short-run and by making prudent long-run investment decisions, managers can contribute to the objective of maximizing the value of the enterprise.

MANAGERIAL CHALLENGE

US AIRWAYS' COST STRUCTURE

US Airways Corporation (formerly US Air) was formed through the merger of several diverse regional airlines including Allegheny Airlines, Mohawk Airlines, Lake Central Airlines, Pacific Southwest Airlines, and Piedmont Airlines. Although these mergers led to a "national" competitor in the airline industry, US Airways's market strength was in the Northeast. In that region it faced relatively little direct competition. In 1994, US Airways had a major or dominant presence in Pittsburgh, Charlotte, Philadelphia, the Baltimore/Washington area, New York, and Boston.

The mergers that ultimately led to the establishment of US Airways did not come without difficulties. US Airways possesses a diverse fleet of aircraft, unlike the much more successful Southwest Airlines, which flies only one type of plane, the Boeing 737. US Airways' diversity results in higher costs of maintenance and crew training and in a much more complex crew scheduling problem. In addition, US Airways is burdened with very restrictive work rules that increase labor costs, which account for 40 percent of US Airways' operating costs. The net result is that US Airways' cost per available seat mile was the highest in the industry in 1993—in excess of 11 cents. This compared with a cost of slightly over 9 cents for United Airlines, about 7.5 cents for Continental Airlines, and 7 cents for Southwest.

Because of the traditionally weak competition in its Northeast market stronghold, US Airways had the highest yield in the airline industry in 1993. Yield is the average passenger revenue received for each revenue passenger mile flown. US Airways's 1993 yield was 18.8 cents, compared with 12.76 cents for Continental, 14.21 cents for United, 15.18 cents for American, and 12.37 cents for Southwest.

The combination of high yields and very high costs per available seat mile invited competition. During 1994 after emerging from bankruptcy with a new, lower cost structure, Continental announced a major restructuring of its route system to compete head-on with US Airways in much of its core business area. In addition, Southwest Air began to enter some of US Airways' traditional markets (particularly Baltimore/Washington), as did a host of new discount airlines. By early 1995, the combination of this competitive pressure and US Airways' own very high costs led to mounting losses that threatened its viability as an ongoing enterprise. The stock price tumbled from a high of $15⅜ to $4⅞ in early 1995.

With the cloud of a potential bankruptcy hanging over it, US Airways looked for ways to control its costs in order to restore its financial health. For example, it sought wage concessions from its employees in excess of $1 billion; few were granted. However, unprofitable routes were abandoned, planes were sold, and a host of other cost-reducing measures were successful. Cost control is a difficult problem in any corporation. It is, however, especially difficult in a capital-intensive industry such as this.

In this chapter we consider many of the important cost relationships that are essential to a firm's long-term competitive success.

www . . . .

The annual report for the U.S. Airways Corporation can be found at:

http://www.usair.com/company/financial/indexj.htm

THE MEANING AND MEASUREMENT OF COST

Cost
The sacrifice incurred whenever an exchange or transformation of resources takes place.

In its most elementary form, **cost** simply refers to the sacrifice incurred whenever an exchange or transformation of resources takes place. Many of the difficulties and controversies associated with the concept of cost arise when one attempts to measure this sacrifice. The appropriate manner to measure costs is a function of the purpose for which the information is to be used.

Accounting versus Economic Costs

Accountants have been primarily concerned with measuring costs for *financial reporting* purposes. As a result, they define and measure cost by the *historical outlay of funds* that takes place in the exchange or transformation of a resource. Thus, whenever A sells a product or commodity to B, the *price* paid by B, expressed in dollars, measures the cost of the product to B. When A exchanges labor services for money or other items of value, the *wages* that A receives represent the cost of A's services to the employer. Similarly, the *interest* paid to the bondholder or lending institution is used to measure the cost of funds to the borrower.

Economists have been mainly concerned with measuring costs for *decision-making* purposes. The objective is to determine the present and future costs of resources associated with various alternative courses of action. Such an objective requires a consideration of the opportunities forgone (or sacrificed) whenever a resource is used in a given course of action. Cost is a function of the value of a resource in its best alternative use. First best and second best use changes over time. Consequently, the outlay of funds incurred in obtaining a resource at some earlier date may not always be the appropriate measure of cost in a decision problem today.

Opportunity Cost
The value of a resource in its next best alternative use. Opportunity cost represents the return or compensation that must be forgone as the result of the decision to employ the resource in a given economic activity.

The **opportunity cost** of using a given quantity of resources (inputs) to produce a unit of Good A is the number of units of the *next best* alternative that must be sacrificed or forgone as a result of the decision to produce A. If the resources (labor, materials, equipment) needed to build 10 houses (of a specified size and quality) can also be used to build one office building (likewise of a specified size and quality), then the opportunity cost of the decision to build the office building is equal to the 10 houses that have to be forgone. With a fixed quantity of resources available to the organization, inputs used in the production of one good cannot be used in the production of other goods.

In calculating the cost to the firm of producing a given quantity of output, economists include some additional costs that are typically not reflected in the cost figures appearing in the financial reports of the firm. Both the accounting cost and the economic cost of a product will include such *explicit* costs as labor, raw materials, supplies, rent, interest, and utilities. Economists also include several *implicit* costs. The implicit costs consist of the opportunity costs of time and capital that the owner-manager has invested in producing the given quantity of output. The opportunity cost of the owner's time is measured by the most attractive salary or other form of compensation that the owner could have received by operating or managing a similar kind of firm for another investor. The opportunity cost of the capital employed in producing the given quantity of output is measured by the profit or return that could have been received if the owner had chosen to employ capital in the best alternative investment of comparable risk.

Relevant Cost Concept

The cost that should be used in a given decision-making problem is known as the *relevant cost*. The concept of relevant cost is illustrated with the following examples dealing with depreciation, inventory, unutilized facilities, and the measurement of profitability.

Depreciation Cost Measurement   The production of a good or service, in addition to labor, raw materials, and other resources, typically requires the use of capital assets; that is, patents, licenses, and plant and equipment. As these assets are used in producing output, their service life is expended; the assets wear out or become obsolete. Depreciation is the cost of using these assets in producing the given output. If the Phillips Tool Company owns a machine that has a current market value of $8,000 and that is expected to have a value of $6,800 after one more year of use, then the opportunity cost of using the machine for one year (the depreciation cost) is $8,000 − $6,800 = $1,200. Assuming that 2,000 units of output were produced during the year, the depreciation cost would be $1,200 ÷ 2,000 units = $.60 per unit. Ideally, this is the depreciation cost that the economist would include in calculating the cost to Phillips of the output produced. Unfortunately, it is often very difficult, if not impossible, to determine the *actual value* of the service life of an asset that is consumed in producing a given quantity of output.[1] Some assets are unique (patents); others are not traded in liquid resale markets (plants), and still others are rendered obsolete with little predictability (computers). To overcome these measurement problems, accountants have adopted certain procedures for allocating a portion of the acquisition cost of an asset to each accounting time period and in turn to each unit of output that is produced within the time period. This is typically done by estimating the service life of the asset and then charging a portion of the cost of the asset against income during each year of the service life. If the machine was purchased by Phillips for $10,000 and was expected to have a 10-year life and no salvage value, using the straight-line method of depreciation,[2] $10,000 ÷ 10 = $1,000 would be the depreciation cost of this asset each year. Assuming that 2,000 units of output are produced in a given year, then $1,000 ÷ 2,000 = $.50 would be allocated to the cost of each unit produced by Phillips. Note from this example that the method described for allocating depreciation costs is arbitrary and the calculated depreciation cost may not represent the actual depreciation cost incurred.

Inventory Valuation   Whenever materials are stored in inventory for a period of time before being used in the production process, the accounting and economic costs may differ if the market price of these materials has changed from the original purchase price. The accounting cost is equal to the actual acquisition cost, whereas the economic cost is equal to the current *replacement* cost. As the following example illustrates, the use of the acquisition cost can lead to incorrect production decisions.

Assume that Westside Plumbing and Heating Company is offered a contract for $100,000 to provide the plumbing for a new building. The labor and equipment costs are calculated to be $60,000 for fulfilling the contract. Also suppose that Westside has the materials in inventory to complete the job. The materials originally cost the firm $50,000; however, prices have since declined and the materials could now be purchased for $37,500. Material prices are not expected to increase in the near future and hence no gains can be anticipated from holding the materials in inventory. The question is: Should Westside accept the contract? An analysis of the contract under both methods for measuring the cost of the materials is shown in Table 9.1. Assuming that the materials are valued at the acquisition cost, the firm would not accept the contract, because an apparent loss of $10,000 results. By using the replacement cost as the value of the materials, however, the contract would be accepted, because a profit of $2,500 results. To see which method is

---

[1]This cost of the portion of the asset consumed should be measured in terms of the *current replacement cost* of the asset rather than the *historical acquisition cost* of the asset.

[2]The *straight-line* depreciation method allocates an equal amount of the cost of the asset to each period during the life of the asset. Other *accelerated* depreciation methods are also used. See R. Charles Moyer, James R. McGuigan, and William J. Kretlow, *Contemporary Financial Management*, 7th ed. (Cincinnati, OH: South-Western, 1997).

	Acquisition Cost		Replacement Cost	
TABLE 9.1				
Effect of Inventory Valuation Methods on Measured Profit— Westside Plumbing and Heating Company				

	Acquisition Cost	Replacement Cost
Value of contract	$100,000	$100,000
Costs		
Labor, equipment, and so on	$60,000	$60,000
Materials	50,000	37,500
	110,000	97,500
Profit (or loss)	$(10,000)	$ 2,500

correct, examine the income statement of Westside at the end of the accounting period. If the contract *is not* accepted, then at the end of the accounting period the firm would have to reduce the cost of its inventory by $12,500 ($50,000−$37,500) to reflect the lower market value of this unused inventory. The firm would thus incur a loss of $12,500. If the contract *is* accepted, then the company would make a profit of $2,500 on the contract, but would also incur a loss of $12,500 on the materials used in completing the contract. The firm would thus incur a *net* loss of only $10,000. Hence, acceptance of the contract results in a smaller overall loss to Westside than does rejection of the contract. In this example, replacement cost is the appropriate measure of the cost of materials for decision-making purposes.

Unutilized Facilities   The Dunbar Manufacturing Company recently discontinued a product line and is left with 50,000 square feet of unused and unneeded (for the foreseeable future) warehouse space. The company rents the entire warehouse (200,000 square feet) from the owner for $1,000,000 per year (i.e., $5 per square foot) under a long-term (10-year) lease agreement. A nearby company that is expanding its operations offered to rent the 50,000 square feet of unneeded space for one year for $125,000 (i.e., $2.50 per square foot). Should Dunbar accept the offer to rent the unused space? (Assume that no other higher offers for the warehouse space are expected to be received in the foreseeable future and that no additional costs will be incurred if the space is rented.)

One could argue that Dunbar should reject the offer because the additional rent (revenue) of $2.50 per square foot is less than the lease payment (cost) of $5 per square foot. Such reasoning, however, will lead to an incorrect decision. The lease payment ($5 per square foot) represents a **sunk cost** that must be paid regardless of whether or not the manufacturing company rents the unneeded warehouse space. As shown in Table 9.2, renting the unneeded warehouse space *reduces* the net cost of the warehouse from $1,000,000 to $875,000, a savings of $125,000 per year to Dunbar. The relevant comparison is between the incremental revenue ($125,000) and the incremental costs ($0 in this case). Thus, sunk costs (such as the lease payment of $5 per square foot in this example), which are independent of the alternative action chosen, should not be considered in making the optimal decision.

Sunk Cost

A cost incurred regardless of the alternative action chosen in a decision-making problem.

Measurement of Profitability   Suppose that Robert Bentley owns and operates the Bentley Clothing Store. A traditional income statement for the business is shown in Panel (a) of Table 9.3. The mortgage on the store has been paid and therefore no interest expenses are shown on the income statement. Also, the building has been fully depreciated and thus no depreciation charges are shown. From an *accounting* standpoint and from the perspective of the Internal Revenue Service, Bentley is earning a *positive accounting profit* of $40,000 (before taxes).

TABLE 9.2

Warehouse Rental Decision—Dunbar Manufacturing Company

	Decision	
	Do Not Rent	**Rent**
Total lease payment	$1,000,000	$1,000,000
Less: Rent received on unused space	—	125,000
Net cost of warehouse to Dunbar Manufacturing Company	$1,000,000	$ 875,000

TABLE 9.3

Profitability of Bentley Clothing Store

(a) Accounting Income Statement

Net sales		$500,000
Less: Cost of goods sold		250,000
Gross profit		250,000
Less: Expenses		
Employee compensation*	150,000	
Advertising	30,000	
Utilities and maintenance	20,000	
Miscellaneous	10,000	
Total		210,000
Net profit before taxes		$ 40,000

(b) Economic Profit Statement

Total revenues		$500,000
Less: Explicit costs		
Cost of goods sold	250,000	
Employee compensation*	150,000	
Advertising	30,000	
Utilities and maintenance	20,000	
Miscellaneous	10,000	
Total		460,000
Accounting profit before taxes		40,000
Less: Implicit costs		
Salary (manager)	30,000	
Rent on building	18,000	
Total		48,000
Economic profit before taxes		$−8,000

*Employee compensation does not include any salary to Robert Bentley.

However, consider the store's profitability from an *economic* standpoint. Economic profit is defined as the difference between total revenues and total economic costs. Algebraically, economic profit is given by

$$\text{Economic profit} = \text{Total revenues} - \text{Explicit costs} - \text{Implicit costs} \quad [9.1]$$

As indicated earlier in the chapter, implicit costs include the opportunity costs of time and capital that the entrepreneur has invested in the firm. Suppose that Bentley could go to work as a clothing department manager for a large department or specialty store chain and receive a salary of $30,000 per year. Also assume that Bentley could rent his building to another merchant for $18,000 (net) per year. Under these conditions, as shown in Panel (b) of Table 9.3, Bentley is earning a *negative economic profit* ($-8,000 before taxes). By renting his store to another merchant and going to work as manager of a different store, he could make $8,000 more than he is currently earning from his clothing store business.[3] Thus, accounting profits, which do not include opportunity costs, are not always a valid indication of the economic success of an enterprise.

Conclusions   Several conclusions can be drawn from this discussion of the concept of cost:

1. Costs can be measured in different ways, depending on the purpose for which the cost figures are to be used.
2. The costs of an economic activity (production), which are obtained for financial reporting purposes, are not always appropriate for decision-making purposes. Typically, changes and modifications have to be made to reflect the opportunity costs of the various alternative actions that can be chosen in a given decision problem. The *relevant cost* in economic decision making is the opportunity cost of the resources rather than the outlay of funds required to obtain the resources.
3. Sunk costs, which are incurred regardless of the alternative action chosen, should not be considered in making the optimal decision.
4. The opportunity cost of a given action in a decision problem is sometimes very difficult to measure. Cost estimates can be highly subjective and arbitrary.

SHORT-RUN COST FUNCTIONS

In addition to measuring the costs of producing a given quantity of output, economists are also concerned with determining the behavior of costs as output is varied over a range of possible values. The relationship between cost and output serves as an important building block in theories of resource allocation and pricing within the firm. The behavior of costs is expressed in terms of a **cost function**—a schedule, graph, or mathematical relationship showing the minimum achievable cost of producing various quantities of output. The shape of the firm's long-run cost function has important implications for decisions to expand the scale of operations, and the shape of its short-run cost function has a crucial impact on decisions about the quantities of inputs that are employed in the production process at any point in time.

Cost Function

A mathematical model, schedule, or graph that shows the cost (such as total, average, or marginal cost) of producing various quantities of output.

www..............
You can access a slide show on cost functions and their relationship with production at the following Internet site:
http://price.bus.okstate.edu/archive/Econ3113_963/Shows/Chapter6/index.htm

The discussion in Chapter 8 concerning the inputs used in the production process distinguished between fixed and variable inputs. A fixed input was defined as an input that is required in the production process but whose quantity used in the process is constant over a given period of time regardless of the level of output produced. A variable input was defined as an input whose amount is varied in response to the desired quantity of output to be produced. Short-run questions relate to a situation in which one or more of the inputs to the production process is fixed or incapable of be-

[3] In deciding whether to continue operating the clothing store, Bentley may feel that noneconomic factors, such as the "desire to be one's own boss," outweigh the profitability issue.

ing varied. Long-run questions relate to a situation in which *all* inputs are variable; that is, no restrictions are imposed on the amount of a resource that can be employed in the production process.

The actual period of time corresponding to the long run for a given production process will depend on the nature of the inputs employed in the production process. Generally, the more capital equipment used relative to labor and other inputs (that is, the more capital intensive the process), the longer will be the period of time required to increase significantly all the factors of production and the scale of operations. A period of five or more years may be required for a new or expanded electric utility generating facility, steel mill, or oil refinery to be constructed and put into operation. Before completion of the expansion (the short run), increases in production output can only be achieved by operating existing production facilities at higher rates of use through the utilization of greater amounts of labor and other inputs. In comparison, a service-oriented production process (such as an employment agency, trucking company, consulting firm, or government agency), which uses a relatively small amount of capital equipment, may have a long-run planning horizon of only a few months. This is especially true if the company rents or short-term leases much of its equipment. A significant expansion of the scale of operations can be achieved in a relatively short period of time by leasing additional office space and equipment and by hiring and training additional personnel.

Associated with the short-run and long-run planning periods are short-run and long-run cost functions. This section discusses the development and interpretation of short-run costs and cost functions. The next section contains a similar discussion of cost functions associated with long-run decisions.

Total Cost Function

Fixed Costs
The cost of inputs to the production process that are constant over the short run.

Variable Costs
The costs of the variable inputs to the production process.

The total cost of producing a given quantity of output is equal to the sum of the costs of each of the inputs used in the production process. In discussing short-run cost functions, it is useful to classify costs as either *fixed* or *variable costs*. **Fixed costs** represent the costs of all the inputs to the production process that are fixed or constant over the short run. These costs will be incurred regardless of whether a small or large quantity of output is produced during the period. **Variable costs** consist of the costs of all the variable inputs to the production process. Whereas variable costs may not change in direct proportion to the quantity of output produced, they will increase (or decrease) in some manner as output is increased (or decreased).[4]

EXAMPLE

SHORT-RUN COST FUNCTIONS: DEEP CREEK MINING COMPANY

To illustrate the nature of short-run costs and show how the short-run cost function can be derived from the production function for the firm, consider again the Deep Creek Mining Company example that was discussed in Chapter 8. It was assumed that two inputs, capital and labor, are required to produce or mine ore. Various-sized pieces of capital equipment, as measured by their horsepower rating *Y*, are available to mine

---

[4] A third category, *semivariable costs* can also be considered. Semivariable costs are costs that increase (decrease) in a stepwise manner as output is increased (decreased). Semivariable costs are constant when output varies within a given range. They increase or decrease only when output moves outside this range. The rental cost of a fleet of delivery trucks is an example. Over a wide range of output, delivery expenses are fixed. At some output level, however, the firm requires bigger delivery trucks. In general, cost theory can be developed without employing semivariable costs in the analysis. Such costs can be included with fixed costs.

the ore. Each of these pieces of equipment can be operated with various-sized labor crews X. The amount of output (tons of ore) that can be produced in a given period with each capital-labor input combination is shown again in Table 9.4. It was also assumed that the rental cost of using the mining equipment per period is $.20 per horsepower and that the cost of each worker (labor) employed per period is $50. This yielded the following total cost equation for any given combination of labor X and capital Y (Equation 8.21):

$$C = 50X + .20Y$$

Suppose that Deep Creek has signed a lease agreeing to rent, for the next year, a 750-horsepower piece of mining equipment (capital). During the ensuing year (the short run), the amount of capital that the company can employ in the ore-mining process is fixed at 750 horsepower. Therefore, for each period a fixed cost of $.20 × 750 = $150 will be incurred, regardless of the quantity of ore that is produced. The firm must operate the production process at one of the capital-labor combinations shown in the "Y = 750" column of Table 9.4. Output can be increased (decreased) by employing more (less) labor in combination with the given 750-horsepower capital equipment. Labor is thus a variable input to the production process.

The short-run cost functions for Deep Creek are shown in Table 9.5.[5] The various possible output levels Q and the associated capital-labor input combinations X and Y are obtained from Table 9.4. The short-run variable cost VC is equal to $50 times the number of workers (X) employed in the mining process. The short-run fixed cost FC is equal to the rental cost of the 750-horsepower equipment ($150). The total cost in the short run is the sum of the fixed and variable costs:

$$TC = FC + VC \qquad\qquad [9.2]$$

In Figure 9.1 the three curves from the data given in Table 9.5 are plotted. Note that the TC curve has an identical shape to that of VC, being shifted upward by the FC of $150.

---

[5] The rational producer would not employ more than seven workers in the short-run, because the use of additional workers will not result in any increase in the quantity of ore that is produced.

TABLE 9.4									
Production Function— Deep Creek Mining Company					Capital Input Y (Horsepower)				
		250	500	750	1,000	1,250	1,500	1,750	2,000
	1	1	3	6	10	16	16	16	13
	2	2	6	16	24	29	29	44	44
	3	4	16	29	44	55	55	55	50
Labor Input X	4	6	29	44	55	58	60	60	55
(Number of	5	16	43	55	60	61	62	62	60
Workers)	6	29	55	60	62	63	63	63	62
	7	44	58	62	63	64	64	64	64
	8	50	60	62	63	64	65	65	65
	9	55	59	61	63	64	65	66	66
	10	52	56	59	62	64	65	66	67

TABLE   9.5   Short-Run Cost Functions—Deep Creek Mining Company

Output	Variable Cost		Fixed Cost		Total Cost	Average Fixed Cost	Average Variable Cost	Average Total Cost	Marginal Cost
Q	Labor Input X	$VC=$ $\$50 \cdot X$	Capital Input Y	$FC=\$150$	$TC=$ $FC + VC$	$AFC = \dfrac{FC}{Q}$	$AVC = \dfrac{VC}{Q}$	$ATC = \dfrac{TC}{Q}$	$MC = \dfrac{\Delta TC}{\Delta Q}$
0	0	$\$ 0$	750	$\$150$	$\$150$	—	—	—	—
6	1	50	750	150	200	$\$25.00$	$\$8.33$	$\$33.33$	$\dfrac{50}{6} = \$8.33$
16	2	100	750	150	250	9.38	6.25	15.63	$\dfrac{50}{10} = 5.00$
29	3	150	750	150	300	5.17	5.17	10.34	$\dfrac{50}{13} = 3.85$
44	4	200	750	150	350	3.41	4.55	7.95	$\dfrac{50}{15} = 3.33$
55	5	250	750	150	400	2.73	4.55	7.27	$\dfrac{50}{11} = 4.55$
60	6	300	750	150	450	2.50	5.00	7.50	$\dfrac{50}{5} = 10.00$
62	7	350	750	150	500	2.42	5.65	8.06	$\dfrac{50}{2} = 25.00$

FIGURE   9.1

Short-Run Variable, Fixed, and Total Cost Functions—Deep Creek Mining Company

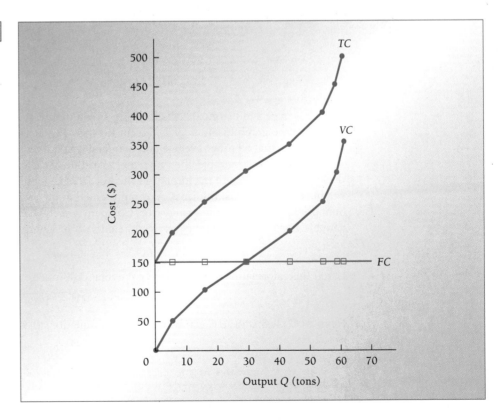

Average and Marginal Cost Functions

Once the total cost function is determined, one can then derive the average and marginal cost functions. The average fixed cost *AFC*, average variable cost *AVC*, and average total cost *ATC* are equal to the respective fixed, variable, and total costs divided by the quantity of output produced:

$$AFC = \frac{FC}{Q} \qquad [9.3]$$

$$AVC = \frac{VC}{Q} \qquad [9.4]$$

$$ATC = \frac{TC}{Q} \qquad [9.5]$$

Also,

$$ATC = AFC + AVC \qquad [9.6]$$

Marginal Cost
The incremental increase in total cost that results from a one-unit increase in output.

Marginal cost is defined as the incremental increase in total cost that results from a one-unit increase in output, and is calculated as[6]

$$MC = \frac{\Delta TC}{\Delta Q} \qquad [9.7]$$

$$= \frac{\Delta VC}{\Delta Q}$$

or, in the case of a continuous *TC* function, as

$$MC = \frac{d(TC)}{dQ} \qquad [9.8]$$

$$= \frac{d(VC)}{dQ} \qquad [9.9]$$

The average and marginal costs for Deep Creek that were calculated in Table 9.5 are plotted in the graph in Figure 9.2. Except for the *AFC* curve, which is continually declining, note that all other average and marginal cost curves are U-shaped.

The Deep Creek example illustrated the derivation of the various cost functions when the cost data are given in the form of a schedule (that is, tabular data). Consider another example where the cost information is represented in the form of an algebraic function. Suppose fixed costs for the Manchester Company are equal to $100, and the company's variable costs are given by the following relationship (where Q = output):

$$VC = 60Q - 3Q^2 + .10Q^3 \qquad [9.10]$$

Given this information, one can derive the total cost function using Equation 9.2:

$$TC = 100 + 60Q - 3Q^2 + .10Q^3$$

Next, *AFC*, *AVC*, and *ATC* can be found using Equations 9.3, 9.4, and 9.5, respectively, as follows:

[6] The ratio $\Delta TC/\Delta Q$ represents the *incremental* cost rather than the true *marginal* cost associated with *one* additional unit of output; however, we will use the term *marginal cost* even though the ratio is presented here on an incremental basis.

FIGURE   9.2

Short-Run Average and
Marginal Cost
Functions—Deep Creek
Mining Company

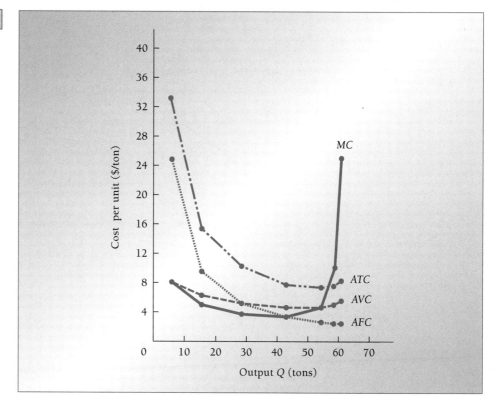

$$AFC = \frac{100}{Q}$$

$$AVC = 60 - 3Q + .10Q^2$$

$$ATC = \frac{100}{Q} + 60 - 3Q + .10Q^2$$

Finally, Manchester's marginal cost function can be obtained by differentiating the variable cost function (Equation 9.10) with respect to Q:

$$MC = \frac{d(VC)}{dQ} = 60 - 6Q + .30Q^2$$

Relationships among the Various Cost and Production Curves

To investigate further the properties of and relationships among the various cost and production curves, assume now that the cost and production curves can be represented by smooth continuous functions as shown in Figure 9.3. Also assume that input X is the variable factor, with an associated variable cost VC; that the per-unit price of each of the factors of production (i.e., C_X and C_Y) is *constant* over all usage levels;[7] and that input Y is the fixed factor, with an associated fixed cost FC. First, note that

[7] This is the same assumption that was employed in the section, "Determining the Optimal Combination of Inputs," in Chapter 8.

FIGURE   9.3

Short-Run Cost and
Production Functions

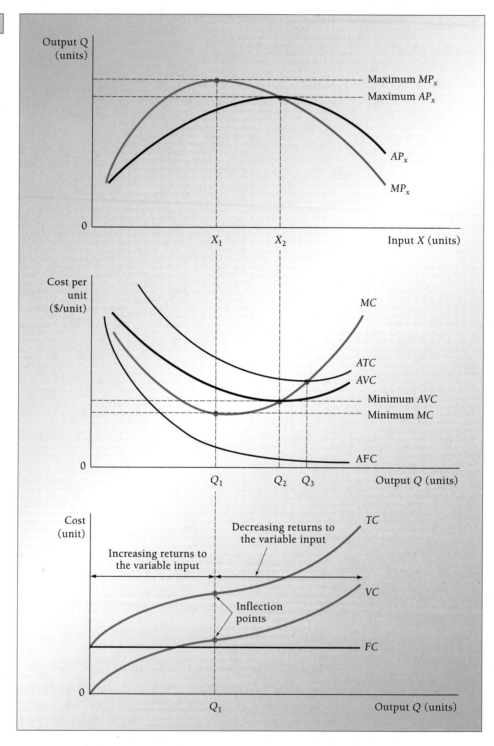

www . . . .
For further reading on the relationship between various cost and product curves see David Friedman's Internet textbook at:
http://www.best.com/ ~ddfr/Academic/Price_ Theory/PThy_Chapter_9/ PThy_Chapter_9.html

variable costs (and total costs) initially increase at a decreasing rate as output Q is increased up to Q_1. Correspondingly, the marginal cost function MC is declining. Over this range of output, the marginal product of the variable input X is increasing. Because it has been assumed that the unit cost of X is constant, an increasing marginal product for input X necessarily implies that the marginal cost function must be declining.[8] The minimum point on the MC curve at Q_1 corresponds to the maximum point on the MP_X curve at X_1. Beyond Q_1, variable (and total) costs increase at an increasing rate and, correspondingly, the marginal cost curve is increasing. Over this range of output, the marginal product of X is decreasing and, for reasons analogous to those just noted, marginal cost must necessarily be rising.

Examining the average variable cost curve, AVC, note that it is declining over output levels to Q_2 and is increasing thereafter. The shape of the average variable cost function, like the shape of the marginal cost function, is closely related to the production function defined in Chapter 8. *Given that the unit cost of the variable input is constant,* an increasing (or decreasing) average product for input X necessarily implies that the average variable cost will be decreasing (or increasing).[9] The minimum point on the AVC curve at Q_2 corresponds to the maximum point on the AP_X curve at X_2. Note also in Figure 9.3 that the marginal cost curve intersects the average variable cost function at its minimum value. This necessarily follows because the marginal product curve intersects the average product curve at its maximum value.

The average total cost curve, which is equal to the sum of the vertical heights of the average fixed cost and average variable cost curves, likewise initially declines and subsequently begins rising beyond some level of output. At a level of output of Q_3 the average total cost curve is a minimum.

As discussed in the previous chapter, more intensive use of the variable inputs (specialization) in combination with fixed inputs to the production process is believed to yield initially more than proportionate increases in output. Subsequently, due to the law of diminishing returns, more intensive use yields less than proportionate increases. This reasoning is used to explain the U-shaped pattern of the ATC, AVC, and MC curves. Initially, specialization in the use of the variable resources results in increasing returns and declining average and marginal costs. With one or more fixed inputs in the production process, increased specialization will begin to yield successively smaller returns, and then marginal and average costs will begin increasing. The actual shape of the cost functions for a specific production process is a question that can best be answered by attempting to measure empirically the functions for a given set of cost-output observations. Chapter 10 continues the discussion of this topic.

----

[8] The relationship can be shown algebraically in the following way: MC is defined as $\Delta TC/\Delta Q$, which is also equal to $\Delta VC/\Delta Q$. ΔVC is equal to $C_X \Delta X$, where C_X is the unit cost of the variable input X. Thus, $MC = C_X(\Delta X/\Delta Q)$. However, the marginal product of input X, MP, was defined in Equation 8.3 as $\Delta Q/\Delta X$, or, in reciprocal form, $1/MP = \Delta X/\Delta Q$. Substituting $1/MP$ in the relationship for MC, we obtain $MC = C_X(1/MP)$. Because the marginal productivity of X is increasing, the marginal cost must be decreasing for the equation to be valid.

[9] This relationship can be shown using the previously defined expressions for the average product AP and average variable cost AVC. AVC is equal to VC/Q. VC is equal to $C_X \cdot X$ where C_X is the unit cost of the variable input. Thus $AVC = (C_X \cdot X)/Q$. In the previous chapter the average product was defined as Q/X (Equation 8.7) or, in reciprocal form $1/AP = X/Q$. Substituting this in the expression for AVC, we obtain $AVC = C_X(1/AP)$. Thus if the average product is increasing, the average variable cost must be decreasing and vice versa.

LONG-RUN COST FUNCTIONS

Over the long-run planning horizon, the firm can choose the combination of inputs that minimizes the cost of producing a desired level of output. Using the available production methods and technology, the firm can choose the plant size, types and sizes of equipment, labor skills, and raw materials that, when combined, yield the lowest cost of producing the desired amount of output. Once the optimum combination of inputs is chosen to produce the desired level of output at least cost, some of these inputs (plant and equipment) become fixed in the short run. If demand increases unexpectedly and the firm wishes to produce not Q_1, as planned, but rather Q_2, it may have little choice but to lay on additional variable inputs like overtime labor and rush-order supplies to meet its production goals. Short-run average cost would be high in such circumstances (e.g., cost C_2 in Figure 9.4). Should this demand persist, a larger fixed input investment in plant and equipment is warranted. Then, unit cost can be reduced to C_2'. Correspondingly, a short-run average cost function like SAC_2 exists for this new set of inputs. In theory, there exists an optimum combination of inputs and a minimum total cost for each level of output. Associated with the fixed inputs in each of these optimum combinations is a short-run average cost function. Several of these other short-run average cost functions (SAC_3, SAC_4) are shown in Figure 9.4.

The long-run average cost function shown consists of the *lower boundary* or *envelope* of all the (infinitely many) short-run curves. No other combination of inputs exists for producing each level of output Q at an average cost below the cost that is indicated by the *LAC* curve. From the graph one can see that the long-run average cost of producing any given level of output, in general, does *not* occur at the point where short-run average costs are minimized. Only at the output level Q_3, corresponding to the minimum cost point on the *LAC* curve, does the long-run average cost equal the minimum short-run average cost.

Optimal Capacity Utilization

The relationship between the short-run and long-run average cost functions can be further illustrated by examining in more detail the effect on costs of an expansion in output from Q_1 to Q_2 in Figure 9.4. Assume that the firm has been producing Q_1 units of output using a plant of size "1," having a short-run average cost curve of SAC_1. The average cost of producing Q_1 units is therefore C_1, and Q_1 is the **optimal output for**

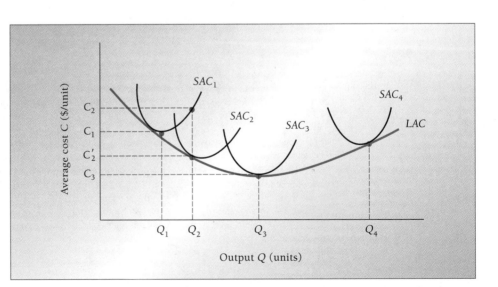

the plant size represented by SAC_1. Optimal output for given plant size is a short-run concept of capacity utilization. Suppose that the firm wishes to expand output to Q_2. What will the average cost of producing this higher volume of output be? In the short run, as we saw earlier, the average cost would be C_2. However, in the long run, it would be possible for the firm to build a plant of size "2," having a short-run average cost curve of SAC_2. With this larger plant, the average cost of producing Q_2 units of output would be only C_2'. Thus, because the firm has more options available to it in the long run, average total cost of any given output generally can be reduced. SAC_2 represents the **optimal plant size for the output rate** Q_2. However, even these inputs and costs of production that are fixed in the short run can be altered in the long run to obtain a still more efficient allocation of resources. Only when optimal output increases to Q_3, where the firm will build the universally least-cost **optimal plant size** represented by SAC_3, will further opportunities for cost reduction cease. This is a long-run concept of capacity utilization for the technology in place at this plant.

Optimal Plant Size for an Output Rate
Plant size that results in lowest average total cost for a given output.

Optimal Plant Size
Plant size that achieves minimum long-run average total cost.

AVERAGE COST PER KILOWATT HOUR[10]

Under pressure from regulators, the electric power industry will open its customer distribution systems to freewheeled electricity. That means that a hospital in North Carolina, traditionally served by Carolina Power and Light, can choose to buy contract electricity from Tennessee, Ohio, or Virginia power companies. The price of electricity is certain to decline, and consumption will increase. Excess capacity is present in much of the power industry today, but lower-cost electric utilities will soon find themselves expanding. After all, price per kilowatt hour ranges from 4 cents in some states to almost 12 cents in others. As more efficient power plants are constructed, some estimates show the price of electricity falling by 1.8 cents using conventional coal-fired steam turbine technology and by as much as 3.0 cents using nuclear and other technologies. These savings imply an $18.00 to $30.00 reduction per month in the residential electricity bill for the same amount of power.

The long-run cost function can also be obtained directly from the production function by first finding the *expansion path* for the given production process. The *expansion path* for a production process consists of the combinations of inputs X and Y for each level of output Q that satisfy the optimality criterion

$$\frac{MP_x}{C_x} = \frac{MP_y}{C_y} \qquad [9.11]$$

developed in the previous chapter (see Equations 8.26 and 8.27). This condition must be satisfied for a given input combination to be an optimal solution to either the output-maximization or cost-minimization problem. In a graphic analysis, the optimal input combination occurs at the point where the production isoquant is tangent to the isocost line (see Figures 8.10 and 8.11).[11]

As shown in Figure 9.5, the expansion path can be represented by a line that connects these various tangency points between the isoquants and isocost lines. After the expansion path is determined, the long-run total cost function can be obtained from the corresponding cost and output values of each tangency point along the expansion path. Thus, for example, from Point 1 in Figure 9.5 one obtains the cost-output combination

---

[10] Based on M. Maloney, R. McCormick, and R. Sauer, Customer Choice, Consumer Value: An Analysis of Retail Competition in America's Electric Industry (Washington, D.C.: Citizens for a Sound Economy, 1996).

[11] As in the development of the short-run cost functions in the previous section, it is assumed that the per-unit price of each factor is constant regardless of the quantity used in the production process. We comment further on this assumption in the next section.

$(C_1, Q^{(1)})$, which is then plotted in Figure 9.6. The cost-output combinations $(C_2, Q^{(2)})$ and $(C_3, Q^{(3)})$ are obtained in a similar manner. Connecting these points yields the long-run total cost (*LTC*) curve shown in Figure 9.6. The long-run average cost (*LAC*) and long-run marginal cost (*LMC*) curves are defined and calculated in a manner similar to their short-run counterparts:

$$LAC = \frac{LTC}{Q} \tag{9.12}$$

$$LMC = \frac{\Delta LTC}{\Delta Q} \tag{9.13}$$

The long-run cost function also can be derived algebraically from the production function. The derivation of the long-run cost function from the Cobb-Douglas production function is examined in the appendix to this chapter.

FIGURE   9.5

Expansion Path

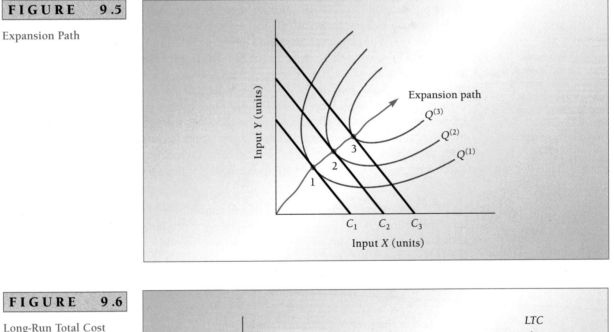

FIGURE   9.6

Long-Run Total Cost Function

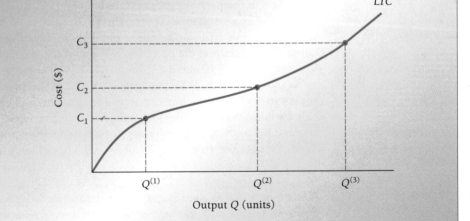

ECONOMIES AND DISECONOMIES OF SCALE[12]

The long-run average cost function of economic theory is hypothesized to be U-shaped—long-run average costs decline over lower ranges of output and rise over higher ranges of output.

Economies of Scale

Declining long-run average costs over the lower part of the range of possible outputs are usually attributed to **economies of scale.** The possible sources of economies of scale can be divided into three categories:

Economies of Scale
Declining long-run average costs as the level of output for a product, plant, or firm is increased.

- Product-specific economies—economies of scale related to the output of one product
- Plant-specific economies—economies of scale related to the total output (of multiple products) of one plant
- Firm-specific economies—economies of scale related to the total output of a firm's operations.

www
Access information on scale economies in rail-based transit systems at the following Internet site: http://nutcweb.tpc.nwu.edu/RESEARCH/carrier/carrier.html

Product-Specific Economies   A number of different sources of scale economies are associated with producing large volumes of a single product. As discussed in the previous chapter, increasing physical returns to scale can be realized from *greater specialization in the use of capital and labor.* As the scale of production is increased, special-purpose equipment (capital), which is more efficient in performing a limited set of operations, can be substituted for less efficient general-purpose equipment. Likewise, as the scale of production is increased, the production process can be broken down into a series of small tasks, and workers (labor) can be assigned to the tasks for which they are most qualified. Workers are then able to acquire additional proficiency through repetition of the tasks to which they are assigned. Generally, the productivity of workers who specialize in performing a given task repetitively is greater than that of more versatile workers who perform a variety of different tasks. Also, in manufacturing multiple units of a product, a *learning curve effect* is often observed; that is, the amount of inputs, such as labor, and associated costs required to produce each unit of output decreases for successive units of output. The learning curve concept is discussed further in Appendix 10A.

Plant-Specific Economies   Sources of scale economies at the plant level include capital investment, overhead, and required reserves of maintenance parts and personnel. With respect to *capital investment,* capital costs tend to increase less than proportionately with the productive capacity of a plant, particularly in such process-type industries as petroleum refining and chemicals. For example, a pipeline with twice the radius of another pipeline can be constructed for less than twice the cost yet have four times the capacity (i.e., $\pi(2r)^2 = 4\pi r^2$ versus πr^2) of the smaller one. Another source of scale economies is *overhead costs,* which include such items as administrative costs (e.g., management salaries) and other indirect expenditures (e.g., heating and lighting expenses). Overhead costs can be spread over a higher volume of output in a larger plant, thus reducing average costs per unit. Finally, scale economies can be realized in equipment maintenance. *Reserves of replacement parts and maintenance personnel* needed to deal with randomly occurring equipment breakdowns normally increase less than proportionately with increases in the size of the plant.

[12] For a more detailed discussion of scale economies, including a summary of the empirical evidence, see F.M. Scherer and David Ross, *Industrial Market Structure and Economic Performance,* 3d ed. (Boston: Houghton Mifflin, 1990), chap. 4.

REFUSE COLLECTION AND DISPOSAL IN ORANGE COUNTY

Private for-profit trash collectors in California have demonstrated the scale economies of landfills. The environmental safety issues at a landfill require enormous investment in environmental impact studies, lining the site, monitoring for seepage and leeching of toxins, and scientific follow-up studies. Spreading these overhead costs across a larger volume of output has led an Orange County company to seek refuse as far away as the northern suburbs of San Diego, almost an hour down the California coast. The trucks from Orange County pass right by several municipal landfills en route. However, the fees charged for dumping at these intermediate sites are much higher. Apparently, the variable transportation costs of hauling a ton of trash prove to be less than the higher start-up costs and environmental monitoring costs per ton at smaller-scale landfills. Municipalities are requiring that these landfills charge a dumping fee that covers the fully-allocated cost, so reduced long-run average total cost provides an advantage for the large-scale sites.

Economies of Scope

Economies that exist whenever the cost of producing two (or more) products jointly by one plant or firm is less than the cost of producing these products separately by different plants or firms.

The cost of a particular product can be affected by the interactions between product-specific and plant-specific economies. **Economies of scope** are present whenever the cost of producing two (or more) products jointly by one plant or firm is less than the cost of producing these products separately by different plants or firms.[13] Economies of scope occur whenever inputs, such as labor and capital equipment, can be shared in the production of different products. One commonly cited example of economies of scope is the airline industry, where the cost of transporting both passengers and freight on a single airplane is less than the cost of using two airplanes to transport passengers and freight separately.

www . . . .
Access information on economies of scope in the German railroad industry at the following Internet site: http://nutcweb.tpc.nwu. edu/RESEARCH/carrier/ carrier4.html

Firm-Specific Economies   In addition to product-specific and plant-specific economies of scale, there are other scale economies associated with the overall size of the firm. Often these latter scale economies can only be realized by the large multiproduct, multiplant firm. One possible source of scale economies to the firm is in *production and distribution*. For example, multiplant operations may permit the firm to maintain lower peak-load capacities at each geographically dispersed plant because products can be manufactured and shipped from plants with unutilized capacity to areas where demand exceeds the capacity of the local plant. Also, delivery costs are often lower for a geographically dispersed multiplant operation compared with one (larger) plant.

A second possible source of scale economies to the firm is in *raising capital funds*. Because flotation costs increase less than proportionately with the size of the security (stock or bond) issue, average flotation costs per dollar of funds raised is smaller for larger firms.[14] Also, the securities of larger firms are generally less risky than those of smaller firms. Statistical studies have shown that both the relative variability in profits and the relative frequency of bankruptcy and securities default tend to vary inversely with the size of firms. Most investors are averse to risk, so they are often willing to pay a higher price (relative to earnings) for the less risky securities of larger firms. Hence, all other things being equal, the larger firm will have a lower cost of capital than the smaller firm.

Possible scale economies also exist in *marketing and sales promotion*. These scale economies can take such forms as quantity discounts in securing advertising media space and time and the ability of the large firm to spread the fixed costs of advertising preparation over greater output volumes. In addition, the large firm may be able to

---

[13] See William J. Baumol, John C. Panzer, and Robert D. Willig, *Contestable Markets and the Theory of Industry Structure* (New York: Harcourt Brace Jovanovich, 1982), chap. 4.

[14] *Flotation costs* are the costs paid to the investment underwriter or securities dealer who arranges the sale of the securities issue to investors.

achieve a relatively greater degree of brand recognition and brand loyalty from its higher level of sales promotion expenditures over an extended period of time.

Another possible source of scale economies is in *technological innovation*. Unlike smaller firms, large firms can afford sizable research and development (R&D) laboratories and costly specialized equipment and research personnel. Also, the large firm is better able to undertake a diversified portfolio of R&D projects and can thus reduce the risk associated with the failure of any one (or small number) of the projects. The smaller firm, in contrast, may be unwilling to undertake a large R&D project, because failure of the project could result in bankruptcy. Finally, the costs of many R&D projects may be so high that only large firms, which are in a position to capture a sizable share of the market for the product, can justify the initial R&D investment.

One other possible source of scale economies is *management*. Compared with a small firm, a large firm can normally make greater use of various specialized types of such in-house managerial talent as tax accountants, market researchers, and labor contract negotiators. The smaller firm must either hire outside consultants as the need arises or do without these specialized managerial skills.

EXAMPLE

ECONOMIES OF SCALE: THE CASE OF VERY LARGE BANKS

Early studies of scale economies in banking have generally been limited to relatively small banks (less than $1 billion in assets). Some of these studies have found dis–economies for banks larger than $25 million[15] and $50 million.[16] These results have been surprising, given the growing number of very large banks in the United States and the persistent financial viability of banks that are more than 1,000 times larger than the supposedly most efficient size.

However, much of the research on banking scale economies has omitted the so-called superscale banks from analysis because of data problems. Shaffer and David[17] have overcome these early data problems and examined the economies of scale in superscale banks (banks ranging in size from $2.5 billion to $120.6 billion in assets as of June 1984). The results of their analysis indicate that the minimum efficient scale among these superscale banks is between $15 billion and $37 billion in assets. The superscale banks also had lower average costs than those estimated for smaller banks.

These results suggest that diseconomies of scale will not prevent increased bank size expansion associated with interstate banking or with the consolidation of existing institutions. Indeed, society may well be better off with such growth in the size of banking organizations because the costs of providing banking services may be reduced, especially if the banks that are involved are not among the very largest.

Diseconomies of Scale

Diseconomies of Scale
Rising long-run average costs as the level of output is increased.

Rising long-run average costs at higher levels of output are usually attributed to **diseconomies of scale.** A primary source of diseconomies of scale associated with an individual production plant is *transportation costs*. If the firm's customers are geographically scattered, then the transportation costs of distributing output from one

---

[15]G. Benston, G. A. Hanweck, and B. Humphrey, "Scale Economies in Banking: A Restructuring and Reassessment," *Journal of Money, Credit and Banking* 14(1982), pp. 435–456.

[16]T. Gilligan, M. Smirlock, and W. Marshall, "Scale and Scope Economies in the Multi-Product Banking Firm," *Journal of Monetary Economics* 13(1984), pp. 393–405.

[17]S. Shaffer and E. David, "Economies of Superscale in Commercial Banking," *Applied Economics* 23(1991), pp. 283–293.

large plant will be greater than the transportation costs of distributing output from a series of strategically located smaller plants. Another possible source of plant diseconomies is *imperfections in the labor market*. As a plant expands and its labor requirements increase, the firm may have to pay higher wage rates or engage in costly worker recruiting and relocation programs to attract the necessary personnel, particularly if the plant is located in a sparsely populated area.

For some industries like textile and furniture manufacturing, long-run average costs for the firm remain constant once scale economies are exhausted; many plant sizes are consistent with least cost production. In other industries like steel ingot production, long-run average costs rise at very large scale. The existence of diseconomies of scale for the firm is hypothesized by some economists to result from *problems of coordination and control encountered by management* as the scale of operations is increased. These coordination and control problems impose rising costs on the firm in a number of different ways. First, the size of management staffs and their associated salary costs may rise more than proportionately as the scale of the firm is increased. Also, less direct and observable costs may occur, such as the losses arising from delayed or faulty decisions and weakened or distorted managerial incentives. Contemporary examples of these problems include General Motors and AT&T.

Overall Effects of Scale Economies

In summary, the possible presence of economies and diseconomies of scale leads to the hypothesized long-run average cost function for a typical manufacturing firm being U-shaped, with a flat middle area as shown in Figure 9.7. Up to some **minimum efficient scale (MES),** that is, the smallest scale at which minimum costs per unit are attained, or up to Q_A in Figure 9.7, economies of scale are present. It also may be possible to increase the size of the firm significantly beyond the MES, from Q_A to Q_B in Figure 9.7, without incurring diseconomies of scale. Over this range, average costs per unit are relatively constant. However, expansion beyond Q_B in Figure 9.7 eventually will result in managerial inefficiencies and rising long-run average costs.

The degree to which an actual production process, plant, or firm is subject to economies or diseconomies of scale is a question that can probably best be answered by examining the empirical evidence. The next chapter discusses some of the techniques that have been used in attempting to answer this question.

Minimum Efficient Scale (MES)

The smallest scale at which minimum costs per unit are attained.

FIGURE 9.7

Long-Run Average Cost Function and Scale Economies

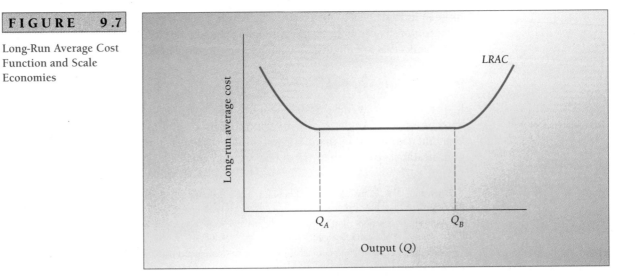

The following two examples examine the problems associated with size—the first one looks at diseconomies of scale at the plant level and the second one (in the International Perspectives section) focuses on the issue of coordination and control in large multiproduct, multiplant corporations.

EXAMPLE

FLEXIBILITY AND OPERATING EFFICIENCY: FORD MOTOR COMPANY'S FLAT ROCK PLANT[18]

Ford Motor Company spent an estimated $200 million in the early 1970s to construct a plant in Flat Rock, Michigan, to build engine blocks. The plant was built exclusively to manufacture engine blocks in the fastest, most efficient manner possible. In fact, it could produce 500,000 tons of cast iron blocks per year. The plant was designed to take advantage of economies of scale—the principle that large-scale production would result in lower costs per unit of output.

In 1981, however, Ford executives decided to close the plant and move the production of engine blocks to a much older plant in Cleveland. The Flat Rock plant originally was built to make V-8 engine blocks on five ultra-high-speed production lines. As George Booth, iron-operations manager for the casting division at Ford, explained, "Flat Rock was built to make a few parts at very high volumes. But the plant turned out to be very inflexible for conversion to making new types and different sizes of engine blocks. It wound up costing us a lot of money."

During the 1970s, cars started getting smaller and fuel efficient four- and six-cylinder engines became more popular. In 1978 Ford spent $36 million to convert just one of the five production lines at the Flat Rock plant to begin making four-cylinder engines for its Escort and Lynx subcompact models. After these changes were made, however, the plant's efficiency declined because much of the remaining machinery was designed to handle larger amounts of iron than required by the smaller, lighter engines.

Compared with the Flat Rock plant, Ford's Cleveland plant had 10 smaller and slower production lines. When operating at full capacity, the Cleveland plant was the less efficient of the two factories; however, Ford executives decided to keep it operating rather than the Flat Rock plant for two reasons. First, it would cost less to convert its smaller production lines into lines for building new engines. Second, with 10 production lines, it had the ability to produce more than five types of engines at one time.

The Flat Rock plant is a rare example of what can occur when a plant is too highly specialized. As David Lewis, a University of Michigan business professor noted, "Flat Rock was efficient at producing what it was originally designed to make, but as soon as the product changed, the plant became outmoded by its own size. It was just too big to convert to other uses. Its closing is a lesson in mass production. Sometimes you really can be too big."

INTERNATIONAL PERSPECTIVES

HOW JAPANESE COMPANIES DEAL WITH THE PROBLEMS OF SIZE[19]

Many large, successful U.S. corporations, such as General Electric, Hewlett-Packard, Sara-Lee, and Johnson and Johnson, are attempting to deal with the problems associated with size by decentralizing their operations. These companies are setting up independent business units, each with its own profit-and-loss responsibility, thereby giving managers more flexibility and freedom in decision making.

---

[18] Based on an article in the *Wall Street Journal*, 16 September 1981.

[19] Based on an article entitled "Is Your Company Too Big?," *Business Week*, 17 March 1989, pp. 84–94.

Like their counterparts in the United States, the better-run Japanese corporations are largely collections of hundreds of individual companies. For example, Matsushita Electrical Industrial Company consists of 161 consolidated units. Another example is Hitachi, Ltd., which is composed of 660 companies, with the stock of 27 of these companies being publicly traded. James Abegglen, an expert on Japanese management, has observed that "As something new comes along, . . . it gets moved out to a subsidary so the elephant does not roll over and smother it. If all goes well, it becomes a successful company on its own. If not, it gets pulled back in."

SUMMARY

- *Cost* is defined as the sacrifice incurred whenever an exchange or transformation of resources takes place.
- Different approaches are used in measuring costs, depending on the purposes for which the information is to be used. For financial reporting purposes, the historical outlay of funds is usually the appropriate measure of cost, whereas for decision-making purposes, it is often appropriate to measure cost in terms of the opportunities forgone or sacrificed.
- A *cost function* is a schedule, graph, or mathematical relationship showing the minimum achievable cost (such as total, average, or marginal cost) of producing various quantities of output.
- Short-run *total costs* are equal to the sum of *fixed* and *variable costs*.
- *Marginal cost* is defined as the incremental increase in total cost that results from a one-unit increase in output.
- The theoretical short-run average variable and marginal cost functions of economic theory are hypothesized to be U-shaped, first falling and then rising as output is increased. Falling costs are attributed to the gains available from specialization in the use of capital and labor. Rising costs are attributed to diminishing returns in production.
- The theoretical long-run average cost function, like its short-run counterpart, is also postulated to be U-shaped. This is due to the presence of economies and diseconomies of scale. *Economies of scale* are attributed primarily to the nature of the production process or the factor markets, whereas *diseconomies of scale* are attributed primarily to problems of coordination and control in large-scale organizations.

EXERCISES

1. Kay Evans has just completed her BS degree and is considering pursuing doctoral (Ph.D.) studies in economics. If Kay took a job immediately after graduation, she could earn $30,000 during the first year, with an anticipated raise of $4,000 per year over the next five years. If Kay pursues the doctorate, five more years of school are required. Kay has been offered an assistantship paying $9,500 per year plus tuition. Books and computer purchases needed for her study will cost an average of $1,500 per year. These costs would not be incurred if Kay took a job immediately. Upon graduation, Kay expects an annual income level of $45,000 during her first year of teaching. The growth rate in Kay's teaching salary is expected to equal the growth rate of her income if she had not pursued the Ph.D. How should Kay evaluate her decision to pursue a Ph.D.? What other information do you need? What factors other than salary should be considered?

2. US Airways owns a piece of land near the Pittsburgh International Airport. The land originally cost US Airways $375,000. US Airways is considering building a

new training center on this land. US Airways has determined that the proposal to build the new facility is acceptable if the original cost of the land is used in the analysis, but the proposal does not meet the airline's project acceptance criteria if the land cost is above $850,000. A developer has recently offered US Airways $2.5 million for the land. Should US Airways build the training facility at this location? (Ignore taxes.)

3.   Howard Bowen is a large cotton farmer. The land and machinery he owns has a current market value of $4,000,000. Bowen owes his local bank $3,000,000. Last year Bowen sold $5,000,000 worth of cotton. His variable operating costs were $4,500,000; accounting depreciation was $40,000, although the actual decline in value of Bowen's machinery was $60,000 last year. Bowen paid himself a salary of $50,000, which is not considered part of his variable operating costs. Interest on his bank loan was $400,000. If Bowen worked for another farmer or a local manufacturer, his annual income would be about $30,000. Bowen can invest any funds that would be derived, if the farm were sold, to earn 10 percent annually. Ignore taxes.
  a.   Compute Bowen's accounting profits.
  b.   Compute Bowen's economic profits.

4.   Mary Graham has worked as a real estate agent for Piedmont Properties for 15 years. Her annual income is approximately $100,000 per year. Mary is considering establishing her own real estate agency. She expects to generate revenues during the first year of $2,000,000. Salaries paid to her employees are expected to total $1,500,000. Operating expenses (i.e., rent, supplies, utility services) are expected to total $250,000. To begin the business, Mary must borrow $500,000 from her bank at an interest rate of 15 percent. Equipment will cost Mary $50,000. At the end of one year, the value of this equipment will be $30,000 even though the depreciation expense for tax purposes is only $5,000 during the first year.
  a.   Determine the (pretax) accounting profit for this venture.
  b.   Determine the (pretax) economic profit for this venture.
  c.   Which of the costs for this firm are explicit and which are implicit?

5.   In the ore-mining example described earlier in the chapter (Table 9.4), suppose again that labor (X) is a variable input and capital (Y) is a fixed input. Specifically, assume that the firm has a piece of equipment having a 500-horsepower rating.
  a.   Complete the following table.
  b.   Plot the variable, fixed, and total cost functions on one graph.
  c.   Plot the marginal, average variable, average fixed, and average total cost functions on another graph.

Output Q	Input X	Variable Cost VC	Input Y	Fixed Cost FC	Total Cost TC	Avg. Variable Cost AVC	Avg. Fixed Cost AFC	Avg. Total Cost ATC	Marginal Cost MC
___	0	___	___	___	___	___	___	___	___
___	1	___	___	___	___	___	___	___	___
___	2	___	___	___	___	___	___	___	___
___	3	___	___	___	___	___	___	___	___
___	4	___	___	___	___	___	___	___	___
___	5	___	___	___	___	___	___	___	___
___	6	___	___	___	___	___	___	___	___
___	7	___	___	___	___	___	___	___	___
___	8	___	___	___	___	___	___	___	___

6. From your knowledge of the relationships among the various cost functions, complete the following table.

Q	TC	FC	VC	ATC	AFC	AVC	MC
0	125						
10							5
20				10.50			
30			110				
40	255						
50						3	
60							3
70				5			
80			295				

7. Economists at General Industries have been examining operating costs at one of its parts manufacturing plants in an effort to determine if the plant is being operated efficiently. From weekly cost records, the economists developed the following cost-output information concerning the operation of the plant:

a. AVC (average variable cost) at an output of 2,000 units per week is $7.50.

b. At an output level of 5,000 units per week AFC (average fixed cost) is $3.

c. TC (total cost) increases by $5,000 when output is increased from 2,000 to 3,000 units per week.

d. TVC (total variable cost) at an output level of 4,000 units per week is $23,000.

e. AVC (average variable cost) decreases by $.75 per unit when output is increased from 4,000 to 5,000 units per week.

f. AFC plus AVC for 8,000 units per week is $7.50 per unit.

g. ATC (average total cost) decreases by $.50 per unit when output is decreased from 8,000 to 7,000 units per week.

h. TVC increases by $3,000 when output is increased from 5,000 to 6,000 units per week.

i. TC decreases by $7,000 when output is decreased from 2,000 to 1,000 units per week.

j. MC (marginal cost) is $16 per unit when output is increased from 8,000 to 9,000 units per week.

Given the preceding information, complete the following cost schedule for the plant. *Hint:* Proceed sequentially through the list, *filling in all the related entries before proceeding to the next item of information in the list.*

Output (Units Per Week)	TFC	TVC	TC	AFC	AVC	ATC	MC
0				x	x	x	x
1,000							
2,000							
3,000							
4,000							
5,000							
6,000							
7,000							
8,000							
9,000							

8. Consider the following variable cost function (Q = output):

$$VC = 200Q - 9Q^2 + .25Q^3$$

Fixed costs are equal to $150.

a. Determine the total cost function.

b. Determine the (i) average fixed, (ii) average variable, (iii) average total, and (iv) marginal cost functions.

c. Determine the value of Q where the average variable cost function takes on its minimum value. *Hint:* Take the first derivative of the *AVC* function, set the derivative equal to 0, and solve for Q. Also use the second derivative to check for a maximum or minimum.

d. Determine the value of Q where the marginal cost function takes on its minimum value.

9. Consider Exercise 8 again.

a. Plot the (i) *AVC* and (ii) *MC* functions on a single graph for the values of $Q = 2, 4, 6, \ldots, 24$.

b. Based on the cost functions graphed in part (a), determine the value of Q that minimizes (i) *AVC* and (ii) *MC*.

c. Compare your answers in part (b) with those obtained earlier in 8(c) and 8(d).

10. Suppose a firm's variable cost function is given by the relationship

$$VC = 150Q - 10Q^2 + .5Q^3$$

where Q is the quantity of output produced.

a. Determine the output level Q where the *average* variable cost function takes on its minimum value.

b. What is the value of the variable cost and average variable cost functions at the output level in part (a)?

c. Determine the output level Q where the *marginal* cost function takes on its minimum value.

d. What is the value of the variable cost and marginal cost functions at the output level in part (c)?

11. A manufacturing plant has a potential production capacity of 1,000 units per month (capacity can be increased by 10 percent if subcontractors are employed). The plant is normally operated at about 80 percent of capacity. Operating the plant above this level significantly increases variable costs per unit because of the need to pay the skilled workers higher overtime wage rates. For output levels up to 80 percent of capacity, variable cost per unit is $100. Above 80 and up to 90 percent, variable costs on this *additional* output *increase* by 10 percent. When output is above 90 and up to 100 percent of capacity, the *additional* units cost an *additional* 25 percent over the unit variable costs for outputs up to 80 percent of capacity. For production above 100 percent and up to 110 percent of capacity, extensive subcontracting work is used and the unit variable costs of these *additional* units are 50 percent above those at output levels up to 80 percent of capacity. At 80 percent of capacity, the plant's fixed costs per unit are $50. Total fixed costs are not expected to change within the production range under consideration. Based on the preceding information, complete the following table.

Q	TC	FC	VC	ATC	AFC	AVC	MC
500	———	———	———	———	———	———	———
600	———	———	———	———	———	———	———
700	———	———	———	———	———	———	———
800	———	———	———	———	———	———	———
900	———	———	———	———	———	———	———
1,000	———	———	———	———	———	———	———
1,100	———	———	———	———	———	———	———

12. The Blair Company has three assembly plants located in California, Georgia, and New Jersey. Currently, the company purchases a major subassembly, which becomes part of the final product, from an outside firm. Blair has decided to manufacture the subassemblies within the company and must now consider whether to rent one centrally located facility (for example, in Missouri, where all the subassemblies would be manufactured) or to rent three separate facilities, each located near one of the assembly plants, where each facility would manufacture only the subassemblies needed for the nearby assembly plant. A single, centrally located facility, with a production capacity of 18,000 units per year, would have fixed costs of $900,000 per year, and a variable cost of $250 per unit. Three separate decentralized facilities, with production capacities of 8,000, 6,000, and 4,000 units per year, would have fixed costs of $475,000, $425,000, and $400,000, respectively, and variable costs per unit of only $225 per unit owing primarily to the reduction in shipping costs. The current production rates at the three assembly plants are 6,000, 4,500, and 3,000 units, respectively.

   a. Assuming that the current production rates are maintained at the three assembly plants, which alternative should management select?
   b. If demand for the final product were to increase to production capacity, which alternative would be more attractive?
   c. What additional information would be useful before making a decision?

13. Kitchen Helper Company has decided to produce and sell food blenders and is considering three different types of production facilities ("plants"). Plant A is a labor-intensive facility, employing relatively little specialized capital equipment. Plant B is a semiautomated facility that would employ less labor than A but would also have higher capital equipment costs. Plant C is a completely automated facility using much more high-cost, high-technology capital equipment and even less labor than B. Information about the operating costs and production capacities of these three different types of plants is shown in the table on the following page.

   a. Determine the average total cost schedules for each plant type for annual outputs of 25,000, 50,000, 75,000, . . . , 350,000. For output levels beyond the capacity of a given plant, assume that multiple plants of the same type are built. For example, to produce 200,000 units with plant A, three of these plants would be built.
   b. Based on the cost schedules calculated in part (a), construct the long-run average total cost schedule for the production of blenders.

14. Sisneros has just completed his MBA degree and is considering pursuing doctoral (Ph.D.) studies in economics. If Sisneros took a job immediately after his MBA, he could earn $50,000 during the first year, with an anticipated raise of $5,000 per year over the next four years. If Sisneros pursues the doctorate, four more years of school are required. Sisneros has been offered an assistantship

Table for Excercise 13

	Plant Type		
	A	B	C
Unit variable costs			
Materials	$3.50	$3.25	$3.00
Labor	4.50	3.25	2.00
Overhead	1.00	1.50	2.00
Total	$9.00	$8.00	$7.00
Annual fixed costs			
Depreciation	$60,000	$100,000	$200,000
Capital	30,000	50,000	100,000
Overhead	60,000	100,000	150,000
Total	$150,000	$250,000	$450,000
Annual capacity	75,000	150,000	350,000

paying $14,000 per year plus tuition. Books and computer purchases needed for his study will cost an average of $2,000 per year. These costs would not be incurred if Sisneros took a job immediately. Upon graduation, Sisneros expects an annual income level of $65,000 during his first year of teaching. The growth rate in Sisneros' teaching salary is expected to equal the growth rate of his income if he had not pursued the Ph.D. How should Sisneros evaluate his decision to pursue a Ph.D.? What other information do you need? What factors other than salary should be considered?

15. The ARA Railroad owns a piece of land along one of its right-of-ways. The land originally cost ARA $100,000. ARA is considering building a new maintenance facility on this land. ARA has determined that the proposal to build the new facility is acceptable if the original cost of the land is used in the analysis, but the proposal does not meet the railroad's project acceptance criteria if the land cost is above $500,000. An investor has recently offered ARA $1 million for the land. Should ARA build the maintenance facility at this location?

www exercise

Stranded Costs and
Electric Utility Deregulation

16. One of the most controversial policy issue in the area of electric utility deregulation is the treatment of so-called "stranded costs." There are several sites on the Internet that describe stranded costs, including:

http://www.rapmaine.org/stranded.html
http://ee.notes.org/minnesota/stranded.htm
http://www.local.org/stranded.html
http://www.afce.org/position/p&p.htm
http://www.eia.doe.gov/cneaf/electricity/chg_str/chapter8.html

Describe how the different treatments of stranded costs (shareholders pay, ratepayers pay) affect an electric utility's cost structure.

CASE EXERCISE   COST ANALYSIS

The Leisure Time Products (LTP) Company manufactures lawn and patio furniture. Most of its output is sold to wholesalers and to retail hardware and department store chains (for example, True Value and Montgomery Ward), who then distribute the products under their respective brand names. LTP is not involved in direct retail sales. Last year the firm had sales of $35 million.

One of LTP's divisions manufactures folding (aluminum and vinyl) chairs. Sales of the chairs are highly seasonal, with 80 percent of the sales volume concentrated in the January–June period. Production is normally concentrated in the September–May period. Approximately 75 percent of the hourly workforce (unskilled and semiskilled workers) is laid off (or take their paid vacation time) during the June–August period of reduced output. The remainder of the workforce, consisting of salaried plant management (line managers and supervisors), maintenance, and clerical staff, are retained during this slow period. Maintenance personnel, for example, perform major overhauls of the machinery during the slow summer period.

LTP planned to produce and sell 500,000 of these chairs during the coming year at a projected selling price of $7.15 per chair. The cost per unit was estimated as follows:

Direct labor	$2.25
Materials	2.30
Plant overhead*	1.15
Administrative and selling expense*	.80
TOTAL	$6.50

*These costs are allocated to each unit of output based on the projected annual production of 500,000 chairs.

A 10 percent markup ($.65) was added to the cost per unit in arriving at the firm's selling price of $7.15 (plus shipping).

In May, LTP received an inquiry from Southeast Department Stores concerning the possible purchase of folding chairs for delivery in August. Southeast indicated that they would place an order for 30,000 chairs if the price did not exceed $5.50 each (plus shipping). The chairs could be produced during the slow period using the firm's existing equipment and workforce. No overtime wages would have to be paid to the workforce in fulfilling the order. Adequate materials are on hand (or can be purchased at prevailing market prices) to complete the order.

LTP's management was considering whether to accept the order. The firm's chief accountant felt that the firm should *not* accept the order because the price per chair was less than the total cost and contributed nothing to the firm's profits. The firm's chief economist argued that the firm should accept the order *if* the incremental revenue exceeds the incremental cost.

The following cost accounting definitions may be helpful in analyzing this decision:

- Direct labor—labor costs incurred in converting the raw material into the finished product.
- Material—raw materials that enter into and become part of the final product.
- Plant overhead—all costs other than direct labor and materials that are associated with the product, including wages and salaries paid to employees who do not work directly on the product but whose services are related to the production process (such as line managers, maintenance, and janitorial personnel), heat, light, power, supplies, depreciation, taxes, and insurance on the assets employed in the production process.
- Selling and distribution costs—costs incurred in making sales (for example, billing and salespeople's compensation), storing the product, and shipping the product to the customer. (In this case the customer pays all shipping costs.)

☐ Administrative costs—items not listed in the preceding categories, including general and executive office costs, research, development, engineering costs, and miscellaneous items.

QUESTIONS

1. Calculate the incremental (that is, marginal) cost per chair to LTP of accepting the order from Southeast.

2. What assumptions did you make in calculating the incremental cost in Question 1? What additional information would be helpful in making these calculations?

3. Based on your answers to Questions 1 and 2, should LTP accept the Southeast order?

4. What additional considerations might lead LTP to reject the order?

The Cobb-Douglas Production Function and the Long-Run Cost Function

THE COBB-DOUGLAS PRODUCTION FUNCTION

The Cobb-Douglas production function is given by (see Equation 8.32)

$$Q = \alpha L^{\beta_1} K^{\beta_2} \qquad [9A.1]$$

where L is the amount of labor, K is the amount of capital used in producing Q units of output, and α, β_1 and β_2 are constants. The total cost of employing L units of labor and K units of capital in a production process is equal to

$$C = C_L L + C_K K \qquad [9A.2]$$

where C_L and C_K are the per-unit prices of labor and capital, respectively. Using Lagrangian multiplier techniques, one can determine the total cost (C) of producing any level of output.

The objective is to minimize the total cost (C) of producing a given level of output $Q = Q_0$. We begin by forming the Lagrangian function

$$L_C = C + \lambda(Q - Q_0) \qquad [9A.3]$$

$$= C_L L + C_K K + \lambda(\alpha L^{\beta_1} K^{\beta_2} - Q_0) \qquad [9A.4]$$

Differentiating L_C with respect to L, K, and λ and setting these derivatives equal to zero yields

$$\frac{\partial L_C}{\partial L} = C_L + \lambda(\beta_1 \alpha L^{\beta_1 - 1} K^{\beta_2}) = 0 \qquad [9A.5]$$

$$\frac{\partial L_C}{\partial K} = C_K + \lambda(\beta_2 \alpha L^{\beta_1} K^{\beta_2 - 1}) = 0 \qquad [9A.6]$$

$$\frac{\partial L_C}{\partial \lambda} = \alpha L^{\beta_1} K^{\beta_2} - Q_0 = 0 \qquad [9A.7]$$

Solving these equations yields the following cost-minimizing values of L and K:

$$L^* = \left(\frac{Q_0}{\alpha}\right)^{1/(\beta_1 + \beta_2)} \left(\frac{\beta_1 C_K}{\beta_2 C_L}\right)^{\beta_2/(\beta_1 + \beta_2)} \qquad [9A.8]$$

$$K^* = \left(\frac{Q_0}{\alpha}\right)^{1/(\beta_1 + \beta_2)} \left(\frac{\beta_2 C_L}{\beta_1 C_K}\right)^{\beta_1/(\beta_1 + \beta_2)} \qquad [9A.9]$$

Substituting Equation 9A.8 for L and Equation 9A.9 for K in Equation 9A.2 and doing some algebraic operations gives the total cost (C) of producing any level of output (Q):

$$C = C_L^{\beta_1/(\beta_1 + \beta_2)} C_K^{\beta_2/(\beta_1 + \beta_2)} \left[\left(\frac{\beta_2}{\beta_1}\right)^{\beta_1/(\beta_1 + \beta_2)} + \left(\frac{\beta_2}{\beta_1}\right)^{-\beta_2/(\beta_1 + \beta_2)}\right] \left(\frac{Q}{\alpha}\right)^{1/(\beta_1 + \beta_2)}$$

This cost equation indicates that total costs are a function of the output level (Q), the per-units costs of labor (C_L) and capital (C_K), and the parameters (α, β_1, and β_2) of the Cobb-Douglas production function.

Several examples can be used to illustrate the cost-output relationship. In the following examples, assume that $\alpha = 4.0$ and that the per-unit costs of labor (C_L) and capital (C_K) are \$2 and \$8, respectively.

Constant Returns

$\beta_1 = .50, \beta_2 = .50$ (Because $\beta_1 + \beta_2 = 1.0$, this is an example of *constant* returns to scale.)

$$C = (2)^{.50}(8)^{.50} [1 + 1] \left(\frac{Q}{4.0}\right)^1$$

$$= 2.0Q$$

$$ATC = \frac{C}{Q} = \frac{2.0Q}{Q}$$

$$= 2.0$$

These total cost and average total cost functions are graphed in Panel (a) of Figure 9A.1. Note that when the Cobb-Douglas production function exhibits constant returns to scale, total costs increase linearly with output and average total costs are constant, or independent, of output.

Decreasing Returns

$\beta_1 = .25, \beta_2 = .25$ (Because $\beta_1 + \beta_2 < 1.0$, this is an example of *decreasing* returns to scale.)

$$C = (2)^{.50}(8)^{.50} [1 + 1] \left(\frac{Q}{4.0}\right)^2$$

$$= .50Q^2$$

$$ATC = .50Q$$

These cost functions are graphed in Panel (b) of Figure 9A.1. Note that when the Cobb-Douglas production function exhibits decreasing returns to scale, total costs increase more than proportionately with output and average total costs rise as output increases (i.e., decreasing returns to scale).

Increasing Returns

$\beta_1 = 1.0, \beta_2 = 1.0$ (Because $\beta_1 + \beta_2 > 1.0$, this is an example of *increasing* returns to scale.)

$$C = (2)^{.50}(8)^{.50} [1+1] \left(\frac{Q}{4.0}\right)^{.50}$$

$$= 4.0\, Q^{.50}$$

$$ATC = \frac{4.0}{Q^{.50}}$$

These cost functions are graphed in Panel (c) of Figure 9A.1. Note that when the Cobb-Douglas production function exhibits increasing returns to scale, total costs increase less than proportionately with output and average total costs fall as output increases (i.e., increasing returns to scale).

FIGURE   9A.1   Total Cost and Average Total Cost Functions for a Cobb-Douglas Production Function

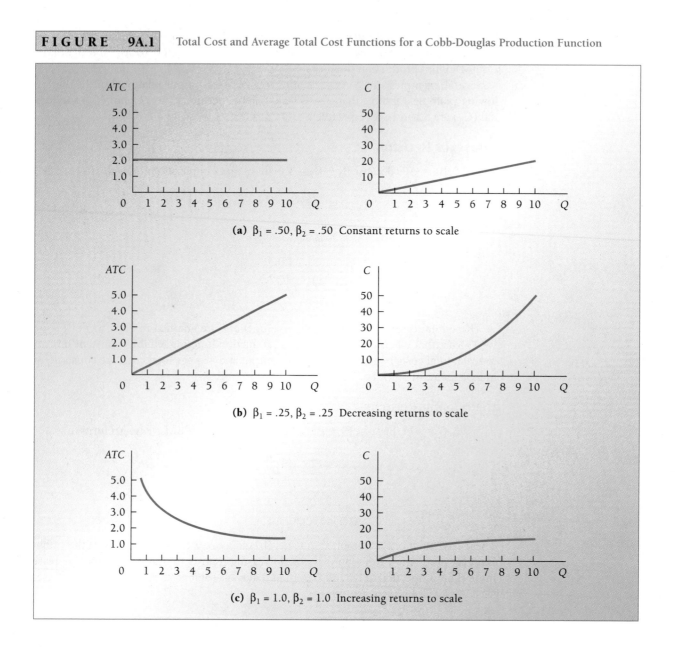

(a) $\beta_1 = .50, \beta_2 = .50$ Constant returns to scale

(b) $\beta_1 = .25, \beta_2 = .25$ Decreasing returns to scale

(c) $\beta_1 = 1.0, \beta_2 = 1.0$ Increasing returns to scale

EXERCISES

1. Determine how many units of labor (L^*) and capital (K^*) are required to produce five units of output (Q_0) for the production function given in the
    a. Constant returns example.
    b. Decreasing returns example.
    c. Increasing returns example.

2. Recompute your answers to Exercise 1 assuming that the per-unit cost of labor increases from $C_L = \$2$ to $C'_L = \$4$. How has the increase in the labor rate affected the optimal proportions of labor and capital used in the production process?

3.   Determine the total cost (C) of producing five units of output (Q_0) for the production function given in the
     a.   Constant returns example.
     b.   Decreasing returns example.
     c.   Increasing returns example.
4.   Use the data in Table 9.4 and a multiple regression analysis program on your computer to estimate a Cobb-Douglas production function of the form shown in Equation 9A.1. Do you observe increasing, decreasing, or constant returns to scale?

Applications of Cost Theory

CHAPTER PREVIEW

To make wealth-maximizing decisions based on the costs of operation, a manager must have good estimates of the cost structure facing the firm. This chapter examines some of the techniques that have been developed for estimating the cost functions of actual production processes and firms. In the short run, a knowledge of the firm's cost function is essential when deciding whether to accept an additional order, perhaps at less than "full cost," whether to schedule overtime for workers, whether to temporarily close the plant, and similar short-run decisions. In the long run, a knowledge of cost-function relationships will determine the capital investments that the firm makes, the production technology the firm chooses, the markets that the firm may choose to enter, and the new products the firm may produce. Because capital expenditures often cannot be reversed without significant losses, it is essential that a wealth-maximizing manager gather the cost information needed to make these long-term investment decisions. The first part of the chapter examines various techniques for empirically estimating short-run and long-run cost functions. The second part of the chapter deals with break-even analysis—an application of cost theory that is useful in examining the profitability of a firm's operations. Appendix 10A discusses learning curves—a cost estimation technique.

ESTIMATION OF COST FUNCTIONS

Recall from Chapter 9 that a *cost function* is a schedule, graph, or mathematical relationship showing the total, average, or marginal cost of producing various quantities of output.[1] In that chapter two different cost functions were defined and derived—the *short-run* and the *long-run* cost functions. The short-run cost function is relevant to decisions in which one or more of the inputs to the production process are fixed or incapable of being altered. To make optimal pricing and production decisions, the firm must have a knowledge of the shape and characteristics of its short-run cost function. That is, to decide whether to accept or refuse an order offered at some particular price, the firm must identify exactly what variable cost and direct fixed cost the order entails. The long-run cost function is associated with the longer-term planning period in which all the inputs to the production process are variable and no restrictions are placed on the amount of an input that can be employed in the production process. Consequently, all costs including indirect fixed costs like facility costs are avoidable. To make optimal investment decisions in new production facilities or new product introductions, the firm must have a knowledge of the behavior of its long-run cost function.

As was shown in Chapter 9, the behavior of production input-output relationships and the factor markets yield hypotheses about the shape of the *theoretical* short-run and long-run cost functions of a typical production process, plant, or firm. Determination of the shape of the *actual* cost functions for a specific individual production process, plant, or firm requires the collection and analysis of cost-output data. Because different approaches are used to empirically estimate short-run and long-run cost functions, the two cases should be considered separately. After completing our discussion of the estimation of short-run cost functions, we return to a discussion of the estimation of long-run cost functions.

SHORT-RUN COST FUNCTIONS

This section discusses the problems inherent in the statistical estimation of short-run cost functions, hypothesized cost-output relationships, and some examples of short-run cost functions.

Problems in Estimating Short-Run Cost Functions[2]

The cost function of economic theory is a *static* relationship that shows, at a given point in time, the costs that will be incurred for various output levels. The actual cost function of a firm is a *dynamic* relationship that is continually shifting throughout time. In seeking to measure statistically the static cost function of economic theory, one usually attempts to take observations of the dynamic actual cost function at different points in time. These observations must be taken in a way that allows one to estimate the average relationship between cost and output over a wide range of out-

---

[1] Once any *one* of the total, average, or marginal cost functions is obtained, the other two can be derived by arithmetic or algebraic methods.

[2] Much of this discussion is based on the work of Joel Dean, who pioneered the development of statistical cost functions. See Joel Dean, *Statistical Cost Estimation* (Bloomington, Ind.: Indiana University Press, 1976), pp. 3–35, for a more expanded treatment of the problems associated with the measurement of cost functions.

MANAGERIAL CHALLENGE

PRODUCT COSTING AND CAM-I[3]

Measurement of a company's costs and cost-output relationships is one of the most important and difficult tasks faced by managers. Accurate cost information is crucial in making all resource-allocation decisions within the company—such as the number of workers to employ, the amount of capital to invest in plant and equipment, and the prices to charge for products. Traditional cost management systems currently in use by many companies, which were established in the 1930s when labor was the chief variable cost, frequently are no longer adequate in generating the cost data required to make resource-allocation decisions that maximize shareholder wealth. As the result of automation, direct labor at many companies today represents less than 15 percent of total production costs.

Several years ago, Computer-Aided Manufacturing-International (CAM-I), a research cooperative set up initially in 1972 to develop software standards for factories, formed a cost management group to look at such issues as investment justification, product costing, total life-cycle costs of products, and measurement of manufacturing performance. Members of the cost management group included large U.S. and European manufacturers, large accounting firms, and the Department of Defense.

The new cost accounting methods promoted by CAM-I differ significantly from traditional methods. For example, consider the general overhead rate. This cost category includes everything except direct labor and materials. Components of overhead include engineering, administration, energy, and depreciation of capital equipment. Overhead costs typically account for 50 percent or more of production costs. In most companies overhead costs are allocated over all products manufactured by the company. The problem with this approach is that companies that make many different products do not know how much it costs to make any one product. The solution is to attempt to determine the costs of every operation, including overhead functions, and allocate them according to how much time a product gets processed by each operation.

When this activity-based cost system was implemented at an automobile stamping plant (which did not want to be identified publicly), it was found that the calculated total production costs for individual products were off by as much as plus or minus 60 percent. As a consequence, the plant was making a number of components it could have bought more cheaply, and it was outsourcing and purchasing several components it would have been cheaper to produce. Management of the stamping plant feels that the new accounting methods may be one of its most potent competitive weapons.

This example of make-or-buy decisions illustrates just one way in which effective cost measurement and analysis is important in making optimal resource-allocation decisions.

www..
You can learn more about the CAM-I Cost Management Systems Program on the Internet at:
http://biz.onramp.net/cami/cmsintro.htm

---

[3] Based on an article entitled "How the New Math of Productivity Adds Up," *Business Week*, 6 June 1988, pp. 100–113.

put values. Most of the problems in cost studies are associated with the methodology for obtaining these cost-output observations. These problems include the following:

- Differences in the methods by which firms define and measure costs
- Accounting for other variables (in addition to the output level) that influence costs, like total (cumulative) volume or the costs associated with batch production runs or change orders

Differences in Cost Definition and Measurement   Recall from the discussion of the meaning and measurement of cost in Chapter 9 that differences exist between the economic and accounting concepts of cost. Economic cost is represented by the value of opportunities forgone, whereas accounting cost is measured by the outlays that are incurred. Some oil and mining companies like Deep Creek Mining record the cost of their own crude oil, coal, or gas shipped downstream to their refining and processing operations at the world market price of those resources (i.e., at their opportunity cost). Other companies account for these same resources at their out-of-pocket cost. If extraction costs are low (e.g., with West Texas intermediate crude oil), the two cost methods will diverge since the higher cost of the marginal producer (e.g., an oil platform in the North Sea) sets the market price.

Because the shape of the short-run variable and total cost functions is similar,[4] either variable costs or total costs can be used to measure the cost function of the firm. One procedure is to attempt to measure costs that vary with output by means of direct accounting costs. "Direct" costs include materials, supplies, direct labor costs, and any direct fixed costs avoidable by refusing the batch order in question—e.g., the lawn furniture rented by a caterer for a client's garden party. Direct costs exclude all overhead and any other (indirect) fixed cost—i.e., any fixed cost that must be allocated. This approach may give unsatisfactory results if a significant portion of overhead costs (for example, staff labor costs in the head office) does indeed vary with the output level. But for batch decisions about whether to accept an order for a proposed charter air flight, a special production run, or a change order, these estimates of variable plus direct fixed costs are just what is needed.

Another procedure is to use total accounting costs in estimating the short-run variable costs of the firm. Although accounting costs may overstate or understate true economic short-run variable costs, one can argue that the two costs should behave similarly over a wide range of output levels. Given that accounting and variable costs do correlate closely over different output levels, then the cost function derived from accounting data will provide an accurate determination of the shape of the short-run cost function for the firm. Particularly troublesome accounting cost categories that must be given careful attention in a cost study are depreciation and, in the case of the multiproduct firm, overhead and joint costs.

Economic depreciation measures the decline in value of a capital asset. Conceptually, depreciation can be divided into two components—the decline in value associated with the passage of *time* and the decline in value associated with *use*. *Time* depreciation represents the physical deterioration of an asset over time (that is not due to use). For example, annual body style change in the automobile industry or technical progress in speed and memory of personal computers renders products and production processes obsolete. Time depreciation is completely independent of rate of output at which the asset (for example, plant and equipment) is operated. *Use* depreciation is the decline in value that occurs as a result of the operation of the asset in producing output.

Because only use depreciation varies with the rate of output, only use depreciation is relevant in determining the shape of the cost-output relationship. However, accounting data on depreciation are seldom broken down into the two components, and it is therefore usually impossible to measure use depreciation costs separately. Also, the depreciation of the value of an asset over its life cycle is usually determined by tax regulations rather than by economic criteria. As a result, the depreciation costs allocated to any period may misstate true economic depreciation costs. Finally, capital asset values (and their associated depreciation costs) are stated in terms of historical costs rather than in terms of replacement costs. In periods of rapidly increasing price levels, this will tend to

---

[4] See Figure 9.3 in the preceding chapter.

understate true economic depreciation costs. These limitations need to be kept in mind when interpreting the cost-output relationship.

In the multiproduct firm, it is common practice to allocate overhead and joint costs among the various product lines and individual products. Because of the arbitrary nature of these accounting allocations, further processing of the accounting cost data may be required before the data can be used in the cost-output equation.

Accounting for Other Variables   Like most other dependent variables in economics, cost is a function of more than just one independent variable. In addition to being a function of the output level of the firm, cost is a function of such factors as output mix, the size of manufacturing lots, employee absenteeism and turnover, production methods, factor prices, and managerial efficiency. Letting C represent cost, Q represent output, and $X_1, X_2, \ldots, X_n$ represent these other factors, the cost function can be written as

$$C = f(Q, X_1, X_2, \ldots, X_n) \qquad [10.1]$$

In estimating the cost-output relationship, the objective is to isolate the influence of these other factors in the relationship. A number of methods can be used in achieving this objective:

- Selecting an appropriate time period for analysis in which the other independent variables remain constant
- Altering the cost-output data to remove the effects of these other variables
- Using multiple regression analysis to hold constant the effects of these other variables

Each of these methods is examined below in more detail.

Selecting an Appropriate Time Period for Analysis   The cost-output observations should be collected during a period in which the variation in the other influencing variables is as small as possible. The data should be collected during a period in which no major changes in the product, plant, equipment, or work methods took place. Likewise, managerial methods and policies should remain constant during the collection period; for example, no major cost-cutting programs should have been instituted during the period.

Once the time period for analysis has been selected, it must be divided into a series of observation periods for collection of cost-output data. The length of an observation period can, in theory, vary from a week or less to a year or more. Several factors have to be *balanced* in choosing the length of the observation period. Use of a short observation period will ensure that the output rate within the period will be approximately constant throughout the period and that the effects (on costs) of fluctuations in the output rate will be captured in the data. Also, the use of a short observation period will permit a large number of cost-output observations to be collected. A large number of observations will improve the reliability of the statistical results. The use of a long observation period will minimize any errors and discrepancies that occur in allocating costs to the various time periods and matching output with its associated costs. The ideal length of the observation period will vary with different situations and will depend in part on the detail and frequency of accounting records that are maintained by the firm and that are available to the investigator.

Altering the Cost-Output Data   The effects of some of the other influencing variables can be removed from the cost-output data through various rectification procedures.

One rectification procedure involves the careful definition and measurement of the output variable. In defining the theoretical cost function, output is assumed to consist of a single homogeneous product. Most plants, however, produce a variety of products if one takes into account differences in sizes, style, and quality. The effects of variations in the product mix from period to period can be reduced by constructing an output variable that is a weighted combination of the different products. Determining the weights to assign to each of the products can sometimes be difficult, particularly when the various products are significantly heterogeneous.

Another somewhat standard adjustment procedure, which can be used whenever wage rates or raw material prices change significantly over the period of analysis, is the deflation of cost data to reflect these changes in factor prices. Provided suitable price indices are available or can be constructed, costs incurred at different points in time can be restated as dollars of equivalent purchasing power. It is preferable to use separate indices to deflate each of the various cost categories (for example, wages, raw materials, and utilities) rather than using a single index to deflate total costs. Two assumptions are implicit in this approach: No substitution takes place between the inputs as prices change and changes in the output level have no influence on the prices of the inputs. For more automated plants that incorporate only maintenance personnel, plant engineers, and material supplies, these assumptions fit the reality of the production process.

Adjustments are sometimes required to match costs with output if a time lag exists from the time a cost is incurred to the time it is reported. Maintenance cost is an example. Maintenance to equipment during peak periods of production can sometimes be postponed until subsequent periods of normal or below-normal operation. As a result, the higher costs of maintenance, which are incurred during periods of peak output due to more wear and tear on equipment, will not be recorded until later periods. A procedure for reallocating costs among different reporting periods is required in these situations.

Using Multiple Regression Analysis   If the effects of some of the other variables that influence costs cannot be removed by either of the preceding methods, a third possible method is to hold constant the effect of these variables using multiple regression techniques. One simple procedure is to use additional explanatory (independent) variables in the statistical cost equation to separate the effects of these other factors from the effect of output on costs. For example, suppose a firm believes that, all other influencing factors remaining constant, costs should decline gradually over time as a result of better production methods and increased managerial efficiency. One way to incorporate this effect into the cost equation would be to include time t as an additional explanatory variable:

$$C = f(Q, t)$$
[10.2]

Other possible explanatory variables include the number of product lines, the number of customer segments, and the number of distribution channels.[5]

Having concluded the discussion of some of the problems associated with measuring short-run cost functions, now consider some of the various cost functions that have been hypothesized to describe the behavior of cost-output relationships.

---

[5] Other more advanced econometric procedures, which are beyond the scope of this text, have been used in dealing with the methodological problems encountered in cost studies. See, for example, A. Sinan Cebenoyan, "Scope Economies in Banking: The Hybrid Box-Cox Function," *The Financial Review* 25, no. 1 (February 1990), pp. 115–125, and H. Fried, C. A. Knox Lovell, and S. Schmidt, *The Measurement of Productive Efficiency: Techniques and Applications* (Cambridge: Oxford University Press, 1993).

www . . . .
To see how economic cost concepts are applied in the military, access the Defense Resources Management Institute's handbook of unit cost management at the following site maintained by the Naval Postgraduate School:
http://web.nps.navy.mil/~drmi/unitcost.htm

Hypothesized Short-Run Cost-Output Relationships

Most empirical cost studies use either a polynomial or logarithmic function to represent the relationship between costs and output.

Polynomial Function   The total cost function, as hypothesized in economic theory, is an S-shaped curve that can be represented by a cubic relationship:

$$TC = a + bQ + cQ^2 + dQ^3 \qquad [10.3]$$

The familiar U-shaped marginal and average cost functions then can be derived from this relationship. The associated marginal cost function is

$$MC = \frac{d(TC)}{dQ} = b + 2cQ + 3dQ^2 \qquad [10.4]$$

and the average total cost function is

$$ATC = \frac{TC}{Q} = \frac{a}{Q} + b + cQ + dQ^2 \qquad [10.5]$$

The cubic total cost function and associated marginal and average total cost functions are shown in Figure 10.1(a). The use of a polynomial function allows one to test statistically for effects of including higher powers of the output variable (Q^2 or Q^3) in the equation.[6]

---

[6] Polynomial functions are easy to fit using standard least-squares techniques. These techniques are described in Chapter 5.

FIGURE   10.1   Polynomial Cost-Output Relationships

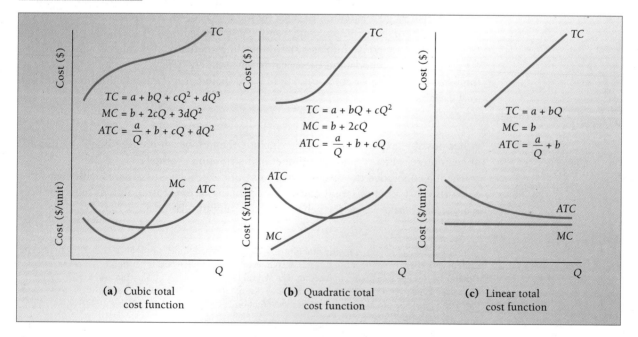

$$TC = a + bQ + cQ^2 + dQ^3$$
$$MC = b + 2cQ + 3dQ^2$$
$$ATC = \frac{a}{Q} + b + cQ + dQ^2$$

(a) Cubic total cost function

$$TC = a + bQ + cQ^2$$
$$MC = b + 2cQ$$
$$ATC = \frac{a}{Q} + b + cQ$$

(b) Quadratic total cost function

$$TC = a + bQ$$
$$MC = b$$
$$ATC = \frac{a}{Q} + b$$

(c) Linear total cost function

If the results of a regression analysis indicate that the cubic term (Q^3) is not statistically significant, then a quadratic cost relationship is obtained:

$$TC = a + bQ + cQ^2 \qquad [10.6]$$

and total costs increase at an increasing rate throughout the typical operating range of output levels. The associated marginal and average cost functions are

$$MC = \frac{d(TC)}{dQ} = b + 2cQ \qquad [10.7]$$

$$ATC = \frac{TC}{Q} = \frac{a}{Q} + b + cQ \qquad [10.8]$$

As can be seen from Equation 10.7, this relationship implies that marginal costs increase linearly as the output level is increased. The quadratic cost relationship generates the cost functions shown in Figure 10.1(b).

If the regression analysis results indicate that both the cubic (Q^3) and quadratic (Q^2) terms are not statistically significant, then a linear relationship is obtained:

$$TC = a + bQ \qquad [10.9]$$

From this relationship, we can derive the marginal and average total cost functions:

$$MC = \frac{d(TC)}{dQ} = b \qquad [10.10]$$

$$ATC = \frac{TC}{Q} = \frac{a}{Q} + b \qquad [10.11]$$

A linear total cost function, as illustrated in Figure 10.1(c), produces some interesting economic implications. First, from Equation 10.10, note that a *constant* marginal cost function is implied by the hypothesized total cost relationship. Second, Equation 10.11 indicates that average total costs are continually decreasing as output increases. Both of these implications are contrary to the law of diminishing marginal returns. Clearly, with one or more fixed inputs, short-run marginal costs will eventually begin increasing.

These implications point out an important limitation of *all* statistically derived cost-output equations, namely, that the relationship embodied in the equation may be valid only over a limited intermediate range of output values. Typically, the cost-output observations from which the cost function is statistically estimated are clustered in the middle range of output levels. Consequently, drawing conclusions based on this function about the behavior of costs at extremely high or low levels of output can be hazardous.

Logarithmic Function   A logarithmic function also can be used to examine empirical cost-output relationships. A simple cost relationship could take the form

$$\ln TC = a + b \ln Q \qquad [10.12]$$

where $\ln TC$ and $\ln Q$ are the respective natural logarithms of total cost and output, respectively, and a and b are the parameters to be estimated by regression analysis. (*Note:* A *natural* logarithm, $\ln X$, is a logarithm to the base "e," where $e = 2.71828. \ldots$ A logarithm to the base 10 is represented as $\log X$.) Such a relationship is shown in Figure 10.2. In actual applications, for a multiproduct, multi-input firm or production

Logarithmic Cost-
Output Relationship

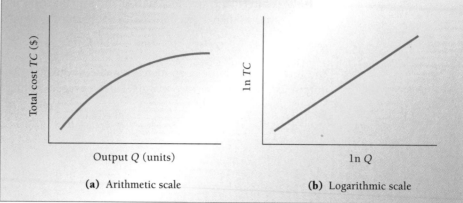

Total cost *TC* ($)

Output *Q* (units)

(a) Arithmetic scale

ln *TC*

ln *Q*

(b) Logarithmic scale

process, the equation can become much more complex with the addition of linear, quadratic, and cross-product terms for all the different products and input prices.

Examples of Statistically Estimated Short-Run Cost Functions

Short-run cost functions have been developed statistically for firms in a large number of different industries—for example, furniture, railways, gas, coal, electricity, hosiery, steel, and cement.[7] Though this discussion will not attempt to survey the results of these investigations, it may be useful to illustrate the methodology employed and the results obtained in a couple of these studies.

EXAMPLE

SHORT-RUN COST FUNCTIONS: MULTIPLE-PRODUCT FOOD PROCESSING

In a study of a British food processing firm, Johnston constructed individual cost functions for 14 different products and an overall cost function for the firm.[8] Weekly data for the period from September 1950 to June 1951 were obtained on the physical production of each type of product and total direct costs of each product (subdivided into the four categories of materials, labor, packing, and freight). Indirect costs (such as salaries, indirect labor, factory charges, and laboratory expenses) remained fairly constant over the time period studied and were excluded from the analysis. A factor price index for each category of direct costs for each product was constructed and used to deflate all four sets of costs, yielding a weekly total deflated direct cost for each product. For the individual products, output was measured by physical production (quantity). For the firm as a whole, an index of aggregate output was constructed by weighting the quantities of each product by its respective selling price and summing over all products produced each period.

For each of the 14 different products and for the overall firm, the linear cost function gave an excellent fit between direct cost and output. (In a few of the regressions, autocorrelation was found to be present, but it was removed through the use of various transformations.) Therefore, Johnston concluded that total direct costs were a linear function of output and marginal costs were constant over the observed ranges of output.

---

[7] See A.A. Walters, "Production and Cost Functions: An Econometric Survey," *Econometrica* 31, no. 1–2 (January-April 1963), pp. 1–66, for a summary of these studies.

[8] See Jack Johnston, *Statistical Cost Analysis* (New York: McGraw-Hill, 1960), pp. 87–97.

EXAMPLE

SHORT-RUN COST FUNCTIONS: ELECTRICITY GENERATION

A study by Johnston of the costs of electric power generation in Great Britain developed short-run cost functions for a sample of 17 different firms from annual cost-output data on each firm for the period 1928–1947.[9] To satisfy the basic conditions underlying the short-run cost function, only those firms whose capital equipment remained constant in size over the period were included in the sample. The output variable was measured in kilowatt-hours (kwh). The cost variable was defined as the "working costs of generation" and included (1) fuel, (2) salaries and wages, and (3) repairs and maintenance, oil, water, and stores. This definition of cost does not correspond exactly with either variable costs or total costs of economic theory. It includes some fixed costs (for example, maintenance costs at zero output) and excludes some variable costs (for example, capital costs). Neither of these problems was considered serious enough to invalidate the results. Each of the three cost categories was deflated using an appropriate price index. A cubic polynomial function with an additional linear time trend variable was fitted to each of 17 sets of cost-output observations.

The results of this study did *not* lend support to the existence of a nonlinear cubic or quadratic cost function, as postulated in economic theory. The cubic term, Q^3, was not statistically significant in any of the regressions, and the quadratic term, Q^2, was statistically significant in only 5 of the 17 cost equations. Among the five regressions with statistically significant quadratic terms, the sign of the Q^2 term was negative in four cases. This result is contrary to economic theory, which postulates steadily increasing *AVC* and *MC* functions for a quadratic total cost function.

A typical linear total cost function (for firm 8) is given by

$$C = 18.3 + 0.889Q - 0.639T$$

where C = working costs of generation (measured in thousands of British pounds), Q = annual output (millions of kilowatt-hours), and T = time (years). The equation "explained" 97.4 percent of the variation in the cost variable.

The results of the two preceding studies are similar to those found in many other cost studies—namely, that short-run total costs tend to increase *linearly* over the ranges of output for which cost-output data are available. In other words, short-run average costs tend to decline and marginal costs tend to be constant over the "typical" or "normal" operating range of the firm. In interpreting these results, one should keep in mind that they are not necessarily inconsistent with the traditional nonlinear cost function of economic theory. If the curvature of the cost function is very slight over the typical operating output range of the firm, random variation in the cost-output data may make it impossible to detect this curvature by the usual statistical methods.

LONG-RUN COST FUNCTIONS

This section discusses several alternative methods for empirically estimating long-run cost-output relationships. When suitable actual cost-output data are available, *statistical methods* analogous to those used in estimating short-run cost functions can be employed in analyzing long-run cost behavior. Long-run cost functions have also been examined using *engineering cost techniques* and the *survivor technique*. These three methods are now discussed in more detail.

---

[9] Ibid., pp. 44–63.

Statistical Estimation of Long-Run Cost Functions

In addition to many of the cost definition and measurement problems that arise in a short-run cost analysis, further difficulties of a conceptual nature are also encountered in estimating the long-run cost-output relationship by statistical methods. The long-run cost function consists of the least-cost combination of inputs for producing any level of output when *all* the inputs to the production process are variable. As is indicated in Figure 10.3, the theoretical long-run average cost function (*LRAC*) consists of the lower boundary, or envelope, of the various short-run average cost functions (*SRAC*).

The long-run cost function can be estimated by using either time-series cost-output data collected on a plant (or firm) whose size has been variable over time or cross-sectional cost-output data collected on a sample of various-sized plants (or firms) at a given point in time. Both approaches involve certain assumptions about technological and operating conditions that must be satisfied before the results give valid estimates of the long-run cost function.

With time-series cost-output data, one encounters the usual problems of holding constant or accounting for various factors (other than output) that affect costs. Estimating the long-run cost function from time-series data requires that observations be taken over a fairly long period of time, usually a number of years, to allow for sufficient variation in plant size. Over a long period of time, however, changes in the product and production technology are likely to occur. Such changes cause the long-run cost curve to shift over time. Without suitable methods for holding constant the effects of changes in products and technology, the cost-output data will be measuring points on *different* long-run cost functions rather than on the *same* function. Also, using time-series data requires that costs be deflated to reflect changes in prices over long periods of time.

For these reasons, the use of cross-sectional data tends to be more prevalent in estimating long-run cost functions. The use of cross-sectional data in the estimation process assumes that each firm in the sample, with its given fixed plant and equipment inputs, is operating at a point along the true long-run cost function. In effect, one is assuming that the four firms having the four short-run average cost functions labeled $SRAC_1$, $SRAC_2$, $SRAC_3$, and $SRAC_4$ in Figure 10.3 are operating at points A, B, C, and D, respectively. If, in fact, the four firms are operating at points such as E, F, G, and H, respectively, then substantial distortion of the shape of the function may occur in the estimation process. Other potential problems encountered when using cross-sectional

FIGURE   10.3

Long-Run Average Cost Function

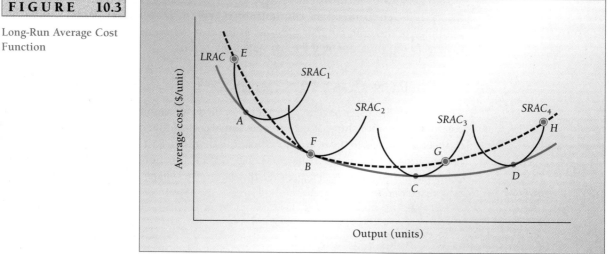

data include merging data from firms that use different accounting techniques and deflating data for regional cost differences.

Examples of Statistically Estimated Long-Run Cost Functions

Numerous empirical studies have been undertaken in an attempt to measure long-run cost functions in a wide variety of industries.[10] Two of these studies are examined below.

LONG-RUN COST FUNCTIONS: ELECTRICITY GENERATION

In the study of electrical power generation by British firms, which was discussed in the previous section, Johnston developed long-run cost functions using both time-series and cross-sectional data. In the time-series analysis, a cubic cost function with a linear trend variable was fitted to each of 23 firms whose capital equipment had *not* remained constant over the 1928–1947 period. The cubic term was not statistically significant in any of the regression equations and the quadratic term was statistically significant in only six of the regression equations. Among these six equations, the sign of the Q^2 term was positive in three cases and negative in three cases. Regardless of whether a trend (time) variable was included in the regression model, a linear model between cost and output tended to give the best fit.

In a study of U.S. electric utility companies, Christensen and Greene used a logarithmic model to test for the presence of economies and diseconomies of scale.[11] The long-run average cost curve (*LRAC*) using 1970 data on 114 firms is shown in Figure 10.4. The bar below the graph indicates the number of firms in each interval. Below 19.8 billion kwh (left arrow in graph), significant economies of scale were found to exist. The 97 firms in this range accounted for 48.7 percent of the total output. Between 19.8 and 67.1 billion kwh (right arrow in the graph), no significant economies of scale were present. The 16 firms in this range accounted for 44.6 percent of the total output. Above 67.1 billion kwh, diseconomies of scale (one firm and 6.7 percent of total output) were found.

Optimal Scale of Operation

The size at which a company should attempt to establish its operations depends on the extent of the scale economies and the extent of the market. Some firms can operate at minimum unit cost with very small scale. Consider a street vendor of leather coats. Each additional sale by a licensed street vendor entails variable costs for the coat, a few minutes of direct labor effort to answer potential customers' questions, and some small allocated cost associated with the step-van or other vehicle where the inventory is stored and hauled from one street sale location to another. [Ninety percent or more of the operating cost is the variable cost of an additional leather coat per additional sale.] Consequently, 10 sales will incur costs dominated by 10 leather coats, 100 sales will incur costs dominated by 100 leather coats, and 1,000 sales will still incur costs dominated by the 1,000 leather coats required to make the sales. Long-run average cost will be constant at approximately the wholesale cost of a leather coat, and a small-scale operation will be just as efficient as large-scale operations.

In hydroelectric power plants, however, few variable costs of any kind occur. Instead, essentially all the costs are fixed costs associated with buying the land that will be

---

[10] See F. M. Scherer and David Ross, *Industrial Market Structure and Economic Performance,* 3d ed. (Boston: Houghton Mifflin, 1990), chap. 4, for a discussion of many of the more significant studies of economies of scale.

[11] L. R. Christensen and W. H. Greene, "Economies of Scale in U.S. Electric Power Generation," *Journal of Political Economy* 84, no. 4 (August 1976).

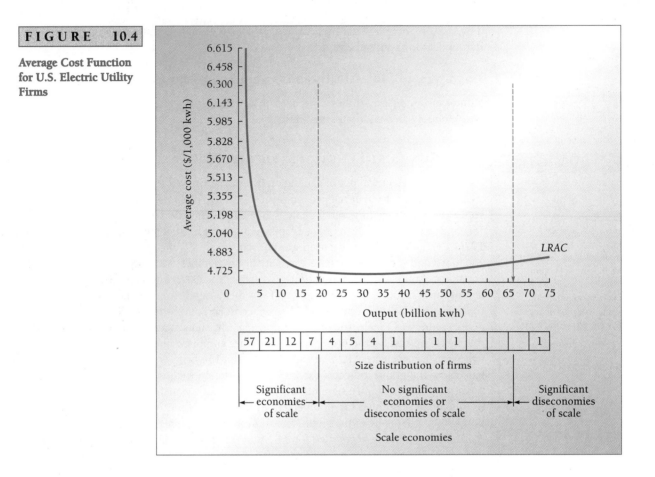

flooded, constructing the dam, and purchasing the huge electrical generator equipment. Thereafter, all the variable inputs required are a few engineers and maintenance workers. Consequently, a hydroelectric power plant has long-run average total costs that decline continuously as the company spreads its fixed cost over additional sales by supplying power to more and more households. Similarly, the distribution lines (the high tension power grids and neighborhood electrical conduits) are a high-fixed and low-variable cost operation. In the electrical utility industry, large-scale operations therefore incur lower unit cost than small-scale operations, as demonstrated in Figure 10.4.

Cable-related businesses like telephone and traditional cable TV have cost characteristics similar to electric utilities. Once the fixed cost of the cable has been put in place, the incremental cost of extending TV or telephone service to another household is very small. The extent of the scale economies in such industries may warrant licensing only one cable company or one local telephone service provider. Municipalities have historically issued an exclusive service contract to such public utilities. The rationale was that one firm could service the whole market at much lower cost than several firms dividing the market and failing therefore to realize all of the available scale economies. However, remember that the optimal scale of operation of any facility, even a declining cost facility, is limited by the extent of the market. The cable TV industry has always been limited by the availability of videocassette recorders as an inexpensive convenient entertainment substitute. As a result, the potential scale economies suggested by industrial engineering studies of cable TV operations have never been fully realized.

In addition, both telephone and cable TV companies are now facing new wireless alternative technologies. Satellite-based digital television and cell phones will cut deeply into the market once reserved exclusively for monopoly-licensed communications companies. As a result, the average unit cost in these cable-based businesses will increase as volume declines (see Figure 10.5), and the price required to break-even will necessarily rise. Of course, the higher the cost-covering price, the more customers cable TV and telephone companies will lose. "Freewheeling" in the electrical utility industry will have the same effect. When industrial and commercial electricity buyers (e.g., a large assembly plant or hospital) are allowed to contract freely with low-cost power suppliers many states away, the local public utility will experience "stranded costs." That is, the high initial fixed costs of constructing dams, power plants, and distribution lines will be left behind as sales volume declines and local customers choose to do business elsewhere. If the costs involved were mostly variable, the local power utilities could simply cut costs and operate profitability at smaller scale. Unfortunately, however, the costs are mostly fixed and unavoidable; consequently, unit costs will rise as the number of customers served declines. Consequently, the advantages of additional competition are projected at only $9 per month savings per household in electricity and $2 per month in cable television.

www . . . .
The following Internet site provides a policy analysis of economies of scale in electricity distribution in the context of electric utility deregulation:
http://www.local.org/compfran.html

EXAMPLE

Long-Run Cost Functions: Banking

A number of empirical studies have attempted to estimate economies of scale and scope in the banking industry, which includes commercial banks, savings and loan associations, and credit unions. A recent article by Clark surveyed the results of 13 of these studies.[12] Possible sources of production economies in financial institutions include:

- Specialized labor—A larger depository institution may be able to employ more specialized labor (e.g., computer programmers, cash managers, investment

---

[12]Jeffrey A. Clark, "Economies of Scale and Scope at Depository Financial Institutions: A Review of the Literature," Federal Reserve Bank of Kansas City, *Economic Review* (September-October 1988), pp. 16–33.

FIGURE   10.5

Fixed Costs Stranded by Freewheeling Electricity and Satellite-Based Digital TV

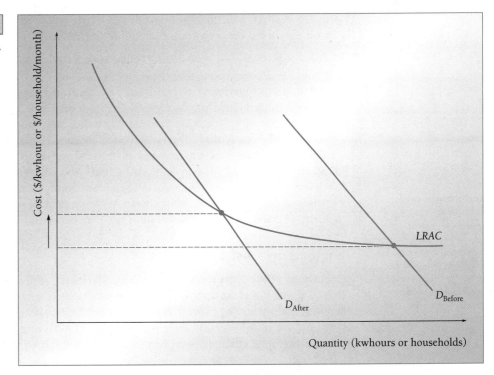

specialists, and loan officers) in producing its services. If the expertise of these workers results in the processing of a higher volume of deposit and loan accounts per unit of labor, then there will be lower per-unit labor costs at larger institutions as compared with smaller ones.

- Computer and telecommunications technology—Once the large setup, or fixed, costs are incurred, computer and electronic funds transfer systems can be used to process additional transactions at small additional costs per transaction. Spreading the fixed costs over a higher volume of transactions may permit the larger firm to achieve lower average costs. Also, economies of scope may be present if any excess capacity of the systems can be used to process other types of accounts at a small additional cost per transaction.

- Information—Credit information about loan applicants must be gathered and analyzed before lending decisions are made. However, once gathered, this credit information can be reused, usually at little additional cost, in making lending decisions to the institution's customers. For example, credit information gathered in making mortgage loans can also be used in making automobile and other personal loans. Thus, larger financial institutions, which offer a wide array of different types of credit, may realize economies of scale and scope in information gathering.

All the studies reviewed by Clark employed a logarithmic cost function. The following conclusions were derived from these studies:

- There are significant overall (i.e., firm-specific) economies of scale only at low levels of output (less than $100 million in deposits).

- There does not appear to be empirical evidence of *global* economies of scope (i.e., savings in total costs from the joint production of *all* products in the product mix).

- There is some evidence of *product-specific* economies of scope (i.e., savings in total costs from the joint production of a *particular* product with other products in the product mix). For example, one study found evidence of cost complementarities (i.e., a decline in the marginal cost of producing one product when it is produced with the other) between consumer and mortgage loans.

These results suggest that smaller, more specialized depository institutions may be at a cost disadvantage and that these institutions may need to expand and diversify their operations to remain competitive. The results also suggest that very large, highly diversified financial institutions probably will not dominate the industry based on cost considerations.

These results are typical of most statistical studies of cost-output behavior in both regulated industries and unregulated manufacturing industries. Most studies have found an L-shaped long-run average cost curve—the average cost curve falls steeply at low levels of output and then tends to flatten out and becomes horizontal with further increases in the level of output. Significant diseconomies of scale are observed in only a minority of the statistical studies of long-run cost behavior.

Engineering Cost Techniques

Engineering Cost Technique

Using a knowledge of production technology, this method of estimating cost functions attempts to determine the lowest cost combination of labor, capital equipment, and raw materials required to produce various levels of output.

Engineering cost techniques represent an alternative approach to statistical methods (least-squares) in estimating long-run cost functions. Using knowledge of production facilities and technology (such as machine speeds, worker productivity, and physical input-output transformation relationships), the engineering approach attempts to determine the most efficient (lowest average cost) combination of labor, capital equipment, and raw materials required to produce various levels of output. Engineering methods have a number of advantages over statistical methods in examining economies of scale. First, it is generally much easier with the engineering approach to hold constant such factors as input prices, product mix, and product efficiency, allowing one to isolate the effects on costs of changes in output. Second, the long-run function obtained by the engineering method is based on the production technology currently available, whereas the function obtained by the statistical approach mixes old and current production technology. Finally, use of the engineering method avoids some of the accounting cost-allocation and resource-valuation problems encountered when using statistical methods to estimate long-run cost functions.

The primary disadvantage of engineering methods is that they deal only with the technical aspects of the production process or plant. The managerial and entrepreneurial aspects, such as recruiting and training workers, marketing the product, financing the operation, and administering the organization, are not included in the analysis.

In a study designed to isolate the various sources of scale economies within a plant, Haldi and Whitcomb collected data on the cost of individual units of equipment, the initial investment in plant and equipment, and operating costs (namely, labor, raw materials, and utilities).[13] They noted that "in many basic industries such as petroleum refining, primary metals, and electric power, economies of scale are found up to very large plant sizes (often the largest built or contemplated). These economies occur mostly in the initial investment cost and in operating labor cost, with no significant economies observed in raw material cost."[14]

Survivor Technique

Survivor Technique
A method of estimating cost functions in which firms are classified by size within an industry and the shares of industry output coming from each size class over time are calculated. Size classes whose shares of industry output are increasing (decreasing) over time are presumed to be relatively efficient (inefficient) and have lower (higher) average costs.

The **survivor technique** was first put forth by Stigler as an alternative method of determining the optimum size (or range of sizes) of firms within an industry.[15] This method involves classifying the firms in an industry by size and calculating the share of industry output coming from each size class over time. If the share of industry output of a given class decreases over time, then this size class is presumed to be relatively inefficient and to have higher average costs. Conversely, an increasing share of industry output over time indicates that the size class is relatively efficient and has lower average costs.

The rationale for this approach is that competition will tend to eliminate those firms whose size is relatively inefficient, leaving only those size firms with lower average costs to survive over time. According to Stigler, "An efficient size of firm . . . is one that meets any and all problems the entrepreneur actually faces: strained labor relations, rapid innovation, government regulation, unstable foreign markets, and what not."[16] The survivor technique has some appealing characteristics. The technique is more direct and simpler to apply than are alternative techniques for examining scale economies. It avoids the accounting cost-allocation and resource-valuation problems

---

[13] J. Haldi and D. Whitcomb, "Economies of Scale in Industrial Plants," *Journal of Political Economy* 75, no. 1 (August 1967), pp. 373–385.

[14] Ibid, p. 373.

[15] G.J. Stigler, "The Economies of Scale," *Journal of Law and Economics* 1, no. 1 (October 1958), pp. 54–81. [Reprinted as chapter 7 in G. Stigler, *The Organization of Industry* (Homewood, Ill.: Richard D. Irwin, 1968).] For other examples of the use of the survivor technique, see also William G. Shepherd, "What Does the Survivor Technique Show About Economies of Scale?" *Southern Economic Journal* (July 1967), pp. 113–122, and H. E. Ted Frech and Paul B. Ginsburg, "Optimal Scale in Medical Practice: A Survivor Analysis," *Journal of Business* (January 1974), pp. 23–26.

[16] Stigler, "The Economies of Scale," p. 73.

associated with statistical methods and the hypothetical aspects of engineering cost approaches.

Despite its appeal, the survivor technique does have serious limitations. First, the technique does not use actual cost data in the analysis, so there is no way to assess the *magnitude* of the cost differentials between firms of varying size and efficiency. Also, because of legal factors, the long-run cost curve derived by this technique may be distorted and may not measure the cost curve postulated in economic theory. As McGee points out, "In some instances, law favors larger firms, especially in regulated industries. On the other hand, antitrust and other laws discourage larger firms even though "economies," as normally construed, persist beyond present firm sizes."[17] Such constraints limit the firm sizes observed by researchers employing the survivor technique.

EXAMPLE

SURVIVOR TECHNIQUE: STEEL PRODUCTION

The survivor technique has been used to examine the long-run cost functions in a number of different industries. One such study is Stigler's analysis of steel ingot production by open-hearth or Bessemer processes.[18] Based on the data in Table 10.1, Stigler developed the U-shaped long-run average cost function for steel ingot production shown in Figure 10.6. Because of the declining percentages, Stigler concluded that both low levels of output (less than 2.5 percent of capacity) and extremely high levels of output (25 percent or more) were relatively inefficient size classes. The intermediate size classes (from 2.5 to 25 percent of capacity) represented the range of optimum size because these size classes grew or held their shares of capacity. Stigler also applied the survivor technique to the automobile industry and found an L-shaped average cost curve indicating that there was no evidence of diseconomies of scale at large levels of output.

---

[17] J. S. McGee, "Efficiency and Economies of Size," in *Industrial Concentration: The New Learning,* ed. H. Goldsmid, H. Mann, and J. Weston (Boston: Little, Brown, 1974), pp. 82–83.

[18] Stigler, "The Economies of Scale," pp. 75–78.

TABLE 10.1	Company Size (Percentage of Total Industry Capacity)	Percentage of Industry Capacity			Number of Companies		
Distribution of Steel Ingot Capacity by Relative Size of Company		1930	1938	1951	1930	1938	1951
	Under ½	7.16	6.11	4.65	39	29	22
	½ to 1	5.94	5.08	5.37	9	7	7
	1 to 2½	13.17	8.30	9.07	9	6	6
	2½ to 5	10.64	16.59	22.21	3	4	5
	5 to 10	11.18	14.03	8.12	2	2	1
	10 to 25	13.24	13.99	16.10	1	1	1
	25 and over	38.67	35.91	34.50	1	1	1

SOURCE: J. S. McGee, "Efficiency and Economies of Size," in *Industrial Concentration: The New Learning,* ed. H. Goldsmid, H. Mann, and J. Weston (Boston: Little, Brown, 1974), p 76. [Adapted from George J. Stigler, "The Economies of Scale," *Journal of Law and Economics* (October 1958). Reprinted by permission.]

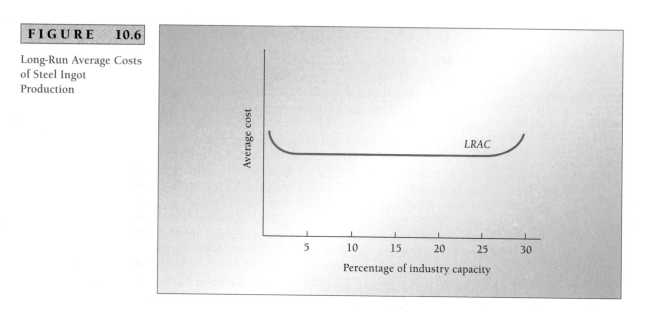

FIGURE   10.6

Long-Run Average Costs
of Steel Ingot
Production

**INTERNATIONAL
PERSPECTIVES**

ECONOMIES OF SCALE AND INTERNATIONAL JOINT VENTURES IN CHIPMAKING[19]

Approximately one dozen large electronics companies in the United States, Europe, and Japan are involved in developing the next generation (64-megabit) of memory chips. The cost of developing the 64-megabit memory chip design and production technology is estimated to range from $600 million to $1 billion. Once this investment is made and the new memory chip is developed, a company will have to invest an additional $600 million to $750 million in a plant that can produce up to 10 million chips a month.

Many of the semiconductor companies involved in these research and development efforts have formed international joint ventures to share the huge fixed costs and risks involved. Some of these partnerships include:

U.S. Company	Foreign Partner
IBM	Siemens (Germany)
Texas Instruments	Hitachi (Japan)
Motorola	Toshiba (Japan)
AT&T	NEC (Japan)

These joint ventures take various forms. For example, AT&T and NEC have an agreement to swap basic chipmaking technologies. The agreement between Texas Instruments and Hitachi specifies that the two companies will develop a common design and manufacturing process for the chips and do low-volume production together, with mass production and marketing to be done separately by each company. Finally, Motorola and Toshiba have entered into a partnership to manufacture memory (and logic) chips in Japan.

---

[19] Based on "The Costly Race Chipmakers Cannot Afford to Lose," *Business Week,* 10 December 1990, pp. 185–187, and "Two Makers of Microchips Broaden Ties," *Wall Street Journal,* 21 November 1991, p. 84.

Break-Even Analysis and Operating Leverage

Break-Even Analysis
A technique used to examine the relationship among a firm's sales, costs, and operating profits at various levels of output.

Many of the planning activities that take place within a firm are based on anticipated levels of output. The study of the interrelationships among a firm's sales, costs, and operating profit at various output levels is known as *cost-volume-profit analysis,* or **break-even analysis.** The use of assets by a firm having fixed operating costs (e.g., depreciation) results in *operating leverage*—that is, an increase in the possible returns (as well as risks) to the owners of the firm. The measurement and implications of operating leverage will be examined after the discussion of break-even analysis is completed.

The term *break-even analysis* is somewhat misleading, because this type of analysis is typically used to answer many other questions besides those dealing with the break-even output level of a firm. For example, break-even analysis is also used to evaluate the financial profitability of new marketing plans or product lines. In addition, it is a valuable analytical tool for measuring the effects of changes in selling prices, fixed costs, and variable costs on the output level that must be achieved before the firm can realize operating profits.

Break-even analysis is based on the revenue-output and cost-output functions of microeconomic theory. These functions are shown together in Figure 10.7. Total revenue is equal to the number of units of output sold multiplied by the price per unit. Assuming that the firm can sell additional units of output only by lowering the price, the total revenue curve *TR* will be concave (inverted U-shaped), as is indicated in Figure 10.7. The total cost curve *TC* shown is a static short-run cost function analogous to that shown earlier in Figure 9.3. It indicates the relationship between costs and output for a given production process in which one or more of the factors of production (for example, plant and production technology) are fixed. Short-run total costs consist of a fixed-cost component and a variable-cost component.

FIGURE   10.7

Generalized Break-Even Analysis

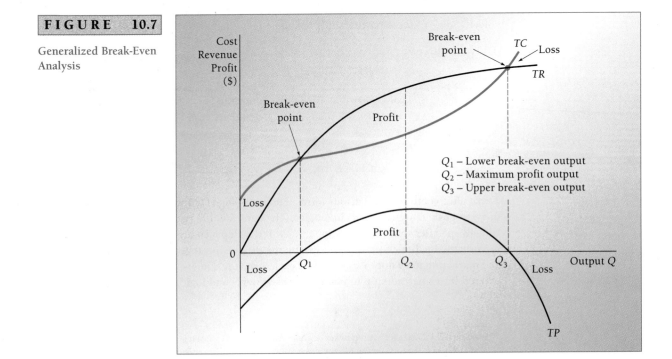

The difference between total revenue and total cost at any level of output represents the total profit that will be obtained.[20] In Figure 10.6, total profit *TP* at any output level is given by the vertical distance between the total revenue *TR* and total cost *TC* curves. A break-even situation (zero profit) occurs whenever total revenue equals total cost. In Figure 10.7, note that a break-even condition occurs at two different output levels—Q_1 and Q_3. Below an output level of Q_1, losses will be incurred because $TR < TC$. Between Q_1 and Q_3, profits will be obtained because $TR > TC$. At output levels above Q_3, losses will occur again because $TR < TC$. Total profits are maximized within the range of Q_1 to Q_3, where the vertical distance between the *TR* and *TC* curves is greatest, that is, at an output level of Q_2.

LINEAR BREAK-EVEN ANALYSIS

In the application of economic break-even analysis to practical decision-making problems, the nonlinear revenue-output and cost-output relationships of economic theory are often replaced by linear functions.[21] A linear break-even analysis can be developed either graphically or algebraically (or as a combination of the two).

Graphic Method

Figure 10.8 shows a basic linear break-even analysis chart. Costs and revenues (measured in dollars) are plotted on the vertical axis and output (measured in units) is plotted on the horizontal axis. The *total revenue* function *TR* represents the total revenue that the firm will realize at each output level, given that the firm charges a constant selling price *P* per unit of output. Similarly, the *total (operating) cost* function *TC* represents the total cost the firm will incur at each output level. Total cost is computed as the sum of the firm's fixed costs *F*, which are independent of the output level, plus the variable costs, which increase at a constant rate of *V* per unit of output. Earnings before interest and taxes, or *EBIT*, is equal to the difference between total revenues (*TR*) and total (*operating*) costs (*TC*). Note that this measure of profits *excludes* financing costs (e.g., interest on debt) as well as taxes.[22]

The assumptions of a constant selling price per unit *P* and a constant variable cost per unit *V* yield *linear* relationships for the total revenue and total cost functions. These linear relationships are valid, however, only over some *relevant range* of output values, such as from Q_1 to Q_2 in Figure 10.8. (The relevant range of output is that range where the linearity assumptions of break-even analysis are assumed to hold.)

The break-even point occurs at point Q_b in Figure 10.8 where the total revenue and the total cost functions intersect. If a firm's output level is below this break-even point—that is, if $TR < TC$—it incurs *operating losses*, defined as a *negative EBIT*. If

---

[20] An additional assumption of break-even analysis is that all the units produced during the period are sold during the period or that all production is in response to firm orders; that is, no inventories exist.

[21] In addition, there is a shift in objectives of the analysis. In economic theory the cost-output and revenue-output relationships are used primarily to determine the profit-maximizing price and output levels. In contrast, the main objective of linear break-even analysis is usually to determine the output level required to either "break even" or earn a "target profit."

[22] See R. Charles Moyer, James R. McGuigan, and William J. Kretlow, *Contemporary Financial Management*, 7th ed. (Cincinnati, OH: South-Western Publishing Company, 1998), chap. 13, for a discussion of how financial leverage (i.e., use of fixed cost sources of financing) can be incorporated into the analysis.

FIGURE   10.8

Linear Break-Even
Analysis Chart

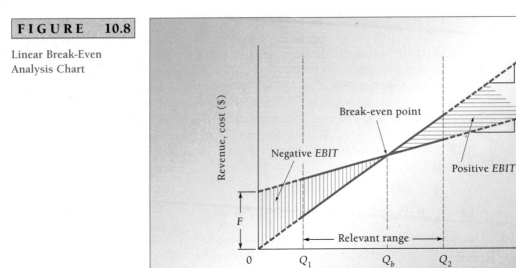

FIGURE   10.8

Linear Break-Even
Analysis Chart

the firm's output level is above this break-even point—that is, if $TR > TC$—it realizes
operating profits, defined as a *positive EBIT.*

Determining a firm's break-even point graphically involves three steps:

1. Drawing a line through the origin with a slope of P to represent the TR function
2. Drawing a line that intersects the vertical axis at F and has a slope of V to
   represent the TC function
3. Determining the point where the TR and TC lines intersect, dropping a
   perpendicular line to the horizontal axis, and noting the resulting value of Q_b

Algebraic Method

To determine a firm's break-even point algebraically, one must set the total revenue and
total (operating) cost functions equal to each other and solve the resulting equation for
the break-even volume.

Total revenue is equal to the selling price per unit times the output quantity:

$$TR = P \times Q \qquad [10.13]$$

Total (operating) cost is equal to fixed plus variable costs, where the variable cost is the
product of the variable cost per unit times the output quantity:

$$TC = F + (V \times Q) \qquad [10.14]$$

Setting the total revenue and total cost expressions equal to each other and substituting
the break-even output Q_b for Q results in

$$TR = TC$$

or

$$PQ_b = F + VQ_b \qquad [10.15]$$

Finally, solving Equation 10.15 for the break-even output Q_b yields

$$PQ_b - VQ_b = F$$

$$(P - V)Q_b = F$$

$$Q_b = \frac{F}{P - V} \qquad [10.16]$$

Break-even analysis also can be performed in terms of dollar *sales* rather than units of output. The break-even dollar sales volume S_b can be determined by the following expression:

$$S_b = \frac{F}{1 - V/P} \qquad [10.17]$$

where V/P is the variable cost ratio (that is, the variable cost per dollar of sales).

The *difference* between the selling price per unit and the variable cost per unit, $P - V$, is referred to as the **contribution margin per unit.** It measures how much each unit of output contributes to meeting fixed costs and operating profits. Thus, the break-even output is equal to the fixed cost divided by the contribution margin per unit.

Occasionally the analyst is interested in determining the output quantity at which a *target profit* (expressed in dollars) is achieved. An expression similar to Equation 10.16 can be used to find such a quantity:

$$\text{Target volume} = \frac{\text{Fixed cost} + \text{Target profit}}{\text{Contribution margin per unit}} \qquad [10.18]$$

Contribution Margin
The difference between price and variable cost per unit in break-even analysis.

EXAMPLE

BREAK-EVEN ANALYSIS: ALLEGAN MANUFACTURING COMPANY

Assume that Allegan manufactures one product, which it sells for $250 per unit ($P$). Variable costs ($V$) are $150 per unit. The firm's fixed costs (F) are $1,000,000. Substituting these figures into Equation 10.16 yields the following break-even output:

$$Q_b = \frac{\$1,000,000}{\$250 - \$150}$$

$$= 10,000 \text{ units}$$

Allegan's break-even output can also be determined graphically, as shown in Figure 10.9.

Another illustration would be to use break-even analysis to approve or reject a batch sale promotion. Suppose in the previous example, the $1,000,000 is a trade rebate to elicit better shelf location for Allegan's product. If the estimated effect of this promotion is additional sales of 9,000 units, less than the break-even output, the change in total contributions will fall below the $1 million promotion cost—i.e., ($250 − $150) × 9,000 < $1,000,000. Therefore, the promotion plan should be rejected.

Because a firm's break-even output is dependent on a number of variables—in particular, the price per unit, variable (operating) costs per unit, and fixed costs—the firm may wish to analyze the effects of changes in any one (or more) of the variables on the break-even output. For example, it may wish to consider either of the following:

1. Changing the selling price
2. Substituting fixed costs for variable costs

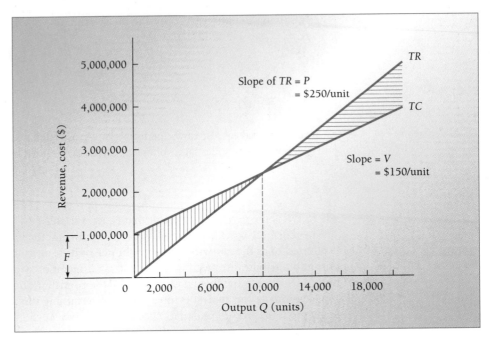

Assume that Allegan increased the selling price per unit P' by $25 to $275. Substituting this figure into Equation 10.16 gives a new break-even output.

$$Q_b' = \frac{\$1,000,000}{\$275 - \$150}$$

$$= 8,000 \text{ units}$$

This can also be seen in Figure 10.10, in which an increase in the price per unit increases the slope of the total revenue function TR' and reduces the break-even output.

Rather than increasing the selling price per unit, Allegan's management may decide to substitute fixed costs for variable costs in some aspect of the company's operations. For example, as labor wage rates increase over time, many firms seek to reduce operating costs through automation, which in effect represents the substitution of fixed-cost capital equipment for variable-cost labor. Suppose that Allegan determines that it can reduce labor costs by $25 per unit by leasing $100,000 of additional equipment. Under these conditions, the firm's new level of fixed costs F' would be $1,000,000 + $100,000 = $1,100,000. Variable costs per unit V' would be $150 − $25 = $125. Substituting $P = $250 per unit, $V' = $125 per unit, and $F' = $1,100,000 into Equation 10.16 yields a new break-even output:

$$Q_b' = \frac{\$1,100,000}{\$250 - \$125}$$

$$= 8,800 \text{ units}$$

As we can see in Figure 10.11, the effect of this change in operations is to raise the intercept on the vertical axis, decrease the slope of the total (operating) cost function TC', and reduce the break-even output.

FIGURE 10.10

Linear Break-Even Analysis Chart for the Allegan Manufacturing Company Showing the Effects of a Price Increase

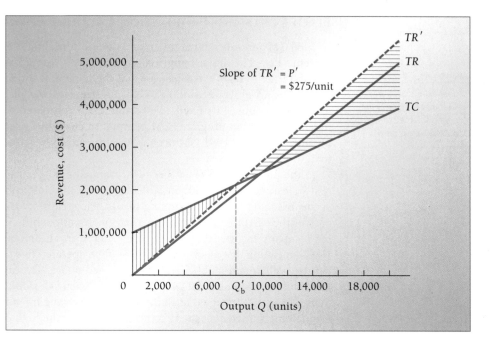

FIGURE 10.11

Linear Break-Even Analysis Chart for the Allegan Manufacturing Company Showing the Effects of Substituting Fixed Costs for Variable Costs

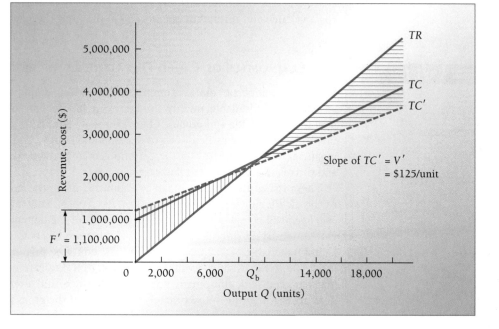

FIXED COSTS AND PRODUCTION CAPACITY AT GENERAL MOTORS[23]

In 1988 GM announced that it would reduce automobile production capacity to match current sales. The downsizing was to take place over a 5-year period. It represented the first time in its 80-year history that the company had significantly shrunk its capacity. As part of its decision to reduce its size, GM was planning to cut $12.5 billion to $13 billion out of its fixed-cost base in 1990 compared with 1986 levels. As part of this cost-reduction program, GM planned to close five of its U.S. automobile assembly lines. (*Note:* In 1991 GM decided to close additional assembly plants, bringing the total to 10.)

In the past GM alternated between producing all the cars it could and then using costly clearance sales to attract buyers (e.g., $3.3 billion in buyers' incentives in 1988) versus reducing output by running plants below capacity through a slow-down in the pace of the assembly line or elimination of an entire shift. The new strategy called for the company to use 100 percent of its American automobile production capacity by 1992—meaning that all of its plants would be operated five days a week with two shifts per day. When automobile demand increased above this capacity level, overtime and third-shift operations and new production efficiencies would be used to boost production. This is the strategy that Ford had been following for some time. Ford, rather than maintaining sufficient capacity to meet demand at the high end of the cycle and laying off workers when demand was low, geared its capacity to the low end of the cycle and strained to meet demand when sales were high.

In effect, GM and Ford were trading off lower fixed costs over the entire business cycle versus (the possibility of) having to incur higher variable costs (e.g., use of higher cost overtime and third-shift operations) at the high end of the business cycle.

THE ECONOMICS OF CHILD DAY CARE CENTERS[24]

With large numbers of mothers employed (or seeking employment) in the economy, the availability of affordable, quality child day care has become an issue of concern to many people—both inside and outside of government. The issues of affordability and quality involve economic considerations of demand and supply, and they can be examined using linear break-even analysis. Key questions involve the perceived high price of day care and the relatively low pay of day care workers.

These issues and questions can be examined using the three components of the linear break-even model, namely, revenues, fixed costs, and variable costs. The gross *revenue* received by a day care center is a function of the demand for such services. Faced with a negatively sloping demand curve, there are limits to the price it can charge. At an annual charge of $10,000, most families would be priced out of the market for day care. The *fixed costs,* or overhead expenses, of a day care center include the costs of management, rent, equipment, supplies, insurance, and a return on investment. Overhead costs constitute approximately 50 percent of the gross revenues in a well-run day care center. Most of these expenses are determined by government laws and regulations, so reducing these costs significantly is difficult. The *variable costs* consist primarily of the wages paid to day care workers. For example, given annual revenues of

---

[23] Jacob M. Schlesinger, "GM to Reduce Capacity to Match Its Sales," *Wall Street Journal,* 25 April 1988, p. 2, and Lawrence Ingrassia and Joseph B. White, "GM Plans to Close 21 More Factories, Cut 74,000 Jobs, Slash Capital Spending," *Wall Street Journal,* 19 December 1991, p. A3.

[24] Victor R. Fochs, "Economics Applies to Child Care Too," *Wall Street Journal,* 2 April 1990, p. A12.

$5,000 per child, a ratio of five children per worker, and profit plus overhead of 50 percent of revenue, the remaining revenue to pay for a full-time worker is $12,500 [i.e., (100% − 50%) × 5 children/worker × $5,000/child]. Typically, day care workers earn about 40 percent less per hour than female kindergarten or elementary school teachers with similar levels of education. Furthermore, although the wages of teachers rise appreciably with each additional year of education, child care workers with college degrees earn only slightly more than those with high-school diplomas.

Analyzing day care operations with the break-even model allows one to focus on the trade-offs among the various decision variables—such as the fees (or costs) to parents, the child-to-worker ratio, and the pay and qualifications of child care workers.

Break-Even Analysis and Risk Assessment

The information generated from a break-even analysis can be used to assess the operating risk to which a firm is exposed. If one adds to this set of information the *expected* (mean) level of sales (in units) for some future period of time, the standard deviation of the distribution of sales, and the assumption that actual sales are normally distributed, one can compute the probability that the firm will have operating losses (that is, it will sell fewer units than the break-even level) and the probability that the firm will have operating profits (that is, it will sell more units than the break-even level).

The probability of having operating losses (that is, the probability of selling fewer than Q_b units) can be computed using the following equation:[25]

$$z = \frac{Q_b - \overline{Q}}{\sigma_Q} \tag{10.19}$$

and the probability values from Table 1 (Appendix B at the back of the book), where $\overline{Q}$ is the expected unit sales, σ_Q is the standard deviation of unit sales, and Q_b is (as defined earlier) the break-even unit sales. The probability of operating profits (that is, the probability of selling more than Q_b units) is equal to one minus the probability of operating losses.

EXAMPLE

RISK ASSESSMENT: ALLEGAN MANUFACTURING COMPANY (CONTINUED)

For the Allegan Manufacturing Company discussed earlier, suppose that expected sales are 15,000 units with a standard deviation of 4,000 units. Recall that the break-even volume was 10,000 units. Substituting $Q_b = 10,000$, $\overline{Q} = 15,000$, and $\sigma_Q = 4,000$ into Equation 10.19 yields

$$z = \frac{10,000 - 15,000}{4,000}$$

$$= -1.25$$

In other words, the break-even sales level of 10,000 units is 1.25 standard deviations *below* the mean. From Table 1, the probability associated with −1.25 standard deviations is .1056 or 10.56 percent. Thus, there is a 10.56 percent chance that Allegan will incur

---

[25] This equation is equivalent to Equation 2.5 discussed in Chapter 2, where Q is the variable of interest rather than r.

operating losses and an 89.44 percent chance (100 percent minus the 10.56 percent chance of losses) that the firm will record operating profits (that is, it will sell more than the break-even number of units of output).

Some Limitations of Break-Even Analysis

Break-even analysis has a number of limitations that arise from the *assumptions* made in constructing the model and developing the relevant data. The application of break-even analysis is of value only to the extent that these assumptions are valid.

Constant Selling Price and Variable Cost per Unit   In the break-even analysis model the assumptions of a constant selling price and variable cost per unit yield *linear* relationships for the total revenue and total cost functions. In practice these functions tend to be nonlinear for the reasons discussed earlier. The assumption of a constant selling price and variable cost per unit is probably valid over some relevant range of output levels; however, consideration of output levels outside this range will normally require modifications in the break-even chart.

Composition of Operating Costs   Another assumption of break-even analysis is that costs can be classified as either fixed or variable. In fact, some costs are partly fixed and partly variable (e.g., utility bills). Furthermore, some fixed costs increase in a stepwise manner as output is increased—they are *semivariable*—and are constant only over relatively narrow ranges of output. For example, machinery maintenance is scheduled after 10 hours or 10 days or 10 weeks of use. These direct fixed costs must be considered variable if a batch production decision entails this much use.

Multiple Products   The break-even model also assumes that a firm is producing and selling either a *single* product or a *constant mix* of different products. In many cases the product mix changes over time, and problems can arise in allocating fixed costs among the various products.

Uncertainty   Still another assumption of break-even analysis is that the selling price and variable cost per unit, as well as fixed costs, are known at each level of output. In practice these parameters are subject to uncertainty. Thus the usefulness of the results of break-even analysis depends on the accuracy of the estimates of these parameters.

Inconsistency of Planning Horizon   Finally, break-even analysis is normally performed for a planning period of one year or less; however, the benefits received from some costs may not be realized until subsequent periods. For example, research and development costs incurred during a specific period may not result in new products for several years. For break-even analysis to be a dependable decision-making tool, a firm's operating costs must be matched with resulting revenues for the planning period under consideration.

Operating Leverage
The use of assets having fixed costs (e.g., depreciation) in an effort to increase expected returns.

Degree of Operating Leverage (DOL)
The percentage change in a firm's earnings before interest and taxes (EBIT) resulting from a 1 percent change in sales or output.

OPERATING LEVERAGE

Operating leverage involves the use of assets having fixed costs. A firm uses operating leverage in the hope of earning returns in excess of the fixed costs of the assets, thereby increasing the returns to the owners of the firm. A firm's **degree of operating leverage** (DOL) is defined as the multiplier effect resulting from the firm's use of fixed operating costs. More specifically, DOL can be computed as the *percentage change* in earnings before interest and taxes (EBIT) resulting from a given *percentage change* in sales (output):

$$\text{DOL at } X = \frac{\text{Percentage change in EBIT}}{\text{Percentage change in Sales}}$$

This can be rewritten as follows:

$$\text{DOL at } X = \frac{\dfrac{\Delta \text{EBIT}}{\text{EBIT}}}{\dfrac{\Delta \text{Sales}}{\text{Sales}}} \qquad [10.20]$$

where ΔEBIT and ΔSales are the changes in the firm's EBIT and Sales, respectively. Because a firm's DOL differs at each sales level, it is necessary to indicate the sales point, X, at which operating leverage is measured. The degree of operating leverage is analogous to the elasticity of demand concept (for example, price and income elasticities) because it relates percentage changes in one variable (EBIT) to percentage changes in another variable (sales). Equation 10.20 requires the use of two different values of sales and EBIT. Another equation (derived from Equation 10.20) that can be used to compute a firm's DOL more easily is

$$\text{DOL at } X = \frac{\text{Sales} - \text{Variable costs}}{\text{EBIT}} \qquad [10.21]$$

The variables defined in the previous section on break-even analysis can also be used to develop a formula for determining a firm's DOL at any given output level. Because sales are equivalent to TR (or $P \times Q$), variable cost is equal to $V \times Q$, and EBIT is equal to total revenue (TR) less total (operating) cost, or $(P \times Q) - F - (V \times Q)$, these values can be substituted into Equation 10.21 to obtain the following:

$$\text{DOL at } Q = \frac{(P \times Q) - (V \times Q)}{(P \times Q) - F - (V \times Q)}$$

or

$$\text{DOL at } Q = \frac{(P - V)Q}{(P - V)Q - F} \qquad [10.22]$$

EXAMPLE

OPERATING LEVERAGE: ALLEGAN MANUFACTURING COMPANY (CONTINUED)

In the earlier discussion of break-even analysis for the Allegan Manufacturing Company, the parameters of the break-even model were determined as $P = \$250$/unit, $V = \$150$/unit, and $F = \$1,000,000$. Substituting these values into Equation 10.22 along with the respective output (Q) values yields the DOL values shown in Table 10.2. For example, a DOL of 6.00 at an output level of 12,000 units indicates that, from a base output level of 12,000 units, EBIT will increase by 6.00 percent for each 1 percent increase in output.

Note that Allegan's DOL is largest (in absolute value terms) when the firm is operating near the break-even point (that is, where $Q = Q_b = 10,000$ units). Note also that the firm's DOL is negative below the break-even output level. A negative DOL indicates the

Output Q	Degree of Operating Leverage DOL
0	0
2,000	−0.25
4,000	−0.67
6,000	−1.50
8,000	−4.00
10,000	(undefined) Break-even level
12,000	+6.00
14,000	+3.50
16,000	+2.67
18,000	+2.25
20,000	+2.00

percentage *reduction* in operating *losses* that occurs as the result of a 1 percent *increase* in output. For example, the DOL of −1.50 at an output level of 6,000 units indicates that, from a base output level of 6,000 units, the firm's operating *losses* will be *reduced* by 1.5 percent for each 1 percent *increase* in output.

A firm's DOL is a function of the nature of the production process. If the firm employs large amounts of equipment in its operations, it tends to have relatively high fixed operating costs and relatively low variable operating costs. Such a cost structure yields a high DOL, which results in large operating profits (positive EBIT) if sales are high and large operating losses (negative EBIT) if sales are depressed.

Business Risk

Business Risk

The inherent variability or uncertainty of a firm's operating earnings (earnings before interest and taxes).

Business risk refers to the inherent variability or uncertainty of a firm's EBIT. It is a function of several factors, one of which is the firm's DOL. The DOL is a measure of how sensitive a firm's EBIT is to changes in sales. The greater a firm's DOL, the larger the change in EBIT will be for a given change in sales. Thus, *all other things being equal,* the higher a firm's DOL, the greater the degree of business risk.

Other factors can also affect a firm's business risk, including the variability or uncertainty of sales. A firm with high fixed costs and very stable sales will have a high DOL, but it will also have stable EBIT and, therefore, low business risk. Public utilities and pipeline transportation companies are examples of firms having these operating characteristics.

Another factor that may affect a firm's business risk is uncertainty concerning selling prices and variable costs. A firm having a low DOL can still have high business risk if selling prices and variable costs are subject to considerable variability over time. A cattle feedlot illustrates these characteristics of low DOL but high business risk; both grain costs and the selling price of beef at times fluctuate wildly.

In summary, a firm's DOL is only one of several factors that determine the firm's business risk.

SUMMARY

- In estimating the behavior of short-run and long-run cost functions for firms, the primary methodological problems are (1) differences in the manner in which economists and accountants define and measure costs, and (2) accounting for other variables (in addition to the output level) that influence costs.

- Many statistical studies of *short-run* cost-output relationships suggest that total costs increase linearly with output, implying constant marginal costs over the observed ranges of output. Although the evidence is not conclusive, it tends to refute the existence of U-shaped average and marginal cost functions as postulated in economic theory.

- Many statistical studies of *long-run* cost-output relationships indicate that long-run cost functions are L-shaped. Economies of scale (declining average costs) occur at low levels of output. Thereafter, long-run average costs remain relatively constant over large ranges of output. Diseconomies of scale are observed in only a minority of the studies.

- *Engineering cost techniques* are an alternative approach to statistical methods in estimating long-run cost functions. With this approach, knowledge of production facilities and technology is used to determine the most efficient (lowest cost) combination of labor, capital equipment, and raw materials required to produce various levels of output.

- The *survivor technique* is a method of determining the optimum size of firms within an industry by classifying them by size and then calculating the share of industry output coming from each size class over time. Size classes whose share of industry output is increasing over time are considered to be more efficient and to have lower average costs.

- *Break-even analysis* is used to examine the relationship among a firm's revenues, costs, and operating profits (EBIT) at various output levels. Frequently the analyst constructs a break-even chart based on linear cost-output and revenue-output relationships to determine the operating characteristics of a firm over a limited output range.

- The *break-even point* is defined as the output level at which total revenues equal total (operating) costs. In the linear break-even model, the break-even point is found by dividing fixed (operating) costs by the difference between price and variable cost per unit.

- *Operating leverage* occurs when a firm uses assets having fixed operating costs. The *degree of operating leverage* (DOL) measures the percentage change in a firm's EBIT resulting from a 1 percent change in sales (or units of output). As a firm's fixed operating costs rise, its DOL increases.

- *Business risk* refers to the variability of a firm's EBIT. It is a function of several factors, including the firm's DOL and the variability of sales. All other things being equal, the higher a firm's DOL, the greater its business risk.

EXERCISES

1. Suppose one estimates, from cost-output data using multiple regression techniques, the following total cost function:

$$TC = \$140,000 + \$250Q + \$1.50Q^2$$

Explain why one cannot necessarily infer that fixed costs are equal to $140,000.

2. A study of 86 savings and loan associations in six northwestern states for 1975 yielded the following cost function:[26]

$$C = 2.38 - .006153Q + .000005359Q^2 + 19.2X_1$$
$$\quad\ (2.84)\quad\ (2.37)\qquad\quad (2.63)\qquad\quad (2.69)$$

where C = average operating expense ratio, expressed as a percentage and defined as total operating expense ($ million) divided by total assets ($ million) times 100 percent

Q = output, measured by total assets ($ million)

X_1 = ratio of the number of branches to total assets ($ million)

Note: The number in parentheses below each coefficient is its respective t-statistic.

a. Which variable(s) is(are) statistically significant in explaining variations in the average operating expense ratio?

b. What type of cost-output relationship (e.g., linear, quadratic, cubic) is suggested by these statistical results?

c. Based on these results, what can we conclude about the existence of economies or diseconomies of scale in savings and loan associations in the Northwest?

3. Referring to Exercise 2 again:

a. Holding constant the effects of branching (X_1), determine the level of total assets that minimizes the average operating expense ratio.

b. Determine the average operating expense ratio for a savings and loan association with the level of total assets determined in part (a) and

(i) 1 branch

(ii) 10 branches

4. A study of the costs of electricity generation for a sample of 56 British firms in 1946–47 yielded the following long-run cost function.[27]

$$AVC = 1.24 + .0033Q + .0000029Q^2 - .000046QZ - .026Z + .00018Z^2$$

where AVC = average variable cost (that is, working costs of generation), measured in pence per kilowatt-hour. (A pence was a British monetary unit, being equal to (at that time) two U.S. cents.)

Q = output, measured in millions of kilowatt-hours per year

Z = plant size, measured in thousands of kilowatts

a. Determine the long-run variable cost function for electricity generation.

b. Determine the long-run marginal cost function for electricity generation.

c. Holding plant size constant at 150,000 kilowatts, determine the short-run average variable cost and marginal cost functions for electricity generation.

d. For a plant size equal to 150,000 kilowatts, determine the output level that minimizes short-run average variable costs.

e. Determine the short-run average variable cost and marginal cost at the output level obtained in part (d).

[26]J. Holton Wilson, "A Note on Scale Economies in the Savings and Loan Industry," *Business Economics* (January 1981), p. 45–49.

[27]Johnston, *Statistical Cost Analysis,* chap. 4.

5. Assuming that all other factors remain unchanged, determine how a firm's break-even point is affected by each of the following:

   a. The firm finds it necessary to reduce the price per unit because of increased foreign competition.

   b. The firm's direct labor costs are increased as the result of a new labor contract.

   c. The Occupational Safety and Health Administration (OSHA) requires the firm to install new ventilating equipment in its plant. (Assume that this action has no effect on worker productivity.)

   Refer to the following data when working Exercises 6–9 below.
   East Publishing Company is doing an analysis of a proposed new finance text. The following data have been obtained:

Fixed costs (per edition):	
Development (reviews, class testing, etc.)	$15,000
Copy editing	4,000
Selling and promotion	7,500
Typesetting	23,500
Total	$50,000
Variable costs (per copy):	
Printing and binding	$ 6.65
Administrative costs	1.50
Salespeople's commission (2% of selling price)	.55
Author's royalties (12% of selling price)	3.30
Bookstore discounts (20% of selling price)	5.50
Total	$ 17.50
Projected selling price	$ 27.50

6. Using the data presented above:

   a. Determine the company's break-even volume for this book in
      (i) Units
      (ii) Dollar sales

   b. Develop a break-even chart for the text.

   c. Determine the number of copies East must sell to earn an (operating) profit of $30,000 on this text.

   d. Determine total (operating) profits at sales levels of
      (i) 3,000 units
      (ii) 5,000 units
      (iii) 10,000 units

7. Determine the degree of operating leverage (DOL) and give an economic interpretation of the value at the following sales levels:

   a. 3,000 units

   b. 7,000 units

8. Suppose expected sales (per edition) are 10,000 units with a standard deviation of 2,000 units:

   a. Determine the probability that East will incur operating losses on the finance text.

   b. Determine the probability that East will have operating profits on the proposed text.

9. Suppose East feels that $27.50 is too high a price to charge for the new finance text. It has examined the competitive market and determined that $25 would be a better selling price. What would the break-even volume be at this new selling price?

10. Cool-Aire Corporation manufactures a line of room air conditioners. Its break-even sales level is 33,000 units. Sales are approximately normally distributed. Expected sales next year are 40,000 units with a standard deviation of 4,000 units.
    a. Determine the probability that Cool-Aire will incur an operating loss.
    b. Determine the probability that Cool-Aire will operate above its break-even point.

11. McKee Corporation has annual fixed costs of $12 million. Its variable cost ratio is .60.
    a. Determine the company's break-even dollar sales volume.
    b. Determine the dollar sales volume required to earn a target profit of $3 million.

12. Smithton Company's sales in 19X1 were $5 million. Its fixed costs were $1.5 million and its variable cost ratio was .60.
    a. Determine the company's DOL.
    b. Based on your answer to part (a), forecast the percentage change in Smithton's EBIT for 19X2 assuming that fixed costs and the variable cost ratio remain the same and that sales increase by 3 percent.

www exercise

The Structure of Airline Costs

13. Airline deregulation in the U.S. has resulted in a change in airline cost structure. Access the following Internet site to learn how: http://nutcweb.tpc.nwu.edu/RESEARCH/ regulatory/ regulatory1.html. The Air Transport Association of America has produced an on-line Airline Handbook that provides information on airline economics and the structure of airline costs. Access this Internet site at http://www.air-transport.org/ handbk/chaptr04.htm. Summarize the major components of airline costs.

COST FUNCTIONS

CASE EXERCISE

The following cost-output data were obtained as part of a study of the economies of scale in operating a public high school in Wisconsin:[28]

Pupils in Average Daily Attendance (A)	Midpoint of Values in Column A (B)	Operating Expenditure Per Pupil (C)	Number of Schools in Sample (D)
143–200	171	$531.9	6
201–300	250	480.8	12
301–400	350	446.3	19
401–500	450	426.9	17
501–600	550	442.6	14
601–700	650	413.1	13
701–900	800	374.3	9
901–1,100	1,000	433.2	6
1,101–1,600	1,350	407.3	6
1,601–2,400	2,000	405.6	7

[28] John Riew, "Economics of Scale in High School Operation," *Review of Economics and Statistics* 48, no. 3 (August 1966), pp. 280–287.

QUESTIONS

1. Plot the data in columns B and C in an output (enrollment)-cost graph and sketch a smooth curve that would appear to give a good fit to the data.

2. Based on the scatter diagram in Question 1, what kind of mathematical relationship would appear to exist between enrollment and operating expenditures per pupil? In other words, do operating expenditures per pupil appear to (i) be constant (and independent of enrollment), (ii) follow a linear relationship as enrollment increases, or (iii) follow some sort of nonlinear U-shape (possibly quadratic) relationship as enrollment increases?

As part of this study, the following cost function was developed:

$$C = f(Q, X_1, X_2, X_3, X_4, X_5)$$

where C = operating expenditures per pupil in average daily attendance (measured in dollars)

Q = enrollment (number of pupils in average daily attendance)

X_1 = average teacher's salary

X_2 = number of credit units ("courses") offered

X_3 = average number of courses taught per teacher

X_4 = change in enrollment between 1957 and 1960

X_5 = percentage of classrooms built after 1950

Variables X_1, X_2, and X_3 were measures of "educational quality," that is, teacher qualifications, breadth of curriculum, and the degree of specialization in instruction, respectively. Variable X_4 measured changes in demand for school services that could cause some lagging adjustments in cost. Variable X_5 was used to reflect any differentials in the costs of maintenance and operation due to the varying ages of school properties. Statistical data on 109 selected high schools yielded the following regression equation:

$$C = 10.31 - .402Q + .00012Q^2 + .107X_1 + .985X_2 - 15.62X_3$$
$$ (.063)^* \quad (.000023)^* \quad (.013)^* \quad (.640) \quad (11.95)$$

$$+ .613X_4 - .102X_5$$
$$(.189)^* \quad (.109)$$

$$r^2 = .557^*$$

Notes:

(1) The numbers in parentheses are the standard deviations of each of the respective coefficients (b's).

(2) An asterisk (*) indicates that the result is statistically significant at the .01 level.

3. What type of cost-output relationship (linear, quadratic, cubic) is suggested by these statistical results?

4. What variables (other than enrollment) would appear to be most important in explaining variations in operating expenditures per pupil?

5. Holding constant the effects of the other variables (X_1 through X_5), determine the enrollment level (Q) at which average operating expenditures per pupil are minimized. (*Hint:* Find the value of Q that minimizes the $\partial C/\partial Q$ function.)

6. Again, holding constant the effects of the other variables, use the $\partial C/\partial Q$ function to determine, for a school with 500 pupils, the reduction in per-pupil operating expenditures that will occur as the result of adding one more pupil.

7.   Again, holding the other variables constant, what would be the saving in per-pupil operating expenditures of an increase in enrollment from 500 to 1,000 students?

8.   Based on the results of this study, what can we conclude about the existence of economies or diseconomies in operating a public high school?

The Learning Curve

In manufacturing multiple units of a product, the quantity of resources (inputs) required to complete each successive unit of output is often observed to decrease as the *cumulative* volume of output increases. This reduction in inputs, and hence associated costs, is known as the **learning curve effect.**[29] This learning phenomenon is most commonly observed in the behavior of labor inputs and costs. The number of work-hours necessary to obtain one unit of output may decline for a variety of reasons as more units of the product are produced. These factors include increased familiarization with the tasks by workers and supervisors, improvements in work methods and the flow of work, reductions in the amount of scrap and rework, and the need for fewer skilled workers as the tasks become more repetitive. Raw material costs per unit may also be subject to the learning curve effect if less scrap and waste occur as workers become more familiar with the production process. Not all inputs and associated costs are subject to the learning process however. For example, transportation costs per unit normally do not decline for successive units of output.

The learning curve principle was first applied in airplane manufacturing during the 1930s. Since then the technique has been applied in many other assembly-type production processes, including shipbuilding and appliance manufacturing. Forecasts of personnel, equipment, and raw material requirements and their associated costs based on the learning curve have been used in scheduling production, determining prices for products sold, and evaluating suppliers' price quotations.

LEARNING CURVE RELATIONSHIP

The learning curve relationship is usually expressed as a constant percentage. This percentage represents the proportion by which the amount of an input (or cost) per unit of output is reduced each time production is doubled. For example, consider a production process in which labor input and costs follow an 80 percent learning curve. Assume that the *first* unit requires labor costs of $1,000 to produce. Based on the learning curve relationship, the *second* unit costs $1,000 \times .80 = $800, the *fourth* unit costs $800 \times .80 = $640, the *eighth* unit costs $640 \times .80 = $512, the *sixteenth* unit costs $512 \times .80 = $409.60, and so on.

This learning curve relationship is shown in Figures 10A.1 and 10A.2. When plotted on an *arithmetic scale,* as shown in Figure 10A.1, the cost-output relationship is a curvilinear function. When plotted on a *logarithmic scale,* as shown in Figure 10A.2, the cost-output relationship is a linear function.

The learning curve relationship can be expressed algebraically as follows:

$$C = aQ^b \qquad [10A.1]$$

---

[29] Other names given to this relationship include learning-by-doing, progress curve, experience curve, and improvement curve.

Learning Curve:
Arithmetic Scale

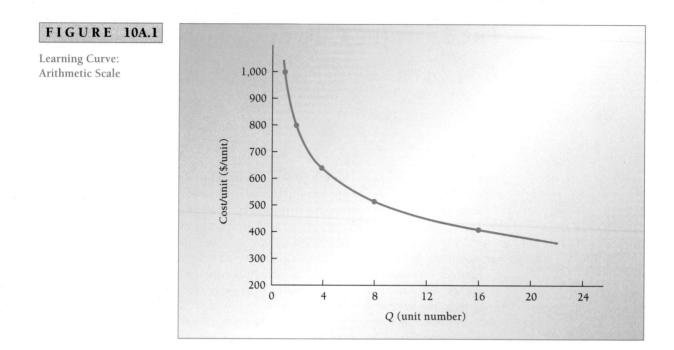

Learning Curve:
Logarithmic Scale

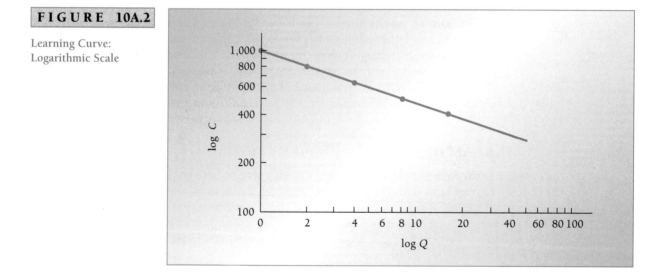

where C is the input cost of the Qth unit of output, Q is consecutive units of output produced, a is the theoretical (or actual) input cost of the first unit of output, and b is the rate of reduction in input cost per unit of output. Because the learning curve is downward sloping, the value of b is normally negative. It should be noted that b is *not* the same as the learning curve percentage. Taking logarithms of both sides of Equation 10A.1 yields

$$\log C = \log a + b \log Q \qquad [10\text{A}.2]$$

When the learning curve is expressed in logarithmic form, b represents the slope of the function.

ESTIMATING THE LEARNING CURVE PARAMETERS

Application of the learning curve in forecasting costs requires that one first determine the values of the log a and b parameters in Equation 10A.2. In the absence of any historical cost-output data for the production process, one would have to make subjective estimates of these parameters based on prior experience with similar types of production operations. For a production process that has been operating for a period of time and for which historical cost-output data are available, however, statistical methods can be used to estimate the parameters. [30] One such method is the *least-squares* technique of regression analysis. [30] In the learning curve equation (Equation 10A.2), log C is the dependent variable and log Q is the independent variable. Applying the least-squares procedure to the series of cost-output observations yields the following equations for estimating the learning curve parameters:

$$b = \frac{n\Sigma(\log Q_i \log C_i) - (\Sigma\log Q_i)(\Sigma\log C_i)}{n\Sigma(\log Q_i)^2 - (\Sigma\log Q_i)^2} \qquad [10A.3]$$

$$\log a = \frac{\Sigma\log C_i - b\Sigma\log Q_i}{n} \qquad [10A.4]$$

where n is the number of observations.

EXAMPLE

LEARNING CURVES: EMERSON CORPORATION

The Emerson Corporation, a manufacturer of airplane landing gear equipment, is trying to develop a learning curve model to help forecast labor costs for successive units of one of its products. From past data, the firm knows that labor costs of the 25th, 75th, and 125th units were $800, $600, and $500, respectively. Develop the learning curve equation from this data and use the resulting model to predict labor costs for the 200th unit of output. The preliminary calculations needed to determine log a and b are shown in Table 10A.1. Substituting the column totals from the last row of Table 10A.1 into Equations 10A.3 and 10A.4 provides the following estimates of the learning curve parameters:

$$b = \frac{3(14.92704) - (5.36991)(8.38021)}{3(9.86711) - (5.36991)^2}$$

$$= -.28724$$

$$\log a = \frac{8.38021 - (-.28724)(5.36991)}{3}$$

$$= 3.30755$$

---

[30] The *least-squares* technique is described in Chapter 5 of this text and in the regression chapter of any basic statistics book.

TABLE   10A.1

Learning Curve:
Preliminary Calculations

Observation i	Q_i (Unit No.)	C_i (Dollars)	Log Q_i	Log C_i	(Log Q_i)^2	(Log C_i)^2	(Log Q_i) $\times$(Log C_i)
1	25	800	1.39794	2.90309	1.95423	8.42793	4.05834
2	75	600	1.87506	2.77815	3.51585	7.71811	5.20920
3(=n)	125	500	2.09691	2.69897	4.39703	7.28444	5.65950
Sum			5.36991	8.38021	9.86711	23.43048	14.92704

The learning curve equation for labor costs is

$$\log C = 3.30755 - .28724 \log Q \qquad [10A.5]$$

Using this model, the estimated cost of the 200th unit of output is obtained as follows:

$$\log C = 3.30755 - .28724 \log 200$$

$$= 3.30755 - .28724(2.30103)$$

$$= 2.64660$$

$$C = \$443.20$$

THE PERCENTAGE OF LEARNING

The percentage of learning, which is defined as the proportion by which an input (or its associated cost) is reduced when output is doubled, can be estimated as follows:

$$L = \frac{C_2}{C_1} \times 100\% \qquad [10A.6]$$

where C_1 is the input (or cost) for the Q_1 unit of output and C_2 is the cost for the $Q_2 = 2Q_1$ unit of output.

EXAMPLE

PERCENTAGE OF LEARNING: EMERSON CORPORATION (CONTINUED)

To illustrate the calculation of the percentage of learning, consider the Emerson Corporation example again. Using the learning curve model developed earlier (Equation 10A.5), labor costs for the $Q_1 = 50$th unit of output are $C_1 = \$659.98$ and labor costs for the $2Q_1 = 100$th unit of output are $C_2 = \$540.84$. Substituting these values into Equation 10A.6 yields

$$L = \frac{\$540.84}{\$659.98} \times 100\%$$

$$= 81.9\%$$

The percentage of learning for labor costs in the production of these landing gear units is thus approximately 82 percent—indicating that labor costs decline by about 18 percent each time output is doubled.

EXERCISE

1. Ajax Controls Company uses a learning curve to estimate labor costs for its products. The firm recently introduced a new line of process control devices and has collected the following cost data:

Unit No.	Labor Cost
100	$1,250
300	1,000
600	850

a. Determine the learning curve for the labor costs required to produce this product.
b. What is the percentage of learning for labor costs?
c. Estimate the labor costs of the 800th unit based on the learning curve developed in part (a).

Linear-Programming Applications

CHAPTER PREVIEW

Most business resource-allocation problems require the decision maker to take into account various types of constraints, such as capital, labor, legal, and behavioral restrictions. Linear-programming techniques can be used to provide relatively simple and realistic solutions to problems involving constrained resource-allocation decisions. A wide variety of production, finance, marketing, and distribution problems have been formulated in the linear-programming framework.[1] Consequently, managers should understand the linear-programming model so they may allocate the resources of the enterprise most efficiently, particularly in situations where important constraints are placed on the actions that may be taken. The chapter begins by developing the formulation and graphical solution to a profit-maximization production problem. The following section discusses the concept of dual variables and their interpretations. A computer solution to a cost-minimization problem is presented next. Finally, the formulation and solution of two problems from finance and distribution are presented.

---

[1] For an extensive bibliography of linear-programming applications, see David Anderson, Dennis Sweeney, and Thomas Williams, *Quantitative Methods for Business,* 6th ed. (St. Paul, Minn.: West Publishing Company, 1995).

MILITARY AIRLIFT COMMAND[2]

The United States Air Force's Military Command (MAC) uses approximately 1,000 planes (of varying capacity, speed, and range) to ferry cargo and passengers among more than 300 airports scattered around the world. Resource constraints, such as the availability of planes, pilots, and other flight personnel, place limitations or constraints on the capacity of the airlift system. Additionally, MAC must determine whether it is more efficient to reduce cargo and top off the fuel tanks at the start of each flight or to refuel at stops along the way and pay for the costs of shipping fuel. The airlift system also requires that cargo handlers and ground crews be available to service the aircraft. Furthermore, schedulers must be able to deal with disruptions caused by bad weather and emergency changes in shipping priorities. Adding just a couple of percentage points to the efficiency of the airlift system can save the Air Force millions of dollars annually in equipment, labor, and fuel costs. Major commercial airlines, such as American and United, face similar scheduling problems. Complex resource-allocation problems such as these can be solved using linear-programming techniques.

---

[2] Based on articles in *Business Week,* 21 September 1987, pp. 69–76, and 13 March 1989, p. 77.

A PROFIT-MAXIMIZATION PROBLEM

This section discusses the formulation of linear-programming problems and presents a graphical solution to a simple profit-maximization problem.

Statement of the Problem

A multiproduct firm often has the problem of determining the optimal *product mix,* that is, the combination of outputs that will maximize its profits. The firm is normally subject to various constraints on the amount of resources, such as raw materials, labor, and production capacity, that may be employed in the production process.

EXAMPLE

PROFIT MAXIMIZATION: WHITE COMPANY

Consider the White Company, a manufacturer of gas (Product 1) and electric (Product 2) clothes dryers. The problem is to determine the optimal level of output (X_1 and X_2) for two products (1 and 2). Information about the problem is summarized in Table 11.1. Production consists of a machining process that takes raw materials and converts them into unassembled parts. These are then sent to one of two divisions for assembly into the final product—Division 1 for Product 1 and Division 2 for Product 2.[3] As listed in Table 11.1, Product 1 requires 20 units of raw material and 5 hours of machine-processing time, whereas Product 2 requires 40 units of raw material and 2 hours of machine-processing time. During the period, 400 units of raw material and 40 hours of machine-processing time are available.

---

[3] This problem ignores any scheduling difficulties that may exist in the production process.

TABLE 11.1		Quantity of Resources Required Per Unit of Output		Quantity of Resources Available During Period
Resource and Profit Data for the White Company Profit-Maximization Problem		Product		
	Resource	1	2	
	Raw material (units)	20	40	400
	Machine-processing time (hours)	5	2	40
	Capacity of Assembly Division 1 (units)	1	0	6
	Capacity of Assembly Division 2 (units)	0	1	9
		Product		
		1	2	
	Profit contribution ($/unit)	100	60	

The capacities of the two assembly divisions during the period are 6 and 9 units, respectively. The operating profit contribution per unit or, more accurately, the per-unit contribution to profit and overhead (fixed costs) is $100 for each unit of Product 1 and $60 for each unit of Product 2. The contribution per unit represents the difference between the selling price per unit and the variable cost per unit. With this information, the problem can be formulated in the linear-programming framework.

Formulation of the Linear-Programming Problem

www
The following Internet site, maintained by Jiefeng Xu of the University of Colorado, provides access to a large number of public-domain computer programs designed to solve linear programming and other optimization problems: http://ucsu.colorado.edu/~xu/software.html

Objective Function   The objective is to maximize the total contributions π from the production of the two products, where total profit contribution is equal to the sum of the contribution per unit of each product times the number of units produced. Therefore, the objective function is

$$\text{Max } \pi = 100X_1 + 60X_2 \qquad [11.1]$$

where X_1 and X_2 are, as defined earlier, the output levels of Products 1 and 2, respectively.

Constraint Relationships   The production process described has several resource constraints imposed on it. These need to be incorporated into the formulation of the problem. Consider first the raw material constraint. Production of X_1 units of Product 1 requires $20X_1$ units of raw materials. Similarly, production of X_2 units of Product 2 requires $40X_2$ units of the same raw material. The sum of these two quantities of raw materials must be less than or equal to the quantity available, which is 400 units. This relationship can be expressed as

$$20X_1 + 40X_2 \leq 400 \qquad [11.2]$$

The machine-processing time constraint can be developed in a like manner. Product 1 requires $5X_1$ hours and Product 2 requires $2X_2$ hours. With 40 hours of processing time available, the following constraint is obtained:

$$5X_1 + 2X_2 \leq 40 \qquad [11.3]$$

The capacities of the two assembly divisions also limit output and consequently profits. For Product 1, which must be assembled in Division 1, the constraint is

$$X_1 \leq 6 \qquad\qquad [11.4]$$

For Product 2, which must be assembled in Division 2, the constraint is

$$X_2 \leq 9 \qquad\qquad [11.5]$$

Finally, the logic of the production process suggests that negative output quantities are not possible. Therefore, each of the decision variables is constrained to be nonnegative:

$$X_1 \geq 0 \qquad X_2 \geq 0 \qquad\qquad [11.6]$$

Equations 11.1 through 11.6 constitute a linear-programming formulation of the profit-maximization production problem.

Economic Assumptions of the Linear-Programming Model

In formulating this problem as a linear-programming model, one must understand the economic assumptions that are incorporated into the model. Basically, one assumes that a series of linear (or approximately linear) relationships involving the decision variables exist over the range of alternatives being considered in the problem. For the resource inputs, one assumes that the *prices of these resources to the firm are constant* over the range of resource quantities under consideration. This assumption implies that the firm can buy as much or as little of these resources as it needs without affecting the per unit cost.[4] Such an assumption would rule out quantity discounts. One also assumes that there are *constant returns to scale* in the production process. In other words, in the production process, a doubling of the quantity of resources employed doubles the quantity of output obtained, for any level of resources.[5] Finally, one assumes that the *market selling prices of the two products are constant* over the range of possible output combinations.[6] These assumptions are implied by the fixed per-unit profit contribution coefficients in the objective function. If the assumptions are not valid, then the optimal solution to the linear-programming model will not necessarily be an optimal solution to the actual decision-making problem. Although these relationships need not be linear over the entire range of values of the decision variables, the linearity assumptions must be valid over the full range of values being considered in the problem.

Graphical Solution of the Linear-Programming Problem

Various techniques are available for solving linear-programming problems. For larger problems involving more than two decision variables, one needs to employ algebraic methods to obtain a solution. Further discussion of these methods is postponed until later in the chapter. For problems containing only two decision variables, graphical methods can be used to obtain an optimal solution. To understand the nature of the

---

[4] This assumption involves the concept of an atomistic buyer in a competitive factor or *input* market. See Chapter 12 for a discussion of this type of market.

[5] "Doubling the quantity of resources" is used as an example. More generally, one would say that a given percentage increase in each of the resources would result in an equivalent percentage increase in output for any given level of resources. See Chapter 8 for a further discussion of the concept of returns to scale.

[6] This assumption is satisfied in a perfectly competitive market for the two final products. Further discussion of this type of market is in Chapter 12.

objective function and constraint relationships, it is helpful to solve the preceding problem graphically. This is done by graphing the feasible solution space and objective function separately and then combining the two graphs to obtain the optimal solution.

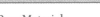

PROFIT MAXIMIZATION: WHITE COMPANY (CONTINUED)

Graphing the Feasible Solution Space   Note from Equation 11.6 that each of the decision variables must be greater than or equal to zero. Therefore, one needs only graph the upper right-hand (positive) quadrant. Figure 11.1 illustrates the raw material constraint as given by Equation 11.2. The upper limit or maximum quantity of raw materials that may be used occurs when the inequality is satisfied as an equality; in other words, the set of points that satisfies the equation

$$20X_1 + 40X_2 = 400$$

Because it is possible to use less than the amount of raw materials available, any combination of outputs lying *on or below* this line (that is, the shaded area) will satisfy the raw materials constraint.

Similarly, the constraint on the amount of machine-processing time (in hours) available (Equation 11.3) yields the combinations of X_1 and X_2 that lie on or below the line (that is, the shaded area) shown in Figure 11.2. Likewise, one can determine the set of feasible combinations of X_1 and X_2 for each of the remaining constraints (Equations 11.4 and 11.5).

FIGURE   11.1

Raw Materials
Constraint

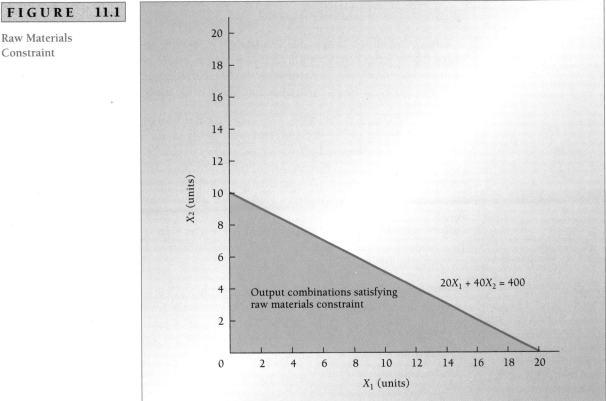

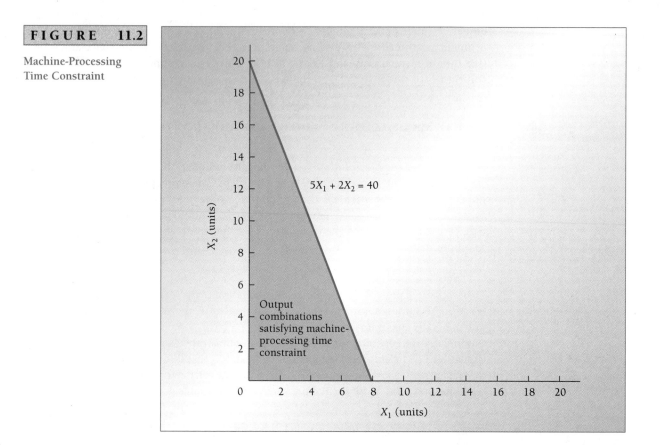

FIGURE 11.2

Machine-Processing Time Constraint

$5X_1 + 2X_2 = 40$

X_2 (units)

Output combinations satisfying machine-processing time constraint

X_1 (units)

Feasible Solution Space
The set of all possible combinations of the decision variables that *simultaneously* satisfies all the constraints of the problem.

Combining all the constraints (Equations 11.2–11.6) yields the **feasible solution space** (shaded area) shown in Figure 11.3, which *simultaneously* satisfies all the constraints of the problem. All possible production combinations of X_1 and X_2 that simultaneously satisfy all the resource constraints lie in or on the boundary of the shaded area.

Graphing the Objective Function   The objective function given by Equation 11.1 specifies the profit that will be obtained from any combination of output levels. The profit function can be represented graphically as a series of parallel *isoprofit* lines. Each of the lines shown in Figure 11.4 is an isoprofit line, meaning that each combination of output levels (that is, X_1 and X_2) lying on a given line has the *same* total profit. For example, the $\pi = \$1,200$ isoprofit line includes such output combinations as ($X_1 = 6$, $X_2 = 10$) and ($X_1 = 9, X_2 = 5$). The objective of profit maximization can be interpreted graphically to find an output combination that falls on as high an isoprofit line as possible. The resource constraints of the problem obviously limit us from increasing output and profits indefinitely.

Graphical Solution   Combining the graphs of the feasible solution space and objective function yields the output combination point within the feasible solution space that lies on the highest possible isoprofit line. The two graphs have been combined in Figure 11.5. From the graph it can be seen that the optimal output combination at point C is $X_1^* = 5$ units and $X_2^* = 7.5$ units, yielding a profit of

$$\pi^* = 100 \times 5 + 60 \times 7.5$$

$$= \$950$$

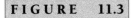

FIGURE 11.3

Feasible Solution Space:
Profit-Maximization
Problem

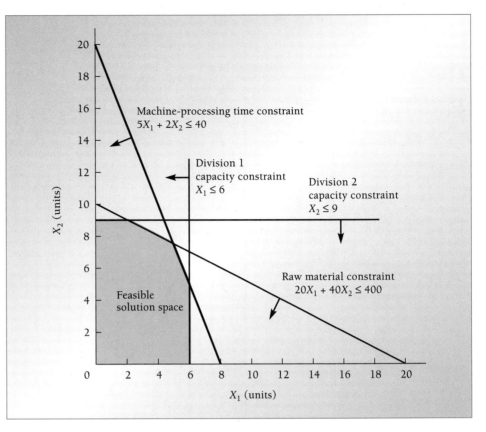

FIGURE 11.4

Isoprofit Lines: Profit-
Maximization Problem

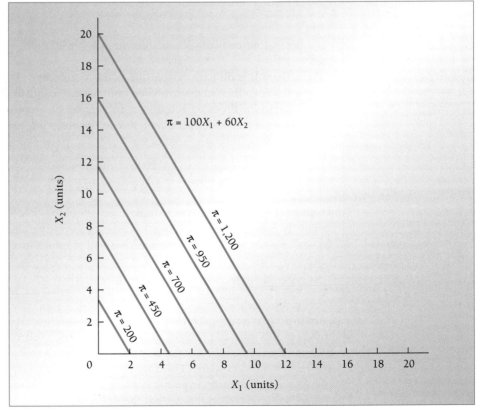

FIGURE   11.5

Optimal Solution: Profit-Maximization Problem

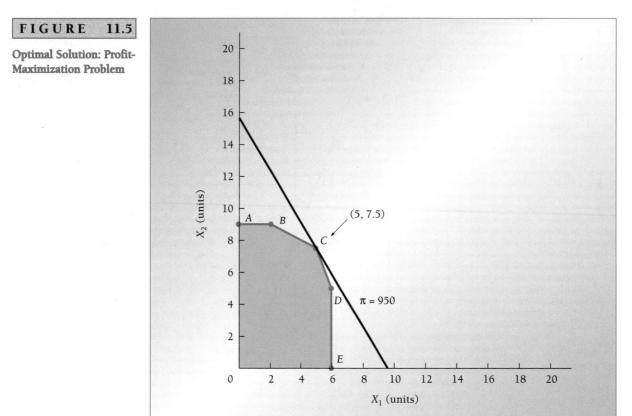

No other output combination within the feasible solution space will result in a larger profit.

Optimal Solution

A feasible solution that maximizes or minimizes the value of the objective function.

Sometimes it is difficult to read the exact coordinates of the **optimal solution** from the graph. When this occurs (or when one wants to confirm the solution algebraically), we can determine the exact solution by solving simultaneously the equations of the two lines passing through the optimum point. In the preceding example, the equations of the two lines passing through point C are

$$20X_1 + 40X_2 = 400$$

$$5X_1 + 2X_2 = 40$$

which correspond to the raw materials and machine-processing time constraints, respectively. Solving these two equations simultaneously does indeed yield $X_1^* = 5$ and $X_2^* = 7.5$ —the same result that was obtained graphically.

Extreme Points and the Optimal Solution

This example demonstrates two important general properties of an optimal solution to a linear-programming problem. These properties are useful in developing algebraic solutions to this class of problem, and they form the foundation for computer (algorithmic) solution techniques. First, note that the optimal solution lies on the *boundary* of the feasible solution space. The implication of this property is that one can ignore the infinite number of interior points in the feasible solution space when searching for an optimal solution. Second, note that the optimal solution occurs at one of the **extreme**

Extreme Point

Graphically, a corner point of the feasible solution space.

points (corner points) of the feasible solution space. This property reduces even further the magnitude of the search procedure for an optimal solution. For this example it means that from among the infinite number of points lying on the boundary of the feasible solution space, only six points—A, B, C, D, E, and zero—need to be examined to find an optimal solution.

Multiple Optimal Solutions

A problem also can have *multiple* optimal solutions if the isoprofit line coincides with one of the boundaries of the feasible solution space. For example, if the objective function in the production problem were equal to

$$\pi' = 100X_1 + 40X_2 \qquad [11.7]$$

then the isoprofit line $\pi' = \$800$ would coincide with the *CD* boundary line of the feasible solution space as illustrated in Figure 11.6. In this case both corner points *C* and *D*, along with all the output combinations falling along the *CD* line segment, would constitute optimal solutions to the problem.

Slack Variables

In addition to the optimal combination of output to produce (X_1^* and X_2^*) and the maximum total profit (π^*), we are also interested in the amount of each resource used in the production process. For the production of 5 units (= X_1^*) and 7.5 units (= X_2^*) of

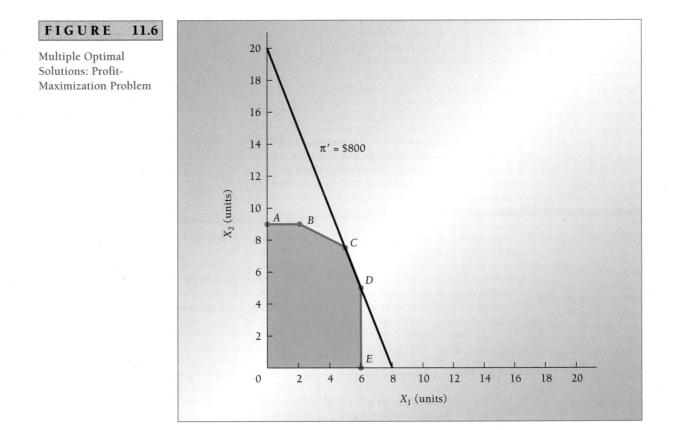

FIGURE   11.6

Multiple Optimal
Solutions: Profit-
Maximization Problem

products 1 and 2, respectively, the resource requirements (from Equations 11.2–11.5) are as follows:

$$20(5) + 40(7.5) = 400 \text{ units of raw materials}$$

$$5(5) + 2(7.5) = 40 \text{ hours of machine-processing time}$$

$$1(5) = 5 \text{ units of Division 1 assembly capacity}$$

$$1(7.5) = 7.5 \text{ units of Division 2 assembly capacity}$$

This information indicates that all available raw materials (400 units) and all available machine-processing time (40 hours) will be used in producing the optimal output combination. However, 1 unit of Division 1 assembly capacity $(6 - 5)$ and 1.5 units of Division 2 assembly capacity $(9 - 7.5)$ will be unused in producing the optimal output combination. These unused or idle resources associated with a less than or equal to constraint $(\leq)$ are referred to as *slack*.

Slack variables can be added to the formulation of a linear-programming problem to represent this slack or idle capacity. Slack variables are given a coefficient of zero in the objective function because they make no contribution to profit. Slack variables can be thought of as representing the difference between the right-hand side and left-hand side of a less than or equal to inequality $(\leq)$ constraint.

In the preceding profit-maximization problem (Equations 11.1–11.6), four slack variables (S_1, S_2, S_3, S_4) are used to convert the four (less than or equal to) constraints to equalities as follows:

$$\text{Max } \pi = 100X_1 + 60X_2 + 0S_1 + 0S_2 + 0S_3 + 0S_4$$

$$20X_1 + 40X_2 + 1S_1 \qquad\qquad\qquad = 400$$

$$5X_1 + 2X_2 \qquad + 1S_2 \qquad\qquad = 40$$

$$X_1 \qquad\qquad\qquad + 1S_3 \qquad = 6$$

$$X_2 \qquad\qquad\qquad\qquad + 1S_4 = 9$$

$$X_1, X_2, S_1, S_2, S_3, S_4 \geq 0$$

As shown later in the chapter, a computer solution of a linear-programming problem automatically provides the optimal values of the slack variables along with the optimal values for the original decision variables.

Slack Variable
A variable that represents the difference between the right-hand side and left-hand side of a less than or equal to $(\leq)$ inequality constraint. It is added to the left-hand side of the inequality to convert the constraint to an equality. It measures the amount of an unused or idle resource.

THE DUAL PROBLEM AND INTERPRETATION OF THE DUAL VARIABLES

The solution of a linear-programming problem, in addition to providing the optimal values of the decision variables, contains information that can be very useful in making *marginal* resource-allocation decisions. This marginal information is contained in what are known as the **dual variables** of the linear-programming problem.

The Dual Linear-Programming Problem

Associated with every linear-programming problem is a related *dual* linear-programming problem. The *originally formulated* problem, in relation to the dual problem, is known

Dual Variable
A variable that measures how much the objective function (for example, profit or cost) will change if a given constraint is increased by one unit, provided the increase in the resource does not shift the optimal solution to another extreme point of the feasible solution space.

as the *primal* linear-programming problem.[7] If the objective in the primal problem is *maximization* of some function, then the objective in the dual problem is *minimization* of a related (but different) function. Conversely, a primal minimization problem has a related dual maximization problem. The dual variables represent the variables contained in the dual problem.

EXAMPLE

PROFIT MAXIMIZATION: WHITE COMPANY (CONTINUED)

Primal Problem
The original formulation of the linear-programming problem.

Dual Problem
A linear-programming problem that is associated with the primal problem. Solution of the primal problem (by the simplex method) automatically provides a solution to the dual problem.

Before indicating how the dual variables can be used as an aid in marginal decision making, it may be useful to illustrate, using the White Company profit-maximization problem, the relation of the dual problem to the primal problem. One way to show the relationship is by means of a matrix diagram, such as the one in Figure 11.7. The **primal problem** is contained in the *rows* of the figure. For example, the first row (W_1) of numbers in the figure contains the Equation 11.2 constraint; that is, $20X_1 + 40X_2 \leq 400$. The last row (Constants) contains the objective function (Equation 11.1); that is, max $\pi = 100X_1 + 60X_2$.

Associated with each constraint of the primal problem is a dual variable. Because the primal problem had four constraints,[8] the **dual problem** has four variables—W_1, W_2, W_3, and W_4. The dual problem is contained in the *columns* of the figure. The objective of the dual problem is contained in the Constants column:

$$\text{Min } Z = 400W_1 + 40W_2 + 6W_3 + 9W_4 \qquad [11.8]$$

Similarly, the constraints of the dual problem are contained under the X_1 and X_2 columns:

$$20W_1 + 5W_2 + W_3 \geq 100 \qquad [11.9]$$

$$40W_1 + 2W_2 + W_4 \geq 60 \qquad [11.10]$$

---

[7] By symmetry, the dual of the dual problem is the primal problem.

[8] The constraints requiring each of the primal variables to be greater than or equal to zero (that is, $X_1 \geq 0$, $X_2 \geq 0$) are not included when determining the number of dual variables.

FIGURE   11.7

Primal and Dual Problems

		PRIMAL				
Variables		X_1	X_2	Relation	Constants	
DUAL	W_1	20	40	$\leq$	400	Equation 11.2
	W_2	5	2	$\leq$	40	Equation 11.3
	W_3	1	0	$\leq$	6	Equation 11.4
	W_4	0	1	$\leq$	9	Equation 11.5
Relation		$\geq$	$\geq$	min Z		
Constants		100	60	max π		Equation 11.1

Equation 11.9   Equation 11.10   Equation 11.8

One also requires

$$W_1 \geq 0, W_2 \geq 0, W_3 \geq 0, W_4 \geq 0 \qquad [11.11]$$

In general, a primal problem with n variables and m constraints will have as its dual a problem with m variables and n constraints.

Economic Interpretation of the Dual Variables

Shadow Price
Measures the value (that is, contribution to the objective function) of one additional unit of a resource. It is equivalent to the dual variable.

In the preceding resource-constrained profit-maximization problem, a dual variable existed for each of the limited resources required in the production process. In such a problem the dual variables measure the "imputed values" or **shadow prices** of each of the scarce resources. Expressed in dollars per unit of resource, they give an indication of how much each resource contributes to the overall profit function. With this interpretation of the dual variables, the dual objective function (Equation 11.8) is to minimize the total cost or value of the resources employed in the process. The two dual constraints (Equations 11.9 and 11.10) require that the value of the resources used in producing one unit each of X_1 and X_2 be at least as great as the profit received from the sale of one unit of each product. An important linear-programming theorem, known as the *duality theorem,* indicates that the maximum value of the primal profit function will also be equal to the minimum value of the dual "imputed value" function.[9] The solution of the dual problem in effect apportions the total profit figure among the various scarce resources employed in the process.

The interpretation of the dual variables and dual problem depends on the nature and objective of the primal problem. Thus a completely different interpretation is involved whenever the primal problem is one of cost minimization.[10]

EXAMPLE

PROFIT MAXIMIZATION: WHITE COMPANY (CONTINUED)

The preceding example illustrates how the dual variables can be used to make marginal resource-allocation decisions. The values of the dual variables, *which are obtained automatically in an algebraic solution of the linear-programming problem,* are $W_1^* = \$.625$ per unit, $W_2^* = \$17.50$ per unit, $W_3^* = \$0$ per unit, and $W_4^* = \$0$ per unit. Each dual variable indicates the rate of change in total profits for an incremental change in the amount of each of the various resources. In this way they are similar to the λ values used in the Lagrangian multiplier technique. The dual variables indicate how much the total profit will change (i.e., marginal profit) if one additional unit of a given resource is made available, provided the increase in the resource does not shift the optimal solution to another corner point of the feasible solution space. For example, $W_2^* = \$17.50$ indicates that profits could be increased by as much as $17.50 if an additional unit (hour) of machine capacity could be made available to the production process. This type of information is potentially useful in making decisions about purchasing or renting additional machine capacity or using existing machine capacity more fully through the use of overtime and

---

[9] See any standard linear-programming text, such as the previously cited Anderson et al., and George B. Dantzig, *Linear Programming and Extensions* (Princeton, N.J.: Princeton University Press, 1963); see G. Hadley, *Linear Programming* (Reading, Mass.: Addison-Wesley, 1962), for a complete discussion of the concept of duality and the duality theorem.

[10] See Hadley, *Linear Programming,* pp. 485–487; and J. G. Kemeny, H. Mirkil, J. L. Snell, and G. L. Thompson, *Finite Mathematical Structures* (Englewood Cliffs, N.J.: Prentice-Hall, 1959), pp. 364–366, and the next section, for examples of the interpretation of other types of dual problems.

multiple shifts. A dual variable equal to zero, such as W_3^* and W_4^*, indicates that profits would *not* increase if additional resources of these types were made available; in fact, excess capacity in these resources exists. (Recall in the discussion of slack variables, portions of these resources were unused or idle in the optimal solution.) This discussion only indicates the type of analysis that is possible. Much more detailed analysis of this nature can be performed using parametric-programming techniques.[11]

A COST-MINIMIZATION PROBLEM

This section develops a cost-minimization problem and illustrates the use of computer programs for its solution.

Statement of the Problem

Large multiplant firms often produce the same products at two or more factories. Often these factories employ different production technologies and have different unit production costs. The objective is to produce the desired amount of output using the given facilities (that is, plants and production processes) to minimize production costs.

EXAMPLE

COST MINIMIZATION: SILVERADO MINING COMPANY

Suppose that the Silverado Mining Company owns two different mines (A and B) for producing uranium ore. The two mines are located in different areas and produce different qualities of uranium ore. After the ore is mined, it is separated into three grades—high-, medium-, and low-grade. Information concerning the operation of the two mines is shown in Table 11.2. Mine A produces .75 tons of high-grade ore, .25 tons of medium-grade ore, and .50 tons of low-grade ore *per hour.* Likewise, Mine B produces .25, .25, and 1.50 tons of high-, medium-, and low-grade ore *per hour,* respectively. The firm has contracts with uranium-processing plants to supply a minimum of 36 tons of high-grade ore, 24 tons of medium-grade ore, and 72 tons of low-grade ore *per week.* These figures are shown in the Requirements column of Table 11.2. Finally, as shown in the bottom row of Table 11.2, it costs the company $50 per hour to operate Mine A and $40 per hour to operate Mine B. The company wishes to determine the number of hours per week it should operate each mine to minimize the total cost of fulfilling its supply contracts.

---

[11] See Hadley, *Linear Programming,* pp. 379–400, for an explanation of such an analysis.

TABLE   11.2

Output and Cost Data for the Silverado Mining Company Cost-Minimization Problem

Type of Ore	Output (Tons of Ore Per Hour) Mine		Requirements (Tons Per Week)
	A	**B**	
High-grade ore	.75	.25	36
Medium-grade ore	.25	.25	24
Low-grade ore	.50	1.50	72
	Mine		
	A	**B**	
Operating cost ($/hour)	50	40	

Formulation of the Linear-Programming Problem

Objective Function   The objective is to *minimize* the total cost per week (*C*) from the operation of the two mines, where the total cost is equal to the sum of the operating cost per hour of each mine times the number of hours per week that each mine is operated. Defining X_1 as the number of hours per week that Mine A is operated and X_2 as the number of hours per week that Mine B is operated, the objective function is

$$\text{Min } C = 50X_1 + 40X_2 \qquad [11.12]$$

Constraint Relationships   The Silverado Mining Company's contracts with uranium-processing plants require it to operate the two mines for a sufficient number of hours to produce the required amount of each grade of uranium ore. In the production of high-grade ore, Mine A produces .75 tons per hour times the number of hours per week (X_1) that it operates, and Mine B produces .25 tons per hour times the number of hours per week (X_2) that it operates. The sum of these two quantities must be greater than or equal to the required output of 36 tons per week. This relationship can be expressed as

$$.75X_1 + .25X_2 \geq 36 \qquad [11.13]$$

Similar constraints can be developed for the production of medium-grade ore

$$.25X_1 + .25X_2 \geq 24 \qquad [11.14]$$

and low-grade ore

$$.50X_1 + 1.50X_2 \geq 72 \qquad [11.15]$$

Finally, negative production times are not possible. Therefore, each of the decision variables is constrained to be nonnegative:

$$X_1 \geq 0, X_2 \geq 0 \qquad [11.16]$$

Equations 11.12 through 11.16 represent a linear-programming formulation of the cost-minimization production problem.

Surplus Variable
A variable that represents the difference between the right-hand side and left-hand side of a greater than or equal to ($\geq$) inequality constraint. It is *subtracted* from the left-hand side of the inequality to convert the constraint to an equality. It measures the amount of a product (or output) in excess of the required amount.

Slack (Surplus) Variables

Recall from the discussion of the maximization problem earlier in the chapter that slack variables were added to the less than or equal to inequality ($\leq$) constraints to convert these constraints to equalities. Similarly, in a minimization problem, **surplus variables** are *subtracted* from the greater than or equal to inequality ($\geq$) constraints to convert these constraints to equalities. Like the slack variables, surplus variables are given coefficients of zero in the objective function because they have no effect on the value.

EXAMPLE

COST MINIMIZATION: SILVERADO MINING COMPANY (CONTINUED)

In the preceding cost-minimization problem, three surplus variables (S_1, S_2, S_3) are used to convert the three (greater than or equal to) constraints to equalities as follows:

$$\text{Min } C = 50X_1 + 40X_2 + 0S_1 + 0S_2 + 0S_3$$

$$\text{s.t.} \quad .75X_1 + .25X_2 - 1S_1 \qquad\qquad = 36$$

$$.25X_1 + .25X_2 \qquad -1S_2 \qquad = 24$$

$$.50X_1 + 1.50X_2 \qquad\qquad -1S_3 = 72$$

$$X_1, X_2, S_1, S_2, S_3 \geq 0$$

Computer Solution of the Linear-Programming Problem

Simplex Method
A step-by-step mathematical procedure for finding the optimal solution to a linear-programming problem.

www.............
LINDO Systems, Inc., is a leading supplier of optimization software. You can download free versions of their linear programming software at the following Internet site:
http://www.lindo.com/download.html

The solution of large-scale linear-programming problems typically employs a procedure (or variation of the procedure) known as the **simplex method**. Basically, the simplex method is a step-by-step procedure for moving from corner point to corner point of the feasible solution space in such a manner that successively larger (or smaller) values of the maximization (or minimization) objective function are obtained at each step. The procedure is guaranteed to yield the optimal solution in a finite number of steps. Further discussion of this method is beyond the scope of this chapter.[12]

Most practical applications of linear programming use computer programs to perform the calculations and obtain the optimal solution. Although many different programs are available for solving linear-programming problems, the output of these programs usually includes the optimal solution to the primal problem as well as the optimal values of the dual variables. The particular program illustrated here is known as SIMPLX.[13] (Similar programs are likely to be readily available on your personal computer or school's computer system.

EXAMPLE

COST MINIMIZATION: SILVERADO MINING COMPANY (CONTINUED)

Putting the objective function and constraints (Equations 11.12 through 11.16) along with the appropriate control statements into the SIMPLX program yields the output shown in Figure 11.8. The optimal values of the decision variables are shown in the Primal Solution column—$X_1^* = 24$ and $X_2^* = 72$. The firm should operate Mine A for 24 hours per week and Mine B for 72 hours per week to *minimize* total operating costs. This yields a minimum total cost of \$4,080 per week.

Note also that the optimal value of the surplus variable S_3^* [that is, $X(5)$ on the computer output] is 48. This indicates that a surplus of 48 tons of low-grade ore (that is, 120 tons versus the required amount of 72 tons) is being produced in the optimal solution. Similarly, S_1 and S_2 are zero (all variables not listed in the primal solution are equal to zero), indicating that exactly the required amounts of high-grade and medium-grade ore (36 and 24 tons, respectively) are being produced in the optimal solution.

Recall from the earlier discussion of the dual problem and dual variables that a dual variable is associated with each constraint equation in the primal problem (excluding nonnegativity constraints). The ore-mining problem has three constraint equations—one for each of the three types of uranium ore. Consequently, it has three dual variables—W_1, W_2, and W_3—associated with each of the respective constraint equations. The optimal values of the dual variables are shown in the Dual Solution column of Figure 11.8—$W_1^* = \$20$, $W_2^* = \$140$, and $W_3^* = \$0$. Each dual variable measures the

---

[12] Any basic linear-programming textbook, such as the previously cited Anderson et al., Dantzig, and Hadley books, contains detailed discussions of this procedure.

[13] "SIMPLX" is a terminal-oriented computer program. See E. Pearsall and B. Price, *Linear Programming and Simulation* (No. MS(350)), CONDUIT (Ames: Iowa State University).

```
:RUN "SIMPLX"

DO YOU WANT INSTRUCTIONS FOR THIS PROGRAM: YES OR NO?$NO

NUMBER OF CONSTRAINTS:              M = 3
NUMBER OF VARIABLES:               N = 2
NUMBER OF SLACKS CREATED:          S = 3
OBJECTIVE IS TO MINIMIZE COST
PRINT CONSTRAINT COEFFICIENTS: YES OR NO?$YES
PRINT OBJECTIVE ROW COEFFICIENTS: YES OR NO?$YES
PRINT RIGHT HAND SIDE ENTRIES: YES OR NO?$YES

C(1) = 50, C(2) = 40, B(1) = 36, B(2) = 24.
B(3) = 72, A(1, 1) = 0.75, A(1, 2) = 0.25, A(2, 1) = 0.25,
A(2, 2) = 0.25, A(3, 1) = 0.5, A(3, 2) = 1.5,

START WITH GIVEN BASIS: YES OR NO?$NO
SUPPRESS THE PIVOT RECORD: YES OR NO?$NO
```

PIVOT	ENTERS	LEAVES	COST	DELTA
INVERSION PERFORMED				
BEGIN PHASE I				
1	X(2)	X(0)	1920	−2
2	X(1)	X(0)	3240	−0.8333333
3	X(3)	X(0)	4560	−0.25
BEGIN PHASE II				
4	X(5)	X(3)	4080	−10

```
REINVERT BEFORE TERMINATION: YES OR NO?$YES
INVERSION PERFORMED
SOLUTION IS OPITMAL
```

SOLUTION COST IS	4080

PRIMAL SOLUTION		DUAL SOLUTION	
VARIABLE	VALUE	VARIABLE	VALUE
X(1)	24	W(1)	20
X(5)	48	W(2)	140
X(2)	72	W(3)	0

change in total cost (i.e., marginal cost) that results from a one-unit (ton) increase in the required output, provided that the increase does not shift the optimal solution to another corner point of the feasible solution space. For example, $W_1^* = \$20$ indicates that total costs will increase by as much as \$20 if the firm is required to produce an additional ton of high-grade uranium ore. Comparison of this value to the revenue received per ton of ore can help the firm in making decisions about whether to expand or contract its mining operations.

Next, consider the interpretation of $W_3^* = \$0$. This zero value indicates that surplus low-grade ore is being produced by the firm. (Recall that $S_3^* = 48$.) At the optimal solution (operating Mines A and B at 24 and 72 hours per week, respectively), the cost of producing an additional ton of low-grade ore is \$0.

A New Technique for Solving Large-Scale Linear-Programming Problems[14]

Since its development in 1947 by operations research pioneer George Dantzig, most linear-programming problems have been solved using the simplex method (or variations thereof). Approximately 80 to 90 percent of these constrained optimization problems can be solved on computers using this algorithm. However, when solving extremely large problems or problems that are changing rapidly, the simplex method often is too slow to be practical.

An AT&T Bell Laboratories researcher, Narendra Karmarkar, developed an alternative solution technique that is potentially 50 to 100 times faster than the simplex method in solving large, complex linear-programming problems. For example, Bell Laboratories (now Lucent Technologies) is using Karmarkar's algorithm to forecast the most cost-effective way to satisfy the future needs over a 10-year horizon of the telephone network linking 20 countries on the rim of the Pacific Ocean. The resulting linear-programming problem contains 42,000 variables. Solving this problem using the simplex method would require 4 to 7 *hours* of mainframe computer time to answer each "what-if" question, whereas this new technique would require less than 4 *minutes*.

In another application, Karmarkar's algorithm was used to solve the Military Airlift Command's scheduling problem described in the *Managerial Challenge* section at the beginning of the chapter. Solving this linear-programming problem, which involves 321,000 variables and 14,000 constraints, required only one hour of computer time—just a fraction of the time that would be required using the simplex method. Given the new method's ability to solve large problems quickly, the Military Airlift Command, as well as commercial airlines such as American and United, should be able to solve complex scheduling problems and make efficient adjustments rapidly in response to changing operating constraints.

Additional Linear-Programming Examples

Linear programming is useful in a wide variety of managerial resource-allocation problems. This section examines some additional applications in finance, marketing, and distribution.

EXAMPLE

Capital Rationing
A situation that exists when a firm has more acceptable investment projects than it has funds available to invest.

The Capital-Rationing Problem: Aspen Ski Company

Rather than letting the size of their capital budgets (expenditures that are expected to provide long-term benefits to the firm, such as plants and equipment) be determined by the number of profitable investment opportunities available (all investment projects meeting some acceptance standard), many firms place an upper limit or constraint on the amount of funds allocated to capital investment. **Capital rationing** takes place whenever the total cash outlays for all projects that meet some acceptance standard exceed the constraint on total capital investment.

For example, suppose that the Aspen Ski Company is faced with the set of nine investment projects shown in Table 11.3, requiring the outlay of funds in each of the next two years (shown in columns 2 and 3) and generating the returns (net present values) shown in column 4.[15] Furthermore, suppose the firm has decided to limit total capital expenditures to $50,000 and $20,000 in each of the next two years, respectively. The prob-

---

[14] Based in part on articles in *Business Week,* 21 September 1987, and 13 March 1989, and *Wall Street Journal,* 3 May 1985.

[15] This problem was first formulated and solved in the mathematical programming context by Weingartner. See Martin Weingartner, *Mathematical Programming and the Analysis of Capital Budgeting Problems* (Englewood Cliffs, N.J.: Prentice-Hall, 1963).

TABLE 11.3

Two-Period Capital-
Rationing Problem—
Aspen Ski Company

Investment j (1)	Present Value of Outlay in Year 1 C_{1j} ($000) (2)	Present Value of Outlay in Year 2 C_{2j} ($000) (3)	Net Present Value of Investment b_j ($000) (4)
1	12	3	$14
2	54	7	17
3	6	6	17
4	6	2	15
5	30	35	40
6	6	6	12
7	48	4	14
8	36	3	10
9	18	3	12

lem is to select the combination of investments that provides the *largest possible return* (net present value) without violating either of the two constraints on total capital expenditures. This problem can be formulated and solved using linear-programming techniques.

Begin by defining X_j to be the fraction of project j undertaken (where $j = 1,2,3,4,5,6,7,8,$ and 9). The objective is to maximize the sum of the returns (net present value) of the projects undertaken:

$$\text{Max } R = 14X_1 + 17X_2 + 17X_3 + 15X_4 + 40X_5 \\ + 12X_6 + 14X_7 + 10X_8 + 12X_9 \qquad [11.17]$$

The constraints are the restrictions placed on total capital expenditures in each of the two years:

$$12X_1 + 54X_2 + 6X_3 + 6X_4 + 30X_5 + 6X_6 + 48X_7 \\ + 36X_8 + 18X_9 \leq 50 \qquad [11.18]$$

$$3X_1 + 7X_2 + 6X_3 + 2X_4 + 35X_5 + 6X_6 + 4X_7 \\ + 3X_8 + 3X_9 \leq 20 \qquad [11.19]$$

Also, so that no more than one of any project will be included in the final solution, all the X_j's must be less than or equal to 1:

$$X_1 \leq 1 \qquad [11.20]$$
$$X_2 \leq 1 \qquad [11.21]$$
$$X_3 \leq 1 \qquad [11.22]$$
$$X_4 \leq 1 \qquad [11.23]$$
$$X_5 \leq 1 \qquad [11.24]$$
$$X_6 \leq 1 \qquad [11.25]$$
$$X_7 \leq 1 \qquad [11.26]$$
$$X_8 \leq 1 \qquad [11.27]$$
$$X_9 \leq 1 \qquad [11.28]$$

Finally, all the X_j's must be nonnegative:

$$X_1 \geq 0, X_2 \geq 0, X_3 \geq 0, X_4 \geq 0, X_5 \geq 0, X_6 \geq 0, X_7 \geq 0, X_8 \geq 0, X_9 \geq 0 \; [11.29]$$

	Primal variables	X_1^* 1.0	X_2^* 0	X_3^* 1.0	X_4^* 1.0	X_5^* 0	X_6^* .970	X_7^* .045	X_8^* 0	X_9^* 1.0

TABLE   11.4

Optimal Solution: Two-Period Capital-Rationing Problem

Dual variables	W_1^* .136	W_2^* 1.864	Total net present value (R^*) = $70.27 (000)

Equations 11.17 through 11.29 represent a linear-programming formulation of this capital-rationing problem.

The optimal solution to this problem is shown in Table 11.4. Aspen should adopt in their entirety Projects 1, 3, 4, and 9, and fractional parts of two others—97 percent of Project 6 and 4.5 percent of Project 7. There will be at most one fractional project for each budget constraint; that is, two fractional projects in this problem. The total return (net present value) of the optimal solution is $70.27 or $70,270.

Fractional parts arise from the manner in which the linear-programming model was formulated. By allowing the X_j's to vary from 0 to 1, it was implicitly assumed that the projects were divisible; that is, the firm could undertake all or part of a project and receive benefits (cash flows) in the same proportion as the amounts invested. This assumption is somewhat unrealistic because most investments must either be undertaken in their entirety or not at all. One possible way to eliminate these fractional projects is to adjust the budget constraints upward to be able to include the entire project. Generally, total capital expenditure limits are flexible enough to allow slight upward adjustments to be made. Another method for eliminating fractional projects in the solution is to use an *integer*-programming formation of the problem. This would be done by adding constraints to the model that require the X_j's to have integer values:

$$X_j \text{ an integer } j = 1, \ldots, 9$$

that is $X_1, X_2, X_3, X_4, X_5, X_6, X_7, X_8, X_9$ are integers. Requiring the X_j's to be integers and also to be between 0 and 1 forces these variables to take on the values of either 1 or 0; that is, the projects would have to be accepted either in their entirety or not at all.

The solution to this primal linear-programming problem also yields a solution to the *dual* problem. There is one dual variable for every constraint in the primal problem. The optimal values of the dual variables associated with the two budget constraints (Equations 11.18 and 11.19) are shown in Table 11.4. In this problem these dual variables indicate the amount that the total present value could be increased if the budget limits (constraints) were increased to permit an additional $1 investment in the given period. In the example, if the budget constraint in Year 1 were increased from $50,000 to $51,000, then the total net present value would increase by W_1^* = $.136 × 1,000 or $136. Similarly, if the budget constraint in Year 2 were increased from $20,000 to $21,000, the total net present value would increase by W_2^* = $1.864 × 1,000 or $1,864. Because the dual variables measure the opportunity cost of not having additional funds available for investment in a given period, they can be used in deciding whether or not to shift funds from one period to another.[16] If the values of the dual

---

[16] The formulation of the capital-rationing problem in a linear-programming framework creates a difficulty in interpreting the dual variables associated with budget constraints. A problem arises because two interdependent measures of the opportunity cost of investment funds are available—the dual variable value and the cost of capital (discount rate), which is used in finding the net present values (b_j's) of the investment projects. For a further discussion of the problem, see William J. Baumol and Richard E. Quandt, "Investment and Discount Rates Under Capital Rationing—A Programming Approach," *Economic Journal* 75 (June 1965), pp. 317–329.

variables are fairly large, indicating that total net present value could be increased significantly through additional investment, the firm may decide to increase its capital expenditure budget through such methods as new borrowing or equity financing.

EXAMPLE

THE TRANSPORTATION PROBLEM: MERCURY CANDY COMPANY

Large multiplant firms often produce their products at several different factories and then ship the products to various regional warehouses located throughout their marketing area. The objective is to minimize shipping costs subject to the constraints of meeting the demand for the product in each region and not exceeding the supply of the product available at each plant.

Suppose that the Mercury Candy Company has two production plants located in New England (1) and the Gulf Coast (2), and three warehouses located in the East Coast (1), Midwest (2), and West Coast (3) regions (see Figure 11.9). Shipping costs per unit of the product from each of the two plants to each of the three warehouses are shown in the center box in the figure. *Demand* for the product at each of the regional warehouses is shown in the bottom row and the *supply* of the product available at each plant is shown in the far right column. The firm wants to minimize its shipping costs.

Begin the linear-programming formulation of the problem by defining X_{ij} to be the number of units of the product shipped from Plant i to Warehouse j. This problem has six X-variables—namely, X_{11}, X_{12}, X_{13}, X_{21}, X_{22}, X_{23}. For example, X_{21} indicates the amount of the product shipped from the Gulf Coast plant to the East Coast warehouse. Similar interpretations apply to the other X-variables.

Total shipping costs are the sum of the number of units of the product shipped from each plant to each warehouse times the respective shipping cost per unit. The objective function is therefore

$$\text{Min } C = 20X_{11} + 35X_{12} + 65X_{13} + 25X_{21} + 15X_{22} + 50X_{23} \qquad [11.30]$$

There are two sets of constraints (plus nonnegativity constraints) in a standard transportation problem such as this one. The first set has to do with meeting the demand for the product at each of the three regional warehouses. Total shipments *to* each warehouse must be greater than or equal to demand in the region:

$$X_{11} \quad + X_{21} \qquad \geq 2{,}000 \qquad [11.31]$$

$$X_{12} \quad + X_{22} \qquad \geq 1{,}500 \qquad [11.32]$$

$$X_{13} \quad + X_{23} \geq 1{,}000 \qquad [11.33]$$

FIGURE   11.9

Transportation Problem
Data—Mercury Candy
Company

		Regional Warehouse			
		East Coast (1)	Midwest (2)	West Coast (3)	Supply
Plant	New England (1)	$20	35	65	2,000
	Gulf Coast (2)	25	15	50	2,500
	Demand	2,000	1,500	1,000	

	X_{11}^*	X_{12}^*	X_{13}^*	X_{21}^*	X_{22}^*	X_{23}^*	C^*
	2,000	0	0	0	1,500	1,000	$112,500

TABLE   11.5

Optimal Solution:
Transportation Problem

The second set of constraints is concerned with not exceeding the supply of the product at each plant. Total shipments *from* each plant must be less than or equal to the supply of the product *at* the plant:

$$X_{11} + X_{12} + X_{13} \leq 2,000 \qquad [11.34]$$

$$X_{21} + X_{22} + X_{23} \leq 2,500 \qquad [11.35]$$

Finally, all the X-variables are required to be nonnegative:

$$X_{11} \geq 0, X_{12} \geq 0, X_{13} \geq 0, X_{21} \geq 0, X_{22} \geq 0, X_{23} \geq 0 \qquad [11.36]$$

Equations 11.30 through 11.36 constitute a linear-programming formulation of the transportation problem.

The optimal solution to this problem is shown in Table 11.5.[17] From the New England plant, Mercury should ship 2,000 units to the East Coast regional warehouse (X_{11}^*). From the Gulf Coast plant, the firm should ship 1,500 units to the Midwest regional warehouse (X_{22}^*) and 1,000 units to the West Coast regional warehouse (X_{23}^*). Total shipping costs of the optimal solution are $112,500.

SUMMARY

☐ Linear-programming problems constitute an important class of constrained optimization problems for which efficient solution techniques have been developed.

☐ Linear programming has an advantage over classical optimization techniques because it can be applied to problems with inequality constraints.

☐ Despite the need for expressing the objective and constraint functions as linear relationships, a wide variety of problems can be formulated and solved in the linear-programming framework.

☐ Virtually all practical linear-programming problems are solved using computer programs that employ algebraic techniques. Graphical solution techniques are used in problems involving two decision variables to illustrate the basic linear-programming concepts.

☐ An important part of the solution of a linear-programming problem is the value of the *dual variables*. The dual variables are useful in making marginal resource-allocation decisions. They provide information on the resources that limit the value of the objective function and help make return-versus-cost comparisons in deciding whether to acquire additional resources.

EXERCISES

1. Maytag, a manufacturer of gas dryers, produces two models—a standard (*STD*) model and a deluxe (*DEL*) model. Production consists of two major phases. In the first phase, stamping and painting (*S & P*), sheet metal is formed (stamped) into

---

[17] Special-purpose computational algorithms are available for solving the transportation problem. See Dantzig, *Linear Programming and Extensions*, pp. 308–310, for a discussion of these algorithms.

the appropriate components and painted. In the second phase, assembly and testing (A & T), the sheet metal components along with the motor and controls are
assembled and tested. (Ignore any scheduling problems that might arise from the
sequential nature of the operations.) Information concerning the resource requirements and availability is shown in the following table:

Resource	Quantity of Resources Required per Unit of Output		Quality of Resources Available During Period
	Dryer Type		
	STD (1)	DEL (2)	
S & P (hours)	1.0	2.0	2,000
Motors (units)	1	1	1,400
STD controls (units)	1	0	1,000
DEL controls (units)	0	1	800
A & T (hours)	0.333	1.0	900
Profit contribution ($/unit)	100	125	

Each dryer (STD or DEL) requires one motor and a respective control unit. Define
X_1 and X_2 to be the number of STD and DEL dryers manufactured per period, respectively. The objective is to determine the number of STD and DEL dryers to produce so as to maximize the total contribution.

a. Formulate the problem in the linear-programming framework.
b. Solve for the optimal values of X_1 and X_2 graphically.
c. Determine the amount of each of the five resources that are used in producing the optimal output (X_1^* and X_2^*).
d. Based on the answer to part (c), determine the values of the five slack variables.

2. Suppose that a computer solution of Exercise 1 yielded the following optimal values of the dual variables: $W_1^* = \$25$ (S & P constraint), $W_2^* = \$75$ (Motors constraint), $W_3^* = \$0$ (STD controls constraint), $W_4^* = \$0$ (DEL controls constraint),
and $W_5^* = \$0$ (A & T constraint). Give an economic interpretation of each of the
dual variables.

3. Rework Exercise 1 (a and b), assuming that the profit contributions are $75 for
each standard (STD) dryer and $150 for each deluxe (DEL) dryer.

4. The MTA, an urban transit authority, is considering the purchase of additional
buses to expand its service. Two different models are being considered. A small
model would cost $100,000, carry 45 passengers, and operate at an average speed
of 25 miles per hour over the existing bus routes. A larger model would cost
$150,000, carry 55 passengers, and operate at an average speed of 30 miles per
hour. The transit authority has $3,000,000 in its *capital* budget for purchasing new
buses during the forthcoming year. However, the authority is also restricted in its
expansion program by limitations imposed on its *operating* budget. Specifically, a

hiring freeze is in effect and only 25 drivers are available for the foreseeable future to operate any new buses that are purchased. To plan for increased future demand, the transit authority wants at least one-half of all new buses purchased to be the larger model. Furthermore, certain bus routes require the use of the small model (because of narrow streets, traffic congestion, and so on), and there is an immediate need to replace at least five old buses with the new small model. The transit authority wishes to determine how many buses of each model to buy to maximize additional capacity measured in passenger-miles-per-hour while satisfying these constraints. Using the linear-programming framework, let X_1 be the number of small buses purchased and X_2 the number of large buses purchased.

    a. Formulate the objective function.

    b. Formulate the constraint relationships.

    c. Using graphical methods, determine the optimal combination of buses to purchase.

    d. Formulate (but do not solve) the dual problem, and give an interpretation of the dual variables.

5. Consider the cost-minimization production problem described in Equations 11.12 through 11.16.

    a. Graph the feasible solution space.

    b. Graph the objective function as a series of isocost lines.

    c. Using graphical methods, determine the optimal solution. Compare the graphical solution to the computer solution given in Figure 11.8.

6. Assume that the Agrex Company, a fertilizer manufacturer, wishes to determine the profit-maximizing level of output of two products, Alphagrow (X_1) and Better-grow (X_2). Each pound of X_1 produced and sold contributes $2 to overhead and profit, whereas X_2's contribution is $3 per pound. Additional information:

    ☐ The total productive capacity of the firm is 2,000 pounds of fertilizer per week. This capacity may be used to produce all X_1, all X_2, or some linear proportional mix of the two.

    ☐ Because of the light weight and bulk of X_2 relative to X_1, the packaging department can handle a maximum of 2,400 pounds of X_1, 1,200 pounds of X_2, or some linear proportional mix of the two each week.

    ☐ Large amounts of propane are required in the production process. Because of an energy shortage, the firm is limited to producing 2,100 pounds of X_2, 1,400 pounds of X_1, or some linear proportional mix of the two each week.

    ☐ On the average, the firm expects to have $5,000 in cash available to meet operating expenses each week. Each pound of X_1 produced requires an initial cash outflow of $2, whereas each pound of X_2 requires an outflow of $4.

    a. Formulate this as a profit-maximization problem in the linear-programming framework. Be sure to clearly specify all constraints.

    b. Solve for the approximate profit-maximizing levels of output of X_1 and X_2, using the graphical method.

7. Suppose a nutritionist for a United Nations food distribution agency is concerned with developing a *minimum-cost*-per-day balanced diet from two basic foods—cereal and dried milk—that meets or exceeds certain nutritional requirements. The information concerning the two foods and the requirements are summarized in the following table.

Nutrient	Fortified Cereal (Units of Nutrient Per Ounce)	Fortified Dried Milk (Units of Nutrient Per Ounce)	Minimum Requirements (Units)
Protein	2	5	100
Calories	100	40	500
Vitamin D	10	15	400
Iron	1	0.5	20
Cost (cents per ounce)	3.0	2.0	

Define X_1 as the number of ounces of cereal and X_2 as the number of ounces of dried milk to be included in the diet.

   a. Determine the objective function.

   b. Determine the constraint relationships.

   c. Using graphical methods, determine the optimal quantities of cereal and dried milk to include in the diet.

   d. Determine the amount of the four nutrients used in producing the optimal diet (X_1^* and X_2^*).

   e. Based on your answer to part (d), determine the values of the four surplus variables.

8. Suppose that a computer solution of Exercise 7 yielded the following optimal values of the dual variables: $W_1^* = 0$ (protein constraint), $W_2^* = 0$ (calories constraint), $W_3^* = .05$ cents (vitamin D constraint), and $W_4^* = 2.5$ cents (iron constraint). Give an economic interpretation of each of the dual variables.

9. The government of Indula, in an effort to expand and develop the economy of the country, has been allocating a large portion of each year's tax revenues to capital investment projects. The Ministry of Finance has asked the various government agencies to draw up a list of possible investment projects to be undertaken over the next three years. The following list of proposals was submitted.

Investment	Present Value of Outlay Year 1 (In $ Million)	Present Value of Outlay Year 2 (In $ Million)	Present Value of Outlay Year 3 (In $ Million)	Net Present Value of Investment (In $ Million)
1. Steel mill	20	80	50	50
2. Automobile manufacturing plant	75	150	100	100
3. Ship-docking facility	25	25	40	75
4. Irrigation system in Region 1	200	75	50	20

Investment	Present Value of Outlay Year 1 (In $ Million)	Present Value of Outlay Year 2 (In $ Million)	Present Value of Outlay Year 3 (In $ Million)	Net Present Value of Investment (In $ Million)
5. New hydroelectric dam in Region 3	75	100	50	40
6. New hydroelectric dam in Region 1	100	110	75	75
7. Oil refinery	25	40	25	60
8. Copper-smelting plant	20	50	50	50

The Ministry of Finance estimates that the present values of the amount (in millions of dollars) available for investment in each of the next three years will be 300, 325, and 350, respectively, and wishes to maximize the sum of the net present value of the projects undertaken.

a. Formulate (*but do not solve*) this problem in the linear-programming framework.

Suppose that a computer solution of this problem yields the following optimal values:

$X_1^* = 0.0$ $X_2^* = .667$ $X_3^* = 1.0$ $X_4^* = 0.0$ $X_5^* = 0.0$ $X_6^* = 1.0$
$X_7^* = 1.0$ $X_8^* = 1.0$ $W_1^* = 0.0$ $W_2^* = .667$ $W_3^* = 0.0$

Note: X_1–X_8 are the primal variables (i.e., proportion of each project undertaken) and W_1–W_3 are the dual variables associated with the capital budget constraints in each of the next three years.

b. Which of the investment projects should the government undertake? How should we deal with the fractional projects in the optimal solution?

c. Give an economic interpretation of the dual variables.

10. American Steel Company has three coal mines located in Pennsylvania, Tennessee, and Wyoming. These mines supply coal to its four steel-making facilities located in Ohio, Alabama, Illinois, and California. Monthly capacities of the three coal mines are 6,000, 8,000, and 12,000 tons, respectively. Monthly demand for coal at the four production facilities is 6,000, 5,000, 7,000, and 8,000 tons, respectively. Shipping costs from each of the three mines to each of the four production facilities are shown in the table below:

		Production Facilities			
		Ohio (1)	Alabama (2)	Illinois (3)	California (4)
Coal	Pennsylvania (1)	3	12	12	30
Mine	Tennessee (2)	6	3	18	25
	Wyoming (3)	20	24	15	15

The company desires to minimize its shipping costs. Let X_{ij} be the amount of coal shipped from Mine i to Production Facility j (for all i and j). Formulate (*but do not solve*) this problem in the linear-programming framework.

11. Mountain States Oil Company refines crude oil into gasoline, jet fuel, and heating oil. The company can process a maximum of 10,000 barrels per day at its refinery. The refining process is such that a maximum of 7,000 barrels of gasoline can be produced per day. Furthermore, there is always at least as much jet fuel as gasoline produced. The wholesale prices of gasoline, jet fuel, and heating oil are $50, $40, and $30 per barrel, respectively. The company is interested in maximizing revenue.

   a. Formulate (*but do not solve*) this problem in the linear-programming framework. *Hint:* There should be three constraints in this problem.

   b. Suppose that a computer solution of this problem yields an optimal value of $45 for the dual variable associated with the capacity constraint of the refinery. Give an economic interpretation of this dual variable.

12. Given the following profit-maximization problem:

$$\text{Max } 10X_1 + 9X_2 \qquad \text{Total profit contribution (\$)}$$

$$\text{s.t. } .70X_1 + X_2 \leq 630 \quad \text{Raw materials constraint (units)}$$

$$.50X_1 + .833X_2 \leq 600 \quad \text{Skilled labor constraint (hours)}$$

$$X_1 + .667X_2 \leq 708 \quad \text{Unskilled labor constraint (hours)}$$

$$.10X_1 + .25X_2 \leq 135 \quad \text{Storage capacity constraint (units)}$$

$$X_1, X_2 \geq 0$$

where X_i = amount of product i manufactured per period, and the following optimal computer solution:

Solution Profit is 7,668			
Primal Solution		**Dual Solution**	
Variable	**Value**	**Variable**	**Value**
$X(2)$	252	W (1)	4.375
$X(4)$	120	W (2)	0
$X(1)$	540	W (3)	6.9375
$X(6)$	18	W (4)	0

determine the following:

   a. Amount of each product that should be manufactured each period
   b. Maximum total profit
   c. Amount of each resource used to obtain the optimal output
   d. Amount that total profit will change if one additional unit of raw material is made available to the manufacturing process
   e. Amount that total profit will change if skilled labor input is increased by one hour

13. How could your university make use of linear programming to schedule courses, professors, and facilities? Try to develop explicitly the objective function and to identify the important constraints within such a linear-programming model.

14. Obtain a copy of a management science textbook (such as the Anderson et al. book referenced in footnote 1 of this chapter) that describes and illustrates the step-by-step procedure involved in solving linear-programming problems using the simplex method. After studying this algorithm, apply it to one or more of the linear-programming problems presented above (such as 1, 4, 6, and 7). Compare your answers with the graphical solutions.

Note: The following exercises require the use of a computer program to solve the linear-programming problems.

15. Solve Exercise 1 using a computer program. Compare the computer solution with the graphical solution.

16. Solve Exercise 4 using a computer program. Compare the computer solution with the graphical solution.

17. Solve Exercise 6 using a computer program. Compare the computer solution with the graphical solution.

18. Solve Exercise 7 using a computer program. Compare the computer solution with the graphical solution.

19. Solve Exercise 9 using a computer program.

20. Solve Exercise 10 using a computer program.

21. Solve Exercise 11 using a computer program.

www exercise

Learning to Download and Use Free Linear Programming Software

22. Access the LINDO Systems, Inc. Internet site at http://www.lindo.com/download. html There are several different programs that you can download; the activity below is based on downloading the What's Best! software, which plugs in to Excel. Once you download What's Best!, double-click on the downloaded file (the one used here is wb30) to install the program. Once the program is installed, you can learn how to use What's Best! by accessing "A Simple Tutorial" by way of the "What's Best! Help" file. What's Best! comes with a number of sample linear programming sample spreadsheets, including a cost-minimizing shipping problem and a profit-maximizing product mix problem.

PRICING AND OUTPUT DECISIONS: STRATEGY AND TACTICS

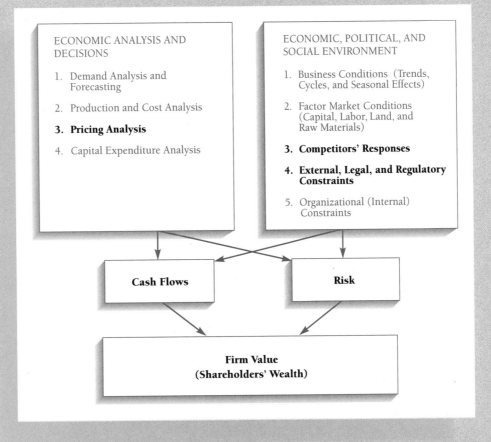

ECONOMIC ANALYSIS AND DECISIONS

1. Demand Analysis and Forecasting

2. Production and Cost Analysis

3. **Pricing Analysis**

4. Capital Expenditure Analysis

ECONOMIC, POLITICAL, AND SOCIAL ENVIRONMENT

1. Business Conditions (Trends, Cycles, and Seasonal Effects)

2. Factor Market Conditions (Capital, Labor, Land, and Raw Materials)

3. **Competitors' Responses**

4. **External, Legal, and Regulatory Constraints**

5. Organizational (Internal) Constraints

Cash Flows

Risk

Firm Value (Shareholders' Wealth)

In the previous chapters we developed the theories and measurement techniques useful in analyzing demand, production, and cost relationships in a firm. In this part we consider the profit-maximizing price-output decisions facing firms in pure competition and monopolistic competition (Chapter 12). Chapter 13 considers the role played by information asymmetries in pricing and contracting decisions. Chapter 14 considers price and output determination in monopoly markets, and Chapter 15 examines these issues in oligopoly markets. Chapter 16 presents a game-theoretic framework for analyzing rival response tactics in oligopoly markets. Appendix 16A discusses optimal mechanism design in serving a queue, conducting an auction, or in vertical requirements contracting with franchise distributors or independent dealers.

Chapter 17 examines specialized pricing problems including pricing for the multi-product firm, pricing of joint products, price discrimination, and pricing techniques used in practice by many firms. Appendix 17A presents the pricing concepts from yield management analysis. Chapter 18 considers the extent, rationale for, and consequences of government regulation of the private sector of the economy. Appendix 18A looks more closely at the problem and solution of economic externalities.

12

Prices, Output, and Strategy: Pure and Monopolistic Competition

CHAPTER PREVIEW

Stockholder wealth-maximizing managers seek a pricing and output strategy that will maximize the present value of the future profit stream to the firm. The determination of the wealth-maximizing pricing strategy depends on the production capacity and technology available to the firm in the short run, the potential for future changes in this production capacity, the cost of producing various levels of output, the nature of the demand for the firm's products, and the potential for immediate and longer-term competition. In this chapter we develop the traditional static partial equilibrium models of price and output determination under certainty for purely competitive markets and monopolistically competitive markets. We also relate these static partial equilibrium models to Michael Porter's Five Forces Strategic Framework for managers facing a wide range of market conditions.

MANAGERIAL CHALLENGE

ANTI-TICKET-SCALPING LAWS[1]

Ticket scalping is the practice of buying tickets at one price and reselling them at a higher price. Some estimates indicate that ticket scalping is a $600 million industry. The practice of ticket scalping is an emotional issue that has motivated nearly half of the states in the United States to regulate it or to forbid it. For example, in New York State ticket scalpers are subject to fines and jail terms of up to one year. North Carolina limits the maximum profit on a ticket resale to $3. Billy Joel has been quoted as saying, "For someone to have to pay more than $30 to see my show is outrageous. My show isn't worth $150."

Contrary to the moral tone of laws enacted to limit or prohibit scalping, many economists have criticized anti-scalping laws as an inefficient and otherwise unwarranted interference with the operation of a free market. Indeed some suggest that these laws have been enacted not to protect the public but rather to protect entrenched business interests.

Williams (see footnote 1) has examined these issues in the context of NFL game tickets. Williams found that anti-scalping laws do make a difference. In states with anti-scalping laws, NFL ticket prices tend to be lower. When scalping is permitted, there is strong evidence that ticket prices are higher. For example, the presence of ticket scalping in California appears to permit the San Francisco 49ers to charge $1.95 more per ticket than would be the case if scalping were outlawed. In his study, Williams controlled for the impact of team quality, team salaries, population, competition, seating capacity, and income in the city of the team.

Why are ticket prices higher in areas where scalping is permitted? One possible explanation is that when legal scalping is permitted, this "shadow market" provides important information to the team whose tickets are being scalped about the real market-clearing price for its tickets. This information can be used to justify ticket price increases from time to time.

From a policy perspective, it appears that economic interests of team owners would be best served if the markets in which they operate permit ticket scalping. In the light of this information, it is not clear why many team owners have been strong proponents of anti-scalping legislation.

www . . . .
To read about another recent anti-ticket-scalping case in Connecticut, access the following Internet site:
http://www.cslnet.ctstateu.edu/attygenl/metro1.htm

---

[1] Based on Andrew T. Williams, "Do Anti-Ticket Scalping Laws Make a Difference?" *Managerial and Decision Economics* (September-October 1994), pp. 503–509.

THE RELEVANT MARKET CONCEPT

The concept of a *relevant market* is important to the consideration of price and output determination. *A relevant market is a group of economic agents (individuals and/or firms) that interact with each other in a buyer-seller relationship.* This interaction results in transactions between the demand (buyer) side of the market and the supply (seller) side of the market. The sellers and buyers are members of the relevant market's strategic group.

Markets often have both spatial and product characteristics. For example, the market for Microsoft's Windows 97 may include individuals around the world, whereas the market for Minneapolis-origin air travel is confined to suppliers in the upper Midwest. Similarly, the market for large, prime-rate commercial loans includes large banks and corporations from all areas of the United States, whereas the market for personal banking services is geographically localized. The market for rare coins, often sold at auctions, includes relatively few individual buyers and sellers, but both groups are drawn from a broad geographic region.

Markets are the focal point for economic activity. Because of the important role played by markets in pricing and allocating resources in a competitive economy, managers whose principal responsibility is strategic planning and public policy analysis should focus considerable attention on the *market structures* that have developed for various goods or services. For example, the four largest firms in the cigarette industry control about 90 percent of the output of that industry. Similarly, the four largest producers of breakfast cereals control 86 percent of the output of that market. In contrast, the market for concrete block and brick is more fragmented—with the largest four firms accounting for only 8 percent of the total output. Even the largest 20 firms account for only 19 percent of total output. Recently, the share of the total output produced by the largest four firms in the women's hosiery industry has grown from 32 percent to 58 percent. These differences in market structures and changes in market structures over time have important implications for the determination of price levels, price stability, resource-allocation efficiency, technological progress, and the likelihood of sustained profitability in these relevant markets.

PORTER'S FIVE FORCES STRATEGIC FRAMEWORK

Michael Porter[2] has developed a conceptual framework for identifying the sources of competitive advantage in a relevant market. Incumbent firms attempt to secure these competitive advantages through their choice of management strategy. Porter conceptualizes management strategy in terms of the likelihood of profitability for a particular industry or line of business. Figure 12.1 displays Porter's five forces that determine the likelihood of sustained profitability: the threat of substitutes, the threat of entry, the power of buyers, the power of suppliers, and the intensity of rivalry.

Threat of Substitutes

First, incumbent profitability is determined by the threat of substitutes. Is the product generic like AAA grade January wheat, two bedroom apartments, and office supplies or is it branded like Jordache Jeans, Coca-Cola, and Marlboros? The more brand loyalty the less the power of substitutes and the higher the incumbent's profitability. Also, the more distant the substitutes outside the relevant market, the less price-responsive will be demand, and the larger will be the optimal mark-ups and profit margins. Iced tea, coffee, and fruit drinks are not perceived by consumers as offering the lifestyle choice associated with "the Pepsi Generation." However, flavored and unflavored bottled water products may erode the loyalty of cola drinkers. If so, cola profitability will decline.

The closeness or distance of substitutes often hinges not only on consumer perceptions created by advertising but also on segmentation of the customers into separate distribution channels. L'Eggs pantyhose distributed through grocery and convenience stores has many fewer substitutes at 9 P.M. the night before a business trip than does pantyhose sold through the department store distribution channels. Consequently, the power of substitutes is reduced, and the profit margin on L'Eggs pantyhose is high. Similarly, one-stop service and non-stop service in airlines are different

---

[2] Michael Porter, *Competitive Strategy* (Cambridge, MA: Harvard University Press, 1980). See also Cynthia Porter and Michael Porter, eds., *Strategy: Seeking and Securing Competitive Advantage* (Cambridge, MA: Harvard Business School Publishing, 1992).

FIGURE   12.1   Porter's Five Forces Strategic Model

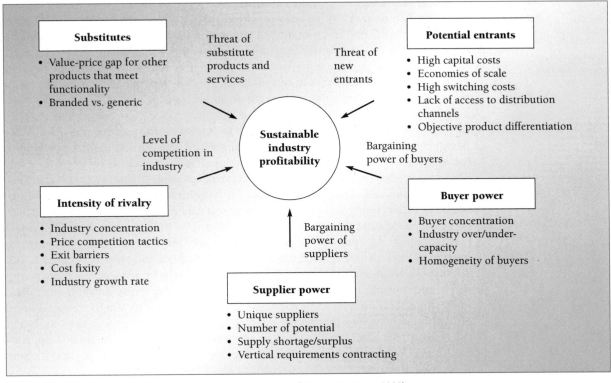

Source: *M. Porter,* Competitive Strategy *(Cambridge, MA: Harvard University Press, 1980).*

products with different functionality. United's hub at Chicago provides a geographically segmented substitute for Minneapolis-origin air travelers.

Geographic and product segmentation can reduce but not eliminate the power of substitutes. Frequent one-stop service through United's Chicago hub may limit the profitability of Northwest Airline's non-stop service at its Minneapolis hub. A large percentage change in quantity demanded of one-stop service when non-stop fares rise (i.e., a positive sign and large absolute size of the cross-price elasticity of demand) would suggest that the relevant market should be defined as all air travel in the upper Midwest, not just non-stop service out of Minneapolis.

EXAMPLE

www
Read the latest on Microsoft's experiences with U.S. antitrust law at the following Internet site maintained by FindLaw: http://www.findlaw.com/01topics/01antitrust/microsoft.html

RELEVANT MARKET FOR WEB BROWSERS: MICROSOFT'S INTERNET EXPLORER[3]

One of the recurring antitrust policy questions in the 1990s has been the definition of the relevant market for computer software. In 1996, Netscape's user-friendly and pioneering product had an 82 percent share in the Internet browser market. But

[3] Based on "U.S. Sues Microsoft over PC Browser," and "Personal Technology," *Wall Street Journal*, 21 and 30 October 1997, "Microsoft's Browser: A Bundle of Trouble," *The Economist*, 25 October 1997, and *U.S. News and World Report*, Business and Technology, 15 December 1997.

during 1996–97, Microsoft's Internet Explorer made swift inroads. Bundling Explorer with its widely adopted Windows 95 operating system, Microsoft marketed an integrated software package pre-installed on PCs. Microsoft quoted higher prices for Windows 95 alone than for Windows with Internet Explorer and threatened PC assemblers like Compaq and Gateway with removal of their Windows 95 license unless they mounted Explorer as a desktop icon. Because most PC customers do want Windows pre-installed on their machines, Explorer penetrated deep into the browser market very quickly. By the start of 1998, some estimates showed Explorer's market share as high as 39 percent.

If the relevant market for these products is an integrated PC operating system (OS), then Microsoft has simply incorporated new technology into an already dominant Windows OS product. An analogy might be the interlock between an automobile's ignition and steering system to deter auto theft. If, on the other hand, Internet browsers are a separate relevant market, like stereo equipment for an automobile, then Microsoft is not entitled to employ anticompetitive practices like tying arrangements to extend their dominance of PC operating systems into this new software market.

Microsoft's spectacular growth in sales of Windows 95 is not the issue. Winning a near monopoly of 85 percent market share in the previously fragmented OS software industry indicates a superior product, a great business plan, and good management. But allowing Microsoft to extend that market power into a new line of business using tactics that would be ineffective and self-defeating in the absence of the dominant market share in the original business, is just what the antitrust laws were intended to prevent. Future Microsoft products may thoroughly integrate the OS and Internet web browser, but at the moment, the latter appears to be an application program separate from the operating system. As such, Microsoft will have to cease any marketing practices that illegally tie the two products.

Threat of Entry

A second force determining the likely profitability of an industry or product line is the threat of potential entrants. The higher the barriers to entry, the more profitable an incumbent will be. Barriers to entry can arise from several factors. First, consider high capital costs. The bottling and distribution business in the soft drink industry necessitates a $50 million investment. Although a good business plan with secure collateral will always attract loanable funds, unsecured loans become difficult to finance at this size. Few potential entrants with the necessary capital implies a lesser threat of entry and higher incumbent profitability.

Second, economies of scale can provide another barrier to entry. In the traditional cable TV industry, the huge infrastructure cost of laying wire throughout the community deterred multiple entrants. The first-mover had a tremendous advantage in spreading fixed cost across a large customer base. Of course, new wireless technology for satellite-based TV may soon lower this barrier, and then numerous suppliers of TV content will exhibit similar unit cost.

Third, if customers are brand loyal, the costs of inducing a customer to switch to a new entrant's product may pose a substantial barrier to entry. Year after year, hundreds of millions of dollars of cumulative advertising in the cereals industry maintains the pulling power of the Tony the Tiger Frosted Flakes brand. Unadvertised cereals go unnoticed. To take another example, airlines raise the switching costs for their regular customers when they issue frequent flyer give-aways. Committing seat capacity to promotional give-aways raises barriers to entry. New entrants therefore have a very high cost of becoming an effective entry threat in these markets.

POTENTIAL ENTRY AT OFFICE DEPOT–STAPLES[4]

In 1997 Office Depot and Staples proposed to merge. Their combined sales in the $13 billion office supply superstore industry totaled 76 percent. Potential competitors include not only Office Max but all small paper goods specialty stores, department stores, discount stores like K-Mart, warehouse clubs like Sam's Club, office supply catalogs, and some computer retailers. This larger office supply industry is very fragmented, easy to enter, and huge; 1996 sales topped $185 billion. By this latter standard, the proposed merger involved a combined firm with only 9 percent market share.

The profit margins of Office Depot, Office Max, and Staples are significantly higher where only one superstore locates in a town. This would suggest that the small-scale office suppliers offer little threat of entry into the superstore market. The exceptional ease of entry (and exit) at small scale moderates the markups and profit margins of incumbent specialty retailers like stationery stores but not of superstores. High capital requirement and scale economies in warehousing and distribution appear responsible for the barriers to entry in the office supply superstore market.

Access to distribution channels is another potential barrier that has implications for the profitability of incumbents. The shelf space in grocery stores is very limited; all the slots are filled. A new entrant would therefore have to offer huge trade promotions (i.e., free display racks or slot-in allowances) to induce grocery store chains to displace one of their current suppliers.

Finally, a barrier to entry may be posed by product differentiation. If the differences between products are objective (e.g., reliability in a copier or ingredients in Coca-Cola's syrup), the entrant must first reverse engineer the copier or attempt to duplicate the syrup characteristics. All that takes time and expense; meanwhile the incumbent is rolling out a new product. In sum, the higher these barriers to entry, the less the threat of potential entrants and the greater the industry profitability.

OBJECTIVE VERSUS PERCEIVED PRODUCT DIFFERENTIATION: XEROX

Shielded from competition by patents on its landmark dry paper copier, Xerox enjoyed a virtual monopoly and 20 percent compound earnings growth through the 1960s and early 1970s. During this period, its research lab in Palo Alto, California, spun off one breakthrough device after another. One year it was the graphical user interface that Apple later brought to market as a user-friendly PC. In 1979, Xerox scientists and engineers developed the Ethernet, a first local area network for connecting computers and printers. Yet, Xerox was able to commercialize almost none of these R&D successes. As a result, Japanese copier companies like Canon and Ikon reverse engineered the Xerox product, imitated its processes, and ultimately developed better and cheaper copiers. Especially with the increasing globalization of commerce, objective product differentiation is always subject to reverse engineering, violations of intellectual property, and offshore imitation even of patented products. In contrast, product differentiation based on customer perceptions of lifestyle images and product positioning (e.g., Coca-Cola) can continuously reduce the power of substitutes and better survive a competitive attack.

---

[4] Based on "FTC Rejects Staples' Settlement Offer," *Wall Street Journal,* 7 April 1997, p. A3.

Power of Buyers and Suppliers

The profitability of incumbents is determined in part by the bargaining power of buyers and suppliers. Buyers may be highly concentrated like Boeing, Lockheed, and Airbus in the purchase of large aircraft engines or extremely fragmented like the restaurants who are customers of wholesale grocery companies. If industry capacity approximately equals or exceeds demand, concentrated buyers can force price concessions which reduce incumbent profitability. On the other hand, fragmented buyers have little bargaining power unless excess capacity and inventory overhang persist.

Unique suppliers may also reduce industry profitability. The Coca-Cola Co. establishes exclusive franchise arrangements with independent bottlers. No other supplier can provide the secret ingredients in the concentrate syrup. Bottler profitability is therefore rather low. In contrast, Coke's own suppliers are numerous; many potential sugar and flavoring manufacturers would like to win the Coca-Cola account, and the syrup inputs are nonunique commodities. These factors raise the likely profitability of the concentrate manufacturers.

Intensity of Rivalrous Tactics

In the global economy, few companies can establish and maintain dominance in anything beyond niche markets. Reverse engineering of products, imitation of advertising images, and offshore production at low cost imply General Motors (GM) cannot hope to rid themselves of Ford and Chrysler, Coca-Cola cannot hope truly to defeat Pepsi, and American Airlines cannot kill off United and Delta. Instead, to sustain profitability in such a setting, companies must avoid intense rivalries and elicit passive more cooperative responses from close competitors. The intensity of the rivalry in an industry depends on several factors: industry concentration, the degree of price competition, exit barriers, and the industry growth rate.

What firms and what products offer close substitutes for potential customers in the relevant market determines the degree of industry concentration. One measure of industry concentration is the sum of the market shares of the four largest or eight largest firms in an industry. The larger the market shares and the smaller the number of competitors, the more interdependence each firm will perceive, and the more intense the rivalry. The ready-to-eat cereal industry has intense rivalry in part because Kelloggs (37 percent), General Mills (25 percent), Post (15 percent), and Quaker Oats (8 percent) together enjoy 85 percent of the market.

Intensity of rivalry is also reduced by tactics that focus on non-price rather than price competition. Airlines are more profitable when they can avoid price wars and focus their competition for passengers on service quality—e.g., delivery reliability, change-order responsiveness, and schedule convenience. But trunk route airlines between major U.S. cities provide generic transportation with nearly identical service quality and departure frequency. Consequently, fare wars are frequent, and the profitability of trunk airline routes is therefore low. In contrast, long-standing rivals Coca-Cola and Pepsi have never discounted their cola concentrates. This absence of "gain-share discounting" and a diminished focus on price competition tactics in general increases the profitability of the concentrate business.

EXAMPLE

PRICE COMPETITION AT THE SODA FOUNTAIN: PEPSICO INC.[5]

Soft drinks are marketed through several distribution channels. Independent and company-owned bottlers supply supermarkets, convenience stores, and vending machines which accounted for 31 percent, 12 percent, and 11 percent, respectively, of all soft drink sales in 1996. Shelf slots in these channels are full, and bottlers compete on stocking services and retailer rebates for prime shelf space and vending machine locations in an attempt to grow their brands. With 34 percent and 32 percent market shares, the Coca-Cola and Pepsi bottlers attempt to avoid head-to-head price competition, which would simply lower profits for both firms, and instead seek predictable patterns of company-sponsored once-every-other-week discounts. Where independent bottlers have established a practice of persistent gain-share discounting, the Coca-Cola Company and PepsiCo have often attempted to purchase the franchises and replace them with company-owned bottlers.

Price competition is heating up, however, in the fountain drink side of the business. As more and more families eat more and more meals outside the household, the fountain drink channel accounted for 27 percent of total sales in 1996 up from 17 percent in 1993. Coca-Cola has long dominated the fountain drink business. At restaurants and soda shops in 1993, Coke enjoyed a 59 percent share to Pepsi's 27 percent. By 1996 Coca-Cola's market share was 64 percent to Pepsi's 21 percent. Recently, PepsiCo declared an intent to vigorously pursue fountain drink sales through discount pricing tactics if necessary. This development threatens continuing profitability in this important channel of the soft drink industry.

Break-Even Sales Change Analysis
A calculation of the percentage increase in unit sales required to justify a price discount, given the gross margin.

The incidence of price competition is determined in part by the cost structure prevalent in the industry. Where fixed costs as a percentage of total costs are high, margins will tend to be larger. If so, every additional customer represents a substantial contribution to covering the fixed costs. All other things the same, gain-share discounting will therefore tend to increase the greater the fixed cost. For example, gross margins in the airline industry reflect the enormous fixed costs for aircraft leases and terminal facilities, often reaching 80 percent. Consider the following **break-even sales change analysis** for an airline that seeks to increase its total contributions by lowering its prices 10 percent:

$$(P_0 - MC)\, Q_0 < (0.9\, P_0 - MC)\, Q_1. \qquad [12.1]$$
$$< (0.9\, P_0 - MC)\, (Q_0 + \Delta Q).$$

If discounting is to succeed, the change in sales ΔQ must be great enough to more than offset the 10 percent decline in revenue per unit sale. Rearranging Equation 12.1 and dividing by P_0 yields,

$$\frac{(P_0 - MC)\, Q_0}{P_0} < \frac{[(P_0 - MC)}{P_0} - 0.1\, \frac{P_0\,(Q_0 + \Delta Q)}{P_0}$$

$$PCM\, Q_0 < [PCM - 0.1]\, (Q_0 + \Delta Q)$$

where PCM is the price-cost margin percentage. That is,

$$\frac{PCM}{[PCM - 0.1]} < \frac{(Q_0 + \Delta Q)}{Q_0}$$

$$\frac{PCM}{[PCM - 0.1]} < 1 + \frac{\Delta Q}{Q_0} \qquad [12.2]$$

---

[5] Based on "Cola Wars Continue," Harvard Business School Case Publishing, 1994 and "Pepsi Hopes to Tap Coke's Fountain Sales," *USA Today,* 6 November 1997, p. 3B.

For airlines, an 80 percent price-cost margin implies that a sales increase of just 15 percent is all that one requires to warrant cutting prices by 10 percent:

$$\frac{0.8}{[0.8 - 0.1]} < 1 + \frac{\Delta Q}{Q_0}$$

$$1.14 \quad < 1 + \frac{\Delta Q}{Q_0}$$

In contrast, in paperback book publishing, a price-cost margin of 12 percent implies sales must increase by better than 500 percent in order to warrant a 10 percent price cut—i.e., $0.12/0.02 < 1 + 5.0^+$. Because a marketing plan that creates a 15 percent sales increase from a 10 percent price cut is much more likely than one that creates a 500 percent sales increase from a 10 percent price cut, the airline industry is more likely to focus on pricing competition than the paperback book publishing industry.

Barriers to exit also reduce the intensity of rivalry in a tight oligopoly. If remote plants specific to a particular line of products (e.g., aluminum smelting plants) are nonredeployable, tactics will be less aggressive because no competitor can fully recover their sunk cost should margins collapse. In addition to capital equipment, nonredeployable assets can include product-specific display racks (L'Eggs), product-specific showrooms (Ethan Allen), and intangible assets that prove difficult to carve up and package for resale (unpatented trade secrets and basic research). Trucking companies, on the other hand, own very redeployable assets—i.e., trucks and warehouses. If a trucking company attacks its rivals, encounters aggressive retaliation, then fails and must liquidate its assets, the owners can hope to receive nearly the full value of the economic working life remaining in their trucks and warehouses. As a result, competitive tactics in the trucking industry are often intensely rivalrous, implying reduced profitability.

Finally, industry demand growth can influence the intensity of rivalry. When sales to established customers are increasing and new customers are appearing in the market, rival firms are often content to maintain market share and realize high profitability. When demand growth declines, competitive tactics sharpen in many industries especially if capacity planning failed to anticipate the decline. Furniture companies discount steeply when housing demand slows. Airline prices and profits declined sharply when demand for air travel leveled off unexpectedly after the Gulf War. Between 1965 and 1975, soft drink consumption in the United States grew by 49 percent. Again, between 1975 and 1985, demand growth was 53 percent. However, from 1985 to 1995, U.S. demand grew by only 24 percent. Sales in the United States flattened out by 1992; annual consumption had reached a plateau of approximately 50 gallons per person (i.e., a gallon per week). Porter's model predicts that flat soft drink demand would lead to more intense rivalry and the lower profitability that PepsiCo Inc. and Coca-Cola Co. are experiencing. Recently, Coke has undertaken many initiatives in its fast-growing international division in an attempt to reduce the likelihood of intense rivalry with PepsiCo.

EXAMPLE

INTENSITY OF RIVALRY AT NORTHWEST AIRLINES[6]

The Minneapolis hub of Northwest Airlines is a very concentrated terminal facility; Northwest has over 80 percent of the flights. Thus, Northwest's market share is comparable to Microsoft's dominance of the operating system business with Windows 95.

---

[6] Based on "Mergers, Monopolies, and the Soaring Cost of Flying," *The Margin,* March/April 1990, p. 19 and "Flying to Charlotte Is Easy," *Wall Street Journal,* 14 June 1995, p. S1.

www . . . .
You can learn more about
a recent U.S. Department
of Transportation study of
entry issues associated
with fortress hubs at the
following Internet site
maintained by AirportNet:
http://www.airportnet.org
/depts/publicat/express/
1996htm/3-11-96.htm

However, high indirect fixed costs for aircraft leases and facilities imply high margins that make it very tempting for airlines to attract incremental customers through price discounting. In contrast, Windows is seldom, if ever, discounted. Consequently, in one-stop flights from Minneapolis, Northwest is subject to intense price competition. Also, exit barriers are low in airlines but rather high in computer software where massive sunk cost expenses for research and development create largely unpatentable trade secrets that are not easily packaged for resale. Finally, industry demand growth is low in airlines but extremely high in computer software.

Frequent price competition, low exit barriers, and flat growth all imply tremendous rivalrous intensity in the airline industry and downward competitive pressure on Northwest Airline's net profit margins. The opposite is true in Microsoft's OS software business. Windows 95 is seldom discounted and remains extremely profitable. In short, airlines have industry characteristics that incline the performance results of even a dominant firm to be more nearly competitive, whereas a dominant firm in computer operating systems faces few of these competitive forces.

The one exception to this reasoning occurs in fortress hubs like Northwest's Minneapolis, and in Charlotte where USAir has 94 percent of the flights. Fortress hubs have few gates remaining for new entrant operations. And new hubs entail high capital investment that may be difficult to liquidate if the new carrier decides to exit. Since the barriers to entry are considerable and the exit barriers nontrivial, fares for nonstop service to and from fortress hubs are very high despite slow demand growth and intense price competition on other routes. In 1994, the 45-minute 227-mile trip between Charlotte and Atlanta on USAir (or Delta) averaged $301 per round-trip with last-three-day bookings exceeding $400. Southwest Airlines offers many round-trip flights of this length for $150 and less.

INDIVIDUAL, FIRM, AND RELEVANT MARKET DEMAND FUNCTIONS

Recall from Chapter 4 that a *demand function* describes the relationship that exists during some period of time between the number of units of a good or service that consumers are willing to buy and a set of factors that influence the willingness to purchase, such as price, income, and advertising. Many times a demand function is represented by a *demand schedule* and/or a *demand curve* that specifies the relationship between prices and the quantities that will be demanded at those prices, holding constant the influence of all other factors.

As discussed in Chapter 4 and illustrated in Figure 4.3, the relationship between the demand curve of various individuals for a specific good or service at some point in time and the market (aggregate) demand curve for that good or service is straightforward. The market demand curve is obtained by laterally summing the demand curves of all individual consumers.

The relationship between the demand function for the single firm and the industry or market demand function is more complex. The nature of the demand function for the individual firm is largely dependent on these conditions:

1. The number and relative size of firms in the industry.
2. The similarity of the products sold by the firms of the industry; that is, the degree of product differentiation.
3. The degree to which decision making by individual firms is independent not interdependent or collusive.
4. The conditions of entry and exit.

On the basis of the nature of these conditions, four specific market structures traditionally have been defined: atomistic competition, monopoly, monopolistic competition, and oligopoly.

Atomistic or Pure Competition

Atomistic or Pure Competition
A market structure characterized by a very large number of buyers and sellers of a homogeneous (nondifferentiated) product. Entry and exit from the industry is costless, or nearly so. Information is freely available to all market participants, and there is no collusion among firms in the industry.

The **atomistic competition** industry model has the following characteristics:

1. A very large number of buyers and sellers, each of which buys or sells such a small proportion of the total industry output that a single buyer's or seller's actions cannot have a perceptible impact on the market price.
2. A homogeneous product produced by each firm; that is, no product differentiation, as with temporary typing services or AAA-grade January wheat.
3. Complete knowledge of all relevant market information by all firms, each of which acts totally independently as, for example, the 117 home builders of standardized three-bedroom subdivision homes in a large city.
4. Free entry and exit from the market, that is, minimal barriers to entry and exit.

The single firm in a purely competitive industry is, in essence, a price taker. Because the products of each producer are perfect substitutes for the products of every other producer, the single firm in pure competition can do nothing but offer its entire output at the going market price. As a result, the individual firm's demand curve approaches perfect elasticity at the market price. It can sell nothing at a higher price because all buyers (assuming rationality) will shift to other sellers. If the firm sells at a price slightly below the long-run market price, its quantity demanded approaches infinity. In the long run, at a price below the market price the firm will lose money, as is demonstrated below. In addition, the firm has no motivation to sell below the market price because each firm may sell its entire output at the market price without having any perceptible influence on that price.

Figure 12.2 indicates the nature of the industry and firm demand curves under pure competition, as, for example, in wheat production. Line *DD'* represents the total industry or market demand curve for bushels of wheat and *SS'* is the market supply curve. At

FIGURE   12.2

Atomistic or Pure
Competition

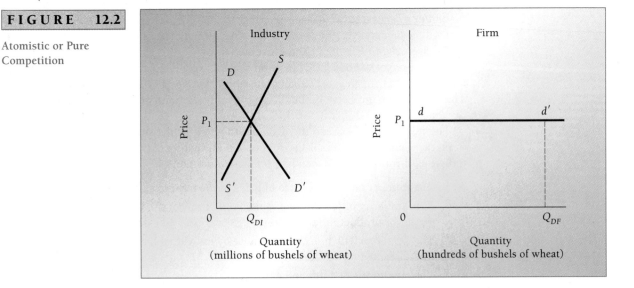

price P_1, the market price, a total of Q_{DI} bushels of wheat will be demanded by the sum of all firms in the industry. Line dd' represents the demand curve facing each individual firm. The individual firm sells its entire output, Q_{DF}, at the market price P_1. By definition the quantity Q_{DF} represents only a small (atomistic) fraction of the total industry demand of Q_{DI}.

THE SUPPLY FUNCTION

The supply function of a good or service is defined as the quantities of that good or service that sellers are willing to make available to purchasers at all possible prices during some period of time. Some of the most important factors that influence the willingness of suppliers to offer goods or services to the market are (1) the price of the commodity; (2) the prices of the resources that must be used to produce the commodity, such as land, labor, and capital resources; and (3) the technology available to produce the product.

By holding constant the prices of resources used to produce the commodity and the technology available for production, we can represent the supply curve as the relationship between the quantity producers are willing to offer for sale and the various asking prices that could be charged. At lower asking price levels, less of a commodity is offered for sale because fewer producers find it profitable to sell the product at the low price. In contrast, as prices increase producers are willing to sell more of the product because their potential profits are enhanced as a result of this higher asking price (if the effects of all other factors are held constant). Thus, in Figure 12.3 we see that a positive relationship exists between price and quantity supplied as indicated by the curve labeled SS.

Movement *along* the supply curve is referred to as a *change in the quantity supplied.* In contrast, a movement *of* the entire supply curve is referred to as a *change in supply.* For example, curve S_1S_1 represents an increase in supply. For any price, such as P_1, the quantity that producers are willing to supply is greater on curve S_1S_1 than it is on curve SS. This supply increase may reflect a technological advance that has lowered the cost of production, a reduction in the cost of one or more of the inputs in the production of the commodity, or simply an increase in the number of firms willing to produce the good or service in question.

FIGURE   12.3

Supply Curves

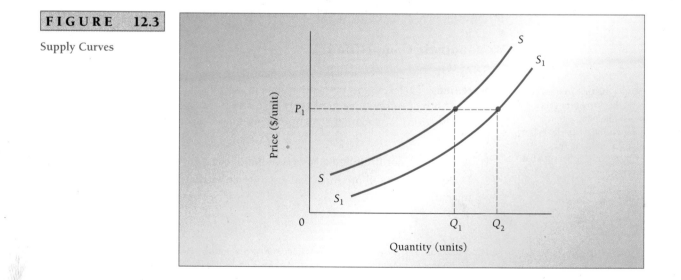

Monopoly

Monopoly
A market structure characterized by one firm producing a highly differentiated product in a market with significant barriers to entry.

The **monopoly** model, the other extreme in market structure from atomistic competition, of an industry is characterized as follows:

1. Only one firm producing some specific product line (in a specified market area), like an exclusive cable TV franchise.
2. Low cross elasticity of demand between the monopolist's product and any other product; that is, no close substitute products.
3. No interdependence with other competitors because the firm is a monopolist in its relevant market.
4. Substantial barriers to entry that prevent competition from entering the industry. These barriers include the following:
   a. Absolute cost advantages of the established firm, resulting from economies in securing inputs or from patented production techniques.
   b. Product differentiation advantages, resulting from consumer loyalty to established products.
   c. Scale economies, which increase the difficulty for new firms in financing an efficient-sized plant or building up a sufficient market. The need to build a large plant to compete effectively is also likely to lead to excess capacity in the industry, depressed prices, and reduced profits for all firms. The new lower prices may not be high enough to permit the new entrant to survive and generate profits. This prospect may deter many potential entrants from actually entering a market where scale economies are substantial.
   d. Large capital requirements, exceeding the financial resources of potential entrants.
   e. Legal exclusion of potential competitors, as is the case for public utilities and patents and licensing arrangements, are some of the most effective barriers to entry.
   f. Information that is not available to potential competitors.

By definition the demand curve of the individual monopoly firm is identical with the industry demand curve, because the firm is the industry. As we will see in Chapter 14, the identity between the firm and industry demand curves allows decision making for the monopolist to be a relatively simple matter, compared to the complexity of rivalrous tactics with few close competitors in tight oligopoly groups.

Monopolistic Competition

Monopolistic Competition
A market structure very much like pure competition, with the major distinction being the existence of a differentiated product.

In 1933 E.H. Chamberlin and Joan Robinson developed the theory of **monopolistic competition.**[7] The term was coined because monopolistic competition includes characteristics both of competitive markets (e.g., many firms) and of monopoly (e.g., product differentiation). The market structure of monopolistic competition is characterized as follows:

1. A few dominant firms and a large number of competitive fringe firms.
2. Dominant firms sell products that are differentiated in some manner, real or imagined.

---

[7] E.H. Chamberlin, *The Theory of Monopolistic Competition* (Cambridge: Harvard University Press, 1933), p. 56. See also Joan Robinson, *The Economics of Imperfect Competition* (New York: Macmillan, 1933).

3. Independent decision making by individual firms.

4. Ease of entry and exit from the market as a whole but very substantial barriers to effective entry among the leading brands.

By far the most important distinguishing characteristic of monopolistic competition, however, is that the outputs of each firm are differentiated in some way from those of every other firm. In other words, the cross elasticity of demand between the products of individual firms is high, but not perfect. Product differentiation may be based on exclusive features (Disneyworld), trademarks (Nike's swosh), trade names (Bass Weejuns), packaging (L'Eggs hosiery), quality (Coach handbags), design (Sony Walkman), color and style (Swatch watches), or the conditions of sale. These conditions may include such factors as credit terms, location of the seller, congeniality of sales personnel, after-sale service, warranties, and so on.

In the world of monopolistic competition it is difficult to define an industry demand curve because each firm produces a product differentiated in some manner from the products of other firms. Thus, rather than well-defined industries, one tends to get something of a continuum of products. Generally, it is rather easy to identify groups of differentiated products that fall in the same industry, like light beers, after shave colognes, or perfumes.

The demand curve for the product of any one firm is expected to have a negative slope. Because there are, by definition, a large number of close but not perfect substitute products, the curve usually will be quite elastic (see Figure 12.4).

The more a firm differentiates its product from that of its competitors, the less elastic will be the demand curve for the differentiating firm's output (that is, the more latitude the firm has in pricing its product). The case of the monopolistic competitor's demand curve has been well summarized by Baumol:

> Under monopolistic competition the demand curve for the product of the firm may be expected to have a negative slope, even though the firm is as small as one operating under conditions of pure competition, for customers will have different degrees of loyalty to the firms from whom they make their purchases. A small reduction in one firm's price may only attract its competitors' most mercurial customers. But, as larger and larger price reductions are instituted, it may acquire more and more customers from its rivals by drawing on customers who are less anxious to switch.[8]

---

[8] W.J. Baumol, *Economic Theory and Operations Analysis*, 4th ed. (Englewood Cliffs, N.J.: Prentice-Hall, 1977), p. 320.

FIGURE   12.4

Demand and Marginal Revenue Curves for the Firm under Monopolistic Competition

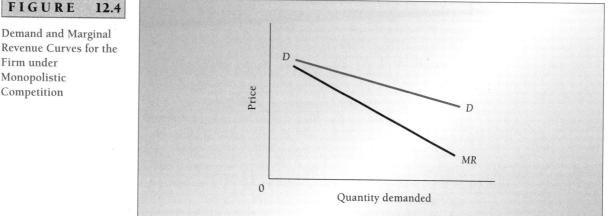

Oligopoly

Oligopolistic Competition
A market structure in which the number of firms is so small that the actions of any one firm are likely to have noticeable impacts on the performance of other firms in the industry.

The **oligopoly** model of an industry describes a market having a few closely related firms. The number of firms producing any commodity is so small that actions by an individual firm in the industry with respect to price, output, product style or quality, terms of sale, and so on, have a perceptible impact on the sales of other firms in the industry. In other words, oligopoly is distinguished by a noticeable degree of *interdependence* among firms in the industry. The products or services that are produced by oligopolists may be homogeneous—as in the cases of air travel, 40 ft. steel I-beams, aluminum, and cement—or they may be differentiated—as in the cases of automobiles, cigarettes, home appliances, cruise ships, colas, and cereals.

Although the degree of product differentiation is an important factor in shaping the single oligopolist's demand curve, the degree of interdependence of firms in the industry is of even greater significance. Primarily because of this interdependence, defining a single firm's demand curve is complicated. The relationship between price and output for a single firm is determined not only by consumer preferences, product substitutability, and level of advertising, *but also by the responses that other competitors may make to a price change by the firm.*

Because of the conceptual difficulty in defining a demand curve for oligopoly, we defer a discussion of this matter until Chapter 14.

PRICE-OUTPUT DETERMINATION UNDER ATOMISTIC (PURE) COMPETITION

As discussed above, the individual firm in an atomistically (or "purely") competitive industry is effectively a price taker because the products of every producer are perfect substitutes for the products of every other producer. Price takers cannot charge a price higher than their competitors because no one would buy from them. Although they can conceivably charge a price lower than the going price, they accept the going price to maximize profits. This leads to the familiar horizontal or perfectly elastic demand curve of the purely competitive firm. Although we rarely find instances where all the conditions for pure competition are met, securities exchanges and the commodity markets approach these conditions. For instance, the individual wheat farmer has little choice but to accept the going price for wheat; however, imperfections creep into even this case because the government provides price supports for farm commodities. In spite of the limited existence of purely competitive markets, individuals and smaller firms are often forced to act as price takers in their economic decisions. Atomistic competition also gives a basis for comparison of pricing and performance of firms in the more typical, imperfectly competitive market structures, such as oligopoly and monopolistic competition.

Short Run

A firm in a purely competitive industry may either make transitory profits or operate at a loss in the short run. In our discussion of price and output decisions, we use the term *profits* to mean returns in excess of a normal return to compensate the entrepreneur for interest on funds invested in the firm and the value of his or her labor services plus an additional amount that is *just sufficient* to keep the entrepreneur producing the same product, given the special risks associated with its production and sale. In the competitive long run, all firms will operate at an equilibrium output where all such profit and losses have disappeared. By definition, the competitive firm in long-run equilibrium just breaks even against all costs, implicit and explicit. As more firms enter (leave) the industry in the long run, supply will increase (decrease) and the market price will be driven downward (upward), helping to eliminate profits (losses) for the remaining firms.

In addition to price changes that occur in the long run, another force also drives all firms toward this break-even equilibrium as firms enter and leave the industry. A firm more efficient than its competitors may temporarily exist because some resources, such as managerial talent, firm location, and quality of raw material inputs, are not homogeneous among firms. But if Firm X has a manager whose extraordinary skills generate $5,000 more in cost savings for Firm X than a similar manager does for Firm Y, it will be in the Firm Y's interest to bid for Firm X's more efficient manager by offering a salary that fully compensates for this extraordinary effectiveness. In the world of pure competition where all firms operate under conditions of certainty and with access to full and complete markets, all savings resulting from the use of more efficient input factors will be eliminated by the competitive bidding process. In equilibrium, therefore, all firms that survive the competitive process have identical costs even though they may adopt different production and operating techniques.

The notion of a competitive long-run equilibrium may seem contrived. We should note that although the equilibrium conditions described here may never in fact occur, they nevertheless represent a condition toward which an atomistically competitive market would *tend to move* in the long run. Figure 12.5 illustrates possible short-run conditions for a competitive firm and thereafter long-run adjustment process is explained.

In atomistic or pure competition the firm must sell at the market price (p_1 or p_2), and its demand curve is represented by a horizontal line (D_1 or D_2) at the market price. In the purely competitive case, marginal revenue MR is equal to price P, because the sale of each additional unit increases total revenue by the price of that unit (which remains constant at all levels of output). For instance, if

$$P = \$8/\text{unit}$$

then

$$\text{Total revenue} = TR = P \cdot Q$$

$$= 8Q$$

FIGURE   12.5

Firm in Pure
Competition: Short Run

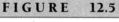

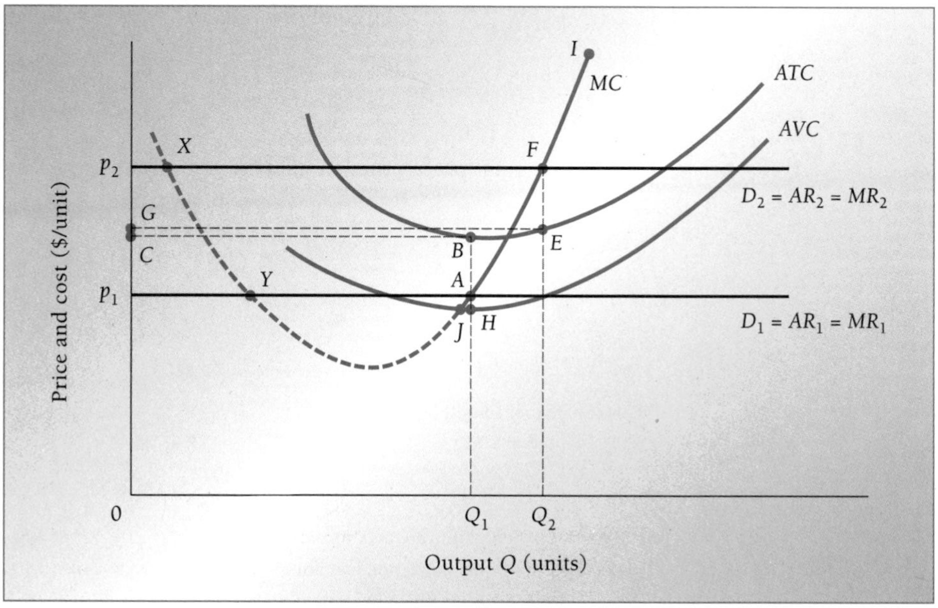

Marginal revenue is defined as the change in total revenue resulting from the sale of one additional unit, or the derivative of total revenue with respect to Q:

$$MR = \frac{dTR}{dQ} = \$8/\text{unit}$$

and marginal revenue equals price.

The profit-maximizing firm will produce at that level of output where marginal revenue equals marginal cost. Beyond that point, the production and sale of one additional unit would add more to total cost than to total revenue ($MC > MR$), and hence total profit ($TR - TC$) would decline. Up to the point where $MC = MR$, the production and sale of one more unit increases total revenue more than total cost ($MR > MC$), and total profit would increase as an additional unit is produced and sold. *Producing at the point where marginal revenue MR equals marginal cost MC is equivalent to maximizing the total profit function.*[9]

The individual firm's supply function in Figure 12.5 is equal to that portion of the MC curve from point J to point I. At any price level below point J the firm would shut down because it would not even be covering its average variable costs (i.e., $P < AVC$).

PROFIT MAXIMIZATION IN PURE COMPETITION (SHORT RUN): ADOBE CORPORATION

EXAMPLE

This example illustrates the profit-maximization conditions for a firm operating in a purely competitive market environment in the short run. Assume Adobe Corporation faces the following total revenue and total cost functions:

$$\text{Total revenue } TR = 8Q$$

$$\text{Total cost } TC = Q^2 + 4Q + 2$$

Marginal revenue and marginal cost are defined as the first derivative of total revenue and total cost, or

$$\text{Marginal revenue } MR = \frac{dTR}{dQ} = \$8/\text{unit}$$

$$\text{Marginal cost } MC = \frac{dTR}{dQ} = 2Q + 4$$

Similarly, total profit equals total revenue minus total cost:

$$\text{Total profit } (\pi) = TR - TC$$
$$= 8Q - (Q^2 + 4Q + 2)$$
$$= -Q^2 + 4Q - 2$$

---

[9] This can be proven as follows:

$$\pi = TR - TC$$
$$\frac{d\pi}{dQ} = \frac{dTR}{dQ} - \frac{dTC}{dQ} = MR - MC = 0$$

or, $MR = MC$ when profits are maximized.

Check for profit maximization by taking the second derivative of π with respect to Q, or $\frac{d^2\pi}{dQ^2}$. If it is less than zero, then π is maximized.

To maximize total profit we take the derivative of π with respect to quantity, set it equal to zero, and solve for the profit-maximizing level of Q. (It is also necessary to check the second derivative to be certain we have found a maximum, not a minimum!)[10]

$$\frac{d\pi}{dQ} = -2Q + 4 = 0$$

$$Q^* = 2 \text{ units}$$

But because $MR = \$8/\text{unit}$ and $MC = 2Q + 4 = [2(2) + 4] = \$8/\text{unit}$, when total profit is maximized, we are merely setting $MC = MR$.

Returning to Figure 12.5, if price $P = p_1$, the firm would produce the level of output Q_1, where $MC = MR$ (profits are maximized or losses minimized). In this case the firm would incur a loss per unit equal to the difference between average total cost ATC and average revenue or price. This is represented by BA in Figure 12.5. The total loss incurred by the firm at Q_1 level of output and price p_1 equals the rectangle $p_1 CBA$. This may be conceptually thought of as the loss per unit (BA) times the number of units produced and sold (Q_1). At price p_1 losses are minimized, because average variable costs AVC have been covered and a contribution remains to cover part of the fixed costs (AH per unit times Q_1 units). If the firm did not produce, it would incur losses equal to the entire amount of fixed costs (BH per unit times Q_1 units). Hence we may conclude that in the short run a firm will produce and sell at that level of output where $MR = MC$, as long as the variable costs of production are being covered ($P > AVC$). If price were p_2, the firm would produce Q_2 units and make a profit per unit of EF, or a total profit represented by the rectangle $FEGp_2$.[11]

Long Run

In the long run, illustrated in Figure 12.6, all inputs are free to vary. Hence no differentiation exists between fixed and variable costs. Under long-run conditions, average cost will tend to be just equal to price and all excessive profits will be eliminated. If price exceeds average costs, more firms will enter the industry, supply will increase, and price will be driven down toward the equilibrium, zero-profit level. In addition, as more firms bid for available factors of production (labor, capital, managerial talent), the cost of these factors will tend to rise. As mentioned earlier, if some inputs for some firms are especially productive, the competitive mechanism will result in their cost being bid up to the point where all cost savings are paid to the more productive input that made initial cost savings possible. The net result is that in the long-run equilibrium all firms will tend to have identical costs, and prices will tend to equal average costs (that is, the average cost curve AC will be tangent to the horizontal price line p_2).

---

[10] The check for profit maximization goes as follows:

$$\frac{d^2\pi}{dQ^2} = -2$$

Because the second derivative is negative, we know we have found a maximum value for the profit function.

[11] As was shown in Figure 12.5, it is possible for the marginal cost function to intersect marginal revenue at more than one place. In this case MC intersects D_2 at points X and F, and D_1 at points Y and A. In the graphic case we may eliminate the X and Y intersections because it is apparent that losses exceed those incurred under the F and A solutions. An algebraic solution to this problem would indicate that X and Y do not satisfy the required second-order condition.

FIGURE   12.6

Long-Run Equilibrium
under Pure Competition

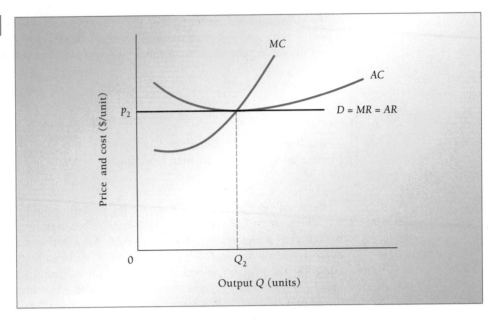

Thus we may say that at the long-run profit-maximizing level of output under pure competition, equilibrium will be achieved at a point where $P = MR = MC = AC$. At this point the firm is producing at its *most efficient* (that is, lowest average cost) level of output.

EXAMPLE

DYNAMICS OF COMPETITION AT AMAZON.COM[12]

On-line retailing has started very slowly in clothing and other search goods that buyers want to "touch and feel," but has excelled in one experience good—namely, books. One of every $27 spent on the Internet last year went to Amazon Books, the first on-line retailer in this industry. Amazon stocks less than 1,000 bestsellers but displays and provides reviews on 2.5 million popular titles. Using Ingram Book Co., the world's largest book wholesaler, Amazon is able to ship most selections in one to three days. Sales have doubled each quarter, and in 1996 topped $16 million. The potential growth for electronic booksellers is enormous because the two largest bookshop chains Barnes and Noble and Borders earned 1996 pre-tax profits of $84 million on $2.45 billion sales and $96 million on $1.96 billion sales, respectively.

The difficulty for Amazon.com, however, is that Internet retailing is a classic example of a business with low barriers to entry and exit. As soon as Amazon's business systems for display, order taking, shipping, and payments stabilize, if profits are present, one should expect substantial entry activity. For example, Barnes and Noble has entered into an exclusive contract with America Online to pitch electronic book sales to AOL's 8.5 million subscribers. Borders then quickly announced plans to enter electronic retailing. And many specialist booksellers of Civil War books, jet plane books, history books, auto books, and so forth, have already begun to flood onto the Internet search

[12] Based on "Web Browsing," *The Economist*, 29 March 1997, p. 71.

sites. Even Amazon's wholesale supplier has entered the fray; for $2,500, Ingram Support Services will set up a web site on behalf of any new book retailer.

Amazon.com has responded by offering customized notification and book discussion services to add value for readers with special interests. The information revolution has made relationship marketing to established customers a pivotal element in securing repeat purchases. Nevertheless, the numerous open opportunities for fast, easy, and cheap entry likely will keep the profits in electronic book retailing tamped down to the competitive rates of return on time, talent, and investment.

MARKET PRICE DETERMINATION

We have spoken generally about the market price that a firm in pure competition is forced to accept. Let us now examine how this price is determined. Recall that the market demand curve shows the amount of a commodity that consumers would be willing to buy at some point in time at a set of specified prices (holding constant the effects of all other factors). The market supply curve may be given a similar interpretation, indicating the quantity of a product sellers *would* be willing to offer for sale at some point in time at a set of specified prices (holding constant the effects of all other factors).[13] The supply curve may be interpreted in terms of the cost functions of firms in the industry. The short-run supply curve for any individual firm may be represented by that portion of the marginal cost curve above average variable cost AVC. If price P ($P = MR$) intersects the marginal cost curve below AVC, the firm will shut down.

Plant shutdown under these circumstances is clearly the best alternative because losses will be limited to the total amount of fixed charges incurred. To operate when average revenue or price is less than average variable costs would result in additional losses equal to the difference between average variable cost and price times the number of units sold. When price exceeds average variable cost (even if price is less than average total cost), losses will be minimized by operating (not shutting down) because some contribution is made (the difference between price and average variable cost times the number of units sold) to covering fixed costs. At any point above AVC, the firm will be maximizing profit or minimizing losses by producing and selling that level of output where $MR = MC$ (remembering that in pure competition $P = MR$). In Figure 12.5 the supply curve for the firm is represented by the segment of the marginal cost curve labeled JI. The industry supply curve is merely the summation of all individual firm supply curves.[14] The interaction between supply and demand curves is illustrated in Figure 12.7.

---

[13] The notion of a market supply curve will not be encountered in our discussion of price-output determination for firms in oligopoly or monopolistic competition. Because the market supply curve is a representation of how much firms will produce and sell if faced with a market price of X dollars per unit, it is not a generally useful concept to develop rigorously for market structures in which firms possess considerable discretion over the prices to be charged. In addition, the market supply curve concept loses its meaning as we talk of products that are increasingly differentiated from one another.

[14] This condition only holds under pure competition when there is a rather wide range of outputs under which approximately constant cost conditions prevail. Under increasing or decreasing cost conditions, this simple additivity property is not strictly correct. Under either condition, the fundamentals of the market price-equilibrium mechanisms, illustrated here, do apply.

FIGURE   12.7

Effects of
Nonequilibrium Pricing

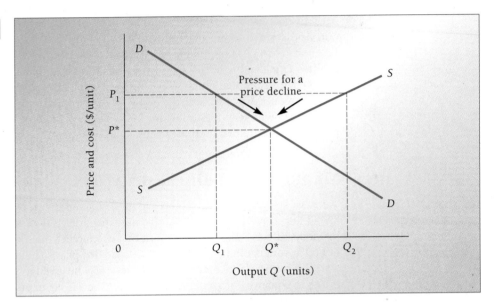

The market price will tend toward an equilibrium where the quantity demanded equals quantity supplied, for example, Q^* in Figure 12.7.

EXAMPLE

MARKET PRICE DETERMINATION: SUPPLY AND DEMAND

Assume that the market supply curve in Figure 12.7 can be expressed as

$$P = 9 + .4Q_S$$

where P is the price per unit in dollars and Q_S is the quantity supplied (in millions of units). Similarly, assume that the market demand curve in Figure 12.7 can be expressed as

$$P = 30 - .3Q_D$$

where Q_D is the quantity demanded (in millions of units).

In equilibrium, the quantity demanded, Q_D, will equal the quantity supplied, Q_S. Equating the price on the demand and supply side of the market yields

$$30 - .3Q = 9 + .4Q$$

$$21 = .7\,Q$$

$$Q = 30 \text{ (million)}$$

The quantity demanded and supplied in equilibrium equals 30 million units. Substituting 30 into either the market demand or supply equations yields an equilibrium market price of $21.

$$P = 30 - .3(30) = \$21$$

$$P = 9 + .4(30) = \$21$$

Hence in this purely competitive market, the market price would be $21 and the total quantity of output supplied and demanded in equilibrium would be 30 million units. If there are 100,000 firms in the industry, each firm would produce an average output of

300 units. Any individual firm's actions to increase or decrease its output would have an insignificantly small impact on the market price.

Effects of Disequilibrium Prices

If a price above the initial equilibrium price (P^*) were charged, such as P_1 in Figure 12.7, the quantity consumers are willing to buy, Q_1, at that price would be less than the number of units producers would be willing to sell, Q_2, and there would be strong market pressure for a price reduction. This is often evident in local real estate markets when there is an economic downturn. The market becomes flooded with homes and prices are reduced.

Similarly, if a market price below the equilibrium price were charged, there would be upward pressure on the price back toward an equilibrium condition. Anyone who has been to a sellout athletic event, such as the Super Bowl, and has been forced to buy tickets at scalpers' prices knows what happens when demand exceeds supply at a given price and upward-pricing pressure is brought to bear.

If the market price that is established, say p_1, results in excessive profits to firms in the industry, more firms will enter the industry, increasing supply to S_1S_1', and driving prices down to p_3. This is illustrated in Figure 12.8(a). In contrast, if some firms are operating at a loss they may cease production, reducing industry supply to S_2S_2' and boosting the price to a level where normal profits are made by the remaining firms. The supply-demand curve analysis shows why shifts in the demand curve (because of changing consumer tastes, changes in prices of complementary and substitute goods, and changes in income) will result in higher or lower prices. This is illustrated in Figure 12.8(b). If real consumer income were to increase, the demand curve for most commodities might be expected to shift upward and to the right by some amount (determined by the income elasticity of demand) to D_1D_1'. This would result in a new equilibrium level of output, Q_2, with a price increase from p_1 to p_2. Because a new, higher price has been established, it is likely that some firms will be making excess profits. As a result, new firms will enter the industry, supply will increase, and prices will decline.

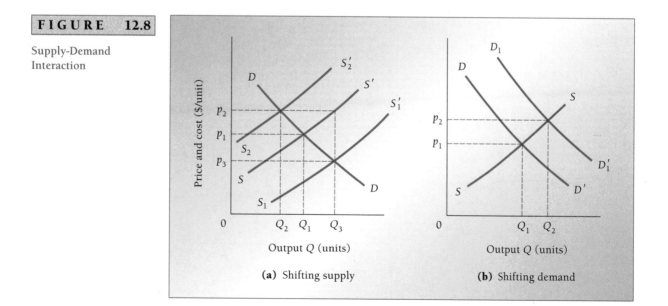

FIGURE   12.8

Supply-Demand Interaction

(a) Shifting supply

(b) Shifting demand

www . . . .
A RAND Corporation study
of the economics of
cocaine and other drug
control laws, particularly
mandatory minimum
sentencing, is available on
the Internet at:
http://www.rand.org/
publications/MR/MR827/

EXAMPLE

MARKET PRICE DETERMINATION: THE COCAINE MARKET

The rules of supply and demand analysis affect all markets, including the market for drugs. When cocaine prices increased dramatically in the early 1980s, huge crops of coca leaf, the raw material used in the production of cocaine, were planted in the producing countries. As these plants reached maturity, there were record harvests. As a result, the price of the raw crop declined by as much as 80 percent from its historically high levels. Although U.S. demand for cocaine also increased substantially, demand did not keep pace with supply. In 1983–84, a gram of 35 percent pure cocaine cost between $100 and $125. In 1985, the price declined to $100, but purity rose to about 55 percent. In 1987, the price declined to a low of $50, with purity as high as 75 percent. Thus, by 1987 the marketplace had dramatically squeezed the profits of cocaine producers.

In summary, while holding constant the effects of all other factors, an *increase* in demand leads to a new equilibrium point where both the equilibrium price and quantity are *higher* than they were at the original equilibrium point. In contrast, a *decrease* in demand results in a new equilibrium point where price and quantity are *lower* than they were at the original equilibrium point. Similarly, while holding constant the effects of all other factors, an *increase* in supply results in a new equilibrium point where the price is *lower* and the quantity is *greater* than they were at the original equilibrium point. In contrast, a *decrease* in supply results in a new equilibrium point with a *higher* price and *lower* quantity than those at the original equilibrium point.

Effects of a Price Ceiling or Price Floor

Figure 12.9 illustrates the impact of a price ceiling or price floor on market equilibrium conditions. If a price ceiling, p_c, is set below the market clearing price, p^*, quantity demanded (Q_2) will exceed the quantity supplied (Q_1) and some sort of rationing process will come into existence. For example, during the 1970s energy crises, price ceilings were set for many oil products, including gasoline. Many crude oil producers withheld production and/or reduced drilling activity, thereby further reducing supply. Rationing for the available gasoline developed in the form of long lines at gas stations.

FIGURE   12.9

Effects of a Pricing
Ceiling or Price Floor

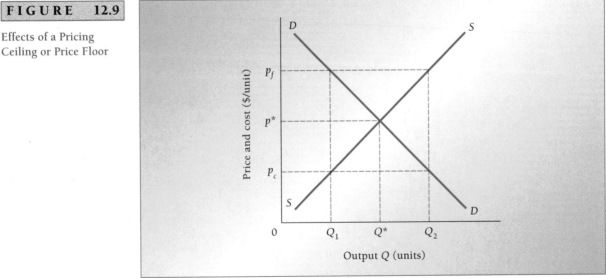

Similarly, if a price floor, p_f, is established above the market clearing price, p^*, then the quantity supplied (Q_2) will exceed the quantity demanded (Q_1), and product surpluses will result. This has happened for many agricultural products, including milk, in the United States.

<table>
<tr><td>

**INTERNATIONAL·
PERSPECTIVES**

</td><td>

THE DETERMINATION OF CURRENCY EXCHANGE RATES

The determination of currency exchange rates is a complex issue which we addressed at length in Chapter 7. However, the essential nature of this problem can be understood in the context of supply and demand analysis. The price for a foreign currency is determined by the interaction of supply and demand. This is illustrated in Figure 12.10.

</td></tr>
</table>

The price on the vertical axis is called the exchange rate. It is the price of a dollar in French francs (FF). Because the FF price of a dollar of foreign currency is measured on the vertical axis, the horizontal axis indicates the quantity of dollars that are traded at various prices. In the foreign currency markets, one must recognize the reciprocal nature of supply and demand relationships. For example, on the vertical axis we have indicated the FF price of a dollar. However, by taking the reciprocal of this price, we would have the dollar price of a FF, and the horizontal axis would measure the quantity of FF. Hence we can say that the supply of FF is the same as the demand for dollars and the supply of dollars is equal to the demand for FF.

What are the primary sources of supply and demand for dollars as shown in Figure 12.10? Assume that you are analyzing this problem from the perspective of the French government. A French *exporter* sells goods to a U.S. firm. In return the exporter receives either dollars or FF that were purchased by the U.S. firm with dollars. This transaction affects the supply of dollars in the foreign currency market. In contrast a French *importer* may purchase goods from a U.S. firm. This purchase will be paid for either with FF (which the U.S. firm will want to convert to dollars) or dollars (which the French importer purchased on the currency market). This transaction affects the demand for dollars in the foreign currency market.

Similarly, *foreign investors* may sell dollars for FF to buy shares in assets such as a French winery or a French company's bonds. This transaction affects the supply of dollars. *French investors* will sell FF for dollars to be able to purchase U.S. government securities, shares of stock in U.S. firms, and the like. The transaction affects the demand for dollars.

FIGURE   12.10

Determination of
Foreign Currency
Exchange Rates

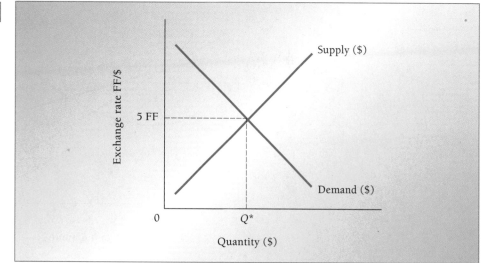

The third major set of players in the foreign exchange markets are *speculators*. Speculators are (generally short-term) traders in the foreign currency market. A speculator's objective is to make profits from buying and selling foreign currency. Speculators form expectations about the future price of a currency. However, given these expectations, speculators will be less willing to hold dollars if their value is high and vice versa.

In summary, regardless of whether we are considering exporters, importers, investors, or speculators, the interactions of these agents in the marketplace will ultimately lead to an equilibrium price, such as the 5 FF/$ price indicated in Figure 12.10 where supply and demand will be equal.

MONOPOLISTIC COMPETITION

Monopolistic competition is an industry with a relatively large number of firms, each selling a product that is differentiated in some manner from the products of its competitors. In such a situation it is increasingly difficult to specify precisely the bounds of an appropriate industry because no two firms produce exactly homogeneous goods or services. Instead of an easily recognizable industry, we tend to find a continuum of more or less closely substitutable products.

Product differentiation may be based on special product characteristics, trademarks, packaging, quality, design, or conditions surrounding the sale, such as location of the seller, warranties, and credit terms. The demand curve for any one firm is expected to have a negative slope and be extremely elastic because of the large number of close substitutes. The firm in monopolistic competition has limited discretion over price (as distinguished from the firm in pure competition) because of customer loyalties arising from real or perceived product differences. A price decline will attract some of the competitors' customers, and a price increase will result in a substantial loss of customers as some will shift to the close substitute offered by competitors. Profit maximization (or loss minimization) occurs when the firm produces at that level of output and charges that price where marginal revenue equals marginal cost (Figure 12.11).

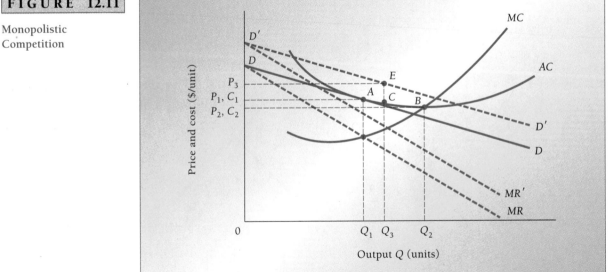

FIGURE 12.11

Monopolistic
Competition

Short Run

Just as in the case of pure competition, a firm may or may not generate a profit in the short run. For example, in the short run a firm may face a demand curve such as $D'D'$, with marginal revenue equal to MR'. Such a firm will set its prices where $MR' = MC$, resulting in price P_3 and output Q_3. The firm will earn a profit of EC dollars per unit of output. However, the low barriers to entry in a monopolistically competitive industry will not permit these short-run profits to be earned for long. As new firms enter the industry, industry supply will increase causing the equilibrium price to fall. This is reflected in a downward movement in the demand curve facing any individual firm. As in the case of pure competition, the existence of profits, such as EC/unit in Figure 12.11 will also result in cost pressures, resulting in a rising average cost curve. Any firm possessing productive inputs that are relatively more efficient in producing output will be bid away by competing firms.

Long Run

With relatively free entry and exit in monopolistically competitive industries, average costs and a firm's demand function will be driven *toward* tangency at a point such as A in Figure 12.11. At this price, P_1, and output, Q_1, marginal cost is equal to marginal revenue. Hence the firm is producing at its optimal level of output. Any price lower or higher than P_1 will result in a loss to the firm, because average costs will exceed price.

A comparison of the price-output solution in monopolistic competition with that in pure competition indicates that because of the negatively sloping demand curve, the point of tangency A occurs at a lower level of output, Q_1, than would occur in pure competition, Q_2. Also, ceteris paribus, the price P_1 charged and the cost C_1 of producing the equilibrium level of output in monopolistic competition will be higher than that of a firm in pure competition, because the purely competitive firm is in equilibrium at output level Q_2, charging a price of P_2 and incurring cost of C_2.

Because the monopolistic competitor produces at a level of output where average costs are still declining, it has been argued that society may reap savings by combining existing firms so that each of the remaining firms are producing a higher level of output (although total output of all firms remains constant) at lower costs (somewhere between points A and B in Figure 12.11). It is conceptually possible for the same level of output to be produced at a lower cost. Hence, a net saving may accrue to society if the number of existing firms is reduced and the equilibrium level of output for each firm thereby increases. This is called the "excess capacity theorem" of monopolistic competition.

EXAMPLE

LONG-RUN PRICE AND OUTPUT DETERMINATION: VIDEO MAGIC, INC.

The market for video rentals in Charlotte, North Carolina, can best be described as monopolistically competitive. The demand for video rentals is estimated to be

$$P = 10 - 0.004\,Q$$

where Q is the number of weekly video rentals. The long-run average cost function for Video Magic is estimated to be

$$LRAC = 8 - 0.006Q + 0.000002Q^2$$

Video Magic's managers want to know the profit-maximizing price and output levels, and the level of expected total profits at these price and output levels.

First, compute total revenue (TR) as

$$TR = P \cdot Q = 10Q - 0.004Q^2$$

Next, compute marginal revenue (MR) by taking the first derivative of TR:

$$MR = \frac{dTR}{dQ} = 10 - 0.008Q$$

Compute total cost (TC) by multiplying LRAC by Q:

$$TC = LRAC(Q) = 8Q - 0.006Q^2 + 0.000002Q^3$$

Compute marginal cost (MC) by taking the first derivative of TC:

$$MC = \frac{dTC}{dQ} = 8 - 0.012Q + 0.000006Q^2$$

Next, set MR = MC and solve for Q:

$$10 - 0.008Q = 8 - 0.012Q + 0.000006Q^2$$

$$0.000006Q^2 - 0.004Q - 2 = 0$$

Use the quadratic formula to solve for Q. Q is equal to 1,000.[15] At this quantity, price is equal to

$$P = 10 - 0.004(1,000)$$

$$= 10 - 4$$

$$= \$6$$

Total profit is equal to the difference between TR and TC, or

$$\pi = TR - TC$$

$$= 10Q - 0.004Q^2 - [8Q - 0.006Q^2 + 0.000002Q^3]$$

$$= 10(1,000) - 0.004(1,000)^2 - [8(1,000) - 0.006(1,000)^2 + 0.000002(1,000)^3]$$

$$= \$2,000$$

The MR and MC at these price and output levels are $2.

The fact that Video Magic expects to earn a profit of $2,000 suggests that the firm can anticipate additional competition, resulting in price cutting, that will ultimately eliminate this profit amount.[16]

---

[15] The solution of quadratic formula, $aQ^2 + bQ + c = 0$, is

$$Q = \frac{-b \pm \sqrt{b^2 - 4ac}}{2a} = \frac{-(-.004) \pm \sqrt{(-.004)^2 - 4(0.000006)(-2)}}{2(0.000006)}$$

$$= 1,000; -333.33$$

Only the positive solution is feasible.

[16] Recall that the TC function includes a "normal" level of profit. Hence this $2,000 represents an economic *rent* above a normal profit level.

A Critique of the Monopolistic Competition Model

The model of monopolistic competition has come under increasing attack with the passage of time.[17] Cohen and Cyert's attacks center around the empirical void created by the model. They conclude that markets that contain a large number of small firms are nearly always markets selling such standardized or near-standardized products as wheat and lumber. Even a moderate degree of product differentiation would likely leave demand curves for the firm so nearly horizontal that the purely competitive model is an adequate approximation. They further argue that markets where customers have strong brand preferences are typically markets better classified as oligopolies where the number of sellers is few.

The retail sector in any city (for example, grocery stores, clothing stores, gas stations, shoe stores, cleaners, and fast-food outlets) is the most frequently cited example of monopolistically competitive markets. But Chamberlin assumes that any price adjustment by one firm will spread its influence over so many firms that there will be no perceptible impact on any of the other firms and hence no readjustment by them. This assumption is clearly not realistic. The effects of price changes by one firm will not be spread evenly over all other retailers but will be concentrated on those retailers in closest proximity to the initiating firm. The impact on these firms is likely to be perceptible and evoke a response. Under these circumstances the oligopoly model of chapters 15 and 16 furnishes a better basis for analysis.

SELLING AND PROMOTIONAL EXPENSES

In addition to varying price and quality characteristics of their products, firms may also vary the amount of their advertising and other promotional expenses in their search for profits. This kind of promotional activity generates two distinct types of benefits. First, demand for the general product group may be shifted upward to the right as a result of the individual firm and industry advertising activities. This general benefit of a higher level of demand presumably comes at the expense of other general product classes. As a result, a higher market price may prevail (at least until new competitors enter the market). This general demand-increasing effect of advertising is probably a major source of incentive for advertising when the market is more highly concentrated, as in monopoly or oligopoly. The greater the number of firms in an industry, the more diffused will be the effects of a general demand-increasing advertising campaign by any one firm. In contrast, a monopolist such as an electric utility, or a highly concentrated oligopoly such as the computer operating systems, will be more inclined to undertake an advertising campaign, partially in the hope of expanding demand for the general product class, of which the individual firm (Microsoft) provides a large share.

The second, more widespread incentive for advertising is the desire to shift the demand function of a particular firm at the expense of other firms offering similar products. This strategy will be pursued both by oligopolists like Philip Morris and General Mills and by firms in more competitive industries like AT&T, MCI, and Sprint as long as an opportunity exists for product differentiation of some form. The level of advertising pursued by oligopolists is determined by the same considerations of mutual interdependence that influence price-output decisions.

---

[17] An excellent discussion of attacks on Chamberlin's theory is in Kalman Cohen and Richard Cyert, *Theory of the Firm*, 2d ed. (Englewood Cliffs, N.J.: Prentice-Hall, 1975), pp. 225–230.

Determining the Optimal Level of Selling and Promotional Outlays

Selling and promotional expenses, often collectively referred to as advertising, are one of the most important tools of nonprice competition employed by profit-maximizing firms in monopoly, oligopoly, and monopolistic competition markets. Other nonprice competition strategies employed by firms in these markets include quality assurance programs and customer service programs. In this section we develop a simple marginal analysis rule that can be used by firms considering additional advertising outlays. The rule also applies to other types of nonprice competition.

To illustrate the effects of advertising expenditures and to determine the optimal selling expenses of a firm, consider the case where price and product characteristics already have been determined. The liquor retailing industry is an important example of such a case. In many states either prices are set by a state board, or manufacturers are permitted to set fixed regulated prices at which their products can be sold. Also, where some form of resale price maintenance is practiced resulting in all retailers selling a product at the manufacturer's suggested retail price, the following model offers interesting insights.

The determination of the optimal advertising outlay is a straightforward application of the marginal decision-making rules followed by profit-maximizing firms. Define MR to be the change in total revenue received from a one-unit increase in output (and the sale of that output). For fixed price settings, MR just equals the price, P. Define MC to be the change in total costs of producing and distributing (but not of advertising) an additional unit of output. The marginal profit *contribution* from one additional unit of output is

$$\text{Contribution} = P - MC \qquad [12.3]$$

The marginal cost of advertising (MCA) associated with the sale of an additional unit of output is defined as the change in advertising expenditures (ΔAk) where k is the unit cost of an advertising message, A, or

$$MCA = \frac{\Delta Ak}{\Delta Q} \qquad [12.4]$$

The optimal level of advertising outlays is the level of advertising where the marginal profit contribution is equal to the marginal cost of advertising, or

$$\text{Contribution} = MCA \qquad [12.5]$$

As long as a firm receives a greater contribution than the MCA it incurs to sell an additional unit of output, the advertising outlay should be made. If MPC is less than MCA, the advertising outlay should not be made and the level of advertising should be reduced until $MPC = MCA$.

EXAMPLE

OPTIMAL ADVERTISING: FLOW MOTORS FORD

The marginal profit contribution from selling Ford automobiles at Flow Motors averages $1,000 across the various models it sells. Flow Motors estimates that it will have to incur $500 of additional promotional expenses to increase its sales by one unit over the current level. Should the outlay for promotion be made?

Because $MPC > MCA$ (i.e., $1,000 > 500$), Flow's profit will be increased by $500 if it incurs an additional $500 of promotional expenses. Flow should continue to make additional promotional outlays up to the point where the marginal cost of advertising equals the marginal profit contribution.

If Flow had found that *MCA* was greater than *MPC*, Flow should cut back on its promotional outlays until *MPC* = *MCA*.

Optimal Advertising Intensity

Optimal expenditure on demand-increasing costs like promotions, couponing, direct mail, and media advertising can be compared across firms using the techniques of marginal analysis. Although intermittent and lagged in their effects on future sales, such marketing costs are accounted as a current expense. For example, the total contributions from incremental sales generated by an ad campaign can be compared to the advertising cost. Advertising is often placed in five media (network TV, local TV, radio, newspapers, and magazines). The "reach" of a TV ad is measured as audience thousands per minute of advertising message; reach is directly related to the advertising message's cost (k). A manager should fully fund in his or her marketing budget any ad campaigns for which

$$(P - MC)\,(\Delta Q/\Delta A) > k \qquad\qquad [12.6]$$

where $(P - MC)$ is the contribution margin and $(\Delta Q/\Delta A)$ is the increase in demand (i.e., a shift outward in demand) attributable to the advertising.[18]

Expanding Equation 12.6 identifies the two determinants of optimal advertising intensity across product lines. The optimal advertising expenditure per dollar sales (Ak/PQ) is determined by the gross margin $(P - MC)/P$ and by the advertising elasticity

$$\frac{(P - MC)}{P}\,\frac{A}{Q}\,(\Delta Q/\Delta A) = \frac{Ak}{PQ} \qquad\qquad [12.7]$$

$$\frac{(P - MC)\,E^a}{P} = \frac{Ak}{PQ} \qquad\qquad [12.8]$$

of demand E^a. Both factors are important. With high margins and very effective ads, the Kellogg Co. spends 30 percent of every dollar of sales revenue on cereal advertising. In contrast, the jewelry industry has 92 percent margins, the highest of all four-digit industries, but Zales' advertising inserts in the weekend paper simply do not trigger many jewelry sales. The advertising elasticity of jewelry is low; consequently, a company like Zales spends less than 10 percent of sales revenue on advertising. Campbell Soup has relatively high advertising elasticity of demand given its strong brand name, but the margins on canned goods are very low (less than 5 percent); consequently, Campbell Soup spends just one tenth of what Kellogg spends on advertising—just 3 percent of sales revenue. Another industry with huge advertising budgets is automobiles, but as a percentage of dollar sales the advertising intensity at GM is only about 7 percent. While automobile demand is sensitive to ads, the profit margin on autos is nowhere new Kellogg's 70 percent.

EXAMPLE

OPTIMAL ADVERTISING INTENSITY AT KELLOGG AND GENERAL MILLS[19]

The ready-to-eat (RTE) cereal industry spends 55 percent of its sales revenue on marketing and promotion—40 percent on advertising alone. In part, this resource commitment reflects the fact that cereal demand is very sensitive to successful ad campaigns

---

[18] Sometimes, the price points at which the product can be sold change after a successful ad campaign. If so, the appropriate valuation of the incremental sales in Equation 12.3 is the new contribution margin.

[19] Based on "Cereals," *Winston-Salem Journal*, 8 March 1995, p. A1 and "Denial in Battle Creek," *Forbes*, 7 October 1996, pp. 44–46.

www . . . .
For more information on food marketing, access the Food Institute Report at the following Internet site: http://www.foodinstitute.com/nonpages/mainnon.htm

like Kellogg's Tony the Tiger or General Mills' Wheaties, The Breakfast of Champions. In addition, however, RTE cereal margins are among the highest of any four-digit industry. Kellogg's Raisin Bran sells for $4.49 and has a direct fixed plus variable manufacturing cost of $1.63. That calculates as a $(4.49 - 1.63)/4.49 = 70$ percent gross margin. Frosted Flakes' margin is 72 percent, and Fruit Loops' margin is 68 percent. These margins reflect brand loyalties built up over many years of advertising investments as well as Kellogg's 37 percent market share. In the highly concentrated RTE cereal industry, Quaker Oats (8 percent), Post (15 percent), General Mills (25 percent), and Kellogg control 85 percent of the market.

Until recently, advertising and retail display promotions were the predominant form of competition in cereals. Like Coca-Cola and Pepsi, the dominant RTE cereal companies had concluded that price discounting would be mutually ruinous and ultimately ineffective. Therefore, each company decided independently to refrain from discounting to attempt to gain market share. However, in June 1996, 20 percent price cuts swept through the industry in part in response to the growth of private-label cereals (e.g., Kroger Raisin Bran) which had collectively grabbed close to 10 percent of the market. Margins on some leading brand-name products fell to 50 percent with ingredients (15 percent), packaging (10 percent), wages (10 percent), and distribution (15 percent) accounting for the rest of the selling price. By late 1997, the price war had ended and traditional advertising competition resumed.

Advertising Resource Allocations across Various Advertising Media

In addition to deciding on the total amount of selling expenses it should incur, the firm also must decide on an appropriate allocation of these selling expenses to different advertising media. Let ΔS_A, ΔS_B, and ΔS_C represent the increase in sales from advertising media A, B, and C, respectively. Similarly, denote ΔA_A, ΔA_B, and ΔA_C as the additional expenditures made in advertising media A, B, and C. Under these conditions an optimal advertising mix is indicated when

$$\frac{\Delta S_A}{\Delta A_A} = \frac{\Delta S_B}{\Delta A_B} = \frac{\Delta S_C}{\Delta A_C} \qquad [12.9]$$

If this were not true and $\Delta S_A/\Delta A_A > \Delta S_B/\Delta A_B$, the firm would profit by reducing its advertising in medium B and increasing it in medium A until an equilibrium is reached.

The Value of Advertising

Traditional economic analysis has tended to conclude that the primary impacts of advertising are to raise prices to consumers and to lead to the creation and maintenance of monopoly power.[20] Other research has focused on the impact of advertising on consumer tastes and preferences. Whether advertising is effective in changing consumer desires remains largely an empirically untested proposition because of the wide range of influences on consumer preferences. The analysis of the effect of advertising on the molding of consumer tastes and preferences tends to imply that this result is undesirable. This conclusion is, however, largely based on intuition. Hard evidence is scarce.

More recently, economic research has focused on the potential value of advertising from a consumer's perspective. Although it is true that advertising costs may be passed

---

[20] Evidence in support of this view is presented in William Comaner and Thomas Wilson, *Advertising and Market Power* (Cambridge, Mass.: Harvard University Press, 1974).

on to consumers, these increased costs may be offset by the beneficial effects of advertising. For example, if advertising is successful in expanding the market for a firm's product, and if that product is produced under conditions where the firm's average cost function is declining, then the saving in unit production costs may more than offset the unit advertising cost.

Both Stigler[21] and Nelson[22] have used the theory of the economics of information to analyze the value of advertising. By giving consumers price information, advertising is expected to reduce the price paid by consumers. In the absence of cheaply available price information, consumers may not find the best price for a product they seek to purchase. This is because the discovery of price information may be costly and time consuming in the absence of price advertising. If, for example, it costs a consumer $10 in time to discover the store that will offer a saving of $8 on the price of an item, the search for price information is not worthwhile. But if price advertising makes all consumers aware of the lowest price supplier of an item at an additional cost of only $1, then the great majority of consumers will be better off as a result of this advertising. For example, Benham found the price of eyeglasses to be substantially lower in states that permitted price advertising than in those that prohibited such advertising.[23] Similar results have been found for dental, medical, and legal services.

In addition, Nelson found that advertisers of all products have substantial incentives to provide useful and truthful information to customers. High-quality information can reduce the search cost for consumers as they seek to make a choice between alternative goods. Because consumers can assess the truthfulness of the information contained in an advertisement and because advertising creates brand awareness (both for good and inferior brands), advertisers who misrepresent their product will not be successful in generating future (and repeat) business.

Finally, both Nelson and Stigler have found that advertising tends to increase demand elasticities of goods. The demand for products that are not widely advertised tends to be price inelastic. The more extensive the advertising effort, the more price elastic the demand for a product becomes. In general, the more elastic the demand for a product, the more competitive is the market for that product—and frequently lower prices result.

SUMMARY

- ☐ A relevant market is a group of economic agents that interact with each other in a buyer-seller relationship. Relevant markets often have both spatial and product characteristics.
- ☐ The Five Forces model of business strategy identifies threat of substitutes, threat of entry, power of buyers, power of suppliers, and the intensity of rivalry as the determinants of sustainable incumbent profitability in a particular industry.
- ☐ The threat of substitutes depends upon the number and closeness of substitutes as determined by the product development, advertising, brand-naming, and segmentation strategies of pre-existing competitors.
- ☐ The threat of entry depends upon the height of barriers to potential entrants including capital requirements, economies of scale, switching costs, access to

[21] George J. Stigler, "The Economics of Information," *Journal of Political Economy* (June 1961), pp. 213–225.

[22] Philip Nelson, "The Economic Consequences of Advertising," *Journal of Business* (April 1975), pp. 213–241.

[23] Lee Benham, "The Effect of Advertising on the Price of Eyeglasses," *Journal of Law and Economics* (October 1972), pp. 337–352.

distribution channels, and trade secrets and other difficult-to-imitate forms of product differentiation.

- The bargaining power of buyers and suppliers depends upon their number, their size distribution, the relationship between industry capacity and industry demand, and the uniqueness of the inputs.

- The intensity of rivalry depends upon the number and size distribution of sellers in the relevant market, the relative frequency of price versus non-price competition, the proportion of fixed to total cost, the barriers to exit, and the growth rate of industry demand.

- The *demand* for a good or service is defined as the various quantities of that good or service that consumers are willing and able to purchase during a particular period of time at all possible prices. The *supply* of a good or service is defined as the quantities that sellers are willing to make available to purchasers at all possible prices during a particular period of time.

- The intersection of the supply and demand curves represents the equilibrium price and quantity that should prevail in the marketplace, given these supply and demand curves. An increase (or decrease) in demand leads to a new equilibrium point where both the new equilibrium price and quantity are higher (or lower) than they were at the original equilibrium point. An increase (or decrease) in supply results in a new equilibrium point where the price is lower (or higher) and the equilibrium quantity is greater (or less) than those at the original equilibrium point.

- In general, a profit-maximizing firm will desire to operate at that level of output where marginal cost equals marginal revenue.

- In a purely (atomistically) competitive market structure, the firm will operate in the short run as long as price is greater than average variable cost.

- In a purely (atomistically) competitive market structure, the tendency is toward a long-run equilibrium condition in which firms earn just normal profits, price is equal to marginal cost and average total cost, and average total cost is minimized.

- In a monopolistically competitive industry, a large number of firms sell a differentiated product. In practice, few market structures can be best analyzed in the context of the monopolistic competition model. Most actual market structures have greater similarities to the purely competitive market model or the oligopolistic market model.

- Advertising expenditures were shown to be optimal from a profit-maximization perspective if they are carried to the point where the marginal profit contribution from an additional unit of output is equal to the marginal cost of advertising. The optimal level of advertising intensity (the advertising expenditure per sales dollar) varies across products and industries and is determined by the marginal profit contribution from incremental sales and by the advertising elasticity of demand.

EXERCISES

1. How are above-normal profits eliminated from a purely competitive or a monopolistically competitive industry?

2. Firms in competitive markets are often viewed as being price takers, that is, they must simply accept the market price as their own. Can you give examples outside of purely competitive industries where firms act as price takers?

3. How do changes in factor prices affect the short-run supply curve for the typical firm in a purely competitive market? If the same firm experiences an increase in its fixed costs, what effect will this have on its short-run supply curve?

4. What effect do you think a state law requiring gasoline stations to post their prices prominently will have on the average price of gasoline charged in the state? How can consumers benefit from such a law requiring the posting of gasoline prices?

5. At one point during the energy crisis of the 1970s, gasohol was viewed as one part of a solution to the problem of shortages of petroleum products. Gasohol was made from a blend of gasoline and alcohol derived from corn. What would you expect the impact of this program to be on the price of corn, soybeans, and wheat?

6. If the government sets a floor price for milk, would you expect that a need would arise for restrictions on the number of cows farmers can milk? In the absence of these restrictions, what outcome would you expect?

7. The demand function for propane is

$$Q_D = 212 - 20P$$

The supply function for propane is

$$Q_S = 20 + 4P$$

a. What is the equilibrium price and quantity?
b. If the government establishes a price ceiling of $6, what quantity will be demanded and supplied?
c. If the government establishes a price floor (minimum price) of $9, what quantity will be demanded and supplied?
d. If supply increases to

$$Q_S' = 20 + 6P$$

what is the new equilibrium price and quantity?
e. If demand increases to

$$Q_D' = 250 - 19P$$

and the supply is as given in part (d), what is the new equilibrium price and quantity?

8. Assume that a firm in a perfectly competitive industry has the following total cost schedule:

Output (Units)	Total Cost ($)
10	$110
15	150
20	180
25	225
30	300
35	385
40	480

a. Calculate a marginal cost and an average cost schedule for the firm.
b. If the prevailing market price is $17 per unit, how many units will be produced and sold? What are profits per unit? What are total profits?
c. Is the industry in long-run equilibrium at this price?

9. During several past wars, and more recently under programs designed to curb inflation, the government has imposed price ceilings on certain commodities. This is done to keep prices from rising to the natural level that would prevail under supply-demand equilibrium. The result is that the quantity that sellers are willing to supply at the ceiling price often falls short of the quantity demanded at that price. To bring supply and demand more into equilibrium, ration coupons are sometimes issued.

   a. Show graphically, using both supply and demand curves, the effects of a ceiling price.
   b. On the black market how much would you be willing to pay for a ration coupon good for the purchase of one unit of the rationed commodity?
   c. If the aggregate demand curve for Commodity X is $P = 100 - 5Q$, and the industry supply curve for that product is $P = 10 + 10Q$, calculate the following:
      (i) The equilibrium price and quantity for Commodity X
      (ii) The quantity that will be sold if a ceiling price of $60 is established
      (iii) The black market price of a ration coupon good for the purchase of one unit of X

10. Royersford Knitting Mills, Ltd. sells a line of women's knit underwear. The firm now sells about 20,000 pairs a year at an average price of $10 each. Fixed costs amount to $60,000, and total variable costs equal $120,000. The production department has estimated that a 10 percent increase in output would not affect fixed costs but would reduce average variable cost by 40 cents.

   The marketing department advocates a price reduction of 5 percent to increase sales, total revenues, and profits. The arc elasticity of demand is estimated at -2.

   a. Evaluate the impact of the proposal to cut prices on (i) total revenue, (ii) total cost, and (iii) total profits.
   b. If average variable costs are assumed to remain constant over a 10 percent increase in output, evaluate the effects of the proposed price cut on total profits.

11. The Jenkins Tool Company has estimated the following demand equation for its product:

$$Q_D = 12,000 - 4,000P$$

where

$$P = \text{price/unit}$$

$$Q_D = \text{quantity demanded/year}$$

The firm's total costs are $4,000 when nothing is being produced. These costs increase by 50 cents for each unit produced.

   a. Write an equation for the total cost function.
   b. Specify the marginal cost function.
   c. Write an equation for total revenue in terms of Q.
   d. Specify the marginal revenue function.
   e. Write an equation for total profits, π, in terms of Q. At what level of output are total profits maximized (that is, find the maximum of the total profit function)? What price will be charged? What will total profit be?
   f. Check your answers in part (e) by equating marginal cost and marginal revenue and solving for Q.
   g. What model of market pricing behavior has been assumed in this problem?

12. A firm operating in a purely competitive environment is faced with a market price of $250. The firm's total cost function (short run) is

$$TC = 6{,}000 + 400Q - 20Q^2 + Q^3$$

   a. Should the firm produce at this price in the short run?
   b. If the market price is $300, what will total profits (losses) be if the firm produces 10 units of output? Should the firm produce at this price?
   c. If the market price is greater than $300, should the firm produce in the short run?

13. The Poster Bed Company believes that its industry can best be classified as monopolistically competitive. An analysis of the demand for its canopy bed has resulted in the following estimated demand function for the bed:

$$P = 1760 - 12Q$$

   The cost analysis department has estimated the total cost function for the poster bed as

$$TC = \tfrac{1}{3}Q^3 - 15Q^2 + 5Q + 24{,}000$$

   a. Calculate the level of output that should be produced to maximize short-run profits.
   b. What price should be charged?
   c. Compute total profits at this price-output level.
   d. Compute the point price elasticity of demand at the profit-maximizing level of output.
   e. What level of fixed costs is the firm experiencing on its bed production?
   f. What is the impact of a $5,000 increase in the level of fixed costs on the price charged, output produced, and profit generated?

14. Assume that a firm sells its product in a perfectly competitive market. The firm's fixed costs (including a "normal" return on the funds the entrepreneur has invested in the firm) are equal to $100 and its variable cost schedule is as follows:

Output (Units)	Variable Cost Per Unit
50	$5.00
100	4.50
150	4.00
200	3.50
250	3.00
300	2.75
350	3.00
400	3.50

   a. Find the marginal cost and average total cost schedules for the firm.
   b. If the prevailing market price is $4.50, how many units will be produced and sold?
   c. What are total profits and profit per unit at the output level determined in part (b)?
   d. Is the industry in long-run equilibrium at this price? Explain.

15. Exotic Metals, Inc., a leading manufacturer of zirilium, which is used in many electronic products, estimates the following demand schedule for its product:

Price ($/Pound)	Quantity (Pounds/Period)
$25	0
18	1,000
16	2,000
14	3,000
12	4,000
10	5,000
8	6,000
6	7,000
4	8,000
2	9,000

Fixed costs of manufacturing zirilium are $14,000 per period. The firm's variable cost schedule is as follows:

a. Find the total revenue and marginal revenue schedules for the firm.
b. Determine the average total cost and marginal cost schedules for the firm.
c. What are Exotic Metal's profit-maximizing price and output level for the production and sale of zirilium?
d. What is Exotic's profit (or loss) at the solution determined in part (c)?
e. Suppose that the federal government announces it will sell zirilium, from its extensive wartime stockpile, to anyone who wants it at $6 per pound. How does this affect the solution determined in part (c)? What is Exotic Metal's profit (or loss) under these conditions?

Output (Pounds/Period)	Variable Cost (Per Pound)
0	$0
1,000	10.00
2,000	8.50
3,000	7.33
4,000	6.25
5,000	5.40
6,000	5.00
7,000	5.14
8,000	5.88
9,000	7.00

16. Wyandotte Chemical Company sells various chemicals to the automobile industry. Wyandotte currently sells 30,000 gallons of polyol per year at an average price of $15 per gallon. Fixed costs of manufacturing polyol are $90,000 per year and total variable costs equal $180,000. The operations research department has

estimated that a 15 percent increase in output would not affect fixed costs but would reduce average variable costs by 60 cents per gallon. The marketing department has estimated the arc elasticity of demand for polyol to be −2.0.

   a.   How much would Wyandotte have to reduce the price of polyol to achieve a 15 percent increase in the quantity sold?
   b.   Evaluate the impact of such a price cut on (i) total revenue, (ii) total costs, and (iii) total profits.

17.   Tennis Products, Inc., produces three models of high-quality tennis racquets. The following table contains recent information on the sales, costs, and profitability of the three models:

Model	Average Quantity Sold (Units/ Month)	Current Price	Total Revenue	Variable Cost Per Unit	Contribution Margin Per Unit	Contribution Margin*
A	15,000	$30	$ 450,000	$15.00	$15	$225,000
B	5,000	35	175,000	18.00	17	85,000
C	10,000	45	450,000	20.00	25	250,000
Total			$1,075,000			$560,000

*Contribution to fixed costs and profits.

The company is considering lowering the price of Model A to $27 in an effort to increase the number of units sold. Based on the results of price changes that have been instituted in the past, Tennis Products' chief economist has estimated the arc price elasticity of demand to be −2.5. Furthermore, she has estimated the arc cross elasticity of demand between Model A and Model B to be approximately 0.5 and between Model A and Model C to be approximately 0.2. Variable costs per unit are not expected to change over the anticipated changes in volume.

   a.   Evaluate the impact of the price cut on the (i) total revenue and (ii) contribution margin of Model A. Based on this analysis, should the firm lower the price of Model A?
   b.   Evaluate the impact of the price cut on the (i) total revenue and (ii) contribution margin for the entire line of tennis racquets. Based on this analysis, should the firm lower the price of Model A?

18.   Industry demand has been estimated as

$$Q = 5,000 - 10P + 350(T - 1)$$

Industry supply has been estimated as

$$Q = 2,200 + 18P$$

   a.   What will the market price be in Year $T = 1$?
   b.   What will the market price be in Year $T = 5$?

19.   Jordan Enterprises has estimated the price elasticity of demand for its Air Express model of basketball shoes to be 2.5. Based on market research and past experience, Jordan estimates the following relationship between the sales for Air Express and advertising/promotional outlays:

Advertising/Promotional Outlays	Sales Revenue
$ 500,000	$4,000,000
600,000	4,500,000
700,000	4,900,000
800,000	5,200,000
900,000	5,450,000
1,000,000	5,600,000

a.   What is the marginal revenue from an additional dollar of spending on advertising if the firm is currently spending $1,000,000 on advertising?

b.   What level of advertising would you recommend to Jordan's management?

www exercise

Alternative Policies for
Reducing Drug
Consumption

20.   As was discussed in this chapter, the rules of supply and demand also apply to drug markets. There have been a number of different policy alternatives advocated for reducing drug demand, including mandatory sentencing, enhanced enforcement, and drug treatment. But which policy is more likely to reduce drug demand, and at what cost? Access the RAND Corporation study of mandatory drug sentencing policy at the following Internet site: http://www.rand.org/publications/MR/MR827/.

What are the key findings of this report as they relate to cost-effective reductions in drug demand? How would you relate them in a supply/demand diagram?

13

Competitive Markets under Asymmetric Information

CHAPTER PREVIEW

This chapter distinguishes competitive markets under ideal information conditions, in which you get what you pay for, from competitive markets under asymmetric information, sometimes called "lemons markets." One prominent example of asymmetric information in a lemons market is a used car whose true quality often is known only to the seller. Goods whose quality is unobservable to the buyer at the point of purchase characterize everything from used cars to house paint to mail-order computer components.

In a lemons market, the buyers discount any and all unverifiable claims by the sellers, who therefore market only lower-quality products (i.e., lemons) at the reduced offer prices available. This disappearance of higher-quality products from the marketplace illustrates the concept of adverse selection: "The bad apples have driven out the good."

To resolve the problem of adverse selection requires bonding mechanisms such as warranties, brand name reputations, collateral, or price premiums for reliable repeat-purchase transactions with regular customers. Creating incentives to reveal asymmetric information is important in joint ventures and partnerships as well. We will see how carefully designed incentive contracts can induce the revelation of proprietary cost information in joint ventures.

Profit sharing is another mechanism for handling the problems posed by asymmetric information. In principal-agent contracts, profit sharing helps owners provide appropriate incentives to managers who contribute their unobservable work effort and creative ingenuity to the maximization of firm value. At the end of the chapter we discuss the use of optimal profit-sharing contracts in sorting managerial job applicants by their degree of risk aversion.

ASYMMETRIC INFORMATION EXCHANGE

In competitive markets for newsprint, crude oil, auto rentals, and delivered pizza, both buyers and sellers have full knowledge of the capabilities and after-sale performance of the standard products. Equilibrium price just covers the supplier's cost of production for a product of known reliable quality. If suppliers were to charge more, rival offers and entry would quickly erode their sales. If suppliers were to charge less, they could not afford to stay in business. This was the message of Chapter 12; in competitive markets under ideal information conditions, you get what you pay for.

In many other competitive markets, however, the symmetry of information between buyer and seller cannot be taken for granted. For example, mail-order suppliers of computer components or personal sellers of used cars often have an informationally advantaged position relative to the buyers. The sellers know the machine's capabilities, deficiencies, and most probable failure rate, but these are difficult matters for the buyer to assess from reading magazine ads or kicking the tires. As a result, equilibrium price in such markets does not convey the same meaning it did in Chapter 12, and reputational assets and other credible commitment mechanisms take on added importance. It is these effects of information asymmetries on competitive market exchange that we now wish to examine.

Incomplete Versus Asymmetric Information

Incomplete Information
Uncertain knowledge of payoffs, choices, etc.

One distinction that can sharpen our understanding of these complicating factors is that between asymmetric information and **incomplete information.** Incomplete information is associated with uncertainty, and uncertainty is pervasive. Practically all exchanges, whether for products, financial claims, or labor services, are conducted under conditions of uncertainty. On the one hand, decision makers often face uncertainty as to the effect of random disturbances on the outcome of their actions. This uncertainty typically leads to insurance markets. On the other hand, decision makers are sometimes uncertain as to the choices or payoffs or even types of opponents they face. This condition typically leads to intentionally incomplete contracting and may result in incomplete markets, even incomplete insurance markets.

Asymmetric Information
Unequal, dissimilar knowledge.

Asymmetric information exchange, in contrast, refers to situations in which either the buyer or the seller possesses information which the other party cannot verify or to which the other party does not have access. For example, sellers of mail-order computer components know considerably more than the buyers about a hard disk's likely performance and durability. And the typical 90-day warranty does nothing to alter this information asymmetry. Both buyer and seller face uncertainty against which they may choose to insure, but one has more information or better information than the other.

In the next section, we discuss further the incomplete contracting and occasional incomplete markets that arise from incomplete information. Thereafter, we return to problems presented by asymmetric information.

Incomplete Contracting and Incomplete Markets

Potential losses from repetitive risks such as workplace injuries and weather hazards are often insured for a small periodic cash flow. Risk spreading is the primary purpose of insurance markets, which pool such casualty risks and thereby reduce the loss exposure to any individual business or household. Randomly occurring injuries at a consumer electronics assembly plant seldom coincide with injuries in a firm's delivery trucks or severe weather disruptions at a textile mill. As a result, modest insurance premiums easily cover the anticipated claims. In this sense, uncertainty and incomplete information are routine business problems handled in routine ways by insurance contracting.

MANAGERIAL CHALLENGE

DEBUGGING COMPUTER SOFTWARE: INTEL[1]

Debugging has been a way of life in the computer industry from its inception. Indeed, the origin of the term *debugging* derives from the daily process of removing dead moths from the thousands of electronic tubes in the ENIAC, the first electronic computer. Every piece of computer hardware or software ever shipped likely had logic faults. Indeed, most popular software programs contained thousands of known "bugs" in their first-generation products. In 1994, incomplete debugging of the floating point division calculator in the new Pentium computer chip caused a massive product recall that cost Intel $475 million dollars.

Why do computer component manufacturers release products with known bugs? One obvious answer is that delayed release may allow competitors to preempt the market with new technologies that render your product obsolete. Another important answer is a central insight of managerial economics that everything worth doing is not necessarily worth doing well. Computer design and manufacturing firms face a rising marginal cost of correcting thousands of bugs detected by their beta testing process. At some point, each firm must balance the lost sales and replacement costs from product

recalls against the ever-increasing cost of design perfection. A somewhat surprising third answer may, however, hold the key; fixing bugs in subsequent generations of software sells upgrades. Microsoft Windows 3.0 had a nasty bug that caused the program to crash with the finality of a hopeless error message—"unrecoverable application error." Microsoft fixed the bug in version 3.1 and proceeded to sell millions of copies of the upgrade.

The message in all this is that buyers and sellers often have very different information about the performance characteristics of the products they exchange. Sometimes this works to the firm's advantage, but oftentimes, buyers penalize a firm for unverifiable claims about what a product can and cannot accomplish. Then, the supplier must incur the additional costs of a bonding mechanism that provides prospective buyers with the assurances they require.

WWW . . . .
Current financial information on the Intel Corporation is available on the Internet at the following site:
http://www.intel.com/intel/finance/index.htm

[1] Based on "It's Not a Bug, It's a Feature," *Forbes,* 13 February 1995, p. 192.

However, in some business environments, such as oil pipelines, nuclear power plants, or skyscraper development on an earthquake fault, the contracting parties may find insurance simply unavailable. That is, no reliable company may wish to undertake to write an insurance contract that accepts a premium now in exchange for covering the losses from a highly uncertain and possibly catastrophic loss sometime later. Incomplete information as to what tiny probabilities one should assign to the catastrophic events may warrant setting premiums that are prohibitively expensive. Consequently, some insurance markets are incomplete.

Furthermore, incomplete information as to what possible outcomes might occur may prevent the affected parties from writing a series of contracts that apportion the gains and losses under any and all contingencies. Consider the **full contingent claims contract** you and your surgeon would need to write before an organ transplant operation. Or alternatively, consider the full contingent claims contract two pharmaceutical companies would need before one licensed the rights to produce a pregnancy-related drug to the other. To develop all the accurate information required for a full contingent claims contract involving multigenerational cumulative health hazards is simply prohibitively expensive. Consequently, few transplant patients and few business partners attempt to

Full Contingent Claims Contract

An agreement about all possible future events.

Postcontractual Opportunistic Behavior
Actions that take advantage of another party's vulnerabilities.

negotiate full contingent claims contracts. The fact that information costs can be prohibitively large leads to the important insight that contracts are often incomplete by design.

One immediate consequence of incomplete contracts is that after signing, some parties may engage in **postcontractual opportunistic behavior** not specifically prohibited by the few restrictive covenants contained in their incomplete contract. Surgical patients may go fishing in swampy bacteria-infested water before their incisions fully heal. Employees who receive on-the-job training (OJT) may take their newly honed skills elsewhere. Managers may reconfigure assets following a labor contract concession in ways their employees did not anticipate. Baseball players may attempt a holdup at the time of contract renewals just before a World Series. Knowing this, surgeons must defend against more accidental injury suits, companies provide less OJT, workers agree to fewer wage concessions, and owners develop more farm team players than they otherwise would. So, the incompleteness of contracts results in inefficient behavior that is the inescapable consequence of costly and therefore incomplete information. To reduce these inefficiencies companies adopt **governance mechanisms** to help resolve postcontractual disputes. Examples of corporate governance mechanisms include monitoring by independent directors, rank order tournaments for promotion, and mandatory arbitration agreements. In the last section of this chapter, we explore the complementary roles of governance mechanisms and pay-for-performance incentive systems for managers.

Governance Mechanisms
Processes to detect, resolve, and reduce postcontractual opportunism.

Asymmetric Information in a "Lemons Market"

WWW . . . .
Read more about how the concept of a lemons market can be applied to the assessment of loan quality and the performance of the Resolution Trust Corporation at the following Internet site:
http://www.fdic.gov/databank/bkreview/1995summ/art1full.html

In services, retailing, and many manufacturing industries, buyers generally search the market to identify low-price suppliers. Sometimes this search is accomplished by asking recent purchasers, by scouring the catalogs and ads, or by visiting showrooms and sales floors. In selecting a supplier many customers are also intensely interested in multiple dimensions of product and service quality, including product design, durability, image, conformance to specifications, order delay, delivery reliability, change order responsiveness, and after-sale service. Customers often spend as much time and effort searching the market for the desired quality mix as they do searching for lowest price. Retailers and service providers understand this and often offer many quality combinations at various prices to trigger a purchase of these **search goods.** Consider, for example, the many price-quality alternatives available from your favorite clothing, sporting goods, furniture, or package delivery business.

Search Goods
Products and services whose quality can be detected through market search.

Search Goods Versus Experience Goods

On the other hand, some products and services have important quality dimensions that *cannot* be observed at the point of purchase. Consider used cars and other resale machinery, nonprescription remedies for the common cold, house paint, and mail-order computer components. The quality of these items can be detected only through experience in using the products. Hence, products and services of this type are termed **experience goods** and are distinguished from search goods.

Ultimately the problem with experience goods in competitive market exchange is the unverifiability of asymmetric information. The seller knows how to detect the difference between high- and low-quality products (e.g., between lemons and cream puffs in the used-car market), but cannot credibly relay this information to buyers, at least not in chance encounters between strangers. Fraudulent sellers will claim high quality when it is absent, and realizing this, buyers discount all such information. Because of the private, impacted nature of the product quality information, the seller's claims and omissions can never be verified without experiencing the reliability of the auto, the efficacy

Experience Goods
Products and services whose quality is undetectable when purchased.

of the common cold remedy, the durability of the house paint, or the capability of the computer component.

All of this is not to say that the buyers of experience goods are without recourse or that the sellers are without ingenuity as to how to market their products. Warranties and investments in reputations provide mechanisms whereby the sellers of house paint and computer components can credibly commit to delivering a high-quality product. The essential point is that in the absence of these bonding or hostage mechanisms, the experience-good buyer will rationally disbelieve the seller's claims. Consequently, the honest seller of truly high-quality experience goods will find little market for his or her higher-cost, higher-priced product. The "bad apples drive out the good" in many experience-good markets.

Adverse Selection and the Notorious Firm

Suppose customers recognize that unverifiable private information about experience-good quality is present, yet knowledge of any fraudulent high-price sale of low-quality products spreads almost instantaneously throughout the marketplace. Is this extreme reputational effect sufficient to restore the exchange of high-quality/high-price experience goods? Or, can the notorious firm continue to defraud customers here and elsewhere? The answer, as you may have already discerned from the discussion of competitive market forces in Chapter 12, depends on the conditions of entry and exit, but not in the way you might expect.

Consider the cost structure and profits of such a notorious firm depicted in Figure 13.1. If offered the low price P_l, the firm operates in competitive equilibrium at Q_1 where the price just covers the marginal cost and average total cost ($SRATC_{low}$) for Q_1 units of the low-quality product. Alternatively, if offered the high price P_h, the firm can either competitively supply Q_1 of the high-quality experience good and again just break even

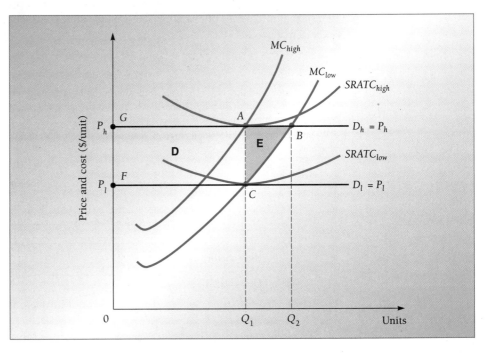

against the higher costs of $SRATC_{high}$,[2] or the firm can deliver a low-quality experience good at Q_2 and continue to incur the lower costs $SRATC_{low}$. The second alternative entails an expansion of output along MC_{low} in response to the price rise and generates profits. That is, the incremental output $(Q_2 - Q_1)$ earns incremental profit equal to the difference between P_h and MC_{low}—namely, the shaded area ABC (labeled bold E)—and in addition, the original output Q_1 earns a fraudulent rent of area $GACF$ (labeled bold D). Although the supplier observes his own cost directly and therefore detects the availability of $D + E$, the problem for the experience-good buyer is that in terms of point-of-sale information, high-price transactions at Q_2 on MC_{low} and at Q_1 on MC_{high} are indistinguishable.

Of course, the supplier is not indifferent between the two alternatives. The high-quality transaction offers a cash flow from operations just sufficient to cover capital costs and break even at point A, whereas the fraudulent transaction (a low quality product at a high price at point B) offers a net profit for at least one period. Table 13.1 depicts this interaction between experience-good buyers and a notorious firm as a payoff matrix.[3] The seller can produce either low or high quality, and the buyer can offer either low or high prices. The row player (the seller) gets the below-diagonal payoffs in each cell, and the column player (the buyer) gets the above-diagonal payoffs in each cell. The buyer prefers to cover the high cost of high-quality products (in the northwest cell) rather than pay less and only cover the lower cost of low-quality products (in the southeast cell). However, the buyer is worst off when the seller defects from delivering an allegedly high-quality product for which the buyer has paid a high price (in the southwest cell). The buyer also recognizes that getting more than she pays for (in the northeast cell) would impose losses on the seller who would then prefer to break even with a low-price/low-quality transaction in the southeast cell.

Each player attempts to predict the other's behavior and respond accordingly. Knowing that the seller prefers profits to breaking even at high prices and that the seller prefers breaking even to losses at low prices, the buyer predicts that low-quality product will be forthcoming independent of the price offered. Therefore, the buyer makes only low-price offers. Just as only dupes maintain their quotas when price begins to erode in a cartel, so too only dupes offer high prices for one-shot transactions with strangers offering experience goods.

---

[2] The minimum cost output for the plant configuration and cost structure associated with high quality could shift right or left, but to simplify assume that it remains the same and that the $SRATC$ just increases vertically from point C to point A.

[3] We analyze the experience-goods strategy game as a two-person, simultaneous-play, one-shot prisoner's dilemma in Chapter 16.

TABLE 13.1

Experience-Good Payoff Matrix

		Buyer			
		Offer High Price		**Offer Low Price**	
Seller	**High Quality**	Break even	Better	Loss ($-D$)	Best
	Low Quality	Profit ($D + E$)	Worst	Break even	Worse

Note: Column-player payoffs are above diagonal. Row-player payoffs are below diagonal.

Adverse Selection
A limited choice of lower quality alternatives attributable to asymmetric information.

This reasoning motivates **adverse selection** by the rational seller in an experience-good market. Because sellers can anticipate only low-price offers from buyers, the sellers never produce high-quality products. That is, the market for experience goods will be incomplete in that not all product qualities will be available for sale. Anticipating that buyers will radically discount their unverifiable high-quality "cream puffs," individual sellers of used cars choose to place only low-quality "lemons" on the market. Similarly, jewelers in vacation locations, anticipating that out-of-town buyers will radically discount high-grade, uncertified gemstones, chose to sell only lower quality gemstones. And unbranded mail-order computer components are inevitably lower quality. Adverse selection always causes competitive markets with asymmetric information to be incomplete. The bad apples drive out the good.

Insuring and Lending under Asymmetric Information

This same adverse selection reasoning applies beyond experience-good product markets whenever asymmetric information is prominent. Consider the transaction between a bank loan officer and a new commercial borrower, or between an insurance company and a new auto insurance policyholder. Through an application and interview process and with access to various databases and credit references, the lender or insurer attempts to uncover the private, impacted information about the applicant's credit or driving history. Nevertheless, just as in the case of claims made by the itinerant seller of an experience good, verification remains a problem. The applicant has an incentive to omit facts that would tend to result in loan or insurance denial (e.g., prior business failures or unreported accidents) and knowing this, the lender may offer only higher rate loans and the insurer higher rate policies.

The problem is that higher rate loans and expensive insurance policies tend to affect the composition of the applicant pool resulting in adverse selection. Some honest, well-intentioned borrowers will now drop out of the applicant pool because of concern about their inability to pay principal and interest on time as promised. On the other hand, applicants who never intended to repay (or drive carefully), or more problematically, those who will try less hard to avoid default or accidents, are undeterred by the higher rates. The asymmetric information and higher rates have adversely selected out precisely those borrowers and drivers the lender and auto insurance company wanted to attract to their loan portfolio and insurance risk pool. Recognizing this problem, the creditors and insurers offer a restricted and incomplete set of loan and insurance contracts. Credit rationing that excludes large segments of the population of potential borrowers and state-mandated protection against uninsured motorists are reflections of the adverse selection problem resulting from asymmetric information in these markets.

SOLUTIONS TO THE ADVERSE SELECTION PROBLEM

In both theory and practice there are two approaches to eliciting the exchange of high-quality experience goods, loans to new borrowers, or insurance policies to strangers. The first involves regulatory agencies such as the Federal Trade Commission, the Food and Drug Administration, and the Consumer Product Safety Commission. These agencies attempt to set quotas (e.g., on minimum feather content in down pillows), impose restrictions (e.g., on the sale of untested pharmaceuticals), enforce product safety standards (e.g., on the flammability of children's sleepwear), and monitor truth in advertising laws. We discuss regulation at greater length in Chapter 18.

Mutual Reliance: Hostages Support Exchange

Reliance Relationship
Long-term, mutually
beneficial agreements, often
informal.

Bonding Mechanism
A procedure for
establishing trust by
assigning valuable property
contingent on your
nonperformance of an
agreement.

A second, quite different approach involves self-enforcing private contracts where each party relies on the other. Such **reliance relationships** often involve the exchange of some sort of hostage, such as a reputational asset or an escrow account. In general, **hostage or bonding mechanisms** are necessary to induce unregulated asymmetric information exchange. For this second approach to the adverse selection problem to succeed, buyers, lenders, or insurers must be convinced that fraud is more costly to the seller, borrower, or insured than the cost of delivering the promised product quality, divulging one's loan defaults, or revealing one's accidents. Then and only then will the customers pay for the seller's additional expected costs attributable to the higher quality products.

One simple illustration of the use of a hostage mechanism to support asymmetric information exchange is a product warranty, perhaps for an auto tire. Tires are an experience good in that blowout protection and tread wear life are product qualities not detectable at the point of purchase. Only through driving many thousands of miles and randomly encountering many road hazards can the buyer ascertain these tire qualities directly. However, if a tread wear replacement warranty and a tire blowout warranty make the sellers conspicuously worse off should they fail to deliver high-quality tires, then buyers can rely on that manufacturer's product claims. As a consequence, buyers will be willing to offer higher prices for the unverifiably higher-quality product.

Hostage mechanisms can be either self-enforcing or enforced by third parties. Like warranties, a seller's representations about after-sale service and product replacement guarantees are ultimately contractual agreements that will be enforced by the Courts. However, other hostage mechanisms require no third-party enforcement. Suppose DuPont's industrial chemicals division reveals to potential new customers the names and addresses of several satisfied current customers. This practice of providing references is not only to assist potential buyers in gauging the quality of the product or service for sale but also to deliver an irretrievable hostage. Once new customers have the ability to contact regular customers to warn about product malfunctions or misrepresentations, the seller has an enhanced incentive to deliver high quality to both sets of buyers. Connecting all suppliers and customers in a real-time information system is a natural extension of this familiar practice of providing references. The total quality movement's ISO 9000 standards recommend that companies insist on just such information links to their suppliers.

EXAMPLE

CREDIBLE PRODUCT REPLACEMENT CLAIMS: DOONY BURKE

The women's handbag market has a wide selection of brand names, prices, and qualities. Leather products have several search goods characteristics in that one can touch and feel the material in order to assess the fineness or coarseness of the grain, the evenness of the tanning process, and the suppleness of the leather, etc. In these respects, one can search for just that quality for which one is willing to pay. However, the susceptibility to discoloring with age or exposure to the elements and the quality of the stitching is much harder to detect at the point of purchase. As a result, some aspects of handbag purchase are an experience-good exchange. Therefore, one wonders how the wide variety of prices and qualities can be sustained. Doony Burke resolves this question by offering an almost preposterous replacement guarantee. Like Bevo sunglasses, Doony Burke offers to replace any handbag for the life of the customer. Because each State Attorney General will assist any customer in enforcing this promise, the commitment is credible, and the replacement guarantee provides a hostage that supports high price–high quality exchanges. In particular, customers can easily discern that Doony Burke is better off producing an exceptionally high-quality handbag to deliver at the first transaction rather than an unlimited series of replacements.

Another illustration of a hostage mechanism occurs in lending to new borrowers. Recall that with uncertain returns and asymmetric information about the bankruptcy potential of loan applicants, a higher interest rate causes adverse selection; some reliable borrowers who intend to repay their debt are induced to switch from safer investment projects to projects with large expected returns but a greater probability of default. Other well-intentioned borrowers simply drop out of the applicant pool because of their concern about an inability to repay at such high rates. To resolve these moral hazard and signaling problems, the lender may employ collateral as a hostage mechanism. Collateral may consist of real property, such as private residences, escrow accounts, and machinery, or intangible intellectual property, such as patents, copyrights, and trademarks. New and unknown, but reliable, borrowers would be attracted by higher collateral requirements and a lower interest rate for any given loan size, whereas bad risk borrowers would refuse such a contract. Giving the collateral as a hostage signals in an irrevocable manner the otherwise unverifiable intent of the borrower to avoid actions that might prevent repayment of the loan.[4] Again, one sees how hostage mechanisms support asymmetric information exchange.

Brand Name Reputations as Hostages

A marketing mechanism that supports asymmetric information exchange is brand name reputations such as Sony Trinitron color televisions, Apple Macintosh computers, and Toyota Lexus automobiles. Branding requires a substantial investment over extended periods of time. Moreover, brand names are capital assets that provide future net cash flows from repeat-purchase customers as long as the brand reputation holds up. To defraud customers by delivering less quality than the brand reputation promised would destroy the capitalized market value of the brand name. Buyers anticipate that value-maximizing managers will not intentionally destroy brand name capital. Brand names therefore deliver a hostage, providing assurances to buyers that the seller will not misrepresent the quality of an experience good.

Ultimately, brand name capital provides such a hostage because the brand name disreputation for delivering fraudulent product quality cannot be separated from the salable brand asset. Successful brands can be extended to sell other products; Nestlé's original hot chocolate brand can be extended to sell cereal-based candy bars, and Oreo cookies can be extended to sell ice cream. But the product failure of Texas Instruments (TI) personal computers means that now the TI brand name cannot be easily extended to other consumer electronic products. All the potential buyers have to figure out is whether the seller would be worse off sacrificing the value of the brand name but economizing on production expenses rather than simply incurring the extra expense to produce a high-quality product while retaining the asset value. A brand name asset such as Overnight Auto Repair may suggest one answer, whereas Midas Muffler suggests another.

---

[4] For a supplemental reading on asymmetric information in financial contracting, see "Lessons on Lending and Borrowing in Hard Times," Federal Reserve Bank of Philadelphia, *Business Review* (July-August 1991), or A. Thakor, "Strategic Issues in Financial Contracting: An Overview," *Financial Management* (Summer 1989).

EXAMPLE

CUSTOMERS FOR LIFE AT SEWELL CADILLAC[5]

The most profitable luxury automobile dealership in the United States is operated in Dallas, Texas, by Carl Sewell. Several decades ago Mr. Sewell realized that the critical success factor in his business was establishing repeat purchase transactions with regular customers. Many potential buyers shop for lowest price in the new automobile market sometimes with no more inconvenience than the fingertip browsing of the Internet. And because the alternatives are many, and the information on posted prices is great, many dealerships spend several hundred dollars per car on selling costs with little prospect of repeat business. Carl Sewell decided instead to expend similarly large amounts attracting "customers for life." He began by making the apparently preposterous claim that he would dispatch Sewell Cadillac emergency roadside service to any Sewell Cadillac customer experiencing car trouble anywhere in the state of Texas. To economize on the need for such trips, Sewell developed an extensive dealer-based maintenance schedule and instituted one of the first total quality management (TQM) programs in his service department. These policies cost plenty, but the word-of-mouth reputation effects every time the dealership delivered on its promise spread the name and quality image of Sewell Cadillac across North Texas. Soon customers were driving in from surrounding cities for the privilege of doing high-margin business with Carl Sewell. And even more importantly, these same customers came back time and time again with very little additional cost to the dealership.

If brand name assets could be sold independent of their reputations (or disreputations), then this hostage mechanism would cease to support experience-good exchange. Assets that can be redeployed at the grantor's wish are not hostages in this reliance contracting sense. The implication is that easy entry and exit, which worked to ensure break-even prices just sufficient to cover costs in normal competitive markets, may have undesirable consequences here in asymmetric information experience-good markets.

Price Premiums with Nonredeployable Assets

Recall that if sellers are offered prices that just cover high-quality cost, sellers of experience goods prefer the profit from defrauding customers by delivering low-quality products. But suppose buyers offered reliable sellers a continuing price premium above the cost of high-quality products. At P_{hh} in Figure 13.2, the non-notorious firm produces Q_1' high-quality product and earns a continuous stream of profits ($IJAG + JKA$) labeled $(T + U)$. This perpetuity may now exceed (in present value) the notorious firm's one-time-only fraudulent rent from production at Q_2'—namely, $(D + T)$ plus incremental profit $(E + U + V)$. That is,

$$(T + U)/d > [(D + T) + (E + U + V)] \qquad [13.1]$$

where d is an appropriate discount rate (e.g., the firm's weighted average cost of capital, perhaps 11%). Lower discount rates or faster rising marginal cost (i.e., a smaller incremental profit from the expansion of output) decreases the likelihood of fraudulent behavior. If reliable delivery of a high-quality product now earns long-term net profit in excess of the one-time-only profit from fraud, sellers will offer both low- and high-quality products at P_l and P_{hh}, respectively, and some buyers will purchase in each market.

---

[5] See Carl Sewell and Paul B. Brown, *Customers for Life,* (New York: Simon and Schuster, 1992).

FIGURE   13.2

High-Quality Experience
Goods Earn a Price
Premium

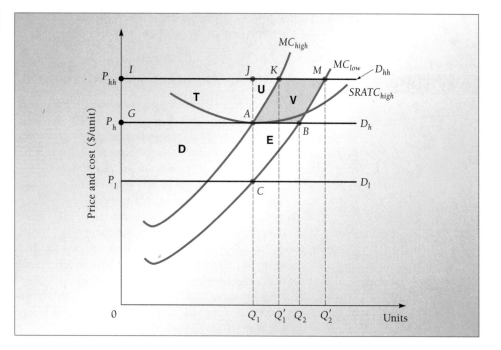

However, transitory profits alone do not allow an escape from adverse selection. Because profits attract entry in competitive markets, the price premiums will erode, and
notorious firm behavior will then return. What is missing is a mechanism to dissipate
the rent from the price premiums. If the sellers invest the high-quality price premiums
in firm-specific assets, such as L'eggs retail displays or a Thomasville Furniture show-
room, then new entrants will encounter a higher entry barrier than previously. Such barriers cause potential entrants to perceive zero expected profit and therefore deter entry.
Profits in excess of the production cost can then persist, and high-quality/high-price experience goods can survive in the marketplace.

The rent-dissipating investments must not be in generic commercial sites easily redeployable to the next tenant or capital equipment easily redeployable to the next manufacturer. If that were the case, hit-and-run entry would recur each time high-quality
prices rose above cost. Then, again, competitive equilibrium would induce adverse selection in experience-good markets. Instead, the investment that dissipates the operating profit from high-quality products must be investment in nonredeployable assets.

Nonredeployable Assets
Assets whose value in
second-best use is near
zero.

Asset Specificity
The difference in value
between first-best and
second-best use.

Nonredeployable assets are assets whose liquidation value is very low, perhaps zero.
Usually this occurs when the assets depend on a firm-specific input such as a L'eggs or
Thomasville brand name. Without the brand name, nobody has a use for the egg-shaped
retail racks or furniture-specific coordinated drapery and wallpaper interiors. Many
such nonredeployable assets have high value in their first best use. The difference between value in first best use and liquidation value is a measure of the **specificity of the
asset.** Highly specific assets make the best hostages to convince customers that asymmetric information transactions will be nonfraudulent.

In summary, asymmetric information causes competitive markets for experience
goods to differ rather markedly from the competitive markets of Chapter 12. Long-run
equilibrium for high-quality experience goods requires revenues in excess of total unit
cost. These profits are invested by reliable sellers of experience goods in highly specific assets. Potentially notorious firms with redeployable assets attract only customers

seeking low-price/low-quality experience goods. In experience-good markets, at best you get what you pay for, never more.

<table>
<tr><td>EXAMPLE</td></tr>
</table>

EFFICIENT UNCUT DIAMOND SORTING: DEBEERS[6]

Another illustration of experience-good exchange is the DeBeers diamond cartel, which controls over 80 percent of the uncut wholesale diamond business. DeBeers offers groupings of diamonds of various grades to approved wholesale buyers. Because buyers are not allowed to cull the less valuable stones, the quality of the diamonds in any given grouping is unverifiable at the point of purchase—hence, the term *sights*. If these arrangements were one time only, no buyer would purchase high-price sights or agree to the culling restrictions. But because DeBeers invests its positive expected profits in careful diamond sorting and therefore can consistently offer its sights below the value at which the diamonds grade out, buyers have a reason for purchasing high-quality experience goods from DeBeers. If a competitor offered no culling restrictions and lower prices, the diamond merchants would carefully weigh the additional cost of sorting the diamonds themselves against the price premiums at DeBeers and might well decide to continue doing business with DeBeers. Knowing this, very few potential entrants into the uncut diamond wholesale business decide to challenge DeBeers despite its high mark-ups and margins.

COST REVELATION IN JOINT VENTURES AND PARTNERSHIPS

One of the most frequent asymmetric information settings many firms encounter is in joint ventures with suppliers and customers. Consider a joint venture to develop several new personal computer products between a PC designer-manufacturer, such as Apple Computer, and Motorola, a leading supplier of computer chips.[7] The Apple operating system depends on the capabilities of the Motorola chips, and the chips are produced in anticipation of the future requirements of the operating system. The partners believe they can better sustain a competitive advantage in this fast-moving technology by jointly developing new products. After the joint venture covers development and production costs, they agree to split the profits equally.

Each partner in the joint venture has private, impacted information about cost to which the other partner does not have access. For example, as it develops the Power PC, Apple knows its operating system development costs, and Motorola knows its computer chip design and production costs. The complication inherent to joint ventures and partnerships is that neither can independently verify the other partner's asymmetric information. Yet, the success of a joint venture often depends on each partner's ability to generate operating profits so as to recover development costs. This necessitates an accurate revelation of true costs. Let's see why and what can be done to achieve this goal.

---

[6] Based on R. Kenney and B. Klein, "The Economics of Block Booking," *Journal of Law and Economics* 26 (1983), pp. 497–540.

[7] The general structure of this section relies on A. Dixit and B. Nalebuff, *Thinking Strategically* (New York: Norton, 1991), pp. 306–319. The illustration here is based on "Apple Wants Other PC Makers to Build Computers to Use Macintosh Software," *Wall Street Journal*, 28 January 1994, p. B5, and "IBM, Apple in PC Design Accord," *Wall Street Journal*, 8 November 1994, p. B5.

The study of optimal incentive contracts under asymmetric information can provide some answers. Each partner faces random disturbances in the determinants of its costs.[8] Sometimes software development is delayed by inconspicuous but debilitating bugs in the programming, which increase the cost from, say, $80 to $120 million. Similarly, sometimes chip development and production necessitates redesign (e.g., Intel's problems with the Pentium chip) increasing that cost, say, from $50 to $70 million. Neither partner can hope to discover and rectify all such problems in advance. However, each can detect early warning signals of cost overruns and, if need be, cancel that particular one of their several joint projects.

Cost Overruns with Simple Profit-Sharing Partnerships

Suppose that when both cost overruns happen simultaneously the product development joint venture should shut down, because the variable costs of proceeding to full-scale production will exceed the projected revenue available, say, $180 million. Consider the payoff matrix of operating profits in Table 13.2. If Apple experiences $120 million cost (the column labeled High Costs), the partnership will cancel the project whenever Motorola also experiences high cost of $70 million (the row labeled High Costs) because proceeding would result in a $10 million operating loss. By the same token, when only one partner or neither partner experiences higher than expected costs, the joint venture project should go forward and realize profits of $30 million, $10 million, and $50 million, respectively. Only with correct shutdown and operate decisions can the joint venture generate its maximum value.

The problem is that initially each partner has an incentive to overstate true costs in order to be overcompensated from the joint venture revenues. For example, in Table 13.2, if Apple reveals true costs of $80 million and Motorola claims costs of $70 million when in fact its true costs are $50 million, Motorola's joint profit share declines by $10 million from one-half of $50 million to one-half of $30 million. But with $20 million extra reimbursement from overstating its cost, Motorola ends up with (1/2) $30 million + $20 million—i.e., ahead by $10 million. Similarly, if Apple overstates its costs, the Apple profit share falls from $25 million to $5 million, but this decline is more than offset by the $40 million extra reimbursement for overstating the $80 million actual cost to $120 million.

If low cost and cost overruns are equally likely at Motorola and if the probability of a cost overrun at Apple is 0.3, then each partner's expected costs are $60 million at Motorola and $92 million at Apple. When true revelation of costs occurs, expected net profit from the joint venture is then (0.5×0.7) $50 million + (0.5×0.3) $10 million + (0.5×0.7) $30 million + (0.5×0.3) $0 = $29.5 million—namely, $14.75 million for each partner.[9] However, if one or both partners overstate costs, the projects with

---

[8] Similar arguments can be made about asymmetric information regarding random disturbances in demand.

[9] Note that the project in the southeast cell is canceled because of mutual early warnings of high cost and therefore a projected operating loss.

TABLE 13.2			Apple	
Joint Profits (in millions) from a Simple Profit-Sharing Partnership with $180 Million in Revenue			Low Costs ($80)	High Costs ($120)
	Motorola	Low Costs ($50)	$50	$10
		High Costs ($70)	$30	−$10

mixed costs in the southwest and northeast cells of Table 13.2 will be canceled, and the expected net profit from the joint venture then declines. For example, if Apple falsely reveals $120 million when low costs of $80 million are present, the joint development project is canceled whenever Motorola experiences $70 million cost. This cancellation results in the partners forgoing the $30 million profit on the mixed cost project in the southwest cell and reduces the expected value of the joint venture to $19 million—i.e., $9.5 million per partner.[10] Value-maximizing managers facing asymmetric information seek some revelation mechanism that will provide appropriate incentives to induce the revelation of true costs and thereby preserve and capture the full $14.75 million per partner expected value of both the low cost and the mixed cost projects.

An Incentive-Compatible Revelation Mechanism

One such revelation mechanism is known as the Clarke tax mechanism.[11] Edward Clarke's pathbreaking idea was that to create appropriate incentives in a partnership, each party's cost or demand revelation should entail an imposition of the expected costs imposed on (and opportunity losses suffered by) the other partners. In this way, the maximizing incentives of each of the asymmetrically informed partners could be made compatible. For our PC product development example, Table 13.3 indicates the profit shares each partner would receive under a Clarke tax mechanism. The row player Motorola gets the below-diagonal payoffs in each cell, and the column player Apple gets the above-diagonal payoffs in each cell. After the other party's expected costs are covered, each partner's payoff is calculated as the residual or net profit from all noncanceled projects triggered by its own cost revelation.

To illustrate, if Motorola reveals Low_m cost, the project will proceed independent of Apple's cost, and Motorola will realize $88 million, which is $180 million revenue minus the $92 million expected cost of Apple.[12] However, if Motorola announces $High_m$ cost, the project is canceled whenever Apple detects early warning signs that its own cost is $High_a$. Consequently, should Motorola decide to reveal high cost when low cost is present, its realized profit share falls off from $88 million to 0.7($180 million − $80 million) + 0.0($180 million − $120 million) = $70 million because of a zero probability

---

[10] This expected value is calculated as (0.5 × 0.7)$50 million + (0.5 × 0.3)$10 million = $19 million.

[11] This revelation mechanism is also referred to as the Clarke-Groves-Ledyard revelation mechanism after T. Groves and J. Ledyard who formalized and refined the concept.

[12] This expected profit number may also be calculated as 0.7($180 million − $80 million) + 0.3($180 million − $120 million).

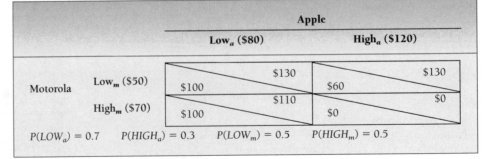

TABLE 13.3		Apple	
Individual Profit Shares (in millions) with an Incentive-Compatible Revelation Mechanism		Low_a ($80)	$High_a$ ($120)
Motorola Low_m ($50)		$100 $130	$60 $130
Motorola $High_m$ ($70)		$100 $110	$0 $0
$P(LOW_a) = 0.7$ $P(HIGH_a) = 0.3$		$P(LOW_m) = 0.5$	$P(HIGH_m) = 0.5$

Note: Column-player payoffs are above diagonal. Row-player payoffs are below diagonal.

of realizing the $60 million residual profit in the northeast cell. The false overstatement of cost by Motorola results in that project being canceled, and everyone loses. Under a Clarke tax mechanism, not just actions but information revelations themselves have consequences. And, as we shall see, these consequences can induce the true revelation of partnership costs.

Incentive-Compatible Revelation Mechanism
A procedure for eliciting true revelation of privately-held information.

The importance of the discovery of such **incentive-compatible revelation mechanisms** can hardly be overemphasized; they have led to many pathbreaking applications. Clarke first developed the concept in the context of the true demand revelations needed in partnerships to finance a jointly consumed public good such as a park, pool, or playground. To build the appropriate size urban park or swimming pool requires private, impacted information about use value and willingness to pay. But if one asks potential demanders who assume their answer will determine their tax share, the respondents will understate their willingness to pay. The demand revelation problem in assessing an optimal tax share in a consumption partnership is analogous to the cost revelation problem in assessing an optimal profit share in a product development partnership.[13]

INTERNATIONAL PERSPECTIVES

www..............
You can read a DRI-McGraw-Hill study of the globalization of the semiconductor industry at the following Internet site maintained by the Electronic Industries Association of Japan: http://www.eiaj.org/study /executive.html

JOINT VENTURE IN MEMORY CHIPS: IBM, SIEMENS, AND TOSHIBA[14]

After years of lobbying for nationalistic industrial policies that would subsidize the design and production of semiconductors in the United States, IBM entered into an agreement in July 1993 with Siemens and Toshiba to co-produce computer memory chips. At the same time, AMD and Intel announced similar joint ventures to develop flash memory chips with Fujitsu and Sharp, respectively. Flash chips retain the information needed to restart computer operating systems when the power is interrupted. In all three cases, the Japanese firm will contribute its superior manufacturing capability, and the American and German firms will contribute their design and innovative research capabilities.

The key question in such joint ventures is whether the Western companies will simply give away their technological knowledge while their Japanese partners deliver little in exchange. This happened once before in the computer chip industry of the 1960 and 1970s. To ensure a more evenly balanced partnership this time, the manufacturing know-how of the Japanese will be dissected as production cost information under various market conditions is revealed and analyzed by the joint venture partners. AMD and Fujitsu also undertook to establish a hostage mechanism by negotiating to purchase 5 percent of each other's stock.

AN OPTIMAL INCENTIVES CONTRACT

Optimal Incentives Contract
An agreement about payoffs and penalties that creates appropriate incentives.

To organize a joint venture around a Clarke tax revelation mechanism usually involves the implementation of a so-called **optimal incentives contract.** Each party agrees in advance to a set of partnership profit shares associated with the expected payoffs from a revelation mechanism (see Table 13.4). The important thing to appreciate is that the problem of independently verifying asymmetric information has not gone away. A third party attempting to enforce the contract (e.g., a district court) would still have just as

---

[13] For more on the public sector applications of revelation mechanisms, see R. Cornes and T. Sandler, "Clarke's Demand-Revealing Mechanism," *Theory of Externalities, Public Goods, and Club Goods* (New York: Cambridge University Press, 1986), pp. 105–108, or N. Tideman and G. Tullock, "A New and Superior Process for Making Social Choices," *Journal of Political Economy* 84 (1976), pp. 1145–1160.

[14] Based on "Pragmatism Wins as Rivals Start to Cooperate on Memory Chips," *Wall Street Journal,* 14 July 1993, p. B1.

TABLE 13.4	**Apple**			
	Probability	Expected Receipts	Expected Costs	Net Profit
Low$_a$	0.7	$120	$80	$28
High$_a$	0.3	$ 65	$60	$ 1.5
		$103.5	$74	$29.5

	Motorola			
	Probability	Expected Receipts	Expected Costs	Net Profit
Low$_m$	0.5	$88	$50	$19
High$_m$	0.5	$70	$49	$10.5
		$79	$49.5	$29.5

TABLE 13.4

Expected Net Profit Shares (in millions) with True Cost Revelation under an Optimal Incentives Contract

much trouble verifying the claims for cost reimbursement arising under this contract as the parties had in trying to verify their own partner's cost. Entering into a partnership incentives contract does not define away the asymmetric information problem. Instead, the revelation mechanism creates incentives for a **self-enforcing reliance relationship** between the partners, not unlike the reliance relationship we described earlier between repeat-purchase customers and high-reputation, premium-priced sellers of experience goods.

That is, the structure of incentives underlying Table 13.4 is fully capable of inducing the partners to reveal their true costs; each would be worse off not doing so. We have already seen how Motorola would be worse off overstating its cost. Similarly, if Apple were to overstate its cost, profitable projects in the southwest cell of Table 13.3 would be canceled. Rather than realizing 0.5($130 million) + 0.5($110 million) = $120 million from the good fortune of incurring Low$_a$ cost, Apple would instead realize only 0.5($130 million) = $65 million, which fails to cover its own low-cost realization of $80 million. In addition, this false overstatement of cost and the cancellation of the profitable project in the southwest cell reduces Apple's expected receipts from the partnership to just (0.5 × 0.7)($130 million) + (0.5 × 0.3)($130 million) = $65 million, whereas with true revelation it realizes $103.5 million = (0.5 × 0.7)($130 million) + (0.5 × 0.7)($110 million) + (0.5 × 0.3)($130 million) = 0.7($120 million) + 0.3($65 million). Truthtelling dominates false revelation for both partners.

We can now also explain why both Apple and Motorola would adopt an optimal incentives contract that credibly commits each partner to a true revelation of asymmetric cost information. Apple realizes an expected net profit with true revelation of $103.5 million expected receipts minus expected costs of $74 million—i.e., $29.5 million. And similarly, Motorola realizes an expected net profit of $79 million expected receipts minus $49.5 million expected costs—i.e., $29.5 million. Each of these amounts equals the $29.5 million joint profits potentially available in the original simple profit-sharing contract of Table 13.2. However, recall that each party knows in advance that the other party will have private, impacted information about cost overruns. Each could therefore predict that the simple profit-sharing partnership would lead to cost overstatement, cancellation of the mixed cost projects, and loss of value. This proactive reasoning implies that only the mutual low-cost outcome in Table 13.2 will escape cancellation and actually generate profit. Therefore, only a much smaller expected profit is assured by the simple profit-sharing contract—i.e., just $0.5 \times 0.7(\$50$ million$) = \$17.5$ million. This smaller amount from simple profit sharing is what rational parties choosing among partnership contracts would compare to the $29.5 million expected net profit from an optimal incentives contract.

The application of incentive-compatible revelation mechanisms and optimal incentive contracts has led to many exciting new types of asymmetric information partnerships. The same principles also underlie the concept of efficient breach of contract in the economics of contract law—i.e., one partner's termination of a contractual relationship necessitates taking into account the opportunities forgone and other expectation damage costs imposed on the partner who does not breach.[15] These concepts have become a key for achieving partnership or joint venture success in both small firms and large corporations under asymmetric information.

JOINT VENTURES IN APPLIANCES: MAYTAG AND WHIRLPOOL[16]

Sometimes joint ventures are designed to increase the value of assets sold through a phased partnership rather than an immediate sale. As a potential buyer of Philips' European appliance division, Whirlpool sought access to more private information than due diligence by their merger and acquisition attorneys could uncover. Philips had a consumer franchise of nine appliance brands and a pan-European network of retail dealers who were second only to Electrolux in market share. But like other intangible assets (e.g., pivotal human resources and technical know-how), brands and distribution relationships are notoriously hard to value. In a new corporate organization and culture, could the Philips brands be redeployed without Philips' extremely strong reputation in European electronics? Would the fragmented network of independent dealers remain loyal once Whirlpool's name was substituted for Philips? And most importantly, what cost savings could be realized by sourcing all of the design, procurement, and production of Whirlpool and Philips components globally to achieve economies of scale?

These questions were best answered by a joint venture in which Philips retained a 47 percent ownership stake, and Whirlpool immediately assumed management control in exchange for $381 million. After both parties shared information for three years and fully assessed potential value, the remainder of the business was sold to Whirlpool for $610 million.

In contrast, Maytag satisfied their strategic plan to enter the European market by purchasing outright Chicago Pacific Corporation whose Hoover Appliance division had a substantial retail dealer network in Britain. However, Maytag knew little about the growing retail power of superstore chains near British shopping malls and still less about the marketing research on British households. Consequently, Maytag stumbled from one promotional blunder to another and eventually sold the Hoover European subsidiary at a $130 million loss. Again, with carefully designed incentives, a joint venture could have elicited the revelation of valuable asymmetric information to better ensure the success of Maytag's European initiative.

---

[15] A good supplemental reading on efficient breach of contracts is R. Cooter and T. Ulen, *Law and Economics* (Glenview, Ill.: Scott, Foresman, 1988), pp. 288–325.

[16] Based on A. Nanda and P. Williamson, "Use Joint Ventures to Ease the Pain of Restructuring," *Harvard Business Review*, November-December 1995, pp. 119–128.

THE PRINCIPAL-AGENT PROBLEM IN MANAGERIAL LABOR MARKETS

Many types of owner-principals hire manager-agents to stand in and conduct their business affairs in exchange for a claim on some of the residual income. Parent companies set up subsidiaries. Bondholders retain independent directors. Manufacturers employ retail distributors and dealers. And, most importantly, equity owners hire corporate executives. The stockholders' objective in such relationships is to preserve value-maximizing incentives while compensating risk-averse managers for a risky income stream and forgone alternative employment opportunities.

The Efficiency of Alternative Hiring Arrangements

Managerial hiring contracts may take on several pure or hybrid forms, including straight salary, wage rate, or profit sharing. In straight salary contracts, the manager and firm agree on a total compensation package and specific conditions of employment. In other contexts, such as management consulting, the manager may receive an hourly wage rate W_a equal to the best alternative employment opportunity in the competitive labor market for his or her type of consulting services. In Figure 13.3, the managerial consultant is hired for, say, 50 hours per week at wage rate W_a. D_l is the firm's input demand, which is the marginal revenue product of these labor services—namely, the marginal output of additional hours times the marginal revenue from selling the resulting additional output. Because each firm is atomistic in the labor market for these management consulting services, S_l is the perfectly elastic supply facing any given employer at the going market wage. Beyond 50 hours, the declining D_l no longer exceeds the incremental input cost along S_l.

Managers also may secure employment under a pure profit-sharing contract. Like pure commission-based salespeople or manufacturer's trade representatives, the manager may accept a percentage (say 40 percent) of the receipts directly attributable to his or her efforts in lieu of wage or salary income. Think of the percentage finder's fee sometimes offered for cost-saving suggestions in big corporations or the federal government. Again in Figure 13.3, we can represent this third alternative hiring arrangement as the

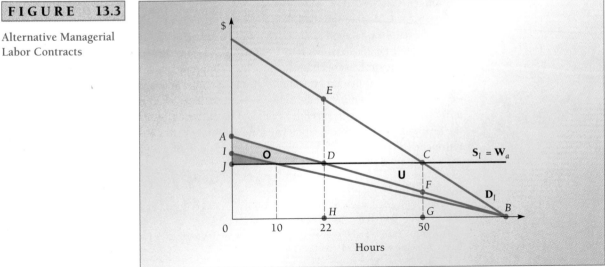

FIGURE   13.3

Alternative Managerial Labor Contracts

ray *AB*, wherein the manager receives 40 percent of the owner's willingness to pay for each hour of management services. Initially, this profit share will exceed the wage rate alternative. For example, during the first 22 hours of work, the profit-sharing contract will overcompensate by area ADJ (labeled area *O*). Thereafter the profit share falls below the manager's market wage rate per hour.

If 40 percent proves to be an equilibrium profit share, the overcompensation (area *O*) will just equal the undercompensation for the last 28 hours of work (area DCF labeled area *U*). This leaves both the manager and the owners indifferent between this hiring arrangement and the alternative 50 hour per week wage rate contract at W_a. If the profit share were reduced to, say, 35 percent (represented by the ray *IB*), the dark-shaded amount of overcompensation for the first 10 hours would fail to offset the massive undercompensation for hours 10 to 50. The manager would then reject the profit-sharing contract in favor of the wage rate offer. By raising the profit share back to 40 percent, the firm appears able to restore the attractiveness of each contract, at least for certain types of workers. In reality, as we shall now see, the situation in hiring managerial talent is often rather different.

Work Effort, Creative Ingenuity, and the Moral Hazard Problem

Pure profit-sharing contracts contain the seeds of their own destruction. Suppose several individuals are involved in generating pharmaceutical sales, and the input the profit sharer contributes to team production is largely unobservable. No time card can successfully monitor the input, perhaps because a measure of work effort rather than work hours is really what is required. The rational employee then considers his or her alternatives. As long as the profit-sharing compensation exceeds the alternative wage rate, he or she dedicates unobservable work effort to this job. Beyond 22 hours of work effort, however, the employee can earn more by working for someone else at the alternative wage rate W_a. Therefore, the disloyal (but rational) trade representative underworks the territory; he or she moonlights. This predictable response is referred to as the **moral hazard problem.** Only a *moral* sense of duty to one's employer prevents this problem from becoming a real *hazard* to the business.

Moral Hazard Problem
A failure to comply with the expected but unobservable aspects of an agreement.

Predicting such behavior, the employer may decide to withdraw the offer of a pure profit-sharing contract. Let's see why. If the territory is underworked by 28 hours, the employer saves profit-sharing payments equal to area *DFGH* in Figure 13.3, but loses output valued at *ECGH* and therefore is out the net value [*ECGH* − *DFGH* − the overpayment *ADJ* = *EDC*] relative to a wage contract that just paid piece rates for 50 hours of work at an implicit wage rate of W_a per hour. The fact that work effort is largely unobservable makes the pure profit-sharing contract unattractive to the employer relative to a piece-rate contract. This is not always so. For example, in hiring attendants for parking garages, the time clock and customer complaints (e.g., horn blowing and broken parking gate barriers) monitor the required input quite well. A dismissal policy in the employment contract making time-on-task a condition of employment elicits the required input. Similar time-on-task constraints and output quotas are employed in hiring sharecroppers and retail sales clerks. In these instances, the firms and their employees have evolved ways to resolve the moral hazard problem. As the Coase theorem emphasizes, private voluntary bargaining will regularly and expeditiously find ways to contract around such problems.[17]

---

[17] For an insightful condensation of the voluminous literature on the Coase theorem, see J. Farrell, "Information and the Coase Theorem," *Journal of Economic Perspectives* (Fall 1987), pp. 113–129.

Benchmarking
A comparison of
performance in similar
jobs, firms, plants,
divisions, etc.

The debilitating problem of moral hazard arises then only when an action such as work effort is unobservable except at a prohibitive cost. Consider again the pharmaceutical sales representative for whom appointment logbooks and random follow-up monitoring simply cannot detect the persuasive effort necessary to secure orders from physician customers. One could trail around after the sales representatives and interview each physician after the sales calls were completed, but quite obviously, this monitoring practice would be prohibitively expensive. Instead, the pharmaceutical company is more likely to jettison the pure profit-sharing contract in favor of some other performance-based incentive contract involving benchmarking. During a period of **benchmarking,** the employer reassigns previously low productivity sales territories to above-average trade representatives to see whether their effort can alter the success rate per sales call. If so, the employer concludes that lack of effort by prior sales representatives was responsible for the low sales. After several such benchmarkings, the employer is able to identify those sales representatives it wishes to keep and those it wishes to dismiss. Importantly, the "keepers" are then allowed to retain all the productive accounts they have developed.

For managerial jobs, however, the moral hazard problem is significantly harder to resolve. The input senior management contributes to team production is not time-on-task at the desk, but rather what we might call "creative ingenuity"—i.e., creative ingenuity in formulating and solving problems that may not even have arisen as yet. Managers are paid to think and think hard, not to shuffle papers. The difficulty is that there is very little way to detect when creative ingenuity is being applied to the employer's business, rather than another business for whom the manager may be mentally moonlighting. Of course, eventually the difference will show up in performance, but over how long a period and how big a difference? These are tough questions to answer satisfactorily to stockholders after a senior manager has shirked his or her duties and finally been let go.

More problematically, the shirking manager may never be let go, and the hard-working manager may never be rewarded. If random disturbances affect the company's performance, it is difficult even after the fact to separate unobservable shirking from negative random disturbances. How then are owners to know when to blame senior managers for downturns in company performance and when to give them credit for upturns? One mechanism often employed to analyze these variances is the company audit. Managers are required to report on the sources and uses of funds in accordance with generally accepted accounting principles (GAAP). Independent auditors can then attempt to verify the managers' explanations for the period-to-period variances by sampling company records.[18] Despite dedicated efforts and substantial auditing fees, separating the effects of management decisions from random disturbances in company performance remains an elusive goal. That is, the moral hazard problem is much harder to solve when combined with the performance uncertainty most firms face.

The Principal-Agent Problem

As we have seen, unobservability and performance uncertainty warrant careful study by owner-principals hiring manager-agents. In isolation, neither characteristic poses any special difficulty for the efficient hiring of management. The moral hazard resulting from the unobservability of a manager's input is resolvable by assigning the manager lagged residual income claims (e.g., deferred stock options). Settling up ex post with a manager, after all the effects of his or her effort and ingenuity have had time to influence performance, creates just the performance-based incentives required.

---

[18] This audit mechanism is explored at greater length at the end of the chapter in the Case Exercise.

STOCK OPTIONS AT ADOBE SYSTEMS[19]

To align managerial incentives with equity owner interests, most companies regularly award deferred stock options to their managers. These performance-based bonuses entitle the holder to purchase company stock at a slight discount to its current value. If the firm's performance subsequently improves, capitalized value rises and both shareholders and the managers stand to gain. To exercise their options, managers often must wait 3 to 5 years, but they sometimes realize gains of 50 to 80 percent or more.

To acquire the stock for these deferred compensation programs, some companies dilute equity by issuing new shares while other companies repurchase shares on the open market. To reduce the cost of these "buybacks" especially in a rising market, companies like Adobe Systems and Interneuron Pharmaceutical as well as giants Dow Chemical and General Motors write "put" contracts. A put contract on Adobe stock entitles the option holder to sell shares to Adobe within a given time frame (e.g., 90 days) at an agreed upon exercise price (often close to the current value, say $29). If the stock price rises and remains above $29 (at say $31), the put option will expire with no further transactions. The holder of a "covered put," who owns both the option and the underlying stock, prefers to keep the appreciated stock. The "naked put" option holder also would not wish to execute the option to sell because $31 would be required to acquire a share that can be "put" to Adobe for only $29. In either case in a rising market, the steep cost of Adobe's acquiring stock for its deferred executive compensation plan is reduced by the cash receipts from selling the "puts." Another company, Intel, has received over $420 million from selling put options since 1991.

Of course, writing put options on company stock has a downside. If the stock price falls (say, to $25), the "puts" will be exercised, and Adobe will have to purchase their own $25 shares for $29. The option holders were willing to pay an option premium in anticipation of this opportunity to realize a net $4 in a declining market and thereby insure the original value of Adobe shares in their portfolios. The deeper the potential collapse of Adobe stock value, the larger the option premium. However, writing put options is hazardous to a company's financial health if managers know that disappointing cash flow surprises and a collapse of shareholder value are likely. Some companies like Adobe, Intel, and Microsoft therefore view the writing of put options as a certification to investors that further growth opportunities abound and that managers remain committed to building shareholder value.

Similarly, performance uncertainty taken alone creates a risk-allocation problem that may be easily resolved with insurance. Managers are somewhat less able to diversify than owners because of the specific human capital the former often invests in a long-term relationship with his or her corporate employer. This usually results in risk-averse owners and risk-averse managers structuring some sort of risk-sharing agreement to accomplish internally the manager's desire for at least partial insurance. A guaranteed baseline salary combined with a performance-based bonus is just such a risk-sharing agreement.

The real difficulty arises when both input unobservability and performance uncertainty are present simultaneously. The coexistence of these problems constitutes the so-

---

[19] Based on "More Firms Use Options to Gamble on Their Own Stock," *Wall Street Journal*, 22 May 1997, p. C1.

Principal-Agent Problem
An incentives conflict in delegating decision-making authority.

called **principal-agent problem** most firms face. Settling up ex post facto with management teams then no longer creates the desired incentives. Some managers get unlucky and receive blame they did not deserve, and others get lucky and receive credit they did not earn. Many companies often attempt to address the problem of managerial moonlighting by benchmarking one manager against another (say, in comparable plants or geographic divisions). They hope that the effects of business cycle factors and random time-series disturbances will be highly correlated across plants and divisions, and that the manager's effort and creative ingenuity will therefore correspond with the plant or division's differential performance. Unfortunately, they are usually wrong. Other companies rely on intense loyalty-building exercises, peer pressure, and lifetime employment contracts to reduce shirking. The Japanese, for example, use these approaches.

Incentive Compatibility Constraint
An assurance of incentive alignment.

Participation Constraint
An assurance of ongoing involvement.

The principal-agent problem can be formalized as an optimization problem subject to dual constraints. The company's choice of a profit-sharing rate and a manager's salary guarantee maximizes the expected utility of the risk-averse owner-principals' profit where profit depends on the manager-agent's effort, on the cost of the managerial incentives contract, and on random disturbances. An **incentive compatibility constraint** then aligns the effort chosen by the manager in response to the share and salary offer with that effort which maximizes the expected utility of the owner-principals. That is, an incentive-compatible profit share and salary elicits the managerial effort and creative ingenuity required to maximize the owner's value. Third and finally, the **participation constraint** ensures that the manager will reject his or her next best offer of alternative employment (e.g., at the certain wage rate). In the next section, we illustrate the meaning of each of these three elements with a linear optimal incentives contract, which can solve the principal-agent problem. However, do not be misled; an optimal managerial incentives contract is easier to describe than to attain.[20]

SIGNALING AND SORTING MANAGERIAL TALENT WITH OPTIMAL INCENTIVES CONTRACTS

Asymmetric information arises in all hiring decisions, but often plays an especially prominent role in managerial hiring decisions. Job applicants know all the information, but potential employers have access only to the information that applicants select for their resumés. Thus, among perhaps 19 resumé facts that the personnel department might like to know, the applicant only discloses 14. Let's see how linear share contracts can be used to sort managerial talent based on one of these undisclosed characteristics—namely, a manager's risk aversion.

Suppose a large bank has two openings for which it desires managers of very different risk aversion. One position is the assistant vice president for commercial construction loans in a city with overbuilt office developments and, consequently, very high vacancy rates. The other position is an assistant vice president to manage the venture capital loan portfolio, to interact with owners of new start-up businesses, and to represent the bank at the entrepreneurship club of the city. As you might suspect, the bank has two rather different people in mind as ideal candidates for these openings. In the commercial construction area, the bank seeks an instinctively cautious and safety-

---

[20] Even the solution we describe is limited to separable functions in effort and money income. The general principal-agent problem with risk-averse owners and managers has multiple solutions and requires *nonlinear* incentive contracts relating salary and profit share to company performance. See Jean Tirole, *The Theory of Industrial Organization* (Cambridge, Mass.: MIT Press, 1988), pp. 35–54, and David Kreps, *A Course in Microeconomic Theory* (Princeton, N.J.: Princeton University Press, 1990), chap. 16.

conscious manager who will take every opportunity to reduce the very large default risk already present in this portion of the bank's business. Both jobs are simply listed as assistant vice president positions; no further details are given.

Two managers with the requisite training and experience apply for the bank positions. Their resumés are very similar. However, unbeknownst to the bank, one drives an old Porsche, not insured against collision damage, and has skydiving as an undisclosed former hobby. Instead of skydiving, this individual (let's call him Dashing) now prefers bungee jumping, which he understandably decides would be inappropriate to list as a hobby on an application for a bank job. The other individual (you guessed it, Smooth) drives a dealer-serviced Land Rover on which she carries the maximum auto insurance coverage. Despite never leaving town, Smooth keeps the Rover in four-wheel drive at all times to secure the extra traction. Once while attending a formal cocktail party with a few close friends, Smooth revealed that she spent her Christmas bonus on "more insurance, of course." Thinking none of this of any real significance to the bank, she too omits the information from the job application.

The bank's problem is to sort these two types of individuals, both of whom are well qualified, into the jobs appropriate for their very different risk aversions. In Figure 13.4, we display the guaranteed base salary and profit-sharing rate, the two components of a **linear incentives contract.** On the horizontal axis are various percentages that represent what additions to *or subtractions from* one's pay occur as a result of the profit-sharing agreement. A greater share rate initially elicits more effort and creative ingenuity and results in greater expected profit contribution from the manager's activities. Eventually, at still higher share rates the profit contribution actually declines. The two hill-shaped loci of points in Figure 13.4 represent expected profit-sharing payouts that would allow the firm to just break even on its incentive payments to the two managers. The lower expected profit hill corresponds to the commercial construction loans job, and the higher hill corresponds to the venture capital loans job.

Let's suppose that the company has expected sales of $100 million and a net cash flow from sales of 12 percent. Hence, expected profits available for distribution to owners and managers run $12 million. The bank first elicits responses to two tentative contract offers for their assistant vice president jobs. Contract A offers $48,000 salary plus or mi-

Linear Incentives Contract
A linear combination of salary and profit share intended to align incentives.

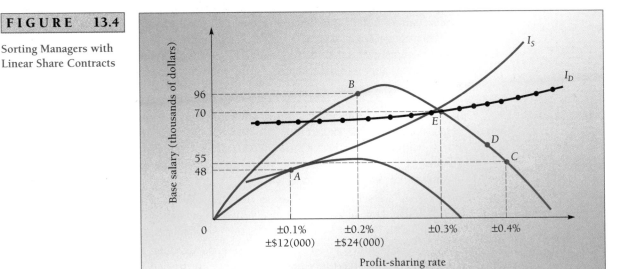

nus 0.1 percent of the net cash flow or $12,000, which implies a $36,000 to $60,000 possible range of income outcomes. Contract B offers $96,000 salary plus or minus 0.2 percent or a $72,000 to $120,000 range. Contracts A and B are not equally attractive. One dominates the other in that minimum outcomes under contract B exceed the maximum outcomes under contract A. Because risk increases only modestly from 0.1 percent to 0.2 percent, both prospective employees are likely to select B, and therefore, contract B is

Pooling Equilibrium
A decision setting that elicits indistinguishable behavior from two or more individuals, firms, etc.

said to result in a **pooling equilibrium.** Such an outcome is illustrated in Figure 13.4 where the indifference curves for both Smooth (I_s) and Dashing (I_d) indicate that contract B would be preferred by both applicants.

To elicit a separation of the two applications in accordance with their risk-aversion necessitates withdrawing contract B and instead introducing a more significant risk-return trade-off. We begin by indicating on Figure 13.4 the indifference curve for Smooth (I_s) that establishes a line of demarcation between contracts to the northwest, which are more preferred than A, and those to the southeast, which are less preferred. To induce a revelation of the risk-aversion differences between Smooth and Dashing, the bank then offers a contract pair such as A and C. Contract C imposes a much larger 0.4 percent profit share and offers only $55,000 expected base salary, just $7,000 above contract A. Smooth finds C much less preferred than the original contract A and immediately says so. In contrast, if Dashing is sufficiently close to being risk neutral (i.e., with almost flat indifference curves between expected salary and profit share), then Dashing may well prefer contract C.

Separating Equilibrium
A decision setting that elicits distinguishable behavior.

This **separating equilibrium** in which Smooth reveals her stronger risk aversion by rejecting C in favor of A, whereas Dashing does just the reverse, attains several of the employer's objectives. First, the linear profit-sharing contract has sorted Dashing as the manager to head up the venture capital group and Smooth as the manager for the commercial construction group. In addition, these profit-sharing contracts may be incentive-compatible contracts in that they elicit appropriate effort and creative ingenuity from both managers while maximizing the owner's value. However, one aspect of an optimal incentives contract remains unaddressed. The participation constraint has not yet been satisfied. An alternative employer can offer contract D, which attracts Smooth with both more expected salary and lower profit risk while retaining the separating properties of the (A,C) contract pair. As long as such improvements in both risk and return are possible, Smooth will continue to resign and move. Only with contract pair (A,E) will both the incentive compatibility and participation constraints be satisfied; Dashing selects contract E while Smooth selects contract A, and both remain in the bank's employ. In addition to resolving the sorting of managerial talent, if the incentives contract induces the appropriate effort from both managers and prevents their being bid away to alternative employment opportunities, that constitutes a solution to the principal-agent problem in managerial contracting.

SUMMARY

- Exchange under incomplete information and under asymmetric information differ. *Incomplete information* refers to the uncertainty that is pervasive in practically all transactions and motivates insurance markets. *Asymmetric information,* on the other hand, refers to private information one party possesses, which the other party cannot independently verify.

- Contracts are seldom complete because full *contingent claims contracting* is often prohibitively expensive. Intentionally incomplete contracting allows *postcontractual opportunistic behavior* and necessitates the use of *governance mechanisms.*

- Asymmetric information in *experience-good* markets leads to *adverse selection* whereby high-price/high-quality products are driven from the market by low-quality products indistinguishable at the point of sale. Buyers in such *lemons markets* refuse to offer prices high enough to cover the cost of high quality because under competitive conditions suppliers will predictably commit fraud, and then perhaps move on to conduct business with unsuspecting customers under other product or company names. Similar problems occur in lending to new borrowers where, again, the good borrowers are driven out of the applicant pool by the high loan rates required to cover the defaults of borrowers who never intended to repay.

☐ To escape adverse selection and elicit high-quality experience goods necessitates either intrusive and expensive regulation or some sort of bonding mechanism to induce *self-enforcing reliance relationships* between buyers and sellers. Warranties, collateral, irrevocable money-back guarantees, and brand names all provide assurance to buyers that the seller will not misrepresent the product quality. Hostages support asymmetric information exchange.

☐ Another way to escape adverse selection is for buyers to offer price premiums and repeat-purchase transactions to firms that resist fraudulently selling low-quality experience goods for high prices. These profits are invested by reliable sellers in *nonredeployable, highly specific assets*. Potentially *notorious firms* with redeployable assets continue to attract only customers seeking low-price/low-quality products. Under asymmetric information, at best you get what you pay for, never more.

☐ Joint ventures and partnerships face an asymmetric information problem in reimbursing each member for privately known costs that are unverifiable. As in demand revelation problems for funding public goods, so too in *cost revelation problems* for partnerships, each member has an initial incentive to falsely reveal (overstate) his or her private (cost) information.

☐ Both understatement of demand and overstatement of cost result in the cancellation of profitable partnership projects. Yet, each individual member may be better off with exaggerated cost reimbursement than with a simple profit share. Preserving the maximum value of the partnership requires an *incentive-compatible revelation mechanism*.

☐ Under an incentive-compatible mechanism, cost revelations incur the expected costs imposed on and opportunities forgone by the other partners. Each partner agrees that not just actions, but information revelations themselves, have consequences for profit-share payout. Such a governance mechanism must be self-enforcing, however, because the asymmetric information problem has not disappeared. A court would have just as much trouble verifying the claims for reimbursement under this incentives contract as it would under the initial simple profit-sharing contract. These incentive-compatible revelation mechanisms do induce the true revelation of partnership costs.

☐ Managerial labor can be hired in several ways—for example, straight salary, wage rate, or profit sharing. Pure profit sharing results in moonlighting, however, because the manager's inputs—namely, effort and creative ingenuity—are largely unobservable. Unobservable effort leads to the *moral hazard problem*, which can be resolved by settling up ex post facto (e.g., with deferred stock options).

☐ In combination, random disturbances in firm performance and unobservable managerial effort present a more difficult *principal-agent problem* to resolve. Owner-principals do not know when to blame manager-agents for weak performance or give credit for strong performance. *Optimal incentives contracts* involving some guaranteed salary and a profit-sharing bonus can, in principle, resolve the principal-agent problem.

☐ Linear combinations of salary and profit sharing can also be used to elicit asymmetric information about managerial preferences and sort managers by their own personal risk aversion.

EXERCISES

1. Which of the following products and services are likely to encounter adverse selection problems: golf shirts at traveling pro tournaments; certified gemstones from Tiffany's; graduation gift travel packages; mail-order auto parts? Why or why not?

2. Without employing a tread wear warranty contract, how could the sellers of tires credibly commit to the delivery of high-quality products with long tread wear life?

3. If a particular supplier in Table 13.1 succeeds in reducing the cost of low-quality products and now earns a profit on the low-price transactions, is the likelihood of fraud by that firm greater or less?

4. If notorious firm behavior (i.e., defrauding a buyer of high-priced experience goods by delivering low quality) becomes known throughout the marketplace only with a lag of three periods, profits on high-quality transactions remain the same, and interest rates rise slightly, are customers more likely or less likely to offer high prices for an experience good? Explain.

5. Show that not just overstatement but also understatement of cost is also dominated by truth-telling in the joint venture of Motorola and Apple.

6. What payoffs would be required under an optimal incentives contract like that in Table 13.4, if the cost overruns at Apple became as likely as those at Motorola?

7. In benchmarking sales representatives against one another, what problems arise from continuing to reassign the above-average trade representatives to previously unproductive sales territories?

8. Explain how the optimal incentives contract would differ if the more risk-averse bank officer (Dashing in Figure 13.4) had generated the smaller expected profit (i.e., the lower hill-shaped locus).

www exercise

Lemons, Loan Quality, and the Resolution Trust Corporation

9. Access the following Internet site maintained by the Federal Deposit Insurance Corporation: http://www.fdic.gov/databank/bkreview/1995summ/art1full.html.

How is the concept of a lemons market applied to the assessment of loan quality and the performance of the Resolution Trust Corporation (RTC)? What are representations and warranties, and how might they mitigate the "lemons market" problem?

CASE EXERCISE

DESIGNING A MANAGERIAL INCENTIVE CONTRACT[21]

One of your consulting clients asks you to implement an incentive scheme for their CEO. The CEO can either work hard (with a personal cost to the CEO of $20,000) or shirk (no cost to the CEO). The CEO faces three possible circumstances: she experiences good luck with 30 percent probability, she has medium luck with probability of 40 percent, or she suffers from bad luck with 30 percent probability. The following table relates the CEO's effort and luck to the company's profit:

	Good Luck (30%)	Medium Luck (40%)	Bad Luck (30%)
High Effort	$1,000,000	$800,000	$500,000
Low Effort	$800,000	$500,000	$300,000

---

[21] This exercise was suggested by B. Ramy Elitzur of Tel Aviv University.

Although company profits are observable and not subject to manipulation, both the CEO's effort and luck are unobservable.

a. Design a cash bonus scheme to elicit managerial behavior congruent with shareholders' interests. Show that this scheme improves shareholder value.

b. Design an option package to elicit managerial behavior congruent with shareholders' interests. Show that this scheme improves shareholder value.

c. Financial audits are basically sampling procedures to verify with a predetermined accuracy the company receipts and expenditures; the larger the sample the higher the audit fee. What's the maximum amount shareholders of this firm would be willing to pay if it were possible for the auditors to distinguish good from medium luck? Medium from bad luck?

14

Price and Output Determination: Monopoly

CHAPTER PREVIEW

In this chapter we develop the static partial equilibrium model for price and output determination under certainty for firms operating in monopoly markets. Monopoly markets have only one firm operating in the industry. The most important implication of monopoly markets is that the monopolist does not have to accept the market price as a given. Rather, monopolists have substantial latitude in establishing price and output levels. In addition to considering price and output determination for "unregulated" monopolies, we also look at these decisions for regulated industries. The regulation of a small number of industries, known as public utilities—electric power, natural gas distribution and transmission, communication, and some elements of transportation—is intense and includes regulation of prices, outputs, profits, and the quality of service provided. The regulation of these industries raises many challenging economic and legal issues. A consideration of these issues is important for a managerial economist for two reasons. First, the public utility industries are an important element of the American economy in their own right. As public debate is focused on regulatory reform, it is important that reform be consistent with basic economic principles to avoid the problems inherent in the current system of utility regulation. Second, because public utility regulation covers nearly all aspects of economic decision making in an enterprise, it provides an interesting laboratory to integrate our understanding of demand analysis, forecasting, production and cost analysis, price-output decisions, cost of capital determination, and capital expenditure analysis.

MONOPOLY DEFINED

In Chapter 12 *monopoly* was defined as a market structure characterized by one firm producing a highly differentiated product in a market with significant barriers to entry. Because there are no close substitutes for the product of a monopolist, the demand curve facing a monopolist will have a significant negative slope (that is, a greater negative slope than is observed under monopolistic competition). A monopoly market structure may be thought of as the opposite extreme from pure competition in terms of the range of observable market structures.

Just as purely competitive market structures are rare, pure monopoly markets are also rare. All goods and services have some substitutes available for them. The more distant the substitutes that are available, the closer a market is to being a pure monopoly.

<table>
<tr><td>

EXAMPLE

WWW . . . .
Read more about intellectual property law as it relates to copyright at the following Internet site:
http://www.intelproplaw.com/

</td><td>

MONOPOLY PRICING: EAST PUBLISHING

East Publishing Company is the producer and distributor of a text, *Managerial Economics*, seventh edition. Because East holds the copyright on the book, no other publisher may legally sell this text in competition with East. In that sense, East has a monopoly position on the market for this text. Why then doesn't East charge you $500 per book? The reason is that although there are no *perfect* substitutes for this book, there are other books that can be used in its place. If the price of this book were raised too much relative to the price of alternatives, many customers would shift to an alternative. In virtually all markets, there are (imperfect) substitutes available for the monopolized product. The number and closeness of these substitutes determines the elasticity (relative steepness) of the demand curve facing a monopolist. The relationship between price elasticity and monopoly price and output determination is discussed below.

</td></tr>
</table>

SOURCES OF MARKET POWER FOR A MONOPOLIST

<table>
<tr><td>

WWW . . . .
The following Internet site (maintained by the Berkeley Technology Law Journal) contains an amicus brief on the economics of intellectual property prepared for the U.S. Supreme Court case of *Lotus Development Corporation* v. *Borland International*:
http://www.server.berkeley.edu/BTLJ/lvb/econprof.html

</td><td>

Several sources of market power can be enjoyed by monopolists. First, a firm may possess a *patent* or *copyright* that prevents other firms from producing the same product. For example, Upjohn, Inc. has a patent on the product Rogaine, the hair growth stimulator for balding men. Until government-approved and effective alternative products are developed, Upjohn has monopoly control over this product. The long and expensive governmental approval process for competing products creates a significant barrier to entry for potential competitors.

Second, a firm may *control* the *critical resources* needed to produce the product. DeBeers Consolidated Mines Limited owns or controls the vast majority of diamond production in South Africa and has marketing agreements with other major diamond-producing countries, including the former Soviet Union. This control of raw materials has enabled DeBeers to maintain high world prices for cut diamonds. Prior to World War II, Alcoa enjoyed a similar position because it controlled nearly all known bauxite deposits, the essential raw material for the production of aluminum.

</td></tr>
</table>

<table>
<tr><td>

EXAMPLE

</td><td>

IMPERMANENT CONTROL OF DENVER AIRPORT HUB: UNITED AIRLINES[1]

The market power attributable to the control of critical resources is typically quite transient. After the deregulation of airlines in 1979, some major carriers developed fortress hubs. In the mid 1980s, USAir (now US Airways), United, Delta, and Northwest controlled

</td></tr>
</table>

---

[1] "Air Fares Decline in Denver," *Wall Street Journal,* 6 February 1996.

MANAGERIAL CHALLENGE

PUBLIC SERVICE COMPANY OF NEW MEXICO: RISKS OF A MONOPOLY MARKET POSITION

The Public Service Company of New Mexico (PNM) provides electric power service (generation and distribution) and natural gas distribution services to the majority of the population of New Mexico. This monopoly position is regulated by the Public Service Commission of the State of New Mexico and, to a lesser extent, by the Federal Energy Regulatory Commission. These commissions determine the rates the company may charge its various classes of customers for the services that are provided. The rates are intended to be based on the cost of providing service, including a "fair return" on the capital invested.

PNM earned a 4.9 percent return on common equity during 1992. In 1995 it was projected to earn 8.0 percent on common equity, and 7.5 percent on common equity between 1997 and 1999. The 1992 industry average return on equity was 11.4 percent according to *Value Line.* The 1997–1999 industry projected return on common equity is 11.6 percent. PNM's extraordinarily low returns are anticipated even though PNM is authorized by its regulatory commission to charge rates consistent with its earning a return of 12.5 percent on common equity. Why has this monopoly supplier of utility services (and many other utility companies) been unable to earn its authorized return?

The regulatory process facing utilities does not ensure that a company will earn its authorized returns. Indeed, in the case of PNM, the regulatory process almost guarantees that PNM will not earn its authorized return. The primary reason in this case is the very high levels of surplus generating capacity that it has accumulated. PNM embarked on an aggressive construction program during the 1970s and 1980s to meet surging demand for electric service in the face of the oil crisis and the rapid growth of the uranium mining industry in New Mexico. Before this capacity came on line, the uranium mining industry in New Mexico virtually shut down, leaving PNM with approximately 50 percent more generating capacity than is presently needed to serve its customer base. The state regulatory commission has refused to permit PNM to recover the costs of this excess capacity in rates charged to its present customers. Even in the absence of regulation, PNM would probably be unable to fully recover the costs of this excess capacity.

Although monopolists enjoy a protected position from competition, they still face significant risks, such as the demand forecasting risks illustrated above. In addition, regulated monopolists, such as public utilities, also face risk associated with the regulatory process. For example, during most of the 1970s and the early 1980s virtually no utility company earned a return on common equity equal to its cost of equity capital.

In this chapter we examine the price and output decisions of both regulated and unregulated firms operating in a monopoly market environment.

www . . . .
Financial information on the Public Service Company of New Mexico, and on electric industry restructuring in New Mexico, is available on the following Internet site:
http://www.pnm.com/

78 percent, 70 percent, 72 percent, and 80 percent of the gates at their hubs in Charlotte, Denver, Atlanta, and Minneapolis, respectively. These dominant carriers effectively barred rival entry by entering into long-term leases with airport authorities. Local customer loyalty then supported 19–27 percent price premiums based on the delivery reliability, change order responsiveness, and nonstop scheduling convenience at these hubs.

By the mid 1990s, however, small start-up airlines threatened to break into the hubs of these market leaders. Delta encountered strong challenges from Kiwi and ValueJet whose presence in Atlanta has caused margins on competing routes to dwindle. Taking customers away from United, Frontier Airlines and Western Pacific have attracted discount and drive-in traffic at Denver and Colorado Springs. Consequently, United fares to and from Denver have declined substantially since 1995.

A third source of monopoly power may be a *government-authorized franchise*. In most U.S. cities, one firm is chosen to provide cable TV services to the community. The local government may regulate rates that can be charged and service quality. Other examples of government franchises include trash collection and the U.S. Postal Service. One important licensing arrangement has been the Federal Communications Commission's plan to give an extra TV channel to each current operating channel, so that they can transition from offering standard TV programming to offering high-definition TV programming. It has been estimated that if these licenses were sold, they could bring nearly $1 billion.

Monopoly power may also arise because there are significant *economies of scale* over a wide range of output. Thus, the monopoly firm will enjoy declining long-run average costs. Under these circumstances it is natural for there to be only one supplier of the good or service, because that one supplier can produce the output more cheaply than can a group of smaller competitors. These so-called natural monopolies are usually closely regulated by government agencies to restrict the profits of the monopolist. Natural monopoly arguments have been used to justify having only one supplier of electric utility distribution services, telephone services (in the past), natural gas distribution services, urban transportation services, and water services.

Advertising and brand loyalties established over a long time period may make it prohibitively expensive for competitors to enter a market. Strong brand loyalties often are associated with high-quality products and an implied guarantee of performance that is difficult for competitors to overcome. For example, for many years Clorox was virtually the only national brand of liquid bleach for laundry. Some potential competitors attempted to enter the market, but they invariably found the requisite promotional costs of entry to be too expensive relative to potential returns. Advertising campaigns and customer service programs are designed to enhance the market power of a firm. When success is achieved in these programs, the firm often is able to profit from the increased pricing flexibility that market power affords.

PRICE AND OUTPUT DETERMINATION FOR A MONOPOLIST

Recall that the demand curve facing a pure monopolist is the same as the industry demand curve because one firm constitutes the entire industry. The price-output decision for a profit-maximizing monopolist is illustrated in Figure 14.1.

Just as in pure competition, profit is maximized at the price and output combination where $MC = MR$. This corresponds to a price of P_1, output of Q_1, and total profits equal to BC profit per unit times Q_1 units. For a negative-sloping demand curve, the MR function is not the same as the demand function. In fact, for any linear, negatively sloping demand function, the marginal revenue function will have the same intercept on the P axis as the demand function and a slope that is twice as great as that of the demand function. If, for example, the demand function were of the form

$$P = a - bQ$$

then

$$\text{Total revenue} = TR = P \cdot Q$$
$$= aQ - bQ^2$$

FIGURE   14.1

Price and Output
Determination: Pure
Monopoly

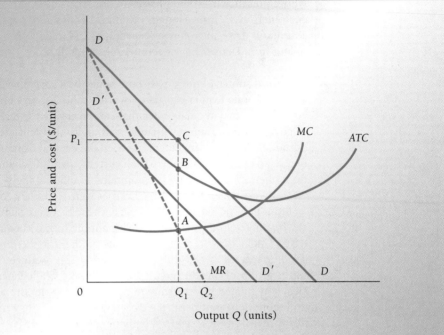

and

$$MR = \frac{dTR}{dQ} = a - 2bQ$$

The slope of the demand function is −b, and of the MR function −2b.

EXAMPLE

PROFIT MAXIMIZATION: MONOPOLY

Assume a monopolist is faced with the following demand function:

$$Q = 400 - 20P$$

and long-run total cost function:[2]

$$TC = 5Q + \frac{Q^2}{50}$$

To maximize profits it would produce and sell that output where $MC = MR$, and charge the corresponding price:

$$MC = \frac{dTC}{dQ} = 5 + \frac{Q}{25}$$

MR may be found by rewriting the demand function in terms of Q:

$$P = \frac{-Q}{20} + 20$$

---
[2] Because the cost function does not possess a fixed-cost component (that is, all terms contain Q), this must represent a long-run cost function.

and then multiplying by Q to find TR:

$$TR = P \cdot Q$$

$$= -\frac{Q^2}{20} + 20Q$$

$$MR = \frac{dTR}{dQ} = -\frac{Q}{10} + 20$$

Setting $MR = MC$, yields

$$-\frac{Q^*}{10} + 20 = 5 + \frac{Q^*}{25}$$

$$Q^* = 107 \text{ units}$$

Substituting Q^* back into the demand equation we may solve for P^*:

$$P^* = \frac{-107}{20} + 20$$

$$= \$14.65/\text{unit}$$

Hence the profit-maximizing monopolist would produce 107 units and charge a price of $14.65 each. This yields a profit of

$$\pi^* = TR - TC$$

$$= (P^* \cdot Q^*) - \left(5Q^* + \frac{Q^{*2}}{50}\right)$$

$$= 14.65(107) - \left(5(107) + \frac{(107)^2}{50}\right)$$

$$= \$803.57$$

Monopoly versus Atomistic/Pure Competition

A close check in Figure 14.1 shows that the monopolist produces at a level of output that is smaller than the industry output would be under pure competition because equilibrium is reached in pure competition at a point where the *ATC* curve is minimized for each firm (that is, the aggregate industry average cost curve is minimized). The profit-maximizing monopolist, faced with a negative-sloping demand curve, will always produce at an output short of that output at which average costs are minimized. As Baumol has observed, some cautions are in order when one concludes that a monopoly will produce less than a purely competitive industry, *all other things being equal*.[3] All conditions are not likely to remain equal. Both demand and cost may change when a monopolist takes over a competitive in-dustry. For instance, the monopolist's cost function may reflect economies of scale that were not possible for the smaller firms in pure competition. Such economies might relate to more efficient plant sizes, the centralizing of inventories, and the centralizing of such functions as financing, purchasing, and legal services. Because of the possibility of making large prof-its, the monopolist may find it advantageous to advertise, possibly increasing aggregate

---

[3] William J. Baumol, *Economic Theory and Operations Analysis*, 4th ed. (Englewood Cliffs, N.J.: Prentice-Hall, 1977), p. 402.

market demand. However, a large monopolist might require a huge administrative structure where coordination and effective communication become increasingly difficult, and diseconomies may result. On balance, a simple comparison between monopoly and pure competition can furnish little more than a possible clue about the levels of output that might be expected under each market structure.

Even if pure competition does result in a larger output than results from a monopoly, it cannot be concluded, especially under conditions of full employment, that breaking up a monopoly (which would lead to an increase in that industry's output) will be in society's best interest. Under full employment, an increase in output in the liquor industry, for example, would require that resources be drawn away from other industries and prices in those industries would possibly rise. To take an extreme example, assume that the liquor industry is a monopoly, the economy is operating under conditions of full employment, and the government seeks to break the liquor monopolist into a large number of smaller competitive firms. As a result, output in the industry increases. The new small liquor companies bid for the services of chemists to work on product development. Some chemists are attracted from drug firms, and those who remain, work at a higher wage. May we conclude that society is better off because more liquor is produced? Prices of liquor perhaps are lower, but the cost of drugs may have risen. Under conditions of full employment, we must be very careful to analyze the impact of reallocating resources from one industry to another before concluding that greater output in any one industry necessarily makes society better off.

The Importance of Price Elasticity

As we have seen, a monopolist wishing to maximize profits should follow the familiar marginal decision rule, that is, set price (or output) at a level where marginal revenue equals marginal cost. The monopolist can choose to establish the price, but the price chosen determines the quantity that will be sold because of the constraint imposed by the demand curve. Alternatively the monopolist can establish the quantity to produce, but the price at which this output can be sold will be determined from the demand curve.

Recall from Chapter 4 that marginal revenue (MR) can be expressed in terms of price (P) and the price elasticity (E_D), or

$$MR = P\left(1 + \frac{1}{E_D}\right) \qquad [14.1]$$

Equating MR with MC (as shown in Figure 14.1) yields the profit-maximizing relationship in terms of price and price elasticity, or

$$MC = P\left(1 + \frac{1}{E_D}\right) \qquad [14.2]$$

For the monopoly case, price will be greater than marginal cost. For example, if price elasticity $E_D = -2.0$, price will equal

$$MC = P\left(1 + \frac{1}{-2}\right)$$

$$MC = .5P$$

$$P = 2MC$$

Note from Equation 14.2 that a monopolist will never operate in the area of the demand curve where demand is price inelastic (i.e., $|E_D| < 1$). If the absolute value of price elasticity is less than 1 ($|E_D| < 1$), then the reciprocal of price elasticity ($1/E_D$) will be

less than minus 1 and marginal revenue $\left[P\left(1 + \dfrac{1}{E_D}\right) \right]$ would be negative. In Figure 14.1,

the inelastic range of output is output beyond level Q_2. A negative marginal revenue means that total revenue can be increased by reducing output (through an increase in price). But we know that reducing output must also reduce total costs, thus resulting in an increase in profit. Hence a firm would continue to raise prices (and reduce output) as long as the price elasticity of demand is in the inelastic range. Hence, for a monopolist the price-output combination that maximizes profits must occur where $|E_D| \geq 1$.

Equation 14.2 also can be used to show that the more elastic the demand (suggesting the existence of better substitutes), the lower the price (relative to marginal cost) that any noncompetitive firm will charge. This relationship can be illustrated with the following example.

EXAMPLE

PRICE ELASTICITY AND PRICE LEVELS FOR MONOPOLISTS

Consider a monopolist with the following total cost function:

$$TC = 10 + 5Q$$

The marginal cost (*MC*) function is

$$MC = dTC/dQ = 5$$

The price elasticity of demand has been estimated to be -2.0. Setting $MC = MR$ (where *MR* is expressed as Equation 14.1) results in the following pricing rule for a profit-maximizing monopolist:

$$MC = \$5 = P(1 + 1/-2.0) = MR$$

$$P = 5/(0.5) = \$10/\text{unit}$$

If, however, demand is more price elastic, such as $E_D = -4.0$, the profit-maximizing monopolist would set the price at

$$P = \$5/(0.75) = \$6.67/\text{unit}$$

OPTIMAL MARK-UP, CONTRIBUTION MARGIN, AND THE GROSS PROFIT MARGIN PERCENTAGE

Sometimes it proves useful and convenient to express these relationships between optimal price, price elasticity, and marginal cost as a mark-up percentage or gross profit margin percentage. Rearranging Equation 14.2 to solve for optimal price yields

$$P = \frac{E_D}{(E_D + 1)} MC \qquad [14.3]$$

Gross Profit Margin
The difference between the profit-maximizing price and incremental variable cost, often expressed as a percentage of the price.

where the multiplier term ahead of *MC* is 1.0 plus the percentage mark-up. For example, the case of $E_D = -3$ is a product with a $-3/(-3 + 1) = 1.5$ multiplier—that is, a 50 percent mark-up. The optimal profit-maximizing price recovers the marginal cost and then marks up *MC* another 50 percent. If $MC = \$6$, this item would sell for $1.5 \times \$6 = \$9$ and the profit-maximizing mark-up is $3 or 50 percent more than the cost.

The difference between price and marginal cost (i.e., the absolute dollar size of the mark-up) is often referred to as a **gross profit margin** or *contribution margin* because having already covered incremental variable cost, these additional dollars are available to contribute to covering fixed cost and earning a profit. They are often expressed as a percentage of the total price. In the previous example, the $3 mark-up above and beyond the $6 marginal cost represents a 33 percent contribution to fixed cost and profit, that is, a 33 percent gross margin on the $9 item. To summarize, an elasticity of -3.0 implies that the profit maximizing mark-up is 50 percent and that 50 percent mark-up implies a 33 percent gross margin. Using Equation 14.3,

$$\frac{(P - MC)}{P} = \frac{1.5\ MC - 1.0\ MC}{1.5\ MC}$$

$$\text{Gross Margin } \% = 0.5\ /\ 1.5 = 33\%$$

Price elasticity information captures all these implications for the marketing plan. Combining the gross margin percentage (33 percent) with incremental variable cost information then yields dollar prices and dollar mark-ups.

<table>
<tr><td>EXAMPLE</td></tr>
</table>

MARK-UPS AND GROSS MARGINS ON CHANEL #5, OLE MUSK, AND WHITMAN'S SAMPLER

Consider three products available at the typical drugstore counter: Chanel #5, Whitman's Sampler, and store brand fragrance Ole Musk. Chanel has a loyal following of regular buyers and a price elasticity of -1.1. Whitman's has some rather close substitutes but substantial name recognition and packaging familiarity; its price elasticity measures -1.86. Finally, customers perceive many close substitutes for the generic fragrance Ole Musk whose price elasticity is therefore -12.0.

Table 14.1 shows the optimal prices, mark-ups, and gross profit margins for these three products. Using Equation 14.3, the multiplier on MC for Chanel #5 is $-1.1/(-1.1 + 1) = 11.0$, and the optimal mark-up is therefore 1000 percent (i.e., ten times the incremental variable cost of the essences and the bottle). Because optimal price is $11.0\ MC$, the gross margin on Chanel #5 calculates as $10.0\ MC/11.0\ MC = 91\%$. Whitman's Sampler has a multiplier of $-1.86/(-1.86 + 1) = 2.16$, an optimal mark-up therefore of 116 percent and a gross margin of $1.16\ MC/2.16\ MC = 54\%$. In contrast, Ole Musk with the greatest price elasticity has a multiplier of $-12/(-12 + 1) = 1.09$, a mark-up of 9 percent and a gross margin of $0.09\ MC/1.09\ MC = 8\%$.

Thus, the more elastic the demand function for a monopolist's output, the lower the price that will be charged, ceteris paribus. At the limit, consider the case of a firm in pure competition with a perfectly elastic (horizontal) demand curve. In this case the price elasticity of demand approaches $-\infty$, hence, one divided by the price elasticity approaches zero and marginal revenue in Equation 14.1 becomes equal to price. Thus, the profit-maximizing rule in Equation 14.2 becomes "Set price equal to marginal cost" and the profit-maximizing mark-up in Equation 14.3 is zero. Of course, this is the same solution developed in Chapter 12 in the discussion of price-output determination under pure competition.

<table>
<tr><td>TABLE   14.1</td></tr>
</table>

Optimal Prices, Mark-Ups and Margins

	E_D	Price	(P − MC) Contribution	Mark-Up %	Gross Margin %
Chanel #5	−1.1	11.0 MC	10.0 MC	1000%	91%
Whitman's Chocolate	−1.86	2.16 MC	1.16 MC	116%	54%
Ole Musk	−12.0	1.09 MC	0.09 MC	9%	8%

Components of the Gross Margin

Gross profit margins differ across industries and across firms within the same industry for a variety of reasons. First, some industries are more capital intensive than others. Airlines have 70–80 percent gross profit margins not because they are particularly profitable relative to other industries but because airlines have high fixed costs; the aircraft are a large proportion of the total cost structure. An essential distinction arises therefore between operating profits and net cash flow available to owners after interest and other fixed costs for capital assets have been paid. The first component of the gross profit margin percentage, then, is capital costs per sales dollar.

Secondly, differences in gross margins reflect differences in advertising, promotion, and selling costs. Leading brands in the ready-to-eat cereal industry have 70 percent margins but half of that price-incremental cost differential (fully 35 percent of every sales dollar) is spent on advertising and promotion. The automobile industry also spends hundreds of millions of dollars on advertising but only 9 percent per sales dollar. The second component of the gross profit margin percentage is advertising and selling expenses per sales dollar.

Third, differences in gross margins arise because of differential overhead in some businesses. The pharmaceutical industry has very high gross margins in large part because of the enormous expenditures on research and development to find new drugs. To conduct business in that product line, other pharmaceutical firms then incur patent fees and licensing costs which raise their overhead costs and set the industry-level prices. Overhead costs also may differ if headquarters salaries and other general administrative expenses are high in certain firms but not others. In that case, usually the cost-disadvantaged firms are eventually forced to cut overhead or abandon doing business in that industry.

Finally, after accounting for any differences in capital costs, selling expenses, or overheads, the remaining differences in gross margins do reflect differential profitability.

EXAMPLE

COMPONENTS OF THE MARGIN AT KELLOGG CO.[4]

The largest box of Kellogg's Raisin Bran sells for $4.49 and has a direct fixed plus variable manufacturing cost of $1.63. That calculates as a (4.49 − 1.63)/4.49 = 70 percent gross margin. The margin on Frosted Flakes is 72 percent, on Fruit Loops 68 percent, and across all brands 55 percent. These high margins reflect brand loyalties built up over many years by massive and continuous advertising investments. On the leading brands, Kellogg spends 30 percent of each sales dollar on advertising, and adds another 5 percent on couponing, slot-in shelf space allowances, rebates, and other promotional expenses. Capital costs entail approximately 22 percent per sales dollar. Expenditures on headquarters, general administrative, R&D, and all other overheads total 8 percent. That leaves a net profit margin of about 5 percent.

Monopoly and Economic Profits

A common misconception is that monopolists always earn economic profits (rents); that is, returns above those required to keep capital in the industry, given the risks being assumed by the investors. Although economic profits are more likely to be earned by monopolists than by firms operating in more competitive market structures, they are not guaranteed to the monopolist in the short run. A monopolist can face a situation where

---

[4] Based on "Cereals," *Winston-Salem Journal,* 8 March 1995, p. A1 and "Denial in Battle Creek," *Forbes,* 7 October 1996, pp. 44–46.

the demand curve for the monopolist's product is located everywhere below the monopolist's average total cost function, such as demand curve $D'D'$ in Figure 14.1. With a demand curve such as $D'D'$, average cost always exceeds average revenue. Consequently, there is no price the monopolist can charge that will result in a profit. This situation can persist in the short run, but in the long run the monopolist will have to lower its costs and/or take actions designed to increase demand. If this cannot be accomplished, the monopolist will cease operating and leave the business.

For example, the public transit system in most major cities operates as a monopolist. For many years these systems were operated by private, regulated companies; however, as automobiles and freeways became more generally available, demand for public transportation decreased and costs increased. Many of these companies were faced with average cost functions that were higher than average revenue functions, and losses were generated. Ultimately, these monopoly public transportation systems were taken over and operated by city or regional governments—and most continue to incur significant operating losses. In this case, no price will result in profitable operations as long as broad service standards are retained.

Monopoly and Efficiency

In the long run, a monopolist can end up operating an optimum scale plant. An optimum scale plant is the plant size that will lead to a maximum level of profits for the firm, but this result is not assured. The monopolist does not face the discipline of strong competition so the monopolist may install excess capacity, or alternatively, fail to install enough capacity. Indeed, a monopolist seeking to restrain entry of new competitors into the industry may install excess capacity that can be used to credibly threaten to flood the market with supply and lower prices, thus making entry less attractive to potential competitors. Even in regulated monopolies, such as electric utility companies, considerable evidence shows that regulation often provides incentives for a firm to overinvest or underinvest in generating capacity. Because utilities are regulated so that they have an opportunity to earn a "fair" rate of return on their assets, if the allowed return is greater (less) than the firm's true cost of capital, there is an incentive to overinvest (underinvest) in new plant.

Limit Pricing

Recall that the monopolist firm's *short-run* profits are maximized by setting marginal revenue equal to marginal cost. As shown in Figure 14.2, this yields an optimal output of Q_1 and an optimal price of P_1. Such a solution, however, may not necessarily maximize the *long-run* profits (or shareholder wealth) of the firm. By keeping prices high and earning monopoly profits, the monopolist firm encourages potential competitors to commit resources in an effort to obtain a share of these profits. For example, if a monopoly is based on a patented product (or production process), potential competitors may invest funds in research and development in order to design an alternative to the monopolist firm's product (or production process). Instead of charging the short-run profit-maximizing price, the monopolist firm may decide to engage in *limit pricing*, where it charges a lower price, such as P_L in Figure 14.2, in order to discourage entry into the industry by potential rivals. With a limit-pricing strategy, the firm forgoes some of its short-run monopoly profits in order to maintain its monopoly position in the long run. The limit price, such as P_L in Figure 14.2, was set below the minimum point on a potential competitor's average total cost curve, (ATC_c). The appropriate limit price is a function of many different factors.[5]

---

[5] The limit-pricing model illustrates the importance of *potential* competition as a control device on existing firms. This concept is examined further in the discussion of contestable markets in Chapter 18. See F. H. Scherer and David Ross, *Industrial Market Structure and Economic Performance*, 3d ed. (Chicago: Rand McNally, 1990), chap. 10, for an expanded discussion of the limit-pricing concept.

FIGURE 14.2

Limit-Pricing Strategy

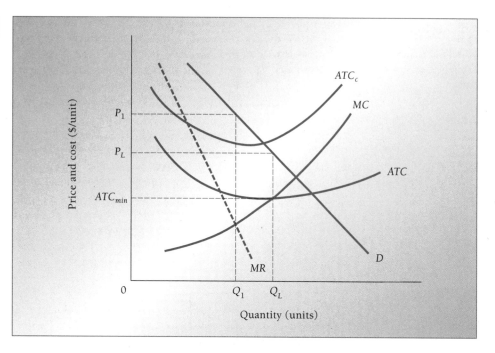

The effect of the two different pricing strategies on the monopolist firm's profit stream is illustrated in Figure 14.3. By charging the (higher) short-run profit-maximizing price, the firm's profits are likely to decline over time at a faster rate (Panel *a*) than by charging a limit price (Panel *b*). The firm should engage in limit pricing if the present value of the profit stream from the limit-pricing strategy exceeds the present value of the profit stream associated with the short-run profit-maximization rule of equating marginal revenue and marginal cost. Such a decision is a function of the discount rate used in calculating the present values. Choosing a high discount rate will place relatively higher weight on near-term profits and relatively lower weight on profits that occur further into the future. A high discount rate is justified when the firm's long-term pricing policy, and hence profits, are subject to a high degree of risk or uncertainty.[6]

Finally, it should be noted that limit pricing can be practiced by firms in oligopolistic industries as well as by firms in monopolistic industries. In an oligopolistic industry, limit pricing can be used by a dominant firm to discourage expansion by smaller firms in the industry as well as to deter entry by firms outside the industry.

EXAMPLE

www . . . .

Current financial information on Bristol-Myers-Squibb is available on the Internet at:
http://www.bms.com/financial/index.htm

LIMIT PRICING TO DISCOURAGE GENERIC DRUGS: BRISTOL-MYERS-SQUIBB[7]

Patent protection is the key to financial success in the pharmaceutical industry. The typical patented drug emerges from tests on 250 chemical compounds, requires 15 years of research and FDA approval processes, and accumulates total costs of entry averaging $350 million. Capoten is Bristol-Myers-Squibb's (BMS) hypertension drug for use in reducing heart-attack risk. Rather than limit pricing, BMS maintained Capoten's 57-cents-per-pill price right to the

---

[6] Recall from Chapter 2 that the relevant rate employed in calculating the present value of future cash (or income) flows is a function of the risk associated with these flows—namely, the greater the risk, the higher the discount rate.

[7] Based on "Too Clever by Half," *The Economist,* 20 September 1997, p. 68, and "Time's Up," *Wall Street Journal,* 12 August 1997, p. A1.

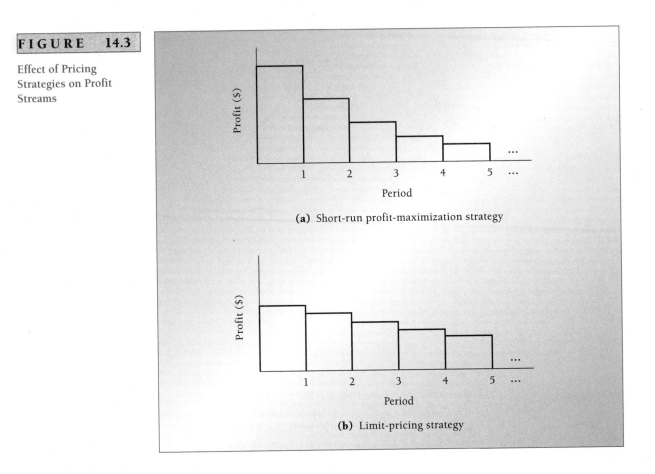

FIGURE   14.3

Effect of Pricing Strategies on Profit Streams

(a) Short-run profit-maximization strategy

(b) Limit-pricing strategy

end of its 20-year patent protection in February 1996. Competition from generics selling for 3 cents per pill was swift and disastrously effective. BMS introduced its own generic product which cannibalized sales of the branded product still further. By the fourth quarter of 1996, Capoten sales collapsed to $25 million from $146 million the year before.

In contrast, Eli Lilly and Schering-Plough recently began limit pricing and advertising heavily their leading antidepressant Prozac and allergy treatment Claritin, which lose patent protection in 2001 and 2002, respectively. One reason these companies chose a different pricing strategy is that new biotechnologies have allowed imitation pharmaceuticals to appear much faster in the 1990s than in earlier decades. Indeed, the first hypertension drug, Inderal, enjoyed almost a decade from 1968–77 of pure monopoly sales before Capoten was introduced. Prozac, on the other hand, met competition from imitators within four years of its 1988 introduction. And Recombinate, a breakthrough drug for hemophiliacs newly patented in 1992, encountered copycat products by 1994. Tactics like limit pricing become all the more important in the presence of quick and relatively easy imitation.

Public Utilities
A group of firms, mostly in the electric power, natural gas, and communications industries, that are closely regulated by one or more government agencies. The agencies control entry into the business, set prices, establish product quality standards, and influence the total profits that may be earned by the firms.

REGULATED MONOPOLIES[8]

Several important industries in the United States operate as regulated monopolies. In broad terms, the regulated monopoly sector of the American economy includes **public utilities** such as electric power companies, natural gas companies, and communications

---

[8] A major portion of this and the following sections was prepared by Professor John Crockett of George Mason University.

companies. In the past, much of the transportation industry (airlines, trucking, railroads) also were regulated closely, but these industries have been substantially deregulated over the past 10 to 15 years.

Electric Power Companies

Investor-owned electric power companies make up one large industry subject to economic regulation. Electric power is made available to the consumer through a production process characterized by three distinct stages. First, the power is generated in generating plants. Next, in the transmission stage, the power is transmitted at high voltage from the generating site to the locality where it is used. Finally, in the distribution stage, the power is distributed to the individual users. The complete process may take place as part of the operations of a single firm, or the producing firm may sell power at wholesale rates to a second enterprise that carries out the distribution function. In the latter case, the distribution firm often is a department within the municipal government serving the locality or a consumers' cooperative.

Firms producing electric power are subject to regulation at several levels. Integrated firms carrying out all three stages of production are usually regulated by state public utility commissions. These commissions set the rates to be charged to the final consumers. The firms normally receive exclusive rights to serve individual localities through franchises granted by local governing bodies. As a consequence of their franchises, electric power companies have well-defined markets within which they are the sole provider of output. Finally, the Federal Energy Regulatory Commission (FERC) has the authority to set rates on power that crosses state lines and on wholesale power sales. Presently efforts are being made to partially or totally deregulate the power production and transmission elements of this industry. The 1992 Energy Policy Act provided much of the impetus for this deregulation. The next question will be the desirability of competition at the retail (distribution) level.[9]

Natural Gas Companies

A second energy industry with extensive regulation is the natural gas industry. The furnishing of natural gas to users also includes a three-stage process. The first stage is the production of the gas in the field. Transportation to the consuming locality through pipelines is the second stage. Distribution to the final user makes up the third stage. The FERC historically set the field price of natural gas that is to be moved out of the production stage. The regulation of natural gas prices at the wellhead has been effectively phased out. In addition, the FERC oversees the interstate transportation of gas by approving pipeline routes and by controlling the wholesale rates charged by pipeline companies to distribution firms. The distribution function may be carried out by a private firm or by a municipal government agency. In either event, the rates charged to final users also are controlled because the distribution firm often has a monopoly in its service area.

Communications Companies

In the communications industry, the most important regulated activity is the provision of telephone service. Interstate telephone service, furnished largely by American Telephone and Telegraph (ATT), is subject to rates set by the Federal Communications Commission (FCC), but competitors of ATT are essentially unregulated. Local service in the

---

[9] See M. Maloney, R. McCormick, and R. Sauer, Consumer Choice, Consumer Value: An Analysis of Retail Competition in America's Electric Utility Industry, Washington, D.C., Citizens for a Sound Economy, 1996.

intrastate markets, which may be provided either by one of the former Bell System companies or by one of the so-called independents, is regulated by state commissions. As in other public utilities, authority to provide service in a locality is granted by a franchise from a local government.

THE ECONOMIC RATIONALE FOR REGULATION

The preceding brief survey of the regulated sector reveals the crucial nature of the regulated industries: They furnish services that are critical to the functioning of the other elements in the economic system. Apart from this factor, do the regulated industries share any other common characteristics that account for the regulation imposed on them? This question can be answered by considering the major reasons cited as justifications for instituting economic regulation.

Natural Monopoly Argument

Natural Monopoly
An industry in which maximum economic efficiency is obtained when one firm produces, distributes, and transmits all of the commodity or service produced in that industry. The production of natural monopolists is typically characterized by increasing returns to scale throughout the range of output demanded by the market.

It is asserted frequently that the firms operating in the regulated sector are **natural monopolies,** indicating that a tendency exists for a single supplier to emerge in a given market. If this were the case, then the implementation of regulation would represent an acknowledgment of this trend. The presence of a single supplier would be sanctioned, and regulatory overview would be imposed to ensure that the firm granted a monopoly position did not behave in the fashion characteristic of an unregulated monopolist, who tends to charge high prices and restrict output.

On economic grounds, the situation that can best be termed a "natural monopoly" is found in the case of a product whose production process is characterized by increasing returns to scale. By recalling the discussion of returns to scale in Chapters 8, 9, and 10, increasing returns to scale imply that as all inputs are increased by a given percentage, the average total cost of a unit of output decreases. Alternatively, the long-run marginal cost of output declines throughout the range of output levels that are relevant. This situation is illustrated in Figure 14.4 for a firm in long-run stable equilibrium.

Suppose that the market demand curve for output is represented by the curve DD in Figure 14.4. The socially optimal level of output would then be Q^*; at that level of output, price would be equal to short-run and long-run marginal cost, and the average total cost per unit would be C^*. In this case the firm and the market cost curves are the same; if more than one firm supplies output, the average total cost for the quantity of output produced and sold in the market would be higher than the average cost of the same level of output of a single firm. A single producer is able to realize economies of scale that are unavailable to firms in the presence of competition. From a social perspective, competition would result in inefficiency in the form of costs above their minimum level. It often is argued that if production relations exist like those in Figure 14.4, a single supplier will eventually emerge. Competing firms will realize that their costs decrease as output expands. As a consequence, they will have an incentive to cut prices to increase quantity demanded. During this period, prices will be below average cost, resulting in losses for the producing firms. Unable to sustain such losses, the weaker firms will gradually leave the industry, until only a single producer remains. Thus competitive forces will contribute to the emergence of the natural monopoly. The airline industry often exhibits this behavior in certain markets, although the end result is more often oligopolistic than monopolistic.

If a monopolistic position were to exist in the absence of regulation, the monopolist would maximize profit by equating marginal revenue and marginal cost, leading to a

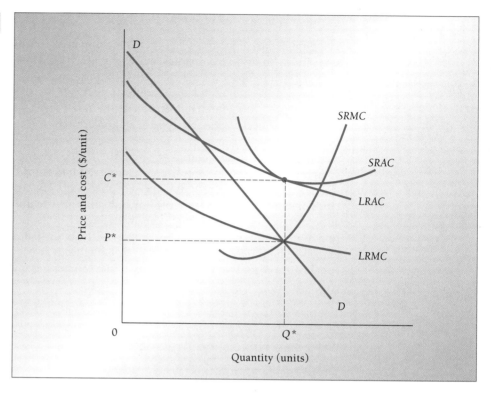

FIGURE   14.4

Natural Monopoly:
Price-Output
Determination

higher price and lower output. Thus intervention through regulation is required to achieve the benefits of the most efficient organization of production. In its simplest form, this is the explanation of regulation based on the existence of natural monopolies.

Figure 14.4 illustrates one final problem that arises in the presence of a genuine natural monopoly. Suppose that a regulatory agency succeeds in establishing the socially optimal price for output, P^*. As the cost curves indicate, this price would lead to losses for the producing firm, because price would be below average total cost. This is obviously an unsustainable result. In this situation the regulating agency normally sets prices at average cost, ensuring revenues sufficient to cover all costs.

Increasing returns to scale, the economic source of a natural monopoly, raise many issues in the theory of optimal pricing. These issues remain controversial among economists. Also, empirical analysis of the cost curves of firms operating in several regulated industries indicates that the natural monopoly argument of declining long-run average costs does not offer a fully adequate explanation for regulation.

Duplication of Facilities Arguments

www . . . .
Read about the role of
duplication of service in the
restructuring of the electric
utility industry in Wyoming
at the following Internet site
maintained by the Public
OnLine Group:
http://eerr.notes.org/
wyoming/restructuring.
htm

Other economic reasons exist for preferring that a single supplier serve a particular market. For example, there would be an undesirable duplication of facilities if electric power, natural gas, or telephone service were provided by several firms in a given locality. The physical network required to connect the producer and user of these services requires a substantial investment before service can be provided. It would be uneconomical to have competing networks of these facilities in a locality. As a consequence, individual firms are granted franchises to furnish service. The franchise gives some assurance to the firm that demands for service will be forthcoming once the capacity is in place, justifying the investment.

DUPLICATION OF FACILITIES: LUBBOCK, TEXAS

The duplication of facilities arguments in support of grants of monopoly service responsibility to utility companies are widely accepted. However, when one considers the very small impact on the cost per *kwh*, for example, the benefits of competition may exceed the costs of facility duplication. There are over 20 communities in the United States with some competition at the retail level for electric service. For example, in Lubbock, Texas, a city with a population of about 200,000, each household and business is served by at least two power companies—Southwestern Public Service, an investor-owned company, and Lubbock Power and Light, a municipal power company. Some sections of town are also served by a third firm, South Plains Electric Cooperative. The electric rate experience in Lubbock, compared with neighboring cities of similar size that are served by only one electric utility, suggests that the benefits of price competition may exceed the higher costs associated with the duplication of distribution systems. This example illustrates that monopoly justification arguments should be evaluated broadly, looking both at cost and price effects, before conclusions regarding the desirability of government grants of monopoly power are reached.

Price Discrimination Arguments

The distribution network in many regulated industries is characterized by a physical link between the producer and users. Many of these services cannot be inventoried. Rather, production and consumption take place simultaneously. Examples of these characteristics include the use of electric power, travel by commercial air carrier, and with minor exceptions, telephone use. The physical connection makes it feasible for the producer to charge different prices for virtually identical service to different users; that is, to engage in price discrimination. The physical link makes it impossible for consumers eligible for lower prices to resell output to users who would otherwise pay the higher charges imposed by the producer. In fact, various types of price discrimination are common in regulated industries. For instance, residential users of electric power and telephones are billed according to rates that are different from those paid by industrial users.

In view of the ability of these firms to engage in price discrimination, one of the justifications for regulatory control over pricing is to ensure that these practices do not result in abuses. One of the functions of regulation is to see that no consumer is made worse off under a scheme of discriminatory pricing than he or she would be in the absence of price discrimination. The economics of price discrimination is discussed in Chapter 17.

The natural monopoly, duplication of facilities, price discrimination, and other arguments that have been advanced to explain the existence of regulated monopolies all contain some elements of truth. Taken individually, they are useful in calling attention to some of the characteristics of the regulated industries that raise questions about how the industries would perform in the absence of regulation. However, no single factor or set of factors clearly distinguishes all regulated industries from all nonregulated industries. The line between the two sectors is often not distinct. For example, timber and logging companies access raw materials in the national forests at below market prices, and *wholesale* electricity is auctioned to the highest bidder at quarter 'til every hour.

THE REGULATORY PROCESS[10]

The agencies that carry out tasks of economic regulation are specialized bodies consisting of a small number of formal decision makers supported by a professional staff of economists, lawyers, accountants, and engineers. At the federal level the members of the various regulatory commissions are appointed by the president, whereas at the state level the commissioners may be elected or appointed officials. The formal proceedings used by the regulatory agencies for determining rates are quasijudicial in character, involving an adversary process. The utilities' adversaries may be the regulatory commission's staff, consumer groups, or in some cases the state attorney general's office. Because these rate hearings are costly and time consuming, many commissions have adopted informal procedures for making periodic adjustments in rates. Finally, the decisions of regulatory agencies are subject to the review of the courts. As a result, the U.S. Supreme Court has established many of the doctrines under which regulation is carried out.

Within this general framework, the regulatory agencies control entry by firms into the regulated industries, set prices that consumers are to pay, and oversee the quality of service provided. Of these basic functions, the determination of prices accounts for the largest proportion of regulatory activity. In many of the regulated industries, the questions of the entry of new firms and the extension of service by established firms into new markets are closed. In other industries, such as in airline transportation and trucking, the regulation of new entrants has been almost eliminated.

Rate Determination

When carried out as part of a formal rate hearing, the process of determining the rates to be charged by a regulated firm takes place in two stages. In the first phase, the total revenue that the firm is to be allowed in a period is calculated. This sum is called the **rate level.**

In the second stage, the specific prices to be charged various users for particular services are set to produce the target revenue, assuming that users purchase estimated quantities of output. The resulting set of prices is called the **rate structure.**

In actual practice, the rate-level phase of a regulatory proceeding consumes the bulk of attention. Once the rate level is determined, the issues of the rate structure are addressed.

The calculation of the total revenue requirement of a firm is organized around the following formula:

$$R = C + (V - D)k \qquad [14.4]$$

where R represents the total revenue requirement, C represents all operating costs including taxes, V is the gross value of the firm's assets, D is accumulated depreciation of the assets, and k is the **rate of return** allowed on assets. The quantity $V - D$ is called the firm's **rate base.** The firm is entitled by law to have the opportunity to earn a reasonable rate of return on this rate base. As the formula suggests, the determination of a firm's revenue can be separated into three steps: estimation of operating costs, identification of the rate base, and calculation of a reasonable rate of return.

Rate Level
The actual dollar amount of revenue a utility is authorized to collect; also called the *total revenue requirement.*

Rate Structure
A set of prices that may be charged to various users of a regulated utility's services.

Rate of Return
The percentage of the rate base a utility is allowed to collect to pay the cost of capital.

Rate Base
The dollar value established by a regulatory commission of a company's plant, equipment, and intangible capital used and useful in serving the public; invested capital minus depreciation.

---

[10] An excellent overview of the regulatory process is found in U.S. Department of Energy, *A Consumer's Guide to the Economics of Electric Utility Ratemaking,* DOE/RG/09154 (Springfield, Va.: NTIS, May 1980). See also Alfred E. Kahn, *The Economics of Regulation: Principles and Institutions* (Cambridge, Mass.: MIT Press, 1988), J.C. Bonbright, A.L. Danielson, and D.R. Kamerschen, *Principles of Public Utility Rates,* 2d ed. (Arlington, Va.: Public Utilities Reports, 1988), and Charles F. Phillips, Jr., *The Regulation of Public Utilities,* 3d ed (Arlington, Va.: Public Utilities Reports, 1993).

A full-scale rate-determination proceeding normally occurs no more frequently than annually for most firms, primarily because of the high costs that such a proceeding imposes on the firm and on the regulatory agency. A rate proceeding can be initiated by either the firm or the regulatory commission. The information required to determine the magnitudes of the various quantities in the formula for computing revenues to be allowed the firm is obtained by analyzing the record of a firm's actual experience over a recent period, called the *test period*. Once the magnitudes for the test period, commonly a year, have been identified, adjustments may be made to reflect forecasted changes in conditions between the test year and the period during which the new rates will be in effect. Each of the elements in the allowed revenue formula raises different issues, so we discuss them separately.

Operating Costs   The operating costs that regulated firms are allowed to recover from consumers include the usual operating expenses, depreciation, and taxes. Regulatory commissions have the power to examine operating costs to ensure that users are not penalized through higher prices as a consequence of a firm's incurring expenses that are higher than necessary. If the commission excludes certain expenses from operating costs, the allowed level of revenue is correspondingly reduced, resulting in lower profits available for common stockholders. Thus the focus of many issues involving operating costs is whether the expenses should be borne by users or by stockholders.

The Rate Base   The rate base of a regulated firm includes the property that the firm has acquired to make service available to its users, less accrued depreciation charges on the property. The firm is entitled to rates that provide an adequate rate of return on the investment required to obtain this property. To have any lower rate would mean that the utility's property was being confiscated. In principle, the role of the rate base in determining the revenues allowed a firm is straightforward. But in practice, the rate base has been a source of continuing controversy in rate proceedings.

www . . . .
Read more about the transition away from rate-of-return regulation in the electric utility industry at the following Internet site maintained by the U.S. Energy Information Administration:
http://www.eia.doe.gov/oiaf/elepri97/comp.html

The Rate of Return   The idea of a reasonable rate of return reflects the need to compensate suppliers of capital for investing in utility securities. Determining the rate of return involves the identification of an appropriate return on these investments; that is, the firm's costs of various types of capital must be estimated. In accomplishing this, information obtained from the capital market about returns available on alternative investments is an important factor.

The existence of regulation does not in itself guarantee that investors will realize an adequate rate of return on their investment, as is evident in the Managerial Challenge at the beginning of this chapter. Regulation is not intended to eliminate the risks inherent in making financial investments. This fact introduces an additional element of judgment into the process of calculating the required rate of return. As a result of this and other factors that make determining the rate of return imprecise, it is common to interpret the required return in terms of an interval encompassing a range of reasonable returns rather than as a single value.

SPECIAL ISSUES IN UTILITY REGULATION

The process of determining the total revenue required by a regulated firm follows a sequence quite different from that used by nonregulated firms. Usually, we think of firms setting prices, selling quantities of output at those prices, and collecting whatever amount of revenue results. In the regulated case, a target level of total revenue is identified before specific prices are set. In a rate proceeding, the individual prices charged by a firm make up the rate structure. The selection of a rate structure raises interesting economic problems, however. In this section we consider two of these. First, the general problem of price discrimination is discussed, and then the so-called peak-load pricing problem is described.

Price Discrimination

It has long been common in the regulated sector to categorize users of the services provided by a single regulated firm on the basis of well-defined characteristics. Each of these categories then constitutes a separate market for output, which is sold at prices unique to that market. For example, markets for electric power and telephone services are divided between residential and commercial users. In railway and truck freight transportation, separate markets on a single route are defined by the commodities shipped. As a result, users in different markets, as defined by the producer, pay different prices for what is essentially the same output. The practice of charging different prices for the same output is called *price discrimination*.

As is evident in Table 14.2, price discrimination is common in the electric power industry. As this table shows, the average price charged per kilowatt-hour ranged from 4.7 cents for industrial customers to 7.8 cents for residential consumers.

Cost Justifications   One justification for price discrimination by regulated firms lies in the fact that users in different markets may differ in the costs they impose on the supplier in providing service to them. It is argued that these cost differentials should be reflected in price differentials so that the information given by prices is accurate and can thus contribute to desirable patterns of resource allocation. In the electric power industry, for example, it may be much less costly per unit of output to serve a large industrial user than it is to serve a typical residential customer. The costs incurred in distributing power to the industrial user may be spread over a substantially larger volume of output, resulting in a lower average cost of output and justifying a lower price per unit for the larger user. The differences in costs such as these are properly a basis for price differences. To charge a uniform price to all customers would be inefficient—encouraging high-cost users to take too much output—and unfair—penalizing low-cost users in the form of prices above cost-justified levels. In fact, narrowly defined, the term *price discrimination* does not apply to situations where cost-of-service differentials are present.

Demand Justification   Cost considerations are not the only source of price discrimination in the regulated sector. Price differentials also are designed to reflect differing demand characteristics of various user groups. In particular, differences in what are called "values of service," which basically reflect differences in elasticities of demand, also lead

TABLE 14.2	Customer Classification	Average Price Per KWH (Cents)
Average Price per kwh Charged by Investor-Owned Utilities to Various Customer Classifications	Residential	7.8
	Commercial	7.3
	Industrial	4.7

Source: Energy Information Administration, *Annual Energy Review,* 1990, Table 100 (Washington, D.C.: U.S. Government Printing Office, 1991).

to differences in price among consumer categories. The basic pattern is that consumers with relatively inelastic demands are charged higher prices. This produces small decreases in quantity demanded by these users. In contrast, users with relatively elastic demands pay lower prices, resulting in what may be substantial increases in output demanded. In the electric power industry, residential users, with no realistic substitutes for purchased power, have relatively inelastic demands. On the other hand, large industrial users presumably have the option of producing their own power and thus have more elastic demand. The demand or value-of-service considerations thus reinforces the pattern of price differentials based strictly on cost factors.

Regulated firms practicing value-of-service discrimination point out that this technique promotes greater use of their services. In turn, this may lead to a more efficient use of a given level of capacity by reducing the excess capacity present at a point in time, spreading the capacity costs over a larger quantity of output and reducing average total costs. In addition, the promotional aspect of discriminatory pricing may lead to the realization of economies of scale in the long run as larger and more efficient plants are installed. The result is that costs for all users may be lower than they would be in the absence of price discrimination. This makes possible prices for all users that are lower than the prices they would otherwise pay. This is true of higher prices for more "costly" consumers as well as lower prices for consumers whose service is less costly to provide.

The challenge raised to regulatory agencies by price discrimination is to ensure that the practice is not abused. The overall rate structure of a regulated firm must be analyzed to see that the users who receive the lowest prices actually pay the full costs of their service. It is conceivable that their prices could be set below cost, with the high-price users subsidizing the low-price consumers through excessive prices. The results of such a pattern would clearly be inefficient as well as inequitable. On the other hand, properly designed rate schedules can promote efficiency without making any users worse off than they would be in the absence of price discrimination.

Block Pricing

The price discrimination discussed thus far involves the segmentation of a firm's total market into submarkets with separate rates for each submarket. This form of price discrimination is referred to as *third-degree price discrimination*. Many regulated firms also use second-degree price discrimination: The customers in a particular category pay differing prices for various units of output based on the quantity of output used per billing period. For example, electric power is typically sold under rates similar to the following pattern:

Price	Quantity
16¢ per kilowatt-hour	First 100 kilowatt-hours
12¢ per kilowatt-hour	Next 300 kilowatt-hours
9¢ per kilowatt-hour	Next 800 kilowatt-hours
5¢ per kilowatt-hour	All over 1,200 kilowatt-hours

This type of price discrimination, called block pricing, involves a type of quantity discount as use increases.

Block pricing was introduced in the early stages of the development of the electric power industry. The justification for its use was that the price pattern embodied in block pricing reflected the behavior of the costs of supplying power as produced quantity increased. Again, by spreading costs of a given level of capacity over more units of output, larger production is associated with lower unit costs. In addition, the promotional aspect of block rates, it was argued, contributes to the development of the industry by justifying the installation of larger, more efficient plants.

Peak-Load Pricing

The characteristics of production in some regulated industries may give rise to another form of price discrimination. In situations where output cannot be stored in inventory, and where the producing firm ordinarily stands ready to satisfy whatever level of demand is imposed by users, the cost of producing a unit of output varies according to a time dimension associated with the demand for that unit of output. To see this, consider the case of an electric power company that faces varying demands for power over the course of a day. For simplicity, suppose that there are only two levels of demand, an afternoon period when the demand is high and the rest of the day when the demand is below the level of afternoon demand. Because of the way in which electricity is produced, the generating capacity required to produce power for the afternoon period stands idle for the remainder of the firm's operating cycle; that is, there is excess generating capacity except during the period when demand is at its peak. The firm can produce additional output during the morning, for instance, at a relatively low marginal cost. The only expense for additional output would be the cost of fuel used. In contrast, to produce an additional unit of output during the afternoon period, the firm would have to install an additional unit of generating capacity, implying that the marginal cost of that unit of output would be quite high.

This example illustrates the essential features of what is called the *peak-load phenomenon*. When demand levels fluctuate over some time period and when the same capacity produces output over this time period, excess productive capacity will exist during some phases of the cycle, called "off-peak" periods. During other phases, the "peak" periods, the system will be fully used. To expand output in the peak period requires the expansion of productive capacity and the costs associated with this expansion. The basic principle of equating prices to marginal costs suggests that peak and off-peak output be priced differently to reflect the differences in marginal cost associated with producing output in each period. The time periods appropriate here are not determined by chronological time, but are rather defined by patterns of demand for output.

A number of regulated industries face demand patterns that vary more or less regularly over a cycle. Electric power, telephone, and transportation services are all produced under conditions characterized by peak loads. In some cases, capacity may be unavailable to serve all users at the peak. If this is the case, the available output is typically rationed by some nonprice mechanism such as queuing.

To see what type of pricing policy is appropriate in the presence of peak loads, consider the situation shown in Figure 14.5 where two independent demand periods are assumed. In the peak period (day), demand is represented by curve D_1, whereas in the off-peak period (night), demand is shown by D_2. All units of output require the use of fuel at a constant rate, assumed to be b per unit. In addition, capital or generating capacity, which costs β per unit, is also required to produce all output; however, the capacity is not fully used except in the peak period.

The supply curve relevant for determining price and output during the day is the curve $b + \beta$, which reflects the marginal (and average) cost of supplying an additional unit of output during the peak period. At price $P_1 = b + \beta$, day users are just willing to pay the cost of producing a unit of output, so this is the appropriate price for peak

FIGURE   14.5

Peak-Load Pricing

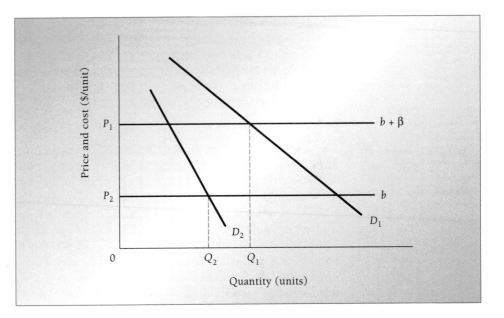

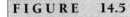

service. At this price, Q_1 units of output are produced, implying that Q_1 is the level of capacity installed. At what price should off-peak output be sold? Given the existence of capacity Q_1, the appropriate price of off-peak output is P_2, equal to the marginal cost of fuel. Providing off-peak service imposes no other costs. As a result, the price should be no higher than b per unit at which Q_2 units of output are sold.[11]

This simplified example illustrates the basic principles of peak-load pricing. Peak users should bear all the costs of capacity, a rule that ensures that the optimal level of capacity is installed. At any lower price, peak service would be sold at a price not completely covering all the costs of production. In contrast, off-peak output should be priced to cover only the costs incurred in producing output, given capacity sufficient to do so. This policy encourages the most efficient use of existing capacity. Notice that in the usual case, users would be expected to purchase both peak and off-peak output.

SUMMARY

- ☐ Monopoly is a market structure with one firm producing a differentiated product in a market with significant barriers to entry.

- ☐ In a pure monopoly market structure, firms will generally produce a lower level of output and charge a higher price than would exist in a more competitive market structure. This conclusion assumes no significant economies of scale that might make a monopolist more efficient than a large group of smaller firms.

- ☐ The primary sources of monopoly power include patents and copyrights, control of critical resources, government "franchise" grants, and economies of scale.

---

[11] If base-load generation has high capital costs, peak-load pricing can induce many consumers to shift their loads to off-peak times, for example, through the use of interruptible service, or highly efficient water heaters that allow customers to heat water at night, rather than on demand. If this occurs, the peak period may be shifted to the current off-peak period. Of course, under these circumstances, the original peak-load prices will be incorrect. The solution would be to charge a fraction of the capital cost during each period, such that demand is the same throughout the day. In the determination of the appropriate peak- and nonpeak-load prices, demand elasticities in the two periods are very important.

▢ Monopolists will produce at that level of output where marginal cost equals marginal revenue if their goal is to maximize profits.

▢ The price charged by a profit-maximizing monopolist will be in that portion of the demand function where demand is elastic (or unit elastic). The greater the elasticity of demand facing a monopolist, the lower will be its price relative to marginal cost, ceteris paribus.

▢ *Contribution margins* and *mark-ups* are inversely related to the price elasticity of demand.

▢ *Gross margins* recover capital costs, selling costs, and overhead as well as earn profits.

▢ Limit pricing is a strategy followed by some monopolists to discourage rivals from entering an industry. The monopolist prices its product below the short-run profit maximizing level to forestall new entry in the long-run.

▢ Public utilities are a group of firms, mostly in the electric power, natural gas distribution, natural gas pipeline, and communications industries, that are closely regulated with respect to entry into the business, prices, service quality, and total profits.

▢ Regulation is designed to fairly compensate investors for the risks assumed on their investment in the assets of a utility. In a properly functioning regulatory environment, no utility should consistently earn a rate of return on its assets that is either above or below that required by investors. Regulation can be thought of as a process that is designed to make all investment projects undertaken by utilities have a net present value equal to zero (rate of return equals cost of capital).

▢ The rationales for public utility regulation are many. The *natural monopoly* argument is applied in cases where a product is characterized by increasing returns to scale. The one large firm can theoretically furnish the good or service at a lower cost than a group of smaller competitive firms.

▢ The *duplication of facilities* argument is applied in cases where it would be undesirable to have more than one provider of a service because that would result in unnecessary duplication of facilities, such as phone, gas, or electric lines in a city.

▢ Because of the potential for *price discrimination* by many utilities, regulation is often justified to protect consumers from abuses that may be associated with unregulated price discrimination.

▢ The regulatory process requires the determination of the *level* of rates as well as the *structure* of rates that will be charged to various user groups. Public utility regulatory commissions have wide latitude in the determination of rate levels, allowable costs, and rate structures.

▢ Price discrimination by utilities is often economically desirable on the basis of cost justifications and demand justifications.

▢ *Peak-load pricing* is designed to charge customers a greater amount for the services they purchase, if these services are used during periods of greatest demand. Long-distance phone services typically have been priced on a peak-load basis.

EXERCISES

1. What impact is a subsidy paid to a monopolist likely to have on consumer prices and output if
    a. The subsidy is a fixed amount that does not vary with the level of output;
    b. The subsidy is paid as a fixed amount on each unit produced; or
    c. The subsidy increases per unit as output increases?

2. You have been retained as an analyst to evaluate a proposal by your city's privately owned water company to increase its rates by 100 percent. The company has argued that at the present rate level, the firm is earning only a 2 percent rate of return on invested equity capital. The company believes a 16 percent rate of return is required in today's capital markets.

   Assume that you agree with the 16 percent rate of return proposed by the company.

   a. What factors need to be considered when setting rates designed to achieve this objective?
   b. Would your analysis differ if you knew that individuals were prohibited by law from drilling their own wells? What impact would this have on the price elasticity of demand?
   c. Water companies have a large proportion of fixed costs as compared with variable costs. How does this fact influence your analysis?
   d. Do you believe this firm (a monopolist) can earn its required 16 percent rate of return even if the public utility commission agrees this is a reasonable rate of return?

3. Evaluate the statement. "The reason monopolists always make excessive profits is that they face a nearly perfectly inelastic demand curve and are thus able to charge an excessively high price."

4. If the regulatory process is working effectively, the aggregate of all projects undertaken by a nondiversified electric utility firm should have a net present value that equals zero. Why is this true?

5. Southwestern Power Company has a cost of equity capital of 16 percent. The firm has consistently been authorized a return on equity capital below this cost. Also, the effects of regulatory lag and attrition have further reduced the realized return to the 13 percent range. If the utility expects this problem to continue, what actions would you expect Southwestern to take?

6. Northwestern Power Company has a cost of equity capital of 12 percent, but it has been continuously successful in earning a 17 percent return on the portion of its equity capital that is committed to utility operations. If Northwestern expects this situation to continue for the foreseeable future, would you expect its next power plant to be a large coal plant or a series of several smaller natural gas-fired plants? Why?

7. What are the major differences between industrial users of natural gas and residential users that allow natural gas utilities to discriminate between the two groups of customers in price?

8. Suppose that the royalties received by an author for writing a college text are set at a rate of about 15 percent of the publisher's total revenue.

   a. Demonstrate graphically that this creates an inherent conflict between the interests of a profit-maximizing publisher and those of a royalty-maximizing author.
   b. As the student consumer, whose interests would you like to see prevail?
   c. Does the magnitude of this conflict between author and publisher diminish in the case of a highly inelastic demand curve? Demonstrate graphically.

9. Ajax Cleaning Products is a medium-sized firm operating in an industry dominated by one very large firm—Tile King. Ajax produces a multi-headed tunnel wall scrubber that is very similar to a model produced by Tile King. Ajax has decided to charge the same price as Tile King to avoid the possibility of a price war. The price charged by Tile King is $20,000.

Ajax has the following short-run cost curve:

$$TC = 800,000 - 5,000Q + 100Q^2$$

   a.   Compute the marginal cost curve for Ajax.
   b.   Given Ajax's pricing strategy, what is the marginal revenue function for Ajax?
   c.   Compute the profit-maximizing level of output for Ajax.
   d.   Compute Ajax's total dollar profits.

10.   One and Only, Inc., is a monopolist. The demand function for its product is estimated to be

$$Q = 60 - .4P + 6Y + 2A$$

where Q = quantity of units sold
        P = price per unit
        Y = per capita disposable personal income (thousands of dollars)
        A = hundreds of dollars of advertising expenditures

The firm's average variable cost function is

$$AVC = Q^2 - 10Q + 60$$

Y is to equal 3(thousand) and A is equal to 3(hundred) for the period being analyzed.

   a.   If fixed costs are equal to $1,000, derive the firm's total cost function and marginal cost function.
   b.   Derive a total revenue function and marginal revenue function for the firm.
   c.   Calculate the profit-maximizing level of price and output for One and Only.
   d.   What profit or loss will One and Only earn?
   e.   If fixed costs were $1,200, how would your answers change for (a) through (d)?

11.   The Lumins Lamp Company, a producer of old-style oil lamps, has estimated the following demand function for its product:

$$Q = 120,000 - 10,000P$$

where Q is the quantity demanded per year and P is the price per lamp. The firm's fixed costs are $12,000 and variable costs are $1.50 per lamp.

   a.   Write an equation for the total revenue (TR) function in terms of Q.
   b.   Specify the marginal revenue function.
   c.   Write an equation for the total cost (TC) function in terms of Q.
   d.   Specify the marginal cost function.
   e.   Write an equation for total profits (π) in terms of Q. At what level of output (Q) are total profits maximized? What price will be charged? What are total profits at this output level?
   f.   Check your answers in part (e) by equating the marginal revenue and marginal cost functions, determined in parts (b) and (d), and solving for Q.
   g.   What model of market pricing behavior has been assumed in this problem?

12.   A monopolist faces the following demand function for its product:

$$Q = 45 - 5P$$

The fixed costs of the monopolist are $12 and the monopolist incurs variable costs of $5.00 per unit.

   a.   What is the profit-maximizing level of price and quantity for this monopolist? What will profits be at this price and output level?

    b. If the government imposes a franchise tax on the firm of $10, what will be the profit-maximizing level of price, output, and profits?

    c. If the government imposes an excise tax of 50 cents per unit of output sold, what is the impact on the profit-maximizing level of price, output, and profits?

    d. If the government imposes a ceiling of $6 on the price of the firm's product, what output will the firm produce and what will be total profits?

13. Unique Creations has a monopoly position in the production and sale of magnometers. The cost function facing Unique has been estimated to be

$$TC = \$100,000 + 20Q$$

    a. What is the marginal cost for Unique?

    b. If the price elasticity of demand for Unique is currently -1.5, what price should Unique charge?

    c. What is the marginal revenue at the price computed in part (b)?

    d. If a competitor develops a substitute for the magnometer and the price elasticity increases to -3.0, what price should Unique charge?

14. Given the demand function $P = 20 - Q$, prove that a nondiscriminating monopolist will maximize *total revenue* if the quantity sold is exactly one-half the amount that would be demanded if the good were provided free; that is, $P = 0$.

15. What motivation does a monopolist have to overinvest in plants and equipment? What factors might restrain the monopolist from such overinvesting?

16. The Public Service Company of the Southwest is regulated by an elected state utility commission. The firm has total assets of $500,000. The demand function for its services has been estimated as

$$P = \$250 - \$.15Q$$

The firm faces the following total cost function:

$$TC = \$25,000 + \$10Q$$

(The total cost function does not include the firm's cost of capital.)

    a. In an unregulated environment, what price would this firm charge, what output would be produced, what would total profits be, and what rate of return would the firm earn on its asset base?

    b. The firm has proposed charging a price of $100 for each unit of output. If this price is charged, what will be the total profits and the rate of return earned on the firm's asset base?

    c. The commission has ordered the firm to charge a price that will provide the firm with no more than a 10 percent return on its assets. What price should the firm charge, what output will be produced, and what dollar level of profits will be earned?

17. A firm faces a demand function per day of

$$P = 29 - 2Q$$

and a total cost function of

$$TC = 20 + 7Q$$

    a. Calculate the profit-maximizing price, output, and profit levels for this firm if it is not regulated.

    b. If regulators set the maximum price the firm may charge equal to the firm's marginal cost, what output level will be produced and what will be the level of profits?

    c.   If regulators seek to equate total costs (including a fair return to invested capital) with total revenues, what output level will be produced and what price will be charged?

18.   The Odessa Independent Phone Company (OIPC) is currently engaged in a rate case that will set rates for its Midland-Odessa area customer base. OIPC has total assets of $20 million. The Texas Public Utility Commission has determined that an 11 percent return on its assets is fair. OIPC has estimated its annual demand function as follows:

$$P = 3,514 - 0.08\,Q$$

Its total cost function (not including the cost of capital) is

$$TC = 2,300,000 + 130\,Q$$

    a.   OIPC has proposed a rate of $250 per year for each customer. If this rate is approved, what return on assets will OIPC earn?

    b.   What rate can OIPC charge if the commission wants to limit the return on assets to 11 percent?

    c.   What problem of utility regulation does this exercise illustrate?

19.   In the text example "Profit Maximization: Monopoly," show that the price elasticity of demand is in the elastic region of the profit-maximizing price and output levels of $14.65 and 107 units, respectively.

www exercise

Monopoly and U.S.
Antitrust Law

20.   In this chapter you have learned about conditions that support the formation of a monopoly, as well as monopoly pricing behavior. Since 1890 monopolization has been illegal in the U.S. At the following Internet site maintained by Anthony Becker you can read a variety of different summaries of U.S. Supreme Court cases that have helped refine antitrust law: http://www.stolaf.edu/people/becker/ antitrust/subject.html.

    This site contains summaries of U.S. Supreme Court cases involving antitrust; scroll down to the material on monopoly and read summaries of the seminal cases, including Standard Oil of New Jersey v. U.S. (1911), and U.S. v. American Tobacco (1911). What tests were developed by the Supreme Court to establish monopolization?

CASE EXERCISE   A MARKET SOLUTION TO CROWDED AIRSPACE[12]

The summer 1986 midair collision between an Aeromexico jetliner and a private plane over Los Angeles brought increased attention to the problem of crowded airspace, especially around the nation's busiest airports. A Federal Aviation Administration survey of the country's 23 busiest airports found that in a 6-hour period, private planes intruded on restricted airspace 175 times.

    The problem of crowded airspace, particularly around the busiest airports, can be viewed as a failure to use the pricing system to allocate this scarce resource. The Federal Aviation Administration (FAA) may be considered a monopolist offering a scarce resource for sale. If this resource is not priced correctly, it will be overconsumed. The result is crowded and unsafe airspace. Unfortunately, the FAA has not treated the problem with the discipline of the pricing system. Rather, the FAA has adopted new rules designed to increase the capacity of the airspace around busy airports. Even if these rules are successful, they can provide only a short-term solution to the problem. Surplus de-

---

[12] Based on J. Gregory Sidak, "Marketplace Solution to Midair Collisions," *Wall Street Journal*, 2 March 1987.

mand for flights through crowded airspace will continue to exist unless this limited resource is priced appropriately.

In the near term, takeoffs and landings at the most crowded airports can be limited by increasing landing and takeoff fees until a market clearing price is reached, which provides a reasonable balance between the demand for landing and takeoff slots and the limited supply. More importantly, however, is the need for a system that would allow air traffic controllers to charge a toll for any flight passing through crowded airspace. A system of fees for airspace access would send many flights to less crowded airspace and less congested airports. Airspace access at these alternative airports would then be priced at lower levels. To implement this system, all planes would have to be equipped with transponders, which identify the plane's altitude and location.

So far the nation's air traffic control system has made only limited use of the price system in allocating its scarcest resource—airspace in crowded air corridors. As demand for this airspace grows, the monopolistic provider of air traffic control services, the FAA, will ultimately be forced either to administratively ration access to this airspace or to use the price system to ration access for them. Like auctioning of wholesale electricity, market mechanisms have an important role to play in allocating scarce resources even in regulated airports.

QUESTIONS

1.   What factors do you feel have resulted in the FAA's unwillingness to use the price system to allocate access to the nation's air traffic control system?

2.   Discuss the pros and cons of an administrative rationing system versus the use of the price system to control access to the crowded airspace.

Price and Output Determination: Oligopoly

CHAPTER PREVIEW

The previous three chapters analyzed price and output decisions of firms that competed in markets where there were either a large number of sellers (i.e., pure competition and monopolistic competition) or no other sellers (i.e., monopoly). In pure competition and monopolistic competition, the firm made its price and output decisions independently of the decisions of other firms. In a monopoly, the firm did not need to consider the actions of rival firms, because it did not have any competitors. This chapter examines price and output decisions by firms in market structures where there are a small number of competitors and each firm's decisions are likely to evoke a response from one (or more) of these rival firms. The maximization of shareholder wealth requires that a firm attempt to take into account these responses in its own decision making. Game-theoretic analysis is introduced to assist in the prediction of rival response.

MANAGERIAL CHALLENGE

AMERICAN AIRLINES RESTRUCTURES ITS FARES[1]

During 1991, American Airlines lost $284.1 million. Other major airlines, including USAir (now US Airways), United, and Delta, also experienced major losses during the year. These losses reflected low demand because of the economic recession and the impact of cutthroat price competition from some of the failing or failed competitors (TWA, Continental, Pan American, Midway, Eastern, and America West). The only major airline that remained profitable during this period was Southwest, a regional carrier known for its low fares and no-frills service. In addition, during this time the fare structure in the industry had become almost incomprehensibly complex. Full-coach class fares (the fares that most often apply to business travelers) between New York and Los Angeles, for example, were $1,504, whereas 21-day advance-purchase (with a Saturday layover) fares on the same route were $549.

Faced with this record of poor performance, large pricing discrepancies, and increasing traveler dissatisfaction with the level and structure of air fares, American Airlines announced a major fare restructuring plan on April 9, 1992. Under the new system, there were only four fares: first class, unrestricted coach, 7-day advance-purchase discount fares, and 21-day advance-purchase discount fares. The goal of the new fare structure was to increase the average price paid by people who fly by lowering the price of full-fare tickets and hopefully getting more people to fly using these tickets instead of discount/promotional fares. The cost of this new fare plan was expected to be $100 million during the first year, as full-fare travelers took advantage of the lower rates. Over the long run, Chairman Robert L. Crandall expected the plan to increase profits by $350 million per year.

The decision to implement the new fare plan was a risky one. Although there was a high degree of certainty associated with the immediate cost of the plan ($100 million), the long-term benefits of the plan were less certain. For example, the actual benefits received depended on the nature of the price elasticity of demand over the new range of fares. If demand turned out to be less price elastic over this fare range than anticipated by American, then the hoped-for benefits probably would not be achieved. A related issue was the response of competitors. If competitors chose to follow the lead of American, as Crandall expected, then there was a greater chance that the program would be effective. On the other hand, if one or more significant competitors did not follow, but rather used it as an opportunity to undercut American's fares in competitive markets, then the plan was less likely to be successful.

Some of the weaker competitors, notably USAir and TWA, responded aggressively and cut their fares even lower than American, United, and Delta. American Airlines (and other airlines) responded by matching or undercutting these lower fares. As a result, most airlines registered increases in the number of passenger seats sold. However, profits declined (or losses increased) because the increase in passenger traffic did not offset the lower fares. In October 1992, American Airlines announced the termination of its new pricing structure.

www . . . .

Current financial information on American Airlines, including quarterly earnings reports, are available at the following Internet site:

http://www.amrcorp.com/amr/investor/investor.htm

---

[1] Based on articles in the *Wall Street Journal,* 10 April 1992, p. B1; 13 April 1992, p. C18; 14 April 1992, p. B8; 22 April 1992, p. B1, and 9 October 1992, p. B1.

OLIGOPOLISTIC MARKET STRUCTURES

An oligopoly is characterized by a relatively small number of firms offering a product or service. The product or service may be differentiated, as in automobiles, televisions, and athletic shoes, or relatively undifferentiated, as in oil, aluminum, and cement. The distinguishing characteristic of oligopoly is that the number of firms is small enough that actions by any individual firm in the industry on price, output, product style or quality, introduction of new models, and terms of sale have a perceptible impact on the sales of other firms in the industry. Thus, the distinctive feature of oligopoly is the recognizable interdependence among the firms in the industry. Each firm is aware in its decision making that any new move, such as introducing a price cut or launching a large promotional campaign, is likely to evoke a countermove from its rivals.

In oligopoly markets like soft drinks, cereals, and airlines, rival response expectations are therefore the key to firm-level analysis. If rival firms match price increases and price cuts, a share-of-the-market demand curve may characterize adequately the sales response to an oligopolist's pricing initiatives. If rival firms are slow to match price increases and cuts, oligopolist's may be tempted to discount to gain share and will lose share or price hikes. In some markets like I-beam steel, rivals match price cuts but ignore price hikes.

| EXAMPLE |

OLIGOPOLY IN THE UNITED STATES: RELATIVE MARKET SHARES

Much of U.S. industry is best classified as oligopolistic in structure. By its very definition, oligopolistic market structures cover a wide range of industry configurations. Some examples are shown in Table 15.1. At one extreme is the market for microprocessor chips, which are the "brains" of many IBM-compatible personal computers sold by Compaq, Packard Bell, and other computer companies. As shown in the table, Intel had a dominant market share of approximately 86 percent of this market, with only one other firm (AMD) having an appreciable share. In 1996, Intel had a virtual monopoly on the newer Pentium processor. In other industries, such as beer, ready-to-eat cereals, and soft drinks, a couple of firms have relatively large market shares with the remainder of the firms in the industry having much smaller shares. Among the major U.S. airlines (excluding regional airlines), although American and United have the largest market shares, market share is more evenly divided among the various firms than in the industries cited above. Finally, in the U.S. gasoline market, a dozen or more firms have sizable market shares, with no one firm having a dominant share.

When analyzing the market structure of industries using national or international market share data, one must keep in mind that relevant markets are often regional. For example, although no airline has a dominant market share nationally, a number of airlines have dominant positions at various airports around the country. For example, American has a 64 percent share at Dallas/Fort Worth, Northwest an 80 percent share at Minneapolis/St. Paul, and US Airways a 94 percent share at Charlotte.

INTERDEPENDENCIES IN OLIGOPOLISTIC INDUSTRIES

The nature of interdependencies in oligopolistic industries can be illustrated using the airline pricing example discussed in the Managerial Challenge at the beginning of the chapter.

TABLE   15.1

Examples of
Oligopolistic U.S.
Industries

www...............
Beverage Digest Online
provides current world-wide
market share statistics on
the carbonated soft drink
industry:
http://www.beverage-
digest.com/datastats.html

Microprocessor (486 and Pentium) Chips[a]	
Intel	86%
Advance Micro Devices (AMD)	9
Others	5

U.S. Beer Sales[b]	
Anheuser-Busch	44.8%
Miller	22.5
Adolph Coors	9.9
Stroh's	8.3
G. Heilman	6.4
Pabst	3.3
Genessee	1.1
Others	3.7

Ready-to-Eat Cereal[c]	
Kellogg	35%
General Mills	25
Post	12
Ralston	7
Quaker	6
Nabisco	4
Private Label	10
Others	1

Soft Drinks[d]	
Coca-Cola	42%
Pepsi	31
Dr. Pepper	8
Seven-Up	4
Schweppes	3
Others	12

Major U.S. Airlines[e]	
American	20.6%
United	20.4
Delta	15.8
Northwest	14.0
Continental	10.5
USAirways	9.5
TWA	9.3

U.S. Gasoline Market[f]	
Shell	8.9%
Chevron	8.3
Texaco	7.8
Exxon	7.8
Amoco	7.5
Mobil	6.8
BP America	5.9
Citgo	5.4
Marathon	5.2
Sun	4.2
Phillips	3.5
Unocal	3.5
Arco	3.1
Conoco	2.6
Others	19.5

Music (Albums)[g]	
Sony	23%
Warner	16
BMG	14
EMI	13
Universal	11
Polygram	10
Others	13

[a] *Business Week,* 6 November 1995, p. 40
[b] *Pittsburgh Press Sunday Magazine,* 1 March 1992, pp. 14–19.
[c] *Reuters,* 15 May 1996.
[d] *Wall Street Journal,* 12 September 1996, p. B9.
[e] *Wall Street Journal,* 14 January 1992, p. A1.
[f] *Wall Street Journal,* 21 January 1992, p. B6.
[g] *Investors' Business Daily,* 13 January 1998, p. A8.

EXAMPLE

AIRLINE PRICING: THE PITTSBURGH MARKET

Consider the case of the airline route between Pittsburgh and Dallas. One can fly this route on a number of different airlines, but only American and US Airways offer non-stop service between these cities. (Flights on other airlines require a stopover and change of planes, which many travelers prefer to avoid, if possible.) Prior to the introduction of American's new fare structure, both airlines were charging $1,054 for a round-trip coach-class ticket. American's new fare was $640, a reduction of $414. US Airways was then faced with the decision of whether to maintain its current $1,054 fare (or some other fare above American's new fare), match American's new $640 fare, or undercut American's $640 fare. American's demand function (and revenues) in the Pittsburgh-Dallas market depended on the reaction of US Airways to the fare reduction. A decision by US Airways to charge a higher fare (e.g., current $1,054 fare) will result in additional market share for American, because many travelers will choose American's lower-priced service.[2] A decision by US Airways to match American's new fare will result in American retaining its existing market share on the Pittsburgh-Dallas route. However, depending on the price elasticity of demand and the mix of full fare and discounted tickets sold, the price reduction could actually increase American's revenues and profits. Finally, a decision by US Airways to undercut American's new $640 fare would lead to a lower market share and a likely further price reduction by American. The above analysis obviously can get much more complicated when there are more than two competitors under consideration.

These recognizable interdependencies can lead to varying degrees of competition and cooperation among the oligopolistic firms. At one extreme is the case of intense rivalry (i.e., no cooperation), where a firm may seek to become a monopolist by driving its competitor(s) out of business. Alternatively, some form of informal, or tacit, cooperation may take place among the oligopolistic firms—"conscious parallelism of action"—with respect to pricing and other decisions.[3] This type of cooperative pricing has been charged with respect to the establishment of bid-ask spreads by securities dealers on Nasdaq stocks.[4] At the other extreme is a formal collusive agreement among the firms to act as a monopolist by setting prices to maximize total industry profits. Because of the wide scope of industry configurations that fall under the oligopoly classification and the difficulty of predicting the response that rivals will take to the competitive moves of other firms, no single normative model can unambiguously describe oligopolists' competitive behavior regarding price, output, and other conditions surrounding the sale of their products.

IGNORING INTERDEPENDENCIES

The easiest approach to the interdependency problem is merely to ignore it; that is, to act as if it does not exist at all and assume that your competitors will do likewise. In actual practice this probably describes the way oligopolists act in making a wide variety of routine decisions or decisions that are likely to have a rather small impact on the entire industry. In these cases tracing through the complex effects of such decisions may not be worth the time and expense required.

Cournot Model

One oligopoly model, which "ignored" the interdependencies among firms, was published by the French economist Augustin Cournot in 1838. According to the Cournot model, each of the two firms (duopoly),[5] in determining its profit-maximizing output level, *assumes that the other firm's output will not change.*

For example, suppose that two duopolists (firms A and B) produce identical products. If firm A observes firm B producing Q_B units of output in the current period, then

---

[2] US Airways may be able to maintain a sizable market share even with a higher fare as the result of brand loyalty. Airlines seek to establish brand loyalty in a number of different ways, such as frequent-flyer programs, timely flights (e.g., early morning for business travelers), and in-flight service (e.g., meals, movies).

[3] See F.M. Scherer and David Ross, *Industrial Market Structure and Economic Performance,* 3d ed. (Chicago Ill.: Rand McNally, 1990), pp. 339–346, for a discussion of the conscious parallelism doctrine.

[4] "U.S. Examines Alleged Price-Fixing on Nasdaq," *Wall Street Journal,* 20 October 1994, p. C1.

[5] The Cournot model can be extended to any number of sellers.

firm A will seek to maximize its own profits assuming that firm B will continue producing the same Q_B units in the next period. Firm B acts in a similar manner. It attempts to maximize its own profits under the assumption that firm A will continue producing the same amount of output in the next period as firm A did in the current period. In the Cournot model this pattern continues until long-run equilibrium is reached—a point where output and price are stable and neither firm can increase its profits by raising or lowering output. The following example illustrates the determination of the long-run Cournot equilibrium.

EXAMPLE

COURNOT OLIGOPOLY SOLUTION: SIEMENS AND THOMSON-CSF

Suppose that two European electronics companies, Siemens (firm S) and Thomson-CSF (firm T), jointly hold a patent on a component used in airport radar systems. Demand for the component is given by the following function:

$$P = 1,000 - Q_S - Q_T \qquad [15.1]$$

where Q_S and Q_T are the quantities sold by the respective firms and P is the (market) selling price. The total cost functions of manufacturing and selling the component for the respective firms are

$$TC_S = 70,000 + 5Q_S + .25Q_S^2 \qquad [15.2]$$

$$TC_T = 110,000 + 5Q_T + .15Q_T^2 \qquad [15.3]$$

Suppose that the two firms act independently, with each firm seeking to maximize its own total profit from the sale of the component.

Siemens's total profit is equal to

$$\pi_S = PQ_S - TC_S$$

$$= (1,000 - Q_S - Q_T)\,Q_S - (70,000 + 5Q_S + .25Q_S^2)$$

$$= -70,000 + 995\,Q_S - Q_T Q_S - 1.25Q_S^2 \qquad [15.4]$$

Note that Siemens's total profit depends on the amount of output produced and sold by Thomson (Q_T). Taking the partial derivative of Equation 15.4 with respect to Q_S yields

$$\frac{\partial \pi_S}{\partial Q_S} = 995 - Q_T - 2.50Q_S \qquad [15.5]$$

Similarly, Thomson's total profit is equal to

$$\pi_T = PQ_T - TC_T$$

$$= (1,000 - Q_S - Q_T)\,Q_T - (110,000 + 5Q_T + .15Q_T^2)$$

$$= -110,000 + 995Q_T - Q_S Q_T - 1.15Q_T^2 \qquad [15.6]$$

Note also that Thomson's total profit is a function of Siemens's output level (Q_S). Taking the partial derivative of Equation 15.6 with respect to Q_T yields

$$\frac{\partial \pi_T}{\partial Q_T} = 995 - Q_S - 2.30Q_T \qquad [15.7]$$

Setting Equations 15.5 and 15.7 equal to zero yields

$$2.50Q_S + Q_T = 995 \qquad [15.8]$$

$$Q_S + 2.30Q_T = 995 \qquad [15.9]$$

Solving Equations 15.8 and 15.9 simultaneously gives the optimal levels of output for the two firms— $Q_S^* = 272.32$ units and $Q_T^* = 314.21$ units. Substituting these values into Equation 15.1 yields an optimal (equilibrium) selling price of $P^* = \$413.47$ per unit. The respective profits for the two firms are obtained by substituting Q_S^* and Q_T^* into Equations 15.4 and 15.6 to obtain $\pi_S^* = \$22,695.00$ and $\pi_T^* = \$3,536.17$.

The Cournot model has been criticized for the unrealistic assumption made by each duopolist about the behavior of its competitor. The assumption that the other firm will keep its output constant, particularly when this independence assumption has proved incorrect on earlier decision-making rounds is not consistent with rational economic behavior. Normally, one would expect the duopolist to learn from past mistakes and either make some alternative assumption about the behavior of the competitor or, if possible, enter into a (formal or informal) collusive agreement with the other firm to raise prices and increase profits.

Despite the shortcomings of the Cournot model, it provides insights into the nature of the interdependencies among oligopolists and the necessity to make *some* assumption about how competitors will react to the firm's price-output decisions.

CARTELS AND OTHER FORMS OF COLLUSION

Cartel
A formal or informal agreement among firms in an oligopolistic industry. Cartel members may agree on such issues as prices, total industry output, market shares, and the division of profits.

Oligopolists may seek to reduce the inherent risk that exists because of the interdependencies of the industry structure by either formally or informally agreeing to cooperate or collude in decision making. Formal agreements of oligopolists are called **cartels.** In general, collusive agreements of any sort are illegal in the United States under the Sherman Antitrust Act of 1890; however, some important exceptions exist. For example, prices and quotas of various agricultural products (e.g., milk, lemons) are set by growers in many parts of the country with the approval of the federal government. The International Air Transport Association (IATA), comprised of airlines flying transatlantic routes, sets uniform prices for these flights. And ocean shipping rates are set by hundreds of collusive "conferences" on each major transoceanic route. Illegal collusive arrangements, however, have also existed from time to time in this country. One of the best-known modern documented cases of this type of illegal cooperation was in the electrical equipment manufacturing industry during the 1950s. Several large firms—including General Electric, Westinghouse, and Allis Chalmers—along with some of their top executives were convicted of engaging in agreements to fix prices and divide up the markets for such items as switchgear and circuit breakers.[6] Cement and paving companies as well as cardboard box manufacturers also are regularly indicted for price fixing. In a celebrated 1994 indictment, General Electric was accused of conspiring with De-Beers Centenary AG to fix industrial diamond prices.[7]

EXAMPLE

OCEAN SHIPPING CONFERENCES[8]

Since the Shipping Act of 1916, ocean freight companies have been exempted from the antitrust laws of the United States. Shipping rates on a transoceanic route are set jointly

---

[6] See "Collusion among Electrical Equipment Manufacturers," *Wall Street Journal,* 10 and 12 January 1962, reprinted in Edwin Mansfield, *Monopoly Power and Economic Performance* (New York: W.W. Norton, 1964).

[7] "GE Price-Fixing Case Won't Be Easy for Government," *Wall Street Journal,* 20 October 1994, p. B3.

[8] Based on "Making Waves," *Wall Street Journal,* 7 October 1997, p. A1 and J. Yong, "Excluding Capacity-Constrained Entrants through Exclusive Dealing: Theory and Applications to Ocean Shipping," *Journal of Industrial Economics,* Vol. 46, No. 2, June 1996.

by 10 to 50 competitors acting as a "shipping conference." Recent studies in 1993 and 1995 by the U.S. Agriculture Department and the FTC found that rates were 18 or 19 percent lower when ocean-shipping companies broke out of these conference arrangements and negotiated as independents. Nevertheless, the conferences maintain their market power by signing exclusive-dealing contracts with large volume customers. The enormous capacity of the shipping conferences allows more schedule frequency and greater reliability than the independents can offer. And liquidated-damages penalty clauses in these exclusives contracts remove much of the incentive for even price-sensitive cargo to seek out independent shippers. Instead, circuitous transportation plans avoid the highest rates. Polaroid, for example, ships film to Europe by first trucking 300 miles to the port of Montreal despite the fact that the product is manufactured 20 miles from the port of Boston.

Factors Affecting Oligopolistic Collusion

The ability of oligopolistic firms to engage successfully in some form of formal (or informal) cooperation depends on a number of different factors. Several of these factors are examined below.[9]

Number and Size Distribution of Sellers   Effective collusion generally is more difficult as the number of oligopolistic firms involved increases. As the number of firms increases, individual firms are more likely to ignore the effects of their pricing and output decisions on the actions of rival firms. Likewise, as the number of firms increases, the chance is greater that one (or more) firm(s) will act independently and cut prices in an attempt to increase market share and profits. Finally, as the number of firms increases, a greater likelihood exists for disagreements concerning the most advantageous pricing and output policies. The DeBeers diamond cartel in South Africa is effective in part because Russia agreed in 1995 to sell 95 percent of their total wholesale supply through DeBeers. DeBeers's central selling organization and Russia alone account for over 75 percent of world supply.[10]

Product Heterogeneity   Products manufactured by different firms are said to be *homogeneous* if they are alike in all significant physical and subjective characteristics and are viewed by customers as virtually perfect substitutes for one another. With perfect homogeneity, price is the only characteristic that differentiates the competing firms' products. In general, when the firms' products are *heterogeneous* (or differentiated), cooperation is more difficult because competition is occurring over a broad array of product characteristics, such as durability, fashion timing, warranty, and after-sale policies. The state of Florida recently accused the leading producers of toilet tissue of illegally fixing prices for this homogeneous product.

Cost Structures   Various firms within an industry are often faced with differing cost functions. Generally, the more cost functions differ among competing firms, the more difficult it will be for firms to collude on pricing and output decisions. Also, successful collusion is more difficult in industries where fixed costs (i.e., overhead) are a high percentage of total costs. This is particularly true during cyclical or secular declines in demand, when firms are operating well below plant capacity. With high fixed costs and cor-

---

[9] See Scherer and Ross, *Industrial Market Structure,* pp. 277–315, for an expanded discussion of these factors and the factual contexts of several price-fixing conspiracies (especially pp. 317–352).

[10] See "Disputes Are Forever," *The Economist,* 17 September 1994.

respondingly low marginal (variable) costs, firms that are operating below capacity can increase profits significantly by cutting prices and increasing output; hence, enforcing pricing agreements under such conditions can be difficult. Consequently, breakdowns in cooperation are most notable in industries that employ highly capital-intensive production processes, such as petroleum refining, steel making, and airlines.

Size and Frequency of Orders   Successful oligopolistic cooperation also depends on the size distribution over time of customer orders. Effective collusion is more likely to occur when orders are small, frequent, and received regularly. When large orders are received infrequently at irregular intervals as in the purchase of aircraft engines, it is more difficult for firms to collude on pricing and output decisions.

Secrecy and Retaliation   An oligopolistic firm will be tempted to grant secret price concessions to selected customers if it feels that these price reductions will not be detected by its competitor(s). By keeping price concessions secret, a firm can forestall retaliation by its competitor(s) and hence earn additional profits. Because secret price cutting interferes with the maximization of total industry profits, oligopolistic industries sometimes attempt to make it difficult to conceal price concessions. One way this can be done is to have an industry trade association collect sales data and publish periodic reports of transactions between firms and their customers. Under such a system, information concerning price cutting by one firm will be quickly disseminated to the other firms in the industry and they can take swift retaliatory action. In general, knowledge of competitors' actions provides a favorable environment for some form of collusion to take place. The toilet paper manufacturers' collusive agreement, mentioned earlier, allegedly operated through public bids for institutional customers like schools and hospitals.

Social Structure of the Industry   Business and social contacts among industry executives at trade association and other meetings often can lead to friendship and mutual understanding that facilitates collusion among oligopolistic firms; however, such contacts do not guarantee cooperation. Personal animosity and distrust among the executives of competing firms may prevent effective collusion.

Profit Maximization and the Division of Output

Under both legal cartels and formal secret collusive agreements, an attempt is made to increase industry profits above the level that would prevail in the absence of collusion. If the control board or directors of the cartel have a reasonably good understanding of the demand relationships for the product being controlled, then the cartel can act as a *monopolist* and *maximize total industry profits.*

The profit-maximization solution for a two-firm, E and F, cartel is shown graphically in Figure 15.1. The *industry* demand, D, marginal revenue, MR, and marginal cost, ΣMC, curves are shown in the right-hand panel of Figure 15.1. The industry marginal cost curve is obtained by summing horizontally across outputs the marginal cost curves of the individual firms in the center and left-hand panels—that is, $\Sigma MC = MC_E + MC_F$. Total industry profits are maximized by setting total industry output (and consequently price) at the point where industry marginal revenue equals industry marginal cost. This yields the solution shown in the right-hand panel of Figure 15.1—the cartel should produce and sell Q^*_{Total} units of output at a price of P^* per unit.

If the cartel seeks to maximize its profits, the market share (or quota) for each firm should be set at a level such that the marginal cost of all firms is identical. In Figure 15.1 the market share for each firm is found at the point where a horizontal line, drawn from

FIGURE   15.1

Price-Output
Determination for a
Two-Firm Cartel

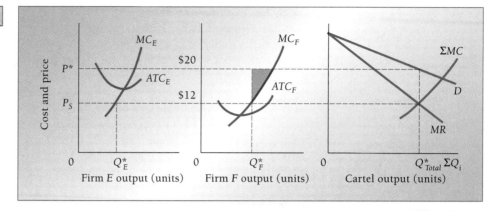

the intersection of the ΣMC and MR curves in the right-hand panel, crosses the MC_E and MC_F curves in the left-hand and center panels, respectively. The optimal output allocation is for firm E to produce a quota of Q_E^* units and for firm F to produce a quota of Q_F^* units. If firm E were producing at a level where its marginal costs exceeded firm F's, cartel profits could be increased by shifting output from E to F until marginal costs are equal.[11]

Cartel pricing agreements are hard to reach, but the central problem for a cartel lies in monitoring these output shares or quotas. Detecting quota violations and effectively enforcing punishment schemes are nearly impossible. Consequently, most cartels are very unstable. Currently, the two longest running cartels are the Organization of Petroleum Exporting Countries (OPEC) and the DeBeers diamond cartel. They have received enormous attention precisely because their longevity is so exceptional. Most cartels are like the price-fixing agreements among cardboard box manufacturers. The collusive agreements form approximately once a quarter and break up within a few weeks. Let's return to Figure 15.1 and see why. Suppose you are firm F facing a cartel-determined price for crude oil P^* of $20 per barrel. Your marginal costs are presently running $12 per barrel at your assigned quota of Q_F/Q_{Total}. The Aramco pipelines, which once consolidated all your throughput from the production wells to shipping terminals, have now been superseded by numerous independent shipping terminals, many within your own nation. In addition, your crude is relatively undifferentiated from that of many other OPEC members. Should you follow your quota commitment? Is it in your best interest to do so? The answer depends on whether your additional sales beyond quota are detectable and whether your additional output will increase total supply enough to place downward pressure on the cartel price. If the answer to both questions is no, then because a 40 percent gross margin ($8) awaits your selling another barrel, a profit maximizer will be tempted to expand output and capture the hatched area of incremental profit in the middle panel of Figure 15.1. Of course, the problem is that other cartel members may think exactly the same way. If everyone takes the cartel price as given and independently profit maximizes, then cartel supply increases to ΣQ_i, and price must fall to the suboptimal level P_s just to clear the market. Enforcement of the ideal quotas Q_F and Q_E is the Achilles' heel of every cartel. In the later discussion of OPEC, we pay particular attention to the swing producer role of Saudi Arabia in absorbing quota violations by other OPEC members and thereby stabilizing the cartel.

---

[11] Note that the average total costs of the two firms are not necessarily equal at the optimal (profit-maximizing) output level. Note also that firm E is given a sizable share of the total output even though its average total costs are higher than firm F's.

In actual practice the ideal allocation of output among firms in a cartel is rarely achieved. Each firm's share of industry output is determined by a process of negotiation, so the strongest firms with the best bargaining position are likely to receive larger market shares than an optimal solution might suggest. In addition, more inefficient producers may be allocated larger shares of total profits than the optimum to convince them to participate in the cartel arrangement without "cheating." Evidence shows that often the level of output of each cartel member is based on historical patterns of sales, productive capacity, or profitability. Sometimes cartels will divide output geographically, giving each member an exclusive license to operate in a certain region.

<table>
<tr><td>EXAMPLE</td></tr>
</table>

CARTEL PRICING AND OUTPUT DECISIONS: SIEMENS AND THOMSON-CSF

The determination of the profit-maximizing price and output levels for a two-firm cartel can also be determined algebraically when the demand and cost functions are given. Consider again the Siemens (firm S) and Thomson-CSF (firm T) example discussed in the previous section. The demand function was given by Equation 15.1 and the cost functions for the two firms were given by Equations 15.2 and 15.3. Suppose that Siemens and Thomson decide to form a cartel and act as a monopolist to maximize total profits from the production and sale of the components.

Total industry profits (π_{Total}) are equal to the sum of Siemens's and Thomson's profits and are given by the following expression:

$$\pi_{Total} = \pi_S + \pi_T$$

$$= PQ_S - TC_S + PQ_T - TC_T \qquad [15.10]$$

Substituting Equations 15.1, 15.2, and 15.3 into this expression yields

$$\begin{aligned}
\pi_{Total} &= (1{,}000 - Q_S - Q_T)\,Q_S - (70{,}000 + 5Q_S + .25Q_S^2) \\
&\quad + (1{,}000 - Q_S - Q_T)\,Q_T - (110{,}000 + 5Q_T + .15Q_T^2) \\
&= 1{,}000Q_S - Q_S^2 - Q_S Q_T - 70{,}000 - 5Q_S - .25Q_S^2 \\
&\quad + 1{,}000Q_T - Q_S Q_T - Q_T^2 - 110{,}000 - 5Q_T - .15Q_T^2 \\
&= -180{,}000 + 995Q_S - 1.25Q_S^2 + 995Q_T \\
&\quad - 1.15Q_T^2 - 2Q_S Q_T \qquad [15.11]
\end{aligned}$$

To maximize π_{Total} take the *partial* derivatives of Equation 15.11 with respect to Q_S and Q_T:

$$\frac{\partial \pi_{Total}}{\partial Q_S} = 995 - 2.50Q_S - 2Q_T$$

$$\frac{\partial \pi_{Total}}{\partial Q_T} = 995 - 2.30Q_T - 2Q_S$$

Setting these expressions equal to zero yields

$$2.5Q_S + 2Q_T - 995 = 0 \qquad [15.12]$$

$$2Q_S + 2.3Q_T - 995 = 0 \qquad [15.13]$$

Solving Equations 15.12 and 15.13 simultaneously gives the optimal output levels: Q_S^* = 170.57 units and $Q_T^* = 284.29$ units.

Substituting these values into Equations 15.10 and 15.11 gives an optimal selling price and total profit for the cartel of $P^* = \$545.14$ per unit and $\pi^*_{Total} = \$46,291.43$, respectively. The marginal costs of the two firms at the optimal output level are equal to

$$MC^*_S = \frac{d(TC_S)}{dQ_S} = 5 + .50Q_S$$

$$= 5 + .50(170.57) = \$90.29$$

$$MC^*_T = \frac{d(TC_T)}{dQ_T} = 5 + .30Q_T$$

$$= 5 + .30(284.29) = \$90.29$$

As in the graphical solution illustrated earlier in Figure 15.1, the optimal output (or market share) for each firm in the cartel occurs where the marginal costs of the two firms are equal.

Comparison of Cartel Pricing and Cournot Equilibrium: Siemens-Thomson Example

Table 15.2 summarizes the results of the Siemens and Thomson example for the cases discussed above (a) where the two companies acted independently to maximize their own company profits (Cournot equilibrium) and (b) where they formed a cartel to maximize total industry profits. Several conclusions can be drawn from this comparison. First, total industry output (Q^*_{Total}) is lower and selling price (P^*) is higher when the firms collude than when there is no collusion. Also, total industry profits (π^*_{Total}) are higher when the firms set prices and output jointly than when they act independently. Finally, although this may not be true in all collusive agreements, one firm's profits (i.e., Siemens's) is actually lower under the cartel solution than when it acts independently. Therefore, to get Siemens to participate in the cartel, Thomson probably would have to agree to share a significant part of the cartel's additional profits with Siemens.

TABLE 15.2		(a) *No Collusion:* Siemens and Thomson Act Independently to Maximize Their Own Company's Profits	(b) *Collusion:* Siemens and Thomson Form a Cartel to Maximize Total Industry Profits
Comparison of Pricing, Output, and Profits for Siemens and Thomson	**Optimal Value**		
	Q^*_S (Siemens's output)	272.32 units	170.57 units
	Q^*_T (Thomson's output)	314.21 units	284.29 units
	$Q^*_{Total} = Q^*_S + Q^*_T$ (Total industry output)	586.53 units	454.86 units
	P^* (Selling price)	\$413.47/unit	\$545.14/unit
	π^*_S (Siemens's profit)	\$22,695.00	\$14,858.15
	π^*_T (Thomson's profit)	\$3,536.17	\$31,433.28
	$\pi^*_{Total} = \pi^*_S + \pi^*_T$ (Total industry profit)	\$26,231.17	\$46,291.43

The remainder of this section and the following International Perspectives section examine two organizations that engage in collusion and effectively act as cartels.

AN INTERCOLLEGIATE SPORTS CARTEL: THE NCAA[12]

The National Collegiate Athletic Association (NCAA) is an organization of nearly 800 colleges and universities and more than 100 related conferences (e.g., Big Ten, Atlantic Coast Conference, and Big East). Although membership in the NCAA is voluntary, schools must belong to the organization to participate in major intercollegiate sports competition and receive a share of the more than $1 billion in revenue generated annually by these activities. Many of the rules of the NCAA have the effect of reducing economic competition among member schools, thus increasing profits (or reducing losses) that schools realize from their athletic programs. The regulations have permitted the NCAA to act like a cartel, controlling to a certain degree both the revenues and costs of its member schools.

In the past, the NCAA negotiated contracts with the major television networks. These contracts limited the number of football games that could be televised each week as well as the number of times a school could appear on television each season. In 1984, however, the U.S. Supreme Court ruled that these restrictions on televised football games were an illegal conspiracy in violation of the Sherman Antitrust Act. This ruling has significantly increased the number of college football games televised on the networks and cable carriers and has reduced the average fees per game paid to the schools. Likewise, schools such as Notre Dame have increased their share of televised games (and revenues) at the expense of schools whose games draw lower television ratings.

Although the NCAA has lost much of its power to control television revenues, it still retains control over costs through restrictions on the compensation of student athletes. Scholarships granted to athletes are limited to tuition, room and board, and textbooks. Without this limitation, schools would undoubtedly compete openly to recruit top athletes by paying them additional money to play for their teams. Like professional athletes, the best student athletes would tend to receive the largest incomes. Under-the-table payments and other forms of cheating, which occur under the current NCAA rules, would tend to disappear. Recruiting scandals, such as the ones that led to the suspension of the football program at Southern Methodist University in 1986, would not occur.

Most economists argue that cartels raise prices, lower output, and are generally not beneficial to society. The effects on output and prices of explicit cartels, such as OPEC, are readily observable. The effects of a cartel such as the NCAA, which claims that its regulations are designed to protect student athletes and promote the financial stability of its members' athletic programs, are much more difficult to detect. Unless the courts rule that the NCAA's restraint on payments to athletes is an unlawful conspiracy, it is unlikely that the NCAA will change the present system.

THE INTERNATIONAL OIL PRODUCERS' CARTEL (OPEC)

The Organization of Petroleum Exporting Countries (OPEC) is a group of the major oil-producing nations.[13] OPEC was founded in 1960 by five large oil-producing countries that were experiencing declining oil revenues as a result of the pricing practices of the major

---

[12] Based on articles in *Business Week,* 14 September 1987, and *Wall Street Journal,* 20 August 1988 and 21 June 1991.

[13] Member countries include Algeria, Ecuador, Gabon, Iran, Iraq, Kuwait, Libya, Nigeria, Qatar, Saudi Arabia, United Arab Emirates, and Venezuela.

www ....
The Organization of
Petroleum Exporting
Countries (OPEC) is one of
the most famous
international cartels. Access
the OPEC Internet site at:
http://www.opec.org/

international oil companies who had organized in 1947 as ARAMCO, a joint venture for exploration and development of the Mideast oil fields. At that time the international oil companies, which produced and marketed a large percentage of the world's oil, set the price of oil and paid taxes and royalties to the governments of countries in which that oil was produced. Under the terms of the ARAMCO agreement, the host nations gradually purchased the oil field assets at pre-arranged terms, concluding their purchase in 1972.

Among OPEC's long-range goals, as set forth in a 1968 document, were that member governments should (1) determine oil prices and (2) own and control their oil resources directly.[14] This first goal was achieved by 1973, when the OPEC countries were able to increase oil prices unilaterally. During late 1973 and 1974, OPEC was able to achieve a fourfold increase in the price of petroleum from $3 to $12 per barrel. In 1975 OPEC produced 55 percent of the world's supply of oil and more than 80 percent of the oil traded on world markets. The second goal, that of government ownership and control, has been either partially or fully achieved in most OPEC countries through takeovers and nationalization of the oil companies' operations. The multinational integrated oil companies continue to be in charge of many of the technical aspects of production and to act as worldwide distributors of OPEC oil.

OPEC is a cartel in the sense that it sets prices for oil. Prices are set at regular meetings of the oil ministers from the OPEC countries. Saudi Arabia is the most influential member of OPEC because of the tremendous size of its production capacity—almost one-half of OPEC's total output. All pricing decisions are voted on by the oil ministers and are supposed to be unanimous; however, during the early 1980s, the OPEC members were unable to agree on a uniform price. The benchmark price of oil ranged from $32 to $36 per barrel among the various producing countries, with actual prices ranging from $32 to $41.[15] The conservative oil producers of the Persian Gulf (for example, Saudi Arabia and Kuwait), having large reserves expected to last well into the next century, attempted to hold prices at the low end of this range to retard the development of substitute fuels. Other countries with lesser petroleum reserves (such as Libya and Iran), along with Algeria, priced their oil at the high end of the range in an attempt to maximize their returns before their oil runs out.

Unlike many other cartels, OPEC had *not,* until recently, resorted to setting production quotas or allocating export shares among its members.[16] Despite this relatively limited amount of central direction and control, OPEC was effective in maintaining the market price of oil during the 1970s. However, during the 1980s, when OPEC's share of the world market output fell by almost one-third, both overt and covert price cutting occurred. Because of the world oil glut during this period (due in part to conservation by consuming nations, substitution of coal for oil, and increased production from such sources as the North Sea), OPEC countries were forced to cut their prices and output. Covert price cutting took several different forms.[17] Nigeria, for example, engaged in secret price cutting by reducing royalties and income taxes for the oil companies working there. Other forms of covert price reductions included bartering and extending payment terms for oil pur-

---

[14] See Dankwart A. Rustow and John F. Mugno, *OPEC: Success and Prospects* (New York: New York University Press, 1976), appendix C, for the full text of this document.

[15] The larger spread in actual prices compared with benchmark prices is due in part to differences in the quality of oil from various producing countries and their proximity to Western markets.

[16] Some OPEC members have individually set quotas on their own oil production to prevent geologically premature depletion or to preserve a vanishing economic asset for future generations. See J. Griffin and W. Xiong, "The Incentive to Cheat: An Empirical Analysis of OPEC," *Journal of Law and Economics,* Vol. 60, No. 2, 1997.

[17] *Wall Street Journal,* 8 September 1981 and "Why the Saudi's Won't Back Down Soon," 8 April 1986.

chases. Under a bartering agreement, Country *A* sells oil to Country *B* at a high price and agrees in return to purchase commodities from Country *B* at above-market, inflated prices. The net effect is that Country *B* actually pays less than the official price for the oil. Extending the payment period from the normal 15–30 days to 3–6 months reduces the effective cost of the oil to the buyer by reducing interest expenses on the funds required to finance the purchase.

During the early 1980s, Saudia Arabia supported oil prices by acting as a "swing producer," cutting its production to as low as 2 million barrels per day (from a high of 10 million barrels per day in 1980). This was less than one-half of its authorized quota of 4.35 million barrels per day. In October 1985, however, Saudia Arabia changed its policy and began increasing its output to as much as 6 million barrels per day—which was well in excess of its quota. The objectives of this policy change were as follows:

1. To increase their own oil revenues (for example, selling twice as many barrels at 30 percent less per barrel would still yield a revenue increase of 40 percent)

2. To encourage consumers worldwide to use more oil and to discourage substitutes

3. To discipline other oil-producing countries, such as Britain, Norway, and Mexico, by making them feel the consequences of falling oil revenues

4. To force competitors in the United States, Canada, Britain, and other countries to shut down their higher-cost oil wells

Over the long run, the Saudia Arabian policy was intended to increase demand for oil, reduce oil reserves and production capacity, and induce greater cooperation on pricing and output decisions among OPEC (as well as non-OPEC) producing countries. As a result of the increase in Saudia Arabia's oil output, prices fell to as low as $12 per barrel during this period. After many months of negotiations, OPEC members (excluding Iraq who refused to participate in OPEC's quota system) agreed in July 1986 to cut oil production significantly and adopted a target price of $18 per barrel. Saudia Arabia again became OPEC's swing producer through its willingness to reduce oil output in order to support the new fixed price.

During the last several years speculation has continued about an OPEC cartel collapse because of weak oil demand, surplus production capacity, rampant price and output quota cheating by member countries, and two wars among OPEC member states that resulted in widespread casualties and damage. OPEC now controls less than 30 percent of world oil output, and Venezuela has publicly challenged the role of Saudia Arabia as swing producer and price leader, especially in the Western hemisphere.[18] In spite of these problems, OPEC has managed to survive.

An awareness of cartel pricing practices is important to business managers for a number of reasons. As noted in some of the examples cited earlier, some industries operate legally as cartels. Also, as more firms become multinational in scope, they will be forced to make decisions in an environment where cartels are permitted. Finally, an understanding of explicit cartel price-output decisions furnishes a good deal of insight into the more common domestic practice of price leadership.

Price Leadership
A pricing strategy followed in many oligopolistic industries. One firm normally announces all new price changes. Either by an explicit or an implicit agreement, other firms in the industry regularly follow the pricing moves of the industry leader.

PRICE LEADERSHIP

Another model of price-output determination in some oligopolistic industries is **price leadership.** Many industries exhibit a pattern where one or a few firms normally set a price and others tend to follow, frequently with a time lag of a few days. The price

---

[18] *The Economist*, 16 March 1996, p. 68, and "Jump Start," *Wall Street Journal*, 14 August 1997.

www ....
Read a speech by the
Director of the Bureau of
Economics, Federal Trade
Commission, on horizontal
price fixing and price
leadership in cyberspace at
the following Internet site:
http://www.ftc.gov/
speeches/other/confbd4.
htm

pattern that is ultimately established depends very much on the degree to which products of the various firms are differentiated. In the case of basic steel products, for example, the price that finally prevails is generally uniform from one producer to another. For more differentiated products, such as automobiles, the uniform price may give way to a pricing structure among firms where recognizable differentials (within a limited range) may persist over time.

Effective price leadership exists when price movements initiated by the leader have a high probability of sticking and no maverick or nonconforming firms exist. The fewer the number of firms in the industry (that is, the greater the interdependencies of decision outcomes among firms), the more effective price leadership is likely to be. As the number of firms expands, the relative dominance of any one firm is likely to decline, as will the interdependencies that exist among firms in the industry. Just as in cartels or illegal explicit collusion, implicit price leadership agreements may break down over time, especially in the face of substantial shifts in demand or costs that the price leader fails to reflect adequately in its established price.

Two major price leadership patterns have been observed in various industries from time to time: These are *barometric* and *dominant price leadership.* Other price leadership models not discussed in this section are based on differential plant sizes, factor costs, technologies, and unequal market share conditions.

Barometric Price Leadership

In barometric price leadership, one firm announces a change in price that it hopes will be accepted by others. The leader need not be the largest firm in the industry. In fact, this leader may actually change from time to time. The leader must, however, be reasonably correct in its interpretation of changing demand and cost conditions so that suggested price changes will be accepted and stick. In essence, the barometric price leader merely initiates a reaction to changing market conditions that other firms find in their best interest to follow. These conditions might include such things as cost increases (or decreases) and sluggish (or brisk) sales accompanied by inventory buildups (or shortages) in the industry.

EXAMPLE

BAROMETRIC PRICE LEADERSHIP: AMERICAN AIRLINES AND CONTINENTAL AIRLINES

On 18 September 1989 American Airlines announced a fare increase beginning September 29 tied to the number of days tickets are purchased before departure—fourteen days $10 to $20, seven days $30 to $80, and two days $60 to $80.[19] On the following day, these fares appeared in the Airline Tariff Publishing Company's computerized database. The other major airlines soon followed American Airlines' lead and raised their fares by a similar amount. On September 20, Midway and TWA increased their fares in line with the new American Airlines fares. On September 21, Delta, Pan Am, and Continental posted identical increases. Then, over the next several days, United, Northwest, and US Airways matched the increases.

If other firms do not agree with the leader's assessment of market conditions and changing cost patterns, a series of higher or lower prices may be announced by competitors until general agreement (via trial-and-error or explicit collusion) on a new price range is reached by all firms.

---

[19] *Wall Street Journal,* 14 December 1989.

In April 1989 Continental Airlines proposed a price increase of between $20 and $80 on round-trip excursion fares beginning May 27.[20] Various carriers, including TWA, United, and Northwest, initially matched Continental's higher fares. However, the industry was divided when other airlines—namely, American, Delta, and US Airways—declined to go along with the price changes. Subsequent to this action, several airlines, including Northwest, which had followed Continental's lead, scrapped their previously announced increases. Continental was then forced to withdraw its proposed increase if it wanted to remain competitive with the other airlines. Various reasons were suggested for why the other airlines failed to go along with the Continental proposal, including weak demand for summer air travel (based on advance bookings), the desire by other airlines to put financial pressure on debt-burdened Continental (the airline eventually filed for bankruptcy protection in December 1990), and concerns expressed by government officials over rising fares and airline industry mergers.

Dominant Price Leadership

In the case of dominant price leadership, one firm establishes itself as the leader because of its larger size, customer loyalty, or lower cost structure in relation to other competing firms. The leader may then act as if it were a monopolist in its segment of the market, setting prices at a level that maximizes its profits (that is, where its marginal cost equals marginal revenue in that segment). In adopting this strategy, however, the leader must be reasonably certain that other firms will respond to the price change by bringing their prices in line with those of the leader.

What is the incentive for followers to accept the established price? In some cases it may be a fear of cutthroat retaliation from a low-cost dominant firm that keeps smaller firms from attempting to undercut the prevailing price. In other cases, following a price leader may be viewed as simply a convenience resulting in an accepted pattern of price leadership and followership that may operate as effectively as a formal cartel. This poses significant antitrust problems because no explicit, illegal collusion is apparent, even though the performance of the industry closely parallels what would prevail if explicit and illegal collusion had taken place.

The price-output solution for the dominant-firm model is shown in Figure 15.2. D_T shows total market demand for the product, MC_L represents the marginal cost curve for the dominant (leader) firm, and ΣMC_F constitutes the horizontal *summation* of the marginal cost curves for the follower firms, each of which may well have costs higher than MC_L. In the following analysis, *assume that the dominant firm sets the price knowing that follower firms will sell as much output as they wish at this price. The dominant firm then supplies the remainder of the market demand; i.e., the residual demand in the dominant firm's segment of the market.*

Given that the follower firms can sell as much output as they wish at the price established by the dominant firm, they are faced with a horizontal demand curve and a perfectly competitive market situation. The follower firms view the dominant firm's price as their marginal revenue and, desiring to maximize profits, produce that level of output where their marginal cost equals the established price. The ΣMC_F curve therefore shows the total output that will be *supplied* at various prices by the follower firms. The dominant firm's residual demand curve D_L is obtained by subtracting the amount supplied by the follower firms ΣMC_F from the total market demand D_T at each price. For

---

FIGURE   15.2

Dominant Price
Leadership

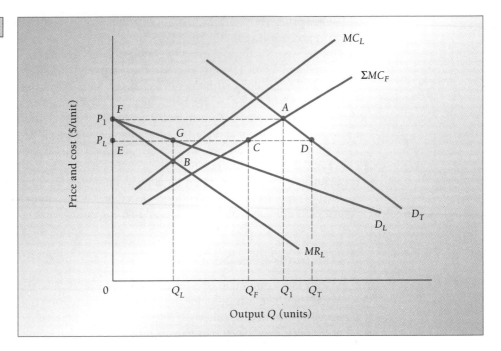

example, at a price of P_L, point G on the D_L curve is obtained by subtracting EC from ED. Other points on the D_L curve are obtained in a similar manner. At a price of P_1 the quantity supplied by the follower firms Q_1 is equal to total market demand (point A) and the dominant firm's residual demand is therefore zero (point F). The dominant firm's marginal revenue curve MR_L is then obtained from its residual demand curve D_L.

The dominant firm maximizes its profits by setting price and output where marginal cost equals marginal revenue. As shown in Figure 15.2, $MR_L = MC_L$ at point B. Therefore, the dominant firm should sell Q_L units of output at a price of P_L per unit. At a price of P_L, total demand is Q_T units, and the follower firms supply $Q_T - Q_L$ units of output.

The following two examples illustrate the application of these concepts. The first example examines Intel's dominant price leadership position in the microprocessor market, and the second one involves the algebraic determination of a dominant price leader's optimal output and selling price.

EXAMPLE

DOMINANT PRICE LEADERSHIP: INTEL

Intel makes microprocessor chips, which are the "brains" of many IBM-compatible personal computers sold by Compaq, Packard Bell, and other computer companies. In the mid-1980s Intel developed a chip called the 80386 (also known as the "386"). For approximately five years, until early 1991, the company was the sole supplier (i.e., 100 percent market share) of this chip. Intel's monopoly was broken when Advanced Micro Devices (AMD) developed a clone of the 386 chip (i.e., a microprocessor chip that performs all the functions of the original chip) and began selling them to computer manufacturers. AMD's share of the market for these chips in 1991 was in the range of 12 percent.[21] Early in 1992 Intel cut the price of its 386 chips from $152 to $99. In addition to stimulating demand, part of the reason for the price cut was to remain the dominant player

---

[21] *Business Week*, 15 April 1991, pp. 69–70, and *Wall Street Journal*, 8 January 1992, p. A3.

in the market for these chips, while attempting to get personal computer manufacturers to build more computers using Intel's faster and more profitable 486 microprocessor chip. Based on its dominant position in the microprocessor market, Intel, in effect, set the price for the 386 chips and let AMD sell as many of its clones as it could at the established price.

EXAMPLE

PRICE LEADERSHIP: AEROTEK

Aerotek and six other smaller companies produce an electronic component used in small planes. Aerotek (L) is the price leader. The other [follower (F)] firms sell the component at the same price as Aerotek. Aerotek permits the other firms to sell as many units of the component as they wish at the established price. The company supplies the remainder of the demand itself. Total demand for the component is given by the following function:

$$P = 10,000 - 10Q_T \qquad\qquad [15.14]$$

where

$$Q_T = Q_L + Q_F \qquad\qquad [15.15]$$

that is, total output (Q_T) is the sum of the leader's (Q_L) and followers' (Q_F) output. Aerotek's marginal cost function is

$$MC_L = 100 + 3Q_L \qquad\qquad [15.16]$$

The aggregate marginal cost function for the other six producers of the component is

$$\Sigma MC_F = 50 + 2Q_F \qquad\qquad [15.17]$$

We are interested in determining the output for Aerotek and the follower firms and the selling price for the component given that the firms are interested in maximizing profits.

Aerotek's profit-maximizing output is found at the point where

$$MR_L = MC_L \qquad\qquad [15.18]$$

Its marginal revenue function (MR_L) is obtained by differentiating the firm's total revenue function (TR_L) with respect to Q_L. Total revenue (TR_L) is given by the following expression:

$$TR_L = P \cdot Q_L \qquad\qquad [15.19]$$

Q_L is obtained from Equation 15.15:

$$Q_L = Q_T - Q_F \qquad\qquad [15.20]$$

Using Equation 15.14, one can solve for Q_T:

$$Q_T = 1,000 - .10P \qquad\qquad [15.21]$$

To find Q_F we note that Aerotek lets the follower firms sell as much output (i.e., components) as they wish at the given price (P). Therefore the follower firms are faced with a horizontal demand function. Hence

$$MR_F = P \qquad\qquad [15.22]$$

To maximize profits, the follower firms will operate where

$$MR_F = \Sigma MC_F \qquad\qquad [15.23]$$

Substituting Equations 15.22 and 15.17 into Equation 15.23 gives

$$P = 50 + 2Q_F \qquad [15.24]$$

Solving this equation for Q_F yields

$$Q_F = .50P - 25 \qquad [15.25]$$

Substituting Equation 15.21 for Q_T and Equation 15.25 for Q_F in Equation 15.20 gives

$$Q_L = (1,000 - .10P) - (.50P - 25)$$

$$= 1,025 - .60P \qquad [15.26]$$

Solving Equation 15.26 for P, one obtains

$$P = 1,708.3333 - 1.6667Q_L \qquad [15.27]$$

Substituting this expression for P in Equation 15.19 gives

$$TR_L = (1,708.3333 - 1.6667Q_L)Q_L$$

$$= 1,708.3333Q_L - 1.6667Q_L^2 \qquad [15.28]$$

Differentiating this expression with respect to Q_L, one obtains Aerotek's marginal revenue function:

$$MR_L = \frac{d(TR_L)}{dQ_L}$$

$$= 1,708.3333 - 3.3334Q_L \qquad [15.29]$$

Substituting Equation 15.29 for MR_L and Equation 15.16 for MC_L in Equation 15.18 gives the following optimality condition:

$$1,708.3333 - 3.3334Q_L^* = 100 + 3Q_L^* \qquad [15.30]$$

Solving this equation for Q_L^* yields

$$Q_L^* = 253.945 \text{ units}$$

or an optimal output for Aerotek of 253.9 units of the component. Substituting this value of Q_L into Equation 15.27 gives

$$P^* = 1,708.3333 - 1.6667 (253.945)$$

$$= \$1,285.083$$

or an optimal selling price of $1,285.08. The optimal output for the follower firms is found by substituting this value of P into Equation 15.25:

$$Q_F^* = .50 (1,285.083) - 25$$

$$= 617.542 \text{ units}$$

or an optimal output of 617.5 units.

THE KINKED DEMAND CURVE MODEL

One very popular model of oligopoly price-output behavior, is Paul Sweezy's *kinked demand curve* model. This model sought to explain rigidities observed in prices in oligopolistic industries. For instance, the price of steel rails had remained at $28 per ton between 1901 and 1916 and at $43 per ton between 1922 and 1933. Similarly, the price of sulphur remained at $18 per ton between 1926 and 1938, except for changes of 2 cents and 3 cents a ton in two of those years.[22]

Sweezy assumed that if an oligopolist cut its prices, competitors would quickly feel the decline in their sales and would be forced to match the price reduction. Alternatively, if one firm raised its prices, competitors would rapidly gain customers by maintaining their original prices and hence would have little or no motivation to match a price increase. In a situation such as this, the demand curve facing an individual oligopolist would be far more elastic for price increases than for price decreases. If a firm *raises* its price and others do not follow, the increase in price will be more than offset by the decrease in sales, and total revenue received will decline. A price *reduction* that is matched by competitors would not be sufficiently offset by an increase in sales. Consequently, the total revenue received by each firm after the price reduction would be less than its original receipts. This is illustrated in Figure 15.3.

The oligopolist's demand curve is represented by DKD', with the prevailing price as P and output as Q. The marginal revenue curve is discontinuous because of the kink in the demand curve at K. Hence marginal revenue is represented by the two line segments MRX and $MR'Y$. If the marginal cost curve MC passes through the gap XY in the marginal revenue curve, the most profitable alternative is to maintain the current price-output policy.[23] The profit-maximizing level of price and output remains constant for the firm, which perceives itself to be faced with a kinked demand curve, even though costs may change over a rather wide range (for example, MC_2 and MC_1). Similarly, shifts in the demand curve either to the right (an increase in demand) or to the

---

[22] Marshall R. Colberg, William C. Bradford, and Richard M. Alt, *Business Economics: Principles and Cases,* rev. ed. (Homewood, Ill.: Richard D. Irwin, 1957), p. 276.

[23] Profit may not be increased by increasing price (and decreasing output), because $MR > MC$, and this difference would increase with a price increase. Similarly, profit may not be increased by decreasing price (and increasing output), because $MR < MC$, and this difference would also increase with a price decrease.

FIGURE   15.3

The Kinked Demand
Curve Model

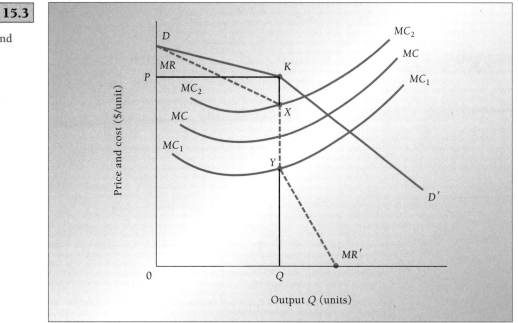

Output Q (units)

left (a decrease in demand) may not change the price decisions of the firm. Because the kink is determined at the *prevailing price,* a shift in demand shifts the gap *XY* in the marginal revenue curve to the right or left.[24] If *MC* still passes through the gap, the prevailing price is maintained, although output will either increase or decrease.

A number of criticisms have been made of the kinked demand curve model as a general model of oligopoly behavior. Although the model does provide a theoretical explanation for why stable prices have been observed to exist in some oligopolistic industries, it takes the prevailing price as given and offers no justification for why that price level rather than some other is the prevailing price. For this reason alone, the kinked demand model of oligopolistic pricing must be viewed as incomplete. Stigler has tested the kinked demand model empirically on seven oligopolies.[25] He found that oligopolistic rivals are just as likely to follow price increases as price decreases, indicating little empirical support for the kinked demand curve. Nevertheless, as Cohen and Cyert have suggested,[26] although the empirical evidence of Stigler indicates the theory may have little credence as a long-run explanation of oligopoly pricing, it may be a valid explanation of the way firms behave when they have little or no knowledge of how competitors will react to price changes. The cases of a new industry in its early stages of development and of an industry in which new rivals enter the market are cited by Cohen and Cyert as instances where the kinked demand model is likely to furnish a satisfactory description of pricing behavior in the short run. But as firms learn what responses to expect from their competitors and as information sources become better developed in the industry, the perceived kink in the demand curve is likely to vanish. In that case, price stability will break down when cost changes or demand shifts occur.

Both the ready-to-eat (RTE) cereal and cigarette industries have recently experienced price wars. In each case, the catalyst for the price war was the fast rising market share of generic products in what had previously been a heavily branded category. In the last decade, generic cigarettes (e.g., a brand named appropriately "Basic") have taken substantial market share from premium brands like Marlboro, Winston, Merit, and Salem. Similarly in RTE cereals, Ralston supplies many grocery store chains with private label cereals (e.g., Kroger Raisin Bran) that sell at price points 30 percent less than the premium brands. The market share of these private label storebrands has grown rapidly capturing 9.7 percent of the market in 1995 relative to only 5.4 percent in 1990.

EXAMPLE	## PRICE WARS AT KELLOGG AND PHILIP MORRIS[27]

In both cereals and cigarettes, the price cut that triggered a price war was a full $1 off. This amount represented a 19 percent price discount on the $4.80 average price for a full-size box of RTE cereal, and a whopping 33 percent discount off the $2.99 average price per pack of premium brand cigarettes. In cigarettes, the 1992 price war was started by the price leader, Philip Morris, who controls a 47 percent market share. The 1995

---

[24] The gap actually can shift down or up as well as to the left or right if there is a parallel (as opposed to proportional) shift in demand.

[25] George J. Stigler, "The Kinky Oligopoly Demand Curve and Rigid Prices," *Journal of Political Economy* 55 (1947), pp. 432–449. See also George J. Stigler, "The Literature of Economics: The Case of the Kinked Oligopoly Demand Curve," *Economic Inquiry* (April 1978), pp. 185–204.

[26] Kalman Cohen and Richard Cyert, *Theory of the Firm: Resource Allocation in a Market Economy* (Englewood Cliffs, N.J.: Prentice-Hall, 1965), pp. 251–254.

[27] Based on "Denial in Battle Creek," *Forbes,* 7 October 1996, "Cereal Thriller," *The Economist,* 15 June 1996, and P. Cummins, "Cereal Firms in Cost-Price Squeeze," Reuters News Service, 15 May 1996.

price war in cereals was started by Post Cereals, the distant third player in the industry with a 15 percent market share. At the same time, Quaker Oats with a 7 percent market share began selling branded cereals like Cap'n Crunch and Life in large "value-priced" bags for $3.50. Post had carefully analyzed the tactical situation and decided it could better maintain regular customers and compete for price-sensitive new customers if Kellogg and General Mills reduced advertising in response to a massive industrywide price cut.

General Mills was experiencing a slowly eroding 25 percent market share, while Kellogg faced a rapidly declining 35 percent market share. As recently as 1988, Kellogg had controlled 41 percent of the market. Every share point in the U.S. ready-to-eat cereal industry is worth $80 million in sales. In part because of a panic-stricken determination to arrest the erosion of their market shares, both Kellogg and General Mills quickly decided to match the Post price cut. Full-size boxes of branded products like General Mills' Wheaties and Kellogg's Frosted Flakes were cut in price from $4.80 to $3.88. Just as Post had predicted, each of the leading firms then scaled back their advertising campaigns. And cereals like Post Raisin Bran and Post Grape Nuts gained share rapidly.

In contrast, in cigarettes the motives for the price war were more benign. Philip Morris's largest competitor, R.J. Reynolds, had undergone a leverage buyout (LBO) 5 years earlier. Reynolds was much less strapped for cash at the time of the price war than they had been at the time of the LBO. If Philip Morris had intended by its $1 price cut to ruin its competitor financially, 1987 would have been a better time to do it. In 1987, fully 97 percent of the Reynolds company's projected future cash flow was committed to debt repayments. By 1992, the accelerated early paydown of the debt repayment schedule had brought the debt commitment at Reynolds down to 64 percent of the expected cash flow. Instead, Philip Morris appears to have become persuaded that; at the all-time-high price of $3 per pack, the heavy smoker who quit had $50 per week expenditure with which to buy many attractive substitutes. Health clubs with smoker cessation programs seldom cost that much.

Avoiding Price Wars

Knowing how to avoid a price war has become a critical success factor for many high-margin businesses in tight oligopolistic groups. Recall from our discussion of the intensity of rivalry in Chapter 14 that the higher the margin, the more tempted companies are to employ price discounting to increase incremental sales. Because each additional sale imposes few additional costs, high margins encourage price discounting to gain market share. So building a business plan or adopting a strategy that reduces the power of substitutes, entrants, buyers, and suppliers and thereby generates high profit margins is no guarantee of success. To sustain profitability, managers also must avoid the gainshare discounting that would otherwise permeate the tactics in a high-margin business.

One key to avoiding price wars in tight oligopolies is to recognize the ongoing nature of the pricing rivalry and attempt to mitigate the intensity of the price competition by growing the market. United Airlines cannot hope to get rid of American Airlines. Kodak foresees a perpetual rivalry with Fuji Film. And Pepsi is stuck with Coke. Consequently, each rival must anticipate retaliation for aggressive discounting designed to attract away the other company's regular customers. Better to maintain high prices and expect your rivals to do the same. Then, each company can focus on opening new markets and selling more volume to established customers. Coke Classic's regular customer consumes an average of six servings per day. In the last 5 years, Coke has introduced dozens of new soft drinks to countries throughout the world. As a result, the concentrate syrup has never been discounted in 80 years.

Customer segmentation with differential pricing is another way to avoid price wars. If low-cost new entrants attack a major airline, one effective response that avoids initiating a price war with other major carriers involves matching prices to a very targeted customer segment and then carefully controlling how much capacity is released for sale to that segment. "Fencing" restrictions like 10-day advance-purchase requirements and Saturday night stay-overs prove crucial in segmenting the price-sensitive discretionary traveler from the regular business expense-account customer. The incumbent carriers can "meet the competition" in these restricted fare classes while reserving sufficient capacity for those who desire to pay for the reliability, convenience, and change order responsiveness of business class and full-coach seats. And most importantly, the incumbent's established competitors can maintain high prices on unaffected departures, segments, and routes. In Appendix 17A, we discuss how yield management techniques can help accomplish these goals.

Another way to avoid or at least mitigate the effects of price wars is to differentiate and innovate. In the 1980s and early 1990s, Interlink sold replacement hypodermic syringes by the thousands to hospitals for 10 cents per syringe. Each time a catheter was changed, a new hypodermic syringe would be inserted into the patient's vein. A Japanese company entered the market with an identical product for 3 cents each. Interlink promptly introduced a replacement device that only needs insertion one time; that is, any new saline or pharmaceutical drip lines can be hooked directly to an Interlink syringe device that need not be removed and replaced. This new process reduces the risk of patient infection and the inherent hazard to the nursing staff of exposure to patient blood. Interlink again dominates the market, and prices have stabilized at high levels.

<table>
<tr><td>EXAMPLE</td></tr>
</table>

NONPRICE TACTICS IN A PRICE WAR: KELLOGG[28]

Kellogg has the strongest brands in the cereals industry with 12 of the 15 top-selling cereals. Rather than match Post's price cuts in 1995, Kellogg might have poured not two but three scoops of raisins into every box of Kellogg's Raisin Bran. In the first two months after the price cuts by Post and General Mills, Kellogg lost three share points (from 35 percent to 32 percent) and Post gained four (from 16 percent to 20 percent). At $80 million per share point and 55 percent average margins, Kellogg's contributions on the lost sales totaled $132 million ($-3 \times \$80$ million $\times 0.55$). To retrieve that operating profit, Kellogg slashed prices 19 percent on two-thirds of its brands sacrificing $305 million ($-0.19 \times \$2.4$ billion sales $\times 0.66$).

Within two years, Kellogg had recaptured its 35 percent share. Nevertheless, many observers have wondered whether expending $305 million a year for two years on product innovation or on advertising would have accomplished even more.

Perhaps the best way to avoid a price war in a small oligopolistic rivalry group is to not start one in the first place. If someone else does start a price war, often the best response is simply to match the competition and then accentuate nonprice elements of the marketing mix by increasing services or advertising brands. Rather than furthering the downward price spiral, Reynolds matched the Philip Morris price cut on its premium brands, Winston and Salem, and ignored the discounting elsewhere. Kellogg matched the Post price cut on only two-thirds of its premium brands. Two years later, cereal prices in the all-important grocery store distribution channel have begun to return to their 1995 levels prior to the price war.

---

[28] Based on "Cereal Thriller," *The Economist,* 15 June 1996.

A final key to avoiding price wars is to recognize the tactical insights often available from game-theoretic analysis of various actions. With effective competitor surveillance to identify a rival's payoffs, the respone of a competitor to one's own price cuts is often predictable based on unilateral self-interest. In other circumstances, cooperative high-price outcomes may emerge from a convergence of mutual interest. In addition, simply recognizing the detailed structure of the pricing "game" can be a first step toward modifying the competitive environment to increase profitability. In the next section and the following chapter, we present game-theoretic techniques that have proven very useful for generating managerial insights in real-world decision making.

OLIGOPOLISTIC RIVALRY AND GAME THEORY

www . . . .
Learn more about game theory at Al Roth's game theory and experimental economics Internet site: http://www.pitt.edu/ ~alroth/alroth.html

Most oligopolistic competition takes place today in product-line submarkets between a few rival incumbents, each with some market power over price. Consider Bayer Aspirin, Bufferin, Excedrin, and St. Joseph's in pain relievers; Pepsi and Coke in colas; Six Flags and Disney in theme parks; and United, Delta, US Airways, and American in air travel to Florida. Smaller competitors selling generic products are often present in fringe markets, but what distinguishes these oligopolists is the presence of some brand name or other barrier to effective entry. A small number of well-established, profitable, and highly interdependent incumbents is often the result. This oligopolistic market structure leads to some quite different forms of competition than we have previously encountered.

Recall that in a competitive industry, such as tract home building or video rentals, each competitor can and must act independently. Each atomistic competitor takes price as "given," that is, determined externally in the open market, because any decision to expand or embargo his or her own supply has no appreciable effect on the industry supply. Even if one firm were to purchase all the video rental outlets in a community, the barriers to entry are so low that any price above cost will surely attract enough new competitors to restore the price-taking equilibrium. In contrast, each firm in an oligopolistic market must pay very close attention to the moves and countermoves of its rivals, and often fiercely defends its market share. Ultimately, competitor surveillance is important in all market structures because quickly adaptive behavior is preferable to reactive behavior. But the intense interdependence of oligopolistic rivalry makes proactive behavior best of all. Each oligopolist must try to predict well in advance the actions, responses, and counterresponses of all rivals and then choose optimal strategies accordingly. Modern **game theory** was invented for precisely this purpose.[29]

Game Theory
A mathematical theory of decision making by the participants in a conflict-of-interest situation.

A Conceptual Framework for Game-Theoretic Analysis

A general definition of a **strategy game** is any consciously interdependent choice behavior by purposeful individuals or hierarchical groups who share a common goal (e.g., tribes, amateur sports teams, or value-maximizing companies). As such, strategy games have always been a part of human endeavors from the very beginnings of prehistory. Some of the earliest formal analyses of strategy games involve voting games, bargaining games, and games of defense. Pliny the Younger, a first-century historian, records the pivotal role of strategic voting in the trial of a Roman senator, whose suicide was assisted

Strategy Game
A decision-making situation with consciously interdependent behavior between two or more of the participants.

[29] Two useful volumes on game theory are R. Duncan Luce and Howard Raiffa, *Games and Decisions* (New York: John Wiley, 1957), and Eric Rasmussen, *Games and Information*, 2d ed. (Cambridge, Mass: Basil Blackwell, 1993).

by several freedmen. The accused preferred death to banishment and almost won acquittal despite a majority in favor of the conviction. Only by strategically voting a second-choice punishment of banishment, did those senators in favor of execution prevent a minority control of the agenda from obtaining the acquittal.

Another example suggests that private property rights for one's personal effects evolved from a strategy game in which prehistoric tribes of hunter-gathers had to decide between guarding consolidated property or marauding against targets of opportunity. The private property consolidators won out; let's see why. In Table 15.3 two competing players (Randle and Kahn) compete for resources by selecting between two actions: Maraude, which occasionally yields unguarded windfall treasures, but leaves one's own possessions vulnerable to counterattack; or Guard, which frees time between defensive struggles for consolidating and multiplying the fruits of one's labors. Kahn has a tactical advantage against anything but strongly guarded positions, but knows too little about defense to be effective in guarding against attack. However, no matter what action Kahn decides to take, an examination of the payoff matrix in Figure 15.3 reveals Randle is always better off selecting Guard. Guard is a **dominant strategy** for Randle in that Randle's outcomes from Guard exceed the outcomes from any alternative strategy, independent of the opponent's behavior. Knowing this or discovering it through trial and error, Kahn predicts his rival Randle will continue to Guard. On that condition, Kahn then prefers Guard himself. {Guard, Guard} therefore emerges as the strategic equilibrium—i.e., a *dominant strategy equilibrium.*

Dominant Strategy
An action rule that maximizes the decision-maker's welfare independent of the actions of other players.

Components of a Game

The essential elements of all strategy games are present in the above example and include: players, actions, information sets, payoffs, an order of play, focal outcomes of interest, strategies, and equilibrium strategies. Let's illustrate with another example taken this time from service quality competition. Suppose two *players*, Xerox and Sharp, must choose whether to discontinue copier repair service that is seven territories removed from their respective regional headquarters located in two different East Coast cities 300 miles apart. Six or seven territories of full service repair are the *actions*. The *payoffs* from the decisions, which must be announced simultaneously at next week's industrial trade show, are shown in Table 15.4. This payoff matrix is the **normal form of the game,** which is an appropriate way of representing any simultaneous-play (versus sequential-play) game.

Normal Form of the Game
A representation of payoffs in a simultaneous-play game.

Sharp finds that full service repair on demand in the more distant seventh territory is very expensive. Cutting back to six territories reduces cost by $15 per week per customer and raises Sharp's profit from $55 to $70 when Xerox also cuts back and from $45 to $60 when Xerox does not. The improved effectiveness of Sharp's service in the remaining six territories lowers the prices rival Xerox can charge and reduces its profit

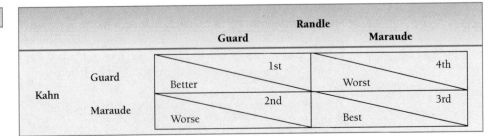

TABLE   15.3

Privitization of Personal Effects

		Randle		
		Guard		Maraude
Kahn	Guard	Better / 1st		Worst / 4th
	Maraude	Worse / 2nd		Best / 3rd

Notes: Randle ranks outcomes from 1st to 4th. Kahn ranks outcomes from best to worst.

<table>
<tr><td rowspan="2" colspan="2"></td><td colspan="2">Sharp</td></tr>
</table>

TABLE   15.4

Six or Seven Territories?

		Sharp	
		Six Territories	**Seven Territories**
Xerox	**Six Territories**	$40 \ $70	$35 \ $55
	Seven Territories	$30 \ $60	$45 \ $45

Notes: Payoffs are profits. Sharp payoffs are above the diagonal, and Xerox payoffs are below the diagonal.

from an initial $45 down to only $30 should Xerox continue servicing all seven territories. By cutting back to six territories itself, Xerox can restrict its losses to just $5 ($45 now to $40). The common *information set* known to both players includes knowledge of all these effects.

What strategy should Xerox adopt? First, using the concept of *dominant strategy* it is clear that Sharp will discontinue service in the seventh territory. Sharp is better off cutting back to six territories independent of what Xerox does. For Sharp, seven territories is *dominated* (unambiguously less preferred than six territories). Xerox wishes it were not so, because its most successful operation entails head-to-head, seven-territory competition against Sharp. Nevertheless, predictable reality lies elsewhere, and Xerox must predict six-territory behavior on the part of its rival and proceed to reexamine its remaining options. Having eliminated Sharp's dominated strategy in the second column, Xerox now has an unambiguously preferred *strategy* of providing full service repairs in only six territories itself. {Six, Six} is therefore the *equilibrium strategy* pair. That is, by applying the concept of a dominant strategy equilibrium to the prediction of its rival's behavior, Xerox can iterate back to analyze its own best action. {Six, Six} is therefore referred to as an **iterated dominant strategy** equilibrium.

Iterated Dominant Strategy
An action rule that maximizes self-interest in light of the predictable dominant-strategy behavior of other players.

The strategic equilibrium concept of eliminating dominated strategies in simultaneous games first appeared in *The Theory of Games and Economic Behavior* (1944) by John von Neumann and Oskar Morgenstern. Von Neumann and Morgenstern confined their analysis primarily to cooperative games, in which players can form coalitions, arrange side payments, and enter into binding agreements. John Nash, Reinhard Selten, and John Harsanyi won the 1994 Nobel Prize in economics for their extension of strategic equilibrium concepts to noncooperative games, sequential games, and games of imperfect information.

EXAMPLE

WWW . . . .
Read more about Harsanyi, Nash, and Selten at the Nobel Prize Internet Archive:
http://www.almaz.com/ nobel/economics/1994a. html

NOBEL GOES TO THREE GAME THEORISTS

Nash, Selten, and Harsanyi won the 1994 Nobel Prize for their work on equilibrium strategies in sequential games ranging from chess and poker to central bank interventions, research and development competitions, and the auctioning of the radio magnetic spectrum. Not infrequently, multiple equilibria arise in such games—e.g., when either duopoly competitor will initiate price cuts and find the other party will only match, but not discount further. Another implication of their work is that the order of play can have determinate effects on strategic decisions. Moving first in a preemptive product development can often foreclose a later competitor's threatened entry. In other circumstances, making the last response in the endgame, as dynamic technology changes to a new direction, can secure a strategic advantage. In addition, under incomplete information about opponent types, behaving like a "crazy" firm, who predatorily prices below cost when there is no later chance of recovering the losses, may deter an opponent's entry. Distinguishing between these and other complex paths to the most profitable strategy is the role of equilibrium strategies.

Cooperative and Noncooperative Games

The fact that in a *cooperative game* players can form coalitions, make side payments, and communicate to one another their private information about their own prices, profit margins, or variable costs has limited the usefulness of cooperative game theory in business settings. An illustration of a side payment in cooperative games is the mandatory compensation scheme a manufacturer might impose when one sales representative violates another's exclusive territory. Or, suppose in the previous Xerox and Sharp example that the two firms got together to arrange a side payment for Sharp that would ensure a strategic equilibrium of {Seven, Seven}. Also in cooperative games, a cartel might decide to enter into binding (i.e., third-party enforceable) contracts to segment the demander nations involved in a global diamond, coal, or coffee market. As you may already suspect, most such cooperative game agreements between arms-length competitors to exchange price information or arrange side payments are per se violations of the antitrust laws in the United States and Western Europe.[30] For these reasons, business strategists paid relatively little attention to game theory until noncooperative strategic equilibrium concepts were developed.

Noncooperative games prohibit collusive communication, side payment schemes, and third-party enforceable binding agreements. Instead, such games focus on self-enforcing reliance relationships to characterize strategic equilibrium and predict rival response. One example we have already encountered in Chapter 13 is the mutual reliance between sellers with nonredeployable assets and buyers of high-priced experience goods. Other examples include computer companies who build operating systems to a common standard that can communicate across PC platforms or competing airlines who announce high fares day after day despite the quick but short-lived attraction of breaking out as a renegade discounter. Clearly, these noncooperative games differ from cooperative games in important ways that make them more applicable to business strategy. Chapter 16 is devoted to an analysis of noncooperative games, with particular attention given to sequential equilibrium concepts such as first-mover/second-mover advantages and credible threats/credible commitments.

Other Types of Games

Games are also classified according to the number of players involved, the compatibility of their interests, and the number of replays of the game. We analyzed both the above games as *single-period ("one-shot") games*. Clearly, however, the ongoing rivalry between the players in "Guarder-Marauder" and in "Six or Seven Territories" is highly pertinent to the strategic situation. In the next chapter, we turn our attention to the distinct and somewhat paradoxical implications of so-called *repeated games*. In a *two-person game*, each player attempts to obtain as much as possible from the other player through whatever methods of cooperation, bargaining, or threatening are available. *n-person games* are

---

[30] For example, the antitrust opinions in U.S. v. National Gypsum, 428 U.S. 422 (1978) and U.S. v. Airline Tariff Publishing Co., et al., 92-52854 (1992) expressly prohibited the exchange of preannouncement price lists between competitors.

more difficult to analyze because subsets of players can form coalitions to impose solutions on the rest of the players. Coalitions can be of any size and can break up and reform as the game proceeds. Parliamentary government is the classic example of *n*-person games. Although the possibility of coalitions adds greatly to the richness of the types of situations that can be considered by game theory, coalition-proofness is an equilibrium concept that adds complexity to the theory required to analyze such games.

In a *two-person zero-sum game,* the players have exactly opposite interests; one player's gain is the other player's loss and vice versa. "Guarder-Marauder" serves as an intuitive example. Although a number of parlor games and some military applications can be analyzed with zero-sum games, the great preponderance of real-life conflict-of-interest situations do not fit within this model. In contrast, in a *two-person non-zero-sum game,* both players may gain or lose depending on the actions each chooses to take. "Six or Seven Territories" is a non-zero-sum game; limiting competition to six territories raises the total profit from the interaction to $110 rather than $90. In all such games at least one outcome is jointly preferred, and consequently, the players may be able to increase their payoffs through some form of cooperation. Perhaps the most famous generic structure for non-zero-sum games is the *Prisoner's Dilemma.* Many real-world conflict-of-interest situations, such as duopoly pricing between Pepsi and Coke, experience good purchase transactions, urban renewal decisions among adjacent landowners, and bargaining policy with terrorists, can be represented as a Prisoner's Dilemma game.

In a Prisoner's Dilemma, two suspects are accused of jointly committing a crime.[31] To convict the suspects, however, a confession is needed from one or both of them. They are separated such that no information can pass between them, so this is a noncooperative game. If neither suspect confesses, the prosecutor will be unable to convict them of the crime and each suspect will receive only a short-term (1-year) prison sentence. If one suspect confesses (that is, turns state's evidence) and the other does not, then the one confessing will receive a suspended sentence and the other will receive a long-term (15-year) prison sentence. If both suspects confess, then each will receive an intermediate-term (6-year) prison sentence. Each suspect must decide, under these conditions, whether or not to confess. This conflict-of-interest situation can be represented in a game matrix such as the one shown in Table 15.5.

This game can be examined by using the concept of a security level, or minimum payoff. For Suspect 1, the minimum payoff of the two alternative actions "Not Confess" and

---

[31] This example is discussed in more detail in Luce and Raiffa, *Games and Decisions,* section 5.4.

TABLE   15.5

Prisoner's Dilemma Payoff Matrix

		Suspect 2	
		Not Confess	**Confess**
Suspect 1	**Not Confess**	One-year prison term for each suspect	Fifteen-year prison term for Suspect 1; suspended sentence for Suspect 2
	Confess	Suspended sentence for Suspect 1; fifteen-year prison term for Suspect 2	Six-year prison term for each suspect

"Confess" are a 15-year and a 6-year prison sentence, respectively. The maximization of his security level would therefore motivate Suspect 1 to choose the second alternative action by confessing. Similar reasoning holds true for Suspect 2, and she also would be motivated to choose the alternative of confessing her guilt. Thus, the second alternative for each player (that is, "Confess") dominates the other strategy (that is, "Not Confess") and constitutes an equilibrium strategy pair and, in this sense, represents the solution of the game. A dominant strategy is one that provides a player with a larger payoff, regardless of what strategy the other player chooses. In this game both suspects would clearly receive a larger payoff (that is, a shorter sentence) if they both would decide to choose their first alternatives ("Not Confess"). However, in seeking to maximize their predictable payoffs (or, more accurately, to maximize their security levels), the first alternative is not a rational choice for either suspect.

As discussed above, in cooperative games the players have complete freedom of communication with the opportunity to make threats and enter into binding and third-party enforceable agreements. Examining the Prisoner's Dilemma game again, assume that the two players (that is, suspects) are able to communicate with each other and are able to enter into a binding agreement on which strategy each player will choose. In this case, because the cooperative outcome associated with both suspects not confessing is preferred to the noncooperative solution, the suspects would have an incentive to enter into a binding agreement for each to choose the strategy of not confessing. Without strong legal or moral sanctions to force the suspects to adhere to the agreement, however, each suspect would be tempted to double-cross the other suspect by confessing his or her guilt. The suspect that breaks the agreement has the possibility of reducing his or her sentence from a six-year prison term to a suspended sentence, as can be seen in Table 15.5. In a cooperative game, however, all such agreements are binding and enforceable.

The analogy to pricing and output decisions among firms in oligopolistic industries is striking. In some instances, cooperation may take the form of price leadership, where one firm takes on the role of price leader and the other firms act as followers. In other instances, the firms may enter into illegal price-fixing agreements and form a cartel. However, just as each of the suspects in the Prisoner's Dilemma game has an incentive to double-cross the other suspect, firms in oligopolistic industries have an incentive to depart from agreed-upon prices or output quotas in any price-fixing agreement. As a result, these price-fixing agreements often break down quickly as one (or more) of the firms attempt to increase its (their) profits through secret price reductions to customers.[32] The Prisoner's Dilemma structure of many such pricing games predicts that the representative cartel member will have a dominant strategy to cheat on the cartel agreements.

EXAMPLE

COFFEE CARTEL DISSOLVES[33]

In October 1991, the 17 top Colombian and Brazilian coffee producers announced an agreement to set up a coffee cartel. Each country and several African and Central American smaller producers agreed in principle to take millions of tons of coffee beans off the market in an effort to drive up wholesale prices. Brazilian producers would hold back 2 million bags of a projected 18 million bag crop. Colombian producers would hold back 1.3 million bags. However, both countries opposed a formal quota system with assigned production ceilings, monitoring mechanisms, and penalization of violators. In July

---

[32] See Scherer and Ross, *Industrial Market Structure*, pp. 244–248.

[33] Based on "Non-zero-sum Strategic Game," *Financial Times*, 2 July 1995.

1989, the previous International Coffee Agreement had collapsed over the refusal to accept assigned quotas.

When the 1992 harvest proved more plentiful than expected, coffee bean prices plummeted. Prisoner's Dilemma is less a "game" than a paradox about cooperation. If all major coffee bean producers could rely upon one another to withhold production, all would have higher profitability. However, each cartel member maximizes self-interest by releasing excess supplies to the world market at just below the cartel official price. Because numerous fellow members think the same way, equilibrium market price will decline. Only dupes then continue to restrain output when prices signal that other members are violating the agreement. Coffee bean producers observed market price dropping precipitously in 1992 and concluded correctly that the cartel agreements to restrain output had dissolved.

We shall see in the next chapter that raising the stakes from noncooperation or entering into a long-term, continuing relationship with opponent/cooperators can diminish this incentive to cheat. Nevertheless, most cartels are like the frequent price-fixing agreements that evolve several times a year among the manufacturer sales representatives for cardboard packaging. Within two or three weeks, the collusive uniform pricing across alternative regional suppliers breaks down, often before the ink on Justice Department indictments can dry.

SUMMARY

- An *oligopoly* is an industry structure characterized by a relatively small number of firms in which recognizable *interdependencies* exist among the actions of the firms. Each firm is aware that its actions are likely to evoke countermoves from its rivals.

- No one normative model of oligopoly behavior adequately describes the optimal behavior (that is, price and output decisions) for firms in oligopolistic industries. Each of the models offers *some* insights that are useful in *some* decision-making situations. It is doubtful, however, whether any comprehensive model will ever be developed.

- In the *Cournot* model of oligopoly behavior, each of the firms, in determining its profit-maximizing output level, assumes that the other firm's output will remain constant.

- A *cartel* is a formal or informal agreement among oligopolists to cooperate or collude in determining outputs, prices, and profits. If the cartel members can enforce agreements and prevent cheating, they can act as a monopolist and maximize industry profits.

- A number of factors affect the ability of oligopolistic firms to engage successfully in some form of formal (or informal) cooperation. These include the number and size distribution of sellers, product heterogeneity, cost structures, size and frequency of orders, secrecy and retaliation, and the social structure of the industry.

- *Price leadership* is a pricing strategy in an oligopolistic industry in which one firm sets the price and, either by explicit or implicit agreement, the other firms tend to follow the decision. Effective price leadership exists when price movements initiated by the leader have a high probability of sticking and there are no maverick or nonconforming firms.

- In the *kinked demand curve* model, it is assumed that if an oligopolist reduces its prices, its competitors will quickly feel the decline in their sales and will be forced to match the reduction. Alternatively, if the oligopolist raises its prices, competitors will rapidly gain customers by maintaining their original prices and will have little or no motivation to match a price increase. Hence, the demand curve facing individual oligopolists is much more elastic for price increases than for price decreases and may lead oligopolists to maintain stable prices.

☐ In a *game-theoretic* analysis of oligopolistic firms' decision making, the firm assumes that its competitor(s) will choose its (their) optimal decision-making strategy. Based on this assumption about its competitor(s), the firm chooses its own best counterstrategy.

☐ Business strategy games may be classified as simultaneous-play or sequential-play, one-shot or repeated, zero-sum or non-zero-sum, two-player or *n*-player, and cooperative or noncooperative.

☐ *Cooperative games* allow communication, coalition formation, binding sidepayment agreements, and third-party enforceable contracts.

EXERCISES

1. Assume that two companies (*C* and *D*) are duopolists that produce identical products. Demand for the products is given by the following linear demand function:

$$P = 600 - Q_C - Q_D$$

where Q_C and Q_D are the quantities sold by the respective firms and P is the selling price. Total cost functions for the two companies are

$$TC_C = 25{,}000 + 100\,Q_C$$

$$TC_D = 20{,}000 + 125\,Q_D$$

Assume that the firms act *independently* as in the Cournot model (that is, each firm assumes that the other firm's output will not change).

   a. Determine the long-run equilibrium outputs and selling price for each firm.
   b. Determine the total profits for each firm at the equilibrium output found in part (a).

2. Assume that two companies (*A* and *B*) are duopolists who produce identical products. Demand for the products is given by the following linear demand function:

$$P = 200 - Q_A - Q_B$$

where Q_A and Q_B are the quantities sold by the respective firms and P is the selling price. Total cost functions for the two companies are

$$TC_A = 1{,}500 + 55Q_A + Q_A^2$$

$$TC_B = 1{,}200 + 20Q_B + 2Q_B^2$$

Assume that the firms act *independently* as in the Cournot model (that is, each firm assumes that the other firm's output will not change).

   a. Determine the long-run equilibrium output and selling price for each firm.
   b. Determine Firm *A*, Firm *B*, and total industry profits at the equilibrium solution found in part (a).

3. Consider Exercise 2 again. Assume that the firms form a *cartel* to act as a monopolist and maximize total industry profits (sum of Firm *A* and Firm *B* profits).

   a. Determine the optimum output and selling price for each firm.
   b. Determine Firm *A*, Firm *B*, and total industry profits at the optimal solution found in part (a).

c. Show that the marginal costs of the two firms are equal at the optimal solution found in part (a).

4. Compare the optimal solutions obtained in Exercises 2 and 3. Specifically:

   a. How much higher (lower) is the optimal selling price when the two firms form a cartel to maximize industry profits compared with when they act independently?

   b. How much higher (lower) is total industry output?

   c. How much higher (lower) are total industry profits?

5. Alchem (L) is the price leader in the polyglue market. All 10 other manufacturers [follower (F) firms] sell polyglue at the same price as Alchem. Alchem allows the other firms to sell as much as they wish at the established price and supplies the remainder of the demand itself. Total demand for polyglue is given by the following function ($Q_T = Q_L + Q_F$):

$$P = 20{,}000 - 4Q_T$$

Alchem's marginal cost function for manufacturing and selling polyglue is

$$MC_L = 5{,}000 + 5Q_L$$

The aggregate marginal cost function for the other manufacturers of polyglue is

$$\Sigma MC_F = 2{,}000 + 4Q_F$$

   a. To maximize profits, how much polyglue should Alchem produce and what price should it charge?

   b. What is the total market demand for polyglue at the price established by Alchem in part (a)? How much of total demand do the follower firms supply?

6. Chillman Motors, Inc. believes it faces the following segmented demand function:

$$P = \begin{cases} 150 - .5Q & \text{when } 0 \le Q \le 50 \\ 200 - 1.5\,Q & \text{for } Q > 50 \end{cases}$$

   a. Indicate both verbally and graphically why such a segmented demand function is likely to exist. What type of industry structure is indicated by this relationship?

   b. Calculate the marginal revenue functions facing Chillman. Add these to your graph from part (a).

   c. Chillman's total cost function is

$$TC_1 = 500 + 15Q + .5Q^2$$

   Calculate the marginal cost function. What is Chillman's profit-maximizing price and output combination?

   d. What is Chillman's profit-maximizing price-output combination if total costs increase to

$$TC_2 = 500 + 45Q + .5Q^2$$

   e. If Chillman's total cost function changes to either

$$TC_3 = 500 + 15Q + 1.0Q^2$$

   or

$$TC_4 = 500 + 5Q + .25Q^2$$

what price-output solution do you expect to prevail? Would your answer change if you knew that all firms in the industry witnessed similar changes in their cost functions?

7. Suppose that two Japanese companies, Hitachi and Toshiba, are the sole producers (i.e., duopolists) of a microprocessor chip used in a number of different brands of personal computers. Assume that total demand for the chips is fixed and that each firm charges the same price for the chips. Each firm's market share and profits are a function of the magnitude of the promotional campaign used to promote its version of the chip. Also assume that only two strategies are available to each firm—a limited promotional campaign (budget) and an extensive promotional campaign (budget). If the two firms engage in a limited promotional campaign, each firm will earn a quarterly profit of $7.5 million. If the two firms undertake an extensive promotional campaign, each firm will earn a quarterly profit of $5.0 million. With this strategy combination, market share and total sales will be the same as for a limited promotional campaign, but promotional costs will be higher and hence profits will be lower. If either firm engages in a limited promotional campaign and the other firm undertakes an extensive promotional campaign, then the firm that adopts the extensive campaign will increase its market share and earn a profit of $9.0 million, whereas the firm that chooses the limited campaign will earn a profit of only $4.0 million.

   a. Develop a payoff matrix for this decision-making problem.
   b. In the absence of a binding and enforceable agreement, determine the dominant advertising strategy and minimum payoff for Hitachi.
   c. Determine the dominant advertising strategy and minimum payoff for Toshiba.
   d. Explain why the firms may choose not to play their dominant strategies whenever this game is repeated over multiple decision-making periods.

8. Consider the following payoff matrix:

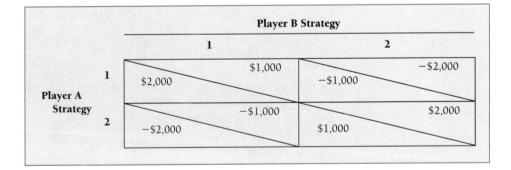

   a. Does player A have a dominant strategy? Explain why or why not.
   b. Does player B have a dominant strategy? Explain why or why not.

9. Suppose that two mining companies, Australian Minerals Company (AMC) and South African Mines, Inc. (SAMI), control the only sources of a rare mineral used in making certain electronic components. The companies have agreed to form a cartel to set the (profit-maximizing) price of the mineral. Each company must decide whether to *abide* by the agreement (i.e., not offer secret price cuts to customers) or *not abide* (i.e., offer secret price cuts to customers). If both companies abide by the agreement, AMC will earn an annual profit of $30 million and SAMI will earn an annual profit of $20 million from sales of the mineral. If AMC does not

abide and SAMI abides by the agreement, then AMC earns $40 million and SAMI earns $5 million. If SAMI does not abide and AMC abides by the agreement, then AMC earns $10 million and SAMI earns $30 million. If both companies do not abide by the agreement, then AMC earns $15 million and SAMI earns $10 million.

a. Develop a payoff matrix for this decision-making problem.

b. In the absence of a binding and enforceable agreement, determine the dominant strategy for AMC.

c. Determine the dominant strategy for SAMI.

d. If the two firms can enter into a binding and enforceable agreement, determine the strategy that each firm should choose.

10. *Library Research Project.* Examine the literature on the price-fixing agreements that occurred in the electrical equipment industry during the 1950s. For example, see the article in the *Wall Street Journal* cited in footnote 7, as well as Richard Austin Smith, "The Incredible Electrical Conspiracy," *Fortune* (April, May 1961) and scattered references (see the index) to the economic aspects of this episode in F.M. Scherer and David Ross, *Industrial Market Structure and Economic Performance,* 3d ed. (Chicago: Rand McNally, 1990). Attempt to answer the following questions:

a. What firms and products were involved in the conspiracy?

b. What measures did the executives use to keep their meetings secret?

c. How did the companies determine who should get contracts and orders?

d. What market-sharing formulas (quotas) were used in allocating demand?

e. What were some of the problems encountered in maintaining the price-fixing agreements?

www exercise

Information-Sharing Among Oligopolists

11. It was observed in the chapter that collusion among oligopolists can be facilitated in part by information sharing. As a consequence, the sharing of price information among rival oligopolists can violate U.S. antitrust laws. You can see how the U.S. Supreme Court has interpreted antitrust law as it pertains to sharing price information by reading a summary of the case of U.S. v. U.S. Gypsum Co. et al. (438 U.S. 422), which is available at the following Internet site maintained by Anthony Becker: http://www.stolaf.edu/people/becker/antitrust/summaries/438us422.htm.

In what manner was price information shared, and why did the court find this to be an antitrust violation?

16

Game-Theoretic Rivalry: Best-Practice Tactics

CHAPTER PREVIEW

When incumbents and potential entrants in product-line submarkets compete against a few rivals, effective decision making necessitates effective tactics. Effective tactics in turn require methods for anticipating rival initiatives, rival response, and counterresponse. Most such predictions of rival behavior can be obtained by analyzing oligopolistic competition as a noncooperative sequential game or as a noncooperative, repeated, simultaneous game. Prominent examples of the former include entry deterrence and accommodation games, bidding games, and product development or research and development (R & D) games, whereas pricing and promotion decisions often involve simultaneous play.

All such noncooperative games prohibit side payments and binding contracts between rivals and instead depend on self-enforcing reliance relationships to secure strategic equilibrium. For example, each airline in a posted pricing game must decide whether it is in its own best interest to resist discounting to gain market share, in light of the best reply responses the airline should anticipate from its rivals. In many circumstances, mutual discounting proves to be a dominant strategy that provides protection from the inroads of a renegade discounter, but forgoes the profits from all firms maintaining higher prices. This is the Prisoner's Dilemma of Chapter 15. The order of play can matter in such games if credible threats and commitments influence the endgame outcomes.

In this chapter we explore the role nonredeployable assets, credible punishment schemes, hostage mechanisms, and imperfect information can play in helping oligopolists escape the repeated Prisoner's Dilemma. In the Appendix, we discuss optimal mechanism design including queue service rules, auctions, and vertical requirements contracting between manufacturers and retail distributors.

MANAGERIAL CHALLENGE

PRICE DIFFERENTIALS IN COMPUTERS[1]

For a decade IBM and Compaq maintained a $1,000 or more price differential over the no-name PC makers and second-tier firms such as Zenith, Dell, and AST. Both competitors always had the opportunity to attract sales away from their rivals by renegade discounting but neither wished to start a price war. Predictably, all discounting would be matched, and both firms would then be worse off. Margins were large and profits high, but sales growth declined precipitously. PC assembly and retailing became subject to enormously effective grassroots entry, and the PC market fragmented. From 1987 to 1991 approximately 300 PC makers below the top 100 vendors increased their share of the market from 4 percent to 16 percent. That volume exceeded both IBM's 12 percent and Apple's 13 percent. IBM's much-lauded systems solutions for mainframe computing never proved effective in the PC market. Niche marketing to hospitals one day, to computer-aided design firms another day, and to airline revenue management systems a third day suited the small no-name manufacturers who incur very low overhead. Basically, these firms just buy components such as disk drives, motherboards, monitors, and memory chips on the spot market and assemble to order.

In 1993–94 Compaq and IBM slashed prices, promoted the discounts, and the price differential between the leading, second-tier, and no-name companies all but disappeared. Even Apple followed suit. The growth of the no-name segment stopped, and the no-names' combined share of the market declined to 12 percent. However, profitability at the leading firms plummeted and remained low. Now that a new generation of more powerful PCs is emerging, what pricing strategy should the leading firms follow?

WWW . . . .
The following Internet site, maintained by PC Week, contains additional information on price competition in the PC industry:
http://www8.zdnet.com/pcweek/news/0714/17ecuts.html

---

[1]Based on "PC Giants' Price War Hurts Tiny Makers," *Wall Street Journal*, 2 November 1992, p. B1.

BUSINESS STRATEGY GAMES

In many oligopolistic industries today, change has become the norm. Correctly anticipating changes in entry and exit, technology, product development, pricing, and promotions several steps ahead of actual events and at least one step ahead of the competition is often the key to a successful business. Despite one's best efforts, sometimes a competitor takes the lead, and then quickly adaptive behavior is preferable to reactive behavior. Unquestionably, however, proactive behavior is best of all, and proactive behavior requires accurate and reliable predictions of rival initiatives and rival response. The managerial purpose of game theory is to predict rival behavior. To execute defensive strategy as well as plan strategic initiatives, business managers must thoroughly understand game-theoretic reasoning.

The predictive capability of game theory proves valuable to Coca-Cola and Pepsi, for example, in deciding whether to maintain high prices or announce discounts for their competing promotions each week in grocery and convenience stores. If both discount, they each earn $8,000 and forgo $4,000 profit relative to the $12,000 per week per store available when they both maintain high prices. However, if one discounts while the other maintains high prices, the discounter earns $17,000, and the rival earns only $6,000. As a value-maximizing manager, what should you do? Think about it. Use the normal form of the game and the techniques of the last chapter to sketch out a strategy. Have you settled for a second-best outcome? Suppose the $6,000 were instead $9,000? Is there now a way to secure the win-win $12,000 outcome? The Prisoner's Dilemma facing Pepsi and Coca-Cola is a noncooperative positive-sum game of coordination. In this chapter we will study how to escape the dilemma and solve such games.

Simultaneous and Sequential Games

www. . . . .
To learn more about various types of games, access the following Internet site containing lecture materials by Marek Kaminski of New York University:
http://www.nyu.edu/projects/kaminski/games strategyandpolitics.html

Sequential Game
A game with an explicit order of play.

Simultaneous Game
A game in which players must choose their actions simultaneously.

In Chapter 15 we saw that strategy games can be classified into several types: cooperative versus noncooperative, two-person versus n-person, zero-sum versus non-zero-sum, and one-play versus repeated games. All strategy games can also be subdivided further into either **sequential games** in which the order of play is specified and often pivotal to the strategic equilibrium, or **simultaneous games** such as the airline fare announcements, which take place concurrently on an electronic bulletin board at 7:00 A.M. each morning. In this chapter we address both simultaneous and sequential games and continue our focus from Chapter 15 on noncooperative, self-enforcing relationships between arm's-length competitors.

To illustrate the importance of the sequential order of play in many tactical situations, consider a two-player coordination game that often arises between manufacturers and independent retail dealers. The payoffs for the promotion and sale of a heavy truck like those sold by Volvo-GM Truck are displayed in normal form in Table 16.1. Let's first examine the actions and payoffs in the left-hand column. The manufacturer wants the retail dealers to continue providing personal selling efforts and after-sales service rather than discontinue these activities and thereby increase their retail margins. In return, the manufacturer agrees to advertise the product. If services continue and advertising occurs, the customers will tolerate the pass-through of a higher wholesale price. The manufacturer will also assist in the realization of this higher revenue by announcing an increase in the manufacturer's suggested retail price (i.e., the MSRP). In that case, the retail dealer and the manufacturer can earn additional profits per sale of $2,000 and $5,000, respectively. However, if MSRP increases and retail services are discontinued (in the northwest cell of Figure 16.1), sales volume declines enough that neither party receives any incremental profit.

Independent dealers may feel tempted to deliver less service than they promise. Although sales will decline, their lack of reasonable efforts in personal selling, for exam-

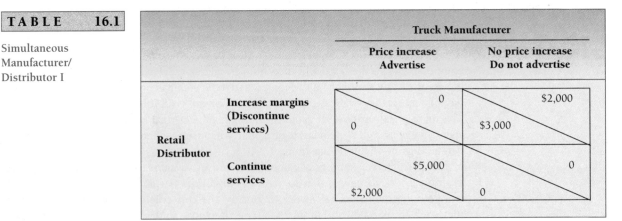

TABLE   16.1

Simultaneous Manufacturer/ Distributor I

		Truck Manufacturer	
		Price increase **Advertise**	**No price increase** **Do not advertise**
Retail Distributor	**Increase margins (Discontinue services)**	0 0	$2,000 $3,000
	Continue services	$5,000 $2,000	0 0

Note: Column-player payoffs are above the diagonal. Row-player payoffs are below the diagonal.

ple, may be difficult for the manufacturer to observe directly and therefore may be indistinguishable from bad luck. A few quarters of apparently bad luck at a substantially higher margin may be in the retail distributor's best interests. This outcome is represented in the northeast cell of Figure 16.1. If retail services *are* discontinued, the manufacturer will not advertise and will leave the MSRP unchanged. Since both parties would then incur fewer expenses, both would again realize incremental profit—i.e., $3,000 for the retailer but only $2,000 for the manufacturer. If the MSRP remains unchanged and the services continue (i.e., the southeast cell), both parties barely cover variable plus direct fixed costs. Therefore, no incremental profit is available on an additional sale.[2]

What would you do as the dealer/distributor in this situation? Would you try for the increased margin by economizing on selling expenses and after-sale services? Remember that your best payoff arises when the manufacturer anticipates your discontinuation of services and does not raise prices. And the manufacturer's best payoff occurs when you provide the expected dealer services and he raises prices. Perhaps you could take turns? One period you could cut services and he would maintain prices; the next period he could raise prices and you would maintain services. How would you coordinate this on again–off again business relation, assuming that merging the two entities into one vertically integrated firm is infeasible? What if your reputation for sharp dealing and misleading manufacturers as to your reliability caused you to miss future distributorship or dealership opportunities? What if it didn't?

As these questions multiply, one quickly comes to the realization that the coordination of business activities in a simultaneous game can be a real challenge. In this chapter, we will analyze the optimal strategies for playing Manufacturer/Distributor I. And at the end of the chapter, we will see how these coordination problems can be resolved by and indeed motivate private voluntary contracting, contract default rules, and the social invention of contract law. For now, simply note how much predictability of rival behavior emerges in this coordination game if we introduce a small but pivotal change in the structure of the game—in particular, a sequential order of play.

---

[2] Manufacturer/Distributor I is an adaptation of the Battle of the Sexes coordination game, a standard variant of the two-player simultaneous games in the Prisoner's Dilemma tradition. E. Rasmussen, *Games and Information*, 2nd ed. (Cambridge, Mass.: Basil Blackwell, 1993) discusses other coordination games.

FIGURE 16.1
Sequential Manufacturer/Distributor I

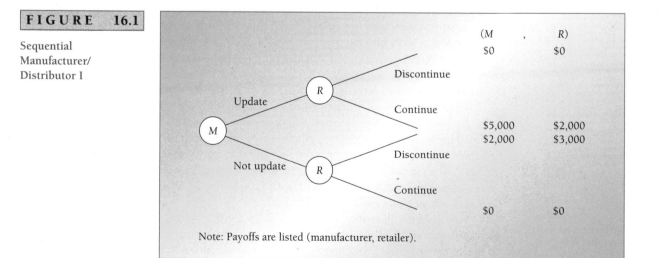

Note: Payoffs are listed (manufacturer, retailer).

A Sequential Coordination Game

Suppose the manufacturer (M) must commit first to either increase the MSRP or leave prices unchanged. And suppose this decision is easily observable and irreversible. For example, suppose the price increase is tied to the release of a product update by the manufacturer. If the manufacturer updates the product, the retail distributor (R) can anticipate with certainty that MSRP will increase and that manufacturer advertising will follow. No longer must the distributor wonder whether the business opportunity is best represented by the first or the second column of Table 16.1. If the product update is released, thereafter the retail distributor knows that the first column is in play. And the retail distributor then has an obvious choice—for example, to continue providing services and receive $2,000 rather than discontinue service and receive zero. That is, the mere introduction of a sequential order to the decision making made it possible to predict the optimal strategic behavior by both parties and resolve the ambiguity present in the simultaneous game.

The new structure of the game can be represented in extensive form as follows. Figure 16.1 is referred to as a **game tree** or *decision tree.* The order of the decisions is read from left to right, and each circle represents a decision node. Update or Not Update identifies possible *actions* that the *player M* can take at the first decision node. (M, R) refer to the *payoffs* for the manufacturer and the retailer, respectively, associated with each sequence of possible actions.

Since the manufacturer can look ahead and foresee that an *Update* of the product will make it advantageous for the retail distributor to *Continue,* the manufacturer finds it in his own best interest to commit to an update, then increase wholesale and MSRP prices, and follow through with advertising. Each party is able to look ahead and reason back using the concept of best-reply response to predict the rival's behavior. None of this sequential reasoning was available in the simultaneous-play version of the game.

To take another example of sequential games, suppose two insurance companies, who manage benefit programs, are bidding for additional business in their area of expertise at a market rate of $200 per hour. The potential customers refuse to leave their current suppliers and award benefit management contracts to the new firms unless billing rates are cut by $50. Abbott, Abbott & Daughters (AA&D) decides to do just that. Your firm, Zekiel, Zekiel & Sons (ZZ&S), must decide whether to match the price cut and then allow customers to choose randomly between the two firms, or whether to lower rates still further to $100 per hour. Past experience suggests, however, that the price cutting may well not stop there. The clients will surely take their best current offer back and forth between the two firms, thereby forcing a downward price spiral. The question therefore is "How low will you go?" Importantly, there is some penultimate stopping rule—i.e., at a price below your $40 cost, the additional business becomes unprofitable and must be refused. AA&D has higher costs—namely, $66 per hour.

Again, your decision depends on an analysis of the sequence of predictable future events, which can be represented with a *game tree* or *decision tree,* such as in Figure 16.2. To simplify, assume that all rate cuts must be in $50 increments, that customers choose quickly between equal rate quotes using fair coin tosses, that once a rate quote has been matched it cannot be lowered, and that many potential customers are present in the market. It is now your turn at node Z1 with rates at the $150 per hour level. What should you do? Match rates or cut rates further?

First, as with all sequential games, ZZ&S needs to predict the subsequent best reply response of its rival at $100, look ahead to its own counter at $50, and finally analyze the endgame below $50. Then ZZ&S will be in a position to reason back to the question at hand. **Endgame reasoning** always entails looking ahead to the last play in an ordered

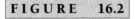

How Low Will You Go?

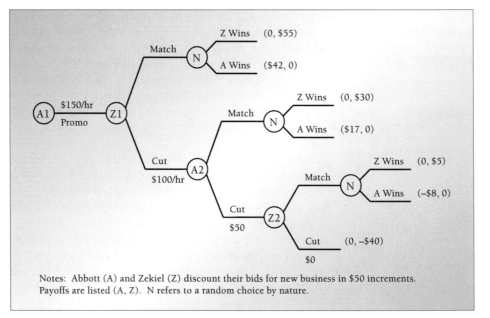

Notes: Abbott (A) and Zekiel (Z) discount their bids for new business in $50 increments. Payoffs are listed (A, Z). N refers to a random choice by nature.

Backwards Induction

Reasoning in reverse time sequence from later consequences back to earlier decisions.

sequence of plays, identifying the player whose decisions will control the outcome of the endgame, and then predicting that player's most preferred choice.

In this instance, knowing that AA&D would lose money at the $50 per hour rates in the lowest branch of Figure 16.2, you predict that at node A2 they will simply match your offer of $100 per hour and take their chances on a coin flip. Consequently, no decision by ZZ&S about a counter at $50 per hour will be required. However, your analysis is far from finished. Realizing all this allows you to employ **backwards induction** and rethink whether your plan to cut rates initially from $150 to $100 is, in fact, in your best interest. Because the endgame reasoning indicates that AA&D will quote a matching $100 rate and split the market at that price, why not on the previous play simply match their current offer of $150 and split the market at a higher price. Realizing that your own price cut from $150 to $100 will not attract new customers, but instead will simply lower the price at which the market is split, you decide to match AA&D's $150 offer, pass the customer a fair coin to toss, and be done with it.

The strategy pair for AA&D and ZZ&S that provides an equilibrium for this sequential bidding game is then {$150, Match}. That is, after the initial price cut to elicit external business, the competitors in effect take turns selling their services at $150 per hour, each randomly winning 50 percent of the new business. This pricing strategy results in an expected profit of 0.5($150 − $40) = $55 per hour. Neither firm prefers the alternatives—namely, a 50 percent market share of the new business at $100 per hour or $50 per hour—so, a noncooperative, self-enforcing agreement to share the market at higher prices emerges. Insurance companies, accountants, optometrists, and other suppliers of homogenous professional services seem to recognize that gainshare discounting even in the presence of a cost advantage often proves counterproductive.

Strategic Equilibrium in Sequential Games

Looking ahead to the rival's best-reply responses in the endgame and then reasoning back to each prior question is Reinhard Selten's concept of an equilibrium strategy for sequential games, a concept for which he and John Nash won the 1994 Nobel Prize in

Nash Equilibrium Strategy
An equilibrium concept for noncooperative games.

Subgame Perfect Equilibrium Strategy
An equilibrium concept for noncooperative sequential games.

economics. Like many other pathbreaking ideas, this very intuitive strategic equilibrium concept is actually deceptive in its simplicity. A **Nash equilibrium strategy** is a decision maker's optimal action such that the payoff, when all other players make best-reply responses, exceeds that decision maker's payoff from any other action, again assuming best-reply responses. Selten applied this Nash equilibrium concept to sequential play and invented the concept of Nash equilibrium in a proper subgame. Selten's **subgame perfect equilibrium strategy** always involves looking ahead to the best-reply responses in all proper subgames and then reasoning back to your preferred strategy at earlier decision points.

As we saw in analyzing "How low will you go?" some nodes of a decision tree, such as Z2 in the bottom half of Figure 16.2, and the endgames thereafter can be eliminated from consideration if they cannot be reached by best-reply responses. Selten's idea was that only in the proper subgame nodes would the Nash equilibrium concept hold. From Z2, AA&D need not consider the effect of ZZ&S matching $50 prices rather than discounting to zero. The reason is that AA&D's cutting rates to $50 in the first place is not a best-reply response for AA&D; that action at node A2 results in losses (−$16) for AA&D with 0.5 probability and zero profits with 0.5 probability, whereas matching the $100 rate results in $34 or zero profits, each with a probability of 0.5—i.e., expected profits of $17. Consequently, the nodes beyond an AA&D price cut to $50 are not a proper subgame; they cannot be reached by best-reply responses.[3] Subgame perfect equilibrium strategy therefore entails analyzing the outcomes associated with actions and best-reply responses at A1 and Z1, the only proper subgame nodes of Figure 16.2.[4] Again, {$150, Match} proves to be the subgame perfect equilibrium strategy.

Sometimes this identification of proper and improper subgames can get quite complicated when there can be many possible endgames. To illustrate, consider the three-way comparative advertising duel in Exercise 3. With varying degrees of success, three firms attack one another with comparative advertising in pairwise, sequential competitions until just one firm remains. It can take two complete rounds of advertising attacks and almost 20 endgames to analyze the subgame perfect equilibrium strategy for that problem.

EXAMPLE

WWW ....
Access current financial information on Bell Atlantic at the following Internet site:
http://www.bell-atl.com/invest/

BUSINESS GAMING AT BELL ATLANTIC[5]

Bell Atlantic Chairman Ray Smith employs the techniques, exercises, and lessons of game theory throughout his organization. In "war games," teams of Bell Atlantic managers assume the role of major competitors and explore tactics that could defeat Bell Atlantic's business plans. Other teams detail future contingencies in a large game tree that allows Bell Atlantic to map its future moves and countermoves as well as uncover the competitive effects of new technological developments (like digital voice and video

---

[3] By analogous reasoning, the subgame at A2 itself is eliminated because ZZ&S's best-reply response to the initial promotional discount is to match at $150 per hour, not to cut rates to $100. Thus, the decisions from node A2 onward cannot be reached by best-reply responses and cannot therefore be involved in subgame perfect equilibrium strategy.

[4] The reader may wonder about the relevance of A2 and matching prices at $100 per hour if there is a miscommunication or mistake by ZZ&S at node Z1. These are valid questions because mistakes and miscommunication do happen in the reality of business rivalry. Indeed, a refinement of subgame perfect strategy allows for just such mistakes and describes equilibrium strategy for either player in this game less uniquely as {Match any price below $200}.

[5] Based on "Business As A War Game: Report from the Battlefront," *Fortune,* 30 September 1996, pp. 190–193.

transmission) before they happen. Traditional planning models lock managers into assumptions the importance of which they can only gauge through sensitivity analysis. But sequential game analysis constantly reminds mangers to shape the game, not just play it. That can mean reversing the order of play by highlighting the value of preemptive strikes in some circumstances (e.g., in merging with Nynex) but the value of "fast second" best reply responses in other circumstances (e.g., in basic research and product development by Lucent Technologies).

In addition, Bell Atlantic has learned to recognize endgames unfavorable to the company and reshape the structure of the competitive rivalry in those businesses. Bell Atlantic recently redefined the scope of the telephone industry's local network strategy game by winning approval in the courts for telephone companies to own the content transmitted over their phone lines. Bell Atlantic managers are now hard at work analyzing the new larger game that includes business directories, digitized movies, and video production.

BUSINESS RIVALRY AS A SEQUENTIAL GAME

It is important to emphasize that the subgame perfect equilibrium concept is self-enforcing. It predicts stable rival response, not because of effective monitoring and third-party enforcement, but because each party would be worse off departing from the equilibrium strategy pair than it would be implementing it. Thus, Abbott, Abbott & Daughters and Zekiel, Zekiel & Sons have, in effect, made credible commitments to one another not to lower rates below the $150 per hour necessary to attract the new business. Credibility mechanisms are the key to securing subgame perfect strategies. And credibility can work both ways; credible commitments can also become credible threats. Let's see how.

Consider a well-established pharmaceutical manufacturer of ulcer relief medicine, who presently markets the only effective curative therapy possessing no known side effects and earns $100,000. This incumbent (let's call the firm Pastense) faces an entry challenge from a small potential entrant new to the industry (Potent). Potent has discovered a new therapeutic process that also has the potential to cure stomach ulcers. Potent must decide whether to enter the monopoly market or stay out and license its trade secrets to any one of several interested buyers. Pastense must decide whether to maintain its present high prices, moderate its prices, or radically discount its prices. The payoffs are displayed in Table 16.2. If Potent enters, and Pastense does not moderate or discount, suppose all the ulcer relief business goes to the new entrant and the incumbent realizes nothing. In contrast, with entry and discount prices, suppose the incumbent's product enjoys a slight cost advantage and earns a $10,000 greater payoff (i.e., $50,000 and $40,000 in the bottom right corner of Table 16.2). Moderate incumbent prices result in $35,000 payoff for Pastense and $50,000 payoff for Potent.

To prevent the reduction of its profit from $100,000 as a monopolist to $50,000 post-entry, Pastense itself might be a prime candidate for the purchase of Potent's trade secret. Realistically, however, it is liable to run up against antitrust constraints that restrict mergers between dominant incumbents and new entrants. Note also that what another established pharmaceutical manufacturer will pay to license the trade secret, with all the attendant technology transfer problems and yet significantly more extensive distribution and marketing experience, bares little correspondence to what Potent itself could hope to earn upon entry. Potent receives its second highest payoff ($60,000) when it licenses its trade secret and Pastense maintains moderate prices. Potent earns the least ($20,000) when it stays out, licenses, but Pastense discounts.

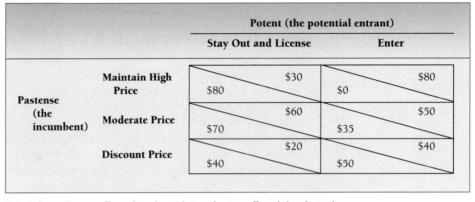

TABLE   16.2

Payoffs (in thousands)
from Entry Deterrence
or Accommodation in
Ulcer Relief
Pharmaceuticals

		Potent (the potential entrant)	
		Stay Out and License	Enter
Pastense (the incumbent)	**Maintain High Price**	$80 $30	$0 $80
	Moderate Price	$70 $60	$35 $50
	Discount Price	$40 $20	$50 $40

Note: Column-player payoffs are above diagonal. Row-player payoffs are below diagonal.

First-Mover and Second-Mover Advantages

www ....

Read a RAND article
relating first-mover
advantage to the decline of
the U.S. machine tool
manufacturing industry in
the 1980's at the following
Internet site:
http://www.rand.org/
publications/RB/RB1500/

As is now obvious, "Who can do what, when?" is the essence of any such sequential strategy game. The order of play is pivotal, because it determines who initiates and who replies, and this determines the best-reply response in the endgame, and thus the strategic equilibrium. As is natural in the present case, suppose the new entrant must choose first whether or not to enter, and the incumbent selects a pricing response thereafter. Figure 16.3 displays the game tree for this order of play. The endgame appears in the two nodes to the right, each labeled I for Incumbent. If Potent enters, Pastense strongly prefers a Discount pricing response, because $50,000 far exceeds the zero or $35,000 outcomes from either the High or Moderate alternatives. This analysis of the incumbent's best-reply response allows Potent to predict that its own $80,000 and $50,000 outcomes should be eliminated from further consideration. Even though each is theoretically associated with its entry, neither can be obtained if Pastense does what is in its own best interest (i.e., makes a best-reply response in this proper subgame).

Similarly in the bottom endgame node, if Potent stays out, its royalty payoffs of $60,000 cannot be obtained, because Pastense will price High to secure $80,000 for itself rather than accept its lower $70,000 and $40,000 alternatives. This means that there are only two **focal outcomes of interest** to Potent in making its entry decision: the shaded payoffs of $40,000 from entering and $30,000 from staying out. Being a value-maximizing firm, Potent decides to enter, predictably, and the events of the starred subgame perfect strategic equilibrium {Enter, Discount} then unfold. Notice that both players could be better off with the {$70,000, $60,000} outcome, but Potent cannot expect Pastense to respond with Moderate rather than High prices should Potent stay out and try to secure the $60,000 payoff from licensing. Consequently, with the present structure of the game, {$50,000, $40,000} is the best they can hope to do.

Focal Outcomes of Interest
Payoffs involved in an
analysis of equilibrium
strategy.

However, to illustrate the pivotal importance of the order of play, let's mix things up a bit. From the incumbent's point of view too, the outcomes {$50,000, $40,000} are not entirely satisfactory. Given its second-mover timing, Pastense did as well as could be expected. But the incumbent may wonder whether seizing the first-mover initiative would have worked to its advantage. The fact of the matter is that no general rule on this point exists; sometimes it will, and sometimes it will not. Each sequential game situation is in this way unique.

To analyze the question, in Figure 16.4 we reverse the order of play. Now, the potential entrant controls the endgame, and the incumbent must announce irreversible pricing policies in advance. Saying they are irreversible does not make it so, but more on that in the next section. Analyzing the three endgame nodes, Pastense realizes that Potent

FIGURE   16.3

Entry Deterrence I:
Incumbent Pricing (in
thousands) in Response
to Entry Threat

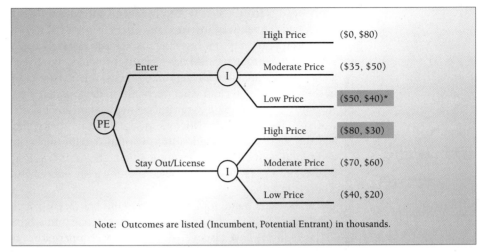

Note: Outcomes are listed (Incumbent, Potential Entrant) in thousands.

will choose to enter when high prices are precommitted, stay out when moderate prices are precommitted, or enter when discount prices are precommitted. Knowing this, Pastense prefers to announce a moderate pricing policy, and the starred {Moderate, Stay Out} strategic equilibrium eventuates. Not only has the potential entrant's behavior changed, but in addition, the payoff to Pastense has risen from $50,000 to $70,000. In this instance, a first-mover advantage proved to be just what the name implies.

EXAMPLE

TECHNOLOGY LEADER OR FAST SECOND: IBM[6]

Whether to secure first-mover advantages in the development of new computing technologies or instead engage in a pattern of quick imitation (i.e., a "fast second" strategy) poses a more difficult choice than one might think. In the absence of sunk-cost investments as a barrier to entry, hit-and-run entry often proves very effective. Apple commercialized the graphical user interface that Xerox invented. Microsoft quickly

FIGURE   16.4

Entry Deterrence II:
Entry Deterrence in
Response to Incumbent
Price Commitment (in
thousands)

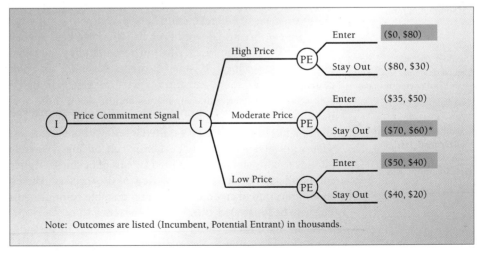

Note: Outcomes are listed (Incumbent, Potential Entrant) in thousands.

---

[6] Based on "Einstein and Eraser-Heads," *Wall Street Journal,* 6 October 1997, p. 1.

challenged Netscape's early dominance of Internet browsers. And Sun Microsystems developed the reduced instruction-set computing (RISC) that IBM pioneered.

By restraining upfront investments in basic research and focusing instead on the development of products, IBM has recently switched from a technology leader to a "first of a kind" problem-solver for high-margin customers. One example has been the marriage of computer imaging and voice-recognition devices that allow hospital radiologists and surgeons to superimpose X-ray images and text on any PC throughout the local-area network in a medical center. Doctors speak to one another while viewing PC-based images, and the IBM hardware and software automatically transcript their diagnostic findings and expert opinions. Other examples would be IBM's wireless modem for the cellular industry and eraser-heads to replace the unwieldy and easily damaged trackball cursor controls in PCs.

On the other hand, IBM Microelectronics has recently leveraged the company's long-standing basic research effort in materials science into a breakthrough in silicon chips. IBM's engineers have discovered how to form copper rather than aluminum circuits and yet prevent the copper atoms from bleeding into the surface of the silicon. Copper is a more conductive material and therefore can be laid down in narrower circuits than aluminum. The more circuits etched on a square centimeter of silicon, the more powerful and cost effective the computer chip. IBM's breakthrough in copper-on-silicon circuitry promises to increase computing power 40 percent for any given size chip.

Credible Threats and Commitments

www . . . .
The following Internet site maintained by the World Bank contains an article describing why regulators must have the capacity to make credible policy commitments in order to provide a stable environment for investors: http://www.worldbank. org/html/fpd/notes/50/ 50Tenenbaum.html

Credible Threat
A mechanism for establishing penalties in a noncooperative game.

Credible Commitment
A mechanism for establishing trust in a noncooperative game.

In multiperiod games, all threats and commitments derive their credibility ultimately from whether or not the threat maker or commitment maker successfully identifies and adopts subgame perfect strategies. In Entry Deterrence I (see Figure 16.3), Pastense's threat to discount the ulcer relief medicine if Potent entered was credible precisely because discounting was, in fact, a best-reply response. Any other response would have made Pastense worse off (i.e., lowered its payoff). A **credible threat** is therefore defined as a conditional strategy that the threat maker is worse off ignoring than implementing. By the same token, a commitment by Pastense to maintain high or moderate prices (i.e., not to discount and thereby spoil the royalty value of Potent's trade secret) if Potent would stay out of the market is a **credible commitment.** Again, this action is the incumbent's best-reply response to Potent's staying out. Therefore, without any monitoring or third-party enforcement whatsoever, one can fully rely on Pastense to honor its commitment, because it would not be in its own best interest to do otherwise.

You can now begin to see why purposeful individual behavior and a shared objective in groups is so critical to game-theoretic reasoning. To predict choices of highly interdependent players, one must know what makes them tick, what true goals they seek, and what the consequence of various actions is on those goals. Sometimes this is easier than it sounds; for example, performance-based incentives and takeover threats often align management objectives quite closely with stockholder value. On the other hand, what motivates a closely held, family-run business is sometimes difficult to fathom. Moreover, consistently transmitted signals of business strategy are often jammed or miscommunicated from the point of view of the receiver. Therefore, to ensure the effective communication of credible threats and credible commitments requires some guidelines. This can be illustrated with Entry Deterrence II.

As we have seen, Pastense found the switch to first-mover status highly advantageous. By promising to maintain moderate prices rather than discount, its profits increased from $50,000 to $70,000 when Potent sold out rather than entered. The question we must now examine, however, is "Why did Potent believe Pastense?" After all, it is clear from the game tree in Figure 16.4 that once Potent licensed its trade secret to another less capable potential entrant (let's call the new firm Impotent), Pastense was better off raising its price back to the high level it had once enjoyed. Although this could not restore the $100,000 profits prior to Potent's threat, the $80,000 payoff from high prices and entry certainly would make Pastense better off. Thus, Pastense's promise to maintain a Moderate Price was not a credible commitment because Pastense is worse off making good on the commitment than ignoring it. One might be inclined to respond that likewise Potent can renege on its commitment to stay out of the ulcer relief business. Licensing a trade secret for royalty revenue today need not preclude Potent's entry tomorrow. Indeed, such royalty agreements seldom include a no-competition clause. However, there is a difference. Potent's payoff is maximized by staying out! Its commitment to stay out if the incumbent maintains moderate prices *is* a credible commitment.

Mechanisms for Establishing Credibility[7]

As second mover, Potent controls the endgame and therefore finds itself in a position to insist on the necessary assurances. The issue then is how to secure a credible commitment mechanism for Pastense. Several alternatives present themselves. Pastense might establish a bond or contractual side payment, which would be forfeited if Pastense raised prices. Some such contracts, referred to as maximum resale price maintenance agreements, do exist between retailers and their suppliers, but any kind of restrictive pricing agreement between arm's-length competitors is generally illegal per se. Another possible credibility mechanism, then, would be for Pastense to invest heavily in a reputation for moderate prices. Loss of this **nonredeployable reputational asset** would discourage reneging on its commitment to maintain moderate prices. Third, Pastense could short-circuit or interrupt the repricing process by preselling its ulcer relief medicine with forward contracts. Fourth, Pastense could enter into teamwork or an alliance relationship with Potent that would sufficiently dilute the rewards from reneging on its commitment. Fifth, Pastense could change the structure of the game to require that both he and Potent only "take small steps." In the next section, we analyze leasing as a way to pursue this alternative.

And finally and most practically in this situation, Pastense could arrange an irreversible and irrevocable **hostage mechanism,** whereby likely future customers were granted a low price guarantee. Sometimes referred to as "most favored nation" clauses, these low price guarantees promise double refunds if the customer discovers any lower-price Pastense transaction during the next or the previous year. As long as Potent observed at least one moderate price transaction before licensing its trade secret, it could rest assured that Pastense had now offered a credible commitment not to raise prices. The resulting double refunds should Pastense raise prices and the sacrifice of future transactions with its own repeat-purchase customers should it renege on the refunds ensure that Pastense will finally be better off honoring its commitment than ignoring it. And again, notice that these are entirely self-enforcing agreements.

Nonredeployable Reputational Asset
A reputation whose value is lost if sold or licensed.

Hostage Mechanism
A mechanism for establishing the credibility of a threat or commitment.

EXAMPLE

DOUBLE-THE-DIFFERENCE PRICE GUARANTEES: CIRCUIT CITY

At times, Circuit City offers to rebate twice the differential purchase price of a VCR to preferred customers should those customers find the same VCR selling for less anywhere in the local area over the next three months. This rebate guarantee will be enforced by the courts. As in the simultaneous-play pricing game between Pepsi and Coca-Cola,

---

[7] This section relies heavily on A. Dixit and B. Nalebuff, *Thinking Strategically: The Competitive Edge in Business, Politics, and Everyday Life* (New York: Norton, 1991), especially chaps. 5 and 6.

www . . . .

For another real-world
example of a double-the-
difference price guarantee,
see the following Internet
site:
http://www.modecomput
ers.com.au/guarantee.
html

Circuit City normally would be better off discounting (maybe even steeply discounting) when competitors like Sound Warehouse maintain high prices. But in the face of this double-the-difference low-price guarantee, Circuit City would lose more money on rebates than it could possibly gain from any amount of incremental business it could reasonably expect to take away from Sound Warehouse. In effect, Circuit City has given its competitor a hostage.

In Figure 16.5, Circuit City provides a bond of its intentions to maintain high prices by preannouncing the double-the-difference price guarantee. Sound Warehouse must then decide whether to discount or maintain high prices in light of the Circuit City rebate program. Like all good hostage mechanisms, the unused hostage is worth more to the giver than its value in use to the recipient. That is, Sound Warehouse *could* trigger double-rebate payments at Circuit City by discounting its own price. And harming a competitor is a reasonable secondary goal, but it's only secondary. Securing your own highest payoff perhaps through legal cooperation with a competitor is the primary goal. Because Circuit City would respond to a Sound Warehouse discount by just matching the lower price point, Sound Warehouse would gain nothing by "executing" the hostage in this way. Indeed, for the hostage recipient such a decision would lead to the payoff labeled "WORSE" in the top right of Figure 16.5.

Knowing that Circuit City controls the endgame and that it would be in Circuit City's best interest after announcing the rebate program to match a discount price, Sound Warehouse finds itself preferring to maintain high prices. Because Circuit City is also best off by maintaining high prices, the payoff {BEST*, BETTER} results. Thus, by introducing a price guarantee that limited its own ability to take advantage of its opponent's vulnerability at high prices, Circuit City secured first-best outcomes when the alternative was WORSE (i.e., compare the shaded and unshaded boxed payoffs in Figure 16.5). A hostage mechanism establishing one's credible commitment to maintain high prices if

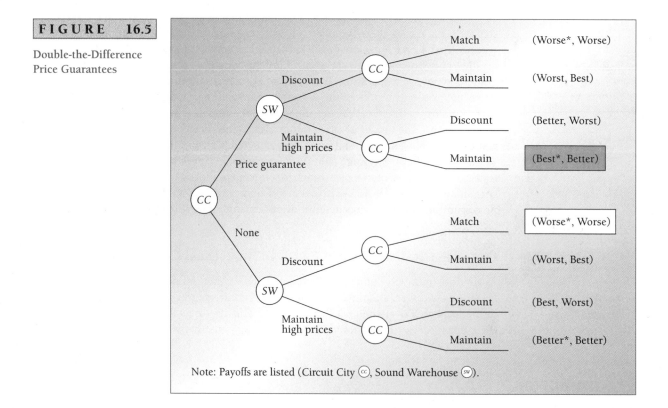

FIGURE   16.5

Double-the-Difference
Price Guarantees

Note: Payoffs are listed (Circuit City ©, Sound Warehouse ⓢⓌ).

the rival maintains high prices, will often elicit high prices from that rival. Thus, from the point of view of both companies, double-the-difference low-price guarantees are unambiguously preferred. Of course, consumer advocates will not prefer these high price outcomes, but complaining about double-the-difference price guarantees attracts few sympathizers to the consumer cause.

As we discussed in Chapter 13, all buyers rationally discount experience goods like used cars and computer components if they can not verify independently at the point of purchase the seller's quality claims. A replacement guarantee or a product performance repair warranty are other good examples of hostage mechanisms—in this case, hostage mechanisms that establish the credibility of a seller's commitment to deliver high-quality goods. Should the seller violate his or her commitment, a third party (usually the courts) will impose on the seller agreed-upon penalties that are larger than the incremental cost of upgrading from lower to higher quality inputs in the first place. Therefore, the buyer is assured of a higher quality machine when the seller offers to include a replacement guarantee or repair warranty for the same (or a slightly higher) price. These guarantees and warranties illustrate a *credible commitment* mechanism—i.e., third-party-enforceable promises that the promise-giver would be worse off violating than keeping.

EXAMPLE

NONCREDIBLE COMMITMENTS: BURLINGTON INDUSTRIES

Classic examples of noncooperative business strategies that malfunction because of the absence of credible commitments include the quota commitments in a cartel and the commitment not to compete after purchasing surplus equipment in a declining industry. Burlington Industries has experienced many problems with the overseas buyers of old looms, which were acquired in mergers and then liquidated at scrap value. The foreign competitors restore the old equipment and then backship their production into the United States despite no-competition clauses in the equipment purchase contracts. Burlington has now begun to destroy old equipment, not just dismantle it, especially in declining product lines where it wishes to pursue a niche strategy as "the last iceman."[8]

As to the quota commitments, recall from Chapter 15 that every cartel must accomplish a restriction of output in order to sustain monopoly cartel prices. If every atomistic cartel member were to take the cartel price as a given and then individually profit maximize, the total industry output would far exceed the supply that maximizes joint cartel profits. Therefore, although reaching a pricing agreement often gets the most public attention when OPEC or other cartels meet, the really difficult work begins afterwards, when the cartel attempts to monitor, detect, and punish quota violations. Commitments by member firms to restrain their output to their assigned quotas are simply not credible commitments. As a consequence, despite many attempts to build teamwork, to secure hostages (both economic and political), and to employ other credibility mechanisms, almost all cartels prove to be highly unstable. The experience in the corrugated cardboard industry is typical. Price-fixing indictments suggest cartels among the cardboard manufacturers within a sales region form approximately quarterly and break up usually within a week to 10 days. In this case, the inability to secure credible commitments serves a desirable public purpose.

---

[8] Kathryn Harrigan has written about this superficially very curious strategy in "Endgame Strategy," *Forbes,* July 1987, pp. 181–196.

Credibility Advantages of Leasing and Renewable Licenses

What buyers will pay for a capital equipment purchase like a corporate jet, a mainframe computer, or a business license depends in part on how well the seller resolves some credible commitment issues. If a piece of equipment has working life that will extend over several market periods, an early buyer of a new model worries about obsolescence and falling prices. What competitive advantages IBM's newest mainframe or minicomputer might offer an information technology user like a direct marketer will be seriously compromised whenever IBM introduces a still newer model and makes the direct marketer's machine obsolete. In addition, other potential buyers who discern somewhat less advantage in the new equipment will likely receive the benefit of a reduced price promotion from IBM at some later date. Knowing this, the first buyer hesitates and offers to pay less than she otherwise would for the new technology. To overcome this persistent problem that will recur with every new generation of equipment, IBM must somehow credibly commit to maintaining high prices and to a planned rate of obsolescence that allows early buyers time to recover their investment costs.

In an industry with very slowly moving technology, a dominant firm could make contractual commitments to phase in new updated equipment only on a preset (delayed) schedule. At times, tractor-trailer trucks have been sold this way, and to a certain extent, the limited body style change from year to year in some automobile models reflects the same idea. However, in the computer industry, even IBM cannot afford such a straitjacket; technology simply moves too fast. So what alternatives remain? Buyers of updated capital equipment can't be expected to risk a lot of capital soon after the roll-out of a new product; yet, companies producing computer equipment cannot lock themselves into delays.

EXAMPLE

LEASING OF MAINFRAMES AND AIRCRAFT: IBM AND LEARJET

One approach is to ask buyers to take small steps by leasing the equipment one market period at a time. Although this fails to slow (and may quicken) the pace of new product introductions, buyers risk less up-front capital and therefore can be induced more easily to take on the new model and update their capital equipment more frequently *at higher prices*. IBM employed exactly this approach for many years by only offering to lease their mainframe computers. The Lear Corporation employs the same techniques in leasing their corporate jets. Although purchase is an option, the lease contracts prove especially attractive to many companies whose business is dependent upon rapidly changing technology.

Careful analysis of the asymmetric information involved in planned obsolescence and in price promotions reveals the tactical advantage of leasing. Because the manufacturer knows the marketing plans and can estimate the pace of technology and the risk of obsolescence much better than the end-user, one would think lease terms can be more favorable when the seller undertakes to absorb the risk of price promotions and planned obsolescence. That is, in a competitive marketplace for capital equipment leases (like the corporate jet lease market), one would expect sellers to offer closed-end leases with residual values that reflect their very accurate estimates of what a two-year-old corporate jet will be worth. This residual value is what really establishes the credibility of the manufacturers' commitment over the lease period to refrain from discounting or introducing a new model that would render the current model obsolete. Were the leasewriter (the lessor) to violate this promise, the asset returned at the end of the lease would be worth less than the residual value at which the manufacturer-lessor has agreed to take it back. In effect, the manufacturer has given a hostage to the leaseholder (the lessee). By agreeing to take back the capital equipment for a preset amount and dispose of it in the resale market themselves, the manufacturer-lessors have credibly committed to a limited set of price promotions and to a limited rate of planned obsolescence.

Of course, there still remains the risk of technological developments that the manufacturer cannot control. The lessor and lessee have credibly committed some things and left others to chance. All remaining risks will be priced into the terms of the residual value lease. As a result, over the lifetime of the equipment it will not be cheaper to lease rather than to buy. To take another example, the buyer who insists on a product warranty imposes the estimable risk of product failure on the seller-lessor; therefore this risk allocation gets priced into a higher lease payment. Nevertheless, manufacturers need some way of credibly committing themselves to maintaining high asking prices and a limited rate of planned obsolescence over the buyer's holding period. Only then will buyers pay the higher prices at which manufacturers wish to transact in the early mature phase of a product's life cycle. **Closed-end leases that declare a residual value** offer such a credible commitment because they demonstrate and certify just what the manufacturer's best estimates of forward value truly are. Leases therefore shore up purchase prices for durable equipment.

Closed-End Lease with Residual Values
A credible commitment mechanism for establishing planned obsolescence and delays in price promotion.

EXAMPLE

LICENSING OF TAXI MEDALLIONS AND CELL PHONES

Similarly, by selling a taxi medallion or a cellular phone authorization as a renewable license, a municipality can credibly commit to a planned increase in supply of the city's transportation and communication infrastructure. If the city were to insist on an outright purchase, taxi and cellular entrepreneurs would be concerned that soon thereafter the city would flood the market with additional taxis and cell phone companies. Consequently, the amounts bid for the right to do business would decline substantially. The point is not that potential license holders wish to avoid being duped, although of course all of us *are* motivated to choose tactics which avoid such embarrassments. Instead, it's that licenses authorizing a business are a property right that the license holders may need to resell. Random disturbances befall every company, and license holders cannot assume that they will be able to realize the cash flows authorized by the license forever. Licenses are durable capital assets, and the preservation of their resale value is of no less concern than would be the case for an owner of a mainframe computer or corporate jet. Municipalities can raise more money therefore with renewable leases for all business licenses.

What occurs in business licensing by municipal and state governments also occurs in the licensing of trade secrets and patents. Again, credible commitments by seller-lessors to actions that will maintain forward asset values are the key to eliciting buyer-lessee willingness to pay. Certainly, at times, a patent holder will maximize value by retaining the patent for its own exclusive use. Manufacturing capacities can be expanded, advertising bought, and distribution systems built. Fungible capital is always available to support promising business plans whatever the stage of development of the patented or patentable products. Nevertheless, the unique manufacturing capabilities, product designers, brand names, or distribution channels of another company may increase the capitalized value of a patent. Taking small steps through renewable leasing and offering residual values as hostages is the mechanism design that maximizes the profitability of releasing many trade secrets and patents.

This section has argued that renewable licensing and leasing offers tactical advantages in establishing credible commitments not obtainable with outright sales. Again, this does *not* imply that leasing will be generally cheaper than buying. Any costs imposed on the seller by the credibility mechanisms (e.g., a higher residual value) will be priced into the lease. The point is simply that some credible commitments impose lower cost on the asymmetrically informed manufacturer as a lessor than would be the discount to the buyer required to achieve the same ends through an outright sale. Consequently, lessor profitability increases with renewable licensing and leasing relative to the alternative profitability available from the sale of durable equipment, business licenses, or patents.

Excess Capacity, Scale of Entry, and Entry Deterrence

In this section we introduce another type of credible threat or commitment, which can markedly influence the subsequent competition—namely, an investment in nonredeployable excess capacity. Irreversible investment in excess capacity credibly commits a high-priced incumbent to serve the price-sensitive new customers who might be attracted into the market by a potential entrant's discounting. If these and other regular customers can be expected to favor doing business with the incumbent, then excess capacity investment can substantially enhance the deterrent effect of an incumbent's threat to cut prices in response to entry.

Why exactly does excess capacity enhance an incumbent's threat to reduce prices should low-price entrants appear in the market? Is it that the incumbent can thereby prevent the new entrant from acquiring a large market share? Is it that the incumbent can deny the new entrant a unique reputation for low prices? Is it that the incumbent can become more profitable than before the entry threat? The answer to all these questions is no. The sole reason any action or communication is credible is if it makes the threat-maker worse off ignoring the threat than carrying out the threat. In Figure 16.6, the competitive firm who invests in excess capacity by expanding from plant 1 to plant 2 is worse off with output Q_1 and unit costs of \$450 at A than selling the larger output Q_2 with unit

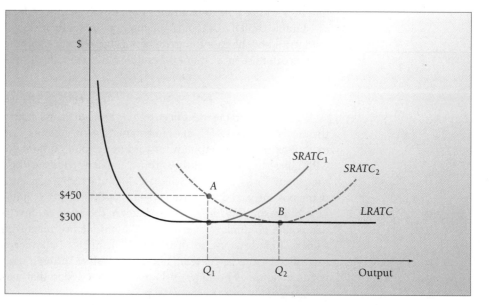

FIGURE   16.6

Excess Capacity
Enhances Credibility in
Entry Deterrence Games

costs of perhaps $300 at B. A noncompetitive firm who must lower price to carry out a threat thereby increases sales and also moves from Q_1 to Q_2. Ignoring the threat would leave the incumbent worse off with higher unit costs at A now that plant 1 has been replaced by plant 2.

Excess Capacity Precommitments

Consider the capacity decision of a well-established medical center hospital that faces an entry threat from an outpatient clinic specializing in obstetrics and elective plastic surgery. The hospital is constructing a new surgical wing. The hospital's business manager can build a facility to meet the future demand projected at their currently high prices, or she can expand the new facility plans to include some considerable excess capacity. Suppose that the birthing rooms and type of operating theater used in obstetrics and plastic surgery are not redeployable to general surgical or other specialized uses. Instead, the excess capacity, if built, will serve as a nonredeployable excess capacity precommitment by the hospital to compete for all the new price-sensitive business that a lower-priced clinic might attract into the market.

The structure of this game is presented in the decision tree in Figure 16.7. The hospital chooses excess capacity or not; the clinic chooses thereafter to enter or stay out, and the hospital then controls the pricing endgame. If the hospital builds excess capacity, it is more likely to cut prices in the face of entry, and the clinic is then better off staying out. If the hospital does not build excess capacity, it is more likely to accommodate the entrant by maintaining high prices, and the clinic is then better off entering. Therefore, looking ahead to predict the hospital and the clinic's best-reply responses in the various proper subgames and endgames, the hospital's likely choices may narrow to two strategies shaded in Figure 16.7: {Excess Capacity, Stay Out, Limit Prices to Forestall Further Entry} and {No Excess Capacity, Enter, Accommodate with Moderate Prices}. Clearly, business as usual is no longer an option. In particular, the very profitable prior business with high prices, no excess capacity, and no competition in the top row of the

Excess Capacity
Precommitment Game

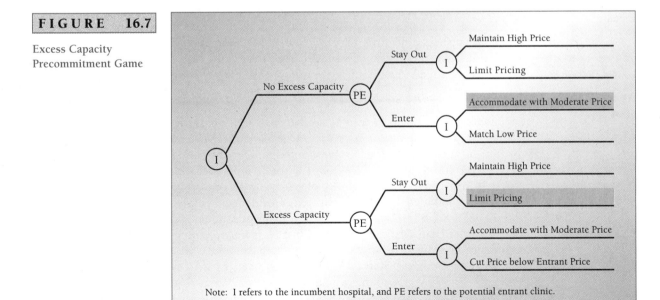

Note: I refers to the incumbent hospital, and PE refers to the potential entrant clinic.

game tree is no longer a focal outcome of interest. The entry threat may require that the hospital now maximize its remaining profit by precommitting itself to constructing some excess capacity. In one scenario, then, the clinic will consider hit-and-run entry while the construction is underway, but decide instead to stay out and enter the same market in another community with less capacity present or projected.

In general, whether incumbents will choose to deter potential entrants (e.g., in the top half of the game tree in Figure 16.7) by the use of excess capacity precommitments or will actually prefer to accommodate (in the bottom half of the game tree) by retaining their smaller capacities and moderate prices is a complex question that depends on several factors. As we saw in both Entry Deterrence I and II, the answer depends in part on whether the incumbent can secure a first-mover advantage. There, the incumbent discounted in one case and maintained moderate prices in the other. It also depends on whether the post-entry competition will be in prices among differentiated product sellers, each with some market power over price, or in quantities among homogeneous product sellers with no market power over price. In addition, the decision to deter or accommodate depends on how old and new customers in various segments of the market sort between an incumbent with excess capacity and a capacity-constrained lower-priced entrant. If the entrant attracts only new price-sensitive customers, that's one thing. If, on the other hand, the new entrant takes away higher willingness-to-pay regular customers of the incumbent, that's something else. Not surprisingly, the former situation more typically leads to accommodation; the latter often leads to deterrence.

Customer Sorting Rules

Brand Loyalty
A customer sorting rule favorable to incumbents.

Efficient Rationing
A customer sorting rule favorable to low-price entrants.

Random Rationing
A customer sorting rule reflecting randomized buyer behavior.

Inverse Intensity Rationing
A customer sorting rule for segmented markets.

Several other alternative sortings are possible. Probably the simplest customer sorting pattern (or rule) is extreme **brand loyalty** to incumbents. In this case, even in the face of differentially higher prices, customers reject the new entrant's offered capacity and instead backorder and reschedule when denied service at the incumbent. Inexorable competitive pressure from imitators normally erodes this degree of market power, but Microsoft might be an example of the exception. At the other extreme, **efficient rationing** allocates the fixed-priced capacity of new entrant discounters in a manner that achieves maximum consumer surplus. This customer sorting rule implies that those with the highest willingness to pay will exert the effort, time, and inconvenience to seek out, queue up, and order early to secure low-priced capacity. Of course, the obvious qualification is that these customers are also likely to have the highest opportunity cost of their time. A third alternative, then, is **random rationing** of the low-priced capacity. Under random rationing, all customers willing to pay the low prices—i.e., both regular customers of the incumbent and the new customers attracted into the market by the entrant's discounting—have an equal chance of securing the low-priced capacity. For example, if 70 customers were present in the market at the incumbent's original high price, and 30 additional customers appear in response to the discounts, the probability of any 1 of the 100 securing service from 1 of the 40 units of low-priced capacity is $40/100 = 0.4$. Conversely, the probability of not being served is $(1 - 0.4) = 0.6$, and under random rationing the incumbent's expected demand falls as a result of the entry from 70 to $70 \times 0.6 = 42$. Finally, a less threatening customer sorting pattern posed by new low-priced capacity in a segmented market is **inverse intensity rationing.** In this instance, the lowest willingness-to-pay customers quickly absorb all the capacity of the low-priced entrant. Starting with that customer just willing to pay the entrant's low price, one proceeds up the demand curve only as far as required to stock out the new entrant. In this instance, the demand of the incumbent may be largely unaffected if the discounter's capacity remains relatively small.

Because of the pivotal nature of the customer sorting patterns, the decision timing, and the nature of the product in predicting deterrence versus accommodation behavior, game-theoretic analysis must often be intertwined with an industry study in order to discriminate among the many possible implications. Otherwise, the rational business decisions of incumbents in these models may vary, from the relatively passive acquisition of enough capacity to absorb the market share of rivals all the way to the aggressive incumbent who occasionally predates in order to be indistinguishable from "crazies"— for example, firms who price below cost with no prospect of later recovering the loss. For the purpose of predicting rival behavior, this state of game-theoretic knowledge presents something of an embarrassment of riches. Hence, we reiterate the importance of doing sufficient field research to discover the particulars of the industry or firm-specific situation.

In the example below, we explore the entry deterrence and accommodation game between Piedmont Airlines (PI) and People Express (PX) between 1984 and 1986. Detailed cost, price, and realized revenue data allow us to distinguish among several pricing and capacity choice implications of sequential game theory. As we shall see, the analysis lends support to the importance of customer sorting patterns in explaining why PX met with little resistance and indeed was accommodated by incumbents in PX's initial mid-Atlantic city-pair markets, but encountered effective deterrence behavior from Piedmont in the Southeastern city-pair markets.

Large-Scale Entry Accommodation of a Low-Cost Competitor

During early 1981 People Express became one of the first new entries into the deregulated interstate airline industry. PX's entry strategy was to offer a uniform low-price, no frills, high-frequency regionwide service to 13 peripheral mid-Atlantic cities using a hub and spoke system out of Newark, New Jersey. By unbundling all services, adopting quick turnaround times, working longer crew shifts, and converting all first-class and galley space into additional coach-class seats, PX achieved a 31 percent reduction relative to the industry average in direct fixed costs per flight (e.g., crew costs) and a 25 percent reduction in variable costs per seat (e.g., cabin service). Having secured the lowest operating cost structure in the industry, PX set out to attract customers who saw air travel as a commodity and would regularly fly rather than drive. The prototypical target customer was a manufacturer's trade representative who often needs to travel on short notice, but is seldom on the company expense account.

In essence, People Express had created a new segment of the market not previously served by much more expensive and infrequent Mohawk and Allegheny flights (the predecessors of US Airways). Importantly, inverse intensity rationing of the cheap capacity ensued. That is, the new low-willingness-to-pay customers attracted into the market by PX's discounting quickly secured all PX's capacity, leaving almost none available to other air travelers. As a result, PX failed to take regular customers away from the higher price point incumbents. Figure 16.8 displays the strategy game this entry presented to the mid-Atlantic regional airlines. The incumbents had to decide whether to match PX's deeply discounted fares or accommodate PX by maintaining high fares. PX had to decide whether to enter with a large-capacity 120-seat Boeing 737 or a small-capacity 30-seat DeHaviland 128.

As in Entry Deterrence I, the new entrant had to decide first, but prediction of the equilibrium strategy was easy because PX had a dominant strategy. No matter what the incumbents' pricing response to the mid-Atlantic markets, PX had higher payoffs from a large-capacity entry. PX's payoffs of $3,877 and $2,068 per flight with frequently scheduled larger capacity aircraft dominated $969 per flight with frequently scheduled

FIGURE   16.8

Large-Scale Entry
Accommodation with
Inverse Intensity
Rationing

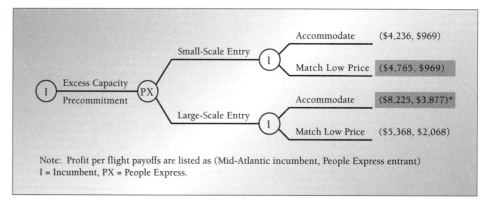

Note: Profit per flight payoffs are listed as (Mid-Atlantic incumbent, People Express entrant)
I = Incumbent, PX = People Express.

small- capacity aircraft. Examining the payoffs resulting from large-capacity entry, the incumbents prefer to accommodate with $8,225 operating profit per flight rather than match and earn only $5,368 per flight. Even though by matching PX's discount, incumbents could pick up extra seats in overflow demand from People's customers, the loss of margin was sufficient to induce the incumbents to prefer to accommodate large-scale entry. {Large Capacity, Accommodate} therefore proved to be the subgame perfect equilibrium. Using leaseback purchases to leverage its modest start-up capital into 17 large capacity planes, People Express intensively developed a dozen peripheral mid-Atlantic routes and thereby managed to avoid retaliation from either the regional or major carriers.

In the Southeast regional markets, the situation was entirely different. Piedmont was the second fastest growing airline in the postderegulation era. By serving small- to medium-size cities ignored by the major carriers and by connecting through hubs with little or no competition, Piedmont retained a record 95 percent of its passengers on connecting flights. Piedmont knew that its reputation with business travelers was high and rising, but also knew that measuring tactical success against a new entrant would require hard data. Piedmont therefore proceeded to count and categorize every passenger on every PX flight into Piedmont cities. From this competitor surveillance data, Piedmont determined that several travel segments sorted randomly to the low-price supplier when substantial price differentials were present, but loyalty to the incumbent prevailed when prices were identical. This brand preference for the incumbent was almost universal at $79 prices, but remained strong even with the new lower-willingness-to-pay customers attracted into the market by People's discounting to $49, $39, $29, and even $19.

Large-Scale Entry Deterrence of a Low-Cost Competitor

Figure 16.9 displays the entry deterrence and accommodation game with random rationing that presented itself to Piedmont and People Express in early 1985; the boxed data lists the common information. On a typical 400-mile route, Piedmont had to decide whether to Match PX's $49 one-way fares or Accommodate the new entrant by maintaining its own $79 one-way fares. Again, PX had to decide whether to enter with a Large Capacity 120-seat Boeing 737 or a Small Capacity 30-seat DeHaviland 128. And again, PX had to decide first; the incumbent's (i.e., Piedmont's) pricing decision controlled the endgame.

Analysis of the subgame perfect equilibrium strategy is straightforward. First, let's examine the payoffs resulting from small capacity entry in the top half of the diagram. The incumbent (PI) prefers to accommodate with $6,979 operating profit per flight rather than match and earn only $5,365 per flight. Even if by matching PX's discount, the incumbent picks up 30 extra seats from People's customers, the loss of margin from ($79 − $16.69) to ($49 − $16.69) is sufficient to reduce the operating profit from $6,979 to

FIGURE   16.9   Matching Price Response with Random Rationing

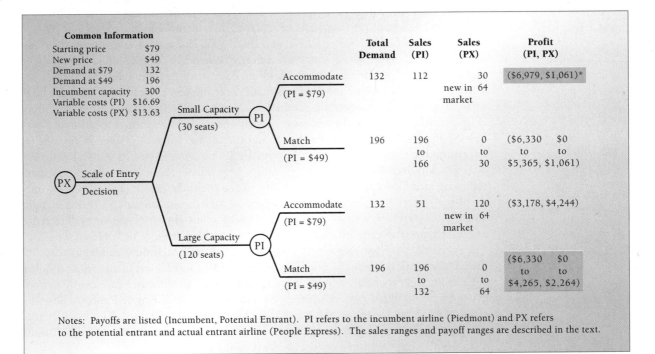

Common Information					
Starting price	$79				
New price	$49				
Demand at $79	132				
Demand at $49	196				
Incumbent capacity	300				
Variable costs (PI)	$16.69				
Variable costs (PX)	$13.63				

	Total Demand	Sales (PI)	Sales (PX)	Profit (PI, PX)
Small Capacity (30 seats)				
Accommodate (PI = $79)	132	112	30 new in market 64	($6,979, $1,061)*
Match (PI = $49)	196	196 to 166	0 to 30	($6,330 $0 to to $5,365, $1,061)
Large Capacity (120 seats)				
Accommodate (PI = $79)	132	51	120 new in market 64	($3,178, $4,244)
Match (PI = $49)	196	196 to 132	0 to 64	($6,330 $0 to to $4,265, $2,264)

Notes: Payoffs are listed (Incumbent, Potential Entrant). PI refers to the incumbent airline (Piedmont) and PX refers to the potential entrant and actual entrant airline (People Express). The sales ranges and payoff ranges are described in the text.

$6,330. Consequently, the second row of endgame outcomes must be eliminated by PX from further consideration; Piedmont would never select it.

Turning then to the large capacity payoffs, the situation is a bit different. With its 120-seat capacity a 737 PX can satisfy all 64 new demanders attracted into the market at price points between $79 and $49 and in addition can offer 56 seats of remaining capacity to the incumbent's price-sensitive customers. In PX's mid-Atlantic markets, this had not proven a problem for incumbents because inverse intensity rationing of PX's cheap capacity described the customer sorting pattern. In contrast, in Piedmont's Southeastern markets, PX's capacity was randomly rationed. With accommodative differential prices of $79 and $49, every customer willing to pay at least $49 would then have an equal probability of securing service from the low-price entrant. For large-scale entry, this meant that 120 seats would be rationed among 196 customers so each of the 132 customers willing to pay the incumbent's $79 accommodating price faces a $(1 - (196 - 120)/196) = 0.61$ chance of being served and a 0.39 chance of being denied service at the low-price entrant. Therefore, the expected demand at Piedmont from accommodating large-scale entry was $132 \times 0.39 = 51$ seats, which implied an expected operating profit of only $3,178.

Responding to the large-scale entry by matching prices offered the potential for much greater Piedmont profit (i.e., $6,330). Again, to ascertain the payoffs in the face of large-scale entry, the incumbent employed extensive competitor surveillance and tracking of target customers, such as the regional headquarters personnel flying regularly back and forth to corporate headquarters in New York. This data allowed Piedmont to conclude that at worst, with matching $49 prices, People Express would attract all 64 new customers who had entered the market in response to discounting, but none of Piedmont's regular customers. At worst, then, Piedmont would receive $(\$49 - \$16.69) \times 132 = \$4,265$ from matching PX's discount and only $3,178 from accommodating prices. Consequently, PX should have eliminated from further consideration its otherwise very attractive $4,244 per flight outcome associated with Piedmont's accommodation of PX's large-scale entry. Predictably, Piedmont would never go for it. Then, from People's perspective, the profit per flight from Large Capacity entry, using PX's lower incremental variable cost of $13.63, was at best ($49 − $13.63) × 64 = $2,264 and could go as low as zero. In contrast, the profit per flight from Small Capacity entry was a nearly certain $1,061. PX should have realized that the subgame perfect equilibrium was {Small Capacity, Accommodate}.

Instead, what actually happened was that People Express entered with the same large capacity employed in its peripheral mid-Atlantic routes. Piedmont was surprised, but of course matched prices, and a price war quickly ensued. At one point, the fares got down to $19, and residents of the Carolinas found themselves invited to "tavern lunches" at Tavern on the Green in New York. Eventually PX's operating profits fell so low it was forced to withdraw. People Express appears to have failed to recognize that with random rationing at differential prices and loyalty to the incumbent at matching prices, only small-scale entry could induce accommodation and the sustainable $1,061 per flight payoffs that were available in this market. This basic insight of several entry deterrence and accommodation games is sometimes humorously referred to as "judo economics." The subgame perfect strategic equilibrium in which mid-Atlantic incumbents were induced to accommodate large-scale entry presumed, of course, inverse intensity rationing such as PX had experienced in its original markets. When the customer sorting pattern changed, the subgame perfect strategic equilibrium changed. People Express chose the right strategy, but for the wrong game and ended up being deterred. The fundamental and generalizable managerial insight here is that differences in customer sorting patterns alter the best-reply responses of incumbents facing entry.

A Role for Sunk Costs in Decision Making

In both theory and practice, sequential games of entry deterrence and accommodation have uncovered a very rich variety of strategic incumbent behavior in response to entry or potential entry. These include the excess capacity precommitments just discussed as well as the credible price discount threats of the previous section. However, they also include price discrimination and capacity allocation schemes based on customer loyalty (e.g., frequent flyer mileage) and advance purchase requirements. Such yield management or revenue management systems can provide incumbents with an effective way to deter new entrant discounters. We discuss the tactical role of revenue management in the next chapter. Finally, entry deterrence and accommodation strategy may also be expressed through advertising campaigns or other promotional investments in nonredeployable assets. Some examples would be reputational investments in company logos (such as Beatrice), or showrooms specially coordinated to enhance only Thomasville Furniture, or L'eggs retail displays unusable for selling anything other than egg-shaped products. All three investments precommit the incumbent to aggressively defend market share and cash flow in order to recover the cost of these nonredeployable investments.

Nonredeployable investments are a reality in many industries. Industrial machinery is often specialized to the purpose at hand and sometimes even to a particular supplier. For decades, Sara Lee Hosiery bought twisted nylon fiber for their highest quality hosiery from a sole source supplier; the upstream nylon production equipment and the downstream hosiery spinning equipment were only usable in this one application. Much of the trade secret knowledge discovered by Microsoft programmers is not easily packaged and separated out for redeployment and sale to another firm. Even airplanes can not be redeployed to routes and trip distances for which they are not designed. Markets in which nonredeployable, sunk cost assets are common will deter entry.

Contestable Market
An industry with exceptionally open entry and easy exit where incumbents are slow to react.

Contestable markets are strategic industry groups in which new firms can enter and exit on short notice without anticipating losses due to sunk costs. Even if only a few firms dominate such a market, prices seldom stay above break-even levels because of the constant "hit and run" tactics. Rival firms jump in and scallop off the profits whenever prices rise and then escape quickly once the profits are dissipated. This ensures little divergence from cost-covering competitive equilibrium. In the perfectly contestable markets scenario, incumbents react more slowly to entry threats than their regular customers who chase after the most inexpensive supplier of the moment. Clearly, this is an unusual "strategic group." More typically, proactive incumbents invest in excess capacity and nonredeployable assets in order to deter entry.

That may sound like sunk-cost reasoning, and indeed that is exactly what it is. Recognizing the sequential interdependence of rivalrous strategy and the role of credible threats and credible commitments therein has led to a rehabilitation of the role of sunk costs in managerial decision making. In fact, it is because firms can do nothing about their sunk-cost investments, precisely because they are irreversible, irrevocable, and otherwise unrecoverable, that a particular threatened plan of action involving the return on these assets is credible. The player with sunk-cost investments has burned bridges; no better alternatives exist. Again, best-reply reasoning is the key to credibility, and credibility is the key to subgame perfect equilibrium strategy.

EXAMPLE

CONTESTABLE MARKET IN BICYCLE HELMETS: BELL SPORTS[9]

Bell Sports began as a motorcycle helmet manufacturer with a small side-bet business in bicycle helmets and accessories. In 1986 sales in the bicycle line were $2 million per year. Today Bell has sales of bicycle helmets nearing $100 million, 85 percent of which occur in the United States. So far, only nine states have initiated regulations making bicycle helmets mandatory for young riders. The potential growth in Europe, where Bell helmets have become a fashion statement, is even greater. Prices range from $29 for colorful hard-shell designs to $80 for ultra-lightweight infant helmets.

The trouble with running a fast-growing niche business is that without sunk-cost investments Bell inevitably attracts many new competitors. Bicycle helmets are easy to fabricate and quickly sell themselves. All one needs is plastic molding machines and a foam extrusion process. These technologies are easily converted from many other industries, and more importantly, can be redeployed to those other uses upon exit. The product sells well in bike shops and such discount stores as Kmart and Wal-Mart without any significant sales force, point-of-sale actions, or after-sale service required of the retail distributors. Consequently, the bicycle helmet market is a classic case of *contestable markets*. Bell Sports is constantly subject to hit-and-run entry from other niche manufacturers—for example, American Recreation, Troxel Cycling, and Giro Sports.

The theory of contestable markets suggests that with no barriers to entry or exit and low customer costs of switching manufacturers, Bell Sports can never make more than a competitive profit in this business. As soon as prices rise above cost, temporary competitors enter the business, customers switch their allegiance, and Bell must lower prices. As a consequence, gross margins are low (averaging 8 percent) and fluctuate by as much as 50 percent from year to year. Bell's only alternatives are to outquick the hit-and-run entrants on new designs or to commit enough marketing investment dollars to establish a nonredeployable brand asset "Bell Helmets," known for safety with style. Until then, entry deterrence will prove infeasible, and entry accommodation must continue.

---

[9] Based on "Bell Sports," *Forbes*, 13 February 1995, pp. 67–68.

SIMULTANEOUS GAMES

Although sequential game reasoning is critical to the successful conduct of business strategy, some decisions must be made simultaneously with one's rivals. Consider offers in a sealed-bid auction for mineral rights or cellular phone licenses, release dates for fashion clothing collections, sales territory assignments, contract bids for new business, promotional ads to meet a newspaper deadline, and posted price announcements. We have already seen one setting in which rival firms must reveal their prices quite literally one moment apart. Every morning at 7:00 A.M. each airline announces all its fares for all its routes at an electronic clearinghouse sponsored by the airline industry.

The same problem also exists for cruise ship operators. Suppose that two cruise lines, Carnival and Royal Caribbean, operate the only three-day Caribbean cruises from Miami. If each firm acts independently to maximize its own profits, the long-run (Cournot equilibrium) profit-maximizing price is $300 per person. If two firms act jointly (e.g., form a cartel) to maximize total industry profits, the profit-maximizing price is $450. Assume that these are the only two prices under consideration.

The payoffs or profits to each firm are shown in Table 16.3. The below diagonal number in each cell is the payoff to Carnival, and the above diagonal number is the payoff to Royal Caribbean. Each firm is reluctant to choose the (jointly) more profitable $450 price. If either firm reneges and discounts to $300, then the firm that charges $450 will earn significantly lower profits than the rival. This game has a typical Prisoner's Dilemma ordering of outcomes. As we have seen, only a sucker unilaterally cooperates by announcing high prices under such circumstances. For example, the payoff for Royal Caribbean from unilateral defection ($375,000) exceeds the payoff from mutual cooperation at high prices ($275,000), which itself exceeds the payoff from mutual defection at low prices ($185,000), which finally exceeds the payoff from unilateral cooperation ($60,000). This ensures that Royal Caribbean has a dominant strategy—for example, to defect. Carnival, on the other hand, has no such dominant strategy. However, because Carnival can predict Royal Caribbean's behavior, by eliminating the prospect of Royal Caribbean's dominated $450 strategy, Carnival can iterate to a preferable strategy itself. Therefore, Carnival's behavior is also quite predictable, and the **iterated dominant strategy** equilibrium proves to be {$300, $300} or {Defect, Defect} just as in Prisoner's Dilemma itself.

Iterated Dominant Strategy
An equilibrium concept independent of rival response and therefore strongly predictive of strategic behavior.

Note that both cruise ship companies could have had dominant strategies, but that is unnecessary for **iterated dominant strategy** equilibrium. The reason is that a dominant strategy requires no particular optimal or suboptimal response behavior on the part of anyone else. It is defined as an action for player i that is an optimal action $\{a_i^*\}$ in the

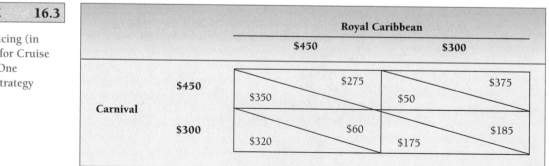

TABLE   16.3

Duopoly Pricing (in thousands) for Cruise Ships with One Dominant Strategy

		Royal Caribbean	
		$450	**$300**
Carnival	**$450**	$350 / $275	$50 / $375
	$300	$320 / $60	$175 / $185

Notes: Column-player payoffs (in thousands) are above the diagonal. Row-player payoffs are below the diagonal.

strong sense that no matter what other players do, the payoff for player i $\Pi_i \{a_i^*, a_{-i}\}$ exceeds the payoff for player i from any other action $\Pi_i \{a_i, a_{-i}\}$:[10]

$$\Pi_i \{a_i^*, a_{-i}\} > \Pi_i \{a_i, a_{-i}\}. \qquad\qquad [16.1]$$

Consequently, one dominant strategy is quite enough to predict rival behavior and therefore strategic equilibrium in any two-person game. Once Royal Caribbean's dominant strategy (i.e., to defect and cut prices to $300) has been identified, Carnival's behavior (i.e., to also defect) is easily predictable. We have seen this twice before in "Six or Seven Territories?" and in "Marauder-Guarder." Recall that Kahn had no dominant strategy but was able to predict his rival's behavior based on her dominant strategy, and that was enough for him to identify an optimal strategic equilibrium response.

Nash Equilibrium Strategy

What about games without any dominant strategy? To examine this question we now return to the problem at the beginning of the chapter concerning Pepsi and Coca-Cola. If unilateral defection by one's rival (i.e., low rival prices in the face of your high prices) should result in $6,000 payoffs, then the problem is simple and each firm has a dominant strategy to defect to the new lower prices. But what if that circumstance now pays off $9,000 for Pepsi as in Table 16.4?[11] Then, there is no dominant strategy. Pepsi wants to discount when Coca-Cola maintains higher prices ($14,000 > $12,000), but just as clearly Pepsi wants to maintain higher prices when Coca-Cola discounts ($9,000 > $6,300). And, the same ambiguity is present for Coca-Cola. What criteria allow the prediction of rival behavior in this game of "Renegade Discounting"?

The answer lies in a reflexive application of the concept of best-reply response. If an action were the best reply to a rival's action, which in turn was the best reply to the original action, the parties would have identified an equilibrium strategy. More formally, a **Nash equilibrium strategy** is defined as an action for player i that is conditionally optimal $\{a_i^*\}$ in that the payoff for player i, given best-reply responses by rivals $\Pi_i \{a_i^*, a_{-i}^*\}$, exceeds the payoff for player i from any other action $\Pi_i \{a_i, a_{-i}^*\}$ given best-reply responses of rivals:

$$\Pi_i \{a_i^*, a_{-i}^*\} > \Pi_i \{a_i, a_{-i}^*\} \qquad\qquad [16.2]$$

Nash Equilibrium Strategy
An optimal action rule or criterion based upon an assumption of best-reply rival responses.

---

[10] A starred action refers to a maximizing choice—namely, here, an action that results from maximizing profit.

[11] The rest of the payoff matrix has been altered to more readily identify the moves and countermoves of each party. Nevertheless, the qualitative structure of the game's outcomes remains the same.

TABLE   16.4

Renegade Discounting in Soft Drinks with No Dominant Strategy

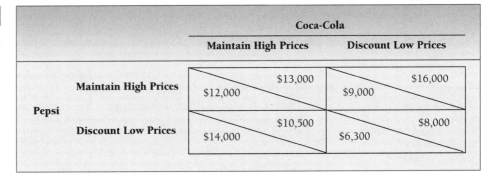

		Coca-Cola	
		Maintain High Prices	**Discount Low Prices**
Pepsi	**Maintain High Prices**	$12,000 / $13,000	$9,000 / $16,000
	Discount Low Prices	$14,000 / $10,500	$6,300 / $8,000

In Renegade Discounting there are two such pure Nash equilibria: {Maintain$_p$*, Discount$_c$*} and {Discount$_p$*, Maintain$_c$*} where the subscripts refer to Pepsi and Coca-Cola. Recall that here there is no order of play; we could have just as easily reversed the recording of the actions in these strategy pairs listing Coca-Cola rather than Pepsi first. The actual rivals appear to have perceived precisely this point because, for 42 weeks in 1992, they took turns discounting their grocery store merchandise.

What is notable about these Nash strategies is that they are nonunique. The multiple equilibria occur because Nash equilibrium is weaker (i.e., easier to satisfy) than dominant strategy equilibrium. The latter requires that an action be optimal for every possible rival response, whereas Nash equilibrium requires only that an action be optimal for a best-reply rival response. That is a less demanding requirement of the equilibrium strategy set and therefore easier to satisfy. However, this knowledge does not help solve Pepsi's problem as to what price to announce. Remember that each bottler is announcing its price without knowing until afterwards what its rival announced. If Pepsi believed Coca-Cola would discount half the time and maintain half the time, the expected value of Pepsi's maintaining is $10,500, whereas the expected value of Pepsi's discounting is smaller (i.e., only $10,150). This would seem to suggest a preference for maintaining high prices, but again, predictably high Pepsi prices allow Coca-Cola to unilaterally defect and earn $16,000, whereas Pepsi would then realize only $9,000. So how can Pepsi avoid tipping its hand and ending up with the $9,000 outcome rather than its own $14,000 defection outcome too often?

The answer lies in Pepsi's randomizing the pricing process. Pepsi must figure out what automated pricing response would make Coca-Cola indifferent between maintaining and discounting and thereby willing to randomize its own price announcement. That is, what probability of discounting by Pepsi will equate Coca-Cola's expected payoff from maintaining high prices to its expected payoff from discounting? Interestingly, because the payoffs are asymmetrical, the desired probability is not 0.5. Let's see what the solution is. Using p and $(1-p)$ to represent the probabilities of Pepsi's maintaining and discounting, respectively, we calculate

$$(p)\ \$13,000 + (1-p)\ \$10,500 = (p)\ \$16,000 + (1-p)\ \$8,000 \qquad [16.3]$$

where the Coca-Cola payoffs have been arranged to correspond to the columns of Table 16.4. The solution probabilities $p = 0.454$ and $(1-p) = 0.546$ accomplish the objective of making Coca-Cola indifferent and therefore its choice unpredictably random.

Note, however, there is a mirror-image Nash reflexivity associated with this solution concept. Coca-Cola faces a comparable payoff structure and strategy dilemma to that of Pepsi, and presumably therefore would want to know what probabilities of maintaining and discounting would make Pepsi indifferent between the two choices. Calculating as before

$$(p')\ \$12,000 + (1-p')\ \$9,000 = (p')\ \$14,000 + (1-p')\ \$6,300 \qquad [16.4]$$

where the Pepsi payoffs have been arranged to correspond to the rows of Table 16.4, we obtain $p' = 0.574$ and $(1-p') = 0.426$. If randomized choice by Pepsi is a best-reply response to randomness by Coca-Cola, and if Coca-Cola can then do no better, this renegade discounting game must have a third Nash equilibrium strategy—namely, {Maintain by Pepsi with $p = 0.454$, Maintain by Coca-Cola with $p' = 0.574$}. This strategy pair is called a **mixed Nash equilibrium strategy**. A 0.454 probability weight on maintaining and a 0.546 probability weight on discounting by Pepsi yields $11,634 expected value for each of Coca-Cola's price announcement strategies. Similarly, a 0.574 probability weight on maintaining and a 0.426 probability weight on discounting by Coca-Cola yields $10,720 expected value for each of Pepsi's price announcement strategies. There

Mixed Nash Equilibrium Strategy
A strategic equilibrium concept involving randomized behavior.

are therefore two pure and one mixed Nash strategy in the strategic equilibrium solution for this game.[12]

The adoption of a conspicuous automated mechanism to implement this mixed Nash strategy (e.g., a computer mechanism to replicate the appropriate unfair coin toss) is a way of implementing the mixed strategy. In principle, however, none of these three Nash equilibrium strategies is preferable to any other. In a one-shot play of Renegade Discounting, all four cells in Table 16.4 still arise. The {$6,300, $8,000} outcome in the southeast cell and the {$12,000, $13,000} outcome in the northwest cell as well as the two asymmetric outcomes that correspond to our two pure Nash strategies will all sometimes arise. In a noncooperative simultaneous game incorporating no communication in advance, no side payments, and no binding agreements, there is simply no way to avoid this multiplicity of possible strategic equilibria. In practice, therefore, a one-shot play of any of the three Nash strategies in the renegade discounting game can work out very well or very badly.

Of course, the {$12,000, $13,000} outcome is best of all. In the next section we will see how to secure this win-win outcome by introducing repeated plays, imperfect information, and credibility mechanisms to convert this simultaneous game to a sequential game.[13] In conclusion, Nash equilibrium strategies are optimal strategies when information about payoffs is complete and certain and when one player's actions cannot influence another player's choices. Sometimes business managers are simply stuck with those conditions.

EXAMPLE

KODAK TAKES A PROMOTIONAL DISCOUNT[14]

To avoid price wars, Eastman Kodak Co. constantly rolls out new products and segments photographic film into several tiers. Kodak Regular film sells at one price point. Kodak Instacolor sells at a higher price point. And Kodak Gold sells at the highest price point. Recently, at Christmastime 1997, Kodak Gold was replaced by a new line called Family of Gold. Between September and Christmas, Kodak decided to discount Gold film 10 percent in some distribution channels and 20 percent in others. Although the original list prices would have made more money for Kodak if competitor prices had remained high, Fuji Photo Film Co. correctly anticipated this short-term promotion of the product Kodak was retiring and proceeded to cut its prices 35 percent. Both companies perceived a one-shot Prisoner's Dilemma simultaneous pricing game.

ESCAPE FROM PRISONER'S DILEMMA

In this section, we relax the assumptions of single-play, complete and perfect information games. Let's return to the Prisoner's Dilemma payoff structure of the opening situation posed in this chapter. Recall that both Pepsi and Coca-Cola were in that case worse off if either unilaterally defected from maintaining high prices. The payoff matrix is presented in Table 16.5. These are operating profits per week per store. Each soft drink bottler would like to pursue the $12,000 payoff, but the only way to avoid the vulnerability of a unilateral defection is by defecting oneself! Dominant strategy drives both

---

[12] The simultaneous manufacturer/distributor game in Table 16.1 also can be solved using mixed strategy. If the manufacturer increases prices with probability 0.60 and the retailer discontinues services with probability 0.71, the two companies will each have made their opponent's decision unpredictably random.

[13] Barry Nalebuff calls this "changing the nature of competition" and sharply distinguishes the conduct from "collusion" that would violate the antitrust laws. See "Businessman's Dilemma," *Forbes*, 11 October 1993, p. 107.

[14] Based on "Kodak Cuts Price on Film," *ABC News and Starwave Co.*, 26 September 1997.

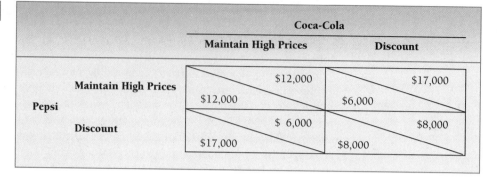

TABLE 16.5

A Repeated Prisoner's Dilemma in Soft Drinks (in thousands)

		Coca-Cola	
		Maintain High Prices	**Discount**
Pepsi	**Maintain High Prices**	$12,000 / $12,000	$17,000 / $6,000
	Discount	$6,000 / $17,000	$8,000 / $8,000

players to discount their 12-packs in the one-shot game. However, surely Pepsi and Coca-Cola recognize they are engaged in an ongoing competitive process, not a one-shot (i.e., single-play) game. Week after week, they will encounter one another in many future replays of this pricing game at grocery and convenience stores all across the nation. Consequently, tacit cooperation rather than dogmatic price cutting has a chance to evolve.

Suppose Coca-Cola begins the process by announcing that a high price will be maintained in period one. The intention is to play that price continuously until Pepsi defects and thereafter to never announce High again. This is a so-called **grim trigger strategy.** One perturbation by Pepsi away from cooperative High pricing, and Coca-Cola's punishment is immediate and never-ending. Multiperiod punishment schemes are a key to inducing cooperation in Prisoner's Dilemma games whether it is film prices, airline fare wars, or soft drink pricing. In this case, Pepsi compares the perpetuity opportunity loss of ($12,000 − $8,000) discounted at the rate d to the one-time gain from defection of ($17,000 − $12,000):

$$\$4,000/d > \$5,000$$

Grim Trigger Strategy
A strategy involving infinitely long punishment schemes.

At any discount rate less than 80 percent, the forgone future gains from cooperatively maintaining high prices outweigh the one-time gains from defection. At any lower rate of discount, the dominant strategy to defect in one-shot games is no longer determinative in perpetual games. This calculation and conclusion reflect a generalizable **Folk theorem,** which states that for any payoff structure a discount rate always exists that is small enough to induce cooperation in an infinitely repeated Prisoner's Dilemma.

Folk Theorem
A conclusion about cooperation in repeated Prisoner's Dilemma.

Because companies do not last forever, the Folk theorem raises an obvious question, "What about for shorter periods, say 20 weeks?" The 20-period calculation is easily done; d now must be less than 79 percent. But if 20 weeks, what about for 2 weeks? Suppose it is now the beginning of week 2. We know we are out of this competitive structure next week (i.e., week 3), so our remaining incentive to maintain high prices is only $\$4,000/(1 + d)$, and our incentive to defect is $5,000. Now all of a sudden, for any discount rate, we're better off defecting. This, too, is a generalizable result. The last play of a repeated Prisoner's Dilemma has the same incentives as a one-shot Prisoner's Dilemma; everybody defects. Therefore, one period away from the endgame of a repeated play Prisoner's Dilemma, neither party has an incentive to maintain its reputation for cooperating. This proposition is even true when rivals adopt grim trigger strategies. If the endgame is at hand, any scheme for punishing defection has little sting.

Unraveling and the Chainstore Paradox

In fact, the prospects for cooperation in any finitely repeated Prisoner's Dilemma are very poor indeed. What is true for a 2-period game must be true by backwards induction for a 3-period game, a 4-period game, and even a 20-period game. Reinhard Selten investi-

Unraveling Problem
A failure of cooperation in games of finite length.

gated this **unraveling problem** for finitely repeated Prisoner's Dilemmas in the context of chainstore incumbents facing repeated entry threats from rivals.[15] In a Prisoner's Dilemma setting just like those we've been examining, the incumbent has a dominant strategy to accommodate the new entrant, even though fighting entry would be preferable if only the potential entrant would stay out. But one's intuition says that in the face of enough repetitions of the chainstore competition, the incumbent's reputation for fighting entry can pay off. And in the extreme this intuition is correct. In **infinitely repeated games,** the Folk theorem does apply. However, in any fewer repetitions, in even the number of chainstore competitions that might face a MacDonalds or a Wal-Mart, the cooperative equilibrium unravels.

Infinitely Repeated Games
A game that lasts forever.

Selten invented the concept of subgame perfect strategic equilibrium to show this paradoxical result and to emphasize the sequential nature of reputation effects and the pivotal role of endgame reasoning. In Figure 16.10 we have a chainstore Incumbent (I) who accommodates or fights in response to a Potential Entrant (PE) who stays out or enters. Accommodation forgoes some of the incumbent chainstore's profit ($100,000 − $80,000) and induces future entry, but fighting entry to acquire a reputation for toughness entails actual losses now (−$10,000). Conceive of the displayed game tree as the last three encounters of a 20-chainstore competition perceived by both players from the start. Looking ahead to the endgame, it is clear that the incumbent will accommodate in the last submarket where it is presently located or at least in the last submarket where it hopes to locate in the future. Eighty thousand dollars exceeds $60,000, and there is no future payoff thereafter to a tough reputation for fighting (or anything else). There is no thereafter! Because the Potential Entrant also knows this, entry will surely take place in that last submarket.

Now, in looking back to the previous submarket (i.e., the nineteenth store), the incumbent realizes that its rival's subsequent entry in the twentieth submarket is certain and therefore that, again, there is no return to reputation for fighting in that nineteenth submarket. Accommodate is therefore the best-reply response in the proper subgame from node B onward to the endgame. Because the entrant can predict this decision as well, entry occurs in the nineteenth submarket at node A. But what is true of the nineteenth must therefore be true of the eighteenth, and the seventeenth, and so forth right back to the start of the game.

Chainstore Paradox
A prediction of always accommodative behavior by incumbents facing entry threats.

This is the backwards induction reasoning that leads to the **chainstore paradox.** We can calculate in submarket 1 that at reasonable rates of discount the incumbent has sufficient NPV from future deterrence to justify fighting rather than accommodating. Yet, the credibility of the incumbent's present fighting is jeopardized by the predictability of its future accommodation. And because of that predictability of accommodation as a best-reply response all the way out to the endgame, the reputation effects of any present fighting unravel. Accommodation therefore occurs in every submarket or every period in the 20-submarket/20-period game just as we argued earlier it would in the 2-submarket/2-period game.

Cooperative Equilibrium in Repeated Prisoner's Dilemma

www . . . .
You can access a recent working paper on the chainstore paradox at the following Internet archive site maintained by Washington University in Saint Louis:
http://econwpa.wustl. edu/eprints/mic/papers/ 9701/9701005.abs

Perhaps the most exciting recent development in noncooperative game theory has been the pursuit and discovery of exceptions to this unraveling result in the chainstore paradox. One way to short-circuit the reasoning of the chainstore paradox is to introduce an uncertain ending of the game. If the incumbent can never be sure whether future encounters beyond submarket 20 will arise, then the reputational effect of fighting in the

---

[15] See J. Harsanyi and R. Selten, *A General Theory of Equilibrium Selection in Games* (Cambridge: MIT Press, 1988), or for a less technical treatment, E. Rasmussen, *Games and Information*, 2d ed. (Cambridge: Blackwell, 1994), chap. 5.

FIGURE 16.10   The Chainstore Paradox

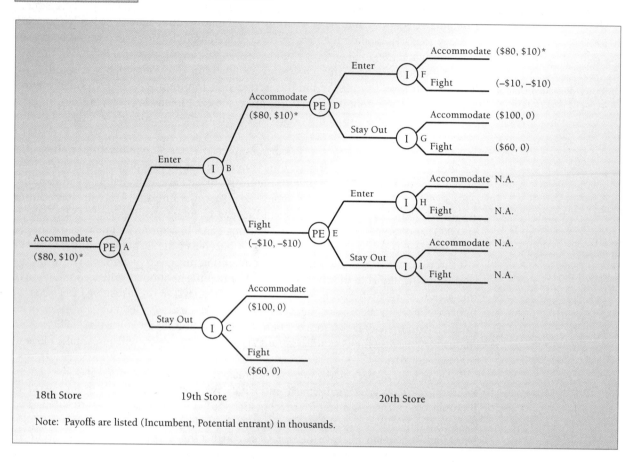

Note: Payoffs are listed (Incumbent, Potential entrant) in thousands.

nineteenth period returns. Any positive probability that the game will continue is sufficient (again, at low enough discount rates) to restore the deterrent effect of fighting in period 20. If fighting is rational in period 20, then the incumbent is willing to fight in 19, 18, and so forth back to period 1. And if it is willing in period 1, then it may not have to because the other firm will not enter. The analogous implication in a finitely-repeated pricing game such as Renegade Discounting is that the rivals will cooperate by maintaining high prices as long as the endgame is uncertain. Therefore, infinite repetition is not required to induce cooperation in Prisoner's Dilemmas; an uncertain ending will suffice.

EXAMPLE

VIOLATION OF THE CHAINSTORE PARADOX: SEMICONDUCTOR PRICING AT INTEL, NEC, AND MOTOROLA[16]

These insights seem especially important in industries with fast-changing technology, such as computer chips and consumer electronics, where cost disadvantages that might end an incumbent's business are seldom permanent because the technology changes so often. One illustration is the semiconductor industry where Intel and Motorola have recently returned to dominance after almost being displaced by Japanese firms such as Hitachi, NEC, and Toshiba 10 years ago.

[16] Based on *Investor's Business Daily*, 13 January 1998, p. A8.

With each successive generation of chips, the market leaders practice life cycle pricing techniques. After a period of high target pricing and value-based pricing, Intel with 26 percent of the worldwide market limits price rather than accommodate NEC with 13 percent, Motorola with 10 percent and numerous small competitors. That is, chip prices are slashed in an attempt to deter entry by the imitators. Then, with uncertain timing, the whole process repeats itself. New chips are introduced at high prices, imitators reverse engineer the design, and limit pricing again ensues. The uncertain endpoint of the successive chip generation games leads to a violation of the chainstore paradox.

Another ingenious escape from Prisoner's Dilemma incorporates the Bayesian probability concept of estimating opponent types based on the forecast provided by past events. If some irrational "crazies" who do not always maximize payoff profit are known to exist in a market, a perfectly sane incumbent may take actions that seem crazy. The intent of the incumbent is to secure an asymmetric information pooling equilibrium in which the incumbent is indistinguishable from the crazies.[17] An example would be an automobile manufacturing incumbent who predates—for example, prices below variable cost—even though the operating losses from such a strategy may not be recoverable in excess profits later. Japanese automobile manufacturers are often accused of such "dumping" in the offshore auto markets, especially in Europe.

EXAMPLE

PREDATION REPUTATION AT BROWN AND WILLIAMSON

The U.S. Supreme Court has recently addressed these issues in promulgating a new standard for judging predatory pricing behavior by U.S. firms. In *Brooke Group Ltd. v. Brown and Williamson Tobacco Company 113 U.S. 2578 (1993),* the Court held that pricing generic cigarettes below cost was not evidence of an undesirable predatory intent to monopolize a market because Brown and Williamson had no opportunity thereafter to earn excess profits. Whether the Court looked deeply enough into the long-term effect of deterring effective entry through a pricing policy that left Brown and Williamson indistinguishable from "crazies" is a hotly debated antitrust issue today.

Winning Strategies in Evolutionary Computer Tournaments

We have seen that a grim trigger strategy can induce cooperation in an infinitely repeated Prisoner's Dilemma. Let's analyze what characteristics of multiperiod, but not perpetual, punishment schemes appear most successful at promoting cooperation. One transparent disadvantage of grim triggers is that cooperative outcomes cannot survive a single small mistake or miscommunication by either player. Selten's concept of a **trembling hand trigger strategy** seeks to improve on this issue by allowing one grace period misplay by the other party before the grim punishment of defection forever is imposed. Of course, a wily rival understanding this strategy will take advantage of its opponent by claiming just as many one-period "mistakes" of defection as it can get away with.

Robert Axelrod has been intrigued by why in long-term interactions, when people are ardently pursuing their own goals, they often end up cooperating with competitors.[18]

Trembling Hand Trigger Strategy
A punishment mechanism that forgives random mistakes and miscommunications.

www
The following Internet site provides further information and software related to Robert Axelrod's book *The Evolution of Cooperation:* http://pscs.physics.lsa.umich.edu/Software/CC/ECHome.html

---

[17] See R. Gibbons, "An Introduction to Applicable Game Theory," *Journal of Economic Perspectives,* 11(1), Winter 1997, pp. 140–147.

[18] Robert Axelrod, *The Evolution of Cooperation* (New York: Basic Books, 1984). See also "Evolutionary Economics," *Forbes,* 11 October 1993, p. 110 and Jill Neimark, "Tit for Tat: A Game of Survival," *Success,* May 1987, p. 62.

He investigated the question of optimal strategy in repeated Prisoner's Dilemma by conducting a computer simulation in which 151 strategies competed against one another 1,000 times. He discovered that those strategies that finished highest in the computer tournament had several characteristics in common. First, winning strategies have great clarity to avoid fewer mistakes by their opponents; simpler is better. Second, winning strategies make unilateral attempts to cooperate; they are initiators of niceness. Third, as we would expect, all winning strategies are provokable; they have credible commitments to some punishment rule. But limited punishment rules displaying forgiveness won out over maximal punishment grim trigger strategies. The reason seems to be that, fourth, winning strategies can recover from misperceptions and mistakes; reprisals need not be self-perpetuating. What types of actual strategies would you guess best fit these five criteria? Surprisingly, "tit for tat" won the tournament! Repeating what your opponent did on the last round is simple and clearly provokable, but consistent with initiating cooperation. And perhaps most importantly, "tit for tat" is forgiving. After a single-period punishment, it reverts to cooperating as soon as the opponent/cooperator does so.

Conspicuous Focal Point
An outcome that attracts mutual cooperation.

For example, one possible approach to cooperation for cruise ship companies Carnival and Royal Caribbean in Table 16.3 is to follow a "tit-for-tat" decision rule. Royal Caribbean, who has a dominant $300 strategy, could signal a **conspicuous focal point** by promoting "staterooms" (rather than smaller, less well-appointed "cabins") as an industry standard and then choosing the $450 pricing strategy in the first period. Thereafter, Royal Caribbean would select the same pricing strategy in the next period as the other firm chose in the previous period. For example, if Carnival charges $450 in the current period, then Royal Caribbean would do likewise in the next period. On the other hand, if Carnival defects and charges $300 in the current period, then Royal Caribbean would retaliate by charging the same $300 price next period. Through repeated plays, the participants may "learn" the "tit-for-tat" decision rule being applied by their competitor.

Since the ($450, $450) actions yield $90,000 more for Royal Caribbean than the iterated dominant strategy equilibrium ($300, $300), Royal Caribbean may well initiate cooperation and thereafter play "tit for tat." With rational, unconfused, and well-informed competitors, communication of conspicuous focal points and multiperiod punishment schemes can elicit conditional cooperation in repeated Prisoner's Dilemma.

Perhaps for this reason, the Third Federal Circuit Court has prohibited airlines from signalling such coordination information to one another through their centralized reservation systems. Self-enforcing reliance mechanisms are often utilized to establish credible commitments between business rivals precisely because arms-length competitors are limited by the antitrust statutes in their ability to contract to assure cooperation.

EXAMPLE

SIGNALLING A PUNISHMENT SCHEME: NORTHWEST[19]

In the summer of 1989, America West announced a $50 fare reduction for 21-day advance purchase tickets on the busy Minneapolis–Los Angeles route. Rather than cutting its own $308 fare from its Minneapolis hub to match the America West $258 fare, Northwest announced a $40 reduction (from $208 to $168) for 21-day advance purchase tickets on the busy Phoenix–New York route. America West's hub is in Phoenix. The retaliatory fare was labeled on the Airline Tariff Publishing computer system as available for

---

[19] Based on "Fare Game," *Wall Street Journal,* 28 June 1990, p. A1 and "Fare Warning," *Wall Street Journal,* 9 October 1990, p. B1.

Price Signalling
A communication of price change plans, prohibited by antitrust law.

only the next 2 days, with possible renewal thereafter. Five days later, America West canceled its $50 promotion on West Coast travel.

Antitrust law makes it illegal for companies to conspire to fix prices. Signalling the particulars of a multiperiod punishment scheme to elicit cooperation in maintaining high prices is seen as a violation of the law. Northwest defended its actions as "competitive initiatives and responses consistent with independent self-interest" and therefore thoroughly legal. However, signalling limited duration punishment schemes is not. *U.S. v. Airline Tariff Publishing Co. et al.,* 92-52854 (1992) expressly prohibited the preannouncement of price changes that might facilitate price coordination.

Industry Standards and Regulatory Constraints

Unlike chess or poker, in business strategy games the players are free to change the rules—for example, the very structure of the game itself. Third-party enforcement of industry standards or regulatory constraints are often a way of changing the structure of a simultaneous-play business rivalry into a sequential-play game. Java programming language for the Internet and digital signal specifications for high-definition television are examples of industry standards used in this way. By restricting the flexibility of one another's best-reply responses, rivals can often secure an escape from the dominant strategy payoffs of a Prisoner's Dilemma and achieve more profitable outcomes.

Consider the business-to-business sale of electrical equipment illustrated in Figure 16.11. General Electric would like to manufacture and distribute a high specifications ("gold-plated") product, perhaps a large transformer for factories and hospitals. Unfortunately, however, the GE distributor has higher payoffs from not providing full installation. Under those circumstances, GE is better off manufacturing a transformer that meets only minimal specifications. Because of the distributor's dominant strategy, the two companies earn payoffs {Worse, Better} and find themselves in a Prisoner's Dilemma. They would both prefer the northwest cell {Better, Best}, but each would then be vulnerable to a defection by the other company resulting in their Worst outcome. By enlisting third parties (TP) like Underwriters' Laboratory in specifying an installation standard or local building codes in enacting an installation regulation, General Electric and its distributors can escape the Prisoner's Dilemma. Since a General Electric distributor would then be engaged in an illegal ("below code") sale should it provide anything less than full installation, General Electric can anticipate full installation and will therefore proceed to manufacture the high specifications product. The payoffs will then improve to {Better, Best}.

The same argument is often made by manufacturers who wish to limit the discounting of their distributors. Resale price maintenance (RPM) agreements prohibit retailers from cutting the price at which they resell the product below a manufacturer's suggested retail price. Most such restrictions on the vertical relationship between manufacturers and distributors or distributors and retailers are illegal, especially when they appear motivated by the desire of competing retail dealers for less price competition. Occasionally, however, a manufacturer or distributor can demonstrate a "legitimate manufacturer's interest" in regulatory or industry standards which place a floor under the resale prices of their products (e.g., a rare book distributor). When one of these special exceptions is made and an RPM agreement is allowed, the parties have succeeded in using a regulatory mechanism to escape a Prisoner's Dilemma analogous to Figure 16.11.[20]

---
[20] See L. Telser, "Why Should Manufacturers Want Fair Trade II?," *Journal of Law and Economics,* 33 October 1990, pp. 409–417.

FIGURE   16.11

Electrical Industry
Standard Escapes a
Prisoner's Dilemma

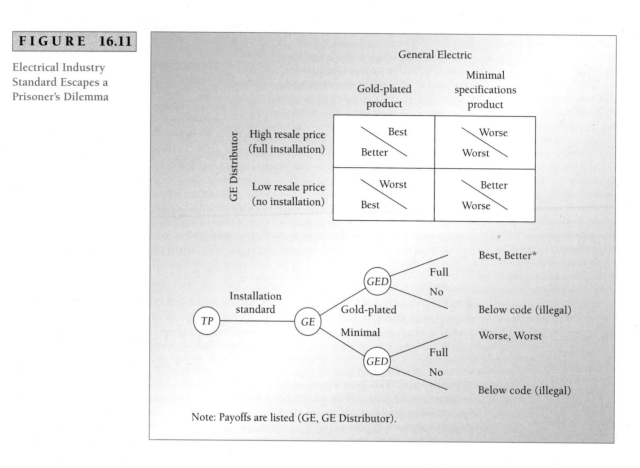

Note: Payoffs are listed (GE, GE Distributor).

RESALE PRICE MAINTENANCE AGREEMENT: STRIDERITE[21]

Nintendo, New Balance Athletic, and StrideRite have all recently paid multimillion dollar fines to settle charges that the manufacturers cut shipments to retail outlets that refused to charge full list price. In StrideRite's case, leading retailers were cut off if they refused to sell six styles of women's Keds at MSRP prices from \$20–\$45. Although StrideRite insisted that it could suspend contracts with distributors who violated other company marketing policies and procedures, the government found that particular stores had been pressured by StrideRite to raise prices. Vertical requirements contracting about matters *other than resale price* is widespread and perfectly legal.

Hostages Support Cooperative Exchange

In Chapter 13 we encountered another noncooperative mechanism for securing cooperation in a repeated Prisoner's Dilemma. Potentially notorious firms selling low-quality experience goods (e.g., PC components) for high prices were identifiable in Table 13.1 as firms with entirely redeployable assets. That is, firms selling out of temporary locations, with unbranded products, and no company reputation were firms that one could reasonably expect to follow the dominant strategy of producing low quality. Consequently, these were firms to whom no customer would offer a high price.

---

[21] Based on "StrideRite Agrees to Settle," *Wall Street Journal,* 28 September 1993, p. A5.

On the other hand, we argued that firms who asked high prices but also exhibited verifiable sunk-cost investments that dissipated the rent from such prices, were much better bets. Reputational advertising of nontransferable company logos (say, Apple) or investment in nonredeployable transaction-supporting assets, such as product-specific showrooms and unique retail displays, presented a hostage to buyers. Recall that the buyers had easy access to information about fraud and punished violators with grim trigger strategies. Otherwise, customers sorted randomly across all the reliable firms. Because sellers offering hostages are worse off if they fail to deliver on the promise of high quality, a buyer can rely on these credible commitments even if unable to verify them at the point of purchase. Although the credible commitments are noncontractual in nature, the reliance relationships they establish are no less predictable than if these were enforceable contracts.

Finally, then, we have cooperative game mechanisms, involving binding (third-party-enforceable) agreements. In Appendix 16A, we analyze coordination games designed to illustrate the role of private contractual agreements such as warranties, bonds, and refund guarantees. These contractual mechasims can also allow escape from defection outcomes in a Prisoner's Dilemma. They, too, offer hostages that support win-win exchange despite a dominant strategy that would otherwise lead players to mutual defection. The key to the credibility of such mechanisms remains exactly the same as in noncooperative games. First, in the light of the warranty obligations, is the promisor better off fulfilling his or her promise than ignoring it? And second, is the warranty or bond irrevocable other than for just causes the promise-giver cannot control? If both features characterize the "hostage" given, then the commitments are credible, and the players in both cooperative and noncooperative games can allow themselves to be vulnerable to defection and yet escape the Prisoner's Dilemma.

SUMMARY

- ▢ Proactive oligopolists require accurate predictions of rival initiatives and rival response. The managerial purpose of game theory is to predict just such rival behavior.

- ▢ Simultaneous play games occasionally arise in pricing and promotion rivalry, but the essence of business strategy is sequential reasoning. The order of play matters in sequential games of coordination between manufacturers and distributors, entry deterrence and accommodation, service competition, R&D races, product development, and so on, because rivals must predict best-reply responses and counterresponses all the way out to an endgame. Endgame reasoning entails looking ahead to the last play in an ordered sequence of plays, identifying the player whose decisions control the available outcomes in the endgame, and then predicting that player's preferred action.

- ▢ Subgame perfect equilibrium strategy looks ahead to analyze endgame outcomes and then reasons back to prior best-reply responses. Credible threats and credible commitments are the key to endgame reasoning, and therefore credibility mechanisms are the key to subgame perfect equilibrium strategy.

- ▢ Nash equilibrium and dominant strategy equilibrium differ in important ways. Nash equilibrium strategy entails actions that maximize each decision maker's payoff, given best-reply responses of the other players. In contrast, dominant strategy equilibrium entails actions that maximize at least one decision maker's payoff, no matter what any other player chooses to do.

- ▢ Advantages may accrue to either first-movers or fast-seconds in a business rivalry. The former can credibly threaten or credibly precommit and therefore preempt some outcomes, whereas the latter replies and can determine the best-reply response in the endgame. Which is more advantageous depends on the particulars of the tactical and strategic situation.

☐ Threats and commitments ultimately derive their credibility from the threat maker adopting subgame perfect strategy. A credible threat is a conditional strategy the threat maker is worse off ignoring than implementing. A credible commitment is an obligation the commitment maker is worse off ignoring than fulfilling.

☐ Mechanisms for establishing credibility include establishing a bond or contractural side payment, investing in a nonredeployable reputation asset, short-circuiting or interrupting the response process, entering into a profit-sharing alliance, taking small steps, or arranging an irreversible and irrevocable hostage mechanism.

☐ Closed-end leases with preset residual values are a mechanism for establishing a durable goods manufacturer's credible commitments to early buyers of new models.

☐ Incumbents may seek to deter potential entrants through the use of excess capacity precommitments or credible threats of advertising campaigns and price discounts. Whether incumbents deter or accommodate potential entrants depends in general on the presence or absence of first-mover advantages, on the structure of competition in prices versus quantities, and on how customers sort across alternative firms when the low-priced capacity stocks out.

☐ Customer sorting patterns include the following: random rationing in which all customers are equally likely to obtain the low-priced capacity; efficient rationing in which the highest (then next highest) willingness-to-pay customers obtain the low-priced capacity until it is exhausted; extreme brand loyalty in which none of the regular customers seek the low-priced capacity; and inverse intensity rationing in which the lowest (then next lowest) willingness-to-pay customers obtain the low-priced capacity until it is exhausted. With inverse intensity rationing, the customer sorting implies a segmented market and is most likely to lead to accommodation of entry.

☐ Mixed strategy provides an optimal rule for randomizing one's actions among multiple Nash equilibrium strategies.

☐ Mutual cooperation in a repeated Prisoner's Dilemma game can be secured with the adoption of an industry standard, multiperiod punishment schemes, and strategic hostage or bonding mechanisms for establishing credible commitments and threats.

☐ Cooperation in noncooperative games is more likely if strategies are clear, provokable, take cooperative initiatives unilaterally, and are forgiving so as not to perpetuate mistakes. The "tit-for-tat" strategy has these characteristics.

EXERCISES

1. Identify the dominant strategy equilibrium if Pepsi and Coca-Cola each earn $12,000 per week per store when both maintain high six-pack prices, $8,000 per week per store when both promote a low discounted price, $17,000 per week per store for either party that defects successfully alone to low prices, and $6,000 per week per store for either party that maintains high prices when the other party defects. What pricing action will Pepsi choose? What about Coca-Cola?

2. How does the analysis and the strategic equilibrium outcome differ in Figure 16.2 if the other firm enjoys a cost advantage—for example, $35 at AA&D? Then does the order of play (i.e., who goes first in making price cuts) matter in this bidding game with asymmetric costs?

3. Consider an ongoing sequence of pairwise marketing competitions between three companies with promotional campaigns of varying degrees of success. Each cam-

paign involves comparative advertising belittling the target company. The company with the most loyal customers (call this firm Most) enjoys 100 percent success when it attacks either of the others. The company with the least loyal customers (i.e., Least) has a 30 percent success rate when it belittles either Most or More. More, itself, experiences an 80 percent success rate. The firms each launch their advertising attacks one at a time in an arbitrary sequence. Least goes first and can attack either Most or More. More attacks second, and Most attacks third. If more than one of the opponents survive the first round of competition, the order of play repeats itself: Least, then More, then Most. Any player can skip his or her turn; that is, the three actions available to Least to initiate the game are as follows: attack More, attack Most, or do nothing and pass the turn.

Try to diagram the game tree and employ subgame perfect equilibrium analysis to identify the strategic equilibrium. What should the most vulnerable firm with the least loyal customers do to initiate play? What would be More's best-reply response if attacked and More survives? What if Least did nothing? What would Most do when and if its turn arose?

4. Why is knowing just one dominant strategy in the two-person People Express entry game against mid-Atlantic incumbents sufficient to predict rival behavior and identify the strategic equilibrium?

5. In the entry deterrence and accommodation game between Piedmont and People Express, explain why Piedmont's expected demand following small-scale entry in Figure 16.9 is 112.

6. Identify all the Nash equilibria for simultaneous Manufacturer/Distributor I in Table 16.1. Calculate the mixed strategy equilibrium. Show your work.

7. The outcomes in the bottom half of the game tree describing the last (the twentieth) submarket of the chainstore paradox in Figure 16.10 are labeled N.A. (not applicable). Why? What specific equilibrium concept in sequential games rules out the applicability of these outcomes? Hint: How would you describe the game tree from node E onwards as opposed to the game tree from node D onwards?

www exercise

The Changing Antitrust Treatment of Resale Price Maintenance

8. The U.S. Supreme Court and other federal courts have ruled on a number of cases involving resale price maintenance. Access the following Internet site maintained by Anthony Becker: http://www.stolaf.edu/people/becker/antitrust/subject.html.

Find the section that summarizes U.S. Supreme Court cases having to do with resale price maintenance, and read the summary for Albrecht v. Herald Co. (1968), and State Oil v. Khan (1997). Describe how the antitrust doctrine applied by the Court to resale price maintenance has changed, and relate this change to the economic analysis of resale price maintenance in the chapter you have just read. What economic arguments did the Supreme Court use in overturning the earlier Albrecht decision?

INTERNATIONAL CASE EXERCISE

RECIPROCATING PROTECTIONISM: BOEING V. AIRBUS[22]

First-mover advantages are often established by up-front investments in nonredeployable (sunk cost) assets. Boeing made sunk cost investments in the development of the Boeing 727 aircraft that were recovered on previous Boeing models. Airbus thereafter was playing catch-up and found that protectionism by the European Economic Com-

---

[22] Based on A. Dixit and B. Nalebuff, "Boeing, Boeing, Gone," *Thinking Strategically* (New York: Norton, 1991), "Airbus Takes Off," *Fortune*, June 1992, and "Uncle Sam's Helping Hand," *The Economist*, April 1994.

munity (EEC) was required to recover its $1 billion development cost. If the North American and EEC markets each offer potential sales with net present value of $900 million, and Boeing and Airbus split each market in the absence of protectionism but win two-thirds of the market in the presence of protectionism, show that protectionism by the EEC is a dominant strategy. Was the threat by the U.S. International Trade Commission to impose tariffs and protect Boeing if the EEC imposed tariffs and protected Airbus a credible threat? What is the subgame perfect equilibrium for this commercial aircraft development game? What will be required if, for geopolitical or technology reasons, the European Union today wishes to maintain an aircraft manufacturing capability? What could the EEC have done earlier to change the structure of this game?

Optimal Mechanism Design: Contracting, Queues, and Auctions

Institutional choices play an extensive role in eliciting efficient behavior. For example, relaxing the institutional constraints to allow free-wheeling of electricity from one public utility to another's customers has put a premium on low-cost operations and will, over time, improve substantially the efficiency of the electric utility industry. Similarly, privatizing Conrail, British Telecom, Japan Air Lines, Telefonos de Mexico, and Societe Generale improved the incentives to maximize capitalized value in these formerly bloated public monopolies. However, the role of institutions in motivating efficient behavior goes far beyond deregulation and privatization initiatives.

In Chapter 13, we saw how incentive-compatible cost revelation procedures could increase the market value of a joint venture. These institutional features of the relationship between joint venture partners like IBM, Siemens, and Toshiba illustrate the concept of *optimal mechanism design*. Institutional choices also involve the form of organization companies adopt and the design of allocation mechanisms like auctions. For example, some firms like Volvo-GM Trucks, IBM, and Firestone Tires develop franchise dealerships rather than attempt to contract over selling procedures and warranty service with the independent retailers preferred by manufacturers like Apple and Michelin. Other firms adopt stand-alone subsidiaries as independent divisions but centralize the production of common components (e.g., General Motors' Chevrolet, Cadillac, and Buick divisions buy from Fisher Body Co.). Selling the radio magnetic spectrum in metropolitan zones to cellular phone companies using multi-round open bidding simultaneous auctions also illustrates the concept of optimal mechanism design. In contrast, the Federal Reserve banks have experimented with auctioning T-Bills using single-round second-highest sealed bid auctions. All these alternative choices of institutional arrangements address the need for coordination and control, twin issues that every successful organization must resolve.

CHOICE OF ORGANIZATIONAL FORM

The Role of Business Contracting in Cooperative Games

At the start of this chapter, we saw that once a manufacturer commits to updating a product, distributors may find that their best-reply response is to continue providing extensive selling effort and postsale services. If so, the required coordination of manufacturer and distributor actions in Figure 16.1 can be achieved by a self-enforcing reliance relationship. At times, however, the payoffs are such that coordination requires something more than the voluntary, self-enforcing mechanisms that secure equilibrium in noncooperative games. Consider the decisions in Table 16A.1. These are the same actions and payoffs with one exception. The distributor payoff in the northwest cell has been changed from breakeven to $2,500 per truck. That is, the distributor is now better off discontinuing some of the selling effort associated with presale services. Sales volume declines, so the manufacturer is clearly worse off. But the distributor who economizes on selling costs may actually do better than with full service and high prices in the

TABLE   16A.1

Simultaneous
Manufacturer/
Distributor II

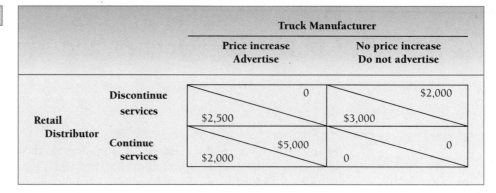

		Truck Manufacturer			
		Price increase Advertise		No price increase Do not advertise	
Retail Distributor	Discontinue services	$2,500	0	$3,000	$2,000
	Continue services	$2,000	$5,000	0	0

southeast cell. Knowing that the distributor now has a dominant strategy to defect and discontinue services, the manufacturer will decide not to raise prices or advertise the product. The payoffs to the distributor now increase still further from $2,500 to $3,000, and the manufacturer earns $2,000.

However, this outcome is not value-maximizing. Higher prices with an advertised full-service product generate total operating profits summed across both players of $7,000— i.e., $2,000 more per truck than the dominant strategy equilibrium {Discontinue, No Price Increase}. To elicit full services in either a one-shot or repeated version of Table 16A.1 requires some sharing of this $2,000 cooperative surplus with the distributor. That is, rather than suspending shipments and changing distributors frequently as one after another pursues the dominant "Discontinue" strategy, the manufacturer may enter into a cooperative game of credible promises and sidepayments—i.e., a relational contract. For example, a franchise contract offering 40 percent of the profits to the distributor (or penalizing the distributor $600 for nonperformance, if detected) can elicit a continuation of full services. Since 0.4 × $7,000 = $2,800 exceeds the $2,500 profit from discontinuing services, the manufacturer who offers such a contract can expect to realize both an acceptance from the chosen distributors and a ($2,800, $4,200) profit outcome.

Contracts

Third-party enforceable agreements designed to facilitate deferred exchange.

Contracts are binding, third-party enforceable agreements designed to facilitate deferred exchange. A *promisee* undertakes some costly action in exchange for and relying upon the *promisor's* promise of a subsequent performance. Here, recalling the sequential version of the above game, the manufacturer updates the product relying upon the retail distributor to subsequently perform presale selling efforts. In Figure 16A.1 we specify one step further in the sequence of probable events and allow the manufacturer to then decide about manufacturer-sponsored advertising. With such delays in transaction comes the possibility of opportunistic behavior and an attendant increase in risk. Distributors can promise one thing and then deliver another. For example, the distributor finds that after the manufacturer commits to a product update, the discontinuance of some selling effort results in higher payoffs ($120,000) than continuing the full expected selling effort ($100,000). The retail distributor therefore selects "Discontinue" (as signified by the starred payoff). Knowing this, the manufacturer may "Advertise" (the double starred payoff) but underinvest in product updates relative to his or her optimal investment when the distributor can be induced to make a credible commitment.

Contracts are one method of establishing such credibility. A contract provides a hostage beyond the mere reputational asset that prospective distributors might offer. In exchange for an agreed consideration, the promisee receives a credible promise. The promisor's commitment to perform is credible because the default rules of contract interpretation and enforcement (in the courts) provide assurance that any expectations

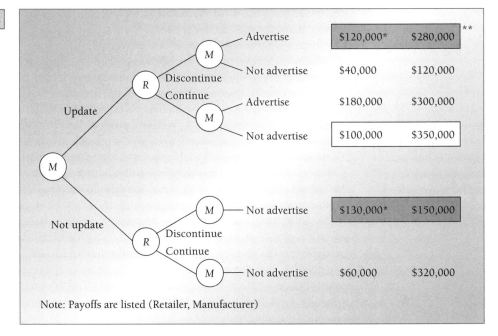

FIGURE   16A.1

Vertical Requirements
Contracting is Required
to Maximize Value

Note: Payoffs are listed (Retailer, Manufacturer)

which the parties clearly spell out (i.e., stipulate) will be met. This stipulation procedure works exceptionally well for fully anticipated events. Moreover, the default rules of contract law reduce the costs of renegotiation and settlement when unanticipated events do occur. For example, the market price that can be realized on the trucks in Figure 16A.1 can change dramatically between the time period of the reliance investment in a manufacturing facility to produce the updated truck and the subsequent promotion and sale of the truck itself. Every contract must therefore allocate these risks (at least implicitly) as well as provide incentives to induce both efficient reliance and efficient performance.[23]

In contrast to these deferred exchanges of a consideration for a promise, spot market transactions pose relatively few information and incentive problems. For example, buying electricity off the grid at quarter 'til the hour for delivery on the hour avoids pricing risk and the possibility of opportunistic behavior. However, these frequent transactional relationships between buyers and sellers engaged in immediate delivery of standardized goods at fixed prices fail to solve an important issue that arises, for example, in long-term uranium supply contracts. What happens when Westinghouse promises to supply uranium fuel rods to public utilities at a fixed price over the next several years, and then finds that the market price of uranium raw material quadruples? Again, deferred exchange requires contractual mechanisms to allocate such risks and provide incentives for efficient reliance and performance.

Vertical Requirements Contracts

In the sequential game in Figure 16A.1, the subgame perfect equilibrium strategy is {Update, Discontinue, Advertise} at the extreme top of the diagram. This odd combination of actions dominates all other sequential patterns and meets the conditions of

---

[23] An excellent discussion of the role of contract remedies as incentives for efficient reliance and performance appears in R. Cooter and T. Ulen, *Law and Economics,* 2nd ed., (Reading, MA: Addison-Wesley, 1997), pp. 214–232.

best-reply response for each player at each proper subgame node in the decision tree. In particular, the manufacturer controls the endgame, preferring to Advertise when the distributor Discontinues and to Not Advertise when the distributor Continues. The payoffs for these choices are boxed in Figure 16A.1. The unboxed payoffs are no longer feasible payoff possibilities because they conflict with best-reply responses of the manufacturer in the endgame. Choosing from the feasible set of best-reply responses in the endgame, the retail distributor prefers the shaded $120,000 payoff from discontinuing services for an updated and advertised product, as we noted earlier, and the shaded $130,000 payoff from discontinuing services for a not-updated unadvertised product. Therefore, moving by backward induction one more step (to the first node), the manufacturer will choose between the shaded outcomes consistent with best-reply responses of the distributor. Therefore, the manufacturer can be predicted to Update the product (i.e., the double-starred outcome).

The subgame perfect equilibrium strategy {Update, Discontinue, Advertise} generates total profits of $120,000 + $280,000 = $400,000. As in Simultaneous Manufacturer/Distributor II in Table 16A.1, this self-enforcing strategic equilibrium is *not* value-maximizing. Since two alternatives generate more profit—i.e., {Update, Continue, Not Advertise} generates $450,000 total profits and {Update, Continue, Advertise} generates $480,000 total profits, one might expect some contract or organizational form to emerge to realize this additional value. One alternative is vertical integration. By buying the distributor firm (for something slightly more than $120,000), the manufacturer could impose the value-maximizing actions and resolve coordination and control with internal monitoring and incentive systems within the consolidated firm.

Alternatively, a vertical requirements contract that offers the distributor $120,000 plus half of the $80,000 cooperative surplus (i.e., $480,000 − $400,000) to provide full services if the manufacturer updated and advertised the product, would increase the manufacturer's payoff from $280,000 to $320,000. Assuming alternative distributors were available, this contract would be accepted by the present distributor, and both players would be $40,000 better off than in the subgame perfect equilibrium {Update, Discontinue, Advertise}, which made no use of contracting. Again, as in our earlier discussion of contracting to maximize value in simultaneous Manufacturer/Distributor II, the contract here is likely to be structured around an offer of a percentage of the profits. A vertical requirements contract that offered to grant 33 percent ($160,000/$480,000) of the profits to an authorized distributor in exchange for full selling effort and after-sale service of an updated product that was advertised by the manufacturer would maximize the value of this business opportunity.

Alternative Organizational Forms[24]

Whether firms decide to employ spot markets, relational contracting, fixed profit-share franchise contracts, or vertical integration depends on the relative degree of coordination and control required to maximize value and on several characteristics of the assets involved. At one end of the spectrum, spot market recontracting is efficient for fully redeployable durable assets not dependent upon other complementary assets. Rental cars provide a good illustration of such assets that may be allocated through spot markets with no loss of efficiency. The limiting feature of this "organizational" form, however, is the potential for "hold-up" inherent in the frequent renewal of spot market contracts. Should one party have nonredeployable assets (e.g., a major league sports franchise and stadium), spot market recontracting provides too

---

[24] An excellent synthesis on this topic is Oliver Williamson, "Economics and Organization: A Primer," *California Management Review*, Winter 1996.

many opportunities for players with mobile skills and marketable talent to appropriate the surplus value in any business relationship.

Reliant Assets
Partially nonredeployable durable assets.

Reliant assets are nonredeployable durable assets sold in thin markets for less than their value in first-best use. These assets are highly specific to their current use because of substantial unrecoverable sunk cost investments either in acquisition, distribution, or promotion. Specialized equipment is the most common reliant asset. When reliant assets are dependent on unique complements in order to achieve any substantial value added, one has the maximum potential for hold-up in spot market recontracting. These dependency relations may be either one-way or bilateral. Manufacturers with independent distributors are a good example of a bilateral dependent relationship involving reliant assets. Each party in a Volvo-GM Truck manufacturer/distributor relationship is equally dependent on the other. In such cases, franchise contracts with a fixed profit share are highly efficient.

Relational Contracts
Promisory agreements of coordinated performance among owners of highly interdependent asset.

When assets are dependent on unique complements but not reliant because of their substantial redeployability, the parties often adopt long-term performance-based **relational contracts.** Redeployable corporate jets and pilots provide a good illustration. Pilots need not own the planes nor secure franchise contracts to operate the planes. Instead, the organizational form of a jet charter company is normally one of long-term standby relationships with contract pilots who report on short notice for piecemeal assignments. This system works well, and both the pilots and plane owners understand that the longevity and reliability of the relationship enhances value.

Finally, when reliant assets are one-way dependent on unique complementary resources, the most efficient organizational form is vertical integration. Remote aluminum plants are one-way dependent on nearby bauxite mines. In contrast, because the bauxite can be shipped anywhere, the mine owners are not dependent on the local aluminum plant. Both assets entail substantial sunk cost investment, but only the remote aluminum plant is a nonredeployable durable asset—for example, one with little value to other companies should the nearby bauxite source disappear. This is the situation in which upstream vertical integration by the manufacturer is required in order to prevent opportunistic hold-up and maximize the manufacturer's capitalized value.

EXAMPLE

Vertical Integration at Web TV[25]

Enormous business opportunities loom on the horizon for companies operating at the intersection of Web-based Internet services and the TV. Personal computers have penetrated into 40 percent of American households but televisions are present in literally every household, with a measured penetration now reaching 98 percent. Over the next 5 to 10 years, 220 million analog television sets may be replaced by $150 billion worth of television-enabled PCs and digital televisions. The lure for customers will be Internet-based interactive services and much higher digital picture quality.

Microsoft has invested heavily in digital entertainment programming for these "smart televisions" and television-enabled PCs. Their know-how and trade secret investments are largely nonredeployable and include the operating system and user interface backbone for everything from interactive museum tours to distance learning virtual courses to Web page construction. However, all these investments may be focused on the wrong distribution channel. WebTV Networks Inc. has recently perfected a system that allows consumers to surf the Internet through their low-end TVs. The core of WebTV's tech-

---

[25] Based on "Why Microsoft Is Glued to the Tube," *Business Week*, 22 September 1997, p. 96 and "Microsoft to Buy Web TV for $425 Million," *Wall Street Journal,* 7 May 1997, p. A8.

nology is a patented signal compression chip that crams the capabilities of a TV tuner, cable modem, and high-speed video modem into one $50 unit. WebTV's technology has freed content providers of the bandwidth limitations that currently prevent the Net from transmitting high-speed Web images and video. It may also have freed consumers of the need to upgrade to digital TV. Most households are able to connect the device to their analog TV set and begin surfing the Internet within 15 minutes.

If twenty-first-century households will be able to cruise the Net and download video with inexpensive network PCs or old televisions, Microsoft's huge investment in digital entertainment will decline exponentially in value. And because WebTV has successfully patented their technology, WebTV has many partners and end-product users like the giant consumer electronics manufacturers Sony and Philips. Consequently, Microsoft decided to vertically integrate and bought WebTV for $425 million. Microsoft intends to combine its one-way dependent and reliant digital entertainment assets with WebTV's technology to produce digital consumer products for cell phones, pagers, and hand-held PCs.

Vertical Integration[26]

Technological interdependencies can themselves motivate competitive firms to purchase other stages of production and vertically integrate. For example, in order to reduce handling and set-up costs, the blast furnaces, converters, reduction and rolling mills are all vertically integrated into one continuous process in the hot-rolled steel industry. Otherwise, the intermediate metal products would require costly reheating. Search, bargaining, and hold-up costs are also reduced when internal transfers and the monitoring and incentive systems within the firm replace the spot market contracting and recontracting necessitated by operating at arms length with outside suppliers and independent distributors. Nobel laureate Ronald Coase argued that these factors explain why the firm emerged as an organizational form despite the diseconomies of ever wider spans of managerial control.[27] However, the usual motive for a manufacturer to vertically integrate upstream to suppliers or vertically integrate downstream to retail distributors involves successive monopolization (i.e., the presence of market power over price at more than one stage of production).

Consider, first, an upstream yarn supplier who operates in a competitive intermediate product market and a downstream hosiery manufacturer who enjoys the market power to mark-up the wholesale price for pantyhose above its marginal cost. Figure 16A.2 illustrates the situation each firm faces when the yarn inputs are combined in fixed proportions with manufacturing labor and machinery to yield hosiery output. The outside demand curve and its marginal revenue capture the hosiery manufacturer's revenue opportunities in the wholesale pantyhose product market. Given the marginal cost of hosiery production (MC_h) and the competitive price of yarn ($P_y = MC_y$), the manufacturer sets summed marginal cost of hosiery production and yarn inputs ($MC_h + MC_y$) equal to hosiery marginal revenue (MR_h) at output Q^*. This proves to be a joint profit-maximizing output decision because the output that maximizes hosiery profits also sets the marginal cost of yarn equal to the net marginal revenue product of the yarn supplier. That is, subtracting the downstream marginal cost (MC_h) from the downstream marginal revenues (MR_h) leaves the *net* revenue opportunity available to the upstream yarn supplier—i.e., ($MR_h - MC_h$). Setting this derived demand for yarn inputs equal to upstream marginal costs (MC_y) identifies Q^*

---

[26] For more extensive discussion of this topic, see "Theory of Vertical Integration," chapter 12 in R. Blair and D. Kaserman, *Antitrust Economics* (Homewood, IL: Irwin, 1985).

[27] The complex issues in achieving coordination and control with internal firm-level monitoring and incentive systems are related to the principal-agent problem we discussed in Chapter 13. See P. Milgrom and J. Roberts, *Economics, Organization, and Management* (New York: Prentice-Hall, 1992).

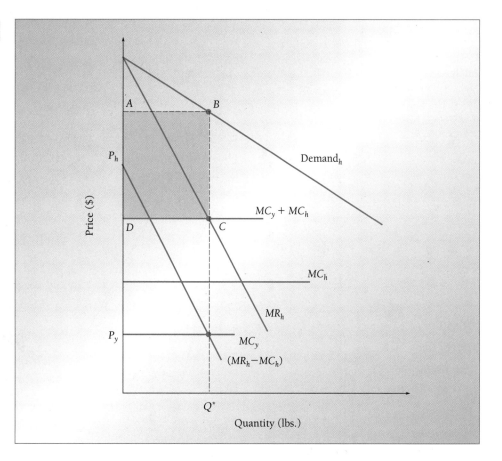

as the yarn supplier's preferred thruput rate as well as the hosiery manufacturer's preferred output rate. Thus, the upstream supplier who prices yarn so as to just recover marginal cost imposes no thruput constraint on downstream hosiery operations.

Since the hosiery manufacturer in Figure 16A.2 would change neither the yarn input prices, nor the wholesale output prices, nor the thruput quantity if the manufacturer were to vertically integrate upstream and operate the yarn supplier, vertical integration can only result in disadvantages associated with a wider span of managerial control. For profits ABCD to remain unchanged, these disadvantages would need to be offset by some other factor like reduced transaction costs. In general, in the absence of other factors, we would conclude that in Figure 16A.2, the hosiery manufacturer has no profit motive for backwards integration into the competitive yarn supplier's business.

In contrast, however, consider the case in which the yarn supplier has a proprietary process that is unique and adds substantial value to the hosiery manufacturing process. In Figure 16A.3, the derived demand for the yarn input is again $(MR_h - MC_h)$ and everything else about the hosiery operations remains the same as Figure 16A.2, except that now the upstream firm has the market power to mark-up its own marginal cost (MC_y). Taking then a second marginalization of the revenue, subtracting off the hosiery production cost, and setting $(MMR_h - MC_h) = MC_y$, the yarn supplier maximizes upstream profits EFGH by choosing a price P'_y at thruput Q'. Since P'_y exceeds the upstream marginal cost MC_y, the summed marginal cost facing the hosiery manufacturer is now higher, and consequently, the desired output declines from $Q*$ to Q'. Although hosiery prices rise to P'_h, the higher costs and smaller output of hosiery operations cause the profits of the downstream firm (the manufacturer) to decline— i.e., IJKL in Figure 16A.3 < ABCD in Figure 16A.2. The presence of profit margins

Hosiery Integration
Analysis with Upstream
Market Power

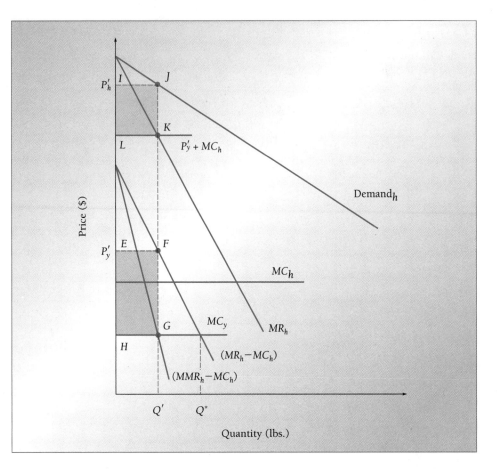

upstream results in a thruput constraint that unambiguously reduces downstream profitability.[28]

Backwards vertical integration by the hosiery manufacturer can squeeze out the margins upstream by simply setting an internal transfer price for yarn $P_y = MC_y$. This change will return the optimal thruput to Q^*, the profit-maximizing level for the consolidated yarn and hosiery operations. That is, even after paying the upstream profits *EFGH* to secure the control rights from the yarn company, the downstream hosiery manufacturer has higher net profits (*ABCD* − *EFGH*) than its profit from independent operations *IJKL*. Consequently, we would expect these two firms to coordinate their operations either as a joint venture or as a vertically integrated firm.

THE CONCEPT OF AN OPTIMAL MECHANISM DESIGN

In Chapter 13, we saw how particular institutional arrangements could elicit true revelation of cost information in a joint venture. An incentive-compatible contract induced the partners to reveal their asymmetric information because each party incurred the cost of his or her own information revelation on the other party. That is, the contract imposed a mechanism for sharing profits that aligned the self-interest of each partner with revelation of true

---

[28] This implication holds without qualification here because of fixed proportions production, i.e., the efficient input mix remains unchanged despite the reduction in output. Under variable proportions, vertical integration may be motivated or not, depending on the input substitutability and possible cost savings.

and complete information to the other partner. This incentive-compatible revelation mechanism provided a complex example of the concept of optimal mechanism design.

In contrast, consider the apparently simpler question of how to divide a deceased individual's personal possessions fairly. Mechanism design focuses on the process or procedure that will create incentives to elicit the desired behavioral objective. In so-called **fair division games,** the key insight of mechanism design reasoning is the need for open communication and role reversal. This suggests letting one party divide the estate and the other choose which half they prefer. Under the incentives created by this procedure, the person dividing the estate will offer larger or more numerous possessions in one parcel if another parcel contains particularly valuable possessions. In short, the first party "cuts the cake" and the other party then chooses first which piece they wish to consume.

Fair Division Games
Procedures for dividing assets by consensual agreement.

EXAMPLE

FAIR DIVISION OF A DECAYING PRIZE

The optimal mechanism design for fair division becomes less obvious when the prize is decaying with the passage of time as the players renegotiate. Suppose a donor offers to divide $3 million between two charitable foundations. The only catch is that the donor wants the recipients to agree upon the division of the gift which declines by $1 million each time either party refuses the proposed division. The two foundations flip a coin to see who should make the first offer of how to split the $3 million. Suppose the Getty Foundation wins the toss. How much should they offer to the Phillips Foundation who will structure a second-round division should this first one be refused and who will also respond to a third and final offer should the second be refused? Notice there definitely is a penultimate endgame to this problem in that after three rounds the donor rescinds his or her conditional gift. Think about how little the Phillips Foundation would be willing to accept in the third and final round. Can they hold out for more than this in the second round? What therefore is the maximum Getty needs to offer to trigger an acceptance in the first round? Does this game have a first-mover advantage, or is it better to play second and be the respondent in the third and final round?

Optimal Queue Service Rules

A frequent business application of optimal mechanism design is the queue service rule for filling customer orders from those waiting to purchase tickets for a popular event, perhaps a concert. The traditional first-come-first-served procedure induces an inefficient pattern of customer arrivals. If the box office opens at 9 A.M. a few potential customers arrive three hours earlier or even the night before. Others stand on queue two hours, and many more show up to wait in line at 8 A.M. What one's customers are willing to pay for tickets may be affected by the inconvenience of this wait. And the subpopulation of customers who have low opportunity cost of time (and are therefore willing to arrive the earliest, wait the longest, and obtain tickets with the greatest probability) may not be the subpopulation who will pay the most for tickets. This is why many ticket agencies have no objection to a wealthy patron paying someone with lower opportunity cost of time to stand on queue, purchase the ticket, and transfer it at face value to the higher-willingness-to-pay customer.[29] In any case, all this waiting time is time wasted; other queue service rules may be much more efficient.

---

[29] Scalpers, of course, charge higher prices still, but note that such grey markets reveal to the ticket agency what those customers, not willing to show up at the ticket window and wait, are in fact willing to pay. This information helps the ticket agency set an optimal price.

First-Come First-Served versus Last-Come First-Served

As a provisional alternative, consider last-come first-served. Under this queue service rule, a customer has no incentive to stand on queue and wait. Indeed, anytime a queue forms, all those in front of the last person to arrive have an incentive to leave and go about their other business, returning later when fewer people are likely to show up. In essence, the last-come first-served mechanism design has removed the incentives for inefficient behavior artificially created by first-come first-served. Customers did not prefer to arrive early and peak-load their demands. Instead, it was the nonoptimal queue service rule that artificially created incentives to arrive early, stand around, and wait. With last-come first-served, in contrast, customers have an incentive to spread their arrivals throughout the ticket window's normal hours of operation. Once a more or less uniform distribution of customer arrivals throughout the day can be established, the ticket agency can adjust its capacity and set its service rate to deal with the steady stream of customers who arrive and purchase with no waiting.

EXAMPLE

CONTAINERIZED SHIPPING AT SEA-LAND

Historically, ocean shipping rates were heavily regulated based on categories of cargo (e.g., paper, film, frozen fish) and shipping lanes (e.g., Rotterdam to New York, Liverpool to Jacksonville, Seoul to San Francisco). Conferences of ocean shipping companies announced common carrier shipping rates for first-come first-served customers. More than half the world's cargo still moves under publicly announced ocean shipping contracts at these uniform shipping rates. With no ability to adjust prices, sales people maximized the volume of cargo. The only good ship was a full ship. Since empty slots on a container ship perish as a revenue opportunity the moment the ship sails, companies queued up large volumes of containers and cargoes in anticipation of each ship's departure. Waiting time became a substantial implicit cost totaling millions of dollars a day.

Today, deregulation is fast approaching the ocean shipping industry. Deregulation bills have been drafted, and a spot market for space in containerized ships has emerged to operate alongside the regulated contract cargo allocation rules of first-come first-served. The immediate consequence has been delays in low-priority shipments from one voyage to the next in favor of higher-rate cargo. Shippers are no longer compelled to take a common carrier contract cargo awaiting shipment instead of charging what the market will bear for an expedited delivery of fresh shrimp or perishable pharmaceuticals.

In response to this new business environment, since 1993 Sea-Land Service, Inc., of Charlotte, North Carolina, has optimized the placement of their containers around the world. Each empty container at each freight terminal is assigned a forecasted net revenue opportunity at that location and at other potential locations along the shipping route. Balancing capacity at locations where it may be needed for increased demand or higher-rate cargo has markedly reduced the waiting time of cargo in the Sea-Land system. Shippers who offer less waiting time can charge higher rates and earn higher profits in the deregulated ocean shipping industry of the near future.

Few ticketing operations have adopted a last-come first-served queue service rule. One apparent reason and one subtle reason seem involved. First, the power of custom should not be underestimated. Customs like first-come first-served have evolved not randomly but rather to serve some useful purpose. One purpose may be that popular items sold at fixed prices create lots of ill will among those denied access. If I can't observe the person who got the last ticket paying a premium market-clearing auction price higher than what I would have paid, some sense of fairness is provided by the first-come first-served queue service rule. And that sense of fairness may be important to prevent fighting in ticket lines. Customs often reduce precisely these kinds of inconspicuous but potentially ruinous transaction costs.

A second more subtle reason, however, is that still another queue service rule may be the optimal mechanism design. Under last-come first-served, recall that any customer should leave the queue whenever a later arrival preempts his or her priority ranking as last in line. But customers will not wish to return many times to the ticket window. Again, time is money. So, customers ahead in line are likely to offer side payments to late arrivals to induce *them* to leave. Predictably those with the highest opportunity cost of time will end up bribing those with lower opportunity cost to leave and return. This side payment system may again reduce the ticket agency's receipts because in many ways it has just replaced the inefficiency of arriving early and waiting with the inefficiency of arriving often, departing, and returning. The recipients of the side payments are no worse off since they voluntarily decide to leave and return later, but those who make the side payments now turn to the window and surely offer less than they otherwise would have paid to secure good seats.

Stratified Lotteries

How can the ticket agency's mechanism design deal with this subtle complication? One obvious answer is to employ advance reservations and price discrimination in segmented customer submarkets. Most scarce capacity subject to random demand arrivals is allocated in precisely that way, and we discuss using such differential pricing schemes in Chapter 17. Remember, however, that here the problem was one of allocating scarce capacity at uniform prices across all the customers.

EXAMPLE

STRATIFIED LOTTERY: TICKETMASTER

Suppose rather than announcing in advance what position in the customer queue would be served first, the ticketing agency picked a position at random. In effect, that's exactly what a lottery for the right to purchase a ticket does. Anytime prior to the day of sale, a customer stops by to pick up a lottery number. Since those customers with low willingness to pay are equally likely to get the winning lottery numbers as those with high willingness to pay, Ticketmaster and other companies adopt a **stratified lottery** scheme. Rights to purchase high-price seats are distributed in one lottery, medium-price seats in another, and low-price seats in a third. At a designated date, the winning numbers are chosen at random and posted perhaps on public access cable TV channels. Only those customers holding the winning lottery numbers arrive to buy tickets, and since seat availability is assured, there is no reason to arrive early, queue up, and wait. This lottery mechanism design does then optimally reduce waiting time while allowing the ticket agency to secure higher uniform prices for each class of seats than customers might otherwise pay.

Stratified Lottery
A randomized mechanism for allocating scarce capacity across demand segments.

AUCTION DESIGN AND INFORMATION ECONOMICS

Perhaps one of the most prominent applications of mechanism design theory has been in the design of auctions. Everything from *Monday Night Football* to mineral rights, forest land, and the electromagnetic spectrum have been allocated recently to their highest valued use through auctions. The choices in auction design are numerous. Bidding can be *simultaneous* open outcry like most estate auctions or *sequential* like the private placement auctions for newly issued securities. Bid prices can be *continuous* or constrained by minimum *discrete* bid improvements. The New York Stock Exchange has recently debated continuous decimalization of their auction prices or a continuation of the one-eighth tick size restrictions on minimum bid improvements. Bids may be *sealed* and the bidders remain anonymous or bids may be *posted*. Bidding can be *one-time only* or repeated in *multiple rounds* with cancellation and amendment of prior bids allowed (so-called *open bidding*). **English auctions** ascend to higher and higher prices until the last bidder to make an offer exceeding all other offers is declared the winner. Winning bidders may be required to pay their *highest* bid or the *second-highest* bid. **Dutch auctions** work in the opposite direction by identifying the first bidder to register an acceptance as the auctioneer announces a succession of descending asking prices. In ascending price auctions, the winner takes all, but in descending price auctions the winner is often given the opportunity to purchase less than the total capacity available for sale and the auction then continues downward. Finally, owners can place minimum reservation prices below which the item will not sell or allow an auction to proceed with *no minimum*.

Which of these and other auction design characteristics maximize the revenue to the seller and which allocate resources to their highest-valued use are important business questions and public policy issues. One well-understood insight from mechanism design theory is that asymmetric information will lead to timid bidding in ascending price auctions because of the winner's curse. To illustrate the winner's curse, consider the following auction situation.[30] You are developing a bidding strategy for an asset whose value to the seller is distributed uniformly between $0 and $100. The seller knows this value and desires some profit on the transaction to cover the auction expenses, but places no minimum reservation price on the auction. You anticipate that a rational seller will refuse all offers below his or her personal value. The asset might be a baseball player's labor contract or a set of maps of the subterranean geological formations in a petroleum-rich area. Because of different complementary assets and skill, your value is certain to be 50 percent higher than the seller's personal asset value. What offer should you make?

Winner's Curse in Asymmetric Information Bidding Games

If neither party knows the true value, an expected value of $50 plus a small premium (i.e., well below $75) is a reasonable offer that will be accepted. However, if the seller knows the true value, consider what reasonable offers will be accepted and what reasonable offers will be refused. To simplify the analysis, suppose just three realizations of the seller's value are possible: $0, $50, and $100. In Figure 16A.4, we see that should the true value be zero, only offers that overpay for the asset will be accepted. These payoffs are shown in the shaded boxes at the right of the decision tree. Should the true value be $50, $50 offers will be refused and again only $100 offers that overpay (even relative to the $75 value to the bidder) will be accepted (see the lowest boxed payoff). If the assets have the maximum possible value to the seller of $100, offers of $0, $50, *and* $100 will be refused. In short, all reasonable offers will be refused. Therefore, surprisingly, you should offer nothing at all! If you win such an auction, you are cursed with having overpaid for the asset.

English Auction
An ascending price auction.

Dutch Auction
A descending price auction.

---

[30] Adapted from M. Bazeman and W. Samuelson, "I Won the Auction But Don't Want the Prize," *Journal of Conflict Resolution*, December 1983, pp. 618–634. See also R. McAfee and J. McMillan, "Auctions and Bidding," *Journal of Economic Literature*, September 1987, pp. 699–738.

FIGURE 16A.4

Winner's Curse in an
Asymmetric Information
Bidding Game

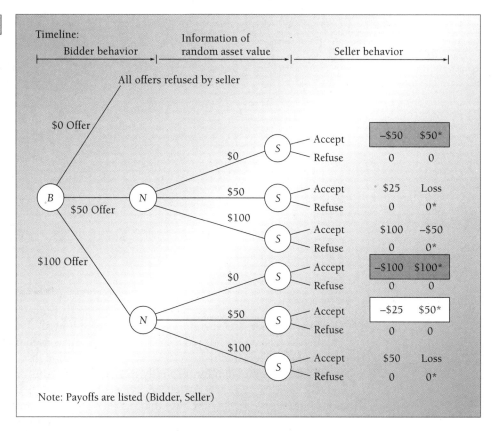

Note: Payoffs are listed (Bidder, Seller)

EXAMPLE

WINNER'S CURSE AT ABC[31]

When bids for the right to televise *Monday Night Football* for the next eight years reached $4 billion recently, NBC decided that the winner would be cursed with losses of $100 million to $125 million per year and dropped out of the auction. ABC continued bidding and eventually won the "prize" for $4.4 billion. Since NBC last televised this show and sold its ad slots, they were in the best position to know its true current value. Viewership has tumbled 33 percent since the peak interest in professional football in the early 1980s. The new television rights do allow for more TV time-outs in which to sell 30-second spot commercials. And football can increase other prime-time ratings as CBS demonstrated by successfully shifting the Sunday NFL Game of the Week audience right into their highest-rated show *60 Minutes*. When the Fox Broadcasting network won the rights to the Sunday NFL games, the *60 Minutes* audience shrank back to its original size. Nevertheless, we agree with NBC's assessment of the winner's curse. ABC may be hard pressed to come close to recovering their investment.

Table 16A.2 lists several auction price sequences for offshore oil tracts and FCC spectrum rights. The huge gaps between the winning bid and the second highest bid suggest that a winner's curse was present. Bidding sequences for star players in professional sports look very similar.

Mechanism design theory reveals several insights about this asymmetric information bidding game. First, most bidders will figure out the winner's curse in an auction design

---

[31] Based on "Thrown for a Loss By the NFL," *Time*, 26 January 1998, p. 52.

TABLE 16A.2		Offshore Oil[1]		FCC Spectrum[2]	
Bids for Offshore Oil Tracts and FCC Spectrum Rights		Santa Barbara Channel	Alaska North Slope	Miami Metro Area	Dallas Metro Area
		$43.5[1]	$10.5[1]	$131.7[2]	$84.2[2]
		32.1	5.2	126.0	72.0
		18.1	2.1	125.5	68.7
		10.2	1.4	119.4	
		6.3	0.5	119.3	
			0.4	113.8	
				113.7	
				108.4	

[1] In millions, 1969 dollars.

[2] In millions, 1995 dollars.

Source: Adapted from Tables II and IV in R. Weber, "Making More for Less," *Journal of Economics and Management Strategy,* 6(3), Fall 1997, pp. 529–548.

like Figure 16A.4, and therefore bid very timidly, if at all.[32] To induce more aggressive bidding in repeated, multiple-round versions of such asymmetric information games, sellers like DeBeers find they must sort carefully their rough-cut diamonds, grading them into "sights." Reputation for reliability in grading the sights more economically than the bidders could is what brings DeBeers' buyers back, auction after auction. DeBeers then has a minimum participation rule that insists on a certain number of bids if one wishes to be asked back. Secondly, if the asymmetric information is discoverable by appraisals, marketing research, or other similar investments, another insight from auction design theory is that the seller should conduct a multiple-round auction with open bidding. Open bidding allows the bidders to react to asymmetric information revealed in prior rounds and therefore reduces the winner's curse. Most recently, this idea was used by the Federal Communications Commission in the spectrum auctions for personal communication systems (PCS) like cell phones, mobile fax and data service, and voice-mail pagers.

Information Revelation in Common-Value Auctions

To illustrate this role of open bidding, consider two PCS bidders: Wireless Co., an alliance of Sprint and several large cable TV companies who spent $2.1 billion and won the rights to serve 145 million customers in 29 metropolitan service areas, and PCS PrimeCo., an alliance of three regional Bell companies who spent $1.1 billion and won the rights to serve 57 million customers in 11 metropolitan service areas. Several winning bids are listed in Table 16A.3. For example, Wireless paid $46.6 million for the Louisville, Kentucky, service area. How did Wireless decide what to bid?

Suppose that both bidders know that the net present value of the rights to transmit PCS services in Louisville is a random variable uniformly distributed from $10 million to $60 million with six discrete values possible—for example, $10 million, $20 million, $30 million, $40 million, $50 million, and $60 million. Also assume (provisionally) that both parties value the asset identically, a so-called **common-value auction.** The problem then from the bidders' point of view is to elicit sufficient information from the

Common-Value Auction
Auction where bidders have identical valuations when information is complete.

---

[32] Notice the same conclusion applies to a continuous-bid version of this auction, though experimental evidence suggests that most first-time players misperceive the asymmetric information nature of the seller's right of refusal and incorrectly bid $50 to $75. See C. Camerer, "Progress in Behavioral Game Theory," *Journal of Economic Perspectives,* 11(4), Fall 1997, pp. 167–188.

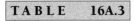

TABLE   16A.3

Winning Bids in
Broadband PCS Auction

Market	Population[1]	Winner	Second Highest	Bid[2]	Price/Pop.
New York	26.4	Wireless	Alaacr	$442.7	$16.76
San Francisco	11.9	PacTel	AmerPort	$202.2	$17.00
Charlotte	9.8	BellSouth	CCI	$70.9	$7.27
Dallas	9.7	Wireless	Alaacr	$88.4	$9.12
Houston	5.2	PrimeCo	Wireless	$82.7	$15.93
New Orleans	4.9	PrimeCo	Powertel	$89.5	$18.17
Louisville	3.6	Wireless	PrimeCo	$46.6	$13.10
Salt Lake City	2.6	Wireless	GTE	$46.2	$17.95
Jacksonville	2.3	PrimeCo	GTE	$44.5	$19.56

[1]In millions from the 1990 Census.

[2]Price paid for 30 MHz Block B spectrum rights, March 1995.

(Source: P. Cramton, "The FCC Spectrum Auctions," *Journal of Economics and Management Strategy,* 6(3), Fall 1997, pp. 431–496.)

market environment and from the offers of other bidders to correctly identify the value and ensure a profit (i.e., not overpay for the asset). In advance, each company conducts marketing research experiments to narrow the possible outcomes and thereby better inform its own bid. Suppose Wireless Co.'s marketing research results are unable to exclude the two tails of the uniform distribution of possible values (i.e., $10 million and $60 million) but can exclude with certainty $20 million and $30 million as well as $50 million. Taken by itself, this information allows Wireless to narrow its probability assessments to $10 million, $40 million, and $60 million. Weighting each outcome equally yields an expected value bid of $36.7 million as follows:

$$\frac{1}{3}\,(\$10\ million) + \frac{1}{3}\,(\$40\ million) + \frac{1}{3}\,(\$60\ million) = \$36.7\ million. \quad [16A.1]$$

Similarly, PCS Prime Co. conducts its own marketing research which, let's assume, excludes $10 million, $30 million, and $50 million as possible outcomes for the Louisville service area. That is, PCS PrimeCo. has access to separate information that causes it to calculate a different expected value bid,[33]

$$\frac{1}{3}\,(\$20\ million) + \frac{1}{3}\,(\$40\ million) + \frac{1}{3}\,(\$60\ million) = \$40\ million. \quad [16A.2]$$

---

[33] The equally weighted probabilities of 1/3 are actually Bayesian probabilities of each possible remaining value based on a perfectly accurate forecast that $10 million, $30 million, and $50 million (the prime numbers in the set of possible asset values) have been ruled out. It is helpful if we think of the marketing research as identifying Prime and Not Prime numbers between one and six. Then, the Bayesian probability ($20 million/Perfect Forecast of Not Prime) = (0.167 × 1.0)/(0.167 + 0.833 × 0.4) = 0.33 where 0.167 is the prior probability before the marketing research is conducted that $20 million will be the realized asset value. The number 1.0 is the accuracy of the forecasting instrument—for example, the conditional probability that when $20 million is the true value, the conclusion from the marketing research will be that the value is Not Prime, meaning "not a prime number between one and six." The number 0.833 is the prior probability that the asset value will be something other than $20 million. And finally, the number 0.4 is the probability that when something other than $20 million is the true asset value, the perfectly accurate forecasting instrument will still say Not Prime. That happens with $40 million and $60 million—i.e., twice in five possibilities.

The analysis here is easily modified to incorporate less than perfect forecasts from the marketing research. That is fortunate indeed because imperfect forecasts are the reality of business. See E. Rasmussen, *Games and Information,* 2nd ed. (Cambridge: Basil Blackwell, 1993), Chapter 12, section 4.

These are the best estimates of the common value based on the asymmetric information available to the two firms. Consequently, in a simultaneous sealed-bid auction, the most a seller could hope to realize is $40 million. With sealed bids, there is no information conveyed to the competitor, and an optimal bidding strategy is therefore simply to shade your bid slightly below the Bayesian expected value based on your own information set. PCS PrimeCo. would therefore bid something just under $40 million and win the spectrum rights for the Louisville service area.

Open Bidding

Notice, however, from the seller's point of view ex post facto (after receiving the sealed bids) that the joint information set of the two parties suggests PCS PrimeCo. has underpaid. To review, the union of the two sets of marketing research outcomes excludes $10 million, $20 million, $30 million, and $50 million. Said another way, the *combined* marketing research results have narrowed the possible outcomes for the value of the Louisville service area to $40 million and $60 million. Neither firm has access to this much information. Each simply knows a subset of all the marketing research available. But as a seller in such a setting, the FCC wished to elicit full revelation of *all* asymmetric information because it affects the winning bid. If $40 million and $60 million are equally likely, and the bidders can somehow discern this information, the Louisville service area is worth just under $50 million, not PCS PrimeCo's bid of just under $40 million.

One way to bring all the asymmetric information into play is to adopt a sequential open-bidding auction design. Then, whichever company bids first, the other company will deduce the first bidder's additional marketing research results and proceed to increase their bid in light of the more complete information available. For example, if PCS PrimeCo bids first, and bids $40 million based on its own asymmetric information, Wireless Co. will then be in a position to deduce that PCS PrimeCo's marketing research excluded $10 million, $30 million, and $50 million as possible values. That's the only information that would be consistent with a bid of $40 million in a simultaneous sealed-bid auction over an asset with a uniform distribution from $10 million to $60 million with only these six possible outcomes. Knowing from its own marketing research that $20 million, $30 million, and $50 million have also been ruled out, Wireless will immediately place a winning bid of just under $50 million:

$$\frac{1}{2} (\$40 \text{ million}) + \frac{1}{2} (\$60 \text{ million}) = \$50 \text{ million}. \qquad [16A.3]$$

If there were other service areas in which Wireless could be required to bid first, and PCS PrimeCo had a turn playing the fast second, this sequential open-bidding auction design would work well. Winning bids would rise to the Bayesian expected asset values reflecting all available information, and highest value users would receive the assets. However, with not two but many bidders eligible for the auction, a rotation of the bidding sequence becomes cumbersome and, in any case, the delay in asking bidders to wait their turn is problematic in any industry with fast-moving technology. Moreover, open bidding with a structured sequence of role reversals on multiple auctions allows bidders to signal and punish one another (e.g., with "tit for tat") and therefore increases the likelihood of tacit collusion.

EXAMPLE

OPEN BIDDING SIMULTANEOUS AUCTION OF PCS SPECTRUM RIGHTS[34]

Thirty firms ultimately participated in the broadband spectrum auctions. The FCC specified two 30-MHz blocks for each of 51 metropolitan service areas. A special feature of these metropolitan service areas was strong interdependencies in providing service in contiguous service areas. Bidders were encouraged therefore to assemble and reassemble efficient bundles of licenses as the auction progressed. Consequently, multiple-round simultaneous auctions with open bidding were adopted by the FCC to allocate spectrum rights. Each bidder was told there would be several rounds of bidding, all bids in each round were announced, and each bidder was allowed to cancel or amend bids from round to round. All bids in every metro area remained open as long as any bidding activity continued in any service area. The auction lasted 112 rounds over a four-month period in early 1995. Using this auction design, the FCC raised $7.7 billion. AT&T paid $49.3 million and Wireless Co. paid $46.6 million for the A block and B block spectrum rights in Louisville.

As new technologies become available, the FCC intends to conduct additional auctions periodically to continue placing spectrum rights in the hands of the highest-value users. For example, in March 1998, 139 companies bid $578 million for UHF microwave transmission rights to broadcast wireless Internet access service.

Strategic Underbidding in Private-Value Auctions[35]

Private Value Auction
Auction where the bidders have different valuations when information is complete.

One serious drawback of highest-bid open outcry auctions is the strategic reticence bidders exhibit. If the bidders have common information but different valuations (i.e., a so-called **private value auction**), those with high willingness to pay have an incentive to refrain from aggressive bidding in an attempt to just exceed the bid of the player with the second highest valuation. For example, in the FCC's spectrum auctions, the cellular phone incumbents already established in a metropolitan area had higher valuation than other bidders. In the early rounds of any such open bidding auction over private values, eventual high bidders hold back. Analysis of the FCC data suggests only 53 percent of the eventual winners were the high bidders after the early rounds. Sellers worry that this strategic reticence dampens the overall level of bidding throughout the auction and may well reduce final revenue.

Underbidding in a private-value auction is rational only if bidders can be assured of winning in the final round. One way to reduce strategic underbidding in private-value auctions is to seal the bids. A less extreme approach is to end the auction without warning, after several preliminary rounds, thereby in effect sealing the bids unpredictably. Of course, any mechanism that prevents communication may have a significant disadvantage when asymmetric information is present among the bidders—for example, in a common-value auction setting. As we saw in the previous section, it can be in the seller's interest to induce the revelation of all such asymmetric information. In fact, sellers

---

[34] Based on "Market Design and the Spectrum Auctions," A Special Issue of *Journal of Economics and Management Strategy*, 6(3), Fall 1997 and "Sale of Wireless Frequencies," *Wall Street Journal*, 25 March 1998, p. A3.

[35] Two excellent elaborations of this and the next topic are J. McMillan, "Bidding in Competition," *Games, Strategies, and Managers* (New York: Oxford University Press, 1992), Chap. 11 and E. Rasmussen, "Auctions," *Games and Information*, 2nd ed. (Cambridge, Mass: Basil Blackwell, 1993), Chap. 12.

often have an incentive to preannounce expert estimates of value (as Christie's and Sotheby's auction houses do) in order to reduce the winner's curse.

This concern is important in auction design, but not always controlling. The reason is that some asymmetrically held information can, if revealed, lower the rational bid (see the Case Exercise below). So, sealing bids is a design alternative that becomes more attractive the greater the variation in private values and the more common (symmetric) the information pertaining to valuation among the bidders. Open bidding or preannouncing estimates and appraisals is more attractive whenever favorable information about the common value is known to the seller. Even when the seller is in the dark, open bidding has a positive expected value for the seller because the exchange of common-value information always reduces the winner's curse.

Second-Highest Sealed Bid Auctions

Incentive Compatible Auction Mechanism
A procedure for eliciting full value bids.

Strategic reticence (underbidding) is especially troubling, of course, if the seller is collecting bid revenue from all participants in the auction. A "seller" may be attempting to assess whether there exists sufficient total willingness to pay to justify investment in a new facility (e.g., a ballpark, a pool, a set of tennis courts, or a clubhouse). Each potential user is asked what he or she would pay for access. If sufficient demand exists, the facility manager then builds the facility and collects the highly divergent, discriminatory prices from each "bidder." As we saw in Chapter 13, the key to such an assessment is designing an **incentive-compatible auction mechanism.** The same thing is true in designing a private-value auction. If as an auction designer, I could remove the incentive to underbid and at the same time prevent a winner's curse, I would have aligned your incentives with true revelation of value. Think through the following illustration of an ingenious incentive-compatible auction mechanism that won William Vickery a considerable prize, the Nobel prize![36]

Suppose two bidders each value a service or asset between $0 million and $10 million. No information about the actual net present values is known. That is, there is no common-value information, asymmetric or otherwise. This is a purely private value auction. The auction will last only one round, the bids are sealed, and the highest bid wins. Your valuation is $6 million—what should you bid?[37]

With two bidders present, each must assume that the other will offer something less than his or her private value, say k times v where k is a proportion and v is the private value. Bid prices by Aaron (P_a) greater than k times Bob's value (v_b) will win. That is, anytime $P_a/k > v_b$, Aaron wins the auction and realizes a profit of ($v_a - P_a$). With uniform density, the probability that Bob's value is any given number between $0 and $10 million is 1/10 million. Again, Aaron wins when this value is between $0 and P_a/k dollars. Therefore, Aaron's cumulative probability of winning is P_a/k events, each of which has a marginal probability of 1/10 million—i.e., Aaron's cumulative probability of winning is $P_a/(k \times 10$ million). Aaron's expected profit from the auction may therefore be written,

$$E(\text{Profit}_a) = (v_a - P_a) \frac{P_a}{k \cdot 10,000,000} \qquad [16A.4]$$

---

[36] Every game theory and mechanism design theory book describes the Vickery auction, also known as the second-highest sealed-bid auction, or the uniform-price auction. Vickery's original article is also revealing and insightful; see W. Vickery, "Counterspeculation, Auctions, and Competitive Sealed Tenders," *Journal of Finance*, 16(8), 1961, p. 37.

[37] This example relies on McMillan, *op. cit.,* pp. 138 and 208–209.

Differentiating Equation 16A.4 with respect to P_a and setting the derivative equal to zero, Aaron's expected profit from the auction is maximized when

$$(v_a - 2P_a) \frac{1}{k \cdot 10,000,000} = 0 \qquad [16A.5]$$

—i.e., when $P_a = v_a/2$. That is, Aaron will maximize her expected profit from participating in the auction, conditional on Bob's choosing a kv_b bidding rule, by choosing to reduce her own private value by 1/2. Since Aaron and Bob are symmetrically situated in this bidding game, Bob too should reduce his private value by 1/2. With $k = 1/2$, the players are in a Nash equilibrium. Each maximizes self-interest, conditional on the other player's bidding $v/2$, by bidding half of his or her own private value. In a two-player simultaneous highest-price-wins-and-pays sealed-bid auction, the rational underbidding is fully 50 percent!

If there are five bidders, it is easy to show that you should reduce your private value by 1/5th, and if n bidders, by $1/n$th.[38] Quite intuitively, therefore, the more bidders, the smaller the rational underbidding. Sellers understand this and therefore provide sorting services (in DeBeers' case) and handsome catalogs and live exhibitions (in Christie's case) to draw bidders into the auction process. If sellers expend enough resources to expand the pool of bidders, in the limit the seller can realize $(n-1)/n$ of the maximum private value (v_{max}). Five bidders implies 80 percent of v_{max}. Ten bidders implies 90 percent of v_{max}. Twenty bidders implies 95 percent of v_{max}. Increasing the number of bidders from two to five resulted in a 30 percent increase in value, doubling the number of bidders from five to ten resulted in a 10 percent increase in value, and doubling them again resulted in only a 5 percent increase in value. Diminishing returns to these efforts by sellers to expand the pool of bidders implies that the fundamental problem of strategic underbidding will be mitigated but never eliminated.

EXAMPLE

EXPONENTIAL VALLEY INC. AUCTIONS A CHIP PATENT[39]

Exponential Valley Inc., a Silicon Valley microprocessor start-up, has decided to auction its portfolio of 45 issued and pending patents rather than move into production. The computer chip patents include features that would allow a competitor to match forthcoming chip products from industry leader Intel Corp. Intel regularly sues companies who make clones of their chips and has been very effective in deterring entry with this strategy. The Exponential Valley patents appear to offer an opportunity to provide protection from Intel's patent infringement suits. Digital Equipment, Advanced Micro Devices, and a division of National Semiconductor have all expressed interest in bidding on the patents. At considerable expense, Exponential has developed a large prospectus of technical and bidding information that it targeted to other possible bidders: Rambus, Inc., Chromatic Research Inc., and Texas Instruments. The larger the number of bidders, the less the strategic underbidding.

But now suppose that we make one small additional change in the auction design. What if, rather than requiring the winning bidder to pay the high bid, the auction rules specified in advance that the highest bid wins but that the winner would pay the second-highest bid? Notice that the winner's curse is no longer present. By defi-

---

[38] See Rasmussen, *op. cit.,* p. 296.
[39] Based on "An Auction of Chip Patents May Ignite Bidding War," *Wall Street Journal,* 1 August 1997, p. B5.

nition, under the rules of a second-highest sealed-bid auction, the payment triggered by bidding one's true private value cannot exceed the next best alternative selling price. This use of a verifiable outside option (an exit option) to shore up the bidder's protection from suffering a winner's curse was the key insight of William Vickery's mechanism design.

Vickery Auction

An incentive-compatible revelation mechanism for eliciting sealed bids equal to private value.

To sum up, every bidder in a **Vickery auction** over private values has no incentive to underbid. Reducing your bid below your private value has no effect on the payment due should you win. Underbidding in a second-highest sealed-bid auction when you are the highest willingness-to-pay participant increases the probability of losing an auction asset that it would have been possible to acquire for less than it is worth to you. And if someone else values the asset more than you, no payment is triggered by bidding up to your own private value. Therefore, for all possible cases, true revelation of private values dominates underbidding as an auction strategy. And because bids are sealed and the auction lasts only one round, no strategic bidding, false carding, or signalling can have any effect on other participants in the auction. Therefore, No Underbidding is a dominant strategy equilibrium for all bidders.[40]

What auction design to adopt is often a complex trade-off between the above results and the particulars of the business generating the asset value. In the spectrum auctions, open bidding in multiple rounds with the winner paying the highest-price bid met the needs of the telecommunication companies to reconfigure their contiguous service areas as the auction proceeded. Careful analysis and application of the managerial insights from mechanism design reasoning can better inform these choices and increase capitalized value.

EXAMPLE

SECOND-HIGHEST SEALED-BID AUCTION: U.S. TREASURY BILLS[41]

Auction design decisions in security markets often focus on what auction mechanisms raise the most revenue for sellers. On this question, debate currently rages about the optimal design of Treasury bill new-issue security auctions. Denmark and Sweden adopt diametrically opposed designs. The Swedes sell government bills and bonds at discriminatory prices; the Danes sell at a uniform second-highest sealed-bid price. Given this diversity of expert opinion and practice, the Federal Reserve has authorized the New York Federal Reserve Bank to experiment with both designs for two-year and five-year notes. The preponderance of Treasury auctions in the United States (and indeed around the world) are discriminatory descending-price (Dutch) auctions; buyers pay whatever they bid for quantities of T-bonds along a demand schedule submitted by each bidder. If the market-clearing price implies a yield of 5.03 percent, a typical bidder may get $5 million worth of T-bills at a considerably higher price yielding 5.01 percent, $10 million worth of T-bills at a slightly higher price yielding 5.02 percent, and perhaps $10 million at the market-clearing price yielding 5.03 percent.

Uniform price second-highest sealed-bid auctions are very different. Every bidder in this auction might pay the uniform slightly higher price associated with a yield of 5.02 percent. If so, the Treasury's revenue from the auction will increase, or said another way, the Treasury's marginal cost of raising debt capital will decline from 5.03 percent to 5.02 percent.

---

[40] The bidder's degree of risk-aversion has no bearing on this result. However, more risk-averse bidders do ensure against no-win outcomes in winner-take-all highest-price sealed-bid auctions by increasing their bid relative to winner-take-all second-highest sealed-bid auctions, and this can result in a still further increase in seller revenue.

[41] Based on "Bidding Up Debt Auctions," *Business Week,* 8 September 1997, p. 26 and S. Nandi, "Treasury Auctions: What Do the Recent Models and Results Tell Us?" *Federal Reserve Bank of Atlanta Economic Review,* Fourth Quarter 1997.

However, the recent Vickery auction experiments have raised nearly identical revenue to the traditional Treasury auction methods. This result highlights the insight that the principal advantages of second-highest sealed-bid auctions are to reduce strategic underbidding and bidder collusion among small numbers of bidders in private-value auctions. In contrast, security markets are efficient with numerous potential buyers willing to pay a common value of these T-bond and T-bill assets. Therefore, second-highest sealed-bid mechanism design is largely inappropriate. Indeed, recent research suggests that Vickery auction mechanisms may actually facilitate collusion because of the peculiarities of submitting an entire demand schedule of bids in the new issue security markets. Again, combining managerial insight with a careful analysis of the particulars proves important.

CASE EXERCISE

SPECTRUM AUCTION

Suppose that two bidders know that the net present value of the rights to transmit PCS services in Louisville is a random variable uniformly distributed from $10 million to $60 million with six discrete values possible—i.e., $10 million, $20 million, $30 million, $40 million, $50 million, and $60 million. Also assume that both parties value the asset identically, making this a common-value auction. In advance, each company conducts marketing research experiments to narrow the possible outcomes and thereby better inform its own bid. Suppose Wireless Co.'s marketing research results exclude the two tails of the uniform distribution of possible values (i.e., $10 million and $60 million) as well as $40 million. Similarly, PCS PrimeCo conducts its own marketing research which, let's assume, excludes $10 million, $30 million, and $50 million as possible outcomes for the Louisville service area.

a.   What should Wireless Co. bid in a single-round sealed-bid common-value auction? What should PCS PrimeCo bid in this same auction?

b.   If Wireless goes first in a sequential announced bid auction with multiple rounds to follow, what should PCS PrimeCo respond in round 2? In round 3, will Wireless then wish to amend its earlier bid? Why?

c.   What auction design would be in the seller's best interest—single-round sealed-bid or multiple-round open bidding?

d.   Identify other factors that could affect the optimal auction design.

Pricing Techniques and Analysis

CHAPTER PREVIEW

This chapter builds on the price and output determination models developed in Chapters 12 through 16 as it considers more complex pricing issues. The first two sections examine models and applications of price discrimination that assume the firm sells a product at different prices to different buyers at the same time. Next, we consider cases in which the firm produces multiple products, some that are independent in the production process, others that are jointly produced. Another section deals with the problems of transfer pricing, that is, the pricing of intracompany sales of products between different divisions within the firm. Finally, we characterize value-based as opposed to cost-based pricing and discuss the product life cycle including penetration pricing, target pricing, limit pricing, price skimming, prestige pricing, and price lining. Together, the pricing practices presented in this chapter provide an extensive overview of the way managers apply the pricing principles from economic models to maximize shareholder wealth. Appendix 17A develops the powerful yield management concepts of price discrimination and capacity allocation.

CONCEPTUAL FRAMEWORK FOR PROACTIVE VALUE-BASED PRICING

In the past, pricing decisions were often treated as an afterthought and made in ad hoc fashion as a reaction to competitor initiatives. When pricing rivalry was more stable, many firms simply routinely marked up cost. Today, pricing proactively with systematic analysis of which orders to accept (and which to refuse) at particular value-based prices has become a critical success factor for many businesses. Proactive pricing is tactically astute and internally consistent with operations strategy. A high-cost airline cannot slash prices dramatically even if 10 or 20 percent increases in market share are thereby achievable. It must anticipate not only a matching price reaction by its lower-cost rivals but perhaps further price cuts below its own cost. Knowing all this in advance renders gain-share discounting much less attractive despite the temptation of additional incremental sales in a high-margin business.

To take another example, in the men's aftershave industry, an incumbent recently encountered a new entrant whose product Vibrance was introduced with a penetration price 40 percent below the leading brand. The incumbent increased advertising but maintained its original price point and was astounded to observe a 50 percent decline in market share through the grocery store distribution channel. Only afterwards was systematic analysis completed. Estimations showed that demand was very price elastic and advertising inelastic. All pricing decisions must be systematic and analytical, based on hard facts not ad hoc hunches.

Finally, the appropriate conceptual framework for setting prices is an analysis of the determinants of customer value. What triggers a customer's purchase is value in excess of asking price or a ratio of value to price greater than a competitor. Firms must begin their pricing decisions by identifying the value-drivers in each customer segment. Business air travelers value delivery reliability, the ability to change itineraries on short notice (i.e., change order responsiveness), and schedule convenience more than attentive cabin personnel, wide seats, or quick flights. Because such value drivers are harder to imitate, sustainable price premiums are often associated with these order processing characteristics rather than the product or service itself. On the other hand, Prestone and Zerex have leading anticorrosive radiator fluids whose produce characteristics warrant a price premium. Under apparent price pressure, Zerex often simply meets the competition as long as competing prices on generic radiator fluid cover cost. A thorough value analysis reveals, however, that this cost-based pricing fails to realize about one-third of Zerex's sustainable profit margin.

Cost-based pricing has been called one of the "five deadly business sins"; what firms should do instead is "price-based costing." That is, firms should segment customers, perform extensive value analysis, and then develop products whose costs allow substantial profitability in each product line the firm chooses to enter. Each firm's marketing and operations capabilities are the key to then sustaining that profitability. Costs are not irrelevant. Indeed, a key to effective revenue management is knowing with great precision just what activity-based costs are associated with each type of order from each customer segment. Knowledge of differential costs supports the adoption of differential pricing, and even more importantly, allows value-based pricing managers to discern *which orders to refuse*. But costs should be the consequence of a value-based pricing and product development strategy that integrates marketing, operations, and financial analysis.

In sum, pricing decisions should be proactive and systematic-analytical not reactive and ad hoc. And, most importantly, pricing should be value-based, not cost-based. This value-based conceptual framework leads naturally to a differential pricing environment in which mass-produced products or services are customized to the requirements of individual customer classes.

www . . . .
Read an article by Kevin M. Guthrie on value-based pricing at the following Internet site for the Andrew W. Mellon Foundation's recent Scholarly Communication and Technology conference:
http://www.arl.org/scomm/scat/guthries.html

MANAGERIAL CHALLENGE

PRICING OF APPLE COMPUTERS: MARKET SHARE VERSUS PROFITABILITY[1]

Apple Computer manufactures and sells the Macintosh line of personal computers (PCs). Apple PCs compete against PCs produced and sold by a number of other companies, including IBM, Compaq, and Packard Bell. Apple uses microprocessor chips designed by Motorola as the "brains" of its PCs, whereas most of the other PC makers use Intel (or Intel clone) microprocessor chips in their machines.

Historically, Apple has priced its Macintosh computers higher than similar models of other PC makers. For example, despite price cuts in early 1995 by both Apple and other computer companies, Macintosh systems were still priced $500 to $1,000 higher than some comparable Intel microprocessor-based systems. Partly as the result of its higher prices, Apple's share of the worldwide PC market dropped from 9.4 percent in 1993 to 8.1 percent in 1994. Also, although total unit sales of the PC industry grew 32 percent in the fourth (calendar) quarter of 1994, Apple's sales were flat. Offsetting this decline in market share, Apple's gross profit margin increased from 24 percent earlier in the year to 29 percent in the fourth quarter of 1994, and its quarterly earnings per share more than quadrupled to $1.46 during the fourth quarter from $0.34 in the last quarter of 1993. (*Gross profit margin* measures profit as a percentage of sales before deducting capital costs, research, development, selling, general, and administrative expenses.)

One computer industry analyst observed, "I believe Apple sacrificed market share in the interest of profitability." By emphasizing profit over market share, Apple risks losing more market share over time. Software developers prefer to write and sell application programs for PCs with larger market shares, such as those based on Intel microprocessors. A lack of a wide range of application programs could further depress demand for Macintosh PCs. Some Apple managers believe that the company must increase its market share to about 20 percent, or roughly double its 1995 market share, to motivate software companies to write application programs for Macintosh PCs.

Ian Diery, Apple's sales vice president, defended the company's high prices saying that Apple had to improve its balance sheet so that it could continue research and marketing efforts. He claimed that "It's much better to gamble on market share growth from a strong balance sheet than from a weak one." The question of whether Apple's strategy of charging premium prices for products will be successful over the long run remains unanswered.

This chapter focuses on a variety of different pricing strategies, including the decision by companies, such as Apple, to charge premium prices for their products.

www . . . .
Access financial information on Apple Computer, including quarterly earning reports, at the following Internet site:
http://www.apple.com/investor/

[1]Jim Carlton, "Apple's Choice: Preserve Profits or Cut Prices," *Wall Street Journal,* 22 February 1995, p. B1.

DIFFERENTIAL PRICING

One of the simplest examples of differential pricing is congestion-based pricing at peak demand periods on roadways, bridges, and subway systems as well as in hotels, rental car companies, and airlines. In Figure 17.1, peak-period drivers place demands on a Los Angeles toll road between 6 A.M. and 9 A.M. far in excess of its carrying capacity (Q_C). Charging peak-period commuters a toll equal to just the minuscule cost of wear and tear maintenance (MC_{OP}) induces many more cars to enter the highway (Q_P) than can be accommodated (i.e., $Q_P > Q_C$). The result is slowdowns, stoppages, and a

FIGURE   17.1

Congestion Tolls with
Peak–Off Peak Demand

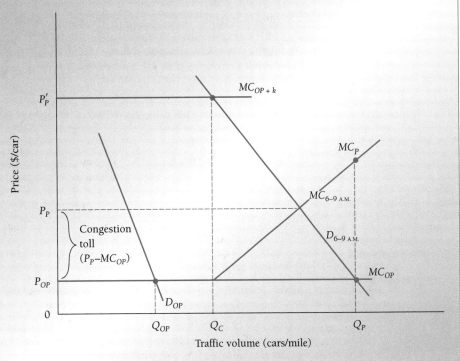

markedly increased travel time for each commuter. Beyond the traffic volume at which this congestion begins, MC_P represents the incremental fuel and time costs imposed (by one additional car) on all the other drivers along a 10-mile stretch of toll road. A congestion toll of $(P_P - MC_{OP})$ induces discretionary peak period travelers to switch to other travel times and alternative modes of transportation. If a toll road authority set peak-period prices just sufficient to cover this congestion cost, traffic volume would decline and the equilibrium differential prices P_P and P_{OP} would emerge.

EXAMPLE

www . . . .
Read about a recent poll
showing that a majority of
southern Californians
support congestion tolls at
the following Internet site
maintained by Resources
for the Future:
http://www.rff.org/news/
transp.htm

CONGESTION TOLLS IN ORANGE COUNTY, CALIFORNIA[2]

In 1985 the typical American spent 22 hours per year in traffic jams due to peak-period congestion. By 1995, this figure had doubled to over 40 hours per year. In 2005, the forecast is 80 hours per year. Is the answer simply more highways? One community in Southern California thinks not. Congestion tolls which charge commuters for the congestion their car's presence imposes on other drivers have been adopted by a private toll road in Orange County, near Los Angeles. Every day, 24,000 drivers pay a peak-period congestion toll of $2.75 per trip for an uncongested 10-mile stretch of true expressway. Toll booths, which themselves cause delays, have been replaced by credit-card-size transponders mounted in dashboards from which overhead computers deduct tolls as the cars speed along. Although the congestion toll expenses of a typical commuter mount up quickly, the cost of additional road capacity per car (k in Figure 17.1) would necessitate a still higher price P'_p. And time is money, so faced with the convenience of the private toll road versus the slow commute on "freeways," many peak-period travelers are opting for the differential pricing of a congestion toll.

[2] Based on "How to Make Traffic Jams a Thing of the Past," *Fortune*, 31 March 1997, p. 34.

Like peak–off peak roadway pricing, many examples of differential pricing do not entail charging differential prices for the same capacity. Differential pricing at matinee and evening movie theatres, for example, involves optimizing behavior for demanders not in rivalry for the same theatre seats. Matinee and evening showings of first-run movies are different product lines. Similarly, seasonal discounts in the resort and cruise ship businesses are reflective of different product lines. However, if two customer classes are in rivalry for the same capacity (e.g., the seats on a particular airplane flight), then differential pricing involves price discrimination.

PRICE DISCRIMINATION

Price Discrimination

The act of selling the same good or service, produced by a single firm, at different prices to different buyers during the same period of time.

Price discrimination is defined as the act of selling the same product (a good or service), produced under single control (that is, by one firm), at different prices to different buyers during the same period of time. This basic definition, which assumes a homogenous product, can be broadened to a more operational level if we also include cases in which differences between prices of a firm's products exceed the differences in costs of production. Examples of price discrimination include the following:

- ▦ Doctors, dentists, hospitals, lawyers, tax consultants, and economic consultants who charge the rich more than the poor for the same quality of service
- ▦ Producers who offer large purchasers quantity discounts that exceed the difference in marginal selling costs between large and small purchasers
- ▦ Firms that sell the exact same product (e.g., appliances or tires) under two different labels at widely varying prices
- ▦ Athletic teams that sponsor family nights and ladies' nights at discount prices, while others pay the full price
- ▦ Hotels, restaurants, and other businesses that offer discounts to senior citizens
- ▦ Airlines that offer discounted fares based on the day of the week (or time of day) of travel and the length of stay (e.g., a stayover Saturday night is normally required for the most heavily discounted "super saver" fares)
- ▦ State-supported universities that charge higher tuition to students who are not state residents
- ▦ Academic journals that charge a lower price to individuals and a higher price to institutional subscribers (e.g., libraries)
- ▦ University bookstores that offer faculty members a discount on books, which is not available to students or other customers
- ▦ Korean TV manufacturers who may sell products at a lower price in the United States than in Japan

A determination of whether price discrimination is actually being practiced requires that cost differentials be evaluated in conjunction with price differentials. The term *price discrimination* has a strictly neutral connotation in economic jargon. A determination of whether the exercise of this business practice, under any given set of circumstances, should be considered bad or good is a distributive question that depends on your point of view.

As far as the individual firm and its shareholders are concerned, the practice of charging different prices to different individuals (if it is done with a proper recognition of demand elasticities) will always result in a level of profits at least as high as would occur if only one price were charged, and usually profits may be increased through price discrimination. This is so because the price that a consumer pays for a product will never exceed that which he or she is willing to pay rather than do without it, and in many cases it does not equal this amount. As a consequence, the satisfaction or utility gained from the purchase of the product often exceeds that which is lost from paying the prevailing price. This results in a surplus of satisfaction or *consumers' surplus* that a customer may derive from the purchase. For example, if a coffee aficionado were willing to pay $6.00 for a morning cup of java, but found that the neighborhood Starbuck's charged only $2.00, the consumer surplus would be $4.00. Price discrimination aims at transferring part or all of the consumers' surplus from the consumer to the producer.

Conditions Required for Successful Price Discrimination

Before examining the various degrees of price discrimination that may be practiced, consider the conditions that will enable a firm (or any organization charging a price for goods or services provided) to engage successfully in this strategy. The two basic conditions are the following:

1. It must be possible to segment the market and to prevent the transfer of the seller's product from one segment to another (i.e., to prevent arbitrage).
2. Differences in the elasticity of demand from one segment to another must exist at the same price.

The illustrations presented at the beginning of this section indicate some of the bases of price discrimination. One case is that of consumer ignorance, where Consumer A pays more than Consumer B for the same good or service, but where there is little or no communication between consumers, so one consumer does not know he or she is paying a higher price. One example is an automobile dealer who charges different prices to different customers, depending on the relative negotiating strength of each buyer. The nature of personal services, such as medical and dental care, also permit effective price discrimination, because it is generally impossible to resell these services to a third party once they have been performed; for example, it is impossible for a patient paying low Medicare rates to resell a kidney transplant operation. Similarly, a hockey team may charge different prices to groups than to individuals. Advance purchase requirements and evidence of group affiliation are used to enforce this segmentation. Other criteria used to effect price discrimination are age, sex, educational status, income levels, and military status of the buyers. Geographical differences in buyers' locations, alternative uses to which a product is put (for example, electric power rates for households versus industrial users), product labeling or branding, and peak versus off-peak rates (for example, discounted long-distance direct dialing telephone rates during the evening and weekends) are also used to segment the market and facilitate price discrimination. The actual basis used for market segmentation is relatively unimportant as long as it is effective (that is, little leakage occurs among segments) and as long as different price elasticities exist between the resulting segments.

First-, Second-, and Third-Degree Price Discrimination

In the limiting case of perfect or *first-degree price discrimination*, the monopolist presumably knows not only the market-clearing price but also the maximum each individual is willing to pay for any quantity.[3] The monopolist then charges each customer the

---

[3] In the discussion assume that the price-discriminating firm is a monopolist who knows the entire demand schedule for each customer. The practice has been frequently observed in other imperfectly competitive market structures as well. Only in highly competitive markets, where new sellers may move rapidly into higher-priced market segments thereby undermining price differentials charged, is discrimination unlikely.

highest price that purchaser is willing to pay for each unit purchased (providing this price exceeds the marginal cost of production). In this manner, the entire consumers' surplus is captured by the producer. Conditions such as these are extremely rare, but do occur in particular markets—for example, the auction market for T-bills (discussed at the end of Appendix 16A) where bidders each submit their entire demand schedule of bids at various quantities.

EXAMPLE

BLOCK RATE-SETTING: TRI-STATE GAS COMPANY

Figure 17.2 illustrates second-degree price discrimination as practiced by the Tri-State Gas Company. Let DD_1 represent the household demand for natural gas in a community. If the gas company charged P_1, Q_1 cubic feet of natural gas would be demanded. If, however, the firm wished to sell Q_3 cubic feet of gas, a price of P_3 would have to be charged. In second-degree discrimination, consumers would be charged a set of prices rather than a single price. For instance, as shown in Panel (a), the first Q_1 cubic feet used would be priced at P_1; the next block of usage, $Q_2 - Q_1$, would be priced at P_2; and the last block, $Q_3 - Q_2$, at P_3. If as shown in Panel (b), only one price were charged—for example, P_3—total revenue received by the gas company would equal the price P_3 times Q_3 units sold. Consumer's surplus in this case is given by the triangle DP_3C. By charging three separate prices, total revenue is now represented by rectangles P_1P_2AE plus P_2P_3BF in addition to the original amount $0P_3CQ_3$. The remaining consumer's surplus, which the utility was unable to appropriate, is represented by the small triangles DP_1A, AEB, and BFC. As can be seen, consumers' surplus (shaded area) is much smaller when a set of prices is charged than when only one price is charged.

Two-Part Tariff

One effective method of implementing first- or second-degree price discrimination is to charge both a lump sum entry fee and a user fee, a so-called two-part tariff. Amusement parks, nightclubs, golf and tennis clubs, cellular phone providers, and computer and rental car companies often charge a lump-sum fee plus user fees. The lump-sum monthly

FIGURE   17.2

Second-Degree Price
Discrimination: Tri-State
Gas Company

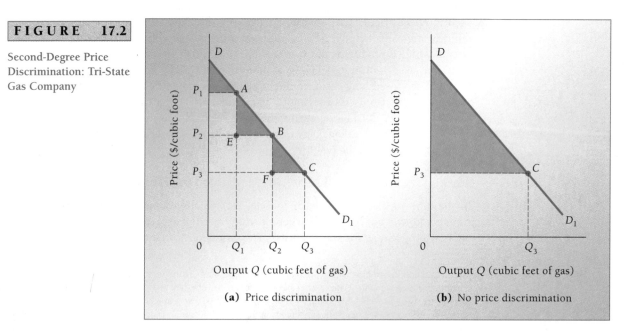

(a) Price discrimination   (b) No price discrimination

or daily fee provides access to the facility, phone, computer, or car independent of use, and the per hour or per minute or per mile fee varies with usage. Heavy demanders pay more through higher user fees. In principle, each supplier can set user fees equal to marginal cost and then ask for lump-sum entry fees equal to the entire consumer surplus (e.g., *ABC* in Figure 17.3). In practice, such first-degree price discrimination is seldom possible, so suppliers must decide whether to set uniformly high or low entry fees and whether to charge high or low user fees. Cellular phone companies like AT&T Wireless and men's toiletries producers like Gillette practically give away the requisite telecommunications and shaving equipment and then charge steep prices for the cell phone calls and the blades. Golf and tennis clubs, in contrast, have substantial membership fees and annual dues but often price the tennis courts at a trivial user fee (e.g., $5 per hour).

Consider the two-part pricing depicted in Figure 17.3 for two customer segments with relatively elastic and relatively inelastic demand for rental autos. These might be young couples who are renting cars for vacationing (D_1) and manufacturers' trade representatives renting cars for sales calls. The challenge is to find a uniform daily rate (the lump sum access fee) and a mileage charge that maximize profit and keep both segments in the market. One alternative would be to price the mileage at its marginal cost (*MC*) and elicit Q_1 and Q_2 usage while realizing from both customer segments the maximum daily rate the D_1 demanders will pay (namely, *AEF*). Perhaps, however, a better alternative is available. Suppose the car rental agency raises the price to *P** and reduces the daily access fee to the shaded area in Figure 17.3. Mileage will decline in both segments, and area *P*DEA* will be net revenue lost by virtue of the reduced daily access fee in both segments. However, the additional net revenue from mileage charges (*P*DGA* in one segment and *P*HIA* in the other segment) will more than offset these lost access fees. Consequently, in addition to charging positive lump-sum access fees, a monopolist will adopt two-part tariffs that price usage above its marginal cost.

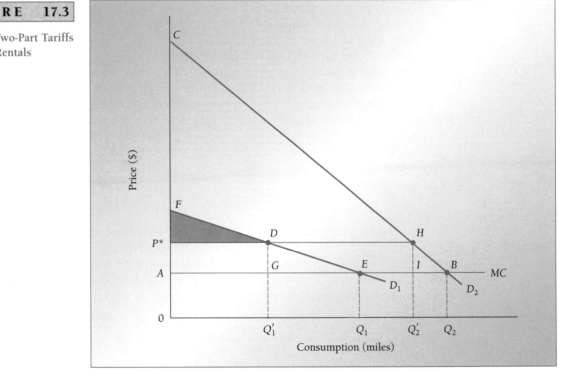

FIGURE   17.3

Optimal Two-Part Tariffs
for Auto Rentals

EXAMPLE

$19.95 FOR "UNLIMITED ACCESS" AT AMERICA ONLINE[4]

In qualifying for and winning purchase orders, customer service and availability are often as important as low price. Internet on-line providers like America Online (AOL), Prodigy, and CompuServe provide computer help by phone and downloadable help files as well as Internet access. Internet access is a limited-capacity service for which assured availability may be expensive. Seven million subscribers to AOL discovered this dose of reality last year when a user charge per hour was replaced by a flat fee. For $19.95 a month, AOL users became entitled to an unlimited amount of attempted access to the Net. As customers quickly discovered, however, "unlimited access" did not mean unlimited use. The need to make 20 sign-on attempts before achieving an Internet connection led to frustrated customers and a "D" service rating in *PC World*'s poll.

Most on-line providers have infrastructure costs for high-speed modems, routers, servers, and other equipment that run 80 cents to $1.30 an hour per customer. The larger the established customer base, the lower these direct fixed costs per customer. With 7 million subscribers, AOL had a direct fixed cost of only 25 cents per customer per hour. In contrast, help lines and other on-line customer support impose a variable cost of $25 to $30 per customer per hour. Neophyte users are therefore big money losers; the profit margins are associated with providing access to cyberspace veterans.

In February 1996, AT&T's WorldNet took advantage of the potential scale economies inherent in such a cost structure by offering the first flat-rate fee (i.e., $19.95 per month) for up to five hours per month of on-line access. The rest of the industry (MCI Internet, Microsoft Network, CompuServe, AOL) quickly followed suit, and a battle for market share erupted. With radical degradation of service quality (i.e., access) and few ways to impose switching costs on customers who sought service from other providers, AOL initially lost share despite matching the lowest lump-sum access fee in the industry.

More recently, customers have encountered new pricing packages that tie the total expense to the desired degree of availability and intensity of use. MCI Internet offers $3 for 3 hours per month plus $1.80 for each additional hour. Prodigy offers $9.95 for 10 hours plus $2.50 for each additional hour. CompuServe offers 5 hours for $9.95 plus $2.95 for each additional hour or $24.95 for 20 hours plus $1.95 for each additional hour. All these services have adopted two-part pricing—for example, a lump-sum entry fee plus a user charge to cover variable cost and discourage trivial uses. Where capacity is insufficient to absorb peak demand, two-part pricing is an efficient way to recover capacity cost and provide for additional capital equipment investment. Using such mechanisms, CompuServe is delivering Internet connection on the customers' first try 97 percent of the time. Even AOL itself has now decided to offer several levels of reliability of Internet access at increasingly higher ($29.95, $39.95, $49.95) per-month access charges. Without at least a small user fee to discourage trivial use, excess demand will continue to plague their business.

Third-degree price discrimination is probably the most common form of price discrimination. In addition to practicing second-degree price discrimination within markets, the utilities, for example, frequently segment their customers into several smaller groups—such as household, institutional, commercial, and industrial users—and establish a different rate schedule for each one of these groups.

---

[4] Based on "Shopping for Web Access," *USA Today*, 3 February 1997, p. 8D and "Rivals Target AOL Users," *USA Today*, 3 February 1997, p. 1D, "Why Internet Deals May Not Last," *Wall Street Journal*, 24 December 1996, p. B1, and "Waiting for the Call," *The Economist*, 5 April 1997, p. 72.

Milk producers, such as the Blue Ridge Dairy Cooperative, charge different prices for milk, depending on whether it is to be sold as fluid milk for retail sales in a local market (where the producers' associations have a virtual monopoly) or whether it is to be sold in the more competitive surplus market, where it is used to make cheese, ice cream, powdered milk, and butter. The price of the monopoly-marketed fluid milk invariably exceeds the price in the more competitive surplus market.[5] The reasons for this are examined below.

To maximize profits, discriminating monopolists, such as the Blue Ridge Dairy Cooperative, must allocate their capacity to produce output in such a way as to make identical the marginal revenue in all markets. If marginal revenue derived from the fluid milk market exceeded marginal revenue derived from the surplus market, profits could be increased by transferring output from the surplus market to the fluid market. When the price rise in the surplus market (resulting from the output reduction) and the price decline in the fluid market (resulting from the output expansion) settle to such a level that MR is equal in both markets, the monopolist is at a profit-maximizing equilibrium allocation of capacity. The total capacity to be allocated among the two or more market segments is determined by setting the combined marginal revenue of all markets equal to marginal cost. This is illustrated in Figure 17.4. The marginal revenue curves for fluid milk sales (MR_1) and surplus sales (MR_2) are added together horizontally to yield the total marginal revenue curve $MR_1 + MR_2$. Total capacity is set at the point where total marginal revenue equals total marginal cost (that is, point A). Total capacity at this point is Q_T gallons of milk. Because marginal revenue must be equal in each market to achieve profit maximization, one can determine the price and output combination that will prevail in each market at the profit-maximizing level of marginal revenue. In the fluid milk market, output will be Q_1 gallons at a price of P_1, because this is the price-output combination that corresponds to the profit-maximizing level of marginal revenue required to cover the marginal cost of the last gallon sold. Similarly, in the surplus market output equals Q_2 gallons at a price of P_2 (determined from the demand curve D_2D_2). The sum of the outputs in these two markets equals total output ($Q_1 + Q_2 = Q_T$). Not surprisingly, one finds that the price is higher in the less competitive fluid milk market, where the price elasticity of demand is less, than in the more competitive surplus market. As a general rule, one would expect to find an inverse relationship between the price elasticity of demand and price in markets served by discriminating monopolists.

[5] Edmond S. Harris, *Classified Pricing of Milk,* Technical Bulletin no. 1184, U.S. Department of Agriculture (Washington, D.C.: U.S. Government Printing Office, 1958).

FIGURE   17.4

Third-Degree Price
Discrimination: Blue
Ridge Dairy Cooperative

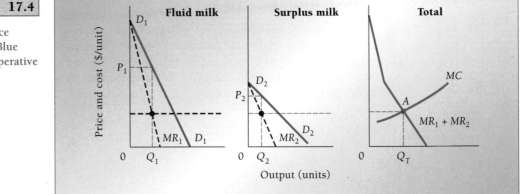

MATHEMATICS OF PRICE DISCRIMINATION

This section develops the mathematics of price discrimination using some numerical examples.

Price Discrimination and the Price Elasticity of Demand

An inverse relationship must exist between price and price elasticity in the separate markets served by a discriminating monopolist. Recall that marginal revenue must be equal in each market served by the monopolist and must equal total marginal cost for profits to be maximized. If the marginal revenues are not equal, total revenue could be increased (with no impact on total cost) by shifting sales from the low marginal revenue market to the high one. In Chapter 4 the relationship between marginal revenue (MR) and price (P) was shown to be (Equation 4.7) the following:

$$MR = P\left(1 + \frac{1}{E_D}\right) \tag{17.1}$$

where E_D is the price elasticity of demand. If there are two markets such that P_1, P_2, E_1, and E_2 represent the prices and price elasticities in the two markets, we may equate marginal revenue in each market:

$$MR_1 = MR_2 \tag{17.2}$$

However,

$$MR_1 = P_1\left(1 + \frac{1}{E_1}\right) \quad \text{and} \quad MR_2 = P_2\left(1 + \frac{1}{E_2}\right)$$

Hence

$$P_1\left(1 + \frac{1}{E_1}\right) = P_2\left(1 + \frac{1}{E_2}\right)$$

$$\frac{P_1}{P_2} = \frac{\left(1 + \dfrac{1}{E_2}\right)}{\left(1 + \dfrac{1}{E_1}\right)} \tag{17.3}$$

EXAMPLE

PRICE DISCRIMINATION AND THE PRICE ELASTICITY OF DEMAND: TRANS-AMERICA AIRLINES

Trans-America Airlines has determined that the price elasticity of demand for New York to Los Angeles unrestricted coach and Super Saver (stayover Saturday night required) coach services are -1.25 and -2.50, respectively. Determine the relative prices (P_1/P_2) that Trans-America should charge if it is interested in maximizing profits on this route. Substituting $E_1 = -1.25$ and $E_2 = -2.50$ into Equation 17.3 yields

$$\frac{P_1}{P_2} = \frac{\left(1 + \dfrac{1}{-2.50}\right)}{\left(1 + \dfrac{1}{-1.25}\right)}$$

$$= 3.0$$

or

$$P_1 = 3.0\, P_2$$

Thus the price of an unrestricted coach seat (P_1) should be 3.0 times the price of a Super Saver coach seat (P_2). We see that when the elasticity in Market 1 (unrestricted coach) is less (in absolute value) than that in Market 2 (Super Saver coach), the price in Market 1 will exceed the price in Market 2.

Price Discrimination and Profitability of the Firm

The advantages to a monopolist of engaging in price discrimination can be illustrated with the following example. Two cases are considered—Case I where the firm charges different prices for the same product in the two different markets and Case II where the firm charges the same price in the two different markets (i.e., does not engage in price discrimination).

EXAMPLE

PRICE DISCRIMINATION AND PROFITABILITY: TAIWAN INSTRUMENT COMPANY

Taiwan Instrument Company (TIC) makes computer memory chips in Formosa, which it ships to computer manufacturers in Japan (Market 1) and the United States (Market 2). Demand for the chips in the two markets is given by the following functions:

$$\text{Japan: } P_1 = 12 - Q_1 \qquad [17.4]$$

$$\text{United States: } P_2 = 8 - Q_2 \qquad [17.5]$$

where Q_1 and Q_2 are the respective quantities sold (in *millions* of units) and P_1 and P_2 are the respective prices (in dollars per unit) in the two markets. TIC's total cost function (in millions of dollars) for these memory chips is

$$C = 5 + 2\,(Q_1 + Q_2) \qquad [17.6]$$

Case I: Price Discrimination TIC's total combined profit in the two markets equals

$$\pi = P_1 Q_1 + P_2 Q_2 - C \qquad [17.7]$$

$$= (12 - Q_1)Q_1 + (8 - Q_2)Q_2 - [5 + 2(Q_1 + Q_2)]$$

$$= 12Q_1 - Q_1^2 + 8Q_2 - Q_2^2 - 5 - 2Q_1 - 2Q_2$$

$$= 10Q_1 - Q_1^2 + 6Q_2 - Q_2^2 - 5 \qquad [17.8]$$

To maximize π with respect to Q_1 and Q_2, find the partial derivatives of Equation 17.8 with respect to Q_1 and Q_2, set them equal to zero, and solve for Q_1^* and Q_1^*:

$$\frac{\partial \pi}{\partial Q_1} = 10 - 2Q_1 = 0$$

$$Q_1^* = 5 \text{ (million) units}$$

$$\frac{\partial \pi}{\partial Q_2} = 6 - 2Q_2 = 0$$

$$Q_2^* = 3 \text{ (million) units}$$

Substituting Q_1^* and Q_2^* into the appropriate demand and profit equations yields

$$P_1^* = \$7 \text{ per unit}$$

$$P_2^* = \$5 \text{ per unit}$$

$$\pi^* = \$29 \text{ (million)}$$

The optimal solution is illustrated graphically in Figure 17.5 (a).

FIGURE   17.5   Demand and Cost Functions for Memory Chips: Taiwan Instrument Company

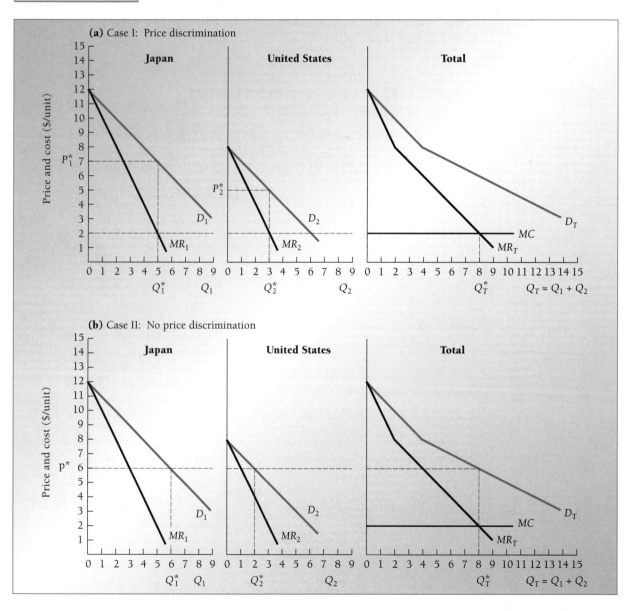

Maximizing π with respect to Q_1 and Q_2 is equivalent to setting $MR_1 = MR_2$. The equivalence of MR_1 and MR_2 may be proved by taking the partial derivatives of the TR function:

$$TR = P_1 \cdot Q_1 + P_2 \cdot Q_2$$
$$= (12 - Q_1)\, Q_1 + (8 - Q_2)\, Q_2$$
$$= 12Q_1 - Q_1^2 + 8Q_2 - Q_2^2 \qquad [17.9]$$

with respect to Q_1 and Q_2, and substituting the solution values, $Q_1^* = 5$ and $Q_2^* = 3$:

$$MR_1 = \frac{\partial TR}{\partial Q_1} = 12 - 2Q_1$$
$$MR_1^* = 12 - 2(5) = \$2 \text{ per unit}$$
$$MR_2 = \frac{\partial TR}{\partial Q_2} = 8 - 2Q_2$$
$$MR_2^* = 8 - 2(3) = \$2 \text{ per unit}$$

which equals the total marginal cost, that is, the derivative of Equation 17.6 with respect to $(Q_1 + Q_2)$.

The respective elasticities in the Japanese and U.S. markets at the optimal solution are

$$E_1 = \frac{dQ_1}{dP_1} \cdot \frac{P_1}{Q_1}$$
$$= -1\left(\frac{7}{5}\right) = -1.40$$

and

$$E_2 = \frac{dQ_2}{dP_2} \cdot \frac{P_2}{Q_2}$$
$$= -1\left(\frac{5}{3}\right) = -1.67$$

Hence we see that, as in the Trans-America Airlines example, when the elasticity of demand is less in Japan (Market 1) than in the United States (Market 2), the price in Japan is greater than in the United States.

Case II: No Price Discrimination   Suppose that protectionist (antidumping) trade laws in the United States prohibit foreign computer chip manufacturers from selling these products for less than the prices charged in Japan. In other words, assume that TIC is not permitted to engage in price discrimination.

To determine the profits TIC will earn if it does not discriminate between the two markets, solve the two demand equations for Q_1 and Q_2 and add them to get a total demand function:

$$Q_1 = 12 - P_1$$
$$Q_2 = 8 - P_2$$
$$Q_T = Q_1 + Q_2$$
$$= 12 - P_1 + 8 - P_2$$

Because price discrimination is no longer possible, P_1 must equal P_2, and

$$Q_T = 20 - 2P$$

or

$$P = 10 - \frac{Q_T}{2}$$

Total profit is now

$$\pi = PQ_T - C$$

$$= 10Q_T - \frac{Q_T^2}{2} - 5 - 2Q_T$$

$$= 8Q_T - \frac{Q_T^2}{2} - 5 \qquad\qquad [17.10]$$

To find the profit-maximizing level of Q_T, differentiate Equation 17.10 with respect to Q_T, set it equal to zero, and solve for Q_T^*:

$$\frac{d\pi}{dQ_T} = 8 - Q_T = 0$$

$$Q_T^* = 8 \text{ (million) units}$$

Substituting Q_T^* into the appropriate equations yields

$$P^* = 10 - \frac{Q_T}{2} = \$6 \text{ per unit}$$

$$\pi^* = 8Q_T - \frac{Q_T^2}{2} - 5 = \$27 \text{ (million)}$$

$$Q_1^* = 12 - 6 = 6 \text{ (million) units}$$

$$Q_2^* = 8 - 6 = 2 \text{ (million) units}$$

$$MR_1^* = 12 - 2(6) = \$0 \text{ per unit}$$

$$MR_2^* = 8 - 2(2) = \$4 \text{ per unit}$$

The optimal solution is illustrated graphically in Figure 17.3 (b).

The two cases are summarized in Table 17.1. Note that TIC's profits ($29 million) are higher when it engages in price discrimination than when it does not engage in price discrimination ($27 million).

TABLE 17.1 Taiwan Instrument Company: Effects of Price Discrimination		Case I Price Discrimination		Case II No Price Discrimination	
Market		*1 (Japan)*	*2 (U.S.)*	*1 (Japan)*	*2 (U.S.)*
Price P* ($/unit)		7	5	6	6
Quantity Q* (million units)		5	3	6	2
Marginal Revenue MR ($/unit)		2	2	0	4
Profit π* ($ million)			29		27

The example developed above shows that by charging different prices to different groups of customers, monopolists may always increase their profits above the level achieved if no market segmentation is attempted, as long as the groups of customers have differing demand elasticities.

PRICING OF MULTIPLE PRODUCTS

Most firms produce or sell more than one product; therefore, we will reexamine the basic model of a one-product firm, which maximizes profits by setting the marginal cost of production for the item equal to the marginal revenue derived from its sale. This model breaks down if the firm has idle capacity, which may be used to produce completely new products, new models of existing products, or new and different styles, sizes, and so on.

When idle capacity exists, either as unused or only partially used plant facilities and equipment or as underused technical knowledge and organizational capabilities, the firm is faced with the challenge of making profitable use of these resources. As long as the new product (or modification of an existing product) may be sold at a price that exceeds the true marginal cost of producing and selling it, the profitability of the firm will be enhanced by its adoption. A range of alternative uses for idle resources should be examined when choosing the most profitable alternatives.

In an analysis of the cost of adopting various alternatives, one must consider true marginal costs, because the decision to add new or different products or drop some existing lines may well have an impact on the sales of a firm's remaining outputs. For instance, new products may compete with existing ones, raising the implicit cost of the new product. Let us examine the nature of these demand interdependencies in more detail.

Products with Interdependent Demands

Consider the case of a firm that produces only two products (A and B). Total revenue (sales) for the firm can be represented as

$$TR = TR_A + TR_B \qquad [17.11]$$

where TR_A and TR_B are the respective revenues for the two products. Marginal revenue for each of the products is given by

$$MR_A = \frac{\partial TR}{\partial Q_A} = \frac{\partial TR_A}{\partial Q_A} + \frac{\partial TR_B}{\partial Q_A} \qquad [17.12]$$

$$MR_B = \frac{\partial TR}{\partial Q_B} = \frac{\partial TR_A}{\partial Q_B} + \frac{\partial TR_B}{\partial Q_B} \qquad [17.13]$$

The MR_A formula (Equation 17.12) shows that the marginal revenue associated with a change in the quantity sold of Product A is composed of two parts. The first term, $\partial TR_A/\partial Q_A$, measures the change in total revenue for Product A associated with a marginal increase (or decrease) in the quantity sold of Product A. The second term, $\partial TR_B/\partial Q_A$, represents the demand interdependency between the two products—that is, the change in total revenue for Product B associated with a marginal increase (or decrease) in the quantity sold of Product A. The MR_B formula (equation 17.13) is interpreted in a similar manner with respect to a marginal increase (or decrease) in the quantity sold of Product B.

The interdependency terms, $\partial TR_B/\partial Q_A$ and $\partial TR_A/\partial Q_B$, can be positive, negative, or zero. If the two products under consideration are *complements,* then these terms will be *positive,* that is, an increase in the quantity sold of one product will result in an *increase* in total revenue for the other product. If the products are *substitutes,* then the terms will be *negative,* meaning that an increase in the quantity sold of one product will result in a *decrease* in total revenue for the other product. Finally, if there are no demand interdependencies between the two products, then the terms will be equal to zero.

EXAMPLE

INTERDEPENDENT DEMANDS: THE GILLETTE COMPANY

Table 17.2 lists many of the products sold by the Gillette Company. Although most of Gillette's products have independent demands, several demand interdependencies are likely to exist. For example, the interdependency terms between Waterman pens and Braun electric shavers would likely be equal to zero, indicating that changes in demand for one product would have no effect on the demand for the other. However, one would expect the interdependency terms between the Sensor and Trac II razors to be negative, because these products are substitutes for one another. Indeed this is the case for these products. When Gillette introduced the Sensor in the United States in 1990, sales (total revenues) of the Trac II razor declined below the level of the previous year. Conversely, one would expect the interdependency terms between Foamy shaving cream and Gillette razors (and/or razor blades) to be positive, because these products are complements to one another.

As this example illustrates, managers must be aware of and take into account demand interdependencies when making price and output decisions. Failure to recognize these interdependencies may lead to decisions that do not maximize shareholder wealth.

TABLE   17.2

Gillette Company Products

Razors and Blades	**Braun Personal Care Appliance Products**
Sensor	Electric shavers
Atra	Electric hair epilators
Trac II	Hair dryers
Good News	Electric curling wands
Daisy Plus	Electric toothbrushes
Toiletries and Cosmetics	Oral irrigators
Deodorants/Antiperspirants	**Braun Household Appliances**
Right Guard	Steam irons
Dry Idea	Travel/alarm clocks
Shaving Cream	Toasters
Foamy	Coffee makers
Hair Care	Food processors
White Rain	Hand blenders
Skin Care	Juicers
Jafra	**Oral-B Preventive Dentistry Products**
Stationary Products	Toothbrushes
Writing Instruments	Dental floss
Waterman	Interdental brushes
Paper Mate	Professional dental supplies
Flair	
Correction Fluid	
Liquid Paper	

Products with Independent Demands

In this section we develop a model that can be used in allocating resources when a firm produces multiple products whose demands are *independent*.[6] This analysis assumes that the productive resources of the firm can be transformed rather easily from one product to another, facilitating adaption to changing market and product demands. The market conditions that the firm faces for each of its products may range from pure competition to a near monopoly. When the firm has excess personnel, organizational resources, and capacity, it may increase output with only a small additional cost. Instead of reducing prices and increasing output for an existing product, it may decide to invade new markets where price is greater than marginal cost. New markets are assumed to be invaded in order of their profitability. Hence the firm does not reach an equilibrium situation until no more markets are available where the price of a product exceeds its marginal cost.

Starting from a point where the firm is producing one product, marginal revenue equals marginal cost, and 60 to 70 percent of capacity is being used, we may now examine the decision to add additional products. Figure 17.6 illustrates a situation of a firm with five products, although that number might well be greater or less. D_1 represents the demand for Product 1, D_2 for Product 2, and so on. The number of units of Product 1 that are sold equals Q_1, of Product 2, $Q_2 - Q_1$, and so on. Profits are maximized when the firm produces and sells quantities of the five products such that marginal revenue is equal in all markets and equal to marginal cost. The line *EMR* represents a new line of *equal marginal revenue*. Because it is assumed that new product markets were entered in order of their profitability, the prices charged for the five products are arranged in declining order, from P_1 to P_5, and the elasticity of demand increases from D_1 to D_5. The *EMR* line is determined by the intersection of the firm's marginal cost curve

---

[6] The assumption that the demands for the various products produced by the firm are not significantly interrelated (i.e., independent) is not necessary because the demand curves for each product could be adjusted for such interdependence.

FIGURE   17.6

Multiple-Product Pricing

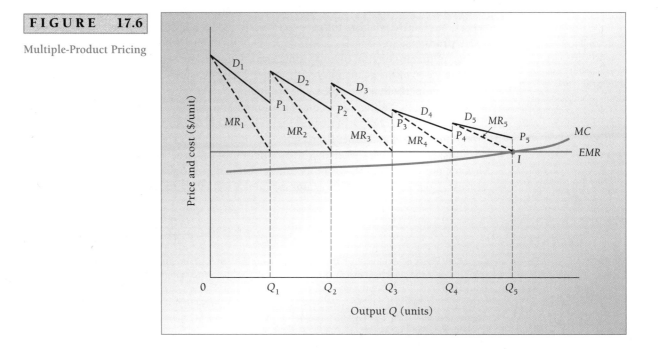

MC and the marginal revenue curve for the last product market that may be profitably served. Theoretically, this would be the one with the most elastic demand, D_5.[7] If D_5 is perfectly elastic, this then is the marginal market or last profitable new-product market. In such a case Price $= MR = MC$. If the marginal market is less than perfectly elastic, the possibility exists of some remaining market that may be entered where price exceeds MC.

The equilibrium condition where there is virtually an equivalence between P, MR, and MC in the marginal market illustrates the well-known fact that nearly all firms produce some products that generate little or no profit and are on the verge of being dropped or replaced. In some cases, such as the railway and utility industries, zero-profit products may be produced to keep the organization intact.

EXAMPLE

MULTIPLE-PRODUCT PRICING: SUPERMARKET PRICING

Supermarkets provide an illustration of this multiple-product pricing model. One of the primary productive resources of a supermarket is shelf space, which can be allocated among a wide variety of product categories—such as meat, dairy products, canned goods, frozen foods, and produce. Generally the markups and profit margins on staple items, such as bread, milk, and soap, are lower than on nonstaple items, such as imported foods and specialty items. In an effort to increase their overall profitability, many supermarkets have added higher profit-margin categories, such as delicatessens, in-store bakeries, and floral departments, to the mix of products they sell.[8] This can be accomplished either by reallocating existing shelf space through the reduction of the amount of shelf space assigned to lower profit-margin items or by expanding the overall size of the store. Obviously, expanding the size of the store will increase marginal costs much more than the reallocation of shelf space to higher profit-margin product categories.

PRICING OF JOINT PRODUCTS

Joint Products
Products that are interdependent in the production process, such as gasoline and fuel oil in an oil refinery. A change in the production of one produces a change in the cost or availability of the other.

Thus far our concern has been with price and output decisions for firms that produce several *alternative* products that are technically independent in the production process. **Joint products,** in contrast, are interdependent in the production process; that is, a change in the production of one produces a change in the cost (or more specifically, the marginal cost) or the availability of the other. Many examples exist of joint products that have the property that the process of producing two or more products is technically interdependent, including the production of liquid oxygen and nitrogen from air, beef and hides from steers, and gasoline and fuel oil from crude oil. In some cases, such as the production of beef and hides from cattle, the outputs are obtained in relatively fixed proportions. In other cases, such as the production of gasoline and fuel oil from crude oil, variable proportions of the outputs can be obtained through changes in the production process. Each of these cases is examined on the following pages.

---

[7] The *EMR* line is determined by horizontally summing the marginal revenue curve for each product. The intersection of the combined marginal revenue curve (note that the combined marginal revenue curve is not shown in Figure 17.4) with the marginal cost curve (Point *I* in Figure 17.4) establishes the *EMR* line.

[8] Allocation of shelf space within each product category also involves a consideration of profit margins when making decisions about stocking private-label versus national-brand canned goods, prepackaged versus fresh-cut meat, and so on.

Joint Products in Fixed Proportions

When outputs are produced in fixed proportions, they should be analyzed as a *product package*. Because the products are jointly produced, all costs are incurred in production of the package and no conceptually correct method exists for allocating these costs to the individual products. Determination of the optimal output and prices of the products involves a comparison of the total marginal revenue from all the products with the marginal cost. In the following analysis, each unit of the product package consists of the output obtained from one unit of input. For example, the slaughtering of a steer might yield a product package consisting of 500 pounds of beef and one hide.

Figure 17.7 (a) shows the demand functions and their respective marginal revenue functions for two products (*A* and *B*) that make up a product package, along with the marginal cost function for the production process. The total marginal revenue function (MR_T) for the product package is obtained by *vertically* summing the marginal revenue functions for the individual products (MR_A and MR_B). The net revenue gain to the firm of producing one more unit of the product package is the additional (marginal) revenue from Product *A* plus the inseparable additional (marginal) revenue from Product *B*. The intersection of the total marginal revenue function (MR_T) and the marginal cost function (*MC*) determines the optimal output of the product package (*Q**) along with the optimal prices of the two individual products (i.e., P_A^* and P_B^*).

EXAMPLE	**PRICING OF JOINT PRODUCTS: WILLIAMS COMPANY**

Suppose the Williams Company is faced with the following demand functions for two joint products produced in fixed proportions:

$$P_1 = 50 - .5Q \qquad [17.14]$$

$$P_2 = 60 - 2Q \qquad [17.15]$$

FIGURE 17.7	Optimal Price and Output Determination of Joint Products *A* and *B* Produced in Fixed Proportions

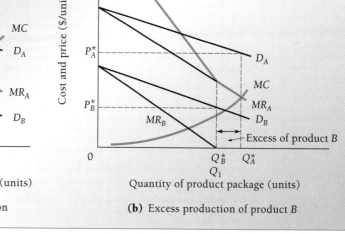

(a) No excess production   (b) Excess production of product B

Furthermore, suppose that the marginal cost function for the joint products is

$$MC = 38 + Q \qquad [17.16]$$

The two marginal revenue functions are obtained as follows:

$$TR_1 = P_1 Q = (50 - .5Q)Q = 50Q - .5Q^2$$

$$MR_1 = \frac{dTR_1}{dQ} = 50 - Q$$

$$TR_2 = P_2 Q = (60 - 2Q)Q = 60Q - 2Q^2$$

$$MR_2 = \frac{dTR_2}{dQ} = 60 - 4Q$$

Summing the two inseparable marginal revenue functions vertically yields

$$MR_T = MR_1 + MR_2$$
$$= (50 - Q) + (60 - 4Q)$$
$$= 110 - 5Q \qquad [17.17]$$

Setting the total marginal revenue function equal to the marginal cost function and solving for Q yields the optimal output

$$MR_T = MC$$
$$110 - 5Q = 38 + Q$$
$$72 = 6Q$$
$$Q^* = 12$$

or 12 units of the product package. Substituting this value into the demand functions (Equations 17.14 and 17.15) gives the optimal prices of the two products:

$$P_1^* = 50 - .5(12)$$
$$= \$44 \text{ per unit of Product } A$$
$$P_2^* = 60 - 2(12)$$
$$= \$36 \text{ per unit of Product } B$$

One complication in the preceding analysis can occur if the marginal cost function (MC) intersects the total marginal revenue function (MR_T) at an output in excess of Q_1 in Figure 17.7 (a). Above Q_1, the marginal revenue of Product B is negative and the firm would not want to sell more than Q_1 units of Product B. When this situation occurs, as shown in Figure 17.7 (b), the optimal solution is to *produce* Q_A^* units of the product package. This is determined at the intersection of the MR_A and MC functions. Q_A^* units of Product A should be *sold* at a price of P_A^*. However, only Q_B^* ($= Q_1$) units of Product B should be sold at a price of P_B^*. The *excess output* of Product B, namely $Q_A^* - Q_B^*$ should be destroyed or discarded so as not to depress the market price.

When solving a numerical problem, one can check to see if the marginal cost function intersects the total marginal revenue function at an output greater than Q_1 by substituting the optimal output (Q^*) into the MR_A and MR_B functions. If either marginal revenue value is negative, then the marginal cost function should be set equal to the marginal revenue function of the other product in determining the optimal price and output combination.[9] For example, if the MR_B function is negative, then one would use MR_A (rather than MR_T) to determine the optimal solution.

Joint Products in Variable Proportions

When the outputs can be produced in variable proportions, the analysis is somewhat more complex than the fixed proportions case.

EXAMPLE

PRICING OF JOINT PRODUCTS: SLUSSER CHEMICAL COMPANY

The decision facing the Slusser Chemical Company is illustrated in Figure 17.8. The quantities of two chemicals (X and Y) that may be produced are indicated on the vertical and horizontal axes. The isocost or production possibility curves (labeled TC) indicate the amounts of X and Y that may be produced for the same total cost. For instance, looking at the isocost curve labeled $TC = 8$, we see that the firm may produce Q_x units of X and Q_y units of Y, Q_x' units of X and Q_y' units of Y, or any possible combination along that curve at an equivalent total cost of $TC = 8$. Hence there are two ways of increasing the output of, say, Product X. One way is to move along the isocost curve increasing the

---

[9] Note in the Williams Company example that when $Q^* = 12$, $MR_1 = 50 - 12 = \$38 > 0$ and $MR_2 = 60 - 4(12) = \$12 > 0$. Hence, no excess output of either product was being produced.

FIGURE 17.8

Joint Products Produced in Variable Proportions: An Optimal Price-Output Mix—Slusser Chemical Company

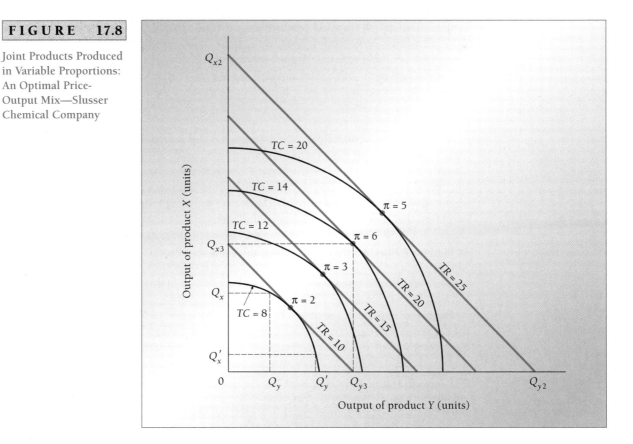

output of X at the expense of Y. The other is to increase the amount of the inputs or factors (e.g., capital and/or labor) in the production process; that is, move in a northeast direction to a higher isocost curve. The only requirement of isocost or production possibility curves is that they be concave to the origin, indicating an imperfect adaptability of the firm's productive resources in producing X and Y.

The isorevenue lines (labeled TR) take into account the prices received by Slusser for its two outputs. Each line is of equal revenue, indicating that any combination of X and Y along any particular line will yield the same total revenue. The *straight* isorevenue lines in Figure 17.8 indicate that products X and Y are being sold in *purely competitive markets;* that is, the prices of X and Y do not change as output changes. (If this were not the case, the isorevenue lines would no longer be straight; nevertheless, the general tangency solution for an optimal output combination does not change.) Line $TR = 25$ is constructed such that Q_{y2} times the price of Y (P_y) equals Q_{x2} times the price of X (P_x). The slope of each isorevenue line is equal to $P_y \div P_x$, because the slope of $TR = 25$ equals $Q_{x2} \div Q_{y2}$, and $P_x(Q_{x2}) = P_y(Q_{y2})$; therefore

$$\frac{P_y}{P_x} = \frac{Q_{x2}}{Q_{y2}}$$

A whole family of isorevenue lines exists that is defined by the prices and levels of output for X and Y. The further one moves in a northeast direction, the greater the total revenue associated with any isorevenue line.

The solution for an optimum combination of outputs requires a point of tangency between the isocost and isorevenue curves. This may be illustrated with the $TC = 14$ isocost curve. Under the conditions depicted in Figure 17.8 Slusser should produce Q_{x3} units of X and Q_{y3} units of Y because total profit, π (the difference between TR and TC), is maximized at that point. To produce any other possible output combination along the $TC = 14$ isocost curve would result in the same costs (14), but would place the firm on a lower isorevenue curve thereby reducing profit. Because profits are maximized at the point of tangency ($\pi = 6$), the marginal cost of producing each product must be exactly equal to the marginal revenue each product generates.

The analysis presented here could be expanded considerably by dropping some of the assumptions. For instance, the two-product case could be expanded to a more general n-product case. One could also assume a far greater number of variable factors of production than the one factor (or bundle of factors) implicitly assumed. In addition, the assumption that the prices of input factors are not a function of their use and the assumption that the prices of outputs are independent of the quantity produced could be dropped. Cases such as these are capable of mathematical analysis, but in many instances the simplified model presented provides an adequate framework for analysis.[10] Linear programming also has proved to be an extremely useful tool for examining problems of allocating common productive facilities among two or more products to maximize profits.

In conclusion, the decision to add (or delete) products to (from) a firm's product line must consider true marginal benefits as well as true marginal costs. If a new product is a reasonably close substitute for an existing product, the addition of the new product is

---

[10] The interested reader may wish to explore some of these more advanced models. See, for example, William Mauer and Thomas Naylor, "Monopolistic-Monopsonistic Competition: The Multi-Product Multi-Factor Firm," *Southern Economic Journal* 31 (July 1964), pp. 38–43 and Frederick Warren-Boulton, "Vertical Control with Variable Proportions," *Journal of Political Economy,* 1974, pp. 783–802.

likely to reduce sales of the existing product. This reduction must be considered in the marginal decision analysis. In addition, complementarities in demand between two or more products (that is, when a lower price or increased availability of one product stimulates an increase in demand for another) must also be considered in a multiproduct firm's price and output decisions.

Finally, in deciding whether to add, delete, or change the relative output of any one product, the impact of that action on the cost of producing the firm's other outputs must be taken into consideration. Only after true marginal costs and benefits have been accounted for may optimal strategies about the makeup of a firm's product line be adopted.

TRANSFER PRICING[11]

www . . . .
Read more about transfer pricing and multinational firms at the following Internet site maintained by the Organization for Economic Cooperation and Development:
http://www.oecd.org/daf/fa/wp6.htm

Associated with the tremendous growth in the size of corporations has been a trend toward decentralized decision making and control within these organizations. Because of the exceedingly complex coordination and communication problems within the large multiproduct national or multinational firm, such firms typically are broken up into a group of semiautonomous operating divisions. Each division constitutes a profit center with the responsibility and authority for making operating decisions. Combined with an appropriate set of rewards and incentives, division managers presumably will be oriented toward making decisions that maximize the profitability of the profit center. With all the divisions operating in this manner, it is believed that such a system will maximize the overall profitability of the firm.[12] This section examines the conditions under which such a decentralized system will in fact lead to optimal price and output decisions; that is, decisions that maximize the overall profit of the firm. Because of the complex nature of this problem, the analysis is limited to several somewhat simplified cases.

In practice, a number of conditions cause the price-output decisions made by one division of the decentralized firm to be dependent on (that is, influenced by) the price-output decisions of another division. One source of dependence occurs whenever the external demand functions of the two divisions are interrelated. For example, a degree of dependence presumably exists between the demand functions of the Chevrolet and Pontiac divisions of General Motors. In the analysis of this section, however, it is assumed that the external demand functions of each division are independent.

Another source of dependence occurs whenever the production processes of two divisions are cost dependent either through technological interdependence or through the effects of output changes on the costs of inputs employed in the production process. An example of the former type of interdependence would be the case of an oil refinery in which the mix of outputs (for example, gasoline, kerosene, heating oil, and lubricants) is limited by the production process. An example of the latter type would be two divisions that are bidding for a raw material or labor skill that is in short supply and that are, as a result, causing the price to rise. In the ensuing analysis, it is assumed that the production processes are cost independent.

A third source of dependence, and the only one considered in this section, occurs whenever one division sells all or part of its output to another division of the same firm.

---

[11] This section draws heavily on the contributions of J. Hirshleifer to the transfer pricing problem. See his classic articles "On the Economics of Transfer Pricing," *Journal of Business* 29 (1956), pp. 172–184 and "Economics of the Divisionalized Firm," *Journal of Business* 30 (1957), pp. 96–108.

[12] Mathematical programming techniques have been proposed to analyze these decentralized resource-allocation systems. See, for example, George Dantzig, *Linear Programming and Extensions* (Princeton, N.J.: Princeton University Press, 1963), chap. 23 and William J. Baumol and Tibor Fabian, "Decomposition Pricing for Decentralization and External Economies," *Management Science* 11 (September 1964), pp. 1–32.

For example, within the Ford Motor Company a multitude of internal transfers of goods and services takes place. The Engine and Foundry Division, Transmission and Chassis Division, Metal Stamping Division, and the Glass Division among others transfer products to the Automotive Assembly Division. The Automotive Assembly Division in turn transfers completed cars to the Ford and Lincoln-Mercury Divisions.

The price at which each intermediate good or service is transferred from the selling to the buying division affects the revenues of the selling division and the costs of the buying division. Consequently, the price-output decisions and profitability of each division, as determined by the standard profit-maximization rule (that is, marginal cost equals marginal revenue), will be affected by the transfer price.

A **transfer price** serves two functions in the decentralized firm. One function is to act as a measure of the *marginal* value of resources used in the division when making the price and output decisions that will maximize profits. The other is to serve as a measure of the *total* value of the resources used in the division when analyzing the performance of the division. It is sometimes possible for these functions to conflict.[13] The emphasis in this section is on determining the correct transfer price to use in making optimal (that is, profit-maximizing) price-output decisions.

Transfer Price

The price at which an intermediate good or service is transferred from the selling to the buying division within the same firm.

---

www . . . .
Access financial information on Bell Atlantic at the following Internet site: http://www.bell-atl.com/invest/

PRICING OF INTERDEPARTMENTAL SERVICES AT BELL ATLANTIC[14]

Bell Atlantic has taken the transfer pricing concept and applied it on an experimental basis to the pricing of interdepartmental services, such as information services, business research, medical services, and training and development. Each of 10 client-service departments charges other departments of the company for the services it renders. For example, a manager who uses an in-house speech writer would have to pay for this service out of his or her department's budget. The speech writer's department would then be credited with the amount charged for providing the service. From these revenues, each client-service department is expected to pay all its expenses, including salaries and benefits, rent, office equipment, and electricity. A department that fails to cover its costs could be faced with some difficult choices, such as replacing the manager, reducing its staff, or even possible elimination by giving the work to an outside vendor.

One of the most difficult problems in implementing such a transfer pricing system is determining the costs and market value of a department's services. Most departments ended up pricing their services in line with what outside vendors charge. Some departments billed for their services on an hourly basis, whereas others charged a set amount for each project. To prevent overcharging by the client-service departments, in-house users were allowed to use outside vendors when they could obtain a better price from the vendor.

The benefits from such a pricing system are twofold. First, some client-service departments found that they were overstaffed and were required to reduce the scale of their operations. For example, the communications-services group eliminated 11 positions. Second, users of these services were forced to scale back their requests to more realistic levels if the price quote was too high. Under the old system, service requests were sometimes excessive because the costs were being borne by the department doing the work rather than by the clients. Annual savings with the new system of more than $4 million were reported for four of Bell Atlantic's client-service groups.

---

[13] See C. Horngren and G. Foster, *Cost Accounting: A Managerial Emphasis,* 9th ed. (Englewood Cliffs, N.J.: Prentice Hall, 1997), Chap. 25.

[14] Based on "At Bell Atlantic, Competing Is Learned from the Inside," *Wall Street Journal,* 12 July 1989, p. B1.

In the following analysis, assume that a decentralized firm consists of two separate divisions that form a two-stage process to manufacture and market a single product. The production division manufactures an intermediate product, which is sold internally to the marketing division at the transfer price. The marketing division converts the intermediate product into a final product, which it then sells in an imperfectly competitive (that is, monopolistic) external market.

Given the assumptions of demand and cost independence discussed above, there are three possible cases to consider:

- *No* external market for the intermediate product.
- *Perfectly competitive* external market for the intermediate product.
- *Imperfectly competitive* external market for the intermediate product.

The first two cases are examined in the remainder of this section. The third case of an imperfectly competitive external market can be analyzed using the third-degree price discrimination model discussed earlier in the chapter. It is not examined here.

No External Market for the Intermediate Product

With no external market for the intermediate product, the production division would be unable to dispose of any excess units over and above the amount desired by the marketing division. Likewise, if demand for the final product should exceed the capacity of the production division, the marketing division would be unable to obtain additional units of the intermediate product externally. Therefore, the quantity of the product manufactured by the production division must necessarily be equal to the amount sold by the marketing division.[15] The determination of the profit-maximizing price-output combination and the resulting transfer price are shown in Figure 17.9. The marginal cost

---

[15] This analysis assumes that all units produced during the period must be sold during the period; that is, no inventories of the intermediate product can be carried over into the next period.

FIGURE   17.9

Determination of the Transfer Price with No External Market for the Intermediate Product

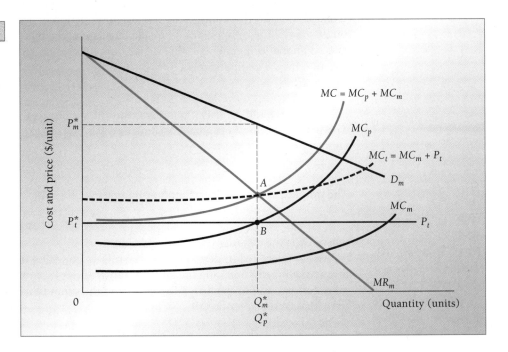

per unit to the firm, MC, of any level of output is the sum of the marginal costs per unit of production, MC_p, and marketing, MC_m. By equating marginal cost MC to external marginal revenue MR_m (point A), one obtains the firm's profit-maximizing decisions— P_m^* as the optimal price and Q_m^* as the optimal quantity of the final product to be sold by the marketing division in the external market. Therefore, the optimal transfer price, P_t^*, is set equal to the marginal production cost per unit, MC_p, at the optimum output level Q_p^* (Point B). This will cause each division, when seeking to maximize its own division profit, to maximize the overall profit of the firm. This result can be demonstrated in the following manner.

Once the transfer price is established, the production division will face a *horizontal* demand curve (and corresponding marginal revenue curve) at the given transfer price for the intermediate product. The profits of the production division will be maximized at the point where its divisional marginal cost equals divisional marginal revenue—in this case where the P_t line intersects the MC_p curve. This condition yields Q_p^* as the optimum quantity of the intermediate product, which is identical to the optimum quantity of the final product Q_m^* determined previously. Similarly, once the transfer price is established, the marketing division is faced with a marginal cost curve MC_t, which is the sum of the marginal marketing cost per unit, MC_m, and the given transfer price, P_t. The profits of the marketing division will be maximized at the point were its divisional cost is equal to its divisional marginal revenue—in this case, where the MC_t and MR_m curves intersect. This condition yields the same optimal price and output decision (that is, P_m^* and Q_m^*) as was obtained previously in maximizing the overall profits of the firm.

DETERMINING THE OPTIMAL TRANSFER PRICE: PORTLAND ELECTRONICS

The production division (p) of the Portland Electronics Company manufactures a component that it sells internally to the marketing division (m), which promotes and distributes the product through its own domestic retail outlets. Assume that there is no external market for this component (i.e., the production division cannot sell any excess production of the component to outside buyers and the marketing division cannot obtain additional components from outside suppliers). The marketing division's demand function for the component is

$$P_m = 100 - .001Q_m \qquad [17.18]$$

where P_m is the selling price (in dollars per unit) and Q_m is the quantity sold (in units). The marketing division's total cost function (in dollars) is (excluding the cost of the component)

$$C_m = 300,000 + 10Q_m \qquad [17.19]$$

The production division's total cost function (in dollars) is

$$C_p = 500,000 + 15Q_p + .0005Q_p^2 \qquad [17.20]$$

where Q_p is the quantity produced and sold.

We are interested in determining the profit-maximizing outputs for the production and marketing divisions and the optimal transfer price for intracompany sales. The marginal cost per unit to the firm, MC, is equal to the sum of the marginal costs of production, MC_p, and marketing, MC_m:

$$MC = MC_p + MC_m \qquad [17.21]$$

The marginal cost of the production division is equal to the first derivative of C_p (Equation 17.20):

$$MC_p = \frac{dC_p}{dQ_p}$$

$$= 15 + .0010Q_p \qquad [17.22]$$

The marginal cost of the marketing division is equal to the first derivative of C_m (Equation 17.19):

$$MC_m = \frac{dC_m}{dQ}$$

$$= 10 \qquad [17.23]$$

Substituting Equations 17.22 and 17.23 into Equation 17.21 and recognizing that

$$Q_m = Q_p$$

we obtain

$$MC = 15 + .0010Q_m + 10$$

$$= 25 + .0010Q_m \qquad [17.24]$$

The marketing division's total revenue function is equal to

$$TR_m = P_m Q_m$$

$$= (100 - .001Q_m)Q_m$$

$$= 100Q_m - .001Q_m^2 \qquad [17.25]$$

Taking the first derivative of TR_m (Equation 17.25) gives

$$MR_m = \frac{d(TR_m)}{dQ_m}$$

$$= 100 - .002Q_m \qquad [17.26]$$

Setting Equation 17.24 equal to Equation 17.26, gives the optimal output for the marketing division:

$$MC = MR_m$$

$$25 + .0010Q_m = 100 - .002Q_m$$

$$Q_m^* = 25,000 \text{ units}$$

Because $Q_p = Q_m$, the optimal output for the production division is

$$Q_p^* = 25,000 \text{ units}$$

Therefore the optimal transfer price for intracompany sales of the component is equal to the marginal production cost per unit at the optimal output level of $Q_P^* = 25,000$ units, or

$$P_t^* = MC_p$$

$$= 15 + .0010(25,000)$$

$$= \$40 \text{ per unit}$$

Thus, to maximize profits, Portland's production division should produce and sell 25,000 units of the component to the marketing division. The marketing division should distribute 25,000 units of the component through its retail outlets. The optimal transfer price for intracompany sales is $40—the production division's marginal cost per unit at an output of 25,000 units.

Perfectly Competitive External Market for the Intermediate Product

With an external market for the intermediate product, the outputs of the production and marketing divisions are no longer required to be equal. In the following analysis assume that the external market for the intermediate product is perfectly competitive. Two different situations involving supply and demand for the intermediate product are examined below:

- *Excess internal supply.* The production division has the capacity to produce more of the intermediate product than is desired by the marketing division and sells the excess output externally in the competitive market.
- *Excess internal demand.* The marketing division requires more of the intermediate product than can be supplied internally by the production division and buys additional units externally in the competitive market.

Excess Internal Supply   The derivation of the optimal price-output decisions for the firm is shown in Figure 17.10. With a perfectly competitive market for the intermediate product, the production division is faced with a horizontal external demand curve D_p for its output at the existing market price P_t. Setting divisional marginal revenue MR_p equal to the divisional marginal cost MC_p (point C) yields a profit-maximizing output of Q_p^* units of the intermediate product. The marketing division, which must purchase the intermediate product either internally or externally at a price of P_t, will have a marginal cost curve MC_t, which is the sum of the marginal marketing cost per unit MC_m, and the

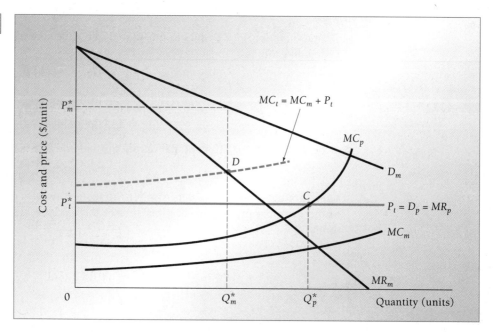

given transfer price P_t. Again, equating divisional marginal revenue MR_m to divisional marginal cost MC_t (point D) shows that profits will be maximized when Q_m^* units of the final product are sold externally at a price of P_m^* per unit. The solution indicates that the production division should produce Q_p^* units of the intermediate product and sell Q_m^* units of its output to the marketing division and sell the difference, $Q_p^* - Q_m^*$, externally, in the intermediate product market.

A clear-cut transfer price emerges from this analysis. The competitive market price P_t becomes the optimal transfer price (P_t^*) for intracompany sales of the intermediate product. The production division can sell as much output as it wishes externally at this price and therefore would have no incentive to sell internally to the marketing division at a price less than P_t^*.

EXAMPLE

DETERMINING THE OPTIMAL TRANSFER PRICE: PORTLAND ELECTRONICS (CONTINUED)

Consider again the Portland Electronics Company discussed earlier. Suppose that the production division (p) of Portland Electronics Company manufactures a component that it can sell either internally to the marketing division (m), which promotes and distributes the product through its own domestic retail outlets, or externally in a perfectly competitive wholesale market to foreign distributors. The production division can sell the component externally to these distributors at $50 per unit.

The task is to determine the profit-maximizing outputs for the production and marketing divisions and the optimal transfer price for intracompany sales. The production division's optimal output occurs at the point where divisional marginal revenue equals divisional marginal cost. Because the production division can sell as much output as it wishes (externally) at the competitive market price of $50, its marginal revenue is equal to

$$MR_p = 50$$

As we saw earlier, the production division's marginal cost relationship is (Equation 17.22)

$$MC_p = 15 + .0010Q_p$$

Setting $MC_p = MR_p$ yields the optimal output for the production division:

$$15 + .0010Q_p = 50$$

$$Q_p^* = 35,000 \text{ units}$$

The marketing division's optimal output occurs where divisional marginal revenue equals divisional marginal cost. Marginal cost for the marketing division (MC_t) is equal to the sum of its own marginal marketing costs (MC_m) plus the cost per unit of the components purchased from the production division (P_t) or

$$MC_t = MC_m + P_t \qquad [17.27]$$

Because the external wholesale market for the component is perfectly competitive, the production division would not be willing to sell components to the marketing division for less than the market price of $50 per unit. Therefore, the optimal transfer price (P_t^*) is the competitive market price of $50 per unit.

$$P_t^* = \$50 \text{ per unit}$$

As was shown earlier, marginal marketing costs (MC_m) were

$$MC_m = 10$$

Hence, by Equation 17.27, MC_t is given by

$$MC_t = 10 + 50$$
$$= 60$$

The marketing division's marginal revenue function (MR_m) was given earlier as (Equation 17.26)

$$MR_m = 100 - .002Q_m$$

Setting $MR_m = MC_t$ yields the optimal output for the marketing division:

$$100 - .002Q_m = 60$$
$$Q_m^* = 20,000 \text{ units}$$

Thus to maximize profits, Portland's production division should produce 35,000 units of the component and sell 20,000 units internally to the marketing division and the remaining 15,000 units (35,000 − 20,000) externally to other (foreign) distributors. The marketing division should distribute 20,000 units of the component through its retail outlets. The optimal transfer price for the intracompany sales is the competitive market price of $50 per unit.

Excess Internal Demand   The derivation of the optimal price-output decisions for the firm under excess internal demand is shown in Figure 17.11. Similar to the excess internal supply situation discussed above, the production division will attempt to maximize its profits by setting divisional marginal revenue MR_p equal to divisional marginal cost MC_p (point E). This yields an optimal solution of Q_p^* units of the intermediate product. The marketing division, with a marginal cost curve MC_t equal to the sum of

FIGURE 17.11

Determination of the Transfer Price with a Perfectly Competitive External Market for the Intermediate Product— Excess Internal Demand

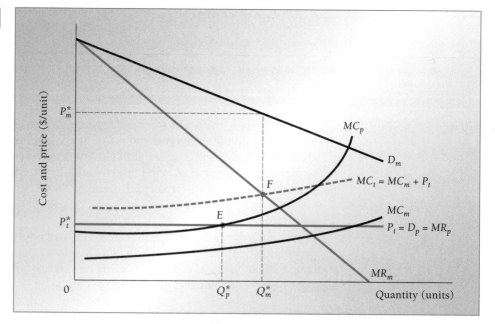

the marginal marketing costs per unit MC_m and the given transfer price P_t, will attempt to maximize profits by equating divisional marginal revenue MR_m to divisional marginal cost MC_t (point F). This yields an optimal solution of Q_m^* units of the final product being sold externally at a price of P_m^* per unit. The solution indicates the production division should produce and sell its entire output of Q_p^* units of the intermediate product to the marketing division. The marketing division should purchase an additional $Q_m^* - Q_p^*$ units of the intermediate product externally in the intermediate product market.

As in the situation of excess internal supply discussed earlier, the optimal transfer price (P_t^*) for intracompany transfers of the intermediate product is equal to the competitive market price P_t. The marketing division can purchase as much of the intermediate product as it wishes externally at this price and therefore would be unwilling to make purchases from the production division at a price more than P_t^*.

INTERNATIONAL
PERSPECTIVES

TRANSFER PRICING, TAXES, AND ETHICS[16]

Multinational corporations have a great deal of flexibility in setting transfer prices, because there are often no external market standards for setting these intrafirm prices. In the absence of differential tax rates between the various countries in which a firm does business, the establishment of appropriate transfer prices involves application of microeconomic decision rules and cost accounting principles. However, because large multinational firms operate in several different countries, each with its own system of taxation and its own unique corporate income tax rates and policies, the use of transfer pricing to aggressively manage and reduce tax liabilities is common and profitable. For example, the IRS recently charged Toyota with systematically overcharging its U.S. subsidiary for most of the vehicles and parts sold in the United States. The effect of these actions was to transfer profits that would have been booked (and taxed at high rates) in the United States to Japan, where tax rates are much lower. Toyota has denied any wrongdoing but has agreed to pay the IRS $1 billion in a settlement of these claims.

Westinghouse Electric booked 27 percent of its 1986 domestic profit in Puerto Rico, where it has very few sales. The corporate tax rate in Puerto Rico is set at 0 percent to stimulate the economy. Yamaha Motor's U.S. subsidiary paid only $5,272 in taxes in the early 1980s, whereas IRS accountants claim that proper accounting of transfer prices would have resulted in $127 million in taxes.

The issue of setting proper transfer prices is extremely complex. Many differences between company policies and IRS regulations arise because of the complexity of the issue. However, as can be seen above, the IRS has become increasingly aggressive in prosecuting blatant cases of abuse. Financial managers of multinational firms will have to give this issue greater attention in coming years, if they expect to achieve the goal of maximizing shareholder wealth within the bounds of legal and ethical standards of business practice.

PRICING IN PRACTICE

To this point the pricing chapters have been concerned with normative models of firm behavior. With the exception of the limit-pricing model discussed in Chapter 14, the basic underlying assumption of these traditional models is that the firm seeks to maximize

---

[16] Based on L. Martz, "The Corporate Shell Game," *Newsweek*, 15 April 1991, pp. 48–49.

(short-run) profits. Recall that Chapter 1 discussed some of the weaknesses and criticisms of decision making based on the profit-maximization objective. Two of the most substantive objections are the following:

1. The firm is assumed to have the information necessary to make the marginal calculations and decisions that profit maximization demands. In a world where information is not free and uncertainty is more the rule than the exception, one should not be surprised to see some divergence between normative theory and actual business practice.

2. The model has an inherent short-run bias in that no time dimension is placed on the profits being maximized. Yet, the firm's value-maximization objective is explicitly the maximization of the net present value of the net cash flows *over time*. In spite of this, many problems may be analyzed using the calculus of profit maximization when the long-run profitability impacts are either insignificant or nonexistent. However, many decisions *do* have longer-run implications, accounting for some of the observed divergence between business practice and normative short-run theory.

Product Life-Cycle Framework[17]

www . . . .
Read about the development of product life-cycle theory by Conrad Jones at the following Internet site maintained by Booz-Allen and Hamilton: http://www.bah.com/wcb/productlife.html

Life Cycle Pricing
Pricing that varies throughout the product life cycle.

Pricing is one of the areas where this longer-run life-cycle view of the firm's decision making proves very helpful. In the early stages of a **life cycle pricing,** the marketing, operations, and financial managers decide what the customer will value, how the firm can manage the supply chain to consistently deliver those characteristics, and how much it will cost, including the financing costs. If the value-based prices can cover this long-run full cost, the product becomes a prototype. Each proposed product or service then proceeds to marketing research where the demand at various price points in several distribution channels usually is explored. Marketing research will identify a *target price* that the cross-functional product manager or the general managers will know is required on average over the product life cycle in order for the new product to provide sufficient revenue to cover fully allocated cost.

Once a product or service roll-out takes place (usually at target price levels), the marketing plan often authorizes promotional discounts. In this stage of the life cycle, the firm is interested in penetrating the market. To do so requires coupons, free samples, name recognition advertising, and slot-in allowances on retail shelves. *Penetration pricing* therefore characterizes an early stage of the product life cycle at which net prices to the manufacturer fall below the firm's target price.

In the mature stage of the product or service life cycle, the product managers focus on adding value in both product refinements and order management processes. These initiatives might include warranty service, brand-name advertising, product updates, or increased flexibility in accepting change orders from regular customers. Each decision at this mature stage is motivated by a desire to realize the highest *value-based pricing* allowed by the competitive conditions and potential entry threats. Although at times this view of pricing as a component of the product life-cycle investment decision can be overwhelmed by short-term tactical firefighting, the product life cycle remains a planning framework to which the pricing manager often returns.

At a late mature stage of the product or service life cycle, product managers may decide to limit price in order to deter entry. *Limit pricing* appears to be inconsistent with

---

[17] On the conceptual framework of value-based pricing over a product's life cycle, see T. Nagle, *The Strategy and Tactics of Pricing* (Englewood Cliffs, N.J.: Prentice-Hall, 1987), Chap. 6.

profit maximization but in fact is motivated by a long-term profitability objective. Eli Lilly limits the price of Prozac to variable plus direct fixed costs in order to arrest or at least slow the onslaught of imitators into a very lucrative product line. Since competitors are constantly devising lower-cost ways of imitating leading products, limit pricing often has only temporary success. If the entry threat materializes into a real live new entrant, many incumbent firms then accommodate by raising prices in a particular high-price high-margin market niche. This pricing practice is often referred to as *niche pricing*. Concluding that declining market share from entry into the mass market is inevitable, the incumbent moves upmarket and sells its experience and expertise at high prices in the top-end segments of the market much as it did at the start of the product life cycle.

EXAMPLE	## NICHE PRICING OF NETPCS: IBM[18]

Traditional personal computers with ever larger hard drives and faster chips have become a commodity business dominated by component assemblers like Gateway. Recent product introductions by IBM, Dell, Compaq, and Hewlett-Packard suggest that the days of the one- to two-year-old $3,000 personal computer on every company desktop are numbered. Corporate America is returning to a concept of networked computer terminals and timesharing pioneered by Hewlett-Packard and Dartmouth College in the late 1960s. These diskless machines are basically terminals linked to a central server that sends them programs and data which then load and run locally. At $500–$750, these networked computers are much less costly to update than PCs. Nevertheless, a niche market remains for desktop machines that include a hard disk and can still have programs installed and run locally. IBM and other manufacturers intend to serve this corporate market with NetPCs costing about $1,000. In addition to niche pricing these network products and other system solutions like Internet security systems, IBM has announced its intent to exit traditional PC manufacturing.

Full-Cost Pricing Techniques

Full Cost (or Cost-Plus) Pricing
A method of determining prices in which a charge to cover overhead, plus a percentage markup or margin, is added to variable production and marketing costs to arrive at a selling price.

Full-cost pricing requires that estimates be made of the variable costs of production and marketing. A charge to cover overhead, plus a percentage markup or margin, is then added to variable costs to arrive at a final price. Overhead or indirect costs may be allocated among a firm's several products in a number of ways. One typical method is to estimate total indirect costs assuming the firm operates at a standard level of output. This is frequently set in the range of 70 to 80 percent of capacity. These standard costs are then allocated among the various products on some basis such as a percentage of average variable cost. For example, suppose that Hewlett-Packard's average variable cost of producing and selling an electronic calculator is $50. The company might add a charge of 120 percent of variable costs to cover indirect or overhead charges. To this full average cost of $110, a markup of, say, 20 percent is added, yielding a final price of $132. This could be modified slightly to reflect traditional industry pricing practice or the firm's own standard pricing rules.

It is immediately apparent that full-cost pricing violates the marginal pricing rules of traditional theory, because fixed costs enter explicitly into the price determination formula. It has been argued, however, that when average (unit) costs remain nearly con-

---

[18] Based on "NetPCs Having a Hard Time Booting Up," *Business Week,* 22 September 1997, p. 102.

stant over the relevant output range and when the price elasticity remains fairly constant over time, the use of cost-plus pricing may lead to nearly optimal decisions. These conditions are frequently encountered in the retail trades. Furthermore, as we have seen in Chapter 14, the size of the markup employed for different products is a function of demand elasticities and degree of competition. So it *may* be that in its responsiveness to varying demand conditions, full-cost pricing approaches the marginal solution.

Markup or full-cost pricing rules have also been criticized for being based on historical accounting costs and marketing plans rather than costs actually incurred at the time prices are set and the product is sold. To the extent that actual costs vary from the historical standard used in determining prices, full-cost pricing necessarily results in a suboptimal set of prices.

Target (or Target Return-on-Investment) Pricing
A method of pricing in which a target profit, defined as the desired profit rate on investment times total gross operating assets, is allocated to each unit of output to arrive at a selling price.

Under **target return-on-investment pricing,** or simply *target pricing,* the firm selects an acceptable profit rate on investment. This is usually defined as earnings before interest and depreciation divided by total gross operating assets. This return is then prorated over the number of units expected to be produced over the planning horizon. Target pricing rules may be expressed in equation form as

$$P = VC_l + VC_m + VC_{mk} + \frac{F}{Q} + \frac{\pi K}{Q} \qquad [17.28]$$

where

P = price per unit
VC_l = unit labor cost
VC_m = unit material cost
VC_{mk} = unit marketing cost
F = total fixed or indirect costs
Q = number of units to be produced during the planning horizon
K = total gross operating assets
π = desired profit rate on investment

At least three advantages have been enumerated for the use of target return-on-investment pricing. It has been argued that it leads to price stability because it is based on cost standards that vary much less than actual costs. Price stability is advantageous for two reasons. First, price changes are costly. New price lists must be prepared and salespersons informed. Second, in an oligopolistic market structure, explicit price changes are likely to evoke unknown competitive responses. A second advantage of target return pricing is that it is well suited to use in an industry where price leadership is prevalent. As variations between actual and standard costs increase, the price leader feels increasing pressure to either raise or lower prices.

Full-Cost Pricing versus Marginal Analysis

Let us attempt to resolve the conflict between those who advocate the use of *marginal pricing rules* and those who argue for the use of such "short-cut" rules as *full-cost pricing* and *target pricing.* Advocates of full-cost and target pricing argue that it is important to allocate all fixed costs among the various products produced by the firm and that each product should be forced to bear its fair share of the fixed-cost burden. In contrast, marginalists say that any allocation of fixed costs between products is impossible to carry out adequately and that requiring each product to cover a fair share of fixed costs may be clearly suboptimal. Each product should instead be viewed in the light of the proportion that it contributes to fixed costs and profits of the firm as a whole. This provides a sounder basis for considering whether the manufacture and sale of a product should be expanded, maintained, or discontinued in favor of some alternative that may make a greater contribution to covering company overhead and making a profit.

EXAMPLE

FULL-COST PRICING VERSUS MARGINAL ANALYSIS: PHONEMATE COMPANY

If PhoneMate's model 7200 telephone answering machine accounts for 40 percent of sales but only 10 percent of the contribution to fixed costs and profits, the firm should seek ways to increase its contribution or replace it with a more profitable alternative. In this example, the full-cost pricing criteria might indicate that the product should be quickly discontinued because it is not covering a fair share of fixed costs and is not providing an adequate profit margin. In the short run, however, any contribution to fixed costs is more consistent with profit maximization (although ways should be sought to increase this contribution) than dropping the product and merely shifting the burden of covering fixed costs to the remaining products of the firm. A longer-run analysis *might* indicate that dropping the 7200 model will result in actual fixed-cost savings that are greater than the maximum fixed-cost contribution that the 7200 model may be expected to generate. Also, in the long run the firm has the flexibility of altering its product line by substituting more profitable models for some of the firm's poorer performers.

One criticism that advocates of full-cost pricing aim at the marginalists is that if fixed costs are not allocated in some manner among products, some products are likely to be overlooked and prices for them set too low. This can happen only if the firm lacks an effective control system in which a general manager continually monitors the overall contribution of a firm's complete product line. This person can then ensure that value-based prices are set sufficiently high in relation to both the variable cost of each product and the total fixed costs of the firm. In addition, marginal pricing gives the firm far more flexibility in setting appropriate prices, evaluating offers to buy below this price, and comparing alternative uses for the firm's productive capacity. Remember that target pricing must be met only on average across the product's entire life cycle.

Incrementalism: Marginalism in Practice

In the real world, demand and cost functions are not known with certainty but must be approximated. In addition, accumulating better information on the exact nature of these functions and their variations can be quite costly. These costs must be weighed against the benefits to be realized from more complete knowledge. In such a case, it is impossible (or impractical) to estimate the marginal impact of the last dollar spent on advertising or to calculate precisely the marginal cost of each unit which is produced, and then to attempt to produce up to a point where estimated marginal cost equals estimated marginal revenue.

Incremental Analysis
The real-world counterpart to marginal analysis. Incremental analysis requires that an estimate be made of the changes in total cost and revenue that will result from a price change or from a decision to add or delete a product, accept or reject a new order, or undertake a new investment.

Faced with these limitations, many business decisions are based on **incremental analysis.** In its broadest sense, incrementalism requires that an estimate be made of *changes in total cost, changes in total revenues, or changes in both total costs and revenues* that are likely to result from a decision to change prices, drop or add a product, accept or reject a new order, or undertake an investment. The concept of incremental reasoning is simple, but its application requires care. For instance, the decision to drop an item from the firm's product line requires that the loss in revenue from this action should be evaluated in the light of the total *actual* cost savings that may occur. The following questions must be addressed:

1. How much, if any, will sales of other items in the firm's product line increase because this item is dropped?
2. To what extent will some overhead or fixed costs be reduced?

3. Are there more profitable alternative uses for the firm's productive capacity?
4. What is the long-run sales and profit outlook for this item versus the alternatives being considered?

Successful use of incremental analysis requires that all these factors be considered in relation to their impact on total revenues received and total costs incurred by the company. Only then can decisions be made that will lead to greater profits.

EXAMPLE

CONTINENTAL AIRLINES

One frequently cited example of the business use of incremental reasoning is the case of Continental Airlines.[19] At one point Continental was filling only about 50 percent of its available seats, or about 15 percent less than the industry average. Eliminating only 5 percent of its flights would have resulted in a substantial increase in this load factor, but would have reduced profits as well. The airline industry is characterized by extremely high fixed costs, which are incurred whether a plane flies or not. There are depreciation costs, interest charges, and the cost of maintaining ground crews, not to mention headquarters staff overhead. Consequently, Continental has found it profitable to operate a flight as long as it covers variable or out-of-pocket costs plus a small contribution to fixed costs.

The analysis of whether to operate a flight proceeds as follows: First, management examines the majority of scheduled flights to be certain that depreciation, overhead, and insurance expenses are met for this basic schedule. Then the possibility of scheduling additional flights is considered, based on their impact on corporate net profit. If revenues on a flight exceed *actual operating costs,* the flight should be added. Actual operating costs are determined by soliciting inputs from every operating department that specify exactly what extra expenses are incurred as a result of the additional flight's operation. For instance, if a ground crew that can service the additional flight is already on duty, none of the costs of this service are included in actual operating costs.

Another example of such analysis is the case of a late-night Continental flight from Colorado Springs to Denver and a very early morning return flight. Even though the flight often goes without a passenger and very little freight, the cost of operating it is less than an overnight hanger rental in Colorado Springs. Hence the flight is maintained.

In performing this type of incremental analysis, two important points must be stressed. First, someone in management must have coordinating authority to ensure that overall objectives are met before facing decisions based solely on incremental analysis. In the case of Continental, the vice president of economic planning assumed this task. Second, every reasonable attempt must be made to identify *actual* incremental costs and revenues that are associated with a particular decision. Once this has been accomplished, incremental analysis becomes a useful and powerful tool in considering a wide range of decision problems facing the firm. Appendix 17A considers these issues in further detail.

WWW . . . .
Read more about pricing strategies in an article by Gene Koprowski in *Marketing Tools* magazine, available on the Internet at the following site: http://www.demographics.com/publications/MT/95_mt/9509_mt/mt330.htm

OTHER PRICING STRATEGIES

In addition to marginal, incremental, and full-cost pricing strategies, several other pricing methods are used under certain circumstances. *Skimming* is often used in pricing new products. Also some goods are deliberately priced very high to increase their prestige demand (*prestige pricing*). Finally, *price lining* is used in pricing certain categories of goods. These techniques are considered next.

---

[19] This example is adapted from "Airline Takes the Marginal Route," *Business Week,* 20 April 1963.

Skimming

When a new product is introduced by a firm, pricing for that product is a difficult and critical decision, especially if the product is a durable good—one that has a relatively long useful life. The difficulty of pricing the new product arises from the fact that demand may not be known with confidence. If the price is initially set too low, some potential customers will be able to buy the product at a price below what they are willing to pay. These lost profits will be gone forever. This problem is accentuated when the firm initially has limited production capacity for the new product. In contrast, if the firm sets a high price and maintains this price over a long time period, new competition will be encouraged.

Skimming

A new-product pricing strategy that results in a high initial product price. This price is reduced over time as demand at the higher price is satisfied.

Under these circumstances, many firms have adopted a strategy of **skimming,** or pricing down along the demand curve. The initial price is set at a high level, even though the firm fully intends to make later price reductions. When the product is first introduced, there will be a group of customers who are willing to pay the high price established by the firm. Once this source of demand has been exhausted, the price is reduced and a new group of customers is attracted. This strategy is readily apparent in mainframe computers and explains the prevalence of capital leasing in that industry. As we discussed in Chapter 16, manufacturers who engage in a predictable pattern of price skimming need credibility mechanisms to assure early full-price customers that later discounting will be limited.

EXAMPLE

IBM PERSONAL COMPUTER

Since its initial introduction, several price reductions have been made on the IBM PS/2 personal computer. This pricing strategy can be illustrated using Figure 17.12. Panel (a) shows the estimated demand curve DD and the marginal revenue curve MR for the IBM-PS/2 computer as well as the marginal cost curve MC. As a monopolist for the IBM-PS/2, IBM would set price P_1 and produce output Q.

FIGURE 17.12   Example of Demand Skimming: IBM Personal Computer

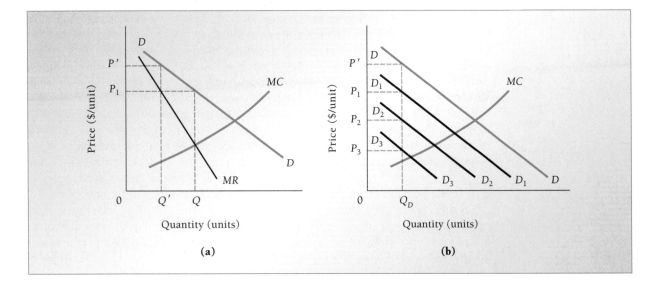

(a)   (b)

Suppose, however, that IBM chooses to follow the skimming strategy for its personal computer. It could initially set a price higher than P_1, such as P'. At that price, only Q' units would be demanded and sold. By setting the initial price at P', all consumers who are willing to pay that price or more will buy the product. Once this has occurred, IBM can then lower the price to capture the demand from the next segment of customers.

Panel (b) shows new demand curves, such as D_1D_1. The new demand curve is less than the initial demand curve DD—it is shifted to the left—by an amount equal to the Q' units that have already been purchased at price P'. A new lower price is now established, such as P_1, and Q_D units are sold at this price. The new price P_1 may be set in such a manner that it approximately matches the firm's production capacity. When demand has been exhausted at this price, the price is lowered again, to a level such as P_2. The new demand curve D_2D_2 is lower and to the left of D_1D_1 by an amount equal to the Q_D units that were sold at the previous price. (Although Panel (b) shows quantity demanded to be the same amount for each price level, this is not necessary. The figure is merely drawn that way for ease of presentation.)

This strategy can be continued many times to capitalize on the unique product characteristics and availability until competition forces the firm to a "permanently" more competitive price level. The rate at which reductions are made may depend on production capacity, the speed of competitive product introductions, and the trade-off between receiving profits now and deferring them into the future by use of the skimming strategy. In the case of IBM, price reductions were strongly resisted until true IBM "clone" PCs became available from competitor firms such as Compaq and Packard-Bell.

Prestige Pricing

Prestige Pricing

The practice of charging a high price for a product to enhance its perceived value.

Some products are priced to increase their perceived value to potential consumers. **Prestige pricing** is the practice of charging a high price so as to limit potential buyers and create the impression that the product is higher quality than similar, lower-priced products. For example, in the automotive market the sporty European sedans, such as the Mercedes, Audi, and BMW, are priced in the $25,000 to $75,000 range. These cars have been highly successful in attracting a loyal, prestige-oriented clientele. At the same time, a car such as the Toyota Camry has received wide acclaim from such impartial panels as the Consumers Union when it was compared with these more expensive vehicles. Its price is considerably less than the European alternatives, yet it has not attracted the loyal following of prestige-oriented consumers that the European sedans have.

The DeBeers diamond cartel, which controls at least 80 percent of the world's uncut diamond market, effectively sets prices for diamonds by greatly restricting their availability. For example, in the early 1980s, it appeared that the South African cartel might collapse. A sharp decline in demand, coupled with the withdrawal of Zaire (the world's largest producer of diamonds) from the cartel and huge new discoveries in Australia threatened to undercut the cartel. But by holding nearly $1 billion in diamonds off the market, DeBeers was able to avoid a price decline and bring Zaire and Australia back into the cartel. This pricing strategy has assured potential diamond buyers of the value of their investment and it has prevented diamonds from becoming too commonplace.

Prestige pricing is sometimes abused by selling firms. In many cases customers equate price with quality, particularly in those instances where objective product quality information is difficult or expensive to acquire. Two physically identical products may be packaged differently and priced differently to take advantage of the tendency of consumers to equate high price with high quality. The pages of *Consumers Reports* are full of examples suggesting that this relationship between high price and high quality does not always exist.

Price Lining

Price Lining

The practice of producing a product that will fit in a particular price range for similar, competitive products.

In normal circumstances, profit-maximizing firms will attempt to set a price that maximizes the profits the firm generates from the sales of a particular product. The product and its particular quality characteristics are assumed to be known, but in some circumstances this process is reversed. For example, a price target may be established and the firm attempts to develop a product with a set of quality characteristics that will allow it to maximize profits at the target price; that is, given a price constraint, the firm attempts to develop a product with a set of quality characteristics that will lead to maximum profits in that product price line. Japanese automobile and electronics firms have been very successful with this strategy. This practice is called **price lining.** It is not inconsistent with the notion of profit maximization. Price lining simply reverses the typical profit-maximization decision process.

The automobile industry has a set of price lines that have been established over time among the major producers. In the case of the Ford Motor Company, it sells its Ford-brand vehicles as the basic car with broad appeal. The Mercury brand is designed to appeal to a somewhat more affluent group of customers. The Lincoln brand is aimed at the wealthiest or most prestige-conscious group of consumers. Within the Ford brand are a number of sublines. The subcompact line, the Escort, competes with subcompacts of other U.S. and foreign producers. The compact line is represented by the Contour; the sporty line is represented by the Mustang; the mid-size line is represented by the Taurus; and the full-size line is represented by the Crown Victoria. In each of these lines, Ford competes with similar cars from General Motors. Each subline in the Ford model group is priced closely in line with the price of similar-sized General Motors vehicles. The objective of each auto producer is to create a distinctively high-quality vehicle in that price and model range. If price must be increased significantly, the product will not sell well, regardless of its quality.

Other examples of strong price lining exist in the pricing of snack foods for vending machines and canned soft drinks. Vending companies will be reluctant to sell a product that requires special machines for dispensing. As a consequence, candy makers often compete on product quality and product size, rather than on price.

SUMMARY

- All pricing decisions should be proactive systematic and value-based—for example, related to careful detailed assessment of customer value.
- *Price discrimination* is the act of selling the same good or service produced by a given firm at different prices to different customers. Two conditions are required for effective price discrimination:
  1. One must be able to segment the market and prevent the transfer of the product (or service) from one segment to another.
  2. There must be differences in the elasticity of demand at a given price between the market segments.

To maximize profits using price discrimination, the firm must allocate output in such a way that marginal revenue is equal in the different market segments.

☐ Price discrimination is often implemented through two-part pricing. Optimal two-part prices entail a lump-sum access fee and a user charge that exceeds marginal cost and varies per unit consumed.

☐ For firms selling multiple products with interdependent demands, decisions to add or delete products in existing product lines may have (positive or negative) impacts on the sales of the firm's current outputs. In the analysis of such decisions, it is necessary to include the costs of these impacts in the marginal cost calculations.

☐ *Joint products* are products that are technically interdependent in the production process; that is, a change in the production of one produces a change in the cost or availability of another. When the joint products are produced in *fixed proportions,* the optimal output of the product package (consisting of the individual products) and optimal prices of the individual products is found at the intersection of the total marginal revenue function and the marginal cost function of producing the product package. When joint products are produced in *variable proportions,* the optimal output occurs where the marginal cost of producing each product is equal to the marginal revenue of each product. This occurs at the point of tangency between the isocost and isorevenue curves for the products.

☐ A firm is often faced with the problem of pricing items that are produced and used internally in the firm. This is the emphasis of *transfer pricing* analysis. When the external market for the intermediate product is perfectly competitive, the firm should use the market-determined price on intracompany sales. In other cases an appropriate profit-maximizing transfer price is a function of the marginal costs and revenues of the respective divisions in the firm.

☐ Pricing strategy varies throughout the product or service life cycle. A frequent pattern is target pricing, followed by penetration pricing, value-based pricing, limit pricing, and finally niche pricing.

☐ Many actual business pricing practices, such as *full-cost pricing,* can be consistent with the marginal pricing rules of economic theory. *Incrementalism* is a widely applicable method of economic analysis that may help management to achieve a more efficient and profitable level of operation.

☐ When new products are introduced, firms may use the *skimming* strategy to price the product and increase total profits. *Prestige pricing* is often used in segmenting markets. *Price lining* requires the firm to develop products with specific product quality characteristics that will maximize profits, given a price constraint.

EXERCISES

1. Why does the phone company offer different pricing structures for business and personal phone lines? Compare this with the reasons why a bank has a different pricing structure for business and personal checking accounts.

2. East Publishing has best-selling textbooks in both managerial economics and corporate finance. Each book accounts for roughly 60 percent of the estimated yearly market in its field. Text *A* sells about twice as many copies as Text *B* each year.

   East has recently completed a series of market pricing experiments in which it estimated that the price elasticity of demand, E_D, for both texts is about equal. In addition, East believes that the marginal cost of production for these two books is about constant over the current range of sales.

   In spite of the fact that about twice as many copies of Text *A* than Text *B* are sold, the firm charges the same price for both books.

As economist for the firm, you have been asked to prepare an analysis of the firm's pricing policy. $\left[\text{Hint: Remember the relationship } MR = P\left(1 + \dfrac{1}{E_D}\right).\right]$

3. The price elasticity of demand for a textbook sold in the United States is estimated to be -2.0, whereas the price elasticity of demand for books sold overseas is -3.0. The U.S. market requires hardcover books with a marginal cost of $6; the overseas market is normally served with softcover texts, having a marginal cost of only $4.50. Calculate the profit-maximizing price in each market. $\left[\text{Hint: Remember that } MR = P\left(1 + \dfrac{1}{E_D}\right).\right]$

4. What types of price discrimination are often used by electric utility firms? Does this amount to an abuse of their monopoly power?

5. American Export-Import Shipping Company operates a general cargo carrier service between New York and several Western European ports. It hauls two major categories of freight: manufactured items and semimanufactured raw materials. The demand functions for these two classes of goods are

$$P_1 = 100 - 2Q_1$$
$$P_2 = 80 - Q_2$$

where Q_i = tons of freight moved. The total cost function for American is

$$TC = 20 + 4(Q_1 + Q_2)$$

a. Calculate the firm's total profit function.
b. What are the profit-maximizing levels of price and output for the two freight categories?
c. At these levels of output, calculate the marginal revenue in each market.
d. What are American's total profits if it is effectively able to charge different prices in the two markets?
e. If American is required by law to charge the same per-ton rate to all users, calculate the new profit-maximizing level of price and output. What are the profits in this situation?
f. Explain the difference in profit levels between the discriminating and nondiscriminating cases. To do this one should calculate the point price elasticity of demand under the nondiscriminating price-output solution.

6. Phillips Industries manufactures a certain product that can be sold directly to retail outlets or to the Superior Company for further processing and eventual sale by them as a completely different product. The demand function for each of these markets is

$$\text{Retail Outlets: } P_1 = 60 - 2Q_1$$
$$\text{Superior Company: } P_2 = 40 - Q_2$$

where P_1 and P_2 are the prices charged and Q_1 and Q_2 are the quantities sold in the respective markets. Phillips' total cost function for the manufacture of this product is

$$TC = 10 + 8(Q_1 + Q_2)$$

a. Determine Phillips' total profit function.
b. What are the profit-maximizing price and output levels for the product in the two markets?

    c.   At these levels of output, calculate the marginal revenue in each market.

    d.   What are Phillips' total profits if the firm is effectively able to charge different prices in the two markets?

    e.   Calculate the profit-maximizing level of price and output if Phillips is required to charge the same price per unit in each market. What are Phillips' profits under this condition?

7.   a.   Many university bookstores offer to professors price discounts that are generally not available to students. What conditions make this sort of price discrimination feasible and profitable for the bookstore?

    b.   Similarly, students are often given discounts to attend cultural and athletic events, whereas professors do not receive these discounts. What conditions make this sort of price discrimination possible and desirable?

8.   In the face of stable (or declining) enrollments and increasing costs, many colleges and universities, both public and private, have found themselves in progressively tighter financial dilemmas. This has led to a basic reexamination of the pricing schemes used by institutions of higher learning. One proposal advocated by the Committee for Economic Development (CED) and others has been for the use of more nearly full-cost pricing of higher education, combined with the government provision of sufficient loan funds to students who would not otherwise have access to reasonable loan terms in private markets. Advocates of such proposals argue that the private rate of return to student investors is sufficiently high to stimulate socially optimal levels of demand for education, even with the higher tuition rates. Others have argued against the existence of significant external benefits to undergraduate education to warrant the current high levels of public support.

    As with current university pricing schemes, proponents of full-cost pricing generally argue for a standard fee (albeit higher than at present) for all students. Standard-fee proposals ignore relative cost and demand differences among activities in the university.

    a.   Discuss several possible rationales for charging different prices for different courses of study.

    b.   What are the income-distribution effects of a pricing scheme that charges the same fee to all students?

    c.   If universities adopted a system of full-cost (or marginal cost) pricing for various courses, what would you expect the impact on the efficiency of resource allocations within the university to be?

    d.   Would you complain less about large lecture sections taught by graduate students if these were priced significantly lower than small seminars taught by outstanding scholars?

    e.   What problems could you see arising from a university that adopted such a pricing scheme?

9.   Explain why you feel that the interdependency terms between each of the following pairs of products would tend to be either positive (complements), negative (substitutes), or zero (independent):

    a.   Polaroid: Instant cameras and film

    b.   RJR Nabisco: Fleishmann's and Blue Bonnet margarine

    c.   RJR Nabisco: Ritz crackers and Oreo cookies

    d.   RJR Nabisco: Oreo cookies (regular size) and Mini Oreos

    e.   RJR Nabisco: Camel and Winston cigarettes

    f.   General Motors: Saturn compact cars and Chevrolet compact cars

    g.   General Motors: Buick full-size cars and Chevrolet compact cars

10. A company produces both oil and natural gas from a well in the panhandle of West Texas. If these products are produced from the well in fixed proportions, what would one expect the impact of an increase in the price of oil to be on the rate of gas production?

11. Refer to the Williams Company joint products example (Equations 17.14–17.16) discussed in the chapter:

   a. On a graph with quantity on the horizontal axis and price (and cost) on the vertical axis, plot the demand and marginal revenue functions for the two products and the marginal cost function for the product package.

   b. From the graph in part (a), determine the optimal output and price for each of the two products. Compare the graphical solution with the algebraic solution in the chapter.

12. Referring again to the Williams Company joint products example (Equations 17.14–17.16) discussed in the chapter, assume that the marginal cost function (Equation 17.16) is replaced with the following one:

$$MC = 22 + .5Q$$

Determine the optimal output and selling prices for each of the two products.

13. Referring back to the Portland Electronics Company transfer pricing example discussed in the chapter, where there was a competitive external market for the intermediate product, complete the following table (based on the optimal solution):

	Production Division	Marketing Division
Total revenue		
Total cost		
Total profit		

14. Referring again to the Portland Electronics Company transfer pricing example discussed in the chapter, where there was a perfectly competitive external market for the intermediate product, assume that the company can buy (or sell) additional units of the component at $30 per unit. Determine the optimal price and output decisions for the production and marketing divisions and compare them with the solution obtained in the chapter.

15. Consolidated Sugar Company has two divisions: a farming-preprocessing (p) division and a processing-marketing (m) division. The farming-preprocessing division grows sugar cane and crushes it into juice, which it may sell to the processing-marketing division or sell externally in the perfectly competitive open market. The processing-marketing division buys cane juice, either from the farming-preprocessing division or externally in the open market, and then evaporates and purifies it and sells it as processed sugar.

   The processing-marketing division's demand function for processed sugar is

$$P_m = 24 - Q_m$$

where P_m is the price, in dollars per unit, and Q_m is the quantity sold, in units, and its cost function (excluding cane juice) is

$$C_m = 8 + 2Q_m$$

The farming-preprocessing division's total cost function for cane juice is

$$C_p = 10 + 2Q_p + Q_p^2$$

where Q_p is the quantity produced, in units. Assume that one unit of cane juice is converted into one unit of processed sugar. Furthermore, assume that the open market price for cane juice is $14.

a. What is the profit-maximizing price and output level for the farming-preprocessing division?

b. What is the profit-maximizing price and output level for the processing-marketing division?

c. How much of its output (cane juice) should the farming-preprocessing division sell (i) internally to the processing-marketing division and (ii) externally on the open market?

d. How much of its input (cane juice) should the processing-marketing division buy (i) internally from the farming-preprocessing division and (ii) externally on the open market?

e. What is the minimum price at which the farming-preprocessing division would be willing to sell cane juice to the processing-marketing division? Explain.

f. What is the maximum price that the processing-marketing division would be willing to pay to buy cane juice from the farming-preprocessing division? Explain.

g. To maximize the overall profits of Consolidated Sugar, what price should the company use for intracompany transfers of cane juice from the farming-preprocessing division to the processing-marketing division?

16. General Medical makes disposable syringes, which it sells to hospitals and doctor supply companies. The company uses cost-plus pricing and currently charges 150 percent of average variable costs. General Medical has learned of an opportunity to sell 300,000 syringes to the Department of Defense if they can be delivered within three months at a price not in excess of $1 each. General Medical normally sells its syringes for $1.20 each.

    If General Medical accepts the Defense Department order, it will have to forgo sales of 100,000 syringes to its regular customers over this time period, although this loss of sales is not expected to affect future sales.

a. Should General medical accept the Defense Department order?

b. If sales for the balance of the year are expected to be 50,000 units less because of some lost customers who do not return, should the order be accepted (ignore any effects beyond one year)?

17. Cullinary Products, Inc. (CPI) performs a target return pricing calculation as part of its analysis of any proposed new products. CPI's research and development department has provided the following information concerning a new food processor it has designed:

☐ Labor costs (per unit) $22

☐ Material costs (per unit) $11

☐ Marketing costs (per unit) $2

☐ Fixed overhead costs (per year) $1,500,000

☐ Gross investment (operating assets) $6,000,000

☐ Required rate of return on investment (per year) 25%

Determine the target price based on projected sales per year of

a.   80,000 units
b.   100,000 units
c.   60,000 units

18. The Pear Computer Company has just developed a totally revolutionary new personal computer. It estimates that it will take competitors at least two years to produce equivalent products. The demand function for the computer has been estimated to be

$$P = 2,500 - .0005Q$$

The marginal (and average variable) cost of producing the computer is $900.

a.   Compute the profit-maximizing price and output levels assuming Pear acts as a monopolist for its product.
b.   Determine the total contribution to profits and fixed costs from the solution generated in part (a).

Pear Computer is considering an alternative pricing strategy of sliding down the demand curve. It plans to set the following schedule of prices over the coming two years.

Time Period	Price	Quantity Sold
1	$2,400	200,000
2	2,200	200,000
3	2,000	200,000
4	1,800	200,000
5	1,700	200,000
6	1,600	200,000
7	1,500	200,000
8	1,400	200,000
9	1,300	200,000
10	1,200	200,000

c.   Calculate the contribution to profit and overhead for each of the 10 time periods and prices.
d.   Compare your results in part (c) with your answer in part (b).
e.   Explain the major advantages and disadvantages of "sliding down the demand curve" as a pricing strategy.

www exercise

Congestion Pricing

19. During times of peak usage of network resources such as highways, mainframe computers, and power transmission lines, providing access to an additional user can have negative impacts on all other users. Congestion or peak-load pricing systems at least partially internalize the external costs of congestion. But while congestion pricing may make economic sense, how can charging commuters higher prices be made politically viable? Access the following Internet site maintained by Resources for the Future (RfF): http://www.rff.org/news/transp.htm. How did RfF economists Winston Harrington, Alan Krupnick and Anna Alberini pose the question of congestion pricing in their commuter survey? What were the congestion prices they used, and what alternative solutions did they provide? What were their results?

CASE EXERCISE   TRANSFER PRICING

DeSoto Engine, a division of International Motors, produces automobile engines. It sells these engines to the automobile assembly division within the corporation. A dispute has arisen between the managers of the DeSoto division and the assembly division concerning the appropriate transfer price for intracompany sales of engines. The current transfer price of $385 per unit was arrived at by taking the standard cost of the engine ($350) and adding a 10 percent profit margin ($35), based on an estimated volume of 450,000 engines per year. The manager of the DeSoto division argues that the transfer price should be raised because the division's average profit margin on other products is 18 percent. The manager of the assembly division claims that the transfer price should be lowered because an assembly division manager at a competing automobile company indicated that engines only cost his division $325 per unit. The corporation's chief economist has been asked to settle this intracompany pricing problem.

The economist collected the following demand and cost information. Demand for automobiles is given by the following function:

$$P_m = 10,000 - .01Q_m$$

where P_m is the selling price (in dollars) per automobile and Q_m is the number of vehicles sold. (Assume for simplicity that price is the only variable that affects demand.) The total cost function for the assembly division is (*excluding* the cost of the engines)

$$C_m = 1,150,000,000 + 2500Q_m$$

where C_m is the cost (in dollars). The DeSoto division's total cost function is

$$C_p = 30,000,000 + 275Q_p + .000125Q_p^2$$

where Q_p is the number of engines produced and C_p is the cost (in dollars).

QUESTIONS

Assume that no external market exists for these engines (that is, the DeSoto division cannot sell any excess engines to outside buyers and the assembly division cannot obtain additional engines from outside suppliers).

1.   Determine the profit-maximizing output (vehicles) for the assembly division.
2.   Determine the profit-maximizing output (engines) for the DeSoto division.
3.   Determine the optimal transfer price for intracompany sales of engines.
4.   Calculate (a) total revenue, (b) total cost, and (c) total profits for each division at the optimal solution found in questions 1, 2, and 3.

The manager of the DeSoto division is dissatisfied with the solution to the transfer-pricing problem. On further investigation, he finds that a *perfectly competitive external market exists for automobile engines*, with many automobile manufacturers and suppliers willing to sell or purchase engines at the going market price. Specifically, a large German automobile company (BW Motors) has offered to purchase all of DeSoto's engine output (up to 700,000 engines per year) at a price of $425 per unit.

5.   Determine the profit-maximizing output for the assembly division.
6.   Determine the profit-maximizing output for the DeSoto division.
7.   Determine the optimal transfer price for intracompany sales of engines.
8.   Determine how many engines the DeSoto division should sell (a) internally to the assembly division and (b) externally to BW Motors.
9.   Calculate (a) total revenue, (b) total costs, and (c) total profits for each division at the optimal solution found in questions 5, 6, 7, and 8.

Yield Management

THE CONCEPT OF YIELD MANAGEMENT

Most competition takes place today in product-line submarkets between highly interdependent rivals each with some market power over price. Consider Delta and US Airways in air travel to Florida, and Busch Gardens, Disney, and Universal Studios in theme parks. To gain and sustain market share, each firm must secure competitive advantages by raising perceived value to customers or by lowering production, distribution, or selling cost. Then, by segmenting customers and preventing arbitrage, such firms may seek to raise revenue with price discrimination—for example, airlines charge larger markups for weekday business travelers who forego fewer close substitutes than vacationers staying over a Saturday night.

Customer segmentation and price discrimination are frequently complicated by prohibitive stocking costs and capacity choices that must be made before demand is known. Consider an airline, printing business, or hospital, which must acquire and schedule capacity before the respective demands for the 11 A.M. flight, the press run next Thursday, or tomorrow's elective surgeries are known. Scheduling decisions and the marketing mix can influence the order flow of these businesses, but can never remove entirely the random character of their demand.

If no revenue can be realized after departure from empty airline seats, from underutilized printing presses, or empty surgical theatres, random customer arrivals force a firm with fixed capacity to choose between underutilizing excess capacity or imposing service denials and stockouts on regular customers. The "spoilage" from unsold capacity and the "spill" of high-margin repeat customers are serious problems that may affect the firm's financial success and indeed its survival. In Figure 17A.1, a reduction in capacity from Q^{d_1} to a level just sufficient to meet mean demand at P_0 reduces the spoilage for low demand events (Q^{d_2}) from AB to CD, but introduces spill for high demand events (Q^{d_1}). Yield management (YM) is an integrated set of managerial economics techniques designed to deal with these pricing and capacity allocation problems under fixed capacity and random demand.[20]

SPILL AND SPOILAGE AT SPORTS OBERMEYER[21]

The selling season in fashion retailing is short (lasting no more than several months), and customer demand at the product line level is very fickle and hard to forecast. Consequently, buyers for retail merchants like Nieman-Marcus, Bloomingdale's, Saks Fifth Avenue, Rich's, and Marshall Fields must place orders far in advance of actual sales without really knowing which fashion trends will sell well and which will sell poorly. Sports Obermeyer faces this problem with ski clothes. In a particular winter ski season, Pan-

---

[20] F. Harris and P. Peacock provide a thorough overview of YM techniques and potential industry applications in "Hold My Place Please: Yield Management Improves Capacity Allocation Guesswork," *Marketing Management,* 4(2), Fall 1995, pp. 34–46.

[21] Based on M. Fisher et al., "Making Supply Meet Demand In An Uncertain World," *Harvard Business Review,* May–June 1994, pp. 83–93.

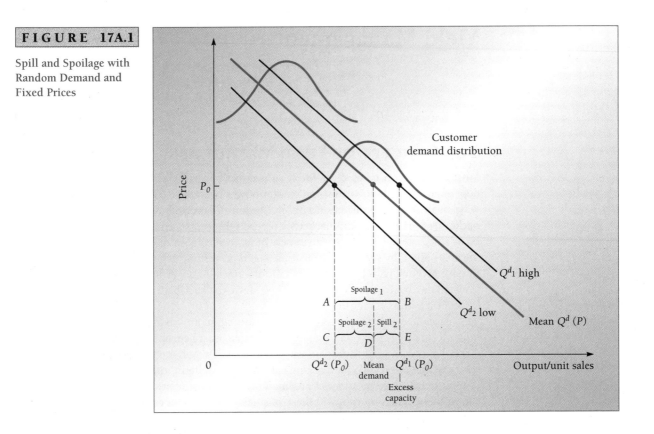

dora ski parkas may become a fashion statement and quickly sell out. If Pandora parkas go on back order, creating frustrated buyers, the store will lose that customer's goodwill and future sales. In addition, the lost retail contribution margin every time Sports Obermeyer "spills" one of these customers is $15.

On the other hand, Pandora's line of ski parkas may not "catch on" this season. Instead, they may end up as spoilage (i.e., a large inventory overhang of unsold winter clothes). The merchant would then incur losses on the unsold merchandise and forego the opportunity to sell another Champion sweatshirt that could have occupied the ski parka's shelf space. Sports Obermeyer can use the tools of yield management to balance these costs of spill and spoilage and thereby determine how many parkas to order and what shelf space to devote to parkas versus sweatshirts.

A Cross-Functional Systems Management Process

Firms might respond to unanticipated demand fluctuations in the presence of capacity constraints by simply auctioning off their scarce product to the highest bidder or by holding massive clearance sales when faced with inventory overhang. Much to their detriment, department store retailers have taken this myopic marketing view of what prices can accomplish. Fashion conscious customers shop numerous stores to "win" the trendy items and do so with little repeat purchase loyalty. Everyone else has become habituated to wait for the inevitable and deep discount sales. The proportion of department store revenue earned through transactions at clearance sale prices rose from 39 percent in 1964 to 58 percent in 1984.[22] Even regular customers of leading department stores report buying at discount prices almost as often (46 percent) as at regular prices (54 percent). Not surprisingly, profitability in department store retailing has collapsed, and consolidation mergers have taken some of the best known retailers out of business. What might these stores have done differently?

One alternative would be for the retail merchant's suppliers to develop flexible manufacturing systems (FMSs) so they could respond to demand fluctuations more quickly. If reorder cycles could occur several additional times within the fashion season, merchants could stockpile less inventory and yet experience fewer stockouts. This sounds almost too good to be true. An FMS is often too myopic an approach to the problem, one that attempts to use operations alone to solve a problem that is really cross-functional. Some manufacturing environments are simply inappropriate for the application of FMS technology. The economies from large production runs in textile manufacturing or metal working imply that designer jeans and refrigerator manufacturing operations should adopt transfer lines that minimize new setups in order to realize massive cost savings. A flexible manufacturing system will not provide the answer to unpredictable demand fluctuations in these types of production environments.[23]

Another alternative to resolve the problems posed by high-margin spill is simply to acquire more capacity. Of course, no company can afford to build additional capacity ad infinitum. Aggregate capacity planning incorporates a careful financial analysis of the capital budgeting problem that identifies the optimal fixed capacity for any line of business. Reserving some of this fixed capacity for late-arriving high-margin customers is a key to successfully addressing the problem of demand fluctuations. One of the insights of yield management analysis is that reserving capacity as the moment of delivery approaches should not be interpreted as "excess capacity" but rather as a sustainable revenue opportunity. Every company has some orders that it should refuse. **Yield management** is fundamentally an order acceptance and refusal process that links marketing, operations, and finance to decide which orders to accept at particular prices and which to refuse.

Sources of Sustainable Price Premiums

Practitioners of yield management believe that the sources of sustainable price premiums lie in these cross-functional systems management processes. In this view, innovative products and successful advertising campaigns are quickly reverse engineered and readily imitated. Advertising and product design cannot therefore provide sustainable competitive advantage. Process advantages, on the other hand, prove much more difficult for competitors to imitate.

Yield management processes add value for which customers gladly pay higher prices. In most cases, the added value arises through customizing and optimizing the account and order management. In the airline industry, for example, some customers want extensive flexibility of reservations that allows frequent changes in departure and arrival times. If an airline has the operations capability and information technology to provide this service, business travelers with unconfirmed meeting schedules will offer large price premiums to secure this *change order responsiveness*. To take another example, Disney offers substantial price premiums to gift product suppliers who can deliver first-quality

Yield Management
A cross-functional order acceptance and refusal process.

---

[22] B. P. Pashigian, "Demand Uncertainty and Sales," *American Economic Review,* 78(5), December 1993, pp. 936–953.

[23] For a more extensive discussion of yield management techniques and managerial insights applied to manufacturing, see F. Harris and J. Pinder, "A Revenue Management Approach to Demand Management and Order Booking in Assemble-to-Order Manufacturing," *Journal of Operations Management,* 12(4), December 1995, pp. 299–309.

on-time as promised. When Disney order clerks submit an error-laden request that needs to be changed within the normal 30-day reorder cycle, Disney volunteers to pay even more. Such supplements to revenue go exclusively to firms that have the systems management processes that can handle extraordinary change order requests.

Firms compete on other aspects of order processing as well. Some customers want short *scheduling delay* (e.g., just-in-time retailers without warehouses). Others want high *delivery reliability* and a very small probability of being denied service in the event of a stockout (e.g., business executives traveling to a stockholders' meeting). Still others value *conformance to product or service specifications*. For time-sensitive deliveries of organ transplants, for example, excellent on-time service records warrant paying very high airfares. The alternative would be a much more expensive jet charter service. Manufacturers as well as service firms can establish sustainable price premiums based on these same order processing characteristics of change order responsiveness, minimal scheduling delay, delivery reliability, and conformance to specifications.

YIELD MANAGEMENT DECISIONS

www . . . .
To learn more about yield management, and to access information on yield management programs and expert systems, go to the following Internet site: http://www.cqu.edu.au/~farrellk/

Yield management (YM) can be divided into three decisions: (1) a proactive pricing decision, (2) an inventory or capacity reallocation decision, and (3) an overbooking decision. What all three decisions have in common is a tactical focus heavily dependent on anticipated rival responses; a systems management philosophy integrating marketing, operations, and finance; and finally a multiproduct orientation that continuously reconfigures the firm's product offerings. We now address the managerial economics of each YM decision in turn.

Proactive Price Discrimination

Proactive price discrimination involves maximizing profits in the light of anticipated late-arriving demand and rival firm responses. In principle, computerized decision support systems (DSS) make it possible to reauction the remaining seats on a flight or the remaining runs on the printing press each time a new customer arrives on a reservation system. Conceivably, each customer would then experience third-degree price discrimination and pay a unique price reflecting his or her time of delivery, service costs, and price elasticity. Few YM practitioners have adopted bid price systems. Instead, most set prices and initially allocate capacity with the familiar techniques of marginal analysis.

Demand is estimated by market segment (e.g., for each of two customer classes—say, business and nonbusiness air travel). The expense account business traveler tends to make less flexible travel plans and reserve space later and thus faces fewer close alternatives than the nonbusiness traveler. Average revenue and marginal revenue schedules for business travelers therefore prove to be less elastic than for nonbusiness travelers, as indicated in Figure 17A.2. Previously, the airline's capacity planning department will have summed all the expected marginal revenues $E(MR)$ from the various segments and determined an optimal total capacity by setting summed marginal revenue $[\Sigma E(MR)]$ equal to the marginal cost of the last seat sold (MC_{lss}).[24] The result in Figure 17A.2 is that a plane with 170 seats should be scheduled for the Thursday 11 A.M. flight departure.

One may think of the optimal price discrimination decision as determining how this total capacity of 170 seats should be allocated across the customer segments. Because at

---

[24] To find aggregate demand, remember that individual demands (and *MRs*) are horizontally summed for rivalrous goods that cannot be shared (such as airplane seats and bite-sized candy bars), whereas demands for nonrivalrous goods (such as outdoor statues, tennis courts, and national defense) are vertically summed.

Price Discrimination and
Optimal Capacity
Allocation (45 Days in
Advance) for Thursday
11 A.M. Flight from
Dallas to Los Angeles

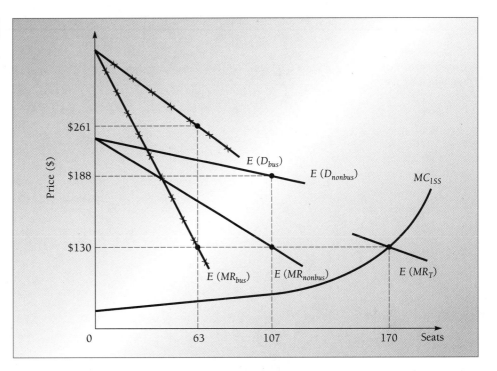

the margin a firm forgoes revenue unless the last customer in each segment contributes
a marginal revenue equal to the marginal cost of the last seat sold (MC_{lss}), the optimal
allocation results from equating the segment-level MRs to one another:

$$MR_{bus} = (MC_{lss}) = MR_{nonbus} \qquad [17A.1]$$

which in Figure 17A.2 is at $MR = \$130$. Consider a case in which this condition did not
hold. Suppose the 62nd seat sold in the business class contributed $150 of marginal rev-
enue and the 108th seat sold in the nonbusiness class contributed $120. Clearly, one
could raise $30 additional revenue for unchanged costs by selling one less seat in non-
business and one more in business leaving both classes with, say, a $MR = \$130$.[25]

What prices can achieve the initial capacity allocation of 63 seats to the business class
and 107 seats to the nonbusiness class? The answer is deceptively simple. Optimal price-
discriminating prices are whatever asking prices will clear the market if the firm supplies 63 and 107 seats in these two fare classes. In Figure 17A.2 the answer appears to
be $261 and $188 with some effective barrier or "fencing," which prevents resale from
the lower to the higher fares. The trick, of course, is predicting demand sufficiently well
to know what prices will have this effect for the 11 A.M. flight next Thursday.

OPTIMAL CAPACITY ALLOCATION: 11 A.M. FLIGHT TO LAX

Table 17A.1 shows the data on which such a decision would be based in practice. The
first three columns show number of seats demanded, fares, and marginal revenue for
business-class travelers. For example, at a fare of $1,084, only one seat on the entire

---

[25] Note that the MR of each segment is not set equal to MC. Rather, the summed MR of all segments has
been set equal to MC. The individual MRs are set equal to the MC of the last unit sold (i.e., $130), and
therefore to one another.

TABLE   17A.1

Allocating Airline
Capacity with Price-
Discriminating Fares

Business Class			Leisure Class			Total Seats	Marginal Cost
Seats	Fare	Marginal Revenue	Seats	Fare	Marginal Revenue		
1	$1,084	$1,084				1	$87
2	1,032	980				2	87
3	974	858				3	87
4	907	705				4	87
5	835	550				5	87
10	613	390				10	87
			1	$342	$342		87
			2	331	320		95
			3	319	294		95
			4	311	288		95
20	456	280	5	305	280	25	95
			10	280	256		95
			20	260	240		95
30	381	230	30	250	230	60	100
			40	240	210		100
			50	231	194		100
40	331	180	60	222	180	100	112
			70	214	162		112
50	295	150	80	206	150	130	112
			90	198	140		120
60	268	133	100	192	133	160	125
63	261	130	107	188	130	170	130
			110	186	128		140
70	252	122	120	181	122	190	155
			130	176	115		170
80	235	110	140	173	110	220	190

plane would be sold, and it would go to a business-class passenger. If the fare falls to $1,032, two seats are taken by business-class passengers. At a fare of $974, three seats are taken, and so on. Expected marginal revenue is the increase in total revenue realized from selling one more seat in the business class. For example, when a single seat is sold at $1,084, total revenue is also $1,084. When two seats are sold at a fare of $1,032, however, total revenue jumps to $2,064, and marginal revenue, which is the difference in total revenue realized from selling one more seat, is $2,064 minus $1,084, or $980. Similarly, the marginal revenue associated with the third seat sold is $2,922 minus $2,064, or $858.

Table 17A.1 also shows corresponding information for leisure class passengers. Note that the first leisure class seat is sold at $342, the second at $331, and so on. The last two columns depict total seats sold and marginal cost, which is the variable cost associated with serving one additional passenger in either class.

Using this simple two-booking-class example, marginal revenue equals rising marginal cost at $130 per seat. (Marginal cost increases by steps with additions of flight attendants needed to serve additional passengers and the additional fuel consumed because of worsening aerodynamics at high load factors.) At MC = \$130, optimal fares are obtained by equating individual marginal revenues of both segments and the marginal cost of the last seat expected to be sold (the 170th seat in this example). Business and leisure traveler marginal revenues equal \$130 at 63 and 107 seats, respectively, and fares of \$261 and \$188 are optimal at these seat allocation levels.

Capacity Reallocation

The second step in yield management is to *reallocate capacity* as delivery times approach in the light of advance sales and confirmed orders. Suppose you forecasted advance sales for business class on Thursday departures from Dallas to Los Angeles in accordance with the exponential function (tickets purchased = aB^t) estimated in semilog form as

$$\ln(\text{tickets}) = \ln a + \ln B(t) = \alpha + \beta t \qquad [17A.2]$$

where t is a simple time trend variable. Similarly, suppose you forecasted all nonbusiness travel with a sales saturation function such as

$$\text{Tickets purchased} = e^{k_1 - k_2(1/t)} \qquad [17A.3]$$

estimated as

$$\ln(\text{tickets}) = k_1 - k_2(1/t). \qquad [17A.4]$$

where k_1 and k_2 are constants defining the rate of sales growth throughout the advance sales period. These forecasted business and nonbusiness "booking curves" are plotted in Figure 17A.3. Note that the curves exhibit the early- and late-arriving characteristics of demand in the nonbusiness and business markets, respectively.

The forecasted booking curves reflect new demand arrivals and cancellations and are, in that sense, net bookings. Moreover, assume they reflect substantial nonrefundable

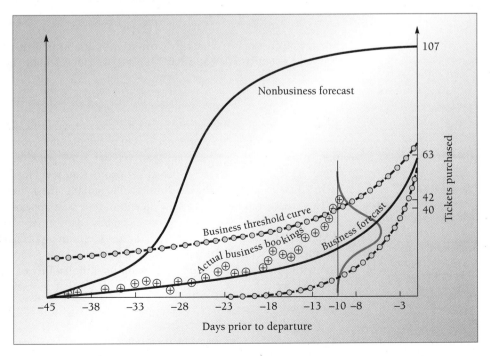

FIGURE   17A.3

Advance Sales Forecasts, Bookings, and Threshold Curves

deposits on advance sales and therefore imply realized revenue rather than just potential sales.[26] For the 11 A.M. flight to Los Angeles, the final demand target in Figure 17A.3 is 63 business and 107 nonbusiness passengers. This is an *initial* allocation of total capacity when customer reservations open 180, 120, 60, or in our case 45 days prior to departure. It is subject to (and in fact often is) change(d) by the yield managers.

Confidence intervals based on the different demand arrival distributions are then used to determine when actual bookings have deviated so far from forecast as to warrant an exception report. For example, business travel appears to be above forecasted ticket sales at day $t - 10$ by a statistically significant amount. This violation of the threshold sales level raises the question of whether to stop sales in the nonbusiness class where contribution margins $[(P_{nonbus} - MC) = (\$188 - \$130) = \$58]$ are clearly lower than in the business class segment, where $(P_{bus} - MC) = (\$261 - \$130) = \$131$.

The answer to this capacity reallocation question lies in applied statistics and in the initial profit-maximizing capacity choice under risk. Marginal capacity expansions are warranted as long as the expected incremental revenue minus marginal cost (i.e., the additional expected contribution to fixed cost) exceeds the incremental cost of additional capacity. In capacity reallocation, the cost of additional capacity in the business class is an opportunity cost—namely, the foregone contribution from selling one less seat in the nonbusiness class. At the margin, we would reallocate capacity as long as the expected contribution margin from allocating another seat to business travelers would exceed the lost contribution margin from a boarding denial in nonbusiness. That is,

$$(P_{bus} - MC)(Prob\ Shortage_{bus}) = (P_{nonbus} - MC)$$

$$\$131\ (Prob\ Shortage_{bus}) = \$58 \qquad [17A.5]$$

where the *Prob Shortage*$_{bus}$ is the probability that the business class will in fact stockout and, therefore, the probability that the extra business-class seat will realize its $180 marginal contribution.

Using the preannounced prices and resulting contribution margins of $58 and $131, and solving Equation 17A.5, high yield spill should occur 44.1 percent of the time:

$$(Prob\ Shortage_{bus}) = \$58/\$131 = 0.441$$

For any business-class demand distribution (say, normally distributed with a mean of 60 seats and a standard deviation of 20 seats), we can calculate the optimal capacity choice as

$$\mu_{seats} + z_\alpha \sigma_{seats} = 60 + 0.148 \times 17 = 63\ seats \qquad [17A.6]$$

where z_α is the absolute value of the standard normal critical value for one-tailed alpha = 0.148 from Table 1 in Appendix B. These calculations correspond to the initial situation in which business-class capacity was set at 63 seats (see Figure 17A.2). On this flight, 63 seats is often referred to as the **protection level** for business-class seats. Similarly, 107 seats is the **authorization level** for nonbusiness-class seats.

Now that we have received an exception report, it appears that the arrival distribution for next Thursday's flight is not normally distributed with mean 60 and standard deviation 20, that is, N(60,20). Instead, the exception report may indicate mean demand has increased such that the new demand distribution is N(52,17). Again, using the fact that with prices of $261 and $188 the optimal probability of stockout in business class is 0.148, we can calculate using Equation 16A.6 that the new optimal capacity alloca-

Protection Level

Capacity reserved for sale in higher margin segments.

Authorization Level

Capacity authorized for sale in lower margin segments.

---

[26] In the last YM decision, we will consider the effect of no-shows on authorized overbookings.

tion will be 62 seats + 0.148(20) seats = 65 seats. This implies that at present a stop-sales policy of 105 seats should apply to the bookings accepted in nonbusiness travel and that the extra two seats (107 − 105) should be reallocated to business class. Continued monitoring of bookings relative to the forecast thresholds may result in a return of these seats to nonbusiness class or a still further allocation toward business travelers.

The same questions and analyses we have examined in airlines apply in assemble-to-order manufacturing when a sport apparel manufacturer or a customized paper products manufacturer must decide which orders to accept and which to refuse (i.e., how to allocate fixed total capacity). As yield management moves out of the service sector (e.g., airlines, hotels, rental cars, advertising agencies, hospitals, professional services) and into manufacturing, these managerial economics techniques will become increasingly important.[27]

EXAMPLE

OPTIMAL PROBABILITY OF STOCKOUT AT SPORTS OBERMEYER

Recall that Sports Obermeyer must allocate its fixed-retail shelf and display-rack space between Pandora parkas and Champion sweatshirts. The lost retail contribution margin every time Sports Obermeyer "spills" a Pandora parka customer is $15. The lost retail contribution margin on a Champion sweatshirt is $4. Knowing these margins and the relative sales effectiveness of particular shelf space, Sports Obermeyer can use the tools of yield management to balance the costs of spoilage and spill in order to decide the optimal incidence of stockouts in Pandora parkas and allocate their retail space. Using Equation 17A.5, Sports Obermeyer calculates that Pandora parkas should stockout 27 percent of the time—that is, $4/$15 = 0.27.

Optimal Overbooking

The third and final yield management decision is an *optimal overbooking* decision. Here the airline authorizes the reservation clerks to sell more seats than are available on each departure to combat the lost revenue from "no-shows." Of course many tickets entail discount fares that require advance purchase, but some business-class tickets are not purchased until check-in time. This means that a confirmed sale is not realized revenue until delivery time. In some industries orders can be canceled or shipments refused. At times the air carriers have experienced up to 35 percent no-shows in certain city-pair markets during August.

The optimal overbooking decision is an explicit illustration of marginal analysis in practice. Each airline seeks to minimize the summed costs of spoilage and spill. In Figure 17A.4, as expected demand of business travelers approaches planned capacity and the expected load factor approaches 100 percent, the total cost of spoilage (i.e., unsold seats × contribution$_{bus}$) declines geometrically toward zero. In contrast, as the expected load factor approaches 100 percent, the costs of high-yield spill rise for three reasons. First, oversales represent lost contributions, which might have been captured by other service offerings (e.g., later flights); that is, some customers balk and proceed to a competitor. Second, oversales necessitate out-of-pocket expenses to compensate enplaned passengers who volunteer to give up their seats. And third, stockouts sacrifice customer

---

[27] See F. Harris and J. Pinder, "A Revenue Management Approach to Order Booking and Demand Management in Assemble-to-Order Manufacturing," *Journal of Operations Management,* December 1995, pp. 299–309.

goodwill and brand loyalty thereby causing lost future sales. These rising total costs of high-yield spill also are depicted in Figure 17A.4.

Total summed costs are reduced when the load factor increases as long as the rising costs of oversales are more than offset by the falling cost of spoilage. From below 92 to 97 percent load factors, the declining cost of spoilage more than offsets the rising cost of oversales for nonbusiness travel. Beyond 97 percent, the rate of spoilage cost reduction is less than the rate of oversale cost increase. This may be seen in the lower diagram by comparing the $MC_{oversales}$ to the marginal benefit of reduced spoilage, $MB_{spoilage}$, which is the MC of unsold seats *saved* by planning a higher load factor. For the non-business class, the optimal planned load factor appears to be 97 percent. In contrast, in the business class the $MC_{oversales}$ is so much higher as load factor increases that the optimal planned load factor is only 94 percent.

Both decisions are referred to as overbooking decisions because a 97 percent expected load factor for the 105 seats now allocated to nonbusiness travelers may necessitate actually booking not $0.97 \times 105 = 102$ seats but rather 127 seats in periods when no-shows are averaging 20 percent. Similarly, optimal overbooking in business may imply confirming reservations not for 61 seats in heavy (35 percent) no-show periods but rather for 94 seats. On average, the airline enplanes 102 nonbusiness and 61 business

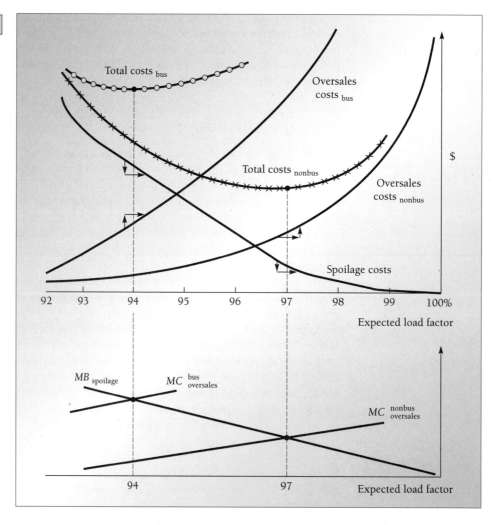

travelers on the Thursday 11 A.M. flight to Los Angeles. Of course, these 163 total passengers expected are only an average of actual passenger counts, which may vary on any particular departure from large spoilage to severe oversales.

EXAMPLE

PINPOINT BOOKING ACCURACY AT AMERICAN AIRLINES[28]

Price differentials on American Airlines' popular 5:30 P.M. flight (Flight 2015) from Chicago to Phoenix are huge, ranging from $238 to $1,404 round trip. American constantly adjusts the capacity allocation to each of seven fare classes as advance sales data deviate from forecast. Four weeks prior to a recent departure, American had already sold 69 of the 125 coach seats at Super Saver fares. With three weeks to departure, all three fare classes below $300 had reached their maximum authorization levels and were closed to further reservations. One day before departure, 130 passengers were booked on the 125-seat flight, but American was still authorizing up to five additional full coach reservations. The yield management computers predicted that cancellations and no-shows might go as high as 10. The next day Flight 2015 departed full with no one denied boarding.

Yield management both continuously reallocates capacity and adjusts these overbooking authorizations as advance sales data roll in. The incremental revenues from effective yield management can be significant. For example, American Airlines recently calculated its additional revenue from attending to these problems at $467 million per year.

Marriott International estimates that revenue management contributes as much as $200 million each year to its revenue stream. And the Canadian Broadcasting Corporation realized a $2 million revenue gain the first two weeks after it adopted revenue management techniques.[29]

EXAMPLE

REVENUE MANAGEMENT IN BASEBALL: THE BALTIMORE ORIOLES[30]

Recent applications of revenue management have taken the techniques out of travel services and into elective surgeries, radio and television advertising, opera and symphony concerts, law firms, consulting firms, golf courses, and now baseball. Like airlines, all these businesses have fixed capacity with perishable inventory; once the last out has been called (or, some would say, the seventh inning stretched), empty seats offer no realizable value. Although season ticket holders are prominent in the planning of any professional sports franchise, single-game and three-game ticket packages remain a substantial source of revenue. And unstable demand makes prediction of sales in these segments a challenging and continuous process, especially in baseball.

Most professional teams celebrate their sellouts, but fail to realize that some spare capacity (however slight) as game time approaches is a substantial revenue opportunity. Allowing discount ticket packages and promotions to displace last-minute walk-in customers often sacrifices high-margin repeat purchase business. At the same time, overall

---

[28] Based on "High-tech Pricing Boosts Business Fares," *Charlotte Observer,* 9 November 1997, p. 1D.

[29] As cited in R. Cross, *Revenue Management: Hardcore Tactics for Market Domination* (New York: Broadway Books, 1997).

[30] Based on "Managing Baseball's Yield," *Barron's,* 11 September 1995, p. 50.

attendance in professional baseball remains below pre-strike levels, and many games are played in ballparks only half full. The Baltimore Orioles revenue manager attempts to balance both these errors of understocking and of overstocking. Single-game seats purchased well in advance are available at a discount. However, a substantial capacity of well-placed seats is protected in anticipation of late-arriving high-willingness-to-pay customers. Advance sales are tracked, and variances are noted relative to previous sales histories for that homestand against similar opponents. As game day approaches, authorization levels for release of discount tickets gradually adjust to reflect the probability of stockout in higher-margin segments. Ideally, on game day, perhaps 97 percent of the seats are filled with fans in a variety of different segments paying a variety of different prices each reflecting the location, customer responsiveness, reliability, timing, and other ticketing services that particular customers preferred, thereby adding maximum value.

EXERCISES

1. Explain the effect on capacity reallocations of advance sales data implying mean demand of 55 rather than 60 during a slow travel week for business class, using the information in Figures 17A.2 and 17A.3, and Equation 17A.6.

2. Suppose the frequent-flyer program has raised the cost of high-yield spill twofold because business customers who are denied boarding now take their business to other carriers for several future trips, not just the current one. Reanalyze the overbooking decision in Figure 17A.4 under these circumstances. Will overbooking of business class service increase or decrease?

18

Government Regulation

CHAPTER PREVIEW

As managers make decisions designed to lead to the maximization of shareholder wealth, they are faced with many constraints. Some of these constraints are external social pressures that may be brought to bear on the firm. Those that have not been codified into law but are loosely described as "moral obligations" have been referred to as the social responsibilities of business. Other constraints have been codified into legal obligations of all firms in a similar industry or class. These constraints include a wide array of government regulations designed to ensure a smooth, efficient, and competitive functioning of the economy. Government intervention into the functioning of the economy is a very important element in the resource-allocation decisions made by managers in nearly every firm. To allocate efficiently the resources of an enterprise and to make wealth-maximizing price-output decisions, managers must fully understand both the competitive and the regulatory aspects of their environment. This chapter explores some of these regulatory issues. Appendix 18A examines the solution to problems arising from the existence of economic externalities.

MANAGERIAL CHALLENGE

THE COASE THEOREM AND GOVERNMENT REGULATION

The 1991 Nobel Prize in economics was awarded to Professor Ronald Coase from the University of Chicago Law School. Professor Coase is best known for his work on the relationship among property rights, transactions costs, and the role of government. Coase challenged the prevailing view that economic externalities, such as air pollution, were "problems" in need of governmental action, because, it had been argued, firms will not consider these "external" costs when making choices regarding output levels and technology choices.

Coase argued that externalities should not be viewed as one party inflicting harm on another party. Rather, he viewed the externalities as a problem of allocating a scarce resource. For example, a factory may desire to use the air to emit pollutants from its production process. The owners of a nearby amusement park might desire clean air in the area so that they can attract more tourists. Coase claimed that this externalities problem would be resolved without government intervention if the transaction costs of arriving at the solution are kept low. The issue is one of arriving at the appropriate assignment of property rights.

For example, in air pollution control, the Coase approach to allocating "rights to pollute" finally has been adopted on a widespread basis. Under the conditions of the Clean Air Act of 1990, the Environmental Protection Agency (EPA) is directed to set allowances for sulphur emissions from electric utility plants on a plant-by-plant basis. Congress gave polluters the right to trade these rights among themselves. For example, if one firm already has emission levels at its plants that are within acceptable bounds, it can sell its excess rights to pollute to another firm. Depending on the price of these "pollution rights," firms that do not meet the emissions standards can choose either to buy the pollution rights at a market price, or to install the needed pollution control equipment—whichever is cheaper. In May 1992, the Tennessee Valley Authority (TVA) announced the purchase of a substantial block of pollution rights from Wisconsin Power and Light Company, a firm that already met the EPA standards for its plants. The Chicago Board of Trade has recently created a market on which these pollution rights can be traded. Such a development greatly reduces the transaction costs associated with these sales.

In the broadly defined arena of government regulation of business, there has been a resurgence of interest in allowing market forces to operate, rather than relying on governmental regulators. Deregulation of most aspects of the transportation industries is complete; natural gas pipelines and telephone companies have been greatly deregulated; and there is substantial movement toward deregulation of the electric utility industry. The trend toward greater deregulation will open new opportunities for future managers and confront them with new challenges.

www . . . .
Read an autobiography of Ronald Coase at the following Internet site maintained by the Nobel Foundation:
http://nobel.sdsc.edu/laureates/economy-1991-1-autobio.html

MARKET STRUCTURE, CONDUCT, AND PERFORMANCE[1]

Much government regulation of business is designed to increase the plane of competition by eliminating monopoly and attempts to monopolize an industry, as well as by attacking certain patterns of market conduct that are believed to have deleterious effects

---

[1] An excellent reference on the relationships among market structure, conduct, and performance is F. M. Scherer and D. Ross, *Industrial Market Structure and Economic Performance,* 3d ed. (Boston: Houghton-Mifflin, 1990).

on a workably competitive market structure. Attempts to regulate business in this manner are discussed in this and the following section. The rationale for this type of regulation is the belief, founded on economic theory, that the more competitive the market structure, the greater the efficiency with which resources are allocated and the better the public interest will be served.

Market Performance

Ultimately what society would like from the producers of goods and services is that they perform in a satisfactory manner. *Good performance* is a multidimensional concept which includes these elements:

1. Resources should be allocated in an *efficient* manner within and among firms such that these resources are not needlessly wasted and that they are responsive to consumer desires. Therefore, a balance must be drawn between potential scale economies of production and distribution and the output restrictions (and higher prices) that are assumed to be characteristic of monopoly power.

2. Producers should be *technologically progressive;* that is, they should attempt to develop and adopt quickly new techniques that will result in lower costs, improved quality, or a greater diversity of new and better products.

3. Producers should operate in a manner that encourages continued *full employment* of productive resources. It can be argued that unused resources are wasted resources, especially when they are perishable, as in the case of human capital.

4. Productive resources should be organized in such a way as to encourage an *equitable distribution of income.* Although the notion of equity is a value-laden concept, we can say that profits should be no higher in the long run than necessary to invoke the productive use of resources in a particular endeavor. In addition, price stability should be encouraged because of the perverse ways in which inflation changes the distribution of income.

Other aspects of good performance can be enumerated, including the extent to which a firm or industry promotes the conservation of natural resources and the performance and safety characteristics of products that are supplied.

Unfortunately, these elements of good market performance are not always completely compatible with one another or agreed on by everyone. This prevents the development of an unambiguous index that might be used to assess the performance characteristics of a firm or an industry. Consequently, research on market performance has tended to focus on certain specific, measurable aspects of market performance such as profit rates, price-cost margins, actual costs versus technologically possible costs, selling cost in relation to price or total costs, relative price flexibility, stability of employment throughout the business cycle, and improvements in the productivity of labor.

Market Conduct

With good performance as the ultimate objective, it is important to develop a conceptual model that will help explain the causes of good or bad performance. Both Edward Mason[2] and Joe Bain[3] have provided a general model of the factors influencing market

---

[2] Edward S. Mason, "Price and Production Policies of Large-Scale Enterprise," *American Economic Review,* Supplement (March 1939), pp. 61–74, and "The Current State of the Monopoly Problem in the United States," *Harvard Law Review* (June 1949), pp. 1265–1285.

[3] Joe S. Bain, *Industrial Organization* (New York: John Wiley, 1959).

performance. This model is illustrated in Figure 18.1. Performance is viewed as dependent on the market conduct of firms in an industry. In general, market conduct includes the patterns of behavior followed by firms in the industry when adapting to a particular market situation. Included in market conduct are such things as the following:

1. *Pricing behavior of the firm or group of firms*—This includes a consideration of whether prices charged tend to maximize individual profits, whether collusive practices in use tend to result in maximum group profits, or whether price discrimination is followed.

2. *Product policy of the firm or group of firms*—For example, is product design frequently changed (as with auto style changes)? Is product quality consistent or variable? What variety of products is made available?

3. *Sales promotion and advertising policy of the firm or group*—How important are sales promotions and advertising in the firm's or industry's market policy? How is the volume of this activity determined?

4. *Research, development, and innovation strategies employed by the firm or group*—How substantial are expenditures for these purposes? To what extent is new technology available to smaller firms?

5. *Legal tactics used by the firm or group*—Are patent and trademark rights strictly enforced or defended? Are patent rights licensed to others at fair rates?

Although the distinction between conduct and performance may sometimes be blurred, it is important to remember that performance refers to the *end results* of the

FIGURE   18.1   A Conceptual Market Performance Model

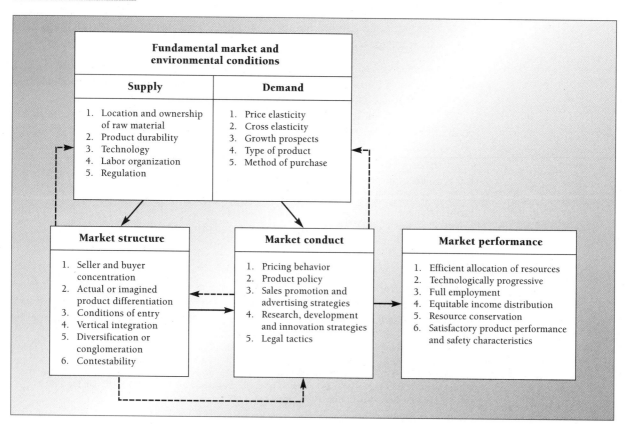

policies or processes of adjustment pursued by a firm, whereas market conduct encompasses the *processes* whereby the end results are reached.

Market Structure

Market conduct is to some extent dependent on the structure of a particular market. The concept of market structure refers to three main characteristics of buyers and sellers in a particular market:

1. The degree of *seller* and *buyer concentration* in the market, as well as the size distribution of these sellers or buyers—On the seller side this determines whether an industry is classified as monopoly, oligopoly, pure competition, or some variant thereof. It is also important to know if there is a significant "fringe" of potential competitors confronting the larger firms in a concentrated industry.[4] Buyer concentration is also important because the bargaining power of buyers determines in part the gross margin sellers can earn.

2. The degree of actual or imagined *differentiation* between the products or services of competing producers—When buyers perceive the product of one firm to be different from that of another, these buyer preferences will impart a degree of market power to the seller that ultimately affects that seller's market conduct and performance.

3. The *conditions surrounding entry* into the market—This refers to the relative ease with which new sellers may enter a market. When significant barriers to entry exist, competition may cease to become a disciplining force on existing firms, and we are likely to see performance that departs from the competitive ideal.

Other related aspects of market structure include the extent to which firms are vertically integrated back to their sources of supply or forward to the final markets, and the degree of diversification of individual firms, because that is also likely to impart market power and lead to unsatisfactory conduct and performance.

Condition of Entry

The condition of entry gives clues about potential rivals. The condition of entry is a measure of the height of the barriers that exist against new competitors and that protect existing firms from potential competition. The condition of entry, or the barriers to entry in an industry, may be measured conceptually as "the largest percentage by which established sellers can persistently elevate their prices above the minimized or competitive average costs of production and distribution without inducing new sellers to enter the industry."[5] The importance of entry barriers may be seen in a simple example. Consider the case of a monopolist who knows that raising prices above a level that just yields a normal rate of return on the investment will result in a large influx of new competitors in the industry. The monopolist may choose no competitors and normal profits in the short run to preserve a long-run position. Alternatively, when substantial barriers to entry exist or when entry is completely blocked, as in the case of the possession of patent rights, the monopolist may be expected to charge the highest price consistent with short-run profit maximization and still maintain the preferred position over the long run (or at least the useful life of the patent). We can see that the relative

---

[4] For example, see Stephen A. Rhoades, "Market Performance and the Nature of a Competitive Fringe," *Journal of Economics and Business* (May 1985).

[5] Bain, *Industrial Organization*, p. 237.

ease or difficulty of entry for new firms in an industry can have a significant impact on industry performance.

When firms are able to raise their prices somewhat above those that would prevail under competition without inducing the entry of new firms, some barriers to new entry must exist. These may be classified into three types. These general types of entry barriers and how they arise are summarized on the left side of Table 18.1; the consequences of the entry barrier on new competitors are enumerated on the right.

Contestable Markets and the Structure-Performance Relationship

William Baumol, J. C. Panzar, and R. D. Willig[6] have developed a theory of *contestable markets* that provides additional useful insights into the structure, conduct, and performance relationship. The theory of contestable markets can be best considered as a generalization of the theory of perfect competition. It yields the same results as the theory of perfect competition

---

[6] William J. Baumol, J. C. Panzar, and R. D. Willig, *Contestable Markets and the Theory of Industry Structure* (New York: Harcourt Brace Jovanovich, 1982).

TABLE 18.1

Type and Consequences of Barriers to Entry

Type	Consequences for New Entrants
A. Product differentiation barriers arise from 1. Buyer preferences, conditioned by advertising, for established brand names 2. Patent control of superior product designs by existing firms 3. Ownership or control of favored distribution systems (for example, exclusive auto dealerships)	A. 1. New entrants cannot sell their products for as high a price as existing firms can. 2. Sales promotion costs for new entrants may be prohibitive. 3. New entrants may be unable to raise sufficient capital to establish a competitive distribution system.
B. Absolute superiority of established firms in the matter of production and distribution costs arise from 1. Control of superior production techniques by patent or secrecy 2. Exclusive ownership of superior natural resource deposits 3. Inability of new firms to acquire necessary factors of production (management, labor, equipment) 4. Superior access to financial resources at lower costs	B. 1. Costs of new entrants are higher than for existing firms. Hence, while existing firms may charge a price which results in above-normal profits, new entrants may be unable to make even a normal profit at that price.
C. Economies of large-scale production and distribution (or sales promotion) arise from 1. Capital-intensive nature of industry production processes 2. High initial start-up costs	C. 1. The entry of a new firm at a sufficient scale will result in an industry price reduction and a disappearance of the profits anticipated by the new entrants. 2. New firms may be unable to acquire a sufficient market share to sustain efficient operations.

SOURCE: Joe S. Bain, *Industrial Organization* (New York: Wiley, 1959), pp. 237–265.

but requires substantially fewer assumptions than the perfectly competitive model. The theory of contestability provides a substitute for the theory of perfect competition in a market characterized by the existence of single- or multiproduct scale economies.

A perfectly contestable market is one that is accessible to potential entrants. Freedom of entry and exit is the central behavioral postulate of contestable markets. In a perfectly contestable market, potential competitors have the same cost function as the incumbent firm(s). These potential competitors can enter and leave the market without a loss of capital. The potential competitors use the incumbent firms' pre-entry price as the basis for evaluating the profitability of entry. With freedom of entry and exit, potential competitors need not fear the pricing reactions of competitors. If profit potential disappears after initial entry, the new entrants can simply leave the industry. The possibility of hit-and-run profits by potential entrants will cause incumbent firms to set prices equal to cost, because at any higher price there will be an opportunity for profitable entry.

The theory of contestable markets has shifted the focus of attention in market structure, conduct, and performance relationships to the conditions of entry and exit. The lower the barriers to entry and exit, the more nearly a market structure fits the perfectly contestable market model, and consequently, the more likely the resulting set of prices and outputs will meet the perfectly competitive market norm of price equal to marginal cost.

Market and Environmental Conditions

Market structure, conduct, and ultimately performance are also influenced by certain *fundamental market and environmental conditions*. These may be divided into factors primarily influencing the *supply* or *input side* of the production equation and those whose primary impact is on the *demand side*. The supply side includes the location and ownership distribution of essential raw materials, the durability of the product, the available technology and production techniques commonly used, the degree to which labor inputs are readily available and organized (unionized), and the extent to which the firm's activities are regulated by government. On the demand side, such factors as the price elasticity of demand, the number of close substitutes that are available (measured by the cross elasticity of demand), the growth prospects of the industry, the type of good or service being produced (intermediate, consumer, specialty, convenience, and so on), and the method of purchase by buyers (list price acceptance, negotiation or haggling, sealed bid) must be included in an analysis of fundamental conditions influencing market structure, conduct, and performance.

The solid arrows in Figure 18.1 indicate flows that are primarily causal in the model, resulting ultimately in some observable market performance. As the dotted arrows indicate, however, some secondary and feedback flows are also involved. The major concern of studies in the field of market structure, conduct, and performance is to develop the capability to predict market performance, based either on observations of the fundamental market and environmental conditions, market structure and conduct, or on some contemplated and controllable changes in these factors.

Before moving to a further discussion of the characteristics of market structure, we wish to emphasize one final point about the usefulness of this model in providing guidance for developing regulatory policies. The point is that there is no one place in the causal chain, from fundamental conditions to market performance, at which regulation will always work best. In some cases direct control of market structure may be an effective and efficient means of achieving desired performance. In other cases direct control over certain business practices (that is, over market conduct) will be more effective. The essential ingredient in any good regulatory policy is developing the logical chain of events between fundamental market conditions and market performance and then imposing any necessary constraints at the most appropriate point.

Market Concentration

The purpose of measuring market concentration is to indicate the extent to which market exchanges take place in a competitive atmosphere. Market concentration is related directly to the degree of competition that exists in an industry. Our concern with market concentration is based on the fact that both economic theory and empirical evidence indicate that when industry sales, assets, or contributions to value added are concentrated in a few hands, market conduct and performance are more likely to be monopolistic than competitive in nature.

Market Concentration Ratio
The percentage of total industry output produced by the 4, 8, 20, or 50 largest firms.

One widely used index of market concentration is the **market** (or *industry*) concentration ratio. It may be defined as the percentage of total industry output (measured, for instance, in terms of sales, employment, value added, or value of shipments) attributable to the 4, 8, 20, or 50 largest companies. Data on market concentration ratios are regularly made available from the Bureau of the Census, based on the *Census of Manufacturers*. The Bureau of the Census defines industries in terms of SIC (Standard Industrial Classification system) product categories. Under this system, an industry is defined as a group of establishments producing a single product or a more or less closely related set of products. The SIC system consists of up to a seven-digit category code, indicating increasing specificity of industry and product as the number of digits increases. All manufacturing, for example, is specified by the first digit, food and kindred products by a two-digit category, candy and other confectionary products by a four-digit category, and salted nuts and other confectionary type of products by a five-digit category. For the purpose of furnishing concentration ratios, the Bureau of the Census provides data at the four- and five-digit levels of specificity. Thus, a four-digit industry may be rather narrowly defined, such as printing ink (SIC 2893), or more broadly defined, as in the case of agricultural chemicals (SIC 2879).

It is necessary to use care in interpreting Bureau of the Census concentration ratios. In some cases the four-digit SIC industry designation will be too broad, including many products that do not serve the same function and hence are not substitutable. In other cases they are too narrow, failing to include ready substitutes. For example, metal, glass, and paper containers are classified as separate industries. Another problem with the census concentration ratios is that in many instances they understate the true level of concentration. For example, many bulky, low-value, or highly perishable commodities cannot be economically transported far from their places of production. This occurs in such industries as cement, brewing, milk supply, brick making, and newspaper publishing. The SIC industrial classifications, however, are based solely on the product and ignore the market area, implicitly assuming the entire nation to be the market. Thus newspapers show a four-firm concentration level of 16 percent, whereas on any regional basis this might very well be more on the order of 90 percent. When imports make up a large percentage of the supply of any product, reported concentration ratios tend to overstate the monopoly power present in the industry.

Table 18.2 provides concentration ratios for selected industries. Some industries have become highly concentrated, such as cereal breakfast foods, malt beverages, turbines, and motor vehicles. In the case of motor vehicles, the existence of substantial foreign competition has made that industry more competitive than the concentration ratios indicate. Some industries, such as concrete block and brick, are very fragmented at the national level, but tend to be much more concentrated in local geographical markets. Since 1978, concentration has increased in women's hosiery, malt beverages, and burial caskets,

| **TABLE** **18.2** | | | | | | |

Concentration Ratios and Herfindahl-Hirschman Index for Selected Industries

| Four-digit SIC | Industry Name | Year | Share of Value of Shipments Accounted for by the 4, 8, and 20 Largest Companies in Each Manufacturing Industry | | | Herfindahl-Hirschman Index |
			4-Firm Ratio	8-Firm Ratio	20-Firm Ratio	
2043	Cereal breakfast foods	1987	87	99	99^+	2,207
2026	Fluid milk	1987	21	32	48	195
2082	Malt beverages	1987	87	98	99^+	*
		1982	77	94	99	2,089
		1977	64	83	98	†
		1972	52	70	91	†
2251	Women's hosiery, except socks	1987	61	72	88	1,501
		1982	58	66	81	1,539
		1977	50	62	78	†
		1972	35	49	69	†
2841	Soap and detergents	1987	65	76	84	1,698
2911	Petroleum refining	1987	32	52	78	435
3211	Flat glass	1987	82	*	*	1,968
		1982	85	*	*	2,032
		1977	90	99	99^+	†
		1972	92	*	100	†
3271	Concrete block and brick	1987	7	12	21	33
3353	Aluminum sheet, plate, and foil	1987	74	91	99^+	1,719
3511	Turbine and turbine generator sets	1987	80	95	99	2,162
		1982	84	92	98	2,602
		1977	86	97	99	†
		1972	90	96	99	†
3711	Motor, vehicles and car bodies	1987	90	95	99	*
3949	Sporting and athletic goods	1987	13	21	35	94
		1982	17	28	44	140
		1977	21	28	41	†
		1972	28	37	50	†
3995	Burial caskets	1987	59	66	77	1,820
		1982	52	60	71	1,247
		1977	36	48	62	†
		1972	25	34	47	†

Notes: * withheld to avoid disclosing data for individual companies. † Not available.

SOURCE: 1987 Census of Manufacturers, MC87-S-7, U.S. Department of Commerce, February 1992, Table 4.

suggesting the presence of economies of scale and/or scope in these industries. In contrast, concentration has decreased in flat glass, turbine and turbine generator sets, and sporting and athletic goods.

Another measure of market concentration is the **Herfindahl-Hirschman Index,**[7] or *HHI*:

$$HHI = \sum_{i=1}^{N} S_i^2$$

where S_i is the market share of the ith firm and N is the number of firms in the industry. When an industry is composed of one firm with a 100 percent market share (pure monopoly), the *HHI* is equal to its maximum value of 10,000 (or 1.0 if market share is measured in its decimal equivalent, 1.0). The *HHI* value decreases as the number of firms (N) increases and increases as inequalities in market shares among a given number of firms rises. The *HHI* is generally highly correlated with other measures of market concentration, such as the four-firm sales concentration ratio.[8] *HHI* values for selected industries are shown in Table 18.2.

ANTITRUST: GOVERNMENT REGULATION OF MARKET CONDUCT AND STRUCTURE

Since 1890, a number of federal laws have been passed with the intent of preventing monopoly and of maintaining competition in U.S. industry. The ultimate objective of these laws is to protect the public from the abuses and inefficiencies that are thought to flow from the possession of monopoly power. These laws have come to be known as **antitrust laws** because they were initially directed at the large voting trusts such as Standard Oil, American Tobacco, and several coal and railroad trusts. Under a trust agreement, the voting rights to the stock of a number of directly competitive firms were conveyed to a legal trust, which managed the firms as if they were one big multiplant monopoly, thereby maximizing profits. Although extremely successful on the bottom line of the income statement, these trusts were viewed with increasing dismay because of the high price and restricted outputs that resulted. In this section we summarize the provisions of the most important of these antitrust laws and their effects on business decisions.

The Sherman Act (1890)

The Sherman Act was the first national antitrust law designed to regulate monopoly and the use of monopoly power. Its important provisions are brief, but they are wide-ranging. First, it declares illegal

> every contract, combination in the form of a trust or otherwise, or conspiracy in restraint of commerce among the several States, or with foreign nations . . .

This provision applies only to agreements in which two or more persons are involved. The second important provision is more general, in that it also applies to individual efforts to monopolize. It declares that

> every person who shall monopolize, or attempt to monopolize, or combine or conspire with any other person or persons, to monopolize any part of the trade or commerce among the several States, or with foreign nations, shall be deemed guilty of a misdemeanor.

Herfindahl-Hirschman Index

A measure of market concentration equal to the sum of the squares of the market shares of the firms in a given industry.

www . . . .

An excellent source of information on antitrust on the Internet is found at the following address: http://www.antitrust.org/

The Internet site for the Antitrust Division of the Department of Justice can be found at: http://www.usdoj.gov/atr/index.html

The following Internet site maintained by FindLaw provides a comprehensive set of links to antitrust resources on the Internet, including relevant U.S. Code, case summaries, journals, and access to the Federal Trade Commission and the Department of Justice: http://www.findlaw.com/01topics/01antitrust/index.html

Antitrust Laws

A series of laws passed since 1890 to limit monopoly power and to maintain competition in most American industries.

---

[7] O. Hirschman, "The Paternity of an Index," *American Economic Review* 54 (September 1964), pp. 761–762.

[8] See Scherer and Ross, *Industrial Market Structure,* pp. 72–73.

www . . . .
You can read the full text of
the Sherman Act, Clayton
Act, and other laws
pertaining to monopolies
and the restraint of trade in
Title 15 of the U.S. Code at
the following Internet site
maintained by Cornell
University:
http://www.law.cornell.
edu/uscode/15/ch1.html

This act turned the already existing common-law prohibitions against restraint of trade and monopolization into federal offenses, requiring federal enforcement. In the years following the passage of the Sherman Act, dissatisfaction with the generality of its provisions, as well as with the lack of vigor with which it was enforced, led to pressure for additional legislation.

The Clayton Act (1914)

An attempt to develop a comprehensive list of forbidden monopolistic practices was largely a failure in Congress. It was difficult to enumerate precisely and define all existing unfair business practices and guard against future practices that might evolve. Hence the Clayton Act enumerated only four such unfair practices:

1. *Price discrimination* between purchasers of commodities was illegal, except to the extent that it was based on differences in grade, quality, and quantity of the product sold. Lower prices were permitted only where they made "due allowances for differences in the cost of selling or transportation" and where they were offered "in good faith to meet competition." To discriminate otherwise in pricing was illegal if the effect was to substantially lessen competition or tend to create a monopoly. It was this section of the Clayton Act, Section 2, that was amended and strengthened by the Robinson-Patman Act during the era of the rise of the chain store.

2. Section 3 of the act forbade sellers from leasing or making "a sale or contract for the sale of . . . commodities . . . on the condition that the lessee or purchaser thereof shall not use or deal in the . . . commodity . . . of a competitor." This is commonly referred to as a prohibition against "exclusive and *tying contracts*." As with the price discrimination section, the prohibition was not absolute but only applied to the extent that the practice substantially lessened competition or tended to create a monopoly.

3. Section 7, the *antimerger* section, forbade any corporation engaged in commerce from acquiring the shares of a competing firm or from purchasing the stocks of two or more competing firms. As with Sections 2 and 3, the prohibition was not absolute but applied only in cases where substantial damage to competition could be proven or where it tended to create a monopoly.

4. *Corporate interlock,* defined as cases where the same person is on the board of directors of two or more firms, was declared illegal in Section 8, if (a) the corporations were competitive, (b) if any one had capital, surplus, and undivided profits in excess of $1 million, and (c) where "the elimination of competition . . . between them would constitute a violation of any of the provisions of the antitrust laws."

The Federal Trade Commission Act (1914)

The Federal Trade Commission Act (FTC) was passed as a supplement to the Clayton Act. Its major antitrust provision, found in Section 5, merely states "that unfair methods of competition in commerce are hereby declared illegal." A determination of what constitutes unfair methods of competition beyond those specified in the Clayton Act is left to the Federal Trade Commission, which the act established as an independent government antitrust agency with the goal of attacking unfair practices. The creation of a specific government antitrust agency with appropriated funds needed to initiate cases under the acts was the most significant aspect of the 1914 acts. No longer did enforcement have to be initiated at private expense and risk to curb the excesses of unfair and monopolistic practices.

The Robinson-Patman Act (1936)

The Robinson-Patman Act can be discussed both as antitrust legislation aimed at controlling the pricing aspects of market conduct and as an expression of a government policy aimed at restricting certain forms of price competition, thereby benefiting a special group of sellers.

The act, which amended Section 2 of the Clayton Act has both a criminal and a civil section. The criminal part (Section 3) specifies three offenses, which are punishable by fine or imprisonment:

1. Selling more cheaply to one buyer than another, on sales that are otherwise identical
2. Charging different prices in different parts of the country when the intent is that of "destroying competition or eliminating a competitor"
3. Selling at "unreasonably low prices" when the intent is to destroy or eliminate competition or a competitor

In terms of usefulness, Section 3 is of little significance because the first offense is too narrowly defined to be of any practical importance and the third is too vague (unreasonably low prices) and it is too difficult to prove the qualifying "intent," so the section is of limited use. Only the second offense has been of any help in restraining unbridled price discrimination.

Section 2, the civil section, has had the greatest impact. Its provisions are summarized below:

1. Section 2(a) makes it illegal to discriminate in price when selling goods of "like grade and quality" where the effect may be to "substantially lessen competition or tend to create a monopoly" or "to injure, destroy, or prevent competition with any person who either grants or knowingly receives the benefits of such discrimination, or with customers of either of them." This section not only declares price discrimination to be illegal when it *injures competition,* but also when it tends to *injure competitors.* In addition, it applies not only to injury to competition with respect to the one who grants the lower price but also to the one who receives it.

   A seller who is charged with price discrimination under Section 2(a) has two legal defenses. First the "cost defense" permits differentials in price that "make only due allowance for differences in the cost of manufacture, sale or delivery." The "good faith" defense permits a lower price to be charged to meet "an equally low price of a competitor." These defenses are outlined in Section 2(b).

2. Section 2(c) prohibits the payment of a brokerage commission to anyone but an independent broker. This section has been interpreted to make such payments illegal per se, without having to show proof of competitive injury.

3. Sections 2(d) and 2(e) prohibit the seller from allowing discounts to a buyer for merchandising services rendered the seller by the buyer. It also prohibits the seller from rendering such services to the buyer, unless these services or allowances are "accorded to all purchasers on proportionately equal terms." Advertising or promotional allowances, for example, must be made available to all sellers, not just a few selected large firms. Generally, these services have had to be made available proportionate to the dollar volume of purchases made by individual customers.

The Wheeler-Lea Act (1938)

In addition to its function of protecting consumers from unfair methods of competition, the Wheeler-Lea Act also serves an important antitrust role. Before Wheeler-Lea was passed as an amendment to Section 5 of the FTC Act, the courts had severely restricted the interpretation of unfair methods of competition. In several key cases the courts required not only proof of damaging deception to a buyer but also strong evidence that the deceptive firm had competitors who were also damaged and who were not engaging in similar deceptive practices themselves. By making illegal not only unfair methods of competition but also unfair or deceptive acts or practices, whether harm to competition is proven or not, the act provides for expanded consumer protection and also makes the prosecution of such cases far easier by removing the restrictive court interpretations.

The Celler-Kefauver Antimerger Act (1950)

Several court decisions following the passage of the Clayton Act substantially weakened its antimerger prohibition as contained in Section 7. The original statute dealt only with horizontal mergers, those between directly competing companies; others were not prohibited.

Another serious weakness in the original statute was that it applied only to mergers via *stock* acquisition. Mergers via the acquisition of *assets* were not affected. The Celler-Kefauver amendment was passed to close these loopholes. Under the amended Section 7, acquisition of another corporation's *stock or assets* is prohibited where "in any line of commerce in any section of the country, the effect of such acquisition may be substantially to lessen competition, or to tend to create a monopoly." Thus the two major weaknesses of the antimerger section of the Clayton Act were overcome.

The Hart-Scott-Rodino Antitrust Improvement Act (1976)

The Hart-Scott-Rodino law requires larger companies (i.e., those with assets and sales over $100 million and $10 million, respectively) that are planning to merge to provide notification and information concerning the proposed merger to the Antitrust Division of the Department of Justice and to the Federal Trade Commission. After notification of the proposed merger, a waiting period of 30 days ensues, during which these government antitrust enforcement agencies review the information submitted by the companies and examine the competitive effects of the merger proposal. The initial waiting period often is extended by enforcement officials in order to seek additional documents from the companies. After reviewing the information submitted, the government can either challenge the proposed merger in federal court or allow the merger to be completed, possibly with some modifications.

Enforcement of the Antitrust Laws

Within the federal government, both the Antitrust Division of the Department of Justice and the Federal Trade Commission FTC share responsibility for enforcing the antitrust laws. The Antitrust Division can file both criminal and civil cases against companies that it believes are violating the antitrust laws, whereas the FTC does not have the authority to prosecute criminal cases. Rulings of the FTC can be appealed by companies to the federal courts. Private individuals and companies can also file antitrust cases in the federal courts. These cases constitute the majority of antitrust suits filed each year.

Government antitrust agencies can use various methods to enforce the laws. Most antitrust cases are settled with *consent decrees* negotiated between the company and enforcement officials. Under a consent decree, a company agrees to take certain actions (or not engage in other actions) in return for the government agreeing not to seek additional penalties in the courts. In cases filed by antitrust agencies against a company, the courts may issue an *injunction* requiring (or prohibiting) certain actions by the company. The courts may also impose *fines* and *prison sentences* if the defendants are found guilty of violating the antitrust laws. In cases involving charges of monopolization, the courts may require *divestiture* of certain assets by the company. Finally, in antitrust cases filed by private individuals and companies, the party filing the suit is entitled to *treble damages* if the defendant is found guilty.

Antitrust Laws and Business Decisions

A wide variety of business decisions are affected by the antitrust laws.

Collusion   Explicit agreements among competitors to fix prices, along with other overt forms of collusion, such as market-sharing agreements, are illegal under the Sherman Act. The courts generally have ruled that such agreements are illegal, regardless of whether they cause injury to competitors. The legality of other less explicit forms of collusion is not as clear-cut. For example, in 1994 six major airlines agreed to settle price-fixing allegations that they used their jointly owned, computerized ticket information systems to provide advance notification of price changes to their competitors and thereby raise fares. On the other hand, other implicit forms of collusion, such as price leadership practiced in some industries, normally are not prosecuted under the antitrust laws. In a few cases, such as the dairy industry, producers have been legislatively exempted from the antitrust laws and are legally permitted to jointly set prices and allocate output (quotas).

www . . . .
Read the full text of the 1992 horizontal merger guidelines issued by the U.S. Department of Justice at the following Internet site:
http://www.usdoj.gov/atr/Guidelines/merger.txt

Mergers   A number of difficult legal and economic issues are encountered in attempting to determine whether a proposed merger will be challenged by government antitrust agencies. First is the issue of what is meant by the term *substantially lessening competition*. Every horizontal merger reduces competition by eliminating at least one competitor, by definition. The Antitrust Division of the Department of Justice issued merger guidelines in 1982 (revised in 1984), based on the Herfindahl-Hirschman Index (HHI), that it uses in deciding whether to challenge a proposed merger:

1. For markets with an HHI above 1,800, the government is likely to challenge a merger that increases the index by 50 to 100 (percentage) points.
2. For markets with an HHI between 1,000 and 1,800, a merger challenge by the government is unlikely unless the index increases by 100 or more (percentage) points.
3. For markets with an HHI below 1,000, the government is unlikely to challenge a merger.

The merger guidelines also list other factors that are considered in the analysis, including the ease with which competitors can enter the industry, likely failure of the to-be-acquired firm without the merger, and possible gains in efficiency for the (combined) firm.

A second important issue is the relevant product market to be used in computing statistics of market control, such as the HHI. The number of close substitutes that a product has is an important determinant of market power. The fewer and poorer the number of close substitutes a product has, the greater is the amount of monopoly power that is possessed by the producing or selling firm.

In addition to defining the relevant product market, the geographical market is also important in determining market control or power. Is the market local, regional, national, or international? Generally, a wider definition of the market will reduce the incidence of monopoly power and lower the probability of a merger substantially lessening competition.

Rather than filing a lawsuit to prevent a merger between large competing firms, antitrust enforcement agencies sometimes negotiate a consent decree that permits a merger to take place provided certain conditions are met to minimize the anticompetitive effects of the merger. For example, in the case of AT&T's $12.6 billion acquisition of McCaw Cellular (the largest U.S. cellular telephone company), the consent decree contained provisions requiring AT&T to operate McCaw as a separate subsidiary and allowing McCaw customers to pick any long-distance carrier to handle long-distance calls made on their cellular telephones. In another instance, the antitrust commission of the EC insisted that British Airways divest itself of 353 landing slots at London's Heathrow Airport if BA and American Airlines wished to merge. Rather than lose this many of its choice assets, BA decided to continue competing with American.

Monopolization   As we saw earlier, firms engaged in overt forms of collusion with other companies can be successfully prosecuted under the Sherman Act. Companies acting alone also can be charged under the act with illegally attempting to monopolize a market or engaging in monopolistic practices. However, proving such alleged violations of the laws often is quite difficult. The last large monopolization case brought by the antitrust enforcement officials resulted in the breakup of AT&T back in 1982.

www...............
Access the full text of the 1994 Microsoft consent decree, the 1997 Order to unbundle Internet Explorer from Windows 95, various court proceedings and rulings, and extensive commentary at the following Internet site maintained by FindLaw:
http://www.findlaw.com/01topics/01antitrust/microsoft.html

| EXAMPLE |

POTENTIALLY ANTICOMPETITIVE PRACTICES: MICROSOFT[9]

More recently, it was alleged that Microsoft, a company that develops software for personal computers, used its dominant position in the market for computer operating systems to gain an unfair advantage in the market for applications software. Netscape had complained that Microsoft illegally tied its Internet access software (Microsoft Explorer) to sales of Windows 95, which provides the operating system for 80 percent of the personal computers in the U.S. Microsoft distributed Explorer free with every sale of Windows 95 to Compaq and Dell Computers, priced Windows 95 without Explorer much higher, and threatened to remove the Windows 95 license if any Web browser other than Microsoft Explorer was pre-installed on the PCs Compaq shipped. Over four quarters in late 1996 and 1997, Microsoft's share of the Web browser market grew from 20 percent to 39 percent. Tying arrangements that extend the monopoly power of a dominant firm in one market to another distinct product and relevant market are per se illegal. Because these sales practices precluded Netscape from selling its Web browser, Microsoft was required to unbundle the two products and change its pricing practices.

Despite the difficulties of proving that an individual firm is engaged in monopolistic practices, companies must take into account in their decision making the possibility of legal challenges by either their competitors or government regulators.

---

[9] Based on "Browse This," *U.S. News & World Report,* 5 December 1997, p. 59, "U.S. Sues Microsoft Over PC Browser," *Wall Street Journal,* 21 October 1997, p. A3, "Knowing the ABCs of the Antitrust Case Against Microsoft," *Wall Street Journal,* 30 October 1997, p. B1, and "Microsoft's Browser: A Bundle of Trouble," *The Economist,* 25 October 1997, p. 74.

Price Discrimination   A large company that operates in two (or more) different geographic (or product) markets and cuts prices in one market and not in the other market can be accused under the Robinson-Patman Act of engaging in illegal price discrimination. To see why such pricing behavior could be judged illegal, consider the following situation. Assume that a large company has a high degree of monopoly power in one market (A) and earns monopoly profits, whereas the other market (B) is more competitive and the company does not have such power. The large company can cut prices (possibly below cost) in the more competitive market (B) with the intent of driving smaller firms out of the market, while keeping prices high in the market (A) where it already has a monopoly position. Profits from its monopoly position in the one market (A) could be used to subsidize the losses in the more competitive market (B). Once the smaller firms have been driven out of the competitive market (B), the larger company can then raise prices and earn monopoly profits in this market also.

Differentiating between the normal operation of a competitive market and illegal price cutting with the intent of eliminating current or potential competitors is a complex issue. Proving that a company has engaged in illegal price discrimination can be quite difficult. In the discussion of the Robinson-Patman Act in the previous section, we saw that a company accused of illegal price discrimination has two lines of defense. First, the company can argue that the price differences reflected differences in the costs of serving different customers. Second, the company can claim that any price differences were done to meet equally low prices by competitors.

Because of the complexity of the law and the difficulty of proving such violations, very few cases were filed by the antitrust agencies during the 1990s. Most of the price discrimination cases filed under the Robinson-Patman Act have been initiated by private individuals and companies.

REGULATORY CONSTRAINTS: AN ECONOMIC ANALYSIS

Federal, state, and local governments are involved in the regulation of business enterprises. Table 18.3 contains a (partial) listing of the federal government agencies and departments, in addition to the Federal Trade Commission and Antitrust Division of the Department of Justice discussed earlier, that impose regulations on the operating decisions of firms. State regulations encompass a wide range of activities, including regulation of public utility companies and licensing of various businesses, such as health-care facilities, and numerous professions, such as law and accounting. Local governments frequently impose on businesses such regulations as zoning laws and building codes. Regulatory constraints can be imposed on individual firms, entire industries, or on all businesses. These constraints can affect a firm's operating costs (both fixed and variable), capital costs, and revenues. The following example illustrates the scope and effect of environmental regulations on one large company.

EXAMPLE

REGULATION AND ECONOMIC PERFORMANCE: THE CASE OF DUPONT[10]

DuPont's vice president for environmental affairs said at the time the 1990 Clean-Air Bill was in the final stages of consideration in Congress that, "From a legislative standpoint, it has probably as significant an effect on the company as anything else ever has." The

---

[10] Based on "How Clean-Air Bill Will Force Du Pont into Costly Moves," *Wall Street Journal*, 25 May 1990, p. 1ff.

TABLE   18.3

Partial Listing of Federal
Government Regulatory
Agencies*

Department/Agency	Purpose
Environmental Protection Agency (EPA)	Regulates pollution of air, water, and land
Consumer Product Safety Commission (CPSC)	Protects against unreasonable risks of injury associated with consumer products
Equal Employment Opportunity Commission (EEOC)	Enforces laws on employment discrimination based on race, religion, and sex
Labor—Employment Standards Administration	Enforces minimum wage and overtime laws
Labor—Occupational Safety and Health Administration (OSHA)	Regulates safety and health conditions in the workplace
Labor—National Labor Relations Board (NLRB)	Regulates labor relations between employers and employees (and their unions)
Interstate Commerce Commission (ICC)	Regulates interstate surface transportation
Nuclear Regulatory Commission (NRC)	Regulates civilian use of nuclear energy
Securities and Exchange Commission (SEC)	Regulates issuance of new securities and trading of existing securities
Federal Communications Commission (FCC)	Regulates radio and television broadcasting and interstate telephone service
Federal Reserve System	Regulates commercial banks and bank holding companies
Agriculture—Food Safety and Inspection Service	Regulates meat and poultry industry for safety and accurate labeling
Health and Human Services—Food and Drug Administration (FDA)	Regulates safety of food, drugs, and cosmetics
Energy—Federal Energy Regulatory Commission (FERC)	Regulates interstate rates for transportation and sale of natural gas and transmission and sale of electricity
Transportation—Federal Aviation Administration (FAA)	Regulates safety of airplanes, airports, and airline operations
Transportation—National Highway Traffic Safety Administration (NHTSA)	Regulates safety of motor vehicles and tires
Labor—Mine Safety and Health Administration	Regulates safety and health in mines
Treasury—Office of Comptroller of the Currency	Regulates national banks
Treasury—Bureau of Alcohol, Tobacco, and Firearms (BATF)	Regulates manufacture and sale of alcoholic beverages, tobacco, explosives, and firearms

*For a complete listing and description of all federal regulatory agencies, see *United States Government Manual 1994/5,* Office of Federal Register, National Archives and Records Administration.

bill is intended to force factories, power plants, automobiles, gasoline, and other products to be less polluting. The estimated total cost to the economy is $21.5 billion annually by the year 2005. The bill has among its objectives to make areas such as Los Angeles essentially smog-free within 15 years.

DuPont has been identified as the nation's fifth largest air polluter. Consequently, the impact of the act on DuPont is expected to be enormous. The firm's environmental equipment budget is expected to double to $500 million per year under the act. DuPont estimates that the bill's acid-rain controls will put up to 1,000 of its miners out of jobs because they work in coal mines that produce coal with a high sulphur content. Because operating pollution control equipment is energy intensive, DuPont estimates that its annual electricity bill will increase by $40 million under the bill.

DuPont supplies half of the chlorofluorocarbons (CFCs) in the United States. It had pledged to phase out production of these ozone-depleting chemicals by 2000, but was counting on replacing CFC production with HCFCs. The bill, however, sets deadlines for phasing out HCFCs as well. Hence, DuPont will have to redirect its planned HCFC investments. Under the bill, DuPont's Conoco subsidiary will have to invest substantial sums in its refineries to produce a new, cleaner burning gasoline. Industrywide, the cost of this investment could come to $20 billion.

As indicated in this example, government regulations can impose substantial costs on individual firms. These costs have major impacts on the product lines a firm chooses, the technology employed in producing the product, and the prices charged to consumers.

Rather than attempt to exhaustively enumerate the various regulations placed on businesses, the primary focus of this section is on the usefulness of economic analysis in assessing the impact of operating controls. In some instances, a linear-programming model may help to assess the impact of a constraint on the firm.[11] In other cases, a reasonably straightforward use of our knowledge of the market structure and the relevant firm or industry demand and cost functions can offer helpful insights. The following example is an illustration of the usefulness of this latter type of analysis.

| EXAMPLE |

The Palladium Metal-Casting Industry[12]

The palladium metal-casting industry is composed of about 25 firms that operate foundries engaged in making palladium castings. These foundries have recently been under attack because of the heavy pollution they cause in the communities where they operate. Consequently, the EPA is considering standards to force a reduction in particulate emissions.

The industry makes various sizes and shapes of castings; however, production levels in individual firms are measured by hundred-pound weights of castings poured, and prices and costs vary roughly in accordance with the weight of the casting. Current industry employment is about 12,000 workers.

In an effort to assess the impact of proposed standards on the industry, the EPA has agreed to work with the trade association's economists to make these estimates. Industry demand has been estimated at

$$P = \$15,000 - .3Q$$

where P = price per hundred pounds of castings poured
Q = hundreds of pounds of castings poured

Hence, total revenue TR equals

$$TR = P \cdot Q$$
$$= \$15,000Q - .3Q^2$$

---

[11] Linear programming was discussed in Chapter 11.

[12] The palladium metal-casting industry is a hypothetical example of the type of economic analysis that may be useful in assessing the impact of a wide variety of constraints. The data presented in this example are not intended to be associated with any particular industry.

and marginal revenue *MR* equals

$$MR = \frac{dTR}{dQ}$$

$$= \$15,000 - .6Q$$

Similarly, the industry's total cost function *TC* has been estimated as

$$TC = \$100,000,000 + 6Q + .05Q^2$$

Hence marginal cost *MC* equals

$$MC = \frac{dTC}{dQ}$$

$$= 6 + .1Q$$

Because of a history of price leadership in the industry, the price-output solution that has generally evolved in the industry has been very close to that of a profit-maximizing monopoly. Consequently, price and output may be determined for the industry by equating marginal cost with marginal revenue and solving for *Q*:

$$MC = MR$$

$$6 + .1Q = 15,000 - .6Q$$

$$.7Q = 14,994$$

$$Q^* = 21,420$$

Substituting in the demand equation, we find that

$$P^* = 15,000 - .3(21,420)$$

$$= \$8,574$$

Given this price-output combination, total industry profits π are estimated as

$$\pi = TR - TC$$

$$= PQ - TC$$

$$= (8,574)(21,420) - [100,000,000 + 6(21,420) + .05(21,420)^2]$$

$$\pi^* = \$60,585,740$$

This profit of about $60.6 million represents a return on industry investment (*ROI*), estimated at about $840 million, of

$$ROI = \frac{\$60.6 \text{ million}}{\$840 \text{ million}} \times 100 = 7.2\%$$

This return is somewhat below average for U.S. industry, but this is merely an average return. Some firms are more efficient than others, thereby earning a higher return and vice versa.

To reduce smoke pollution within the proposed EPA limits, a total investment of $150 million would be required. This will increase total industry fixed costs by about $15 million (after-tax depreciation plus interest). If no variable costs were associated with the use of this pollution control equipment, the price-output solution would remain the same, but profits would drop by $15 million and the return on investment (assuming no required return on the pollution control investment) would decline to

$$ROI_1 = \frac{\$45.5 \text{ million}}{\$840 \text{ million}} \times 100 = 5.4\%^{13}$$

This is well below the U.S. industry average. If the $150 million pollution investment were considered in the asset base, the ROI would be even less impressive.

It is unrealistic, however, to assume that only fixed costs will change. Variable costs also increase because it is costly to operate and maintain the pollution control equipment. Hence industry economists estimated a new industry total cost function:

$$TC_1 = \$115,000,000 + 8Q + .1Q^2$$

and

$$MC_1 = \frac{dTC_1}{dQ} = 8 + .2Q$$

Equating MC_1 to MR, we get

$$MC_1 = MR$$

$$8 + .2Q = 15,000 - .6Q$$

$$.8Q = 14,992$$

$$Q^* = 18,740$$

Substituting in the demand equation yields

$$P^* = 15,000 - .3(18,740)$$

$$= \$9,378$$

Thus we see that output declines nearly 3,000 units and prices are increased by about $800. Under these circumstances, total industry profits π_2 equal

$$\pi_2 = TR - TC_1$$

$$= (9,378)(18,740) - [115,000,000 + 8(18,740) + .1(18,740)^2]$$

$$\pi_2^* = \$25,475,040$$

and return on investment (ignoring the pollution control investment) slips to

$$ROI_2 = \frac{\$25.5 \text{ million}}{\$840 \text{ million}} \times 100 = 3.0\%$$

Remembering that ROI_2 is an average figure, it is quite likely that some of the less efficient firms would close. Industry and EPA economists make an admittedly crude estimation that the new industry total cost and marginal cost functions, after the exit of some firms, would equal

$$TC_2 = \$85,000,000 + 15Q + .2Q^2$$

$$MC_2 = 15 + .4Q$$

---

[13] Note that if the $150 million pollution control investment is added to the denominator, the computed ROI declines to 4.6 percent.

The profit-maximizing output now becomes

$$MC_2 = MR$$
$$15 + .4Q = 15,000 - .6Q$$
$$Q^* = 14,985$$

and price equals

$$P^* = 15,000 - .3(14,985)$$
$$= \$10,504$$

Thus we see that output will decline about 4,000 more units (from 18,740 to 14,985) and price will increase nearly \$1,150.

New industry profits (π_3) will be

$$\pi_3 = TR - TC_2$$
$$= (10,504)(14,985) - [85,000,000 + 15(14,985) + .2(14,985)^2]$$
$$\pi_3^* = \$27,267,620$$

The resulting industry return on investment ROI_3 will be enhanced by both the increase in profits from \$25 to \$27 million and the reduction in total industry investment as a result of the departure of the inefficient firms. Total industry investment is now estimated to equal only \$630 million. Hence

$$ROI_3 = \frac{\$27.2 \text{ million}}{\$630 \text{ million}} \times 100 = 4.3\%$$

It is also estimated that the departure of the industry's more inefficient firms will reduce total industry employment by about 3,000. The team of economists has determined that about one-half of the output reduction (from 21,420 to 14,985) will be absorbed by shifting demands to substitute domestic metal firms, and the other half will result in a negative balance-of-payments drain. The current foreign price per hundred pounds of casting is about \$10,300. Thus the balance-of-payments impact of the proposed environmental standard is

$$BOP \text{ impacts} = \frac{1}{2}(21,420 - 14,985)(\$10,300)$$
$$= \$33,140,250$$

Armed with this and other data, such as what the regional impacts of plant closings will be on both unemployment rates and overall regional economic development, the EPA is in a far better position to assess the effect of its proposed standards.

Perhaps the EPA will not decide on an across-the-board standard but may impose stricter limitations on firms located in densely populated areas than on those in sparsely inhabited areas. It may also decide to phase the standards in over time so their impacts will not be felt all at once. This would have the benefit of giving local communities, heavily dependent on the palladium foundries for employment, time to make necessary adjustments to expand the base of the area's economy, providing more stability in employment.

This hypothetical example illustrates the insights that economic analysis can furnish in assessing the impact of operating controls on industry. Similar methods can be used to analyze nearly all the areas of operating constraints enumerated at the beginning of this section. The type of model chosen, as well as the complexity of that model, depends on the nature of the problem, the insights and creativity of the analyst, and the precision required in the results.

The Deregulation Movement

www . . . .
Read more about federal regulation of the energy industry at the following Internet site:
http://www.ferc.fed.us/

Beginning in the late 1970s and continuing through the 1980s and 1990s sentiment has increased for relying less on government regulation and more on the marketplace to achieve desired economic objectives. This sentiment for increased deregulation has been felt most significantly in the price regulation of transportation services. Such recent pieces of legislation as the Airline Deregulation Act of 1978, the Railroad Revitalization and Regulatory Reform Act of 1976, and the Motor Carrier Act of 1980 have greatly increased the flexibility of airlines, railroads, and the trucking industries to set prices and determine levels of service and areas of operation *outside* of the regulatory framework. The objectives of these pieces of legislation have been to give the affected industries greater pricing flexibility in exchange for an increased and more open level of competition.

Although the full impact of deregulation in these industries has yet to be felt, most observers believe the impact has been quite favorable. In the airline industry, deregulation has meant greater competition on many routes with fare reductions and promotional fares becoming quite common. In the trucking industry, deregulation has been credited with a reduction in the rate of increase of trucking charges and improvements in service in many areas.

In the communications industry, AT&T has faced increased competition (primarily, but not exclusively) in the long-distance market from such firms as MCI. Customers may also purchase their own phone equipment from a wide range of suppliers other than AT&T. The breakup of AT&T into seven independent regional phone companies and a long-distance company is an important step in deregulation of the telecommunications industry.[14]

Deregulation has subjected electric power generation and transmission companies to additional competition. The National Energy Policy Act of 1992 mandated a more open transmission system, which will provide more power supply options to wholesale customers. Also, the prospect of increased competition at the wholesale level may lead retail customers to pressure utilities and state regulators to reduce prices or allow them to choose supplies. Deregulation of natural gas pipelines is effectively a reality today. Thus, it appears as though the United States has entered an era of less regulation and more reliance on the marketplace to achieve economic objectives.

GOVERNMENT SUPPORT OF BUSINESS

Besides regulating business enterprises, numerous government programs and policies aid and support business. These include:
1. Restricting competition
2. Direct and indirect support

---

[14] For a discussion of the impacts of deregulation, see A. E. Kahn, "Surprises from Airline Deregulation," R. W. Crandall, "Surprises from Telephone Deregulation and the AT&T Divestiture," and E. J. Kane, "Interaction of Financial and Regulatory Innovation," *American Economic Review* (May 1988), pp. 316–334.

Restricting Competition

www..............
Access the U.S. Patent and
Trademark Office at the
following Internet site:
http://www.uspto.gov/

Many examples of public policies pursued by government have the effect, if not always
the intent, of restricting competition. These take numerous forms, including the is-
suance of licenses and patents and the restrictions on price competition. Such import
controls as tariffs and quotas have the same impact of restricting competition.

Licensing   When the government requires and issues a license permitting someone
to practice a particular business, profession, or trade, it is by definition restricting the
entry of some potential new competitors into that practice. Licensing is generally used
to protect the public from fraud or incompetence in those cases where the potential
for harm is quite large. Thus, doctors are required to meet certain educational standards of professional competence; restaurants need to meet public health standards;
real estate agents must meet certain standards of professional knowledge; financial
trustees must be bonded to ensure the public against fraud; and cab drivers are licensed with the intent of protecting the public from problem drinkers, accident-prone
drivers, and the like.

In most of these cases the reason for requiring a license is to protect the public *and*
the industry by establishing some minimal, acceptable criteria for participation in cases
where consumers may find it difficult and/or prohibitively expensive to gather the information needed to make a rational choice. In other cases, however, the rationale for,
or the type of, licensing is not so clear. In fact, in many instances the effect of licensing
is to restrict unnecessarily entry into the trade and therefore to deter competition. In
some cities, such as Washington, D.C., taxicab licensing is intended solely to protect the
public from the dangers of poor or incompetent drivers. The result is that fares are generally low and service is abundant. Other cities have severely restricted the number of
cabs by selling only a small number of cab permits, as is the case in Chicago, or by giving an exclusive franchise to only one or a few companies, as in Houston. In such instances the effect of licensing goes well beyond the bounds of protecting the public.
Those who have been privileged to receive such a license are protected against new competition, and the public pays in the form of poorer service and higher than necessary monopoly prices.

Patent
A legal government grant of
monopoly power that
prevents others from
manufacturing or selling a
patented article.

Patents   **Patents** are by definition a legal government grant of monopoly power. The
holder of a patent may prevent others from manufacturing or selling a patented product
or from using some patented process. The patent holder may grant a license permitting
others to make limited use of the patent, and in exchange some sort of royalty arrangement is usually made. The monopoly granted by a patent is not, however, an absolute
one. First, it is limited to a 17-year period, and no renewal privilege is permitted. Second, competing firms are not prohibited from engineering around an existing patent and
bringing out a closely competitive, alternative design. Third, many patents are successfully challenged by competitors, placing a further limitation on the monopoly grant of
power. Even an unsuccessful legal challenge of a patent, particularly a challenge by a
large firm on patents held by a smaller firm, may be successful in forcing the challenged
firm to relent and perhaps sell or license its patent, because such lengthy legal battles
can be quite expensive for an individual or small firm.

Society pays two definite costs when it grants monopoly power to an individual or
firm. Once an invention is made, it may cost very little for others to duplicate it, except
for the necessary production costs. Yet the monopoly grant entitles the inventor to

receive a premium above the cost of production, either in the form of higher-than-competitive-level prices, or as a royalty payment from licenses for a period of 17 years. Hence we witness the same resource misallocation problems as are evident in any other form of monopoly. It is possible that a shorter patent monopoly period would provide sufficient incentives to encourage a high level of inventive activity in many areas.

Second, it has been observed that critical patents frequently help create strong monopoly positions that remain long after the original patent expires, because of other barriers to entry that are built up in the interim. This has been the case in such industries as aluminum, shoe manufacturing, braking systems, rayon, cigarettes, metal containers, photographic equipment and supplies, and gypsum products.[15]

Offsetting these monopoly costs is the increase in inventive activity that the patent monopoly is alleged to encourage. Unfortunately, it is impossible to assess this impact in any meaningful, quantitative manner. Although doubtlessly some reduction in inventive activity would occur if the patent right were abolished, firms may protect the profits from inventions in other ways, including the following:

1. By keeping the technical aspects of the invention secret

2. By taking full advantage of the lead time over competitors that a new invention provides

Patents are used quite extensively by such industries as electronics, drugs, and chemicals, whereas auto manufacturers, paper, machinery, and rubber processors use them very little.

Restrictions on Price Competition   Restrictions on price competition have taken many forms in various industries. Agricultural prices have long been a function of government-guaranteed parity prices. Similarly, rates for scheduled ocean freight services by U.S. flagships are set by the international shipping conferences and approved and defended by the U.S. Maritime Commission.

Over the years a number of more general pieces of legislation have been enacted that have had the effect of limiting price competition. The most important remaining example of this type of legislation is the Robinson-Patman Act of 1936, which prohibits certain forms of price discrimination. Some of its more important provisions were summarized earlier in the discussion of antitrust laws.

Robinson-Patman arose during the Depression when independent retailers and wholesalers, particularly grocers and druggists, were under strong pressures from the emerging large chain stores. These chain stores, by virtue of their size, possessed certain operating economies not realized by the small independents. More important, the chains were frequently able to wield their economic muscle to secure special low prices or brokerage concessions from sellers. Supported by the threat of moving their sizable orders elsewhere, the chains received special price concessions that were not based on inherent operating economies of scale. For example, A & P received price concessions from food manufacturers by threatening to take its business elsewhere if they were not granted. Wholly owned, nonfunctioning dummy brokerage firms were established by businesses such as A & P to exact additional concessions in the form of a broker's price discount. The broker performed a useful intermediary function as a wholesale distributor for smaller firms, but in the case of A & P no services were pro-

[15] A. E. Kahn, "The Role of Patents," in *Competition, Cartels and Their Regulation*, ed. J. P. Miller (Amsterdam: North Holland, 1962).

vided, yet compensation in the form of brokers' discounts was still received. This situation further threatened the existence of the small independents, and a massive lobbying effort was mounted. The Robinson-Patman Act was finally passed in an attempt to preserve small business by regulating price discrimination.

The Robinson-Patman Act is a curious piece of legislation that has probably deterred many price reductions that otherwise would have been made if it were not for the fear of prosecution. Under the Reagan administration, the act was not aggressively enforced because of the belief that it discourages competition by not encouraging the efficiencies of high volume transactions. Moreover in a May 1988 Supreme Court decision, the Court upheld the right of Sharp Electronics to stop selling its products to a Houston discount retailer who refused to sell them at the higher mark-ups suggested by Sharp. This decision has been described as a green light for high-markup retailers who may pressure manufacturers to stop supplying discount retailers.

Refusals to Deal   In general, a manufacturer can refuse to deal with any retail distributor who fails to follow company policies that are based on legitimate business justifications. However, there are three limitations on this authority. First, the orders of a renegade discounter can be refused if and only if the manufacturer acts independently of compliant dealers whose sales at higher price points are suffering because of the increased competition (*United States v. GM,* 1966). Second, an explicit well-justified policy must be in place in advance; the manufacturer cannot pressure individual dealers, threaten suspension of shipments of new "hot" products, or offer to reinstate if the offending dealers agree to raise their prices (*FTC v. StrideRite,* 1996). Finally, manufacturers cannot lock-in buyers of durable products by refusing to supply parts to independent service organizations (ISOs) especially if the ISO prices are far below the manufacturer's service prices. In *Eastman Kodak v. Image Technical Services* (1992), the Supreme Court argued that buyers of Kodak copiers might not fully estimate the life-cycle repair and maintenance costs of a Kodak-only service contract. Therefore, customers should be able to select independent service and non-warranty repair. Kodak's defense that ISO maintenance and repair failed to meet Kodak's quality standards was disproven by the evidence.

Import Quotas   Another major policy that has supported domestic businesses by restricting competition is the use of import quotas. Faced with tough competition from producers abroad, many U.S. industries have sought restrictions on imports of products from abroad. Most vocal among these industries have been the textile, sugar, steel, and automobile industries. These industries have argued that without restrictions on foreign competition, thousands of U.S. workers would lose their jobs and critical domestic industries could be faced with extinction.

Import quotas inevitably lead to higher prices being paid for goods subject to the import restrictions. For example, in the automobile industry, the U.S. International Trade Commission estimates that the Japanese auto import restrictions had the effect in the early 1980s of increasing the average price for a Japanese car by $1,300, or about 30 percent. Under the import restrictions, the supply of Japanese-made cars fell short of the demand and many dealers were able to charge as much as $1,000 more than the official sticker price for some of the most popular models. In addition, because of the higher prices being charged for Japanese-made vehicles, U.S. manufacturers were able to charge higher prices for their products. Similar restrictions on the importation of microcomputer chips have resulted in significant price increases and shortages of many popular chips.

INTERNATIONAL PERSPECTIVES

The U.S. Sugar Import Quota[16]

www

To learn more about the current U.S. sugar import quota, access the following Internet site maintained by the Foreign Agricultural Service (U.S. Department of Agriculture): http://ffas.usda.gov/itp/imports/sugar-import.html

Since 1982, the United States has imposed quotas on sugar imports to support a domestic price guarantee by the federal government that exceeds world market levels. The high price has stimulated U.S. sugar production and shifts in demand toward other sweeteners, which has necessitated large reductions in sugar import quotas in recent years.

Figure 18.2 illustrates some of the effects of the U.S. trade restrictions in 1983. The lines *SS* and *DD* are the U.S. supply and demand curves for sugar. The world price was 15 cents per pound, and U.S. purchases were assumed to have no effect on this price. With free trade, U.S. production, consumption, and imports would have been 6.14 billion pounds, 19.18 billion pounds, and 13.04 billion pounds, respectively. To raise the internal (U.S.) price to 21.8 cents per pound, a tariff of 2.8 cents per pound and a quota of 5.96 billion pounds were used. The value of the quota is 4.0 cents per pound, because 2.8 cents per pound of the 6.8 cents per pound differential between the U.S. price and the world price is due to the tariff.

The welfare effects of the trade restrictions are indicated by the areas *f*, *g*, *h*, *i*, and *j*. The price-increasing effects of the trade restrictions cause consumers to suffer a loss of consumer surplus equal to $1.266 billion, the sum of areas *f*, *g*, *h*, *i*, and *j*. Producers gain, in the form of producer surplus, area *f*, whose value in $616 million. The U.S. government also gains $167 million in tariff revenue, which is represented by area *i*. Consequently, the net effect for the United States is a loss of $483 million, which is the sum of areas *g*, *j*, and *h*. Area *g* is the loss due to inefficient production and area *j* is the loss due to inefficient consumption. Area *h*, which is equal to $238 million, is the value of the import licenses received by foreign suppliers. In other words, the quota entails a transfer from U.S. consumers to foreign producers of $238 million.

[16] Adapted from C. C. Coughlin and G. E. Wood, "An Introduction to Non-Tariff Barriers to Trade," Federal Reserve Bank of St. Louis, January/February 1989, pp. 32–46.

FIGURE 18.2

The Effects of Trade Restrictions on the U.S. Sugar Market

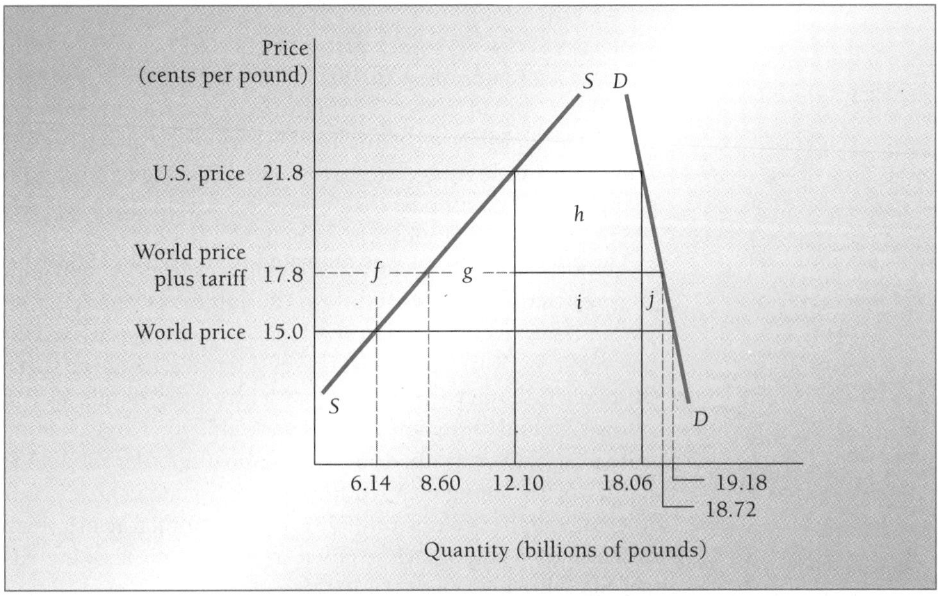

Source: P. Krugman and M. Obstfeld, *International Economics* (Glenview, Ill.: Scott, Foresman, 1988).

The preceding analysis, although effectively highlighting the winners and losers from the U.S. sugar program, is not the entire story. These estimates pertain to one year only. Because the U.S. sugar policy is ongoing, the losses are ongoing as well. In addition, important dynamic interrelationships between policy changes and production and trade changes exist.

There are a number of dynamic consequences of the U.S. sugar program, many stemming from the fact that sugar has several close substitutes. Corn sweeteners, noncaloric sweeteners, honey, and specialty sugars are all close substitutes. Higher sugar prices have induced the production of alternative sweeteners that compete with and, consequently, threaten U.S. sugar producers.

The fact that sugar is used in different goods has set in motion a number of adjustments. Examples abound of the distortions induced by the artificially high U.S. sugar price. For example, the large price differential between U.S. and foreign sugar provides a cost advantage to foreign, especially Canadian, food-processing firms. The sugar policy can be viewed as a tax on U.S. refiners and processors that was not levied on foreign firms.

Trade flows responded to these price changes as a rapid expansion in imports of sugar-containing goods ensued. In fact, the differential between U.S. and world sugar prices became so large at one time that sugar-containing goods were imported solely for their sugar content. For example, during 1985, world sugar prices declined so sharply that, in June 1985, the U.S. sugar price was 776 percent of the world price. This difference induced some firms in the United States to import Canadian pancake mix, which was not subject to the quota, and process it to extract the sugar.

The induced changes in production and trade have forced a number of additional U.S. actions to maintain the sugar prices. For fiscal year 1985, the U.S. sugar import quota was reduced 17 percent. This was followed by reductions of 27.6 percent in 1986 and 45.7 percent in 1987. Trade restrictions on sugar substitutes also have resulted. Two of these are: (1) an emergency ban on imports of certain syrups and blended sugars in bulk in June 1983; and (2) emergency quotas on a broad range of sugar-containing articles in both bulk and retail forms in January 1985.

The increasingly restrictive import barriers have produced tensions with numerous exporters of sugar, most of whom are developing countries. To conform with the General Agreement on Tariffs and Trade (GATT), the import quotas must be applied in a nondiscriminatory fashion. The United States applied this provision by basing its quota allocation on imports during the relatively free-market period of 1975–1981. Attempts to maintain constant shares for most countries, however, ran into practical problems. Countries experiencing rapid growth in sugar exports to the United States between 1975 and 1981 were subjected to substantial cuts between the end of the free-market period and the beginning of the quotas. For example, sugar exports from Honduras were reduced from 93,500 tons in 1981 to 28,000 tons in 1983.

The effect of this cut was mitigated somewhat in 1983 when the United States transferred 52 percent of Nicaragua's quota to Honduras, an action that simultaneously punished the Sandinista regime and rewarded a neighboring state thought to be in danger from the Nicaraguan-supported rebellion. This action violated GATT rules and generated much criticism of the United States. Such a quota system increases the likelihood that trade policy is used for noneconomic reasons.

The lessons from the U.S. sugar program are straightforward. First, significant costs have been imposed on U.S. consumers. Second, the resulting distortions in economic incentives have harmed U.S. producers dependent on sugar. Third, economic responses to the legislation have revealed a number of loopholes that have necessitated additional restrictions and distortions so that U.S. sugar producers could continue to benefit. Fourth, U.S. attempts to ensure fairness have necessitated substantial resources to ascertain production and trade behavior. Finally, the program has been used for political purposes to reward and punish foreign countries.

Direct and Indirect Support

In addition to the assistance that government gives private business by restricting certain forms of competition, it also provides direct and indirect support. These take many forms, including subsidies, government-sponsored research and development programs, and special tax benefits.[17] This kind of support to business occurs at all levels of government and may be granted for a wide variety of motives. The most convincing of these is that the favored activity confers significant external benefits, which firms operating independently in the private sector could not confer or would not take into account in their profit-and-loss performance statements.[18] Nevertheless, these external benefits are deemed appropriate as social benefits by the government and therefore warrant some sort of subsidy support.

Subsidies   The transportation industry has been the recipient of substantial economic subsidies, practically from the beginning of this country. The rationale for this subsidization includes providing common carrier service to all parts of the nation as a stimulus to regional economic development, providing a militarily usable large-scale transportation network in case of war or national disaster, and assisting industrial development by furnishing inexpensive and plentiful logistical support. The earliest recipients of these subsidies were the railroads, and the subsidies were primarily in the form of free land provided along rights of way. Railroad subsidies had all but ceased when the formation of Amtrak to salvage rail passenger service reversed the trend. Other rail subsidies have resulted from the reorganization of six bankrupt Eastern railroads, headed by the Penn Central, into Conrail.

Also, the domestic shipping industry receives substantial aid in the form of largely free operation and maintenance of the navigable waterways.

Government-Sponsored Research and Development   The airline industry is also the recipient of many forms of government subsidy. Airframe manufacturers have long benefited from government-sponsored research and development to discover new technologies for use by the military. Perhaps the most significant such example is the development of the jet engine, which has revolutionized commercial airline transportation.

The electric power industry has received invaluable research and development assistance from the Nuclear Regulatory Commission (and its predecessor, Atomic Energy Commission) as well as generalized R & D aid aimed at developing and perfecting alternative power sources to reduce the impact of the energy crisis.

---

[17] The government also assists private business by entering into partnerships with it, as in the case of Amtrak, the Federal Land Bank (which makes farm loans), the Federal National Mortgage Association (which finances Federal Housing Authority mortgages), the Communications Satellite Corporation, the Federal Deposit Insurance Corporation, the Export-Import Bank, and others. Some of these draw funds solely from the public sector, whereas others tap both the private and public sectors. They all operate in private markets in one way or another, frequently by insuring private risks in the financial markets. The experiences of the FDIC and the now-defunct FSLIC programs indicate just how large these contingent liabilities of the government can be. Losses in the savings and loan program (FSLIC) have exceeded $100 billion, and the final cost to the government is still unknown.

[18] A discussion of externalities is presented later in the appendix to this chapter.

These examples of largely government activities designed to promote private business give some indication of the extent of government involvement.

Tax Benefits   In addition to providing subsidies and research and development aid in support of various industries, tax policy has also been used to support certain industries or economic activities. For example, the extractive industries such as oil, gas, and coal mining have received favorable tax treatment in the form of depletion allowances. Investment in capital equipment has also been encouraged through the provision of investment tax credits and accelerated depreciation allowances to investing firms. And small companies are subject to lower effective tax rates than are large companies, reflecting the government's belief that small business is a valuable institution in a democratic society and that small business provides competition for larger enterprises, thereby keeping prices in check. Also, by permitting individuals to deduct home mortgage interest expenses, tax policy has provided strong support for the housing industry.

Managers must pay close attention to the tax consequences of their actions when making pricing and resource-allocation decisions in their firms.

SUMMARY

- *Market performance* refers to the efficiency of resource allocation within and among firms, the technological progressiveness of firms, the tendency of firms to fully employ resources, and the impact on the equitable distribution of resources.
- *Market conduct* refers to the pricing behavior; the product policy; the sales promotion and advertising policy; the research, development, and innovation strategies; and the legal tactics employed by a firm or group of firms.
- *Market structure* refers to the degree of seller and buyer concentration in a market, the degree of actual or imagined product differentiation between products or services of competing producers, and the conditions surrounding entry into the market.
- Contestable markets are assumed to have freedom of entry and exit for potential competitors. In a perfectly contestable market, the resulting set of prices and outputs approaches those expected under perfect competition.
- Measures of market concentration include
  - Market concentration ratio, defined as the percentage of total industry output attributable to the 4, 8, 20, or 50 largest companies
  - Herfindahl-Hirschman Index (HHI), which is equal to the sum of the squares of the market shares of all firms in an industry
- A group of antitrust laws have been passed to prevent monopoly and to encourage competition in U.S. industry. The most important of these acts are the Sherman Act of 1890, the FTC and Clayton acts of 1914, the Robinson-Patman Act of 1936, the Wheeler-Lea Act of 1938, the Celler-Kefauver Antimerger Act of 1950, and the Hart-Scott-Rodino Antitrust Improvement Act of 1976.
- Federal, state, and local governments all impose regulations on business enterprises. Regulatory constraints can affect a firm's operating costs (both fixed and variable), capital costs, and revenues.
- The current political and economic environment favors a significant reduction in the amount of government regulation and interference in the operation of the private sector of the economy. This has been observable in deregulation in the

banking, transportation, natural gas pipeline, electric utility, and telecommunications industries.

▢ A number of regulatory policies are designed to restrict (or have the impact of restricting) competition. These include licensing; issuing patents, trademarks, and copyrights; and using import controls, such as tariffs and quotas. Price competition has been limited in several industries by various regulatory agencies including the Interstate Commerce Commission, the Federal Energy Regulatory Commission, and the U.S. Maritime Commission.

▢ The Robinson-Patman Act provides a more general form of restriction on price competition. It limits the practice of price discrimination between buyers.

▢ In addition to these activities, government support of business also has taken the more explicit form of direct and indirect subsidies, as in the case of Amtrak, Conrail, and the shipping industries. The rationale for such subsidy support is generally that the favored industry generates significant external benefits for which it would not normally be rewarded in the marketplace. Government-sponsored research and development programs also have benefited certain industries, such as aircraft manufacturers and airlines. Tax policy likewise has been used to support certain industries or economic activities, such as the housing industry.

EXERCISES

1. Under what circumstances would you defend pure competition as the most efficient market structure? What arguments can you make to the contrary?

2. Discuss the proposition that corporate "raiders," such as T. Boone Pickens, Carl Icahn, and Saul Weinberg, are a valuable element in the efficient operation of the economy and that such takeover threats result in long-run benefits to shareholders and more efficient management.

3. An industry is composed of one firm (1) controlling 70 percent of the market, a second firm (2) with 15 percent of the market, and a third firm (3) with 5 percent of the market. Approximately 20 firms of approximately equal size divide the remaining 10 percent of the market. Calculate the Herfindahl-Hirschman Index before and after the merger of Firm 2 and Firm 3 (assume that the combined market share after the merger is 20 percent). Would you view a merger of Firm 2 with Firm 3 as procompetitive or anticompetitive? Explain.

4. How can you justify the existence of government-granted monopolies for such public utilities as local telephone service, natural gas distribution, and electricity in the light of the traditional economic argument that the more competition there is, the more likely it is that an efficient allocation of resources will occur?

5. What are the major factors to be considered, for antitrust purposes, in determining the relevant market in which a firm competes?

6. Suppose an industry is composed of eight firms with the following market shares:

A	30%	E	8
B	25	F	5
C	15	G	4
D	10	H	3

Based on the (revised 1984) merger guidelines, would the Antitrust Division likely challenge a proposed merger between

a. Firms C and D (assume the combined market share is 25 percent)?
b. Firms F and G (assume the combined market share is 9 percent)?
Explain your answer.

7. Evaluate the importance of the concept of price elasticity of demand when attempting to identify the ultimate incidence of the impact of government regulations on business that (a) increase fixed costs and (b) increase variable costs.

8. Discuss the pros and cons of the regulation of oil and natural gas prices.

9. During the 1970s, many banking organizations earned rates of return on common equity that were significantly above the average earned in other U.S. industries. During the mid-1980s, earned returns in the banking industry had declined relative to other U.S. industries. What factors can you identify that might be responsible for this trend?

10. What economic arguments can be made in favor of mandatory seat-belt usage laws in automobiles and mandatory helmet laws for motorcycles?

11. What are the incentives to innovate for a monopoly firm as compared with a firm in a competitive market if patent protection is not available? Does your answer change if patent protection is available?

12. Would you consider the airline industry to be a contestable market? Explain.

13. Specific Motors Corporation is one of the Big Three auto manufacturers in Transylvania. Specific's share of the domestic auto market is 55 percent. The next two closest competitors control 25 and 15 percent of the market, respectively, and the rest may be accounted for by two small, specialized firms. Specific has been under pressure from Transylvania's Justice Department and the State Trade Commission for monopolistic practices. To discourage any attempts to break up Specific, management has decided to maintain its market share below 55 percent of the total domestic automobile sales revenues.

Specific estimates that to stay within its constraint sales of 55 percent of the market, its total sales should not exceed $2.8 billion.

The firm faces the following demand and cost functions:

$$P = 16{,}000 - .02Q$$

$$TC = 850{,}000{,}000 + 4{,}000Q$$

a. Calculate the unconstrained profit-maximizing level of price and output for Specific.
b. At this level, what will total sales revenues be? Total profits?
c. If the firm constrains its sales revenue to $2.8 billion, calculate price, output, and profit levels under the constraint.

(*Hint:* Remember the quadratic formula: $x = \dfrac{-b \pm \sqrt{b^2 - 4ac}}{2a}$

based on the equation $ax^2 + bx + c = 0$.)

d. What is the cost to the firm of this market-share constraint?

14. Seidman Products, Inc. is a manufacturer of chocolate-flavored LTD tablets and aspirin. Each bottle of LTD costs the firm 50 cents in wages and 25 cents in materials to produce. In contrast, the wage and material costs per bottle of aspirin are 25 cents each. All LTD and aspirin that are produced in the period are sold on one-period credit terms. Labor and materials costs for the period must be paid in cash during that period. Liquid resources (cash, collections from previous periods, and bank credit), which are available to pay for labor and material expenses during the

period, are expected to amount to $150. The firm has 60 hours of pill-manufacturing time available during the period and 25 hours of bottling-capacity time.

Each bottle of aspirin requires 9 minutes of manufacturing time and 6 minutes of bottling time. Each bottle of LTD requires 24 minutes of manufacturing time and 3 minutes of bottling time.

Because of the fear of misuse of the LTD if more is produced than is needed to meet pure medical research needs, the Food and Drug Administration has limited LTD output per period to a maximum of 100 bottles.

The selling price of a bottle of aspirin is $2.50. Each bottle of LTD sells for $4.75.

   a.   Formulate this problem in a linear-programming framework. Specify the objective function and all constraints.
   b.   Using the graphic method, solve for the optimal output mix between aspirin and LTD.
   c.   What is the cost to the firm of the FDA output restriction on LTD production?
   d.   As president of Seidman Products, what resources would you seek to increase to expand your firm's profits?

15.   The industry demand function for bulk plastics is represented by the following equation:

$$P = 800 - 20Q$$

where Q represents millions of pounds of plastic.

The total cost function for the industry, exclusive of a required return on invested capital is

$$TC = 300 + 500Q + 10Q^2$$

where Q represents millions of pounds of plastic.

   a.   If this industry acts like a monopolist in the determination of price and output, compute the profit-maximizing level of price and output.
   b.   What are total profits at this price and output level?
   c.   Assume that this industry is comprised of many (500) small firms, such that the demand function facing any individual firm is

$$P = \$620$$

Compute the profit-maximizing level of price and output under these conditions (the industry's total cost function remains unchanged).

   d.   What are total profits, given your answer to part (c)?
   e.   Because of the risk of this industry, investors require a 15 percent rate of return on the investment made in this industry. Total industry investment amounts to $2 billion. If the monopoly solution prevails [parts (a) and (b)], how would you describe the profits of the industry?
   f.   If the competitive solution most accurately describes the industry, is the industry operating under equilibrium conditions? Why or why not? What would you expect to happen?
   g.   The Clean Water Coalition has proposed pollution control standards for the industry that would change the industry cost curve to

$$TC = 400 + 560Q + 10Q^2$$

What is the impact of this change on price, output, and total profits under the monopoly solution?

h. Assume these standards are being proposed only in the state of Texas, which has 50 of the 500 producers. What impact would you expect the new standards to have on Texas firms? The rest of the industry?

16. A product you produce has the following annual demand function:

$$P = 90 - .003Q$$

The marginal cost of producing the product is $30. If the firm pays a fee of $50,000 to the General Drug Research Council, it can have its product's effectiveness certified. The demand function for a certified product is expected to be

$$P = 100 - .003Q$$

a. Calculate the price, output, and profit contribution if the product is not certified.
b. Calculate the price, output, and profit contribution if the product is certified.
c. Should the firm undergo the certification process?

17. Assume an industry produces a relatively homogeneous product, such that all sales must be made at approximately the same price. Assume also that the industry is dominated by one large firm but a fringe of smaller, competitive firms exists. Fringe competitors and potential new entrants are so small in size that they have no perceptible influence on price.

Discuss graphically or verbally the pricing strategies available to the dominant firm:

a. If the profit-maximizing price charged by the dominant firm is below the lowest attainable average total cost (including normal profits) for the smaller existing competitive firms and potential entrants.
b. If the profit-maximizing price charged by the dominant firm exceeds the competitive fringe firms' lowest attainable average costs, including a normal profit. Would you expect a different strategy to be followed if the dominant firm sought to maximize short-run rather than long-run profits?
c. If the dominant firm is relatively unsure of the industry's future or perceives a rapidly changing technology in the industry such that an optimal scale of operation can be achieved with an increasingly small plant size. What strategy would you expect the dominant firm to follow?
d. If the dominant firm adopts a long-run strategy to deter new entry. Explain how the use of full-cost pricing rules can lead to nearly maximum long-run profits.

18. Public Service Company has been disappointed by its failure to be allowed to earn what it considers to be a fair return on its investment in utility assets. The firm has averaged a return on equity of 12 percent over the past 10 years, with a standard deviation of 3 percent. It is considering a series of acquisitions that, when complete, would roughly double the firm's size. The expected return on equity from these new activities is 19 percent, with a standard deviation of 7 percent. Based on past performance, the correlation between returns in the utility business and returns in the other businesses is expected to be +0.3.

a. Calculate the expected return and risk of the returns for the Public Service Company before and after the acquisitions.

[*Hint:* A general formula for the risk (standard deviation) of two assets' returns is

$$\sigma_T = \sqrt{w_A^2 \sigma_A^2 + w_B^2 \sigma_B^2 + 2w_A w_B \rho_{AB} \sigma_A \sigma_B}$$

where w_A and w_B are the proportions invested in assets A and B, respectively, and $w_A + w_B = 1$; σ_A and σ_B are the standard deviations of returns for assets A and B, respectively; and ρ_{AB} is the correlation of returns from assets A and B.]

b. Recalculate the expected return and risk of the Public Service Company after completing the acquisitions if the acquisitions are two times the size of the utility business of Public Service Company; that is, w_A = proportion of utility assets = 0.333 and w_B = proportion of acquired assets = 0.667.

c. What other potential benefits can you see being derived from this program of diversification?

d. What regulatory problems can you perceive when a utility diversifies outside of the regulated sector of the economy?

19. An industry produces its product, Scruffs, at a constant marginal cost of $50. The market demand for Scruffs is equal to

$$Q = 75,000 - 600P$$

a. What is the value to a monopolist who is able to develop a patented process for producing Scruffs at a cost of only $45?

b. If the industry producing Scruffs is purely competitive, what is the maximum benefit that an inventor of a process that will reduce the cost of producing Scruffs by $5 per unit can expect to receive by licensing her invention to the firms in the industry?

20. The demand curve in a competitive industry has been estimated to be

$$P = 1,500 - 9Q$$

The industry's short-run supply curve is

$$P = 80 + 3Q$$

A single firm emerges as the dominant firm in the industry and gradually acquires all of the other firms in the industry. The marginal cost curve for the monopolist becomes

$$MC = 50 + 3Q$$

as a result of effecting a number of operating economies.

a. Calculate the competitive market's price and output levels.

b. Calculate the price and output levels for the industry once the monopolist assumes control, assuming that industry demand remains unchanged.

c. If this monopolist were regulated so that the maximum price the monopolist is allowed to charge is $450, what is the benefit to consumers and the cost to the monopolist?

21. If OPEC agrees to raise the price of oil by $3 a barrel and if all other world oil prices increase by a similar amount, is the economic cost to consumers equal to $3 a barrel, something more, or something less?

www exercise

Price Discrimination

22. In this chapter you have learned about the circumstances under which a firm with market power would engage in price discrimination. Access the following Internet site maintained by Anthony Becker: http://www.stolaf.edu/people/becker/antitrust/ subject.html. This site contains summaries of U.S. Supreme Court cases involving antitrust; scroll down to the material on price discrimination. Learn more about U.S. antitrust law as it relates to price discrimination by reading one or more of the case summaries. The case of Texaco, Inc., v. Ricky Hasbrouk (496 U.S. 543) is particularly useful in illustrating the test applied by the U.S. Supreme Court for illegal price discrimination: http://www.stolaf.edu/people/becker/antitrust/summaries/496us543.html

Economic Externalities and Market Failure

EXTERNALITIES

Economic externalities are one of several causes of the private market mechanism's failure to achieve an efficient allocation of societal resources. This appendix takes a closer look at the problem and examines several proposed public policy remedies.

The Importance of Externalities

Managers in both the public and private sectors are faced with many decisions influenced by economic externalities. The private sector manager needs to be aware that economic externalities are often generated by the firm in the normal course of its business. Such an awareness allows the firm to consciously consider ways of reducing negative externalities in the normal course of its business or of emphasizing to the public the positive externalities (social benefits) that the firm generates and for which it is not compensated by the market. *Furthermore, the private manager has a strong interest in the kinds of remedies adopted by society (the government) for controlling externalities at the least cost.*

The public sector manager also needs to be aware of the nature and sources of economic externalities. Many public enterprises also generate these effects in the normal course of their activities. When these are negative, appropriate actions must be taken to control the problem. More importantly, perhaps, the full extent of positive externalities should be understood by the public manager because these benefits often provide the justification for maintaining or expanding a public program. In the role of a regulator, the public manager must understand the scope of remedies available and the strengths and weaknesses of each.

Externalities Defined

Externalities

Impacts that occur whenever a third party receives benefits or bears costs arising from an economic transaction in which he or she is not a direct participant. An example would be the effects of industrial pollution on area residents.

Externalities *exist when a third party receives benefits or bears costs arising from an economic transaction in which he or she is not a direct participant.*[19] This occurs when *producers* or *consumers* provide benefits to others (the third party) for which the market system does not enable them to receive full payment in return. Thus when a firm provides workers with new skills through job training, the firm is not only furnishing a base for its own increased productivity but also simultaneously expanding the pool of skilled labor from which other firms may benefit; that is, when a worker moves from one employer to another, it is difficult for the first employer to charge the second for skills

---

[19] In viewing the externality problem, one must recognize that externalities exist primarily because of an incomplete definition of property rights in the laws. As we see later in this appendix, one solution to externality problems is to define property rights more completely and to incorporate this expanded definition into the legal structure.

provided to the employee. Similarly, producers or consumers may inflict costs on a third party for which the market does not require them to bear commensurate costs in return. A commuter, for example, may decide to drive rather than use public transportation to get to work in the morning. This results in additional road congestion and costs (in terms of the opportunity cost of lost time as well as greater operating expenses) to all those who had already been using the roads. This commuter, however, looks only at personal costs, both operating costs and the value of commuting time, in deciding whether to drive or use public transportation.

Another way of viewing externalities is to say that they exist when significant interactions occur between the utility functions of individuals and the production functions of firms, or a combination of production and utility functions, not recognized by the market mechanism. For instance, in the case of an individual's utility function, an externality is said to be present if

$$u^x = u^x(W_1, W_2, W_3, \ldots, W_n, Z_1) \tag{18A.1}$$

The utility of individual X is a function of Activities W_1 through W_n, which are under X's control, but also of Activity Z_1, which is under the control of some other individual. In such cases, when each individual pursues his or her own self-interest and attempts to maximize his or her personal utility function or allocate productive resources in the most profitable manner, the individual may end up less well off under the private market solution than under some modified or partially controlled market arrangement. The usual marginal conditions for an optimal allocation of resources do not apply here, and resources will likely be misallocated. That is, the economic system only gives partial signals to producers and consumers regarding their respective profit and utility-maximizing decisions. As a result, society as a whole will be less well off when externalities exist and are not recognized in resource-allocation decisions. In an economy dominated by pure competition, for example, it is easy to see how the existence of externalities will result in a misallocation of resources. As we saw in Chapter 12, the equilibrium condition under pure competition is one in which the long-run marginal costs (the costs to society and the firm) of providing one more unit of output are just equal to price (the value society or consumers place on this additional output). If, however, the producer of a product were to generate by-products or other costs in the production process for which payment did not have to be made, the $P = MC$ solution is no longer ideal. The true marginal costs of production will be somewhat higher and the private market solution will allocate an inappropriately large amount of resources to the production of this commodity. Conversely, when benefits of consumption are conferred with little or no cost on others in addition to the immediate consumer, the price or societal value of this commodity will be artificially low, and output will be set at a suboptimally low level.

Thus, when externalities exist there is a divergence between private returns—those accruing to the *direct* parties in an economic transaction—and social returns—those accruing to the direct plus *indirect* parties in such a transaction.

Production Externalities

External Production Economies   *External production economies* are said to occur when an increase in one firm's production generates benefits accruing to others that may not normally be recaptured through the market mechanism by the producing firm. External economies of this sort may arise, for example, if a firm decides to increase its plant size in some locality. The new, larger plant may require that rail service be provided to handle the increased output of the firm. If this service is provided, it benefits not only the firm that induced the extended rail service but also all other firms and individuals in the community who now have access to a new, lower-cost source of transportation. Another type of external economy of production may arise when the expansion of output of one firm—for example, a large appliance manufacturer—makes it less costly for other metal fabricators to acquire needed raw material. This may occur if the appliance manufacturer buys from a steel firm operating in the range of increasing returns to scale. As a result of the new orders, prices may fall and all other steel purchasers will also benefit from these lower prices.

In both these instances there is a divergence between private and social benefits, with social benefits exceeding those recapturable by the private firm that initially expanded its output and consequently generated the externality.

External Production Diseconomies   *External diseconomies of production* arise when a firm's production results in uncompensated costs or detriments to others. External production diseconomies are real costs of production that, until they are internalized either voluntarily or by legal requirement, are escaped by the private business firm. Thus, although the associated social costs are not "relevant" costs to managerial decision making, they always have the potential to become relevant if management is overcome by social conscience or the law. These costs are borne by others dependent on the same resources for their own production processes. Once again, the market system fails to account for all relevant costs in the resource-allocation decisions of autonomous enterprises or municipalities.

Other common examples of external diseconomies of production are apparent in the case of oil spills, excessive use of dangerous pesticides, airport noise, traffic congestion, and urban renewal.

Consumption Externalities

External Consumption Economies   When the utility functions of individuals are interdependent, as in Equation 18A.1, an increase in consumption by one consumer may have either advantageous or disadvantageous effects on another. When an action taken by one consumer results in uncompensated benefits to other consumers, we say there are *external economies of consumption*. If X provides an excellent education for his children, this presumably makes them better citizens and benefits others in society. Similarly, if Y replaces her noisy, 20-year-old central air conditioner with a new, quieter model or renovates her urban rowhouse that previously posed an eyesore, the benefits largely accrue to the neighbors.

External Consumption Diseconomies   When an action taken by one consumer results in uncompensated detriments or costs to others, we say there are *external diseconomies of consumption*. One example is the traffic congestion externality discussed in Chapter 17. Another example is the standard drainage problem. Mr. Jones's home is next to a vacant lot. Because both lots are very flat, drainage is a problem. Consequently, when Jones built his home he had it placed on a slab much higher than the surrounding land and then graded and filled in his lot so that the water would run onto the vacant property. Some years passed and then Smith built on the vacant lot. Being a reasonably astute man, he built his home even higher than Jones's, reversing the drainage problem. As a result of Smith's action, Jones is now forced to install an underground drain system at considerable expense—a clear case of an external diseconomy of consumption.

Interaction of Production and Consumption Externalities

Thus far we have dealt with externalities of consumption and production as completely separable phenomena. It should be apparent, however, that producers may impose externalities on consumers and vice versa. Indeed, some of our most significant pollution problems are of just this kind. Pollution in the Los Angeles basin may diminish the demand for the Pasadena Sightseeing Company or it may impair the health of a region's residents.

Although the isolated examples of externalities that we have cited may seem rather trivial taken by themselves, the sum of externalities generated in any one economy may assume enormous significance. They help to explain why underdeveloped countries or urban ghettos find it difficult to attract industry from more developed regions where skilled labor, easy access, well-developed financial institutions, and suppliers are all readily available. Likewise, the fact that the market system requires that little or no cost be incurred by those using air and water resources as industrial and municipal sewers explains the increased problem of, and concern with, environmental quality. Consumption externalities also play a significant role in most societies. Housing patterns, eating habits, and dress standards differ widely from country to country because the utility functions of consumers, and hence their consumption patterns, are highly interdependent. Fashion and style trends are frequently visible evidence of such interdependencies.

Public Sector Externalities

Externalities occur in the public as well as the private sector. One local government may dispose of its sewage in a fashion that imposes additional treatment costs on another downstream town. This is the case of many communities located along the Schuylkill River from which Philadelphia draws much of its drinking water. Similarly, a major metropolitan power company may resort to nuclear energy to supply the metropolitan region and then expose both urban and rural areas to the dangers associated with the transportation and storage of nuclear wastes.

At the federal level, spillovers or externalities are often evident between agencies. For example, the Public Health Service Hospital at Staten Island, New York, is said to have been dumping 7,500 gallons of untreated sewage per day into upper New York Bay as well as placing a heavy burden on New York's regular sewage disposal system. In Los Angeles the buses run by the Rapid Transit District are exempt from the same smog checks that private vehicles, buses, and trucks must pass.

Pecuniary Externalities
External effects that are reflected in prices and therefore result in no inefficiency.

Pecuniary Externalities

Caution needs to be exercised in order that the secondary price effects of a transaction are not confused with the true instances of externalities discussed in the preceding two sections. True externalities are effects that are not conveyed through the price system. Remember that the nature of externalities is that they take place outside, or external to, the market price system. Thus when one's preference for meat shifts from beef to mutton, the price of beef will fall and that of mutton will rise. Beef producers will be worse off and mutton producers will be better off because of the price change. At the same time beef consumers will be better off, while mutton consumers will be worse off. But all of these interdependencies have operated through the market price system and no *true* externality exists. In fact, such price impacts (or "pecuniary externalities") are the primary ingredient of the marketplace.

The legal doctrine of "coming to the nuisance" in *Spur Industries v. Del Webb Development* illustrates the principle that pecuniary externalities result in no inefficiency. If the land you purchase for an eventual subdivision development is located next to a cattle feedlot, the price you pay per acre will reflect the stench. The reduced price of the land will internalize the spillover effects. Later, if residents of the subdivision complain about the stench and the feedlot is declared a public nuisance, you the developer may have to pay to relocate the cattle feeding business. Again, when external effects *are* reflected in prices, all affected parties directly participate in the transaction; there is no inefficiency.

Economic Externalities and Resource Allocation

When externalities are present, resources are likely to be misallocated by producers or consumers whether the externality is beneficial to its recipients or not. If producers or consumers make a contribution to society's well-being for which they are not compensated, they are less likely to engage in the action generating the external benefit (social contribution) than if they were fully reimbursed for all benefits generated. Similarly in the case of external diseconomies, a producer or consumer will likely overallocate resources to some production or consumption activity if part of the costs of engaging in this activity is shifted to others. The reason for this likely misallocation of resources is that when externalities exist, the price system fails to provide the correct signals to firms making output and resource-allocation decisions. In the case of external diseconomies, only part of the costs of production or consumption are considered—those that the firm must pay or that it imputes in terms of its opportunity costs. Similarly, when external economies are present, market price is no longer an adequate measure of social benefit.

The Reciprocal Nature of Externalities

One characteristic of externalities that must be emphasized before moving to a discussion of possible solutions is that *it takes at least two to create an externality.* For example, power plants located in the middle of the desert impose only minor social costs on distant areas until people move to the vicinity of the power plant. The more people who live in the area of the plant, the greater are the externalities. Thus if more residents move into the area of the power plant, they may seek an injunction against the power plant to stop polluting. But remember, the power plant imposed little or no cost on anyone until the new residents moved into the vicinity of the plant. Although the plant imposes costs on the residents, the granting of an injunction against the plant imposes costs on the power company. In an instance such as this, it is not altogether clear exactly who has caused the externality and who should bear the liability. Should the power plant be forced to pay to reduce pollution, or should the new residents have to pay the cost of installing pollution-abatement equipment?

The problem of "Who should pay?" may be solved in a number of ways, although it often boils down to who has the greatest negotiating or political strength. Ronald Coase has shown that an efficient solution to externalities can generally be achieved if the creator of the externality (pollution, for example) and the recipient of the externality get together and reach an agreement through bargaining.[20] No matter who pays, however, the general principle of how much of society's resources should be allocated to solving the externality problem is clear. *An external cost, for example, should be reduced up to the point where the marginal costs of any further reduction just equal the marginal benefits to society from the reduction. Similarly, an action that generates external benefits should be expanded to the point where the marginal benefits to all of society from such an expansion just equal the societal marginal costs of gaining the benefit.*

---

[20] Ronald Coase, "The Problem of Social Cost," *Journal of Law and Economics* 2 (October 1960), pp. 1–44.

EXAMPLE

COASE'S RAILROAD

Among the numerous examples in Ronald Coase's famous paper "The Problem of Social Cost," perhaps the most discussed is a reciprocal externality between a spark-throwing railroad and a farmer with adjacent flammable fields. Coase's ingenious and intriguing claim was that under certain conditions involving full information and low transaction costs, the direction of liability assignment had no effect on the resource allocation decisions of these parties. In particular, if the railroad had the property right to throw sparks along its right-of-way, the trains scheduled down this track and the acreage planted along it would be exactly the same as if the railroad had liability for spark-induced damages. To see how compensatory side payments and minimally sufficient bribes operate to achieve this remarkable result through Coasian bargaining, consider the payoffs in Table 18A.1.

If the railroad has the property right (i.e., Table 18A.1a), the farmer incurs $600 worth of crop destruction per train per 10 acres planted along the tracks. Initially, the railroad ignores these external, spillover costs and chooses an activity level of trains that maximizes its own profit (i.e., two trains in the bottom row of Table 18A.1a). The farmer would plant 10 rather than 20 acres along the tracks in order to earn $300 and avoid losing $800 (in the extreme southeast cell). If there were impediments to bargaining, no further action would take place in an unregulated laissez-faire market environment. However, a mutually beneficial private voluntary bargaining opportunity exists. If the railroad were to cut back to one train, the farmer's profit would rise from $300 to $900. Yet, the railroad's profit declines from $1,500 to only $1,000. Accordingly, $501 is a minimally sufficient bribe to elicit the lower train-activity level, and $600 is the savings in fewer crops burned. Thus, Coase predicted that if the parties have few impediments to bargaining, the farmer would offer a sidepayment sufficient to abate the incremental (second) train and its spark hazard, because the second train is worth less (to the railroad) than the incremental agricultural losses cost the farmer. Just how much the farmer will pay and how little the railroad will accept is not addressed, but one thing is clear.

TABLE 18A.1   Coasian Bargaining

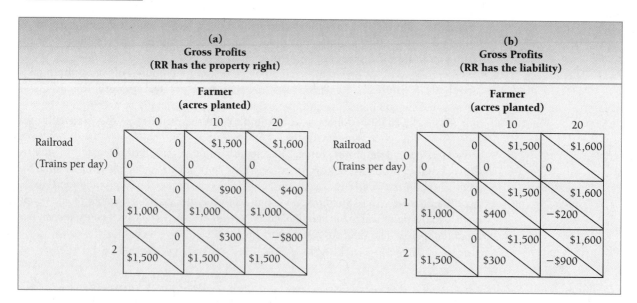

Potential gains from trade do motivate a bargain to reduce railroad activity from two trains to one, and the farmer plants 10 acres.

Now, consider the case in which the railroad has the liability for spark-induced crop damages. Initially, the farmer prepares to plant 20 acres along the tracks as this activity level maximizes his or her independent profit (at $1,600). However, no trains are profitable with this much acreage in production since $600 in damages per train per 10 acres (i.e., $1,200 altogether) is owed when the railroad has $1,000 gross profit with one train, and $2,400 in damages is owed when the railroad has $1,500 gross profit with two trains. But, suppose the railroad offered to compensate the farmer for not only crop damages but also lost profit if the farmer would plant fewer acres. In particular, the railroad can offer the farmer $101 to plant 1 acre rather than 2 acres since the gross profit differs by only $100 (i.e., $1,500 versus $1,600). If the railroad then also compensates the farmer $600 for one train's crop damage on 10 acres, the railroad owes $701 and earns a gross profit of $1,000. Table 18A.1b displays the net profits once crop damages have been compensated. Directing your attention to the middle row of Table 18A.1b, the railroad offers the farmer compensation in excess of $100 to scale back the acreage planted from 20 acres where farmer gross profit is $1,600 to 10 acres where farmer gross profit is $1,500. This reallocation of activities is worth $600 in damage savings to the railroad. Again, Coasian bargaining leads the parties to agree upon one train and 10 acres.

The Coase Theorem

Coase Theorem

A prediction about the role of private voluntary bargaining in reciprocal externalities with low transaction costs.

The **Coase Theorem** makes no claim about the distributional consequences of reversing the direction of a liability assignment. Quite obviously, making the railroad liable in one instance and asking the farmer to cover his or her own crop losses in the other, results in quite different net profit outcomes. However, what the Coase Theorem does assert is that in reciprocal externality settings, resource allocation as to the externality-generating and externality-receiving activity levels will be unchanged independent of the liability assignment. One train will be scheduled, and 10 acres will be planted

Some powerful qualifications are in order, many of which Coase himself recognized. First, technical transaction costs of searching for and identifying the responsible owners and affected parties, of detecting violations of one's property rights, and of internally negotiating the sidepayments or bribes (say, within a group of claimants), all these transaction costs must remain low and be unaffected by the reversal of the liability assignment. Second, neither party can operate in a purely competitive market, for then the profits required for sidepayments and bribes would be nonexistent. And, third, and perhaps most importantly, one party quickly makes an offer the other is just willing to accept only when the information regarding the payoffs in Table 18A.1a or Table 18A.1b is complete, certain and known to both parties. When information is incomplete and impacted, private voluntary bargaining need not lead to resource allocation that is invariant to the direction of liability assignment. And this asymmetric information qualification to the Coase Theorem holds even if property rights are fully specified, completely assigned, and costlessly enforced.

The problem presented by asymmetric information is present in all negligence situations where *reported* damages and the precautionary actions of the plaintiff and the defendant have some bearing on the assignment of liability. For example, the parties in Coase's railroad example would avoid liability in part by employing spark arresters or land set-backs as long as the benefit in crop-loss savings exceeded the cost. However, the problem posed by asymmetric information is that some aspects of precaution are inherently unobservable or unverifiable (e.g., attentiveness to subtle signals of impending hazard) while others are observable but affect accident avoidance in a non-deterministic way (e.g., good brakes may lock up on rain-slickened roads when less effective brakes would not). Uncertainty and unobservability together result in the problem of moral hazard, which we discussed in Chapter 13. There is no incentive-compatible mechanism that can both preserve the voluntary nature of the Coasian bargaining and also elicit true revelation of the unobservable damages. Therefore, contrary to the traditional understanding of the Coase Theorem, disputants in reciprocal externality conflicts might be expected not to engage in private voluntary bargaining but rather to delegate the question of damage assessment and recovery to third-party court systems. Civil procedural rules can be seen as credible commitment mechanisms by which potential disputants bind themselves to liability assignments and wealth transfer remedies that motivate efficient accident avoidance despite frequently asymmetric information.[21]

POSSIBLE SOLUTIONS TO THE EXTERNALITIES PROBLEM

The foregoing discussion leads to the conclusion that when externalities are present, the market mechanism is likely to fail to achieve an efficient allocation of societal resources. In such instances, intervention of some sort or another may be necessary to force firms to internalize negative externalities. Unfortunately, the range of externalities that exists, the constraints of political decision-making processes, the problems of accurately measuring the costs or benefits of any particular externality, and the existence of transaction costs incurred in applying a particular solution to a particular problem make it impossible to identify any one correct solution to the problem. Accordingly, this section enumerates several proposed solutions and discusses their relative merits.

Solution by Prohibition

One simple approach to solving problems created by externalities is merely to prohibit the action that generates the external effects. A little reflection on most externality problems, however, should indicate that in most cases this is at least nonoptimal and frequently impractical. Auto emissions could be cut to zero if autos were banned, but the effects of such a move, at least in the short run, would be disastrous. Pollution in the Houston Ship Channel or the Detroit River could practically be abolished if industries and municipalities were no longer permitted to dump any of their waste products there. But employment would also grind to a halt in the short run in these areas if such a step were taken. Furthermore, an optimal solution does not require that externalities be completely eliminated, but that the *right amount* of them be eliminated. In the case of air and water, both of these resources have the capacity to assimilate wastes up to a certain level. A strict zero-pollution policy would entail a waste of some resources.

Solution by Directive

The problem of controlling externalities is to get just the right amount of them; that is, to attempt to eliminate an externality up to the point where the marginal costs of further reductions are just equal to the marginal benefits derived therefrom. We have seen

---

[21] For further discussion of asymmetric information as a qualification of the Coase Theorem, see J. Farrell, "Information and the Coase Theorem," *Journal of Economic Perspectives,* Fall 1987, pp. 113–137 and F. H. B. Harris, "Economic Negligence, Moral Hazard, and the Coase Theorem," *Southern Economic Journal,* 56(3), January 1990, pp. 698–704.

that outright prohibition may be suboptimal, so another possibility that has been suggested is to let the government decide how much of the externality may be produced. This is the approach that has been used in setting auto emission standards. This approach also suffers from serious weaknesses. First, one problem is determining just how much of an externality should be permitted. This requires in theory that costs and benefits of various levels of reduction be compared. But in many instances, estimating the benefits of various levels of pollution reduction, for example, is nearly impossible. Second, even if an overall standard could be agreed on, when multiple sources of pollution are in an area, each of the polluting entities must in turn be directed how it should act. A simple proportionate distribution of "pollution rights" is likely to be suboptimal because the costs of achieving various levels of pollution reduction may vary dramatically from industry to industry. Optimality, however, requires that the marginal effectiveness of the last dollar spent by each polluter be equated.

Solution by Voluntary Payment

Some have argued that when externalities exist, collective action may not be necessary because it is in the interest of private parties to voluntarily take the appropriate action. If a foul-smelling paper mill plant is located in a community, there is likely to be a divergence between the private and social cost or the private and social benefit of paper production. To avoid the foul smells, the community might seek to pay the plant to reduce or eliminate the odor discharges. Optimality (and good sense) requires that the payment not exceed the value of the damage suffered by the community. The paper mill should accept the payment if it exceeds the costs of reducing the foul odors generated and reject the payment if it is less than the cost of odor reduction. Although the voluntary payment solution is certainly consistent with *Pareto optimality* (everyone is better off and no one is worse off in this case), some problems exist. First, how is the community to value the odor damage? Individual citizens are likely to understate their willingness to pay to reduce the odors in hopes that their neighbors will provide sufficient funds to get the desired reduction. Second, in a dynamic economic system, demand for paper may rise causing the mill to increase output. New and greater payments would have to be offered as demand rose.

Impediments to Bargaining   Several impediments to private voluntary bargaining as a mechanism for resolving externalities are well recognized in the legal system. Information costs regarding sources of the externality and search costs to identify absentee owners and all the affected parties are the justification for certifying class action suits. Class actions prove critical to reducing these transaction costs in the case of oil spills and other large scale disasters affecting many claimants. Voluntary private bargaining about incompatible uses also is impeded by the need for continuous monitoring and enforcement. However, unquestionably the most significant impediment to bargaining in large numbers externality cases is the strategic hold-out or strategic free-rider problem. When a court grants an injunction against a polluter's operation, relief from the injunction may necessitate securing unanimous waiver from the affected parties. If many claimants are certified as possessing such a right of waiver, each claimant has an incentive to hold out for more compensation than would be required to cover his or her damages. The predictable presence of strategic hold-outs short circuits the private voluntary bargaining hypothesized by the Coase Theorem to resolve the externality. In such cases, the courts therefore adopt other mechanisms involving liability rules and the payment of permanent damages.

| EXAMPLE |

BOOMER V. ATLANTIC CEMENT

In the early 1970s, a large cement plant valued at $45 million spewed cement dust regularly across a neighborhood of Albany, New York. Some of the affected households were unable to continue their laundry operations; others suffered the inconvenience of airborne small particulates requiring frequenting washing and repainting of their cars and homes. The Atlantic Cement plant was declared a public nuisance, and the court chose among three types of injunctions: 1) an order to cease operations until the air pollution could be abated, 2) an order to cease operations until a waiver could be obtained from each household in the affected neighborhood, or 3) an order declaring the cement plant liable for $185,000 in permanent damages and requiring a cessation of operations until these court-specified damages were paid. Since the first injunction hinged on undeveloped technology, and the second created strategic hold-outs, the New York Court of Appeals opted for the third alternative. Although the court, in effect, thereby licensed the on-going nuisance for a one-time-only fee of $185,000, no private voluntary bargain to reduce the cement dust could have overcome the strategic free-rider/strategic hold-out problem. And, having to pay court-mandated damages, the plant's owners did begin to internalize the social cost of cement production when establishing plants in other locations.

Solution by Merger

When the entities generating and absorbing the externalities are firms, merger is a very attractive but limited way of internalizing externalities. If a paper mill is polluting a stream so that a chemical firm downstream must make large expenditures on water purification before using the water in its processes, the problem may be eliminated by a merger of the two firms. After the merger, it is in the best interests of the new firm to consider the chemical plant's purification costs in determining what quality of effluent should be emitted from the paper mill. A merger solution has two problems. First, it is feasible only when the entities involved are firms—or perhaps municipal or regional water, air, or transportation authorities. Second, as the number of entities increases, the possibility of effecting a merger decreases.

Solution by Taxes and Subsidies

One solution to externalities problems, which has long been favored by economists, is to provide subsidies (either in the form of cash or tax relief) to those whose activities generate significant external benefits and to tax those whose activities create external costs. Such a tax and subsidy scheme, however, requires a tremendous amount of information if it is to be administered in an optimal fashion. A tax and subsidy approach differs only slightly from the solution-by-directive approach. Rather than issuing directives to individual firms about the quantities of each pollutant (or external benefits, such as clean water) that each is permitted, the tax and subsidy scheme seeks to do this indirectly by setting taxes or providing subsidies that will maximize overall societal benefit. Thus it is subject to the same weaknesses discussed in the case of solution by directive. In spite of these problems, a less than perfect attempt at achieving an optimal allocation of resources may be justified if the societal costs of a continued external diseconomy or of a less than optimal external economy are large enough. In deciding on an approach, the cost of gaining the information necessary to arrive at an optimal solution needs to be weighed against the societal losses that accrue if nothing is done or if some other imperfect solution is adopted.

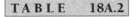

TABLE   18A.2

Interdependent of
Investment Returns:
Two Property Owners

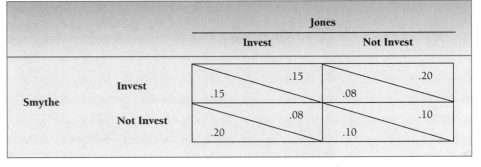

		Jones	
		Invest	**Not Invest**
Smythe	**Invest**	.15 / .15	.20 / .08
	Not Invest	.08 / .20	.10 / .10

properties. They have an additional amount available to invest in the properties. This sum is currently invested in corporate bonds yielding 10 percent. If neither Smythe nor Jones invests additional funds in real estate, they will continue to earn the 10 percent return, as is indicated in the "Not invest–Not invest" cell. Alternatively, if both decide to invest and upgrade their properties, they will each earn a return of 15 percent.

When Smythe invests and Jones does not, or vice versa, the one who redevelops earns only 8 percent because the new building is still in a predominantly old neighborhood, whereas the one who does not invest gets the benefits from the improvement in the neighboring property with no additional required outlay of funds. Let us see why this might occur. If Jones demolishes her old building and builds a new one complete with off-street parking and other attractions, this would mean that Smythe's tenants would, for example, have a better chance to find on-street parking spaces. In addition, Smythe's tenants might value living next to some higher-income people and having their children mix with each other. As a result Smythe may be able to raise his rents somewhat. Jones, however, is not so lucky, because potential renters would have to evaluate the neighborhood (including Smythe's old building). Consequently, Jones could not charge the rents she would like. Thus Jones's return is only 8 percent, whereas Smythe gets a 20 percent return.

Being aware of the possible outcomes indicated in Table 18A.2, both Smythe and Jones might decide not to invest. Let us examine the payoff matrix from Smythe's point of view. If Jones invests, Smythe can get a return of 15 percent if he also invests, but a 20 percent return by not investing. If Jones does not invest, the best Smythe can hope for is a 10 percent return by also not investing. Thus no matter what Jones does, Smythe is better off not investing. Similar logic follows for Jones. Each player, acting in his or her own self-interest in the absence of cooperation, will decide *not to invest* and will thus receive only a 10 percent return. But this solution is not optimal, because they could both receive a 15 percent payoff by getting together and agreeing to redevelop their properties. In the simple two-person case illustrated here, voluntary cooperation is likely. However, as the number of property owners in an area increases, the chances of effecting such voluntary cooperation diminish rapidly.

Another possibility is that some third party might step in, purchase both properties (thereby internalizing the externalities), and receive the 15 percent return on each. This does in fact happen quite often. For instance, Texas Eastern Transmission purchased a 30-square block area in Houston for redevelopment. But without the public right of eminent domain, there is always the chance that some of the property owners will refuse to sell in order to reap the externalities of development themselves, or they may hold out for such a high price that it expropriates part of the expected profits of the developer.

This example illustrates that because of the externalities that exist in the real estate area, there may be serious impediments to privately initiated urban renewal. As the number of properties in need of renewal increases, the impediments to private action also increase. Because of these problems, we often see urban renewal take place under government sponsorship.

In this section we have briefly introduced several of the approaches that have been proposed for, or used in, the solution to externalities problems. It should be apparent that no one best solution exists for all cases. Because of the great diversity of externality problems, appropriate policies must be tailored to meet the specific problem, while comparing the costs and benefits of alternative solutions. Policymakers may then be guided in their decision making to choose that alternative where net benefits are likely to be maximized and the social costs are effectively internalized, forcing firms to treat social costs as a part of their relevant costs for decision-making purposes.

SUMMARY

- Economic externalities exist when a third party receives benefits or bears costs arising from an economic transaction in which he or she is not a direct participant. The impact of economic externalities is felt outside of (external to) the normal market pricing and resource-allocation mechanism.
- When economic externalities exist, resources are likely to be misallocated through the market pricing mechanism.
- Many possible solutions to problems of economic externalities exist. These include solution by prohibition, solution by directive, solution by voluntary payment, solution by merger, solution by taxes and subsidies, solution by sale of rights to create the externality, and solution by regulation.
- Coase has shown that an efficient allocation of resources can generally be achieved in the face of externalities if the creator and recipient of the externality get together and reach an agreement on how to handle the problem through bargaining.
- Impediments to private voluntary bargaining include asymmetric information, large numbers, and an absence of the surpluses required for making sidepayments.

EXERCISES

1. Discuss the problems of aircraft noise around an airport from an externality perspective and a possible solution perspective if (a) housing existed in the airport area before the airport was built and (b) housing was built adjacent to the airport after the airport was built and operating.

2. A sheep rancher has leased the mineral rights to her land to an oil company. The sheep rancher fears that discharges from the oil wells will pollute her underground water resources. Consequently, the contract for the sale of mineral rights requires that the rancher and the oil company reach a mutually agreeable solution to the problem should it occur, or the mineral rights lease will be terminated and the rancher will be required to return a portion of the lease proceeds to the oil company. The portion that must be returned to the oil company is to be determined through a process of binding arbitration. Discuss possible "optimal" solutions should this problem arise.

3. Why do zoning ordinances frequently prohibit the construction of residences near industrial areas and large retail malls?

4. Using game theory, show why two adjacent rental property owners may not make a profit-maximizing level of investment in their properties.

5. Chester County is a rural farm county in southeastern Pennsylvania. It is within 30 miles of the outer reaches of the city of Philadelphia, and as such is somewhat typical of other rural areas being affected by urban growth (sprawl). In recent years, much of the farmland in the country has been sold to real estate developers who have sold small lots ($\frac{1}{2}$ to 1 acre) for new suburban developments. The impact of this development has been significant. Schools became overcrowded as the new, higher-density suburbias filled up. Septic systems were no longer adequate to dispose of the increased volume of sewage. The new suburbanites pushed for a public sewer and treatment system (as well as city, not well, water). Roads previously adequate for farm traffic needed to be widened. The greater volume of traffic found the slow, cumbersome farm traffic to be a dangerous nuisance. Many suburban residents complained of the odor of manure on neighboring fields.

As these and other problems developed, a great strain was placed on the county's tax revenues to meet the growing need for social services. Consequently, taxes have been raised dramatically, largely reflecting increased land values. Until recently, the remaining farms, of which there are still many, had not been assessed for taxes at the same percentage of *actual* market value of the real estate property as the new suburbanites. The new suburbanites complained, arguing that farmers should pay their fair share and that the fair share should be based on real estate values, just as the taxes on the new suburbanites are.

a. Discuss the pros and cons of increasing farm tax assessments to make them in line with other property assessments in the county in terms of (i) economic efficiency and (ii) equity.

b. What are the externalities in this case?

c. How should the problem of compensation for externalities be handled?

6. Before the imposition of mandatory 55-mph speed limits on most of this nation's highways during the 1973–1974 energy crisis, motorists were asked to voluntarily reduce their driving speed to 55 mph. Those who did generally found that the majority of drivers continued along at their customary 65 to 75 mph.

a. Why is a program of voluntary energy conservation, particularly among small consumers, likely to be ineffective?

b. Formulate the problem of voluntary energy conservation compliance in the framework of a game theory problem. Can you show why the desired solution is unlikely to prevail?

7. Branding Iron Products, a specialty steel fabricator, operates a plant in the town of West Star, Texas. The town has grown rapidly because of recent discoveries of oil and gas in the area. Many of the new residents have expressed concern at the amount of pollution (primarily particulate matter in the air and waste water in the town's river) emitted by Branding Iron. Three proposals have been made to remedy the problem:

a. Impose a tax on the amount of particulate matter and the amount of waste water emitted by the firm.

b. Prohibit pollution by the firm.

c. Offer tax incentives to the firm to clean up its production processes. Evaluate these alternatives from the perspective of economic efficiency, equity, and the likely long-term impact on the firm.

8. Middlefield, Ohio, a town with a 50,000 population, is the home of Legco Steel. Legco employs about 20 percent of the town's workforce. Because of an increase in complaints from local environmentalists, the town's city council is considering taking action to reduce the firm's pollution. The following alternatives are being considered:

(1) Pass an ordinance requiring the firm to reduce its discharge of particulates into the air by 95 percent.

(2) Impose a tax of $5 per ton of particulates.

(3) Maintain the status quo.

The expected payoffs to the firm and the town are as follows:

Action	Firm (Impact on Profits)	Town (Impact on Employment)
Reduce discharge with ordinance	−50%	20% reduction in workforce employed in Middlefield
Tax discharge	−10%	5% reduction in workforce employed in Middlefield
Do nothing	0%	0%

a. What action do you think the town should take? Why?
b. What other factors need to be considered?
c. Why do you think Alternative (a) has such a large impact on employment in Middlefield?

9. Lead Weight Refining, Inc., operates a large ore smelter in Junction City, Utah. The firm produces lead ingots that are later used to manufacture batteries for heavy-duty equipment. In the lead-refining process, a substantial amount of air pollution is generated.

A local mothers' organization is concerned about the health hazard posed by the emissions of the firm. After consulting with local officials, the mothers convince the city to impose a pollution tax on the discharges of the firm.

Each unit of output, Q, is comprised of one unit of lead, Q_A, and one unit of air pollution (particulates), Q_B. The total cost function of the firm is

$$TC = 25,000 + 8Q + 4Q^2$$

The demand for lead is

$$P_A = 4,522 - 4Q_A$$

The demand function for the firm's particulate pollution is derived from the use of these pollutants as an input in the battery production process. The demand function for these discharges is

$$P_B = 400 - Q_B$$

a. In the absence of any pollution tax, what price, quantity, and profit levels will prevail for the firm?
b. Compute the marginal revenue for lead output and for pollution output at this price and output level.
c. What is the minimum tax that must be charged to completely eliminate pollution by the firm?

10. **a.** Discuss the reasons why it is necessary to be able to measure the damage from pollution so the affected parties may reach an optimal solution through bargaining.

   b. How does your answer to part (a) relate to the negative reaction of many communities to the location of a nuclear power plant in their area?

11. A local coke works operates in a competitive market where the prevailing price is $100 per ton. The marginal cost of producing coke is $20 + 2.5Q$.

   a. What output will the firm produce?

   b. Pollution from the production of coke causes damage of approximately $10 per ton. If an effluent charge of $10 per ton is imposed, what will be the output of the firm?

12. The demand for specialty glue is given as follows:

$$P = 1,200 - 6Q$$

where P is the price per 100 pounds of specialty glue produced and Q is the amount produced and sold in hundreds of pounds.

   The marginal cost of producing glue for the entire glue industry is

$$MC = 700 + 2Q$$

   a. What will industry output and price be in the absence of regulation?

   b. The production of specialty glue results in marginal pollution costs of

$$MC = 200 + Q$$

   What is the marginal social cost for the production of specialty glue?

   c. If the firms in the industry attempt to achieve a *socially* optimal level of output, what price should be charged and what should be the level of output?

LONG-TERM INVESTMENT DECISIONS AND RISK MANAGEMENT

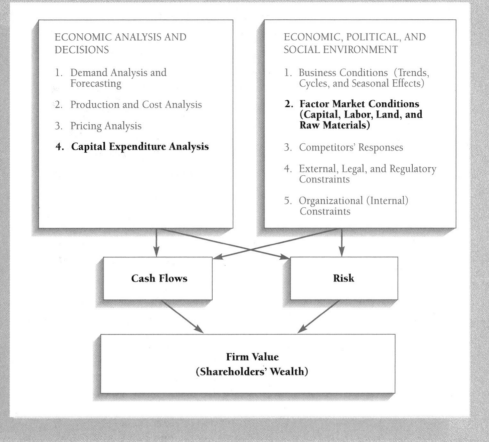

ECONOMIC ANALYSIS AND DECISIONS

1. Demand Analysis and Forecasting

2. Production and Cost Analysis

3. Pricing Analysis

4. **Capital Expenditure Analysis**

ECONOMIC, POLITICAL, AND SOCIAL ENVIRONMENT

1. Business Conditions (Trends, Cycles, and Seasonal Effects)

2. **Factor Market Conditions (Capital, Labor, Land, and Raw Materials)**

3. Competitors' Responses

4. External, Legal, and Regulatory Constraints

5. Organizational (Internal) Constraints

Cash Flows

Risk

Firm Value (Shareholders' Wealth)

This part of the book looks at the capital investment decision for a firm. Investments in new, long-term assets have a major impact on a firm's future stream of cash flows and the risk of those cash flows. As such, the long-term investment decision has a significant impact on the value of the firm. Capital investment decisions can be viewed as the link between the short-run price and output decisions made by managers of a firm and the long-run decisions made by those managers. A capital investment involves a change in the production technology used by the firm and/or a change in the scale of operations of the firm. In Chapter 19, we introduce the concept of a project's net present value. The net present value of a project can be viewed as the increment to shareholder wealth that is expected to accrue as a result of undertaking a capital investment project. The same tools that are relevant to capital investment analysis by private sector managers also can be used, with minor modifications, by managers in public and not-for-profit enterprises. Chapter 20 examines the concept of risk as applied to capital investment decision making and reviews techniques for managing risk.

Long-Term Investment Analysis

CHAPTER PREVIEW

Investment analysis (capital budgeting) is the process of planning for the purchases of assets whose returns (cash flows) are expected to continue beyond one year. When making capital budgeting decisions, the managers of a firm are committing the firm's resources to the expansion of its productive capacity, an improvement in its cost efficiency, or a diversification in its asset base. Each of these decisions has important implications for the future cash flows the firm can be expected to generate and the risk of those cash flows. Capital expenditures are a bridge between the short-term price and output determination decisions facing managers daily and the longer-term strategic decisions that wealth-maximizing managers must make to remain competitive. Public sector managers use the techniques of cost-benefit analysis and cost-effectiveness analysis when analyzing many long-term resource-allocation decisions. These techniques also are presented in this chapter.

M A N A G E R I A L C H A L L E N G E

FORD MOTOR COMPANY'S ACQUISITION OF JAGUAR

For some time, Ford Motor Company has attempted to develop internally a world-class luxury car to compete with Mercedes and BMW. It attempted to introduce such a car in the United States under the Merkur nameplate. That attempt ended in failure when Ford announced the discontinuance of Merkur sales in the United States. Unable to internally develop such a product line, Ford chose to buy an established luxury car line with instant name recognition.

In December 1989 Ford Motor took control of Jaguar PLC, the British luxury car firm, after a difficult hostile takeover bid that ended in Ford paying $2.6 billion. (In contrast, Toyota invested an estimated $900 million to create its successful and very profitable Lexus division.) After taking control, Ford executives undertook a close examination of the operations of the British car firm. Their findings were troubling. They determined that Jaguar production facilities were primitive. Jaguar also had skimped on investments in engineering new products, such that any really new products were many years from reality. The productivity of Jaguar workers was estimated to be only half that of workers at Mercedes and BMW and only one-fourth as good as

Toyota's Lexus division. Losses for 1990 were projected to be $100 million, even after Ford realized up to $100 million in savings in parts purchases because of its greater buying power. Ford concluded that it would have to invest another $2 billion to turn Jaguar around and make it a profitable firm, with profitability expected no sooner than 1995.

Ford's investment in Jaguar represents a long-term commitment to have a successful entry in the world luxury car market that can compete with Mercedes, BMW, and Lexus. In spite of the high cost of the acquisition, Ford managers have expressed optimism that this capital investment ultimately will be successful and create value for Ford's shareholders. However, as Ford has discovered, long-term commitments are fraught with a good deal of risk. Only time will reveal to Ford's managers and investors whether this project really does have a positive net present value.

www . . . .

Access financial information on Ford Motor Company, including annual reports and data on quarterly results, at the following Internet site:
http://www.ford.com/corporate,info/stockholder/

THE NATURE OF CAPITAL EXPENDITURE DECISIONS

Previous chapters in the text have been primarily concerned with analytical tools and decision models that may assist managers in making the most efficient use of existing resources. This chapter considers decisions to replace or expand an enterprise's resource base.

Decisions to replace assets have the effect of changing the technology employed by a firm. This leads to an alteration of the relevant production and cost functions. Most replacement decisions are made with the expectation that a sufficiently lower cost function will prevail after the replacement to justify the required outlays.

Decisions to expand a firm's asset base lead to an increase in the scale or size of the productive facilities. Expansion decisions are based on forecasts of future demand and costs after the expansion. If quantity demanded is suitably high or costs sufficiently low, the resulting profits may justify the expansion decision.

Capital Expenditure
A cash outlay designed to generate a flow of future cash benefits over a period of time extending beyond one year.

A **capital expenditure** is a cash outlay that is expected to generate a flow of future cash benefits lasting longer than one year. It is distinguished from a normal operating expenditure, which is expected to result in cash benefits during the coming one-year period. (The choice of a one-year period is arbitrary, but it does serve as a

Capital Budgeting
The process of planning for and evaluating capital expenditures.

useful guideline.) **Capital budgeting** is the process of planning for and evaluating capital expenditures.

In addition to asset replacement and expansion decisions, other types of decisions that can be analyzed using capital budgeting techniques include research and development expenditures, investments in employee education and training, lease-versus-buy decisions, and mergers and acquisitions.

The importance of capital expenditures to a firm is derived from the fact that current capital outlays, by definition, have a long-range impact on the performance of the enterprise. These current outlays affect future profitability, and in aggregate they plot the future direction of the firm by determining products that will be produced, markets to be entered, the location of plants and facilities, and the type of technology (with its associated costs) to be used. Capital expenditures require careful analysis because they are both costly to make and difficult to reverse without incurring considerable costs.

A BASIC FRAMEWORK FOR CAPITAL BUDGETING

www. . . . .
Read about the State of Rhode Island's experiences with capital budgeting at the following Internet site:
http://www.budget.state.ri.us/capri.htm

Recall from earlier chapters that the economic theory of the firm indicates that a firm should operate at the point where the marginal cost of an additional unit of output just equals the marginal revenue derived from that output. Following this rule will lead to profit maximization by a firm. As we saw in the Sara Lee example in Chapter 2, this principle may be applied to the capital budgeting decisions of the firm. In the context of capital budgeting, the marginal revenue may be thought of as the rates of return earned on successive investments. Marginal cost may be interpreted as the firm's weighted marginal cost of capital—that is, the cost of successive increments of capital acquired by the firm, weighted by the proportions in which these funds are expected to be used in the firm's capital structure.

EXAMPLE

CAPITAL BUDGETING DECISION: CLARK CANDY COMPANY

This basic capital budgeting decision-making framework for the Clark Candy Company is illustrated in Figure 19.1. The company has nine investment projects under consideration, labeled A, B, C, . . ., I. The model assumes that all projects have the same risk. This schedule of projects often is called the *investment opportunity curve*. The projects are indicated by lettered bars on the graph. For example, Project A requires an investment of $2 million and is expected to generate a 24 percent rate of return. Project B will cost $1 million ($3 million minus $2 million on the horizontal axis) and generate a 22 percent rate of return, and so on. Graphically, the projects are arranged in descending order by their rates of return, indicating that no firm has a limitless number of possible investment projects that all generate very high rates of return. As new products are produced, new markets entered, and cost-saving technologies adopted, the number of highly profitable investment opportunities tends to decline. The *marginal cost of capital curve* represents the marginal cost of capital to the firm; that is, the cost of each additional dollar raised in the capital markets.

Using this basic model, the firm should undertake Projects A, B, C, D, and E, because their returns exceed the firm's marginal cost of capital. Although there are some practical difficulties in implementing this conceptual model, it furnishes a guideline for optimal decision making.

A Simplified Capital Budgeting Model

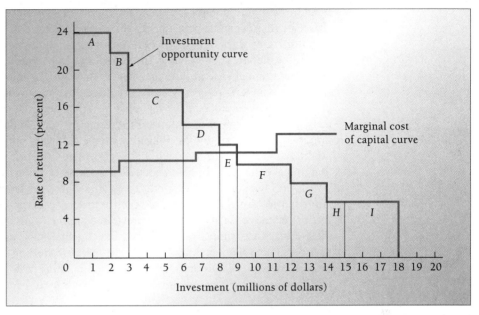

THE CAPITAL BUDGETING PROCESS

The process of selecting capital investment projects consists of the following important steps:

1. Generate alternative capital investment project proposals.
2. Estimate cash flows for the project proposals.
3. Evaluate and choose, from the alternatives available, those investment projects to implement.
4. Review the investment projects after they have been implemented.

Generating Capital Investment Projects

Ideas for new capital investments can come from many sources both inside and outside the firm. Proposals can originate at all levels in the organization, from factory workers all the way up to the board of directors. Most medium- and large-sized firms have staff groups whose responsibilities include searching for and analyzing capital expenditure projects. These staff groups include cost accounting, industrial engineering, marketing research, research and development, and corporate planning personnel.

Capital expenditure projects can be classified into various categories, depending on the nature of the benefits expected. One category includes projects that are designed to *reduce costs*. Like products that become obsolete, technological progress also renders plants, equipment, and production processes obsolete. Normal wear and tear make older plants and equipment more costly to operate due, for example, to more downtime and higher maintenance costs. Obsolescence and deterioration should generate proposals to replace older facilities with new, more efficient plants and equipment.

A second category of capital expenditures includes projects designed to *improve a firm's demand curve,* or to respond to changes in that curve. If increased demand for a product line is forecast, and if existing manufacturing and distribution facilities are inadequate to meet this demand, then the firm must develop proposals for expanding capacity. A firm also may make investments in advertising/product promotion campaigns in an attempt to positively influence the demand for its products. Although often not thought of as traditional capital expenditures, these promotional outlays have all the characteristics of capital investments and can be analyzed in the same way.

A third category of capital expenditure projects includes those that create *future growth options* for the firm. For example, investing in research and development (R&D) can be viewed as a capital expenditure that creates future growth options for the firm. Although any particular R&D project will be very difficult to justify using traditional capital expenditure analysis procedures, one must recognize that the traditional procedures normally do not consider the option value created by R&D outlays. These outlays give the firm the "option," but not the obligation, to make further outlays needed to bring a new product to market. Without the initial R&D outlays, the firm would not possess the option to make the second-phase expenditures and to reap the associated rewards.[1]

A fourth type of capital expenditure includes projects designed to *meet legal requirements and health and safety standards,* such as proposals for pollution control outlays, ventilation, employee safety, and fire-protection equipment. At first glance it may seem that these outlays are "simply required" and thus no analysis is needed. However, managers have the choice of not making these outlays and just shutting down a plant. The decision revolves around the question of whether the remaining cash flows in a project are sufficiently large to justify the additional outlays necessary to keep the plant operating.

CAPITAL EXPENDITURES AT CHRYSLER—THE GRAND CHEROKEE[2]

In early 1992 Chrysler Corporation introduced its new Grand Cherokee sport utility vehicle. The vehicle was developed using an unusual (for Chrysler) "platform team" approach. Instead of developing this new vehicle sequentially, passing it from market research to design to engineering to manufacturing, Chrysler assembled a team of 700 to 800 engineers, marketing research, and design personnel and told them to develop the new vehicle as a team. As a result, the new Cherokee was developed and brought to the market more quickly and at a lower cost than had been typical for other American auto companies. The new Grand Cherokee was developed and a new plant built in Detroit to produce it, all for about $1.1 billion. In comparison, in the early 1980s, General Motors spent $1 billion each, just on the plants it built—not counting any new-product development costs. Chrysler hopes to sell up to 175,000 of these vehicles each year, realizing a profit of $5,500 per unit.

The Grand Cherokee capital expenditures contain elements of both demand curve management and cost reduction. Chrysler has seen sales of its older, smaller Jeep Cherokee decline from a peak of nearly 200,000 units per year to about 125,000, primarily because of stiff competition from the Ford-built Explorer. Chrysler hopes to regain much of this lost market share. In addition, the decision to build the Grand Cherokee in an efficient, new plant in Detroit rather than in its older, underutilized plant in Toledo reflects a commitment to hold costs of production at a minimum. Finally, it is Chrysler's intention to cut the price of its old Jeep Cherokee and market it aggressively as a low-cost sporty utility vehicle alternative. Chrysler is hoping that this strategy will permit it to expand export sales in Europe. Thus Chrysler has created for itself the option either to retain the older model if it sells well at a lower price, or to phase out the older model

---

[1] See Nalin Kulatilaka and Alan Marcus, "Project Valuation under Uncertainty: When Does DCF Fail?" *Journal of Applied Corporate Finance* (Fall 1992), pp. 92–100 and Lenos Trigeorgis, "Real Options and Interactions with Financial Flexibility," *Financial Management* (Autumn 1993), pp. 202–224, for discussion of real options in capital budgeting.

[2] Based largely on "Iacocca's Last Stand at Chrysler," *Fortune,* 20 April 1992, pp. 63ff.

and close the Toledo plant. Thus one can see that in many major capital expenditure projects there may be elements of cost reduction, demand management, and creation of strategic options to be considered in the evaluation process.

EXAMPLE

SARA LEE: CREATING STRATEGIC OPTIONS IN EASTERN EUROPE[3]

Sara Lee Corporation is a large, U.S.-based, multinational manufacturer and marketer of branded, high-quality consumer products. Among other items it produces and sells, Sara Lee is a major producer and marketer of coffee products in Holland, Belgium, Spain, France, and Denmark. During 1991, Sara Lee made a number of strategic acquisitions designed to enhance its long-term international position. With the opening of the economies of the former Soviet satellite states in Eastern Europe, Sara Lee embarked on a strategy designed to give it the needed "options" to expand into the Eastern European market. It acquired a 51 percent interest in Compack Trading and Packing Company, Hungary's largest coffee business. This acquisition gives Sara Lee an opportunity to develop experience operating a firm in the emerging, and somewhat peculiar, business climate of Eastern Europe. Although the acquisition of Compack is unlikely to provide immediate, positive returns to Sara Lee, it will give Sara Lee the expertise needed when it considers other acquisitions and expansions in the Eastern European markets. On the basis of traditional capital investment criteria this acquisition was probably difficult to justify, but when the value of the strategic options it creates for making future investments in the region are considered, Sara Lee found this to be a very attractive acquisition.

EXAMPLE

ALTERNATIVE INVESTMENTS FOR CLEAN AIR[4]

www . . . .
You can read more about how stationary-source polluters can comply by scrapping older cars at the following Internet site maintained by the South Coast Air Quality Management District:
http://www.aqmd.gov/rules/html/r1610.html

The 1990 Clean Air Act placed strict new standards on air pollution. A California program that is being considered at the national level provides polluting firms with a new investment alternative to meet the standards of the act. Prior to the implementation of the new market-based program in California, a polluting firm had two (legal) options—close the plant or make the capital investments needed to bring the plant up to acceptable emission standard levels. The California plan created a market for pollution rights. For example, suppose a factory must reduce its nitrogen oxide emissions by 130,000 pounds per year and that it would cost the firm $1 million to install the necessary equipment. Under the California plan, the firm could buy 1,000 older cars, which emit an average of 130 pounds of nitrogen oxide a year, for a price of $700 per year. The cars would be scrapped, removing them permanently from the roads, and thereby reducing harmful emissions by the required 130,000 pounds. The company would save $300,000. In 1990, Unocal bought 8,376 pre-1971 cars for $700 each. These cars accounted for 13 million pounds of emissions per year, as much as the hydrocarbon emissions from 250,000 new cars or one large oil refinery. As this market-based approach spreads, financial managers will have one more investment alternative available when considering investments to meet pollution standards.

Estimating Cash Flows

One of the most important and difficult steps in the selection process is estimating the cash flows associated with investment projects. Because the cash flows will occur in the

[3] Based on Sara Lee Corporation, *1991 Annual Report.*
[4] Based on "Cold Cash for Old Clunkers," *Newsweek,* 6 April 1992, p. 61.

future, varying degrees of *uncertainty* exist about the values of these flows. In Chapter 20, techniques for dealing explicitly with risk and uncertainty are presented. For now, we assume the decision maker is able to estimate cash flows with sufficient accuracy to use these estimates in deciding whether to undertake the capital investment. Another difficulty arises from the intentional or unintentional introduction of *bias* in cash-flow estimates. Individuals often have difficulty determining objective cash-flow estimates when they have a vested interest in seeing the project undertaken. The natural tendency is for some individuals to be overly optimistic in their estimates; that is, to underestimate the costs and to overestimate the benefits of an investment project. Therefore, it is helpful to have the estimates reviewed by someone outside the department or division proposing the expenditure.

Certain basic guidelines have been found helpful in approaching the analysis of investment alternatives. First, cash flows should be measured on an *incremental* basis. In other words, the cash-flow stream for the project should represent the difference between the cash-flow streams to the firm with and without acceptance of the investment project. Second, cash flows should be measured on an *after-tax* basis, using the firm's marginal tax rate. Third, all the *indirect effects* of the project throughout the firm should be included in the cash-flow calculations. If a department or division of the firm is contemplating a capital investment that will alter the revenues or costs of other departments or divisions, then these external effects should be incorporated into the cash-flow estimates. Fourth, *sunk costs* should not be considered when evaluating the project. A sunk cost is an outlay that has been made (or committed to be made). Because sunk costs cannot be recovered, they should not be considered in the decision to accept or reject a project. Fifth, the value of resources used in the project should be measured in terms of their *opportunity costs*. Recall from Chapter 9 that opportunity cost is the value of a resource in its next best alternative use. In the context of capital budgeting, opportunity costs of resources (assets) are the cash flows that these resources could generate if they are not used in the project under consideration.

For a typical investment project, an initial investment is made in year 0, which generates a series of yearly net cash flows over the life of the project *(n)*. The net investment *(NINV)* of a project is defined as the initial net cash outlay in year 0. It includes the acquisition cost of any new assets plus installation and shipping costs and tax effects.[5]

The incremental, after-tax net cash flows *(NCF)* of a particular investment project are equal to cash inflows minus cash outflows. For any year during the life of the project, these may be defined as the difference in net income after tax $(\Delta NIAT)$ with and without the project plus the difference in depreciation (ΔD):

$$NCF = \Delta NIAT + \Delta D \qquad [19.1]$$

$\Delta NIAT$ is equal to the difference in net income before tax $(\Delta NIBT)$ times $(1 - t)$, where t is the corporate (marginal) income tax rate:

$$\Delta NIAT = \Delta NIBT(1 - t) \qquad [19.2]$$

$\Delta NIBT$ is defined as the difference in revenues (ΔR) minus the differences in operating costs (ΔC) and depreciation (ΔD):

$$\Delta NIBT = \Delta R - \Delta C - \Delta D \qquad [19.3]$$

---

[5] When the new asset is replacing an existing asset, one must also include in the net investment calculation the net proceeds from the sale of the existing asset and the taxes associated with its sale. See R. Charles Moyer, James R. McGuigan, and William J. Kretlow, *Contemporary Financial Management,* 7th ed. (Cincinnati: South-Western, 1997), pp. 328–330 for a discussion of the cash-flow calculations for replacement decisions.

Substituting Equation 19.3 into Equation 19.2 yields

$$\Delta NIAT = (\Delta R - \Delta C - \Delta D)(1 - t) \qquad [19.4]$$

Substituting this equation into Equation 19.1 yields the following definition of net cash flow:

$$NCF = (\Delta R - \Delta C - \Delta D)(1 - t) + \Delta D \qquad [19.5]$$

EXAMPLE

CASH-FLOW ESTIMATION: HAMILTON-BEACH

To illustrate the cash-flow calculations, consider the following example. Suppose that Hamilton-Beach, a manufacturer of small electric appliances, has been offered a contract to supply a regional merchandising company with a line of food blenders to be sold under the retail company's private brand name. Hamilton-Beach's treasurer estimates that the initial investment in new equipment required to produce the blenders would be $1 million. The equipment would be depreciated (using the straight-line method)[6] over five years with a zero (0) estimated salvage value at the end of the five-year contract period. Based on the contract specifications, the treasurer estimates that incremental revenues (additional sales) would be $800,000 per year. The incremental costs if the contract is accepted would be $450,000 per year. These include cash outlays for direct labor and materials, transportation, utilities, building rent, and *additional* overhead. The firm's marginal income tax rate is 40 percent.

Based on the information, *NINV* and *NCF* can be calculated for the project. The net investment (*NINV*) is equal to the $1 million initial outlay for the new equipment. The difference in revenues (ΔR) with and without the project is equal to $800,000 per year and the difference in operating costs (ΔC) is equal to $450,000 per year. The difference in depreciation (ΔD) is equal to the initial outlay ($1 million) divided by 5, or $200,000 per year. Substituting these values, along with $t = .40$, into Equation 19.5 yields.

$$NCF = (\$800,000 - \$450,000 - \$200,000)(1 - .40) + \$200,000$$

$$= \$290,000$$

Hamilton-Beach must decide whether it wants to invest $1 million now to receive $290,000 per year in net cash flows over the next five years. The next section illustrates two of the criteria used in evaluating investment proposals.

Evaluating and Choosing the Investment Projects to Implement

Once a capital expenditure project has been identified and the cash flows have been estimated, a decision to accept or reject the project is required. Acceptance of the project will result in a cash-flow stream to the firm; that is, a series of either cash inflows or outflows for a number of years into the future. Typically, a project will result in an initial (first-year) outflow (investment) followed by a series of cash inflows (returns) over a number of succeeding years. To compare and choose among alternative projects with their associated cash-flow streams, a measure of the desirability of each project must be obtained. The basic problem in measuring and comparing the desirability of investment projects is assessing the value of cash flows that occur at different points in time.

---

[6] This depreciation method is just one of several possible methods that can be used. See Moyer, McGuigan, and Kretlow, *Contemporary Financial Management,* 7th ed., Appendix A, for a discussion of the various depreciation methods.

Internal Rate of Return (IRR)
The discount rate that equates the present value of the stream of net cash flows from a project with the project's net investment.

Various criteria can be employed to determine the desirability of investment projects. This section focuses on two widely used discounted cash-flow methods.[7]

☐ Internal rate of return (r)

☐ Net present value (NPV)

www . . . .
Read more about internal rate of return in an article by consultant Ray Martin at the following Internet site maintained by RiskWorld:
http://www.riskworld.com/Nreports/1997/RMartin/html/nr7aa001.htm

Internal Rate of Return   The **internal rate of return (IRR)** is defined as the discount rate that equates the present value of the net cash flows from the project with the net investment. The following equation is used to find the internal rate of return:

$$\sum_{t=1}^{n} \frac{NCF_t}{(1 + r)^t} = NINV \qquad [19.6]$$

where n is the life of the investment and r is the internal rate of return.

An investment project should be accepted if the internal rate of return is greater than or equal to the firm's required rate of return (cost of capital); if not, the project should be rejected.

EXAMPLE

CALCULATION OF INTERNAL RATE OF RETURN: HAMILTON-BEACH

The internal rate of return for the Hamilton-Beach investment project is calculated as follows:

$$\sum_{t=1}^{5} \frac{280,000}{(1 + r)^t} = 1,000,000$$

$$\sum_{t=1}^{5} \frac{1}{(1 + r)^t} = \frac{1,000,000}{290,000} = 3.4483$$

The term $\left[\sum_{t=1}^{5} 1/(1 + r)^t\right]$ represents the present value of a \$1 annuity for five years discounted at r percent and is equal to 3.4483. Looking up 3.4483 in the Period = 05 row of Table 5 in Appendix B, this value falls between 3.5172 and 3.4331, which corresponds to discount rates of 13 and 14 percent, respectively. Interpolating between these values yields an internal rate of return of

$$r = .13 + \frac{3.5172 - 3.4483}{3.5172 - 3.4331}(.14 - .13)$$

$$= .1382$$

or 13.8 percent.

If Hamilton-Beach requires a rate of return of 12 percent on projects of this type, then the project should be accepted because the expected return (13.8 percent) exceeds the required return (12 percent). Later in this chapter we consider how to determine the required return (i.e., the firm's cost of capital).

Net Present Value   The **net present value** (NPV) of an investment is defined as the present value, discounted at the firm's required rate of return (cost of capital), of the stream

---

[7] For those not familiar with discounting (present value) techniques, Appendix A at the end of this book provides a review of these concepts.

Net Present Value (NPV)
The present value of the stream of net cash flows resulting from a project, discounted at the required rate of return (cost of capital), minus the project's net investment.

of net cash flows from the project minus the project's net investment. Algebraically, the net present value is equal to

$$NPV = \sum_{t=1}^{n} \frac{NCF_t}{(1 + k)^t} - NINV \qquad [19.7]$$

where n is the expected life of the project and k is the firm's required rate of return (cost of capital).

An investment project should be accepted if the net present value is greater than or equal to zero and rejected if its net present value is less than zero. This is so because a positive net present value translates directly into increases in stock prices and increases in shareholder wealth.

EXAMPLE

NET PRESENT VALUE CALCULATION: HERSHEY FOODS

Hershey Foods is considering an investment in a new "Kiss" wrapping machine. The machine has an initial cost (net investment) of $2.5 million. It is expected to produce cost savings from reduced labor and to generate additional revenues because of its increased reliability and productivity. Over its anticipated economic life of five years, the new "Kiss" wrapping machine is expected to generate the following stream of net cash flows (NCF_t):

Year (t)	Net Cash Flow (NCF_t)
1	$600,000
2	800,000
3	800,000
4	600,000
5	250,000

If Hershey requires a return (k) of 15 percent on a project of this type, should it make the investment?

Hershey can solve this problem by computing the net present value of the cash flows from this project (using Equation 19.7) as follows:

Year (1)	Cash Flow (2)	Present Value Interest Factor at 15 Percent* (3)	Present Value (4) = (2) × (3)
0	($2,500,000)	1.00000	($2,500,000)
1	600,000	0.86957	521,742
2	800,000	0.75614	604,912
3	800,000	0.65752	526,016
4	600,000	0.57175	343,050
5	250,000	0.49718	124,295
			($379,985)

*Table 4, Appendix B

Because this project has a negative net present value, it does not contribute to the goal of maximizing shareholder wealth. Therefore, it should be rejected.

Net Present Value versus Internal Rate of Return   Both the net present value and the internal rate of return methods result in identical decisions to either accept or reject individual projects. This is true because the net present value is greater than (less than) zero if and only if the internal rate of return is greater than (less than) the required rate of return k. In the case of *mutually exclusive* projects—that is, projects where the acceptance of one alternative precludes the acceptance of one or more other alternatives—the two methods may yield contradictory results; one project may have a *higher* internal rate of return than another and, at the same time, a *lower* net present value.

Consider, for example, mutually exclusive projects X and Y shown in Table 19.1. Both require a net investment of $1,000. Based on the internal rate of return, Project X is preferred, with a rate of 21.5 percent compared with Project Y's rate of 18.3 percent. Based on the net present value with a discount rate of 5 percent, Project Y ($270) is preferred to Project X ($240). Thus it is necessary to determine which of the two criteria is the correct one to use in this situation. The outcome depends on what *assumptions* the decision maker chooses to make about the *implied reinvestment rate* for the net cash flows generated from each project. The net present value method assumes that cash flows are *reinvested at the firm's cost of capital*, whereas the internal rate of return method assumes that these cash flows are *reinvested at the computed internal rate of return*.[8] Generally, the cost of capital is considered to be a more realistic reinvestment rate than the computed internal rate of return because this is the rate the next (marginal) investment project can be assumed to earn. This can be seen in Figure 19.1. This last project invested in, Project E, offers a rate of return nearly equal to the firm's marginal cost of capital. Consequently the net present value approach is normally superior to the internal rate of return when choosing among mutually exclusive investments. Table 19.2 summarizes the two techniques.

Reviewing Investment Projects after Implementation

A very important but often neglected step in the selection process is the review of investment projects *after* they have been implemented. The purpose of this review should be to provide information on the effectiveness of the selection process. In the review, the actual cash flows from an accepted project are compared with the estimated cash flows at the time the project was proposed. This type of analysis requires the firm to keep some

---

[8] A more thorough discussion of this problem and the underlying assumptions is found in J. Hirshleifer, "On the Theory of the Optimal Investment Decision," *Journal of Political Economy* 66 (August 1958), pp. 95–103 and James H. Lorie and Leonard J. Savage, "Three Problems in Rationing Capital," *Journal of Business* 23 (October 1955), pp. 229–239.

TABLE 19.1		Project X	Project Y
Net Present Value vs. Internal Rate of Return for Mutually Exclusive Investment Projects	Net investment	$1,000	$1,000
	Net cash flows		
	Year 1	667	0
	Year 2	667	1,400
	Net present value at 5%	$240	$270
	Internal rate of return	21.5%	18.3%

| | **TABLE** | **19.2** | Summary of the Capital Budgeting Decision Criteria |

Criterion	Project Acceptance Decision Rule	Benefits	Weaknesses
Net present value (NPV)	Accept project if project has a positive or zero NPV; that is, if the present value of net cash flows, evaluated at the firm's cost of capital, equals or exceeds the net investment required.	Considers the timing of cash flows. Provides an objective, return-based criterion for acceptance or rejection. Most conceptually accurate approach.	Difficulty in interpreting the meaning of the NPV computation.
Internal rate of return (IRR)	Accept project if IRR equals or exceeds the firm's cost of capital.	Easy to interpret the meaning of IRR. Considers the timing of cash flows. Provides an objective, return-based criterion for acceptance or rejection.	Sometimes gives decision that conflicts with NPV. Multiple rates of return problem.*

*See Moyer, McGuigan, and Kretlow, *Contemporary Financial Management,* 7th ed., p. 351, for a discussion of the multiple internal rates of return problem.

additional information in its accounting records to be able to associate specific costs and revenues with various investment projects. Because estimating future cash inflows and outflows is uncertain, one would not expect the actual values to agree perfectly with the estimated values. The analysis therefore should be concerned with checking for any large or systematic discrepancies in the cash-flow estimates by individual departments, plants, or divisions, and attempting to ascertain the reasons for these discrepancies. An analysis such as this will enable decision makers to make better evaluations of investment proposals submitted in the future.

ESTIMATING THE FIRM'S COST OF CAPITAL

A firm's cost of capital is an important input in the capital-budgeting analysis procedure. The theory and measurement of a firm's cost of capital is a complex topic that is more appropriately dealt with at length in financial management texts. The purpose of this section is to provide an introduction to the topic and to summarize some of its most important elements.

The **cost of capital** is concerned with what a firm has to pay for the capital—that is, the debt, preferred stock, retained earnings, and common stock—it uses to finance new investments. It also can be thought of as the rate of return required by investors in the firm's securities. As such, the firm's cost of capital is determined in the capital markets and is closely related to the degree of risk associated with new investments, existing assets, and the firm's capital structure. In general, the greater the risk of a firm as perceived by investors, the greater the return investors will require and the greater will be the cost of capital.

The cost of capital also can be thought of as the minimum rate of return required on new investments undertaken by the firm.[9] If a new investment earns an internal rate of

WWW
Ibbotson Associates publishes *Cost of Capital Quarterly,* which includes industry cost of capital analysis on over 300 industries, at the following Internet site: http://valuation.ibbotson.com/

Cost of Capital
The cost of funds that are supplied to a firm. The cost of capital is the minimum rate of return that must be earned on new investments undertaken by a firm.

___
[9] Technically, this statement assumes that the risk of the new investments is equal to the risk of the firm's existing assets. Also, when used in this context, the cost of capital refers to a weighted cost of the various sources of capital used by the firm. The computation of the weighted cost of capital is considered in this chapter.

return that is greater than the cost of capital, the value of the firm increases. Correspondingly, if a new investment earns a return less than the firm's cost of capital, the firm's value decreases.

The following discussion focuses on the two major sources of funds for most firms—debt and common equity. Each of these sources of funds has a cost. The cost of each of the various component sources of capital is an important input in the calculation of a firm's overall cost of capital.

Cost of Debt Capital

The pretax cost of debt capital to the firm is the rate of return required by investors. For a debt issue, this rate of return k_d equates the present value of all expected future receipts—interest I and principal repayment M—with the offering price V_0 of the debt security:

$$V_0 = \sum_{t=1}^{n} \frac{I}{(1 + k_d)^t} + \frac{M}{(1 + k_d)^n} \qquad [19.8]$$

The cost of debt k_d can be found by using the methods for finding the discount rate (that is, yield to maturity) discussed in Appendix A.

Most *new* long-term debt (bonds) issued by companies is sold at or close to par value (normally $1,000 per bond), and the coupon interest rate is set at the rate required by investors. When debt is issued at par value, the pretax cost of debt, k_d, is equal to the coupon interest rate. Interest payments made to investors, however, are deductible from the firm's taxable income. Therefore, the *after-tax* cost of debt is computed by multiplying the pretax cost by 1 minus the firm's marginal tax rate t:

$$k_i = k_d(1 - t) \qquad [19.9]$$

EXAMPLE

COST OF DEBT CAPITAL: AT&T

To illustrate the cost of debt computation, suppose that AT&T sells $100 million of 8.5 percent first-mortgage bonds at par. Assuming a corporate marginal tax rate of 40 percent, the after-tax cost of debt is computed as

$$k_i = k_d(1 - t)$$
$$= 8.5(1 - .40) = 5.1\%$$

Cost of Internal Equity Capital

Like the cost of debt, the cost of equity capital to the firm is the equilibrium rate of return required by the firm's common stock investors.

Firms raise equity capital in two ways: (1) *internally,* through retained earnings and (2) *externally,* through the sale of new common stock. The cost of internal equity to the firm is less than the cost of new common stock because the sale of new stock requires the payment of flotation costs.

The concept of the cost of internal equity (or simply "equity," as it is commonly called) can be developed using several different approaches, including the *dividend valuation model* and the *capital asset pricing model.*

Dividend Valuation Model   Recall from Chapter 1 that shareholder wealth was defined as the present value, discounted at the shareholder's required rate of return k_e, of the expected future returns generated by a firm (see Equation 1.1). For the typical firm, these future returns can take two forms—the payment of dividends to the shareholder or an increase in the market value of the firm's stock (capital gain). For the shareholder who plans to hold the stock indefinitely, the value of the firm (shareholder wealth, according to the **dividend valuation model**) is

$$V_0 = \sum_{t=1}^{\infty} \frac{D_t}{(1 + k_e)^t} \qquad [19.10]$$

where D_t is the dividend paid by the firm in period t.[10] If the shareholder chooses to sell the stock after n years, his or her wealth (V_0) is

$$V_0 = \sum_{t=1}^{n} \frac{D_t}{(1 + k_e)^t} + \frac{V_n}{(1 + k_e)^n} \qquad [19.11]$$

where V_n is the market value of the shareholder's holdings in period n. However, Equation 19.11 can be shown to be identical to 19.10, because the value of the firm in period n is based on the future returns (dividends) of the firm in period $n + 1, n + 2, \ldots$[11]

If the dividends of the firm are expected to grow *perpetually* at a *constant compound rate* of g per year, then the value of the firm (Equation 19.10) can be expressed as[12]

$$V_0 = \frac{D_1}{k_e - g} \qquad [19.12]$$

where D_1 is the dividend expected to be paid in period 1 and V_0 is the market value of the firm. If D_1 is the dividend *per share* (rather than total dividends) paid in period 1, then V_0 represents the market price *per share* of common stock. Solving Equation 19.12 for k_e yields

$$k_e = \frac{D_1}{V_0} + g \qquad [19.13]$$

The following example illustrates how Equation 19.13 can be applied in estimating the cost of equity capital.

Dividend Valuation Model
A model (or formula) stating that the value of a firm (i.e., shareholder wealth) is equal to the present value of the firm's future dividend payments, discounted at the shareholder's required rate of return. It provides one method of estimating a firm's cost of equity capital.

EXAMPLE

COST OF INTERNAL EQUITY CAPITAL: FRESNO COMPANY

Suppose the current price of the common stock of Fresno Company (V_0) is $32. The dividend per share of the firm next year, D_1, is expected to be $2.14. Dividends have been growing at an average compound annual rate of 7 percent over the past 10 years, and

[10] A profitable firm that reinvests all its earnings and never distributes any dividends would still have a positive value to stockholders because its market value would be increasing and shareholders could sell their stock and obtain a capital gain on their investment in the firm.

[11] The value of the firm in period n is

$$V_n = \sum_{t=n+1}^{\infty} \frac{D_t}{(1 + k_e)^{t-n}}$$

When this expression is substituted in Equation 19.11, Equation 19.10 is obtained.

[12] Equation 19.12 is often referred to as the *Gordon model*, for Myron J. Gordon, who pioneered its use. See Myron J. Gordon, *The Investment, Financing, and Valuation of the Corporation* (Homewood, Ill.: Irwin, 1962). More complicated forms of Equations 19.12 and 19.13 must be used if the constant growth assumption does not apply.

this growth rate is expected to be maintained for the foreseeable future. Based on this information, the cost of equity capital is estimated as

$$k_e = \frac{2.14}{32} + .07 = .137$$

or 13.7 percent.

Capital Asset Pricing Model   Another technique that can be used to estimate the cost of equity capital is the **capital asset pricing model (CAPM).** The CAPM is a theory that formally describes the risk-required return trade-off for securities. According to the CAPM theory, the rate of return required by investors consists of a risk-free return r_f plus a premium compensating the investor for bearing the risk. The risk premium varies from stock to stock.

Obviously less risk is associated with an investment in a stable stock, such as AT&T, than in the stock of a small, wildcat oil drilling firm W. As a result, an investor in the drilling stock requires a higher return than the AT&T investor. Figure 19.2 illustrates the difference in required rates of return (or the cost of internal equity) for the two securities. The relationship illustrated in this figure is called the *security market line* (SML). The SML depicts the risk-return relationship in the market for all securities.

The cost of equity capital can be quantified using the CAPM. The CAPM assumes that a single risk-free rate exists, and the risk-required return trade-off for stocks is characterized by a straight line sloping upward from the risk-free rate. The required return can be obtained by calculating the risk associated with a stock.

Risk is defined as the variability of outcomes (e.g., returns). The variability of returns for individual stocks is closely related to the variability of stock prices. In the context of the CAPM and the SML, *total* variability of returns is not considered to be the relevant measure of risk, however. Instead, total variability can be divided into two components:

☐ The variability of returns that is *unique* to a security. This is called *unsystematic risk.* It includes return variability caused by such factors as differing management skills, strikes, natural disasters, effects of new competition, and so on.

Capital Asset Pricing Model (CAPM)

A theory that formally describes the nature of the risk-required return tradeoff. It provides one method of estimating a firm's cost of equity capital.

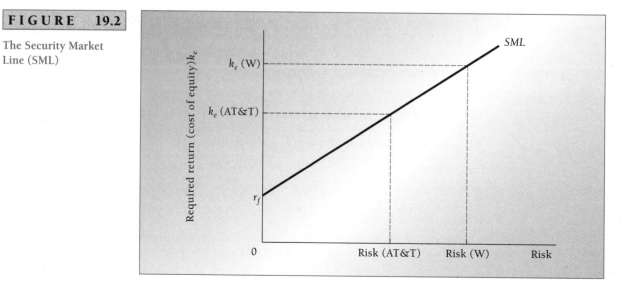

FIGURE   19.2

The Security Market Line (SML)

- The variability of returns that affects *all* securities. This is called *systematic* or *nondiversifiable* risk. It is measured by the co-movement or covariation of a security's returns with the returns of the overall market. The overall market movement is usually measured by some broad market index such as the S&P 500 stock index. Systematic variability is caused by factors such as changes in the level of interest rates, the impact of recessions or business expansions, and so on.

If an investor holds a well-diversified portfolio of individual securities, the variability of returns arising from unique factors affecting individual securities can possibly be diversified away, leaving only systematic risk.

To use the SML to estimate the cost of equity, one must estimate the systematic risk of individual securities. One measure of the systematic risk of a stock is the stock's *beta*, β. (Beta is estimated as the slope of a regression line between an individual security's returns and the returns for a market index.)[13]

The stock market as a whole has a beta of 1.0; stocks whose prices fluctuate less than the market as a whole have betas of less than 1.0; and stocks with price fluctuations greater than the market have betas greater than 1.0. For example, if a stock has a beta equal to 1.0, a 5 percent increase (or decrease) in the returns on the market index would be expected to be associated with a 5 percent increase (or decrease) in that security's returns. If a stock has a beta of 2.0, a 5 percent increase (or decrease) in market returns would be expected to be associated with a 10 percent increase (or decrease) in that security's returns. Finally, a beta of 0.5 implies that a 5 percent increase (or decrease) in market returns would be expected to be associated with a 2.5 percent increase (or decrease) in that security's returns.

Thus, according to the CAPM, the cost of equity calculation can be illustrated as

$$k_e = r_f + \beta(k_m - r_f) \tag{19.14}$$

where k_m is the expected return on the market as a whole. This equation shows that the risk premium portion of a firm's cost of equity is proportional to its beta.

EXAMPLE

COST OF INTERNAL EQUITY CAPITAL: MIDWESTERN POWER COMPANY

To illustrate the k_e calculation using the CAPM, suppose that the Midwestern Power Company common stock has a beta (β) of 0.8 and the present risk-free rate (r_f) is 7 percent. If the expected return on the market (k_m) is 13 percent, substituting these values into Equation 19.14 yields

$$k_e = 7.0 + 0.8(13.0 - 7.0)$$

$$= 11.8\%$$

Cost of External Equity Capital

The cost of external equity is greater than the cost of internal equity for the following reasons:

- Flotation costs associated with new shares are usually high enough that they cannot realistically be ignored.

---

[13] See Moyer, McGuigan, and Kretlow, *Contemporary Financial Management,* 7th ed., chaps. 5 and 11, for a more detailed discussion of the CAPM theory and its use in calculating the cost of equity capital.

▫ The selling price of the new shares to the public must be less than the market price of the stock before announcement of the new issue, or the shares may not sell. Before any announcement, the current market price of a stock usually represents an equilibrium between supply and demand. If supply is increased (all other things being equal), the new equilibrium price will be lower.

When a firm's future dividend payments are expected to grow forever at a constant per period rate of g, the cost of external equity k_e' is defined as

$$k_e' = \frac{D_1}{V_{\text{net}}} + g \tag{19.15}$$

where V_{net} is the net proceeds to the firm on a per share basis.

| EXAMPLE |

COST OF EXTERNAL EQUITY CAPITAL: FRESNO COMPANY

To illustrate, consider the Fresno Company example used in the cost of internal equity discussion, where $V_0 = \$32$, $D_1 = \$2.14$, $g = .07$, and $k_e = 13.7$ percent. Assuming that new common stock can be sold at $31 to net the company $30 a share after flotation costs, k_e' is calculated using Equation 19.15 as follows:

$$k_e' = \frac{-.14}{30} + 0.07$$

$$= 0.141 \text{ or } 14.1\%$$

Because of the relatively high cost of newly issued equity, many companies try to avoid this means of raising capital. The question of whether a firm should raise capital with newly issued common stock depends on its investment opportunities.

Weighted Cost of Capital

Firms calculate their cost of capital to determine a discount rate to use when evaluating proposed capital expenditure projects. Recall that the purpose of capital expenditure analysis is to determine which *proposed* projects the firm should *actually* undertake. Therefore, it is logical that *the capital whose cost is measured and compared with the expected benefits from these proposed projects should be the next or marginal capital the firm raises.* Typically, companies estimate the cost of each capital component as the cost they expect to have to pay on these funds during the coming year.[14]

In addition, as a firm evaluates proposed capital expenditure projects, it normally does not specify the proportions of debt and equity financing for each individual project. Instead, each project is presumed to be financed with the same proportion of debt and equity contained in the company's target capital structure.

Thus the appropriate cost of capital figure to be used in capital budgeting is not only based on the next capital to be raised but also weighted by the proportions of the capital components in the firm's long-range target capital structure. This figure is called the *weighted,* or *overall, cost of capital.*

---

[14] Stated another way, the cost of the capital acquired by the firm in earlier periods—that is, the *historical* cost of capital—is *not* used as the discount rate in determining next year's capital expenditures.

The general expression for calculating the weighted cost of capital k_a is

$$k_a = \begin{bmatrix} \text{equity} \\ \text{fraction} \\ \text{of capital} \\ \text{structure} \end{bmatrix} \begin{bmatrix} \text{cost} \\ \text{of} \\ \text{equity} \end{bmatrix} + \begin{bmatrix} \text{debt} \\ \text{fraction} \\ \text{of capital} \\ \text{structure} \end{bmatrix} \begin{bmatrix} \text{cost} \\ \text{of} \\ \text{debt} \end{bmatrix}$$

$$= \left[\frac{E}{D+E} \right](k_e) + \left[\frac{D}{D+E} \right](k_i) \qquad [19.16]$$

where D is the amount of debt and E the amount of equity in the target capital structure.[15]

EXAMPLE

WEIGHTED COST OF CAPITAL: COLUMBIA GAS COMPANY

To illustrate, suppose that Columbia Gas has a current (and target) capital structure of 75 percent equity and 25 percent debt. (The proportions of debt and equity should be the proportions in which the firm intends to raise funds in the future.) For a firm that is not planning a change in its target capital structure, these proportions should be based on the current *market value weights* of the individual components (debt and common equity). The company plans to finance next year's budget with $75 million of retained earnings ($k_e = 12\%$) and $25 million of long-term debt ($k_d = 8\%$). Assume a 40 percent marginal tax rate. Using these figures, the weighted cost of capital being raised to finance next year's capital budget is calculated using Equation 19.16 as

$$k_a = 0.75 \times 12.0 + 0.25 \times 8.0 \times (1 - 0.40)$$

$$= 10.2\%$$

This is the discount rate that should be used to evaluate projects of average risk.

www . . . .
Legacy Systems Research offers cost-benefit analysis software at the following Internet site:
http://www.costbenefit.com/index.htm

Cost-Benefit Analysis
A resource-allocation model that can be used by public and not-for-profit sector organizations to evaluate programs or investments on the basis of the magnitude of the discounted benefits and costs.

COST-BENEFIT ANALYSIS

The remainder of this chapter is devoted to some techniques of analysis that may be used to assist in public and not-for-profit sector resource-allocation decisions. The primary analytical model examined is cost-benefit analysis, although cost-effectiveness studies are also discussed.

   Cost-benefit analysis is an analytical tool used to evaluate programs and investments based on a comparison of all the benefits and costs arising from a particular program or project. Cost-benefit analysis is the logical public sector counterpart to the capital budgeting techniques discussed earlier. In the following sections of this chapter the focus is on the additional problems that arise in attempting to allocate resources and make other economic decisions in public and not-for-profit sector organizations. These include the measurement of benefits and costs, the determination of an appropriate discount rate, and the uses and limitations of the model.

---

[15] If the target capital structure contains preferred stock, a preferred stock term is added to Equation 19.16. In this case Equation 19.16 becomes

$$k_a = \left(\frac{E}{E+D+P} \right)(k_e) + \left(\frac{D}{E+D+P} \right)(k_i) + \left(\frac{P}{E+D+P} \right)(k_p)$$

where P is the amount of preferred stock in the target capital structure and k_p is the component cost of preferred stock.

Uses of Cost-Benefit Analysis

In general, cost-benefit analysis is a method for assessing the desirability of projects when it is necessary to take both a long and a wide view of the repercussions of a particular program expenditure or policy change. As in private sector capital budgeting, cost-benefit analysis often is used in cases where the economic consequences of a project or a policy change are likely to extend beyond one year in time. Unlike capital budgeting, however, cost-benefit analysis seeks to measure all economic impacts of the project; that is, side effects as well as direct effects.

Accept-Reject Decisions

Cost-benefit analysis may be used for a number of purposes, depending on the nature of the project, the constraints of public policy, and the requirements of the information user or decision maker. One use is to determine whether a specific expenditure is economically justifiable. For instance, one might examine a program designed to eradicate syphilis, considering the current costs of the disease that could be averted by a specific expenditure of funds. Following the framework used by Klarman,[16] benefits (averted costs) may be divided into four categories:

1. Expenditures on medical care, including physician and nurse fees, drug costs, and hospital and equipment charges
2. Loss of gross earnings during the disease
3. Reduction in gross earnings after the disease because of decreased employment opportunities resulting from the social stigma attached to the illness
4. The pain and discomfort associated with having the disease

Suppose a particular program designed to aid syphilis eradication is proposed that requires a one-time outlay of $250 million (Table 19.3). Assume that the total benefits (averted disease costs) of this one-year program are expected to accrue for a period of five years. If one accepts, for the moment, that an appropriate social discount rate is 15 percent for this project, the program may be evaluated in the net present-value analy-

---

[16] H. E. Klarman, "Syphilis Control Programs," in *Measuring Benefits of Government Investments*, ed. Robert Dorfman (Washington, D.C.: Brookings Institution, 1965).

TABLE   19.3

Net Benefit-Cost Analysis

End of Year (1)	Actual Dollar Benefit (Cost) (2)	Present Value Interest Factor at 15 Percent* (3)	Discounted Benefits and Costs ($ Million) (4) = (2) × (3)
0	($250,000,000)	1.000	($250.00)
1	150,000,000	.870	130.50
2	125,000,000	.756	94.50
3	100,000,000	.658	65.80
4	50,000,000	.572	28.60
5	25,000,000	.497	12.43
			Net benefits = $81.83

*Table 4, Appendix B.

sis framework developed in the capital budgeting discussion. The decision rule is to accept the project if the (discounted) benefits are greater than or equal to the (discounted) costs. Because the program has a positive calculated net discounted benefit, in this case $81.83 million, it is an acceptable project.

Alternative decision-making criteria include the internal rate of return and the benefit-cost ratio. According to the internal rate of return criterion, a project is acceptable if the IRR is greater than or equal to appropriate social discount rate. In the case of the syphilis eradication program, the IRR for the benefits and costs shown in Table 19.3 is 32.4 percent. Because this exceeds the social discount rate of 15 percent, the project is acceptable. According to the benefit-cost ratio criterion, a project is acceptable if the benefit-cost ratio is greater than or equal to 1.0, where the **benefit-cost ratio** is equal to the present value of the benefits (discounted at the social discount rate) divided by the present value of the costs (similarly discounted). For the syphilis eradication program, the benefit-cost ratio is equal to

Benefit-Cost Ratio
The ratio of the present value of the benefits from a project or program (discounted at the social discount rate) to the present value of the costs (similarly discounted).

$$\text{Benefit--cost ratio} = \frac{130.50 + 94.50 + 65.80 + 28.60 + 12.43}{250}$$

$$= 1.33$$

Because this ratio exceeds 1.0, the project is acceptable according to this criterion. All three decision criteria will give identical decisions to accept or reject individual projects.

Program-Level Analysis

In addition to being used to evaluate whether an entire program is economically justifiable, cost-benefit analysis may also be used to determine whether the size of an existing program should be increased (or reduced) and, if so, by what amount. This determination may be made using traditional marginal analysis as developed earlier in the text.

Returning again to the syphilis-control program, assume that, because of strong lobbying from antisyphilis groups, a number of expenditure levels beyond the originally proposed $250 million are being considered. Table 19.4 summarizes these proposed programs and their expected benefits. It can be seen that an analysis that looked in isolation at only one of these proposed program expenditure levels would have concluded that any of the program levels was worthwhile because each proposal generates positive expected net program benefits.

If these program levels are analyzed as a group, however, it becomes clear that there is a limit to the economically justifiable expenditure of funds for syphilis control. The required analysis is summarized in Table 19.5. A level of expenditure of $300 million is best because it generates an additional (marginal) $164.17 million in benefits, but the marginal program cost (in comparison to the $250 million program level) is only

TABLE 19.4			
Schedule of Program Benefits for Various Cost Levels	**Program Cost (Millions of Dollars)**	**Discounted Program Benefits (Millions of Dollars)**	**Net Program Benefits (Millions of Dollars)**
	$250	$331.83	$ 81.83
	300	496.00	196.00
	350	540.00	190.00
	400	565.00	165.00

TABLE 19.5			
Marginal Analysis of Benefits and Costs	**Program Cost (Millions of Dollars)**	**Marginal Cost (Millions of Dollars)**	**Discounted Marginal Benefits (Millions of Dollars)**
	$ 0	—	—
	250	$250	$331.83
	300	50	164.17
	350	50	44.00
	400	50	25.00

$50 million. To increase the program to $350 million would be counterproductive, because only $44 million in benefits are generated for the additonal $50 million outlay (marginal costs exceed marginal benefits).

STEPS IN COST-BENEFIT ANALYSIS

The general principles of cost-benefit analysis may be summarized by answering the following set of questions:[17]

1. What is the objective function to be maximized?
2. What are the constraints placed on the analysis?
3. What costs and benefits are to be included and how may they be valued?
4. What investment evaluation criterion should be used?
5. What is the appropriate discount rate?

The decision-making process in cost-benefit analysis may be traced in the flow-chart presentation of Figure 19.3. Program objectives are set by the public through their political representatives. Alternatives are enumerated, explored, and revised in the light of constraints that may be operative in the system. These alternatives are then compared by enumerating and evaluating program benefits and costs in a present-value framework. Discounted benefits are compared with discounted costs, and intangibles are considered so a recommendation may be made about the merits of one or more alternative programs.

OBJECTIVES AND CONSTRAINTS IN COST-BENEFIT ANALYSIS

Cost-benefit analysis is merely an application of resource-allocation theory. As such, we need to examine it in the light of several criteria that have been proposed by welfare economists for evaluating the desirability of alternative social and economic states. One such criterion is Pareto optimality.[18] A change is said to be desirable or consistent with Pareto optimality if at least one person is made better off (in his or her own judgment) and no one is made worse off (in their own judgments). Although this criterion seems to be relatively value free, as well as potentially verifiable, it suffers from the severe weak-

---

[17] The next two sections of this chapter draw heavily on the review article by A. R. Prest and R. Turvey, "Cost-Benefit Analysis: A Survey," *Economic Journal* (December 1965), p. 683.

[18] A further discussion of the Pareto criterion is provided in W.J. Baumol, *Economic Theory and Operations Analysis*, 4th ed. (Englewood Cliffs, N.J.: Prentice-Hall, 1977), chap. 21.

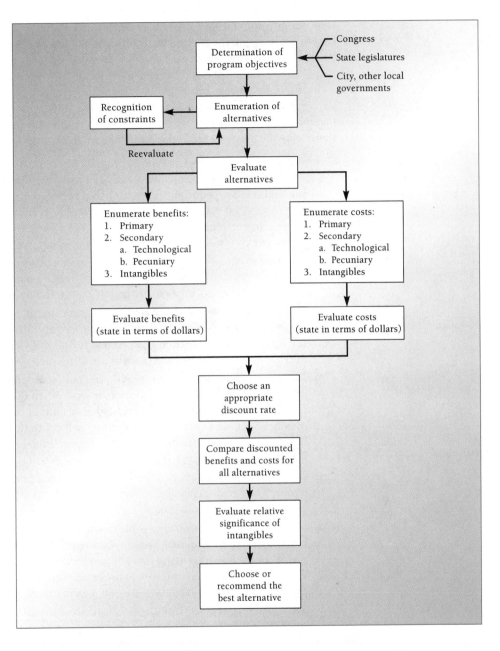

ness that few changes are likely to leave some individuals better off and *no one* worse off. In addition, it assumes that we know, a priori, how people affected by a program will evaluate its effects on them.

Cost-benefit analysis is tied to a weaker notion of social improvement, sometimes called the Kaldor-Hicks criterion, or merely the notion of a "potential" Pareto improvement. Under this criterion, a change (or an economic program) is desirable either (1) if it is consistent with the Pareto criterion or (2) if a potential Pareto improvement may be made by redistributing the gains such that all people in the community are at least as well off as they were before the change. This is the notion of cost-benefit analysis. A project is desirable if the benefits exceed the costs of the project because the project could be completed and the gainers *could* be made to compensate the losers. The fact that there is no compensation from gainers to losers is not a matter of direct consideration in cost-benefit analysis, but the income distributional impacts of a program are an extremely important side issue. All that cost-benefit analysis requires for a project to be acceptable is that total discounted societal benefits exceed the total discounted societal costs.

In addition to recognizing that the maximization of society's wealth is the primary objective function in cost-benefit analysis, it is also important to establish the constraints that may exist or be placed on the achievement of this objective. According to Otto Eckstein's classification system,[19] these include the following:

1. *Physical constraints*—The type of program alternatives considered is ultimately limited by the currently available state of technology and by the production possibilities derived from the relationship between physical inputs and outputs. For example, it is not yet possible to prevent cancer; hence, major emphasis, beyond research programs, must be directed toward early detection and treatment.

2. *Legal constraints*—These may include domestic as well as international laws relating to property rights, the right of eminent domain, due process, constitutional limits on a particular agency's activities, and so on.

3. *Administrative constraints*—Effective programs require that individuals are available, or can be hired and trained, to carry out the program objectives. Even the best-conceived program is worthless unless individuals with the proper mix of technical and administrative skills are available.

4. *Distributional constraints*—Programs affect different groups in different ways because gainers are rarely the same as losers. When distributional impacts are of concern, the objective of cost-benefit analysis might be presented in terms of maximizing total benefits less total costs, subject to the constraint that benefits-less-costs for a particular group reach a prespecified level.

5. *Political constraints*—What may be optimal may not be feasible because of the slowness and inefficiency of the political process. Many times what is *best* is tempered by what is *possible,* given the existence of strong competing interest groups as well as an often cumbersome political mechanism.

6. *Financial or budget constraints*—More often than not, agencies work within the bounds of a predetermined budget. This requires that the objective function be altered to the suboptimizing form of maximizing benefits given a fixed budget. Virtually all programs have some absolute financial ceiling above which the program may not be expanded, in spite of the magnitude of social benefits.

7. *Social and religious constraints*—It is futile to tell Indians to eat sacred cattle to solve their nutritional problems. This is just one example of the social and religious constraints which may limit the range of feasible program alternatives.

ANALYSIS AND VALUATION OF BENEFITS AND COSTS

Cost-benefit analysis is quite similar to traditional private sector profit-and-loss accounting. In the private sector the firm is guided by the criterion that private revenues must be equal to or exceed private costs over the long run for the firm to survive. In contrast, in cost-benefit analysis the economist asks whether society as a whole will be bet-

[19] Otto Eckstein, "A Survey of the Theory of Public Expenditure Criteria," in *Public Finances: Needs, Sources and Utilization,* ed. James M. Buchanan (Princeton, N.J.: Princeton University Press, 1961).

ter off by the adoption or nonadoption of a specific project or by the acceptance of one project to the exclusion of alternatives. As Ezra Mishan points out:

> . . . For the more precise concept of the revenue of the private concern, the economist substitutes the less precise, yet meaningful, concept of the social benefit. For the costs of the private concern, the economist will substitute the concept of opportunity cost . . . or social value foregone elsewhere in moving factors into a projected economic activity.[20]

The starting point for evaluating benefits and costs of a project is the observable market valuations. This assumes that the following conditions are met (or at least approximately met):

☐ Consumers equate the value of the marginal unit of each commodity consumed to the value of foregone alternatives.

☐ Producers operate so that each commodity is produced in a manner that sacrifices the lowest value of foregone alternatives.

These are the conditions present in a competitive economy. With this assumption in mind, benefits may be measured by the market price of the outputs from a public program or by the price consumers would be *willing* to pay if they were charged. Similarly, costs are measured as the monetary expenditures necessary to undertake a project. When the assumed conditions of competition do not exist—for example, when externalities or economies of scale are present—then the estimate of benefits and costs must be modified to take account of this situation.

Direct Benefits

Benefits and costs may be categorized in a number of ways. *Primary* or *direct* benefits of a project consist of the value of goods or services produced if the project is undertaken compared to conditions without the project. The primary benefit of an irrigation project is the value of the additional crops produced on the irrigated land less the cost of seeds, labor, and equipment required to produce the crops. The primary benefits attributable to a college education might be considered as the increase in gross earnings of the graduate over what would have been earned without a college degree. In sum, the value of primary or direct benefits of a project may be taken as the total amount users pay (assuming pure competition) or would be willing to pay (total revenue if a charge is made, plus the consumers' surplus when pure competition does not prevail). Although this principle of evaluating direct benefits may be reasonably straightforward for irrigation projects, the estimation of direct benefits in the valuation of human life, as in health-care or accident prevention[21] programs, poses serious conceptual problems.

Direct Costs

Direct or *primary costs* are generally easier to measure than direct benefits. They include the capital costs necessary to undertake the project, operating and maintenance costs incurred over the life of the project, and personnel expenses. Once again the estimation of these costs is generally much easier for investments in physical assets—such as dams, canals, and so on—than it is for human resource investments. Remember that the costs

---

[20] Ezra J. Mishan, *Cost-Benefit Analysis: An Introduction* (New York: Praeger, 1971), pp. 7–8.

[21] For a summary of this problem, see Ezra J. Mishan, "Evaluation of Life and Limb: A Theoretical Approach," *Journal of Political Economy* (July–August 1971), pp. 687–705. See also *Journal of Risk and Uncertainty* 8, no. 1 (January 1994) for a series of articles dealing with cost-benefit analyses of health and safety regulations and the valuation of human life.

being measured are opportunity costs, or the social value foregone elsewhere because factors of production have been moved into the projected area of activity. If a proposed project will draw 20 percent of the required labor from the ranks of the unemployed, the market cost (wage payments) of these workers' services will overstate the true social cost.[22] A similar conclusion applies for the use of idle land. With *no* alternative use, the opportunity cost of the use of this land is zero (for as long as no productive alternative uses exist), no matter what the government happens to actually pay its owner in compensation. Such compensation to the owner only affects the *distribution* of the benefits derived from land usage.

Indirect Costs and Benefits

In addition to the primary impacts of a project, government investment invariably creates *secondary* or *indirect* effects. Secondary costs and benefits may be of two types: *real* or *technological* effects, and *pecuniary* effects. Real secondary benefits may include reductions in necessary outlays for other government projects, as for example when a glaucoma-detection campaign reduces the number of people who go blind, thereby reducing the need for job retraining as well as the need for future government disability transfer payments. Similarly, an irrigation dam may reduce flooding and create a recreational area. These secondary benefits should be counted in a cost-benefit study. The same argument applies in accounting for secondary costs. For example, the Wallisville Dam Project in Texas was alleged to cause in excess of $500,000 in damages annually to saltwater fishing because of its impacts on the tidal marshlands. This real secondary cost should have been counted in the cost-benefit analysis of the Wallisville Project.

Pecuniary benefits should generally not be included in the enumeration of "countable" benefits in a study. They generally arise in the form of lower input costs, increased volumes of business, or changes in land values resulting from a project. For example, an improved highway may lead to greater business volume and profitability of gas stations, souvenir shops, and restaurants along that road, as well as higher land values and consequently higher rents to the landlords. Many of these benefits are purely distributional in nature because some business will be drawn from firms along other roads once the new road is completed.

If the economy is operating under conditions of full employment, secondary impacts of the multiplier effect and induced investment that may occur as a result of a particular government investment also should not be counted. Under full employment, these benefits must be presumed to occur whether the expenditure of funds is public or private. The objective of a regional project may be to induce local investment, generate multiplier effects, and reduce regional unemployment. Under special circumstances some of these secondary effects may be appropriate to include in the analysis.

Intangibles

A final group of program benefits and costs is intangibles. These are recognizable impacts of a project for which it is either extremely difficult or impossible to calculate a dollar value. Intangibles may include such notions as quality of life, aesthetic contributions (or detriments), and balance-of-payments impacts. Intangibles may be merely listed if it proves impossible to translate them into reasonable estimates of dollar bene-

---

[22] A discussion of this issue is provided by Robert Haveman, "Evaluating Public Expenditures under Conditions of Unemployment," in *Public Expenditures and Policy Analysis,* ed. Robert Haveman and Julius Margolis (Chicago: Markham, 1970).

fits and costs. Alternatively, they may be analyzed by making trade-offs against tangibles in such a manner that the cost of additional increments of intangible improvement, for instance, may be compared with the foregone tangible benefits of a project. An example of this sort of trade-off analysis can be seen in the U.S. Maritime program. One objective of the U.S. Maritime subsidies is to reduce the U.S. balance-of-payments deficit. A comparison of real program costs with balance-of-payments impacts can provide the basis for a choice among the commitment of various levels of real resources to gain foreign exchange savings. As one study of this matter concludes, "It is scarcely credible . . . that the Nation would have been willing to spend $1 to save $1 of foreign exchange."[23]

THE APPROPRIATE RATE OF DISCOUNT

Social Discount Rate
The discount rate to be used when evaluating benefits and costs from public sector investments.

When the benefits or costs of a program extend beyond a one-year time limit, they must be discounted back to some common point in time for purposes of comparison. This is so because most people prefer current consumption to future consumption. The **social discount rate** is used to adjust for this preference.[24] The choice of the appropriate discount rate to evaluate public investments is critical to the conclusions of any cost-benefit analysis. Projects that may appear to be justified at a low discount rate, say 5 percent, may seem to be a gross misallocation of resources at a higher rate, such as 15 percent. The choice of a discount rate is likely to have a profound impact on the type of projects to be accepted. A low rate favors investments with long lives, most of which will be of the durable "bricks and mortar" variety, whereas a high rate favors those whose benefits become available soon after the initial investment. When urgent public needs are apparent, a high rate will tend to be more appropriate. To take an extreme example, when automobile deaths are rising at an alarming rate, it does little good to invest in a dam, even though at a low rate of discount this may appear to be a better alternative than investing to reduce the automobile accident rate.

A higher rate may completely switch investment priorities. In spite of the fact that the choice of a discount rate may completely alter the outcome of a careful benefit-cost analysis, it is given little attention in many studies. In some cases the researcher may select a rate merely because it has been used in the past (probably with equally little justification). Other studies merely select some arbitrary rate, or rates, and perform the analysis, letting the reader decide which is best.[25]

The literature on the social discount rate is extensive and, in many cases, contradictory. Rather than attempt to synthesize and summarize the many points of view that have been expressed, the following discussion focuses on the opportunity cost criterion for estimating the social discount rate. This approach has been most clearly enunciated by Baumol.[26] Baumol's discussion is based on a recognition of the fact that resources

---

[23] Gerald R. Jantscher, "Federal Aids to the Maritime Industries," *The Economics of Federal Subsidy Programs*, Joint Economic Committee (Washington, D.C.: U.S. Government Printing Office, 26 February 1973).

[24] A review of discounting and present-value concepts is provided in Appendix A.

[25] Weisbrod, for example, used both 10 percent to represent the opportunity cost of capital in the private sector and 4 percent to represent the cost of government borrowing to perform his analysis. See Burton A. Weisbrod, *Economics of Public Health: Measuring the Economic Impact of Diseases* (Philadelphia: University of Pennsylvania Press, 1960).

[26] William J. Baumol, "On the Social Rate of Discount," *American Economic Review* (September 1968), pp. 788–802; "On the Discount Rate for Public Projects," in *Public Expenditures and Policy Analysis*, ed. Robert Haveman and Julius Margolis (Chicago: Markham, 1970), pp. 272–290; and "On the Appropriate Discount Rate for Evaluation of Public Projects," statement in *The Planning-Programming-Budgeting System: Progress and Potentials*, Subcommittee on Economy in Government, Joint Economic Committee, 90th Congress, 1st Session (Washington, D.C.: U.S. Government Printing Office, 1967).

invested in a particular manner in one sector could be withdrawn from that sector and invested elsewhere to yield either a higher or a lower rate of return.

Once it is recognized that the discount rate performs the function of allocating resources between the public and private sectors, then a discount rate should be chosen that will properly indicate when resources should be transferred from one sector to another. This simply means that if resources can earn 20 percent in the private sector, then they should not be transferred to the public sector unless they can earn something greater than 20 percent on the invested resources. As Baumol explains:

> The correct discount rate for the evaluation of a government project is the percentage rate of return that the resources utilized would otherwise provide in the private sector.[27]

In calculating the opportunity cost of funds withdrawn from the private sector, one should recognize that funds withdrawn from corporate investment will generally incur a higher opportunity rate than funds taken from consumption. If funds used by a firm generally yield a 20 percent rate of return *before taxes,*[28] then this is the opportunity cost to society of these funds. The cost of funds withdrawn from consumption may be estimated by reference to the rate of return on risk-free bonds, such as U.S. government securities. Consumers investing in such securities which pay, say a 10 percent rate of interest, are actually indicating their preference between current consumption and future consumption. Those consumers who do not invest in these risk-free securities are indicating that they place a higher implied personal opportunity value on current consumption than the risk-free security rate. For nonbondholders, one must conclude that the opportunity cost of present consumption to them is at least as high, if not higher, than that of investors in risk-free securities.

We conclude, as does Baumol, that

> the correct discount rate for a project will be a weighted average of the opportunity cost rate for the various sectors from which the project would draw its resources, and the weight for each such sector in this average is the proportion of the total resources that would come from that sector.[29]

EXAMPLE

COSTS AND BENEFITS OF A TOYOTA AUTOMOBILE PLANT TO KENTUCKY[30]

Toyota built an assembly plant near Lexington, Kentucky, that is able to produce 200,000 automobiles annually. To get Toyota to locate the plant in Kentucky, the state agreed to invest approximately $325 million over a 20-year period. These expenditures include the following:

☐ Land and site preparation $ 33 million
☐ Local highway construction   47 million

---

[27] Baumol, "On the Discount Rate for Public Projects," p. 274.

[28] The opportunity cost of funds withdrawn from corporate investment must be on a before-tax basis, because that is the true rate of return these resources generate. The fact that the corporate income tax may transfer up to 35 percent of this directly to the government is a distributional matter and not an efficiency consideration.

[29] Baumol, "On the Discount Rate for Public Projects," p. 279. Baumol raises a number of other important issues in his development of an appropriate social discount rate, such as the role of risk in public versus private investments, the problem of externalities not accounted for in both the public and private sectors, and income distribution issues. None of these however, alters the fundamental arguments presented above.

[30] Based on an article in the *Wall Street Journal,* 9 June 1987.

▣ Employee training center and education of workers	65 million
▣ Education of Japanese workers and families	5 million
▣ Interest on economic development bonds	167 million

The returns to the state over the 20-year period are estimated at $632 million in income, sales, and payroll taxes from Toyota, its suppliers, and related businesses.

These numbers yield an internal rate of return of 25 percent, according to a University of Kentucky research team. Because the state's economic resources are limited, one must consider whether these resources could be invested in other projects that would generate even higher rates of return. However, as Brinton Milward, director of the university's center for business and economic research, explains, "Could you put these funds into improvements in education and transportation and come up with a better benefit-cost ratio? My guess is no. Manufacturing has a pretty high multiplier" (in terms of the repeated turnover of money in the form of jobs and sales).

COST-EFFECTIVENESS ANALYSIS

Cost-Effectiveness Analysis
An analytical tool designed to assist public decision makers in their resource-allocation decisions when benefits cannot be easily measured in dollar terms but costs can be monetarily quantified.

Although cost-benefit analysis may be beneficially applied in a wide range of areas, in many types of government activity it is simply not feasible because of the problems of measuring the value of program outputs. For instance, program analyses in the fields of defense, environmental protection, crime prevention, industry regulation, and income redistribution are more frequently conducted using the cost-effectiveness framework than the cost-benefit one. Cost-benefit analysis asks the questions: "What is the dollar value of program costs and benefits, and do the benefits exceed the costs by a sufficient amount, given the timing of these outcomes, to justify undertaking the program?" In contrast, the question asked by **cost-effectiveness analysis** is: "Given that some pre-specified objective is to be attained, what are the costs associated with various alternative means for reaching that objective?" In essence, cost-effectiveness analysis *begins* with the premise that some identified program outputs are useful and proceeds to explore (1) how these may be most efficiently achieved *or* (2) what the costs are of achieving various levels of the prespecified output.

In many governmental programs, the outputs can be specified and measured, but difficulty in evaluating these outputs in dollar terms precludes the use of cost-benefit analysis. For example, it is easy to measure or prespecify the number of families placed in adequate housing as a result of low-income housing programs. But it is far more difficult to evaluate the societal benefits accruing from this program because its major impacts are income redistributional. Cost-effectiveness analysis is widely applied in Department of Defense program studies. The benefits of most defense activities may be thought of as providing levels of deterrence. But for any specific program, such as the strategic nuclear bomber force, it is virtually impossible to quantify and evaluate benefits in dollar terms. In cases such as these, cost-effectiveness analysis may be useful.

Constant-Cost Studies

With these general remarks about cost-effectiveness analysis in mind, three more specific types of these studies are examined. *Constant-cost studies* attempt to specify the output that may be achieved from a number of alternative programs, assuming all are funded at the same level (costs are constant between alternatives). In essence, constant-cost studies measure what may be acquired for a specific outlay of funds. Constant-cost studies differ from cost-benefit studies as there is no attempt to place dollar values on the outputs of alternative programs. The greatest use of constant-cost studies is in cases where program outputs have multiple dimensions (there may be income distribution effects, aesthetic effects, or impacts on future economic development). This is the case in many urban renewal programs. Decision makers may examine several alternatives for land provided by urban renewal. They might choose on the basis of what uses—industrial, commercial, or residential—offer the greatest potential profitability. Alternatively, an explicit attempt may be made to provide for planned development considering the esthetics of development, the impacts of current development on surrounding areas and future development potential, and the desire to provide a mix of different cultures and income groups within the city. For projects such as these, all one can do is attempt to spell out all the impacts of several alternative, equal-cost schemes. This in itself is likely to be a monumental task. With impacts clearly identified, it becomes the decision maker's responsibility to weigh (subjectively) the outputs of each alternative and to make a choice.

Least-Cost Studies

The second type of cost-effectiveness analysis is *least-cost studies*.[31] As might be expected, the emphasis of these studies is to identify the least expensive way of generating some quantity of an output. For instance, a city might decide that it wishes to reduce by 20 percent the number of burglaries occurring each year within its jurisdictional limits. One approach could be to expand the size of the police force, increase the number of foot patrol officers, and increase the number of squad cars on the streets at any one time. Another possibility might be to require builders to install security bars on the windows of all new homes and to provide cash or tax incentives for current homeowners to improve their personal security systems. A third alternative might be a community drive supporting Operation Identification, where individuals place permanent identifying marks on their belongings to make "fencing" of this merchandise more difficult. If it is recognized that drugs addicts are responsible for many burglaries, a drug rehabilitation program may be considered. Combinations of these programs are also possible. Each of these alternatives is evaluated in terms of the expenditure required to achieve the desired objective—a 20 percent reduction in burglaries.

Objective-Level Studies

A third type of cost-effectiveness analysis is *objective-level studies*. These studies attempt to estimate the costs of achieving several alternative performance levels of the same objective. This may be illustrated with the case of reducing automobile emission levels. Table 19.6 provides some hypothetical data relating to various emission-control standards.

In addition to the increased fuel and maintenance costs and the added new-car costs, other impacts of a program to reduce auto emissions must be considered. For example, what is the relative impact of such a program on various income groups? In areas where the automobile is a necessity, a program that substantially increases the cost of driving without simultaneously providing feasible alternative means of transportation could be disastrous. Given the current domestic energy situation, one must examine the effects of increased fuel consumption by less efficient engines on the balance of payments. Finally, in performing objective-level studies, we must be aware of the state of technology assumptions that are being made. Although the estimates in Table 19.6 may be realistic

---

[31] The discussion of both constant-cost and least-cost studies is based largely on Neil M. Singer, *Public Microeconomics* (Boston: Little, Brown & Co., 1972), chap. 12.

TABLE 19.6		

Hypothetical Data Relating to the Cost of Achieving Various Levels of Auto Emission Reductions

Percentage of 19X8 Emission Levels	Costs (Millions of Dollars—Including Fuel Consumption, More Frequent Maintenance, and Added New-Car Costs)
90	$200
70	250
40	500
20	2,500
10	7,500
5	38,000
1	140,000

for the reciprocating engine, they may far overstate actual costs if alternative technology were assumed. Table 19.6 *does* illustrate that as the level of objective achievement increases, the associated costs frequently increase at a much more rapid rate. Objective-level studies do not directly measure program benefits, but they do measure intermediate program outputs or objectives. This may give the decision maker the information needed to make more rational decisions. For example, it may be clear that the $2.5 billion expenditure needed to reduce emissions to 20 percent of their 19X8 levels is reasonable. It may be far less clear whether an additional 19 percent (from 20 percent to 1 percent) emissions reduction is worth the required incremental expenditure of $137.5 billion ($140 billion less $2.5 billion).

Thus, in comparison to cost-benefit analyses, cost-effectiveness analyses provide less positive inputs on which economic decisions can be made. They furnish decision makers with disciplined studies relating program costs with some measurable but unvalued estimates of program outputs.

SUMMARY

- A *capital expenditure* is defined as a current outlay of funds that is expected to provide a flow of future cash benefits.

- The capital expenditure decision process should consist of the following steps: generating alternative investment proposals, estimating cash flows, evaluating and choosing the projects to undertake, and reviewing the projects after implementation.

- The *internal rate of return (IRR)* is defined as the discount rate that equates the present value of the net cash flows from the project with the net investment. An investment project should be accepted (rejected) if its internal rate of return is greater than or equal to (less than) the firm's required rate of return (that is, cost of capital).

- The *net present value (NPV)* of an investment is defined as the present value of the net cash flows from the project, discounted at the firm's required rate of return (that is, cost of capital), minus the project's net investment. An investment project should be accepted (rejected) if its net present value is greater than or equal to (less than) zero.

- The *cost of capital* is defined as the cost of funds that are supplied to the firm. It is influenced by the riskiness of the firm, both in terms of its capital structure and its investment strategy.

- The after-tax cost of debt (issued at par) is equal to the coupon rate multiplied by 1 minus the firm's marginal tax rate.
- The cost of equity can be estimated using a number of different approaches, including the dividend valuation model and the capital asset pricing model.
- The weighted cost of capital is calculated by weighting the costs of specific sources of funds, such as debt and equity, by the proportions of each of the capital components in the firm's long-range target capital structure.
- *Cost-benefit analysis* is the public sector counterpart of capital budgeting techniques used in private sector resource-allocation decisions.
- Cost-benefit analysis involves the following steps:
  1. Determining the program objectives
  2. Enumerating the alternative means of achieving the objectives, subject to the legal, political, technological, budgetary, and other constraints that limit the scope of action
  3. Evaluating all primary, secondary, and intangible benefits and costs associated with each alternative
  4. Discounting the benefits and costs using a social discount rate to arrive at an overall measure of the desirability of each alternative (for example, benefit-cost ratio)
  5. Choosing (or recommending) the best alternative based on the overall measure of desirability and the relative magnitude of the nonquantifiable intangibles
- Because of the measurement problems arising from the intangible impacts and economic externalities of many public programs, cost-benefit analysis is most useful in comparing projects with similar objectives and similar magnitudes of intangibles and externalities.
- In cases where it is not feasible to place dollar values on final program outputs, *cost-effectiveness analysis* may be used. Cost-effectiveness analysis assumes a priori that the program objectives are worth achieving and focuses on the least-cost method of achieving them.

EXERCISES

1. A firm has the opportunity to invest in a project having an initial outlay of $20,000. Net cash inflows (before depreciation and taxes) are expected to be $5,000 per year for five years. The firm uses the straight-line depreciation method with a zero salvage value and has a (marginal) income-tax rate of 40 percent. The firm's cost of capital is 12 percent.
   a. Compute the following quantities:
      (i) Internal rate of return
      (ii) Net present value
   b. Should the firm accept or reject the project?

2. A machine that costs $12,000 is expected to operate for 10 years. The estimated salvage value at the end of 10 years is $0. The machine is expected to save the company $2,331 per year before taxes and depreciation. The company depreciates its assets on a straight-line basis and has a marginal tax rate of 40 percent. The firm's cost of capital is 14 percent. Based on the internal-rate-of-return criterion, should this machine be purchased?

3. A company is planning to invest $75,000 (before taxes) in a personnel training program. The $75,000 outlay will be charged off as an expense by the firm this year

(Year 0). The returns estimated from the program in the form of greater productivity and a reduction in employee turnover, are as follows (on an after-tax basis):

Years 1–10: $7,500 per year

Years 11–20: $22,500 per year

The company has estimated its cost of capital to be 15 percent. Assume that the entire $75,000 is paid at time zero (the beginning of the project). The marginal tax rate for the firm is 40 percent.

Based on the net-present-value criterion, should the firm undertake the training program?

4. Alliance Manufacturing Company is considering the purchase of a new, automated drill press to replace an older one. The machine now in operation has a book value of zero and a salvage value of zero. However, it is in good working condition with an expected life of 10 additional years. The new drill press is more efficient than the existing one and, if installed, will provide an estimated cost savings (in labor, materials, and maintenance) of $6,000 per year. The new machine costs $25,000 delivered and installed. It has an estimated useful life of 10 years, and a salvage value of $1,000 at the end of this period. The firm's cost of capital is 14 percent and its marginal income tax rate is 40 percent. The firm uses the straight-line depreciation method.

  a. What is the net cash flow in year zero (that is, initial outlay)?
  b. What are the net cash flows after taxes in each of the next 10 years?
  c. What is the net present value of the investment?
  d. Should Alliance replace its existing drill press?

5. Sam's Cleaners is considering opening a new store. The store will be owned by Sam and will cost $200,000 to build. It will be located on a piece of land that will be leased at a rate of $2,000 per year, payable at the end of each year. For planning purposes, the store is expected to have a maximum 20-year life. Cleaning equipment for the new store will cost an additional $40,000 and have an economic life of 20 years. The equipment will be depreciated on a straight-line basis to an estimated salvage value of $0 at the end of 20 years. The building will be depreciated on a straight-line basis to an estimated salvage value of $40,000.

Operating revenues are expected to be $60,000 per year during the first 10 years. These revenues are expected to equal $100,000 per year for years 11–20. Cash operating costs, exclusive of lease payments, are expected to be $20,000 per year during the first 10 years of operation and to increase to $26,000 per year for years 11–20. The firm's marginal tax rate is 40 percent.

  a. Compute the net investment for the new cleaning store.
  b. Compute the annual net cash flows for the new cleaning store.
  c. Compute the project's net present value assuming a 12 percent cost of capital (required rate of return).
  d. Should Sam's Cleaners open the new store?

6. The Charlotte Hornets, a recent expansion basketball team, has been offered the opportunity to purchase the contract of an aging superstar basketball player from another team. The general manager of the Hornets wants to analyze the offer as a capital budgeting problem. The Hornets would have to pay the other team $800,000 to obtain the superstar. Being somewhat old, the basketball player is expected to be able to play for only four more years. The general manager figures that attendance, and hence revenues, would increase substantially if the Hornets obtain the superstar. He estimates that *incremental* returns

(additional ticket revenues less the superstar's salary) would be as follows over the four-year period:

Year	Incremental Returns
1	$450,000
2	350,000
3	275,000
4	200,000

The general manager has been told by the owners of the team that any capital expenditures must yield at least 12 percent after taxes. The firm's (marginal) income tax rate is 40 percent. Furthermore, a check of the tax regulations indicates that the team can depreciate the $800,000 initial expenditure over the four-year period.

    a. Determine the following measures of the desirability of this investment:
      (i) Internal rate of return
      (ii) Net present value
    b. Should the Hornets sign the superstar?

7. An acre planted with walnut tress is estimated to be worth $15,000 in 25 years. If you want to realize a 12 percent rate of return on your investment, how much can you afford to invest per acre? (Ignore all taxes and assume that annual cash outlays to maintain your stand of walnut trees are nil.)

8. Panhandle Industries, Inc. currently pays an annual common stock dividend of $2.20 per share. The company's dividend has grown steadily over the past 10 years at 8 percent per year; this growth trend is expected to continue for the foreseeable future. The company's present dividend payout ratio, also expected to continue, is 40 percent. In addition, the stock presently sells at eight times current earnings (that is, its "multiple" is 8).

    Calculate the company's cost of equity capital using the dividend capitalization model approach.

9. Panhandle Industries, Inc. (see Exercise 8) stock has a beta, β, of 1.15 as computed by a leading investment service. The present risk-free rate is 7 percent, and the expected return on the stock market is 13 percent. Compute the company's cost of equity capital using the capital asset pricing model. How does this value compare with the one determined in Exercise 8 using the dividend capitalization model?

10. The Gordon Company currently pays an annual common stock dividend of $4.00 per share. Its dividend payments have been growing at a steady rate of 6 percent per year, and this rate of growth is expected to continue for the foreseeable future. Gordon's common stock is currently selling for $65.25 per share. The company can sell additional shares of common stock after flotation costs at a net price of $60.50 per share.

    Based on the dividend capitalization model, determine the cost of

    a. Internal equity (retained earnings)
    b. External equity (new common stock)

11. Baker Manufacturing Company has a beta, β, estimated at 1.10. The risk-free rate is 6 percent and the expected market return is 12 percent. Compute the company's cost of equity capital.

12. The Williams Company has a present capital structure (that it considers optimal) consisting of 30 percent long-term debt and 70 percent common equity. The company plans to finance next year's capital budget with additional long-term debt and retained earnings. New debt can be issued at a coupon interest rate of 10 percent. The cost of retained earnings (internal equity) is estimated at 15 percent. The company's marginal tax rate is 40 percent.

    Calculate the company's weighted cost of capital for the coming year.

13. Several studies have reported very low private and social rates of return on an investment in securing (providing) graduate education in many disciplines. In spite of this evidence, an increasing number of schools have been offering advanced-level degrees. (Surprisingly, in spite of normative prescriptions of economic theory, economics falls into the category of these low-return disciplines.)

    a. How can you explain this seeming contradiction to an efficient allocation of societal resources?

    b. Can you suggest some alternatives that could help direct more resources away from low-return educational programs toward higher-return alternatives?

14. The state of Glottamora has $100 million remaining in its budget for the current year. One alternative is to give Glottamorans a one-time tax rebate. Two proposals have been made for expenditures of these funds.

    The first proposed project is to invest in a new power plant, costing $100 million and having an expected useful life of 20 years. Projected benefits accruing from this project are as follows:

Years	Benefits Per Year (Millions of Dollars)
1–5	$ 0
6–20	20

The second alternative is to undertake a job-retraining program, also costing $100 million and generating the following benefits:

Years	Benefits Per Year (Millions of Dollars)
1–5	$20
6–10	14
11–20	4

The State Power Department has argued that a 5 percent discount factor should be used in evaluating the projects, because that is the government's borrowing rate. The Human Resources Department suggests using a 12 percent rate, because that more nearly equals society's true opportunity rate.

    a. What is implied by the various departments' desires to use different discount rates?

    b. Evaluate the projects using both the 5 percent and the 12 percent rates.

    c. What rate do you believe to be more appropriate?

    d. Make a choice between the projects and the tax-refund alternative. Why did you choose the alternative you did?

15. The Department of Transportation wishes to choose between two alternative accident prevention programs. It has identified three benefits to be gained from such programs:
    a. Reduced property damage, both to the vehicles involved in an accident and to other property (for example, real estate that may be damaged at the scene of an accident)
    b. Reduced injuries
    c. Reduced fatalities

    The department's experts are willing to make dollar estimates of property damage savings that are expected to accrue from any program, but they will only estimate the number of injuries and fatalities that may be averted.

    The first program is relatively moderate in its costs and will be concentrated in a large city. It involves upgrading traffic signals, improving road markers, and repaving some potholed streets. Because of the concentration and value of property in the city, savings from reduced property damage are expected to be substantial. Likewise, a moderate number of traffic-related deaths and injuries should be avoided.

    The second program is more ambitious. It involves straightening long sections of dangerous rural roads and installing improved guardrails. Although the property damage savings are expected to be small in relation to total cost, the reduction in traffic-related deaths and injuries should be substantial.

    The following table summarizes the expected costs and payoffs of the two programs:

Year	1	2	3	4	Total
Alternative #1					
Cost ($000)	200	200	100	50	550
Reduced property damage ($000)	50	100	250	100	500
Lives saved	60	40	35	25	160
Injuries prevented	500	425	300	150	1,375
Alternative #2					
Cost ($000)	700	1,800	1,100	700	4,300
Reduced property damage ($000)	150	225	475	300	1,150
Lives saved	50	75	100	125	350
Injuries prevented	800	850	900	900	3,450

    Assume that a 10 percent discount rate is appropriate for evaluating government programs:
    a. Calculate the net present costs of the two programs.
    b. Generate any other tables that you may find useful in choosing between the programs.
    c. Can you arrive at any unambiguous choice between the two alternatives? What factors are likely to weigh on the ultimate choice made?
16. One study completed for the American Enterprise Institute estimated the cost per life saved in several programs supported or mandated by the government. The following results were reported:

Estimates of cost per life saved	
Recommended for cost-benefit analysis by the National Safety Council for traffic safety	$37,500
Kidney dialysis at home	$99,000
Instructions to military pilots on when to crash-land airplanes	$270,000
Consumer Product Safety Commission's proposed lawn-mower safety standards	$240,000 to $1,920,000
OSHA-proposed acrylonitrile exposure standard	$1,963,000 to $624,976,000
OSHA coke-oven emission standard	$4,500,000 to $158,000,000

Other analyses have indicated that a proposed plan to further reduce carbon monoxide auto emissions would cost $1 billion in increased costs of production and costs to the consumer and that the plan would prolong two lives in 20 years. This could be compared with the $200 it would cost to prevent each of 24,000 premature deaths per year by installing cardiac care units in ambulances.

Some studies of the value of a human life have computed an implicit value in the range of $200,000 to $700,000. These studies have examined wage differentials for hazardous jobs and provide estimates of what people are willing to pay for a small decrease in risk.

a.   Given these estimates of the value of a human life, which of the programs discussed do you think should be pursued?

b.   How can you explain the actions of a mine operator who may spend $5 million to free a trapped miner?

www exercise

Capital Budgeting for the Federal Government

17.   Capital budgeting has been discussed in the context of a profit-maximizing firm, and some argue that many of the same tools can be applied to government budget planning and analysis. To learn more about proposed legislation to utilize capital budgeting for the federal government, access the following Internet site: http://www.house.gov/wise/tcapbud.htm. What are the elements of HR 1233? How are the concepts of capital budgeting applied to government? In what ways are they different than for a profit-maximizing firm? Can you see any possible controversies over what constitutes government investment?

CASE EXERCISE

COST-BENEFIT ANALYSIS[32]

The Michigan State Fairgrounds is centrally located in the Detroit Standard Metropolitan Statistical Area (SMSA), which consists of Wayne, Oakland, and Macomb counties. The population within the SMSA numbered 4,197,931 persons in 19X0—over 47 percent of the state's total population. More than 59 percent and 75 percent of the state's population reside within 60 and 100 miles, respectively, of the fairground site. The site is located near an efficient freeway system that connects many areas of the state. The State Fairgrounds is operated by the Agriculture Department and is currently in a deplorable state of disrepair. Costs have exceeded revenues by a substantial margin every

---

[32] Adapted from an unpublished paper by Eric Hartshom of Wayne State University, "Cost-Benefit Analysis Concerning the Proposed Redevelopment Program for the Michigan State Fairgrounds."

year in the recent past. A redevelopment program has been proposed for the fairgrounds that would serve several purposes:

1. Revitalization of the fairgrounds would prevent further economic deterioration of the existing facilities, increase attendance and consequently revenues, and perhaps make the fairgrounds an economically viable entity.

2. A further benefit to be realized would be an economic stimulus to the area resulting from increased employment from the initial construction program, as well as increased revenues realized from the additional business that the proposed new facilities would generate.

3. Finally, aesthetic value could be realized from the upgrading and redevelopment of what is currently a marginal area of the city.

The redevelopment program would consist of the overall rehabilitation of the grounds and buildings as well as the construction of several income-producing buildings, including a hotel and convention facility and a dog track (providing dog racing is legalized in Michigan and the fairgrounds can obtain the necessary license). Either a new coliseum would be constructed or the present one redesigned and refurbished. The cost of the redevelopment program would be $20 million. Construction would take three years with 50 percent of the cost incurred in year 0, 30 percent in year 1, and 20 percent in year 2. The redevelopment program would require funding by the state and/or federal government. The following estimated benefits would be derived from the project:

1. *Initial construction benefits.* Previous studies showed that 38 worker-years of employment are derived from each $1 million in construction. Assuming an hourly rate of $6, 40 hours per week, and 50 weeks per year, and relating this to the $20 million cost of the redevelopment program, results in $9,120,000 of economic benefit to be derived through increased employment. Like the construction costs, these benefits would be spread over three years ($4.560 million in year 0, $2.736 million in year 1, and $1.824 million in year 2).

2. *Coliseum.* An appropriate coliseum facility could generate, in excess of current levels, an additional $500,000 annually (years 3–20) from shows and events not currently available in the Detroit area.

3. *Increased state fair attendance.* With improved facilities (such as those planned in the redevelopment program), attendance at the state fair is expected to increase from 700,000 presently to 1,000,000 people annually. Assuming present per capita expenditures ($3.33) at the Michigan State Fair, the increased attendance would result in an additional $1 million in revenue annually (years 3–20).

4. *Convention and hotel facility.* It is estimated that a 200-room hotel, convention, and dining facility located at the fairgrounds would generate nearly $1.5 million in additional revenue annually (years 3–20).

5. *Dog-racing track.* It is estimated that an average dog-racing facility will produce $1.5 million in revenue annually. However, it must be realized that dog racing is similar to horse racing, and it is expected that a portion of the revenues generated by a dog track would be realized owing to a transfer of funds from local horse-racing facilities. Because this transfer of funds should not be considered in the analysis, it would be assumed that one-third of the dog-racing revenues will result from the redistribution of funds from local horse-racing tracks. Consequently only $1 million in annual revenues (years 3–20) will be attributed to the proposed dog-racing track.

Type of Cost or Benefit	Year(s)	Annual Benefit (+) or Cost (−) ($ Million)
Construction outlay	0	$−10.000
Construction outlay	1	−6.000
Construction outlay	2	−4.000
Increased employment	0	+4.560
Increased employment	1	+2.736
Increased employment	2	+1.824
Coliseum	3–20	+0.500
State Fair attendance	3–20	+1.000
Convention and hotel facility	3–20	+1.500
Dog-racing track	3–20	+1.000

The cost and benefits of the proposed redevelopment are summarized in the following table. Assume that a 10 percent interest rate is appropriate for discounting the costs and benefits of the proposed project.

QUESTIONS

1. Determine the benefit-cost ratio (defined as the ratio of discounted benefits to costs) for the proposed fairground development.
2. Based on this analysis, should the redevelopment program be undertaken?
3. List some of the secondary benefits and costs, as well as intangibles, associated with the project.

   In calculating the benefits of the fairground redevelopment program, increased employment opportunities were included.

4. What assumption about employment in the Detroit area must be made in associating these benefits with the project?
5. Recalculate the benefit-cost ratio, assuming that these benefits are not included in the analysis. How does this affect the desirability of the project?

   In calculating the benefits of the fairground redevelopment project, it was assumed that $1.5 million in additional annual revenue would be generated from the convention and hotel facility.

6. What assumption is being made about the effects of this facility on other hotel and convention facilities? Is this a realistic assumption?
7. Suppose that only $500,000 of the facility's annual revenues can be attributed to "new" convention and hotel business. Recalculate the benefit-cost ratio under this assumption (also exclude employment benefits). How does this affect the desirability of the project?
8. Suppose that the fairground is unable to obtain a license to operate a dog-racing track. Assume that construction costs are reduced by 15 percent if a dog-racing track is not built. Recompute the benefit-cost ratio under this assumption (also exclude employment and convention facility benefits). How does this affect the desirability of the proposed redevelopment project?

Risk Analysis

CHAPTER PREVIEW

In Chapter 2, shareholder wealth was shown to be a function of both the expected returns and the risk of those expected returns. In general, investors will place a higher value on a more certain future stream of returns (cash flows). Conversely, the less certain (riskier) future returns are perceived to be, the lower the value assigned to these returns by investors. In the financial markets a positive relationship exists between the rate of return required by investors and the risk of the investment. Normally, high returns can only be earned by assuming high risk. In this chapter we develop approaches for making decisions under risk and uncertainty, and examine techniques designed to reduce risk efficiently. An appropriate balance of risk and expected return is an important ingredient in shareholder wealth maximization.

MANAGERIAL CHALLENGE

PLANNING FOR FUTURE POWER NEEDS: PUBLIC SERVICE COMPANY OF NEW MEXICO

The Public Service Company of New Mexico (PNM) is the major producer and distributor of electric power in New Mexico. Its total revenues in 1991 were approximately $845 million. The book value of its plant in service was nearly $2 billion in 1991. Through 1986 PNM was able to earn returns on its common equity investment that were comparable to other firms in the industry—approximately 12 percent. After 1986, and particularly during 1990 and projected into 1991, PNM's returns on common equity plummeted to a level of only about 2 percent. What was the cause of this significant decline in performance?

During the 1970s, PNM experienced high growth in the demand for its services as the Sunbelt prospered and industry grew in the region. One large user of power was the growing uranium mining industry in New Mexico that was serving the needs of nuclear power plants being built by other electric utilities. Faced with rapid growth in demand and increasing costs for its traditional fuel, natural gas, PNM embarked on a major program to expand and modernize its power-generating capacity. As the managers of the utility planned for the future, they made projections of future demand. PNM's managers examined a number of alternatives to meet the growing demand, including purchasing power from nearby utilities, building large coal-fired plants close to New Mexico's abundant coal resources, and building nuclear power plants. The objective of PNM's management was to meet the projected demand at the lowest cost. Having seen what happened to the price of natural gas in the early 1970s, these managers also were aware of the desirability of having a diverse mix of fuel sources. PNM ultimately decided to participate with other regional utilities in the construction of several large coal-fired plants in the Four Corners region of northwest New Mexico, to build additional coal-fired plants of its own, and to participate with other utilities in the construction of a five-unit nuclear power plant called Palo Verde.

As time passed, load growth did not materialize as expected. In the aftermath of the disaster at Three Mile Island, demand for uranium ore declined and lower cost alternative sources were developed. The New Mexico uranium mining industry virtually shut down. The state of New Mexico required that expensive pollution control devices, called scrubbers, be installed at the coal plants being constructed, thereby dramatically increasing their cost and the cost of power produced from these plants. The Palo Verde project was plagued by cost overruns, delays, and extensive and costly safety modifications. Ultimately two of the five units of Palo Verde were canceled. When the construction program was completed, PNM found itself with capacity nearly 80 percent in excess of peak demand (a 20 percent reserve margin is more normal).

This discussion illustrates one of the key concepts discussed in this chapter—the importance of risk analysis in decision making. When long-term investment decisions are made, a firm faces significant risks. In this case, revenue forecasts proved to be in error—not because of the use of faulty forecasting procedures, but because of the high level of uncertainty that accompanies long-term projects. Also, projections of costs that were to be incurred over a more than 10-year period proved to be incorrect because of unexpected increases in inflation and unforeseen changes in construction requirements to meet safety and pollution control standards.

In this chapter we examine the concept of risk in more detail and look at some techniques that are helpful when managers need to assess the risk of various business strategies. In addition, we also consider risk-management practices that can help managers control or eliminate the risk in various business strategies.

WWW . . . .

Financial information on the Public Service Company of New Mexico is at:

http://www.pnm.com/Investors/financials/financials.htm

RISK AND DECISION ANALYSIS

A decision problem has several basic elements. First, there must be an individual or group that is faced with the problem, that is, a *decision maker.* The decision maker must be seeking to achieve some *objective,* or desired outcome. At least two *alternative actions* or strategies, which can possibly achieve the stated objective, must be available to the decision maker. In addition, *a state of doubt* must exist within the decision maker about which alternative action is best in seeking to achieve the desired objective. Finally, the problem exists within an *environment* consisting of all factors that can influence the achievement of the objective or desired outcome but that cannot be controlled completely by the decision maker.

This framework is applicable in a wide variety of decision-making situations ranging from very complex management (resource allocation) problems to relatively simple problems encountered in daily life. The amount of effort expended in analyzing a decision problem using this framework clearly depends on the magnitude of the payoffs (that is, values of the outcomes) involved and the period of time available. Day-to-day routine decisions are not subjected to the same degree of analysis as are decisions that will have a long-term impact on the individual or organization. Some specific examples of decision problems are presented later in the discussions of the solution techniques of decision theory.

For purposes of exposition and analysis, we can divide decision making into several parts depending on the characteristics of the decision problem. A commonly used classification scheme for decision making is described by Luce and Raiffa "according to whether a decision is made by (i) an individual or (ii) a group, and according to whether it is effected under conditions of (a) certainty, (b) **risk,** or (c) **uncertainty.**"[1]

Risk
A decision-making situation in which there is variability in the possible outcomes and the probabilities of these outcomes can be specified by the decision maker.

The distinction between an individual and a group is based on the compatibility of the objectives or interests of the participants in the decision-making situation. If all the participants share the same underlying objectives, then the decision problem can be analyzed *as if* the decision were going to be made by one individual. If, however, conflict exists between the objectives of two or more participants, then the decision-making situation would be analyzed as one of group decision making. Such a group decision-making situation is referred to as a "game" and is analyzed using the techniques of *game theory.*[2]

Uncertainty
A decision-making situation in which the decision maker is either unable or unwilling to specify the probabilities of occurrence of the possible outcomes of the decision.

The classification of decision-making problems among the certainty, risk, and uncertainty categories is determined by the knowledge of the possible outcomes (or payoffs) that will occur when one of the two (or more) alternative actions is chosen in a decision problem. Luce and Raiffa define a situation to be decision making under

1. *Certainty* if each action is known to lead invariably to a specific outcome;
2. *Risk* if each action leads to one of a set of possible specific outcomes, each outcome occurring with a known probability; or
3. *Uncertainty* if each action has as its consequence a set of possible specific outcomes, but where the probabilities of these outcomes are completely unknown or not even meaningful.[3]

---

[1] R. Duncan Luce and Howard Raiffa, *Games and Decisions* (New York: John Wiley, 1957), p 13. A fourth category considered by Luce and Raiffa was "(d) a combination of uncertainty and risk in the light of experimental evidence . . . statistical inference" (p. 13). We limit the analysis to the first three categories; that is, certainty, risk, and uncertainty.

[2] Game theory is examined in Chapters 14 and 15 as part of the discussion of oligopolistic price and output decision making.

[3] Luce and Raiffa, *Games and Decisions,* p. 14.

In a game, or conflict decision-making situation, a condition of uncertainty exists because one decision maker does not know the state of knowledge, motivations, and hence the actions of the other decision makers. Game theory seeks to reduce this element of uncertainty by postulating certain assumptions about the state of knowledge and motivations of the other decision makers in the game situation.

In this chapter, we focus on individual decision making under risk and uncertainty. In addition, we consider the application of risk analysis techniques to long-term decision making (capital budgeting). Finally, we review strategies available to managers to reduce risk.

INCORPORATING RISK INTO THE DECISION-MAKING PROCESS

Recall from Chapter 2 that risk refers to the potential variability of outcomes from a decision alternative. The more variable these possible outcomes are, the greater is the risk associated with a decision alternative.

Numerous approaches have been developed for incorporating risk into the decision-making process. These range from relatively simple methods, such as the use of subjective or informal approaches, to fairly complex ones, such as the use of computerized simulation models. Five of these methods, namely, the *subjective* or *informal* approach, *utility function* approach, *decision tree* approach, *risk-adjusted discount rate* approach, and *simulation* approach are discussed below. This list is not exhaustive; many other risk-adjusted methods are available to the decision maker.

Subjective or Informal Approach

Decisions are frequently based on the decision maker's subjective feelings about risk in relation to expected return. For example, if a firm is evaluating two mutually exclusive investments having approximately equal net returns, the decision maker will probably choose the less risky investment. This informal approach to decision making is commonly used because it is both simple and inexpensive.

If, however, two investments under consideration have significantly different net returns as well as different levels of perceived risk, the decision becomes more complicated. In these cases the decision maker must determine—again subjectively—whether the additional risk will be offset by sufficiently higher returns.

Even though subjective decision making is often useful, more precise methods yield more valuable information in many cases.

Utility Function Approach

In decision problems whose uncertain possible outcomes constitute monetary payoffs (that is, dollars) with known probabilities of occurrence, it has been observed that a simple preference for higher dollar amounts is not sufficient to explain the choices made by many individuals. The classic example, known as the St. Petersburg paradox, was formulated by the seventeenth-century mathematician D. Bernoulli and illustrates the dilemma. The paradox consists of a gamble in which a "fair" coin—that is, a coin in which the probability of a head and tail is one-half—is tossed until the *first head* appears. The player receives or wins 2^n dollars when the first head appears on the nth toss. The question is: How much should the player be willing to pay to participate in this gamble (that is, how much should the player be willing to wager)? The *expected monetary value* of such a gamble is infinite.[4] Therefore, based on the criterion of expected monetary value, the individual should be willing to wager everything he or she owns in return for the chance to receive 2^n dollars. Because most individuals would choose not to participate under these conditions, we conclude that the actual monetary values of the possible outcomes of the gamble do not necessarily reveal a person's true preference for these outcomes and that the maximization of expected monetary value criterion is not necessarily a reliable guide in predicting the actions or strategies a person will choose in a given decision-making situation. Other more commonly observed examples of behavior, such as investment portfolio diversification and the simultaneous purchase of lottery tickets (that is, gambling) and insurance, also lend support to these conclusions.

If we reject maximization of expected monetary value as a valid guide in decision problems involving risky outcomes, what then is the proper criterion for decision making in such situations? In their pioneering work on game theory, Von Neumann and Morgenstern constructed a framework based on the assessment of the "utilities" of the outcomes,[5] which provides an answer to this question.[6] Within their framework it can be shown that the *maximization of expected utility* criterion will yield decisions that are in accord with the individual's true preferences, provided the individual is able to assess a consistent set of utilities over the possible outcomes in the problem. **Expected utility** is calculated by summing, over all the possible outcomes that may result from a decision, the product of the utility of each outcome, U_i, times its respective probability of occurrence, P_i:

Expected Utility
The product of the utility of each outcome times its respective probability of occurrence, summed over all possible outcomes.

$$E(U) = \sum_{i=1}^{n} U_i \times P_i \qquad [20.1]$$

Despite the apparent attractiveness of this decision criterion, a number of difficulties arise in attempting to implement it. First, in a large organization, whose utility function do we use? In the case of a private firm do we use the managers' or the shareholders' utility functions? Suppose we use the shareholders' utility functions; because different shareholders have different utility functions, which one do we use? The utility functions of different individuals are not directly comparable, and hence it is theoretically impossible to arrive at a group utility function. Second, assuming that we have resolved the question of whose utility function to use, serious problems arise in measuring the utility function of

---

[4] This statement can be demonstrated as follows:

$EMV = P(\text{1st head on 1st toss}) \times 2^1 + P(\text{1st head on 2nd toss}) \times 2^2 +$
$\qquad P(\text{1st head on 3rd toss}) \times 2^3 + \ldots$

$\qquad = \left(\frac{1}{2}\right)^1 \times 2^1 + \left(\frac{1}{2}\right)^2 \times 2^2 + \left(\frac{1}{2}\right)^3 \times 2^3 + \ldots$

$\qquad = 1 + 1 + 1 + \ldots$

EMV constitutes the sum of an infinite series of 1's.

[5] Recall from Chapter 4 that *utility* is defined as the satisfaction an individual receives from a good (or combination of goods). The term *good* can refer to a commodity (such as bread), a service (such as haircuts), or, as in the discussion in this section, wealth (money).

[6] See John von Neumann and Oskar Morgenstern, *Theory of Games and Economic Behavior,* 3d ed. (Princeton, N.J.: Princeton University Press, 1953), pp. 15–30, especially pp. 26–27. Their framework consists of a series of axioms that imply the existence of a utility function. These axioms in turn yield a theorem concerning an individual's preferences for combinations of risky outcomes.

an individual. The approaches used in attempting to empirically derive a utility function sometimes result in inconsistent utility assessments.[7] Similarly, theoretical approaches to the derivation of utility functions do not necessarily yield satisfactory results.[8] Nevertheless, if the decision makers' true preferences for the outcomes of the problem are to be incorporated into the decision-making framework, the lack of a better system for accomplishing this task forces us to attempt to make these utility assessments.

Let us illustrate how to use utilities and the maximization of expected utility criterion in decision problems involving risk. Suppose an entrepreneur has developed a new and untested product and is considering whether to invest some capital in an effort to market the product. Suppose extensive studies of the marketing of products belonging to the same general category as this one have shown that 20 percent are successful and the remainder (that is, 80 percent) are failures. Because a subcontractor can be employed to manufacture the product, no investment in production facilities is required. The entrepreneur has determined that the cost of producing and marketing a batch of the product will be $40,000. If the marketing effort is successful, a profit of $160,000 will result. Suppose further that the product can be easily copied and subsequent competition will therefore limit the profitable sales of the product to the initial production run. If the product is not initially successful and the marketing effort fails, the entrepreneur's loss will be limited to the initial $40,000 investment.

The basic characteristics of the decision problem can be summarized in a payoff table format such as Figure 20.1, where the various alternative actions (that is, decisions) are listed down the left-hand side of the payoff table, the various states of nature are listed across the top of the payoff table, and the various outcomes (that is, dollar payoffs) are

---

[7] Frederick Mosteller and Phillip Nogee, "An Experimental Measurement of Utility," *Journal of Political Economy* 59, no. 5 (October 1951), pp. 371–404; Donald Davidson and Patrick Suppes (in collaboration with Sidney Siegal), *Decision Making: An Experimental Approach* (Stanford, Calif.: Stanford University Press, 1957); P. E. Green, "Risk Attitudes and Chemical Investment Decisions," *Chemical Engineering Progress* 59, no. 1 (January 1963), pp. 35–40; C. Jackson Grayson, Jr., *Decisions Under Uncertainty: Drilling Decisions by Oil and Gas Operators* (Boston: Division of Research, Harvard Business School, 1960); Daniel Kahneman and Amos Tversky, "Prospect Theory: An Analysis of Decision under Risk," *Econometrica,* 47, no. 2 (March 1979), pp. 263–291; and Colin Camerer, "An Experimental Test of Several Generalized Utility Theories," *Journal of Risk and Uncertainty* 2, no. 1 (April 1989), pp. 61–104.

[8] One classic theoretical study was done by Milton Friedman and Leonard J. Savage, "The Utility Analysis of Choices Involving Risk," *Journal of Political Economy* 56, no. 4 (August 1948), pp. 279–304.

FIGURE   20.1

Payoff Table for
Investment Decision
Problem

		STATES OF NATURE	
		Product Is Successful	Product Is a Failure
ALTERNATIVE ACTIONS (DECISIONS)	Invest in Product	$160,000	$-40,000
	Do Not Invest in Product	0	0
	Probability of occurrence	.20	.80

listed in the payoff table for each action/state-of-nature combination. Note that the decision "Do Not Invest in Product" results in a zero return or payoff, regardless of the state of nature. The probability of occurrence of each state of nature is shown in the row below the payoff table.

The expected monetary value of the decision to "Invest in Product" is

$$EMV_1 = \$160,000 \times .20 + (\$-40,000) \times .80 = \$0$$

and for the decision "Do Not Invest" it is

$$EMV_2 = 0 \times .20 + 0 \times .80 = \$0$$

Therefore, based on the maximization of expected monetary value criterion, the entrepreneur would be *indifferent* to the two alternative actions in this problem.

Let us now introduce the entrepreneur's utility function for wealth (money) into the decision-making framework and see how it affects preference for the two alternative actions.

Case I   Assume that the entrepreneur has a utility function (see Figure 20.2) that is characterized by *diminishing marginal utility* for money. *Marginal utility* measures the satisfaction the individual receives from a given incremental change in wealth.[9] Marginal utility is given by the *slope* of the utility function at any point on the curve.

$$\text{Marginal utility} = \text{Slope} = \frac{\Delta U(M)}{\Delta M} \qquad [20.2]$$

Diminishing marginal utility indicates that the slope of the utility function is *decreasing* as the stock of money (that is, wealth) increases. It means that as an individual's wealth increases, that individual receives *less additional satisfaction* from each equal increment of wealth.

---

[9] The terms *wealth, money,* and *return* are used interchangeably throughout the discussion of utility in this chapter.

FIGURE   20.2

Utility Function
Exhibiting Diminishing
Marginal Utility

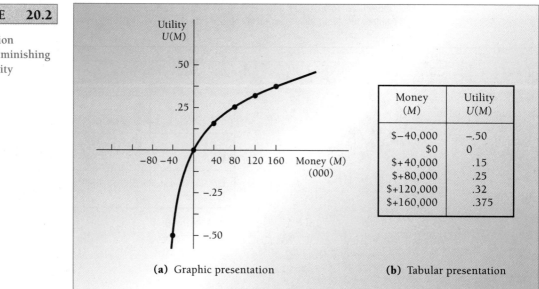

Money (M)	Utility U(M)
$-40,000	-.50
$0	0
$+40,000	.15
$+80,000	.25
$+120,000	.32
$+160,000	.375

(a) Graphic presentation   **(b)** Tabular presentation

www ....
Visit Vanguard Software
Corporation, creator of
DecisionPro, a management
decision analysis software
package with a decision
tree component, at:
http://www.vanguardsw.
com/

By Equation 20.1, the expected utility, based on the utility function in Figure 20.2 of the decision to "Invest in Product," is

$$E(U_1) = U(\$160,000) \times .20 + U(\$-40,000) \times .80$$

$$= .375 \times .20 + (-.50) \times .80 = -.325$$

and for the decision "Do Not Invest" it is

$$E(U_2) = U(0) \times .20 + U(0) \times .80$$

$$= 0 \times .20 + 0 \times .80 = 0$$

The decision "Do Not Invest" has a higher expected utility. Therefore, based on the maximization of expected utility criterion, the entrepreneur would decide *not* to invest in the new product.

In terms of expected value, the investment (that is, gamble) is fair because, as was shown earlier, it has an expected monetary value of zero. An individual who because of a diminishing marginal utility for money exhibits a definite preference for *not* undertaking fair investments such as this one is said to be *risk averse,* or to have an aversion to risk. Also, though not illustrated by this example, it is possible for the risk-averse individual to be unwilling to undertake investments having *positive* expected monetary values.

Case II   Assume that the entrepreneur has a utility function (see Figure 20.3) that is characterized by *increasing marginal utility* for money. *Increasing marginal utility* indicates that the slope of the utility function is increasing as the individual's wealth increases. In other words, it means that as an individual's wealth increases, that individual receives *more additional satisfaction* from each (equal) increment of wealth.

Based on the utility function in Figure 20.3 the expected utility of the decision to "Invest in the Product" is

$$E(U_1) = U(\$160,000) \times .20 + U(\$-40,000) \times .80$$

$$= .65 \times .20 + (-.10) \times .80 = +.05$$

and for the decision "Do Not Invest" it is the same as in the preceding diminishing marginal utility case; that is, $E(U_2) = 0$. Therefore, the optimal decision, based on the maximization of expected utility criterion, would be *to invest* in the product.

FIGURE   20.3
Utility Function Exhibiting Increasing Marginal Utility

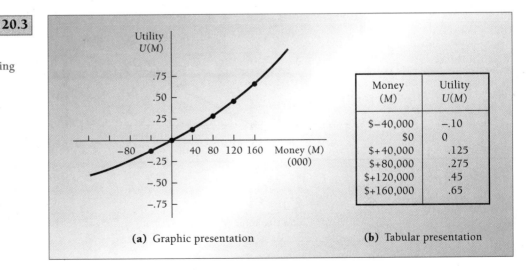

(a) Graphic presentation

Money (M)	Utility U(M)
$-40,000	-.10
$0	0
$+40,000	.125
$+80,000	.275
$+120,000	.45
$+160,000	.65

(b) Tabular presentation

An individual who, because of an increasing marginal utility for money, has a definite preference for undertaking actuarially fair investments such as this one is said to be a *risk preferrer,* or to have a preference for risk. Although not illustrated by this decision problem, it is also possible for an individual with a preference for risk to be willing to undertake investments having *negative* expected monetary values.

Case III   Assume that the entrepreneur has a *linear* utility function (see Figure 20.4). In other words, the individual has a *constant marginal utility* for money, indicating that as wealth increases, the individual receives the *same additional satisfaction* from each given (equal) increment of wealth.

Although we will not illustrate the calculations for this case, it can be demonstrated that the expected utilities of both the decisions to "Invest in Product" and "Do Not Invest" are zero. Therefore, the entrepreneur with a linear utility function would be indifferent to the two alternative actions when seeking to maximize expected utility and would be said to be *risk neutral.* Note this is the same decision (that is, indifference) as was obtained earlier in this section with the maximization of expected monetary value criterion.

We will not prove the result here, but it can be shown that for an individual having a linear utility for money, *the maximization of expected monetary value criterion will generally yield the same decisions as the maximization of expected utility criterion.* This statement has important implications for decision making. It means that if the decision maker feels his or her utility function is linear (or approximately linear) over the range of outcomes in a decision problem, then there is no need to go through the difficult task of attempting to derive his or her utility function for money. In this case, choosing the alternative with the *largest* expected monetary value will yield decisions that are in accord with the decision maker's true preferences.

In summary, we see that individuals' attitudes toward risk affect the shape of their utility function and determine the alternative that will be chosen in a decision problem involving risk.

Decision Tree Approach

Decision problems involving a reasonable number of alternative actions and states of nature can be analyzed using *decision trees.* Decision trees are an alternative approach to

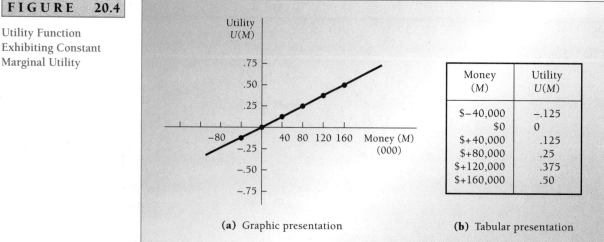

FIGURE   20.4

Utility Function Exhibiting Constant Marginal Utility

(a) Graphic presentation

(b) Tabular presentation

Money (M)	Utility U(M)
$−40,000	−.125
$0	0
$+40,000	.125
$+80,000	.25
$+120,000	.375
$+160,000	.50

the use of payoff tables, such as the one illustrated earlier in Figure 20.1 for the investment decision problem. This decision problem is represented in the decision tree shown in Figure 20.5. In a decision tree, decision nodes (numbered boxes) are used to represent points at which the decision maker must choose among several alternative actions, and state-of-nature nodes (numbered circles) are used to represent possible state-of-nature outcomes. At decision node $\boxed{1}$ are two decision branches (alternative actions)—Invest and Do Not Invest in Product. At the state-of-nature nodes ② and ③ are two state-of-nature branches (outcomes)—Product Is a Success and Product Is a Failure. The probabilities are shown along each state-of-nature branch. The outcome (payoff) is shown at the end of the branch. Using this information, we can calculate the expected monetary value for each decision branch and then select the one with the *largest* value. This yields the same results (that is, EMV and decision) as those shown in the previous section.

In the actual applications, decision trees can be much more complex than the one illustrated in Figure 20.5. They may involve sequential (or multiperiod) decision points with the opportunity to seek additional information (for example, through test market research) about the states of nature and then revise the probabilities.

When a decision tree is constructed with multiple periods, it is possible to recognize the feedback from each branch of the tree into each future period. For example, if a firm invests in a new product, the success or failure of that product in period 1 implies a great deal about its success or failure in future periods. If a product is successful during period 1, the probability of future success is greatly enhanced. Accordingly, the prospect of success in period 2 can be viewed as being closely correlated with the success in period 1. Similarly, the prospect of success in period 3 is enhanced if the product has been successful in periods 1 and 2. These *conditional* probabilities can be explicitly incorporated into a multiperiod decision tree.

Risk-Adjusted Discount Rate Approach

When making long-term capital budgeting (investment) decisions, the risk-adjusted discount rate approach is a commonly used method for dealing with the uncertainty

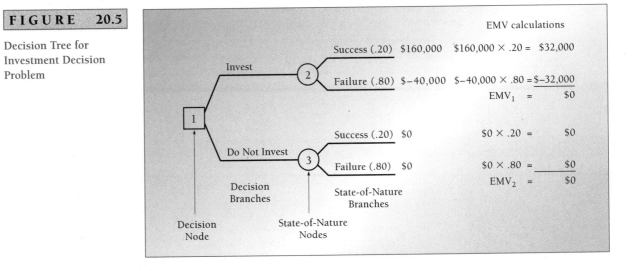

FIGURE 20.5

Decision Tree for Investment Decision Problem

associated with future cash-flow estimates. In the basic net present value decision-making model (which is described in more detail in Chapter 19), net present value (*NPV*) is defined as

$$NPV = \sum_{t=1}^{n} \frac{NCF_t}{(1 + k)^t} - NINV \qquad [20.3]$$

where NCF_t is the net cash flow in period t (for each of n periods). *NINV* is the net investment, and k is the firm's *cost of capital*. An investment project is accepted if its *NPV* is greater than or equal to zero. In the risk-adjusted discount rate approach, the net cash flows for each project are discounted at a **risk-adjusted rate,** k*, rather than the firm's cost of capital (k). The magnitude of k* depends on the risk of the project—the higher the risk, the higher the risk-adjusted discount rate.

Risk-Adjusted Discount Rate

A discount rate that reflects the risk associated with a particular investment project.

The risk premiums (that is, k* − k) applied to individual projects are commonly established *subjectively.* For example, some firms establish a small number of risk classes and then apply a different risk premium to each class. Average risk projects, such as equipment replacement decisions, are evaluated at the firm's cost of capital; above-average-risk projects, such as facility expansions, might be assigned a risk premium of 3 percent above the firm's cost of capital; and high-risk projects, such as investments in totally new lines of business or the introduction of new products, might be assigned a risk premium of 8 percent above the firm's cost of capital. Because the risk premiums for each project are subjectively determined and no explicit consideration is given to the variation in cash flows of the project, this approach can lead to suboptimal decisions. In general, the risk-class method is most useful when evaluating relatively small projects that are frequently repeated. In these cases, much is known about the projects' potential returns, and it is probably not worth the effort to compute more "precise" risk premiums.

EXAMPLE

RISK-ADJUSTED DISCOUNT RATE: HAMILTON-BEACH COMPANY

The Hamilton-Beach Company has been offered a contract to supply private-label food processors to a regional discount store chain. The investment required for this project is $1 million. It is expected to produce annual net cash flows of $290,000 for a period of five years. Hamilton-Beach uses the risk-adjusted discount rates shown in Table 20.1 when evaluating capital investment decisions. The risk premium (θ) for each risk class (determined subjectively) is added to the firm's cost of capital ($k = 12$ percent) to arrive at the risk-adjusted discount rate.

If the investment project (contract for food blenders) is considered to be of average risk, then a risk-adjusted discount rate (k*) of 12 percent is used in the discounted cash-flow analysis.

TABLE   20.1

Risk-Adjusted Discount Rates: Hamilton-Beach Company

Project Risk	Risk Premium (θ)	Risk-Adjusted Discount Rate ($k^* = k + \theta$)
Average risk	0%	12%
Above-average risk	3	15
High risk	8	20

$$NPV = \sum_{t=1}^{5} \frac{\$290,000}{(1 + .12)^t} - \$1,000,000$$

$$= \$290,000(3.6048) - \$1,000,000$$

$$= +\$45,392$$

The NPV for the project at a discount rate of 12 percent is \$45,392 and the project (contract) should be accepted.

However, if management decides that the project is of above-average risk and evaluates it at a rate (k^*) of 15 percent, the NPV is

$$NPV = \sum_{t=1}^{5} \frac{\$290,000}{(1 + .15^t)} - \$1,000,000$$

$$= \$290,000(3.3522) - \$1,000,000$$

$$= \$-27,862$$

Because the NPV of the project is negative at a 15 percent discount rate, it should *not* be accepted.

Thus, the assessment of the project's risk affects its desirability (as measured by NPV) and determines whether it is accepted.

Simulation Approach

Simulation
A decision-making tool that models some event, such as cash flows from an investment project.

Computers have made it both feasible and relatively inexpensive to apply **simulation techniques** to economic decisions. Simulation is a planning tool that models some event. When simulation is used in capital budgeting, it requires that estimates be made of the probability distribution of each cash-flow element (revenues, expenses, and so on). If, for example, a firm is considering introducing a new product, the elements of a simulation might include the number of units sold, market price, unit production costs, unit selling costs, the cost of the machinery needed to produce the new product, and the cost of capital. These probability distributions are then put into the simulation model to compute the project's net present value probability distribution. In any period NCF_t may be computed as

$$NCF_t = [q(p) - q(c + s) - D](1 - t) + D \qquad [20.4]$$

where q is the number of units sold, p the selling price per unit, c the unit production cost (excluding depreciation), s the unit selling cost, D the annual depreciation, and t the firm's marginal tax rate. Using Equation 20.4 and the previously defined NPV equation (Equation 20.3), it is possible to simulate the net present value of the project. Based on the probability distribution of each of the elements that influence the net present value, one value for each element is selected at random.

EXAMPLE

INVESTMENT PROJECT SIMULATION: HOUSE OF CHOCOLATE, INC.

House of Chocolate is considering investing in a new mixing machine that costs \$100,000 and has an expected life of five years. Annual depreciation (D) on the machine is \$20,000 and the firm's marginal tax rate is 50 percent. Annual demand (q), selling price (p), unit production (c), and selling (s) costs are random variables.

Assume, for example, that the following values for the input variables are randomly chosen: $q = 20,000$; $p = \$10$; $c = \$2$; $s = \$1$. Inserting these values along with $D = \$20,000$ and $t = 50\%$ or 0.50 into Equation 20.4 gives the following:

$$\text{NCF}_t = (20,000 \times \$10 - 20,000 \times \$3 - \$20,000)(1 - 0.50) + \$20,000$$

$$= (\$200,000 - \$60,000 - \$20,000) \times 0.50 + \$20,000$$

$$= \$80,000$$

Given that the net investment is equal to the depreciable cost of the machinery ($\$100,000$ in the example), that the net cash flows in each year of the project's life are identical, that $k = 10$ percent, and that the project has a five-year life, the net present value of this particular iteration of the simulation can be computed as follows:

$$NPV = \sum_{t=1}^{5} \frac{\$80,000}{(1 + 0.10)^t} - \$100,000$$

$$= \$80,000 \times 3.791 - \$100,000$$

$$= \$203,280$$

In an actual simulation the computer program is run a number of different times using different randomly selected input variables in each instance. Thus the program can be said to be repeated, or *iterated*, and each run is termed an *iteration*. In each iteration the net present value for the project would be computed accordingly. Figure 20.6 illustrates a typical simulation approach.

The results of these iterations are then used to plot a probability distribution of the project's net present values and to compute a mean and a standard deviation of returns. This information provides the decision maker with an estimate of a project's expected returns as well as its risk. Given this information, it is possible to compute the probability of achieving a net present value that is greater or less than any particular value.

FIGURE 20.6

An Illustration of the Simulation Approach

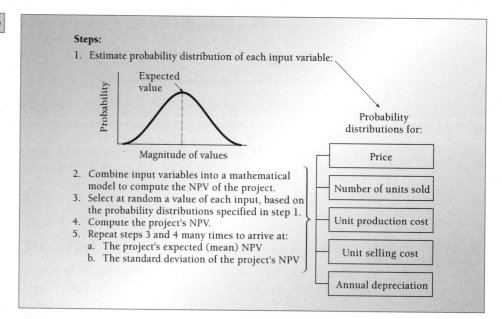

Steps:

1. Estimate probability distribution of each input variable:

   (graph: Probability vs. Magnitude of values, showing Expected value at peak)

   Probability distributions for:
   - Price
   - Number of units sold
   - Unit production cost
   - Unit selling cost
   - Annual depreciation

2. Combine input variables into a mathematical model to compute the NPV of the project.
3. Select at random a value of each input, based on the probability distributions specified in step 1.
4. Compute the project's NPV.
5. Repeat steps 3 and 4 many times to arrive at:
   a. The project's expected (mean) NPV
   b. The standard deviation of the project's NPV

EXAMPLE

INVESTMENT PROJECT SIMULATION: HOUSE OF CHOCOLATE, INC. (CONTINUED)

Assume that the simulation for the previously illustrated project results in a normal distribution with an expected net present value of $120,000 and a standard deviation of $60,000. The probability of the project having a net present value of $0 or less can now be found. The value of $0 is 2.0 standard deviations below the mean:

$$z = \frac{\$0 - \$120,000}{\$60,000}$$

$$= -2.0$$

It can be seen from Table 1 in Appendix B that the probability of a value less than 2.0 standard deviations below the mean is 2.28 percent. Thus there is a 2.28 percent chance that the actual net present value for this project will be negative. Figure 20.7 shows the probability distribution of this project's net present value. The shaded area under the curve represents the probability that the project will have a net present value of $0 or less.

The simulation approach is a powerful one because it explicitly recognizes all the interactions among the variables that influence the outcome. It provides both a mean and a standard deviation that can help the decision maker analyze trade-offs between risk and expected return. Unfortunately, considerable time and effort may be needed to gather the information for each of the input variables and to formulate the model correctly. This limits the feasibility of simulation to large projects. In addition, the simulation example illustrated here assumed that the values of the input variables were independent of one another. If this is not true—if, for example, the price of a product has a large influence on the number sold—then this interaction must be incorporated into the model, introducing even more complexity.

FIGURE   20.7

Illustration of the Probability That a Project's Returns Will Be Less Than $0; House of Chocolate, Inc.

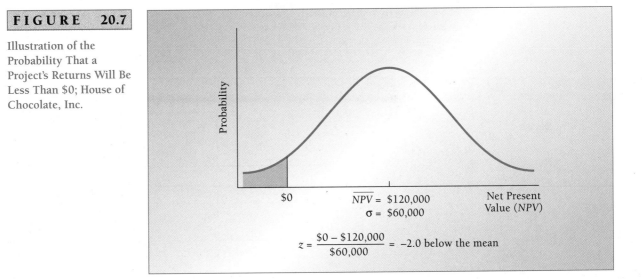

Decision Making under Uncertainty

www ....
Read about the history of decision-making and decision analysis at the Arlington Software Corporation site: http://www.arlingsoft. com/history.htm

Consider now a situation in which the decision maker is either unable or unwilling to specify the probabilities of occurrence for the various possible outcomes. Under these conditions, what is the appropriate decision criterion for choosing among the alternative actions in a decision problem? As we shall see in the following analysis, a number of different decision rules are available and no single best criterion can be specified.

To illustrate various proposed decision criteria, consider again the investment decision example introduced earlier in the discussion of utility functions. Assume now that no information is available on the past success-failure rates for the marketing of similar types of products and that the entrepreneur is unable to furnish a subjective assessment of the chances of success and failure. Furthermore, assume that the entrepreneur's preferences for money are represented by the utility function shown in Figure 20.2. Using this utility function, the monetary payoffs of the investment decision problem shown in Figure 20.1 can be transformed into the utility values shown in Figure 20.8. The two decision criteria, which are illustrated in this section, are the *maximin* criterion and the *minimax regret* criterion.[10]

Maximin Criterion

The maximin criterion concentrates on the worst possible outcome (that is, *minimum* or smallest utility) across all states of nature associated with each alternative action. For the alternative A_1 ("Invest in Product"), the minimum utility in the first row of Figure 20.8 is $-.50$. Likewise, for the alternative A_2 ("Do Not Invest in Product"), the minimum utility in the second row is 0. With the maximin criterion, the alternative action having the *maximum* of these minimum utility values is chosen. Using this criterion, we would decide not to invest in the product (that is, Action A_2) because this alternative has the largest minimum utility value.

The maximin criterion is a very conservative decision-making rule because it evaluates alternative actions solely on the worst possible outcome associated with each ac-

---

[10] Various other decision criteria (namely, Hurwicz criterion, principle of insufficient reason) have been proposed. See Luce and Raiffa, *Games and Decisions*, sec. 13.2–13.5, for a discussion of these criteria and related decision-making concepts.

FIGURE   20.8

Utility (Payoff) Table for Investment Decision Problem

		STATES OF NATURE	
		S_1 Product Is a Success	S_2 Product Is a Failure
ALTERNATIVE ACTIONS	A_1 Invest in Product	.375	−.50
	A_2 Do Not Invest in Product	0	0

tion. Hypothetical decision problems can be constructed in which this criterion will yield choices that many critics find inappropriate or unreasonable.[11]

Minimax Regret Criterion

Regret measures the loss that results from choosing the incorrect alternative action for a given state of nature. The regret associated with an alternative action is the *difference* between the *best possible* payoff (or utility) that could have been received and the *actual* payoff (or utility) that is received. For example, consider the utility entries in Figure 20.8. Suppose S_1 is true (that is, the "Product Is a Success"). The regret associated with Alternative A_2 ("Do Not Invest In Product") is the difference between largest utility in the S_1 column (that is, .375 for A_1) and the utility of A_2 in this column (that is, 0). Thus in the regret table, shown in Figure 20.9, a value of .375 has been entered into the (A_2, S_1) position. Clearly, there is no regret associated with Alternative A_1 ("Invest in Product"), because this is the correct decision when S_1 is true. Hence, a zero has been entered in the (A_1, S_1) position in Figure 20.9. Similar reasoning yields the regret values in the S_2 ("Product Is a Failure") column.

Having specified the regret table, the *maximum* regret for each alternative action is determined. For A_1 the maximum regret (in row 1) is .5. Similarly, for A_2 the maximum regret (in row 2) is .375. The decision maker then chooses the alternative action having the *minimum* of these maximum regret values. In this case he or she would choose not to invest in the product (A_2), because this alternative has the smallest maximum regret value. Although this is the same action that was chosen previously using the maximin criterion, these two decision criteria need not, in general, yield the same decisions.

As with the maximin criterion, serious questions have been raised concerning the applicability of minimax regret as a decision-making criterion. Consideration of these questions, however, is beyond the scope of this chapter.[12]

---

[11] See Luce and Raiffa, *Games and Decisions,* pp. 279–280, for an example of a decision-making situation that illustrates one of the problems associated with the maximin criterion.

[12] See Luce and Raiffa, *Games and Decisions,* p. 281, for a summary of some of the objections that have been raised concerning this criterion.

FIGURE   20.9

Regret Table for
Investment Decision
Problem

		STATES OF NATURE	
		S_1 Product Is a Success	S_2 Product Is a Failure
ALTERNATIVE ACTIONS	A_1 Invest in Product	0	.50
	A_2 Do Not Invest in Product	.375	0

Managing Risk and Uncertainty

www . . . .
Read how the U.S.
Department of the Interior
applies risk management
principles to mitigate risk to
park visitors, employees,
and public-trust resources at:
http://www.mrps.doi.gov/

Many avenues are open to the manager who wishes to reduce the level of risk associated with a particular decision. In this section we briefly consider some of these strategies for managing risk.

Acquisition of Additional Information

In many cases the risk facing a manager arises because of a lack of information. For example, when making the decision to develop and market a new product, there is considerable risk regarding the market's acceptance of this new product. To reduce this risk many firms will "test-market" the product in a limited area or present the product to panels of consumers for their evaluation. These tactics provide important information to the company as it seeks to assess the probable success of the new product.

Information can also be purchased from individuals or firms that possess the knowledge the decision maker seeks. For example, a wildcat oil drilling firm will employ the services of petroleum geologists as it attempts to determine where to drill exploratory wells. Similarly, companies that plan to sell new debt securities often pay to have their bonds "rated" by one of the bond rating services, such as Moody's or Standard and Poor's. The ratings applied to the bonds reduce the risk of determining the yield that will have to be offered to investors when the bonds are sold.

Normally, additional information is costly. Hence, the wealth-maximizing firm would be willing to pay for additional information as long as the marginal value of that information exceeds its marginal cost.

Diversification

Diversification
The act of investing in a set of securities or assets having different risk-return characteristics.

Diversification is the act of investing in a set of securities or assets having different risk-return characteristics. By investing in diverse assets the firm can achieve considerably more stability in returns than is possible by investing in a single asset. When a firm diversifies it holds a *portfolio* of assets or investments. *Portfolio risk* is the risk associated with collections of assets or securities. In the following examples we illustrate diversification through a portfolio of securities. The principles developed in these examples, however, are equally relevant to any collection of different assets. The diversification strategy has been used by many firms to reduce the risk associated with operating in a narrow line of business.

Expected Returns from a Portfolio   When two or more securities are combined into a portfolio, the expected return of the portfolio is equal to the weighted average of the expected returns from the individual securities. For example, assume a portfolio contains Acme Corporation (*A*) securities and Babbo Corporation (*B*) securities, which have expected returns of 12 percent and 8 percent, respectively. If a portion w_A of the available funds (wealth) is invested in Security *A*, and the remaining funds w_B is invested in Security *B*, the expected return of the portfolio $\hat{r}_p$ is as follows:

$$\hat{r}_p = w_A\hat{r}_A + w_B\hat{r}_B, \qquad [20.5]$$

where $\hat{r}_A$ and $\hat{r}_B$ are the expected returns for Securities *A* and *B*, respectively. Furthermore, $w_A + w_B = 1$, indicating that all funds are invested in either Security *A* or Security *B*.

The range of possible expected returns for a portfolio consisting of Securities *A* and *B* is 12 percent (if 100 percent of the portfolio is invested in Security *A* and 0 percent is invested in Security B) to 8 percent (if 100 percent is invested in Security B and 0 percent is invested in Security A). In addition, any linear weighted combination of returns for Securities A and B between 8 and 12 percent is also possible. For example, assume that 30 percent of this portfolio consists of Security A, and Security B constitutes the remaining 70 percent. In this case the expected return on the portfolio is computed as follows:

$$\hat{r}_p = 0.3(12\%) + 0.7(8\%) = 9.2\%$$

In general, the expected return from any portfolio of n securities or assets is equal to the sum of the expected returns from each security times the proportion of the total portfolio invested in that security:

$$\hat{r}_p = \sum_{i=1}^{n} w_i \hat{r}_i \qquad [20.6]$$

where $\Sigma w_i = 1$ and $0 \leq w_i \leq 1$.

Portfolio Risk   Although the expected returns from a portfolio of two or more securities can be computed as a weighted average of the expected returns from the individual securities, it is not sufficient merely to calculate a weighted average of the risk of each individual security to arrive at a measure of the portfolio's risk. Whenever the returns from the individual securities are not perfectly positively correlated, the risk of any portfolio of these securities may be reduced through the effects of diversification. Thus, diversification can be achieved by investing in a diverse set of securities that have different risk-return characteristics. The amount of risk reduction achieved through diversification depends on the degree of correlation between the returns of the individual securities in the portfolio. The lower the correlations among the individual securities, the greater the possibilities for risk reduction.

The risk for a two-security portfolio, measured by the standard deviation of portfolio returns, is computed as follows:

$$\sigma_p = \sqrt{w_A^2 \sigma_A^2 + w_B^2 \sigma_B^2 + 2 w_A w_B \rho_{AB} \sigma_A \sigma_B}, \qquad [20.7]$$

where w_A is the proportion of funds invested in Security A; w_B is the proportion of funds invested in Security B; $w_A + w_B = 1$; σ_A^2 is the variance of returns from Security A (or the square of the standard deviation for Security A, σ_A); σ_B^2 is the variance of returns from Security B (or the square of the standard deviation for Security B, σ_B); and ρ_{AB} is the correlation coefficient of returns between Securities A and B.[13]

For example, consider a portfolio containing Securities A and B as described here:

	Acme (A)	Babbo (B)
Expected return	0.12	0.08
Standard deviation of returns	0.09	0.09
Proportion invested in each security	0.5	0.5

[13] The correlation coefficient measures the extent to which high (or low) values of one variable are associated with high (or low) values of another. Values of the correlation coefficient range from +1.0, for perfectly positively correlated variables, to −1.0, for perfectly negatively correlated variables. The *less* two variables are positively correlated, the *greater* are the potential benefits of portfolio risk reduction. See Chapter 5 for additional discussion of the meaning and measurement of the correlation coefficient.

Given various values for the correlation between the securities' returns, the risk of a portfolio containing equal proportions of the two securities can be computed.

First, consider the case where $\rho_{AB} = +1.0$ (that is, perfect *positive* correlation). The portfolio's risk is calculated as follows:

$$\sigma_p = \sqrt{(0.5)^2(0.09)^2 + (0.5)^2(0.09)^2 + 2(0.5)(0.5)(+1)(0.09)(0.09)}$$

$$= \sqrt{0.002025 + 0.002025 + 0.00405}$$

$$= \sqrt{0.0081}$$

$$= 0.09$$

When the returns from the two securities are perfectly positively correlated, the risk of the portfolio is equal to the weighted average of the risk of the individual securities (9 percent in this example). *Thus, no risk reduction is achieved when perfectly positively correlated assets are combined in a portfolio.*

The returns from most assets are not perfectly positively correlated; this allows for risk reduction through diversification. For example, consider next the case of a low positive correlation of returns, such as $\rho_{AB} = +0.1$. The portfolio risk in this example is as follows:

$$\sigma_p = \sqrt{(0.5)^2(0.09)^2 + (0.5)^2(0.09)^2 + 2(0.5)(0.5)(+0.1)(0.09)(0.09)}$$

$$= \sqrt{0.002025 + 0.002025 + 0.000405}$$

$$= \sqrt{0.004455}$$

$$= 0.067$$

In this case diversification reduces the portfolio risk from 9 percent (the weighted average of the individual security risks) to 6.7 percent.

Finally, consider the case of a perfect *negative* correlation $\rho_{AB} = -1.0$. In this example the portfolio risk is completely eliminated.[14]

Figure 20.10 graphs the relationship between the correlation of returns for securities A and B and the risk (σ_P) of a portfolio containing equal proportions of securities A and B ($w_A = w_B = 0.5$). This figure indicates that the relationship between portfolio risk and the correlation of security returns is not linear.

One of the benefits of diversification is the reduction of total portfolio risk. This risk reduction is often cited as one of the primary reasons for corporate diversification. However, the evidence is mixed regarding the consistency of corporate diversification with the objective of shareholder wealth maximization.

EXAMPLE

DIVERSIFICATION MISAPPLIED: THE CONGLOMERATE MERGER

During the 1960s and 1970s many firms, such as ITT, Gulf and Western, Litton Industries, and LTV, attempted to reduce the risk of their operations by diversifying into a wide range of often unrelated industries. The rationale that was made for these far-flung acquisitions was to reduce the inherent operating risk of the enterprise. For example, U.S. Steel acquired Marathon Oil because of the cyclical risk in the steel industry. Ford

---

[14] When returns from two assets are perfectly negatively correlated, *some* combination of these two assets in a portfolio can completely eliminate portfolio risk. This risk-eliminating combination will only be $w_A = w_B = 0.5$ when the two assets have the same standard deviation of returns. When this is not the case, the weightings of w_A and w_B must be changed from 0.5 to fully eliminate portfolio risk.

FIGURE 20.10

Portfolio Risk versus
Correlation of Security
Returns*

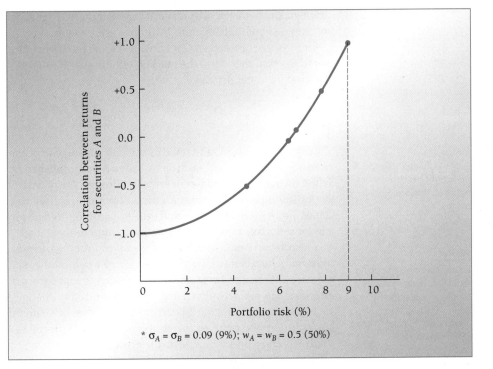

* $\sigma_A = \sigma_B = 0.09$ (9%); $w_A = w_B = 0.5$ (50%)

Motor acquired a network of savings and loan institutions. Reynolds Tobacco diversified into food products, shipping, and oil and gas exploration. To make acquisitions in these unrelated businesses, the acquiring firms paid substantial premiums over the preacquisition market price of the acquired firms. Premiums of 20 to 75 percent or more were not uncommon.

In the late 1970s and early 1980s investors began to question the wisdom of these acquisitions. One issue related to the ability of a company's managers to manage effectively such a diverse collection of corporate assets. Evidence grew that there were no economies in managerial talent. Indeed, the performance of many of the acquired firms suggested that they were less successfully managed as part of the conglomerate than when they were stand-alone enterprises. More importantly, the fundamental rationale for these acquisitions came under closer scrutiny. Why should a firm pay a premium to diversify itself when that same firm's stockholders can diversify at no premium by simply buying a portfolio of stock made up of diverse companies? Individual diversification is a much cheaper alternative to managing business risk than is diversification at the firm level. It appeared that diversification had been undertaken for the benefit of the company's managers (who, by the nature of their jobs, are poorly diversified into the performance stream of their employer).

As the decade of the 1980s progressed, there was significant evidence that these diversified firms were not maximizing the creation of shareholder value. It became evident that in many cases value could be created by acquiring these poorly run firms, selling off their diverse pieces, and refocusing the firm into its core business. This wave of restructuring often took the form of leverage buyouts, where the firm is acquired in a highly debt-levered transaction, often with the managers of the firm taking a substantial ownership interest in the firm. The combination of the discipline of high required debt payments and the alignment of the interests of owners and managers produced dramatically better performance at many of these firms. On average, these transactions increased shareholder wealth by 50 percent or more.

In most circumstances stockholders can diversify better and more cheaply than corporations can; therefore, the market will not place a significant value on diversification undertaken at the firm level.

Hedging

Hedge
A risk-reducing strategy of taking offsetting positions in the ownership of an asset.

A **hedge** is a transaction that limits the risk associated with market price fluctuations for a particular investment position. A hedge is accomplished by taking offsetting positions in the ownership of an asset or security through use of derivative securities, such as buying or selling a futures contract (or an option) to offset risk exposure in the cash market. A *futures contract* is a standardized contract, traded on an organized exchange, to buy or sell a fixed quantity of a defined commodity at a set price in the future. Hedging can also be accomplished using *forward contracts*. A forward contract is a contractual agreement between two parties to exchange a commodity at a set price in the future. The primary differences between futures contracts and forward contracts are that forward contracts are not actively traded on an organized exchange, such as the Chicago Board of Trade; normally forward contracts do not deal in standardized goods; and they carry the risk that one party to the contract may not perform as agreed. In contrast, futures contracts carry no such performance risk because they are essentially guaranteed by the exchange on which they are traded.

www . . . .
Learn more about hedging and other economic reasons for commodity futures trading at the U.S. Commodity Futures Trading Commission site:
http://www.cftc.gov/econpurp.html

Futures and forward contracts create the legal obligation for the buyer (or seller) to purchase (or sell) the goods specified in the contract at the agreed upon price at some future point in time. In contrast, an *option* gives the buyer the *right,* but not the obligation, to either buy or sell the underlying commodity. We will confine our discussion of hedging to futures contracts.[15]

Futures markets exist for many commodities, including minerals (such as copper, gold, silver, and crude oil), agricultural commodities (such as corn, wheat, live hogs, cotton, and cattle), and financial instruments (such as Treasury bills, Treasury bonds, foreign currencies, commercial paper, and broad-based common stock indexes such as the *Standard and Poor's 500 Stock Index*). Any enterprise that normally buys or sells these commodities (or products closely related to these commodities) or is engaged in borrowing or lending operations can make use of futures contracts, forward markets, and options to eliminate, or at least largely offset, the risk of future price fluctuations.

EXAMPLE

HEDGING BORROWING COSTS: WESTEX COMPANY

The corporate treasurer of Westex projects in late September that the company's cash flows will require a $3 million bank loan in mid-December. This loan is expected to be needed for three months. The contractual agreement between the corporate borrower and its bank establishes the rate on loans such as this to be 1.5 percentage points above the three-month Eurodollar rate (also referred to as the LIBOR—London Interbank Offer Rate). The current (September) LIBOR rate is 9.5 percent. The treasurer is concerned that this rate may increase over the next three months. Therefore, the treasurer wishes to "lock in" the current rate (11 percent) as her company's cost of borrowing in mid-December.

---

[15] More advanced treatments of hedging concepts are contained in Alan L. Tucker, *Financial Futures, Options and Swaps* (St. Paul, Minn.: West, 1991), and in David A. Dubofsky, *Options and Financial Futures: Valuation and Uses* (New York: McGraw Hill, 1992).

Eurodollar Time Deposit futures contracts are traded on the International Monetary Market (IMM), a division of the Chicago Mercantile Exchange. These Eurodollar contracts are for $1 million of three-month Eurodollar time deposits. The IMM has a pricing system that quotes these contracts on a discounted percentage basis; that is, the price of a contract is quoted as 100 minus the annualized interest rate on three-month Eurodollar Time Deposits. For example, a contract price of 91 implies an annualized interest rate of 9 percent (100 minus 91 = 9 percent).

In September, the corporate treasurer observes that the December futures contract, which can be used to "lock in" the forward borrowing rate, is trading at 90.30, implying a forward Eurodollar rate of 9.7 percent (100.0 − 90.3). If the treasurer sells three December Eurodollar futures contracts ($1 million each) at 90.3, she can ensure that her cost of funds in December will be 11.2 percent (9.7 percent LIBOR rate plus the 1.5 percentage points spread over LIBOR charged by the bank).

By mid-December the current Eurodollar rate has risen to 12.0 percent. The December futures price has declined to 88.00, reflecting the current 12 percent rate. Because of these higher rates, the company's quarterly interest payments to the bank are $101,250 ($3,000,000 × 13.5 percent × 0.25 years). The decline in the future price, however, produces a profit for the corporate treasurer of $17,250 [(90.3−88.0) × $2,500 × 3 contracts]. (Each one percentage point increase in the price of a Eurodollar futures contract is equivalent to an increase in the value of that contract of $2,500, (that is, $1,000,000 × .01 × 0.25 years). Recall that the corporate treasurer sold three Eurodollar contracts in September at 90.3. The treasurer can cancel her position in the futures market by buying three contracts in December at the new lower price of 88.0.

Thus, the net interest cost to the corporate treasurer is $84,000 ($101,250 interest payment to the bank less $17,250 profit from the futures contracts), giving an effective annual rate of 11.2 percent.

In this example, the treasurer has perfectly hedged her borrowing cost position. In practice, it is usually not possible to perfectly hedge one's position because of (1) differences in the size of standard future contracts and the amount of hedging desired by the firm; (2) the inability to find a futures contract in a commodity or financial instrument that has precisely the same pattern of price movements as the commodity or financial instrument in which the firm is dealing; (3) variations in the difference (called the basis) between the spot or cash market price for a commodity or financial instrument and the futures market price over the life of the futures contract; and (4) the inability to match a firm's period of risk exposure to the expiration time of the futures contract. In spite of these shortcomings, hedging can be used in many situations to reduce the risk of future price changes in goods or financial instruments. Over the past decade many new financial contracts have been developed that permit financial institutions and other firms to control their future financing cost and/or to guarantee their returns on anticipated future investments.

Other Approaches for Managing Risk

In addition to hedging, acquiring additional information, and diversifying, several other techniques can be used to manage risk, such as purchasing insurance, gaining control over the operating environment, and limiting the use of firm-specific assets.

Insurance   When an individual makes a premium payment to an insurance company, that individual is exchanging the premium payment for protection against specified losses, up to the limits identified in the policy. Insurance is commonly available for losses due to fires, natural disasters, accidents occurring in the workplace, the death of key employees, fraud, product liability, and theft. Some financial instruments such as corporate bonds are backed by insurance that guarantees the payment of principal and interest. When deciding which risks should be insured externally, and which should be self-insured, managers are confronted with a trade-off between a certain, small, periodic cost (the payment of the insurance premium), and the uncertainty of bearing the full cost of a loss from time to time. The willingness of managers to assume some insurable risks, the cost of the insurance, and the severity of the consequences of experiencing an uninsured loss will determine whether insurance is purchased or not.

Gaining Control over the Operating Environment   Some business risks can be reduced by actions designed to gain control over the operating environment. For example, to ensure adequate outlets for its products, a firm may establish a network of exclusive dealerships. If access to raw materials is uncertain, a firm may integrate backwards toward the source of supplies. The use of patents and copyrights can protect a firm against immediate competition. Legal action can also reinforce its rights under patents and copyrights. For example, in 1993 Intel, a maker of computer microprocessor chips, filed a suit against a competitor, Advanced Micro Devices (AMD), charging that AMD's "clone" chip violated Intel copyrights. The lawsuit was viewed as an effort by Intel to create fear and uncertainty in the minds of AMD's customers and hence dissuade them from using AMD chips in their personal computers.[16]

Limited Use of Firm-Specific Assets   If a firm builds a plant that can only be used to produce its specific product, that firm has effectively limited its options should the product prove to be unsuccessful. The more general the purpose of the assets employed by a firm, the more flexibility that firm has to redeploy these assets to other uses. A trade-off exists between the use of firm- or product-specific assets, which are likely to be more efficient, and the use of more general-purpose assets, which give the firm increased future flexibility. When planning new investments, this trade-off must be carefully evaluated.

SUMMARY

▢ A decision problem consists of several basic elements—a decision maker, a set of objectives, two or more alternative actions that can possibly achieve the desired objectives, a state of doubt about which alternative is best in achieving the objectives, and an environment consisting of factors beyond the control of the decision maker.

▢ For purposes of exposition and analysis, decision making is divided into several parts: *individual decision making* under *certainty, risk,* and *uncertainty,* and *group decision making.* Decision making under risk refers to the situation where the probabilities of the possible outcomes can be specified by the decision maker. In decision making under uncertainty, the decision maker is either unwilling or unable to specify these probabilities. Group decision making refers to the situation where a conflict exists among the objectives of the participants.

---

[16] "Advanced Micro's 486-Chip Clones Violate Copyrights, Intel Charges," *Wall Street Journal,* 29 April 1993, p. B12.

▦ The decision maker's attitude toward risk affects the shape of his or her utility function and the choices he or she will make in a decision problem involving risk or uncertainty.

▦ Many different approaches are available for incorporating risk into the decision-making process. Five of these methods are the *informal approach, utility function approach, decision tree approach, risk-adjusted discount rate approach,* and the *simulation approach.*

▦ The *maximin* and *minimax regret* decision criteria can be used to choose between alternatives in decision making under uncertainty.

▦ Many techniques are available for managing risk, including investing in additional information, using derivative securities such as options and futures contracts to hedge a position in the cash market, using portfolio risk-reduction techniques when making investment decisions, purchasing insurance, investing in "flexible assets," and making decisions designed to gain some control over the operating environment.

EXERCISES

1. Suppose that a person is considering an investment in a new product. The cost of producing and marketing the product is estimated to be $6,000. Three possible outcomes can result from this investment:
    -   The product can be *extremely successful* and yield a *net* profit of $24,000.
    -   The product can be *moderately successful* and yield a *net* profit of $12,000.
    -   The product can be *unsuccessful,* in which case the loss will be equal to the initial cost of producing and marketing the product (that is, $6,000).

    Additionally, assume that if the person does *not* invest in the new product, the $6,000 can be invested in another venture that is certain to yield a *net* profit of $1,500. Furthermore, suppose that he or she has assessed the chances of the product being extremely successful, moderately successful, and unsuccessful at .10, .20, and .70, respectively.

    a.   Determine the decision alternatives.
    b.   Determine the possible outcomes for each decision alternative.
    c.   Formulate the problem in a payoff table format (such as Figure 20.1) showing the net profit that will result from each alternative action/state-of-nature combination.
    d.   Determine the expected net profit of each decision alternative.
    e.   Assuming that the objective is to maximize expected monetary payoff, which alternative should be chosen?

2. Assume that the decision maker faced with the investment alternatives in Exercise 1 is risk averse in the sense of having a diminishing marginal utility for money (return). Suppose the utility function can be specified as

Money M ($)	Utility U(M)
−6,000	−.75
0	0.0
+1,500	.09
+6,000	.225
+12,000	.375
+24,000	.525

a. Formulate Exercise 1 in a utility (payoff) table format (such as Figure 20.8), showing the utility that will result from each alternative action/state-of-nature combination.

b. Determine the expected utilities of each of the alternative actions.

c. Based on the maximization of expected utility criterion, which alternative should be chosen?

3. Consider Exercise 2 again. Suppose that the decision maker is either unable or unwilling to assess the probabilities of the product being extremely successful, moderately successful, or unsuccessful.

a. Based on the *maximin* decision criterion, which alternative should be selected?

b. Based on the *minimax regret* decision criterion, which alternative should be selected?

4. Shown below is an entrepreneur's utility function for money (return) along with two alternative investment projects (*A* and *B*). Assume that the entrepreneur only has enough funds to undertake one of these investments.

Utility Function		Investment			
Return	Utility	A		B	
		RETURN	PROBABILITY	RETURN	PROBABILITY
$-300,000	-4.00				
0	0.0				
300,000	.60	$-300,000	.40	$-300,000	.10
450,000	.80	1,500,000	.60	0	.20
750,000	1.00			450,000	.40
1,500,000	1.33			750,000	.30

a. Calculate the expected monetary value of each investment.

b. Assuming that the entrepreneur's investment objective is to maximize expected monetary value, which investment should be chosen?

c. Calculate the expected utility of each investment.

d. Assuming that the entrepreneur's objective is to maximize expected utility, which investment should be chosen?

e. Explain why there is a difference in the alternatives chosen in parts (b) and (d).

5. A simulation model similar to the one described in the chapter has been constructed by the HNG Corporation to evaluate the largest of its new investment proposals. After many iterations of the model, HNG's management has arrived at an expected net present value of $4.2 million with a standard deviation of $2.4 million. The net present value probability distribution is approximately normal.

a. Determine the probability that the project will have a negative net present value.

b. Determine the probability that the net present value will be less than $1.0 million.

6. A bakery is considering how many dozen hamburger buns to stock on Saturdays. From past experience, the probabilities of selling 20, 25, 30, 35, or 40 dozen are known to be .15, .20, .30, .25, and .10, respectively. The selling price is $2 per dozen and the cost is $1 per dozen. Any hamburger buns unsold at the end of the day must be sold to a surplus baked goods store for $.30 per dozen, as they can-

not be sold in the bakery the following day. The bakery must decide whether to stock 20, 25, 30, 35, or 40 dozen.

a. Determine the alternative actions under consideration.

b. Determine the states of nature.

c. Formulate the problem in a payoff table format showing the net profit that will result from each alternative action/state-of-nature combination.

d. Determine the expected profit of each alternative action.

e. Based on the maximization of expected monetary value criterion, how many dozen hamburger buns should the bakery stock on Saturdays?

7. An investor is considering investing in two securities. Security A, the less risky security, has an expected return of 12 percent with a standard deviation of 3 percent. Security B has an expected return of 21 percent with a standard deviation of 11 percent. The correlation between the returns for securities A and B is +0.3. The investor plans to put 60 percent of his wealth in A and 40 percent in B.

a. Calculate the expected return from a portfolio made up of securities A and B.

b. What is the standard deviation of this portfolio's returns?

c. What is the probability of receiving a portfolio return of less than 15 percent? (Assume that the distribution of portfolio returns is approximately normal.)

8. Mammouth Mutual Fund of New York has $10 million to invest in certificates of deposit (CDs) for the next 6 months (180 days). It can buy either a Pittsburgh National Bank (PNB) CD with an annual yield of 11 percent or a Frankfurt (Germany) Bank CD with a yield of 13.5 percent. Assume that the CDs are of comparable default risk. The analysts of the mutual fund are concerned about exchange rate risk. They were quoted the following exchange rates by the international department of a New York City bank:

Germany (Deutsche Marks)	
Spot	$0.5200
30-day futures	0.5190
90-day futures	0.5170
180-day futures	0.5155

a. If the Frankfurt Bank CD is purchased and held to maturity, determine the net gain (loss) in U.S. dollars relative to the PNB CD assuming that the exchange rate in 180 days equals today's spot rate.

b. Suppose the German mark declines in value by 5 percent relative to the U.S. dollar over the next 180 days. Determine the net gain (loss) of the Frankfurt Bank CD in U.S. dollars relative to the PNB CD for an uncovered position.

c. Determine the net gain (loss) from a covered position.

9. A corn producer can profitably produce a minimum of 10,000 bushels of corn if he is assured of a price of $2.90 per bushel at the time of planting. The corn will be harvested in late August. At the time of planting the farmer notes that the September futures price for corn is $2.90.

a. What action should the farmer take to hedge his position, that is, to "lock in" an effective price of $2.90 for his corn?

b. By late August the price of cash corn has dropped to $2.50. The September futures price has also declined to $2.50. Ignoring commissions, compute the net profits and losses from the farmer's hedged position, after the farmer closes out the hedge.

c. How does your answer to part (b) change if the late August cash price and the September futures price increase to $3.40?

10. Goody's Drug Company is considering an expansion into a new product line that is more risky than its existing product mix. The new product line requires an investment, *NINV*, of $10 million and is expected to generate annual net cash inflows of $2.0 million over a 10-year estimated economic life. Goody's weighted cost of capital is 12 percent, and the new product line requires an estimated risk-adjusted discount rate of 17 percent, based on the security market line and betas for comparable companies engaged in the contemplated new line of business.

a. What is the project's *NPV* using the company's weighted cost of capital?
b. What is the project's *NPV* using the risk-adjusted discount rate?
c. Should Goody's Drug adopt the project?

11. The managers of U.S. Rubber have analyzed a proposed investment project. The expected net present value (*NPV*) of the project, evaluated at the firm's weighted cost of capital of 18 percent, has been estimated to be $100,000. The company's managers have determined that the most optimistic *NPV* estimate of the project is $175,000 and the most pessimistic estimate is $25,000. The most optimistic estimate is a value that is not expected to be exceeded more than 10 percent of the time. The most pessimistic estimate represents a value that the project's *NPV* is not expected to fall below more than 10 percent of the time. What is the probability that this project will have a negative *NPV*?

www exercise

Accessing Decision
Analysis Software

12. Decision and risk analysis is becoming increasingly sophisticated, and it is important for managers and business economists to have the necessary computer tools. There are a growing number of companies that provide decision analysis software. Many of them offer free demonstration software that can be used or downloaded from the Internet. Two such companies are Vanguard Software Corporation, maker of DecisionPro (http://www.vanguardsw.com/) and Arlington Software Corporation, maker of ERGO (http://www.arlingsoft.com). Access these or other similar sites, download their demonstration software, and compare their performance.

A

The Time Value of Money

INTRODUCTION

Many economic decisions involve benefits and costs that are expected to occur at different future points in time. For example, the construction of a new office complex requires an immediate outlay of cash and results in a stream of expected cash inflows (benefits) over many future years. To determine if the expected future cash inflows are sufficient to justify the initial outlay, we must have a way to compare cash flows occurring at different points in time. Also, recall from Chapter 1 that the value of a firm is equal to the discounted (or present) value of all expected returns. These future returns are discounted at a rate of return, consistent with the risk of the expected future returns. When future returns are more certain, the discount rate used is lower, resulting in a higher present value of the firm, *all other things being equal.* Conversely, when future returns are riskier or more uncertain, they are discounted at a higher rate, resulting in a lower present value of the firm, *all other things being equal.*

An explicit solution to the problem of comparing the benefits and costs of an economic transaction that occur at different points in time requires answers to the following kinds of questions: Is $1 to be received one year from today worth less than $1 in hand today? If so, why is it worth less? How much less is it worth?

The answers to these questions depend on the alternative uses available for the dollar between today and one year from today. Suppose the dollar can be invested in a guaranteed savings account paying a 6 percent annual rate of return (interest rate). The $1 invested today will return $1(1.06) = $1.06 one year from today. To receive exactly $1 one year from today, only $1/(1.06) = $.943 would have to be invested in the account today. Given the opportunity to invest at a 6 percent rate of return, we see that $1 to be received one year from today is indeed worth less than $1 in hand today, its worth being only $.943. Thus, the existence of opportunities to invest the dollar at positive rates of return makes $1 to be received at any future point in time worth less than $1 in hand today.[1] This is what is meant by the *time value of money.* The investor's required rate of return is called the *discount rate.*

PRESENT VALUE OF A SINGLE PAYMENT

We can generalize this result for any future series of cash flows and any interest rate. Assume that the opportunity exists to invest at a compound rate of r percent per annum. Then the *present value* (value today) of $1 to be received at the end of year *n*, discounted at *r* percent, is

$$PV_0 = \frac{1}{(1 + r)^n} \qquad [A.1]$$

---

[1] In this analysis we are abstracting from price level considerations. Changes in the level of prices (the value of the dollar in terms of the quantity of goods and services it will buy) can also affect the worth of the dollar. In theory, future price increases (or decreases) that are *anticipated* by the market will be reflected in the interest rate.

The term, $1/(1 + r)^n$, is often called a Present Value Interest Factor, or $PVIF_{r,n}$. Table 4 in Appendix B contains PVIF values for various interest rates, r, and periods in the future, n.

EXAMPLE

PRESENT VALUE

If an opportunity exists to invest at a compound rate of return of 12 percent, then the present value of $1 to be received four years ($n = 4$) from today is

$$PV_0 = \frac{1}{(1 + .12)^4} = (PVIF_{12\%,4})$$

$$= \$1 (0.6355)$$

$$= \$0.6355$$

As we see in Table A.1, investing $0.6355 today at an interest rate of 12 percent per annum will give $1 at the end of four years.

Alternatively, the PVIF factors from Table 4, Appendix B could be used to find the present value of $1 expected to be received in four years ($n = 4$), assuming an interest rate of 12 percent ($r = 12\%$) as follows:

$$PV_0 = \$1(PVIF_{12\%,4})$$

$$= \$1(0.63552)$$

$$= \$0.6355$$

EXAMPLE

PRESENT VALUE OF A DEFERRED BEQUEST

What is the present value of an expected bequest of $2 million to your university if the expected remaining lifespan of the donor is eight years and the university uses an interest rate of 9 percent to evaluate gifts of this type?

$$PV_0 = \$2,000,000(PVIF_{9\%,8})$$

$$= \$2,000,000(0.50187)$$

$$= \$1,003,740$$

Your university would be indifferent between receiving $1,003,740 today or $2 million in eight years.

TABLE   A.1

Present Value of $1 to Be Received at the End of Four Years

Year	Return Received at End of Year	Value of Investment at End of Year	
0 (present)	—	$.6355	← Initial amount invested
1	.6355(.12) = $.0762	.6355 + .0762 = .7117	
2	.7117(.12) = .0854	.7117 + .0854 = .7971	
3	.7971(.12) = .0957	.7971 + .0957 = .8928	
4	.8928(.12) = .1072	.8928 + .1072 = 1.000	

Solving for the Interest or Growth Rate

Present value interest factors (PVIF) also can be used to solve for interest rates. For example, suppose you wish to borrow $5,000 today from an associate. The associate is willing to loan you the money if you promise to pay back $6,802 four years from today. The compound interest rate your associate is charging can be determined as follows:

$$PV_0 = \$6,802(PVIF_{r,4})$$

$$\$5,000 = \$6,802(PVIF_{r,4})$$

$$PVIF_{r,4} = \frac{\$5,000}{\$6,802}$$

$$= 0.735$$

Reading across the 4-year row in Table 4, 0.735 (rounded to 3 places for simplicity) is found in the 8 percent column. Thus, the effective interest rate on the loan is 8 percent per year, compounded annually.

EXAMPLE

CALCULATION OF EARNINGS GROWTH RATES FOR INTERNATIONAL PAPER

Another common application of the use of PVIF factors from Table 4 is the calculation of the compound rate of growth of an earnings or dividend stream. For example, International Paper Company had earnings per share of $2.56 in 1996. Security analysts have forecasted 2001 earnings per share to be $6.37. What is the expected compound annual rate of growth in International Paper Company's earnings per share? We can use the PVIF factors from Table 4 to solve this problem as follows:

$$\$2.56 = \$6.37(PVIF_{r,5})$$

$$PVIF_{r,5} = 0.40188$$

Looking across the 5-year row in Table 4 we find a PVIF equal to 0.40188 under the 20 percent column. Thus the compound annual growth rate of earnings for International Paper Company is 20 percent. (Interpolation can be used for PVIF values between the values found in the tables. In practice, financial calculators normally are used for these types of calculations.)

PRESENT VALUE OF A SERIES OF EQUAL PAYMENTS (ANNUITY)

The present value of a series of *equal* $1 payments to be received at the end of each of the next n years (an *annuity*), discounted at a rate of r percent, is

$$PV_0 = \frac{1}{(1 + r)^1} + \frac{1}{(1 + r)^2} + \cdots + \frac{1}{(1 + r)^n}$$

$$PV_0 = \sum_{t=1}^{n} \frac{1}{(1 + r)^t} \qquad\qquad [A.2]$$

For example, the present value of $1 to be received at the end of each of the next four years, discounted at 12 percent, is

$$PV_0 = \sum_{t=1}^{4} \frac{1}{(1 + .12)^t}$$

$$= \frac{1}{(1 + .12)^1} + \frac{1}{(1 + .12)^2} + \frac{1}{(1 + .12)^3} + \frac{1}{(1 + .12)^4}$$

$$= .89286 + .79719 + .71178 + .63552 = \$3.0374$$

As shown in Table A.2, investing $3.0374 today at 12 percent will return exactly $1 at the end of each of the next four years, with nothing remaining in the account at the end of the fourth year. Again, rather than perform the present value calculations (Equation A.2), we can use a table to look up the values we need. Table 5 in Appendix B contains the present values at various interest rates of $1 to be received at the end of each year for various periods of time. The values in Table 5 are called Present Value Interest Factors for Annuities, or $PVIFA_{r,n}$, where r is the interest rate per period and n is the number of periods (normally years).

Using the PVIFA factors from Table 5, the present value of an annuity ($PVAN_0$) can be computed as

$$PVAN_0 = PMT(PVIFA_{r,n}) \qquad\qquad [A.3]$$

where PMT = the annuity amount to be received each period.

EXAMPLE

PRESENT VALUE OF AN ANNUITY

You have recently purchased the winning ticket in the Florida lottery and have won $30 million, to be paid in equal $3 million increments (PMT) at the end of each of the next ten years. What are your winnings worth to you today using an interest rate of 8 percent? The PVIFA factors from Table 5 can be used to solve this problem as follows:

$$PVAN_0 = \$3,000,000(PVIFA_{8\%,10})$$

$$= \$3,000,000(6.7101)$$

$$= \$20,130,300$$

Thus your $30 million winnings are worth only $20,130,300 to you today.

TABLE   A.2   Present Value of $1 to be Received at the End of Each of the Next Four Years

Year	Return Received at End of Year	Amount Withdrawn at End of Year	Value of Investment at End of Year	
0 (present)	—	—	$3.0374	←initial amount invested
1	$3.0374(.12) = $.3645	$1.00	$3.0374 + .3645 − 1.00 = 2.4019	
2	2.4019(.12) = .2882	1.00	2.4019 + .2882 − 1.00 = 1.6901	
3	1.6901(.12) = .2028	1.00	1.6901 + .2028 − 1.00 = .8929	
4	.8929(.12) = .1071	1.00	.8929 + .1071 − 1.00 = .0000	

Solving for the Interest Rate

Present value of an annuity interest factors also can be used to solve for the rate of return expected from an investment. This rate of return is often referred to as the internal rate of return from an investment. Suppose the Big Spring Tool Company purchases a machine for $100,000. This machine is expected to generate annual cash flows of $23,740 to the firm over the next five years. What is the expected rate of return from this investment?

Using Equation A.3 we can determine the expected rate of return in this example as follows:

$$PVAN_0 = PMT(PVIFA_{r,5})$$

$$\$100,000 = \$23,740(PVIFA_{r,5})$$

$$PVIFA_{r,5} = 4.2123$$

From the 5-year row in Table 5, we see that a PVIFA of 4.2123 occurs in the 6 percent column. Hence, this investment offers a 6 percent expected (internal) rate of return.

PRESENT VALUE OF A SERIES OF UNEQUAL PAYMENTS

The present value of a series of *unequal* payments (PMT_t, $t = 1, \ldots, n$) to be received at the end of each of the next n years, discounted at a rate of r percent, is

$$PV_0 = \sum_{t=1}^{n} \frac{PMT_t}{(1 + r)^t}$$

$$= \sum_{t=1}^{n} PMT_t(PVIF_{r,t}) \qquad [A.4]$$

The $PVIF_{r,t}$ values are the interest factors from Table 4, Appendix B. Thus, the present value of a series of unequal payments is equal to the sum of the present value of the individual payments.

EXAMPLE

PROJECT EVALUATION FOR INTEL

Intel computer is evaluating an investment in a new chip-manufacturing facility. The facility is expected to have a useful life of five years and yield the following cash-flow stream after the initial investment outlay:

End of Year t	Cash Flow PMT_t
1	+ $1,000,000
2	+ 1,500,000
3	− 500,000
4	+ 2,000,000
5	+ 1,000,000

The negative cash flow in year 3 arises because of the expected need to install pollution control equipment during that year. The present value of this series of unequal payments can be computed using PVIF factors from Table 4 and assuming a 10 percent interest (required) rate on the investment:

$$PV = \$1,000,000(PVIF_{10\%,1}) + \$1,500,000(PVIF_{10\%,2})$$
$$- \$500,000(PVIF_{10\%,3}) + \$2,000,000(PVIF_{10\%,4})$$
$$+ \$1,000,000(PVIF_{10\%,5})$$
$$= \$1,000,000(0.90909) + \$1,500,000(0.82645)$$
$$- \$500,000(0.75131) + \$2,000,000(0.68301)$$
$$+ \$1,000,000(0.62092)$$
$$= \$3,760,050$$

The present value of these cash flows ($3,760,050) would be compared with the required initial cash outlay to determine whether to invest in the new manufacturing facility.

B

Tables

TABLE 1*

Values of the Standard
Normal Distribution
Function

z	0	1	2	3	4	5	6	7	8	9
−3.	.0013	.0010	.0007	.0005	.0003	.0002	.0002	.0001	0001	.0000
−2.9	.0019	.0018	.0017	.0017	.0016	.0016	.0015	.0015	.0014	.0014
−2.8	.0026	.0025	.0024	.0023	.0023	.0022	.0021	.0021	.0020	.0019
−2.7	.0035	.0034	.0033	.0032	.0031	.0030	.0029	.0028	.0027	.0026
−2.6	.0047	.0045	.0044	.0043	.0041	.0040	.0039	.0038	.0037	.0036
−2.5	.0062	.0060	.0059	.0057	.0055	.0054	.0052	.0051	.0049	.0048
−2.4	.0082	.0080	.0078	.0075	.0073	.0071	.0069	.0068	.0066	.0064
−2.3	.0107	.0104	.0102	.0099	.0096	.0094	.0091	.0089	.0087	.0084
−2.2	.0139	.0136	.0132	.0129	.0126	.0122	.0119	.0116	.0113	.0110
−2.1	.0179	.0174	.0170	.0166	.0162	.0158	.0154	.0150	.0146	.0143
−2.0	.0228	.0222	.0217	.0212	.0207	.0202	.0197	.0192	.0188	.0183
−1.9	.0287	.0281	.0274	.0268	.0262	.0256	.0250	.0244	.0238	.0233
−1.8	.0359	.0352	.0344	.0336	.0329	.0322	.0314	.0307	.0300	.0294
−1.7	.0446	.0436	.0427	.0418	.0409	.0401	.0392	.0384	.0375	.0367
−1.6	.0548	.0537	.0526	.0516	.0505	.0495	.0485	.0475	.0465	.0455
−1.5	.0668	.0655	.0643	.0630	.0618	.0606	.0594	.0582	.0570	.0559
−1.4	.0808	.0793	.0778	.0764	.0749	.0735	.0722	.0708	.0694	.0681
−1.3	.0988	.0951	.0934	.0918	.0901	.0885	.0869	.0853	.0838	.0823
−1.2	.1151	.1131	.1112	.1093	.1075	.1056	.1038	.1020	.1003	.0985
−1.1	.1357	.1335	.1314	.1292	.1271	.1251	.1230	.1210	.1190	.1170
−1.0	.1587	.1562	.1539	.1515	.1492	.1469	.1446	.1423	.1401	.1379
− .9	.1841	.1814	.1788	.1762	.1736	.1711	.1685	.1660	.1635	.1611
− .8	.2119	.2090	.2061	.2033	.2005	.1977	.1949	.1922	.1894	.1867
− .7	.2420	.2389	.2358	.2327	.2297	.2266	.2236	.2206	.2177	.2148
− .6	.2743	.2709	.2676	.2643	.2611	.2578	.2546	.2514	.2483	.2451
− .5	.3085	.3050	.3015	.2981	.2946	.2912	.2877	.2843	.2810	.2776
− .4	.3446	.3409	.3372	.3336	.3300	.3264	.3228	.3192	.3156	.3121
− .3	.3821	.3783	.3745	.3707	.3669	.3632	.3594	.3557	.3520	.3483
− .2	.4207	.4168	.4129	.4090	.4052	.4013	.3974	.3936	.3897	.3859
− .1	.4602	.4562	.4522	.4483	.4443	.4404	.4364	.4325	.4286	.4247
− .0	.5000	.4960	.4920	.4880	.4840	.4801	.4761	.4721	.4681	.4641

*Note: Table values give the probability of a value occurring which is *less than* Z standard deviations from the mean.

Note 1: If a random variable X is not "standard," its values must be "standardized": $Z = (X − \mu)/\sigma$. That is:

$$P(X \leq x) = N\left(\frac{x - \mu}{\sigma}\right)$$

Note 2: For $z \geq 4$, $N(z) = 1$ to 4 decimal places; for $z \leq −4$, $N(z) = 0$ to 4 decimal places.

TABLE 1*											
z	0	1	2	3	4	5	6	7	8	9
.0	.5000	.5040	.5080	.5120	.5160	.5199	.5239	.5279	.5319	.5359
.1	.5398	.5438	.5478	.5517	.5557	.5596	.5636	.5675	.5714	.5753
.2	.5793	.5832	.5871	.5910	.5948	.5987	.6026	.6064	.6103	.6141
.3	.6179	.6217	.6255	.6293	.6331	.6368	.6406	.6443	.6480	.6517
.4	.6554	.6591	.6628	.6664	.6700	.6736	.6772	.6808	.6844	.6879
.5	.6915	.6950	.6985	.7019	.7054	.7088	.7123	.7157	.7190	.7224
.6	.7257	.7291	.7324	.7357	.7389	.7422	.7454	.7486	.7517	.7549
.7	.7580	.7611	.7642	.7673	.7703	.7734	.7764	.7794	.7823	.7852
.8	.7881	.7910	.7939	.7967	.7995	.8023	.8051	.8078	.8106	.8133
.9	.8159	.8186	.8212	.8238	.8264	.8289	.8315	.8340	.8365	.8389
1.0	.8413	.8438	.8461	.8485	.8508	.8531	.8554	.8577	.8599	.8621
1.1	.8643	.8665	.8686	.8708	.8729	.8749	.8770	.8790	.8810	.8830
1.2	.8849	.8869	.8888	.8907	.8925	.8944	.8962	.8980	.8997	.9015
1.3	.9032	.9049	.9066	.9082	.9099	.9115	.9131	.9147	.9162	.9177
1.4	.9192	.9207	.9222	.9236	.9251	.9265	.9278	.9292	.9306	.9319
1.5	.9332	.9345	.9357	.9370	.9382	.9394	.9406	.9418	.9430	.9441
1.6	.9452	.9463	.9474	.9484	.9495	.9505	.9515	.9525	.9535	.9545
1.7	.9554	.9564	.9573	.9582	.9591	.9599	.9608	.9616	.9625	.9633
1.8	.9641	.9648	.9656	.9664	.9671	.9678	.9686	.9693	.9700	.9706
1.9	.9713	.9719	.9726	.9732	.9738	.9744	.9750	.9756	.9762	.9767
2.0	.9772	.9778	.9783	.9788	.9793	.9798	.9803	.9808	.9812	.9817
2.1	.9821	.9826	.9830	.9834	.9838	.9842	.9846	.9850	.9854	.9857
2.2	.9861	.9864	.9868	.9871	.9874	.9878	.9881	.9884	.9887	.9890
2.3	.9893	.9896	.9898	.9901	.9904	.9906	.9909	.9911	.9913	.9916
2.4	.9918	.9920	.9922	.9925	.9927	.9929	.9931	.9932	.9934	.9936
2.5	.9938	.9940	.9941	.9943	.9945	.9946	.9948	.9949	.9951	.9952
2.6	.9953	.9955	.9956	.9957	.9959	.9960	.9961	.9962	.9963	.9964
2.7	.9965	.9966	.9967	.9968	.9969	.9970	.9971	.9972	.9973	.9974
2.8	.9974	.9975	.9976	.9977	.9977	.9978	.9979	.9979	.9980	.9981
2.9	.9981	.9982	.9982	.9983	.9984	.9984	.9985	.9985	.9986	.9986
3.	.9987	.9990	.9993	.9995	.9997	.9998	.9998	.9999	.9999	1.0000

Values of the Standard Normal Distribution Function (cont'd)

Source: *Statistical Analysis: With Business and Economic Applications,* by Ya-lun Chou. Copyright © 1969 by Holt, Rinehart and Winston, Inc. Reprinted by permission of Holt, Rinehart and Winston, Inc.

TABLE 2*	Table of "Students" Distribution—Value of t

Degrees of Freedom	Probability												
	0.9	0.8	0.7	0.6	0.5	0.4	0.3	0.2	0.1	0.05	0.02	0.01	0.001
1	0.158	0.325	0.510	0.727	1.000	1.376	1.963	3.078	6.314	12.706	31.821	63.657	636. 619
2	0.142	0.289	0.445	0.617	0.816	1.061	1.386	1.886	2.920	4.303	6.965	9.925	31.598
3	0.137	0.277	0.424	0.584	0.765	0.978	1.250	1.638	2.353	3.182	4.541	5.841	12.924
4	0.134	0.271	0.414	0.569	0.741	0.941	1.190	1.533	2.132	2.776	3.747	4.604	8.610
5	0.132	0.267	0.408	0.559	0.727	0.920	1.156	1.476	2.015	2.571	3.365	4.032	6.869
6	0.131	0.265	0.404	0.553	0.718	0.906	1.134	1.440	1.943	2.447	3.143	3.707	5.959
7	0.130	0.263	0.402	0.549	0.711	0.896	1.119	1.415	1.895	2.365	2.998	3.499	5.408
8	0.130	0.262	0.399	0.546	0.706	0.889	1.108	1.397	1.860	2.306	2.896	3.355	5.041
9	0.129	0.261	0.398	0.543	0.703	0.883	1.100	1.383	1.833	2.262	2.821	3.250	4.781
10	0.129	0.260	0.397	0.542	0.700	0.879	1.093	1.372	1.812	2.228	2.764	3.169	4.587
11	0.129	0.260	0.396	0.540	0.697	0.876	1.088	1.363	1.796	2.201	2.718	3.106	4.437
12	0.128	0.259	0.395	0.539	0.695	0.873	1.083	1.356	1.782	2.179	2.681	3.055	4.318
13	0.128	0.259	0.394	0.538	0.694	0.870	1.079	1.350	1.771	2.160	2.650	3.012	4.221
14	0.128	0.258	0.393	0.537	0.692	0.868	1.076	1.345	1.761	2.145	2.624	2.977	4.140
15	0.128	0.258	0.393	0.536	0.691	0.866	1.074	1.341	1.753	2.131	2.602	2.947	4.073
16	0.128	0.258	0.392	0.535	0.690	0.865	1.071	1.337	1.746	2.120	2.583	2.921	4.015
17	0.128	0.257	0.392	0.534	0.689	0.863	1.069	1.333	1.740	2.110	2.567	2.898	3.965
18	0.127	0.257	0.392	0.534	0.688	0.862	1.067	1.330	1.734	2.101	2.552	2.878	3.922
19	0.127	0.257	0.391	0.533	0.688	0.861	1.066	1.328	1.729	2.093	2.539	2.861	3.883
20	0.127	0.257	0.391	0.533	0.687	0.860	1.064	1.325	1.725	2.086	2.528	2.845	3.850
21	0.127	0.257	0.391	0.532	0.686	0.859	1.063	1.323	1.721	2.080	2.518	2.831	3.819
22	0.127	0.256	0.390	0.532	0.686	0.858	1.061	1.321	1.717	2.074	2.508	2.819	3.792
23	0.127	0.256	0.390	0.532	0.685	0.858	1.060	1.319	1.714	2.069	2.500	2.807	3.767
24	0.127	0.256	0.390	0.531	0.685	0.857	1.059	1.318	1.711	2.064	2.492	2.797	3.745
25	0.127	0.256	0.390	0.531	0.684	0.856	1.058	1.316	1.708	2.060	2.485	2.787	3.725
26	0.127	0.256	0.390	0.531	0.684	0.856	1.058	1.315	1.706	2.056	2.479	2.779	3.707
27	0.127	0.256	0.389	0.531	0.684	0.855	1.057	1.314	1.703	2.052	2.473	2.771	3.690
28	0.127	0.256	0.389	0.530	0.683	0.855	1.056	1.313	1.701	2.048	2.467	2.763	3.674
29	0.127	0.256	0.389	0.530	0.683	0.854	1.055	1.311	1.699	2.045	2.462	2.756	3.659
30	0.127	0.256	0.389	0.530	0.683	0.854	1.055	1.310	1.697	2.042	2.457	2.750	3.646
40	0.126	0.255	0.388	0.529	0.681	0.851	1.050	1.303	1.684	2.021	2.423	2.704	3.551
60	0.126	0.254	0.387	0.527	0.679	0.848	1.046	1.296	1.671	2.000	2.390	2.660	3.460
120	0.126	0.254	0.386	0.526	0.677	0.845	1.041	1.289	1.658	1.980	2.358	2.617	3.373
∞	0.126	0.253	0.385	0.524	0.674	0.842	1.036	1.282	1.645	1.960	2.326	2.576	3.291

*Note: Probabilities given are for two-tailed tests. For example, a probability of .05 allows for .025 in one tail of the distribution and .025 in the other.

Table 2 is taken from Table III of Fisher and Yates: *Statistical Tables for Biological, Agricultural and Medical Research,* published by Longman Group, Ltd., London (previously published by Oliver and Boyd, Edinburgh), and by permission of the authors and publishers.

TABLE 3　The F-Distribution—Upper 5% Points

δ_2 \ δ_1	1	2	3	4	5	6	7	8	9	10	12	15	20	24	30	40	60	120	∞
1	161.4	199.5	215.7	224.6	230.2	234.0	236.8	238.9	240.5	241.9	243.9	245.9	248.0	249.1	250.1	251.1	252.2	253.3	254.3
2	18.51	19.00	19.16	19.25	19.30	19.33	19.35	19.37	19.38	19.40	19.41	19.43	19.45	19.45	19.46	19.47	19.48	19.49	19.50
3	10.13	9.55	9.28	9.12	9.01	8.94	8.89	8.85	8.81	8.79	8.74	8.70	8.66	8.64	8.62	8.59	8.57	8.55	8.53
4	7.71	6.94	6.59	6.39	6.26	6.16	6.09	6.04	6.00	5.96	5.91	5.86	5.80	5.77	5.75	5.72	5.69	5.66	5.63
5	6.61	5.79	5.41	5.19	5.05	4.95	4.88	4.82	4.77	4.74	4.68	4.62	4.56	4.53	4.50	4.46	4.43	4.40	4.36
6	5.99	5.14	4.76	4.53	4.39	4.28	4.21	4.15	4.10	4.06	4.00	3.94	3.87	3.84	3.81	3.77	3.74	3.70	3.67
7	5.59	4.74	4.35	4.12	3.97	3.87	3.79	3.73	3.68	3.64	3.57	3.51	3.44	3.41	3.38	3.34	3.30	3.27	3.23
8	5.32	4.46	4.07	3.84	3.69	3.58	3.50	3.44	3.39	3.35	3.28	3.22	3.15	3.12	3.08	3.04	3.01	2.97	2.93
9	5.12	4.26	3.86	3.63	3.48	3.37	3.29	3.23	3.18	3.14	3.07	3.01	2.94	2.90	2.86	2.83	2.79	2.75	2.71
10	4.96	4.10	3.71	3.48	3.33	3.22	3.14	3.07	3.02	2.98	2.91	2.85	2.77	2.74	2.70	2.66	2.62	2.58	2.54
11	4.84	3.98	3.59	3.36	3.20	3.09	3.01	2.95	2.90	2.85	2.79	2.72	2.65	2.61	2.57	2.53	2.49	2.45	2.40
12	4.75	3.89	3.49	3.26	3.11	3.00	2.91	2.85	2.80	2.75	2.69	2.62	2.54	2.51	2.47	2.43	2.38	2.34	2.30
13	4.67	3.81	3.41	3.18	3.03	2.92	2.83	2.77	2.71	2.67	2.60	2.53	2.46	2.42	2.38	2.34	2.30	2.25	2.21
14	4.60	3.74	3.34	3.11	2.96	2.85	2.76	2.70	2.65	2.60	2.53	2.46	2.39	2.35	2.31	2.27	2.22	2.18	2.13
15	4.54	3.68	3.29	3.06	2.90	2.79	2.71	2.64	2.59	2.54	2.48	2.40	2.33	2.29	2.25	2.20	2.16	2.11	2.07
16	4.49	3.63	3.24	3.01	2.85	2.74	2.66	2.59	2.54	2.49	2.42	2.35	2.28	2.24	2.19	2.15	2.11	2.06	2.01
17	4.45	3.59	3.20	2.96	2.81	2.70	2.61	2.55	2.49	2.45	2.38	2.31	2.23	2.19	2.15	2.10	2.06	2.01	1.96
18	4.41	3.55	3.16	2.93	2.77	2.66	2.58	2.51	2.46	2.41	2.34	2.27	2.19	2.15	2.11	2.06	2.02	1.97	1.92
19	4.38	3.52	3.13	2.90	2.74	2.63	2.54	2.48	2.42	2.38	2.31	2.23	2.16	2.11	2.07	2.03	1.98	1.93	1.88
20	4.35	3.49	3.10	2.87	2.71	2.60	2.51	2.45	2.39	2.35	2.28	2.20	2.12	2.08	2.04	1.99	1.95	1.90	1.84
21	4.32	3.47	3.07	2.84	2.68	2.57	2.49	2.42	2.37	2.32	2.25	2.18	2.10	2.05	2.01	1.96	1.92	1.87	1.81
22	4.30	3.44	3.05	2.82	2.66	2.55	2.46	2.40	2.34	2.30	2.23	2.15	2.07	2.03	1.98	1.94	1.89	1.84	1.78
23	4.28	3.42	3.03	2.80	2.64	2.53	2.44	2.37	2.32	2.27	2.20	2.13	2.05	2.01	1.96	1.91	1.86	1.81	1.76
24	4.26	3.40	3.01	2.78	2.62	2.51	2.42	2.36	2.30	2.25	2.18	2.11	2.03	1.98	1.94	1.89	1.84	1.79	1.73
25	4.24	3.39	2.99	2.76	2.60	2.49	2.40	2.34	2.28	2.24	2.16	2.09	2.01	1.96	1.92	1.87	1.82	1.77	1.71
26	4.23	3.37	2.98	2.74	2.59	2.47	2.39	2.32	2.27	2.22	2.15	2.07	1.99	1.95	1.90	1.85	1.80	1.75	1.69
27	4.21	3.35	2.96	2.73	2.57	2.46	2.37	2.31	2.25	2.20	2.13	2.06	1.97	1.93	1.88	1.84	1.79	1.73	1.67
28	4.20	3.34	2.95	2.71	2.56	2.45	2.36	2.29	2.24	2.19	2.12	2.04	1.96	1.91	1.87	1.82	1.77	1.71	1.65
29	4.18	3.33	2.93	2.70	2.55	2.43	2.35	2.28	2.22	2.18	2.10	2.03	1.94	1.90	1.85	1.81	1.75	1.70	1.64
30	4.17	3.32	2.92	2.69	2.53	2.42	2.33	2.27	2.21	2.16	2.09	2.01	1.93	1.89	1.84	1.79	1.74	1.68	1.62
40	4.08	3.23	2.84	2.61	2.45	2.34	2.25	2.18	2.12	2.08	2.00	1.92	1.84	1.79	1.74	1.69	1.64	1.58	1.51
60	4.00	3.15	2.76	2.53	2.37	2.25	2.17	2.10	2.04	1.99	1.92	1.84	1.75	1.70	1.65	1.59	1.53	1.47	1.39
120	3.92	3.07	2.68	2.45	2.29	2.17	2.09	2.02	1.96	1.91	1.83	1.75	1.66	1.61	1.55	1.50	1.43	1.35	1.25
∞	3.84	3.00	2.60	2.37	2.21	2.10	2.01	1.94	1.88	1.83	1.75	1.67	1.57	1.52	1.46	1.39	1.32	1.22	1.00

δ_1 / δ_2	1	2	3	4	5	6	7	8	9
1	4052	4999.5	5403	5625	5764	5859	5928	5982	6022
2	98.50	99.00	99.17	99.25	99.30	99.33	99.36	99.37	99.39
3	34.12	30.82	29.46	28.71	28.24	27.91	27.67	27.49	27.35
4	21.20	18.00	16.69	15.98	15.52	15.21	14.98	14.80	14.66
5	16.26	13.27	12.06	11.39	10.97	10.67	10.46	10.29	10.16
6	13.75	10.92	9.78	9.15	8.75	8.47	8.26	8.10	7.98
7	12.25	9.55	8.45	7.85	7.46	7.19	6.99	6.84	6.72
8	11.26	8.65	7.59	7.01	6.63	6.37	6.18	6.03	5.91
9	10.56	8.02	6.99	6.42	6.06	5.80	5.61	5.47	5.35
10	10.04	7.56	6.55	5.99	5.64	5.39	5.20	5.06	4.94
11	9.65	7.21	6.22	5.67	5.32	5.07	4.89	4.74	4.63
12	9.33	6.93	5.95	5.41	5.06	4.82	4.64	4.50	4.39
13	9.07	6.70	5.74	5.21	4.86	4.62	4.44	4.30	4.19
14	8.86	6.51	5.56	5.04	4.69	4.46	4.28	4.14	4.03
15	8.68	6.36	5.42	4.89	4.56	4.32	4.14	4.00	3.89
16	8.53	6.23	5.29	4.77	4.44	4.20	4.03	3.89	3.78
17	8.40	6.11	5.18	4.67	4.34	4.10	3.93	3.79	3.68
18	8.29	6.01	5.09	4.58	4.25	4.01	3.84	3.71	3.60
19	8.18	5.93	5.01	4.50	4.17	3.94	3.77	3.63	3.52

δ_1 / δ_2	10	12	15	20	24	30	40	60	120	∞
1	6056	6106	6157	6209	6235	6261	6287	6313	6339	6366
2	99.40	99.42	99.43	99.45	99.46	99.47	99.47	99.48	99.49	99.50
3	27.23	27.05	26.87	26.69	26.60	26.50	26.41	26.32	26.22	26.13
4	14.55	14.37	14.20	14.02	13.93	13.84	13.75	13.65	13.56	13.46
5	10.05	9.89	9.72	9.55	9.47	9.38	9.29	9.20	9.11	9.02
6	7.87	7.72	7.56	7.40	7.31	7.23	7.14	7.06	6.97	6.88
7	6.62	6.47	6.31	6.16	6.07	5.99	5.91	5.82	5.74	5.65
8	5.81	5.67	5.52	5.36	5.28	5.20	5.12	5.03	4.95	4.86
9	5.26	5.11	4.96	4.81	4.73	4.65	4.57	4.48	4.40	4.31
10	4.85	4.71	4.56	4.41	4.33	4.25	4.17	4.08	4.00	3.91
11	4.54	4.40	4.25	4.10	4.02	3.94	3.86	3.78	3.69	3.60
12	4.30	4.16	4.01	3.86	3.78	3.70	3.62	3.54	3.45	3.36
13	4.10	3.96	3.82	3.66	3.59	3.51	3.43	3.34	3.25	3.17
14	3.94	3.80	3.66	3.51	3.43	3.35	3.27	3.18	3.09	3.00
15	3.80	3.67	3.52	3.37	3.29	3.21	3.13	3.05	2.96	2.87
16	3.69	3.55	3.41	3.26	3.18	3.10	3.02	2.93	2.84	2.75
17	3.59	3.46	3.31	3.16	3.08	3.00	2.92	2.83	2.75	2.65
18	3.51	3.37	3.23	3.08	3.00	2.92	2.84	2.75	2.66	2.57
19	3.43	3.30	3.15	3.00	2.92	2.84	2.76	2.67	2.58	2.49

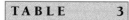

The F-Distribution—Upper 1% Points (cont'd)

δ_2 \ δ_1	1	2	3	4	5	6	7	8	9
20	8.10	5.85	4.94	4.43	4.10	3.87	3.70	3.56	3.46
21	8.02	5.78	4.87	4.37	4.04	3.81	3.64	3.51	3.40
22	7.95	5.72	4.82	4.31	3.99	3.76	3.59	3.45	3.35
23	7.88	5.66	4.76	4.26	3.94	3.71	3.54	3.41	3.30
24	7.82	5.61	4.72	4.22	3.90	3.67	3.50	3.36	3.26
25	7.77	5.57	4.68	4.18	3.85	3.63	3.46	3.32	3.22
26	7.72	5.53	4.64	4.14	3.82	3.59	3.42	3.29	3.18
27	7.68	5.49	4.60	4.11	3.78	3.56	3.39	3.26	3.15
28	7.64	5.45	4.57	4.07	3.75	3.53	3.36	3.23	3.12
29	7.60	5.42	4.54	4.04	3.73	3.50	3.33	3.20	3.09
30	7.56	5.39	4.51	4.02	3.70	3.47	3.30	3.17	3.07
40	7.31	5.18	4.31	3.83	3.51	3.29	3.12	2.99	2.89
60	7.08	4.98	4.13	3.65	3.34	3.12	2.95	2.82	2.72
120	6.85	4.79	3.95	3.48	3.17	2.96	2.79	2.66	2.56
∞	6.63	4.61	3.78	3.32	3.02	2.80	2.64	2.51	2.41

δ_2 \ δ_1	10	12	15	20	24	30	40	60	120	∞
20	3.37	3.23	3.09	2.94	2.86	2.78	2.69	2.61	2.52	2.42
21	3.31	3.17	3.03	2.88	2.80	2.72	2.64	2.55	2.46	2.36
22	3.26	3.12	2.98	2.83	2.75	2.67	2.58	2.50	2.40	2.31
23	3.21	3.07	2.93	2.78	2.70	2.62	2.54	2.45	2.35	2.26
24	3.17	3.03	2.89	2.74	2.66	2.58	2.49	2.40	2.31	2.21
25	3.13	2.99	2.85	2.70	2.62	2.54	2.45	2.36	2.27	2.17
26	3.09	2.96	2.81	2.66	2.58	2.50	2.42	2.33	2.23	2.13
27	3.06	2.93	2.78	2.63	2.55	2.47	2.38	2.29	2.20	2.10
28	3.03	2.90	2.75	2.60	2.52	2.44	2.35	2.26	2.17	2.06
29	3.00	2.87	2.73	2.57	2.49	2.41	2.33	2.23	2.14	2.03
30	2.98	2.84	2.70	2.55	2.47	2.39	2.30	2.21	2.11	2.01
40	2.80	2.66	2.52	2.37	2.29	2.20	2.11	2.02	1.92	1.80
60	2.63	2.50	2.35	2.20	2.12	2.03	1.94	1.84	1.73	1.60
120	2.47	2.34	2.19	2.03	1.95	1.86	1.76	1.66	1.53	1.38
∞	2.32	2.18	2.04	1.88	1.79	1.70	1.59	1.47	1.32	1.00

Source: E. S. Pearson and H. O. Hartley, *Biometrika Tables for Statisticians*, Vol. 1, Table 18 with permission.

TABLE 4   Present Value of $1 (PVIF)

Period	1%	2%	3%	4%	5%	6%	7%	8%	9%	10%	Period
01	.99010	.98039	.97007	.96154	.95233	.94340	.93458	.92593	.91743	.90909	01
02	.98030	.96117	.94260	.92456	.90703	.89000	.87344	.85734	.84168	.82645	02
03	.97059	.94232	.91514	.88900	.86384	.83962	.81639	.79383	.77228	.75131	03
04	.96098	.92385	.88849	.85480	.82270	.79209	.76290	.73503	.70883	.68301	04
05	.95147	.90573	.86261	.82193	.78353	.74726	.71299	.68058	.64993	.62092	05
06	.94204	.88797	.83748	.79031	.74622	.70496	.66634	.63017	.59627	.56447	06
07	.93272	.87056	.81309	.75992	.71063	.66506	.62275	.58349	.54705	.51316	07
08	.92348	.85349	.78941	.73069	.67684	.62741	.58201	.54027	.50189	.46651	08
09	.91434	.83675	.76642	.70259	.64461	.59190	.54393	.50025	.46043	.42410	09
10	.90529	.82035	.74409	.67556	.61391	.55839	.50835	.46319	.42241	.38554	10
11	.89632	.80426	.72242	.64958	.58468	.52679	.47509	.42888	.38753	.35049	11
12	.88745	.78849	.70138	.62460	.55684	.49697	.44401	.39711	.35553	.31683	12
13	.87866	.77303	.68095	.60057	.53032	.46884	.41496	.36770	.32618	.28966	13
14	.86996	.75787	.66112	.57747	.50507	.44230	.38782	.34046	.29925	.26333	14
15	.86135	.74301	.64186	.55526	.48102	.41726	.36245	.31524	.27454	.23939	15
16	.85282	.72845	.62317	.53391	.45811	39365	.33873	.29189	.25187	.21763	16
17	.84436	.71416	.60502	.51337	.43630	.37136	.31657	.27027	.23107	.19784	17
18	.83602	.70016	.58739	.49363	.41552	.35034	.29586	.25025	.21199	.17986	18
19	.82774	.68643	.57029	.47464	.39573	.33051	.27651	.23171	.19449	.16354	19
20	.81954	.67297	.55367	.45639	.37689	.31180	.25842	.21455	.17843	.14864	20
21	.81143	.65978	.53755	.44883	.35894	.29415	.24151	.19866	.16370	.13513	21
22	.80340	.64684	.52189	.42195	.34185	.27750	.22571	.18394	.15018	.12285	22
23	.79544	.63414	.50669	.40573	.32557	.26180	.21095	.17031	.13778	.11168	23
24	.78757	.62172	.49193	.39012	.31007	.24698	.19715	.15770	.12640	.10153	24
25	.77977	.60953	.47760	.37512	.29530	.23300	.18425	.14602	.11597	.09230	25

APPENDIX B   Tables

TABLE   4   Present Value of $1 (PVIF) (cont'd)

Period	11%	12%	13%	14%	15%	16%	17%	18%	19%	20%	Period
01	.90090	.89286	.88496	.87719	.86957	.86207	.85470	.84746	.84043	.83333	01
02	.81162	.79719	.78315	.76947	.75614	.74316	.73051	.71818	.70616	.69444	02
03	.73119	.71178	.69305	.67497	.65752	.64066	.62437	.60863	.59342	.57870	03
04	.65873	.63552	.61332	.59208	.57175	.55229	.53365	.51579	.49867	.48225	04
05	.59345	.56743	.54276	.51937	.49718	.47611	.45611	.43711	.41905	.40188	05
06	.53464	.50663	.48032	.45559	.43233	.41044	.38984	.37043	.35214	.33490	06
07	.48166	.45235	.42506	.39964	.37594	.35383	.33320	.31392	.29592	.27908	07
08	.43393	.40388	.37616	.35056	.32690	.30503	.28478	.26604	.24867	.23257	08
09	.39092	.36061	.33288	.30751	.28426	.26295	.24340	.22546	.20897	.19381	09
10	.35218	.32197	.29459	.26974	.24718	.22668	.20804	.19106	.17560	.16151	10
11	.31728	.28748	.26070	.23662	.21494	.19542	.17781	.16192	.14756	.13459	11
12	.28584	.25667	.23071	.20756	.18691	.16846	.15197	.13722	.12400	.11216	12
13	.25751	.22917	.20416	.18207	.16253	.14523	.12989	.11629	.10420	.09346	13
14	.23199	.20462	.18068	.15971	.14133	.12520	.11102	.09855	.08757	.07789	14
15	.20900	.18270	.15989	.14010	.12289	.10793	.09489	.08352	.07359	.06491	15
16	.18829	.16312	.14150	.12289	.10686	.09304	.08110	.07073	.06184	.05409	16
17	.16963	.14564	.12522	.10780	.09293	.08021	.06932	.05998	.05196	.04507	17
18	.15282	.13004	.11081	.09456	.08080	.06914	.05925	.05083	.04367	.03756	18
19	.13768	.11611	.09806	.08295	.07026	.05961	.05064	.04308	.03669	.03130	19
20	.12403	.10367	.08678	.07276	.06110	.05139	.04328	.03651	.03084	.02608	20
21	.11174	.09256	.07680	.06383	.05313	.04430	.03699	.03094	.02591	.02174	21
22	.10067	.08264	.06796	.05599	.04620	.03819	.03162	.02622	.02178	.01811	22
23	.09069	.07379	.06014	.04911	.04017	.03292	.02702	.02222	.01830	.01509	23
24	.08170	.06588	.05322	.04308	.03493	.02838	.02310	.01883	.01538	.01258	24
25	.07361	.05882	.04710	.03779	.03038	.02447	.01974	.01596	.01292	.01048	25

TABLE	5	Present Value of an Annuity of $1 (PVIFA)

Period	1%	2%	3%	4%	5%	6%	7%	8%	9%	10%	Period
01	.9901	.9804	.9709	.9615	.9524	.9434	.9346	.9259	.9174	.9091	01
02	1.9704	1.9416	1.9135	1.8861	1.8594	1.8334	1.8080	1.7833	1.7591	1.7355	02
03	2.9410	2.8839	2.8286	2.7751	2.7233	2.6730	2.6243	2.5771	2.5313	2.4868	03
04	3.9020	3.8077	3.7171	3.6299	3.5459	3.4651	3.3872	3.3121	3.2397	3.1699	04
05	4.8535	4.7134	4.5797	4.4518	4.3295	4.2123	4.1002	3.9927	3.8896	3.7908	05
06	5.7955	5.6014	5.4172	5.2421	5.0757	4.9173	4.7665	4.6229	4.4859	4.3553	06
07	6.7282	6.4720	6.2302	6.0020	5.7863	5.5824	5.3893	5.2064	5.0329	4.8684	07
08	7.6517	7.3254	7.0196	6.7327	6.4632	6.2093	5.9713	5.7466	5.5348	5.3349	08
09	8.5661	8.1622	7.7861	7.4353	7.1078	6.8017	6.5152	6.2469	5.9852	5.7590	09
10	9.4714	8.9825	8.7302	8.1109	7.7217	7.3601	7.0236	6.7101	6.4176	6.1446	10
11	10.3677	9.7868	9.2526	8.7604	8.3064	7.8868	7.4987	7.1389	6.8052	6.4951	11
12	11.2552	10.5753	9.9589	9.3850	8.8632	8.3838	7.9427	7.5361	7.1601	6.8137	12
13	12.1338	11.3483	10.6349	9.9856	9.3935	8.8527	8.3576	7.9038	7.4869	7.1034	13
14	13.0088	12.1062	11.2960	10.5631	9.8986	9.2950	8.7454	8.2442	7.7860	7.3667	14
15	13.8651	12.8492	11.9379	11.1183	10.3796	9.7122	9.1079	8.5595	8.0607	7.6061	15
16	14.7180	13.5777	12.5610	11.6522	10.8377	10.1059	9.4466	8.8514	8.3126	7.8237	16
17	15.5624	14.2918	13.1660	12.1656	11.2740	10.4772	9.7632	9.1216	8.5435	8.0215	17
18	16.3984	14.9920	13.7534	12.6592	11.6895	10.8276	10.0591	9.3719	8.7556	8.2014	18
19	17.2201	15.2684	14.3237	13.1339	12.0853	11.1581	10.3356	9.6036	8.9501	8.3649	19
20	18.0457	16.3514	14.8774	13.5903	12.4622	11.4699	10.5940	9.8181	9.1285	8.5136	20
21	18.8571	17.0111	15.4149	14.0291	12.8211	11.7640	10.8355	10.0168	9.2922	8.6487	21
22	19.6605	17.6581	15.9368	14.4511	13.1630	12.0416	11.0612	10.2007	9.4424	8.7715	22
23	20.4559	18.2921	16.4435	14.8568	13.4885	12.3033	11.2722	10.3710	9.5802	8.8832	23
24	21.2435	18.9139	16.9355	15.2469	13.7986	12.5503	11.4693	10.5287	9.7066	8.9847	24
25	22.0233	19.5234	17.4181	15.6220	14.9039	12.7833	11.6536	10.6748	9.8226	9.0770	25

| TABLE | 5 | Present Value of an Annuity of $1 (PVIFA) (cont'd) |

Period	11%	12%	13%	14%	15%	16%	17%	18%	19%	20%	Period
01	.9009	.8929	.8850	.8772	.8696	.8621	.8547	.8475	.8403	.8333	01
02	1.7125	1.6901	1.6681	1.6467	1.6257	1.6052	1.5852	1.5656	1.5465	1.5278	02
03	2.4437	2.4018	2.3612	2.3216	2.2832	2.2459	2.2096	2.1743	2.1399	2.1065	03
04	3.1024	3.0373	2.9745	2.9137	2.8550	2.7982	2.7432	2.6901	2.6386	2.5887	04
05	3.6959	3.6048	3.5172	3.4331	3.3522	3.2743	3.1993	3.1272	3.0576	2.9906	05
06	4.2305	4.1114	3.9976	3.8887	3.7845	3.6847	3.5892	3.4976	3.4098	3.3255	06
07	4.7122	4.5638	4.4226	4.2883	4.1604	4.0386	3.9224	3.8115	3.7057	3.6046	07
08	5.1461	4.9676	4.7988	4.6389	4.4873	4.3436	4.2072	4.0776	3.9544	3.8372	08
09	5.5370	5.3282	5.1317	4.9464	4.7716	4.6065	4.4506	4.3030	4.1633	4.0310	09
10	5.8892	5.6502	5.4262	5.2161	5.0188	4.8332	4.6586	4.4941	4.3389	4.1925	10
11	6.2065	5.9377	5.6869	5.4527	5.2337	5.0286	4.8364	4.6560	4.4865	4.3271	11
12	6.4924	6.1944	5.9176	5.6603	5.4206	5.1971	4.9884	4.7932	4.6105	4.4392	12
13	6.7499	6.4235	6.1218	5.8424	5.5831	5.3423	5.1183	4.9095	4.7147	4.5327	13
14	6.9819	6.6282	6.3025	6.0021	5.7245	5.4675	5.2293	5.0081	4.8023	4.6106	14
15	7.1909	6.8109	6.4624	6.1422	5.8474	5.5755	5.3242	5.0916	4.8759	4.6755	15
16	7.3792	6.9740	6.6039	.2651	5.9542	5.6685	5.4053	5.1624	4.9377	4.7296	16
17	7.5488	7.1196	6.7291	6.3729	6.0472	5.7487	5.4746	5.2223	4.9897	4.7746	17
18	7.7016	7.2497	6.8389	6.4674	6.1280	5.8178	5.5339	5.2732	5.0333	4.8122	18
19	7.8393	7.3650	6.9380	6.5504	6.1982	5.8775	5.5845	5.3176	5.0700	4.8435	19
20	7.9633	7.4694	7.0248	6.6231	6.2593	5.9288	5.6278	5.3527	5.1009	4.8696	20
21	8.0751	7.5620	7.1016	6.6870	6.3125	5.9731	5.6648	5.3837	5.1268	4.8913	21
22	8.1757	7.6446	7.1695	6.7429	6.3587	6.0113	5.6964	5.4099	5.1486	4.9094	22
23	8.2664	7.7184	7.2297	6.7921	6.3988	6.0442	5.7234	5.4321	5.1668	4.9245	23
24	8.3481	7.7843	7.2829	6.8351	6.4338	6.0726	5.7465	5.4509	5.1822	4.9371	24
25	8.4217	7.8431	7.3300	6.8729	6.4641	6.0971	5.7662	5.4669	5.1951	4.9476	25

TABLE 6   Durbin-Watson Statistic for 2.5% Significance (one-tail) or 5.0% Significance (two-tail)

	m = 1		m = 2		m = 3		m = 4		m = 5	
n	d_L	d_U	d_L	d_U	d_L	d_U	d_L	d_U	d_L	d_U
15	0.95	1.23	0.83	1.40	0.71	1.61	0.59	1.84	0.48	2.09
16	0.98	1.24	0.86	1.40	0.75	1.59	0.64	1.80	0.53	2.03
17	1.01	1.25	0.90	1.40	0.79	1.58	0.68	1.77	0.57	1.98
18	1.03	1.26	0.93	1.40	0.82	1.56	0.72	1.74	0.62	1.93
19	1.06	1.28	0.96	1.41	0.86	1.55	0.76	1.73	0.66	1.90
20	1.08	1.28	0.99	1.41	0.89	1.55	0.79	1.72	0.70	1.87
21	1.10	1.30	1.01	1.41	0.92	1.54	0.83	1.69	0.73	1.84
22	1.12	1.31	1.04	1.42	0.95	1.54	0.86	1.68	0.77	1.82
23	1.14	1.32	1.06	1.42	0.97	1.54	0.89	1.67	0.80	1.80
24	1.16	1.33	1.08	1.43	1.00	1.54	0.91	1.66	0.83	1.79
25	1.18	1.34	1.10	1.43	1.02	1.54	0.94	1.65	0.86	1.77
26	1.19	1.35	1.12	1.44	1.04	1.54	0.96	1.65	0.88	1.76
27	1.21	1.36	1.13	1.44	1.06	1.54	0.99	1.64	0.91	1.75
28	1.22	1.37	1.15	1.45	1.08	1.54	1.01	1.64	0.93	1.74
29	1.24	1.38	1.17	1.45	1.10	1.54	1.03	1.63	0.96	1.73
30	1.25	1.38	1.18	1.46	1.12	1.54	1.05	1.63	0.98	1.73
31	1.26	1.39	1.20	1.47	1.13	1.55	1.07	1.63	1.00	1.72
32	1.27	1.40	1.21	1.47	1.15	1.55	1.08	1.63	1.02	1.71
33	1.28	1.41	1.22	1.48	1.16	1.55	1.10	1.63	1.04	1.71
34	1.29	1.41	1.24	1.48	1.17	1.55	1.12	1.63	1.06	1.70
35	1.30	1.42	1.25	1.48	1.19	1.55	1.13	1.63	1.07	1.70
36	1.31	1.43	1.26	1.49	1.20	1.56	1.15	1.63	1.09	1.70
37	1.32	1.43	1.27	1.49	1.21	1.56	1.16	1.62	1.10	1.70
38	1.33	1.44	1.28	1.50	1.23	1.56	1.17	1.62	1.12	1.70
39	1.34	1.44	1.29	1.50	1.24	1.56	1.19	1.63	1.13	1.69
40	1.35	1.45	1.30	1.51	1.25	1.57	1.20	1.63	1.15	1.69
45	1.39	1.48	1.34	1.53	1.30	1.58	1.25	1.63	1.21	1.69
50	1.42	1.50	1.38	1.54	1.34	1.59	1.30	1.64	1.26	1.69
55	1.45	1.52	1.41	1.56	1.37	1.60	1.33	1.64	1.30	1.69
60	1.47	1.54	1.44	1.57	1.40	1.61	1.37	1.65	1.33	1.69
65	1.49	1.55	1.46	1.59	1.43	1.63	1.40	1.66	1.36	1.69
70	1.51	1.57	1.48	1.60	1.45	1.63	1.42	1.66	1.39	1.70
75	1.53	1.58	1.50	1.61	1.47	1.64	1.45	1.67	1.42	1.70
80	1.54	1.59	1.52	1.63	1.49	1.65	1.47	1.67	1.44	1.70
85	1.56	1.60	1.53	1.63	1.51	1.66	1.49	1.68	1.46	1.71
90	1.57	1.61	1.55	1.64	1.53	1.66	1.50	1.69	1.48	1.71
95	1.58	1.62	1.56	1.65	1.54	1.67	1.52	1.69	1.50	1.71
100	1.59	1.63	1.57	1.65	1.55	1.67	1.53	1.70	1.51	1.72

m = number of independent variables
n = number of observations

Source: From J. Durbin and G. S. Watson, "Testing for Serial Correlation in Least-Squares Regression," *Biometrika*, Vol. 38 (1951); 159–177. With the permission of the authors and the Trustees of *Biometrika*.

CHAPTER 2

3. Budget = $875 million
5. c. $v = 0.067$
7. a. 0.0062
10. b. $1,714
11. a. 0.0668

CHAPTER 3

3. d. $Q^* = 8$
5. a. $100 - 12Q + 1.5Q^2$
7. b. $Q^* = 5$
9. c. $P^* = \$20$
11. a. $Q^* = 180$
13. a. 25 units newspaper advertising
16. a. $50 - 8Q$
18. b. $\% X^4 - X^2$
20. a. $Q = 25$
24. $-32X^3 + 56X$

APPENDIX 3A

3. a. $X^* = 13$ units newspaper advertising

CHAPTER 4

1. $Q_{A2} = 1,830$
3. 44%
5. a. -0.3
7. Chow: 11.528 million
9. $P = \$90$
11. a. $E_D = -0.59$
15. a. -3%
17. a. i. $E_D = -1.78$
20. -3%
23. a. $E_X = 1.34$
25. Week 2-3: $E_Y = 0.538$
29. $Q_{19X2} = 5169$
31. c. $Q_2 = 505$
33. a. -0.375

CHAPTER 5

2. c. $Y = 11.148 + 1.492X$
4. d. $R^2 = 0.885$
6. a. Income coefficient = 5.9492
10. b. $E_A = 0.98$
13. c. 1.909
15. a. $E_X = d$
20. a. $Y' = 19.6325 + 1.2945X_1 + .3828X_2 - 2.5219X_3$
22. 0.590

CASE EXERCISE

7. $E_D = -0.167$
9. D-W = 1.385

APPENDIX 5A

1. a. $R^2 = 0.93$
3. a. i. $S' = 247.644 + .3926A - .7339P$

CHAPTER 6

1. b. $S_{t+1} = 729,000$
4. b. GNP = 955
6. b. $+6\%$
8. a. $Q_D = 11,450$
10. b. $Y'_{10} = 259.03$
12. a. December 19X6 = 468
14. a. $Q = 10,200(000)$

CHAPTER 7

1. Both increase
3. Outsource abroad and buy foreign assets
6. 50% decline. Relative purchasing power parity

CASE EXERCISE

DM/$ increases

CHAPTER 8

2. $TP_X = 80$ when $X = 4$
4. b. 10 or 11 men
6. b. $AP_X = 6X - .4X^2$
8. b. $Q^* = 44$
12. a. 4.88%
14. a. i. $\beta_L = 0.70$
16. a. Constant returns
17. a. Homogeneous of degree = 0.7

CASE EXERCISE

4. $E_K = 0.415$

APPENDIX 8A

1. d. $Q^* = 43.231$

CHAPTER 9

3. a. $10,000

CHAPTER 8 (continued)

8. a. $TC = 150 + 200Q - 9Q^2 + 0.25Q^3$
10. a. $Q^* = 10$
12. a. TC(one plant) = $4,275,000

CASE EXERCISE

1. $4.55

APPENDIX 9A

1. a. $L^* = 2.5$ units
3. a. $10

CHAPTER 10

3. a. $Q^* = \$574.08$ (million)
6. c. 8,000
8. a. $p = 0.0062$
11. a. $30,000,000

CASE EXERCISE

5. $Q^* = 1,675$

APPENDIX 10A

1. c. $C = \$803.51$

CHAPTER 11

1. b. $X_1^* = 800$(STD)
   $X_2^* = 600$(DEL)
4. c. X_1^* (small) = 12
7. a. Objective function: min $C = 3.0X_1 + 2.0 X_2$
11. a. Objective function: max $R = 50X_1 + 40X_2 + 30X_3$
21. $X_1 = 5,000$ barrels of gasoline

CHAPTER 12

7. a. $P = \$8$
9. c. iii. Ration coupon value = $15
11. d. $MR = 3 - Q/2,000$
13. b. $P^* = \$1,220$
15. d. $\pi = \$9,000$
17. b. i. $\Delta TR = +\$59,395$
19. b. $900,000 on advertising

CHAPTER 13

5. Apple's expected net profit = $1.5 million less from understatement

Case Exercise

c. $54,000 and $112,000

Chapter 14

9.   c. $Q^* = 125$
11. e. $\pi^* = \$263,625$
13. b. $P^* = \$60$
16. a. ROI = 14.2%
18. a. ROI = 12.98%

Chapter 15

2.   a. $P^* = \$145$
        $Q^*_A = 30$
5.   a. $P^* = \$9,666.7$
6.   c. $P^* = \$125$
9.   a. Dominant strategy for AMC
        is to "Not Abide"

Chapter 16

2.   ($150, Match), No
3.   Least should pass
6. $P^r = 5/7$, $P^t = 3/5$

Appendix 16A
Case Exercise

b.   PCS will bid $20 million

Chapter 17

3. $P_{US} = \$12$
5.   a. $\pi = -20 + 96Q_1 + 76Q_2 - 2Q_1^2 - Q_2^2$
12. $P_1^* = \$40.67$
15. c. i. $Q_m^* = 4$ units internally
17. a. $P = \$72.50$

Case Exercise

1. $Q_m^* = 356,790$ units
5. $Q_m^* = 353,750$ units

Appendix 17A

2.   Decrease

Chapter 18

6.   a. HHI before = 1,964
13. a. $P^* = \$10,000$
15. b. $\pi^* = \$450$ million
18. a. σ_T (after) = 4.2%
20. b. $Q^* = 69.05$

Appendix 18A

9.   c. $146
11. b. $Q^* = 28$

Chapter 19

2.   IRR = 9.1%
4.   b. $NCF_{10} = \$5,560$
6.   a. i. IRR = 14.94%
8. $k_e = 13.4\%$
10. b. $k'_e = 13\%$
12. $k_a = 12.3\%$
14. b. Power plant: $NPV_{@12\%} = \$-22.71$ million

Case Exercise

1.   B/C ratio = 1.90

Chapter 20

2.   b. $E(U)$ for $A_1 = -0.3975$
4.   a. $E(V_A) = \$780,000$
6.   e. 30 dozen
8.   c. +$32,620
10. a. NPV = $1.3 million

Internet Addresses

Below is a list of Internet addresses presented in the margins throughout this book for the reader's use. Every attempt was made to ensure that these links were working at the date of publication. However, Internet links are perishable experience goods, and the authors apologize for any unforeseen problems in connecting to these sites.

CHAPTER 1

http://www.salomon.com/investor.htm
http://www.toyota.com/times
http://www.circuscircus.com
http://www.berkshirehathaway.com
http://www.ibm.com/Investor/acquisitions.html
http://www.pepsico.com/web_pages/resource/financial_info
http://www.rjrnabisco.com/
http://www.epa.gov/docs/acidrain/trading.html
http://www.bea.doc.gov/bea/di1.htm
http://www.towers.com

CHAPTER 2

http://www.aeronomics.com/news
http://www.saralee.com/financial/stock/index.htm
http://www.usair.com/company/financial/indexj.htm
http://www.pg.com/docInfo/financial_center/
http://www.moodys.com/index.shtml
http://www.riskview.com

CHAPTER 3

http://www.amrcorp.com/amr/investor/investor.htm
http://www.illinova.com/
http://www.bug.com/finance/financ.htm
http://www.public-policy.org/~~ncpa/studies/
    s171/s171.html
http://www.wto.org/goods/textiles.htm
http://www.cato.org/pubs/pas/pa-140es.html

CHAPTER 4

http://www.public-policy.org/~~ncpa/ba/ba231.html
http://www.taxadmin.org/fta/rate/cigarett.html
http://www.gm.com/index.cgi
http://www.ita.doc.gov/media/
http://quote.yahoo.com/
http://www.uchastings.edu/plri/spr96tex/calgam.html
http://www.rtimarketresearch.com/rt03008.htm
http://www.vw.com/
http://www.census.gov/hhes/www/housing.html

http://www.antitrust.org/
http://www.usdoj.gov/atr/index.html
http://www.ftc.gov/search/search.htm
http://www.seiko-corp.co.jp/
http://www.mot.com/
http://www.ftc.gov/search/search.htm

CHAPTER 5

http://www.casro.org/
http://www.bts.gov/NTL/
http://www.bedsonline.com/simmons.html
http://www.horizonweb.com/pcn/swhome.htm
http://www.mesc.usgs.gov/wildlife-nonmarket-benefits.html
http://www.cif1.com/
http://www.sonic.net/~~punch/guest/browse.htm

CHAPTER 6

http://www.jdpower.com/forecast.html
http://www.dominos.com/info/search.html
http://www.marketsearch-dir.com/html/d2153.htm
http://www.nber.org
http://www.conference-board.org/
http://www.tcb-indicators.org/rev96/rev96.htm
http://www.bea.doc.gov/bea/scbinf.html
http://www.napm.org/indexedfiles/rob/main.html
http://www.isr.umich.edu/src/
http://www.libertynet.org/~fedresrv/econ/liv/
http://weatherhead.cwru.edu/forecasting/
http://www.dismal.com/

CHAPTER 7

http://www.ita.doc.gov/media/
http://quote.yahoo.com/
http://www.cummins.com/news/finance.html
http://www.ny.frb.org/pihome/mktrates/
http://www.cme.com/market/currency/index.html
http://www.americasnet.com/mauritz/mercosur/english/
http://europa.eu.int/en/eu.html
http://www.stls.frb.org/publ/net/
http://www.cme.com/market/cfot/simulation/

CHAPTER 8

http://www.sel.com/retail.html.

http://price.bus.okstate.edu/archive/Econ3113_963/Shows/
Chapter6/index.htm

http://www.pathfinder.com/fortune/magazine/1996/960429/
economy.html

http://www.best.com/~ddfr/Academic/Price_Theory/
PThy_Chapter_9/PThy_Chapter_9.html

http://www.afns.ualberta.ca/wcdairy/wcd96/wcd96333.htm

http://price.bus.okstate.edu/archive/Econ3113_963/Shows/
Chapter7/index.htm

http://www.clev.frb.org/research/may96et/merger.htm

http://medusa.be.udel.edu/WWW_Sites/oo_Micro%20Models!/
Index.html

http://www.sel.com/retail.html

CHAPTER 9

http://www.usair.com/company/financial/indexj.htm

http://price.bus.okstate.edu/archive/Econ3113_963/Shows/
Chapter6/index.htm

http://www.best.com/~ddfr/Academic/Price_Theory/
PThy_Chapter_9/PThy_Chapter_9.html

http://hubcap.clemson.edu/customerchoice/

http://nutcweb.tpc.nwu.edu/RESEARCH/carrier/carrier.html

http://nutcweb.tpc.nwu.edu/RESEARCH/carrier/
carrier4.html

http://www.ford.com/corporate-info/stockholder/

http://www.rapmaine.org/stranded.html

http://ee.notes.org/minnesota/stranded.htm

http://www.local.org/stranded.html

http://www.afce.org/position/p&p.htm

http://www.eia.doe.gov/cneaf/electricity/chg_str/
chapter8.html

CHAPTER 10

http://biz.onramp.net/cami/cmsintro.htm

http://web.nps.navy.mil/~drmi/unitcost.htm

http://www.treasury.nsw.gov.au/etf/etf95_5.htm

http://www.local.org/compfran.html

http://www.gm.com

http://nutcweb.tpc.nwu.edu/RESEARCH/regulatory/
regulatory1.html.

http://www.air-transport.org/handbk/chaptr04.htm

CHAPTER 11

http://ucsu.colorado.edu/~xu/software.html

http://www.melbourneit.com.au/linear.html

http://www.lindo.com/download.html

CHAPTER 12

http://www.cslnet.ctstateu.edu/attygenl/metro1.htm

http://www.findlaw.com/01topics/01antitrust/microsoft.html

http://www.ftc.gov/search/search.htm

http://www.airportnet.org/depts/publicat/express/1996htm/
3-11-96.htm

http://www.rand.org/publications/MR/MR827/

http://www.foodinstitute.com/nonpages/mainnon.htm

http://www.rand.org/publications/MR/MR827/

CHAPTER 13

http://www.intel.com/intel/finance/index.htm

http://www.fdic.gov/databank/bkreview/1995summ/art1full

http://www.eiaj.org/study/executive.html

http://www.WhirlpoolCorp.com/ics/ir/index.html

http://www.adobe.com/aboutadobe/invrelations/main.html

http://www.fdic.gov/databank/bkreview/1995summ/art1full

CHAPTER 14

http://www.pnm.com/

http://www.intelproplaw.com/

http://server.berkeley.edu/BTLJ/lvb/econprof.html

http://www.bms.com/financial/index.htm

http://www.ferc.fed.us/

http://eerr.notes.org/wyoming/restructuring.htm

http://www.eia.doe.gov/oiaf/elepri97/comp.html

http://www.stolaf.edu/people/becker/antitrust/subject.html

CHAPTER 15

http://www.amrcorp.com/amr/investor/investor.htm

http://www.beverage-digest.com/datastats.html

http://www.stolaf.edu/people/becker/antitrust/summaries/
468us085.html

http://www.opec.org/

http://www.ftc.gov/speeches/other/confbd4.htm

http://www.pitt.edu/~alroth/alroth.html

http://www.almaz.com/nobel/economics/1994a.html

http://www.stolaf.edu/people/becker/antitrust/summaries/
438us422.htm

CHAPTER 16

http://www8.zdnet.com/pcweek/news/0714/17ecuts.html

http://www.nyu.edu/projects/kaminski/
gamesstrategyandpolitics.html

http://www.bell-atl.com/invest/

http://www.rand.org/publications/RB/RB1500/

http://www.worldbank.org/html/fpd/notes/50/50Tenenbaum

http://www.modecomputers.com.au/guarantee.html

http://econwpa.wustl.edu/eprints/mic/papers/9701/9701005

http://pscs.physics.lsa.umich.edu/Software/CC/ECHome

http://www.stolaf.edu/people/becker/antitrust/subject.html

CHAPTER 17

http://www.arl.org/scomm/scat/guthries.html

http://www.apple.com/investor/